Foreign Relations
of the
United States
Diplomatic Papers
1936
(In Five Volumes)

Volume IV
The Far East

United States
Government Printing Office
Washington : 1954

DEPARTMENT OF STATE PUBLICATION 5404

DIVISION OF PUBLICATIONS

CONTENTS

LIST OF PAPERS

(Unless otherwise specified, the correspondence is *from* or *to* officials in the Department of State.)

THE FAR EASTERN CRISIS

CHAPTER I: JANUARY 1–APRIL 15, 1936

THE FAR EASTERN CRISIS

Chapter I: January 1–April 15, 1936—Continued

THE FAR EASTERN CRISIS

CHAPTER I: JANUARY 1–APRIL 15, 1936—Continued

THE FAR EASTERN CRISIS

Chapter I: January 1–April 15, 1936—Continued

THE FAR EASTERN CRISIS

Chapter I: January 1–April 15, 1936—Continued

THE FAR EASTERN CRISIS

CHAPTER I: JANUARY 1–APRIL 15, 1936—Continued

THE FAR EASTERN CRISIS

CHAPTER I: JANUARY 1–APRIL 15, 1936—Continued

THE FAR EASTERN CRISIS

Chapter I: January 1–April 15, 1936—Continued

THE FAR EASTERN CRISIS

CHAPTER I: JANUARY 1–APRIL 15, 1936—Continued

CHAPTER II: APRIL 16–JUNE 30, 1936

THE FAR EASTERN CRISIS

CHAPTER II: APRIL 16–JUNE 30, 1936—Continued

THE FAR EASTERN CRISIS

CHAPTER II: APRIL 16–JUNE 30, 1936—Continued

THE FAR EASTERN CRISIS

CHAPTER II: APRIL 16–JUNE 30, 1936—Continued

THE FAR EASTERN CRISIS

CHAPTER II: APRIL 16–JUNE 30, 1936—Continued

THE FAR EASTERN CRISIS

CHAPTER II: APRIL 16–JUNE 30, 1936—Continued

THE FAR EASTERN CRISIS

CHAPTER II: APRIL 16–JUNE 30, 1936—Continued

THE FAR EASTERN CRISIS
Chapter II: April 16–June 30, 1936—Continued

THE FAR EASTERN CRISIS

CHAPTER II: APRIL 16–JUNE 30, 1936—Continued

THE FAR EASTERN CRISIS

CHAPTER II: APRIL 16–JUNE 30, 1936—Continued

THE FAR EASTERN CRISIS

Chapter II: April 16–June 30, 1936—Continued

THE FAR EASTERN CRISIS
CHAPTER III: JULY 1–OCTOBER 15, 1936

THE FAR EASTERN CRISIS

Chapter III: July 1–October 15, 1936—Continued

THE FAR EASTERN CRISIS

CHAPTER III: JULY 1–OCTOBER 15, 1936—Continued

THE FAR EASTERN CRISIS

CHAPTER III: JULY 1–OCTOBER 15, 1936—Continued

THE FAR EASTERN CRISIS

Chapter III: July 1–October 15, 1936—Continued

THE FAR EASTERN CRISIS

Chapter III: July 1–October 15, 1936—Continued

THE FAR EASTERN CRISIS

CHAPTER III: JULY 1–OCTOBER 15, 1936—Continued

THE FAR EASTERN CRISIS

CHAPTER III: JULY 1–OCTOBER 15, 1936—Continued

THE FAR EASTERN CRISIS

CHAPTER III: JULY 1–OCTOBER 15, 1936—Continued

THE FAR EASTERN CRISIS

CHAPTER III: JULY 1–OCTOBER 15, 1936—Continued

THE FAR EASTERN CRISIS

CHAPTER III: JULY 1–OCTOBER 15, 1936—Continued

CHAPTER IV: OCTOBER 16–DECEMBER 31, 1936

THE FAR EASTERN CRISIS

CHAPTER IV: OCTOBER 16–DECEMBER 31, 1936—Continued

THE FAR EASTERN CRISIS

CHAPTER IV: OCTOBER 16–DECEMBER 31, 1936—Continued

THE FAR EASTERN CRISIS

CHAPTER IV: OCTOBER 16–DECEMBER 31, 1936—Continued

THE FAR EASTERN CRISIS

Chapter IV: October 16–December 31, 1936—Continued

THE FAR EASTERN CRISIS

CHAPTER IV: OCTOBER 16–DECEMBER 31, 1936—Continued

THE FAR EASTERN CRISIS

CHAPTER IV: OCTOBER 16–DECEMBER 31, 1936—Continued

THE FAR EASTERN CRISIS

CHAPTER IV: OCTOBER 16–DECEMBER 31, 1936—Continued

THE FAR EASTERN CRISIS

CHAPTER IV: OCTOBER 16–DECEMBER 31, 1936—Continued

THE FAR EASTERN CRISIS

CHAPTER IV: OCTOBER 16–DECEMBER 31, 1936—Continued

THE FAR EASTERN CRISIS

CHAPTER IV: OCTOBER 16–DECEMBER 31, 1936—Continued

CHINA

PROBLEM OF CHINA'S ECONOMIC RECONSTRUCTION AND THE ATTITUDE OF THE
UNITED STATES AND OTHER GOVERNMENTS RESPECTING FINANCIAL ASSISTANCE
TO CHINA

CHINA

PROBLEM OF CHINA'S ECONOMIC RECONSTRUCTION AND THE ATTITUDE OF THE
UNITED STATES AND OTHER GOVERNMENTS RESPECTING FINANCIAL ASSISTANCE
TO CHINA—Continued

CHINA

Problem of China's Economic Reconstruction and the Attitude of the United States and Other Governments Respecting Financial Assistance to China—Continued

CHINA

PROBLEM OF CHINA'S ECONOMIC RECONSTRUCTION AND THE ATTITUDE OF THE
UNITED STATES AND OTHER GOVERNMENTS RESPECTING FINANCIAL ASSISTANCE
TO CHINA—Continued

CHINA

PROBLEM OF CHINA'S ECONOMIC RECONSTRUCTION AND THE ATTITUDE OF THE UNITED STATES AND OTHER GOVERNMENTS RESPECTING FINANCIAL ASSISTANCE TO CHINA—Continued

CHINA

MEASURES TAKEN BY THE UNITED STATES FOR THE PROTECTION OF AMERICAN
LIVES AND PROPERTY IN CHINA—Continued

CHINA

Measures Taken by the United States for the Protection of American
Lives and Property in China—Continued

CHINA

Measures Taken by the United States for the Protection of American
Lives and Property in China—Continued

CHINA

MEASURES TAKEN BY THE UNITED STATES FOR THE PROTECTION OF AMERICAN
LIVES AND PROPERTY IN CHINA—Continued

CHINA

MEASURES TAKEN BY THE UNITED STATES FOR THE PROTECTION OF AMERICAN
LIVES AND PROPERTY IN CHINA—Continued

CHINA

CHINA

ATTITUDE OF THE DEPARTMENT OF STATE ON THE EXPORT TO CHINA OF ARMS
OR MUNITIONS, INCLUDING MILITARY AIRCRAFT—Continued

CHINA

PROBLEM OF CONTROLLING THE TRAFFIC IN OPIUM AND NARCOTIC DRUGS IN CHINA, INCLUDING MANCHURIA AND JEHOL

EFFORTS FOR THE CONSIDERATION OF AMERICAN CLAIMS OUTSTANDING AGAINST CHINA

CHINA

EFFORTS FOR THE CONSIDERATION OF AMERICAN CLAIMS OUTSTANDING AGAINST
CHINA—Continued

CHINA

EFFORTS FOR THE CONSIDERATION OF AMERICAN CLAIMS OUTSTANDING AGAINST
CHINA—Continued

CHINA

CHINA

REPRESENTATIONS BY THE UNITED STATES AGAINST THE ESTABLISHMENT OF MONOPOLIES IN CHINA—Continued

CHINA

REPRESENTATIONS BY THE UNITED STATES AGAINST THE ESTABLISHMENT OF MONOPOLIES IN CHINA—Continued

CHINA

REPRESENTATIONS BY THE UNITED STATES AGAINST THE ESTABLISHMENT OF
MONOPOLIES IN CHINA—Continued

CHINA

REJECTION BY THE UNITED STATES OF APPLICATION OF CHINESE INCOME TAX
TO AMERICAN CITIZENS—Continued

RESERVATION OF AMERICAN RIGHTS IN PROPOSED CHANGES FOR CONTROL OF
PILOTAGE AT SHANGHAI

ASSISTANCE TO PAN AMERICAN AIRWAYS IN SECURING RIGHTS NEEDED TO
EXTEND ITS UNITED STATES–PHILIPPINE SERVICE TO CHINA

CHINA

CHINA

ATTITUDE OF THE DEPARTMENT OF STATE WITH RESPECT TO THE APPLICATION OF CHINESE LAWS TO AMERICAN INSURANCE COMPANIES DOING BUSINESS IN CHINA—Continued

RE-REGISTRATION OF TITLE DEEDS TO REAL PROPERTY OF AMERICANS IN CHINA

CHINA

RE-REGISTRATION OF TITLE DEEDS TO REAL PROPERTY OF AMERICANS IN CHINA—
Continued

CHINESE CENSORSHIP RESTRICTIONS UPON AMERICAN MOVING PICTURES IN
CHINA

CHINA

CHINESE CENSORSHIP RESTRICTIONS UPON AMERICAN MOVING PICTURES IN
CHINA—Continued

CHINA

AMERICAN INTEREST IN PROBLEMS AFFECTING THE INTERNATIONAL
SETTLEMENT AT SHANGHAI

CHINA

AMERICAN INTEREST IN PROBLEMS AFFECTING THE INTERNATIONAL
SETTLEMENT AT SHANGHAI—Continued

JAPAN

POLITICAL DEVELOPMENTS IN JAPAN; THE ASSASSINATIONS OF FEBRUARY 26

JAPAN

POLITICAL DEVELOPMENTS IN JAPAN; THE ASSASSINATIONS OF FEBRUARY 26—
Continued

JAPAN

POLITICAL DEVELOPMENTS IN JAPAN; THE ASSASSINATIONS OF FEBRUARY 26—
Continued

JAPAN

POLITICAL DEVELOPMENTS IN JAPAN; THE ASSASSINATIONS OF FEBRUARY 26—
Continued

JAPAN

POLITICAL DEVELOPMENTS IN JAPAN; THE ASSASSINATIONS OF FEBRUARY 26—
Continued

DISAPPROVAL BY THE AMERICAN GOVERNMENT OF THE EMPLOYMENT OF AMERICAN CITIZENS BY A FOREIGN GOVERNMENT AS PROPAGANDA AGENTS

JAPAN

DISAPPROVAL BY THE AMERICAN GOVERNMENT OF THE EMPLOYMENT OF AMERICAN
CITIZENS BY A FOREIGN GOVERNMENT AS PROPAGANDA AGENTS—Continued

JAPAN

REPRESENTATIONS ON ESTABLISHMENT OF OIL MONOPOLIES IN JAPAN AND
MANCHURIA—Continued

JAPAN

REPRESENTATIONS ON ESTABLISHMENT OF OIL MONOPOLIES IN JAPAN AND
MANCHURIA—Continued

JAPAN

TRADE RELATIONS BETWEEN THE UNITED STATES AND JAPAN; FURTHER DISCUS-
SION OF VOLUNTARY RESTRICTION BY THE JAPANESE OF EXPORTS TO THE UNITED
STATES AND THE PHILIPPINES—Continued

JAPAN

TRADE RELATIONS BETWEEN THE UNITED STATES AND JAPAN; FURTHER DISCUS-
SION OF VOLUNTARY RESTRICTION BY THE JAPANESE OF EXPORTS TO THE UNITED
STATES AND THE PHILIPPINES—Continued

JAPAN

TRADE RELATIONS BETWEEN THE UNITED STATES AND JAPAN; FURTHER DISCUSSION OF VOLUNTARY RESTRICTION BY THE JAPANESE OF EXPORTS TO THE UNITED STATES AND THE PHILIPPINES—Continued

JAPAN

TRADE RELATIONS BETWEEN THE UNITED STATES AND JAPAN; FURTHER DISCUS-
SION OF VOLUNTARY RESTRICTION BY THE JAPANESE OF EXPORTS TO THE UNITED
STATES AND THE PHILIPPINES—Continued

JAPAN

TRADE RELATIONS BETWEEN THE UNITED STATES AND JAPAN; FURTHER DISCUS-
SION OF VOLUNTARY RESTRICTION BY THE JAPANESE OF EXPORTS TO THE UNITED
STATES AND THE PHILIPPINES—Continued

JAPAN

TRADE RELATIONS BETWEEN THE UNITED STATES AND JAPAN; FURTHER DISCUS-
SION OF VOLUNTARY RESTRICTION BY THE JAPANESE OF EXPORTS TO THE UNITED
STATES AND THE PHILIPPINES—Continued

JAPAN

TRADE RELATIONS BETWEEN THE UNITED STATES AND JAPAN; FURTHER DISCUS-
SION OF VOLUNTARY RESTRICTION BY THE JAPANESE OF EXPORTS TO THE UNITED
STATES AND THE PHILIPPINES—Continued

JAPAN

TRADE RELATIONS BETWEEN THE UNITED STATES AND JAPAN; FURTHER DISCUS-
SION OF VOLUNTARY RESTRICTION BY THE JAPANESE OF EXPORTS TO THE UNITED
STATES AND THE PHILIPPINES—Continued

JAPAN

Trade Relations Between the United States and Japan; Further Discussion of Voluntary Restriction by the Japanese of Exports to the United States and the Philippines—Continued

Disinclination of Japan To Negotiate a Convention With the United States Regulating Fisheries off the Coast of Alaska

JAPAN

DISINCLINATION OF JAPAN TO NEGOTIATE A CONVENTION WITH THE UNITED
STATES REGULATING FISHERIES OFF THE COAST OF ALASKA—Continued

SETTLEMENT OF CASE PRESENTED BY THE JAPANESE GOVERNMENT ON BEHALF
OF JAPANESE STEAMSHIP COMPANIES SUBJECT TO UNITED STATES WAR PROFITS
TAX FOR THE YEARS 1918 AND 1919

JAPAN

Settlement of Case Presented by the Japanese Government on Behalf of Japanese Steamship Companies Subject to United States War Profits Tax for the Years 1918 and 1919—Continued

Japan's Proposal That Perpetual Leases in Former Foreign Settlements in Japan Be Canceled in Favor of Ownership Rights

JAPAN

JAPANESE AUTOMOBILE LEGISLATION VIOLATIVE OF THE 1911 TREATY OF COMMERCE AND NAVIGATION BETWEEN THE UNITED STATES AND JAPAN

JAPAN

JAPAN

SIAM

JAPAN

THE FAR EASTERN CRISIS[1]

CHAPTER I: JANUARY 1–APRIL 15, 1936

Japanese dissatisfaction with situation in China and pressure to bring about favorable readjustment; President Chiang Kai-shek's determination to avoid surrender to Japan; possibility of German-Japanese military understanding; recurrence of incidents along Soviet-Outer Mongol borders of "Manchoukuo"; assurance of Soviet aid to Outer Mongolia in event of Japanese attack; Arita–Chang exploratory conversations at Nanking, March 16–19; Chinese protest against Soviet-Outer Mongol mutual assistance pact of March 12

500.A15A5/597 : Telegram

The Chairman of the American Delegation to the London Naval Conference (Davis) to the Secretary of State

LONDON, January 6, 1936—9 p. m.
[Received January 6—5 : 30 p. m.]

34. In the course of a conversation yesterday with Craigie,[2] a full report of which is contained in a memorandum being mailed,[3] he told me in strict confidence that he had learned that the Japanese and Chinese are now actively engaged in negotiating a pact of nonaggression which Chiang Kai Shek [4] had proposed himself, that the Japanese Foreign Office is reported to favor it and to be pressing the matter but that the military group in Japan is opposed because it would put an end to their operations in China.

Craigie added that if such an agreement were reached as would seem probable in the near future, it would automatically settle the Manchurian question if the situation were thus to be accepted by the Chinese.

Craigie said that speaking personally his idea is that if we are to get a naval agreement with Japan,[5] it will be necessary to have some political basis and if such a pact of nonaggression were consummated, the Japanese, British, and ourselves might then enter into a pact of nonaggression in the Pacific which could give to the Japanese justification for entering a naval agreement to maintain the present *status*

---

[1] Continued from *Foreign Relations*, 1935, vol. III, pp. 1–507 ; see also *Foreign Relations*, Japan, 1931–1941, vol. I, pp. 241–246 and 290–299.
[2] Robert Leslie Craigie, British Assistant Under Secretary of State for Foreign Affairs.
[3] Dated January 6, not printed.
[4] President of the Chinese Executive Yuan (Premier).
[5] For correspondence regarding naval discussions, see vol. I, pp. 22 ff.

quo. I told Craigie I doubted if it were practicable now to try to reach any political agreement as it would raise questions that are now insoluble. Furthermore, that his suggestion raised some very serious questions that would require careful consideration before determining whether or not they would have political association, that it was doubtful if the pact of nonaggression would give China anything more than the Nine Power Pact [6] had given in the way of protection, and that it might also seem ridiculous for us to enter into such a treaty with Japan which would in effect approve the past violation of the Nine Power Pact. Craigie stated that the British position is that the Nine Power Pact is still in force in effect and that he thought his suggestion should be carefully considered. He also said that if anything further came of his ideas the Foreign Secretary,[7] himself, would take occasion to talk with me on the subject.

We realize the objections to excluding other interested powers from any nonaggression pact and of course will not give any encouragement to this idea. I seriously doubt if Eden, himself, would entertain such a limited pact which might have such far reaching consequences.

DAVIS

793.94/7623 : Telegram

The Counselor of Embassy in China (Peck) to the Secretary of State

NANKING, January 7, 1936—1 p. m.
[Received 3 : 25 p. m.]

4. My 160, December 31, 11 a. m.[8]

1. Chen Chieh, administrative Vice Minister for Foreign Affairs, told me yesterday that it was expected that the Japanese Government would agree in principle to the proposal for a conference to effect a comprehensive adjustment of Sino-Japanese relations although no official agreement had yet been obtained. Hsu Mo, the political Vice Minister, told me the Chinese plans contemplated some kind of commission with special plenipotentiaries at their head. In regard to the scope of discussion the latter criticized as unreasonable the reported Japanese demand that China advance concrete proposals based on Hirota's "three principles" [9] since Japan not China originated these principles. He added that China had not agreed to avoid any specified subjects such as extraterritoriality.

---

[6] Signed at Washington, February 6, 1922, *Foreign Relations*, 1922, vol. I, p. 276.
[7] Anthony Eden.
[8] *Foreign Relations*, 1935, vol. III, p. 502.
[9] Koki Hirota, Japanese Minister for Foreign Affairs; for his policy, see telegram No. 72, November 11, 1935, 2 p. m., from the Embassy in China, *Foreign Relations*, 1935, vol. III, p. 404.

2. From another Foreign Office source it is confirmed that there has been no change in the status of this matter since its inception. According to a Domei despatch from Tokyo dated January 5 the Japanese Foreign Office will insist upon (1) the prior submission by the Chinese of a concrete list of proposals and (2) prior acceptance by China of Hirota's three point program; and before agreeing to formal discussion will obtain approval of the Japanese Ministries of War, Navy and Finance. This despatch states that the situation in China does not warrant optimism because of the undercurrent of anti-Japanese activity and regretfully expresses belief that the Nanking Government intends to bring up the question of the abrogation of the "unequal treaties."

3. By mail to Peiping.

PECK

500.A15A5/597 : Telegram

The Secretary of State to the Ambassador in China (Johnson) [10]

WASHINGTON, January 7, 1936—7 p. m.

4. 1. Under date January 6 Davis telegraphed from London as follows:

[Here follows the substance of telegram No. 34, printed on page 1.]

2. Department has had no information from any other source indicating that there are in progress negotiations such as Craigie described.

3. Please cable Department your comments and any information pertinent.

HULL

793.94/7631 : Telegram

The Ambassador in China (Johnson) to the Secretary of State

PEIPING, January 9, 1936—4 p. m.
[Received January 9—9 : 30 a. m.[11]]

9. 1. Several incidents have occurred recently which are alleged to have caused dissatisfaction on the part of the Japanese military with General Sung [12] and his men. They are as follows: (*a*) According to Japanese press report, some 40 Chinese soldiers in uniform of Sung's army looted on January 2, two Japanese owned shops at Taku, de-

---

[10] The same telegram was sent on the same date to the Embassy in Japan as No. 2.
[11] Telegram in two sections.
[12] General Sung Che-yuan, Chairman of the Hopei Provincial Government and of the Hopei-Chahar Political Council.

stroyed Japanese flags, and interfered with Japanese consular police. (*b*) As the result of delay by Chinese guards in opening a Peiping city gate at 10 p. m. January 5, to a motor car containing six or seven Japanese military, some ineffective shooting occurred and one or two Chinese guards were allegedly beaten. The entire blame is placed by the Japanese on the Chinese, although reports indicate that the Japanese were by no means blameless. (*c*) General Sung refused some days ago the request of the commandant of the local Japanese guard to call to discuss certain important matters, Sung sending word that the matters were within the province of the mayor. (*d*) Three Koreans attempted to enter the local military headquarters compound to shoot birds. Refusal resulted in a Chinese guard and the three Koreans being beaten.

2. At least the first incidents have been taken up officially. The local assistant to the Japanese Military Attaché informed the foreign press yesterday that demands would be made with regard to the second upon receipt of instructions from Tokyo and that the incident was regarded as an insult to the Japanese Army and as the result of the fundamentally anti-Japanese attitude of Sung's army.

3. These incidents, the Japanese attitude in regard thereto, and alleged Japanese dissatisfaction with Sung's delay in doing what the Japanese want have aroused apprehension that the Japanese will in the near future force Sung and his army out of North China (putting into nominal power Chinese more susceptible to Japanese direction) unless he complies with Japanese desires.

By mail to Tokyo.

JOHNSON

793.94/7630 : Telegram

The Ambassador in China (Johnson) to the Secretary of State

PEIPING, January 9, 1936—5 p. m.
[Received January 9—9 : 40 a. m.]

10. Embassy's 9, January 9, 4 p. m. Consulate General at Tientsin has been informed by Japanese Consul that with regard to anti-Japanese acts of soldiers of General Sung committed at Taku on January 2nd, 3rd, 4th, and 6th, six demands have been made: (1) apology by Sung, (2) strict supervision of troops and staff of the Public Safety Bureau at Taku, or possibly, (3) immediate dismissal of local Chinese authorities responsible for the acts, (4) indemnity for damages suffered by the Japanese residents, (5) immediate cessation of anti-Japanese acts by troops and police, and (6) assurances for the future.

The Japanese Consul does not expect the incident to develop into serious proportions but does regard it as indicative of the anti-Japanese attitude of Sung's army. He stated that, contrary to press reports, there has been no increase of Japanese troops at Tangku.

JOHNSON

500.A15A5/602 : Telegram

The Ambassador in China (Johnson) to the Secretary of State

PEIPING, January 9, 1936—6 p. m.
[Received January 9—10 : 43 a. m.]

11. Department's 4, January 7, 7 p. m.

1. I have heard no hint of any proposal for a non-aggression pact. I have no reason to believe that situation has changed from that set forth in my telegram No. 72 of November 11, 2 p. m., sent from Nanking, [13] setting forth the character of the three-point policy reported at the time to have been accepted by the Japanese Cabinet, communicated to the Japanese diplomatic, military and naval representatives in China and to the Chinese Ambassador to Japan when the latter was about to return to China. I was given to understand while in Nanking in November that the Chinese Government indicated its willingness to discuss these matters with the Japanese Government provided that the Japanese Government would (a), treat China as a sovereign nation, and (b), lay before Chinese Government a concrete proposal elaborating the three points.

2. In his telegram No. 160 of December 31, 11 a.m.[14] Peck reports that a proposal for the fundamental readjustment of Sino-Japanese relations through proper diplomatic channels had been made by the Chinese Government to the Japanese Government. I am instructing Nanking by telegram to make discreet inquiry as to the exact nature of the proposals said to have been put forward by the Chinese Government. If in fact they include a suggestion for a nonaggression pact between China and Japan, I would suspect that a suggestion may have been put forward to counter a claim made by the Japanese that the Chinese have entered into some kind of an agreement with Soviet Russia against Japan. But I am extremely doubtful that the Sino-Japanese controversy can be reduced to such a simple formula as that suggested by Craigie. There is no evidence locally that the Japanese intended to abandon their plans to achieve a portion of domination on the Asiatic Continent, and particularly in China. I doubt whether Japan will use actual military force to accomplish this pur-

---

[13] *Foreign Relations*, 1935, vol. III, p. 404.
[14] *Ibid.*, p. 502.

pose except by way of threat or bluff. Thus far the Japanese military have succeeded in coercing local Chinese authorities to assent orally or in writing to situations [permitting] Japanese encouraged autonomy movements to be undertaken (1st) under the so-called Tangku truce;[15] (2d) under the so-called agreement between Ho Ying Chin and [General Umetsu in 1935?][16] and (3d) under the settlement of the Chahar [dispute?] of June 27th [17] and the Japanese military threaten to meet with force any attempt on the part of the Nationalist Chinese Government to suppress these autonomous movements in North China as being in contravention of the above-mentioned three agreements. The Japanese have thus succeeded in obtaining a certain legalization of their military needs in North China which can be extended more or less indefinitely.

3. Japan, Soviet Russia and Great Britain are the three countries immediately involved. Expansion of Japanese interests on the Asiatic Continent will inevitably clash (1st) with the interests of Soviet Russia in the north and (2d) with the interests of Great Britain as the result of interests spread southward. The Japanese are proceeding with their eyes open and have thrown into the discard the League Covenant,[18] the Nine Power Treaty and the Kellogg Pact [19] in order to be free to carry out their policy. It would be absurd for us or the British to accept a non-aggression [pact?] as guaranteeing Japanese abandonment of ambitious plans on the Asiatic mainland.

4. I agree with Davis. The political basis for Japan's acceptance of the League Covenant was the Shantung provisions of the Versailles Treaty.[20] The political basis for the acceptance by Japan and the United States of the naval agreement of 1922[21] was the Nine Power Treaty and the agreement regarding non-fortification of our possessions in the Pacific.[22] Japan's recent attitude toward the Covenant of the League of Nations, the Nine Power Treaty and the Naval Treaty does not in my opinion offer reasonable ground for belief that the political basis offered by Craigie would be of any value.

JOHNSON

---

[15] Signed May 31, 1933, *Foreign Relations*, Japan, 1931–1941, vol. I, p. 120.
[16] See Embassy's despatch No. 332, March 27, p. 89.
[17] See telegram No. 321, June 27, 1935, 4 p. m., from the Minister in China, *Foreign Relations*, 1935, vol. III, p. 280.
[18] *Foreign Relations*, The Paris Peace Conference, 1919, vol. XIII, p. 69.
[19] Signed at Paris, August 27, 1928, *Foreign Relations*, 1928, vol. I, p. 153.
[20] See articles 156–158 of the peace treaty with Germany signed June 28, 1919, *Foreign Relations*, The Paris Peace Conference, 1919, vol. XIII, pp. 55, 298.
[21] Signed at Washington, February 6, 1922, *Foreign Relations*, 1922, vol. I, p. 247.
[22] See article XIX of the naval treaty, *ibid.*, pp. 247, 252.

500.A15A5/603 : Telegram

The Ambassador in Japan (Grew) to the Secretary of State

Tokyo, January 9, 1936—6 p. m.
[Received January 9—1:40 p. m.]

7. Department's 2, January 7, 7 p. m.[23]

1. The Embassy has no knowledge of the treaty negotiations indicated. (See, however, Embassy's 232, December 7, noon.[24])

2. The Chinese Chargé d'Affaires in Tokyo about 10 days ago is reported to have proposed to the Japanese Foreign Office a meeting in Nanking to discuss the Sino-Japanese situation. The Foreign Office before acceding desired a list of the points to be discussed which the Nanking Government has not yet produced. Suma [Consul General] in Shanghai [*Nanking*], has come to Tokyo for consultation and Ariyoshi[25] is reported due here on January 20.

3. My comments on Craigie's ideas as personally expressed to Davis are as follows:

The Japanese military program in North China has not been moving smoothly. The attempt to include the five provinces in the autonomy movement failed. The professors and students movement has manifested a solidarity and determination which took the military by surprise and although they allegedly discount its importance it has caused embarrassment. The Japanese have failed in their immediate objective. Their determination eventually to dominate North China is no less strong but they do not visualize accomplishing this end by military occupation which would greatly increase expenses and would necessarily weaken their defensive manpower in Manchuria against Soviet Russia as well as inviting possible sanctions by foreign powers. It therefore appears possible that their tactics may now assume a different form in which the conclusion of a nonaggression pact entailing Chinese acceptance of the *status quo* in Manchuria with perhaps some separate agreement for the acceptance of one or more Japanese military advisers at least in Hopei might eventuate. The foregoing is however pure conjecture based on recent developments. I am sceptical as to the likelihood of the conclusion of such a pact.

If such a pact should materialize the present treaty structure in the relation of the powers to China would presumably in effect have become obsolete. It would then be the better part of wisdom to shape our policy having in mind the long future rather than the past and immediate present—in other words to secure the most effective guarantee of the future protection of our interests in the Far East in general and of our relations with Japan in particular.

---

[23] See telegram No. 4 of the same date to the Ambassador in China, p. 3.
[24] Not printed.
[25] Akira Ariyoshi, Japanese Ambassador in China.

I am not prepared without further study to evaluate all the implications of a non-aggression pact with Japan which would presumably be based on the fundamental principles already subscribed to in the Kellogg-Briand Pact. If however as Craigie opines the present naval *status quo* might be secured through the conclusion of bilateral pacts between Japan, Great Britain and the United States, I do not think that the idea should be turned aside without the most careful consideration. The time is obviously coming when we must seriously reconsider our whole future outlook and policy in the Far East and although such a reconsideration may raise questions which now, as Davis stated, appear insoluble I am inclined to feel that their alleged insolubility is predicated more on the difficulties of adjusting ourselves to new facts and conditions, however unwelcome these facts and conditions may be, than upon insuperable obstacles. If the Chinese Government should enter such an agreement as Craigie believes "probable in the near future" the new facts and conditions suggested above would then seem to have definitely materialized.

Repeated to Peiping.

GREW

500.A15A5/605 : Telegram

The Chairman of the American Delegation (Davis) to the Secretary of State

LONDON, January 10, 1936—1 a.m.
[Received January 9—9 : 35 p.m.]

40. Supplementing my 39, Jan. 9, 7 p.m.[26] Eden told me it was his opinion that the so-called negotiations between China and Japan for a non-aggression pact were not as serious a matter as Craigie thought and that in a talk with the Chinese Ambassador he gathered the impression that the Chinese are discussing this idea in order to play for time but without any serious intention of consummating such a pact.

DAVIS

793.94/7635 : Telegram

The Counselor of Embassy in China (Peck) to the Secretary of State

NANKING, January 10, 1936—10 a.m.
[Received January 10—7 : 45 a.m.]

10. The Soviet Ambassador told me last night he had received information that the Japanese intend very shortly to land troops at

---

[26] Vol. I, p. 26.

Foochow and Tsingtau. Jabin Hsu of the Ministry of Finance could not confirm this but said the Japanese are tampering with naval officers under Admiral Shen, the mayor of Tsingtau, in effort to bring about declaration of autonomy by the Tsingtau Special Municipality. Repeated to Peiping.

PECK

793.94/7657 : Telegram

The Ambassador in China (Johnson) to the Secretary of State

PEIPING, January 13, 1936—4 p.m.
[Received January 13—2 : 10 p.m.]

15. 1. Doihara [27] arrived yesterday at Tientsin. Vice Chief of Staff of Kwantung army Itagaki arrived Tientsin January 9. Manchukuo Vice Minister for Foreign Affairs Ohashi arrived in Peiping January 4, subsequently visiting Taiyuanfu and Tsinanfu, and has allegedly returned to Manchuria. According to some reports, Itagaki has visited Tsinanfu and Tsingtau, meeting Military Attaché Isogai at the latter place.

2. These movements of important Japanese have aroused apprehension that fresh developments in the extension of Japanese control are imminent.

3. The following reasonable explanation has been advanced by a junior Japanese diplomatic official. Ohashi's trip is without much significance as he came for the purpose of "explaining" Manchukuo to Chinese leaders and without permission of the Kwantung army. Itagaki came to solve the internal Japanese military problems and will return soon to Manchuria. He confirms reports of jealousy of the Japanese North China garrison of the Kwantung army's direction of affairs in North China. However, Doihara has come to stay until the powers of the Hopei-Chahar Political Council are satisfactorily enlarged, that is, until the desired degree of autonomy has been attained in finance and in foreign affairs, which include closer relations with Manchukuo and agreement for action against Communism, and in economy.

4. Reports continue to be received to the effect that Li Shou Hsin and tractable Mongols are beginning or will shortly begin to separate Inner Mongolia in Suiyuan from Chinese authority as they have apparently done successfully in Chahar.

To Tokyo by mail.

JOHNSON

[27] Maj. Gen. Kenji Doihara, head of the Japanese military mission at Mukden.

793.94/7661 : Telegram

The Ambassador in China (Johnson) to the Secretary of State

PEIPING, January 14, 1936—4 p.m.
[Received January 14—2 : 55 p.m.]

17. Embassy's 15, January 13, 4 p.m.

1. It has been announced that General Sung will appoint (without Nanking's approval) Shih Yu San as commander of the Peace Preservation Corps of Peiping. Sung has asked, however, that the Government cancel the existing order for Shih's arrest. Shih is regarded as a renegade and has frequently caused disturbances.

2. There are reports that Sun Tien Ying, who revolted in 1934, and Liu Kuei-tang, who ravaged the countryside in that year, may be given posts by Sung.

3. The Economic Committee of the Hopei-Chahar Political Council was inaugurated January 11th. It is understood that its first problem is to assist the shopkeepers of Peiping, of whom 5,000 are in difficulties, to tide over Chinese New Year (January 24).

4. It is reported that the Foreign Affairs Committee of the Council will be inaugurated January 15 or 16 with Chen Chung Fu as head. Chen who has been living recently in Tientsin, resided 20 years in Japan where he assisted Sun Yat Sen prior to the revolution. He is said to be a violent opponent of Chiang Kai Shek.

5. It is understood that Sung and Itagaki plan to leave Peiping together today or tomorrow for Tientsin for discussion of the North China situation.

JOHNSON

793.94/7663 : Telegram

The Ambassador in China (Johnson) to the Secretary of State

PEIPING, January 15, 1936—noon.
[Received January 15—9 : 15 a.m.]

18. Embassy's 17, January 14, 4 p.m.

1. In addition to appointments previously reported, Sung Che Yuan has appointed his own men to important posts in several other organizations which control revenue. These posts were previously held by appointees of Nanking.

2. The character of Sung's regime is becoming increasingly autonomous in line with Japanese desires. A junior Chinese official under Sung states that the latter intends to retain all revenues of Hopei and Chahar, remitting none to Nanking, including postal and customs revenue. The local postal authorities received notice yesterday from

Sung that revenue from the sale of revenue stamps should not be forwarded to Nanking. However, the local customs authorities have not yet received a comparable order.

Repeated to Nanking and Tokyo.

JOHNSON

500.A15A5/654

The Ambassador in China (Johnson) to the Secretary of State

No. 180   PEIPING, January 15, 1936.
[Received February 10.]

SIR: I have the honor to refer to the Department's confidential telegram No. 4 of January 7, 7 p.m., and to my telegraphic comments thereon contained in the Embassy's No. 11, January 9, 6 p.m., and to make the following additional comments on the suggestions therein raised.

I must confess that I was somewhat astonished at Craigie's suggestion regarding the possibility of a tripartite non-aggression pact as a political basis for a naval settlement. . . . I know of course that Great Britain is exceedingly worried about the future of British interests in the Far East, in the light of Japanese expansion onto the Asiatic Continent, but it seems to me that the British will be grasping at a straw indeed if they are now brought to the belief that a non-aggression pact will protect those interests from Japanese encroachment. It is possible that the British know something that we do not know, but I am wondering where they get their information and why they are not more open with us. Certainly such conversations as I have had with my British colleague have not revealed any beliefs on his part in regard to the probabilities of Japanese activity which I myself have not entertained.

I do not want to be considered as one who believes that the American Government should bestir itself to use force to save China from probable Japanese conquest. I do not shut my eyes to the possibility that anything may happen here. Even a Sino-Japanese alliance is within the realm of possibilities in this situation, an eventuality which I have suggested as the only alternative to a Sino-Japanese armed conflict, assuming that the present situation is to go on. But a Sino-Japanese alliance would be characterized by the relations of a master to a slave, rather than by the relations which would ordinarily exist between two peoples equal parties to an alliance. I do not wish to be considered as one who clings to a belief in the permanence of the status here and who therefore is unwilling to accept new developments with all that they imply, and unprepared to entertain new understandings more in keeping with the new state of affairs. But it seems to me it is not we who should take the initiative and abandon the past at this moment. It is not we who should anticipate the new situation. Little or no harm will come to us if we await the outcome, for the initiative lies with China. If the outcome is to be a Sino-Japanese alliance, then will be time enough for us to cut our cloth to the new requirements.

It was Japan that pushed into the discard the understandings upon which the Naval Treaty of 1922 was based. What assurance have we that Japan will now be any more ready to accept a new political basis upon which to found agreements insuring the security of the interests of the United States and Great Britain? We are not yet suppliants in the conflict that has begun between the "haves" and "have nots" for a redistribution of the resources so necessary to the security of modern nations. I feel that it is absurd to believe that Sino-Japanese relations can yet be reduced to the simple formula of a non-aggression pact. Living here in the area where the policy of Japan is being persistently and consistently effectuated by the leaders of Japan's military, I do not observe any indication that the said military are abandoning that policy. On the contrary, the Japanese military, particularly the representatives of the Kwantung Army, are as active as ever, perhaps more active; for Peiping had a visit the other day from General Itagaki, who came by air after having visited Tsingtao and Tsinan. He spent four hours with General Sung Che-yuan. He also called personally upon the comparatively unknown Yin Ju-keng who heads the autonomous government at Tungchow. I do not know what they talked of; I can only surmise. But I know that General Itagaki is reputed to be the real brains of the Japanese Army in Manchuria, and he would not be here unless serious and important business of the Kwantung Army was being discussed, and I have no doubt what that business must be. His visit synchronized with a visit from Ohashi, formerly a minor secretary in the Japanese diplomatic service in Peiping but more recently a Vice Minister of Foreign Affairs in the Government of "Manchukuo". These activities on the part of Itagaki and Ohashi may possibly be the Kwantung Army's reaction to this alleged suggestion of a non-aggression pact, but they confirm my belief that the Japanese military are not going to be thwarted in the carrying out of their plans by such a pact.

It will not hurt the United States and Great Britain to await the event. I feel sure that it will be harmful for us to attempt to bury our heads in the sand of a tripartite non-aggression pact at this moment. I accept the statement that Japan does not want to become involved in a military operation here in North China at the present time, because I believe that the Japanese military want to make themselves secure against Soviet Russia before they proceed farther south. The modern airplane has made Japan's situation extremely vulnerable.

It can no longer be considered a ship, but from a military point of view must be looked upon as a missile, and therefore stopped before it is launched. Japan cannot, from a military point of view and in her present state of suspicion, feel secure within her own shores until she has placed herself in a position where she can stop hostile aircraft before they can leave the ground.

Russia, Great Britain, the United States and Holland control the greater part of the world's resources in iron, oil, coal and cotton, which are so necessary to national security in this age. Italy, Germany and Japan have none of these resources; they are dependent upon us. They are over-populated, in debt, desperate, and determined. It is not to their interest, severally or together, to make common cause with Soviet Russia, the United States, Holland and Great Britain to make secure the present control of those resources. I would as soon make an agreement with a starving family next door whereby we would mutually undertake not to seize one another's bread, as enter into an arrangement with any or all of these three countries not to aggress on one another's interests. Some other means of reaching security has to be found.

I confess my inability to know just what basis for such an agreement is open to us, but I feel that there can be no basis of agreement until we can be certain that the powers in question are willing to abandon the obviously aggressive ideas which they now entertain. And nothing but force, economic or physical, seems to be adequate to meet the kind of force which these powers naturally believe in and are ready to use. There is talk in some quarters of the advisability of a redistribution of world resources for the benefit of all, but I have yet to see any worthwhile suggestion as to how this redistribution is to be brought about without involving the more difficult problem of the exploitation of those resources.

The Philippine Islands possess in considerable quantities the resources of oil, coal, iron and gold which Japan needs. Perhaps here in the East these resources of the Philippines are the only remaining unpreempted resources of their kind. We never exploited them, because we did not need them. We were a dog in the manger while we occupied the Islands. I doubt whether the Filipino will ever exploit these resources . . . I understand that Quezon,[28] with the assistance of former Governor Harrison[29] who is now his economic adviser, has some idea of developing these resources by concessions. It should be possible for American ingenuity and American capital to exploit these resources of the Philippines for the benefit of China and Japan and the Filipino, but I wonder whether the American

---

[28] Manuel L. Quezon, President of the Philippine Commonwealth.
[29] Francis Burton Harrison.

can do this with Filipino labor. I do not know. Perhaps the experience of those who have developed the Benguet gold fields with the aid of the mountain tribes holds the answer to this question. But the coal and iron and oil of the Philippines cannot always remain undeveloped; and if the Filipino or the American does not do the job, then the Japanese will and must. This problem of exploitation at the present time is one that is closely allied with the needs growing out of nationalism and national requirements, and must be considered in any suggested redistribution of world resources that may be undertaken for the purpose of bringing about world security.

Respectfully yours,   NELSON TRUSLER JOHNSON

793.94/7784

The Consul General at Canton (Spiker) to the Ambassador in China (Johnson) [30]

No. 92   CANTON, January 15, 1936.

SIR: I have the honor to enclose for the Embassy's information a copy of the Chinese text and this office's English translation of a secret document [31] concerning the alleged activities of the Japanese looking to the establishment of an autonomous government of "South China", with its beginnings in the Province of Fukien. A copy of the secret document was handed to me by a reliable informant upon my assurances that the document would be handled in strictest confidence and that every care would be taken to preserve its secrecy. For this reason, no mention is made in this despatch of the name of my informant who, it is to be observed, is an official occupying a position of authority and who has proved a reliable informant in the past. This office is inclined to accept his assurances that the secret report is an entirely authentic one submitted by secret Government agents in Fukien. I am informed that these agents, posing as enemies of Marshal Chiang Kai-shek and of the Nanking regime, are being accepted by the Japanese agents as malcontents who may be depended upon to join the "Anti-Japanese Associations" which will shortly transfer their opposition to the allegedly "pro-Japanese" Chiang Kai-shek and the present Nanking Government. Those back of the scheme appear to believe that by this subterfuge it will be a comparatively simple matter to arouse local opposition to Nanking's appointees in Fukien and to overthrow the existing government regime there, making room for such of the numerous malcontents

---

[30] Copy transmitted to the Department by the Ambassador in China in his despatch No. 199, January 30; received March 9.
[31] Enclosures not printed.

as may be approved by the Japanese as puppets in the proposed new "autonomous government".

The secret report is of a business-like tenor, admits that full information has not yet been procured by the secret agents and, in general, rings true as compared with the usual flamboyant reports of Chinese subordinates to their superiors in relation to the accomplishment of tasks to which the former have been set.

While the events described in press reports may be entirely disassociated from the scheme described in the secret report, this office has been interested in the possible relationship of recent newspaper reports similar to the following one which appeared in the *South China Morning Post* of January 7, 1936, under a Canton date line:

"Communists in southern Fukien have looted the hamlets around Yung Ting (in southwestern Fukien close to northern border of Kwangtung Province), their leader being 'General' Lee Tien-hui.

"Lee Tien-hui's men are equipped with new rifles and wear smart uniforms. The Communist officers told the villagers that they had instructions from the 'Central Authorities' to summon a big anti-Japanese meeting.

"After plundering the border villages, the Reds escaped back into Fukien taking several hostages with them.

"Another Communist band is in league with pirates in northern Fukien, by whom they are supplied with smuggled arms."

In relation to such news reports, it is to be observed that smuggling activities which have long existed between Taiwan and the Fukien coast, which have involved Taiwanese in Fukien, and which, at times, have resulted in the intervention of the Japanese consular, naval and other authorities, would indicate the feasibility of landing arms and ammunitions for the use of malcontents in Fukien, as described in the secret report.

My informant states that definite information has been received to show that, while the Japanese Army is to have control over the establishment of autonomous governments in the north and the interior of China, this task, in relation to the southern coastal provinces, has been assigned to the Japanese naval authorities in cooperation with the Taiwan Government.

Information is now being gathered in relation to Japanese activities in South China in general and will be transmitted in a subsequent despatch.

A copy of this despatch is being supplied in strict confidence to the American Consulates at Foochow, Amoy and Swatow, and to the Commander of the South China Patrol of the United States Asiatic Fleet.

Respectfully yours,

C. J. SPIKER

793.94/7668 : Telegram

The Ambassador in China (Johnson) to the Secretary of State

PEIPING, January 16, 1936—4 p.m.
[Received January 16—11 : 10 a.m.]

21. 1. Conversations continue at Tientsin with Sung, Hsiao Chen Ying,[32] Doihara, Tada [33] and others participating. Developments are kept secret.

2. Various Japanese observers express the opinion that Yin Ju Keng's area [34] will not be merged with the Hopei-Chahar Political Council until the latter reaches a degree of autonomy comparable to that of the former.

3. It is reported in the press that Sugiyama, Vice Chief of Staff at Tokyo, will shortly visit Manchuria and North China. The informant mentioned in the Embassy's despatch 3235 of January 4, 1935,[35] states that Sugiyama is one of the four or five most influential Japanese military officers and that his primary purpose is to study the Government of China situation from the viewpoint of a possible Russian military advance. The informant states that Japanese military officers believe that Russia is preparing to attack Manchukuo through Outer Mongolia, an opinion which the informant does not hold, and that therefore the Japanese military are now more interested in Chahar and Suiyuan than in other parts of North China. He said that Doihara will remain in Tientsin to advise Sung until March when he will be transferred to Japan to command a brigade. He also states that the Japanese are still dissatisfied with Sung.

To Tokyo by mail.

JOHNSON

793.94/7674 : Telegram

The Counselor of Embassy in China (Peck) to the Secretary of State

NANKING, January 17, 1936—9 a.m.
[Received 11 : 15 a.m.]

19. My 17, January 16, 10 a.m.[35] It is learned from apparently reliable sources that on January 15 the student representatives presented questions and "demands" by delegations from different localities and that the following 10 subjects were those in which the greatest number of delegations concurred:

[32] Mayor of Tientsin.
[33] Maj. Gen. Hajao Tada, commanding the Japanese North China garrison.
[34] East Hopei demilitarized districts.
[35] Not printed.

1. Referring to General Chiang's statement to the Kuomintang Congress on November 19 that "we shall not talk lightly of sacrifices until we are driven to the last extremity which makes sacrifices inevitable", the students inquired at what stage the limit of endurance would be reached and resistance to Japanese aggression would begin.

2. They inquired concerning the exact extent of China's military preparedness. They presented the following "petitions" or "demands".

3. That traitors be punished.

4. That autonomy movements in North China be suppressed.

5. That revision of school textbooks in North China to meet Japanese wishes be opposed.

6. That the freedom of the press be restored.

7. That open diplomacy be practiced instead of secret diplomacy.

8. That the Government do its best to organize the Chinese masses.

9. That the greatest care be taken in readjusting Sino-Japanese relations.

10. That the Hopei-Chahar Political Council be abolished.

General Chiang spoke to the student representatives from January 16, 3 p.m. to January 16, 7 p.m., the seven main points of his address being as follows:

(1) War against Japan is only a question of time and when it comes the whole nation will be mobilized and responsibility will not rest on the students alone.

(2) China at present is inferior to Japan in this detail of preparedness and organization and war cannot be declared recklessly.

(3) Reviewing the history of Sino-Japanese relations, he said that since the Sino-Japanese war in 1894 Japan has been determined to invade China for, in the view of the Japanese, China is Japan's only economic outlet.

(4) The so-called "continental policy" has become the traditional policy of Japan and it means "down with the Kuomintang and down with Chiang Kai Shek".

(5) China, also, has a traditional policy, which is the policy of the Kuomintang, no surrender to Japan. There were no secret clauses in the Tangku truce and no such thing exists as the so-called Ho-Umetsu agreement.[36]

(6) To meet the special situation, education in China will be on an extraordinary basis designed to meet the special needs.

(7) The entire nation should be reassured that Chiang Kai Shek will never surrender to Japan nor sign any agreement injuring the State. He does not fear death for the cause.

The press is under strict orders to publish no information regarding statement made by Chiang and I suggest that this message be treated temporarily as confidential. Repeat to Peking.

PECK

---

[36] Alleged agreement in 1935 between General Ho Ying-chin, Chinese Minister of War, and General Yoshijiro Umetsu, commanding the Japanese North China garrison.

793.94/7677 : Telegram

The Ambassador in China (Johnson) to the Secretary of State

PEIPING, January 19, 1936—noon.
[Received January 19—2 : 37 a.m.]

25. Embassy's 18, January 15, noon.

1. The Consul General at Tientsin reports that he has been informed by the Commissioner of Customs at Tientsin that the latter received written notice January 18 from the Hopei-Chahar Political Council that he turn over to the Council all of the customs revenue for January and his balance.

It is also reliably stated that the Salt Commissioner has received similar instructions.

Repeated to Nanking and Tokyo.

JOHNSON

793.94/7679 : Telegram

The Ambassador in China (Johnson) to the Secretary of State

PEIPING, January 20, 1936—3 p.m.
[Received January 20—10 : 30 a.m.]

26. Embassy's 25, January 19, noon. Local postal official states that his office has received no order from the Hopei-Chahar Political Council to turn over revenue other than revenue obtained from revenue stamps reported in Embassy's 18, January 15, noon.

2. Foreign Affairs Committee of the Council was inaugurated this morning. It has 10 members with Chen Chung Fu as chairman. (See paragraph 4 of Embassy's 17, January 14, 4 p. m.). The chairman of the Economic Committee (reference paragraph 3 of the above-mentioned telegram) is Hsiao Chen Ying.

3. According to one of Sung Che Yuan's subordinates, the office of the special delegate of the Ministry of Foreign Affairs at Peiping will soon be abolished as a result of the inauguration of the Foreign Affairs Committee.

4. The Peiping-Tientsin garrison headquarters was abolished January 15 and the Hopei-Chahar Pacification headquarters, of which Sung is Commissioner, was inaugurated the same day.

5. The Embassy is informed that the dispute between Yin Ju Keng and the Peiping-Mukden Railway over railway revenue from that part of the line which runs through the demilitarized zone has been settled by the railway agreeing to pay Yin $100,000 per month and that Yin's railway office has been abolished.

By mail to Tokyo.

JOHNSON

893.00/13346 : Telegram

The Counselor of Embassy in China (Peck) to the Secretary of State

NANKING, January 21, 1936—4 p.m.
[Received January 21—11 a.m.]

22. 1. Under date of January 17 the National Government *Gazette* published "provisional general principles governing the organization of the Hopei-Chahar Political Affairs Commission" which define the Commission's functions in a general way only and leave the Commission, from a legalistic point of view, an amorphous organ awkwardly superimposed upon the Hopei and Chahar Provincial Governments and the municipalities of Peiping and Tientsin. The "principles" state that the Commission: (1) is established to control "all political affairs" of the two Provinces and two municipalities named; (2) shall have from 17 to 21 members with a chairman to assume general control of its affairs assisted by a standing committee of from three to five persons, all members to be appointed by Nanking; (3) shall temporarily have three departments—a secretariat and departments of political affairs and finance; (4) may establish special committees for special questions and may "engage" the personnel therefor and may also have a "certain number" of advisers, counselors and experts; and (5) may "within the scope of laws and ordinances of the central authorities draft laws and regulations for exclusive use and submit them to the National Government for approval and record".

2. Full translation will go forward by mail.[38]

PECK

762.94/68

The Ambassador in Germany (Dodd) to the Secretary of State

No. 2617　　　　　　　　　　　　　　　BERLIN, January 22, 1936.
[Received February 1.]

SIR: I have the honor to transmit herewith a clipping [39] from the January 20 edition of the (London) *Morning Post*, with regard to an alleged military agreement between Germany and Japan.

We discussed the clipping confidentially with the Berlin correspondent of the *Post*. He stated that his information came from a responsible ministerial source and he had believed it to be substantially accurate when sending it to his paper. Since then the substance matter was denied orally by the Foreign Office in a telephone conversa-

---

[38] Not printed.
[39] Not reprinted; but see quotation in report by Military Attaché in Germany, January 30, p. 31.

tion which the *Post* correspondent had yesterday. Nevertheless, he had now received further confirmation and believed that the possibility of a German-Japanese agreement in some such form is credited in London official circles.

We have been quite suspicious for some time of an arrangement of this character but have had no definite or satisfactory confirmation. Several days ago, however, we learned from an unofficial but extremely well informed German source that some such arrangement was arrived at last October or early November between Ribbentrop[40] and the Japanese, which, our informant said, was at Japanese instigation although not as wide in scope as the Japanese would have desired.

I might also add that the Naval and Military Attachés told us recently that they had been much struck with a dinner party at the Japanese Naval Attaché's a short time ago which all the highest German naval officers attended, a most unprecedented happening in Berlin, we understand, where admirals and the like do not apparently honor naval attachés with their company at dinner, etc.

With these indications supporting our suspicion, we have thought it worth while to send their substance to the American Delegation at the London Naval Conference to see if Mr. Davis can give us any further light on this score. Meanwhile we are pursuing the matter locally in the course of our effort to try and keep the Department currently informed of any developments in German-Japanese relations.

Respectfully yours,   WILLIAM E. DODD

693.94244/2

The Ambassador in China (Johnson) to the Secretary of State

No. 195   PEIPING, January 22, 1936.
                                                [Received February 24.]

SIR: I have the honor to enclose a copy of despatch No. 134 of January 16, 1936, from the Consulate General at Tientsin,[41] regarding a case of sugar-smuggling which occurred at the 15th U. S. Infantry camp at Chinwangtao on the night of January 6–7, 1936. It will be observed that, according to the report of the American Army officer concerned, the persons in charge of the smuggling operations were Japanese.

In this connection it may be remarked that the Taikoo Sugar Refining Company, a British organization which has a very large trade in sugar in China, is reported now to have its warehouse in Tientsin filled with stocks, "without being able to sell a pound" by reason of the activities of sugar-smugglers in North China.

Respectfully yours,   NELSON TRUSLER JOHNSON

---

[40] Joachim von Ribbentrop, Special Ambassador at Large for Adolf Hitler.
[41] Not printed.

793.94/7688 : Telegram

The Counselor of Embassy in China (Peck) to the Secretary of State

NANKING, January 23, 1936—noon.
[Received January 23—9 a. m.]

23. 1. Following statement for the press has been received from the Foreign Office:

"Interview by press correspondents concerning Mr. Koki Hirota's [42] reference, in his speech before the Japanese House of Peers last Tuesday, to alleged concurrence by China to Japanese three principles vis-à-vis China, one of which is stated to be China's recognition of the puppet state of 'Manchukuo', a spokesman of the Waichiaopu stated as follows:

'By the three principles Mr. Hirota must have meant those three points which he put forward to General Chiang Tso Pin, then Chinese Ambassador to Tokyo, in September 1935 by way of reply to the latter's proposals. It will be recalled that in the fall of last year the Chinese Government proposed, through Ambassador Chiang, to the Japanese Government certain fundamental measures for the improvement of the relations of the two countries. In reply, Mr. Hirota informed Ambassador Chiang to the effect that the Chinese proposals, in principle, were not unacceptable to Japan but that before Japan's acceptance of the same China must agree to three things:

1. China must abandon her policy of playing one foreign country against another;
2. China must respect the fact of the existence of the "Manchukuo";
3. China and Japan must jointly devise effective measures for preventing the spread of Communism in regions in the northern part of China.

However, these three points were considered by the Chinese Government as being too vague in their phraseology to serve as a subject for useful discussion. So the Japanese Government was requested to state the concrete terms embodied in these points, but up to the present time Japanese Government have not yet done so. Mr. Hirota's recent statement to the effect that China has indicated her concurrence to these points is, therefore, without foundation. On the other hand, General Chang Chun shortly after assuming his duties as Minister for Foreign Affairs, has proposed that Sino-Japanese negotiations should be conducted according to regular procedure and through diplomatic channels with a view to the fundamental readjustment of the relations between the two countries. Now in his recent speech before the House of Peers, Mr. Hirota not only expressed concurrence to General Chang's proposal but also reiterated Japanese fundamental policy of non-menace and non-aggression against neighboring countries in the hope of restoring the relations of the two countries to normalcy as well as adjusting their mutual

---

[42] Japanese Minister for Foreign Affairs.

interests. From this standpoint, there seems to be no divergence of views between the two sides. With these as a starting point in the negotiations between China and Japan there can be no doubt that the relations between the two countries will be greatly improved'."

PECK

793.94/7685 : Telegram

The Consul General at Shanghai (Davis) to the Secretary of State

SHANGHAI, January 23, 1936—4 p. m.
[Received January 23—7 : 10 p. m.]

51. Mayor Wu told me this morning that the Japanese Consul General called on him recently saying that he had instructions from Tokyo to adopt a stronger attitude in dealing with the local Chinese authorities and that these instructions were issued because the attitude of the Nanking Government toward Japan had changed. See my despatch No. 66, January 10th.[43]

Repeated to Department and Nanking.

DAVIS

793.94/7687 : Telegram

The Ambassador in China (Johnson) to the Secretary of State

PEIPING, January 23, 1936—5 p.m.
[Received January 23—10 a.m.]

33. Embassy's 21, January 16, 4 p. m. Progress of Japanese activities and Sino-Japanese negotiations and conversations in Hopei and other provinces of North China continue to be obscure. It is believed that the Japanese are continuing their efforts to obtain the autonomy of the five provinces but find Sung, Han,[44] and Yen[45] difficult. It is thought that, if Sung does not come to terms with the Japanese, he will be forced out of Hopei. It is possible that the appointment of Shih Yu-san as commander of Peace Preservation Corps of Peiping, presumably at Japanese instance, may be a preparatory measure for removing Sung if necessary. It is said that, disregarding their personal feelings, there are important elements among the subordinates of Sung, Han, and Yen strongly opposed to submitting to the Japanese.

2. Apparently Teh Wang[46] has not yet declared independence. (See Embassy's 24, January 19, 11 a.m.[43]) According to a competent

---

[43] Not printed.
[44] General Han Fu-chu, Chairman of the Shantung Provincial government.
[45] Marshal Yen Hsi-shan, director of peace preservation in Shansi.
[46] Prince Teh, Secretary General of the Inner Mongolian Autonomous Government Committee.

Chinese observer, the drive of Li Shou Hsin into Suiyuan awaits the melting of snows, one purpose of taking Suiyuan being to bring pressure on Yen to obtain his acquiescence to the Japanese program. The rumored appointment of the renegade Sun Tien Ying to a military post in southern Hopei may also be a potential threat directed toward Yen.

3. There are no indications here that the Kwantung army's plans for North China will be altered by possible Sino-Japanese conversations at Nanking.

By mail to Nanking and Tokyo.

JOHNSON

893.01 Outer Mongolia/57

The Ambassador in Japan (Grew) to the Secretary of State

No. 1648   TOKYO, January 23, 1936.
[Received February 10.]

SIR: I have the honor to report that, according to press despatches which have emanated for the most part from Hsinking, clashes between armed "Manchukuo" and Outer Mongolian forces have occurred on January 8, 14, 15, 16, and 17 at various places in the frontier region. On the last named date it is alleged that a group of more than 100 Mongols was involved; on January 15 seven "Manchukuo" soldiers are said to have been carried off by the Mongols, apparently in reprisal for the previous seizure of Mongol soldiers. The cause of these clashes is not clear, but it is apparent that neither the Mongols nor the Manchurians, each of whom is confident of support from the Soviets and the Japanese, respectively, are at present willing to show any sign of weakness or of a willingness to compromise. If the press may be credited, the language of the notes of protest exchanged between Hsinking and Urga has been intemperate and, on the part of Hsinking at least, there have been threats of action to force Mongolian acceptance of "Manchukuo's" views on the location of the frontier. It is not certain, however, whether that is indeed the primary question at issue in these incidents; it is at least possible that the "Manchukuo" side is endeavoring to determine the extent and nature of the support which the Outer Mongolians are likely to receive from the Soviets.

In addition to the foregoing disturbances reports have been current that a Japanese airplane landed on Soviet territory not far from Vladivostok on January 10 and was detained with its two occupants who were wounded in an effort to abduct a local inhabitant. The press states that the Soviet Ambassador has protested to the Foreign Minister against the landing of this plane and that the Foreign Minister, in his reply, recalled the benefits which acceptance of his proposal for the establishment of a Soviet–"Manchukuo" border commission would entail. The Foreign Minister again referred to this question of establishing a border commission when he addressed the Diet on January 21, but his reference was a non-committal one, leaving in doubt whether or not negotiations are pending. The Embassy will endeavor to obtain further information on this matter when opportunity offers.

Meanwhile, with the border question coming to the fore once more, the Army has published an estimate of the land forces of China, Russia, and Japan, showing plainly the numerical inferiority of the Japanese Army. This, together with the speeches which dealt with military preparedness at the recent session of the Central Executive Committee of the U. S. S. R. in Moscow, has been commented on by several of the Japanese papers which suggest that the Soviet troops should be reduced along the Siberian frontier, that the normal development of Soviet-Japanese relations demands a settlement of the border difficulties, and, in the case of the *Nichi Nichi* at least, that a border commission should in fact be established. This paper stated on January 8th that

"Any ray of hope for the future relations of Japan and the Soviet Union must be based on the proposal of Mr. Koki Hirota, the Foreign Minister, for the establishment of a committee for the settlement of border disputes".

Unfortunately, however, for the establishment of a border commission, Japanese references to this idea still tend to be put in the form of recommendations to the U. S. S. R. for acceptance in toto rather than as proposals for negotiations leading to mutual concession and compromise. Moreover the Japanese still emphasize that a commission would be first concerned with the demarcation of the frontier rather than with the settlement of incidents.*

From the foregoing then it is apparent that there has been an increase in the number and apparent seriousness of border incidents. Owing, however, to the general preoccupation with the Naval Disarmament Conference in London, with the dissolution of the Diet here in Tokyo, and with the progress of events in North China, there has not been an equivalent increase of public anxiety. These other issues are more real and more pressing in the public mind.

The difficulty of obtaining authoritative information as to what is going on in the northwestern corner of "Manchukuo" is of course apparent. There is none available in Tokyo at the moment. Any opinions or predictions are therefore subject to more than the usual

---

* Embassy's despatches No. 1467, September 7, 1935, and No. 1536, Confidential, November 1, 1935. [Footnote in the original; despatches not printed.]

qualifications and are necessarily speculative. Nevertheless two possibilities may be noted on this basis.

In the first place frontier incidents are occurring with increasing frequency along the Manchu-Mongol frontier and with diminishing frequency along the Manchu-Siberian frontier. From a region where the Soviet military preparations are admittedly powerful the center of friction has shifted to the poorly defined Outer Mongolian border where the defenses are relatively untried, to say nothing of the loyalty of the Mongolians to their Soviet tutors. Moreover this shift coincides with a general trend of Japanese interest westward and southward and with an intensified fear on the part of the army of the spread of communist influence in East Asia. The current incidents may be preliminary to an attempt by force to open Outer Mongolia to Japanese influence. An attempt by diplomatic means conclusively failed last summer and autumn.

In the second place, the winter climate of Mongolia with its temperatures of 40 and more degrees below zero renders military operations extremely difficult. Therefore, even if the current incidents should indeed be preliminary to large scale efforts to open Outer Mongolia, the winter season must pass before serious trouble is likely. A breathing spell of some three or four months might reasonably be expected.

However, time and time again in the Far East it has been demonstrated that the reasonable may not be counted upon. The Embassy holds to its previously expressed opinion that no serious trouble between Japan and Soviet Russia is foreseen in the near future †, but so long as armed forces confront each other, so long as frontier incidents occur, it must be repeated that the risk of war is always present. The situation in Outer Mongolia described in this despatch cannot but create a certain degree of anxiety.

Respectfully yours,

JOSEPH C. GREW

500.A15A5/652

The Ambassador in Japan (Grew) to the Secretary of State

No. 1655   TOKYO, January 25, 1936.
[Received February 10.]

SIR: With the withdrawal of the Japanese delegation from the London Naval Disarmament Conference,[48] the relations of the Powers, especially the United States and Great Britain, are entering upon a

---

†Embassy's despatch No. 1630, confidential, January 7, 1936. [Footnote in the original; despatch printed on page 706.]

[48] See vol. I, pp. 22 ff.; see also *Foreign Relations*, Japan, 1931–1941, vol. I, pp. 294–297.

new phase the importance of which, as time goes on, will become increasingly and more insistently acute. Without discussing this matter in the present despatch it may be of interest to touch upon what, so far as the Embassy has been able to judge, has been taking place in Tokyo during the course of the Conference.

The main point seems to be the difference in views between the Naval authorities and the Foreign Office.* These differences represent in concrete form the constant struggle between the military and the civilian authorities to which the Embassy has referred frequently in despatches and telegrams. It is a struggle which forces the admission that the military group, though dominant, is not without a persistent and not wholly ineffectual opposition. The Embassy nevertheless wishes to repeat what it so often has emphasized, namely that the divergence in views which exists between these two groups is one which up to the present has been amply demonstrated to have to do with tactics and methods rather than with objectives. The liberal element, if the civilian authorities can be so described, has shown itself to be precisely as nationalistic and chauvinistic in its aims and purposes as the military element but it cannot be successfully denied that the methods differ to an appreciable degree.

Military character, induced by the very nature of its military training, tends to express itself in much the same manner in whatever country it may be. It seeks to reach its objective by the shortest possible route, to slash and cut its way through obstacles and to waste no time in dealing with the niceties of any situation. This is developed to a higher degree in those countries where the military element is subject to the least restraint and in which the country owes its position in world affairs most recently to feats of military prowess. Such is the case in Japan and it is this factor with which the non-military element, ably led by the Foreign Minister, is constantly contending.

If I have somewhat labored the foregoing point it is in order to find a possible explanation for the apparent inconsistencies with which Mr. Hirota can, from time to time, be charged. I refer especially to the statement which he made to me on January 13 † to the effect that he had won out in his contest with the Navy over immediate withdrawal of the Japanese delegation from London, and that while Admiral Nagano [49] might return to Tokyo he hoped and expected that Ambassador Nagai [50] would remain in the Conference. In the

---

*Embassy's telegram No. 9, January 12, 7 p. m. [Footnote in the original; for telegram, see Foreign Relations, Japan, 1931–1941, vol. I, p. 290.]

† Embassy's telegram No. 11, January 13, 11 p. m. [Footnote in the original; for telegram, see vol. I, p. 32.]

[49] Japanese Chief Delegate to the London Naval Conference.

[50] Japanese Ambassador in France and member of the Naval Conference delegation.

face of what happened immediately thereafter it might appear that Mr. Hirota's statement did not conform to the facts. However, during a conversation with him a few days after that date, and after the announced departure of both Nagano and Nagai from London, Mr. Hirota explained to me that his statement represented what he hoped and believed to be true at the time, namely that conditions would be favorable for Ambassador Nagai to remain.

The facts being what they have proven to be, it can only be surmised that the Foreign Minister's statement to me on January 13 was an expression of a hope rather than a confirmation of the facts.

This does not mean, however, that the Foreign Office did not have its way over the Naval authorities in the method of Japan's withdrawal from the Conference. There is little doubt that without the restraining hand of Mr. Hirota the Navy, left to itself, would have quit the Conference in an atmosphere of ill-feeling and acute irritation, to return to Tokyo in a spirit of truculence and bombast supported enthusiastically by the press. This has definitely been avoided. The press has clearly been subject to restraint ‡ and has been marked by an effort to comment objectively upon the departure of Japan from the Conference and to do so with the minimum recrimination and bitterness. There is also an absence of the boastful spirit § which was so evident in the press two years ago and especially during the early days of 1935 when the question of abrogating the Washington Treaty first became the subject of general discussion.

In thus emphasizing the contribution of the so-called liberal element to Japan's international relations, I do not wish to create the impression that the Embassy has in any way altered its opinion on this subject which was expressed on page 9 [51] of the despatch referred to in the foregoing paragraph, an opinion to which I still subscribe. However, it cannot be denied that there are influences at work in Japan with which the military is forced to reckon.

In reviewing the conclusions drawn from Japan's attitude toward the Conference by Japanese public opinion and Government circles, the one fact which stands out is the unanimous conviction here that the plan which Japan offered was the only one which had to do with actual naval disarmament, that the British and American plans, if adopted, would have had no practical effect whatsoever in this direction, and that nothing short of this accomplishment had any merit whatever. The British unilateral declaration formula was in no sense

---

‡ Embassy's telegram No. 14, January 18, noon. [Footnote in the original; telegram not printed.]

§ Embassy's despatch No. 1102, December 27, 1934, p. 11. [Footnote in the original; for despatch, see *Foreign Relations*, 1935, vol. III, p. 821.]

[51] See paragraph beginning "At this point I should like to," *ibid.*, p. 825.

less unpalatable to the Japanese public than the American plan of a general 20% reduction (the practical reduction in armament effect of which was ignored here), but there is a tendency in the press to feel that the American policy is more antagonistic to Japan than that of Great Britain.

Another feature of the present discussions in the press is the evident apprehension of the possibility of an increasing cooperation between Great Britain and the United States against Japan. This is not yet admitted as a probability but the efforts made by some writers to prove the doubtfulness of this as a possibility reveals the existence of the thought. The *Chugai* of January 16, 1935, states: "Japan's withdrawal from the parley would seem to lead to its isolation and to cooperation between Great Britain and the United States. We grant that Japan will find itself isolated but this does not necessarily mean that the bonds between Great Britain and the United States will be strengthened by stiffening their attitude against this country. On the surface, these two countries stand on common ground in matters relative to disarmament. A close study will show, however, that they do not see eye to eye in regard to the more important questions of disarmament. The policy of the United States is directed against this country. That of Great Britain is not necessarily so directed. Thus it would be almost impossible to accord the fundamental policies of the two countries . . ."[52]

As to the causes behind the attitude of Japan at the Conference and her absolute unyielding attitude upon the question of naval parity, they are many and they do not come within the scope of this despatch. However, much light on this question is thrown by the following remarks, also from the *Chugai* article quoted above: "Another important question to this country is the possible effect of the failure of the Conference on China. It has been customary for it to rely more on Great Britain and the United States following every international conference in which this country is represented. In the present conference this country has adopted a policy which does not give China the slightest cause to believe that Japan is subservient to Great Britain and the United States. Japan's policy in the conference has been independence. Thus it would be hard for China to see in it any sign of weakness. . . ."[52]

Respectfully yours,   JOSEPH C. GREW

---

[52] Omission indicated in the original despatch.

793.94/7693 : Telegram

The Counselor of Embassy in China (Peck) to the Secretary of State

NANKING, January 27, 1936—11 a.m.
[Received January 27—10 a.m.]

24. Isogai, Japanese Military Attaché, interviewed Chiang Kai Shek, January 25, prior to returning to Japan. I have reliable information that he produced the impression that he favors the contention of the Chinese Government that negotiations concerning Sino-Japanese relations should be taken out of the hands of military leaders and returned to regular diplomatic channels. The Chinese attributed this attitude to his being a representative of the War Office and his consequent jealousy of the Kwantung army officers now prominent in Northern negotiations. The Chinese authorities believed that the Japanese Government has decided to follow policy of nibbling and continuous moderate pressure for the time being instead of taking any drastic step. They think that this advice was given by Suma during recent Tokyo visit. Suma himself told a foreign news correspondent after his return to Nanking January 22 that the Japanese Government intended to be "very patient" in dealing with the Chinese.

Repeated to Department and Peiping.

PECK

893.01 Inner Mongolia/52 : Telegram

The Ambassador in China (Johnson) to the Secretary of State

PEIPING, January 27, 1936—noon.
[Received January 27—11 a.m.]

34. Embassy's 33, January 23, 5 p. m.

1. According to Chinese and Mongol sources, the National Government decreed January 25 the establishment of an "autonomous" Political Council for the Mongols in Suiyuan Province, the capital to be at a place south of Paotou and the Council's head to be the leader of the Ordos League. A reliable informant states that the Council is to have control of Pailingmiao and other territory in Suiyuan belonging to Teh Wang but that Teh is not to be permitted to participate in the new government.

2. This action on the part of the National Government ought to alienate completely the sympathies for the Chinese of Teh Wang and Mongols in Chahar and cause them to throw in their lot with the Japanese and Li Shou Hsin entirely. Furthermore, the Mongols believe that an agent of the National Government was responsible for the assassination January 23 between Changpei and Kanggan of

an important Mongol representative. It is to be expected that events in Inner Mongolia in China may be accelerated as an outcome of these two occurrences.

By mail to Tokyo.

JOHNSON

793.94/7700 : Telegram

The Ambassador in Japan (Grew) to the Secretary of State

TOKYO, January 30, 1936—noon.
[Received January 30—5 : 17 a. m.]

19. In recent conversation my British colleague asked the Minister for Foreign Affairs as to the truth of the local press report that one of the three Japanese requirements for a Sino-Japanese *rapprochement* was that China should recognize Manchukuo. Hirota replied that such was not the case. He realized that China could not possibly recognize Manchukuo under present circumstances but hoped that the situation could be gradually developed with recognition as an ultimate aim. For the present he merely wished to see an improvement in the factual relations between China and Manchukuo involving customs ports, et cetera. He also hoped that the Chinese Government would cease to refer to Manchukuo as "a puppet state".

In the same conversation Clive [54] said that he considered the alleged autonomous government in East Hopei a farce and that Yin Ju Keng is notoriously a "scalawag". Hirota did not commit himself.

Repeated to Peiping by mail.

GREW

793.94/7701 : Telegram

The Ambassador in China (Johnson) to the Secretary of State

PEIPING, January 30, 1936—4 p. m.
[Received January 30—11 : 30 a. m.]

40. 1. Embassy's 26, January 20, 3 p. m., paragraph 1. Local post office official states that he has been instructed by his Ministry to turn over to them as from January 1st 40 percent of revenue obtained from sale of revenue stamps. There is doubt whether the Council will be satisfied with this.

2. Embassy's 25, January 19, noon. The Embassy has been reliably informed that customs revenues at Tientsin are not being remitted to the Council but are being sent daily to the Inspector General.

3. Reports are conflicting with regard to the situation existing at Changping which is about 30 miles northwest of Peiping on the Peiping–Suiyuan Railway and on the border of the demilitarized zone

[54] Sir Robert H. Clive, British Ambassador in Japan.

in area claimed by Yin Ju Keng. One informant with official sources states today that the magistrate opened the gates to a force which was variously reported as belonging to either Liu Kwei Tang or Yin Ju Keng and that some of Sung's soldiers are outside the town. If the force within the town is being used as an instrument for extension of Yin's or Manchukuo's power, undisputed occupation of Changping would be a step toward gaining control of the railway and would make possible the separation of Sung's troops in Hopei from his one division in Chahar which would probably prevent Sung's taking early action to restrain Li Shou Hsin's forces from taking Kalgan, a probability which is now being rumored.

4. The press reports bandits of Liu Kwei Tang numbering 500 out of a total force of 1,500, have entered the northern tip of Honan. In line with the statements in the Embassy's 33, January 23, 5 p. m., with regard to the possible use of Sun Tien Ying and Shih Yu San to assist in the establishment of an autonomous North China, some observers are of the opinion that Liu may be used to effect the inclusion of Honan north of the Yellow River in such a regime. By mail to Tokyo.

JOHNSON

762.94/69

Report by the Military Attaché in Germany (Smith)[55]

Report No. 14,500 BERLIN, January 30, 1936.

On Jan. 24th in the course of a conversation with the official representative of the German War Ministry, Major von Pappenheim, I casually handed him a copy of the London *Morning Post* of January 20th containing a Tokio dispatch reporting the consummation of a German-Japanese military alliance. This dispatch reads as follows:

"From our own Correspondent Berlin, Jan. 19.

In well-informed German political circles it is stated that a military agreement between Germany and Japan was signed in Tokyo on January 4, by which, in the event of either power being attacked, the other is pledged to come to its assistance. The aggressor in mind is, it need hardly be said, Russia.

The agreement was signed on behalf of the German Government by the German Ambassador in Tokyo and the Military Attaché. Further details are not obtainable."

I stated that I had not as yet read any official German denial of this story, and had thought that probably the German War Ministry would care to take a position in the matter, inasmuch as much loose conversation was going the rounds of Berlin embassies that such a treaty had either been completed or was in preparation.

---

[55] Copy transmitted to the Department on February 19 by the War Department.

The representative of the War Ministry, far from taking my question casually, told me that I had raised a very serious matter in which he had no competence, and that he must seek the approval of higher authority before an official answer could be given me. He said inofficially, however, that the entire story was nonsense, and that there was no firm basis at present for a military agreement, which in its very nature could only be aimed at Russia. Nevertheless, he stated also very definitely, that Japan desired such an alliance, and that the question had been raised by their Berlin representatives lately in a pressing manner (*sogar drückend*).

On January 29, I was asked over the telephone to come to the Ministry of War again. The attaché chief, Major von Pappenheim, was on this occasion not alone, the German G–2, Colonel von Stülpnagel being present. Major von Pappenheim was the speaker throughout the conversation.

He stated that he and the Ministry of War greeted my question, as they desired no shadow of suspicion to disturb their good relations between Germany and the United States. As the question had raised a political as well as a military question, a delay in their reply had been inevitable, as the matter had had to be referred to the Führer himself.

He desired now to state officially:

1. That the matter was essentially a political matter with which the Foreign Office could only deal.
2. Inasmuch, however, as the London *Morning Post* dispatch hinted at a "military alliance", the Ministry of War felt free to make known to an interested foreign attaché the Government's position in the matter.
3. This position was:

(*a*) The statement of the London *Morning Post* was untrue.
(*b*) The German Government attaches no importance to the matter.
(*c*) The German Government felt that no Berlin denial was necessary, inasmuch as such a denial had been issued in Tokio by a spokesman for the Japanese foreign office.

Your attention is called to the rather unusual wording of the denial, which was apparently drawn up only after careful thought by high German officials. The reply can easily be interpreted not as a complete denial of a German-Japanese alliance, but rather only of the London *Morning Post* version of such an alliance.

The United States Ambassador has been consulted with regard to these conversations, and has been furnished a copy of this report.

TRUMAN SMITH
Major, G. S.

761.9315 Manchuria/35 : Telegram

The Chargé in the Soviet Union (Henderson) to the Secretary of State

Moscow, January 31, 1936—4 p. m.
[Received January 31—2 : 55 p. m.]

39. The usual emissary of the Kremlin who in past conversations has been in the habit of minimizing the importance of Soviet-Japanese dissensions in the Far East stated to me yesterday substantially as follows:

The feeling which had hitherto prevailed in the Soviet Union that Japan would be too deeply occupied with completing its conquest of North China to attempt any aggressive action against the Soviet Union in the near future was being replaced with an uneasy feeling that on [*sic*] the outbreak of a Japanese-Soviet conflict in the spring or summer of the present year was quite within the realms of possibility. The desertion into Soviet territory on January 29th (as reported in the *Pravda* of January 30th) of a whole company of Manchurian soldiers, together with a Manchurian lieutenant and several non-commissioned officers, was the very type of an incident which the Soviet Government feared might serve the Japanese as a pretext for opening of hostilities. It seemed that the company after having killed its Japanese officers fled into the Soviet Union with a considerable amount of military equipment. It was disarmed and sent into the interior for internment. The Soviet Government was concerned lest a number of such incidents might result in insistence on the part of the Japanese Government that the deserters be extradited and charges that the disturbances were the result of the activities of the Comintern.

The anxiety of the Soviet governmental circles was sharpened by the fact that they were inclined to believe reports recently published to the effect that Germany and Japan had entered into an alliance directed against "the activities of the Comintern". They feared that if Japan should launch an attack under the pretext that it was crusading against the Comintern this alliance might serve as a basis for a simultaneous German attack from the West. They also felt that it was possible that influential groups in other countries which otherwise would have no sympathy for Japanese or German aggression might be inclined because of their dread of the spread of Communism [to support such attacks.]

The Soviet Government believed that of all the great powers Great Britain was in the best position to exercise restraint upon Germany. Undoubtedly Litvinov [56] while in London would discuss the matter with the British Government.

HENDERSON

---

[56] Soviet Commissar for Foreign Affairs.

893.01 Outer Mongolia/77

The Consul General at Harbin (Adams) to the Ambassador in China (Johnson) [57]

[Extracts]

No. 196   HARBIN, January 31, 1936.

SIR: I have the honor to submit further observations on the opinion, set forth in the Consulate General's despatch No. 192, dated January 27, 1936, (No. 300 to the Department) [58] that the higher authorities of the Kwantung Army do not at the present time desire serious complications with Outer Mongolia and Soviet Russia, although an incident in the hands of an officer on the "front" may cause them to take action.

.   .   .   .

To turn to Manchuria and Soviet Russia, all Japanese civilians, both officials and merchants, to whom the subject has been broached, were agreed that the Kwantung Army does not desire war with Russia at the present time. General Minami and his Chief of Staff, Lieutenant-General Nishio, are said to be of this persuasion. On the other hand, it is common gossip that many of the younger officers in Manchuria, among whom may possibly be included the Vice-chief of Staff, Major-General Itagaki, openly advocate waging war on Soviet Russia at the earliest opportunity. It is believed that many of these malcontents have been sent to Manchuria expressly to get rid of their troublesome activities in Japan, and that as a consequence the ratio of nationalistic zealots among officers of the Kwantung Army is even higher than in the army at home. The theory has been advocated that one reason for the lack of concentration of large bodies of Japanese troops at any one point near the border—as is reported to be the case—is to minimize the possibility of an officer involving the Kwantung Army in large scale operations.

An enlightening incident, illustrating the ideas of this type of officer, and at the same time showing that some officers have different opinions from their superiors and are willing to make public that fact, took place recently. Mr. Impey, Far East correspondent for the *Daily Mail* (London), had an interview with Major Shun Akikusa, second in command of the Harbin Special Service Mission. The Major, upon being asked whether Japan and Soviet Russia would soon be at war, replied most emphatically that the two countries would be at war within a few months. His chief, Major General Rinzo Ando, said the following day, when asked the same question

---

[57] Copy transmitted to the Department by the Consul General in his despatch No. 306, January 31; received March 10.
[58] Not printed.

by the same man, that war was not envisaged by the Kwantung Army; he added, however, that there were many fanatics on both sides. According to rumor in Japanese circles in Harbin, General Ando, who is far from well, has been criticized for not being able to control his subordinates, although he himself has been described as being a conservative. Not only has Major Akikusa publicly expressed opinions on matters of policy opposite to those of the Kwantung Army, but his superiors appear to be powerless either to discipline him, or to have him transferred elsewhere.

The danger of serious developments on the Outer Mongolian frontier has probably increased since the reported military agreement reached at Moscow recently between Soviet Russia and Outer Mongolia, as there has been evidence of an increase in Mongolian resistance to the presumably aggressive tactics of "Manchukuo" border outposts. It has also come to light that they are supplied with automobiles, have at least one airplane, and have developed a rapid system of telegraphic communication from the border to Urga and Moscow.

Thus, although it is believed that the present policy of the Kwantung Army is to avoid hostilities, it remains to be seen whether sufficient discipline can be maintained to keep the younger officers in check.

Respectfully yours,   WALTER A. ADAMS

711.94/1057 : Telegram

The Ambassador in Japan (Grew) to the Secretary of State

TOKYO, February 1, 1936—11 a. m.
[Received February 1—2 : 56 a. m.]

21. 1. The Tokyo *Nichi Nichi*, Japanese edition, this morning published an article to the effect that as a result of conversations between the Japanese Ambassador in Washington [59] and the Secretary of State, and between Hirota and myself, the following principles had been established:

(*a*) There are no American-Japanese problems insoluble by diplomatic means.

(*b*) Both countries should refrain from irritating speech and actions. The article then alleges that steps are now being taken for the conclusion of an American-Japanese political agreement based on the principle of division of the Pacific into American and Japanese spheres of action and including the spirit of the Hull-Hirota mes-

---

[59] Hirosi Saito.

sages.[60]   The article intimates further that this political agreement may lead to a bilateral naval disarmament agreement.

2. The *Jiji* this morning published a short article alleging that Hirota is working toward a tripartite agreement between the United States, Great Britain and Japan whereby each country will undertake the maintenance of peace in its particular sphere; United States in the Americas, Great Britain in Europe and Japan in the Far East, the tripartite agreement to replace the League of Nations as world peace machinery.

3. The Embassy has no knowledge of any negotiations tending to ends outlined in the two articles but as both articles appeared today it is believed possible that they may in fact be trial balloons put out by the Foreign Office.

GREW

711.94/1057a : Telegram

The Secretary of State to the Ambassador in Japan (Grew)

WASHINGTON, February 1, 1936—1 p. m.

16. For your information.   Press reports indicate that Japanese press has widely carried stories affirming comprehensive political negotiations between Grew and Hirota and between Hull and Saito.

Interrogated by press correspondents this morning, the Secretary of State said there were no new developments in relations between the United States and countries of the Far East; and Departmental officers have informally explained to correspondents that there have been held numerous conferences with regard to particular questions of trade but no conferences on political matters have been held or been suggested.

HULL

761.9315 Manchuria/35 : Telegram

The Secretary of State to the Ambassador in Japan (Grew)

WASHINGTON, February 3, 1936—5 p. m.

17. Information received by the Department indicates that in some Soviet circles there is an uneasy feeling that the outbreak of a conflict between Japan and the Soviet Union in the spring or summer of this year is within the realm of possibility.

HULL

---

[60] February 21 and March 3, 1934, *Foreign Relations*, Japan, 1931–1941, vol. I, pp. 127–129.

793.94/7702 : Telegram

The Ambassador in China (Johnson) to the Secretary of State

PEIPING, February 4, 1936—noon,
[Received February 4—7 : 30 a. m.[61]]

44. Embassy's 33, January 23, 5 p. m.

1. Two councilors of Sung Che Yuan state in conversation that the Japanese military are continuing to press Sung hard for a declaration of complete autonomy and that Sung is still loathe to do so.

One of the informants states that Sung definitely will not comply and that this will result in the instigation of disturbances by the Japanese for the purpose of effecting a way out of the seeming deadlock.

2. The Consul at Tsinanfu has sent the following telegram:

"February 3, 11 a. m. Han Fu Chu, said to be inspecting troops at Liaochenghan, and Sung Che Yuan, said to be sweeping tombs at Loling, are reliably reported to have conferred in Tehchow February 1st. Speculation rife in informed circles whether the purpose of the conference was to arrange closer cooperation in resistance to or acceptance of Japanese demands."

3. Details of conversations between Japanese and Yin Ju Keng and Sung's men and between Japanese and Shansi and Shantung officials are lacking. It is understood that Doihara intends to remain in Hopei for some time. The Chief of Staff of the Japanese North China Garrison went yesterday to Yin's so-called capital. Conversations at Tokyo of Japanese military, including Major General Isogai, Japanese Military Attaché, and Lieutenant Colonel Ikeda, staff officer of the North China Garrison, are regarded as having significance in connection with the future course of the Japanese military in North China.

4. Embassy's 40, January 30, 4 p. m., paragraph 1. It is learned from local official source that the post office has received a request from the Hopei-Chahar Political Council for a complete accounting of all receipts and expenditures as from January 1st. The post office has requested instructions from Nanking.

By mail to Tokyo.

JOHNSON

---

[61] Telegram in two sections.

761.9315 Manchuria/36 : Telegram

The Ambassador in Japan (Grew) to the Secretary of State

TOKYO, February 4, 1936—5 p. m.
[Received February 4—1:15 p. m.]

24. Department's 17, February 3, 5 p. m.

1. Siberian-Mongolian border situation.

(*a*) Incidents relating to the Siberian and Mongolian borders are handled by the Kwantung army headquarters in Hsinking with little reference to Tokyo. Consequently War Office here has apparently little information as to current situation. The Military Attaché of the Embassy [62] reports that the War Office continues to refer to the border incidents as "annoying."

(*b*) *Nippon Dempo* in a despatch from Hsinking dated February 2 reports that the Kwantung army has reversed its reported previous decision to take "strong measures" and will now do nothing to aggravate the border situation "for fear that entire Far Eastern situation might take a severe turn for the worse". A Domei report from Moscow dated February 3 states that the Red Army would assist an impartial commission of inquiry into reported mutiny Manchukuo troops near Mishan January 29 during a skirmish between Japan–Manchukuo and Soviet mutineer forces.

(*c*) The Soviet Ambassador and General Rink, the Military Attaché, continue to express confidence that owing to the strength of Soviet defenses the Japanese will not attack. The Soviet Military Attaché told Colonel Crane on January 28 that if the Japanese bring too much pressure to bear against the Outer Mongolians the Soviet Government will aid them by technical means. General Rink has just returned from the U.S.S.R. and his confident attitude contrasts strongly with his evident anxiety of a year and more ago.

(*d*) With regard to the present border situation, although the recent incidents have renewed anxiety, the Embassy foresees no serious trouble in the near future. This does not eliminate possibility of a grave incident rendering it impossible to restrain the opposing armies. (See despatch 1648, January 23 due Washington February 8).

2. Possibility of war this spring or summer.

(*a*) Foreign observers consider recent Japanese trial balloon (Embassy's telegram No. 21 [63]) is an effort to counterbalance Litvinov-Eden [64] and Litvinov–Flandin [65] conversations. They believe the Foreign Office to be apprehensive of negotiations which may strengthen the U.S.S.R. in Europe.

---

[62] Lt. Col. William C. Crane.
[63] Dated February 1, 11 a.m., p. 35.
[64] British Secretary of State for Foreign Affairs.
[65] French Minister without Portfolio and former Premier.

(*b*) The Soviet willingness to resist by force Japanese-Manchukuo violations of Mongolian and Siberian borders has demonstrated to the Kwantung army that immediate objectives of revising boundaries and opening Outer Mongolia can only be reached by war. The question has therefore arisen whether these immediate objectives, plus fundamental desire to eliminate Russia from East Asia, will lead Japanese leaders to favor coming spring or summer as most favorable opportunity to strike. It is generally assumed here that the Soviets will not themselves attack. Those who hold that Japan will attack this year claim that increasing strength of Soviet defenses make it a case of "now or never". The majority, however, feels that the present Government in Japan will not deliberately attack Russia until or unless Russia is also involved in war on her western front. Consequently, the Japanese decision will await developments in Europe.

(*c*) In considering the possibility of war in the spring or summer of this year, it appears likely that the influences surrounding the throne, Hirota, the majority of the business interests and probably the General Staff in Tokyo will be opposed to war under present circumstances. Should hostilities break out in Europe it is difficult at this stage to foretell in what manner the resulting cleavage of opinion among Japanese leaders for and against a war with Russia would be resolved.

To Peiping by mail.

GREW

793.94/7782

The Ambassador in China (Johnson) to the Secretary of State

No. 81   NANKING, February 4, 1936.
[Received March 9.]

SIR: I have the honor to enclose herewith copies of two despatches [66] addressed to the American Ambassador at Peiping, both dated February 3, 1936, and both reporting evidence that there is current in Chinese educational and political circles a belief that hostilities between China and Japan will commence within the next two or three months, and that the Chinese public is paying close attention to the prolonged resistance offered by the Ethiopian forces to the Italian invasion of Ethiopia,[67] on the ground that this is an indication that China would be able to oppose effective military resistance to Japan.

I have the honor to add that in a further conversation held by me yesterday with a Chinese official, Dr. Y. T. Tsur, Administrative Vice

---

[66] Neither printed.
[67] See vol. III, pp. 34 ff.

Minister of Industries, evidence was again given that the idea of the inevitability of hostilities between China and Japan is prevalent and that the conflict in Ethiopia is receiving close attention. Dr. Tsur said he supposed that the "baptism of fire" through which China had been passing must be prolonged to include hostilities with Japan and that "perhaps" China would emerge from the ordeal improved and strengthened. He asked whether I thought that the Ethiopians would be able to continue the struggle against the Italian forces much longer. I called attention to the difference between the reports of these hostilities emanating from Italian and Ethiopian sources, respectively, and remarked that if one were to believe the Italian reports, the Italian forces in Ethiopia had met with practically no difficulty from the opposition of the Ethiopian troops, but only from climatic conditions and the terrain.

My acquaintance with Dr. Tsur began some twenty years ago when he was President of Tsinghua College. So far as I am aware he is still a member of the Board of Trustees of the Foundation for the Promotion of Education and Culture, which handles the American remitted Boxer Indemnity, and has recently been President of Yenching University in Peiping, an American missionary institution. He was appointed to his present post in the Ministry of Industries in December, 1935, and appears to have come at the solicitation of General Chiang Kai-shek. He told me that he had been invited by General Chiang to luncheon on February 1 and he spoke to me in an admiring tone of the high qualities of General Chiang as a national leader.

In view of the fact that Dr. Tsur is new to the political atmosphere of Nanking, I thought it advisable not to endeavor to extract much concrete information from him at this first interview.

Respectfully yours,   For the Ambassador:
                                                  WILLYS R. PECK
                                                  Counselor of Embassy

761.94/876

Memorandum by the Under Secretary of State (Phillips)

[WASHINGTON,] February 7, 1936.

The Soviet Ambassador [68] having just returned from Russia called upon me this morning. In reply to my inquiry as to whether he had any new impressions about the situation in the Far East and in Europe, he said something along the following lines.

---

[68] A. A. Troyanovsky.

The border incidents in the Far East were disturbing but the Russian forces were still so strong that he did not believe that the Japanese Government intended any serious penetration. He admitted that the danger lay in the independent authority and possible action of local Japanese officers. He mentioned the fact that about two months ago a Japanese force of 100 men or so penetrated into Soviet territory to a distance of between three and four miles; that a comparatively small group of Russians fired upon them and killed eight or nine, but that this fracas had never been mentioned by the Japanese press. He thought that possibly the irritation on the border was kept alive by the Japanese in order to concentrate the interest of the Soviet forces in that vicinity and so leave the Mongolian frontier more exposed.

The Ambassador spoke with great enthusiasm about the morale in the Soviet Army, which he described as far superior to what it had been formerly; the modern army was educated, well clothed and disciplined, and which was of especial significance, had learned courtesy to and respect for women. For instance, he said that in the ordinary tramcars in Moscow, the Soviet soldier would always give his seat to a woman, whereas formerly that had never been the case.

In referring to Germany, he mentioned the generous credit which the German Government had offered for a period of ten years; he supposed the explanation lay in the fact that Germany needed raw materials which it could get from Russia, such as manganese, oil etc.; but the fact that Germany was willing to extend such huge credits indicated that there was no early intention at least of making war on Russia, for in such case Germany would incur great financial loss. The Ambassador thought that Czechoslovakia and Rumania were in considerable danger from Germany; he did not seem to feel that the same danger applied to Memel. He mentioned the fact that England and France were offering credits to Russia, and that there had been renewed efforts on their part for the settlement of debts, but he did not indicate that the Soviets had yielded in this respect. The Ambassador felt certain that the Sarraut's Government in France would ratify the treaty of mutual assistance with Soviet Russia and do so in the near future.

I asked whether the Ambassador had returned to us with any renewed hope of a satisfactory disposition of our problems. He indicated that he had more hope now than he had after his previous visit and return, and I gained the impression that he may have new proposals to offer us.

W[illiam] P[hillips]

500.A15A5/678

The Ambassador in Japan (Grew) to the Secretary of State

No. 1665   TOKYO, February 7, 1936.
                                                   [Received February 24.]

SIR: Reference is respectfully made to the Department's strictly
confidential telegram No. 2, January 7, 7 p. m.,[69] and to our strictly
confidential reply No. 7, January 9, 6 p. m., both telegrams on the
subject of rumored negotiations for a non-aggression pact between
Japan and China and a tentative personal proposal made by Mr.
Craigie, British Assistant Under Secretary of State for Foreign
Affairs, to Mr. Norman Davis that we consider the advisability of concluding non-aggression pacts between the United States, Great Britain
and Japan, should a Sino-Japanese pact be consummated, in return
for the acceptance by the Japanese of a naval agreement acceding
to the present naval *status quo*. In our reply I stated that we did
not think that a Sino-Japanese pact was feasible at the present time,
but that should it materialize, the idea advanced by Mr. Craigie should
not be turned aside without careful consideration in view of the
obsolescence of the present Far Eastern treaty structure and the necessity of revising our future outlook and policy in the Far East. It
appears desirable to supplement our telegram with a more detailed
explanation of our thoughts on the question, namely that while doubting the feasibility of a Sino-Japanese non-aggression pact for some
time to come, and further doubting the advisability at present of
bilateral non-aggression pacts between the United States, Great
Britain and Japan, we believe that our Government should lose no
opportunity to explore every avenue which might lead to a political
agreement respecting American rights and interests in the Far East,
in view of the fact that new facts and conditions will eventually
compel us, as well as other peoples of the world, to revise our outlook
upon the political status of the Far East.

It would seem desirable first to examine the "new facts and conditions" in the Far East, mentioned in our telegram No. 7, January
9, 6 p.m., and then consider the course which the United States can
most wisely and profitably follow in this part of the world in future.
This discussion seems for the moment to be hypothetical and academic.

In considering the premises upon which an argument for or against
the conclusion of revised political agreements in respect to the Far
East may be based, the following points might be taken into consideration:

---

[69] See telegram No. 4, of the same date, to the Ambassador in China, p. 3.

PREMISES

(1) The attitude of Japan in the past toward such collective pacts as have been concluded for the security of the world in general and the Far East in particular has not been such as to inspire confidence in the inviolability of such non-aggression pacts as Japan may adhere to in the future.

(2) Nothing save defeat in war (and perhaps in the long run not even that) will arrest the Japanese movement to obtain eventually at least *de facto* political, military and economic control of the northern areas of China. This movement may be accelerated by military operations as in Manchuria, or it may develop slowly behind a facade of alleged autonomous governments subservient to the Japanese, as in Hopei and Chahar.

(3) The movement is based on a three-fold urge: (*a*) to provide broader economic opportunity for Japan's steadily expanding population; (*b*) to control essential raw materials which Japan lacks; and (*c*) to consolidate Japan's strategic position against Soviet Russia and thereby to hold Communism in check. The basic and primary urges are the first and second, but the principal impelling force at the moment, at least among the military, is the third urge, namely, to place themselves in such a position on the mainland of Asia as to prevent the spread of Communism, especially into Japan, to preserve a *Pax Japonica* in the areas adjacent to their own territory, and to consolidate their control of Manchuria by securing a degree of control over Mongolia and North China. These urges in Japan are strong and insistent, and the world cannot expect that they will be eradicated by moral suasion or other peaceful methods.

(4) The Japanese expansionist movement will interfere to a progressively greater extent with American rights and interests in the areas which come under Japanese control, as it has already interfered with our rights and interests in Manchuria. At the same time, it will probably interfere to an even greater degree with British rights and interests which are believed to be more extensive than ours in the areas under consideration.

(5) We as a nation are therefore faced with certain inescapable facts with which it is becoming increasingly impracticable to deal on a legal, moral or idealistic basis—in other words on any of the foundations upon which the policy and acts of the United States in the Far East are traditionally based. This does not mean that the United States should scrap its time-honored belief in the principle of the inviolability of treaties and in the moral and idealistic standards which it has traditionally championed, but it does mean that in dealing with Japan we can no longer rely on those principles and standards and that we must supplement them in whatever effective way may command itself.

(6) If and when China enters into some political agreement with Japan, whether called a non-aggression pact or given some other name, it can be assumed that the agreement would accept, expressly or tacitly, the fact of the existence of "Manchukuo" and of the Japanese political and economic penetration of North China. It is obvious that under such circumstances the present treaty structure governing the relations of the Powers with China, already crumbling, would either juridically or practically have become entirely obsolete. The principle of the maintenance of the territorial and administrative integrity of China would then have lapsed, China herself having accepted the violation of her own territorial and administrative integrity.

(7) The United States would then be confronted with the problem either of endeavoring to uphold an obsolete treaty and to defend a helpless country, or of simply endeavoring to safeguard American rights and interests in the Far East as best we might under the conditions then obtaining. In endeavoring to safeguard our rights and interests we would not have to deal with a general scramble of the Powers for spheres of influence or special privileges as in the past, but exclusively with the activities of one country, Japan.

POSSIBILITY OF A SINO-JAPANESE NON-AGGRESSION PACT

In considering the arguments for and against revised political agreements, based upon the above premises, it might be well first to consider the possibility of a Sino-Japanese non-aggression pact because much of the argument to follow is based upon the existence or non-existence of some such agreement.

In the opinion of this Embassy, it is doubtful if any Sino-Japanese non-aggression or other political pact can be concluded at the present time. The Japanese military, still the dominant force in the Japanese Government, do not wish to have their hands tied by any pacts binding the nation to peaceful methods. They had their experience of such pacts with the Covenant of the League of Nations, the Kellogg-Briand Pact and the Nine-Power Treaty, and they do not desire any more such pacts, except possibly with Great Britain and with the United States, the only nations in the Pacific strong enough to oppose Japan by sea. This attitude on the part of the Japanese military is indicated by their refusal to consider the various non-aggression trial balloons sent up by the Soviet Union. On the other hand, it appears to be extremely doubtful if the Chinese Government would accept a non-aggression or other political pact with Japan. As was pointed out earlier in this despatch, a non-aggression pact implies some sort of political agreement, and any sort of peace-making political agreement between China and Japan at the present time would certainly imply the acceptance, *de facto* or *de jure*, by China of the existence of "Manchukuo" and of the partial loss of sovereignty over North China. It is not believed that any government in China today could or would conclude such a pact. This view is, I believe, shared by our Embassy in China. At the same time, it must be remembered that Japan is pressing China for a political agreement involving acceptance by China of the *status quo*, and therefore the possibility exists that China may eventually be forced to acquiesce in Japan's demands, choosing between acquiescence or war with Japan. In either case, however, as far as can now be foreseen, the result will be the partial or complete domination of China by Japan, and it is this fact which we must take into consideration in mapping our future course in the Far East.

POSSIBLE ADVANTAGES OF ANGLO-AMERICAN-JAPANESE NON-AGGRESSION PACTS

Turning now to the question of a tripartite or a series of bilateral pacts between the United States, Great Britain and Japan in regard to our respective relations in the Far East, it can be argued, as an advantage of such a pact or pacts, that we could stabilize the situation in the Far East to an extent sufficient to warrant the United States and Great Britain in asking Japan to accept the naval *status quo*, thereby giving us a definite naval superiority over Japan for a period of years. It is believed that any pacts or agreements entered into in the future relating to conditions in the Far East should be made to cover only a definite, limited period, probably for not more than, say, ten years and renewable for another similarly limited period at such time as could best be obtained at the time of renewal. The gradual decay of the treaty structure based on the Washington Conference of 1921 and 1922 is evidence of the impracticability of concluding pacts designed to cover an unlimited period such as in the case, for instance, with the Nine-Power Treaty. If, however, for a period of approximately ten years we could obtain naval superiority over Japan and at the same time avoid an expensive and dangerous naval construction race, something worthwhile would have been accomplished. The question of the *quid pro quo*—a very large question—will be discussed later when considering the disadvantages of such a pact or pacts.

It is believed possible that the British Government may be seriously considering some sort of political agreement with Japan whereby in return for Britain's acceptance of the *status quo* on the Asiatic mainland, Japan will agree to respect British rights and interests in Asia. If Great Britain should conclude such an agreement and the United States refuse to consider a similar agreement, we would be confronted with the same situation that the Four-Power Pacific

Pact [70] was designed to eliminate, namely, an Anglo-Japanese Alliance, although in somewhat altered and attenuated form. The position of the United States in the Pacific area in general and in the Far East in particular would thereby be weakened.

The principal argument in favor of the conclusion of a non-aggression or some similar political pact with Japan, however, is the simple one that, if we wish to reduce the permanent danger of conflict with Japan, we shall eventually be compelled to reach some political agreement in respect to the Far East which will take into consideration the new facts and conditions mentioned previously in this despatch. It is certain that nothing short of superior force will stop Japan's advance into Asia, and as the United States and Great Britain are distinctly not inclined to employ force against Japan, while China apparently is not capable of exerting sufficient force to restrain Japan, it would appear that the only effective course which we can pursue will be to endeavor to slow up the Japanese expansionist movement by a series of agreements of limited duration, each of which would be designed to restrain Japan in one direction or another. The situation in the Far East, perhaps to a greater degree than in any other part of the world, is not static, but decidedly dynamic, and therefore does not lend itself to the conclusion of more or less permanent treaties, such as the Nine-Power Treaty was intended to be. We are now, therefore, faced with the problem of searching again for the most effective means whereby Japanese interference with American rights and interests in the Far East can be held in check, while at the same time reducing to a minimum the friction between Japan and the United States which inevitably increases the potential risk of war. A tripartite non-aggression pact, or a series of bilateral non-aggression pacts, between the United States, Great Britain and Japan, would be a step along this road.

DISADVANTAGES OF NON-AGGRESSION PACTS

Turning now to the disadvantages of such non-aggression pact or pacts, the first would appear to be the very meagre security which we would obtain by this means. Our past experience with Japanese observance of such treaties does not conduce to any degree of optimism in regard to the future observance by Japan of any pact designed to secure our rights and interests (or those of China) in the Far East.

We would, moreover, be forfeiting, to the extent that we were bound by the tripartite or bilateral agreements, our right or privilege of cooperating with other Powers in collective action to restrain Japan—a policy which the American Government has previously

---

[70] Signed at Washington, December 13, 1921, *Foreign Relations*, 1922, vol. I, p. 33.

adopted, with indifferent success, in dealing with Sino-Japanese disputes and in endeavoring to implement the Kellogg-Briand Pact in the Far East. We would also to some extent lose our freedom of action and would to that degree increase Japan's freedom of action in the Far East. Against this it can be argued that the United States is already bound by the Kellogg-Briand Pact to abjure war as an instrument of national policy, and that therefore, in concluding a non-aggression or other peace pact with Japan, the United States would lose no freedom of action not already renounced.

The principal argument against the conclusion of a non-aggression or similar pact with Japan, however, is that such a pact implies a political agreement, and any political agreement with Japan made now or in the foreseeable future would have to include our express or tacit acceptance of the *status quo* on the Asiatic mainland. It can be argued that "Manchukuo" is a political entity which does exist, irrespective of the means by which it was brought into being or by which it is being maintained in existence, and that the fact of its existence has been recognized by China and by other countries whenever they have had dealings of any kind with that country. Our recognition or non-recognition of the fact of "Manchukuo's" existence, therefore, would not greatly alter the existing situation, and it is argued that recognition by the United States of the *de facto* existence of "Manchukuo" would be a small price to pay for our security, even for a limited period, in the Far East, for the lessening of the danger of war with Japan, and for obviating the necessity of entering an expensive naval construction race. On the other hand, however, even our tacit acceptance of the *status quo* on the Asiatic mainland would to that extent condone Japan's actions in Asia and would indicate an abandonment of the principles of world peace for the general acceptance and observance of which the United States has struggled for many years. It is not believed that the American Government and the American people are prepared to take this step, now or in the near future.

CONCLUSION

As was stated before, the consensus of opinion in this Embassy is that a Sino-Japanese non-aggression pact is not feasible at the present time and that the disadvantages of a tripartite non-aggression pact, or a series of bilateral non-aggression pacts between the United States, Great Britain and Japan probably outweigh the advantages. Nevertheless it is believed that our Government should not neglect carefully to explore every avenue which might lead to some variety of political agreement with Japan which would tend to protect our interests in this part of the world and to reduce the friction between the United States and Japan. As was expressed by Ambassador

Nelson T. Johnson in 1932 (telegram No. 1078, September 8, 11 a.m.[71]), in discussing a possible conference on the Far Eastern question in Geneva:

"We must sooner or later deal with the situation which those forces (the forces driving Japan into China) have created. It is better that we deal with it now by methods of peace than later by the methods of war . . .[72]

"If the opportunity . . . presents itself the United States could come forward with a plan for an international conference to take up and consider the question of the situation in the East linked with such questions as the limitation of armaments and the modification of promises under the Kellogg Pact . . ."

The Embassy believes that the fact that it does not consider a non-aggression pact to be desirable or feasible at the present moment does not exclude the possibility of some other form of agreement which, while not sacrificing our principles or our rights and interests, would tend to obviate to some extent, at least, the risk of armed conflict with Japan. It may be said that in times past the Japanese have considered the obligations of bilateral treaties as more compelling than those involved in general or multilateral pacts. We must also recognize that any political arrangement with Japan must take into account the fact that the attitude of Soviet Russia is an important consideration in Japanese political calculations.

Pending, however, the possible conclusion of some political agreement with Japan, it is our firm belief that the primary method of supplementing the legal, moral and idealistic principles for which the United States has always stood sponsor in the Far East is to build and maintain our Navy at a strength sufficient for adequate defense in case of Japanese aggression against our rights and interests (see despatch No. 1102, December 27, 1934 [73]). While our Navy is not maintained for purposes of aggression, from which we are restrained by our commitments under the Kellogg-Briand Pact, plus our national policy of non-aggression, plus the practical difficulties of obtaining concrete results by war with Japan, nevertheless it is not believed that we should gratuitously sacrifice the factor of warning inherent in the possession of a strong fleet. Such a factor tends to support and implement our diplomacy if only by its psychological effect. If and when we do negotiate some political agreement with Japan in respect to the Far East, to replace the Nine-Power Treaty, we shall be in a much better position to insist upon our rights and legitimate interests if we possess a strong fleet than if we permit our naval strength to fall below that indicated for adequate defense. We should not lose

---

[71] For telegram No. 1078, dated September 7, 1932, 9 p. m., see *Foreign Relations*, 1932, vol. IV, p. 229.

[72] Omissions indicated in the original.

[73] *Foreign Relations*, 1935, vol. III, p. 821.

sight of the fact, deplorable but true, that no practical and effective code of international morality upon which the world can rely has yet been discovered, and that the standards of morality of one nation in certain given circumstances have little or no relation to the standards of another nation in other circumstances, and little or no relation to the standards of the individuals of the nations in question. To shape our foreign policy on the unsound theory that other nations are guided and bound by our own present standards of international ethics would be to court sure disaster.

Respectfully yours,

JOSEPH C. GREW

711.94/1059a : Telegram

The Secretary of State to the Ambassador in Japan (Grew)

WASHINGTON, February 10, 1936—7 p.m.

19. For your information. When asked this afternoon to comment on Senator Pittman's speech in the Senate today,[74] the Secretary said, only :

"I have not yet had opportunity to read Senator Pittman's speech. Senator Pittman occupies an important position in the legislative branch of the Government. There has been as regards his speech no consultation or collaboration between him and me. There is no reason why I should make any comment."

HULL

793.94/7719 : Telegram

The Counselor of Embassy in China (Lockhart) to the Secretary of State

PEIPING, February 11, 1936—3 p. m.
[Received February 11—1 : 18 p. m.]

59. Embassy's 44, February 4, noon.

1. Doihara arrived February 8 at Peiping from Tientsin reputedly to remain for some time. The conference of military officers at Tokyo continues and Sugiyama's departure for Manchuria and North China (see Embassy's 21, January 16, 4 p. m.) is reported as postponed until February 20. General Sung and the Hopei-Chahar Political Council apparently continue to procrastinate in proclaiming toward that degree of autonomy which the Japanese military desire. However, Doihara in two press interviews stated that the Council will have Japanese advisers; and a Japanese press report

---

[74] Speech on Japanese policy in China by Key Pittman, Democrat, of Nevada, Chairman of the Senate Committee on Foreign Relations; *Congressional Record*, vol. 80, pt. 2, p. 1703.

from Tsitsihar states that Shiro Nagai, director of the General Affairs Board in the Heilungkiang Provincial Government and formerly in the Tokyo Finance Bureau, will be financial adviser to the Council.

2. The Hopei-Chahar Council is considering the establishment of an education commission to supervise education, its duties probably to be restricted at the beginning to middle schools. It is understood that the commission was "suggested" by the Japanese, not "demanded". Local educators are opposed to it, claiming that such a threat to educational liberty would cause students to demonstrate again and would result in schools and universities eventually removing from Peiping.

3. Reports here that Japanese-manufactured text books are to be used in Yin Ju Keng's area are substantiated by Mukden's despatch 222, February 7 [75] which states that the Mukden Chinese press reports that 1,500,000 primary school text books compiled by the East Asia Cultural Society are being printed in Mukden for use in the area under Yin Ju Keng.

By mail to Tokyo.

LOCKHART

747.94/20

The Consul General at Sydney (Moffat) to the Secretary of State

No. 125   SYDNEY, February 11, 1936.
                                                       [Received March 10.]

SIR: There can be no doubt but that recent Japanese moves in the Orient, coupled with the attitude of her delegation at London, have seriously disturbed the Australian Government and to a lesser degree the Australian public. Last October when I visited Canberra the general attitude was that Japan would probably be occupied for many years to come digesting her acquisitions in Manchukuo and that for the time being her energies must be concentrated exclusively in that direction. Of late, however, Australia has made a radical revision in her estimates of future Japanese policy based on reports received from Tokyo, presumably from Sir Robert Clive, supported by those from her own Trade Commissioner, Major Longfield Lloyd.

Both Sir George Pearce, the Minister of External Affairs, and Colonel Hodgson, the Secretary of the Department of External Affairs, told me in Canberra last week that the news from Tokyo was distinctly disquieting: that there was a new and increasing access of megalomania in Japan, coupled with a growing conviction that the greatest single obstacle to the fulfilment of Japanese ambition to become Master of the Western Pacific was the British Empire. Some

---

[75] Not printed.

form of anti-British move in the Orient was accordingly looked for as soon as Japan was less preoccupied with a possible threat from the Soviet.

Sir George Pearce told me that he had never forgotten a conversation he had had during the Washington Conference of 1921–1922 with Prince Tokugawa. The latter had said to him: "There is absolute unanimity in Japan on the proposition that we must expand; but there are two schools of thought as to where we should expand: the first is the Continental school, the second is called the Blue-water school. For the moment, the Continental school has the upper hand, and probably will for years to come, but if ever it should be blocked or thwarted, then it will be a matter of real concern for Australia." Sir George added that he wondered whether each of the two schools of thought referred to was not simultaneously feeling that it was in the ascendant.

So long as we are in the Philippines Australia feels fairly safe, believing that it would be suicidal for Japan to move further south leaving the Philippines on her flank. But if and when we withdraw, whether Japan absorbs the Islands or whether they remain under weak native rule, this feeling of security will vanish. There is accordingly an increasing bitterness at our policy of withdrawal from the Philippines as step succeeds step in its realization. Colonel Hodgson told me that according to the information reaching Canberra as to future developments in the Philippines, American army circles were saying quite openly: "At least the United States will never give up a naval and military base in the Islands", while, on the other hand, civilian opinion was reported to be emphasizing the reluctance of the United States to retain any responsibility whatsoever in the Philippines without full authority.

Meanwhile Japan and Australia continue to be "good friends" and Tokyo goes on buying wool from Australia and pressing for a trade treaty. Australia has by now pretty definitely shown Japan what she will and what she won't give in the way of concessions. The Prime Minister told me that the powerful grazier interests were no longer pressing the Government to "buy" favors from Japan, while Colonel Hodgson said with considerable emphasis of manner: "You can rest assured that Japan is going to be very disappointed at what she actually gets from us."

There is some feeling that the invitation to Mr. Hughes,[76] the veteran war-time Prime Minister, to re-enter the Cabinet from which he had been dismissed three months ago, was in part due to his knowledge of the Japanese problem. I was even told by a journalistic friend, although of course I cannot confirm this, that Mr. Hughes'

[76] William Morris Hughes.

return was informally suggested to Mr. Lyons [77] by Downing Street. In any event, the Australian Government while not yet the victim of a "scare" is definitely worried at the turn events are taking.

Respectfully yours,   PIERREPONT MOFFAT

711.94/1059 : Telegram

The Ambassador in Japan (Grew) to the Secretary of State

TOKYO, February 12, 1936—5 p. m.
[Received February 12—7 : 03 a. m.]

26. Senator Pittman's speech in the Senate has aroused relatively little press comment. Such excerpts as were telegraphed were given a prominent position in the news columns as well as the Secretary of State's speech that he had not been consulted in reference to it. The *Asahi*, the *Nichi Nichi* and the *Hochi* are the only important Tokyo papers as yet to comment on it editorially and they attribute it to anti-Japanism and the Senator's desire to get before the public in election year; they deny the charge that Japan is closing the door in China and regret that a man of Senator Pittman's high position in American public life should be so misled as to make the unfounded charge he does against Japan.

The Spokesman of the Foreign Office has refused to discuss the speech and there is evident a desire in official quarters to minimize its importance.

The *Japan Times* this evening publishes a reasonable editorial pointing out Senator Pittman's place in the American Government and explaining that he does not represent the Administration.

GREW

793.94/7765

Memorandum by the Chief of the Division of Far Eastern Affairs (Hornbeck) to the Secretary of State

[WASHINGTON,] February 12, 1936.

MR. SECRETARY : The Chinese Ambassador asked me last evening to arrange for an appointment for him with you.

The Ambassador said that he had had instruction from his Government, and that the Chinese Ambassadors at London and at Moscow have similar instructions, to state that the Chinese Government has reason to believe that in the near future the Japanese will renew and augment their pressure upon the Chinese Government for an early diplomatic settlement of certain questions; that the Japanese are in-

---

[77] Joseph Aloysius Lyons, Australian Prime Minister since 1932.

sisting upon a negotiation on the basis of the Hirota three-point program (see memorandum attached [78]); that the Chinese Government cannot make that program a basis of negotiation; and that the Chinese Government wishes to inquire what, in the event of augmented Japanese pressure upon China, will be the attitude of the American Government.

I have said to the Chinese Ambassador that this is a pretty broad question, and he has admitted to me that it is a "hypothetical question." I have asked him what he might be prepared to reply in case you were to ask him what will be the attitude and action of the Chinese Government. He replied that he was not in position to say, but that he must present to you his Government's case.

May I suggest that an appointment be made for you to receive the Ambassador on Friday.[79]

793.94/7785

The Ambassador in China (Johnson) to the Secretary of State

No. 234

PEIPING, February 12, 1936.
[Received March 9.]

SIR: I have the honor to refer to the Embassy's strictly confidential despatch No. 184 of January 17, 1936,[80] with regard to the subject of the conflicting policies of China, Japan, and the Soviet Union in Eastern Asia, and to enclose for the information of the Department a copy of an editorial, entitled "Neither Accepted Nor Rejected", published in the *Peking & Tientsin Times* (British) of January 31 1936,[80] discussing the problem of China's present position in the triangle.

[Here follows report on the editorial.]

The initiative, as heretofore, rests with the Japanese. As emphasized by Ambassador Grew in his confidential despatch No. 1630 of January 7, 1936,[81] the moderate group in Japan is loath to have the Japanese Army undertake any adventures on the Asian continent that might check the substantial improvement of economic conditions now being experienced in Japan. The Army, stressing the political aspects of the situation more heavily than the economic, is convinced of the need of establishing the Japanese position in Asia on so strong a base that the Japanese Empire would be free from threat from any quarter, but it recognizes the strength of the argument that a China thrown into disorder would be to the disadvantage of Japan both

---

[78] Not printed; it was based on reports from the Embassy in China.
[79] See memorandum of February 15, by the Chief of the Division of Far Eastern Affairs, p. 60.
[80] Not printed.
[81] *Post*, p. 706.

economically and politically. It is probably primarily because of this realization that the Army has endeavored to achieve its ends in North China and Nanking by the exercise of steady pressure and threats to force acquiescence from the Chinese side without open conflict between the two countries.

The policy of attrition, however, is necessarily slow, and in China forces seem to be gathering which threaten to decrease the pace still further. Japan can hardly view with equanimity the growing radicalism in student circles, weakness of the economic structure, obduracy toward the Japanese program in even "pro-Japanese" officials, and growing strength of Chinese Communism, which threaten to bring the whole thing down upon the Japanese Army's head. And on "Manchukuo's" frontiers, the strength of the Soviet Army grows appreciably from month to month.

In those circumstances, the question would seem to be how long the patience of the Japanese militarists can last under a strain that is increasing. The border incidents arising out of clashes between Japanese-"Manchukuo" and Soviet Russian and Outer Mongolian forces have of late been increasing in number and intensity, and there is now reported in the press the advance of augmented "Manchukuo" forces to the Buir Nor region which has been the scene of frequent pitched battles. (An informed Russian newspaperman states that both Soviet Russian and Mongol sources report that the presumably hostile troops have not yet appeared on the border, and he suggests that the Japanese have perhaps in this case been more interested in creating an alarm than in actually going into action. Consul General Adams of Harbin in his despatch No. 192 of January 27, 1936,[82] also gives evidence indicating that Japan does not contemplate major hostilities with the Soviet Union in the immediate future.) As regards North China, there exists substantial evidence that the Japanese are pressing hard on the local Chinese militarists for a definitive settlement along autonomous lines and that, in the absence of such a settlement, Yin Ju-keng's East Hopei regime and other "autonomous" organizations may be expected to constitute the spearhead of a new Japanese thrust into North China. It is reported by the Military Attaché's Office that Yin Ju-keng is now expanding his military cadres, which were built around the former Peace Preservation Corps, into five divisions of troops totalling 27,000 men; Japanese advisers and instructors are said to have been engaged. At Changpei in Chahar the "Manchukuo" forces of Li Shou-hsin are already in control—and Changpei District extends to Kalgan and includes that part of the city lying northwest of the river traversing its area, so that Kalgan, important both strategically and commercially, would probably

---

[82] Not printed.

fall without a blow. Abandoned to their fate by the National Government, the Mongols of Inner Mongolia in Chahar are apparently being forced into a position which will give them no choice but to throw in their lot with the Japanese, for reasons of self-preservation.

In a well informed quarter in Peiping it is held that the Japanese Army would not dare force war with the Soviet Union prior to the establishment of control firmly in North China; however, as regards the Outer Mongolia-"Manchukuo" border incidents, the same authority stated that it is quite possible that the Japanese Army is preparing at this time to open "the Outer Mongolia problem", and to make an initial test of the Soviet Union's attitude toward the question of that country's defense, by launching a strong attack westward on Ulan Bator (Urga). A simultaneous Japanese advance into Suiyuan, he pointed out, would facilitate a flank attack on the same objective.

In this connection, the recent visit to Moscow of Premier Genbun of Outer Mongolia and the popular importance attached to the visit to the Kremlin of a delegation from the Buriat-Mongolian A. S. S. R. at the end of January may be of significance and are facts attesting to the Soviet Republic's interest in this situation. It is improbable that the Russians view Outer Mongolia indifferently, especially inasmuch as the control of that territory by Japan would not only put the Soviet Union at a grave strategic disadvantage militarily but would result in a serious loss of Soviet prestige both at home and abroad. According to a statement made by a local Russian to a resident British banker, the Soviet Union's attitude regarding Outer Mongolia can be discovered from a careful reading of the speech made on foreign relations by Molotov, Chairman of the Council of People's Commissariat of the Union of Soviet Socialist Republics, at the meeting on January 11 of the Central Executive Committee. This speech, it is said, was meant to be a clear warning to Japan. (There is enclosed, for the ready reference of the Department, a copy of that section of the speech which deals with the Far East, as reported by the Tass News Agency.[83])

The military conferences at present taking place in Tokyo are therefore of more than usual significance. Major-General Isogai (Japanese Military Attaché in China), Lieutenant-General Sugiyama (Vice-Chief of the Tokyo General Staff), Minister of War Kawashima, and other important Japanese militarists are said now to be considering the whole matter of the future of Sino-Japanese relationships. There is enclosed, in English translation, a copy of a news item [83] appearing in the *Yachou Min Pao* (*Asia People's Voice*, Japanese Chinese-language newspaper, Peiping) of January 31 which purports to give the agenda of the discussions. If this report is cor-

---

[83] Not printed.

rect, it will be noted that the present discussions are very comprehensive. After the conference has terminated, Sugiyama is scheduled to make a one month's trip to "Manchukuo" and North China, reputedly for the purpose of coordinating the policies and activities of the Kwantung Army and the North China Garrison with the plans of the War Office; Isogai will return to Shanghai; as already reported, Major-General Doihara intends to take up a permanent residence in Peiping "for the purpose of promoting Sino-Japanese relations".

Respectfully yours,

For the Ambassador:

F. P. LOCKHART
Counselor of Embassy

761.94/873 : Telegram

The Chargé in the Soviet Union (Henderson) to the Secretary of State

Moscow, February 13, 1936—2 p. m.
[Received 8:20 p. m.]

45. Your 19, February 6.[85] It is extremely difficult to ascertain the real views of the Kremlin with regard to the possibility of an attack by Japan during the present year since the statements of responsible Soviet officials frequently differ and sometimes change from day to day. After a careful consideration of all the information which it has been able to obtain from published sources and from Soviet civilian and military officials and competent foreign observers in Moscow, the Embassy nevertheless ventures to set forth these views as follows:

1. The Kremlin does not believe that the Japanese Government is deliberately planning a war against the Soviet Union this spring, although it feels that Japan is energetically making preparations internally and externally for the eventuality of such a war.

2. It feels that although the Japanese Government has no desire for an immediate war with the Soviet Union, there is grave danger that some incident may occur which might strengthen the hands of an aggressive and active minority in Japan which is of the opinion that if the Soviet Union is to be eliminated as an important factor in the Far East that elimination must take place this year. This feeling is reflected in the extreme nervousness with which some of the border incidents are regarded. (See my telegram 39, January 31, 4 p. m.)

3. The Kremlin takes the position that the border incidents which have already occurred have been sufficiently grave to justify the Soviet Union in making war upon Japan. It is determined, however, not to be provoked into a war as long as these incidents do not constitute a serious invasion of Soviet territory or a dangerous threat to the security of the Soviet Far East or as long as they are not of such a nature as to force the Red Army to take defensive military action.

4. The Kremlin is particularly concerned regarding possible developments in Mongolia, since it feels that the Kwantung army might

---

[85] Not printed.

take action in Mongolia which, for military and political reasons, it would hesitate deliberately to take in Soviet territory. It is believed that the extent of assistance which the Soviet Union would give Mongolia in case of invasion would be determined by the internal situation at the time and the type of campaign conducted.

5. Kremlin is hopeful that the Japanese Government will continue to consider that China proper, not the Soviet Union or Mongolia, offers the best field at the present time for Japanese expansion on the Asiatic Continent. Recent announcements regarding the strength of the Red Army are promoted in part by a desire to warn the Kwantung army that the difficulties of penetrating into the Soviet Union or Mongolia would be much greater than those connected with further penetration into China proper and at the same time to convince that section of Japanese opinion which is in favor of driving the Soviet Union from the Far East that it is already too late to engage in such an undertaking without help from other great powers.

6. The Kremlin is convinced that developments in the Far East are dependent to a certain extent on those in Europe and vice versa and feels that Great Britain may be the deciding factor in the maintenance of peace, since, in its opinion, Germany will not embark on an eastern European adventure with an actively hostile Great Britain at its back and Japan will not deliberately go to war if it feels that it cannot count on support from the West, particularly if it cannot depend upon the benevolent neutrality of Great Britain.

In view of the above, one of the main objects of Soviet diplomacy at the present time is to bring about a closer *rapprochement* with Great Britain which it apparently feels may be more valuable over a protracted period than the mutual assistance pact with France. Although the Soviet Government is confident that the pact will be ratified within the next few days, after the experience of the last 2 years, it has grave doubts with respect to French dependability. In general, the statements of officials of the Foreign Office are believed to be somewhat more optimistic than the actual feelings of the Kremlin would justify. Since his return from the West, Litvinov, in particular, is bubbling over with optimism. The Embassy has learned from several sources, believed to be reliable, that he states that his conversations in London were extremely satisfactory and that he feels that with the changed situation in Great Britain, the danger of the Soviet Union being drawn into an armed conflict has been averted for the present, at least.

HENDERSON

893.01 Inner Mongolia/54½ : Telegram

The Chargé in the Soviet Union (Henderson) to the Secretary of State

Moscow, February 14, 1936—noon.
[Received February 14—11 : 13 a. m.]

46. The following is a summary of a Tass telegram from Ulanbator dated February 13th published in today's *Pravda:*

At 7 a. m. on February 12th, a Japanese-Manchurian mixed detachment of 500 men in 20 trucks and 1 passenger car armed with fixed and portable machine guns and 3 field guns, accompanied by 2 tanks and 2 airplanes, crossed the Mongolian frontier and attacked the Mongolian Frontier Guard at a point 7 kilometres from Bulundersun. The Mongolian Frontier Guard, although outnumbered by over 5 to 1, put up a stiff resistance before retreating. They left behind 1 field gun and 1 machine gun which were carried away by the Japanese-Manchurians. The Japanese-Manchurian detachment penetrated into Mongolian territory to a depth of 10 or 12 kilometres. Upon the arrival of reenforcements, Japanese-Manchurians were driven back to Manchukuo. Mongolian losses were 1 killed and 7 wounded and Japanese-Manchurian losses 10 killed and 20 wounded. The Mongolian Government has despatched a telegraphic note to Manchukuo protesting against the incident and demanding immediate investigation.

HENDERSON

893.01 Outer Mongolia/62 : Telegram

The Counselor of Embassy in China (Lockhart) to the Secretary of State

PEIPING, February 14, 1936—7 p. m.
[Received February 14—1 : 38 p. m.]

63. The following telegram has been received from the Consul General at Harbin:

"4. February 14, 5 p. m. The Japanese Mission here confirmed newspaper reports stating that in an engagement on February 12, near Olanhodok on the Outer Mongolian border nine Japanese were killed. The Japanese charge bombardment by two Soviet planes in Manchukuo territory. Indications are that more Japanese troops are moving westward but details are not available".

LOCKHART

662.9331 Manchuria/2½

Memorandum by the Ambassador in China (Johnson) [86]

NANKING, February 14, 1936.

I had a long talk to-day with Dr. Kiep, head of the German Economic Mission, in the course of which he stated that his Mission had come out to the Far East for the purpose of reaching conclusions as

---

[86] Copy transmitted to the Department by the Ambassador in China in his despatch No. 340, March 28; received April 20.

to what opportunities there were for increasing Germany's trade in the Far East. He stated that the visit of the Mission to Manchuria had no political significance whatever; that this was quite well understood by Mr. Hirota; but that later, when they arrived in Manchuria, Mr. Ohashi, Vice Minister of Foreign Affairs of the "Manchukuo" Government, had used their visit for political purposes, for it was from Ohashi and his group that emanated the publicity which hindered the possibility of a German-Japanese military alliance. He stated that he had complained to Hirota of Ohashi's methods.

Dr. Kiep drew a comparison between the situation which developed between Germany and France when the German Army thought of France as a weak neighbor and therefore a threat to Germany, and the situation which now exists between Japan and China.

He spoke of German business in Manchuria, stating that formerly the South Manchuria Railway made some thirty-three per cent of its foreign purchases from the United States, thirty-three per cent from Japan, and spent the remaining thirty-three per cent in Europe and Germany. He said that now this had all changed, as the South Manchuria Railway purchased more than eighty per cent of its requirements from Japan; that recent developments in Manchuria were crowding German as well as other Western business representation in Manchuria; that German representation to-day was only forty per cent of its former strength and that it was still growing weaker. The reason was Japanese political control in Manchuria, aided by the great number of Japanese retailers all over the country. He mentioned also the great number of Japanese advisers employed in the various departments of the Government of "Manchukuo", who were in a position to make it possible for bids to go to Japanese suppliers of goods.

Dr. Kiep stated that Germany was in dire need of Manchurian soy beans which they imported and used as a fertilizer for the farmers' fields of Germany. He ascribed the recent butter shortage in Germany to their inability to purchase the soy bean of Manchuria. Germany was prepared to buy where it could sell. Manchuria was buying more and more from Japan and therefore selling less and less to Germany. He stated that his chief interest in Manchuria was to work out some sort of an arrangement whereby Germany could take soy beans in exchange for German goods. He said that difficulties were in the way, however, as the Yokohama Specie Bank wanted to have a monopoly of the business and to receive guarantees from the German Government covering all credits. He said that he did not know what attitude the Reich Bank would take in regard to this matter.

Dr. Kiep explained in some detail Germany's need and the difficulties which she was now having. He mentioned the fact of the boycott which was current throughout the world and especially effective in the United States. It was his hope that the peoples of the world would forget the Jew in Germany and cease to agitate the matter, as such agitation by outsiders only tended to make the situation worse in Germany itself. He ascribed the recent recrudescence of anti-Jewish activities in Germany to politics, stating that the Party was losing a good deal of prestige because of the rapidly-increasing control over politics exercised by the newly-created German Army. The Party's problem was to keep itself before the eyes of the people.

Reverting again to China, Dr. Kiep stated that Germany's trade with China was too important to Germany for Germany to enter into any kind of an arrangement of a cooperative character with Japan. Germany was not interested in mixing up in the situation here in the Far East and thus sacrificing her hard-won share of world commerce.

NELSON TRUSLER JOHNSON

793.94/7766

Memorandum by the Chief of the Division of Far Eastern Affairs (Hornbeck)

[WASHINGTON,] February 15, 1936.

Reference, memorandum to the Secretary of February 12 hereunder attached.[87]

The Chinese Ambassador called me on the 'phone this morning and said that he had been checking his telegrams and had found a mistake in reading: in connection with his request for an interview with the Secretary, he found that it was not necessary that he see the Secretary, but his instruction was to "keep in touch with the Department of State"; he thought that it would be preferable that he talk the matter over at this stage with me rather than with the Secretary.

The appointment for the Ambassador to see the Secretary at twelve o'clock this day was therefore canceled, and the Ambassador called on me.

The Ambassador repeated substantially what he had said to me as recorded in the memorandum of February 12 under reference. He then added that his Government had reason to believe that the Japanese Government had approached or would approach the American, the British, and the Russian Governments with the objective of keeping those Governments apart and causing them to stand aside while Japan proceeded with Japan's China policy. The Chinese Government wished to know whether the American Government had been thus approached. I said in reply that the Japanese Government had made no approach to us. The Ambassador wished to know what would be our attitude if we were so approached. I replied that I thought the Ambassador could formulate for himself an adequate reply to

---

[87] *Ante,* p. 52.

that question and could give his Government a reply of his own making: that it is perfectly clear to anyone in this country that the American people and the American Government are at present disinclined toward "foreign entanglements", especially anything in the nature of political commitments which would tie this country to other countries or involve us in conflicts between other countries; and that it is also clear that this country remains, as it always has been, well disposed toward China—whence it would be unlikely that we would commit ourselves to or pursue a policy obviously prejudicial to China's interests and in the nature of taking sides with another or other countries against China.

The Ambassador said that he was glad to have what I had said and that he hoped and trusted that the American Government would be on guard. He then inquired whether we had any news of new Japanese activities in China, and I replied that we had not. He made the observation that things appeared comparatively quiet in China and that the Japanese were not pressing expressly upon any one demand.

S[TANLEY] K. H[ORNBECK]

793.94/7725 : Telegram

The Second Secretary of Embassy in China (Atcheson) to the Secretary of State

NANKING, February 18, 1936—10 a. m.
[Received February 18—7:40 a. m.]

35. 1. I am informed by responsible official of Executive Yuan that Chiang Kai Shek has now set the "limit of Japanese aggression" at which the Chinese "must" begin fighting as invasion of or interference in Shantung or Suiyuan. Formerly the "limit" was Chahar; this official states that both regions, Chahar and Hopei, are now considered as effectively lost to China as is Manchukuo, the chief hope of the negotiations in the North being to save the Government's face by continuing as long as possible the lip service of the Hopei-Chahar Council. According to this and other reliable sources, the Yellow River continues [to] be the principal front line in the Chinese plans for defense. However, I learn authoritatively from another source that the general staff's aerial survey section which has been making reconnaissance maps and fire plans along that line has suddenly ceased this work because of intrigue thought to have been inspired by Japanese, thus leaving the Chinese artillery at present without means of conducting indirect fire if fighting should occur.

2. Recent large shipments of motor trucks from Pukow to the northwest and other considerations have tended to confirm belief held in some circles that Chiang is preparing to assist Soviet Russian forces against the Japanese. On the other hand Chiang yesterday told an

American correspondent in confidence and not for publication that
China positively would remain neutral in event of Soviet-Japanese
hostilities.

3. To the Department and Peiping. To Tokyo by mail.

ATCHESON

793.94/7731 : Telegram

The Counselor of Embassy in China (Lockhart) to the Secretary of State

PEIPING, February 18, 1936—9 p. m.
[Received February 18—11 : 20 a. m.]

1. Following apparently a decision of the Japanese military in
North China to try to obtain more satisfactory press reports about
their activities, certain Japanese officers have suddenly become more
communicative than had been the case for some weeks. Among them
is Doihara who told pressmen yesterday at Peiping among other
things that (1) it is not necessary for the National Government to
approve appointments of Japanese advisers to the Hopei-Chahar
Political Council, (2) the Council need not be separated for the
National Government, (3) the Japanese might assist in suppression
of Communism if it should threaten North China, (4) the Japanese
will not invade North China, (5) he does not insist on Asia for the
Asiatics, and (6) Pu-yi [88] will not come to North China in March
(in reply to a question specifying that month).

2. Embassy's 8, January 8, noon, paragraph 5.[89] Although students
in Peiping returned to classes after prolonged winter vacation, they
are creating difficulties in some schools. These movements have not
yet reached important proportions. The student movement in Peiping is in confusion, presumably as the result of efforts of radical students to gain control of the Peiping Students Union [and?] the objectives of the radicals are not clear. In the opinion of one responsible
educator, the radicals may intend to bring about a conflict between
Japanese and Chinese in order to promote Communism.

3. The financial situation of the Hopei-Chahar Political Council is
obscure. It is understood that negotiations between it and the National Government over division of revenues have practically reached
a deadlock.

4. There are lacking concrete signs of dissatisfaction on the part
of Japanese military at the slow progress of the Council toward a
greater degree of autonomy.

---

[88] Manchu ex-Emperor of China, "Emperor Kang-teh of Manchoutikuo" since
1934.
[89] Not printed.

5. Embassy's 44, February 4, noon, paragraph 3. Lieutenant Colonel Ikeda, North China Garrison staff officer, has returned to Tientsin from Tokyo where he was supposedly engaged in significant conversations.

LOCKHART

793.94/7734 : Telegram

The Counselor of Embassy in China (Lockhart) to the Secretary of State

PEIPING, February 20, 1936—5 p. m.
[Received February 20—4:45 p. m.[90]]

79. A reliable official of the local Japanese Embassy has expressed the following views in private conversation.

The present apparent relaxation of Japanese military policy with respect to North China is the outcome of the conversations during the middle of January of such important officers as Doihara, Isogai, and Itagaki (See Embassy's 15, January 13, 4 p. m., paragraph 1). They arrived at an agreement that (1) direction of Japanese military policy in North China is to be removed from the hands of the Kwantung army, (2) Doihara will return to Japan in March, and (3) the policy will be in hands of the North China Garrison. The North China Garrison is to be enlarged (the degree of increase is not yet known but will probably be double the present strength) and will be under the command of a lieutenant-general. This means that Tada will go. His successor is not yet known but it will not be Doihara. This agreement was arrived at because of the international situation, principally the attitude toward Japan of Russia, the United States and Great Britain, and because of the differences of opinion existing between Itagaki and Tada on the one hand and Doihara on the other with regard to policy. There will be quiet for 3 or 4 months not necessarily because of a change of objective but because of a change of method.

3. The Foreign Office policy is the most reasonable explanation available of the seeming pause of the Japanese military with the procrastination of Chinese military in attaining a degree of autonomy desirable to the Japanese military. An unofficial but informed and frank Japanese has also recently stated that Doihara will go to Japan next month and that there will be quiet in North China for some time.

Repeated to Nanking, by mail to Tokyo.

LOCKHART

---

[90] Telegram in two sections.

893.797 Manchuria/5

The Secretary of State to the Ambassador in Japan (Grew)

No. 950   WASHINGTON, February 20, 1936.

SIR: Reference is made to despatch No. 189, December 2, 1935, from the Consul General at Mukden to the Ambassador at Peiping [91] reporting discrimination against American automotive trucks in favor of Dowa trucks. A notation on the despatch indicates that a copy was transmitted to you.

In principle the Department believes that when there occur in Manchuria specific instances of discrimination against American trade and American products the record should be kept clear as to this Government's continued interest in the effective maintenance of the principle of equal opportunity by bringing to the attention of the appropriate Japanese authorities the instances of such discriminatory treatment. The Department has noted that in the case discussed by the Consul General at Mukden, the Consul General does not regard the present time as opportune for the making of formal representations. Having in mind both this fact and the view with regard to principle that is expressed above, the Department raises for the consideration of and decision by the Embassy the question whether it might not be advisable for the Counselor or the First Secretary of the Embassy orally and informally to bring to the attention of the Japanese Foreign Office the fact that the Embassy has received information indicating that the Kwantung Army as well as railways and other organizations in Manchuria are placing obstacles in the way of the purchase of American trucks on a freely competitive basis.

Very truly yours,   For the Secretary of State:

WILLIAM PHILLIPS

761.94/877 : Telegram

The Ambassador in the Soviet Union (Bullitt) to the Secretary of State

Moscow, February 21, 1936—9 p. m.
[Received February 22—7 : 15 a. m.]

58. Litvinov said to me today that he feared the Japanese elections might have resulted in an increase in the strength of the Seiyukai which would strengthen the hands of the Japanese militarists. He asserted, however, that even if the militarists should be strengthened he had no fear of an early Japanese attack on the Soviet Union.

He stated that all the Soviet Government's reports from Manchuria indicated that the Japanese were having great difficulty in controlling the native population; that the resistance to the Japanese in

[91] Not printed.

North China was much greater than anticipated; that the Japanese financial situation was more grave than it appeared to be; that in addition to the Emperor, his closest advisers, the leading businessmen, the navy and at least half the officers of the army were opposed to war on the Soviet Union at the present time. He added that he anticipated Japanese refusal of the Soviet proposal that there should be a neutral member on the border commission to be set up by Japan, Manchukuo and the Soviet Union. He said that if this proposal should be rejected he would be ready to accept the Japanese proposal for a mixed commission consisting of the Soviet Union on one side and Japan and Manchukuo on the other.

Litvinov said that he as well as all the British and French statesmen with whom he had talked had been delighted by the defeat of the proposed American neutrality legislation because they felt that the proposed legislation would have prevented the United States from giving support to England, France and the Soviet Union in case of war with Germany. He made no further reference to the United States and did not bring up Soviet-American relations.

He said that he had just received word that both Eden and Flandin would attend the League meeting on the coordination of sanctions at Geneva on March 2d contrary to their statements to him that they would not attend. He stated that he was uncertain whether or not he would go because he felt that there was nothing important to discuss. He said "sanctions are dead" and added that in view of recent Italian successes he considered it beyond the realm of possibility that the League could make any compromise proposal similar to the Hoare-Laval proposal.[92] He commented further that no one today would be ready to take the moral onus of proposing a reward to the aggressor after the wave of indignation which had greeted the Hoare-Laval proposal.

In this connection it seems pertinent to add that when I saw Attolico, the Italian Ambassador to Germany, on my way through Berlin on February 12th he said to me that he had been in Rome recently and that he felt the moment was approaching when it might be appropriate for the President of the United States to propose mediation along the lines of the Hoare-Laval proposal with certain modifications in favor of Italy. As Attolico spent considerable time with Mussolini in January and as he went on to elaborate his remark most seriously I derived the impression that Mussolini may be deluded enough to hope that he can persuade the President to rush in where the successors of Hoare and Laval now fear to tread.

BULLITT

---

[92] For the Anglo-French proposal, see *Foreign Relations*, 1935, vol. I, pp. 699–723, *passim;* it was arranged between the French Premier, Pierre Laval, and the British Foreign Secretary, Sir Samuel Hoare.

761.9315 Manchuria/40 : Telegram

The Ambassador in the Soviet Union (Bullitt) to the Secretary of State [93]

Moscow, February 23, 1936—8 p. m.
[Received February 23—5 : 05 p. m.]

60–61. My 58, February 21, 9 p. m. second paragraph. The *Moscow Daily News* of today carries the following official statement.

"On February 21, 1936, the Japanese Ambassador M. Ota visited Comrade B. S. Stomonyakov, Assistant Peoples Commissar for Foreign Affairs, and informed him that the Japanese Government does not consider it possible to accept the Soviet Government's proposal to include neutral representatives in a mixed commission for investigating the border incident of January 3 and asked the Soviet Government not to insist on its proposal.

Comrade Stomonyakov stated that the Soviet Government still considers desirable, in the interests of ascertaining the truth, the participation of neutral, disinterested representatives in the Commission. However, if the Japanese side does not consider it possible to accept this proposal the Soviet Government while sincerely regretting this is ready in the interests of peace to meet the wishes of the Japanese Government and agrees to the investigation of the incident by mixed commission consisting of only representatives of the U. S. S. R., Japan and Manchukuo. The commission should be based on parity with equal representation of the U. S. S. R. on the one side and of Japan and Manchukuo on the other side.

BULLITT

793.94/7741 : Telegram

The Counselor of Embassy in China (Lockhart) to the Secretary of State

PEIPING, February 24, 1936—4 p. m.
[Received February 24—6 : 47 a. m.]

87. Embassy's 79, February 20, 5 p.m. Commander of the Japanese North China Garrison Tada informed Chinese newspapermen February 23 that (1), unless the Eastern Hopei anti-Communist autonomous government, whose objects are autonomy and defense against Communism, and the Hopei-Chahar Political Council, which was organized by the National Government, "reached the same water level, they could not flow together"; (2), the Japanese Government has not yet replied to his request, which was made on the suggestion of Sung Che Yuan, that it recommend (additional) Japanese for appointment as advisers to the Hopei-Chahar Political Council, and

[93] The two sections of this message, transmitted as telegrams Nos. 60 and 61, are printed as one document.

(3), the Kwantung army, in whose hands is the Northern Chahar affair, had reached an agreement with the chairman of Chahar by which the area (extending across Chahar north of the Great Wall from Jehol to Suiyuan) taken by Li Shou Hsin should be policed by Li's forces organized into a Mongolian special police.

By mail to Tokyo.

LOCKHART

793.94/7749 : Telegram

The Counselor of Embassy in China (Lockhart) to the Secretary of State

PEIPING, February 25, 1936—5 p. m.
[Received February 25—10 : 55 a. m.]

89. Embassy's 79, February 20, 5 p. m. According to a report of the Tokyo *Asahi* of this morning, the following army changes will occur in March. Lieutenant General Seiji Kozuki, now commanding the 12th division in Japan, will succeed Major General Tada as commander of the North China Garrison. Colonel Seiichi Kita, who reputedly will be promoted on March 1st to major general, will be Kozuki's Chief of Staff. (Kita was chief of the Japanese Military Mission at Shanhaikwan in 1933 when the Japanese occupied that city, was involved in the conclusion of the Tangku truce,[94] visited Chinese Minister twice during last year, and is at present chief of the China section of the Japanese General Staff at Tokyo.) Major General Doihara will be succeeded as chief of the Special Service Mission at Mukden by Colonel Takayoshi Matsumuro, who reputedly will be made on March 1st a major general. (Matsumuro was chief of the Special Military Mission at Chengteh after the Japanese occupation of Jehol and is now in Japan).

2. Replacing of a major general and a colonel by a lieutenant general and a major general as the two principal officers of the North China Garrison would presumably foreshadow a substantial increase in its numerical strength and perhaps in its powers for negotiation with North China Chinese leaders.

3. According to a Japanese Domei report of February 24 from Tokyo, Sugiyama, Vice Chief of Staff at Tokyo, referred to in the Embassy's 21, January 16, 4 p. m., has postponed his tour of Manchuria and North China until the middle of March.

By mail to Tokyo.

LOCKHART

[94] Signed May 31, 1933, *Foreign Relations*, Japan, 1931–1941, vol. I, p. 120.

793.94/7764 : Telegram

The Ambassador in the Soviet Union (Bullitt) to the Secretary of State

Moscow, February 28, 1936—6 p. m.
[Received February 28—12 : 50 p. m.]

74. Dr. Yen, Chinese Ambassador, stated to me today that he had just received a most private letter from Nanking which said that if the Japanese should attempt to compel acceptance of their "three principles" by an ultimatum or if the Japanese should advance into Shantung, General Chiang Kai Shek positively would fight.

BULLITT

793.94/7812

The Consul General at Shanghai (Gauss) to the Secretary of State

No. 43   SHANGHAI, February 29, 1936.
[Received March 23.]

SIR: I have the honor to report that Mr. Hachiro Arita, newly appointed Ambassador to China, arrived in Shanghai aboard the M. V. *Asama Maru* on February 26, 1936, accompanied by his wife and Major General Rensuki Isogai, Japanese Military Attaché. His coming was viewed with mixed feelings locally; some fear that he may sympathize with the army and favor a stronger attitude toward China, while others hope that his strength and prestige will enable him to effect a genuine *rapprochement* without the interference from the military which has been so familiar of late.

In an interview with representatives of the press he stated that he considers it essential to establish Sino-Japanese relations on a firm footing for the sake of peace and prosperity in East Asia, that he has instructions looking to the general readjustment of relations between the two countries, and that he intends to deal with problems in private talks rather than at a formal conference. He announced it as his intention to reside in Nanking. It is understood that the Counselor of Embassy, Mr. K. Wakasugi, newly transferred from Peiping, will continue to live in Shanghai.

[Here follows summary of press views.]

Respectfully yours,   C. E. GAUSS

893.00/13449

The Ambassador in China (Johnson) to the Secretary of State

No. 106   NANKING, March 3, 1936.
[Received April 6.]

SIR: I have the honor to refer to the Embassy's despatch No. 66 of November 7, 1935, from Peiping,[95] regarding the Communist situ-

---

[95] Not printed.

ation in west China, and briefly to outline below certain aspects of current developments in the anti-Communist campaign in the Shensi-Shansi sector. The information on which this account is given has been obtained partly from newspapers, and partly from conversations held by an officer of the Embassy with persons acquainted with conditions in the area concerned.

As has previously been recorded, little occurred in north Shensi subsequent to the arrival there of the forces of Hsü Hai-tung, P'eng Teh-huai and Mao Tse-tung to supplement the Communist strength of Liu Tzu-tan's 26th Army Corps. Liu Tzu-tan, a Communist leader of intelligence and experience, had already, by careful organization over a period of years, developed in north Shensi a Communist organization firmly rooted in the agrarian community; the arrival of the military forces of three other powerful veteran leaders gave a guarantee that the growth of the north Shensi organization would be protected by such force as the Communist militarists had at their disposal. Hsü Hai-tung led the 25th Army Corps, whose history dated back to the period when a Chinese Soviet ruled the area at the junction of the Honan-Hupeh-Anhwei borders. Mao Tse-tung is the Political Commissioner for the Soviet Government in China, with a revolutionary experience dating back to the beginnings of the Kuomintang in Canton and including the term when the Soviets ruled much of Kiangsi and Fukien. His military organization, as led into Shensi from Szechwan after the long trek from Kiangsi, constitutes the "Shensi-Kansu Branch Forces", divided into three main columns led by the able irregular strategists Lin Piao, P'eng Teh-huai and Yeh Chien-ying. In conjunction with the Communist military strength reported by General Yen Hsi-shan as already existing in north Shensi under the leadership of Liu Tzu-tan (see the Embassy's aforementioned despatch of November 7), this accretion of revolutionary strength in the Kansu-Shensi area gave early indications of holding a potential threat, the exact direction of which could not be clearly ascertained, for north China.

In the course of the winter of 1935–6 the Communists had practically undisturbed possession of north Shensi, themselves winning the victories in the few battles occurring with Government troops, and presumably were thus enabled to consolidate their forces and determine on their strategy for the coming year. A move has now been made which may be of significance in this connection. In January, a small Communist force, evidently acting as a vanguard, crossed the Yellow River from Shensi at Sanchiaochen (Chungyang Hsien) and penetrated into west Shansi. The Communist control was established over the fords along the river in the immediate vicinity. Then, beginning on February 22, heavy Communist forces, reputedly under the control of Mao Tse-tung, began to move into west Shansi. More than 10,000 Communist troops are reported already to have entered the western part of the province and to have launched attacks on Chungyang, Shihlou and other district towns in the area. More Communist forces are said to be coming up, while a concentration of troops under Liu Tzu-tan and Hsü Hai-tung is reported to be occurring in the vicinity of Wayaopu, Yungpingchen, Yenchuan and Yenchang, that is, between the Yen and Chingchien Rivers in east-central Shensi. A major move by the Communist forces seems to have been begun.*

The objective of such a military movement is of course difficult to discern, especially in view of the well-known characteristic of the Communist armies of "noising about the east and striking in the west". An immediate maneuver might logically be expected to take the form of an effort to cut off the five Shansi brigades now in northeast Shensi, where they were despatched to assist the 84th and 86th Government Divisions, if the irregulars felt strong enough. These brigades have now been ordered recalled for the protection of their home province, but a successful drive northward by the Communist forces which have penetrated Shansi would block their return and possibly subject them to a disastrous attack by the Communist armies still in Shensi. There seems to be no indication that the Communist forces plan the evacuation of Shensi at this time: the present move seems designed more to be an extension of their activities to new fields than an aimless retreat in search of possible haven.

The Communist penetration into Shansi constitutes a challenge to the leaders of that province that they will have difficulty in meeting by reason of the deterioration that has afflicted the provincial economy. General Yen Hsi-shan, after last July making known to the world the state of affairs existing in North Shensi, announced that village ownership of land would be put into effect in Shansi in order to revive agriculture and thus overcome the threat offered by Communist ideology. The leaders of the National Government were able to convince him upon the occasion of his attendance at the Kuomintang National Congress that the time was not yet ripe for the institution of such sweeping reforms as he proposed (they also gave him Yuan $5,000,000, according to report), with the result that Yen consented to postpone the implementation of his plan.† Nevertheless, reliable

---

*According to the official interpretation of Vice-Commander-in-Chief of Bandit Suppression Chang Hsueh-liang, at present in Nanking, this movement by the Communist forces is the result of the success of the Government's campaign against them in Shensi. This explanation can be dismissed as being highly improbable. [Footnote in the original.]

†Agricultural experts express their doubts regarding 1) the *bona fides* of Yen Hsi-shan's project, which possibly would benefit the governing group in Shansi more than the peasants and 2) the economic wisdom of the proposal in a region where 72% of the peasants are reputed to own their land and the agricultural problems evidently are primarily not those of land tenure. [Footnote in the original.]

reports from observers who have visited Shansi are to the effect that there exists the greatest activity there under Yen's direction, along the lines of education, propagandizing and organization, as preparation for reforms to be effected there at no late date. One of the interesting aspects of the situation is that groups of every political complexion have been drawn into those activities, with "radical" periodicals and literature as readily obtainable as the official Kuomintang interpretation of social economics, with the probable result that the orthodox Communist view, only slightly disguised under the veil of anonymity, has been able to compete freely for converts with other political ideologies.

An interesting commentary on the present state of affairs in Shansi was made by Chairman Hsü Yung-ch'ang in a newspaper interview given on February 24, on the occasion of his recent visit to Suiyuan as Yen Hsi-shan's delegate to the Suiyuan Mongol Political Council.‡ Yen Hsi-shan, Director of the new organ, according to Hsü could not attend because of the veteran general's concern with the threat offered by the Communists of north Shensi, where the situation was described as being "very tense". Hsü stated that the Communist leader P'eng Teh-huai had convinced the other Communist strategists that it was preferable to attack Shansi rather than advance northwards against Yülin, and thus to achieve the weakening of the defense line along the Paotow front. But, continued the Shansi Chairman, the Shansi troops in north Shensi would definitely not be withdrawn, although any threat on Shansi itself would be met by moving up other forces already in the province. (The fact that orders have already been issued for the return of the Shansi troops in north Shensi would seem to indicate that the threat is stronger than at first considered. Nevertheless, the evident fact that the Shansi militarists had prior knowledge of the impending attack should have enabled them to make defense preparations.) The Shansi defenses against Communism, he said, had been strengthened by the organization, under the direction of Yen Hsi-shan, of people's organizations called "Justice Corps" and "Anti-Communist Defense Militia", and Suiyuan was disposed to follow Shansi's example and set up similar organizations. However, when it came to the matter of rendering financial assistance to Suiyuan, Hsü was reported to have viewed the situation very pessimistically, saying,

"Shansi hasn't the slightest chance of doing it. Very shortly, incident upon setting up the Anti-Communist Defense Militia and administering other matters, the people's burdens will be increased by additional assessments. When Shansi has not time to care for itself, naturally it is impossible to discuss assistance to Suiyuan."

‡*Ta Kung Pao* (*L'Impartial*, Tientsin), February 27, 1936. [Footnote in the original.]

Hsü said that he had early recognized the dangers inherent in making new assessments on the people, but "The matter must be taken care of, and the only way is to ask the people for money." But the reporter observed that Hsü was from first to last oppressed by the problems offered by Shansi's finances. However, Yen Hsi-shan's proposal for the circulation of "commodity scrip" as currency had not been yet put into effect, according to Chairman Hsü, and Shansi's currency generally could be considered quite stable. (Independent information is to the effect that Yuan $2,000,000 of the province's Yuan $88,000,000 in currency is in the form of "commodity scrip".)

Hsü Yung-ch'ang treated the subject of village ownership of land at some length, stating that the procedure for putting it into effect had already been settled upon but that the people viewed the project with alarm, while the Communists charged that "Of course this won't be put into effect, it being but a temporary expedient for the deception of the people." The reporter quoted Hsü as continuing:

"Our idea is that the methods of the Communist Party are too violent, leading inevitably to bloodshed. The procedure involved in the village ownership of land can avoid bloodshed; however, as regards the beginning of its application, it is undeniably impossible to avoid disturbances. We have not as yet come to the time for putting the plan into effect, and we do not plan now to do so. However, should it happen that we are pressed to a point where there is no way out, when it is impossible to avoid bloodshed, then we'll disregard popular disturbances (and go ahead with the project) by reason of our wish to avoid the shedding of blood."

It would appear as if the Communist challenge might directly or indirectly bring about interesting events in the sometime "Model Province" of Yen Hsi-shan. The implications those events would hold for Sino-Japanese relations may be readily deduced.

Respectfully yours,   NELSON TRUSLER JOHNSON

793.94/7777 : Telegram

The Ambassador in China (Johnson) to the Secretary of State

NANKING, March 5, 1936—noon.
[Received March 5—9 : 25 a. m.]

50. 1. Chang-Chun [96] yesterday told *New York Times* correspondent, but without as yet giving permission for publication, that (1) China had not agreed and could not agree to Hirota's three points and no written correspondence had been exchanged and nothing has been initialed or signed in this connection; (2) in November 1935 Chiang Kai-shek informed Ariyoshi that China was willing to consider the three points if comprehensively amplified and defined but

---

[96] Chinese Minister for Foreign Affairs.

Chiang was speaking personally and not as a representative of the Government; and (3) a year ago, while en route to Europe, Wang Chung Hui [97] had proposed to Hirota a Chinese three point program involving (a) abolition of unequal treaties, (b) mutual cessation of actions and policies detrimental to the other and (c) settlement of outstanding questions through normal diplomatic means. (Chang-Chun recently remarked to me that he anticipated no immediate discussion of these matters with the new Japanese Ambassador and that he expected that any such discussion when begun would be protracted over a long period.)

2. Two days ago in Shanghai the correspondent interviewed Arita who said that (1) Chiang Kai Shek had given China's agreement to Hirota's three points and the Japanese were determined to hold the Chinese Government to that agreement and (2) the attempted military coup in Tokyo would not cause a stiffening of Japan's attitude toward China because that attitude was already very stiff. (Arita is arriving at Nanking today on a Japanese naval vessel to present his credentials.)

3. T. V. Soong [98] gave the correspondent his confidential opinion, not to be ascribed to him, that continued procrastination by the National Government in dealing with Japanese issues would make hostilities between the two countries inevitable and that acceptance of the Japanese program would mean civil war in China.

Repeated to Peiping, Tokyo.

JOHNSON

894.00/636

Memorandum by the Counselor of Embassy in China (Peck) [99]

NANKING, March 5, 1936.

In the course of a general conversation [1] Dr. Kung said that he was sometimes a little surprised at the lack of appreciation of the United States and of European Powers of the serious threat to international peace and security offered by Japanese imperialistic ambitions.

Dr. Kung remarked that in pursuit of these ambitions China was an instrumentality through which Japanese militarists hoped to acquire the power necessary to extend the beneficent rule of the Japanese Emperor, not only over Asia, but actually over the world. Looking upon the far-flung British Empire, Japanese militarists did not

---

[97] Chinese judge, Permanent Court of International Justice at The Hague.
[98] Former Chinese Minister of Finance.
[99] Copy transmitted to the Department by the Ambassador in China in his despatch No. 112, March 6; received April 6.
[1] Between the Ambassador in China and the Chinese Minister of Finance, Vice President of the Executive Yuan (Kung).

perceive why the Japanese sun should not shine over an equally extensive chain of possessions.

If Japan had taken pains from the beginning to cultivate friendly feelings on the part of the Chinese, the materialization of their dream might have been perceptibly advanced by this time. Admitted to friendly cooperation, the Chinese might have seen something in the idea of "Asia for the Asiatics". Owing to the realities of Japanese operations, however, the Chinese understood that this idea was merely a cloak for Japanese ambition to extend Japanese domination.

Dr. Kung said that the army and navy of Japan have differing ideas regarding the steps which should be taken in the immediate future. The army believes that it would be best to wrest territory on the mainland from the Soviet Union and from China, whereas the navy believes that the next logical expansion should be toward islands in the South Pacific and adjacent to the southeastern coast of Asia, including those in the possession of European countries. Dr. Kung referred to the well-known economic invasion by the products of Japanese industries into the markets of the Occidental Powers, and even into those countries themselves. He said it was being claimed that British workmen in Lancashire were clothed in garments woven in Japan. He prophesied that the armed strength of Japan would some time be utilized to break down the tariff and other barriers with which modern industrialized nations now attempt to preserve their markets. On this account, i. e., the threat to their territorial possessions and to their markets, he could not understand why the western powers seemed so indifferent to the steps now being taken by Japan to consolidate and expand the bases of Japan's military strength.

Dr. Kung expressed the opinion that the policy of providing for "collective security" would require that the nations thus threatened should take steps to curb Japan's present actions and future ambitions.

WILLYS R. PECK

793.94/7778 : Telegram

The Counselor of Embassy in China (Peck) to the Secretary of State

NANKING, March 6, 1936—2 p. m.
[Received March 6—6 : 52 a. m.]

51. My 50, March 5, noon.

1. This office is reliably informed that at an emergency Cabinet meeting called this morning to discuss the Communist situation in Shansi it was announced that a threat had been received from Japanese Military Attaché Isogai to the effect that the Japanese will not permit the sending of Central Government troops into Shansi to oppose the Communists unless the Chinese Government agrees to Hirota's three point

program and even in that case any troops thus despatched must be withdrawn when their mission against the Communists is completed.

2. Repeated to Peiping and Ambassador at Shanghai.

PECK

893.00/13387 : Telegram

The Counselor of Embassy in China (Lockhart) to the Secretary of State

PEIPING, March 7, 1936—5 p. m.
[Received March 7—9 a. m.]

119. Embassy's 116.[2] Following from American Consul General at Canton.

"March 6, 9 a. m. Referring to my telegram of March 5, 4 p. m., rift between Marshal Chen[3] and Hu Han Min[4] group widening. Day before yesterday Chen took over from Tsou Lu[5] control of all local Government educational institutions other than Chungshan University in the control of which institution Tsou has recently had strong backing from Nanking. Chen's action thus appears to be further direct challenge to Nanking authority here.["]

LOCKHART

793.94/7793 : Telegram

The Counselor of Embassy in China (Peck) to the Secretary of State

NANKING, March 14, 1936—9 a. m.
[Received March 14—7 a. m.]

53. 1. This office has been informed by a responsible official of the Executive Yuan that, (1) United Press reports that the Yuan order No. 12 "decided to use armed force for the suppression of Japanese smuggling in North China" are untrue; (2) Executive Yuan, after discussing this problem decided merely to issue instructions to the natives "to employ effective measures"; (3) the Yuan is hoping to inspire commercial and other public opinion against the purchase of smuggled goods some of which are now being shipped south on both the Tientsin-Pukow and Peiping–Hankow Railways; (4) the Chinese authorities are unable to stop the smuggling operations because the Japanese military have refused to permit armed customs troops to proceed against smugglers along the coast on the ground that such action would violate the Tangku truce and have warned the Chinese against

---

[2] Dated March 6, 5 p. m., not printed.
[3] Chen Chi-tang, leading military commander at Canton.
[4] Inactive chairman of the standing committee of the Kuomintang Central Executive Committee.
[5] Chancellor of Chungshan University, Canton.

operations outside the 3 mile limit as being on the high seas beyond Chinese jurisdiction.

2. He said that protests filed with the Japanese Embassy here had elicited official replies that the Japanese authorities in the North would assist in suppressing smuggling into the demilitarized zone but spokesmen of the Embassy had stated unofficially that Japanese civil officials were powerless to act in the matter.

PECK

793.94/7794 : Telegram

The Ambassador in China (Johnson) to the Secretary of State

PEIPING, March 16, 1936—4 p. m.
[Received March 16—11 a. m.]

135. 1. Sino-Japanese relations in North China continue to be quiet as reported in paragraph 1 of the Embassy's 102, March 3, 11 a.m.[6] It would seem that the present period of quiet may continue for some time. There have been some minor developments which ought to be pleasing to at least some of the Japanese military.

2. An agreement was signed March 6th at Tientsin by the Managing Director of the Peiping–Mukden Railway and by an official of the South Manchuria Railway for the establishment from May 1st of through freight car service with Peiping-Mukden Railway. (Conclusion of such an agreement was supposed to have been promised by the Chinese at the time of the Tangku truce.) A local Japanese official states that he expects a through freight car agreement later. According to a Japanese press despatch, the Kwantung army regards the new agreement as "a great contribution to the promotion of close communication between North China and Manchukuo".

3. A total of five Japanese advisers have been appointed to the Hopei–Chahar Political Council. In addition to the two mentioned in paragraph 2 of the Embassy's 62, February 14, 5 p. m.,[6] Nagai, who was mentioned in the Embassy's 59, February 11, 3 p. m. has been definitely assigned to assist the Economic Committee of the Council. Also, an officer of the South Manchuria Railway and an officer of an electric company in Manchukuo have been assigned to advise construction and communication committees which are yet to be inaugurated under the Council.

4. It is reliably reported that Doihara, who has been assigned to Kurume, Kyushu, is to be succeeded as unofficial negotiator in Peiping by Colonel Takayoshi Matsumuro (see Embassy's 89, February 25,

---

[6] Not printed.

5 p. m.) but that Matsumuro will be attached to the North China garrison and not to the Kwantung army. This apparent effort on the part of the Japanese authorities to place Sino-Japanese affairs in North China under the North China Garrison may not, however, be entirely successful in practice because the Kwantung army as negotiator of the Tangku truce will presumably be able to intercede in matters which derive from that truce.

5. Japanese Military Attaché Isogai on a brief visit from Shanghai to Peiping is reported to have informed Japanese press men at Peiping on March 14 that Japan could not much longer tolerate the present unsatisfactory situation in North China and that he had received a most unpleasant impression of the results of General Sung Che Yuan's regime. It is doubted that this speech has much significance. He has made similar fiery statements in the past in Shanghai and he may desire to intrude himself as Military Attaché into Sino-Japanese questions in North China during the present period of suspended activity.

By mail to Tokyo.

JOHNSON

893.00/13410 : Telegram

The Counselor of Embassy in China (Peck) to the Secretary of State

NANKING, March 17, 1936—3 p. m.
[Received March 17—2 p. m.]

56. Following is translation of a note from the Minister of Foreign Affairs dated March 14:

"Some of the foreign diplomatic missions in Nanking have recently inquired of the Ministry of Foreign Affairs regarding the duties and rights of the Foreign Relations Committee of the Hopei-Chahar Political Affairs Commission which on March 7, 1936 issued a circular to the various foreign diplomatic missions in China to the effect that it attends to all diplomatic matters for Hopei, Chahar, Peiping and Tientsin.

The Ministry of Foreign Affairs takes this occasion to state that the provisional general principles governing the organization of the Hopei-Chahar Political Commission provide, when necessary, the Commission may establish different special committees, but that their duties shall be confined to the study and discussion of various problems and such committees shall have no authority to transact any business with foreign authorities.

The Ministry of Foreign Affairs has the honor to indite this third-person note for the Embassy's information."

PECK

761.9315 Manchuria/53

The Ambassador in the Soviet Union (Bullitt) to the Secretary of State

No. 1470   Moscow, March 18, 1936.
                                                 [Received April 2.]

SIR: In connection with my despatch No. 1469 of March 18, 1936,[7] I have the honor to report the following conversation with Mr. Sakoh, Japanese Counselor of Embassy in Moscow. As I have reported repeatedly to the Department, Sakoh is in charge of all important negotiations with the Soviet Government and is a more important figure in the Japanese Embassy here than Ambassador Ohta.

Sakoh from time to time talks with me intimately and with apparent frankness. In the course of a long conversation of this nature on March 16th, he made a number of statements which I consider important.

After giving me the details of Ohta's discussion with Stomoniakoff, which had taken place on the afternoon of our conversation, he said that Stomoniakoff had stated that he personally welcomed the proposal of the Japanese Government [8] but must refer it to Stalin before definite acceptance.

Sakoh went on to say that Ohta had made it clear that the entire question of the deltas of the Amur and Ussuri rivers must be excluded from the scope of action of the proposed commission. He said that in particular the question of the island of Heiheitsu, which composes the delta opposite Habarovsk at the junction of the Amur and Ussuri rivers, had been reserved as not discussable by the commission. He then indicated clearly that the Japanese Government desires the question of Heiheitsu to remain in suspense as it offers an excellent quasi-legal ground for Japan to start war with the Soviet Union at any time she may desire.

Sakoh predicted that both the commission for the redemarcation of the border from Lake Khanka to the Tumen-Ula river and the proposed commission for redemarcation of the Mongolo-Manchurian border would never reach agreement on any point. He said that the Japanese negotiators would draw out the negotiations until the Japanese political, military, and financial situation had improved. He added that the purpose of the Japanese Government in proposing these commissions was simply to gain time for military preparations.

Sakoh then stated flatly that, in the opinion of the Japanese Government, war with the Soviet Union would remain a national necessity so long as Vladivostok should remain in the hands of the Russians.

---

[7] Not printed.
[8] It proposed the formation of a commission for redemarcation of the boundary between the Soviet Union and "Manchoukuo".

In explanation, Sakoh pointed out the familiar fact that Vladivostok today is the exact center of the Japanese Empire and added that the development of the airplane would soon place every inch of Japanese and "Manchukuoan" territory within two hours flight of Russian bombing planes. He asserted, furthermore, that the Soviet Union now has 40 submarines at Vladivostok and is increasing the number of submarines there as rapidly as possible. He added that the threat constituted by these hostile airplanes and submarines at the center of the Japanese Empire was one which could not be removed except by war.

I asked Sakoh when he thought Japan would be ready to attempt to take Vladivostok from the Soviet Union. He replied that, in his opinion, the date for attack would be in 1937—"about a year or a year and a half from now."

Sakoh went on to state that it would be impossible for Japan to attack the Soviet Union with any hope of success until certain conditions precedent had been fulfilled. Specifically, he explained that the strategic railroads which Japan is now building in Manchuria will not be completed until December, 1936. He added that it was the belief of the Japanese Government that an attack on the Soviet Union could not be successful until Outer Mongolia or at least a considerable portion of it should be in the hands of the Japanese.

Sakoh then went on to say that there was a further factor which was becoming increasingly important: the financial position of Japan. He said that in order to make the essential preparations for an attack on the Soviet Union it would be necessary for Japan to obtain loans from either England or the United States. Sakoh expressed the hope that public opinion in the United States and the Government of the United States might soon come to realize that Japan would be entirely justified in attempting to eliminate Vladivostok as a Russian base of operations and that the growth of this realization might cause the United States to adopt a more friendly attitude toward Japan. He referred to the recent address to the United States Senate by Senator Pittman[9] and said that he hoped that it did not represent the views of our Government or American public opinion. He concluded by saying that he hoped the moment had come when relations between Japan and the United States might become more friendly.

Mr. Sakoh enjoys, I believe, the complete confidence of Mr. Hirota and I venture to suggest that his statements may represent the views of at least a portion of the Japanese Government.

Respectfully yours, WILLIAM C. BULLITT

---

[9] For text of speech of February 10 by Senator Key Pittman of Nevada, see *Congressional Record*, vol. 80, pt. 2, p. 1703.

893.797 Manchuria/6

The Ambassador in Japan (Grew) to the Secretary of State

No. 1734   Tokyo, March 18, 1936.
                                            [Received April 6.]

Sir: I have the honor to refer to the Department's instruction No. 950 of February 20, 1936, in regard to reported discrimination in Manchuria against American trucks in favor of Dowa trucks.

The Counselor of the Embassy took occasion, in a recent interview with the Vice Minister for Foreign Affairs to invite attention to the situation as reported. The Vice Minister voluntarily offered to obtain what information he could on the subject, and then stated that as it seemed to relate to a matter under the control of the authorities of "Manchukuo" he thought it might be well for the interested parties to take up the question directly. He added that so far as the Japanese were concerned, it might be that they were acting in accordance with the policy of "Manchukuo". He reiterated, however, that he would see what he could discover, but showed no disposition to discuss the question further.

Respectfully yours,   Joseph C. Grew

761.94/894

The Ambassador in Japan (Grew) to the Secretary of State

No. 1740   Tokyo, March 18, 1936.
                                            [Received April 6.]

Sir: I have the honor to submit the following review of certain developments affecting Soviet-Japanese relations since the Embassy's despatch No. 1716 of March 4, 1936.[10]

SIBERIAN-"MANCHUKUO" BORDER

According to a despatch from Moscow to the *Asahi* on March 9 the Soviet Vice-Commissar for Foreign Affairs, Mr. Stomoniakov, gave to the Japanese Ambassador, Mr. Ota, a "qualified assent" to the Japanese contention that the Manchu-Siberian border must be defined. On the 13th Mr. Stomoniakov is reported to have handed to Mr. Ota a note containing the Soviet Government's views on the scope and task of the projected mixed commission to settle the Chinchangkou Incident* but the contents of the note have not as yet been made public. On the 17th the Foreign Office spokesman in Tokyo confirmed that the Soviet plan for the proposed commission which had been agreed to by

---

[10] Not printed.
*Embassy's despatch No. 1716, March 4, 1936. [Footnote in the original; despatch not printed.]

"Manchukuo", Japan, and Soviet Russia had been received and stated that the plan appeared to be practical.

From a Moscow despatch published in Tokyo on March 18 it now appears that the negotiations between Mr. Ota and Mr. Stomoniakov are being accelerated. Mr. Ota is reported to have proposed the establishment of a commission to be composed of representatives of "Manchukuo" and the USSR and charged with the task of re-demarcating the frontier from Lake Hanka on the eastern border of "Manchukuo" to the Tumen River where the USSR, "Manchukuo", and Korea meet. He is further reported as saying that if this proposition is agreed to, the Japanese Government is ready to accept at once the USSR's proposals regarding the formation of a standing mixed commission for examination of border incidents occurring along this section of the frontier. In reply, Mr. Stomoniakov is believed to have inquired whether Japan is willing to bring about the formation of similar commissions to deal with the conflicts along the Outer Mongolian border. He then told Mr. Ota that he assumed that commissions for the prevention of incidents would be formed for the entire Soviet-Manchurian frontier and not merely for separate sections. The negotiations just outlined have caused the *Asahi* to comment that they are an expression of the "positive diplomacy" to which Mr. Hirota's Cabinet is pledged.

Meanwhile there appear to have been two incidents of minor importance along the frontier. On March 13 a Domei report from Hsinking declared that the "Manchukuo" Foreign Affairs Commissioner at Heiho protested to the Soviet authorities against the armed occupation of the island of Panchantao in the Amur River. On the same day a Moscow report from Habarovsk was published in Tokyo stating that on March 5 a Japanese-"Manchukuo" patrol fired on Soviet workmen across the Amur who were making an excavation. The patrol then crossed the river into Soviet territory and inspected the excavation.

MONGOL-MANCHU BORDER

There have been no reports of fighting along the Outer Mongolian border for a period of more than one month although Japanese reinforcements are said to have been concentrated nearby. There has, however, been an apparent change in the former policy of the USSR not to reveal the nature of the relationship existing between the Outer Mongolian Government and that of Soviet Russia. It will be remembered that on February 23 a report in the *Asahi* alleged that the Japanese Ambassador in Moscow had been definitely informed that the USSR had accepted responsibility for the independence of Outer Mongolia.† This report appears now to have been confirmed in a

†Embassy's despatch No. 1716, March 4, 1936. [Footnote in the original.]

conversation between Mr. Roy Howard of the Scripps-Howard news-papers and Mr. Stalin [11] on March 3.[12] According to the version of this unusual interview which was widely published in Japan Mr. Stalin told Mr. Howard that the USSR must stand ready to help the Mongolians in the event of a Japanese attack. On March 13 a further report from Moscow declared that General Demid, the War Minister of Outer Mongolia, had publicly stated that as a result of the recent visit of Outer Mongolian officials to Moscow, definite assurances had been received that the USSR would aid Outer Mongolia if it should be attacked.

In addition to the new development mentioned above, the cor-respondence between Outer Mongolia and "Manchukuo" concerning the border fights during February continued during the past two weeks. Under date of March 6 "Manchukuo" answered the Mon-golian note of February 29 proposing the establishment of a com-mission of investigation. The reply is said to have given "Man-chukuo's" assent in principle to the proposed commission but to have denied responsibility for the incidents in question, to have inquired as to the location of the proposed commission as well as to which incident would be dealt with, and to have affirmed a desire for a policy of "the good neighbor" vis-à-vis Outer Mongolia. On March 16, according to a Domei report from Hsinking, Outer Mongolia's reply was received with "signs of dissatisfaction" on the part of the "Man-chukuo" authorities. According to a Moscow report which was pub-lished at the same time in Japan the reply reaffirmed Outer Mon-golia's wish to settle the incident of February 12 first and then, if successful, to proceed to the consideration of other incidents. It was further proposed by Outer Mongolia that the commission should meet alternately at Tamskume and Kansurmiao on the Outer Mongolian and "Manchukuo" sides of the border respectively. The dissatisfac-tion of the "Manchukuo" officials with this proposition appears to be caused by its failure to comply with "Manchukuo's" wish to open formal diplomatic relations with Outer Mongolia.

If no other comment is justified at this stage of the negotiations it may, however, be said that the Mongol-Manchu border question is gradually being revealed in its true light as a conflict of interest be-tween Soviet Russia and Japan with each country less reluctant than formerly to acknowledge its concern in the matter.

ARREST OF JAPANESE STAFF OF SOVIET EMBASSY IN TOKYO

Taking advantage of the unusual conditions prevailing in Tokyo as a result of the incident of February 26, the police arrested eleven

---

[11] Secretary General of the Central Committee of the All-Union Communist Party.
[12] See telegram No. 76, March 2, 6 p. m., *Foreign Relations*, The Soviet Union, 1933–1939, p. 288.

Japanese interpreters, translators, and language teachers connected with the Soviet Embassy. The arrests, which became known on March 12, were for alleged subversive activities including the gathering of detailed information during the suppression of the insurgent movement in Tokyo. So far as is known, with the single exception of an employee of the Chinese Embassy, no Japanese connected with other Embassies and Legations in Tokyo were molested. The arrests are reported to have been the subject of immediate but unavailing protests from the Soviet Embassy here and the Vice-Commissar of Foreign Affairs in Moscow. As the men have not been released, the Soviet Embassy has been handicapped in carrying on its normal routine.

According to biographical sketches published in the *Asahi* most of the arrested employees have previously been detained by the police because of radical activities. Several at least have been members of Communist societies in Japan. Members of the Diplomatic Corps have voiced the opinion that the Japanese authorities have been waiting for an opportunity to remove these undesirable elements, and that they determined on the present as a favorable opportunity. Visitors to the Soviet Embassy have long remarked on the unusual type of Japanese to be seen there and it is not difficult to believe the police contention that these people are in fact Communist sympathizers. In connection with this incident reference is made to the Embassy's telegram No. 55, March 3, 6 p. m.,[13] in which the Soviet Ambassador's opposition to the assignment of a private detective to protect him during the present emergency is set forth. As indication of the extraordinary atmosphere which apparently prevails at the Soviet Embassy a member of the British Embassy assured a member of my staff that whenever the Soviet Ambassador leaves his Embassy by car with his Japanese detective seated beside the driver, an armed Russian (rumored to be a GPU man) sits beside the Ambassador to protect him from his protector. This story originated with a member of the Soviet Embassy staff who sought to illustrate thereby the perfidy of the Japanese!

For a brief discussion of the probable course of the relations between Japan and Soviet Russia as affected by the February 26 Incident and the consequent change of Government in Japan, the attention of the Department is invited to the Embassy's Strictly Confidential despatch No. 1741 of March 18, 1936.

Respectfully yours,

JOSEPH C. GREW

---

[13] Not printed.

761.94/895

The Ambassador in Japan (Grew) to the Secretary of State

No. 1741   TOKYO, March 18, 1936.
[Received April 6.]

SIR: In the Embassy's confidential despatch No. 1694 of February 20 [14] the factors were enumerated which led to the conclusion that a recourse to war was not at that time intended by either Japan or Soviet Russia but that the border situation remained menacing. Now, after a change of Government in Japan brought on by the violence of February 26, the situation requires reexamination.

In the main the factors enumerated before the Incident still obtain. The Japanese Army is not equipped to fight the USSR with good prospects of success; its leaders, for this reason if for no other, are believed to remain opposed to a war in the near future. The danger of an imminent war, deliberately provoked by the Japanese, could only be acute if the younger officers were in control of the Government, a condition contrary to fact.

According to a telegram* to the Department from the Embassy at Moscow the "Kremlin feels that although the Japanese Government has no desire for an immediate war with the Soviet Union, there is a grave danger that some incident may occur which might strengthen the hands of an aggressive and active minority in Japan which is of the opinion that if the Soviet Union is to be eliminated as an important factor in the Far East that elimination must take place this year". February 26, however, was not an incident of this kind. Although many of the reforms demanded by the insurgents have been included in the program of the new Government†, a minority which believes that the elimination of the Soviet Union from the Far East must take place this year has not gained control. It is the responsible leaders of the Army who have increased their influence in governing Japan and it is they who have insisted with popular support upon the adoption of a more "positive policy" in foreign affairs. This "positive policy", as the Prime Minister explained it‡ to me, means the acceleration of Japan's policies with respect to China and the USSR. It means that the old policies will be carried on more intensively but it is not a threat of imminent war. The present leaders of the Army may be counted upon not to advocate a war with Russia so long as the present disparity in military preparedness obtains.

---

[14] Not printed.
*Moscow's No. 45, February 13, 1936, 2 p. m., Strictly confidential. [Footnote in the original; telegram printed on p. 56.]
†Embassy's despatch No. 1735, March 19, 1936. [Footnote in the original; despatch printed on p. 761.]
‡Embassy's 74, March 13, 1936, 7 p. m. [Footnote in the original; telegram printed on p. 759.]

Moreover, the implications of the reported *rapprochement* between England and Soviet Russia and the Franco-Soviet pact have been noticed here; a typical comment is that of the *Miyako Shimbun* of March 2, "the pact will facilitate the execution of the Soviet's policy in the Far East". The pact may be said to provide the Foreign Office and the Prime Minister with powerful arguments in favor of prudence and patience in dealing with the USSR while it also provides the War Office with an additional argument for increased military strength. For the present the danger of war now appears little greater than before February 26, although, as heretofore, the discipline of the younger Japanese officers along the Manchurian frontier cannot be relied on with assurance.§

Taking a longer view, however, the situation seems more disquieting. The ordeal which Mr. Hirota went through before being enabled to form his Cabinet has demonstrated where a large measure of control now lies. The Army has committed Mr. Hirota to a more "positive policy"; it is urging upon him (as he told me himself ‖) an increase of the Japanese forces in Manchuria until they more nearly equal those of the Soviets across the border. This desideratum is freely voiced in the press as are other specific requirements. The following are said by the Domei news agency to be the General Staff's plans for expansion to commence with the 1937–1938 fiscal year:

1. Increase in the army in "Manchukuo" as the number of Japanese soldiers there is strikingly small compared with the 230,000 Soviet soldiers in the Far East.
2. Perfection of aviation and air defense. The Soviet Army has 4000 airplanes in contrast to but 1000 for the Japanese army.
3. Light machine guns, heavy machine guns, field guns and "infantry cannon", all inferior to those used by the Soviet Army, will be perfected and as many manufactured as possible.
4. Mechanized equipment will be perfected, for the Soviet Union is one of the leading powers of the world in this branch. Japan is said to have about one tenth as much mechanized equipment as the Soviet Union.
5. Perfection of preparations for chemical warfare is considered important.

The above requirements, it is to be noted, are related to the materiel said to be in the possession of the Russians. Furthermore Mr. Hirota and Mr. Baba, the Finance Minister, are apparently pledged to raise the funds for a program of this nature. It is commonly accepted in Tokyo on the basis of Mr. Baba's own somewhat ambiguous statements that he will not seek to limit the defense appropriations as strictly as did Mr. Takahashi; [15] it is hinted that he holds office on

---

§Mukden's 196, January 31, 1936. [Footnote in the original; despatch not found in Department files.]

‖ Embassy's 74, March 13, 1936, 7 p. m. [Footnote in the original.]

[15] Japanese Minister of Finance, assassinated on February 26.

terms that prevent this. As the *Kokumin Shimbun* of March 13 stated, "The army has been the main factor behind the recent sensational developments. The outlined policies of the Hirota Government to a large extent represent the wishes of the Military. . . .[16] The fact that the Army requested a revision of policy was due to no other reason than that the fighting services were not satisfied with the policy which Mr. Hirota had been following as head of the Foreign Office."

It is difficult to see what Mr. Hirota's "positive diplomacy" can accomplish in dealing with Soviet Russia. Manifestly he will redouble his efforts to solve the border problems, the fishery dispute and such other questions as may come up for negotiation. As reported in the Embassy's despatch No. 1740, March 18, 1936, he is already pressing for a definition of the eastern "Manchukuo" border and for the establishment of a permanent commission for the settlement of border disputes. But the USSR is no longer in the weak position of several years ago; it has entrenched itself securely along the Amur; it has served notice by armed force along the Outer Mongolian border and through the medium of Mr. Roy Howard's newspapers¶ that the Kwantung Army had best direct its ambitions elsewhere. While probably anxious to settle the border questions by negotiation Soviet Russia may no longer be expected to yield important concessions. Meanwhile the Japanese Army has apparently sufficient influence in the Government to undertake a measurable increase of Japanese military strength in Manchuria so that it may more nearly equal that of the Russians across the border. When this increase is brought about the situation will become more dangerous for two reasons: first because war with Soviet Russia would then give greater promise of success and thus be a more reasonable venture and second because of the mere proximity of two large trained fighting forces. Fortunately, however, this is not an immediate consideration because the Army's plans are still in the formative stages and because they would, when adopted, take considerable time to carry out.

For the present, on the other hand, there are Mr. Hirota's assurances that war will not occur while he is in office and his expressed opinion that a Japanese war with Russia would be stupid because both parties would have everything to lose and nothing to gain thereby.** My interpretation of this remark is that Mr. Hirota foresees the fact that while such a war would accomplish immense damage, it might well result in a stalemate so far as permanent advantage is concerned.

---

[16] Omission indicated in the original despatch.
¶ Embassy's No. 1740, March 18, 1936.   [Footnote in the original.]
** Embassy's 74, March 13, 1936, 7 p. m.   [Footnote in the original.]

Furthermore these assurances are fortified first by the inferiority of the Japanese Kwantung Army in numbers and in equipment to the Russian Far Eastern Army and second by the fact that Generals Terauchi and Ueda †† as well as the Chief of Staff, Prince Kanin, are believed to be powerful leaders with a high sense of responsibility.

Respectfully yours,　　　　　　　　　　　　JOSEPH C. GREW

793.94/7808 : Telegram

The Counselor of Embassy in China (Peck) to the Secretary of State

NANKING, March 20, 1936—2 p. m.
[Received March 20—11:05 a. m.[17]]

[59.] My March 18, 4 p. m. to Peiping.[18]　A joint communiqué was issued by the Foreign Office and the Japanese Ambassador late March 19th as follows:

"With reference to the question of readjusting Sino-Japanese relations, General Chang Chun, Minister for Foreign Affairs, and Mr. Hachiro Arita, Japanese Ambassador to China, had a series of four talks in the Waichiaopu between March 16 and March 19. Each conversation lasted from 2½ to 3 hours, nobody else being present besides the two diplomats. The conversations were in the nature of an informal exchange of opinions, both expressing their frank views in a free and sincere manner.

As the object of the parleys was to facilitate satisfactory progress of future negotiations for readjusting Sino-Japanese relations, no definite procedure has been arranged, nor was the scope of discussion limited to any particular subjects. All questions concerning the relations between the two countries were discussed, and no attempt was made to reach any conclusions.

The talks were conducted in a most friendly atmosphere throughout the 4 days and ended at 4:30 o'clock on Thursday afternoon (March 19), as previously arranged. Although a complete agreement on all points has not yet been achieved, the parleys may be considered to be very helpful towards producing a better appreciation of each other's viewpoints."

Chang Chun and Arita have held four lengthy daily conferences from March 16th to 19th inclusive. From such information as is available it appears that these conversations were actually, as reported in the press, more in the nature of an exchange of views than of negotiations and that no basis for future negotiations was agreed upon or any actual progress made toward a readjustment of Sino-Japanese relations. It appears that Arita did not make any definite

---

†† Respectively Minister of War, and Commander in Chief of the Kwantung army. [Footnote in the original. Ueda was also new Japanese Ambassador in "Manchoukuo".]

[17] Telegram in two sections.
[18] Not found in Department files.

proposals, one reason being his uncertainty as to his own future assignment and another reason being, possibly, lack of specific instructions based upon whatsoever "positive" policy may have been adopted in Tokyo as a partial basis for Hirota's press announcement of March 17.

Arita is to talk with Chiang Kai Shek this afternoon and is planning to proceed to Shanghai tomorrow for a conference with Japanese Consuls General from various Chinese posts before going on to Tokyo.

PECK

793.94/7858

The Ambassador in China (Johnson) to the Secretary of State

No. 326　　　　　　　　　　　　　　　　　PEIPING, March 26, 1936.
　　　　　　　　　　　　　　　　　　　[Received April 20.]

SIR: I have the honor to enclose copies of ten memoranda [19] of conversations which I had during February at Nanking with various officials on the subject of Sino-Japanese relations and to summarize them below.

Dr. Lo Wen-kan, former Minister of Justice, indicated that he expects an outbreak of hostilities between Japan and China. Dr. C. T. Wang, former Minister for Foreign Affairs, stated that China is concentrating its forces for a conflict which seems inevitable. Mr. Hallett Abend, correspondent for the *New York Times*, informed me that Mr. Y. Suma, Japanese Consul General at Nanking, had told him that the Japanese Government was much concerned over the quantity of arms which China had been purchasing and which were a waste of money as the Japanese army could crush China in two months. The German Ambassador, Mr. Oscar Trautmann, expressed the opinion that in intellectual and military Chinese circles there was an increasing belief in the inevitability of a Sino-Japanese war, although he was not certain with regard to the attitude of General Chiang Kai-shek in this respect.

The Minister for Foreign Affairs, General Chang Ch'un, in the course of conversations with me on February 13 and 14 stated that he was prepared to discuss all phases of Sino-Japanese relations with the Japanese, that it was difficult to know who was speaking for Japan, and that, although the Japanese military dictate the policies of the Japanese Government, they are divided among themselves. He expressed the opinion that the Japanese were somewhat hesitant about going ahead (in China) in view of the present uncertainty in the world situation.

---

[19] None printed.

With regard to the rebellion of February 26 in Tokyo, General Chiang Tso-pin, the Minister of the Interior, General Yu Fei-peng, the Acting Minister of Communications, and Mr. Wu Ting-ch'ang, the Minister of Industry, expressed the belief that there will be further trouble in Japan as a result of divergence of opinion among Japanese. The Soviet Ambassador, Mr. Dimitri Bogomoloff, stated that he believed the rebellion would result in increased control of the Japanese Government by the military and would bring inflation, increased foreign trade, and greater expenditure for the military who would continue to go ahead in China but who would not dare to attack Soviet Russia because the border defenses of the latter were too strong for Japan to penetrate without great cost in material and men.

Respectfully yours,   NELSON TRUSLER JOHNSON

793.94/7859

The Ambassador in China (Johnson) to the Secretary of State

No. 332   PEIPING, March 27, 1936.
                                           [Received April 20.]

SIR: I have the honor to refer to the alleged agreement reached in June or July of last year between General Ho Ying-ch'in (Minister of War, then Acting Chairman of the Peiping Branch Military Council) and Lieutenant-General Yoshijiro Umetsu (then a Major-General in command of the Japanese North China Garrison), with regard to affairs in North China, and to enclose in English translation and in the Chinese original copies of various documents dated from May 29 to July 6, 1935,[20] purporting to be a record of the negotiations between the Chinese and Japanese sides which led to the written acceptance of the Japanese proposals by General Ho Ying-ch'in on the latter date. This material was obtained recently by Third Secretary O. Edmund Clubb from a foreign source in Shanghai under the injunction of strict secrecy.

Although this text was not obtained directly from a Chinese official source and no definite proof can be obtained of its authenticity in the face of the Chinese official statements that no such document as the "Ho-Umetsu Agreement" exists, nevertheless, it is felt that this record of memoranda of conversations and the purported document itself adhere so closely to what was known of the negotiations at the time as to give the whole an aspect of verity. It is to be observed, in this connection, that the *China Weekly Review* of March 14, 1936, carried a translation of the memorandum (as it is entitled) allegedly as finally presented to General Ho Ying-ch'in by the Japanese side for

---

[20] Enclosures not printed.

signature and that this text is essentially the same as that which is enclosed in more careful translation. The *China Weekly Review's* account, however, does not include General Ho Ying-ch'in's acceptance of the Japanese proposals. As regards the subject of these negotiations, Mr. Clubb was recently informed by an officer of the Japanese Embassy that 1) there was no "agreement" between General Ho and Lieutenant-General Umetsu, but an exchange of communications, 2) the officer believed the substance of this exchange to be substantially as reported at the time (he had not seen the actual documents), 3) the Chinese acceptance of the Japanese proposals was definitely given by General Ho Ying-ch'in after his return to Nanking, and 4) he (the Japanese officer) regarded the evidence as indicating that General Ho Ying-ch'in had given the acceptance only after consultation with General Chiang Kai-shek and by the latter's authority. The statement that the Chinese acceptance was given only after General Ho's return to Nanking, if true, would be in accordance with the impression prevalent at the time that the War Minister left on June 13 from Peiping without accepting the Japanese proposals and also in accordance with the date appearing on the brief note of acceptance as it was alleged to have been sent from Nanking under date of July 6, 1935. The Fengtai disturbance outside the walls of Peiping, occurring as it did between the time of General Ho's departure from Peiping and July 6, may have been the Japanese threat that forced Chinese compliance.

The record of the verbal representations made by the Japanese side beginning on May 29 and continuing until June 11 is not at variance with the information obtained at the time and forwarded to the Department in the Embassy's telegrams 233, June 1, 4 p. m., 236, June 2, 2 p. m., 243, June 5, 2 p. m., 245, June 7 [6], 5 p. m., 259, June 10, 6 p. m., and especially 270 of June 13, 3 p. m.[21] Those telegrams and this record of verbal representations outline the dissatisfaction of the Japanese military with the then existing state of affairs in North China, with particular reference to various activities alleged to be primarily anti-Japanese, and show the development of Japanese measures designed to "correct" those factors felt to be detrimental to the future of Sino-Japanese relations. They indicate also the resistance offered by General Ho Ying-ch'in, under the instructions of the National Government, to the signing of the proposed document, which was described by Mr. Wang Ching-wei, President of the Executive Yuan, as being "actually no different from signing a treaty to give up Hopei".

General Ho's alleged letter of July 6 in reply to the Japanese stated that the items under consideration were all accepted, and

---

[21] Telegram No. 245 not printed; for the other telegrams see, respectively, *Foreign Relations,* 1935, vol. III, pp. 196, 198, 201, 222, and 237.

that General Ho Ying-ch'in on his own part hoped they would be made effective. Subsequent actions of the Chinese authorities have not run counter to the Japanese desires expressed last June, and the circumstantial evidence inclines one to believe in the genuineness of the documents submitted herewith. Any additional information which may come to light regarding this general matter will be forwarded promptly to the Department.

Respectfully yours, NELSON TRUSLER JOHNSON

711.94/1102

The Ambassador in China (Johnson) to the Secretary of State

No. 337 PEIPING, March 27, 1936.
[Received April 20.]

SIR: I have the honor to refer to the Embassy's telegram No. 60 of February 13, 4 p. m.,[22] regarding the local reaction to Senator Pittman's speech of February 10, and to enclose for the information of the Department copies of two memoranda dated February 13 and February 14, 1936, respectively,[23] of conversations with Finance Minister H. H. Kung and Foreign Minister Chang Ch'ün in which both of these gentlemen expressed themselves as pleased with the sentiments of the Senator's speech.

It will be observed that Dr. Kung at the same time indicated that the Chinese would have found the American silver policy more advantageous to themselves if they had been ready to take advantage of the opportunities it offered.

Respectfully yours, NELSON TRUSLER JOHNSON

793.94/7819 : Telegram

The Counselor of Embassy in China (Peck) to the Secretary of State

NANKING, March 28, 1936—9 a. m.
[Received March 28—7 a. m.]

67. 1. An official of the Foreign Office has informed an officer that he thought Chiang Kai Shek had recently met Sung Che Yuan in Kaifeng to discuss the North China situation, the most immediate problem being criticism against Sung by the Japanese military which probably presages an attempt to replace Sung if a suitable substitute can be found. He concurred in the general impression here and in Peiping (see Peiping's 147, March 24, 8 p. m., paragraph 4 [22]) that developments in North China must await clarification of the situation

---

[22] Not printed.
[23] Neither printed.

in Tokyo but he expressed the opinion that a renewal of Japanese pressure upon the Chinese Government could be expected in less than 2 months time.

2. He denied reports that in the March 16–19 conversations between the Japanese Ambassador and the Minister for Foreign Affairs the former had insisted that China had accepted Hirota's so-called three points or insisted that they must form the basis of discussion. He said, however, that Arita had brought up for discussion the "concrete measures" which were implied by the three points and that in general both officials had "laid their cards on the table so that each Government knew where the other stood."

3. He stated that the Japanese Government had not yet made known to the Chinese Government any nominee to replace Arita and assumed that this question awaits Arita's return to Japan.

4. By mail to Tokyo.

PECK

761.93 Outer Mongolia/4 : Telegram

The Ambassador in the Soviet Union (Bullitt) to the Secretary of State

Moscow, March 28, 1936—3 p. m.
[Received March 28—11 : 35 a. m.]

93. A Tass telegram from Ulan-Bator published in today's *Izvestia* states that the 20th session of the small Hural approved the future of the Government of the Mongolian People's Republic, "in particular the agreement between the Soviet Union and the Mongolian People's Republic concerning mutual assistance".

This constitutes the first semiofficial admission by the Soviet Government that an agreement involving mutual assistance between the Soviet Union and the Mongolian People's Republic has been concluded.

The Soviet Government has evaded hitherto all questions on this subject in order to avoid being accused of "imperialism".

Dr. Yen, Chinese Ambassador, before his departure for Berlin (where he is now extremely ill) informed me that he had asked Stomoniakoff how the Soviet Government could reconcile Stalin's statements to Howard anent Outer Mongolia with the Soviet Government's continued assurances to the Government of China that the Soviet Government still respected Chinese sovereignty over Outer Mongolia. On Tuesday Stomoniakoff replied by a question "Would you rather have Outer Mongolia in the hands of the Japanese?"

We are informed today by the Chinese Embassy that the Chinese Government had made no official protest and that no such protest may be expected.

The Japanese Embassy informs us that Japan will continue unalterably to regard Outer Mongolia as an integral part of China under Chinese sovereignty.

There is of course little fundamental difference between the present position of Outer Mongolia and that of the non-Russian Constituent Republics within the Soviet Union.

BULLITT

762.94/72

The Ambassador in Japan (Grew) to the Secretary of State

No. 1753

TOKYO, March 30, 1936.
[Received April 20.]

SIR: I have the honor to refer to the Department's instructions No. 945, dated February 18, 1936, and 958, dated February 24, 1936,[25] both transmitting copies of despatches and reports in regard to an alleged military agreement between Germany and Japan, obviously supposed to be directed against the Soviet Union.

Although the spokesman of the Japanese Foreign Office on January 17, 1936, asserted that the reports of a German-Japanese military alliance were "entirely false", the Embassy has been endeavoring to ascertain what, if anything, lay behind the persistent rumors of some sort of German-Japanese alliance. The First Secretary of the Soviet Embassy in Tokyo recently informed a member of the staff of this Embassy that the Soviet Embassy had received information that an agreement did in fact exist between Germany and Japan, but that it was entirely a military agreement, concluded between military officers of both governments. The Foreign Offices of the two governments, according to the Soviet First Secretary, were not involved in the conclusion of the agreement and may not even be aware of its existence. He did not, however, know the terms of the alleged agreement, except that they were directed at the Soviet Union.

In a recent conversation between a member of the staff of this Embassy and the German Military Attaché in Tokyo, the subject of the alleged military agreement between Germany and Japan was brought up. Although he was not asked directly whether or not such an agreement existed, the Military Attaché implied that no concrete agreement had been concluded and that the only agreement which Germany would consider would be some sort of consultative pact, to become operative should it appear desirable or necessary at some future time to attack Soviet Russia from both the east and the west.[26]

Respectfully yours,

JOSEPH C. GREW

---

[25] Neither printed, but see despatch No. 2617, January 22, from the Ambassador in Germany, p. 19, and report of January 30, by the Military Attaché in Germany, p. 31.

[26] For correspondence concerning the German-Japanese accord of November 25, 1936, against the Communist International, see vol. I, pp. 390 ff.

693.943/5 : Telegram

The Secretary of State to the Ambassador in China (Johnson)

WASHINGTON, April 1, 1936—noon.

70. Reference Dairen's despatch of February 26 addressed to Embassy at Tokyo [27] in regard to reported tariff agreement between the authorities of the "autonomous" area of North China and those of Japan.

Department assumes that you are already studying the situation under reference and that in due course you will inform the Department of the results of your investigation.[28]

HULL

893.01 Outer Mongolia/86 : Telegram

The Ambassador in the Soviet Union (Bullitt) to the Secretary of State

Moscow, April 1, 1936—2 p.m.
[Received April 1—12 : 05 p. m.]

95. The Soviet press this morning reports that fighting is in progress between "Japano-Manchurian detachments and forces of the Mongolian People's Republic" and alleges that the fighting is taking place at a point 45 kilometers inside Mongolian territory.

The Soviet press also publishes a long statement on frontier incidents which concludes "Stomoniakoff reminded the Ambassador (Ohta) of the reiterated statements made by the Soviet Government in Tokyo and in Moscow to the effect that the Soviet Government is interested, from the point of view of the interests of peace as well as the security of its own borders, in the maintenance of peace on the Mongolo-Manchurian border. Stomoniakoff noted that on February 21 he had informed Ohta of the obligation undertaken by the Soviet Union to render assistance to the Mongolian People's Republic in the event of a third party attacking it.

This obligation has been actually in existence since 1921 when the Soviet and Mongolian Governments defending themselves against a common attack on their territories agreed to render each other mutual assistance. This oral obligation took the form of a protocol on mutual assistance signed in Ulanbator on March 13th of this year".

I asked Krestinsky, acting Commissar for Foreign Affairs, if this treaty of mutual assistance would be published. He replied "probably not". I then asked him if the agreement was similar to the agreements

[27] Not printed.
[28] See telegram No. 215, April 30, 11 a. m., from the Ambassador in China, p. 126.

between the Soviet Union and France,[29] and the Soviet Union and Czechoslovakia,[30] or if it involved virtual incorporation of Outer Mongolia as a constituent state of the Soviet Union.

He replied that the agreement was similar to those between the Soviet Union, France and Czechoslovakia, and added that there was no thought at present of incorporating Outer Mongolia in the Soviet Union.

Krestinsky stated that the Commissariat for Foreign Affairs considers the latest incidents an effort of the younger military group in Japan to force the hand of the Government and provoke war with the Soviet Union. He expressed the opinion that serious consequences were not to be feared.

I have been informed by a member of the Soviet hierarchy, however, that the generals of the Red Army are extremely apprehensive that the present clashes may grow into major war. From another fairly reliable source I learned that 2,000 engineers from Moscow have been mobilized during the past week for service in the Far East and that certain of these men have been ordered to Outer Mongolia.

BULLITT

793.94/7879

The Ambassador in China (Johnson) to the Secretary of State

No. 133   NANKING, April 1, 1936.
                                                                  [Received May 4.]

SIR: I have the honor to state that Sir Alexander Cadogan, the retiring British Ambassador, called on me today to say goodbye, and in the course of the conversation told me briefly of the results of recent conversations which he had held with some of the leading persons in Nanking.

Our conversation was, of course, informal and had the nature of an exchange of impressions. Sir Alexander said that he had had farewell interviews with General Chiang Kai-shek, President of the Executive Yuan, Mr. Chang Ch'un, Minister for Foreign Affairs, and others, and had taken pains to inquire whether any progress had been made in the conversations recently held between the two persons just named and Mr. Arita, until recently Japanese Ambassador in Nanking, who has returned to Tokyo to take up the post of Minister for Foreign Affairs.

General Chiang Kai-shek had, as usual, been rather uncommunicative, but he and Mr. Chang Ch'un had both stated, in effect, that the

---

[29] Signed at Paris, May 2, 1936, League of Nations Treaty Series, vol. CLXVII, p. 395.
[30] Signed at Prague, May 16, 1936, League of Nations Treaty Series, vol. CLIX, p. 347.

conversations with Mr. Arita had not resulted in any progress in settling the differences between Japan and China. Mr. Chang Ch'un told Sir Alexander there was still a lack of agreement in regard to a fundamental issue between the two Governments, but it seemed possible that some agreement in regard to various details might possibly be reached. Sir Alexander said that he had observed to Mr. Chang Ch'un that there were two ways of handling such a situation as exists between Japan and China; one way would be to try to reach a basic understanding and leave details for later consideration, while the other way would be to adjust such differences as could be adjusted, hoping thus to reach, ultimately, a settlement of the fundamental issue. To this Mr. Chang Ch'un had said that the second method seemed to be the only one feasible.

I remarked that the fundamental issue which Mr. Chang Ch'un had referred to as still being a point of disagreement between Japan and China was probably the refusal of China to submit to Japanese tutelage, and Sir Alexander concurrred in this supposition.

The British Ambassador said that he had talked with Mr. Suma, Secretary of the Japanese Embassy, and Mr. Suma had confirmed the general feeling that no progress had been made in the conversations between Mr. Arita and General Chiang Kai-shek and Mr. Chang Ch'un. In fact, Mr. Suma said, some of the outstanding questions which were formerly under negotiation had been "discarded" by the Chinese. Sir Alexander said that he had not been able to ascertain clearly what Mr. Suma meant by this statement. My own supposition is that Mr. Suma meant either that the Chinese had refused to carry to a conclusion some of the discussions which were in progress, or that Mr. Suma meant that the Chinese Government had repudiated some of the positions formerly taken by it. For example, the press has carried statements made by Japanese officials that the Chinese Government had "accepted" Mr. Hirota's "three principles", whereas published statements of Chinese leaders assert that these "three principles" have not been accepted by China, except as subjects for discussion.

Sir Alexander inquired what I thought had been the result of the February 26 incident in Tokyo, that is, what phase of Japanese policy toward China had gained the ascendancy in the Japanese Government as the outcome of that incident. I replied that, while my impressions were all gathered at secondhand, I felt that the rather socialistic attitude toward alleged unequal distribution of wealth in Japan had gained some headway and that the plan to expand on the continent through military occupation of territory had probably become more firmly entrenched as the policy of the Japanese Government. Sir Alexander said that nothing important had happened since the February 26 incident in the way of Japanese military activities in north China, and I observed that I had heard several important Chinese express the opinion at the time the incident occurred that China might expect a lull of several months, until normality had been restored in the political scene in Tokyo.

Sir Alexander said that it irritated him to hear Japanese complain of China's lack of friendship for Japan and he intimated that in his conversation with Mr. Suma he had pointed out the unreasonableness of expecting the Chinese to be friendly toward Japan so long as Japan maintained in power a puppet like Yin Ju-keng in the demilitarized zone of eastern Hopei Province, and did not take steps to prevent Japanese smuggling into Hopei Province. During our conversation I referred to a recent informal dissertation I had heard given by Mr. Tai Chi-tao, President of the Examination Yuan, on what he termed the historic urge of Japan to expand on the Asiatic mainland. It was President Tai's opinion that this urge had existed for centuries, would continue to form Japanese foreign policy and would ultimately be the cause of the destruction of Japan. Sir Alexander said that it was all very well to talk about a mere "urge" to expand on the mainland, but doubtless Japan is in a desperate situation and must do something to improve it. This fact must be taken into account. I remarked that this office had recently prepared a translation of an editorial which appeared in a Nanking popular journal, drawing lessons for China from the bold action of Germany in breaking the shackles of "unequal treaties". Sir Alexander said he feared that the writer of the editorial had not carried his argument to its logical conclusion and called attention to the fact that Germany has become powerful through discipline and energy, whereas China seems to remain perpetually an inert mass. I observed in regard to this that General Chiang seemed to be doing his best to create a powerful military machine and that he was reported to be sending large numbers of troops to the region of Haichow, north Kiangsu Province, in apparent fear that the Japanese might attempt to seize the Lung-Hai Railway. Sir Alexander said that he had heard of the Chinese apprehension that the Japanese might seek to seize this railway, beginning at the port of Haichow.

I remarked that the editorial to which I had referred showed that Chinese are beginning to think of China in relation to the general international set-up. For example, they were drawing lessons from the demonstrated ability of Ethiopia, a nation at least as backward as China, to oppose Italy for many months and were beginning to wonder whether if China were to oppose Japan's encroachments actively, other nations would not think more highly of China and would not come to China's assistance. Such Chinese were speculating what would be the attitude of the leading nations, say Great Britain and the United States, if China should begin such active resistance.

Sir Alexander said that "feelers" on this subject had been put to him and he had not hesitated to reply that the Chinese might expect nothing from Great Britain.   I observed that the Chinese might feel themselves warranted in expecting some support from Great Britain, since that country had been, in public opinion, foremost in measures designed to place some restraint on Italy in its imperialistic schemes in Ethiopia. Sir Alexander replied that the Chinese ought to be able to see that the two situations are entirely different; in Europe it was possible for Great Britain to enlist the joint support of other nations, whereas in the Far East there would be no nation to join Great Britain in opposing Japan's encroachments on China.   He pointed out that it would be impossible for Great Britain to exert any military strength of its own in the Far East.   I assented to his general view and admitted that the nearest Great Power, the United States, would be extremely unlikely to take any part in the matter, since American participation in any war is enormously more expensive than participation by any other nation, and there were no American interests in China which would seem to warrant the colossal expenditure that past experience indicated would probably be necessary.

Sir Alexander said that he was glad to have had his experience as Ambassador in China before taking up his new post of Deputy Under-Secretary of State for Foreign Affairs in London, although he felt that his experience in China had been too brief to give him a genuine insight into the problems here.   I replied that I did not feel that this was the case, that Sir Alexander had acquired a thorough comprehension of the psychological factors which mould political events in the Far East and that the details were more or less inconsequential.   Sir Alexander said he hoped to have an interesting talk in Tokyo with the British Ambassador there.

Sir Alexander expressed the hope that if I should pass through London I would establish contact with him, so that our relations might be continued.

Respectfully yours,

For the Ambassador:
WILLYS R. PECK
Counselor of Embassy

793.94/7823 : Telegram

The Ambassador in China (Johnson) to the Secretary of State

PEIPING, April 2, 1936—6 p. m.
[Received 7:35 p. m.]

163. Paragraph 4 of the Embassy's 102, March 3, 11 a. m.[31]

---

[31] Not printed.   In this telegram the Embassy stated: "Angered by recent student activities, Sung Che Yuan has taken severe measures during the past few days, arresting more than 20 students and 3 professors allegedly for Communist leanings. . . . The arrested professors are understood not to be Communists but to have incited students to participate in recent student demonstrations."

1. Some tens of students among those arrested in late February and in March are still in custody. In addition to these, about 50 were arrested March 31 for participating in demonstration at Peiping National University in memory of the one student known to have died (of pneumonia) while in custody. The demonstrators numbered about 1,000 students from various universities.

2. The situation is quiet at present. Many students appear to be aware of the fact that if demonstrations get out of hand, the Japanese may use that as an excuse for interference in educational institutions on the ground that Communism is endangering them. It is reliably reported that the Hopei-Chahar Political Council is not taking steps to obtain control of the administration of the universities and is not interfering other than to arrest demonstrators and alleged agitators. The proposal for the establishment of an education committee under the Hopei-Chahar Political Council for control of education is not being pushed at present.

3. Of the three professors mentioned in the telegram referred to above, two have been released. The whereabouts of the other professor and his wife is not known. No students have been sent to Nanking for discipline.

4. It is possible that the student question may have serious implications for the future for the reasons that, (1), students are restless and dissatisfied and these factors are being made use of by communistic students, that (2), the Chinese authorities may make matters worse by inept handling, and that (3), the Japanese military, although they are merely watching the situation at present, may in the future make use of student troubles to aid their own interests in some way.

By mail to Tokyo.

JOHNSON

893.01 Outer Mongolia/88 : Telegram

The Ambassador in China (Johnson) to the Secretary of State

PEIPING, April 2, 1936—6 p. m.
[Received April 2—5 : 45 p. m.]

164. Embassy's 160, April 1, 7 p. m.[32]

Tass report of April 2 under Moscow dateline states the Mongol forces repulsed the attack in the region of Tomsykbulak with heavy losses, driving the Japanese-Manchurian detachments back over the border.

JOHNSON

---

[32] Not printed.

893.01 Outer Mongolia/89 : Telegram

The Ambassador in the Soviet Union (Bullitt) to the Secretary of State

Moscow, April 3, 1936—9 a. m.
[Received April 3—6:50 a. m.]

97. Last evening in the course of a conversation at which I was present, Voroshilov [33] said to Ohta, Japanese Ambassador, that although the Soviet Union desired peace any attack by Japan against Outer Mongolia would be met by an attack twice as severe.

The Japanese Ambassador answered that the fighting on the Mongol-Manchurian frontier was not to be taken seriously; that it was due purely to the fact that the frontier was not clearly marked.

Voroshilov replied that the frontier was extremely clearly marked and that the Soviet Union would repel any troops which might cross it.

Ohta replied that the new commander of the Japanese Armies in Manchuria was a man who had the complete confidence of Hirota and that he anticipated no further difficulties.

Voroshilov answered that he did anticipate further difficulties and that if war should break out soon Japan unquestionably would be defeated.

BULLITT

793.94/7824 : Telegram

The Ambassador in China (Johnson) to the Secretary of State

PEIPING, April 3, 1936—noon.
[Received April 3—7:20 a. m.]

168. 1. Paragraph 4 of the Embassy's 135, March 16, 4 p. m., and 89, February 25, 5 p. m. Major General Takayoshi Matsumuro arrived March 28 from Tientsin to succeed Doihara as chief Japanese negotiator in North China and since then has been conversing at Tientsin with Sung Che Yuan and other Chinese leaders. The Embassy has been informed that Matsumuro is to establish a special military mission at Peiping which will be directly responsible to the Tokyo General Staff and not to the North China Garrison. Japanese allegations that Sino-Japanese affairs in North China are not to be directed by the Kwantung army lose significance because Matsumuro was formerly of the Kwantung army, is allegedly strongly reactionary and is understood to have obtained his present assignment as the result of representations made at Tokyo by the Kwantung army.

---

[33] Soviet Commissar for Defense.

Doihara has been succeeded as chief of the special military mission at Mukden by Major General Toshiji Miura, formerly of the China Section of the War Ministry. Doihara, now a lieutenant general, has returned to Tokyo where he will be in command of that part of the first division which does not go to Manchuria. It is now said that a new commander may not be appointed to the North China Garrison but that Tada may be promoted to lieutenant general and continue as commander. The newly appointed Japanese Military Attaché relieving Isogai, who has been appointed director of the Military Affairs Bureau at Tokyo, is Seiichi Kita, recently promoted to the rank of major general. Kita is described as being more moderate than Matsumuro. Matsumuro and Sung Che Yuan are expected to arrive at Peiping on April 6.

2. According to Chinese sources, the current conversations at Tientsin concern questions arising from the existence of Yin Ju Keng's regime, the situation in Chahar, the situation in Shansi, and the alleged existence of a secret Sino-Russian treaty. It is doubtful that reports to the effect that the Japanese have requested permission to send Japanese troops to West Hopei near the Shansi border are true. However, the report that they have urged Sung to despatch some of his troops to Shansi may be true as it would be in accord with the Japanese method of extending Sung's influence as a cloak for extension of Japanese influence. Sung is alleged to have refused on the ground that his troops are all needed in Hopei. It is anticipated that the Japanese will continue to insist on an enlargement of the autonomous character of Sung's regime.

3. A sixth Japanese adviser has arrived at Peiping. (Reference paragraph 3 of Embassy's 135, March 16, 4 p. m.) He is a former official of the Manchukuo regime and will be adviser to the Economic Committee of the Hopei-Chahar Political Council.

By mail to Tokyo.

JOHNSON

893.01 Outer Mongolia/90 : Telegram

The Ambassador in the Soviet Union (Bullitt) to the Secretary of State

Moscow, April 4, 1936—8 p. m.
[Received April 4—3 p. m.]

99. Stomoniakoff, Assistant Commissioner for Foreign Affairs in charge of Far Eastern matters, said to me today that the latest Soviet information from Japan, Manchuria and Mongolia indicates that the Japanese Government has no intention whatsoever of making an immediate attack on either Outer Mongolia or the Soviet Union. He

expressed the belief that the recent fighting on the Manchurian-Mongolian frontier had been begun by undisciplined action of younger Japanese officers against the will not only of the Government in Tokyo but also of the new commander-in-chief in Manchuria. He insisted that there had been no Soviet soldiers or officers with the Mongolian troops which repelled the attack.

BULLITT

793.94/7880

The Ambassador in China (Johnson) to the Secretary of State

No. 134   NANKING, April 4, 1936.
                                                  [Received May 4.]

SIR: I have the honor to refer to my despatch No. 131 of March 27, 1936,[34] on the subject "Chinese Press Comment on Germany's Militarization of the Rhineland", with which was transmitted a translation of an editorial in the *Hsin Min Pao*, a newspaper popular in Nanking, drawing certain lessons for China from Germany's self-assertion in international relations.

There is enclosed herewith a translation [34] made in this office of another editorial from the same journal, entitled "Will the United States Help China to Resist Japan?", published on March 26.

The text of the editorial is taken from statements said to have been made by Senator Pittman, in which the Senator is said to have criticized Japan for violation of the "Nine Power Treaty for the protection of China" and to have advocated increase of American armaments "as a means of preserving peace".

The conclusions reached by the writer were that the Senator's reference to Japanese ambitions was merely to justify the expansion of American armaments, that the United States is not devoted to "upholding justice and humanity" to the extent of giving China armed assistance against Japan, and that "it is simply a dream if we expect the United States to help China to resist Japan".

This article is typical of a strain of comment in the Chinese press at the present time. Apparently Chinese editorial writers, even after the experience of the last four or five years since the "Mukden Incident" in 1931, are still reluctant to abandon the hope that there is a world sentiment which will maintain the inviolability of territorial frontiers, overcoming the tendency of vigorous nations to expand at the expense of nations which show ineptitude in the current race to turn the world into a collection of "armed camps".

The Nanking regime seems to fear that, as a Japanese statesman is said to have observed recently, China's efforts to arm are entirely

---

[34] Not printed.

futile, because Japan could crush Chinese resistance in two months, and to see the necessity of enlisting military assistance from some foreign source. The enclosed editorial shows the bitterness with which China relinquishes the hope of such assistance from the United States. In spite of published denials from the Chinese Foreign Office, there are still rumors in Nanking that the Government has made some sort of a military alliance with the Soviet Union, directed against Japan. It appears to be the desire of the Chinese to obtain guarantees of their frontiers similar to the guarantees sought by Belgium and France under the Locarno Treaties,[35] and the sort of assistance which the Soviet Union and France are said to have promised each other in the recently ratified pact. The system of regional pacts of mutual assistance is respectable enough in Europe, and appears to be superseding the League Covenant as a practical factor. It is China's misfortune in attempting to adapt the system to China's needs that (1) the Far East offers only two other Powers with whom to bargain, and (2) China has so little to offer in exchange for aid from another nation.

Respectfully yours,

For the Ambassador:

WILLYS R. PECK

Counselor of Embassy

793.94/7826 : Telegram

The Counselor of Embassy in China (Peck) to the Secretary of State

NANKING, April 6, 1936—noon.
[Received April 6—10:45 a. m.]

82. 1. On April 4th McDaniel of the Associated Press had long interview with Suma for background purposes only. Suma stated he did not think the Japanese military intended to take any decisive step in the near future to overcome Chinese refusal to come to friendly understanding with Japan but he said he was warning the Chinese in a friendly way that so long as the Chinese Government refuses to accept at least in principle Japan's offer of friendly cooperation there will exist the possibility of a grave disaster to China more serious probably than the mere creation of a second "Manchukuo" in North China would be. Japan insists that China shall make its relations with all other nations subordinate to those between China and Japan and until this principle is accepted there can be no settlement of comparatively minor issues such as the smuggling in North China although if China once capitulates such details will be settled at once and easily. Japan regrets and distrusts Chinese Government's continued purchasing of expensive war equipment since possible enemies are few

---

[35] For texts of the treaties with Germany, signed October 16, 1925, see League of Nations Treaty Series, vol. LIV, pp. 289 ff.

and Japan is obviously one of them.   Suma said that while Chinese-Japanese relations are in the present stalemate he is directing all his efforts at the creation of good will through personal contacts with Chinese officials.   Nevertheless it is the personal belief of Suma that Japan will have to use force against China before China will consent to accept Japan as their friend and guide.

2. Referring to the policies of other nations in China Suma said that it seemed to him that the United States is coming to adopt a sensible and satisfactory attitude, that is, one of abstaining from entanglement in Far Eastern issues similar to the policy of Japan in the Western Hemisphere.   Great Britain, however, still seeks to perpetuate a traditional leading position in China and the Japanese Government must devise means of causing Great Britain to recognize that Japan, not Great Britain, is now the leading power in the Far East.   Great Britain does not appear to realize that Japan has powerful means of reenforcing its arguments such as by interfering with textile markets in India.

3. To Peiping by mail.

PECK

761.93 Outer Mongolia/7 : Telegram

The Counselor of Embassy in China (Peck) to the Secretary of State

NANKING, April 7, 1936—6 p. m.
[Received 9 : 49 p. m.[36]]

83. 1. The Embassy has obtained from the Foreign Office a copy in English of the following communiqué issued to the press late this afternoon:

2. "Following official confirmation of the conclusion of a mutual assistance protocol between the Soviet Union and Outer Mongolia, the Waichiaopu has lodged a vigorous protest with the Soviet Government declaring that the Chinese Government can, under no circumstances, recognize such a protocol and is in no wise bound by it.

The Waichiaopu recalls that the Soviet Union unequivocally pledged itself, in article 5 of the Sino-Soviet Agreement of May 31, 1924,[37] to recognize Outer Mongolia as an integral part of China and to respect China's sovereignty therein.

The action of the Soviet Government in concluding the protocol with Outer Mongolia, in the opinion of the Waichiaopu, constitutes not only an infringement of China's sovereignty but also a breach of its solemn pledge to the Chinese Government.

The protocol, it is learned, was signed on March 12.   It provides that the two parties will come to the aid of each other in case of an attack by a third party."

PECK

---

[36] Telegram in two sections.
[37] Signed at Peking, *Foreign Relations*, 1924, vol. I, pp. 495, 496.

761.93 Outer Mongolia/9 : Telegram

The Counselor of Embassy in China (Peck) to the Secretary of State

NANKING, April 8, 1936—noon.
[Received 2 : 55 p. m.]

84. This office's April 7, 6 p. m.

1. It appears likely that the objects of the Foreign Office protest and announcement were (1) to refute indirectly Japanese suspicions that Chinese and the Soviet Union have concluded a pact of mutual assistance, the implication being that (*a*) a Soviet-Mongolian pact would not have been necessary had a Sino-Soviet pact existed and (*b*) a protest so strongly worded would not have been made if the Soviet Union had recently become a formal ally of China; (2) to save the Chinese Government's face as much as possible in a situation in which it cannot afford to act except on paper because Soviet friendship is necessary in the event of war between China and Japan; (3) to answer recent Japanese criticism in the press that China has ignored the alienation of Outer Mongolia by the Soviet Union while protesting to the world over the loss of Manchuria; and (4) to keep the record clear for the future.

2. The Soviet [Embassy] refused to comment on the announcement when approached by an American press correspondent but both Chinese and Japanese officials privately expressed to him views similar to 1 and 2 above and a Chinese official intimated that the Chinese Government would not press for a reply if the Soviet Union should ignore the protest, an analogy being drawn with the Chinese protest against the sale of the Chinese Eastern.

3. To Tokyo by mail.

PECK

761.93 Outer Mongolia/8 : Telegram

The Ambassador in the Soviet Union (Bullitt) to the Secretary of State

Moscow, April 8, 1936—4 p. m.
[Received April 8—10 : 35 a. m.]

100. Moscow press this morning published the text of the Protocol of Mutual Assistance between the Soviet Union and the Mongolian People's Republic, dated March 12, 1936.

The Governments agree that in the event of a threat of attack on either they will discuss immediately the situation created and "adopt all those measures which will be necessary to safeguard the security of their territories."

They further "undertake in the event of a military attack on one of the contracting parties to render each other every assistance, including military assistance".

BULLITT

793.94/7833 : Telegram

The Counselor of Embassy in China (Peck) to the Secretary of State

NANKING, April 9, 1936—9 a. m.
[Received April 9—7 a. m.]

85. 1. A well-informed Chinese who arrived from Tientsin last night and who has recently been an official of the Tientsin municipal government has stated to an officer of the Embassy that General Matsumuro is pressing Tientsin Mayor Hsiao Chen Ying and General Sung Che Yuan for a written agreement providing for Sino-Japanese military cooperation against Communists.

2. Informant stated that large numbers of National Government troops continue to enter Shansi Province and his opinion tends to confirm a general belief here that Japanese objections to the despatch of such troops (reference this office's 51, March 6, 2 p. m.) are based on the probability that they will consolidate Chiang Kai Shek's authority in that province at the border of territory which is under Japanese influence by reason of the jurisdiction of the Hopei-Chahar Council. (Minister of Military Administration General Ho Ying Chin is understood to have flown to Taiyuan several days ago and is reported to be there at present.) Recently a Japanese spokesman here has minimized the number of Central Government forces sent to Shansi (reference this office's 65, March 26, 3 [2] p. m.[38]) and 2 days ago the same spokesman informed a foreign news correspondent that only two Central Government divisions were then actually in that province, according to reports he professed to have received from Japanese military officers in Peiping.

3. To Tokyo and Tientsin by mail.

PECK

793.94/7835 : Telegram

The Secretary of State to the Ambassador in China (Johnson)

WASHINGTON, April 9, 1936—5 p. m.

82. 1. Under date April 6 the American Ambassador at London telegraphs as follows:

"In a casual luncheon conversation today a Foreign Office official intimated that they had received somewhat disturbing reports in the last few days from China, that it was possible that the Chinese were

[38] Not printed.

reaching a point where 'they might do something foolish'. He said that 'Chiang Kai Shek had to decide whether he would take the course of wisdom which was to effect a compromise with the Japanese or take on the role of national hero in leading a fruitless drive against the Japanese'."

2. In the absence of identification of the parties to the conversation the Department is not inclined, in the light of your reports and other data, to attach undue importance to the statement made in the first sentence quoted above but brings London's telegram to your attention for purposes of information and in order that you may have the indication contained in the last quoted sentence of the trend of thought in some British circles.

HULL

761.93 Outer Mongolia/10 : Telegram

The Ambassador in the Soviet Union (Bullitt) to the Secretary of State

Moscow, April 9, 1936—5 p. m.
[Received 8 p. m.]

103. Soviet press this morning publishes a note of the Chinese Minister for Foreign Affairs to Bogomolov, Soviet Ambassador in China, dated April 7, 1936, asserting that the protocol between the Soviet Government and Outer Mongolia forms "undoubtedly a violation of the sovereignty of China and the terms of the Chinese-Soviet Agreement of 1924." The note goes on to state: "It is therefore my duty to declare a strong protest to your Excellency and to state that the conclusion of the above mentioned protocol with Outer Mongolia by the Government of the Union of Soviet Socialist Republics is illegal and the Chinese Government cannot under any circumstances recognize such a protocol and is in no way bound by it."

Litvinov's reply to the Chinese Chargé d'Affaires in Moscow rejecting the protest, dated April 8, is also published. It contains the following statement: "Neither the fact of the signing of the protocol nor its separate articles violate to the slightest degree the sovereignty of China."

Litvinov then asserts: "that the Soviet-Chinese Agreement of 1924 concluded in Peiping did not suffer any harm and retains its force."

I have discussed the situation in the Far East with both Litvinov and Stomoniakoff during the past 2 days. They are exceedingly optimistic. They believe that the Japanese have alienated completely all sympathy among the Mongols not only of Outer Mongolia but also Inner Mongolia and Manchuria and are convinced that Japan's political position in North China, Manchuria and Inner Mongolia is becoming weaker.

A large Mongolian delegation reached Moscow last night for the purpose of arranging further integration between the military and economic systems of the Soviet Union and Outer Mongolia.

BULLITT

761.93 Outer Mongolia/20

The Consul General at Harbin (Adams) to the Ambassador in China (Johnson)[39]

No. 224   HARBIN, April 10, 1936.

SIR: I have the honor to attach hereto, as enclosure No. 1,[40] a copy of a Kokutsu despatch from Hsinking dated April 6, 1936, containing a translation of a statement concerning the reported Soviet-Outer Mongolian agreement. It agrees exactly with the versions which appeared in the Japanese and Chinese press. Although the Commissioner for Foreign Affairs and the Japanese Consulate General were unable to confirm that the Foreign Office actually gave out the statement, they had little doubt that Kokutsu reported correctly. It is believed that the statement may be taken as official.

The statement first assumes that in making the agreement, Soviet Russia broke Article V of the Sino-Soviet Agreement of 1924 regarding China's territorial integrity. It then says that the U. S. S. R. desires to place Outer Mongolia in its power "in fact as well as in name"; that the pact is contrary to the will of the majority of the Mongols; that its real intent is to use Outer Mongolia as a base to Sovietize the Far East; that it is a military alliance against "Manchukuo" and Japan; that the agreement cannot be recognized by "Manchukuo"; that as the Nanking Government has ignored the pact, it must be concluded that it has a secret agreement with Soviet Russia; that hence the Nanking Government may be considered as the public enemy of the Far East; that "Manchukuo" and Japan will be obliged to take independent action if China does nothing; that as Manchuria and Mongolia are racial and geographical neighbors, "Manchukuo" has as much if not more right to speak in Mongolia than the Soviet Union; that as the establishment of the Soviet position in Outer Mongolia increases communist influence, "Manchukuo" is menaced thereby, which may occasion it to take proper measures in Outer Mongolia; and, finally that the recent aggravation of attack on "Manchukuo" frontier guards is worthy of serious attention.

The relations existing between "Manchukuo" and Japan make the above referred to statement sound strange coming as it does from the authorities in Hsinking. The unrestrained tone of the article would

---

[39] Copy transmitted to the Department by the Consul General at Harbin in his despatch No. 346, April 10; received May 18.
[40] Not printed.

appear to indicate that the Kwantung Army is alarmed over the situation.

Attached hereto, as enclosure No. 2,[41] is an English translation of an editorial which appeared in the *Harbin Nichi Nichi*, issue of April 2, 1936, claiming that the Russian policy toward Japan and "Manchukuo" has recently changed from one of passive defense to positive action. This editorial would not have been published in Harbin without the approval of the Japanese Military Mission.

The Harbin press reports of the Chinese protest against the conclusion of an agreement of mutual assistance between Soviet Russia and Outer Mongolia do not carry conviction. The protest was made following an outburst on the part of the Japanese press and probably following serious representations to Nanking by the Japanese.

In this general connection, attention is invited to this Consulate General's despatch No. 134 to the Embassy, October 7, 1935, entitled " 'Manchukuo' and Outer Mongolia".[41] That despatch invited attention to the circumstances that Japanese demands that the soldiers of Outer Mongolia be treated by the Chinese Government as "Chinese communists" might well drive China to jettison Outer Mongolia as a means of resisting Japanese pressure for Chinese military action which would tend to involve China in Japan's clashes with Russian interests.

Respectfully yours, WALTER A. ADAMS

761.93 Outer Mongolia/14 : Telegram

The Counselor of Embassy in China (Peck) to the Secretary of State

NANKING, April 11, 1936—7 p. m.
[Received April 11—3 : 20 p. m.[42]]

89. My 87, April 10, 9 a. m.[41] An official of the Foreign Office has unofficially sent to an officer of the Embassy the text of a note to Soviet Ambassador dated today as follows:

"Your Excellency: With reference to the signing of the Protocol of Mutual Assistance between the Government of the Union of Soviet Socialist Republics and Outer Mongolia, I had the honor to address to Your Excellency, on the 7th of April, a note of protest, stating that the signing of the protocol constituted an infringement of the sovereignty of China and a breach of the Sino-Soviet Agreement of 1924, and that the Chinese Government could under no circumstances recognize such a protocol.

On the 9th of April, I received from Your Excellency a copy of the note addressed to the Chinese Chargé d'Affaires at Moscow by the

---

[41] Not printed.
[42] Telegram in two sections.

Soviet Commissar of Foreign Affairs in reply to the above-stated protest.   The note declared that 'the Soviet Government confirms once more that the above-mentioned agreement (the Sino-Soviet Agreement of 1924), as far as the Union of Soviet Socialist Republics is concerned, remains in force in future'.   I have taken cognizance of the pledge thus again given by the Government of the Union of Soviet Socialist Republics that it recognizes Outer Mongolia as an integral part of Republic of China and respects China's sovereignty therein.

I am, however, obliged to consider as without ground the explanation given by the Soviet Government in regard to the signing of the protocol by the Union of Soviet Socialist Republics with Outer Mongolia.   Particularly, the Mukden–Soviet Agreement, signed at Mukden in 1924,[45] which is cited in the note under reply, cannot be regarded as a precedent for the present protocol.

The contention in the Soviet note that the signing of the Mukden–Soviet Agreement did not elicit a protest from the Chinese Government is just contrary to facts.   It has to be recalled that before the said agreement was submitted by the local authorities to the Central Government and subsequently approved by the latter as an annex to the Sino[-Soviet?] Agreement, the Ministry of Foreign Affairs at Peiping (then Peking) repeatedly made protests to the then Soviet Ambassador to China, on September 25 and October 11, 1924, respectively, and the Chinese diplomatic representative at Moscow also lodged protests with the Soviet Government.   It was not until the said agreement had been approved by the Central Government and all legal procedure has [had?] been complied with that a notification was sent to the Soviet Government in March, 1925 to the effect that the Mukden-Soviet Agreement was to be considered as an annex to the Sino-Soviet Agreement of 1924.   Thus, the signing of the Mukden-Soviet Agreement, which was originally an illegal act on the part of the Soviet Government, an act contrary to international practice, was only rectified subsequently by the Chinese Government. In no sense can it be referred to as a precedent for the Government of the Union of Soviet Socialist Republics to enter into any agreement with Chinese local authorities.

Inasmuch as the present protocol signed by the Government of the Union of Soviet Socialist Republics with Outer Mongolia constitutes an infringement of China's sovereignty and is in complete contradiction with the Sino-Soviet Agreement of 1924, the Chinese Government has to renew its protest in respect of the protocol and to reiterate its stand in that regard as enunciated in its last note of protest on the same subject.

I have to request Your Excellency to transmit the above communication to Your Excellency's Government.

I avail, etc."

PECK

---

[45] See telegram No. 377, October 4, 1924, 5 p. m., from the Chargé in China, *Foreign Relations*, 1924, vol. I, p. 510.

CHAPTER II: APRIL 16–JUNE 30, 1936

Continuation of Japanese economic penetration in North China; German-"Manchoukuo" trade agreement of April 30; informal British and American representations to Japan over smuggling operations in North China; Japanese-"Manchoukuo" treaty of June 10 on abolition of extraterritorial rights; demand by Southwest China for armed resistance to Japan; stiffening of North China against Japanese military pressure

793.94/7847 : Telegram

The Ambassador in China (Johnson) to the Secretary of State

PEIPING, April 16, 1936—3 p. m.
[Received April 16—10:40 a. m.]

191. Embassy's 168, April 3, noon.

1. Major General Matsumuro established his office at Peiping on April 10. The Japanese Embassy now states that this office is under the North China Garrison and not under the Tokyo General Staff. Matsumuro and Sung Che Yuan are in Tientsin.

2. Sung apparently continues his policy of procrastinating to the greatest degree possible in meeting Japanese desires. Sung's purpose is evidently to maintain his present *status quo* as long as possible.

3. Preparations for inauguration of reconstruction and communications committees under the Hopei-Chahar Political Council are being made slowly but the dates of inauguration have not yet been fixed. It is understood that the Japanese military hope that these committees will accelerate Sino-Japanese economic cooperation. It is doubtful, however, whether much can be expected of the committees for the reasons that the committees will probably procrastinate and that neither Chinese nor Japanese capital seems to be available at present for effective support of significant project.

4. The Economic Committee of the Council decided on March 21 to urge the Ministry of Railways at Nanking to issue a permit for the construction of a private narrow gauge railway from Kalgan to Dolonor and referred to economic advisers for study a proposal for readjustment of the Lungyen iron mine in Chahar. The action of General Sung's regime in respect to these projects in which the Japanese are interested illustrates that regime's methods of attempting simultaneously to please the Japanese and to delay.

5. Notwithstanding the situation described above, there is evidence of a steady Japanese economic and social penetration into Hopei and Chahar, such as (1) the continued smuggling of Japanese produce into China through Yin Ju Keng's area, (2) expanding trade by Japanese and Koreans in Hopei in opium and other narcotics, which is being extended to towns in Chahar and Suiyuan Provinces, according to foreigners resident there, (3) establishment of Japanese owned bus lines in northern Hopei, (4) activities for improvement of cotton pro-

duction, (5) establishment of various Japanese investigation organs and (6) intended improvement of the Peiping-Mukden Railway installation at Shanhaikwan at a reputed cost of $600,000 (Chinese currency).

6. The attitude of the Chinese military leaders in North China indicates that the Japanese will be unable to effect the establishment of a regime of the degree of autonomy and geographical scope which they presumably still desire unless they are ready to threaten the Chinese leaders with the use of armed force or to run the risk of using armed force.

7. According to a competent press correspondent who has just visited Kalgan and Kueihwa, the foreign residents of those provinces do not expect a forward movement into Suiyuan by Japanese controlled Mongols of Chahar for some time.

By mail to Tokyo.   JOHNSON

793.94/7846 : Telegram

The Counselor of Embassy in China (Peck) to the Secretary of State

NANKING, April 16, 1936—5 p. m.
[Received April 16—7: 55 a. m.]

92. 1. An officer of the Embassy has just been informed by a Chinese official of Cabinet rank that the Hopei-Chahar Council has agreed to the formation of a Sino-Japanese "anti-Communist" commission including Sung Che Yuan as head and Matsumuro as member and that under the terms of the agreement Japanese troops may proceed as far as Shihchiachuang and Shunteh, Hopei, as Hopei is considered to be threatened by Communist forces. This statement has not been verified by other sources.

2. Repeated to the Department, Peiping, Tokyo.

PECK

893.00/13464 : Telegram

The Counselor of Embassy in China (Peck) to the Secretary of State

NANKING, April 17, 1936—noon.
[Received 1: 50 p. m.]

94. Peiping's 183, April 14, 2 p. m.[46]

1. *Shanghai Evening Post and Mercury* April 16 published in news columns an "explanation of the hitherto completely mysterious" release of Bosshardt[47] as due to change in Communist policy

---

[46] Not printed.
[47] Telegram No. 183, April 14, 2 p.m., from the Ambassador in China reported that this missionery was "understood to be of Swiss nationality" (893.00/13457).

described in a quoted article said to have been written by one Wang Ming, "leading member of the Internationale in Moscow" and to have appeared (date not given) in the London *International Press Correspondence*, "official organ of the Communist Internationale". According to this quoted article the new policy involves (1), concentration of Communist effort against "Japanese imperialism"; (2), establishment of more normal relations with other "imperialist" powers which "should not exclude the possibility under certain conditions of fighting together with them" against Japan; (3), relinquishment of "partisan traditions in relation to foreign diplomatic, trading, cultural and religious institutions and persons, i. e., a stop should be put to their arrest and holding to ransom."

2. Such policy would seem to be complete reversal of that hitherto followed including opportunist attacks upon foreigners as illustrated by the reported statement of the Stams' murderers in December, 1934,[48] that the victims were being killed because being missionaries they were imperialists and had assisted Chiang Kai Shek in anti-Communist acts. That the reported new policy caused Bosshardt's release would not appear to be entirely borne out by Yunnanfu's April 15, 4 p. m., to the Embassy that Bosshardt when freed was told by Communist leader that Father Kellner would be released upon payment of ransom.

3. A change in Communist policy as described in Wang's article would be a logical development in the light of present strained Soviet-Japanese relations because it would tend (1), simultaneously to strengthen the Communist cause in China and build up possible resources against Japan by playing upon and supporting the anti-Japanese feeling in this country: and (2), to weaken Chinese official and popular sentiment against Communists by aligning the latter with other Chinese against the common enemy. Moreover, although the principles of the First International are opposed alike to the furthering of representative democratic institutions and of nationalistic ambitions, nevertheless Russian Communist advisers for their own ends espoused "bourgeois democratic" aims in this country until 1927 and if the reported present plan to direct Chinese Communist strength against Japan is a fact, the change in policy appears to be a reversion to past technique. The opportunity given by the situation in the Far East to use Chinese nationalistic feeling as a weapon against Japanese nationalism with a view to breaking down the latter, thereby permitting the growth of Communism in Japan would also seem to be a logical objective at this time.

4. To the Department and Peiping. By mail to Moscow, London, Tokyo and Shanghai.

PECK

[48] For correspondence concerning this case, see *Foreign Relations*, 1934, vol. III, pp. 479 ff.

701.9493/103 : Telegram

The Counselor of Embassy in China (Peck) to the Secretary of State

NANKING, April 18, 1936—4 p. m.
[Received 5 : 17 p. m.]

99. 1. Press reports that Chinese Government's *agrément* to appointment of Kawagoe[49] would be announced today appear premature. According to responsible official of the Foreign Office, the Government will not act on the nomination before 3 or 4 more days. A Domei (Japanese news agency) despatch dated Nanking, April 15, purports to quote an unnamed high official of the Foreign Office as saying that "China is not in a position to object to Kawagoe's appointment."

2. It seems generally to be regretted in Chinese circles that Shigemitsu was not nominated Ambassador to China.[50] According to one foreign press despatch, the Chinese believe that Kawagoe won the appointment by his sympathetic attitude, as Consul General at Tientsin, toward the acts of the Japanese military in North China and his appointment "is considered a further surrender (presumably of the Japanese Foreign Office) of [*to?*] the Japanese military authorities."

3. Repeated to Department and Peiping, by mail to Tokyo, Tientsin.

PECK

793.94/7860 : Telegram

The Ambassador in China (Johnson) to the Secretary of State

PEIPING, April 20, 1936—2 p. m.
[Received April 20—12 : 30 p. m.]

201. 1. Nanking's telegram to the Department 92, April 16, 5 p. m., and paragraph 2 of the Embassy's 168, April 3, noon. Although joint suppression of Communism has probably been urged recently by Matsumuro, available information here indicates that Sung has not yet entered into an agreement. According to various sources, Sung has recently stated that he is not a traitor to China and that, unlike Ho Ying Chin, he has not entered into any written agreement with the Japanese. Chinese observers state that Sung is deeply averse to yielding to Japanese representations of major importance.

2. There are at present in Peiping two Kuominchun generals who formerly outranked Sung. One of them, Shih Ching Ting, has been here for some time as chief counselor of the Hopei-Chahar pacifica-

---

[49] Shigeru Kawagoe's appointment as Japanese Ambassador was confirmed May 1.
[50] Vice Minister for Foreign Affairs, Mamoru Shigemitsu was appointed Ambassador to the Soviet Union.

tion headquarters. The other, Teng Che-hsi, has only recently arrived from Nanking and has been appointed Chief of Court Martial of the Hopei-Chahar pacification headquarters. A third, Lu Chung Lin, was in Peiping recently as a representative from Feng Yu Hsiang. It seems probable that their advice to their former subordinate Sung has been that he should not yield to Japanese representations. What significance, if any, the movements of these men may have with regard to the Kuominchun as a unit is a matter of speculation.

3. The future of Sung's relations with the Japanese appears to depend upon (1) the courage of Sung in refusing to make important concessions to the Japanese, (2) the degree of pressure which the Japanese may be willing to exert, and (3) the extent of aid, if any, which the National Government may give to Sung.

4. The principal Chinese military of Hopei are expected to return from Tientsin to Peiping within a day or two. The principal Japanese military in the five northern provinces are expected to have a conference soon at Tientsin with Colonel Nagami, Chief of Staff of the North China Garrison, who has just returned from Tokyo where he represented Major [General] Tada at the annual meeting of Japanese commanders. It is anticipated that subsequent to [this?] Sino-Japanese conversations at Peiping will be resumed.

5. According to the Japanese press, there will be a conference at Shanghai of Japanese military officers after the imminent arrival there from Japan of the new Japanese Military Attaché.

6. Tientsin's telegram, November 27, 11 a.m.,[51] the Consulate General at Tientsin reports in despatch 190, April 16,[52] that there is renewed activity in the vicinity of the international race course. Evidence points to construction under supervision of Japanese military of large building or buildings near the land already leveled off for use as airfield. Apparently an aerodrome or barracks is being constructed. A Chinese official stated that the work involves an area of some 700 acres, much of which belongs to the Peiping-Mukden Railway.

7. Yin Ju Keng of the demilitarized zone has sent a "good will envoy" to Hsinking. Information is lacking with regard to developments in Yin's relations with the Japanese.

8. According to press reports, some 250 soldiers of the Japanese Embassy Guard left Peiping April 18 for Japan, replacements of approximately the same strength having arrived April 16.

By mail to Tokyo.

JOHNSON

---

[51] *Foreign Relations*, 1935, vol. III, p. 447.
[52] Not printed.

793.94/7861 : Telegram

The Consul General at Canton (Spiker) to the Secretary of State

CANTON, April 20, 1936—4 p. m.
[Received 4 : 05 p. m.]

Referring to previous correspondence concerning possible cooperation between Japanese and Kwangsi provincial leaders. In a lengthy newspaper statement published in local and Hong Kong press on April 18, Marshal Li Tsung Jen, military spokesman for Kwangsi, urges war resistance against Japan as sole means of salvation of China at this juncture. Li holds there is no likelihood of the United States, Great Britain, or Russia going to war with Japan and that those who urge delay in belief that such war will solve China's problems play directly into Japan's hands. He admits that in Sino-Japanese conflict, Japan will promptly seize China's ports and will blockade her coast but that ensuing extended guerrilla warfare in interior China will require such an expenditure of men and treasure by Japan that under pressure from within and without there will be precipitated economic and political crisis which will make prosecution of foreign war impossible. On the other hand, Li presages that "the impact of foreign aggression and raising of standard of war for national emancipation the Chinese will become more united"; that Japan will suffer "such diplomatic isolation that it would be easy for the powers to help China either morally or materially and to capitalize Japan's war-given exhaustion". Despatch follows.[53] Sent to Department and to Peiping and Nanking.

SPIKER

793.94/7905

The Ambassador in China (Johnson) to the Secretary of State

No. 385   PEIPING, April 20, 1936.
[Received May 18.]

SIR: I have the honor to enclose a copy of a memorandum [54] of a conversation which I had on April 14, 1936, with Dr. S. G. Cheng, who was until recently the Special Delegate of the Ministry for Foreign Affairs for Hopei Province, with regard to Sino-Japanese relations, during which he stated that the Chinese Minister for Foreign Affairs, General Chang Ch'un, regarded Peiping as inevitably lost to China, that he (Dr. Cheng) did not believe that the Japanese would occupy Peiping, although they would probably achieve a greater interest in matters in North China, that he believed that the Japanese were anxious for a more active cooperation, that the Na-

---

[53] Not found in Department files.
[54] Not printed.

tional Government had an incorrect view of the situation in North China, and that General Chang Ch'un was not prepared to assist General Sung Che-yuan with either money or munitions.

Dr. Cheng has recently been transferred from Hopei to the Provinces of Sikang and Szechwan as Special Delegate, his post in Hopei being given to Mr. Lo Chia-heng who continues to hold the post of Special Delegate of the Ministry of Foreign Affairs for Chahar Province. It is believed that the National Government has given the post to Mr. Lo because he speaks Japanese, which Dr. Cheng does not.

Respectfully yours, NELSON TRUSLER JOHNSON

893.00/13469 : Telegram

The Ambassador in China (Johnson) to the Secretary of State

PEIPING, April 21, 1936—2 p. m.
[Received April 21—noon.]

203. 1. Paragraph 3 of Embassy's 191, April 16, 3 p. m. The Reconstruction Committee of the Hopei-Chahar Political Council was inaugurated April 20 with General Men Chih Chung as chairman. Men is a member of the Council and a former divisional commander of Feng Yu Hsiang. Men stated that duties of the Committee will be highway construction, river conservancy, mining, and agricultural works.

2. General Chin Teh Chun, Mayor of Peiping, and General Chen Chi Yen, Peiping Commissioner of Public Safety, both of whom are subordinates of Sung Che Yuan, have been appointed superintendent and assistant superintendent respectively of the National Library of Peiping and of the Palace Museum. These appointments indicate the continuing extension of control by Sung's group over organs in Hopei Province of the National Government. A subordinate of General Sung has told the Embassy that the appointments have been made in order that the Hopei-Chahar Political Council may know what is going on in these two institutions.

Copy by mail to Tokyo.

JOHNSON

893.00/13470 : Telegram

The Ambassador in China (Johnson) to the Secretary of State

PEIPING, April 21, 1936—4 p. m.
[Received April 21—11 : 50 a. m.]

204. The Consul General at Mukden [55] reported in despatch 247, April 14,[56] that he had advised Americans residing at Sinpin to

---

[55] Joseph W. Ballantine.
[56] Not printed.

evacuate. Prior to issuing the warning, Ballantine had been informed by the commander of the gendarmes at Mukden that banditry was rife in the Sinpin area and that there were not enough troops available to afford adequate protection. A part of the danger apparently arose from the attitude of the authorities toward the missionaries at Sinpin, some evidence of which is contained in Mukden's despatch 234, March 12.[56a] It is understood that of the five or six Americans who were at Sinpin, only one or two remain and that those remaining expect to evacuate within 1 or 2 days.

By mail to Tokyo.   JOHNSON

693.943/4 : Telegram

The Counselor of Embassy in China (Peck) to the Secretary of State

NANKING, April 22, 1936—noon.
[Received April 22—6 : 55 a. m.]

103. 1. An officer of the Embassy has been informed by a responsible concerned Chinese official that the Chinese Government has decided, as the only effective means of stopping the smuggling of Japanese goods into North China, to lower the import tariff on rayon, sugar and cigarette papers in order to make smuggling unprofitable. He stated that the new tariff rates will shortly be made effective and intimated that this action was taken partially in order to preclude the Hopei-Chahar Council from carrying into effect an intention, recently reported in the press, of extending "special trading privileges" in North China which would be tantamount to reduction of import duties.

2. Repeated to the Department and Peiping, by mail to Tokyo.

PECK

893.01 Manchuria/1332

The Consul General at Harbin (Adams) to the Secretary of State

No. 349   HARBIN, April 22, 1936.
[Received May 18.]

SIR: I have the honor to state that from time to time, and in more or less disconnected form in various despatches, I have commented on the policy of the Kwantung Army in Manchuria. Because of the outstanding importance of the effects of that policy upon developments in Manchuria and possibly the Far East generally, I believe it advisable, even at the risk of tedious repetition, to embody in one despatch the disconnected observations already made and to report some recent developments.

When the Kwantung Army obtained control in Manchuria through the Mukden incident of 1931 and subsequent military operations it

---

[56a] Not printed.

soon made apparent its intention of reserving to itself the benefits of its enterprise and of building for itself a home or empire in Manchuria where it could rule without hindrance from the Diet or the civil government departments in Tokyo, and where it could raise and appropriate as it pleased its own revenues. It created, as its agency, the government of "Manchukuo" and began to formulate and execute plans for control, by that government, of the development of private manufacturing enterprises through a licensing system, and for control and operation by it of public utilities and essential industries.

The Army found, however, several obstacles to the full and effective exercise by it of control over Manchuria. These obstacles were the Government of the Kwantung Leased Territory, the large Japanese and Korean communities and interests in Manchuria, the Chinese Eastern Railway and the South Manchuria Railway Company. The Kwantung Leased Territory comprised a free port area which occasioned a material loss of customs revenue to "Manchukuo" through extensive smuggling. The Overseas Department in Japan had a considerable voice in the Government of the Kwantung Leased Territory, control over its policing and over the policing of the South Manchuria Railway zone. The large Japanese and Korean communities in Manchuria and the extensive business and industrial interests controlled by them were through their extraterritorial status, immune from the tax agencies and courts created by the Kwantung Army. The Chinese Eastern Railway, carrying with it still the prestige and power of former days, was under effective Soviet control and was in fact in a position to resist taxation. The only direct contributions which it made to "Manchukuo" were sums, whose amounts were decided upon by the railway itself, for bandit suppression work. The South Manchuria Railway Company, representing huge financial interests in Japan, and exercising certain quasi-governmental functions itself, was controlled by a board of directors appointed by the home government in Japan. It possessed extraterritoriality and was therefore immune from taxation by the "Manchukuo" government.

It will thus be seen that the Kwantung Army found that Manchuria, as a revenue producing area, was far from perfect as then organized, and that much work was necessary to develop the country into an efficient producer of revenue. The Army lost no time in beginning that work.

The problem of the Kwantung Leased Territory was partially solved by the creation in Tokyo of the Manchuria Affairs Bureau, under a military chief, with effective power of decision in matters relating to Manchuria. This eliminated the Overseas Department from the Kwantung Leased Territory and the South Manchuria Railway zone. The police of the Kwantung Leased Territory were placed under the control of a *gendarmerie* officer and a Kwantung Bureau was created in the Japanese Ambassador's office in Hsinking where the effective government of the area resided. With respect to the smuggling for which the Kwantung Leased Territory formed a base, Consul Grummon at Dairen had the following to say on April 5, 1935:

" . . . [57] Mr. J. Fukumoto, Commissioner of Customs of 'Manchukuo' at Dairen, informed an officer of this Consulate that serious consideration was being given by the authorities to the advisability of abolishing the freedom of duty of goods entering and leaving the Kwantung Leased Territory. Mr. Fukumoto remarked that in the event that customs duties were to be collected in the Territory the 'Manchukuo' customs tariff would be applied.

". . . The smuggling activities across the borders of Kwantung Leased Territory which are exceedingly difficult to curb effectively and result in a considerable loss of revenue to 'Manchukuo' would undoubtedly cause the Hsinking authorities to look with favor upon such a change of status in the Leased Territory."

There was not even a whisper of demand from the 29 million Chinese in Manchuria for the abolition of extraterritoriality. As soon as the subject came up the Japanese and Korean communities in Manchuria promptly showed that they were opposed to the abolition of their extraterritorial status. Despite the entire absence of demand and the opposition of the civilian Japanese in Manchuria, however, the Kwantung Army through its influence at home caused the Japanese Government voluntarily to bring up the subject. This gesture was naturally favorably received by the Kwantung Army's agency, the "Manchukuo" government. According to a special telegram, dated April 18, 1936, from Hsinking to the *Manchuria Daily News*, Dairen, a virtual agreement has been reached and it is expected that the agreement between "Manchukuo" and Japan providing for the abolition of Japanese extraterritoriality in Manchuria will be signed during the latter part of May, to become partially effective on July 1, 1936. All through the discussions that have occurred the question of taxation was paramount.

After a long fight, full of bitterness and vituperation, "Manchukuo" finally obtained control of the Chinese Eastern Railway by purchase of the Soviet interest therein on March 23, 1935. The railway was promptly absorbed into the "State Railways" system and handed over for management to the South Manchuria Railway Company, giving that company a complete monopoly of rail transportation in Manchuria. In this connection it is interesting to note that the *Japan-Manchukuo Year Book* of 1936 gives the length of the South Manchuria Railway Company's tracks as 1,129 kilometers, and the

---

[57] Omissions indicated in the original.

length of the State Railways (controlled and operated by the South Manchuria Railway Company) as 6,671.6 kilometers. It will thus be seen that the subsidiary has grown to six times the size of the parent and managing company. While the South Manchuria Railway Company financed most of the railway construction in Manchuria, the nominal ownership by "Manchukuo" of six-sevenths of the railways of Manchuria naturally gives the Kwantung Army considerable voice in railway affairs. Of course, the abolition of extraterritoriality will go far towards solving the problem of the South Manchuria Railway Company for the Kwantung Army. The right of "Manchukuo" to tax the South Manchuria Railway Company will destroy the independent position of that company and give "Manchukuo" an effective voice in its management.

It is interesting to note that the army already has sufficient influence over the South Manchuria Railway Company to cause it to work for the destruction of its independence. An instance of this was the election on March 29, 1936, of nine councilors of the Japanese Residents' Association of Harbin. The Japanese Residents' Association is a quasi-municipal enterprise which looks after the interests of the Japanese community. Its main activities consist of the operation of schools for Japanese children and the conduct of measures of sanitation. It also makes representations in matters affecting Japanese interests generally. It is governed by 18 councilors whose term of office is two years; the election of half of this number takes place every year. Shortly before the election the State Railways Office (which is under the control of the South Manchuria Railway) surprised the Japanese community by suddenly putting forward five members of its staff as candidates, besides one former South Manchuria Railway man. It is said that the members of the railway staff were required by the railway management to vote for the railway candidates. About half of the independent voters refrained from voting as a protest against the railway candidates, the stated objection being that most of these candidates were newcomers to Harbin and had little connection with the affairs of the Japanese community. Four of the five railway candidates were elected, and amongst the other five elected was one who was until recently connected with the railway and who is looked upon as a railway man as far as the Council is concerned.

There appears to be little doubt in the minds of local Japanese that the councilors elected by the South Manchuria Railway will use their influence to hinder Japanese civil opposition to the abolition of extraterritoriality.

In connection with the progress of the plans of the army to obtain control of the South Manchuria Railway, I beg to invite attention to Consul Grummon's excellent despatch of April 6, 1936, to the Embassy in Tokyo, entitled "Reorganization Plans of the South Manchuria Railway Company".[58]   The matter was summed up by Consul Grummon in the statement that the South Manchuria Railway is now in the process of being absorbed by its creature, the State Railways, so that it may, according to army plans, function as an instrument of national policy.

The Kwantung Army has steadily pursued its policy of severing all connections between "Manchukuo" and Japan, excepting the link which the army itself affords.   Insofar as the general administrative structure of the Japanese Government is concerned there is something to be said for the claim that "Manchukuo" is an independent country.

The beginning of the Kwantung Army's levies upon Manchuria was extremely moderate.   In the fiscal year 1934–1935 the "Manchukuo" government's contribution to the expenses of the Kwantung Army was stated to be $9,000,000.   For the current fiscal year that contribution was fixed at $19,500,000.   When the measures which the Army has initiated for increased revenues for "Manchukuo" become effective, it may be expected that the contribution of "Manchukuo" to the expenses of the Kwantung Army will increase rapidly.

It seems that the situation outlined in this despatch is worthy of careful future observation because, with its further development, it may in the course of a few years materially affect happenings in Japan as well as in Manchuria and China proper.   I believe that the astonishingly rapid progress which the Kwantung Army is making towards the realization of its aim for an independent position on the continent of Asia is, from a political viewpoint, possibly the most important development that is occurring in Manchuria and north China.

Respectfully yours,   WALTER A. ADAMS

893.00/13478 : Telegram

The Counselor of Embassy in China (Peck) to the Secretary of State

NANKING, April 29, 1936—9 a. m.
[Received April 29—7 : 30 a. m.]

110. Although there has existed some suspicion that the strenuous efforts of the National Government to improve its military position are being exerted primarily to meet criticism of southwestern and other leaders that Chiang Kai Shek does not intend to resist foreign aggression, there is increasing evidence here that preparations for actual warfare are being seriously undertaken.   For example, the

---

[58] Not printed.

Nanking Embassy learns from an authoritative source that the [National] Health Administration for the past 10 weeks has been expending monthly $1,000,000 for the purchase of bandages, cotton, surplus medicines, materials for manufacture of artificial limbs, and other articles required to equip the Chinese Army Medical Corps; 120 trucks have recently been purchased for use as ambulances; 2 recently completed hospitals at Nanchang have been reserved for anticipated use by wounded soldiers; and the military authorities have been discussing a proposed purchase of an electric light plant sufficient to operate all branches of its local establishments.

2. From another reliable source it is learned that an airplane factory similar to that described in my 60, March 21, 9 a. m.[59] is to be constructed at Loyang with assistance of the Eurasia Company, engines to be 1000 horsepower hornet type manufactured in Germany; the Nanking arsenal is working night and day on 3 shifts and has increased its output of heavy machine guns to 120 per month. Woodland, mountain and most elevated places in vicinity of Nanking and as far as Chinkiang have been made military reservations closed to the public; it is understood that they are being utilized for gun emplacements, chiefly anti-aircraft.

3. According to several reliable sources, the principal railways operating in or through the Yangtze Valley region have been ordered to acquire 1 year's supply of fuel and maintenance equipment including couplers, wheels, and similar articles.

4. The Ministry of Industries is reliably reported to have purchased an electric plant for its own use in emergency. Other Government departments, including the Ministry of Finance, have formulated plans for the removal of archives and equipment in case of necessity.

5. Some officials express with apparent sincerity fear that Nanking will be attacked (see paragraph 4, my 91, April 16, 2 p. m.[59]); others scout such possibility and it does not seem reasonable to anticipate any incident here unless one should be caused in order to exert pressure upon the Chinese Government in connection with some serious incident elsewhere. In this connection, a well-informed Chinese who is the confidential assistant of a ranking official of the Government recently stated to an officer of the Embassy that an enemy blockade of the Chekiang, Kiangsu or Shantung coast would definitely result in Chinese resistance from the air. This official anticipated the possibility of an incident at Tsingtau and according to him and other Chinese and foreign sources it is learned that two of Chiang Kai Shek's best divisions have been despatched to the vicinity of Tsingtau, (1) in preparation for possible foreign aggression in Shantung and,

---

[59] Not printed.

(2) in case Han Fu Chu should deviate in his loyalty to the Government (see paragraph 3, Nanking Embassy's 91, April 16, 2 p. m.).

6. To Department.   By mail to Peiping and Tokyo.

PECK

793.94/7874 : Telegram

The Ambassador in China (Johnson) to the Secretary of State

PEIPING, April 29, 1936—3 p. m.
[Received April 29—1 : 20 p. m.]

213.   1. Reference paragraph 1 of Embassy's 201, April 20, 2 p. m., Sung Che Yuan and his self-seeking civilian subordinates are conferring at Tientsin with Japanese military leaders. Available information indicates that Sung is being urged to sign an anti-Communism agreement which is designed for strategic purposes with regard to Soviet Russia, for further separation of the Sung regime from the National Government, and for further extension of Japanese influence in North China.   Details are not obtainable.

2. Japanese advisers suggested recently to the Foreign Affairs Committee of the Hopei-Chahar Political Council that Japanese nationals be granted the privilege of free residence in North China.   All of the Committee except the chairman, allegedly a member of the Kwangsi clique of the Kuomintang and opposed to Chiang Kai Shek, disapproved of the suggestion, which has been referred to Sung Che Yuan. Acceptance of the suggestion would facilitate Japanese penetration and activities as, for example, it might be used as an excuse to bring in additional Japanese police and courts.

3. According to Chinese officials, it has been definitely decided by the Hopei-Chahar Political Council to construct a railway from Shihkiachwang on the Pinghan Railway to Tsangchow on the Tsinpu Railway.   (Reference page 3 of Embassy's despatch 2897, August 10, 1934.[61])   Apparently the project has the approval of the National Government as the Ministry of Railways has appointed the "chief of the engineering bureau of the Tsangchow-Shihkiachwang Railway". It is not known what Japanese interests are involved.

4. The Japanese military are constructing new barracks at Kupeikou to the south of the north gate, apparently on a fairly extensive scale.   At present there are about 100 Japanese troops at Kupeikou.

5. It is reliably reported that all construction of roads, railways, and the like in Jehol Province has ceased since the Tokyo assassinations.   There is a news report about Hsinking, indicating an economy program with regard to Manchukuo.

[61] Not printed.

6. Major General Tada, commander of the North China Garrison, and Major General Itagaki, Chief of Staff of the Kwantung army, have been promoted to the rank of lieutenant general.

7. An unconfirmed report is current in Peiping today that the form and personnel for an autonomous Mongol government under Japanese direction is ready for inauguration "at a suitable time" with Prince Teh as the head and Panhofen in western Chahar as the capital.

By mail to Peiping.

JOHNSON

793.94/7876 : Telegram

*The Second Secretary of Embassy in China (Atcheson) to the
Secretary of State*

NANKING, April 30, 1936—10 a. m.
[Received April 30—7 : 50 a. m.]

113. My 92, April 16, 5 p. m., and 103, April 22, noon.

1. Foreign Office has given to the press official denial of press reports from Peiping that Sung Che-yuan has entered into an agreement with the Japanese military for Sino-Japanese cooperation against Communism.

2. In an informal private conversation last evening a responsible official of the Foreign Office stated to me positively that no such agreement had yet been made. He indicated, however, that he feared Sung eventually would have to meet Japanese wishes in this respect, stated that Japanese military officers had recently been pressing Sung for such agreement, and intimated that Sung is bargaining for the best terms possible and is attempting as a *quid pro quo* to obtain the abolition of the East Hopei regime and the inclusion of the East Hopei area in the territory under the jurisdiction of the Hopei-Chahar Council.

3. Except for threats of a military *démarche*, which he indicated are not being employed by Japanese officers at this time, the principal lever in the hands of the Japanese to force acceptance of the proposal in the Hirota program relating to joint Sino-Japanese action against Communism appears to be the situation arising out of the smuggling through the demilitarized zone of large quantities of Japanese goods (estimated by some to amount in value from two to three hundred million Chinese dollars per annum and to cost the customs daily from ten to twenty thousand in revenues). He feels that the smuggling constituted an attack upon the Customs Administration which might later be directed against the customs at other places and eventually destroy its effectiveness as the Government's chief and most reliable revenue-producing agency. The seriousness of the Chinese predicament in this respect, he intimated, might cause Sung to capitulate if

by so doing the effectiveness of the customs in the North might be maintained. He said that reduction of the import tariff would not in his opinion prove a good solution of the smuggling problem because it would mean reduction not only of duty on items now being smuggled but eventually of all items with consequent great loss of revenue.

4. Repeated to the Department and Peiping. By mail to Tokyo.

ATCHESON

693.943/6 : Telegram

The Ambassador in China (Johnson) to the Secretary of State

PEIPING, April 30, 1936—11 a. m.
[Received April 30—6:40 a. m.]

215. Department's 70, April 1, noon, and paragraph 5 of Embassy's 191, April 16, 3 p. m.

1. The smuggling of Japanese produce into North China through Yin Ju Keng's area has reached such widespread proportions that it is now beginning to affect trade in various parts of China. The Consulate General at Tientsin has obtained from the customs a detailed statement showing the quantities of principal smuggled commodities from August, 1935, to April 18, 1936, and a summary of arrivals at Tientsin and departures therefrom during the week ending April 18, 1936. From April 12 to April 18, inclusive, there arrived from the North at the East Station, Tientsin, 8,044 bags of artificial silk yarn; 46,452 bags of white sugar; 49 bags of cigarette paper; 1,842 bags of piece goods; and 1,591 packages of sundries, all of these goods having been smuggled in through Yin Ju Keng's area. During the same period smuggled goods despatched to other parts of China by the Peiping and Tsinpu Railways from the East, West and Central Stations at Tientsin amounted to 5,198 bags of artificial silk yarn, 34,089 bags of white sugar, 312 bags of cigarette paper, and 20 packages of sundries. These goods were destined to Tsinanfu, Chowchun, Paotou, Tehchow, Hsuchow, Kaifeng, Shunteh and Yutze. From August 1, 1935, to April 18, 1936, the following smuggled goods arrived at the East Station at Tientsin: 82,689 bags of artificial silk; 5,969 bags of cigarette paper; 19,228 bags of piece goods; 398,525 bags of white sugar; and 6,799 bags of sundries. The exact time of delivery of these goods has been checked by the railway authorities and some of the produce delivered to motor trucks and mule carts and taken to places in the Japanese concession in Tientsin.

2. The smuggling operations are now being extended along the coast south of Tangku toward the Shantung border. Smugglers in that area are alleged to be bringing their goods from Dairen and by means of small rivers and roads to make delivery to the Tientsin-Pukow Railway at Tanghsien.

3. Another recent important development which if prolonged will seriously impair an important American trade, is that large quantities of smuggled kerosene and gasoline have now begun to arrive in Tientsin from East Hopei. It is known that shipments of as large as 1,000 cases of Japanese kerosene and as many as 990 cases of gasoline have recently arrived at Tientsin. Shipments of several hundred cases of either kerosene or gasoline are not uncommon. This situation is so menacing that the Standard Vacuum Company has [sent?] its North China manager to Shanghai for a conference.

4. The uncurbed activities of the smugglers are now leading to a complete disorganization of trade and to disastrous impairment of customs revenues in North China. At present there seems to be no prospect of early relief. On the contrary, there are suspicions that the present extraordinary situation may be the result of a studied effort to impair the financial and economic control in North China of the Central Government. General Matsumuro recently remarked to a press representative that from the point of view of China the movement is smuggling, but from the point of view of the East Hopei Autonomous Government the goods are "imports". The fact that smugglers apparently pay a tax to Yin Ju Keng's authorities which is less than rates levied by the regular customs establishment lends a certain amount of color to Matsumuro's reported statement.

5. The smuggling problem is probably now the most serious single factor confronting the Central Government.

By mail to Shanghai and Tokyo.

JOHNSON

761.93 Outer Mongolia/16 : Telegram

The Second Secretary of Embassy in China (Atcheson) to the Secretary of State

NANKING, April 30, 1936—11 a. m.
[Received April 30—10 a. m.]

114. My 90, April 12, 9 [*11*] a. m.[61a]

1. I am informed by a responsible official of the Foreign Office that no reply from the Soviet Government has been received to the Chinese second protest of April 11. He stated that unless the Soviet Government replied, the Chinese Government would send the former no further communication on the subject and would assume that the Soviet Government accepted China's position as set forth in the Chinese notes of April 7 and 11. He did not believe that the Soviet Union would cancel the pact of March 12 with Outer Mongolia but considered that

---

[61a] Not printed.

failure to do so "would not matter because to the Chinese Government the pact is non-existent."

2. Repeated to the Department and Peiping. By mail to Moscow.

ATCHESON

761.93/1570 : Telegram

The Second Secretary of Embassy in China (Atcheson) to the Secretary of State

NANKING, April 30, 1936—noon.
[Received April 30—6 : 40 a. m.]

115. 1. Foreign Office has released following statement in English to the press.

"The persistent reports in the Japanese press of an alleged secret treaty between China and Soviet Russia were deplored by Dr. T. T. Li, director of intelligence and publicity department of the Foreign Office, in the course of a press interview this afternoon.

Declaring that such reports were absolutely groundless, Dr. Li said that their repeated appearance in the Japanese newspapers in spite of China's denials led to the suspicion of some willful purpose.

The circulation by the Japanese papers of such sensational but totally unfounded rumors, he emphasized, would in no way serve the cause of Sino-Japanese understanding."

2. To Department. By mail to Peiping, Moscow and Tokyo.

ATCHESON

793.94/7875 : Telegram

The Ambassador in China (Johnson) to the Secretary of State

PEIPING, April 30, 1936—4 p. m.
[Received April 30—7 : 50 a. m.]

217. Reference paragraph 6 of the Embassy's 213, April 29, 3 p. m. The Embassy is reliably informed that several changes are being made in the status of the Japanese military in Hopei Province for the purpose of showing the Chinese "the fixed determination" of the Japanese military and of enhancing the prestige of Lieutenant General Tada's position vis-à-vis other Japanese military. Appointment of the commander of the North China Garrison will hereafter be made directly by the Emperor, thereby putting the post in the same status as that of commanders of the Kwantung army, the forces in Chosen and Taiwan Districts. Presumably Tada will receive the first appointment as he has recently been raised in rank. As a result of the approaching increase of the strength of the North China Garrison (which Japanese sources state will be double the present number) the Japanese Embassy Guard in Peiping will be raised from the status of a

regiment to that of a brigade. The present commander, a lieutenant colonel, is being replaced by a colonel. At the same time, the brigade will be commanded by a major general who will have under him two lieutenant colonels. There will thus be an exceptional number of high ranking officers in Peiping, including Major General Matsumuro, head of the North China Garrison. Matsumuro is assisted by a major; Assistant Military Attaché continues to be a major.

By mail to Tokyo.

JOHNSON

894.00/647

The Ambassador in Japan (Grew) to the Secretary of State

No. 1798   TOKYO, April 30, 1936.
                                                            [Received May 18.]

SIR: It has been known for a number of years past that there are in Japan two schools of thought in regard to the direction of Japan's national expansion. One school, the "continental school", led by the Japanese Army, advocates advance on the Asiatic continent, principally to the west and north, in order to acquire sources of raw material and markets for manufactured goods in Manchuria, Mongolia, Siberia and China Proper. The efforts of this school have resulted in the annexation by Japan of Korea, the formation of "Manchukuo" and the establishment of the semi-autonomous governments of North China, but they also brought about the abortive expeditions into Shantung and Siberia following the World War. On the whole, however, this school has been reasonably successful in its attempts to contribute to the expansion of the Japanese nation and consequently has held the center of the stage for a number of years past, thoroughly eclipsing the other school of thought.

The second school of thought is the "oceanic" or "blue water" school, which advocates Japanese expansion, not to the frozen wastes of the north, where it is difficult for Japanese to live and work, nor to the over-populated country of China, where Japanese cannot compete with the local labor, but to the south, whence, it is said, the principal portion of the Japanese racial root stock came many hundreds of years ago and where climatic and labor conditions favor Japanese expansion. This second school, as is to be expected, is led by the Japanese Navy, as any expansionist program to the south of Japan would inevitably mean that the primary participant would be the Navy rather than the Army. (In this connection please see strictly confidential despatch No. 125 of February 11, 1936, from the Consul General in Sydney, N. S. W.)

There has been a marked recrudescence of opinion in recent months favoring the southward expansion theory. A large part of this has consisted merely of newspaper rumors, but it is believed that the rumors have been inspired by the younger officers in the Navy who are dissatisfied with the Navy's place in the shade and wish to see the Navy take a more prominent position in the progress of the nation. These newspaper reports of the Navy's opinions, therefore, are entitled to a certain amount of consideration, representing as they do the ideas of a large section of the Navy.

During September 1935, reports appeared in the Japanese press to the effect that the Navy had begun to advocate a general southward advance. The reasons for this proposed southward movement were stated as being both defensive and economic. It was claimed that it would be necessary for the Japanese Navy to offset the strengthening of American defenses in the Pacific Ocean, as represented by the establishment of commercial air routes and the rumored strengthening of the fortifications at Guam, by the extension of Japanese naval activities to the south. It was also claimed that it would be desirable for Japan, for national defense and trade reasons, to endeavor to acquire further supplies of rice, fish, petroleum, cotton, iron ores, wool, and rubber in the South Seas, as well as to provide outlets in that region for excess Japanese population.

In the early part of the year several persons, including naval officers, are reported to have stated, in articles in the magazines and in public speeches, that now that "Manchukuo" is well established, the time had arrived for the Japanese to turn their attention southward, in an effort to obtain concessions and increased trade in the Netherland Indies and the Philippine Islands. On January 22, 1936, at a luncheon given by businessmen of Osaka, Vice Admiral Takahashi, the Commander-in-Chief of the Combined Fleet, is said to have stated that:

> "Manchukuo is experiencing sound development, and her economic basis is firmly established. We should, therefore, turn our attention southward, and strive for the acquisition of new markets . . ."[62] In such a case the cruising radius of the ships of the Japanese Navy will have to be increased to reach such locations as New Guinea, Borneo and the Celebes."

(Note: Admiral Takahashi's speech was never published in Japan, as far as the Embassy is aware, but a summary, which was later claimed to contain misquotations, was cabled to the United States by one of the news agencies and was used by Senator Pittman in his speech before the Senate on February 10, 1936. The above excerpts from Admiral Takahashi's speech were obtained through indirect sources by the Naval Attaché of the Embassy.)

---

[62] Omission indicated in the original.

On March 21, 1936, the *Osaka Mainichi* and *Tokyo Nichi Nichi*, English Edition, published what purported to be the Navy's recommendations to the newly-established Hirota Government for reform of the national administration. Under the heading of "Foreign Policy", the Navy is reported to have suggested the following:

"(1) Establishment of Foreign Policy. Centralization of diplomacy and enhancement of the self-initiative policy through the founding of a national policy of dealing with foreign nations.

(2) Protection of the North and Southern Penetration. As regards Japan's continental development, we should not depend on Asia alone to maintain the life of our nation. We should expect a southward penetration for our national development in the future. But this southward penetration must be carried out by pacific means, rejecting all recourse to force."

On April 17, 1936, the *Yomiuri* and *Miyako* newspapers published reports to the effect that the Premier, Mr. Hirota, had decided to abolish the present South Seas Government (which has jurisdiction over the former German islands north of the equator, now being held by Japan under mandate), and to place the islands under the jurisdiction of a bureau in the Formosan Government-General, "as a step in the execution of the so-called 'southward policy' ". At the same time it was planned to establish a military government of Formosa and the South Seas Islands, the Governor-General to be an Army or Navy officer and the Vice Governor-General a civilian. According to the *Asahi* of April 25, 1936, however, Admiral Nagano, the Minister for the Navy, is opposed to the plan of placing the South Seas Islands under the jurisdiction of the Formosan Government General, because, instead of being abolished, the South Seas Government should be strengthened "to promote the Navy's policy of southward advance". The Admiral based his arguments against the incorporation of the South Seas Government into the Formosan Government General on the grounds that there is little economic connection between the South Seas Islands and Formosa, that the people of the two administrations are different racially and could not well be governed by the same administration, and that, as the islands are held under mandate from the League of Nations, they cannot be regarded as an integral part of the territory of Japan, as is Formosa, and cannot be governed under the same system. It does not appear that any decision has as yet been reached upon the question of the future administration of the South Seas Islands.

There appear to be several reasons for the sudden recurrence of propaganda in Japan for a "southward advance". Some observers believe that the Japanese Navy is envious of the success obtained by the Army in promoting Japanese expansion and wishes to earn credit with the nation by itself undertaking new expansion schemes.

With this is bound up the question of budget appropriations. The further afield the Navy extends its activities, the larger the appropriations which will be necessary for naval defense. Other observers believe that the Navy, in advocating a southward advance policy, is primarily in search of an assured supply of petroleum and is planning to obtain supplies eventually in Netherland India. This is the opinion of the Naval Attaché of the Embassy and of the Netherlands Minister to Tokyo, whose remarks will be given later in this report. The First Secretary of the Soviet Embassy in Tokyo, who naturally regards all developments in Japan from the Soviet point of view, believes that the recent advocacy of a southward advance policy is caused by the fact that the advance of the Japanese in northwestern Asia has been halted and cannot be resumed without serious danger of a major war. He points out that General Chiang Kai-shek has moved a part of his troops up into southern Shansi; that the Chinese Communist troops are advancing eastwards through Shensi and Suiyuan, with the slogan of "Down with Japanese Imperialism"; that Outer Mongolia, backed by the Soviet Union, is offering stout resistance to Japanese penetration; and that the Soviet Union can effectively prevent the Japanese Army from encroaching upon Soviet territory. The Japanese Army on the Asiatic continent is thus fairly thoroughly encircled and cannot advance without the risk of a serious war. Consequently the Japanese nation has turned its attention to the south.

While this Embassy cannot subscribe entirely to the thesis that the Japanese nation as a whole has turned its attention to the south, it does appear probable that the Japanese Navy, finding the efforts of the Army on the continent now being fairly consistently thwarted, believes the time ripe to make a move itself and thereby to draw the attention of the nation to the Navy rather than to the Army. It should be understood that there is in Japan a more or less persistent feud between the Army and the Navy, dating back to the days when one was controlled by the Choshu clan and the other by the Satsuma clan. The feud, of course, does not extend to the point where either party would let their quarrels endanger the Empire, but it is not only possible but probable that the Navy, finding that the Army has extended itself to a point where it is likely to involve the country in a war unless it stops, has taken advantage of the situation to show the nation that "Codlin is the friend, not Short". In addition to that, there is no doubt that the Navy wished to extend its sphere of activities to cover the entire western Pacific north of the Equator and to include, if possible, in that sphere a section of the Pacific south of the Equator from which an assured supply of petroleum can be obtained under any circumstances. The present oil situation in Japan, brought on by the Army's demand that the foreign oil interests carry stocks in the country amounting to six months' supplies, is so uncertain that the Navy undoubtedly will endeavor to find an independent source of supply as soon as possible.

The Embassy has been endeavoring, for some time past, to ascertain exactly what was behind the sudden appearance of propaganda in favor of a "southward advance", what are the objectives of the movement, and what effect the movement will have upon American interests in the Far East and especially in the Philippine Islands. Nothing very definite has yet been learned, but the following summaries of conversations and newspaper articles may serve to throw some light on the question.

On April 25, 1936, General Pabst, the Netherlands Minister to Japan, called on me and stated, in the course of our conversation, that he had telegraphed his Government to the effect that, if conditions in Europe remained in the present state, compelling the British fleet to stay in or near home waters, there was a "fifty-fifty chance" that the Japanese Navy would attempt a "coup de main" within six months, with the objective of taking possession of some part of the Netherlands Indies producing petroleum. The Netherlands Minister, however, is somewhat inclined to take an alarmist view of affairs, and, except for the propaganda in favor of a southward movement, I see nothing to indicate any sudden or drastic move by the Japanese Navy in the near future. I am therefore inclined to discount the Minister's statement.

In a conversation with the First Secretary of the Embassy on April 21, 1936, Admiral Hasegawa, the Vice Minister for the Navy, commented on the "southward advance" policy of the Navy. He said that the policy was largely "newspaper talk" but that the Navy did advocate the extension of Japanese trade to the south. If important trade routes to the islands to the south of Japan were thus established, it would be necessary for the Navy to extend its operations further afield for the purpose of protecting these trade routes. The Navy's policy, however, was purely pacific and implied no threat whatsoever against the Netherlands Indies or the Philippine Islands. It was the erroneous conception of the policy published by the newspapers which had startled various persons.

On April 25, 1936, Mr. Arita, the Minister for Foreign Affairs, received the foreign newspaper correspondents in Tokyo. In the course of the conversation, one of the correspondents asked the Minister to clarify the policy of southward expansion which had been mentioned in the press of Japan. According to the *Japan Advertiser* of April 26, 1936,

"The Foreign Minister said that he knew that the papers were ascribing an alleged intention of southward expansion to naval circles, but he did not know whether they were accurate. He could see nothing beyond economic expansion, for Japan has no ulterior ambitions."

On April 30, 1936, Mr. Shigeru Yoshida, recently appointed Japanese Ambassador to Great Britain, called and stated, in the course of our conversation, that the population problem in Japan was becoming increasingly difficult and that foreign countries should realize the seriousness of the situation and endeavor to help Japan in finding an adequate outlet. He said that it was principally a matter of finding outlets for Japan's trade, with opportunity for Japanese subjects to follow that trade. Upon being asked, he said that it meant peaceful penetration. Again upon being asked, he said that he thought that the "blue-water school" (i. e., the school advocating expansion to the south) would win out eventually over the "continental school".

The Embassy will endeavor to obtain further clarification of this alleged policy of the Japanese Navy.[63]

Respectfully yours,   JOSEPH C. GREW

893.515/1096

Memorandum by the Ambassador in China (Johnson) of a Conversation With Sir Frederick Leith-Ross[64]

PEIPING, April 30, 1936.

Sir Frederick asked me whether I thought there was any likelihood of a war between Japan and China. With regard to Japan and Russia he expressed the opinion that the Japanese had probably decided to lay off, as the Russians were too well prepared. I told Sir Frederick that I found it very difficult to believe that there would be war between Japan and China. I said that of course it was always possible that the Chinese might be forced into some kind of a conflict, but that I thought they would take an awful lot of provocation before this would happen. I said that I had heard a great deal about the possibility of trouble when I was in Nanking in February, but that I did not put much stock in this. I knew that the Chinese were spending a good deal of money upon armaments.

Sir Frederick said that he thought this large expenditure of sums on armaments was very dangerous; that the Chinese were apt to lose the resources which they needed so much for the successful completion of the currency scheme. He stated that the opinion in favor of war

---

[63] A further despatch on this subject was submitted May 15; not printed.

[64] Extract of memorandum transmitted to the Department by the Ambassador in China in his despatch No. 437, May 8; received June 1. Sir Frederick, chief economic adviser to the British Government, was in China temporarily as financial adviser to the British Embassy.

between Japan and China increased proportionately with the distance one traveled toward the south; in North China he found little or no interest in war with Japan; when one got to the Yangtze River one found it fairly strong; but when one arrived at Canton and Kwangsi one found a very active and outspoken war psychology. He said that Li Tsung-jen of Kwangsi had stated that they were prepared to co-operate with Chiang Kai-shek if he would fight the Japanese. Sir Frederick stated that he had a certain amount of sympathy with this point of view, but that he could not convince himself that the Chinese really would fight.

I told Sir Frederick that after all some one had to start a fight, and personally I did not think that the Chinese would start one; that as regards the Japanese it seemed to me that they were having too easy a time for them to change their tactics and begin an open conflict. I said that the present tactics here in North China indicated a certain cynical attitude of the Japanese towards the Chinese, and that the continued connivance of the Japanese at the smuggling operations now being conducted on such a large scale in North China would result eventually in the complete breakdown of the Chinese Customs service. I pointed out that this must eventually bring about the financial starvation of the Government; that troops and Government services were unpaid; and that under the circumstances the Japanese would have every reason to station forces here to protect their people and their interests from the chaos which they had created. Under the circumstances it seemed to me that if the Japanese wanted to ap-propriate territory or desired to take control of the administrative agencies in this area they need only proceed as they were now proceed-ing and that no war was likely to occur. Sir Frederick expressed the belief that to continue a policy of this kind would be as disastrous for the Japanese as for the Chinese, as they would soon find China a rotting carcass on their hands.

I told Sir Frederick that the whole situation here in North China had been changed somewhat, first by the decision of the Japanese Government to increase its military force here in North China and to appoint a commanding officer of rank sufficiently high to make him independent of control by the Kwantung army so that he would come under the direct control of Tokyo; and secondly, by the events of February 26th of this year. I expressed the opinion that the officers who had been retired as the result of the incidents of February 26th would now doubtless constitute a new body of elder statesmen or Genro who would have to be consulted by every person called upon to form a government in Japan. I said that in my opinion these men who really stood for the Army were on the horns of a dilemma: that they must either agree to a reform of the entire economic structure of Japan upon which the great Japanese industrial and commercial houses were built, or seek to extend the Japanese military adventure in China, in order to take the minds of the people and the army off the problems at home. I said that it was a little early yet to determine which path the army and its superiors would take. I pointed out that the first result, apparently, of the change which occurred on February 26th was the cessation of all expenditures on development work in Manchuria. I said that the best explanation I could get for this stoppage of expenditure in Manchuria appeared to be that the new authorities wished to put all available money into an expansion of Japan's armed force.

Sir Frederick stated that he thought the present Japanese authorities were quite capable of attempting to reform the economic situation in Japan and to carry on an extension of their interests in China at the same time. He stated that the Japanese were very anxious for him to return home through Japan, but that he had not made up his mind whether he would go that way or not; he thought that there was little use for him to go through merely to drink a cup of sake.

NELSON TRUSLER JOHNSON

693.94244/45

The Consul General at Shanghai (Gauss) to the Ambassador in China (Johnson) [65]

No. 159   SHANGHAI, April 30, 1936.

SIR: I have the honor to enclose, for the confidential information of the Embassy, a copy of a memorandum of conversation [66] which took place at Shanghai on April 27, 1936, between Mr. K. Wakasugi, Counselor of the Japanese Embassy, and Mr. H. J. Timperley, correspondent for the *Manchester Guardian.*

It will be noted that during the course of a discussion regarding smuggling in North China, and the Japanese attitude thereto, Mr. Wakasugi made the interesting statement that "We are not doing anything to help the Customs people, nor are we doing anything to help the smugglers", and that he added significantly "We would be glad to cooperate with the Chinese in suppressing the smuggling but first of all they must meet our terms." In response to Mr. Timperley's inquiry as to the nature of such terms Mr. Wakasugi stated that in the first place China would have to lower the Customs duties on the principal articles being smuggled. Mr. Timperley adduces from this statement, and probably not illogically, that the Japanese contemplate using China's anxiety concerning the serious loss of revenue resulting

---

[65] Copy transmitted to the Department by the Consul General at Shanghai in his despatch No. 169, April 30; received June 1.
[66] Not printed.

from smuggling in North China and elsewhere as a lever to force a reduction in tariff rates on certain Japanese commodities.

Mr. Wakasugi's belief that Japan's policy vis-à-vis China will probably not be definitely formulated until after the Extraordinary Session of the Diet, which convenes in May, is of particular interest and is at variance with the recent statements attributed to Mr. Arita, the Japanese Minister for Foreign Affairs, and to Colonel Kita, the newly appointed Japanese Military Attaché, whose pronouncements have given the impression that there exists at the present time a coordinated and definite policy.

As regards the general situation in China, Mr. Wakasugi appears to be "optimistic" and believes that so long as Japan does not "press for something which impairs Chinese sovereign rights" there can be no outbreak of hostilities between the two countries because "The Chinese will have nothing to fight about." He added significantly, "After all it is up to us." This appears to be a very shrewd estimate of the point to which Japanese aggression may be carried with impunity and is possibly indicative of a general attitude in Japanese diplomatic circles that the essentials of Japan's program can and should be effected without a technical breach of China's sovereignty.

Respectfully yours,

C. E. GAUSS

662.9331 Manchuria/3 : Telegram

The Second Secretary of Embassy in China (Atcheson) to the Secretary of State

NANKING, May 2, 1936—10 a. m.
[Received May 2—10 a. m.[67]]

118. I am informed by responsible officials of the Foreign Office that (1), the German Chargé on April 29, notified the Foreign Office orally that a "commercial arrangement" lacking any political significance would be concluded next day between Germany and Manchukuo; (2), such agreement was signed in the Manchukuo Embassy in Tokyo April 30 by Dr. Otto Kiep, head of the German Trade Commission in the Far East, but the identity and status of the official acting on behalf of Manchukuo is not yet known; (3), the German embassy has promised to furnish the text but this has not yet been received; (4), Dr. Ritter, head of the economic section of the German Foreign Office informed the Chinese Ambassador in Berlin that the agreement contemplated the purchase by Germany of Manchurian soyabeans on 75% credit and 25% cash, the credit to be used in the purchase by Manchukuo interests of German products.

2. Repeated to Department and Peiping; by mail to Tokyo, Berlin.

---

[67] Telegram in two sections.

3. Although some such development is believed to have been envisaged by the Foreign Office as a probable result of the Kiep mission, the informants indicated that hopes to the contrary had been entertained, particularly because of the efforts put forth by Germany since the war to win Chinese good will and expand German trade in China. The Foreign Office is obviously concerned; it fears the agreement may set a precedent for other countries who have been showing interest in Manchurian trade (the informants named Great Britain, France and Belgium); it considers that the agreement constitutes factual recognition of Manchukuo by Germany. Thus if others follow Germany's example in respect to commercial arrangements it is to be anticipated that diplomatic relations between Manchukuo and some Western Power may later ensue, eventually resulting in a general breakdown of the Western Powers' present policy of nonrecognition of the Manchurian regime.

4. To the Department and Peiping, by mail. To Tokyo, Berlin.

ATCHESON

662.9331 Manchuria/4 : Telegram

The Second Secretary of Embassy in China (Atcheson) to the Secretary of State

NANKING, May 2, 1936—noon.
[Received 2:50 p. m.]

120. My 118, May 2, 10 a. m.

1. According to an officer of the German Embassy: (1) it was realized that the Chinese Government would be "worried" by the agreement but the agreement was necessary for economic reasons; (2) the agreement has not yet been actually signed but will be in a short time, probably by Kiep on behalf of Germany and possibly by the Manchukuo Ambassador on behalf of Manchukuo; (3) negotiations for the agreement have been proceeding for about 6 months and resulted from the Kiep economic mission; (4) the agreement does not in any way imply recognition of Manchukuo and is similar to other agreements such as those relating to through rail traffic between North China and Manchuria and postal communications between Manchuria and various countries; (5) any Chinese objections will be met on those grounds and the further ground that the agreement will make for the economic welfare of Germany and Manchuria because Germany (a) is the largest importer of soya beans which it requires for bean cakes for cattle feed, (b) has the better facilities for the manufacture of bean cake and oil, and (c) under the agreement can sell machinery for industrial plants in Manchuria against purchases of soya beans; (6) any loss to German exports arising from Chinese dissatisfaction with the agreement will be temporary only.

2. Press and other releases indicate to be incorrect the statement that the agreement has not yet been signed.

3. Repeated to Department and Peiping. By mail to Tokyo and Berlin.

ATCHESON

893.01 Outer Mongolia/94 : Telegram

The Second Secretary of Embassy in China (Atcheson) to the Secretary of State

NANKING, May 2, 1936—3 p. m.
[Received May 2—10:05 a. m.]

121. I am informed by spokesman of the Foreign Office that press reports of declaration of autonomy by Teh Wang are not correct and that Teh Wang has telegraphed assurances to this effect.

To the Department and Peiping.

ATCHESON

893.00/13485 : Telegram

The Second Secretary of Embassy in China (Atcheson) to the Secretary of State

NANKING, May 5, 1936—10 a. m.
[Received 3:50 p. m.[68]]

122. 1. In spite of the efforts during April of Wang Chung Hui as mediator and of various emissaries going between Canton and Nanking, relations between the National Government and the Southwest remain obscure. According to Japanese sources one question discussed recently was a Southern proposal, designed to obviate question of increased subsidies, that the Government purchase Kwangtung dollars 30,000,000 at par, the purpose being to provide Kwangtung 10,000,000 dollars profit arising from the higher value of National Government bank notes in relation to foreign exchange. Another Southern proposal was that the Government liquidate 14,000,000 dollars worth of 1925 Northern Expedition bonds. (Japanese interests are reported to have purchased at 15% some of these bonds and "military promises to pay" issued by the expeditionary forces for supplies, and to have asked through the Japanese Embassy for their repurchase by the National Government at 30%).

2. To Department. By mail to Peiping.

3. While ostensibly the general issues between Nanking and the Southwest have continued to center upon question of policy toward Japan and thus symbolized by the persisting failure of Hu Han Min

[68] Telegram in two sections.

(virtually the prisoner of Chen Chi Tang) to come to Nanking and assume office, Southwestern opposition to Nanking is believed actually to be more military than political and to express the traditional dissatisfaction of Southwestern militarists with Chiang Kai-Shek's tendency to dictatorship. Concretely the immediate issues seem to have resolved themselves into questions of (1) financial assistance to Southwestern military leaders; (2) allotment of National Government offices to members of the military and civilian groups of the Southwestern faction; (3) powers to be vested by the draft constitution in the future president who presumably will be Chiang Kai-Shek; (4) the extent to which the National Government recommended a show of resistance to Japan.

4. On the Southern side these questions have been overshadowed by the ambition of Chen Chi-Tang and Li Tsung Jen to perpetuate their authority in Kwangtung and Kwangsi; they have been overshadowed on Nanking's side by Chiang's determination to continue his domination of the Government and expand his personal control. Thus doubt exists (1) whether Chiang sincerely desires Hu to assume office as chairman of the standing committee of the Central Executive Committee (of which Chiang is Vice and Acting Chairman); or (2) whether Hu, if he should enter the Government, could do more than a minor civilian group which is not a determining factor so long as the regional dictatorship of Chen and local government exist. With May 5 set for promulgation of the draft constitution and November 12 as date for its adoption by the party in control, Chiang is thought to prefer the *status quo* in respect to important National Government posts until he is safely elected president.

5. To Department. By mail Peiping.

ATCHESON

793.94/7888 : Telegram

The Ambassador in China (Johnson) to the Secretary of State

PEIPING, May 6, 1936—11 a.m.
[Received May 6—7 a.m.]

229. Embassy's 213, April 29, 3 p.m.

1. According to information obtainable from a Chinese official, the conversations at Tientsin between Sung Che Yuan and Japanese military have reached an impasse. Sung wants northern Chahar and Yin Ju Keng's area returned to him. The Japanese want greater control of railways in Hopei, allegedly requesting permission to station Japanese troops at the strategic railway junction Fengtai, south of Peiping, and at Shihkiachwang. They also want to control Nanyuan airfield (at Peiping).

2. This information is more or less in accord with information obtained from a similar informant in Tientsin by the Consulate General to the effect that the Japanese military are resolved to gain control of the communications in Hopei and Chahar, expand their military forces, gain control of and develop economic and industrial resources, and create an independent North China.

3. Local officials now state that although Sung has approved construction of the Shihkiachwang-Tsangchow Railway, the National Government has not yet done so and that the chief of the engineering bureau of the proposed railway was appointed by Sung and not by the National Government. Wang Jun Chen left for Japan May 4 apparently in conjunction with the proposed railway. Wang has a Japanese mother, was formerly a department chief of the Peiping-Hankow Railway, and is now simultaneously adviser to Sung, adviser to the South Manchuria Railway, and high adviser to Yin Ju Keng.

4. Embassy's 217, April 30, 4 p.m. Lieutenant General Tada has been transferred to the command of the 11th Division in Japan. His successor, Lieutenant General Kanichiro Tashiro, appointed by the Emperor, was formerly Military Attaché to China, Chief of Staff of Japanese forces at Shanghai during the fighting of 1932, and subsequently Commander of the 11th Division.

By mail to Tokyo.

JOHNSON

693.94244/8 : Telegram

The Ambassador in Japan (Grew) to the Secretary of State

TOKYO, May 6, 1936—noon.
[Received May 6—6:40 a. m.]

94. Acting under instructions the British Ambassador called on the Minister for Foreign Affairs on May 2 and invited the Minister's attention orally to the great damage that was being done to legitimate trade by the extensive smuggling operations of Japanese subjects in North China. He said that British traders and others as well were suffering and that there seemed little disposition to curb these activities. It was even reported that Japanese authorities were indifferent to these illicit operations because it was felt that the Chinese tariff was too high and extensive smuggling might result in a reduction in the tariff by the Chinese Government. Further the action of the East Hopei Government in arbitrarily reducing the import duties and then allowing the goods on which reduced tariff had been paid to enter into general commerce in China was resulting in complete demoralization of the Chinese import business. The British Government was concerned not only with the damage being done to British

traders but were also fearful that the situation might so develop that the customs service would be completely demoralized and the Chinese Government would find itself unable to service the loans held by British subjects on the security of the Chinese customs revenue.

The Minister for Foreign Affairs replied on May 4 that Japanese merchants were also suffering from these operations of smugglers but that the Japanese Government had absolutely no political motive and was lending no encouragement to the action of the East Hopei Government in setting up an independent tariff. The Japanese Government, however, felt that little could be done at the moment to ameliorate the general situation because Chinese internal administration was not very effective and the Nanking Government no longer remitted funds to the North China Administration. He added that Japanese interests were also concerned with the service on the Chinese external loans.

The British Ambassador also under instructions asked me whether the American Government would be prepared to authorize me to make a similar approach to the Minister for Foreign Affairs. He said that he had spoken to the French Ambassador here and that the latter was in communication with his Government.

I can see no objection to acceding to this request because while we have no direct interest in the Chinese customs loans we are definitely interested in honest customs administration.

Repeated to Peiping. ———————

GREW

693.94244/8 : Telegram

The Secretary of State to the Ambassador in Japan (Grew)

WASHINGTON, May 8, 1936—6 p. m.

52. Your 94, May 6, noon.

1. The Department authorizes you to make an oral and informal approach, similar to that of the British Ambassador, to the Minister for Foreign Affairs in regard to the smuggling situation in North China, along lines as follows:

The extensive smuggling operations in North China have created a serious situation in that area. It has been reported, with substantial supporting evidence, that Japanese subjects have taken a prominent part in these operations; that there has been little evidence of a Japanese disposition to curb their activities; that Japanese authorities in China have placed obstacles in the way of the enforcement of Chinese preventive measures; and that the eastern Hopei "autonomous" regime has arbitrarily reduced import duties and has permitted goods on which the reduced rates have been paid to pass into general commerce in China. These conditions are leading to extensive disorganization of the Chinese import trade. This Government is concerned not only with the adverse effect of this situation on American import trade but with the impairment of the Chinese Government's income from customs revenue which impairment tends to jeopardize the capacity of the Chinese Government to meet its outstanding financial obligations to American citizens.

2. Inform Department by telegraph in regard to your conversation with the Foreign Minister.

3. Repeat paragraph 1 to Peiping as Department's No. 110, May 8, 6 p. m.

HULL

761.93/1574

The Ambassador in the Soviet Union (Bullitt) to the Secretary of State

No. 1580 Moscow, May 9, 1936.

[Received June 5.]

SIR: In connection with despatch No. 247 of the Embassy in Peiping dated February 20, 1936,[69] reporting a rumored agreement between the Soviet Union and Sinkiang, I had a conversation today with Stomoniakoff, Assistant People's Commissar for Foreign Affairs, who is in charge of the Far Eastern relations of the Soviet Union.

Stomoniakoff denied that there was any truth in the rumor. He said, "I can assure you categorically and officially that there is no secret agreement between the Soviet Union and Sinkiang either written or verbal". I referred to the general belief that the Soviet Union was preparing to establish Sinkiang as an "independent republic" on the lines of Outer Mongolia. Stomoniakoff said that this was absolutely untrue, that the Soviet Union was greatly interested in trade with Sinkiang, that the geographical position of Sinkiang was such that its trade must naturally flow to the Soviet Union, that the Soviet Government had been careful to develop close and most friendly relations with the Government of Sinkiang, but that nothing had been done or would be done which might in any way infringe upon the sovereignty of China.

Respectfully yours, WILLIAM C. BULLITT

[69] Not printed.

894.00/664

Statement by Mr. J. Stowell Wright, Acting Territorial Director in Hawaii of the Federal Housing Administration [70]

[HONOLULU,] May 10, 1936.

1. On Thursday, May 7, at 2:30 p. m., the undersigned [71] as Field Representative of the FHA, paid an official call (the second) on Mr. Teijiro Tamura, Japanese Consulate General, to thank him for his cooperation with the FHA, in that he pointed out to his subjects that loans under Title II of the national housing act were possible for aliens. The subject, as previously reported, is very frank in his discussions. During the course of the conversation, the undersigned suggested that inasmuch as Japan and her motives were so misunderstood, it might be a good idea for Japan to launch a national advertising campaign, explaining her problems, etc. The balance of the interview developed from that one suggestion. Below, I am quoting Mr. Teijiro Tamura almost verbatim:

Subject Speaking: "There was a time when Japan and her people cared what America thought . . ."[72] now the temper of the Japanese is so that they don't care what anyone thinks and they are through explaining. If the time comes to fight, then Japan will fight, the odds be what they may. (Sat straight in chair and slapped desk.) We are going to pursue our course as we see it. Several years ago when I was on duty in Chicago, an American advertising agency with headquarters in N. Y. and offices in Chicago and San Francisco, approached me on an advertising campaign to build good will. I thought it was a good idea and got the Japanese Tea Association to sponsor it. It may have done some good but now it wouldn't.

"America is very difficult to get along with. It is easier to get along with England. In America it is a democracy and anyone in any house may raise his voice in protest and the politicians listen and act even though trade agreements have been made by American ambassadors. Right now on the East Coast, a handful of manufacturers are shouting that the Japanese imports to the United States of cotton goods is hurting business. The United States Government can tell no lie and everyone believes what they say, yet the United States Department of Commerce figures show that we buy far more in raw cotton from the United States than is shipped back in piece goods. Our piece goods, according to the United States figures are less than one half of one per cent of all the goods sold in the United States. They all cry 'The Japanese are shipping in too much. They should be curtailed. What will happen?' The politicians will listen, and even though they know our exports to the United States are low, they will further stifle us just to get votes.

---

[70] Copy received from the War Department on May 28. The statement was an enclosure to a covering report to the War Department by Lt. Col. G. S. Patton, Jr., Assistant Chief of Staff for Military Intelligence at Fort Shafter, Hawaii, as "indicative of a changing attitude in part of the Japanese."

[71] Copy not signed.

[72] Omission indicated in the original.

"America and England say Japan cannot build but a few warships. We will never be satisfied with their orders. Warships are instruments of war, not peace. We have a small, isolated nation. We must protect ourselves. President Roosevelt is a navy man and his interests are there. He says that increases of the Army and Navy in manpower and ships, make for peace. It does not. It makes for war. The people of Japan read in the newspapers about the United States building more ships. To fight against who? No one but Japan. The fleet comes to Hawaii for maneuvers . . .[73] practicing for war . . . against who . . . no one else would be the logical enemy but Japan.

"Admiral Yarnell and General Drum [74] are gentlemen but their interests are military. Yarnell talks of increasing the defenses of Pearl Harbor . . . I read in the newspapers about Kolekole Pass . . . that General Drum believes Oahu needs that to expedite the movement of troops in case of emergency. Both of them have Japan in mind. They talk about possible trouble with aliens. They are talking about my nationals! They are suspicious of us. That is why the temper of the Japanese people is like it is. Everything is aimed at us. No more do we care what America or any other nation thinks of us. We are going to do what necessity compels us to do!

"The United States keeps getting nearer to Japan. The fleet comes all the way here for maneuvers. Then the clipper ship has bases at Midway, Wake and Guam. How much nearer to Japan is America coming, my people ask. All of this is what makes the people of Japan nervous."

793.94/7896 : Telegram

The Counselor of Embassy in China (Peck) to the Secretary of State

NANKING, May 12, 1936—4 p. m.
[Received May 12—9 : 20 a. m.]

133. This office's 92, April 16, 5 p. m.

1. An officer of the Embassy has been confidentially informed by a responsible official of the Foreign Office that (1) reports alleging the conclusion of a Sino-Japanese anti-Communist agreement in the North on May 6 have been received by the Foreign Office but have not been confirmed; (2) the Japanese have been using the smuggling situation in the North as a coercive argument for the conclusion of such an agreement but Hsiao Chen Ying and the other interested Chinese officials have been a stumbling block through their insistence that the East Hopei regime continue to exist; (3) details of the specific Japanese proposals or of the progress of the discussions between them and Sung Che Yuan and latter's associates are not known but the Foreign Office expects to have this information soon.

---

[73] Omissions indicated in the original.
[74] Rear Adm. Harry E. Yarnell, Commandant of Pearl Harbor Naval Station, and Maj. Gen. Hugh A. Drum, Commander of the Hawaiian Department, U. S. Army, respectively.

2. Informant denied that the National Government had given up hope of avoiding the conclusion of such an agreement and said that (1), the Chinese Government was considering the imposition of consolidated taxes on smuggled goods as a preventative against smuggling; (2), the Chinese Government has instructed its Ambassador in Washington to approach the Department in regard to the smuggling situation; (3), loss to the customs revenues now amounted to Chinese dollars 2 million weekly; (4), the Embassy would shortly be furnished reliable statistics and full information concerning smuggling.

3. Repeated to the Department and Peiping.

PECK

693.94244/12

The Chinese Embassy to the Department of State

With the Chinese customs authorities stripped of all powers of prevention as a result of Japanese interference smuggling in North China has assumed incredible proportions. Immense quantities of contraband goods have poured through the demilitarized zone into Tientsin and thence overflowed the trading centers throughout the country. Apart from the serious loss of revenue to the Government illicit traffic has killed trade in several important business lines and impaired China's ability to meet foreign obligations.

That the situation has further grown worse during the last few months is shown by facts. For the week ending April 25, 1936, 374,112 kilograms of artificial silk yarn, 697,862 kilograms of white sugar and 12,564 kilograms of cigarette paper were smuggled into Tientsin by the Peining Railway. The duties leviable are computed to be over two million three hundred thousand dollars at which rate the loss of revenue would amount to over one hundred million yearly which constitutes approximately one-third of the customs gross revenue for 1934.

Having saturated the northern markets contraband goods now flow into the Yangtse area. The American-owned *Evening Post* of Shanghai in a recent survey of the effects of smuggling on import business described the serious predicament of foreign importers and added "they fear complete ruin for local import business" unless illicit trade should soon be curtailed.

The situation as it now stands is a hopeless one for the customs authorities are unable to exercise their normal preventive functions. A brief résumé of how smuggling has reached its present proportion with the connivance and approval of the Japanese authorities will explain the situation.

Smuggling in North China started on a small scale during the early part of 1935. Illicit goods then entered the country mainly through the Great-Wall passes but the customs authorities could still hold smuggling activities in check. Then a great impetus was given to smuggling by the illegal export of silver from North China by bands of Koreans and Japanese *ronins*. Instead of taking steps to curb their activities the Japanese military authorities seemed to do their best to encourage them. In May last year two Japanese silver smugglers injured themselves in an attempt to get away from the customs officers by jumping from the Great Wall. The Japanese authorities subsequently made strong demands for compensation for the injured and for the withdrawal of customs patrols from the Great Wall. The customs authorities accepted these demands under threat that the rejection of them would be followed by steps toward expelling the customs authorities from Shanhaikwan.

The withdrawal of customs patrols was followed shortly afterwards by the disarming of customs officers within the demilitarized zone. The Chief of the Kuan Tung Military Mission at Shanhaikwan notified the customs commissioner at Chinwangtao to the effect that owing to special political conditions customs officers are not allowed to carry revolvers in the demilitarized zone. From then on the situation became one wherein unarmed customs officers had to deal with armed Korean and Japanese smugglers who knew they could attack customs officers with impunity and were thus encouraged to go farther in open lawlessness and audacity.

The Japanese authorities were repeatedly requested by the Chinese authorities to curb their nationals in smuggling activities but all requests were ignored. The Japanese military authorities maintained that the matter did not concern the army authorities but the consular police while the latter took the attitude that smuggling into China was not an offense under the Japanese law. Protests lodged with the Tokyo Foreign Office were equally fruitless and several notes from Nanking have hitherto remained unanswered. On the other hand the Japanese authorities made strong demands if any Japanese or Korean smugglers got hurt in the slightest degree in frays with customs officers.

The position further grew worse in September when the Japanese authorities forced the removal of all customs preventive vessels armed or otherwise from the waters within three miles of the demilitarized zone. This together with the Japanese refusal to recognize the customs' right of search outside the three-mile limit (China's Preventive Law gives the Customs this right within twelve marine miles of the coast) rendered uncontrollable smuggling by sea from Dairen to East-Hopei coast. The chief centers of smuggling are beaches of Peitaiho, Chinwangtao, Nantassu and that near Liushouying, all within the demilitarized zone. At these points illicit goods are brought ashore without fear of seizure and then transported to interior markets via the Peining Railway.

Baulked in every attempt to carry out preventive measures the customs authorities this year restored the measures designed to prevent contraband goods from reaching the markets. An agreement was reached March 21 between the customs and the Peining Railway Administration whereby the Railway agreed not to accept freight or cargo except against the customs' transportation permit. However the Railway was unable to carry out the agreement under pressure from the Japanese military authorities.

Recently the puppet regime of East Hopei, apparently with the approval of the Japanese over-lords, enforced its own dues on incoming cargo which are about one-fourth of the legitimate duties. The Japanese now claim that any goods whereon the required tax [is?] paid to the so-called East Hopei Autonomous Council cannot be regarded as smuggled goods.

In these circumstances the customs authorities are evidently confronted with a hopeless task. The grave situation not only entails a serious loss of revenue but jeopardizes the security of foreign loans and threatens to kill all legitimate trade as cargoes entering the northern frontier easily reach the Yangtse area by means of the Tsinpu and Pinghan Railways and it is from goods consumed in this area that the bulk of customs revenue is derived.

The Japanese authorities contend that smuggling is due to high import duties but nothing is further from the truth. If high duties were the real cause then the amazing smuggling scandal would not be confined to East Hopei and one might expect to find the same conditions along the whole coast. The truth is that the smuggling evil flourishes in North China only with the connivance and approval of the Japanese authorities.

A special correspondent of the *North China Daily News* in a recent article comes to the following conclusion: "All accounts agree that smuggling is being carried on by Japanese transportation companies under the protection of bands of Koreans who are only too aware of the impunity they enjoy thanks to Japanese extraterritorial rights. Indeed Japanese consular authorities openly state that smuggling into China is no offense under Japan's laws. In other words, smuggling is conducted with the connivance and direct approval of the Japanese authorities". The *Shanghai Evening Post* likewise believes—"Japan holds the key position of the North China smuggling picture". An editorial in the issue of May 6 of the same journal declares—"smuggling in North China can be stopped by the Japanese or with Japanese collaboration; otherwise it must go on".

WASHINGTON, May 12, 1936.

893.00/13490 : Telegram

The Consul General at Canton (Spiker) to the Secretary of State

CANTON, May 13, 1936—9 a. m.
[Received 11 a. m.]

It has been reliably confirmed that Hu Han Min died yesterday evening at 7:45 as the result of a paralytic stroke on May 9. Details follow by mail despatch.[75]

His death, together with the serious illness of the aged Hsiao Fo Cheng and the weakened political hold of Tsou Lu, seems to presage at least a temporary disorganization and lessening of the influence of the southwestern civilian Kuomintang group and a corresponding opportunity for the military leaders to strengthen their control. It is generally believed that such a development, which tending [*tends?*] to clarify issues, will probably lessen the prospects of reconciliation with Nanking which according to various recent information obtained locally, are already at least as remote as they have been for many months.

Transmitted to Department, Peiping, Nanking.

SPIKER

693.94244/9 : Telegram

The Ambassador in Japan (Grew) to the Secretary of State

TOKYO, May 13, 1936—11 a. m.
[Received May 13—3 a. m.]

104. Department's 52, May 8, 6 p. m.

1. As the Minister for Foreign Affairs has been obliged to postpone receiving me owing to constant occupation in the Diet and Privy Council I called this morning on the Vice Minister for Foreign Affairs and made the desired oral and informal approach.

2. The Vice Minister said that the smuggling operations in China which were being carried on both in the North and in the South were due in considerable measure to the high Chinese tariff on certain commodities. Japanese firms had also protested against these smuggling operations as well as against the high tariff rates. The Nanking Government on its own volition had withdrawn its coast guard ships from waters adjacent to the demilitarized zone. Meanwhile the Japanese Government is carefully studying the situation. The Vice Minister said that he did not feel competent to discuss the situation in greater detail but that he would report my observations to the Minister for Foreign Affairs as soon as possible.

Repeated to Peiping.

GREW

---

[75] Not printed.

919456—54——16

693.94244/10 : Telegram

The Counselor of Embassy in China (Peck) to the Secretary of State

NANKING, May 13, 1936—2 p. m.
[Received May 13—9 : 15 a. m.]

135. The Minister of Finance during a general conversation this morning informed me that the smuggling operations in the North are becoming an increasingly serious threat to the Government finances and to all legitimate trade and he asked whether the American Government had made representations to the Japanese Government on this subject as the British Government had done. I said I had seen press references to the action of the British Government but I did not know whether the American Government had taken any similar step. He expressed the opinion that it would be desirable for the American Government to make representations both to the Japanese and to the Chinese Governments expressing concern over the damage to American trade and the threat to American interests represented by the decrease in maritime customs receipts which are security for the American portion of the Boxer Indemnity and at least indirect security for other American obligations. Kung said he had been informed of the nature of the representations recently made by the British Ambassador in Tokyo. I recalled that the Embassy had already made oral representations to the Chinese Government on this subject (see my despatch to the Embassy of January 21 [77]) but promised to report his observations.

To the Department and Peiping.

PECK

793.94/7900 : Telegram

The Ambassador in China (Johnson) to the Secretary of State

PEIPING, May 14, 1936—2 p. m.
[Received May 14—6 : 35 a. m.]

241. Embassy's 240, May 13, 1 p. m.[77] First Secretary of Japanese Embassy called on me this morning under telegraphic instructions to inform me confidentially of the approaching increase of strength of the North China Garrison. He stated that the increase will be the minimum needed to cope with the new situation which he described as Communism in Shansi, underground anti-Japanese activities in Hopei, and increase in number of Japanese residents in eastern Hopei and along the Peiping–Shanhaikwan Railway; that the increase is based on treaty rights; that the purpose of the increase was to main-

[77] Not printed.

tain peace in this area for the good of China and Japan and other foreign powers; that it was not for the purpose of bringing pressure on China, encroaching upon Chinese sovereignty or upon interests of other powers; that some of the new troops would arrive tomorrow; that he did not know the percentage of increase.

Repeated to Nanking, by mail to Tokyo.

JOHNSON

693.94244/10 : Telegram

The Secretary of State to the Ambassador in China (Johnson)

WASHINGTON, May 14, 1936—5 p. m.

117. Nanking's 135, May 13, 2 p. m.; Department's 110, May 8, 6 p. m. repeated by Tokyo; [78] and Tokyo's 104, May 13, 11 a. m. to Department.

Please instruct Peck by telegraph to call on the Minister of Finance and inform him orally and in confidence that the smuggling situation in North China has been brought by this Government not only to the attention of the Chinese Foreign Office at Nanking but also to the attention of the Japanese Foreign Office at Tokyo. Peck should also on an appropriate occasion similarly inform the Minister for Foreign Affairs.

With regard to Nanking's No. 133, May 12, 4 p. m., paragraph 2, a secretary of the Chinese Embassy on May 12 left with the Department a memorandum giving a résumé of the smuggling situation in North China. The memorandum contains no request for action. The Department is acknowledging receipt of the memorandum, stating that this situation has had and continues to have careful attention.

The Department is sending you by pouch a copy of the memorandum.

Repeated to Tokyo as Department's No. 56, May 14, 5 p. m.

HULL

793.94/7901 : Telegram

The Ambassador in China (Johnson) to the Secretary of State

PEIPING, May 15, 1936—3 p. m.
[Received 7 : 45 p. m.]

243. 1. Embassy's 229, May 6, 11 a. m. Sung Che Yuan, who has been in Tientsin since the latter part of March, is expected to return to Peiping within a day or two. Available information indicates that his conversations at Tientsin with Japanese military have not yet re-

[78] See telegram No. 52, May 8, 6 p. m., to the Ambassador in Japan, p. 142.

sulted in any signed agreement. It is now anticipated that negotiations await the arrival of Tashiro, the new commander of the North
China Garrison, who has already left Tokyo for Tientsin.

2. Notwithstanding Sung's continuing delay in entering into the
agreement presumably desired by the Japanese military, he continues
to increase the autonomy of his regime step by step. Recent
developments in this direction are given below:

A. Supposedly as the outcome of Japanese representations, Sung
has effected the suspension of all military training in Government
and private universities and higher schools in Peiping and the dismissal of their military instructors. This training was instituted
reputedly as a result of Japanese seizure of Manchuria and the
instructors were mostly military men of the National Government.

B. (Reference paragraph 3 of Embassy's 191, April 16, 3 p. m.)
The Communications Committee of the Hopei-Chahar Political Council was inaugurated May 14 with Chen Chueh Sheng, Managing Director of the Peiping–Mukden Railway, as Chairman. The committee
will allegedly deal with affairs relating to roads, railways, airways,
navigation, posts, and telegraphs. Presumably, it will gradually take
over functions heretofore of the appropriate ministries at Nanking.

C. General Teng Che Hsi, a Kuominchun leader, was appointed
May 15 on Sung's recommendation as President of the Hopei High
Court, a post heretofore occupied by a Nanking official. Teng continues to be Chief of Court Martial. (Reference Embassy's 201, April
20, 2 p. m.) Shih Ching Ting has resigned as Chief Counselor because of a difference with Sung over an internal matter. Lu Chung
Lin is understood to have gone to Tsinanfu to see Han Fu Chu. General Liu Chi, a Kuominchun leader, arrived May 14 at Peiping from
Shanghai. The significance of movements of these generals formerly
senior to Sung and notwithstanding the influence of the views of anti-
Japanese Feng Yu Hsiang with respect to the Kuominchun as a unit
is still speculative.

D. The Hopei political bank which is under Sung's control has
now a note issue reputedly totaling $1,000,000. Confidence in its
notes is allegedly good in Peiping and Tientsin but lacking in the
countryside. The Hopei Silver Currency Bureau, which is under
Sung's control, has issued copper coin notes to an extent of more than
$500,000. Sung's Hsing Yeh Currency Bureau in Chahar has a note
issue of allegedly about $600,000, including copper certified notes.
Hsi Yi Chu money shop in Peiping acts as a clearing house for the
notes of the Chahar Bureau. This situation is inimical to the
monetary policy of the National Government.

E. The post of Special Inspector of Foreign Affairs for Hopei and
Chahar has been abolished by the Nanking Ministry for Foreign

Affairs and its duties will be carried out by the Foreign Affairs Committee of the Hopei-Chahar Political Council.

3. The proposed East Hopei Bank of Yin Ju Keng's regime has not yet been organized. A competent informant stated that the Ta Ching Bank, which has its head office in Tientsin, has come to an agreement with Yin's regime whereby the bank has supplied Yin's regime with $2,000,000 in notes for use in East Hopei in return for an unstated amount of notes of the Central Government. The standing of the Ta Ching Bank is allegedly not good and it is believed that there is little if any collateral for its note issue.

By mail to Tokyo.

JOHNSON

793.94/7902 : Telegram

The Counselor of Embassy in China (Peck) to the Secretary of State

NANKING, May 16, 1936—10 a. m.
[Received May 16—7 a. m.]

140. 1. A responsible official of the Foreign Office has confirmed to an officer of the Embassy a Central News Agency report dated May 15 to effect that Foreign Office on April 7th made oral representations to Japanese Embassy here against increase in Japanese Garrison at Tientsin and that yesterday the Foreign Office instructed Chinese Embassy in Tokyo to make further oral representations in the matter.

2. To Department and Peiping. By mail to Tokyo.

PECK

693.94244/13 : Telegram

The Counselor of Embassy in China (Peck) to the Secretary of State

NANKING, May 16, 1936—6 p. m.
[Received May 16—11 : 50 a. m.]

Department's [telegram] 117, May 14, 5 p. m., to Peiping. I saw the Minister of Finance May 16, 5 p. m., and conveyed message. He said that recently there had been a slight improvement in the attitude of the Japanese military in that they had allowed the customs to seize some smuggling craft. He asserted that the Chinese authorities had good evidence that certain Japanese firms have been protected by the Japanese military presumably not without profit to themselves. He believed that the recent improvement was caused by the foreign protests and that if these are continued in strong terms the Japanese may permit eradication of the abuse. He said Sung Che Yuan had withdrawn his so-called coastal inspection offices in compliance with orders from him, Kung, and that he strongly suspected it had been the intention of Sung to start a rival smuggling enterprise. He said there are many Japanese of good principles who are ashamed of the actions of the military in connection with North China smuggling.

Repeated to Peiping.

PECK

165.559/2

The Consul General at Mukden (Ballantine) to the Secretary of State

No. 105   MUKDEN, May 16, 1936.
                                                    [Received June 17.]

SIR: I have the honor to submit for the Department's consideration certain observations regarding the question of how far it is profitable or wise in view of present conditions in Manchuria to carry trade promotion activities. These observations are made with particular reference to the Department's Mimeographed Instruction of April 11, 1936, (file No. 165.559/1) entitled "Reports Concerning Construction Activity",[80] but they apply generally to the preparation of all reports involving personal field investigation.

It is true that since the Japanese occupation of Manchuria in 1931 there has been considerable activity in construction work here, and on the face of it the situation should be such as to present favorable opportunities for American business. The officially inspired local press and news services carry frequent reports of large projects, of interviews by prominent foreign visitors expressing amazement at the marvelous progress of Manchuria, and of statements tending to show that the principle of the open door is being scrupulously respected. These reports are very misleading, and the significant fact in the situation is that since 1931 there has been a general exodus from Mukden of locally established non-Japanese engineering and import firms. The exception may be noted of a few German firms, which have held on through four lean years, and which see new hope in consequence of the conclusion recently of a "Manchukuo"-German trade agreement, whereby "Manchukuo" will be compelled to take in exchange for Germany's large purchases of Manchurian beans a certain proportionate quantity of German goods. As the United States usually sells more than it buys in Manchuria and is therefore not in Germany's new position to bargain for a share in lines of Manchurian economic activity suited to German industry, such as construction, there is little likelihood of any immediate improvement of the American trade position here in this respect. The position thus of American exporters is not the same as that of the German firms.

---

[80] Not printed.

Japan has made heavy investments in Manchuria since 1931, as is evidenced by the huge adverse balances of Manchurian trade, and indeed much of the construction work is of the nature of an investment for which Japan has not received payment. Every effort is therefore being made by the Japanese in control of the Government to ensure for their nationals such business opportunities as exist here in order that Japan may recoup its outlay. Since a preponderating part of the construction being done is on account of the Government and semiofficial firms, the authorities are in a position effectively to direct business into Japanese channels.

As there is a host of Japanese firms in the field competing among themselves for construction work and equipped for any kind of job that may be offered, and as Japan produces almost everything in the way of manufactured materials and equipment which local specifications call for, there is no room for American enterprise.

Even if for any reason American firms were accorded an equality of opportunity it would be difficult to see how they could compete with the Japanese firms. The American firm unless it were long established here would be subject to a great handicap due to unfamiliarity with the local labor market, language difficulties not only in handling native employees but also in interpreting specifications (which are invariably in Japanese) and in tendering, unsatisfactory conditions relating to meeting credit terms asked and of making collections of payments due, and uncertainty of consular legal protection because of non-recognition.

In regard to the supply of equipment and materials for construction work, preference is almost invariably given to products handled by firms locally represented, since the authorities will not ordinarily make payments until the goods have been delivered (and in the case of equipment, installed) and inspected. The only concern which makes it a regular practice to place orders directly with exporters abroad is the South Manchuria Railway Company, which has an office for that purpose at Room 4004–6, Lincoln Building, 60 East 42 N. B. Street, New York City. Since this company, together with its affiliated and subsidiary companies and the "Manchukuo" State Railways, which it operates, represents the greater part of big business in Manchuria and uses an overwhelming share of the American engineering material and equipment imported, it will be clear that American engineering and export firms are already provided a direct contact in New York with practically all that there is in the way of opportunity for doing business with Manchuria.

Due to the unrecognized status of "Manchukuo" foreign consuls stationed here are in an anomalous position, and are obliged to be unusually circumspect in their activities. The Japanese military, which are in a dominating position, are abnormally suspicious and are inclined to regard as espionage any activities relating to the investigation of construction work. The Consulate General believes that the influence that it has enjoyed here has been of real practical value in protection work, but it is felt that this influence would be jeopardized by any lack of circumspection in meeting local susceptibilities. In connection with inquiries regarding railway construction which have been made in reference to the Department's instruction of February 23, 1935 (File No. 165.363/65),[81] the Consulate General has sensed a distinct feeling that these inquiries were unwelcome, while certain information has been withheld with the flat explanation that it was regarded as a military secret.

The Consulate General believes that the purposes of American trade will be reasonably well served by voluntary trade reports submitted by this office from time to time, based upon published material and observation. In view of these circumstances, the Department may wish to take up with the Department of Commerce the question of the treatment that should be given by consular officers in Manchuria to requests for periodic and special surveys of the type referred to herein.[82]

Respectfully yours,   J. W. BALLANTINE

793.94/7908 : Telegram

The Counselor of Embassy in China (Peck) to the Secretary of State

NANKING, May 18, 1936—noon.
[Received 9:10 p. m.[83]]

143. 1. An official of the Foreign Office this morning read to an officer of the Embassy portion of a telegram stated to have just been received from Chinese Ambassador at Washington to effect that in connection with Japanese activities in North China, presumably including smuggling and increase of Tientsin Japanese Garrison, Under Secretary had issued statement to press reaffirming American position in respect to North China developments as set forth in the Secretary's statement of December 5, 1935.[84]

2. To Department and Peiping.

3. Same official stated that Foreign Office on May 15 or 16 handed to Japanese Embassy a lengthy note concerning smuggling in North

---

[81] Not printed.
[82] The Department on June 29 replied that it "concurs in the Consul General's position that 'circumspection in meeting local susceptibilities' should be carefully observed in the matter of investigating construction work" and suggested a procedure for future trade reports (165.559/2).
[83] Telegram in two sections.
[84] See telegram No. 191, December 5, 1935, 5 p. m., to the Chargé in Japan, *Foreign Relations, 1935*, vol. III, p. 473.

China which is being published in the press and which recapitulates the smuggling activities and previous representations and asks that the Japanese Government take immediate steps to restrain the Japanese military authorities from further interference with the principal functions of the customs and to withdraw the protection "hitherto enjoyed by Japanese and Korean smugglers".

4. We have a translation of this note and if it is not published in the United States and the Department desires to receive the text by radio, instructions to that effect will be appreciated.

5. To Peiping by mail.

PECK

693.94244/14 : Telegram

The Ambassador in Japan (Grew) to the Secretary of State

TOKYO, May 18, 1936—2 p. m.
[Received May 18—6 : 32 a. m.]

108. Embassy's 104, May 13, 11 a. m. The Minister for Foreign Affairs through the Vice Minister this morning transmitted to the Embassy an unsigned and undated memorandum containing his views concerning the smuggling situation in North China. He said that the Foreign Office was now studying the situation and that no formal and definite statement could yet be made but that the following were his views at present. I find that this document quoted below is identical with one handed to the British Embassy and cabled textually to the British Government on May 4th in reply to the Ambassador's approach of May 2nd.

"Smuggling in North China

1. I need scarcely say that the imputation of any political motive to the Japanese Government in connection with the question of smuggling in North China would be quite unfounded. The fact is that this smuggling is attributable partly to a purely economic cause and partly to that which concerns the internal administration of China. As things stand at present I believe that it is hardly possible for any foreign country to take any effective steps in order to prevent that smuggling.

2. Smuggling into China is not confined to North China but is likewise prevalent in South China. The fundamental causes of this traffic lie on the one hand in the Chinese system of unreasonably high tariffs and on the other hand in the fact that for certain reasons relating to the internal administration of China the local authorities are not sufficiently zealous to insure the collection of customs duties, the revenue from which goes *in toto* into the Treasury of the Central Government. As a matter of fact the local authorities of North China owing to the failure of the Nanking Government to defray the administrative expenses promised to them have apparently become disinclined to be

earnest guardians of the customs revenue which is not available for their local purposes. A similar phenomenon has also been discernible in connection with the attitude hitherto assumed by the Canton Government.

3. It is not only other foreign merchants but also the legitimate traders of Japanese nationality who are suffering from the rampancy of smuggling. In fact, the Japanese traders and Chambers of Commerce and Industry in North China have made loud complaints regarding the losses sustained by the Japanese owing to the smuggling in question and have made earnest requests for the control of that illegal proceeding. Accordingly the Japanese Government have had under careful consideration means of controlling smuggling but since this practice is as I have already said ascribable to the high tariffs of China and to the lack of zeal of the local Chinese authorities in regard to the control of smuggling the Japanese Government are unable to find any appropriate measure to control the surreptitious traffic.

Such being the case I trust it will readily be understood that the Japanese Government could give no support whatever to the establishment of special customs tariffs by any local authority in China.

4. As regards the Chinese customs revenue for the service of foreign loans the Japanese Government are as much interested as the British Government and sincerely hope that the Chinese Government will give due consideration to the fundamental causes responsible for the prevalence of the above-mentioned smuggling."

Repeated Peiping.

GREW

693.94244/16 : Telegram

The Counselor of Embassy in China (Peck) to the Secretary of State

NANKING, May 19, 1936—3 p. m.
[Received May 19—9:30 a. m.]

146. 1. A foreign adviser to the Chinese Government has expressed to me the opinion that if the present extensive smuggling were to continue certain indirect unfavorable effects on American and other foreign interests would tend to result.

2. Customs revenue in 1935 was approximately 315,000,000 with expenses of collection say 30,000,000 and cost of loan service say 250,000,000. Up to last autumn the Government had counted upon surplus of customs revenue available for governmental purposes of approximately 50,000,000 yearly. However, during much of the period since last summer customs revenue has failed even to meet debt charges and for the first 4 months of 1936 has been about one-sixth below that for the corresponding period of 1935. Part of this decrease had been occasioned by economic factors such as stocking up of surplus imports during period of favorable exchange with consequent lessening of imports later but these economic causes would tend automatically to adjust themselves. This is not true of decreases in cus-

toms revenue caused by smuggling and since increase of revenue from taxation is difficult to achieve the Chinese Government will be obliged to depend more and more on loans if losses from smuggling continue. Informant observed that hitherto Chinese Government borrowing has largely represented investment of savings by the public but if dependence on loans were to go on independently [*indefinitely?*] there would be a tendency for the Government to expand its bank credit against obligations with inflationary effect. He thought that if this process were not offset by other factors there would ultimately develop a degree of risk threatening the position of Chinese currency in exchange transactions. This in turn would discourage exportation of foreign goods to China and would make it difficult for the Chinese Government to meet its obligations expressed in foreign currency.

3. Informant did not refer to any anxiety of the Chinese Government that the public might become alarmed and begin extensive exchanges of Chinese currency for foreign currency but the reassuring statement issued by the Minister of Finance May 17, (see my 144, May 18, 2 p. m.[85]) seems designed to forestall possibility of such alarm whether occasioned by anticipated results of revenue losses from smuggling or by other causes.

To the Department and Peiping.

PECK

693.94244/19 : Telegram

The Ambassador in China (Johnson) to the Secretary of State

PEIPING, May 19, 1936—4 p. m.
[Received May 19—1:35 p. m.]

249. My 248, May 18, 11 a. m.[85] The devastating effects of smuggling continues to be discussed in the press. No effective anti-smuggling measures have yet been developed. Measures advocated include (1) establishment of customs houses at points along Peiping–Hankow and Tientsin–Pukow Railways, and (2) establishment of separate anti-smuggling organization to which the Inspector General of Customs is reported to have objected on the grounds that the present preventive organization is adequate.

I am informed by Reuter's Peiping correspondent that the following Reuter's report from Shanghai dated May 18 is doubtless an official written statement given to the press by the Inspector General of Customs:

"Sir Frederick Maze, Inspector General of Customs, officially reporting to the Chinese Government on smuggling from Manchuria and Darien into North China states that the varieties of smuggling

---

[85] Not printed.

goods are increasing daily while a progressive decrease in customs
revenue is shown at many ports. For example, during the past 4
months the Tientsin collections have dropped 23 percent, reports Sir
Frederick. He goes on to say that unless the customs preventive department is free to resume normal operations in the North, including
the rearming of vessels and shore stations, and unless the railway
authorities in the North are enabled to cooperate with the customs
authorities 'it is idle to expect any improvement in the existing unprecedented and serious situation.' It is generally believed there that
the Nanking authorities hesitate to rearm the customs vessels in northern waters owing to the risk of incidents."

JOHNSON

693.94244/20 : Telegram

The Ambassador in Japan (Grew) to the Secretary of State

TOKYO, May 20, 1936—noon.
[Received May 20—6 : 54 a. m.]

109. Embassy's 108, May 18, 2 p. m. My British colleague yesterday informally discussed the smuggling situation in China with
Matsudaira, former Ambassador to Great Britain, now Minister of
the Imperial Household. Clive made it clear that there had been no
joint Anglo-American representations but that the practical interests
of both our countries were seriously affected by the situation. He
realized that the Japanese military in China could not be expected
to "climb down" immediately from the position they had taken because this would entail loss of face in view of the British and American *démarches* but he thought that the matter ought to be adjusted
by early and direct negotiation with Nanking. It might be true, he
said, that some of the Chinese tariff schedules were too high but the
action of the East Hopei regime in permitting goods to enter China at
greatly reduced rates with the support of the Japanese military was
disrupting the whole Chinese customs organization and if continued
would lead to increasing friction with Great Britain where questions
were now being asked in Parliament.

Clive said that Matsudaira promised to talk immediately to Arita [87]
and seemed to be considerably impressed with the potential seriousness of the situation. Clive observed to me that the Japanese are "ter-
rified" by any indication of Anglo-American cooperation in the Far
East and he feels that even similar if not joint representations possess
great power of leverage.

An opposite point of view was expressed to me this morning by
Yoshida [88] who said that Arita had been greatly disturbed by the smuggling activities in China and had been trying to find ways and means

[87] Hachiro Arita, Japanese Minister for Foreign Affairs since April 2.
[88] Shigeru Yoshida, appointed Japanese Ambassador in the United Kingdom.

to improve the situation but that the publicity arising out of the American and British *démarches* had rendered his position difficult and embarrassing because whatever he might now do would be interpreted as done under foreign pressure.

These are opposing points of view but they both carry weight. The Japanese undoubtedly are fearful of facing a united front by the United States and Great Britain but the chauvinist element would be inclined to object to anything that could possibly be interpreted as "truckling" to foreign pressure.

Clive is not aware whether the Germans are interested as reported in the press. The British Counsellor mentioned the situation to the German Chargé d'Affaires merely in casual conversation. The French Ambassador said that nothing could be expected from his Government which at present is in a state of crisis.

The German Chargé d'Affaires told me last evening that his Government is not interested in the smuggling situation in North China since German commercial interests in China lie chiefly in the South.

To Peiping by mail.

GREW

793.94/7912 : Telegram

The Ambassador in China (Johnson) to the Secretary of State

PEIPING, May 20, 1936—5 p. m.
[Received May 20—3 : 20 p. m.]

252. 1. Embassy's 241, May 14, 2 p. m. According to the most reliable information obtainable from foreign military observers, there are now 2258 Japanese troops at Tientsin, of which 1200 are new arrivals; 738 at Shanhaikwan, of which 500 are new arrivals; 400 at Tungchow, of which 200 are new arrivals; and 700 at Peiping of which 300 are new; that is, there are now 4,096 at these 4 places, of which 2200 are new arrivals. More troops are expected to arrive by the end of May. The retiring commander of the North China Garrison informed his foreign military colleagues on May 13 in writing that the increase in strength would be "about more than double in number." The actual number is apparently still a military secret.

2. Embassy's 217, April 30, 4 p. m. Colonel Mutaguchi who arrived recently and announced that he had succeeded Lieutenant Colonel Hasegawa as Commandant of the Japanese Embassy Guard has now been succeeded by Major General Masakazu Kawabe, who arrived at Peiping, May 16. Kawabe is in command of an infantry brigade which is part of the North China Garrison and one regiment of this brigade forms the Embassy Guard. Mutaguchi continues in command of that regiment. It is not known what the rest of the brigade con-

sists of nor where it is to be. Kawabe states that he will reside in Peiping, where quarters have been rented for him.

By mail to Tokyo.

JOHNSON

793.94/7908 : Telegram

The Secretary of State to the Counselor of Embassy in China (Peck)

WASHINGTON, May 20, 1936—5 p. m.

34. Your 143, May 18, noon.

1. Referring to paragraph 1 of your telegram, the Under Secretary at the press conference May 16 in response to a question whether this Government had taken any steps to determine whether Japan's action in strengthening its garrison in North China violated the Boxer Protocol [89] replied that in his opinion the Secretary's public statement made on December 5, 1935, covers the situation.

2. A translation of the note referred to in paragraph 4 of your telegram does not appear to have been published in the United States. It is suggested that you send by naval radio a summary of the note and forward the text by mail. However, should you consider that the complete text would be of interest to the Department at this time, please send it by naval radio.

HULL

761.93 Outer Mongolia/25 : Telegram

The Counselor of Embassy in China (Peck) to the Secretary of State

NANKING, May 21, 1936—9 a. m.
[Received 10 : 50 a. m.[90]]

148. 1. The Soviet Ambassador yesterday told an American correspondent, not for quotation, that:

(1) The low point in Russian policy in the Far East was the sale of the Chinese Eastern Railway in 1935 as a concession to avoid war with Japan; (2) the Soviet Government subsequently learned that a policy of conciliation was assumed by the Japanese to be one of weakness; (3) Soviet policy vis-à-vis Japan was now one of defiance based on the theory that a strong attitude would be more likely to prevent Japanese aggression and resultant war than a weak; (4) the Soviet Union-Outer Mongolian Pact of March 12 (see our 114, April 30, 11 a. m.) was a direct notice to Japan that there exists a definite limit beyond which Japanese hegemony cannot advance on continental Asia; (5) Soviet policy toward China is one of helpfulness looking to the building up of China as a bulwark against Japan and has no altruistic implications.

[89] Signed at Peking, September 7, 1901, *Foreign Relations*, 1901, Appendix (Affairs in China), p. 312.
[90] Telegram in two sections.

2. The correspondent gained the impression that Russia's ultimate aims envisage Russian control of Mongolia, Manchuria and part of North China including the coast as far south as Tsingtau which is now the only real ice free harbor on the northern Asiatic coast.

3. To Department. By mail to Peiping, Tokyo, Moscow.

PECK

693.94244/23 : Telegram

The Ambassador in Japan (Grew) to the Secretary of State

TOKYO, May 21, 1936—10 a. m.
[Received May 21—1 : 02 a. m.]

110. Embassy's 109, May 20, noon. Evidence is accumulating that the smuggling situation in North China is causing misgivings in Tokyo. The Foreign Office spokesman yesterday completely altered his tone in discussing the subject with the press correspondents and stated that high officials are being sent to China to observe the situation. As the Japanese military authorities in China are apparently adamant in their determination to prevent patrol of the Hopei coast by armed revenue cutters the inference is that Tokyo intends to bring about some sort of compromise that will improve matters.

The general impression is that the American and British *démarches* have served to focus attention on the issue and to that extent have been helpful.

Repeated to Peiping.

GREW

693.94244/27 : Telegram

The Counselor of Embassy in China (Peck) to the Secretary of State

NANKING, May 22, 1936—10 a. m.
[Received May 23—6 : 28 a. m.[91]]

149. Department's 34, May 20, 5 p. m.

1. The note, dated May 15, would lose character by being summarized. Translation as furnished the press by the Foreign Office is as follows:

2. "In regard to the unwarranted interference to which the Customs Preventive Service has been subjected by the Japanese military at Chinwangtao and the protection afforded to the Japanese and Korean smugglers, the Waichiaopu has had the honor of addressing to you several notes of protest, to which, however, no satisfactory reply has hitherto been received from the Japanese Government. I wish now to reiterate that in taking appropriate measures to prevent smuggling the Chinese Maritime Customs are exercising function inherent in their

[91] Telegram in three sections.

duties of safeguarding the integrity of the state revenue and that the exercise of such powers of prevention admits no interference from any source.

As clearly pointed out in the previous notes, in which the Waichiaopu requested the Japanese Government to take effective steps to restrain their military authorities from further unwarranted and illegal interference with the preventive functions of the Chinese Customs, there is no reference in the Tangku Agreement [92] to the question of armed customs vessels, nor can any article of the said agreement be construed as imposing any restrictions on the anti-smuggling activities of armed customs patrols or preventive vessels."

3. Section 2 follows.

4. "The repeated requests made by the Chinese Government on the ground of China's sovereign rights and for the protection of legitimate trade interests, both Chinese and foreign, have, however, been ignored by the Japanese Government with the result that smuggling has increased to the extent of impairing the integrity of the Chinese national revenue.

According to information received by the Foreign Office, Japanese and Korean smugglers, taking advantage of the serious impairment of the efficacy of the Customs Preventive Service in consequence of Japanese interference, have during recent months engaged in large scale smuggling by sea. A large number of junks and motor driven vessels, some as large as 500 tons, have been employed for smuggling along the coast from Lutai to Chinwangtao, while the landing and transportation of smuggled goods have been carried on without the fear of seizure by the customs. By means of the railways illicit goods have been shipped southward and dumped on the various markets.

As regards the smuggling situation on land, immense quantities of smuggled goods from Chinwangtao have been brought to Tientsin and various places in the interior via Peiping–Liaoning Railway, and a large percentage of these goods have also reached the southern ports via the Tientsin–Pukow Railway. At Shanhaikwan and other places the audacity of armed Japanese and Korean smugglers has been amazing, numerous cases having occurred in which customs officers were attacked with impunity and goods already seized by the customs were recovered by force. As a result of such smuggling, it is estimated that the loss of revenue suffered by the maritime customs from last August to April this year amounted to over 25 million dollars, while the figure for the month of April alone was no less than 8 million dollars, thus indicating the rapid deteriorating of the position."

5. Section 3 follows.

6. ["]The unprecedented seriousness of the situation has been the cause of grave concern to Chinese and foreign traders, as well as far-sighted observers in Japan. As failure to take immediate steps to curb such illegal activities would result in further increase of smuggling, with the consequences of reducing the revenue of the Chinese customs and impairing the national finances of China, the Chinese

---

[92] Signed May 31, 1933; *Foreign Relations, Japan, 1931–1941*, vol. I, p. 120.

Government is constrained to lodge a further protest with the Japanese Government.

I, therefore, ask you to be good enough to transmit to your Government the above views with the request that immediate steps be taken to restrain the Japanese military authorities from further interference with the preventive functions of the customs and to withdraw the protection hitherto enjoyed by Japanese and Korean smugglers. I further request that such smuggling concerns as the 'Shih Ho Transportation Company' mentioned in the previous notes of protest be immediately dissolved and that other prompt measures be taken for the effective suppression of Japanese and Korean smugglers at Chinwangtao and other places".

7. To Peiping by mail. Copy of translation sent to Peiping and Tokyo with copy of this office's despatch to Department, No. 165, May 20.[93]

PECK

693.94244/26 : Telegram

The Counselor of Embassy in China (Peck) to the Secretary of State

NANKING, May 22, 1936—11 a. m.
[Received May 22—9 : 30 a. m.]

150. Department's 117, May 14, 5 p. m. to Peiping.

1. I communicated the Department's message to the Minister for Foreign Affairs during private conversation after a dinner given May 21, 8 p. m., by the Soviet Ambassador. The Minister for Foreign Affairs told me that the smuggling situation is still very serious and that the Chinese Government is now attempting to suppress smuggling through three measures: (1) inflicting severe penalties, (2) control of transportation through permits and (3) control through cooperation with Chamber of Commerce and similar organizations.

2. At this point the Soviet Ambassador joined us and the conversation turned on Japanese activities. The Ambassador expressed the view to the Minister for Foreign Affairs that "Japan is saber rattling". He said that his Government had discovered that the Japanese misunderstood conciliation as weakness and that boldness was probably the best preventive of war. (Compare my May 21, 9 a. m., paragraph 1, points 2 and 3). Referring to Manchurian border incidents, he said that his Government had denied to the Japanese Government the contention of the latter that boundaries were vague and had said that if any military parties crossed them into Soviet territory military action would result; that the Soviet Union would be glad if Japan did not regard such border incidents as *casus belli* but if Japan made them pretext for war then the Soviet Government "could not help it".

---

[93] Not printed.

(These remarks seemed to be in part a repetition also of those reported in telegram number 97, April 3, from the American Ambassador at Moscow to the Department.)

3. The Minister for Foreign Affairs was noncommittal but indicated general concurrence in the Ambassador's description of Japan's attitude and the correctness of the Soviet attitude toward Japan. He said to me that he thought the best way to settle difficulties in the Far East would be to convene a conference of the interested powers including China, the Soviet Union and the United States but he supposed the American Government would not be willing to exclude Japan. I observed that the Washington Conference on Far Eastern Affairs had included nine nations. The Minister for Foreign Affairs and the Ambassador asked me to express my personal opinion concerning the advisability of a conference but I evaded this. The conversation then terminated and the observation of the Minister for Foreign Affairs concerning a conference seemed to have been merely a chance remark and not premeditated.

4. To Department and Peiping.

PECK

893.108 Manchuria/43

The Ambassador in China (Johnson) to the Secretary of State

No. 477   PEIPING, May 22, 1936.
                                            [Received June 15.]

SIR: I have the honor to enclose a copy of despatch No. 261 of May 12, 1936, from the Consulate General at Mukden, on the subject of native communist armies in Manchuria.[94]

Although there have from time to time been reports of communists among the "bandits" of Manchuria, this is the most concrete information yet received in regard to them and their organization. No reports have been received of large-scale encounters between these alleged communist armies and the Japanese military, and it is therefore assumed that if such armies actually exist they have been skillful in avoiding clashes with Japanese military patrols.

Respectfully yours,   NELSON TRUSLER JOHNSON

793.94/7913 : Telegram

The Ambassador in Japan (Grew) to the Secretary of State

                                    TOKYO, May 23, 1936—11 a. m.
                                    [Received May 23—2 : 25 a. m.]

111. According to the best information available to the Military Attaché, the Japanese Garrison in North China will be increased to

[94] Not printed.

about 4300 officers and men, or to 4675 if additional field artillery is to be sent. Japanese officers here deny that an army division is to be organized in North China.

Repeated to Peiping.

GREW

793.94/7915 : Telegram

The Ambassador in China (Johnson) to the Secretary of State

PEIPING, May 25, 1936—noon.
[Received May 25—10 : 30 a. m.]

259. 1. Chinese officials continue to deny that General Sung Che Yuan has entered into any important agreement with the Japanese. They claim that the Japanese are asking for permission to station troops at Fengtai, as well as at Changsintien on the Peiping–Hankow Railway. However, the Japanese military have already taken over a large tract of land at Fengtai and are rapidly constructing buildings on it. It is possible that Hsiao Chen Ying has presumed to make an agreement with the Japanese without reference to Sung.

2. A serious split has allegedly occurred among subordinates of Sung. Sung's division commanders have long disliked Sung's civilian subordinates who negotiated with the Japanese. This feeling has come to a head with the resignation of General Shih Ching Ting from the post of Chief Counselor of the Hopei-Chahar pacification headquarters. (Reference paragraph 2 of Embassy's 201, April 20, 2 p. m.; and subdivision C of paragraph 3 [2] of Embassy's 243, May 15, 3 p. m.) The divisional commanders are favorably disposed toward Shih and partly for this reason Hsiao Chen Ying, Chen Chueh Sheng, and other members of what is now referred to as the Kirin clique brought about Shih's resignation through making misrepresentations to Sung. One official believes that the outcome must be that either (1) Sung will rid himself of these civilians or, (2) the civilians will effect the removal of Sung and act for the Japanese in establishing a regime. This second possibility may have motivated Hsiao in entering into agreements with the Japanese of which Sung is unaware. Sung is said to be attempting now to quiet the dissatisfaction of his military subordinates.

3. The attitude of these civilians is indicated by Chen Chueh Sheng's interview on May 22 to the United Press correspondent in which he said that the National Government is wholly to blame for the smuggling situation in North China, and by an address made a few days ago to Hopei Province magistrates by Pan Yuan Kuei, Chief of the Department of Political Affairs of the Hopei-Chahar Political Council, the address being primarily a veiled attack on Chiang Kai Shek.

4. This so-called Kirin clique is understood not yet formally organized. It allegedly includes General Chin Teh Chun, the Mayor of Peiping, General Men Chih Chun, Chairman of the Reconstruction Committee, and General Fu Chan Kuei, Chief of Staff of the Hopei-Chahar pacification headquarters, presumably because they fear they could not otherwise hold their jobs.

5. Reference subdivision D of paragraph 2 of Embassy's 243, May 15, 3 p. m., the Hopei-Chahar Political Council issued an order May 23 designating the Hopei Provincial Bank as the sole bank of issue in Hopei and Chahar. This runs counter to the monetary policy of the National Government.

[6.] The Embassy has no information about increase of Japanese forces in addition to that contained in Embassy's 252, May 20, 5 p. m. Lieutenant General Tashiro, commanding North China Garrison, arrived at Tientsin, May 19.

7. Many rumors are current and the situation is not clear. Leading educators of Peiping met May 22 to discuss the desirability of a public expression of opinion on the situation but did not act because of their feeling that they did not know enough of the facts about the situation.

8. According to one report, the Japanese are threatening Sung Che Yuan with a new "autonomy movement" if he does not more quickly meet their wishes, the new movement to be an extension of Yin Ju Keng's sphere to include Peiping and Tientsin.

9. According to an informed official, Japanese recently visited post offices in Kueihwa and Paotow in Suiyuan to investigate the organization and administration of those offices. There are unconfirmed reports of a concentration of Japanese Manchukuo troops in northern Chahar.

By mail to Tokyo.

JOHNSON

793.94/7917 : Telegram

The Counselor of Embassy in China (Peck) to the Secretary of State

NANKING, May 25, 1936—5 p. m.
[Received May 26—2:25 p. m.[95]]

157. 1. Embassy has obtained from Foreign Office translation of address on Sino-Japanese relations delivered at weekly memorial service this morning by Minister for Foreign Affairs as follows:

2. "In view of our persistent efforts towards cultivating friendly relations with our neighboring countries, [I] need not emphasize here the importance which we attach to the question of cooperation between China and Japan, which besides being neighbors are also united by

[95] Telegram in seven sections.

the ties of racial and cultural affinities. Since the Mukden 'incident' of September 1931, however, an endless succession of crises of unprecedented gravity have resulted in the estrangement of the two peoples and increased their suspicions. The present abnormal state of their relations has been a cause of deep concern to farsighted persons in both countries, and it has been their common desire to restore the friendly feelings which should exist between the peoples and the Governments of the two countries.

3. "Speaking at the Sixty-Eighth Session of the Imperial Diet held over a year ago, Mr. Koki Hirota, then Foreign Minister in the Japanese Government, enunciated the principle of 'nonaggression and no[n]-menace' towards neighboring countries. Although no clear and concrete measures materialized to give effect to this idea of improving Sino-Japanese relations and no practical results were obtained, his efforts in the case [cause?] of peace created a deep impression abroad. With the assumption of the premiership by Mr. Hirota about a month ago and the subsequent appointment of Mr. Hachiro Arita to the post of Foreign Minister, there did not seem to be any fundamental change in Japan's foreign policy. At the recent Sixty-Ninth Session of the Imperial Diet, the new Foreign Minister declared that it was Japan's national policy 'to insure the stability of East Asia, contributing thereby to the cause of world peace, and at the same time to promote the happiness and welfare of Nanking by upholding firmly international justice!' In other words, Mr. Arita not only stated what he declared to be the policy of his Government but also expressed the common aspirations of the various peoples in eastern Asia.

4. "The situation between China and Japan being what it is today, further failure to achieve a thorough readjustment would not only be detrimental to the interests of the two countries, but concerns the whole question of peace in eastern Asia. Therefore, immediately after the assumption of my duties as Foreign Minister, I made up my mind to do my best to effect the readjustment of Sino-Japanese relations through diplomatic channels, and I am happy to say that a similar desire seems to exist in Japan. Nevertheless, it is a matter for regret that concrete discussions have not yet started as regards the scope of the desired readjustment and the manner in which it is to be brought about. So far as China is concerned, any problems, the solution of which will redound to the mutual welfare of the two countries and the security of peace in eastern Asia, are considered as coming within the scope of readjustment, and any formulas based on equality and reciprocity as well as mutual respect for sovereign rights are regarded helpful means towards achieving our end. The readjustment, which it is our intention to bring about, should not be confined to any local question, or to any particular issues. It is desired not as a temporary policy to ease the present situation, but with the object of ensuring the peaceful coexistence of the two peoples for generations to come.

5. "Nations, as individuals, may become the subjects of deep hatreds and animosities, but, as the Chinese saying goes, no lasting fuel ever lasts a century. The will to restore peace and harmony is bound to triumph, provided it is strong enough. It cannot be denied by seeming obstacles. Such being my firm belief, I consider the task of establishing friendly intercourse between China and Japan an im-

mediate challenge to practical statesmanship in both countries. I appeal to the political foresight of the responsible authorities of both sides, and earnestly hope that they will make a strong effort to remove the cause of hostility and establish a lasting understanding. It is particularly urgent for them to appreciate each other's standpoint and difficulties and to enter promptly into sincere discussions through the proper channels. It does not avail matters to indulge in mutual recriminations, to harp on vague principles, or to utter under [sic] threats of coercion or of reprisals. What is important is to face concrete problems bearing on the mutual interests of the two countries with an honest and sincere resolve to find equitable solutions.

6. "In the furtherance of her national economy, especially in the field of foreign trade, Japan has complained that she is being surrounded by the so-called economic blocs and the artificial barrier of economic nationalism. Now, in view of the intimate economic relations between China and Japan, any true consideration of the latter's economic interests would presuppose a genuine sympathy with China in any situation tending to wreck her economic structure, as well as a desire to see such a situation ameliorated. At present the smuggling in North China has assumed amazing proportions. The flood of contrabands has paralyzed the market and killed the business of legitimate trade, both Chinese and foreign. Apart from the huge loss of revenue, the situation threatens the very foundation of our economic structure. The Customs Preventive Service, on account of the serious obstacles placed in its way, has been powerless to deal with this orgy of smuggling, but we believe that, if it is the real desire of Japan to cooperate with this country, a simple move on her part will instantly put an end to such a deplorable situation.

7. "Japan has frequently professed her concern over the Communist disturbances in certain parts of this country; and such concern is well understood by us inasmuch as the effects of internal agitations in one country are bound to be felt by its neighbors, due to the close interdependence of modern nations. During the last few years the Chinese Government has waged a relentless struggle against the Red menace, and the situation has been pacified to such a large extent that we are confident in the early liquidation of the whole trouble. Under whatever circumstances, China is determined not to relinquish even temporarily her firm hand against the Communists, nor to tolerate within her territory the subversive activities of any organization aiming at the overthrow of the existing political institutions by force.

8. "During the last few years the Chinese people have concentrated their efforts on the rebuilding of their country strictly on the basis of self-salvation and self-help. We are confident in our own strength to bring about a national renaissance. We have never contemplated the possibilities of political alliance, nor have we attempted in the least manner to play off distant powers against neighboring countries. The basis of our policy is: live and let live. In other words, we want the right of national existence for ourselves, as well as the establishment of the principle of coexistence and coprosperity in the comity of nations. While we are making a supreme effort to ensure our own security, we also earnestly desire that all interested powers will jointly strive for the consolidation of peace in eastern Asia."

9. By mail to Peiping and Tokyo.

PECK

693.94244/23 : Telegram

The Secretary of State to the Ambassador in Japan (Grew)

WASHINGTON, May 26, 1936—1 p. m.

64. Your 110, May 21, 10 a. m. Referring to the statement of the Foreign Office spokesman reported in the above-mentioned telegram, the Department suggests that the Embassy orally and informally and at an opportune moment inquire of the Japanese Foreign Office as to the present status of the matter with a view to ascertaining the names of the officials who are to make the investigation and the date of their departure from Japan. In the event the matter is under way and the officials have departed from Japan, it is suggested that the Embassy in its discretion reaffirm the continued interest of this Government in the smuggling situation and indicate that the Embassy and Department would welcome information in regard to the findings and results of the investigation.

HULL

693.94244/30 : Telegram

The Ambassador in the United Kingdom (Bingham) to the Secretary of State

LONDON, May 27, 1936—noon.
[Received May 27—6 : 38 a. m.]

282. Department's 180, May 26, 5 p. m.[96] The following is pertinent portion of Foreign Secretary's answer on May 25.

"The information at the disposal of His Majesty's Government tends to confirm that customs officials at the shore stations in the demilitarized zone, as well as vessels operating in its coastal waters, are prevented by the Japanese military authorities from carrying arms. There is moreover reason to believe that difficulties are experienced by Chinese customs officials on trains in the demilitarized zone. The principal agents engaged in the smuggling traffic in North China are said to be Japanese and Koreans, although some Chinese may be taking part."

"In particular His Majesty's Ambassador at Tokyo in his handling of this matter has kept in close touch with the representatives of the other governments interested. I understand that representations have also been made to the Japanese Government by the United States Ambassador".

Text by pouch yesterday.[96]

BINGHAM

---

[96] Not printed.

693.94244/31 : Telegram

The Ambassador in Japan (Grew) to the Secretary of State

TOKYO, May 27, 1936—6 p. m.
[Received May 27—9 : 25 a. m.]

114. Department's 64, May 26, 1 p. m.   The Vice Minister for Foreign Affairs [97] in informal conversation today stated that the chief of the Eastern Asia Bureau of the Foreign Office would visit Manchuria and North China reaching the East Hopei region about June 15 and would be instructed to make a full report on the smuggling situation.   Preceding him by about 10 days a new Japanese Consul is being assigned to Tientsin with instructions to familiarize himself in regard to conditions in Hopei and to collect data for the use of the chief of the East Asia Bureau upon the latter's arrival.   The Vice Minister said that he would be glad to keep the Embassy currently informed and asked if the Embassy had any data in its possession indicating that specific items of American trade were suffering from the smuggling.   He was informed that while information of this character was not at present available to this Embassy the American Embassy was interested in the general situation and would welcome any data that the Japanese Government could furnish.

Repeated to Peiping by mail.

GREW

793.94/7920 : Telegram

The Ambassador in China (Johnson) to the Secretary of State

PEIPING, May 28, 1936—noon.
[Received May 28—6 : 24 a. m.]

264. Reference paragraph 1 of Embassy's 259, May 25, noon.

1. According to information supplied by a reliable visitor to Fengtai, which is the junction of the three important railways of North China, the Japanese have taken over two pieces of property near the railway station at Fengtai without payment to the owners, are occupying some brick buildings about 650 feet east of the station, are making additions to them which approximately quadruple their capacity, and are constructing at a point some 650 feet south of the station some buildings on a plot of land which they have enclosed in barbed wire and which is about 20 acres in extent.

2. This informant also visited Changsintien, the first station south of Fengtai on the Peiping–Hankow Railway, and states that the Japanese have occupied a piece of ground about 12 or 13 acres in extent and have begun the erection of buildings thereon.

By mail to Tokyo.

JOHNSON

---

[97] Kensuke Horinouchi.

693.94244/36 : Telegram

The Counselor of Embassy in China (Peck) to the Secretary of State

NANKING, May 28, 1936—2 p. m.
[Received 2:20 p. m.]

159. Nanking's 157, May 25, 5 p. m.

1. Japanese news agency Domei from Nanking May 22nd [reports?] that Japanese Chargé from Shanghai had called on Foreign Minister and drawn attention to "unfavorable effect of Chinese allegations regarding Japan's responsibility for smuggling situation upon Sino-Japanese relations".

2. I was today informed by Executive Yuan official that Japanese First Secretary (not Suma) had recently called at the Yuan and stated that "China would suffer" if Chinese Government continued to "mobilize world opinion against Japan" on account of smuggling. Informant stated that it now appeared that one Japanese objective which had emerged from their opportunist use of the smuggling situation to advance their general program, was the allocation to the jurisdiction of the Communications Committee of the Hopei–Chahar Council, of the northern sections of the Peiping–Hankow and Tientsin–Pukow Railways, with a view to alienating those sections from Nanking's control.

3. We have been informed that Foreign Office has ordered Suma to Tokyo to report on Chinese protests concerning smuggling. He left Nanking for Japan May 24. A few days previously an American news correspondent stated to him that the Japanese Government could easily stop the smuggling if it wished and he asked "why should we? What would there be in it for us?["] Another American news correspondent was today informed by an officer of Japanese Embassy that Japan would not attempt to end the smuggling unless the situation in North China were "adjusted" in accordance with Japanese proposals.

4. Repeated to the Department and Peiping, by mail to Tokyo.

PECK

693.94244/38 : Telegram

The Chargé in Germany (Mayer) to the Secretary of State

BERLIN, May 29, 1936—noon.
[Received May 29—7:42 a. m.]

163. Yesterday the British Counsellor [98] spoke to me informally of a recent conversation he had had with the German Foreign Office regarding smuggling in North China. The British Embassy had

---

[98] Basil Cochrane Newton, British Minister at Berlin.

been instructed by their Government to inform the Foreign Office of their representations in Tokyo on this subject in the hope that Germany would feel disposed to take similar action. The Foreign Office said they would telegraph the German Embassy in Tokyo for a report and on its receipt would discuss the matter further with Newton.

Newton also told me that they had just received a "repeat" from the British Embassy at Tokyo indicating that the Japanese authorities were about to undertake an investigation of the matter.

Newton said that he was not instructed to discuss the matter with me but he knew we were interested and wished to let us know the British action taken here with the idea that possibly our Government would want me to speak with the Foreign Office somewhat similarly. I said I would be glad to report this conversation to you.

Apart from the desirability you may feel from a general political point of view of cooperating with the British in Far Eastern affairs, I feel that it might be useful for me to discuss this matter with the Foreign Office here as affording indirectly an opportunity of testing German-Japanese relations.

MAYER

793.94/7922 : Telegram

The Ambassador in China (Johnson) to the Secretary of State

PEIPING, May 29, 1936—4 p. m.
[Received 8 : 10 p. m.]

267. 1. The present trend in Sino-Japanese relations is indicated by the following developments:

(*a*) Evidence accumulates that the civilians or so-called Kirin group of Sung Che Yuan's regime (reference paragraphs 2, 3, and 4 of Embassy's 259, May 25, noon) intend to force Sung to break completely with the National Government. Noncompliance would supposedly result in departure of Sung and his army from northern Hopei. Compliance might possibly result in creation of disturbances by Sung's military subordinates.

(*b*) The Japanese authorities in North China apparently have no intention of rendering that assistance which is necessary for checking smuggling by Japanese nationals.

(*c*) The press reported May 28, that the National Government had "rejected" the Japanese reply to its representations with regard to the increase of Japanese forces in North China (Nanking's 145, May 18, 3 p. m.[99]) and had instructed the Chinese Ambassador in Tokyo to make further representations. The report states that the Chinese deny the Japanese allegations of "instability in North China," an

---

[99] Not printed.

assertion which can and may be met by the instigation by the Japanese of fresh disturbances in Hopei. Rumors of possible fresh "autonomous" movements continue to circulate in Tientsin.

(d) There are indications that oppressive measures by Japanese against so-called anti-Japanese-Chinese in Peiping are being renewed.

(e) Students of Tientsin and Peiping are again becoming restless. 2,000 students demonstrated yesterday in Tientsin and later decided at a mass meeting to strike for 3 days. The immediate cause of the activity is said to be the increase of Japanese forces in North China and a secondary cause commemoration of the Shanghai May 30 incident. One student leader stated in private conversation that one purpose is to render support to Sung in his present differences with Hsiao Chen Ying. Students in Peiping are to meet tonight to decide whether to strike for 3 days.

By mail to Tokyo.

JOHNSON

693.94244/38 : Telegram

The Secretary of State to the Chargé in Germany (Mayer)

WASHINGTON, May 29, 1936—5 p. m.

64. Your 163, May 29, noon.

1. The Department approves your discussing orally and informally with the appropriate official of the Foreign Office the smuggling situation in North China. You should do so as on your own initiative and not as under instruction from the Department. You should not make any request that the German Government make representations in Tokyo on this subject.

2. For your information in discussing this subject with the Foreign Office. Several months ago the diplomatic representatives in China of several governments, including the American and British, made representations to the Chinese Government. During the early part of this month the American and British Governments made representations to the Japanese Government. The American Government's representations took the form of an oral and informal approach by the American Ambassador to the Japanese Foreign Office, wherein the American Ambassador pointed out that the extensive smuggling operations in North China have created a serious situation in that area; that it has been reported, with substantial supporting evidence, that Japanese subjects have taken a prominent part in these operations; that Japanese authorities in China have placed obstacles in the way of the enforcement of Chinese preventive measures; that these conditions are leading to extensive disorganization of the Chinese import trade; and that the American Government is concerned not only with the

adverse effect of this situation on American import trade but with the impairment of the Chinese Government's income from customs revenue which impairment tends to jeopardize the capacity of the Chinese Government to meet its outstanding financial obligations to American citizens.

3. In the light of the facts that this Government has received from no government an official request that this Government approach other governments with a view to the making by them of representations in Tokyo on this subject and that this Government has made no such approach to any other government, it seems advisable to the Department that you not make such an approach to the German Government.

4. Please continue to keep Department informed by telegraph of developments.

HULL

693.94244/39 : Telegram

The Ambassador in China (Johnson) to the Secretary of State

PEIPING, May 29, 1936— 5 p. m.
[Received 7 : 12 p. m.]

268. Embassy's 265, May 28, 4 p. m.[1]

1. There is no evidence that measures of the National Government are effecting any decrease of smuggling in North China. According to a Reuter report which is said by the Consulate General at Tientsin to be correct, 150 Koreans ejected Chinese passengers from several third class coaches of a train of the Tientsin–Pukow Railway on May 27 at Tientsin and themselves entered the coaches with 552 bales of smuggled rayon which they carried as personal baggage. This action was presumably taken to avoid possibility of difficulties from lack of customs documents covering goods shipped by rail out of Tientsin. Japanese police on the scene made no effort to interfere. The Japanese authorities in North China apparently have no intention of rendering that assistance which is necessary for effectively checking smuggling by Japanese nationals. Nor can it be anticipated that railway officials at Tientsin will cooperate with other Chinese authorities in attempting to prevent smuggling.

The local Japanese Assistant Military Attaché informed the press this morning in reply to a quotation [*question?*] that the Japanese are not pressing Sung Che Yuan to establish a customs service independent of Nanking.

By mail to Tokyo.

JOHNSON

---

[1] Not printed.

761.94/905

The Ambassador in Japan (Grew) to the Secretary of State

No. 1866   Tokyo, May 29, 1936.
                                            [Received June 15.]

SIR: I have the honor to submit the following reviews of developments affecting Soviet-Japanese relations that have occurred since the Embassy's despatch No. 1831 of May 13, 1936.[2] There is appended hereto an annex[2] containing comments taken from the press and other sources relating to the chronology of events given in the despatch.

The only new developments of note affecting Soviet-Japanese relations during the period May 13, the date of the last report, to May 27, were the provisional fisheries agreement, the arrival of the first increase in the Japanese Army Garrison in Manchuria and North China, the Anglo-Soviet naval conversations, and the protests over the arrest of the Japanese employees of the Soviet Embassy. The two minor border incidents that took place were apparently not considered developments calculated to cause concern to either Government. The final sessions of the Diet still occupied almost the entire attention of both the press and the public, and those sessions were concerned for the most part with internal affairs.

THE BORDER PROBLEMS

It was reported on May 13 that a clash occurred between Soviet and "Manchukuo" forces at Wuchaiatzu near Changlingtzu when a Soviet patrol crossed the frontier and was fired upon by "Manchukuo" guards after ineffectually warning the Soviet troops to return. The Soviet soldiers were driven back but they returned later with reinforcements and both sides took up strong positions some 500 meters apart. The casualties reported were slight but the Kwantung Army, it is understood, plans to lodge a protest with the Soviet authorities. The news report blames the lack of border demarcation for this latest clash.

The Foreign Office at Hsinking according to the press plans to lodge a protest with the Outer Mongolian Government because of the landing in "Manchukuo" territory on May 8 of an Outer Mongolian plane. The occupants of the plane are understood to have questioned the local inhabitants regarding conditions in that vicinity and subsequently to have flown back to their own territory.

The concentration of Soviet troops along the "Manchukuo" border has finally brought about an increase in the Kwantung Army's strength. Army headquarters in Tokyo have already agreed to an

---

[2] Not printed.

eventual increase and in addition the Kwantung Army has decided at a conference on May 16 on a special program to expand its air forces. Lieutenant General Itagaki recently returned to Hsinking after a conference in Tokyo and apparently brought word that the necessary reinforcements would be forthcoming.   According to the press there is to be a fundamental change in the Kwantung Army. Instead of the present system of replacing Japanese troops stationed in Manchuria with others from Japan there is to be developed a standing army in Manchuria which will not be subject to frequent change. It is understood that the First Regiment which has just left for Manchuria will not replace other troops. The Lieutenant General it is understood reported to Kwantung Army headquarters that the Japanese nation is more keenly concerned over the frontier question than he had anticipated. Another despatch on May 15 reported that Soviet troops along the border were being continually reinforced, apparently in preparation for any emergency, and it was indicated that, therefore, immediate reinforcement of Japanese "Manchukuo" strength is necessary.

Very little progress has been made toward the establishment of the proposed border commissions. Although both nations have agreed in principle on the establishment of commissions to settle the poorly marked section of the eastern "Manchukuo" border, the Soviet Government still advances its proposal for a second general commission for settling border disputes and frontier lines along the entire 4300 kilometers of Soviet Outer Mongolian border. It is reported that during a call on the Foreign Minister Ambassador Yureneff was requested to explain the difference between the special and general commissions for settlement of border disputes called for in the Soviet proposal. The Ambassador explained that his Government desired the establishment of a general commission to deal with all border questions while the special commission would attempt to settle border questions and define the frontier along that part of the eastern frontier specified in the Japanese proposal. The Foreign Minister informed him, according to the report, that the proposal for a general commission was premature and that the Japanese Government was interested first in settling the eastern border problems. During his call the Ambassador also lodged a protest regarding the suspension by the "Manchukuo" Government of retirement payments to former Soviet employees of the Chinese Eastern Railway. It was also reported that he mentioned the recent clash on the border at Wuchaiatzu.

FISHERIES CONTROVERSY

According to the last report the Japanese Ambassador to Moscow succeeded in negotiating a provisional extension to the existing fisheries treaty with the Soviet Government on May 25. The treaty was due to expire on May 27 and as prophesied the extension provided for the continuance of that treaty only until the end of the present calendar year in order to cover the fishing season which has already commenced. A copy of the official English text of the Protocol issued by the Japanese Foreign Office together with a translation of the promulgation order in the *Official Gazette* of May 28 is enclosed.[3]

GENERAL RELATIONS

Colonel Hikosaburo Hata who has recently returned after two years at Moscow to head the War Office Press Section, is understood to have reported that Soviet Government Officials are skeptical of Japan's *soi-disant* Continental policy, believing it one of further aggression. He spoke of the rapid military progress in Russia, construction of many machines and airplanes, but did not believe that the effectiveness of Soviet forces should cause apprehension because their rapidly-built equipment, particularly aircraft, was poorly constructed. He is reported to have said that the USSR is deeply concerned over the Polish and German frontiers as well as over the Soviet and Outer Mongolian borders of "Manchukuo". The frequent clashes along the latter two frontiers he stated, have been worrying Soviet Officials.

On May 19 a press report published what are said to be the Foreign Minister's instructions to Mr. Yoshida, the new Ambassador to London. According to the report the Foreign Minister stated that close understanding with Great Britain is a vital factor in the successful pursuance of Japan's Continental policy in view of the fact that a *rapprochement* between Britain and Soviet Russia would constitute a major obstacle to Japan's plans. He stated that the positive nature of the Soviet Far Eastern policy has caused Japan to desire a readjustment of relations with the USSR and that because of the reported Anglo-Soviet conversations on naval questions it was of great importance that Great Britain understand and sympathize with Japan's aims on the Continent. Ambassador Yoshida will endeavor to convince the British Government that Japan and Britain can pursue their Far Eastern policies amicably, each respecting the others' rights and interests. It is understood that he will also point out to the British Government that Soviet propaganda against Japan, issued in connection with the USSR's entry into the League of Nations, is detrimental to Anglo-Japanese relations and therefore Great Britain must aid Japan in presenting its true Continental policy to the world.

---

[3] Not printed.

The Japanese employees of the Soviet Embassy in Tokyo who were arrested some time ago on espionage charges have not yet been released. The Soviet Vice Foreign Commissar according to the press protested to the Japanese Ambassador against the "persecution" of those employees and stated that the campaign in the Japanese press has been giving the Embassy a bad name and hindering its work of improving relations. Mr. Stomoniakov insisted that the arrested translators were merely doing their legitimate work and that espionage charges are entirely false. It was understood on the 24th that Japan would file a counter protest with the Soviet Government pointing out instances of anti-Japanese propaganda, that the Soviet Embassy's employees were arrested in accordance with domestic law, that the Soviet protest is interference in Japan's domestic administration, and that the newspapers are not conducting an anti-Soviet campaign but are merely reporting the facts. The press stated that the counter protest will shortly be delivered by the Japanese Ambassador, and will also include a protest against the statements in Soviet newspapers attacking Japanese policies in alleging Japan is even threatening British and American territories.

The local press has been very full of news regarding the Anglo-Soviet naval talks and Japanese navy circles are reported to be keenly interested in the alleged Soviet plan of increasing its submarine strength to between 70 and 80 vessels. It appears to be the belief in Tokyo that the USSR will not agree with Britain to weaken its naval forces in the Far East as that would give the Japanese navy a dangerous superiority.

Japan has decided definitely to increase its military forces in both North China and Manchuria in order not only to hasten elimination of bandits but also to provide better protection to the borders of "Manchukuo". As reported by telegraph* it is understood that the North China Garrison will be increased to more than 4500 men. It is not known thus far how many additional troops will be added to the Kwantung Army Garrison in Manchuria but it is understood that steady additions over a period of time will be made.

During the period under review very little attention was paid to Soviet-Japanese relations in the Diet, inasmuch as no new incident had occurred to increase friction and negotiations regarding existing questions were progressing as well as could be expected.

Respectfully yours,   JOSEPH C. GREW

---

*Embassy's telegram No. 111, May 23, 11 a. m.   [Footnote in the original.]

893.01 Manchuria/1336 : Telegram

The Ambassador in Japan (Grew) to the Secretary of State

TOKYO, May 30, 1936—noon.
[Received May 30—6:12 a. m.]

116. Some 2 weeks ago the British Ambassador informed the Minister for Foreign Affairs that many Chinese employees of British concerns in Manchuria including the British-American Tobacco Company and the British Presbyterian Mission had been arrested by the authorities in Manchuria and were being held. Among them was the chief sales agent of the tobacco company in Mukden who had been obliged to sign a check for 60,000 yuan on the alleged ground that he had received that sum from the Chinese Communist Party. The Ambassador told Arita that these arrests were causing serious difficulties to the British concerns and he furthermore protested that Japanese gendarmes in Manchukuo had invaded the premises of the Presbyterian Mission without permission of the British Consul thereby violating extraterritorial rights. The Ambassador's representations occasioned no publicity.

Yesterday the Vice-Minister for Foreign Affairs told the Ambassador that an investigation had been made and that the arrests were in no way directed at British interests but were based on suspicion of Communistic activities on the part of the employees. The Vice-Minister then broached the subject of extraterritoriality in Manchuria but the Ambassador said that he had no authority to discuss that subject. Repeated Peiping.

GREW

693.94244/41 : Telegram

The Ambassador in Japan (Grew) to the Secretary of State

TOKYO, May 30, 1936—1 p. m.
[Received May 30—7:59 a. m.]

117. 1. The British Ambassador this morning informed me that in late April Suma, the Japanese Consul General at Nanking, informed the Commercial Counsellor of the British Embassy in China that the smuggling situation was a political and not an economic issue; that the Japanese Government would do nothing to improve the situation pending Chinese acceptance of Japanese views; that the smuggling was a perfectly reasonable method of bringing pressure to bear on China for revision of the tariff; that the February 26 incident had consolidated and strengthened the determination of the Japanese Army to proceed with a firm hand in China; that the situation could not be stabilized until the five northern provinces of China had become

completely independent of Nanking; and that the efforts of China to strengthen armaments constituted an absurd and dangerous move because any "incident" could lead to open conflict.

2. Clive brought this conversation to Arita's attention who denied Suma's statement of the Japanese Government's attitude toward the smuggling issue and reiterated that there was no political motive behind the smuggling.   Clive believes that Suma's recall to Japan at the present moment may be a result of the above-reported conversation.

3. Domei reports this morning that on landing yesterday at Kobe, in an interview with newspapermen, Suma stated that he had told Chiang Kai Shek that "China must now choose between mutual interdependence with Japan or war with Japan".   Associated Press informs the Embassy that this phrase will not appear in the English translation to be distributed by Domei but that it did appear in the original Japanese version of the interview.   The *Asaki* version of the interview does not contain the threat of war but the *Nichi Nichi* version states that Suma said that "the future course of the Chiang Government must be either to rely upon Japan or to open hostilities against Japan".

Repeated to Peiping.

GREW

793.94/7923 : Telegram

The Consul General at Tientsin (Caldwell) to the Secretary of State

TIENTSIN, May 30, 1936—8 p. m.
[Received May 30—12 : 30 p. m.]

I am reliably informed that shortly after 8 p. m. yesterday explosion occurred beyond third special area under Japanese troop train from Tangku which was not damaged or delayed.   Japanese military authorities reported to be taking serious view of incident, which some attributed to students.   Reports of this incident on the heels of student demonstrations and Japanese Garrison increase have caused very tense situation here.

Nankai University and Middle School and Peiyang University reported under police occupation, ingress and egress prohibited and telephone cut.   Nevertheless student agitation continues; meetings reported held this morning in all schools and colleges in Tientsin; reported to be propagandizing police; no arrests reported.

Undesirable Japanese reported concentrating here; over 100 reported first special area in which many Americans and Europeans.

For some days rumors have been current of impending Japanese demands, removal of Sung and of other changes of all the important Chinese officials in North China.

Japanese troops arriving last night apparently about 1,250. Japanese military and consular officers now state North China Garrison after increase will not exceed 6,000.

By mail to Peiping and Nanking.

CALDWELL

893.00/13508 : Telegram

The Consul General at Canton (Spiker) to the Secretary of State

CANTON, May 31, 1936—10 p. m.
[Received June 1—8 p. m.]

Referring to your telegram of May 27, 4 p. m.,[4] and in supplement to my telegrams of May 20, 8 p. m. and May 27, 9 a. m.,[5] scheduled conference between Southwest leaders and Nanking delegation during the period May 25 to 28, inclusive, was abortive and according to most reliable sources accomplished nothing toward unification. Separate local negotiations by H. T. Tang, Superintendent of Customs, Shanghai, in relation to the adoption by Southwest of national currency believed possibly productive of results due to the perilous state of Southwest currency which today reached new low, paying premium of nearly 65% for Hong Kong dollars.

2. Civilian leaders Tsou Lu and Hsiao Fo Cheng on pleas of ill-health did not attend conference, such absence generally ascribed to their complete lack of sympathy with the aggressively anti-Chiang Kai Shek platform recently proclaimed by the Southwest purportedly under mandate of Hu Han Min's alleged will which has been given greatest publicity and prominence as the creed of the Southwest. Tsou Lu, who had booked passage several weeks ago and canceled it after Hu's death, suddenly left Canton and sailed from Hong Kong on Italian ship for Europe on May 27 accompanied by two leading members of Chung Shan University faculty, ostensibly to attend celebration at Heidelberg University, the Olympic Games, etc. On the day following his departure the press quoted a statement allegedly made to it by Tsou to the effect that his public address of May 4 was expressive of his present political position. It is interesting to note that this address was mainly devoted to the crying primary need of abandonment of factional lines and of unification of all classes in the whole country in order that the entire national energy may be mobilized in resisting Japan, that the address embodies no challenge to Chiang or to Nanking, and that it specifically opposes cooperation with Japan against Communism, this all being in striking contrast to Hu's alleged will which, while demanding resistance against Japan, lays equal

---

[4] Apparently reference to an Embassy instruction.
[5] Neither printed.

stress on the elimination of Chiang Kai Shek and the suppression of Communism. The final item in Chou's alleged statement reads as follows: "It is also essential to act with those powers who treat us on a basis of equality for a common struggle."

3. A typical press report purporting to come from local official sources as to the results of conference reads as follows: "Canton officials have agreed in principle upon the policy of the Central Government that China is not in a position to resist foreign aggression by war and therefore agreed that the period of extensive preparation for ultimate resistance must be prolonged." See my comments in part 2 of this telegram to follow.[6]

4. The only other statements by the strictly censored local press in relation to the conference were to the effect that certain proposals are being carried back to Nanking by its delegation and that the conference discussed the Whampoa port development scheme.

5. According to a statement by Yeh Chu Chang, prior to his departure for return to Nanking, matter of place of Hu's interment has not yet been decided. Local press contains frequent statements as to alleged opposition of Hu's family on ground that Hu declined to go to Nanking while alive so obviously should not go there when dead. There is a local belief that the disposal of the remains is being used by the Southwest as one of its bargaining points.

6. Tsou Lu's departure on May 27 and that of Yeh Chu Chang, Chu Chia Hua and Chu Min Yi on the following day for Nanking without any announcement of the accomplishment of unified measures by that conference, together with the further alarming depreciation of the local currency described in third sentence of this message is interpreted by local observers as indicating that the Southwestern leaders are maintaining a defiant attitude toward Nanking, though some hold that this is a gesture made to secure a better bargaining position.

7. Part 2 of this telegram follows. This telegram is transmitted to the Department, Peiping and Nanking.

SPIKER

893.00/13508 : Telegram

The Consul General at Canton (Spiker) to the Secretary of State

CANTON, June 1, 1936—10 a. m.
[Received 8 : 35 p. m.]

Following comments constitute part 2 of my telegram of May 31, 10 p. m. Document purporting to be Hu Han Min's will believed by local observers to have been formulated on the insistence of Pai Chung Hsi and, in less degree, of Li Tsung Jen, because of their

---

[6] Telegram of June 1, 10 a. m., *infra.*

personal animosity toward Chiang, Pai being considered as chiefly responsible for wrecking of any plans for *rapprochement* between Southwest and Nanking at this time.

2. Reference is made to those portions of this office's political reports for December, 1935, and subsequent months [7] concerning Japanese relations with the Kwangsi and Kwangtung leaders. Blowing up of railway bridge near Tientsin on May 29 has led to general local belief that Japan is once more following its formula of creating a major incident in the North whenever Nanking appears on the eve of possible *rapprochement* with the Southwest. In this relation see the second paragraph on page 6 of this office's political report for April last.[8] Marshal Chen is reported as favorable to closer cooperation with Nanking but under the pressure from Kwangsi seeks to remain on the fence, playing Kwangsi with Nanking. Recruiting is actively going forward in Kwangsi and its military are now seeking to purchase large number of heavy motor trucks for early delivery. Such maneuvers are viewed with suspicion as evidence that the province is relying on some strength other than its own or Kwangtung's.

3. Kwangtung leaders have not yet been able to secure required permission from Nanking to ship 20,000,000 standard dollars to London as means for stabilizing local currency. Central Government reliably reported to be insisting that Kwangtung authorities first announce total of banknotes issued, that all unissued notes be placed in control of a newly established local currency board on which bankers, merchants, et cetera, are adequately represented, and third that the proceeds of the sale be used solely for the stabilization of Kwangtung currency. Steady decline of local currency during the last few days is causing great alarm and there is fear of a crash unless local authorities soon accept Nanking's help on its own terms. Transmitted to Department, Peiping, Nanking.

SPIKER

793.94/7924: Telegram

The Ambassador in China (Johnson) to the Secretary of State

PEIPING, June 1, 1936—11 a. m.
[Received June 1—6: 30 a. m.]

271. Reference section (*e*) of Embassy's 267, May 29, 4 p. m. Student[s] of Yenching, Tsinghua, and the National University of Peiping and of five middle schools at Peiping went on strike May 30 for 5 days. Groups of strikers of Yenching University began to tour the countryside to explain the political situation. Students of the Normal University at Peiping declared a 3-day strike. The primary

---

[7] None printed.
[8] Not printed.

motive of these student activities is opposition to Japanese aggression. There is a danger that such activities may result in an incident or may be made use of by unscrupulous persons to precipitate a situation inimical to China's sovereignty in Hopei Province.

By mail to Tokyo.

JOHNSON

693.94244/31 : Telegram

The Secretary of State to the Ambassador in Japan (Grew)

WASHINGTON, June 1, 1936—noon.

66. Your 114, May 27, 6 p. m. The Department has received a letter from the Standard-Vacuum Oil Company, New York,[9] stating that the smuggling of kerosene and gasoline into North China is seriously affecting its business and threatens the existence of its trade in that part of China extending from the borders of "Manchukuo" to the Yellow River. The letter further states in substance that smuggled oil brought into North China through the east Hopei autonomous area is assessed by the regime in that area a duty of approximately 11 cents Chinese per gallon, or about one-fourth the amount of the Chinese import duty; that arrivals of Japanese smuggled oil into Chinwangtao and vicinity between April 15 and 30 were 15,600 cases and between May 1 and 20 were 40,000 cases; that the company's sales have ceased in the Chinwangtao area and in Tientsin and have been seriously affected in adjacent territory; and that these smuggled oils are being sold at some Yuan 1.70 per case of 10 gallons below the company's official prices.

The Department suggests that the Embassy unless it perceive objection orally and informally approach the Foreign Office and in response to the inquiry of the Vice Minister mentioned in the telegram under reference bring to its attention the above information, as evidence, in regard to the effect of smuggling on American trade in kerosene and gasoline. It is also suggested that this occasion be taken to point out that the sale and distribution of other items of American trade are effected in a similar manner by the influx of smuggled goods and to reaffirm the concern of this Government in the situation which is seriously affecting American interests.

Repeat to Peiping as Department's No. 131, June 1, noon, adding that the Department desires that Peiping currently furnish Tokyo with copies of despatches and telegrams in regard to smuggling in North China and specifically with a copy of Peiping's despatch No. 322 of March 21.[10]

HULL

---

[9] Dated May 27, not printed.
[10] Not printed.

893.00/13509 : Telegram

The Consul General at Canton (Spiker) to the Secretary of State

CANTON, June 1, 1936—4 p. m.
[Received June 1—2 : 35 p. m.]

Following supplements paragraph 1 of my June 1, 10 a. m. There are persistent local reports that Japanese machinations using Kwangsi leaders as dupes or willing tools against Chiang resulted in the document alleged to be Hu's will which document lends support to Japanese so-called anti-Communistic activities in North China and at the same time denounces Chiang as a dictator : the anti-Japanese item in the document serving as a screen. This telegram has been sent to the Department and the Embassy.

SPIKER

761.94/911

The Ambassador in China (Johnson) to the Secretary of State

No. 491   PEIPING, June 1, 1936.
[Received June 29.]

SIR: I have the honor to enclose a copy [11] in English translation of a Chinese translation of an article, entitled "Return from North China", written in Japanese by Lieutenant General Kenji Doihara, which appeared in *The Asia People's Voice* of May 12, 1936 (a pro-Japanese newspaper published in Chinese at Peiping) with regard to the Russo-Japanese problem. In view of General Doihara's connection with autonomous movements in North China, it is believed that the Department will be interested in the views which he expresses.

After pointing out the tenseness in Russo-Japanese relations, which has been brought about by Russia's strengthening of armaments along the "Manchukuo" border, he catalogues the numerous border incidents which have occurred in the past and which he appears to believe will occur with increasing frequency in the future as Soviet-inspired attempts to administer the Orient, or, as he calls them, "vanguard struggles".

Lieutenant General Doihara next touches on the employment by Russia of Chinese communists (an important section of whom is now concentrated in Shensi) to further Russian ambitions, while from various points in Outer Mongolia Russia endeavors to extend its influence south and east. With some justice, it is believed, Lieutenant General Doihara points out that these two facts should make Hopei "an extraordinarily important place". He believes that the Russo-Japanese situation is now an inflammable one, and he contends that he could not possibly predict that war will not be the result.

---

[11] Not printed.

Lieutenant General Doihara then touches on the Great Asia doctrine and, in language restrained and conciliatory and less chauvinistic than that of the so-called "Continental School" of Japanese imperialists (see Embassy at Tokyo's despatch No. 1798 of April 30, 1936), points out that China will be in favor of an Asia for the Asiatics (the Great Asia doctrine) if Japan does not take China for its actual property.

The policy of an Asia for the Asiatics, "the kingly way of Japan", as Lieutenant General Doihara calls it, is in his opinion the only safeguard for permanent peace in the Orient.   He states that the rejection of interference by the United States, Great Britain and Soviet Russia in order to achieve an Oriental land of freedom is the desire of the Chinese.

In conclusion, Lieutenant General Doihara disavows Japanese intention of aggression in China and suggests that as fifty Chinese students were shortly to visit Japan, this opportunity be availed of to instill in them the "real Japanese idea", a policy, which, as he points out, is contrary to the interests of the United States and Great Britain in the Far East.   It would appear that Lieutenant General Doihara is deeply concerned with the progress of the Soviet Union, and he gives the impression of now attempting to placate China in order to save her territories for Japan.

Respectfully yours,   NELSON TRUSLER JOHNSON

693.94244/54 : Telegram

The Chargé in Germany (Mayer) to the Secretary of State

BERLIN, June 3, 1936—1 p. m.
[Received June 3—10 : 05 a. m.]

167. Department's 64, May 29.   Discussed situation with the Foreign Office in accordance with instructions.

German representative at Nanking has just telegraphed suggesting that his Government, through representative at Tokyo, invite Japanese Government's attention to the seriousness of the smuggling situation.   While no decision has been taken as yet, Foreign Office believes that this suggestion will be followed and informal and oral representations will be made at Tokyo shortly.

The Department's instruction afforded an opportunity to further contact with Erdmannsdorf [12] who I feel has no illusions about Japanese plans with regard to North China.   He did not think however that the Japanese designs went further than this section nor did he believe that either the Japanese or the Russians wanted to fight.

---

[12] Dr. O. von Erdmannsdorff, chief of the East Asiatic Section of the German Foreign Office.

It would be useful if from time to time the Department would provide me with information regarding Far Eastern affairs which I could pass on to Erdmannsdorf or discuss with him.

MAYER

693.94244/53 : Telegram

The Ambassador in Japan (Grew) to the Secretary of State

TOKYO, June 3, 1936—6 p. m.
[Received June 3—9 : 57 a. m.]

119. Department's 66, June 1, noon. In compliance with the Department's instructions the Counsellor of the Embassy [13] today called on the Vice Minister for Foreign Affairs and presented the facts as contained in the telegram under reference. The Vice Minister made no comment in regard to any future action or attitude of the Japanese Government in connection with the matter. Neville obtained the distinct impression from the interview that other governments can expect no cooperation from the Japanese Government at this time in the suppression of the smuggling.

Repeated Peiping.

GREW

693.94244/88

The Ambassador in China (Johnson) to the Secretary of State

No. 497   PEIPING, June 3, 1936.
[Received June 29.]

SIR: I have the honor to refer to Nanking's telegram No. 53 of March 14, 9 a. m., in regard to the difficulties experienced by the Chinese authorities in efforts to stop smuggling operations because of the refusal on the part of the Japanese military to permit armed customs cruisers to proceed against smugglers along the coast of the demilitarized zone in northern Hopei Province on the ground that such action would violate the Tangku Truce, and to previous despatches and telegrams in regard to the Tangku Truce, and in that connection to enclose an article from the *Peiping Chronicle* (a Chinese-owned daily newspaper published in English) of May 20, 1936,[14] on this subject. It is stated therein that a spokesman of the Foreign Office declared on May 18, 1936, that there was nothing in the Sino-Japanese Truce Agreement signed on May 31, 1933, at Tangku which would justify the interference by the Japanese with the Customs Preventive Service (ships and launches) in Eastern Hopei. It is stated that following this declaration the spokesman distributed to the pressmen assembled copies of a

[13] Edwin L. Neville.
[14] Not printed.

translation of the text of the agreement. The terms of the truce as set forth in the translation thus distributed, allowing for language differences resulting from translation, are, with one exception, the same as those included in the translation of the text supplied to me by the Vice Minister for Foreign Affairs, Liu Ch'eng-chieh, on June 2, 1933, which was forwarded to the Department under cover of my despatch No. 2153 of June 14, 1933.[14a] The one exception is that in paragraph 4 of the text forwarded by me there was no provision that the police force "shall not be constituted by armed units hostile to Japanese feelings" as provided in section 4 of the text furnished by the spokesman of the Foreign Office. If these texts are authentic and complete, it is apparent that the statement of the Foreign Office spokesman is correct, and there would appear to be nothing in this agreement as published which would justify the Japanese in interfering with the normal functioning of the Chinese Customs authorities south of the Great Wall. There is reason to believe, however, that agreements on various matters were entered into at the time of the signing of the Tangku Truce which have not yet been published and the scope of those agreements is not yet known accurately. The Chinese argument is in part supported by the fact that, according to information available, the attitude of the Japanese authorities did not result in the disarming of the customs preventive officers until the spring of 1935 and the fact that the Japanese military authorities did not insist on the ceasing of operation of customs armed vessels along the coast of the demilitarized zone until September, 1935, two years after the conclusion of the Tangku Truce.

Respectfully yours,

NELSON TRUSLER JOHNSON

793.94/7941 : Telegram

The Counselor of Embassy in China (Peck) to the Secretary of State

NANKING, June 4, 1936—11 a. m.
[Received 6:35 p. m.]

165. 1. National Government officials, including Vice Minister for Foreign Affairs, deny any declaration or threat of war against Nanking by the Southwest as reported by Domei from Canton, June 2, although it is true Southwest Executive Committee and Political Council on June 2, despatched a joint telegram to the National Government (*a*) protesting against increase in Japanese North China garrisons; (*b*) denouncing Japanese aggression; (*c*) expressing fear that Peiping and Tientsin are going the way of Manchuria; (*d*) pledging full support if the National Government resists the Japanese with armed force; (*e*) urging the National Government to "lead the nation in a fight against the aggressors".

[14a] Not printed.

2. We are informed by one Chinese official in the confidence of high National Government leaders that the Domei report that National Government troops were massing on the Kwangsi and Kwangtung borders as a threat against those two provinces was designed as a smoke screen for an autonomous movement in southern Fukien which was now crystalizing, with Japanese assistance, as the result of activities of Formosans and certain "rebel" Chinese. He said that the concentration of National Government troops in areas bordering Kwangsi and Kwangtung was primarily motivated by this autonomous movement, presumably with a view to (a) suppressing it or (b) preventing its spread into Hunan and Kweichow whose loyalty has at times been open to some question. (Domei's statement of troop movements, which he confirmed as being correct in general outline, was that 14 divisions are concentrated in Kiangsi, 5 divisions are [located?] in Hunan on the Kwangsi–Kwangtung border, and further units are being rushed from Chekiang to southern Fukien, the total numbering 350,000, not including air reserves said to have been concentrated in Kweichow although within Hengchow, Hunan.)

3. The stationing of troops on the Kwangsi border for the purpose of action in southern Fukien is difficult to understand and he said in this connection that though troop movements might also act indirectly to persuade the Southwestern leaders to adopt Nanking's point of view concerning [apparent omission] which had been reiterated informally by the delegation of Nanking officials sent to attend funeral rites for the late Hu Han Min. The desiderata in this connection were reported by Domei as "demands" of Chiang Kai Shek: (a) abolition of Southwestern Political Council and Executive Committee; (b) placing of all Southwestern administrative organs under control of Nanking Executive Yuan; (c) incorporation of Southwestern troops into the National Government military organization; (d) unification of currency; (e) remittance to Nanking of national taxes; (f) appointment by Nanking of all high military and civil officials in the Southwest. According to the informants these were not demands but "suggestions" and the joint telegram sent June 2 by the Southwestern Political Council and Executive Committee was part of the process of bargaining between the Southwest and Nanking in connection therewith.

4. To Department, Peiping, Canton. By mail to Tokyo.

PECK

793.94/7942 : Telegram

The Ambassador in China (Johnson) to the Secretary of State

PEIPING, June 4, 1936—3 p. m.
[Received 9 : 03 p. m.[15]]

282. Embassy's 275, June 2, 4 p. m.[16]

1. The Chinese mentioned in Embassy's despatch No. 118, December 6, 1935,[17] returned from Nanking a few days ago and has since then been conversing with local leaders. Information obtained from him this morning is contained in paragraphs 2 to 7 inclusive of this telegram.

2. The crisis of last week in Sung's regime had to do with the question of the independence of Hopei and Chahar from the National Government. Sung Che Yuan had made up his mind to declare independence. As a result of the strong opposition of Sung's military subordinates, Sung was forced to change his mind and decided against independence.

3. Although Hsiao Chen Ying is pro-Japanese he is opposed to independence. The so-called Kirin group is on the side of the military subordinates in this question.

4. However, the traitor group is in favor of independence and its strength comes from having the support of the Japanese. The three chief traitors are Pan Yu Kuei (an Anhwei man), Chen Chueh Sheng (a Kwangtung man), and Chen Chung Fu (a Kwangsi man). Of these three, Pan Yu Kuei is now the most important.

5. Hsiao Chen Ying's opposition to independence was the reason why the Japanese attempted to force his resignation as mayor of Tientsin. (Hsiao returned to Peiping last night and local officials doubt that he will resume his duties in Tientsin.)

6. As Sung has definitely decided against independence, the next move is apparently to be made by the Japanese. This may take the form of subversive activities which will make it difficult for Sung to remain here. If Sung has to fight, his policy will probably be to retreat while fighting in the direction of Honan.

7. Chen Chung Fu (paragraph 6 of above-mentioned telegram) has gone to Canton. (He left Peiping May 27.) His purpose was to inform Canton that Sung would declare independence and to attempt to obtain a simultaneous declaration of Southwestern independence. Chen may have influenced the Southwest in its manifesto of June 2 demanding war with Japan. Sung, however, will not declare independence.

JOHNSON

---

[15] Telegram in two sections.
[16] Not printed.
[17] Dr. Chiang Monlin, Chancellor of Peiping University; for despatch, see *Foreign Relations*, 1935, vol. III, p. 475.

662.9331 Manchuria/16

The Consul General at Mukden (Ballantine) to the Ambassador in China (Johnson)[18]

No. 274   MUKDEN, June 4, 1936.

SIR: I have the honor to refer to my despatch No. 272 of May 28, 1936,[19] concerning the German-"Manchukuo" trade agreement, and in connection therewith to enclose:[20]

(1) The text of this agreement as given out by the Hsinking Foreign Office, and,

(2) A translation, made in this office, of Order No. 14 of the "Manchukuo" Ministry of Finance concerning the regulation of German-"Manchukuo" exchange.

In my despatch under reference, estimates were made of the probable value of trade between Germany and Manchuria following the conclusion of the agreement. The Consul General at Harbin also made such estimates in his despatch No. 358 of May 15, 1936, to the Department.[19] The publication of the agreement, however, removes the need of conjecture on this point, as the agreement stipulates the amount which each country will buy from the other: Germany Yuan 100,000,000 from Manchuria and Manchuria Yuan 25,000,000 from Germany. These amounts represent the business expected to be done between the two countries under normal conditions, but it is agreed that Germany may reduce her purchases to a minimum of Yuan 65,000,-000 (with a proportionate reduction in payment in foreign exchange) in the event of an unforeseen adverse exchange situation in Germany. On the other hand, should Germany's favorable trade balance with Japan exceed Yuan 63,750,000, such excess "shall be made available for additional (viz. above Yuan 100,000,000) German importation from Manchukuo payable in foreign exchange beyond the amount provided for" (Yuan 75,000,000). It would appear from the somewhat involved wording of this paragraph that two-thirds of this excess will be paid for with foreign exchange and the remaining third with Reichsmarks.

In the "Manchukuo" announcement enclosed in my despatch under reference it is stated (Section 2 c and d) that the fund in Germany made up of the one-fourth payment in Reichsmarks for Manchurian imports into Germany may be used to pay for German patents, salaries of Germans, et cetera, in Manchuria and for German products used and consumed outside of Manchuria by firms "related to Manchukuo". These arrangements must be based on some private understanding,

[18] Copy transmitted to the Department by the Consul General at Mukden in his unnumbered despatch of June 4; received June 27.
[19] Not printed.
[20] Neither enclosure printed.

as the agreement not only contains no provisions for them but stipulates very definitely that "Manchukuo" shall take measures to ensure sufficient importation of German products into Manchuria to utilize the whole amount of the Reichsmark fund in question.

The Consulate General does not feel qualified to comment on the degree of recognition of "Manchukuo" accorded or implied in the agreement. It would call attention, however, to the second paragraph of Article 3, wherein, abruptly and without any explanation for this favor, Germany's favorable trade balance with Japan is taken into consideration in the trade arrangements of the two contracting "countries".

Respectfully yours,   J. W. BALLANTINE

793.94/7943 : Telegram

The Counselor of Embassy in China (Peck) to the Secretary of State

NANKING, June 5, 1936—10 a. m.
[Received June 5—3 : 56 a. m.]

167. Cabinet official informed me confidentially June 4, 6 p. m., that Kwangtung does not wish to oppose the National Government actively but that Kwangsi is exerting great pressure to that end. Informant stated that Kwangsi is being supplied by Japan with munitions on liberal terms and with advisers. Object of Japan is to create disunion in China and destroy ability of the National Government to resist Japanese domination. Informant conceded the possibility that the two Kwangsi leaders, while accepting Japanese assistance in opposing Nanking, may have secret intention of using this military aid ultimately against Japan itself. (I infer he foresaw possibility the Chinese Government might accept Kwangsi challenge to lead nation against Japan.) He said Japanese tactics are exemplified by recent disclosures to the Government by Fu Tso Yi, Provincial Chairman of Suiyuan, of secret offers made to him by Japanese military who promised munitions and money in exchange for openly declaring independence or secretly arranging to permit Japanese military dispositions in Suiyuan in preparation for future domination of Mongolia and Japanese hostilities with the Soviet Union. If second course were adopted Fu would be allowed to issue violently anti-Japanese manifestoes. Informant implied that the Kwangsi manifesto demanding that the Chinese Government fight Japan accordingly did not necessarily irritate the Japanese. Informant felt that Fukien is a danger spot of Japanese intrigue and was greatly depressed by the impossibility of foreseeing where Japan's next attack would be. He insisted Japan does not want to deal any mortal blow to China nor goad China

into open war but wants rather to wear down China's powers of resistance through continual undermining.

PECK

893.00/13517 : Telegram

The Consul General at Canton (Spiker) to the Secretary of State

CANTON, June 6, 1936—noon.
[Received 11 p. m.]

Referring to my telegram of June 5, 5 p. m.,[21] and previous communications, local government controlled press today published manifesto issued by Marshals Chen and Li, Pai Chung Hsi and senior officers of the First and Fourth Group Armies. The manifesto is addressed to the Kuomintang Central Executive Committee, the National Government, the Military Affairs Commission, the Southwest Executive Committee and Southwest Political Council and states that Japan's aggression is now at its height, that the two armies have no choice but to rise and offer armed resistance; that their commanders and officers accordingly [beg?] and crave that they be given orders to proceed north under a new standard and face the enemy; that they are "of one heart and mind in this proclamation of the inexorable attitude."

2. Newspapers further publish following resolution adopted at joint meeting yesterday of the Southwest Executive Committee and Southwest Political Council, Marshals Chen and Li and other high military and civil officials participating: "Resolved that instructions be issued to the First and the Fourth Group Armies; that preparations should be made for mobilization against the Japanese; and that the armies shall be renamed the Chinese Revolutionary Anti-Japan National Salvation Army". It is reported that beginning this morning military units in Canton started wearing brassards bearing new designation.

3. Source of information quoted in first sentence of my telegram of June 5, 5 p. m. today insisted that Kwangtung and Kwangsi forces actually moving northward through southern Hunan. No local confirmation of this report obtainable. Source further alleged that Hunan and Yunnan have signified intention to join Southwest in present movement.

4. Local exchange late yesterday depreciated to 204 for Hong Kong dollar then suddenly rose to 177 and has since remained steady.

5. Other details follow by land wire.

SPIKER

---

[21] Not printed.

693.94244/64 : Telegram

The Ambassador in Japan (Grew) to the Secretary of State

Tokyo, June 8, 1936—8 p. m.
[Received June 8—11:25 a. m.]

123. Embassy's 119, June 3, 6 p. m. In conversation today the British Ambassador stated that his Government viewed the Chinese situation seriously. He said that in his judgment there was nothing at present to hope from the Japanese in the way of cooperation to improve things in China; that the smuggling would go on at least for the time being; that it was entirely possible that the Japanese military envisaged a demoralized customs service in China followed by a collapse of all government there due to lack of revenue; that he had tried to impress upon the Japanese that they could not expect the rest of the world to accept the naive statement that Japan had nothing to do with the smuggling in the North; that the British Government did not accept it, a fact which he had asked Leith-Ross to reiterate in any conversations he may have with Japanese officials here; that he had repeated to Arita that the British Government was acting throughout solely to protect British interests on its own initiative without collusion with other governments.

The Ambassador said that the Japanese had insisted on Leith-Ross visiting Japan and that the invitation had come not from financial interests but from the Foreign Office and military officers in China and that Leith-Ross had been met by an emissary of the War Department on arrival. He was emphatic that Leith-Ross had not intended to come to Japan as he had no business to transact here and had come only because he had been so repeatedly urged that the British Government had finally instructed him to come because failure to do so would look like an international slight. The Ambassador added that he was not sure what the Japanese had in mind in asking him but they had been urging the visit since last winter but Leith-Ross had been delayed on account of the February disturbance, the new Government and the session of the Diet.

GREW

893.00/13522 : Telegram

The Counselor of Embassy in China (Peck) to the Secretary of State

Nanking, June 9, 1936—11 a. m.
[Received 10:30 p. m.]

173. This office's 165, June 4, 11 a. m.

1. Situation in Southwest and in respect to relations between Southwest and Nanking continues obscure. Definite information as to

progress of events is lacking. Denials by both sides that civil war threatens appear in direct contradiction to military activities at least on part of the Southwest. Allegations of Japanese intrigue in Kwangsi, combined with fact that Kwangsi has for some time possessed arms including planes furnished by Japanese seems to produce the illogicality of an anti-Japanese expedition furthered by Japanese assistance.

2. Following reports current here are credible:

(1) Considerable number of National Government troops have been stationed along Kwangtung-Kwangsi borders, probably for more than 2 months, in Kiangsi and Hunan and Fukien;

(2) A schism has been developing between Kwangtung military who have desired to maintain the *status quo* for selfish material reasons and Kwangsi military leaders who have,

(*a*) felt threatened by proximity of National Government dictation and possibility that Chen Chi Tang might come to terms with Nanking, which possibility was increased by death of Hu Han Min;

(*b*) [been] growing self-confident by reason of their improved military resources which have been the result of long and arduous effort assisted by Japanese supplies and training at least in aviation;

(*c*) been subject for many months to pressure to break openly with Nanking exerted by Japanese military officers and possibly accompanied by Japanese loans or bribes;

(3) Pai Chung Hsi and Li Tsung Jen engineered the June 2 declaration of the Southwest Political Council and Executive Committee taking by surprise Chen Chi Tang who has joined with them temporarily for the sake of expediency;

(4) Following the declaration, Kwangsi and probably Kwangtung troops moved toward the Hunan border;

(5) Discussions have since been proceeding by telegraph and through personal representatives between National Government's Southwestern leaders.

3. These circumstances make it appear that the proposed northern anti-Japanese expedition is a threat against Nanking being employed in the process of bargaining and that the Domei report of a Southwestern declaration of war against Nanking was a premature report of an intended act held in reserve for later use in bargaining if necessary. Possible explanations of the apparently contradictory developments in respect to the part which alleged Japanese intrigue has played are of:

(*a*) Kwangsi's anti-Japanese actions are with the consent of or by arrangement with the Japanese whose purpose is served if civil war breaks out;

(*b*) Kwangsi has obtained as much assistance as possible from the Japanese and has now no compunction in turning against the Japanese the weapons which Japanese have provided;

(c) lacking means or desire to pay the Japanese for assistance rendered, a "declaration of war" against Japan furnishes a convenient device to avoid payment. (The explanation under (a) seems the most credible.)

4. A peaceful settlement is not unlikely. Chiang Kai Shek yesterday suggested calling the second plenary session of the Central Executive Committee which, if convened, can take steps such as postponement of enforcement of constitution which may plan to meet part way presumable dissatisfaction of Southwest with Chiang's dictatorship and the dissatisfaction which Southwestern leaders are believed to feel with the constitution as a document devised in the proclaimed draft form legalizing that dictatorship by making Chiang President of the Republic. Meanwhile, discussions may lead to solution of specific pending issues including questions of finance and distribution important Government posts.

5. By mail to Peiping and Tokyo.

PECK

893.00/13523 : Telegram

The Consul General at Canton (Spiker) to the Secretary of State

CANTON, June 9, 1936—3 p. m.
[Received 11: 59 p. m.]

Referring to my telegram of June 6, 4 p. m.[22] In an interview given to a foreign press correspondent June 7th by Marshals Chen and Li they admitted that they had moved their troops across the Hunan border some days ago but described movement as natural gesture to demonstrate their readiness to fight Japan. Denying rumors of their intended war against Nanking as malicious rumors spread by Japanese sources, they stated emphatically that "Chinese will never fight Chinese"; that what they seek is a friendly understanding with Nanking which will permit employment of common basic policies but no acceptance of dictatorship and "no common government" and that if such an understanding can be secured, combined anti-Japanese action, Communist suppression and adoption of the national currency will be easily arranged.

2. Hong Kong, Chinese and foreign press on June 6 give prominence to Nanking press report that Japanese Chargé d'Affaires on June 6 formally notified Nanking Government that, whether or not authorized by Nanking, recent actions of the Southwest are provocative and that Japan reserves the right to take such action as she sees fit, including the despatch of Japanese warships to Canton if situation warrants. I am reliably informed two Japanese destroyers

---

[22] Not found in Department files.

arrived Hong Kong today. One on station here as usual. Above press report was not published in Canton newspapers which are strictly censored. Marshal Li answered allegation Japanese threat with bitter anti-Japanese speech before Southwest Political Council yesterday morning. Text of speech as published by government controlled news service contains following statements: "we should not wait to see Nanking move. If Nanking moves to resist Japan, well and good, for we want cooperation in resistance. If not, we ourselves must rise to resist because this is really our last chance of life". "We urge that every drop of our soldiers' blood be shed on a foreign foe and that every rifle be aimed at the Japanese imperialist. Therefore this northern expedition is really a people's revolutionary expedition for saving our country and its last chance of life. It is not a civil war. It cannot and must not be".

3. Yesterday delegation of Canton students signed petition Marshal Li for immediate mobilization of troops to fight Japan, freedom of speech in anti-Japanese campaign and cancellation of examination and military training system imposed by Marshal Chen following last student outbreak here. Li reported to have agreed to the first two requests but hedged on the last, placing responsibility on Kwangtung Department of Education. A large student patriotic demonstration is scheduled for June 13th under the care the Nanking authorities. The latter have suddenly decreed that school examinations, only recently set forward to June 20th, must be completed and the schools evacuated by June 12th, apparently with the motive of insuring completion of examinations and disbandment of students before the latter get out of hand.

4. Direct report from Wuchow, Kwangsi, to this office under date of June 6th reported commandeering of motor boats and all public busses to assist in steady movement of troops northward through city to Kweilin area. Also reported that late that night numerous air craft flew over the city and that Kwangsi currency had depreciated to point where Hong Kong dollar sold for 3 dollars local currency. Report on June 7th from the same source stated that Kwangsi Government had issued orders that death penalty be visited on persons refusing to accept Kwangsi currency. City allegedly flooded with sensational rumors emanating from non-Chinese nationals.

5. Report just received from recent arrival from northeastern Kwangtung to the effect that there was fighting on June 5th and 6th at Chenping, Taipu and Pingtsun in that area between pro-Nanking and anti-Nanking units of the Kwangtung forces. Commissioner Chen Wei Chou, brother of Marshal Chen, is rushing his well equipped salt troops to area named. Forces of Chang Fa Kwei reported as massed on nearby Fukien border. It is definitively known that there

are heavy troop movements from this area to eastern Kwangtung where all busses are being stopped and subjected to thorough search. There is sign of great activity on the part of local military airplanes.

Sent to the Department, Peiping, Hankow and Shanghai.

SPIKER

893.00/13521 : Telegram

The Counselor of Embassy in China (Peck) to the Secretary of State

NANKING, June 10, 1936—9 a. m.
[Received June 10—6 : 35 a. m.]

175. 1. We are reliably informed that yesterday Chiang Kai Shek sent a telegram to Chen Chi Tang appealing for national solidarity.

2. To Department, Peiping, Canton.

PECK

893.00/13526 : Telegram

The Counselor of Embassy in China (Peck) to the Secretary of State

NANKING, June 10, 1936—1 p. m.
[Received 3 : 20 p. m.]

176. 1. Minister for Foreign Affairs this morning told a visiting American news correspondent that the second plenary session of the Fifth Central Executive and Supervisory Committees would be called to resolve the crisis created by the Southwestern militarists. He said that if Southwestern leaders and delegates did not participate they would be failing to cooperate with the country. Following Chiang Kai Shek's suggestion June 8th that the session be convened (see our 173, June 9, 11 a. m., fourth paragraph) Central Executive Standing Committee met yesterday to discuss plans for the session. It therefore appears that the Government is maneuvering to place the Southwestern militarists in such position that they cannot set up an openly independent regime without branding themselves as traitors, the expectation being that if they participate in the session some compromise is likely. Perhaps with this thought in mind the Minister for Foreign Affairs told the correspondent that the Government's foreign policy including policy toward Japan likewise made clear at the sixth plenary session of the Fourth Committee in December 1935 and could not be altered except by another plenary session.

2. He said also in consequence that China was seeking peace and working to solve international issues diplomatically and that other means would be adopted only as the very last resort. He could not, however, predict the future because of recent changes in Japanese diplomatic representation in China the results of which could not be foreseen.

3. He denied that Japanese demand had [approached] the Foreign Office in any way in connection with developments in the South. (Since it is known that the Japanese Chargé d'Affaires has not visited Nanking this month, Suma is in Japan and that Nanking office of the Japanese Embassy is in charge of a Third Secretary, this denial would seem to disprove of the Hong Kong press reports mentioned in second paragraph of Canton's June 9, 3 p. m.)

4. Repeated to Department and Peiping, by mail to Tokyo.

PECK

893.00/13525 : Telegram

The Consul General at Canton (Spiker) to the Secretary of State

CANTON, June 10, 1936—8 p. m.
[Received June 10—1:55 p. m.]

Referring to my telegram of June 10, 7 p. m.,[23] mobilization proclamation of Marshals Pai and Li made public today announcing, first, that wherever their army penetrates there all relations with Japan shall cease and all humiliating agreements made with Japan be null and void; second, that resistance to Japan is the sole purpose of northern expedition since Kwangsi is opposed to all forms of civil strife; third, that all anti-Japanese forces, of whatever province and irrespective of affiliation, are welcome to join Kwangsi in its crusade, and fourth, that no individual or armed force will be molested as the army progresses unless they be traitors to the Chinese people.

2. Marshal Chen continues to avoid any commitments, the Kwangsi leaders being spokesmen and leaders of the advance into Honan. Kwangtung forces believed concentrated on or very near provincial border. It is known that Chen is seeking to purchase very large amount of cement for immediate delivery, presumably for construction of defences. Increasing belief locally that Chen is using every effort not to be drawn into actual conflict with Nanking. Canton remains quiet but apprehensive. Sent to Embassy and Hankow.

SPIKER

793.94/8050

The Ambassador in China (Johnson) to the Secretary of State

No. 510
PEIPING, June 10, 1936.
[Received July 13.]

SIR: I have the honor to enclose a copy of a memorandum [24] of a conversation which I had on June 8 with the Counselor of the Soviet

---

[23] Not found in Department files.
[24] Not printed.

Embassy, Mr. Anatole Bitner, during which he expressed the opinion that the local situation is more dangerous than it was a year ago because of the preparations of the Japanese for the occupation of the five northern provinces, that the process of eliminating the army of General Sung Che-yuan is being carried on quietly, that the Japanese will accomplish their purpose without war, and that Japan is not likely to attack Russia, being too absorbed in preparing the ground in Manchuria and North China .

Respectfully yours,

NELSON TRUSLER JOHNSON

893.00/13531 : Telegram

The Counselor of Embassy in China (Peck) to the Secretary of State

NANKING, June 11, 1936—9 a. m.
[Received 8 : 45 p. m.]

177. My 176, June 10, 1 p.m.

1. Standing Committee of the Central Executive Committee yesterday set July 10 for convening of plenary session and it is expected that an appeal will shortly be made to Southwestern leaders to participate with an ostensible view to adopting a common policy towards Japan, the Southwest and the National Government. A delegation of important leaders may be sent to Canton to make the appeal, and Kung is being mentioned in this connection.

2. We learn from reliable official sources that press reports of the incursion of Kwangsi troops into southern Hunan are in part true and Kwangsi troops have gone north beyond Lingling (Yungchow), south central Hunan, and others at least to Chenhsien (Chenchow), southeastern Hunan. The first body is reported to have passed through Lingling June 8 and to number 2000. Reports that two bodies have converged at and occupied Hengyang (Hengchow) have not been confirmed.

3. Reports concerning any National Government plans for stopping the advance of Southwestern troops northward are conflicting. The official report from official sources is that the first Government line be [is] just south of Changsha.

4. Prior to the present internal crisis some 12 members of Italian air mission were transferred from Nanchang to Nanking and several planes were brought here. A foreign pilot attached to Chiang Kai Shek headquarters has stated that the Italian instructors are to be replaced by Americans, 22 of whom have been engaged in the United States including 2 army reserve officers. (Selection was probably made by Holbrook, formerly in Hangchow school.) Reliably reported that Chiang Kai Shek "has asked the National Aviation Corporation to remove its headquarters from Shanghai to Chengtu ["]

and it is understood that the corporation is still negotiating with his representatives concerning this request.

5. Repeated to Department and Peiping, paragraphs 2 and 3 repeated to Hankow.

PECK

793.943 Manchuria/23 : Telegram

The Ambassador in Japan (*Grew*) *to the Secretary of State*

TOKYO, June 11, 1936—6 p. m.
[Received June 11—9 : 08 a. m.]

125. Treaty between Japan and Manchukuo signed yesterday is published in the English press today.[25] The Foreign Office has confirmed the accuracy of the text which is described as the first step towards abolition of extraterritoriality in Manchuria. This treaty is concerned primarily with questions arising out of the administration of the South Manchuria Railway zone and the payment by Japanese of Manchukuo taxes. It contemplates the withdrawal of special Japanese police by the end of 1937 and is to be followed in due course by other agreements looking to the extension of Manchukuo judicial authority over Japanese subjects resident in Manchuria. Text follows by mail.

Repeated to Peiping by mail.

GREW

893.00/13534 : Telegram

The Counselor of Embassy in China (*Peck*) *to the Secretary of State*

NANKING, June 12, 1936—10 a. m.
[Received June 12—4 : 23 a. m.]

179. The Minister of Finance informed me confidentially yesterday that he received a visit from General Kita, Japanese Military Attaché, a few days ago and the Military Attaché with evident satisfaction inquired how Kung liked the latest political maneuver of the Southwest under the disguise of a pretended anti-Japanese expedition. Kung asked how he knew the anti-Japanese character of the move was only a pretended [expedition?] and the Military Attaché said evasively that the Japanese had means of knowing this. Kung warned that even if the anti-Japanese aspect were only pretended, nevertheless it might fan widespread anti-Japanese feeling in China into activity and thus imperil Japanese subjects scattered throughout China.

Repeated to Peiping.

PECK

---

[25] For text of treaty signed at Hsinking, June 10, 1936, see *The American Journal of International Law*, vol. 30, No. 4 (October 1936, Supplement), p. 188.

793.94/7948 : Telegram

The Chargé in France (Wilson) to the Secretary of State

PARIS, June 12, 1936—10 a. m.
[Received June 12—6 : 08 a. m.]

489. Following is reported as of possible interest to the Far Eastern Division. An officer of the Embassy in conversation with an officer of Chinese Embassy here who is an old friend was informed that Koo [26] was under instructions to sound out the representatives of the principally interested powers at Geneva as to their reaction should the National Government be forced by the action of Canton to go to war with Japan. The informant expressed firm conviction that the National Government would fight Japan rather than engage in civil war with Canton and said that every effort was now being made to restrain Canton until the reaction of the interested powers could be ascertained.

Repeated to Geneva.

WILSON

893.00/13539 : Telegram

The Counselor of Embassy in China (Peck) to the Secretary of State

NANKING, June 12, 1936—3 p. m.
[Received 6 : 50 p. m.]

183. 1. Central Executive Committee last evening notified its members that Chen Chi Tang had agreed to halt advance of his troops temporarily and to ask Li Tsung Jen and Pai Chung Hsi to do likewise. Kung is reliably reported to have stated privately last evening that Hengchow had not yet fallen to the Southwestern forces. Chiang Kai Shek and Chang [Chun?] are reliably reported to have stated privately this morning that the northward advance of the Southwestern troops in Hunan had halted. Central News Agency, Changsha, June 11, cites reports reaching Changsha that advance of Southwestern troops has halted south of Hengchow and states that busses were still running yesterday between Hengchow and Changsha.

2. Repeated to Department and Peiping, repeated to Canton, Hankow.

PECK

---

[26] V. K. Wellington Koo, Chinese Ambassador in France.

793.94/7950 : Telegram

The Ambassador in China (Johnson) to the Secretary of State

PEIPING, June 12, 1936—3 p. m.
[Received June 12—2 p. m.]

301. Embassy's 282, June 4, 3 p. m.

1. The situation in North China is again becoming tense. Sino-Japanese conversations are in progress in Tientsin. Lieutenant General Sugiyama, Vice Chief of the General Staff at Tokyo until March of this year, and Lieutenant Colonel Tanaka, representative of Lieutenant General Itagaki, Vice Chief of Staff of the Kwantung army, arrived at Tientsin June 11. (Sugiyama's visit was originally scheduled to take place early this year. Reference paragraph 3 of Embassy's 21, January 16, 4 p. m.[26a]) Kuwashima, Director of the Bureau of Asiatic Affairs of the Japanese Foreign Office, also arrived at Tientsin yesterday.

2. It is understood that these officers will visit Sung Che Yuan at Peiping within a day or two.

3. Chinese observers believe that Japanese pressure on Sung is being increased for the purpose of causing him to sign an agreement of significant scope. These observers are of the opinion that the Japanese are not pressing at present for the complete independence of the regime but for an autonomy and for a regularization of Japanese relations with the regime.

4. Japanese reports indicate that the Japanese military continue to contend that the situation in North China is still unsatisfactory because of the threat of Communism, anti-Japanese activities, Chinese attitude toward smuggling, and slow rate of progress in carrying out economic schemes of advantage to the Japanese.

5. The uncertainty existing at present with regard to the relations of the National Government and the Southwest is regarded as weakening Sung's power to resist Japanese pressure.

6. The attitude of Sung toward the situation in the South appears to be one of merely watching developments. Representatives of the National Government have visited him during the past few days and he has received, according to a reliable source, two telegrams from Pai Chung Hsi severely critical of Chiang Kai Shek. Some of Sung's civilian subordinates are understood to be in sympathy with the Southwest but it is not known to what end they may attempt to influence Sung.

7. The attitude of Sung's military subordinates is equally doubtful. They are understood to contemplate armed resistance to the

---

[26a] *Ante*, p. 16.

Japanese at some time. Such resistance, however, seems to be doubtful, notwithstanding a report to the effect that Han Fu Chu has recently informed Sung that he will support the latter in armed resistance.

8. These subordinates are presumably displeased that their efforts to prevent Hsiao Chen Ying's resignation from the mayorship of Tientsin under Japanese pressure have failed. Hsiao is now to [*in*] the Western Hills, and it seems to be definite that he will not resume his duties as Mayor. It is reported that he has resigned from his other offices also.

9. Chi Hsieh Yuan is now rumored as a possible successor to Hsiao as Mayor. Chi was Military Governor of Kiangsu at one time and is said to be an enemy of Chiang Kai Shek. Chi is understood to have been participating in the recent Sino-Japanese conversations at Tientsin. It is reliably reported that the Japanese have handed the Chinese authorities a list of 19 Chinese whom they do not wish to become Mayor of Tientsin.

10. The bombing incident of May 29 near Tientsin has not yet been made use of by the Japanese so far as known.

By mail to Tokyo.

JOHNSON

893.00/13535 : Telegram

The Consul General at Canton (Spiker) to the Secretary of State

CANTON, June 12, 1936—4 p. m.
[Received June 12—10:32 a. m.]

Referring to my telegram of June 11, 10 p. m.,[27] and to Nanking's telegram of June 10, 9 a. m., Southwest Political Council has made strong rejoinder to Nanking's telegram of June 9th. Southwest denies it is starting civil war, accuses Nanking of warlike acts against its own people rather than against the Japanese and urges that operations against Japan begin without delay. In second message Southwest requests Nanking indicate route to be followed by Southwest troops, that concentration points be established, and that Nanking adequately and continually supply Southwest anti-Japanese forces with the money, food and munitions.

2. Canton remains quiet but apprehensive.

Sent to the Department, Peiping, Nanking, Hankow.

SPIKER

---

[27] Not printed.

893.00/13551 : Telegram

The Ambassador in China (Johnson) to the Secretary of State

PEIPING, June 15, 1936—4 p. m.
[Received June 15—2 : 15 p. m.]

304. Reference subdivision (*e*) of Embassy's 267, May 29, 4 p. m.

1. Demonstrations of some 4,000 students on June 13, at Peiping, including a considerable number of middle school students, were directed against Japanese aggression and Chiang. A few students sustained minor injuries when police attempted to disperse them. Observer states, however, that the police were unusually lenient with the students and that most of the students arrested, if not all, were released the same day. Some students attribute this leniency to their staff officers having been in support of Sung Che Yuan's army.

2. The Japanese Domei News Agency reports that Major Hamada, Assistant of Major General Matsumuro, called on the Mayor of Peiping June 13, and "drew his attention to the lukewarm attitude taken by the Chinese authorities toward the anti-Japanese student demonstrations" and that an official of the municipal government called on the Japanese Embassy on June 14 and apologized and pledged that measures would be taken for complete cessation of the anti-Japanese student movement.

3. There is evidence that certain of the students at the direction of officials of the National Government are attempting to gain control of the student movement in Peiping allegedly in order to injure reputation of the movement and make it ineffective. Such students are said to be in large measure responsible for the strikes which began today in several universities. According to some reports, radical students are opposed to strikes at present for the reason that strikes just prior to approaching examinations will lose sympathy for the student movement.

By mail to Tokyo.

JOHNSON

893.00/13550 : Telegram

The Consul General at Canton (Spiker) to the Secretary of State

CANTON, June 15, 1936—6 p. m.
[Received June 15—2 : 45 p. m.]

Referring to my telegram of June 14 [*13*], 4 [*5*] p. m.[28] in statement to press yesterday Marshal Chen denied that Southwest thrust into Hunan has as ulterior motive the overthrow of Chiang and asserted that it was solely for purpose of bringing about adoption of national

---

[28] Not printed.

policy of active resistance to Japan; that the basis for agreement between the Southwest and Nanking is their joint adoption of such policy and that following such agreement adjustments in the Government may be effected by political means. Such statement from Chen considered as only confirmation of statement of his mouthpiece Yu Han Mo as reported in paragraph 2 of my telegram of June 13, 5 p. m.

2. Marshals Li and Pai apparently embittered and disappointed at failure of other provinces to show sympathy by action or word when the Southwest gave the signal and threw down the gauntlet to Nanking by advancing into Hunan. In statement to the Chinese Government, Li again stresses his conviction of urgent necessity for realistic policy of resistance to Japan; scornfully refers to futility of Chiang's plan to discuss matter further at second plenary session in Nanking next month; states that attendance of Southwest delegates at session has not been decided upon; and expresses his grievance at Nanking's disregard of the Southwest's loyalty and patriotism and at the manner in which Nanking's censors wrecked the Southwest's effort to make nation-wide appeal by telegrams to all the provinces. Pai has made no statement since Chen broke his long silence.

3. There is undoubtedly much genuine anti-Japanese feeling in Kwangtung and Kwangsi and a feeling that historically Kwangtung is looked to by the rest of China to initiate great national movements in times of crisis. However, such feeling is tempered with feeling of distrust of the good faith of present leaders. Many believe, however, that Southwest has maneuvered Chiang into a position where, if he attacks Southwest forces after they have retired to their provincial borders, they may assume role of martyrs suppressed for their patriotic ardor, this resulting in revulsion of feeling toward Chiang throughout the country.

4. Developments described in my June 13, 5 p. m., and above, have relieved tension generally although next moves of Chiang and the Kwangsi leaders are being watched with much interest and certain apprehension. Local currency has appreciated to 174 to the Hong Kong dollar but business in general remains dead.

5. Sent to the Department, Peiping, Nanking, Hankow and Shanghai.

SPIKER

893.00/13556 : Telegram

The Counselor of Embassy in China (Peck) to the Secretary of State

NANKING, June 17, 1936—11 a. m.
[Received 7: 39 p. m.]

187. 1. We are authoritatively informed that: (1) negotiations are proceeding (*a*) on one hand between National Government and Chen

Chi Tang and (*b*) on other hand between Kwangsi leaders and the Hunan and Kiangsi Provincial Chairmen acting for the Government; (2) negotiations with Chen['s] representatives involving financial transactions and a current report that the Government has recently allotted him China dollars 13 million is "probably true"; (3) negotiations with Kwangsi representatives are being conducted at Hengyang, Hunan, and Hsiung Shih-hui, Chairman of Kiangsi, is now in Hengyang for this purpose; (4) despite the published statements of Southwestern leaders and controlled Chinese press that Kwangsi and Kwangtung troops which penetrated into southern Hunan have been withdrawn south of Hunan border, considerable numbers both of Kwangsi and Kwangtung forces remain in Hunan and Kwangsi troops are "digging in" at Kiyang; (5) when Sun Fo [29] visited Canton in May to attend funeral rites for Hu Han Min he narrowly escaped being kidnapped and held as hostage and reported plan of the Government to send, at present time, a delegation of high leaders to seek a settlement with the Southwest has been abandoned because leaders selected have declined the mission out of fear for their personal safety.

2. According to despatch from Hong Kong dated June 12, a British official concerned in the prosecution of Chinese suspected of implication in the attempted assassination of Wang Ching Wei and others, November 1, 1935, states that investigation has shown that the plot was designed to enable Southern leaders to seize political power and has "definitely established" that the Southwestern leader has accepted money and arms from the Japanese and the present Southwestern *démarche* is backed by Japanese who wish to divert attention from Japanese activities in North China.

3. According to a no less authoritative source, 18 gunboats of the Chinese Navy along the South China coast have been ordered to Nanking.

4. To Department and Peiping. Repeated to Hankow, Canton. By mail to Tokyo, Hong Kong.

PECK

893.00/13555 : Telegram

The Consul General at Canton (Spiker) to the Secretary of State

CANTON, June 17, 1936—4 p. m.
[Received 7 : 22 p. m.]

Referring to my telegram of June 16, 4 p. m.,[30] protest of the Japanese Consul General and reply of local special delegates for foreign affairs published today. Reply gives assurances of protection of life

---

[29] President of the Chinese Legislative Yuan.
[30] Not printed.

and property of Japanese nationals, then bluntly states that "anti-Japanese publicity and counter-Japanese movement are the genuine expression of the people's will as well as the natural reaction to Japan's actions since September 18, 1931 and that, as such, the political and military authorities of Kwangtung find it impossible to suppress them." Reply concluded with statement that the "effective measures", which the Japanese request the Chinese authorities to take, consist of a "fundamental revision by Japan of its policy and actions for the past 5 years." See comments in my June 17, 6 p. m.

Sent to the Department, Peiping, Nanking, Hankow, and Shanghai.

SPIKER

893.00/13557 : Telegram

The Consul General at Canton (Spiker) to the Secretary of State

CANTON, June 17, 1936—6 p. m.
[Received June 18—12 : 40 a. m.]

Referring to my telegram of June 17, 4 p. m., it is to be noted that in spite of recent anti-Japanese demonstrations and propaganda in Kwangsi and in spite of the fact that the Japanese protest mentioned June 2nd manifesto and other unfriendly utterances of the Southwest Political Council, the protest was not addressed to the Council but to Marshal Chen and asked suppression of anti-Japanese activities in Kwangtung, no mention of Kwangsi being made. Tactful inquiries addressed by this office to local authorities and to Japanese Consul General indicate that similar protest has not been made to the Kwangsi authorities in which case Japanese action may be interpreted as possible further evidence of Japanese support of Kwangsi or effecting to divide Kwangtung and Kwangsi.

2. It is generally believed in well-informed quarters that situation remains fundamentally unchanged although probably relieved for a period which will end with meeting of plenary session in Nanking in July unless Nanking decides to take direct action against Southwest before that time. Marshal Li continues to denounce Chiang but there are reports that Li and Pai are much concerned [over?] constantly diminishing support from Kwangsi populace.

3. There are persistent rumors that Nanking has decided that Marshal Chen and his brother Chen Wei Chou should be removed from the local scene by promotion or otherwise while Yu Han Mou is to succeed Chen. In view of these reports, activities of Nanking forces particularly those of Chang Fa Kuei in Fukien are allegedly now being apprehensively watched by Chen.

4. Reports from bankers and other reliable sources indicate that much progress has been made in Nanking's negotiations for adoption

here of national currency and that this may be expected in the very near future.

5. Sent to the Department, Peiping, Nanking, Hankow and Shanghai.

SPIKER

693.94244/116

The Chinese Embassy to the Department of State [31]

Despite repeated Diplomatic protests and censure of the world's public opinion Japanese authorities in North China continue to extend protection to smuggling there on a large scale. The first twenty days of May witnessed further developments for the worse, both in respect of volume of illicit trade and variety of smuggled goods. For the three weeks ending May 17th smuggled goods arriving at Tientsin from the demilitarized zone comprised 448,920 kilograms of artificial silk yarn, 21,595,230 kilograms of white sugar, 49,324 kilograms of cigarette paper, 243,140 gallons of kerosene oil, 9,623 packages of piece goods and 13,110 cases of sundries. The duty lost on this illicit cargo is roughly estimated at six million dollars or on an average of two million dollars a week, which tallies without previous estimate that the loss of revenue would amount to one hundred million dollars a year or approximately one third of the total gross customs revenue. Under the protection of the Japanese Military authorities the smugglers no longer confine their attention to high duty-paying goods, but at the low costs invade almost every line of legitimate business. The expanding list of contraband goods brought in through the demilitarized zone now include sugar, artificial silk yarn, cigarette paper, kerosene oil, lubricating oil, piece goods, dyes of all descriptions, wire netting, bicycle parts, sea products, apples, medicine, cheese, tooth paste, rubber tires, canned goods, wines, isinglass, fruit juice, cosmetics, waterproof coats, aerated waters, candies, tin plates, nails, soft wood planks, alcohol, needles, beans, tins, milk, cotton and silk braids, saccharine, rubber shoes, electric batteries and shellac. Of chief note are increasing quantities of kerosene oil, which if smuggling is unchecked will soon disappear altogether from the customs returns. Furthermore there have been two consignments of arms and ammunition. It is feared that advantage is also being taken of the situation by drug traffickers. Authoritative observers on the spot point out the significant fact that apart from few comparatively small

---

[31] Handed to the Under Secretary of State by the Chinese Ambassador on June 18; Dr. Sze "asked whether we had taken any steps recently vis-à-vis the Japanese Government and I told him that we had not done so", Mr. Phillips noted at the time.

lots all illicit cargo arriving at Tientsin is of Japanese manufacture or origin.[32]

WASHINGTON, June 18, 1936.

893.00/13560 : Telegram

The Consul General at Canton (Spiker) to the Secretary of State

CANTON, June 19, 1936—5 p. m.
[Received June 20—7 a. m.]

Referring to my telegram of June 17, 6 p. m., Marshals Chen, Li and Pai yesterday sent further telegrams direct to Chiang regretting that the purpose of their expedition into Hunan "solely to resist Japan" has been so unfortunately misunderstood and requesting that Nanking's southward advance be stopped. Unconfirmed reports from Chinese sources state that at conference at Hengchow, Hunan, on June 15th and 16th, Ho Chien as representative of Chiang presented Nanking's terms to the two generals representing Kwangtung and Kwangsi, respectively. These terms allegedly contained following stipulations: complete reorganization of civil and military establishments in both provinces; high officials hereafter to be appointed solely by Nanking; Provincial Council's and Party Executive Committees to be allowed to continue functions so long as only Nanking's mandates are carried out; customs receipts and other national taxes to be remitted direct to Nanking. In return, Nanking allegedly proposes to supply irreducible provincial deficits arising from support of military establishments and from reconstruction schemes in the two provinces. Those losing provincial offices as the result of reorganization of two provincial governments will be given appointments at Nanking. Chiang was twice flown to Changsha to direct these parleys. Southwest leaders reported to have rejected terms whereupon Chiang ordered resumption of advance of his troops against Kwangsi.

2. Believedly reliable source having official contacts states that Chiang has long sought chance to subjugate southern states; that Hunan invasion and Kwangsi's rebellious activities has given Chiang justification to crush Pai whom he regards as a menace to be eliminated at all costs; that Chen is now no problem and will accede to such demands as Chiang may care to make at coming plenary session, these including adoption of national currency with surrender of silver reserves, administration, collection and remission of all revenues as else-

---

[32] In a memorandum of June 20, the Under Secretary of State approved a suggestion that "Mr. Hornbeck orally and in confidence inform the Chinese Ambassador that the American Government has approached the Japanese Government on several occasions in regard to smuggling and that this Government continues to follow with care the situation under reference". (693.94244/117)

where in Nanking controlled territory and complete national administration of Canton-Hankow Railway; that Japan has encouraged Kwangsi to take its stand and is now prepared to give expected backing leaving Pai in desperate situation.

3. This Consulate General just informed by Japanese Consulate General that it is this afternoon sending further protest direct to Chen challenging statement that local demonstration on June 13th was one of mass sentiment rather than an obviously officially staged affair; that former protest was similarly addressed but answered personally by the special delegate for foreign affairs, Chen having completely defeated all contingencies of informant to obtain interview or direct reply to written communications; that no written protest was addressed to the Kwangsi leaders; that informant does not consider local situation serious and denied prevalent press reports that his country's gunboats are now en route to Canton.

4. Unconfirmed Chinese press reports appearing in today's Hong Kong papers state Kwangsi forces in southern Kweichow have had to retreat under pressure from Nanking forces, and that efforts to conscript peasants in eastern Kwangsi has resulted in rioting and murder of recruiting officers. Missionary report from Kweichow states that "In no less than four centers soldiers have revolted, robbed parts of cities then fled into the country". Report unfortunately fails to give location or identity of troops involved.

5. Referring to paragraph 3 of my telegram June 17, 6 p. m., one of Chen's commanders today applied for visit [visa?] for travel to the United States after lengthy European visit.

6. Canton appears back to normal conditions. Local currency has appreciated to 172 to the Hong Kong dollar.

7. Sent to the Department, Peiping, Nanking, Hankow and Shanghai.

SPIKER

793.94/7988 : Telegram

The Ambassador in China (Johnson) to the Secretary of State

PEIPING, June 20, 1936—3 p. m.
[Received 4:15 p. m.]

313. Embassy's 301, June 12, 3 p. m.

1. Presumably important meetings of Japanese officials began June 18 at Tientsin. They are understood to include Lieutenant General Tashiro, Major Generals Kawabe and Matsumuro, and officers of the staff of the North China Garrison, as well as resident officers of Taiyuan, Kweihwa, and Tsinanfu and the Vice Chief and a section chief of the Kwantung army staff. The Chief of the Kwantung

army staff is reputedly to arrive at Tientsin within a day or two. (Kuwashima of the Foreign Office allegedly informed the Chinese press at Peiping June 14 that "as the War Ministry knows the (North China) situation better than the other Ministry all problems in the area are being handled by the War Office.")

2. Presumably these meetings are to decide policy with regard to Sung Che Yuan's regime. There are persistent reports that General Sung's attitude toward the Japanese has stiffened since the conferences of the latter part of May with his subordinates (reference Embassy's telegram 275, June 2, 4 p. m.[33] and 282, June 4, 3 p. m.) when his military subordinates (1) persuaded him to reverse his decision to declare independence in accordance with Japanese desires and (2) insisted that Hsiao Chen Ying should not resign the mayorship of Tientsin under Japanese pressure.

3. An indication of this new attitude is Sung's appointment of General Chang Tzu Chung, his senior divisional commander and prievously Chairman of Chahar, to succeed Hsiao as Mayor of Tientsin. Crang's appointment was urged by Sung's military subordinates and was definitely not desired by the Japanese military. Sung was allegedly lead to believe that if he appointed the Japanese favorite, Chi Hsieh Yuan (reference paragraph 9 Embassy's 301, June 12, 3 p.m.), his regime would soon come to an end as Chi would do Japanese bidding more readily than Hsiao Chen Ying had done which would mean that Tientsin, the most important port of Sung's area, would be lost to him.

4. The Japanese military have reputedly yielded on the question of Chang's appointment (Chang assumed office June 18) because (1) Chang's powers as mayor are to be less than were Hsiao['s], (2) Chang is simpler minded than Hsiao and can be handled easily, and (3) the Japanese military are apprehensive that some of Sung's subordinates might otherwise cause trouble which the Japanese wish to avoid.

5. The question of what the Japanese military may decide at these meetings and what will be the form of their subsequent negotiations with Sung, who is now in Tientsin, cannot be answered at present.

6. Rumors of possible cooperation of Han Fu Chu with Sung, either for or against the Japanese, are prevalent. Kuwashima of the dissolution [Foreign Office?] visited Han June 18 and the press reports that Sung will meet Han shortly at Sung's birthplace in Shantung.

7. Although it is evident that Sung is in communication with the Southwest, his intentions in that regard are not known.

By mail to Tokyo.

JOHNSON

---

[33] Not printed.

793.94/7994: Telegram (part air)

The Consul at Geneva (Gilbert) to the Secretary of State

GENEVA, June 22, 1936—noon.
[Received June 23—9 a. m.]

238. With Paris' 489, June 12, 10 a. m., in mind I asked Hoo [34] if China was considering any pertinent action before the League. His reply was in the negative. He stated that Chinese action in Geneva at any time must be predicated on prior assurances of support from the powers and of this there were no evidences. He said that Koo would head the Chinese delegation at the June 30th Assembly and that naturally China's situation would be discussed with representatives of interested powers as occasion suggested. He felt reasonably certain, however, that Koo had no specific instructions . . . [35]

GILBERT

893.00/13563: Telegram

The Consul General at Canton (Spiker) to the Secretary of State

CANTON, June 22, 1936—4 p. m.
[Received June 22—11 a. m.]

Referring to my telegram of June 20, noon,[36] local government controlled press today published message addressed by Marshals Chen, Li and Pai to the "soldiers of the nation" calling upon them to rise and support the war against Japan. In view of the reported strict censorship engaged in by Nanking, it would appear improbable that this message will travel much further than the provincial boundary Kwangtung and Kwangsi. The same press contains a telegram allegedly addressed by the veteran Hsiao Fo Cheng to overseas Chinese stating that the Southwest Political Council deems it futile to call a further conference to deliberate on the issue but deems it imperative that Nanking should act immediately by leading armed resistance against Japan.

2. I am informed by usually reliable official source that all Kwangtung forces have returned to Kwangtung and that main body of Kwangsi troops have withdrawn to Chuanchow, Kwangsi, but that smaller body continues to occupy strategic defensive position at Yungchow, Hunan. Informant alleges that report of recent conference at Hengchow between representatives of Nanking and the Southwest is absolutely unfounded and that Li's appointment of Pai to full con-

---

[34] Victor Chitsai Hoo, Chinese Minister in Switzerland.
[35] The Consul at Geneva in his telegram No. 282, July 3, 4 p. m. reported meeting "Koo today who in what he had to say confirmed my 238". (793.94/8030)
[36] Not printed.

trol of Kwangsi forces was purely routine matter confirming Pai's field command of expedition into Hunan and has no special significance as believed in some quarters.

3. Sent to the Department, Peiping, Nanking, Hankow and Shanghai.

SPIKER

761.9411/40 : Telegram

The Ambassador in Japan (Grew) to the Secretary of State

TOKYO, June 22, 1936—6 p. m.
[Received June 22—9 : 20 a. m.]

133.   1. It is possible that the American press may report a news despatch appearing in the Japanese press today to the effect that the Soviet Ambassador again recently proposed to Premier Hirota the conclusion of a Russo-Japanese non-aggression pact which was again refused by Hirota. The facts as ascertained by the Embassy from the Soviet Embassy today are as follows:

2. Yureneff who had obtained leave of absence but whose leave has since been postponed called on the Premier at the latter's request on June 10 to say farewell. In the course of a general discussion of Russo-Japanese affairs the Premier brought up the question of the large number of Soviet troops stationed on or near the Soviet-Manchukuo-Korean borders. Yureneff stated that a political rather than a military solution might be found for this question and recalled the fact that the Soviet Union in 1931 had proposed a non-aggression pact. The Premier shrugged the suggestion aside with the statement "we shall find some other way".

3. The Counsellor of the Soviet Embassy stated that the Soviet Union will not remove its troops from the border unless a non-aggression pact is concluded; it will in such case move the troops further from the border but will not demolish the border fortifications.

4. It is not clear why the Japanese press gives publicity to this conversation today 12 days after it was held.

GREW

893.00/13568 : Telegram

The Consul General at Canton (Spiker) to the Secretary of State

CANTON, June 23, 1936—noon.
[Received 12 : 20 p. m.]

Referring to my telegram of June 22, 4 p. m., am reliably informed by official that at joint meeting of Southwest Political Council and Kuomintang Central Executive Committee yesterday it was decided to demand satisfactory assurances from Nanking in relation to the following points as prerequisite to Southwest's participation in plenary session at Nanking in July: (1) severance of diplomatic relations with Japan; (2) declaration that all Sino-Japanese secret treaties including Tangku truce are null and void; (3) armed resistance to increase of Japanese troops in North China in violation of Boxer Protocol; (4) mobilization of strength of entire country in readiness for resistance to Japan; and (5) cancellation of all orders of the National Government suppressing freedom of speech, of assembly and of the right to form patriotic associations.

2. Informant states that such demands are expected to make the situation much more tense and serious than heretofore since if Nanking accepts it means hostilities with Japan while if Nanking declines its insincerity is established and the Southwest will probably take independent action, the nature of which has not yet been decided but which may be expected to mark a sharp break in relations of the Southwest leaders with the Japanese. Informant is closely connected with Southwest leaders and his views are colored accordingly although hitherto his information has proved generally reliable.

3. Local government-controlled press today publishes text of a further telegram allegedly sent on June 21st to Chiang Kai Shek by Marshals Chen and Li both of whom are becoming increasingly articulate against Chiang. Telegram taunts Nanking leaders with being brave toward their brethren and cowards toward the foreign foe, urges action without delay against the Japanese and promises that Kwangtung and Kwangsi leaders will follow Chiang "through fire and water, will go at his order to any theatre of war". Chen's sudden activity in issuing personal statements to local press after long period of silence is causing comment but is believed possibly indicative of no more than pressure to support secret bargaining with Nanking.

4. Kwangsi military headquarters which for weeks has repeatedly and most emphatically denied that Japanese advisers were employed by Kwangsi yesterday informed American press correspondent that all Japanese advisers left Kwangsi several days ago and that Kwangsi defied anybody to find a single Japanese adviser in that province. Reliable mail information from Kweilin under date of June 15th showed that city was held by militia only, that all troops had gone to the North, that wholesale conscription was proceeding and that students were very active spreading anti-Japanese propaganda throughout the area.

5. Sent to the Department, Peiping, Nanking, Hankow, Shanghai.

SPIKER

793.94/7996 : Telegram

The Counselor of Embassy in China (Peck) to the Secretary of State

NANKING, June 24, 1936—8 a. m.
[Received June 24—7 a. m.]

198. 1. Foreign Office has issued a denial of Japanese press reports that Suma gave Chinese Minister of Foreign Affairs on June 19th a "stern warning" against the "continuation of malicious propaganda" against Japan.

2. To Department, by mail to Peiping and Tokyo.

PECK

___

793.94/7995 : Telegram

The Ambassador in Japan (Grew) to the Secretary of State

TOKYO, June 24, 1936—6 p. m.
[Received June 24—9 : 25 a. m.]

139. Embassy's 111, May 23, 11 a. m. The Military Attaché was informed today in conversation at the War Department that the movement of troops for the reenforcement of the North China Garrison has been completed and that the garrison now has a strength of slightly under 5,000 men of all branches of the army.

Repeated to Peiping.

GREW

___

893.00/13573 : Telegram

The Counselor of Embassy in China (Peck) to the Secretary of State

NANKING, June 25, 1936—noon.
[Received 5 : 20 p. m.]

203. 1. The Second Secretary was informed this morning by a responsible official of the Foreign Office that the Government's spirit of optimism in respect to the Southwestern situation has changed to one of considerable pessimism, due partly to the assumption by Chen Chi Tang on June 23 of the office of "Commander-in-Chief of the First Group Army of the Anti-Japanese National Salvation Forces" (see Canton's June 24, 9 p. m.[37]) and partly because of difficulties encountered in negotiations with Kwangsi. Another official of the Foreign Office told the Secretary that the Government's attempt to cause a split between Chen and the Kwangsi leaders which had been meeting success as evidenced by the adoption by Kwangtung of legal tender notes (see Canton's June 20, noon, and paragraph 2 of our 193, June 19, noon[38]) has now apparently failed and General Chiang,

___

[37] Not printed.
[38] Neither printed.

who has been planning to attack Kwangsi, has therefore deemed it advisable to alter his plan and is attempting to avert a clash and look for a solution of the crisis in the forthcoming plenary session. The first mentioned informant confirmed reports (see paragraph 4 of our 200, June 24, 1 p. m.[39]) that Kwangsi troops are between Kiyang and Hengyang and between Kwangsi and Paolang Shaoyang). He added his denial to previous official denials of Domei reports of June 21 and 22 of an exchange of ultimatums between Chiang and the Southwestern leaders (see paragraph 1 of our 200, June 24, 1 p. m.) and when the Secretary mentioned hearing a report that the Government controlled press in Canton had published the text of a telegram allegedly sent by Chen and Li to Chiang along the lines of the Domei report (see paragraph 3 of Canton's June 23, noon), he stated that he had access to all the telegrams exchanged and no such message had been received. He added that by means of anti-Japanese propaganda the Southwesterners were creating a Frankenstein's monster because the students and the people in the Southwest took this propaganda seriously and he wondered how they would be able to retreat from their position if and when a settlement with the National Government should be arranged.

2. According to the second mentioned informant, the Kwangsi leaders have now let their requirements for a settlement be known in general and of primary importance among them are (1) subsidies to meet the military and civil government expenses of the provinces and (2) the replacement of officials of the neighboring provinces with officials friendly to Kwangsi.

3. The Government appears to be undertaking a definite campaign in the press to place the Kwangsi leaders in an unpopular position both with a view to assisting its present negotiations and to strengthening itself politically if hostilities occur. The semiofficial Central News Agency reports that an association professedly "representing the vote of 30 million Kwangtungese" yesterday telegraphed to the Central Party Headquarters, the National Government and the Military Affairs Commission a demand for drastic action against the "rebellious Kwangtung and Kwangsi generals". The *Central Daily News*, official organ of the Kuomintang, editorially asked the Government to clarify the situation created by the Liang-Kwang,[40] which it described as tantamount to rebellion, and urged the Government to take punitive action against the Southwestern leaders.

The Secretary was informed by a source close to high military officials that all of the Canton officers attending the Army War College

---

[39] Not printed.
[40] The two Kwang provinces (Kwangtung, Kwangsi).

of Nanking have within the last few days returned to Canton. These officers are of the grade of colonel or higher.

5. To the Department and Peiping. Repeated to Canton, Hankow.

PECK

711.94/1115

Memorandum by the Chief of the Division of Far Eastern Affairs (Hornbeck)

[WASHINGTON,] June 25, 1936.

In Tokyo's despatch No. 1798, April 30, 1936, Ambassador Grew reported as follows:

"On April 30, 1936, Mr. Shigeru Yoshida, recently appointed Japanese Ambassador to Great Britain, called and stated, in the course of our conversation, that the population problem in Japan was becoming increasingly difficult and that foreign countries should realize the seriousness of the situation and endeavor to help Japan in finding an adequate outlet. He said that it was principally a matter of finding outlets for Japan's trade, with opportunity for Japanese subjects to follow that trade. Upon being asked, he said that it meant peaceful penetration. Again upon being asked, he said that he thought that the 'blue-water school' (i. e., the school advocating expansion to the south) would win out eventually over the 'continental school'."

Under date May 20, 1936, Mr. Grew states in his diary that on that day Mr. Yoshida called on him and a conversation was held which covered approximately an hour. In the course of this, Yoshida stated that he was expounding a personal point of view: he said that it was necessary to solve Japan's problem of overpopulation, necessary to find some outlet, as well as important to acquire increased opportunities for obtaining raw materials and especially oil. Grew asked how Japan expected to acquire those things if they already belonged to other nations. Yoshida said he hoped that new sources of raw materials and oil could be exploited and possible contacts be made with countries which already possessed such sources. He said that Japan's thought was only one of peaceful penetration and that in developing this peaceful penetration he hoped that the United States might lend its cooperation and play the part of "honest broker". He said that the talk of war with Soviet Russia or with the United States or with Great Britain was utterly foolish and that Japan's aims and efforts were purely pacific. He wished that Japan and the United States together might solve the whole problem of permanent peace in the Pacific area.

Under date June 12, 1936, the Secretary of State made a memorandum of the conversation held between him and Mr. Yoshida on that day.[41] Yoshida said that he was very desirous of promoting better

---

[41] *Foreign Relations, Japan, 1931–1941*, vol. I, p. 241.

relations and better understanding between his country and the United States. He said that the one big fact which he wanted the American people to recognize was the immense and rapidly growing population of Japan and the absolute necessity for more territory for their existence in anything like a satisfactory way. He referred to the fact that there was misunderstanding and misapprehension on the part of our people in this respect as it related to Japanese movements in and about China; that this also was probably true as to the British; that the Japanese armaments were not intended for war against any particular country, especially us, but that Japanese naval officials were always undertaking to create additional vacancies and additional room for promotion, etc., etc. He expressed an earnest desire for conference, collaboration and, without alliances, such relationships as would work out any questions arising in an amicable and fairly satisfactory way. He expressed his purpose to have a number of conversations with Ambassador Bingham, as well as with the British officials, on these subjects, with the view to the former conversations getting back to the Secretary. . . .[42] He stated that he would like for the Secretary to remember the difficulties of the businessmen and traders of Japan and the necessity for outside trade.

On June 16, 1936, Mr. Yoshida called on Mr. Norman Davis. According to Mr. Davis' record, in a letter of June 17,[43] Yoshida said that he felt he could talk with Mr. Davis with entire frankness. He had endeavored to explain to the Secretary of State the problem confronting Japan of keeping its growing population employed, but he had not entered into details. The Japanese people do not want to leave home and the most practical solution would be to keep them employed at home by expanding their trade abroad. The wiser element in the Army realize that the Army has gone too far. They realize that they have created an impossible situation and are calling upon the diplomats for help. The Army has been surprised to find out how well Russia is prepared. They may need to take a new tack. Japan needs to see to it that no other country join with Russia and, if possible, to get an alignment with some other power. He had conferred with Army leaders in Tokyo and these leaders feel that in regard to China they should cultivate the friendship and cooperation of Great Britain and the United States. In fact, they want to cultivate friendship with Nanking also. He knew that Great Britain would not make any agreement with Japan without the approval of the United States, but his idea was first to approach the British with a view to ascertaining whether they have any definite opinion as to the best way to deal with the China situation. Then,

---

[42] Omission indicated in the original.
[43] Not printed.

if it is found possible to reach a tentative meeting of minds conditional upon American approval and cooperation, he would visit Washington on his way back to Tokyo. He is convinced that the United States holds the key to the whole situation. The liberal elements in Japan have been strengthened and the Army leaders are becoming more moderate in their views: the wiser ones are getting the upper hand over the wild younger officers. The wiser naval officers realize that they made a mistake in leaving the Naval Conference without an agreement; but they are not as yet speaking out and he did not know whether opinion would change sufficiently during the next few months to make the Government feel justified in signing the Naval Treaty. There could be no ultimate solution to the naval question nor to any of the difficult problems in the Far East without a political foundation. It is essential to establish such a foundation.

Comment:

There are two points which, on a basis of these records of conversation, Yoshida appears to reiterate: first, that Japan must expand; second, that the United States or the United States and Great Britain should cooperate with Japan. It happens that a year and a half ago, in the course of an after-dinner conversation at the residence of Mr. William Castle,[44] Yoshida laid emphasis upon the idea that the United States, Great Britain and Japan should cooperate in regard to China. With that fact in mind, scrutiny of the present record gives an impression that Yoshida entertains a hope of bringing about some kind of a tentative agreement with the British authorities in London for British-Japanese cooperation, perhaps conditional upon its proving possible to bring the United States into the arrangement, after which the proposal would be brought here for the American Government's consideration.

It would be interesting to know just what Yoshida said to Colonel House [45] that was in Colonel House's opinion so extraordinarily important. However, without that information, what we have here suffices to indicate that Yoshida is working toward the objective of bringing about some kind of a Japanese-British-American *rapprochement*. As a matter of tactics, he advances the thesis that Japan "must expand", and he suggests that we and the British assist toward rather than place obstacles in the way of that solution of the problem of Japan's needs. Also, he affirms that liberal influence in Japan is increasing in strength and that moderate views among the "wiser officers" in the Army are increasing in effectiveness. He intimates that moderate views in the Navy may in the course of some

---

[44] Under Secretary of State, 1931–33.
[45] Edward M. House, member of the American delegation to the Paris Peace Conference of 1919.

months become effective. In these tactics we find a repetition of the method and the affirmations with which we have become familiar on the part of Japanese diplomats.

In the light of what has been reported with regard to the Leith-Ross conversations in Japan and of the text of Leith-Ross' statement issued this week in Shanghai; and of a newspaper report of some weeks ago that Yoshida was going to make certain proposals to the British Government, it is reasonable for us to suppose that efforts are being made and will be made by some Japanese and some British representatives—with or without the definite approval and authorization of the respective foreign offices—to work up some form of a Japanese-British understanding elaborated with an eye to its being potentially attractive to the United States, the objective envisaged being that of a Japanese-British-American cooperative entente with regard to policy in the Far East (or perhaps even policy in general).

It does not appear, however, that Ambassador Yoshida has disclosed to any of his American collocutors what any of the particular principles or provisions or specifications of such an understanding should be or what plan of action or of operation he has in mind.[46]

S[TANLEY] K. H[ORNBECK]

793.94/8070

The Ambassador in China (Johnson) to the Secretary of State

No. 546   PEIPING, June 25, 1936.
                                                    [Received July 28.]

SIR: I have the honor to enclose a copy of a report [47] written by the Military Attaché, Colonel Joseph W. Stilwell, with regard to Chinese military preparations along the so-called Lung-hai line.

Colonel Stilwell, who recently traveled along this line from Chengchow, the intersection of the Lung-hai Railway and the Ping-han Railway, to the coast, states that there is no evidence of military activity of any kind, that conditions seem to indicate either that the Chinese have made elaborate preparations and concealed them more skilfully than any other military power has yet learned to do or that they have made none at all, that, if no preparation has been made, General Chiang Kai-shek either has no intention of waging war against the Japanese or believes he can wage war without preparations, and that the office of the Military Attaché believes that General Chiang has

---

[46] The Assistant Chief of the Division of Far Eastern Affairs, Hamilton, on June 26 made the following notation: "Very good. Also, no matter how sincere Yoshida may be, will not his efforts in London serve, as did Matsudaira's, to attract the attention and support of some of the British and thus to throw a partial smoke-screen around Japan's continued aggression in China?"

[47] Not printed.

no intention whatever at present of opposing the Japanese along the so-called Lung-hai line.

Respectfully yours,

For the Ambassador:

GEORGE R. MERRELL, JR.

First Secretary of Embassy

893.00/13577 : Telegram

The Ambassador in China (Johnson) to the Secretary of State

NANKING, June 27, 1936—noon.
[Received June 27—10:45 a.m.]

207. 1. On June 25 General Chiang Kai Shek issued a press statement regarding the controversy with the Southwest, the salient features of which were the expressed willingness of the National Government to assist various provincial authorities in matters of administration and finance provided discipline and order are maintained. General Chiang in effect promised that if Kwangtung and Kwangsi leaders withdrew their troops into the respective provinces he would not prosecute them for what has occurred, nor order troops from other provinces into the two provinces named. He also reaffirmed his determination not to be a candidate for the office of President as established in the forthcoming constitution.

2. I have questioned members of the Cabinet regarding the Southwestern situation. The Minister for Foreign Affairs this morning analyzed the situation in brief as follows: the death of Hu Han Min deprived the Southwestern regime of its principal political prop and the present military venture is an attempt, through a specious appeal to a popular cause, to maintain the temper of the Southwestern Central Executive Committee and Central Political Council. Another object has been to remedy the desperate financial situation of the two provinces. The Minister for Foreign Affairs referred to General Chiang's statement of June 25, and stated that the National Government is willing to discuss and compromise with the Southwest in matters of political administration and finance but insists that military insubordination as represented by the invasion of other provinces by Kwangtung and Kwangsi forces must be terminated first. He said that if the Southwestern provinces withdrew their forces and consented to discuss all contentious points at the meeting of the Central Executive Committee on July 10, this whole incident would probably be solved without long delay but he could not prophesy what course events would take if the Southwest leaders refused to recall their forces and he seemed despondent over the outlook.

3. By mail to Peking.

JOHNSON

793.94/8008 : Telegram

The First Secretary of Embassy in China (Merrell) to the Secretary of State

PEIPING, June 27, 1936—4 p.m.
[Received 5 : 32 p.m.]

329. Embassy's 313, June 20, 3 p. m.

1. Major General Matsumuro has stated in private conversation that the conference of Japanese officers at Tientsin decided that the Kwantung army will confine its action to affairs north of the Great Wall and that the North China Garrison will direct affairs south of the Wall. The same statement was recently made to the press by a Japanese military spokesman. There is reason to believe, however, that the Kwantung army regards the policy of the North China Garrison as on trial and that the permanency of the improvement in the spheres of control dated [*depends?*] upon the success of the policy of the North China Garrison.

2. The policy of the North China Garrison is not clearly known except that the Japanese military are determined to extend their control over North China. One well-informed Chinese source states that Sung is being pressed for a declaration of neutrality, that he will, in that event, be given control of Yin Ju Keng's area, and that the Japanese military hope Shantung will join the new regime quickly and Shansi and Suiyuan subsequently. Major General Matsumuro, however, has recently stated in conversation that he is deeply dissatisfied with Sung and would like to see his regime replaced by an intelligent civilian regime. The creation of an intelligent civilian regime appears to be impossible, while the [removal?] of Sung could probably be accomplished only by the creation of disorders and would probably be accompanied by further disorders. The Japanese military seem to be in something of a quandary, especially as they maintain that they do not wish to use military force.

3. Decision of Sung Che Yuan for or against further yielding to Japanese wishes seems to depend on the outcome of relations between the National Government and the Southwest. A military conflict in the South, which observers here regard now as probably unavoidable, will (if it is not a quick success for Chiang Kai Shek) greatly weaken Sung vis-à-vis the Japanese.

4. Delegates from the Southwest are allegedly urging Northern leaders to take simultaneous military action against Chiang. Sung conferred with Han Fu Chu on June 20. It is now anticipated that, in case of conflict in the South, Sung and Han will declare neutrality. Yen Hsi Shan is said to have refused to participate with Sung and Han.

By mail to Tokyo.

MERRELL

793.94/8009 : Telegram

The Ambassador in China (Johnson) to the Secretary of State

NANKING, June 29, 1936—11 a. m.
[Received June 29—10 : 30 a. m.]

209. 1. An officer of the Embassy was informed this morning by a responsible official of the Foreign Office that the North China situation is now causing the Chinese Government much greater concern than is the crisis with the Southwest. He said that if Sung Che Yuan should yield a little longer to the Japanese military, serious developments might be avoided. He did not know what influence in this respect might be exerted upon Sung by the new Tientsin Mayor, Chang Tzu Chung, whom he described as a stronger, more stubborn and more anti-Japanese officer than Sung. He said the Japanese had opposed Chang's appointment but had not made an issue of it although they had wanted Chi Hsieh Yuan given the office and they were now working to eliminate Sung's 29th army (formerly Feng Yu Hsiang's Kuo-minchun) from Hopei. If Sung (and Chang) should not yield in this, it was feared that the Japanese would use force to accomplish their desires. In any event he saw another major crisis looming in the North.

2. Appointments of Chang as Mayor of Tientsin and of Major General Liu Ju Ming as Chairman of Chahar, previously made by the Hopei-Chahar Council, were formally mandated by the National Government June 26.

3. Kawagoe is scheduled to leave Shanghai for Nanking tomorrow by Japanese naval vessel. He will present his credentials as Ambassador July 3. The Foreign Minister expects him to take up the customs incidents as his first important matter of business but Suma, First Secretary of the Japanese Embassy, informed me this morning that he is directing the Japanese Consul General at Tientsin, who is now in Shanghai conferring with his Ambassador-designate and is expected to visit Nanking, to settle the matter locally.

4. To the Department and Peiping. By mail to Tokyo and Shanghai.

JOHNSON

893.00/13578 : Telegram

The Consul General at Canton (Spiker) to the Secretary of State

CANTON, June 29, 1936—4 p. m.
[Received June 29—11 : 20 a. m.]

Referring to my telegram of June 27, 11 a. m.,[48] local government controlled press today publishes text of telegram allegedly addressed

---

[48] Not printed.

to Nanking on June 25th by the Southwest Central Executive Committee. Telegram presents five points mentioned in my telegram June 23, noon, and addressed them as "the irreducible minimum to form agenda of the Central Executive Committee at Nanking and, upon passage, to be put immediately into effect". Telegram concluded by urging that five points be referred to the Standing Committee, that all red tape and formality be dispensed with by that Committee in placing the agenda before the Central Executive Committee, and that under no circumstances should the Southwest's proposal be allowed to fall into the hands of the Secretariat of the Central Executive Committee.

2. The same press publishes an open letter to the public from Marshals Chen and Li excoriating the Japanese and the attitude of the Nanking leaders. The marshals state that "slander has been our reward for patriotism" and they urge that the country appoint an investigation committee to examine into the matter.

3. Veteran Hsiao Fo Cheng in statement issued by local government press agency accuses Chiang of sophistry in his recent statement to the press at Nanking (published in Hong Kong June 26th) and concludes by ridiculing Chiang's alleged announcement that he will not become a candidate for the Presidency of China. Hsiao suggests that the People's Convention is still far distant and that Chiang is presumptuous and highly premature in assuming that he is desired for the office. It is generally believed that military are compelling Hsiao to act as organization's civilian mouthpiece and that he and many other individuals and organizations are being ordered to sign a seemingly unending series of proclamations et cetera prepared by the military.

4. Another informant just arrived from Kwangsi confirms previous reports of heavy troop movements northward. Informant reports tremendous increasing feeling in Kwangsi against Pai because of currency situation and conviction that Pai's challenge to Nanking is suicide. American missionaries at Kweilin, Kwangsi, have telegraphed that they left that city yesterday en route to Canton. Previous letters stated they would evacuate in the event of threatening developments in Kweilin area where there had been persistent but unconfirmed reports of fighting to the north.

5. Reliable information from northwest Kwangtung reports movement of approximately 30,000 Kwangtung troops into Lokchang and Namyung area in northern Kwangtung between June 10th and 20th but none since latter date.

6. At 3 a. m. yesterday sandbag barricades were placed on road in Canton suburb where Marshals Chen, Li, the Provincial Chairman and other high officials reside. Following foreign inquiry as to significance of barricades they were hastily removed with statement that construction was merely practice measure. Authorities apparently

taking special precautions but have not declared martial law.   Canton outwardly quiet though there is apprehension that there may be serious developments about July 10th and persistent rumors that Yu Han Mou will take over local control from Chen.

7. Reuter's Canton correspondent today reports representative as stating that Kwangtung and Kwangsi will send seven delegates to Shanghai July 8th prepared to attend plenary session July 10th if Nanking gives satisfactory assurances of adoption of the five points mentioned in paragraph 1 of this telegram.   Local official has just denied truth of Reuter report and alleges that the two provinces will send two special representatives direct to Nanking to negotiate.

8. Sent to the Department, Peiping, Nanking, Hankow and Shanghai.

SPIKER

793.94/8093

Memorandum by the Ambassador in China (Johnson) of a Conversation With the First Secretary of the Japanese Embassy in China (Suma)[49]

NANKING, June 29, 1936.

In the course of conversation today Mr. Suma stated that the situation in North China was very serious from the point of view of the Japanese.   He felt that the political situation there was particularly uncertain.   He referred to the seizure of two Japanese vessels by the Chinese Customs authorities at Tsingtao and Tientsin.   Mr. Suma stated that the Japanese Consul General at Tientsin was due here in Nanking today or tomorrow to discuss these questions.   He said that acting under instructions from his own Government he had protested to the Nanking authorities in this matter but that it was very difficult to handle such matters here in Nanking and he was therefore going to urge the Japanese Consul General at Tientsin to effect a settlement of these matters locally, but he expressed himself as convinced that conditions in North China were not at all promising.

Mr. Suma went on to state that upon his return to Nanking, after his recent visit in Japan, he regretted to find that conditions here were not changed for the better.   He said that his own Government was determined to find some agreement of a basic character which would permit Japan and China to carry on pacifically but that the Chinese were still talking platitudes, giving them kind words and doing nothing of a concrete nature to help to improve the situation.   Mr. Suma said that the promises of the Chinese meant nothing.   He re-

---

[49] Copy transmitted to the Department by the Ambassador in China in his despatch No. 575, July 13; received August 10.

ferred to the fact that the Chinese were making an "armed camp" of Nanking against Japan; that it was now impossible to walk on the hills around Nanking as they were putting up anti-aircraft guns here, there and everywhere, against Japan; all of which made the situation very difficult and very alarming.

He referred to the situation in Southwestern China and said that the Japanese Consul General at Canton had made two protests to the authorities at Canton against the anti-Japanese demonstrations and activities there, only to be told by General Chen Chi-tang that they could not control the honest feelings of the people. Mr. Suma expressed the feeling that such reactions could only portend difficulties in the future.

I gathered generally that Mr. Suma felt very pessimistic as to the future of Sino-Japanese relations.

NELSON TRUSLER JOHNSON

893.00/13584 : Telegram

The Consul General at Canton (Spiker) to the Secretary of State

CANTON, June 30, 1936—4 p. m.
[Received June 30—3:45 p. m.]

Referring to my telegram of June 29, 4 p. m., Marshal Li Tsung Jen yesterday took oath as Commander-in-Chief of the Fourth Group Army of the Anti-Japanese National Salvation Forces (see paragraph 2 of my telegram June 6, noon; and one paragraph of my telegram June 24, 9 p. m.,[50] concerning Chen's similar assumption of new title June 23rd). Following extracts from Li's speech of acceptance as published by local government news agency are in marked contrast with Chen's conciliatory advices that Nanking's leadership be accepted:

"My armed colleagues and I, having been intrusted with this important mission will make every endeavor to bring the Southwest's policy of resistance and salvation to fruition. At the same time we hope that the revolutionary masses of the country will come into line with us". "While we must do our utmost to resist Japanese, we must at the same time keep diligent vigil over Chinese traitors who are to be ruthlessly crushed. As with fighting the bandits, we must first list the internal traitors in order to strengthen both fronts". "I not only pay my very best regards to all revolutionary people and the soldiers of the whole country but also hereby declare that I am resolved to lead the entire Fourth Group Army to the front in our national and revolutionary campaign".

2. Local authorities continue to endeavor to suppress all discussion of local political situation, most casual remarks apparently being

[50] Latter not printed.

919456—54——21

sufficient cause for numerous arrests by plain-clothesmen who swarm in the city. Anti-Japanese propagandists are addressing street crowds but little interest shown, partly because of fear that plain clothes men using this device to trap listeners into making political comments. Unusually large number of Japanese alleged business men and sightseers have been arriving in Canton during the past week. Canton remains quiet.

3. Financial situation in Kwangsi reported serious, Kwangsi Provincial Bank, which has been designated sole medium for exchange transactions having closed its doors several days ago (see paragraph 3 of my telegram June 11, 1 p. m.[51]). Canton currency has remained fairly steady for past 5 days averaging 180 to the Hong Kong dollar. At least 2 million silver dollars of deposits, referred to in first sentence paragraph 3 of my telegram June 6, 4 p. m.,[52] have been withdrawn believedly for deposit with Government reserve of silver in Canton.

4. Sent to the Department, Peiping, Nanking, Hankow and Shanghai.

SPIKER

CHAPTER III: JULY 1–OCTOBER 15, 1936

Warning of gradual abolition of extraterritoriality in "Manchoukuo"; likelihood of Marshal Chang Hsueh-liang joining anti-Japanese movement; restoration of relations between Southwest China and Central Government at Nanking; fresh incidents menacing Chinese control of Suiyuan Province; anti-Japanese incidents at Chengtu, Pakhoi, Hankow, and Shanghai; deadlock in Japanese-Chinese conversations at Nanking for settlement of outstanding problems; British-American efforts toward moderating Japanese attitude in China; American reply to Belgian inquiry regarding extraterritorial situation in "Manchoukuo"; resumption of conversations at Nanking.

793.003 Manchuria/4 : Telegram

The First Secretary of Embassy in China (Merrell) to the Secretary of State

PEIPING, July 2, 1936—11 a. m.
[Received July 2—7 a. m.]

333. Following telegram has been received from the Consul General at Mukden:

"July 1, 6 p. m. Kokutsu published text of statement issued today in the name of the Minister for Foreign Affairs regarding the future status of extraterritorial nationals other than Japanese. The statement declares that whereas, in practice, Manchukuo has hitherto accorded as a favor to nationals of countries which enjoy extraterritorial rights in China similar treatment, it has been decided to abolish

---

[51] Not printed.
[52] Not found in Department files.

this treatment gradually. The statement concludes with the announcement that Manchukuo desires to reach agreements with interested governments regarding the future status of their nationals on the basis of justice, fairness and equality and that it is prepared to enter into negotiations to that end."

MERRELL

893.00/13636

The Ambassador in China (Johnson) to the Secretary of State

No. 552
PEIPING, July 3, 1936.
[Received July 28.]

SIR: I have the honor to refer to the Embassy's despatch No. 147 of January 3, 1936,[53] reviewing the political, military, economic, and financial developments in China during the last six months of 1935, and to submit a similar review of the first six months of the present year.

The significant developments during the period under review, most of which augmented the precariousness of China's situation, were as follows: (1) intensification of the resolve of Japanese military to extend Japanese economic, military, and perhaps political control in China; (2) elevation of the status and increase in the strength of the Japanese North China Garrison; (3) appointment of new personnel to the principal Japanese military and civilian posts in China; (4) the apparent elimination of the Kwantung Army from participation in affairs of North China; (5) growth of smuggling into North China by Japanese, which weakened China financially; (6) increasing autonomy of General Sung Che-yuan's regime in North China; (7) increasing divergence of views between General Sung's military and civilian subordinates; (8) preparation of Japanese-directed Mongols in Chahar to extend their control over Mongol areas in Suiyuan; (9) anti-Japanese demonstrations by students; (10) tendency of communist forces to assemble in west and northwest China; (11) the death of Mr. Hu Han-min, Southwestern political leader, on May 12; (12) the northward advance of troops of Kwangtung and Kwangsi; (13) partially effective efforts of the National Government to improve economic and financial conditions, including the reorganization of the Central Bank of China; (14) continuing efforts of General Chiang Kai-shek to become dictator over larger areas of China; (15) the extension of his authority into Shansi; (16) the Sino-American monetary understanding, announced May 18;[54] and (17) the departure of Sir Frederick Leith-Ross, British financial expert.

---

[53] *Foreign Relations*, 1935, vol. III, p. 502.
[54] See telegram No. 270, May 18, 4 p. m., from the Consul General at Shanghai, p. 481, and telegram No. 120, May 19, to the Ambassador in China, p. 482.

A. *The position of General Chiang Kai-shek:*

Although General Chiang Kai-shek gave up control of no province over which he had extended control, although he brought additionally the Province of Shansi within his sphere of power, and although his powers as dictator within his sphere increased, his position was more perilous at the end of the period under review than it had been at the beginning. In fact, practically all major developments of the six months were factors working for the disintegration of China, chief among which were those developments promoted by Japanese military and subversive movements of Chinese factional leaders.

B. *Policy of the Japanese:*

The Japanese military in China were comparatively inactive during the early months of 1936, apparently awaiting (1) clarification of the situation created in Tokyo by the assassinations of February 26; (2) the increase of the numerical strength of the North China Garrison, (3) the arrival (March 28) of Major General Takayoshi Matsumuro, successor to Lieutenant General Kenji Doihara as chief Japanese negotiator in North China, and (4) the arrival (May 19) of Lieutenant General Kanichiro Tashiro, the first Commander of the North China Garrison to be appointed by the Emperor. The effect of Lieutenant General Tashiro's appointment appeared to be the removal of the Kwantung Army from participation in affairs of North China and an increase of unity in policy and of determination on the part of Japanese military officers dealing with affairs in North China.

It was evident that the Japanese military were resolved (1) to extend their economic, military, and perhaps political control in China, (2) to cause General Chiang Kai-shek either to come to terms or to fall, and (3) to promote the break-up of China through separatist movements.

There was also evidence of increasing cooperation with the Japanese military on the part of Japanese civilian officials concerned with affairs in China, although there was some reason to believe that the civilians would emphasize particularly during the near future the question of Sino-Japanese economic cooperation.

C. *Smuggling: a new Japanese instrument of coercion:*

The probability of Japanese success in obtaining agreements desired by them was enhanced by the development and fostering of a new instrument of coercion; namely, the excessive smuggling of foreign products, for the most part Japanese, principally through Yin Ju-keng's autonomous area in northern Hopei (established through Japanese aid on November 25, 1935) and thence into other parts of China. As a result of Chinese inability to cope with the situation without Japanese cooperation, which the Japanese authorities obviously had no intention of giving, the revenues of China were seriously impaired. It was evident that Japanese military and civilian officers regarded this smuggling as a policy by means of which agreements could be accelerated with North China and, especially, with the National Government, the latter having come no closer to an understanding with the Japanese by the end of the period under review than it had been at the beginning.

D. Chinese military preparedness:

Meanwhile, the purpose of General Chiang Kai-shek's efforts to reach a state of military preparedness was undefined and observers were uncertain whether he intended to resist Japanese aggression at some time or whether he was preparing for action against disaffected Chinese factions.

E. Separatism in North China:

General Sung Che-yuan's regime in Hopei and Chahar, established December 18, 1935, progressed toward greater autonomy through such methods as gradually taking over control of financial, communication, construction, and cultural organs previously under the direction of the National Government. These acts were apparently in part the result of General Sung's desire to improve his own position and in part the result of Japanese urging. Meanwhile he was pressed by the Japanese military and by his own self-seeking civilian subordinates to enter into agreements with the Japanese which would further separate his area from the National Government, which would give to the Japanese greater political, military, and economic control of that area and render more probable the establishment of a North China regime of five provinces, and which would probably bring about the merging of Yin Ju-keng's autonomous area with that of General Sung. Concrete accomplishments by the Japanese during the period under review were apparently few. Submission to Japanese pressure by General Sung involved the possibility of military disorders on the part of at least some of his military subordinates opposed to the program of the Japanese and of some of General Sung's civilian subordinates. Retreat from Hopei seemed difficult as there was no suitable place in the rest of China for General Sung and his allegedly more than 80,000 troops. Armed resistance to the Japanese was regarded as likely to fail.

Meanwhile, preparations of Japanese-directed Mongols in nominal control of Chahar north of the Great Wall continued for the presumed purpose of gaining control of Mongol areas in Suiyuan and of creating a new Mongol puppet regime.

F. Disaffection in the Southwest:

The long-standing, mutual mistrust of General Chiang Kai-shek and the military leaders of the Southwest (Kwangsi and Kwangtung

Provinces) entered a highly critical phase in the latter part of May. The death of Mr. Hu Han-min on May 12 substantially weakened the peace policy allegedly supported by the Southwestern civilian politicians; and his will, which, according to some evidence, may have been forged by the Southwestern military leaders, gave those leaders a useful political weapon as it expressed strong opposition to General Chiang's policies. Motivated primarily by hatred of General Chiang and fear that General Chiang intended shortly to extend effective control over Kwangsi and Kwangtung and probably influenced in part by Japanese advisers and Japanese assistance, General Pai Ch'ung-hsi was chiefly responsible for the initiation of a northward movement of troops of the two provinces for the alleged purpose of fighting the Japanese but for the evident immediate purpose of overthrowing General Chiang Kai-shek. The forces of the Southwest and the forces of General Chiang had not yet begun at the end of June to fight. In case they were to fight, the question was not so much whether General Chiang could win as whether such a conflict would not result (1) in the breaking away of other parts of China where the leaders were dissatisfied with General Chiang and/or under Japanese pressure, (2) in the rallying of the forces of nationalism against General Chiang Kai-shek, (3) in the development of country-wide chaotic conditions, and (4) in the accelerating of the extension of Japanese control with the concomitant injury to Western interests in China. If a compromise were to be effected, it seemed probable that the general situation would not be materially altered.

G. Communist forces:

The principal communist forces in China were by the end of the period under review in the Provinces of Sikang, Ch'inghai, northern Shensi, southeastern Ningsia, and northeastern Kansu. Although communist forces did not form so immediate a threat to the National Government as at times in the past, it was evident that their activities in the west and northwest might, depending on political developments in the rest of China, hold considerable significance for Chinese domestic policy and for Sino-Japanese relations as well.

H. China's periphery:

While Japanese encroachment continued in the north, there was no known alteration in the tenuous relationship of the National Government with the western areas of Sinkiang Province and Tibet. Nor did the Sino-British Commission for the delimitation of the disputed Burma–Yunnan border reach any conclusion.

I. Finance and Economics:

The stabilization of Chinese currency and the strengthening of Government finance, which were the immediate achievements of the monetary decree of November 3, 1935, were continued during the period under review. A loan of $1,460,000,000 (Chinese currency), secured on the Maritime Customs, was issued in February to convert most of the existing domestic loan bonds, thereby greatly reducing the carrying charges on the Chinese national debt and enabling the National Government to effect a considerable saving. Also, a loan of $340,000,000 (Chinese currency), secured on the Maritime Customs, was approved at the same time primarily for the purpose of strengthening Government finance. Chinese credit and public confidence were further strengthened as the result of efforts to readjust and to meet outstanding loan obligations, the announcement on May 18 that the United States would begin regular purchases of substantial amounts of Chinese silver, and the reorganization in February of the Central Bank of China, which was one of the reforms proposed by Sir Frederick Leith-Ross.

Notwithstanding these developments, however, it seemed probable that any lasting betterment of the situation would depend on (1) the maintenance of civil peace, (2) the satisfactory regularization of Sino-Japanese relations, and (3) a more direct and extensive approach by the National Government to the outstanding economic problems of China. Meanwhile, purchasing power and revenue continued to decline, the adverse trade balance (with smuggled imports taken into consideration) remained dangerously high; the new draft budget was larger than the preceding budget and achieved a technical balance only by the inclusion of certain sums to be obtained by borrowing and from "miscellaneous" revenues; the National Government and provincial governments continued to borrow to meet current expenses; excessive taxation and political corruption showed no significant abatement; the agricultural situation showed no outstanding signs of betterment or of further deterioration; and China's import of food stuffs continued to account for an alarming proportion of total purchases made abroad. As usual, however, some progress continued to be made along lines of public health, development of communications, urban improvements, and education.

J. Sir Frederick Leith-Ross:

The significant visit of Sir Frederick Leith-Ross, British financial expert, who arrived in China September 21, 1935, ended with his departure June 23. Although the Chinese authorities were unable to carry out to the full extent his proposals for reforms, because of the political and financial organization of the country, and although he apparently failed to gain the approval of Japan of his proposals, his mission was successful insofar as it resulted in a partial rehabilitation of China's finances. Whether his mission to the Far East will ultimately prove to have a lasting and important effect in respect to the rehabilitation of financial and economic conditions is as yet a question which cannot be answered.

K. *Western nations:*

The relations of China with western nations did not alter materially during the period under review. Neither the visit of Sir Frederick Leith-Ross nor the decision of the United States to purchase Chinese silver appeared to effect any important alteration in the relations of China with the countries concerned. The agreement, however, concluded on March 12 between Soviet Russia and Outer Mongolia for mutual assistance, brought forth statements of dissatisfaction; and the conclusion on April 30 of a commercial arrangement between Germany and "Manchukuo" caused Chinese officials to express apprehension at the implications of that arrangement. Changes in China's relations with western nations appeared to depend upon future developments in China's internal situation and in Sino-Japanese relations.

Respectfully yours, For the Ambassador:
GEORGE R. MERRELL, JR.,
First Secretary of Embassy

793.94/8029 : Telegram

The Consul General at Canton (Spiker) to the Secretary of State

CANTON, July 4, 1936—4 p. m.
[Received July 4—1: 30 p. m.]

Have just been separately approached by local authorities and by the special delegate for Foreign Affairs with blustering effort to hold Dollar Steamship Company responsible for refusal to transport to Shanghai 300 so-called "representatives of various public organs to insist on immediate anti-Japanese military operations." Delegation scheduled to sail from Hong Kong tomorrow on the *President Jefferson* and consists of individuals hitherto unheard of, all of them travelling steerage. Delegation obviously one for demonstration purposes only. Local agent of Dollar Steamship Company informed me that Nanking Government informed American Consul General at Shanghai that members of delegation will not be permitted to land in Shanghai, that American Consul General so informed Dollar Steamship Company which instructed its Hong Kong office to inform delegation and refuse to sell tickets. This Consulate General has emphatically informed local authorities that the Dollar Steamship Company should be left out of the question which is obviously a political one for settlement between the Southwest and the Nanking Government, the American company being only a commercial firm bound by the well known laws governing steamship companies. Both officials finally admitted their appreciation of situation and desisted from efforts to blame American company. Authorities plan to buy through tickets to Kobe for this proclaimed arch anti-Japanese delegation in the belief that through passengers, delegates may be able to stop off in Shanghai and in any event will be quite free to land in Japan where they need no passports. Local Dollar agent who is proceeding at once to Hong Kong has given fullest details of my conversations with local authorities. Have given similar advice directly to the American Consul General at Hong Kong by telephone.

2. Very serious and increasingly chaotic conditions in Kwangsi is being reported in telegram to follow.

Sent to Shanghai and repeated to the Department, Peiping, Nanking and Hankow.

SPIKER

893.00/13597 : Telegram

The Ambassador in China (Johnson) to the Secretary of State

PEIPING, July 7, 1936—6 p. m.
[Received July 7—2:25 p. m.]

343. The following telegram has been received from the Consul at Tsinanfu.

"July 6, 5 p. m. I am confidentially informed by an unquestionably reliable source that Han Fu Chu [55] is sending an important representative by tonight's express to interview Chiang Kai Shek in Nanking before July 10th. The representative will take a letter and most urgent oral entreaty from Han begging Chiang to refrain from armed conflict with the Southwest at all costs no matter how great the provocation, and warning Chiang that Han has no other alternative than to resign if Chiang wastes the national strength in a civil war at this juncture when every bit of Chiang's strength and undivided attention is needed to provide the support requisite for Han to resist Japanese pressure to force Han to join Sung Che Yuan in the establishment of an independent organ for the preservation of peace and neutrality, to protect their respective territories and people. Han will resign rather than submit to the humiliations Sung has experienced."

JOHNSON

793.94/8046 : Telegram

The Ambassador in China (Johnson) to the Secretary of State

PEIPING, July 10, 1936—4 p. m.
[Received July 10—10:50 a. m.]

353. Embassy's 345, July 8, 2 p. m.[56]

1. Wang Keh Min arrived at Peiping July 9. He was formerly associated with Anfu clique, was Acting Chairman of the Peiping

---

[55] Chairman, Shantung Provincial Government.
[56] Not printed.

Political Affairs Readjustment Committee in 1935 after Huang Fu's [57] departure, and was appointed a member of the Hopei-Chahar Political Council at the time of its inauguration, although he has never entered into his duties in this position. He is to be appointed an economic and financial expert.

2. According to the Chinese press, he will be made Chairman of the Economic Committee of the Council in succession to Hsiao Chen Ying who still holds the post although he has been in retirement allegedly in the summer palace since early June.

3. An officer of the Japanese Embassy stated in conversation this morning that the National Government has been opposed to Wang's coming to Peiping but that General Sung and Major General Matsu-muro have been urging him to come; that it is anticipated that Wang may become the head of civil affairs in Hopei with Sung in charge only of military affairs; that the attitude of Sung's military subordi-nates with regard to this possibility is not yet clear; that it is hoped Wang's presence will accelerate Sino-Japanese economic cooperation in North China with regard to which the Japanese military are now most interested and the Japanese Ambassador most enthusiastic; and that the Japanese believe that if Wang is given a high post he will accomplish a great deal.

4. A Tokyo press report of July 9 states that the Foreign Office and the War Ministry have instructed Japanese consular and military authorities in North China to give absolute support to Wang and to request Sung Che Yuan and other leaders of Sung's army to give Wang absolute support.

5. The above-mentioned informant and another officer of the Jap-anese Embassy do not believe the report that Wang has come with a program approved by the National Government for Sino-Japanese cooperation in North China.

3. [6?] The same informant states that he cannot foretell whether Han Fu Chu will join Sung's regime but that he is confident Yen Hsi Shan will not become Chairman [sic] "the vague political and military influence which Chiang Kai Shek wishes in Shansi."

By mail to Tokyo.

JOHNSON

893.00/13666

The Consul General at Tientsin (Caldwell) to the Ambassador in China (Johnson) [58]

No. 262   TIENTSIN, July 10, 1936.

SIR: I have the honor to refer to this Consulate General's despatch No. 258, dated July 3, 1936,[59] concerning the reported arrangements

---

[57] Chinese Minister of Interior, 1934–35.
[58] Copy transmitted to the Department by the Consul General at Tientsin in his unnumbered despatch of July 10; received August 10.
[59] Not printed.

between General Han Fu-chu and Sung Che-yuan in anticipation of war between the Nanking Government and the Southwest, and in that connection to report that according to information which reached the Consulate General yesterday through a somewhat biased but well-informed source, General Chang Hsueh-liang [60] is preparing to adopt an independent course of action in case of civil war.

The source referred to confirms generally the Domei (Japanese) press despatch of June 30, 1936, which appeared in the *Peking & Tientsin Times* (British) of July 1, 1936, and according to which a conference of the old Northeastern generals at Sianfu presided over by General Chang had heard his report of the course of internal politics and had adopted a six-point program of which the most important items were the suspension of the Anti-Red campaign and the establishment of a "North Western Government".

The anti-communist campaign has definitely been brought to a stand-still, the informant asserts. He states that a verbal, or perhaps a written, truce agreement has been reached terminating actual fighting and permitting the conduct of ordinary commercial relations between the garrisoned areas and those under communist occupation.

General Chang and his subordinates are also veering toward a more definite anti-Japanese stand, according to the individual quoted.

This change of heart on General Chang's part the informant attributes to the General's known liberal tendencies—he is alleged, for instance, to be strongly in sympathy with the student movement—and to the fact that the establishment of Japanese hegemony in North China, and of an opium monopoly in the North paralleling the more rigorously enforced Nanking Government monopoly in the Yangtze, have left the Young Marshal in such straitened circumstances financially that he for some months past been drawing on his personal fortune to support his troops. To a divergence in temperament between Chang and Chiang and the economic motive there is added the consideration that if General Chiang in his present dilemma is forced into closer relations with Japan, General Chang's influence in the National Government must suffer an even more definite recession. Nor are his subordinates content with their present situations: the bitterness of the able and forth-right General Yu Hsueh-chung [61] over his present "exile" to Kansu, only a part of which is actually under his control, is said to be typical of their present temper.

The informant believes that in these circumstances General Chang is likely, in the event of a severe internal test of General Chiang Kai-

---

[60] Vice Commander in Chief of bandit suppression forces in the Northwest at Sian, Shensi; head of the Mukden regime from 1928 to 1931.
[61] Commanding bandit suppression forces in Szechwan and Kansu; formerly Chairman of the Hopei Provincial Government, and more recently of the Kansu Provincial Government.

shek's strength, to become more or less independent of, though not unfriendly to, the "Generalissimo".

Respectfully yours,   J. K. CALDWELL

_____

893.00/13604 : Telegram

The Counselor of Embassy in China (Peck) to the Secretary of State

NANKING, July 11, 1936—9 a.m.
[Received July 12—6 : 55 a.m.]

222. 1. The second plenary session Fifth Central Executive and Supervisory Committees held an opening and preparatory session yesterday morning. The first regular session is scheduled for this morning. Among the officials now here or en route to Nanking for the session are: Yu Han Mou, Commander of Chen Chi Tang's First Army; Chang Hsueh Liang; T. V. Soong; Shanghai Mayor Wu Teh Chen; Wang Chung Hui; the five Southwestern delegates named in Canton's July 7, 4 p. m.[62] who arrived yesterday; the Provincial Chairmen of Chekiang, Fukien, Anhwei, Kiangsi, Hunan, Hupei, Honan and 190 out of 255 regular and reserve members are expected to be in attendance. Tang Shao Yi [63] is also here, reportedly having left Canton to escape being unwillingly involved in the Southwestern revolt.

2. Yu Han Mou arrived by plane July 8 and is reported by Central News Agency as having informed press correspondents that hereafter Kwangtung would "adhere to the policy of the Central Government in all matters affecting the state". We are reliably informed that Yu's alignment with Nanking was arranged by General Tang Sheng Chih, Inspector General of military training, who made a secret visit to Hong Kong where he accomplished his mission (which may have included the deferring of the Cantonese) by a financial [arrangement?] involving needed diversions of several millions of dollars.

3. The situation in the Southwest seems to be changing so rapidly that it is difficult to forecast what may develop in the session. Unless the Southwestern rebels capitulate it is considered likely that the session will formulate some mildly worded resolution concerning the necessity of maintaining discipline in order to give Chiang, if need therefor should arise, a mandate under which to subdue them. The Government is frankly worried about Han Fu Chu and the possibility that Chang would cause him to join with Sung in forming a "neutral" regime in North China including Shantung. Feng Yu Hsiang [64] is

_____

[62] Not printed.
[63] Veteran member of the Kuomintang and first Prime Minister under the Republic in 1912.
[64] Vice Chairman of the Chinese National Military Affairs Commission.

understood to have whole-heartedly aligned himself with Han and it is reliably reported that Government agents discourage visits to Feng and intercept his correspondence. A Japanese inspired report that Chang Hsueh Liang and his commanders are thinking of setting up a Northwestern regime are discredited by reliable sources here and are believed to have arisen from a recent conference with Chiang Kai Shek and Feng Yo Hsiang during which Chang Hsueh Liang and Feng are reliably stated to have very strongly advised Chiang not to embark upon a punitive expedition against the Southwest because they considered that general public sentiment opposed such a course.

To the Department and Peiping; repeated to Canton, Hankow, by mail to Shanghai, Tsinanfu.

PECK

893.00/13603 : Telegram

The Consul General at Canton (Spiker) to the Secretary of State

CANTON, July 12, 1936—11 a.m.
[Received 8:35 p.m.]

Referring to my telegram of July 9, 4 p. m.[65] Marshals Chen, Pai and other leading military and civil members of Southwest Political Council yesterday addressed telegram to second plenary session at Nanking urging adoption of the five point program proposed by Southwest June 22. (See my telegram of June 23, noon, and June 29, 4 p. m.) Situation here remains quiet.

2. Sent to the Department, Peiping, Nanking, Shanghai and Hankow.

SPIKER

701.4193/72

Memorandum by the Counselor of Embassy in the United Kingdom (Atherton), Temporarily in Washington

[WASHINGTON,] July 13, 1936.

The day I left London (July 2) I had an after-lunch talk with Sir Alexander Cadogan, who, at the end of July, will become one of the two permanent Under Secretaries of State in the Foreign Office. (It will be recalled that Sir Alexander was recently recalled to the Foreign Office from his post as British Ambassador to China.) I told him that I had purposely asked him to lunch to discuss the Far East with him and that I felt that he would possibly be able to talk to me more freely as to his personal views before he assumed office rather

---

[65] Not printed.

than later and also that I was on the point of going home and I should be glad to have some idea of how he viewed the Far Eastern situation, particularly in view of the announcement made recently in the House of Commons that the British Embassy was to be removed from Peiping to Nanking.[66]

He said that he had no idea of the British policy in regard to the Far East; he could only tell me the general lines along which he intended to advise his Government; and asked me whether I had any views in the matter. I told him that I felt that the time was coming when western nations must, at least in their own council rooms, clarify their position. Were they prepared to continue a guard at Peiping and Tientsin and maintain all the adherence to the past that such decisions involved or with the removal of embassies from Peiping to Nanking should nations assume a new policy which dropped some of the pomp and circumstance of Peking in the old day? (I made these observations not so much with a view to expressing any definitive ideas but with a view to defining my own reflections and enlisting from Cadogan comments on these phases of the Far Eastern situation.) He told me that he felt that the removal of the British Embassy from Peiping to Nanking would not be effected for four or five years, since the work had not even been seriously undertaken, and that even later he should advise against the abolition of the Peiping Embassy and would favor maintaining it as a residence in north China for the British Ambassador. He said that he felt that outside nations must maintain and uphold their rights insofar as possible, conscious, however, that his country certainly felt, and he was inclined to believe that that sentiment was the same in the United States, that neither nation would fight in the Far East. He had replied to all British interests in China who had sought him out: "Give me a good clear-cut case in which British interests have been destroyed or even jeopardized by the Japanese or the Sino-Japanese influence in China" and he would be prepared to make a strong diplomatic case, but where only border-line questions were involved he thought that a rear guard action should be sought with such limitations as the situation and the nature of the issue necessitated. He was not in favor of attempting to cooperate with Japan for a profitable exploitation of China; neither was he in favor of an attempt to short-circuit Japan in China unless Japanese policy tread on British interests. If the Japanese were concentrating say on trying to persuade China to recognize "Manchukuo", that was an issue he did not feel that he was prepared to meet; it was one that must be left to the Chinese, with the realization that if China recognized "Manchukuo" possibly the Japanese position there would be entrenched by the recognition of "Manchukuo" by other

---

[66] See pp. 531 ff.

countries. He felt that there were economic considerations as well as military ones that would guide Japan in her policy in China, certainly if not at the moment as the months went by, and that it was on that line that one must envisage Japan's interests rather than a permanent occupation of China, which would economically be more of a liability than an asset.

I said to him that I felt that everything he said was very interesting and that of course there was one factor: both countries should realize that in the same way that nature abhorred a vacuum the Japanese would abhor an Anglo-American front against them and they would avoid any action, I thought, that would tend to unite us. I was particularly struck by the fact that Cadogan in no way attempted to inspire me with an idea that he or his Government favored a day-to-day Anglo-American front, which would merely possibly make the Japanese harder to work with.

With particular reference to the withdrawal of troops from China he said much as the British Army would welcome the additional battalions freed by the withdrawal of the Peiping and Tientsin guards he personally was not prepared to advocate such a course to his Government, certainly not at the present time and in the present circumstances.

R[AY] A[THERTON]

793.94/8048 : Telegram

The Ambassador in China (Johnson) to the Secretary of State

PEIPING, July 13, 1936—3 p. m.
[Received July 13—7 a. m.]

356. Reference Embassy's 353, July 10, 4 p. m.

1. Wang Keh Min told the local United Press correspondent July 11 (not for publication) that he came to Peiping at the behest of Chiang Kai Shek; that Sung Che Yuan had been inviting him for several months to come; that the Japanese had sent several representatives urging him to come; that the purpose of his visit had been (1) to ask the Japanese what they insist on with regard to North China and how far they intend to go in respect to economic development; and (2) to ask Sung what he wants and what he intends to do; that he (Wang) thinks the Japanese sincere and reasonable in regard to their aims with respect to economic development; that in his opinion cooperation on some lines is possible and on some lines is not; that he is also investigating the Hopei Provincial Bank; that, according to a statement of the manager of that bank, it has recently increased its note issue from 3 million to close to 100 million dollars with little reserve and without the sanction of the National Government; that he will return to Nanking and report to Chiang Kai Shek; and

that, if Nanking sees its way clear to fall in with the Japanese suggestions which he will take back, then he will return to Peiping to administer economic cooperation.

2. Wang left yesterday for Tientsin and is expected to leave Tientsin for Nanking today.

By mail to Tokyo.

JOHNSON

893.00/13617 : Telegram

The Consul General at Canton (Spiker) to the Secretary of State

CANTON, July 13, 1936—11 p. m.
[Received July 14—12 : 05 a. m.]

Referring to my telegram of July 6, 11 a. m.,[67] the below summarized information received during the past 24 hours seems definitely to dispose of theory that Chen might be attempting to reach peaceful settlement with Nanking through Yu Han Mou and indicates strongly that Nanking's appointment of Yu as Pacification Commissioner for Kwangtung and Kwangsi, reported by the Hong Kong press, has in large measure eliminated Chen politically and narrowed the situation to a struggle between Nanking and Kwangsi for the control of Canton with Chen apparently reduced to the role of helpless tool of the latter:

It is reliably reported that Yu's army is already marching south from Namyung posting placards reading "Down with Chen Chi Tang"; that there have been heavy troop movements up the railway toward Shiukwan; that the railway bridge at Shakou about 35 miles south of Shiukwan was blown up yesterday, allegedly by pro-Nanking soldiers from Pakoahow arsenal following defection of their leader, and further northward troop movements thereby interrupted; and that Waichow is swarming with troops apparently loyal to Chen who are coming down East River, presumably for defense of Canton or under pressure from Yu's easternmost forces.

Other defections of military and civil officials have been reliably reported. Well-informed sources, though admitting indications of some Nanking bribery, report that genuine opposition to and lack of faith in Chen's program is so widespread that wholesale further desertions including his Second Army and Navy are likely. At the same time it is admitted that Yu must obtain support soon if he is to check counter defection among his own troops.

(Part 2 of this message will follow.[68])

Sent to the Department, Peiping, Nanking, Shanghai, and Hankow.

SPIKER

---

[67] Not found in Department files.
[68] *Infra.*

893.00/13617 : Telegram

The Consul General at Canton (Spiker) to the Secretary of State

CANTON, July 14, 1936—11 a. m.
[Received 5 : 30 p. m.]

Following constitutes part 2 of my telegram July 13, 11 p. m.

On the basis of information from trustworthy sources which accords well with Hong Kong press reports and other signs, it appears that the Southwestern military leaders, upon learning of Yu's defection, held an all night conference July 10 at which Chen in desperation agreed to the following program: (1) The "purging" of any remaining pro-Nanking elements from Chen's official personnel; (2) the shortening of Kwangtung's defence lines by withdrawal southward from border; (3) appointment of Chiang Kuang Nai [69] to head new 19th Route Army to be immediately organized with nucleus of 10,000 [from] Chen Wei Chou's [70] salt guards, the best trained and equipped troops in Kwangtung; (4) Kwangsi's despatch of two divisions to North Kwangtung and one to Canton to reenforce Kwangtung forces; (5) compensatory Kwangtung financial assistance to Kwangsi. With the exception of item (2), there are convincing indications that this program is being energetically followed, among which may be mentioned: the fact that Chen is now manifestly filling high posts vacated by deserters with pro-Kwangsi officers; that according to persistent reports by usually well-informed Chinese, Chen has just executed a secretary of Hu Han Min on the ground that secretary plotted with Yu Han Mou; that Chen, hitherto hostile to 19th Route Army, is suddenly making most obvious efforts to curry their favor; and that trustworthy reports indicate practical certainty that Kwangsi troops are already en route for Canton down the West River where, as well as at Canton, Southwest military authorities for the past 3 days have been commandeering large numbers of towboats and other craft for troop transport. In regard to item (2), it is reported that certain officers of the old 19th Route Army are holding out and insisting that Chen Ming Shu [71] be recalled to head army but that Marshal Chen flatly rejects such proposal. With arrival of Kwangsi forces in Canton, Chen's opposition is expected to be swept aside.

2. Local situation tense although there is general belief that there will not be fighting in or in immediate vicinity of Canton.

3. Sent to the Department, Peiping, Nanking, Shanghai and Hankow.

SPIKER

---

[69] Commander at Shanghai in 1932 hostilities with Japanese forces and a leader of rebel regime in Fukien, 1933.
[70] Brother of Marshal Chen Chi-tang.
[71] Vice President of the Chinese Executive Yuan (Vice Premier), January–June 1932, and a leader of rebel regime in Fukien, 1933.

893.00/13612 : Telegram

The Counselor of Embassy in China (Peck) to the Secretary of State

NANKING, July 14, 1936—11 a. m.
[Received 5 : 40 p. m.]

225. My 224, July 13, noon.[72]

1. *Central Daily News* publishes today text of three resolutions passed by the plenary session yesterday:

(1) Organizing a national defense council and appointing 18 members as follows: Li Tsung Jen, Pai Chung Hsi, Chen Chi Tang, Liu Chi, Chang Hsueh Liang, Sung Che Yuan, Han Fu Chu, Ho Cheng Chun, Ku Chu Tung, Liu Hsiang, Lung Yun, Ho Chien, Chiang Ting Wen, Yang Hu Cheng, Chu Shao Liang, Hsu Yung Chang, Fu Tso Yi, and Yu Han Mou;

(2) Appointing Yu Han Mu Pacification Commissioner for Kwangtung to replace Chen Chi Tang, and Li Tsung Jen and Pai Chung Hsi Pacification Commissioner and Vice Commissioner for Kwangsi;

(3) Reappointing the present Provincial Chairmen of Kwangtung and Kwangsi.[73]

2. The plenary session is scheduled to terminate today.

3. Sent to the Department, Peiping, Canton, Shanghai and Hankow.

PECK

893.00/13618 : Telegram

The Counselor of Embassy in China (Peck) to the Secretary of State

NANKING, July 15, 1936—noon.
[Received July 15—11 : 35 a. m.]

226. Central News Agency has today released summarized translation of two speeches made to the Plenary Session by General Chiang Kai-shek on July 13. The translations state that among other things the speaker reiterated the declaration of the Fifth Nationalist Party Congress, November last, to the effect that "We shall not forsake peace until there is no hope for peace and we shall not talk slightly of sacrifice until driven to the last extremity which makes sacrifice inevitable" and explained that "any infringement upon China's sovereign and territorial integrity by a foreign nation will drive her to the last extremity when she will think sacrifice inevitable". In explanation the speaker said, "If any foreign power compels us to sign an agreement in recognition of 'Manchukuo' it will then be the time when we shall not fear any longer and when we shall make our last sacrifice". He said that hope for peace had not been exhausted but was even brighter than before. He declared that China would not be afraid

---

[72] Not printed.
[73] Lin Yun-kai and Huang Sho-chu respectively.

to make sacrifices for world peace and justice like a second Ethiopia though China was quite unwilling to be a conquered nation as Ethiopia is. This fate could be avoided if the whole nation should exert utmost efforts for national salvation. Referring to activities in the Southwest the speaker is quoted as saying, "We should all remember that if your internal administration is unified and our national foundation stabilized, all powers in the world will respect us. Just as when China has achieved real solidarity no nation in the world will dare become our enemy."

PECK

893.79694/12 : Telegram

The Counselor of Embassy in China (Peck) to the Secretary of State

NANKING, July 18, 1936—10 a. m.
[Received July 18—3 : 56 a. m.]

228. My despatch to the Department June 15 [74] reporting that the British Government had invited the Chinese Government to send China National Aviation Corporation planes to Hong Kong.

I have been reliably informed that about July 15 the Japanese Minister for Foreign Affairs summoned the Chinese Ambassador and recalled that the Chinese Government was insisting on an integral settlement of Sino-Japanese differences. Arita observed that this would be difficult to achieve but that agreement might possibly be reached in regard to individual questions. He said no individual agreement would bring such reassurance to the Japanese public as would China's permission for Japanese commercial planes to ply between Fukuoka and Shanghai. The Chinese Government returned a refusal of this request in line with its consistent policy to establish contact with points outside China by means of Chinese planes only.

By mail to Tokyo.

PECK

893.00/13627 : Telegram

The Counselor of Embassy in China (Peck) to the Secretary of State

NANKING, July 18, 1936—11 a. m.
[Received 3 : 15 p. m.]

229. 1. An important official of the Chinese Government questioned by me today said that the Chinese Government has no doubt whatever that Japanese assistance was given to Kwangsi in opposing the Government in the form of supplies of money and arms but the Govern-

[74] *Post*, p. 641.

ment has good reason to believe that even the Japanese military faction now believes this step was unwise because of the popular anti-Japanese sentiment which has been stimulated. It appears that the original slogan of the Southwest was to have been "down with Chiang Kai-shek" and it was Pai Chung Hsi who insisted on the anti-Japanese pretext. In granting their consent to this the Japanese had first received Pai's assurance that the anti-Japanese aspect would not be unduly stressed, the safety of all Japanese nationals would be guaranteed, and the boycott would not be revived.

2. The Government hopes that because of continued defections of Chen Chi Tang's troops, Yu Han Mou will be able to effect speedy conquest of Kwangtung and if the assistance lent by Kwangsi troops to Kwangtung makes this unlikely, the Government is prepared to threaten Kwangsi from Kweichow in order to compel withdrawal of Kwangsi troops from Kwangtung. Informant doubted whether Chen Chi Tang is acting in response either to threats or bribes from Japan and said that thorough investigations failed to show any Soviet assistance extended to the Kwangsi leaders. Informant did not believe that the Nineteenth Route Army would constitute a serious military factor and doubted whether its important leaders had actually gone to Canton.

3. Informant said that relations with Japan are almost ominously quiet. The new Ambassador has advanced only generalities in regard to economic cooperation without specific proposals. The Chinese Government fears that if the fighting with the Southwest is unduly protracted the Japanese will take some step of aggression against Shantung where they are attempting to play upon the discontented feelings of Han Fu Chu. Han is anxious to replace Admiral Shen, present Mayor of Tsingtau, with his own appointee but the Government is attempting to retain Shen because of his proved loyalty in the face of threats and inducements from the Japanese Government to induce fullest compliance with Japanese plans for expansion in Tsingtau.

4. About July 24 Chiang Kai-shek and all Cabinet Ministers will remove to Kuling for about 6 weeks. Ministers of Finance and Foreign Affairs will, however, alternate with their senior Vice Ministers.

5. Repeated to Department, Peiping, Canton, Hankow. By mail to Shanghai.

PECK

893.00/13625 : Telegram

The Consul General at Canton (Spiker) to the Secretary of State

CANTON, July 18, 1936—11 p. m.
[Received July 18—6 : 36 p. m.]

Special delegate for Foreign Affairs has just informed me that existing grave situation has been relieved by the following happenings: Yesterday Marshal Chen was waited on by various of his officers and urged to resign. While Marshal Li was today appealed to by group of Kwangtung generals who entreated him to return to Kwangsi and to promise not to send into Kwangtung a very large Kwangsi force which has been mobilized at Wuchow. Both leaders were informed that failure to act as requested would precipitate ruinous war which no one wants. Li informed the generals that he has never had the slightest desire to interfere in Kwangtung's affairs, that he would remove suspicion by returning to Kwangsi and by promising not to move his troops into Kwangtung. Within the hour Li took an aeroplane for Wuchow, and Chen, upon being informed of this, tendered his resignation to the Southwest Political Council. He had packed his effects last night preparatory for flight and is expected to leave Canton at the earliest opportunity, relinquishing charge to Generals Li Yang Ching of the Kwangtung Third Army and Ho Lok, Chen's recently appointed Chief of Staff and long Commissioner of Public Safety here. They will in turn hand over charge to General Yu Han Mou who has been invited by the Kwangtung generals to succeed Chen and who is expected to arrive in Canton within 48 hours. When queried as to probability of acceptance of Li's action by Pai and other Kwangsi leaders, the Special Delegate stated that they would unquestionably accept since "no one wants to fight". He strongly reaffirmed such belief when attention was called to the fact that Kwangsi's problems of finance, et cetera, remain unsolved and province has large army mobilized at Wuchow with 38 steamers and launches and numerous junks held in readiness to throw this force into Kwangtung.

2. Generals Li and Ho today assured Consuls here that the generals accepted full responsibility for the preservation of law and order in the city and the protection of life and property. During the change-over, situation will, of course, be potentially dangerous. American citizens have been kept appropriately advised of developments and cautioned, women and children having yesterday been warned to withdraw from Tungshan suburb to place of greater safety.

3. Sent to the Department, Peiping, Nanking, Shanghai, Hankow.

SPIKER

893.00/13626 : Telegram

The Consul General at Canton (Spiker) to the Secretary of State

CANTON, July 19, 1936—6 p.m.
[Received 6:45 p.m.]

Referring to my telegram of July 18, 11 p.m. Marshal Chen secretly left for Hong Kong on H. M. S. *Moth.* There were heavy movements of Kwangtung troops westward across city last night which are continuing this afternoon although smaller bodies are moving east. Destination of such forces not yet ascertained; some of them probably occupying points to west as discouragement to possible Kwangsi advance while others are replacements in areas occupied by Yu Han Mou. Gunboat at Wuchow today reports that large number of launches and junks gathered at that city have departed with troops returning up West River, this indicating that Pai and other Kwangsi commanders have agreed to Li's undertakings to Kwangtung leaders as reported in my telegram of July 18, 11 p.m.

2. Aside from marked troop movements, Canton remains outwardly quiet, heavy rains contributing to such situation. Finance Commissioner has made popular concession to public by announcing suspension for 1 month of usual tax on imported rice.

3. There is a general feeling of relief and confidence that removal from Kwangtung of the two marshals marks good stride forward in national political adjustment but responsible Chinese invariably qualify their optimistic beliefs with the words "unless the Japanese now do something."

4. In strictest confidence I am reliably informed that Provincial Chairman and the Mayor who fled to Hong Kong are returning to Canton tomorrow morning but will remain in seclusion until Nanking indicates its desires. Their return interpreted as indicating there is little danger of any disturbance in the city. This information supplied to me on condition that it be held in strict confidence until press reports are published.

5. Sent to the Department, Peiping, Nanking, Shanghai and Hankow.

SPIKER

793.94/8065 : Telegram

The Ambassador in China (Johnson) to the Secretary of State

PEIPING, July 21, 1936—5 p.m.
[Received July 21—3:20 p.m.]

372. Embassy's telegrams 353, July 10, 4 p.m., and 356, July 13, 3 p.m.

1. Developments for Sino-Japanese relations in North China seem still to await the outcome of the situation in the South and the return

or non-return of Wang Keh Min to Peiping to take charge of civil affairs in Hopei Province, leaving military affairs to Sung Che Yuan.

2. Chinese and Japanese observers express the opinion that Japanese efforts have failed for the time being to persuade Han Fu Chu to participate in the Hopei-Chahar Political Council. Han may be influenced by Chiang's present success with Kwangtung or by dissatisfaction with possibility of new officials becoming important in Hopei, as mentioned below.

3. It is understood that if Wang Keh Min returns to Peiping he will be assisted by certain men whom he regards as competent in finance and economics and who are acceptable to the Japanese. These men are reported to be Wang Yi Tang, old Anfu clique member, now a member of Hopei-Chahar Political Council; Tsao Ju Lin, who served in Anfu Ministry with Wang Keh Min and who does not hold office at present; Tang Erh Ho, who was not associated with the Anfu clique but who held Cabinet positions in 1922, '23, and '27 and who speaks Japanese and holds no office at present; and Liu Che, of the old Mukden party, at present a member of the Hopei-Chahar Political Council. According to report, these men, with Wang Keh Min as chairman, will form some sort of an economic committee and its formation may be accompanied by some change in the present form of Sung's regime.

4. The Council recently rescinded the order for the arrest of Shih Yu San for subversive activity favorable to Japanese intrigue in 1933 and he has now come to Peiping and become a member of that Council.

5. Sung Che Yuan is allegedly apprehensive that if Wang Keh Min returns to Tientsin, Wang will reduce Sung's revenues because Wang will need part of Hopei's revenue for use in carrying out Sino-Japanese economic cooperation in this area.

6. Wang Keh Min's position will be difficult as he will have to attempt to please the Japanese military, Sung Che Yuan, and Chiang Kai Shek. By mail to Tokyo.

JOHNSON

793.94/8066 : Telegram

The Ambassador in China (Johnson) to the Secretary of State

PEIPING, July 22, 1936—6 p. m.
[Received July 22—11 a. m.]

375. Reference paragraph 3 of Embassy's 372, July 21, 5 p. m.

1. The semi-official Central News Agency reports July 21 from Nanking that the Executive Yuan appointed on that day Tsao Ju Lin and Tang Erh Ho as members of the Hopei-Chahar Political Council. This has been done presumably in preparation for Wang

Keh Min's return to Peiping and indicates approval of Wang's activities in case he does return. The same agency reports the Executive Yuan also appointed as members of Political Council General Liu Jui Min, the new Chahar Chairman, and Ko Ting Yuan, director of the Changlu salt inspectorate.

2. Pan Yu Kuei, heretofore reputedly most influential civilian next to Hsiao Chen Ying in Sung's regime, resigned his post as chief of the Department of Political Affairs of the Hopei-Chahar Political Council and was put in charge July 14 of "Preparation for construction of Shihkiachwang–Tsingchow Railway." His resignation from the Political Affairs Department was allegedly due to dislike of him on the part of Sung Che Yuan's military subordinates because of Pan's allegedly pro-Japanese activities. His future importance seems to depend upon the degree of resisting of Sino-Japanese economic cooperation.

By mail to Tokyo.

JOHNSON

893.00/13633 : Telegram

The Consul General at Canton (Spiker) to the Secretary of State

CANTON, July 24, 1936—4 p. m.
[Received 9 : 45 p. m.]

Referring to my telegram of July 23, 5 p. m.,[75] General Yu Han Mou, escorted by fleet of 26 Nanking airplanes, arrived in Canton yesterday and issued proclamation announcing his assumption of office as Commander-in-Chief of the Kwangtung forces, and declaring that he will use every effort to preserve peace and order. The exodus of officials of the old regime continues while Nanking's appointees are being besieged by hordes of impoverished job hunters. Final steps in the abolition of the Southwest Political Council and the Southwest Executive [Committee] of the Kuomintang are being carried out by occupation of the whole headquarters by troops and by dismissal of many members of their staffs with payment of extra wages. Admiral Chen Chi Liang, Vice Minister of Navy, arrived in Hong Kong on the cruiser *Haichow* yesterday.

2. Official informant confidentially states that there was fighting yesterday in East River district near Waichow between Canton forces loyal to new Commander-in-Chief and certain units of General Li Yang Ching's Third Army. If true, it is believed such disaffection will be speedily suppressed. Generals Li and Ho Lok (see my July 18, 11 p. m.) are being reported as having resigned and gone to Hong

[75] Not printed.

Kong. There is unconfirmed report that Pai Chung Hsi has fled from Nanning to French Indo-China and that Marshal Li will soon join him. Also that troops of former Fifty-first Division (which recently deserted Nanking command in South Kiangsi and joined Yu Han Mou prior to his departure for Nanking) have been disarmed and disbanded by Yu's forces by this time near Lokchang whence troops were seeking to escape to Kwangsi.

3. There are persistent rumors that Nanking investigators have requested Nanking to issue warrant for arrest of Chen Chi Tang and seek his extradition from Hong Kong on a charge of embezzlement of huge sums of Government funds.

4. Sent to the Department, Peiping, Nanking, Shanghai, and Hankow.

SPIKER

893.00/13634 : Telegram

The Counselor of Embassy in China (Peck) to the Secretary of State

NANKING, July 27, 1936—9 a. m.
[Received July 27—7 a. m.]

234. The National Government made following appointments July 25:

Pai Chung Hsi to be Chairman of Chekiang Province; Huang Shao Hsiung, present Chekiang Chairman, to be Pacification Commissioner of Kwangsi; Li Tsung Jen to be member of Standing Committee of National Defense Council (Li was made member of this newly organized Council July 13 by resolution of the recent Plenary Session as reported in our 225, July 14, 11 a.m.).

2. Press reports that Kwangsi troops are concentrating on Hunan border cannot be confirmed here. With practically all the higher officials of the Government now in Kuling, most of those remaining appear to be without accurate detailed information which might otherwise be in their possession. It is generally felt in Government circles here that Chiang Kai Shek has outwitted his enemies, that Li and Pai will either assume their new posts or abandon official life and that the consolidation of the Government's authority in the Southwest is assured.

3. To the Department and Peiping. Repeated to Canton. By mail to Hankow and Shanghai.

PECK

893.00/13641 : Telegram

The Counselor of Embassy in China (Peck) to the Secretary of State

NANKING, July 29, 1936—8 a. m.
[Received 8 : 40 p. m.]

235. 1. We are reliably informed that Chiang Kai-Shek will fly to Canton from Kuling in about a week, presumably as a gesture to demonstrate the extension of his authority over Kwangtung.

2. According to an official of the Executive Yuan, a regular meeting of the Yuan held Kuling yesterday ordered an exchange of posts between General Huang Mu Sung, Chairman of the Tibetan and Mongolian Affairs Commission, and Lin Yun Kai, Chairman of the Kwangtung Provincial Government, and made the following additional appointments: T. L. Soong, brother of T. V. Soong, to be Finance Commissioner of Kwangtung; Liu Wei Chih, political Vice Minister of Industries, to be Reconstruction Commissioner; and Tseng Yang Fu, political Vice Minister of Railways, to be Mayor of Canton. Huang Shao Hsuing is reported to have declined recent appointment as Kwangsi Pacification Commissioner.

3. Repeated to the Department, Peiping, Canton, Hankow. By mail to Shanghai.

PECK

693.94244/117a : Telegram

The Secretary of State to the Ambassador in Japan (Grew)

WASHINGTON, July 29, 1936—5 p. m.

100. Department's 64, May 26, 1 p. m. and your 114, May 27, 6 p. m., in regard to the smuggling situation in north China.

As it is understood that the Chief of the Eastern Asia Bureau of the Foreign Office, who was sent to north China to investigate the smuggling situation, has returned to Japan, the Department suggests that the Embassy in its discretion informally approach the Foreign Office with a view to reaffirming the continued interest of this Government in that situation and (with reference to the offer of the Vice Minister for Foreign Affairs to keep the Embassy currently informed) making inquiries in regard to the findings and results of the investigation.

HULL

793.003 Manchuria/10

The Ambassador in China (Johnson) to the Secretary of State

No. 610   PEIPING, July 29, 1936.

[Received August 24.]

SIR: I have the honor to refer to despatch No. 291 of July 2, 1936, from the Consul General at Mukden to the Embassy, entitled "Declaration, concerning status of extraterritorial nations in 'Manchukuo', ["] copies of which were forwarded direct to the Department.[76]

The Embassy informed Mr. Ballantine in its instruction of July 25 that it approved his proposal to advise American inquirers that they might pay, in the form of voluntary contributions to the "Manchukuo" government, taxes which are non-discriminatory and no higher than those paid by Japanese subjects, and that it concurred in his opinion that the other immediate measures of "Manchukuo" control over Japanese subjects, relating to industrial supervision and special manufacturing taxes, are not likely to affect American residents. A copy of the Embassy's instruction in question is enclosed.[76]

Respectfully yours,   NELSON TRUSLER JOHNSON

793.94/8109

The Ambassador in China (Johnson) to the Secretary of State

No. 618   PEIPING, July 31, 1936.

[Received August 24.]

SIR: I have the honor to submit information with regard to Japanese penetration in those areas in Chahar and Suiyuan Provinces which are occupied by Mongols and in those areas along the Peiping–Suiyuan Railway which are under Chinese administration.

I. JAPANESE PENETRATION IN MONGOL AREAS

a. Japanese interference with foreigners' movements:

Travel by foreigners in territory north of the Great Wall in Chahar Province has been practically stopped by the Japanese military. Japanese military and consular representatives stationed at Kalgan, the Chahar provincial capital at the Great Wall, inform foreigners that they cannot travel north from Kalgan. Permission from the Japanese military officer resident at Kalgan for such travel is regarded as necessary; and such permission is now consistently refused. The Chinese authorities at Kalgan are extremely reluctant to visa foreigners' passports for travel north of Kalgan, their expressed reason being their fear that foreigners may become involved in difficulties with

---

[76] Not printed.

Japanese military or with Japanese-directed Mongol military. Two foreigners, who went on July 29 north from Kalgan for thirty miles to Changpei on the main road to Outer Mongolia, were forced by the Japanese military to return on the same day to Kalgan. Earlier in July two other foreigners were detained for two days by Japanese authorities at Chapsur, which lies further north on the same road. There are reports from missionaries at work in that area of frequent interference by Japanese with the movements of foreigners. Two American missionaries, however, who left Kalgan on July 29, with only Chinese visas, to visit mission stations in Mongol territory in Chahar Province, passed through Changpei without hindrance, the inference being that foreigners who have work to do and who are well-known in the area are not yet prevented entry. These two foreigners expressed their intention of avoiding Chapsur, however, because of their belief that they would otherwise be interfered with at that point. Chinese are not yet restrained from travel.

With regard to travel by foreigners to Pailingmiao, which is in northeastern Suiyuan Province but under Japanese control, it is believed that the situation is similar. Chinese authorities in Kueihwa, the Suiyuan provincial capital on the Peiping–Suiyuan Railway, are most reluctant to permit foreigners to leave Kueihwa for Pailingmiao, maintaining that difficulties with Japanese would be encountered. It is understood, however, that foreigners who have long been associated with that part of Inner Mongolia in northeastern Suiyuan, where Pailingmiao is located, can still move about in that area.

b. Japanese control of Mongols:

Japanese are apparently in complete control of the Mongols inhabiting the areas referred to above. It is reliably reported that no foreigners are now permitted to see Prince Teh, the leading Mongol in Japanese-controlled Mongol territory and the Chairman of the Mongolian Local Autonomous Political Council, the headquarters of which were formally removed in June of this year from Pailingmiao in Suiyuan Province to Chapsur in Chahar Province on the Kalgan-Outer Mongolia road. The increasing curtailment of Prince Teh's influence is indicated by a reliable report of his recent failure to persuade the Japanese to deal leniently in imposing export duties on goods exported by Prine Teh's friend, "Duke" Larson, the well-known Swedish dealer who lives north of Chapsur. It would now seem that Prince Teh is no more than a puppet and that his former strength, which lay in being able to bargain both with Japanese and Chinese authorities, has been completely dissipated as a result of the action of the National Government and the Chinese provincial authorities which cut him off from China by their establishment of a council of Mongols living in Suiyuan Province.

There are allegedly few Japanese in the Japanese-controlled Mongol area, it being said that there are only some ten or twenty Japanese at Pailingmiao and a similar number at Chapsur and at other important points. These Japanese exert their control through the military strength which is behind them in "Manchukuo" and through the presence in Mongol territory in Chahar and northeastern Suiyuan of Japanese-directed Mongol troops from Jehol Province. There are reputedly from one to two hundred such troops at Pailingmiao and a large force of one to two thousand men, under the Japanese-directed Jehol Mongol leader Li Shou-hsin, in the vicinity of Changpei, thirty miles north of Kalgan.

The Japanese have recently instituted military conscription among Mongols in certain parts of Chahar, apparently as an experiment, and there is at Changpei a school where several hundred Mongols are receiving primarily military training, although the Mongols attending were under the impression when they were enrolled that they were to receive other education. It is understood that the Mongols in the school numbered some 500 in the spring of this year but that the number has now decreased to about 300 because of Mongol dissatisfaction with the institution. According to a 27 year-old Mongol, who was forced to attend the school against his will but who recently obtained release through feigning simple-mindedness, the Mongol students are roughly treated; they are told, when they complain of the poor quality of the food, that the soldiers of Genghis Khan had worse food and yet conquered Europe; and every effort is being made to turn the students against Soviet Russia and communism.

c. Attitude of the Mongols under Japanese control:

All reports from Chinese and foreign sources are to the effect that the Mongols do not want to be under Japanese control and that they are treated badly by the Japanese. As stated in previous despatches, the present plight of the Mongols in Chahar Province and northeastern Suiyuan Province is the result of (1) their own weakness militarily, (2) the unjust and inept handling of the Mongol question by Chinese provincial and national authorities, (3) the military strength of Japan, and (4) the firm intention of the Japanese military to gain control of Inner Mongolia in preparation for a possible war with Soviet Russia and, less importantly, to exploit the area economically.

According to well-informed sources, the younger Mongols of the area under discussion are radical and are sympathetic toward Soviet Russia because of the latter's comparative liberal treatment of Mongols in Outer Mongolia; and the Mongol princes in the area under discussion are still on friendly terms with those Mongols in Outer Mongolia who were princes prior to Soviet control and who are still regarded by Mongols as princes. From this information, it would appear that the Japanese could hope for little real support from the Mongols in Inner Mongolia in case of a conflict in which Outer Mongolia and Japan were on opposing sides.

d. Japanese intentions:

The strict control by the Japanese over the Mongol areas referred to above appears to be for the purpose of establishing themselves firmly there prior to extending their control over Mongol areas in Suiyuan Province. Whether the Japanese intend to extend at the same time their control over those parts of Chahar and Suiyuan Provinces which are under Chinese control is not known. (Japanese penetration in the Chinese areas will be discussed later in this despatch.)

There have been frequent reports during the past twelve months that the Japanese intend to cause the Japanese-directed Mongols in Chahar Province to move westward and take over Suiyuan, the latest rumor being that this will occur in September or October of this year and that Prince Teh will be made the puppet emperor of Inner Mongolia with his capital at Kueihwa, the provincial capital of Suiyuan.

Most observers are at present of the opinion, however, that such a forward movement will not occur in the immediate future. The reasons for the suspension of westward expansion are not known but are probably to be found among the following: (1) the Japanese military are awaiting developments in Sino-Japanese relations with respect to China south of the Great Wall; (2) the Kwantung Army is preoccupied with problems confronting them in "Manchukuo"; (3) westward expansion is not approved at present by the "moderate" military authorities at Tokyo who are now allegedly stronger than formerly; (4) the Kwantung Army is uncertain whether a westward movement might not involve them with unwanted military conflict with General Sung Che-yuan's forces in southern Chahar and General Fu Tso-yi's forces in Suiyuan; and (5) the Japanese wish first to regularize their position in the area in Chahar and northeastern Suiyuan which they already control.

In explanation of this fifth point, the Embassy has been informed that the Kwantung Army is disappointed with the decline of revenue in the area in Chahar Province which they control. For example, the Wostwag, a German company which has long traded with Inner Mongolia, has within the past few weeks entirely stopped trade with the Mongol area under Japanese control, the reason being that the Japanese assessed or caused to be assessed a duty of 11 per cent on goods which the Wostwag purchased in that area and that this was followed by a similar assessment by the Chinese provincial authorities when the goods reached territory under Chinese administration. Jap-

anese have been discussing with Wostwag and with the Chahar Provincial authorities ways to adjust the situation so that the Wostwag
will resume its former trade, but so far without success. (The Wostwag stopped all trade with Outer Mongolia in January of this year,
and now all their shipments go by way of Tientsin to Vladivostok.)

II. JAPANESE PENETRATION ALONG THE PEIPING–SUIYUAN RAILWAY

The influence of the Japanese is constantly increasing along the
Peiping–Suiyuan Railway, penetration being also facilitated by a
Japanese weekly military plane service between Peiping and Paot'ou,
the westernmost station of the Peiping–Suiyuan Railway. The plane
(a 1928 Fokker) uses Chinese airfields at the various towns along the
railway and is not open to the general public. Japanese planes, other
than that on the weekly service, are also said to stop frequently at the
Chinese airfields.

There are more than 300 Japanese and Koreans resident at Kalgan,
the Chahar provincial capital, the number at the beginning of this
year having been 180; there are from 50 to 100 Japanese and Koreans
resident at Kueihwa, the Suiyuan provincial capital; and about ten
at Paot'ou, the end of the line.

There is a Japanese military mission at each of those cities, and each
mission has its own short-wave radio outfit for sending and receiving
messages. According to the local Japanese Embassy, those military
officers are under the Kwantung Army; according to the local Japanese
Assistant Military Attaché, those officers are under the North China
Garrison; according to a Chinese official, it is stated on the calling-
cards of those officers that they are under the North China Garrison
although they claim to be under the Kwantung Army when it suits
their convenience. There is also a Japanese civilian resident at Kalgan who is in the employ of the Kwantung Army and who is referred
to as "in charge of Mongolian affairs in Kalgan".

There is a Japanese consulate at Kalgan, and within the past few
months there has been established at Kueihwa a consulate of peculiar
status. A Chinese official who participated in the negotiations for
the establishment of this consulate has stated that the Chinese authorities objected to the establishment of a Japanese consulate at Kueihwa
and that a compromise was finally arrived at whereby the Chinese
authorities agreed to the residence at Kueihwa of Japanese consular
representatives provided no Japanese flag were flown over the building
occupied and no designation as consulate were on the entrance. (A
member of my staff who visited Kueihwa on July 28 found the Japanese consular people housed in a rather wretched Chinese building
with no name at the entrance and no flag flying.)

There are representatives of the South Manchuria Railway Company resident at Kalgan and at Kueihwa, allegedly pursuing economic

investigations. Those at Kueihwa are housed in the nameless quarters of the Japanese consular representatives.

The presence of Japanese is most noticeable in Kalgan. In one short street near the railway station are the following Japanese establishments: several inns, several restaurants and cafes, a motor-bus company, a toy shop, a printers' and stationery shop, and a manufactory of washing powder. These last two mentioned establishments are presumed to be the two manufactories of heroin which are commonly said to be in Kalgan under Japanese or Korean management.

The situation at Tat'ung, on the Peiping–Suiyuan Railway in northern Shansi Province, is not so clear. There are neither consular nor military representatives resident there, and the principal activity of Japanese dealers appears to be the sale of heroin. It is understood that two Chinese inns near the Tat'ung railway station were recently taken over by Japanese nationals for the promotion of this illicit business.

As for the sale of Japanese products along the Peiping–Suiyuan Railway, no information is obtainable. It is believed, however, that considerable business is done in that area in smuggled Japanese goods, especially since the market in Hopei Province and in places to the south of that province has become glutted.

III. Attitude of Chinese Toward Japanese Penetration

The Chinese authorities along the Peiping–Suiyuan Railway are evidently uneasy with regard to the growing Japanese penetration and with regard to ultimate Japanese intentions. One hears that the Chinese provincial authorities have recently been promised aid by the National Government in case of need in resisting the Japanese and that preparations for resistance are being made in northern Shansi and in Suiyuan Province. The accuracy and the significance of such reports are open, however, to doubt. It seems improbable that Japanese penetration by the present gradual means or by actual military force will receive any real check at the hands of the Chinese provincial authorities concerned whether or not they receive aid from the National Government.

IV. Narcotics Along the Peiping–Suiyuan Railway

There seems to be no doubt that there is at least one heroin factory (probably two) in Kalgan conducted by Japanese or Koreans and that heroin is being sold by Japanese nationals or their Chinese employees in cities and towns along the railway in increasing amounts. Figures in regard to this trade, however, are unobtainable because of the secrecy surrounding the business.

As for opium, considerable areas along the railway between Kueihwa and Paot'ou are planted with poppies, notwithstanding the new regulation of this year that poppies may not be grown within a space of about seven miles on either side of the railway. It is said that the area under such cultivation this year is considerably larger than last year, although only a three mile limit with respect to the railway was fixed by the provincial authorities last year. The trade of the Suiyuan authorities in Kansu and Ningsia opium allegedly continues unabated. Disinterested observers resident in the principal cities along the Peiping–Suiyuan Railway estimate invariably more than half the population smokes opium, some estimates being that 90 per cent of the population are addicted. There is no evidence that the opium trade is in other than Chinese hands.

Respectfully yours,   NELSON TRUSLER JOHNSON

741.94/64

The Ambassador in Japan (Grew) to the Secretary of State

No. 1970   TOKYO, August 6, 1936.
[Received August 24.]

SIR : I have the honor to report several new indications of a Japanese desire for improved relations with Great Britain. First, a press campaign, beginning on July 28 in the Tokyo *Asahi*, and continuing down until today, has featured a wish on the part of Japanese official circles and on the part of prominent men in British political life for a renewal between Japan and Great Britain of some such friendship as characterized the period of the Anglo-Japanese Alliance;[78] and today's newspapers speak of a plan for Anglo-Japanese cooperation reported to be entertained by Sir Samuel Hoare.[79] Second, Foreign Minister Arita, in addressing the Diet in May 1936, took occasion particularly to mention his hope for friendly relations with Great Britain. Third, Ambassador Yoshida, on the way to his new duties in London, expressed, as the Department is aware, the hope that he may succeed in bringing about a renewal of Anglo-Japanese concord into which the United States may then be brought.

The Embassy thinks it probable that all three of these channels of expression have been inspired in the matter by Count Makino, recently retired Lord Keeper of the Privy Seal. Ambassador Yoshida is Count Makino's son-in-law, and Foreign Minister Arita also enjoys Makino's confidence. Informed newspaper men, both Japanese and foreign, are likewise of the opinion that the present agitation for friendship with Great Britain is of Japanese manufacture; and it is believed that the calculated applause in the Diet which met the

---

[78] 1902–21.
[79] British Secretary of State for Foreign Affairs, June–December, 1935.

Foreign Minister's brief remarks on the subject was arranged in advance. Although the initiative is now definitely on the side of Japan and the outcome is consequently more doubtful than if the desire for a new accord were mutual, nevertheless the subject deserves careful consideration.

Recent months have brought a number of new factors into the relations between Japan and Great Britain:

(1) The preliminary statement by Leith-Ross, the economist sent by the British Government to China to study means of improving conditions there, indicates that his report to the British Government will be adversely critical of many Japanese actions with regard to China and will speak optimistically of the value of a British policy aiming at increased future trade and investment in China.

(2) Statements by members of the British Government and by members of Parliament, as well as representations to the Japanese Government by the British Ambassador in Tokyo, have made clear serious British interest in putting an end to smuggling in North China, especially on account of the importance of such smuggling on the future of the Chinese Maritime Customs. The Chinese Maritime Customs is among the institutions of China the support of which has been a cornerstone of British policy. It is an example of the international, impartial, expert services in which Great Britain has seen the greatest hope for China's future, and the British Government does not lightly pass over the serious threat contained in the smuggling situation. Very recently, however, Japanese smuggling in North China has become so highly competitive that it has ceased to be particularly profitable and it therefore seems probable that statements emanating from the Japanese Government to the effect that the problem will be attacked hold definite promise.

(3) The recent years of Japan's expansion have been accompanied by a rapid extension of Japan's foreign trade, and relief from the pressure of Japanese manufactures in various British markets such as Australia and India has become a problem of the first importance.

(4) Failure of the League of Nations with regard to Ethiopia opens the way for British reconsideration of the policy of refusing recognition of "Manchukuo", insofar as that policy was based upon faith in the League.

All these factors have their important bearing on the question, "Will the Foreign Minister be successful in bringing Great Britain to a new period of Anglo-Japanese accord, and what will be the nature of the new relations?" Japan seeks a word from Great Britain to China to convince China of the futility of relying on foreign support and the futility of continuing anti-Japan tactics. Japan would expect recognition of "Manchukuo" by China to follow, with later recognition by other countries. Japan seeks a free hand to develop North

China in the direction which has been pursued since the Tangku Truce.[80] Great Britain, on the other hand, does not seek an ally (as in the days of the Anglo-Japanese Alliance) to defeat Russia whom Great Britain does not now fear; but Great Britain would like to have a friendly Japan willing to guarantee and protect British vested rights and interests in China. And Great Britain seeks relief from the growing danger of Japanese trade in the markets of the British Empire. Is there no ground for agreement as between British and Japanese desires?

The Embassy is of the opinion that a sane facing of the future relations of Japan and Great Britain in China should be predicated upon the possibility of a friendly understanding in the not distant future. To be sure, the British public is not to be jockeyed out of its opinions by the views of the British Government, however carefully considered. The strong public sentiment which forced Sir Samuel Hoare out of the office of Foreign Minister is an example of the independence of British public opinion; but this very example also illustrates the practical, easy-going restraint that rescues the British public from backing up its moral protests. A new accord between Great Britain and Japan would arouse the British supporters of the actions of the League of Nations with regard to nonrecognition of the regime in Manchuria; but the British Government, in the light of the decline of the League in the wake of the Ethiopian problem, might opportunistically and convincingly reply that it would be futile to continue to make sacrifices on behalf of a defunct institution. Again, British policy has, for more than a generation, strongly supported international assistance to China in the form of the Chinese Maritime Customs and similar organizations, and there can be little doubt now that Japanese aims in China include a gradual future Japanese control of such administrative organizations; but the Japanese administration in Manchuria has proven itself orderly and not entirely hostile to foreign interests, and even the old British attachment to impartial, international organizations to assist China, might conceivably give way to the belief that British trade in China in proportions comparable to the present will continue to be safe under virtual Japanese administration. There is still occasional romanticizing about huge future trade possibilities in China if Japan is kept out now (an idea mildly endorsed by Leith-Ross) ; but plenty of sound British business opinion is ready to admit that future foreign trade in China holds no great promise while present political conditions continue to prevail. And strongly tempting Great Britain to an accord with Japan is the immediate and pressing threat of Japanese

---

[80] For text of the agreement signed May 31, 1933, see *Foreign Relations*, Japan, 1931–1941, vol. I, p. 120.

merchandise in the British Empire. Relief from that haunting danger would be worth diverting Japanese energies to the continent, even at some sacrifice there; and it is not a foregone conclusion that increased Japanese trade in China would inevitably be at the expense of British trade with China. In any event, an accord which would tend to direct Japan's economic activities toward China might serve to reduce competition from Japanese goods in British territory.

The initiators of the present move for a new basis of Anglo-Japanese relations are the Japanese, but nevertheless the possibility of awakening British response appears sufficiently plausible to warrant careful watching.

Respectfully yours,   JOSEPH C. GREW

894.00/670½

Memorandum by the Chief of the Division of Far Eastern Affairs (Hornbeck)

[WASHINGTON,] August 8, 1936.

At intervals since 1931, observers of economic and political developments in the Far East have come forward, here and there and now and then, with the thesis that there is approaching a breakdown of Japan's internal and/or external economy. Likewise, at intervals, officers of this Department concerned with Far Eastern relations have given consideration, in the light of such predictions, to the facts in the situation; and, at intervals, we have expressed the view that the facts available give no evidence of a crack in or an impending cracking up of Japan's economy.

During the past year the affirmation has repeatedly been made that Japan's foreign trade has reached or is near to its peak and that there may be expected soon a leveling off or even a decline in the figures of that trade. Officers of the Department are at present studying the evidence with regard to this affirmation. It may be some time before we are ready to submit an expression of our views in that connection.

Meanwhile, however, it may be worth while to give thought at this time to certain of the political implications of recent developments in connection with Japan's foreign trade. During the past five years Japan's trade, both in exports and in imports, with a perfectly logical relationship between those two elements, has increased by leaps and bounds. With an amazing coordination and with consequent great comparative efficiency, the Japanese have shown themselves able to make large purchases from abroad of raw materials, to produce manufactured articles, to export these articles and to sell them abroad at prices which have created a substantial demand for the Japanese product. This has brought the Japanese products into successful competition with similar products of other countries both in the home and in the export markets of the said other countries. In consequence, the producers and the sales agencies of other countries have demanded of their governments protection against the newly developed Japanese competition; and there have been raised all over the world various obstacles to the free and natural flow of Japanese exports.

At the same time, Japan's population has gone on increasing; the Japanese are, like other peoples, resorting to labor-saving devices; the demands of the Japanese population for the essentials of livelihood constantly increase; this population looks more and more to manufacturing and sale of manufactured commodities for its livelihood; Japan's capacity to produce and to export increases. The more the exports of Japan are increased, the greater the fear abroad of Japanese competition and the more the steps taken abroad to protect home industry against the lower-in-price Japanese products.

Thus, while the economic pressure outward of Japan is constantly increasing, there is being developed by other countries an economic iron ring in opposition to that pressure.

At the same time, in the political field, the Japanese militarists have embarked, on behalf of the nation, on a course of imperialistic expansion the principal instrument of which is armed force. In this field, as in the field of trade, the Japanese effort has met with initial successes. But, it has aroused fear—not alone among Japan's immediate neighbors but all over the world. China, the Soviet Union, the British Empire, the Netherland Empire and the United States have viewed with anxiety the military moves and the excessive efforts to create a superior army and a superior navy in which the Japanese have engaged. The Soviet Union has established defensive land, air and submarine forces in the Far East, which forces might readily on occasion be turned to offensive purposes. China is making every effort of which she is capable toward armament, now for defense against Japan, but which might on occasion be turned at some time in the future to offensive purposes. Great Britain and the United States, confronted with the refusal of Japan any longer to be bound by naval limitations constructed on the principle of equality of security, are looking earnestly to the perfection of their armaments. In the cases of China and the United States, the policy of armament flows principally from solicitude in the presence of evidence of predatory inclinations on the part of the Japanese. In the cases of the Soviet Union and the British Empire, the policy of armament flows partly from solicitude with regard to situations and problems in Europe and partly from solicitude with regard to situations and problems in the Far East. The great military establishments at Vladivostok, at Singapore, and in the Hawaiian Islands, however, are establishments which relate primarily to the problem of defense against Japan. And now General MacArthur [81] and President Quezon [82] are arming the Philippines, for defense against Japan. Thus, it may reasonably be said there has been created and there is being hardened a military "iron ring" around Japan.

Both in the economic field and in the military field there exists the phenomenon of a nation that is crowded, dynamically energetic, convinced that it must expand and making every effort to expand, and a world that is limited in area and is filled with other sovereign nations most of which are fearful of that nation's expansion, convinced that they must resist it, and taking steps to resist it.

In such a situation, the obvious question is: Will the forces of expansion prove greater than the forces of resistance? If so, when and at what point will the former break through?

The weakest points in the economic and military rings around Japan are to the southwestward and the southward: China and the Philippines (and the Dutch East Indies).

There was a time when China's natural resources were rated as comparatively limitless and China's military strength as negligible. But, in recent years the estimates of China's resources have been revised downward and China's efforts in the direction of military preparedness have made some impression. The old ideas of China as a potential Eldorado no longer prevail. Meanwhile, estimates of the natural resources of the Philippine Islands and portions of the Dutch East Indies are constantly being revised upward, and there is not within these areas themselves any substantial organization for resistance to possible pressure from without. If and when the aegis of American authority and responsibility is withdrawn from the Philippine Islands, there will lie to the southward from Japan a point in the ring the resources of which will invite pressure from Japan and the power of resistance of which will be comparatively weak—perhaps the weakest point in the whole ring.

S[TANLEY] K. H[ORNBECK]

---

[81] Gen. Douglas MacArthur, Chief of Staff, U. S. Army, 1930–35; director of organization of national defense for the Philippine Commonwealth Government since 1935.

[82] Manuel Quezon, President of the Philippine Commonwealth since November 1935.

893.00/13661 : Telegram

The Ambassador in China (Johnson) to the Secretary of State

PEIPING, August 10, 1936—3 p. m.
[Received August 10—2 : 50 p. m.]

399. Reference pages 8 to 11 of the monthly report for January and pages 15 and 16 of the report for May.[83]

1. Various reports indicate that a number of advanced clashes have occurred during the past 10 days in eastern Suiyuan north and east of Tsining (Pingtichuan) which is on Peiping–Suiyuan Railway between Chinese provincial forces and unidentified opponents. It was thought at first that the attackers were perhaps Japanese directed Mongols but there is now reason to believe that they are Chinese malcontents paid by Japanese to test the situation existing in eastern Suiyuan. All attacks are said to have been unsuccessful.

2. These clashes may be the beginning of an attempt by the Kwantung army, which is in charge of Japanese policy in Inner Mongolia and along the Peiping–Suiyuan Railway, to obtain control of Suiyuan through the use of hired Chinese, Japanese directed Mongol forces, and perhaps eventually Japanese forces. All reports show that the Kwantung army has in Chahar Province several thousand Mongol forces, some of them being from Jehol Province and some being Mongols recruited in Chahar. The immediate intention may be limited to obtaining control of that part of eastern Suiyuan inhabited by Mongols of the Chahar banners. Control of this area would make it easier for the Kwantung army to take over control of the Peiping–Suiyuan Railway when desired.

3. It is open to question whether only hired Chinese and Japanese directed Mongol forces can be successful because of (1) the preparedness of Chinese provincial forces and (2) the alleged dislike of the Japanese directed Mongol forces for the Japanese controlling them.

4. The Kwantung army may be in part motivated by its presumed belief that Japanese policy in China proper is not meeting with success.

By mail to Tokyo. JOHNSON

893.00/13670 : Telegram

The Counselor of Embassy in China (Peck) to the Secretary of State

NANKING, August 12, 1936—9 a. m.
[Received 9 : 20 a. m.]

244. (1) Semiofficial Central News Agency reports that Chiang Kai Shek flew yesterday from Kuling to Canton. An officer of the

---

[83] Neither printed.

Embassy was not informed last evening by the Minister of War that Chiang would proceed to Canton this week and the agency's report is believed to be true since Chiang's movements are rarely announced until made.

(2) Chen Li Fu, party leader and member of the standing committee of the Central Executive Committee, together with Chu Cheng, President of the Judicial Yuan, flew yesterday to Canton from Shanghai to reorganize party affairs in Kwangtung. The Minister of the Navy is now at Amoy or near by ostensibly for routine inspection purposes but reportedly to prepare for naval action on the West River, particularly at Wuchow, Kwangsi, if necessary.

(3) Japanese news agency Domei reports that five additional Central Government divisions (the 11th, 14th, 18th, 50th and 67th) yesterday embarked from Canton for duty along the West and North Rivers and 12 planes of the Central Air Force proceeded to Yunnanfu August 9th in preparation for an attack upon Kwangsi.

(4) Unconfirmed reports are circulating here that negotiations with Li Tsung Jen and Pai Chung Hsi have broken down and that their continued refusal to conform to the Government's wishes is based on a belief that Chiang Kai Shek wants at all costs to avoid civil war and will ultimately agree to an arrangement whereby they will render lip service to the National Government but will remain in actual control in Kwangsi.

(5) To the Department and Peiping. Repeated to Canton. By mail to Hankow, Shanghai.

PECK

693.94244/130 : Telegram

The Ambassador in Japan (Grew) to the Secretary of State

TOKYO, August 17, 1936—6 p. m.
[Received August 17—7 : 36 a. m.]

169. Department's 100, July 29, 5 p. m., smuggling situation in North China. This subject was broached today in the course of a conversation with the Vice Minister for Foreign Affairs. The interest of the American Government in the situation was reaffirmed and questions were asked concerning the results of the investigation conducted by Kuwashima, the chief of the Eastern Asia Bureau of the Foreign Office. The Vice Minister said that nothing startling had resulted from Kuwashima's investigations but that he had found that the smuggling had decreased to only one-sixth or one-seventh of its former proportions partly because of saturation of the North China markets and partly because of the more efficient preventive measures taken by the Chinese authorities especially in regard to transshipment on the railways. The Vice Minister stated that the

Japanese Government considers that the fundamental solution of the situation lies in the lowering of the Chinese tariff rates and that he understood that Dr. Kung was now considering this solution. He did not indicate that the Japanese Government would take any steps to deal with the situation which he said was rapidly being alleviated through natural processes.

Repeated to Peiping.

GREW

793.94/8105 : Telegram

The Ambassador in China (Johnson) to the Secretary of State

PEIPING, August 21, 1936—4 p. m.
[Received August 21—9 : 38 a. m.[84]]

410. Reference paragraph 3 of Embassy's 405, August 17, 5 [4] p. m.[85]

1. The Japanese Ambassador visited Peiping from the evening of August 18th to the afternoon of August 20th. He is now in Tientsin to confer with Japanese diplomatic and military officers, including three representatives of the Ministries of Foreign Affairs, Army and Navy.

2. The Japanese Ambassador informed foreign pressmen yesterday that he had expressed the hope to Sung Che Yuan that Sung would suppress Communism in his two provinces; that he had discussed economic questions in principle with Sung; that he had advised Sung to ask for financial and technical assistance for Japan in the "exploitation of resources"; that Sung had agreed with these views; that he (the Japanese Ambassador) hoped that it would be possible to use Chinese capital although Japan would be prepared to help; that the present conditions in North China were tending toward stability; that he would inform the National Government that the Economic developments of North China was purely a local question; that the National Government was understood to be considering the question of lowering tariffs; and that Japan was prepared if necessary to open negotiations with the National Government whether or not it accepted Hirota's three principles.

3. A member of my staff in confidential conversation with the competent Third Secretary accompanying the Japanese Ambassador received certain information which is contained in paragraphs 4 and 5. together with certain inferences based on that conversation.

4. Japanese diplomats are apparently pessimistic about the future of Sino-Japanese relations. They would like to see two or three agree-

---

[84] Telegram in three sections.
[85] Not printed.

ments of an economic character entered into, not so much for the economic advantages involved, as economic development of North China will be a liability for Japan, but for the purpose of improving the feeling of the people. Chiang Kai Shek is expected to make agreements of an economic nature with the Japanese. He is strong enough to do this because his success in the Southwest weakens opposition to such agreements. The situation in Suiyuan not known to Japanese diplomats, but the Japanese Army definitely intends for strategic reasons to extend its control over Inner Mongolia. It is feared that if the Kwantung army acts in Suiyuan in the near future it will react unfavorably on Sino-Japanese negotiations with regard to North China. The question is asked whether Chiang could not enter into some agreement with the Japanese whereby the aid of the Japanese military with respect to Inner Mongolia could be satisfied and legitimatized. It is evident that the diplomats and the military are not yet united.

5. Not one pound of Changlu salt has yet been shipped to Japan because the Chinese do not yet refine the salt sufficiently and because the tax is still too high.[86] The route of the proposed Shihkiachwang-Tsangchow Railway has not yet been decided on. The development of iron in North China is not regarded hopefully at present because the ingredients needed for the manufacture of steel are too widely scattered and communications are lacking.

6. It seems possible to this Embassy that the Japanese Ambassador hopes that he can persuade the Japanese military to remain quiet for the time being and to suspend political activities, such as those looking toward an amalgamation of Sung's and Han's regimes, in order that he may effect some agreements of an economic nature, perhaps including reduction of the Chinese tariff, which will improve the general Sino-Japanese situation. It is not known whether the successful carrying out of such a program will be permitted by the Japanese military and the opponents of Chiang Kai Shek's compromise.

By mail to Tokyo.

JOHNSON

893.52 Manchuria/20

The Ambassador in Japan (Grew) to the Secretary of State

No. 2001   TOKYO, August 21, 1936.
                                                    [Received September 8.]

SIR: I have the honor to enclose a translation of a leading article which appeared in the *Jiji Shinpo* of today[87] indicating that the

[86] The Ambassador in China in his telegram No. 447, September 15, 4 p. m., informed the Department of reports of an agreement on September 9 by Chinese and Japanese interests for the refining of Changlu salt and its shipment to Japan (793.94/8143).
[87] Not printed.

Army's plan for settling 5,000,000 Japanese emigrants in Manchuria is assuming a more concrete shape.

It is clear from the article that while the project is expected to alleviate agrarian over-population at home its primary purpose is to make secure Japan's military occupation of Manchuria. It is noted that the Army considers a Japanese population of at least ten per cent of the total essential for security. This is an admission that the loyalty of the native Chinese population to "Manchukuo" cannot be relied upon. Also worthy of note is the strategic territorial distribution that is to be made of the Japanese emigrants: they are to be concentrated along the Soviet and Mongolian frontiers and also in areas in the vicinity of the principal industrial centers.

Grandiose as the project sounds, it cannot be doubted that the Japanese Army is in earnest about it. Much more doubtful are the prospects of success, notwithstanding the pronouncement that the period of experimental emigration has passed and that the time for large scale emigration has come. According to reliable information, the 500 Japanese agricultural families despatched to Chiamussu in 1932, the 500 families despatched to Hunanling in 1933, and the 500 families sent to Suiliang near Harbin in 1934 have dwindled respectively to 350, 300 and 300. The rigorous climate of North Manchuria, the difficulties of adjustment to so radical a change in environment, the constant menace of bandits, and above all the necessity of competing against the Chinese with their superior hardihood and lower standard of living, all combine to render the country unattractive to Japanese. Granted even that it is possible to subsidize emigration to an extent necessary to induce Japanese initially to take up life in Manchuria, it is difficult to see how they are to be kept contented there unless they continue to obtain subsidies. While much has been heard of the suggestion that the Japanese would be able to maintain a superior standard of living by the adoption of mechanized agriculture, it should be borne in mind, in view of the fact that farming in Japan is pursued by essentially the same intensive hand methods as in China, that there is no assurance that Japanese farmers in Manchuria would be able to adopt mechanized methods any more readily than would Chinese.

Respectfully yours,   JOSEPH C. GREW

793.94/8110 : Telegram

The Counselor of Embassy in China (Peck) to the Secretary of State

NANKING, August 25, 1936—1 p. m.
[Received August 25—7 a. m.]

249. In an informal conversation with the Secretary General of the Executive Yuan today he informed me that the present Japanese

Ambassador had told the Chinese Government that he would not insist on Hirota's three principles but would try to improve Sino-Japanese relations by taking up first economic questions susceptible of settlement and that the Ambassador had also assured the Chinese Government that he would discuss all pending questions with the National Government rather than with local authorities even including economic projects in North China. The Secretary General expressed satisfaction with the way in which the Japanese Ambassador had acted as to these announced intentions. Repeated to Peiping.

PECK

793.94/8111 : Telegram

The Counselor of Embassy in China (Peck) to the Secretary of State

NANKING, August 26, 1936—noon.
[Received August 26—7:18 a. m.]

250. 1. Suma this morning gave me an oral account of the Chengtu incident of August 24, 6 p. m. briefly as follows:

Following the Mukden incident five Japanese Consular offices in West China were closed and the Consulate General at Chengtu which had been maintained for 18 years has been the last to be reopened. Having duly informed the Chinese Foreign Office of the intention to reopen Chengtu and receiving no objection the Japanese Government recently sent an officer to Szechwan but when he arrived at Chungking about August 18, he was refused transportation on the commercial airline and a garage keeper even canceled contract already concluded to store his motor stock. Moreover this officer was stoned on the streets. On August 24, 4 Japanese comprising 2 newspaper reporters, 1 employee of the South Manchuria Railway and 1 merchant all provided with visaed passports arrived in Chengtu from Chungking presumably by plane and at 6 o'clock were attacked by anti-Japanese mass meeting of about 2000 persons. Chinese reports reaching Suma state that 2 of the party were killed, 1 wounded and 1 missing. Chaucer Wu, representative of the Chinese Ministry of Foreign Affairs at Chungking, telegraphed 24 hours after the event that 2 Japanese were missing and 2 wounded as a result of the attack. Suma instructed 2 officers of the Consulate at Chungking to proceed immediately to Chengtu to ascertain facts and it is thought that they went August 25th by plane.

2. Suma having a presentiment that serious trouble was brewing presented strongly worded *note verbale* to the Foreign Office August 24 just before the attack. This communication described the agitation in Szechwan against the reopening of the Consulate General at Chengtu and the treatment accorded Japanese officials in Chungking as being "assaults" and inconsistent with good relations between

China and Japan. Further representations will be made after the Japanese official report has been received.

3. Suma expressed to me his belief that the agitation against the reopening of the Consulate General has been deliberately fomented by officials of the Nanking Government although Liu Hsiang, Provisional [*Provincial?*] Chairman of Szechwan, being a pro-Kwangsi and anti-Chiang Kai Shek politician may also have been inciting it.

4. Suma informed me that the adjustment of Sino-Japanese relations had been at a standstill since the assassination of Vice Minister Tang Yu Jen December 25 last except for a constant exchange of notes of protest and I received the impression that if the Chengtu incident turns out to have been sufficiently serious it will be utilized as a means of accelerating this. Although of course deploring the incidents at Chungking and Chengtu and the consequent damage to Sino-Japanese friendship, Suma appeared pleased at the opportunity thus presented to bring pressure to bear on Chiang Kai Shek and the National Government.

PECK

711.94/1120

Memorandum by the Ambassador in Japan (*Grew*) [88]

[TOKYO,] August 26, 1936.

In taking leave this morning of the Foreign Minister I told Mr. Arita that I was going to the United States only for a short leave of absence for the primary purpose of attending the Harvard Tercentenary Celebration where I was happy to say that honorary degrees were to be presented to certain Japanese scholars and that the trip would of course give me a valuable opportunity for personal contacts again with the President and the Secretary of State. I asked the Minister if he had any particular thoughts which he would like to have conveyed to the authorities in Washington.

SOVIET RUSSIA

The Minister immediately began to talk about Soviet Russia and asked me whether I felt any anxiety with regard to a possible conflict between the two countries. I said that although I had felt some anxiety two years ago, I had recently believed and had so reported to my Government that the situation had improved and that in spite of frequent incidents on the frontier I did not believe that they would lead to conflict. Mr. Arita said that this diagnosis was correct. When he had returned to Tokyo as Foreign Minister he himself had

---

[88] Copy transmitted to the Department by the Ambassador in Japan in his despatch No. 2005, August 26; received September 21.

felt some anxiety on the basis of reports circulated abroad and he had at once investigated the situation and had found that there was no possibility of Japanese aggression (obviously Mr. Arita was speaking of the Japanese army). He said "we are modernizing our army" and he added that the intention was to strengthen the Japanese forces in Manchuria until they approximated the strength of the Soviet forces in Siberia amounting to some 220,000 to 230,000 men.

The Minister then turned to the question of the demarcation of the frontier and said that definite progress was being made to set up a commission for that purpose. In fact he had negotiated with the Soviet Ambassador on this subject only yesterday afternoon and would continue the negotiations this morning. He said it was not intended that this commission would cover the whole frontier but only the eastern portion from Lake Khanka to the Tumen River because this was the district where incidents most frequently occurred. The commission would have charge not only of demarcating the frontier but also of settling such incidents as might arise from time to time. The number of members of the commission was not yet settled.

The Minister said that I might therefore report in Washington that Soviet-Japanese relations were at present quiet and that no intention of aggression existed, so far as he was aware, on either side. The activities of the Comintern were quite a different matter and the Japanese Government was greatly exercised in combating communistic propaganda and the spread of bolshevism in Manchuria and China.

CHINA

The Minister then on an inquiry from myself turned to Japanese relations with China, and said that while every effort was being made by the Japanese Government to improve them, it was feared that a settlement of conditions could be reached but slowly. He said he hoped that something could be accomplished if Wang Ko-min could go to Peiping as a mediator between Nanking and Hopei. The Chahar-Hopei regime was being given no financial subsidies from Nanking and it was hoped that some kind of understanding along these lines could be reached. Mr. Arita believed that the smuggling situation was improving but he did not comment upon it in detail. I told Mr. Arita that the Prime Minister when I took leave of him yesterday had said that he was no longer Foreign Minister but he could nevertheless give me explicit assurances that American trade and commercial interests would in no way be interfered with by Japanese activities in China and I said that I was very glad to be able to bring these assurances to the attention of my Government. Mr. Arita made no comment.

THE UNITED STATES

I then asked the Minister how he regarded Japanese-American relations at the present time. He said that the Japanese people were thoroughly friendly to the United States and that except for a few minor difficulties he thought that our relations were proceeding very well. Our trade relations were producing some of these difficulties. I talked about the trade policy of our Government and the great pressure under which our Government also labored from various domestic industrial interests. The Minister said he hoped that if Mr. Roosevelt were reelected our Government might find this pressure less impelling. I said that Mr. Hull was doing everything in his power to reduce interference with our trade relations to the least possible degree. I spoke of the general foreign policy of the Administration, especially the good neighbor policy and how it had worked out in practise. Mr. Arita observed that Mr. Roosevelt's policy seemed to be somewhat different from that of his predecessor.

After an exchange of personal amenities the interview terminated with marked cordiality.

793.94/8114 : Telegram

The Ambassador in China (Johnson) to the Secretary of State

PEIPING, August 28, 1936—11 a. m.
[Received 3 : 50 p. m.[89]]

422. Reference Embassy's 410, August 21, 4 p. m.

1. The Japanese Ambassador left Tientsin August 24 after conferring there with Japanese military and diplomatic officials. He stopped at Tsinanfu August 25 and saw Han Fu Chu and went from there to Tsingtau on his way to Shanghai.

2. A competent Attaché of the local Japanese Embassy commented yesterday confidentially as follows.

3. The prevailing accomplishment of the Japanese Ambassador's visit to North China was an increase of his own understanding of the situation. He aroused the apprehension of the Japanese military as they feared that he was going to enter into agreements with the Chinese. He did, however, gain the understanding of the Commander of the North China Garrison and he made a good impression on Chinese officials. The Kwantung army is still irritated.

4. Economic agreements await the Japanese Ambassador's conversation with Chiang Kai Shek. Kawagoe prepared his program of economic cooperation while he was stationed in Tientsin and it has the approval of the military. The first start will be the building of

---

[89] Telegram in three sections.

two railways, one being the Shihkiachwang–Tsangchow Railway, although this will probably not go to Tsangchow but will run direct from Shihkiachwang to Tientsin, thereby cutting short the route, the other being the Tsinanfu–Shunteh Railway. Final agreements on railways await the conversations of the Japanese Ambassador with Chiang. The Japanese insist on their financial participation in the construction work of both railways. The first railway will open up the coal fields of Shansi, although this will depend on agreements made with the Shansi authorities, with whom it is difficult to make agreements. National Government influence is increasing there. The second railway will not only open up Shansi coal fields but will also open up a cotton and agricultural area. The second step of the program will be the development of agricultural products, including cotton. The Shansi authorities have refused to permit the Japanese to establish a cotton experimental station at Taiyuan. However, the Japanese intend to establish such stations next spring at Tungchow and at Tientsin. The cotton growing plan has progressed no further than this. The third step will be development of mining, which will be confined to coal and iron, the latter not being very hopeful, and possibly gold. The whole program will be expensive for Japan. It is believed that the Foreign Office official Kuwashima, who has gone to Osaka to persuade Japanese there to invest in North China, will be successful because such investment is a matter of national policy although it may not be regarded by them optimistically.

5. The new Chief of Staff of the North China Garrison, Major General Gun Hashimoto, arrived at Tientsin August 18. In accordance with the present policy of the central authority, he is a moderate. He has had no Kwantung army experience and although clever it is feared he may be unable to control his subordinates.

6. There is no change in the North China situation and a five province regime is no nearer than it was 2 months ago.

By mail to Tokyo.

JOHNSON

393.1163 Seventh Day Adventist/25 : Telegram

The Ambassador in China (Johnson) to the Secretary of State

PEIPING, September 1, 1936—noon.
[Received September 1—7 a. m.]

427. Reverend Otto Christensen, Seventh Day Adventist Mission at Kalgan, informs me that his mission has for some years maintained activities between [*sic*] north of Changpei; that up until recently he has been able to maintain contact with this activity without interference from Japanese and Mongols under Japanese supervision who

now hold Changpei and Chapsur; but that recently he encountered difficulty in trying to get from the Mongols permit to continue and enlarge the mission work to which they have hitherto been friendly. He was unable to see any one in real authority, but has heard from Mongol conversations reports which he believes to be true that the Mongols under Japanese instigation are preparing to force all foreigners out of area immediately north of Kalgan except of course Japanese. He believes that this act of exclusion will include even Larson, who is understood to be a Mongol citizen. He stated that an American named Wardell, formerly a missionary but now employed by Larson in charge of his gardens at Chapsur had been told to leave. I understand that such exclusion if carried out would affect some four Americans resident in that area.

He informed me that it has been currently reported among Mongols that the Japanese are enlisting and arming Chinese bandits for the purpose of sending them west to make trouble, and that it is these people, and the Mongol soldiers from Jehol who are being pushed into Chahar by the Japanese, [who?] only make trouble. He has visited the Japanese military mission at Kalgan and Japanese in Mongolia to obtain permits, but had been invariably informed that they, the Japanese, have nothing to do with permits in that area, although Mongols told them that they cannot issue permits without Japanese approval.

I have told Christensen whose residence is in Kalgan that I feel it would be unsafe for him and other Americans to attempt to remain in that area without permits. I have told him that there is little or nothing I can do to guarantee the continuance of his liberty to go and come in that area. I suggested to him that he give me in writing, a statement of the activities of his mission in that area, as well as a list of their properties. If and when I receive this I propose to send it to the Japanese Embassy here with a request that orders be issued to Japanese in that area to look out for and protect Americans there.

JOHNSON

893.01 Inner Mongolia/78 : Telegram

The Ambassador in China (Johnson) to the Secretary of State

PEIPING, September 1, 1936—2 p. m.
[Received September 1—11 : 30 a. m.]

429. Reference Embassy's 427, September 1, noon.

(1) Information has been obtained with regard to conditions in Inner Mongolia in Chahar and eastern Suiyuan under Japanese control from two Mongol-speaking foreigners who have just returned from that area after a 3 months' and 1 month's visit respectively.

Their information, which is contained in paragraph 2, is not conflicting and it substantiates information submitted by the Embassy in previous telegrams.

(2) There are apparently not Japanese troops in the area in question, but there are Japanese officers and some thousands of Manchukuo and Mongol forces. The Mongols do the bidding of the Japanese only and admit their fear of the Japanese and because Prince Teh is heavily in debt to them as the result of purchases of military supplies. Chinese renegades and bandits, together with some Mongols of similar character, continue to gather in the vicinity of Shangtu in the extreme west of Chahar northeast of Pingtichuan and are allegedly and presumably receiving arms and money from Japan.

(3) An American resident of Suiyuan states that residents of Suiyuan are apprehensive of the allegedly impending westward movement of the above-mentioned elements and that definite preparations are being pushed.

(4) The attitude of Fu Tso Yi, however, is not known. The Chief of Staff of the Kwantung army visited Fu at Kueihwa on August 25 and 26. The purpose and outcome of the visit are not known. Itagaki also visited Yin Ju Keng but did not see Sung Che Yuan. His visit to Yin has aroused speculation in connection with the Japanese Ambassador's alleged statement to the Chinese press that East Hopei and North Chahar should be united. By mail to Tokyo.

JOHNSON

893.01 Manchuria/1362

The Consul at Mukden (Langdon) to the Ambassador in China (Johnson) [90]

No. 18   MUKDEN, September 2, 1936.

SIR: I have the honor to acknowledge the receipt of the Embassy's instruction of August 28, 1936, directing that I report on the present status of the question of residence in Sinpin of American citizens.

As was reported by the Consulate General on April 22, all citizens except Father Haggerty of the Catholic Mission and all British subjects had withdrawn from Sinpin. In the meantime, Rev. W. T. Cook, head of the American Presbyterian Mission at Sinpin, has inquired several times whether conditions permitted his return there. A copy of his letter of August 3 in this connection and of my reply is enclosed.[91] As will be noted in my reply, Dr. Cook was discouraged from resuming work at Sinpin. At the present moment only Father

---

[90] Copy transmitted to the Department by the Consul at Mukden in his unnumbered despatch of September 2; received October 6.
[91] Neither printed.

Haggerty remains in Sinpin, the other American and the British (Presbyterian) missionaries staying in Korea or Mukden awaiting developments.

I have little hope of any early change in the situation that might allow the return of the missionaries to Sinpin. Conditions in the Sinpin region are most disturbed and insecure. In fact, guerilla warfare of a desperate nature has been going on there in the past few months. The insurgents of that area, Chinese political "bandits" and Korean communists and irredentists, are the most numerous and best organized in Manchuria. On August 17, for example, a mixed force of 2000 of them attacked the walled town of Fusung, a little over 100 miles east of Sinpin, killed 9 and wounded 6 of the defence forces, in addition to some townsmen, burned 24 government offices and 261 private houses,* and were only driven off by superior land and air forces rushed from the closest Japanese garrisons.

Apart from the personal danger of living in such a disturbed zone, there is the likelihood that Korean insurgents may use the mission servants and native helpers, all Koreans, as instruments for espionage and communication. In any event, this is what the Japanese military and consular authorities at Sinpin are afraid of, to judge by their refusal at the time to recommend any Korean, even a baby amah, for domestic service at the mission (see previous correspondence). In this connection, I may state that not long ago Colonel Kato, Commander of the Japanese Gendarmes at Mukden, told Consul General Ballantine and me that we should not judge his command too harshly for the examinations and arrests it had made of native employees of foreign companies and missions, as we had no idea of how much seditious activity was going on under the unwitting cloaks of foreigners.

In view of the sinister state of affairs in the Sinpin area, of the evident distrust of every Korean there, and of the fact that the American Presbyterian mission works exclusively among the Korean population, I feel that it would be unsafe, if at all feasible, for members of that mission to resume work before the area has been reasonably pacified. I shall therefore advise Dr. Cook and his associates to stay away from Sinpin for the time being.

As has already been said, Father Haggerty remains in Sinpin despite the Consulate General's advice to him that he come away. His work, however, is among Chinese and he has reported no arrest or treatment of his servants or native assistants suggesting official suspicion of their character. Nevertheless, the fact that his colleague Father Burns was kidnapped by insurgents last February at Tunghwa, fifty miles or

---

*Official release August 30, 1936, Kokutsu. [Footnote in the original.]

so to the east, and is still held captive,[92] shows that he too is running a risk in remaining in Sinpin.

Very respectfully yours,

WM. R. LANGDON

393.1163 Seventh Day Adventist/26 : Telegram

The Secretary of State to the Ambassador in China (Johnson)

WASHINGTON, September 4, 1936— 5 p. m.

215. Your 427, September 1, noon.   With regard to the last paragraph of the telegram under reference, the Department perceives no objection to sending to the Japanese Embassy the statement and list referred to but feels that you should avoid expressly asking that Embassy to issue orders to protect American citizens.   It is suggested that in sending the above-mentioned statement and list to the Japanese Embassy you might indicate that this information is supplied for the purpose of acquainting it with the location of American citizens and their property in that area in order that Americans may not be interfered with or their property damaged.

HULL

893.00/13692 : Telegram

The Second Secretary of Embassy in China (Atcheson) to the Secretary of State

NANKING, September 5, 1936—noon.
[Received September 5—10 : 50 a. m.]

260. My 255, September 1, 10 a. m.[93]

1. According to the press, Wang Chung Hui did not accompany the Peace Mission to Nanning on account of illness and the mission's journey was delayed by weather.   Reuter at Canton reports September 4 that the Peace Conference at Nanning has come to a deadlock because Li Tsung Jen and Pai Chung Hsi insist that, (1) they remain at Kwangsi as Pacification Commissioner and Vice-Commissioner and, (2) Li Chi Sen be appointed Kwangsi Chairman.   It is stated that Chiang Kai Shek's representatives were to return to Canton yesterday.

2. We have so far been unable to obtain reliable information concerning the Nanning negotiations or the plans of the Government if the deadlock continues.   As opposed to the statement of a Foreign Office official under cover in paragraph 3 of the telegram under reference, I am informed by a senior officer of the Executive Yuan that the Government will in no circumstances, other than an attack by Japanese, launch into contests, although its position is legally and

---

[92] Father Burns was released in mid-November 1936.
[93] Not printed.

ethically correct, because it fears that it cannot rely upon Han Fu Chu, Sung Che Yuan, Feng Yu Hsiang, Liu Hsiang and possibly others to maintain an attitude of support.

3. Sent to the Department, Peiping and Canton.

ATCHESON

893.00/13693 : Telegram

The Second Secretary of Embassy in China (Atcheson) to the Secretary of State

NANKING, September 7, 1936—1 p. m.
[Received September 7—9:40 a. m.]

261. My 260, September 5, noon.

1. I am informed by responsible official of the Foreign Office that the impasse with the Southwest has been practically dissolved. Government mandates dated September 6th appoint Li Tsung Jen Pacification Commissioner of Kwangsi and Pai Chung Hsi member of the standing committee of the Military Affairs Commission and Huang Shao Hsiung Chairman of Chekiang. My informant states that word of Pai's acceptance of new post has not been received but his acceptance is assumed and he will proceed to Canton to meet with Chiang Kai Shek and discuss other details to be settled.

2. To Department and Peiping. Repeated to Canton by mail, to Hankow, Shanghai.

ATCHESON

793.94/8129 : Telegram

The Second Secretary of Embassy in China (Atcheson) to the Secretary of State

NANKING, September 9, 1936—2 p. m.
[Received September 9—1:52 p. m.]

262. Penultimate paragraph of Canton's September 8, 11 a. m.[94]

1. Japanese Embassy states that it has no details other than that a Japanese merchant, the only Japanese resident of Pakhoi who has lived there many years and has a Chinese wife, was killed several days ago at Pakhoi by a Chinese mob. (Reuter's at Canton quoting the Japanese Consulate General there gives the date of the alleged murder as September 3.) Suma intimated this morning to a foreign news correspondent that the affair involved members of the former 19th Foreign [*Route*] Army part of which is reported to have been in occupation of Pakhoi on behalf of the Kwangsi rebels. He said that this was one more instance of anti-Japanism and is equivalent to the

---

[94] Not printed.

Chengtu incident in importance and he mentioned the Shanghai murders as previous instances concerning which Japan had shown great patience. He said that Japanese patience was now exhausted and it would be "immediately necessary" for the Chinese Government to take adequate steps to suppress the vicious anti-Japanese feeling which the Government had allowed to grow throughout the country.

2. He said that he opened yesterday preliminary negotiations with the Minister for Foreign Affairs over the Chengtu incident but the conversation was general, he had offered no demands or proposals for settlement and the Japanese Government had not yet formulated its demands. He said he told Chang Chun that the suppression of anti-Japanese feeling in China was essential to a settlement of the Chengtu murder and to the adjustment of Sino-Japanese relations. He said the date of Kawagoe's arrival in Nanking had not yet been set.

3. I am informed by responsible official of the Foreign Office that the Chinese Government has not yet received any official information of the Pakhoi incident.

4. To Department and Peiping. Repeated to Canton, by mail to Shanghai, Tokyo.

ATCHESON

793.94/8128 : Telegram

The Consul at Hankow (Jarvis) to the Secretary of State

HANKOW, September 9, 1936—5 p. m.
[Received September 9—10:05 a. m.]

There are now six vessels of the Japanese Yangtze River forces (11th Squadron) at Hankow (the *Ataka, Katata, Atami, Toba, Futami* and *Kotaka*) and two at Chungking (the *Hozu* and *Hira*). Five of the six vessels at Hankow arrived on September 7th, 8th and 9th. The 11th Squadron numbers 12 vessels.

2. Chaucer Wu, the Foreign Office's special delegate for Szechuan and Sikang, flew through Hankow yesterday on his way from Chengtu to Nanking to report.

3. In Chengtu, according to a reliable foreign source there, the authorities are trying to curb anti-Japanese expressions, there is now little evidence of anti-foreign feeling, and students are politer than they have been for years. Sent to Peiping, Nanking, Shanghai.

JARVIS

793.003 Manchuria/11

The Belgian Ambassador (Van der Straten-Ponthoz) to the Secretary of State

[Translation]

D. 5038   WASHINGTON, September 9, 1936.
No. 3303

MR. SECRETARY OF STATE: By direction of the King's Government, I have the honor to avail myself of Your Excellency's kindness with a view to ascertaining, if possible, the sentiment of the American Government with regard to the declaration made, on July 1st last, by the Minister of Foreign Affairs at Hsinking, concerning the status of foreigners residing in Manchuria. The matter under discussion relates in particular to those belonging to countries still enjoying the privilege of extraterritoriality in Manchuria, as a consequence of the fact that they have it in China.

The declaration in question appears to take the form of an invitation to a group of powers to engage in *pourparlers* with respect to the status of their nationals in the new empire.

The enclosed note sets forth the different considerations which have received the attention of my Government.

It would be happy to learn the intentions of the American Government as to the action to be taken on the overtures of the Manchukuo Government.

The King's Government would especially appreciate it if it could receive such information as soon as possible.

I avail myself [etc.]   R. V. STRATEN

[Enclosure—Translation]

The Belgian Embassy to the Department of State

NOTE

The following points will certainly not have escaped the attention of the American Government. The King's Embassy states them here only to define clearly the circumstances under which the Belgian Government would be interested in ascertaining the intentions of the United States Government as to the action to be taken on the overtures of the Manchukuo Government.

For more than three years, the Japanese military party sought to obtain the elimination of the privilege of extraterritoriality for Japanese nationals in Manchukuo, but always encountered a strong opposition on the part of the civilian elements who dreaded this change and preferred to remain subject to their own consular and judicial authorities, knowing that the final consequence of elimination of the privilege would be a considerable increase of the taxes and imports that they would have to pay, and the largest part of which they had succeeded in eluding up to the present, under the protection of the privilege.

On its part, the military element saw in the subjection of Japanese nationals to the laws of Manchukuo a means of increasing the budgetary receipts of the new Empire which it has created, and thus indirectly, the participation of the latter in the military expenses of the Japanese army in Manchuria, so burdensome for the home government.

The two parties finally arrived at a compromise, as shown by the conclusion of the Treaty of June 10, 1936, signed by His Excellency Mr. Chang Yen Ching, Minister of Foreign Affairs of Manchukuo and His Excellency General K. Uyeda, Ambassador of Japan at Hsinking, concerning the residence and the taxation of Japanese subjects in Manchukuo; this treaty is accompanied with an Interpretative Accord of the same date.   As these acts went into force on July 1st, it is therefore officially from that date that the Japanese and Koreans ceased to enjoy extraterritoriality in Manchuria.

Thus, as the United States Government is aware, the elimination of extraterritoriality will be gradual and will be effected in three stages.   Beginning with July 1st of this year, Japanese nationals will be subject to taxes collected by the various Manchu authorities, but on the basis of a reduced schedule.

As a second stage, on a date not yet fixed, Japanese and Korean persons and firms will be subject to Manchu laws on industry and commerce.   The third stage, the time for which is also undetermined, will place Japanese nationals entirely under the jurisdiction of the laws and courts of the Manchu Empire.   With respect to the application of legal penalties, a comparative scale of the various Japanese and Manchu terms of imprisonment has been published, which permits the assumption that Japanese prisoners will serve their prison terms in Japanese penitentiaries, whether in Manchukuo or Japan.

It is estimated that the accomplishment of this whole program will not exceed a period of five years.

But while the elimination of the privilege is only to be effected very gradually, on the other hand, the advantages that will result therefrom for Japanese nationals will be immediate; hereafter, they will have the right to reside and travel, engage in commerce, industry and agriculture, to own lands and real estate throughout the Manchu Empire. They already had these rights *de facto*, but they now obtain legal sanction of them.

These reforms are the result of labors of various commissions which have held sessions either at Hsinking, or Tokio, since March, 1933.

As the special zone of the South Manchurian Railway enjoys a special régime, which it is also necessary to eliminate gradually, the Japanese Government has published a series of regulations which will remain in force until January 1, 1938, on which date the administration and police rights will be transferred to the Hsinking Government.

With a view to subjecting the inhabitants of this zone to the same taxes as those imposed on the inhabitants of the Manchu territory, the Japanese Government has established four new taxes by these regulations, on wheat flour, tobacco, alcoholic beverages and cement.

The Treaty will not affect Japanese jurisdiction over Kwantung Leased Territory, in which the Cities of Dairen and Port Arthur are situated.

On July 1, the very day on which the new treaty went into force, the Minister of Foreign Affairs at Hsinking made a declaration concerning the status of foreigners residing in Manchuria and belonging to a country still enjoying the privilege of extraterritoriality in Manchuria, as the result of that which they still have in China.

Although by the note addressed, on March 12, 1932, by Manchukuo to seventeen countries,[95] and to which there has been no reply, the new Government undertook to respect the obligations contracted by the Republic of China toward these different countries, the fact is now established that in principle, at least, it refuses to continue to respect one of them. According to certain commentaries, it takes as a basis the circumstance that by their failure to reply, these same powers have reduced this declaration to the level of a unilateral act, and that they cannot claim to continue enjoying a privilege by virtue of a document which they do not recognize as a communication from an independent state.

Nevertheless, the Manchukuo Government will continue, as a favor, and pending a solution of the question, to apply with certain restrictions, to the nationals of those countries, a treatment similar to that which they would have enjoyed if they still really had the privilege of extraterritoriality.

In comparison with the number of Japanese subjects—about 300,000 Japanese and 1,000,000 Koreans—the number of such foreigners in Manchukuo is insignificant; indeed, it must not be forgotten that the Russians (40,000), the Poles (4,000), the Germans, the Austrians, the Czechoslovaks, the Estonians, Latvians, etc., do not have this privilege, either because their countries lost it as a consequence of the World

---

[95] For text of note, see telegram of this date from Mr. Hsieh Chieh-shih, *Foreign Relations*, 1932, vol. III, p. 579.

War, or because they never had it, being succession States of the Russian and Austrian Empires.

The countries still possessing extraterritoriality are listed, with the number of their nationals, in the table below:

(Statistics of the Hsinking Government)

	Manchukuo	Special Zone of the South Manchurian Railway
England	398	11
Canada	72	3
British India	9	0
United States	212	21
France	187	3
Belgium	25	1
Italy	39	0
Switzerland	42	0
Denmark	141	0
Portugal	5	0
Netherlands	33	0
Norway	7	1
Sweden	18	0
Spain	0	0
Mexico	0	0
Peru	0	0

So far as the Belgians are concerned, this official figure is certainly less than the actual number, for in the province of Jehol there are already more than 50 Belgian missionaries, and probably as many more in the province of Chahar which seems to be completely occupied now by the Japanese-Manchu army.

We see from these figures, even if they are somewhat below the actual figure, that the number of foreigners still enjoying extraterritoriality is very small; moreover, a large number of those are Catholic or Protestant missionaries; although France continues to protect the Missions the presence of an Apostolic Delegate at Hsinking permits the direct settlement of many questions concerning the Catholic religious institutions; as to the Protestant missionaries, the tendency among them is to avoid availing themselves of their privilege of extraterritoriality in their relations with the authorities; so far as other cases are concerned the consuls have in general tried to settle each matter in a friendly way with the local authority, according to the particular circumstances; nevertheless the English consular court has continued to function in the last few years to try certain insurance cases or usury cases, of which offense the Hindus commonly render themselves guilty.

The Manchu courts are still in full course of reorganization, which renders their operation very slow; the young Japanese magistrates who form a framework for the Manchu judges are animated, it is said, by a spirit of good will, but are still lacking in local experience.

The declaration of the Ministry of Foreign Affairs will perhaps not have a very great practical bearing but it constitutes, for a group of Powers, an invitation to break a silence of over four years and to enter into *pourparlers* on the subject of the status of their nationals in the new Empire; these *pourparlers*, the utility of which is making itself felt more than formerly, seem bound, however, to remain subject to a prior settlement, or at least the adoption of a *modus vivendi*, between Japan and China, concerning the Manchurian question, which would permit of a modification of the point of view of this group of Powers concerning this question, by at least an implicit "*de facto*" recognition of the young Empire.

The German-Manchu Trade Agreement of April 30, with the presence, soon, of a German Trade Commissioner at Hsinking, already gives German trade a privileged situation; without being able to claim such a situation, which is explained not only by the fact that Germany is the chief European buyer of Manchurian products, but also by political reasons sufficiently known to the American Government, arrangements pursuant to the recent declaration of the Ministry of Foreign Affairs could not but be favorable to the development of the interests of such countries as might conclude them with Manchuria.

An arrangement dealing only with the régime applicable to the nationals of such countries would obviously not justify the claim to obtain the inclusion of the most-favored-nation clause; it is even probable that it would never be obtained in any case, for it would be for Japan the abandonment of her theory of "her special interests" in Manchuria which she has been invoking so frequently for the past 30 years; nevertheless, it is allowable to think that in exchange for the official abandonment of the privilege, rights would be obtained analogous to those of foreigners in Japan proper.

Furthermore, the representatives of those Powers would have officially, as have the German representatives already, an easy access to the authorities of the capital in order to effect all steps and negotiations relative to the interests of their nationals.

793.94/8130 : Telegram

The Consul General at Canton (Linnell) to the Secretary of State

CANTON, September 10, 1936—3 p. m.
[Received September 10—1 : 45 p. m.]

Regarding Pakhoi incident, my telegram September 8, 11 a. m.,[96] it is now learned that the killing of a Japanese occurred on the border

---

[96] Not printed.

on September 3rd.   The Japanese gunboat *Saga* has sailed from Canton for Pakhoi carrying two officials of the Canton Japanese Consulate General who will investigate case.   Dr. Tyau, special delegate for Executive Department's Foreign Affairs states he advised Japanese Consul in charge not to send delegate to Pakhoi for fear of possible mob incidents but they proceeded nevertheless.   Tyau has sent his assistant to Pakhoi to make an investigation.   The Japanese Consul in charge states that they will investigate especially whether the alleged position was given out by 19th Route Army forces while carrying on anti-Japanese demonstration.   If this is found to be the case Japanese attitude will become much firmer.

Sent to the Department, Peiping, Nanking.

LINNELL

741.94/69

The Ambassador in China (Johnson) to the Secretary of State

No. 710   PEIPING, September 11, 1936.
                                        [Received October 5.]

SIR: I have the honor to refer to despatch No. 1970 of August 6, 1936, from the American Ambassador at Tokyo in regard to Anglo-Japanese relations.   Mr. Grew points out that, although Great Britain does not at this time seek an ally in the Far East she would like to have a friendly Japan willing to guarantee and protect her interests in China and from whom she might seek relief from the growing danger of Japanese trade in the markets of the British Empire.   The Ambassador considers whether there is ground for agreement between British and Japanese desires and mentions indications of a *rapprochement* between the two countries.

There are also suggestions of such a *rapprochement* in China.

British interests in China are considerable, particularly in South China, and her investments alone are valued at six times those of the United States.   Should Japanese advocates (including the Japanese Navy) of Japanese expansion to the south gain control of Japan's policy of expansion, as Mr. Yoshida, the Japanese Ambassador to England, believes they will,* such Japanese expansion would be a serious threat to the interests of Great Britain, especially those in Hongkong and the vicinity.   Already Great Britain has suffered from Japanese trade rivalry.   Following the Great War, Japanese cottons made such steady inroads in the markets of India, long monopolized by Lancashire, that by 1932 Japanese exports to that country actually

---

* See Department's strictly confidential instruction No. 205, June 29, 1936, to the Embassy.   [Footnote in the original.   Instruction No. 205 not printed; see memorandum of June 25 by the Chief of the Division of Far Eastern Affairs, p. 220.]

exceeded British exports by some 45,000,000 square yards. The result was the raising of the tariff wall against Japanese goods not only in India, but throughout the Empire. However, contrary to expectations, the total purchases of Japanese goods by India for the first half of 1934 were much much greater than for the first half of 1933 and in spite of the restrictions imposed by the Indian authorities the volume of cotton goods exported to India by Japan for the same period showed a considerable increase over the first six months of 1933.

It is not only on exporting cotton to India that Japan has concentrated, but so successful has been the drive for export trade which she started in 1932 that her total exports of all sorts for the following year showed an increase of 63%. Her exports since that date have increased annually, although not at quite so rapid a rate. Obviously this is at the cost of other manufacturing nations. The visible Japanese trade with China (smuggling activities excluded) appears to have remained static during the last three years, but when one realizes that the value of her total trade with Manchukuo showed an increase in 1934 of approximately 44 million Yen over 1932, some 42 million of which represented exports, it is obvious that this is not the case. British exports to China on the other hand have shown a gradual decrease from 108,258,100 H. K. taels in 1930 to 80,004,000 H. K. taels in 1934. It would appear that it is British trade that is paying to a large extent the cost of Japanese trade expansion and of the many points at which the interests of Great Britain and Japan are in direct conflict, the most serious is their competition for markets in the Far East, particularly in China. When Japan seized Manchuria, the British Foreign Office, under the leadership of Sir John Simon, appeared to think that Japan would stop at the Great Wall and not disturb British interests in China proper. The extension of influence over Hopei and Chahar by Japan and the recent smuggling activities which that nation has condoned in North China have gone far to prove the fallacy of this belief. Great Britain's stake in North China, however, is not great: certain tobacco interests, approximately a 50% interest in the Kailan Mining Administration, and a share in the former Peiping-Mukden and the Peiping-Pukov Railways constitute her outstanding commitments. Of course she has the British Concession interests in Tientsin and various coastal shipping lines such as Jardine, Matheson, & Co. Ltd., and Butterfield and Swire, whose ships call at Tientsin. However, if it came to a question of going to war over these interests she would perhaps be willing to sacrifice them, but her southern sphere of influence is another question and from the long-term point of view the situation for Great Britain presents many difficulties.

The sending of Sir Frederick Leith-Ross, Chief Economic Adviser to the British Government to China, was doubtless due to a feeling of a need for serious study of these conditions. It is also noteworthy that the newly appointed British Ambassador to China has stopped over in Tokyo for a visit with his Colleague there before proceeding to his post in China.

Whether Great Britain has evolved a policy for dealing with her Far Eastern questions, it is difficult to say. Sir Alexander Cadogan, recently said that he had no idea of the British policy in regard to the Far East. Sir Alexander added, however, that he was inclined to believe that British sentiment and American sentiment were similar in that neither nation would fight in the Far East.† From the British point of view, the troubled situations closer at home would appear to preclude any other stand. Confronted with grave European problems, she is presumably attempting to evolve some other method of protecting her interests in China short of war. It is as yet unknown what this method is, but as Great Britain has always appeared to steer the course of an opportunist, some solution by compromise may present itself. There appears to be evidence that this solution entails a more friendly attitude towards Japan.

In my despatch No. 584 of July 17, 1936,[97] I pointed out that the members of the British Embassy staff here expressed the belief that they had gone much farther in the Sasaki Case [98] than they would have done in the course of normal events to comply with the wishes of the Japanese and to prove to their own satisfaction that the British soldiers implicated were not guilty.

The Consul General at Shanghai, in a letter to me dated August 17, 1936, a copy of which is enclosed,[97] citing the fact that the British forces in Shanghai took no action in reference to the functioning of Japanese patrols in the British Defense Sector in Shanghai, says that he cannot escape the impression that a definite effort is being made by the British authorities to avoid any differences of opinion with the Japanese and to defer to them in local matters.

In the same letter Mr. Gauss points out that he has good reason to believe that the British Consul General consulted with the Japanese Consulate General and agreed upon a text of a letter to the Municipal Council in regard to the question of Factory Law and Factory Inspection in Shanghai before proposing as Senior Consul at the Consular Body meeting the letter in question. The question was one which entailed a change on the part of the British Consul General from the course he had previously given Mr. Gauss the impression

---

† Memorandum of conversation held on July 2, 1936, between Sir Alexander Cadogan and Mr. Ray Atherton enclosed in the Department's strictly confidential instruction No. 223, of July 22, 1936. [Footnote in the original. Instruction No. 223 not printed; see memorandum of July 13, by the Counselor of Embassy in the United Kingdom, p. 241.]

[97] Not printed.

[98] British Embassy guard members were accused of killing a Japanese at Peiping in a brawl.

he intended to follow. Mr. Gauss gained the impression that his action was prompted by a desire to show solidarity with the Japanese. In speaking of these incidents, Mr. Gauss says:

"And, running along from day to day, observing the play-up of news in the British press in China, their editorials, et cetera, one gets an impression of a change of attitude; not so much one of conciliation or of support of the Japanese, but of avoidance of criticism of Japanese policy.

"As I said, I may be mistaken; but this is my impression—the 'feel' of the situation—here . . ." [99]

Sir Alexander Cadogan in his conversation with Mr. Atherton on July 2 said that he "was not in favor of attempting to cooperate with Japan for a profitable exploitation of China; neither was he in favor of an attempt to short-circuit Japan in China unless Japanese policy tread on British interests." That such an attitude would prove pleasing to Japan there seems little doubt, especially if credence is to be given to the statement of Mr. Yoshida to Mr. Norman Davis that the Japanese Army leaders now think they should cultivate the friendship and cooperation of Great Britain and the United States and particularly not alienate the British any further by their Chinese policy.

When the interests of two countries clash as directly as do those of Japan and Great Britain there must either be a complete break or there must be an agreement to cooperate in a division of the spoils. The overtures of Japan at this time would appear to indicate that Japan wants a breathing interval and that she feels that she has achieved a position sufficiently strong vis-à-vis England to force a compromise very favorable to her needs for a larger market for the products of her factories. The question is, is Great Britain ready to make the concession which Japan will demand. As indicated above, there is evidence of a British desire to be conciliatory but there is as yet little evidence that she feels the situation is so serious as to make a truce an immediate necessity.

Respectfully yours,

NELSON TRUSLER JOHNSON

793.94/8139 : Telegram

The Ambassador in China (Johnson) to the Secretary of State

PEIPING, September 14, 1936—noon.
[Received September 14—6 : 30 a. m.]

445. The following telegram has been received from the Consul General at Shanghai.

"September 11, 4 p. m. Japanese news agency Domei reports that at conference convened by Japanese Ambassador yesterday afternoon at which the Commander of the Third Fleet and Japanese Military

---

[99] Omission indicated in the original.

and Naval Attachés were present a decision was reached to the effect that 'should the Nanking Government lack the authority to facilitate the investigation by Japanese officials of the Pakhoi mob murder of Mr. Nakano the Japanese authorities on the spot should take whatever measures that are considered appropriate to perform their task'.

Confirmation of the above has been obtained from reliable source.

Unconfirmed reports from fairly reliable sources indicate that should Nanking fail to take immediate and effective steps to suppress anti-Japanese activities the Japanese Government will take action and will deal with local authorities rather than with Central Government.

Repeated to Nanking, by mail. By mail to Tokyo."

JOHNSON

793.94/8140 : Telegram

The Consul General at Canton (Linnell) to the Secretary of State

CANTON, September 14, 1936—4 p. m.
[Received September 14—12 : 03 p. m.]

Reports in local press and confirmed by Japanese Consulate that Japanese gunboat *Saga* arrived at Pakhoi afternoon of 12th but local commander 19th Route Army refused investigating party permission to land. Chinese investigating party landed from Chinese gunboat *Foo Kon*. Dr. Ling Shih Feng in charge of the Chinese investigators asked the *Saga* to leave but ship remains at Pakhoi. All quiet there at last reports.

Press reports today that martial law has been lifted at Wuchow and Kwangsi Government has ordered cessation of all forms of military activities.

Sent to the Department, Peiping, Nanking.

LINNELL

793.94/8142 : Telegram

The Chargé in Japan (Dickover) to the Secretary of State

TOKYO, September 15, 1936—5 p. m.
[Received September 15—9 : 10 a. m.]

186. 1. Vernacular press reports that Pakhoi case is assuming a more serious aspect consequent upon the opposition of the 19th Route Army to the landing there of Japanese investigators, that Nanking is now being pressed to take measures to enable investigation to proceed in security, and that if Nanking fails to act the Japanese Government is prepared to take independent action "in self defense".

2. Notwithstanding strong tone adopted by press, which may have been purposely inspired with a view to producing an effect in China,

there are reasons to believe that Japan would be reluctant to precipitate hostilities at Pakhoi for in doing this, according to opinion in navy circles, Japan would be fighting Chiang Kai Shek's battles for him. Naval Attaché has been informed that only a small gunboat, a destroyer, and a light cruiser have been despatched to Pakhoi, Military Attaché has been told by the War Office liaison officer that no particular preparations have been made for despatching an expeditionary force but that the Taiwan army is watching the situation.

3. According to the *Asahi*, Japanese Ambassador will insist in connection with the settlement of the Chengtu and Pakhoi incidents upon China taking measures for the elimination of anti-Japanese activities which Japan regards as the underlying cause of these incidents, as otherwise settlement of the pending issues and the adjustment of the relations between the two countries will be impossible.

Repeated to Peiping.

DICKOVER

793.94/8146 : Telegram

The Ambassador in China (Johnson) to the Secretary of State

PEIPING, September 15, 1936—5 p. m.
[Received 5 : 57 p. m.]

448. Reference Embassy's telegram 440, September 11, 1 p. m.[1]

1. Wang Keh Min has definitely decided not to accept a post in North China. This decision is presumably the result of opposition by Sung Che Yuan and other Chinese elements supported by Japanese elements opposing Wang.

2. A high Japanese official states that approval was given in July to Wang by Japanese authorities on the understanding that he would be invested by the National Government with wide powers for negotiations but that the failure of the National Government to grant Wang such powers had caused the Japanese authorities to alter their attitude. It is also possible that Wang's going to Dairen to confer with Lieutenant General Itagaki of the Kwantung army may have offended the Japanese North China Garrison and given it further cause to turn against Wang.

3. Wang's decision would appear to weaken somewhat the possibility of future nominal participation by the National Government in Sino-Japanese "economic cooperation" in North China, thereby contributing to some degree to greater autonomy in the North. Also, Sung's gratitude for Japanese support in eliminating Wang at least for the time being may make Sung more amenable to Japanese suggestions in the future.

---

[1] Not printed.

4. The press reports today that Chang Hu and Li Shih Hao are being considered for the post of Chairman of the Economic Committee of the Hopei-Chahar Political Council to act as principal Chinese negotiator for Sino-Japanese economic cooperation. Both these men formerly held Government positions in the Anfu regime when they allegedly made princely fortunes. Neither has a reputation for any special economic or financial ability but they are said to be obedient to orders.

By mail to Tokyo.

JOHNSON

793.94/8149 : Telegram

The Counselor of Embassy in China (Peck) to the Secretary of State

NANKING, September 16, 1936—11 a. m.
[Received 7 : 34 p. m.²]

266. 1. The Japanese Ambassador came to Nanking September 13 accompanied by his Military and Naval Attachés and opened yesterday at 4 p. m. negotiations on the Chengtu incident in conference with the Chinese Minister for Foreign Affairs. (Both the Foreign Office and Japanese Embassy deny that the Pakhoi incident was discussed.) Prior to coming to Nanking, Kawagoe informed press correspondents that he would conduct the negotiations "on a lofty plane." According to a Foreign Office communiqué issued last night which was substantially duplicated by Japanese Embassy spokesmen in statements to press correspondents, the Japanese Ambassador inquired during the conversation concerning the Chinese Government's attitude toward the Chengtu incident and the Foreign Minister expressed "deep regret" and "gave a detailed account of the measures taken by the Chinese Government both before and after the incident and expressed the hope that a satisfactory settlement would soon be reached." The communiqué added "opinions were subsequently exchanged on general Sino-Japanese problems, the special bearing on the Chengtu incident" and that the conversation was concluded in 2½ hours with no arrangements for subsequent conversations having been made.

2. Both Chinese and Japanese officials deny that the Japanese Ambassador presented any demands or made any threats and we believe this is true.

4 [3?]. An officer of the Embassy has been confidentially informed by a responsible official of the Foreign Office:

5 [4?]. That the Japanese Ambassador called the attention of the Foreign Minister to the extreme gravity of the Chengtu incident and

---

² Telegram in five sections.

the situation in general. The informant denied a report that the Japanese Government had set a limit to the time within which the Nineteenth Route Army must be withdrawn from Pakhoi but handed the officer a Reuter telegram just received from Tokyo stating that (1) the Japanese Cabinet deliberated yesterday on the movement of the Chinese squadron and the Navy Minister and Naval Chief of Staff handed the Emperor a report to the effect that shallow waters in the neighborhood of Pakhoi necessitated the use of Hoihow, Hainan Island, as rendezvous for the Japanese fleet and (2) "this foreshadows the possibility of Hainan becoming Japan's base of operations in the event of actual hostilities."

6 [5?]. The obvious and extraordinary caution with which the Japanese are proceeding in their negotiations with the Chinese Government over the Chengtu and Pakhoi incidents is causing much speculation. One explanation is that the Japanese are genuinely concerned lest impossible demands or overt action on their part cause a widespread outburst of anti-Japanese agitation and they wish, because of the domestic situation in Japan and the unsatisfactory state of Soviet-Japanese relations, to preclude developments which might involve Japan in a major conflict.

7 [6?]. The refusal of the Chinese military at Pakhoi to permit Japanese investigators to land has created a situation from which such developments might flow and which is becoming more delicate by reason of a growing belief held by more than one highly placed and responsible official that the stationing of the Nineteenth Route Army at Pakhoi, its reinduction into the national forces and the subsequent incident were deliberately engineered by Li Tsung Jen and Pai Chung Hsi with a view to placing Chiang Kai Shek in an inextricable position vis-à-vis Japan and bringing about his political downfall.

8 [7?]. Repeated to Department and Peiping.

PECK

793.94/8148 : Telegram

The Consul General at Canton (Linnell) to the Secretary of State

CANTON, September 16, 1936—4 p. m.
[Received 4:48 p. m.]

Regarding Pakhoi incident. Chinese gunboat *Fookon* returned to Canton yesterday bringing Dr. Ling and the other investigators sent to Pakhoi by the special delegate for Foreign Affairs. Investigators on landing at Pakhoi September 12 were met by threatening mob including Nineteenth Route Army soldiers and carrying anti-Japanese banners. Being unable to carry on any useful investigation they returned to *Fookon* and to Canton. Nineteenth Route Army Chief of Staff is said to have told Dr. Ling that a Japanese landing party would be resisted with force.

Press reports today stated that several Japanese war vessels are en route to Pakhoi and the gunboat *Saga* is evidently remaining off that port. Japanese Consul in charge [at] Canton, however, stated that so far as he is aware only the *Saga* is in the vicinity of Pakhoi.

Special delegate for Foreign Affairs told Japanese Consul that the Chinese authorities had taken all possible steps to get the Nineteenth Route Army out of Pakhoi but it is not known here whether they are leaving.

It does not appear that any further investigation will be undertaken by the local authorities until the Nineteenth Route Army has left Pakhoi.

Sent to the Department, Peiping, Nanking.

LINNELL

894.001H61/109a : Telegram

The Secretary of State to the Chargé in Japan (*Dickover*)

WASHINGTON, September 16, 1936—6 p. m.

119. 1. On September 14 the Japanese Embassy informally brought to the attention of the Department the intention of a radical organization known as "American Friends of the Chinese People" to hold in New York on September 17, a mock trial of the Emperor of Japan for "crimes committed against China" and on September 18 an anti-Japanese demonstration.

2. There being no Federal statute which would afford warrant for intervention by the Federal Government, an officer of the Department yesterday proceeded to New York to consult with the municipal authorities. The municipal authorities after careful consideration expressed the opinion that they also had no basis in law for taking action to prevent the carrying out of the plans above mentioned, and that any informal action on their part directed toward persuading those responsible for the plans to abandon their projects would not accomplish the desired end and would only be seized upon as a means of obtaining further publicity.

3. Please orally and informally convey the substance of the foregoing to the Foreign Office. You should add that we do not anticipate that the meetings will attract sufficient attention to make likely any violence, but that every precaution is being taken to protect the persons and property of Japanese nationals in New York against any threatened violence which might arise.

4. Please emphasize to the Foreign Office that the Department is treating as confidential the approach made to it by the Japanese Embassy.

5. It is desired that you express your personal view that it is a matter for regret whenever any incident arises calculated to give offense to a friendly nation.

6. A statement along the foregoing lines is being made orally to the Japanese Embassy in response to the initiative taken by that Embassy mentioned in paragraph 1 above.

HULL

793.94/8150 : Telegram

The Counselor of Embassy in China (Peck) to the Secretary of State

NANKING, September 17, 1936—9 a. m.
[Received September 17—6 : 30 a. m.]

267. My 266, September 16, 11 a. m.

1. Kawagoe made yesterday afternoon his second call on Chang Chun and is reliably reported to have asked, under instructions from Tokyo, that prompt measures be taken by the Chinese authorities to enable the Japanese investigators sent to Pakhoi to carry out their mission. The Foreign Minister is said to have promised to telegraph the Kwangtung authorities and to have asked that the Japanese be patient. It is stated that no other questions were discussed.

2. To Department and Peiping.

PECK

793.94/8153 : Telegram

The Consul at Hankow (Jarvis) to the Secretary of State

HANKOW, September 17, 1936—4 p. m.
[Received September 17—1 : 33 p. m.]

My September 9, 5 p. m. The departure down river yesterday of three Japanese gunboats reduced Japanese naval strength at Hankow to three vessels. There is now only one Japanese gunboat at Chungking.

2. A meeting of Japanese residents of Hankow, on September 14th, was addressed by Seto, the Hankow Japanese injured at Chengtu, and Watari and Nakatsu, the resident Japanese naval and military officers. The meeting was orderly and the speeches were earnest and patriotic but not provocative. Both officials referred to the Pakhoi as well as the Chengtu incident.

3. The Pacification Commissioner and the Governor of Hupeh issued yesterday a joint proclamation, quoting instructions from Chiang Kai Shek, warning against disturbances and enjoining the protection of foreigners and the strict maintenance of order.

Sent to the Department, Peiping, Nanking. By cable to Shanghai.

JARVIS

894.001H61/110 : Telegram

The Chargé in Japan (Dickover) to the Secretary of State

Tokyo, September 17, 1936—5 p. m.
[Received September 17—8:43 a. m.]

187. Department's 119, September 16, 6 p. m. Department's instructions carried out today. The Vice Minister for Foreign Affairs in reply said that he appreciated the interest of the Department in the matter, that he realized that the Department was doing everything possible under our laws but that he hoped that something could be done to prevent the news agencies from telegraphing the story of the mock trial to Japan as no feeling would be aroused here if the story could be kept out of the Japanese newspapers. He also said that such action would defeat the aims of the "American Friends of the Chinese People" which organization depended upon publicity for its existence.[3]

DICKOVER

793.94/8151 : Telegram

The Chargé in Japan (Dickover) to the Secretary of State

Tokyo, September 17, 1936—6 p. m.
[Received September 17—8:55 a. m.]

188. Embassy's 186, September 15, 5 p. m. In an informal conversation with me today the Vice Minister for Foreign Affairs stated that "it appeared that" the Japanese defense forces had been bringing pressure on the Foreign Office to compel that office to make strong demands on China in connection with the Chengtu and Pakhoi incidents; that the situation was quiet at the moment as Kawagoe was conducting negotiations in Nanking and the 19th Route Army was reported in the press as evacuating Pakhoi; but that if the diplomatic negotiations "failed to bear fruit" the pressure from the Japanese defense forces might be renewed.

Repeated to Peiping.

DICKOVER

711.0012 Anti-War/1511a : Telegram

The Secretary of State to the Ambassador in Japan (Grew) [4]

Washington, September 17, 1936—6 p. m.

120. In an article appearing in the *New York Times* today, a Washington correspondent of that paper referred to the statement made in

---

[3] The Department's instruction No. 1112, October 1, to the Embassy in Japan stated that at the meeting on September 17 "the proceedings did not include a mock trial of the Emperor of Japan." (894.001H61/112)
[4] A similar message was sent on the same date to the Embassy in China as telegram No. 225.

the Secretary's speech at New York, September 15,[5] to the effect that the Kellogg Pact had been greatly impaired and the correspondent made the deduction that this statement forecast abandonment by this Government of the non-recognition principle. At the press conference today the Secretary stated in substance, in response to a question, that in his New York address he referred to the fact that the Kellogg-Briand Pact on account of disregard by a number of countries had been seriously impaired. The Secretary further stated that there was no purpose in mind to suggest the idea that because international treaties in many instances had been violated this Government would abandon such treaty relations or abandon the policy of entering into international agreements; that on the contrary he sought in the most effective way possible to keep alive and perpetuate the doctrine of the Kellogg Pact. See Radio Bulletin of September 17.

HULL

793.94/8154 : Telegram

The Counselor of Embassy in China (Peck) to the Secretary of State

NANKING, September 17, 1936—8 p. m.
[Received September 17—4 : 18 p. m.]

271. Our 267, September 17, 9 a. m.

1. An officer of the Embassy has been informed by an official of the Japanese Embassy that Chiang Kai Shek this morning ordered Yu Han Mou's army to proceed to Pakhoi and that it is believed therefore that the Japanese investigators will shortly be enabled to land at that place and investigate the murder of September 3.

2. To the Department and Peiping. Repeated to Canton.

PECK

893.01 Manchuria/1377

Report by the Military Attaché in China (Stilwell) [6]

G–2 Report No. 9462 [PEIPING,] September 18, 1936.

On Saturday, August 29, 1936, the Military Attaché interviewed Mr. Ohashi, Vice-Minister of Foreign Affairs of Manchoukuo, at Hsinking. Among other questions on similar lines, Mr. Ohashi was asked his opinion on the following matters, and replied as indicated:

Q. Is banditry in Manchoukuo now under control?

A. Banditry is still a serious question in Manchoukuo. All along the eastern and north-eastern borders, in the difficult wooded and mountainous country there, groups of bandits exist under a com-

---

[5] For text of speech, see Department of State, *Peace and War: United States Foreign Policy, 1931–1941*, p. 333.
[6] Copy transmitted to the Department by the War Department; received October 28.

munist organization. They are hard to get at on account of the nature of the country, and they are supplied with arms and ammunition by Russia. They even have Russian instructors, and follow Russian tactics when in action. As long as this support is available to them, they will be a menace, although their numbers are not large. Perhaps 20,000 would be an ample estimate, although we have no definite information. Banditry will probably be a serious matter in this region for some years. Elsewhere, it is well under control.

Q. Can the Manchoukuo Army now handle the bandit question, or must the Japanese Army assist in combating it?

A. The Manchoukuo Army is not yet in condition to do it alone. Perhaps after five years or so they may be able to.

Q. In your opinion does Russia still hope to expand farther in the Orient?

A. Most certainly. Everything that has happened goes to prove it. Stalin calls himself an Asiatic. Europe offers no such easy road to expansion as does Asia, and the communist party has definitely decided to expand toward the east. Already the center of gravity of Russian industry is being moved east of the Urals. The Tashkent railway has been finished, and feeders for it are reaching out toward Sinkiang. The colonization and industrialization of Siberia are proceeding at a rapid pace. The trans-Siberian railway is now double-tracked throughout. The Siberian garrison has been heavily reinforced and large quantities of stores accumulated for it. Soviet influence has been extended over Outer Mongolia. Great secrecy is maintained east of Lake Baikal,—no one is allowed to see anything. The Russians are so unreasonable about such things that when I went to Khabarovsk and Chita recently, General Blücher refused to see me at all. Of course the Russians intend to expand farther,— what do you imagine motivated the Chinese revolution in 1926? The Russian Bear wants to disrupt Manchoukuo, and if that should come to pass, then Korea would go too, and Japan, defeated, would have a revolution. This situation is extremely critical for Japan. We must unite the nation. We are all that stands between Russia and her goal of the sovietization of Asia; Manchoukuo gone and Japan defeated, China would fall an easy victim. Japan now faces a terrible crisis,— in the next five years I expect to see this matter decided one way or the other. Cannot the world see how Japan simply must go to the limit of her strength to defend Manchoukuo in order to save herself as well as China from communism?

Q. Do you believe there is now any determined effort being made by Russia to extend communism in the Far East?

A. Certainly. The Russian Communist Party has some understanding with the Kuomintang. How far it goes we do not know. Probably a promise from Russia to keep her hands off China proper and even to give assistance to Chiang Kai-shek in consolidating his power, as a return for inaction on the part of China in Sinkiang and Outer Mongolia. Russia is prepared to make big concessions in Europe to get a free hand in Asia; her dream is a big Asiatic Russia, not a European Russia.

The communist armies in China are the puppets of Moscow. Moscow pulls the strings and they respond. They were ordered out of Kiangsi Province to help Chiang Kai-shek. Their whole long trek has been planned and ordered. They went to Szechwan to give Chiang an excuse to consolidate his power there. They went to Shensi for the same purpose. They crossed to Shansi for the same purpose. I told Yen Hsi-shan last fall that they would come to his province and in March they arrived. (And you notice that the Central Government put its troops in Shansi, and that they are still there.) Then Moscow ordered them out and sent them west. They will go where they are sent,—poor deluded idiots. A sorry crew who cannot see how they are being used.

Oh, yes, the Russian purpose is quite plain and the crisis is approaching rapidly. In Japan we can see this cloud gathering and we realize that it will take all our strength to withstand it. And it is of course directed first against us. Until the Manchurian incident, Great Britain was marked out as the principal enemy, but now we have become the target and the propaganda is all directed against us. Do you know how much money Russia is about to spend on propaganda in your country to poison your people against Japan? I am surprised that the Americans cannot see through them.

Q. What is the future of the Mongol race?

A. Independence. Even though apparently dominated by Russia, the Outer Mongols feel their identity as a people. All Mongols remember Genghiz Khan and long to re-establish themselves as a unit. They are intensely obstinate, though stupid and slow, and ultimately they will drift together. Why not? Who wants their country? There is nothing there—no grass, no wood, no water. Nothing. Why should Russia want them? We don't. Let them get together and be a nation again if they want to.

Q. Will continued Chinese immigration into Manchoukuo be encouraged?

A. There is still plenty of room here. The country could support 300 million people. About 500,000 a year are coming in now. Yes, they can come; we expect them, because we have established law and order.

Q. Has Japanese influence been extended far enough in North China to make that flank secure in case of a war with Russia?

A. That is a strategic question about which I do not know anything. But any Japanese control in North China is for defensive purposes only—no one is going to cross the Gobi desert to attack,—an army could not exist there.

(Note: Mr. Ohashi's meaning was that the Japanese would go as far as they thought necessary in North China to ensure that no action direct north from Central China could threaten the left flank while a major effort was being made in the north of Manchoukuo.)

In this talk Mr. Ohashi conveyed the impression that in the Japanese mind a war with Russia is inevitable within five years, that it will be a most serious matter requiring every resource available, and that Japan considers herself the champion of constitutional government in the struggle with communism. The Chinese situation by comparison is insignificant, and can be handled at any time; although they would like to have it settled now on a basis of co-operation, if not Japanese domination, they consider it very secondary in view of the Russian threat.

Mr. Ohashi has had long experience in foreign relations and has probably studied these matters as seriously as any Japanese. His conclusions may appear extreme, but they are, I believe, his real opinions, and as such are a clue to future Japanese policy.

JOSEPH W. STILWELL
Colonel, Infantry

793.94/8156 : Telegram

The Consul at Hankow (Jarvis) to the Secretary of State

HANKOW, September 19, 1936—7 p. m.
[Received September 19—10: 07 a. m.]

A Japanese policeman named Yoshioka was shot dead while on duty in the Japanese concession at Hankow at 11:50 this morning. His assailant, according to the Japanese Consulate General, is unknown. The Japanese police allege confidentially that he was a Chinese noncommissioned officer belonging to a military unit now passing through Hankow on its way north. The Chinese version has not yet been disclosed.

Japanese patrols were landed an hour after the shooting and are posted in the Japanese concession, which is quiet. Sent to the Department, Peiping, Nanking, Shanghai.

JARVIS

793.94/8157 : Telegram

The Ambassador in China (Johnson) to the Secretary of State

PEIPING, September 19, 1936—7 p. m.
[Received September 19—5 : 29 p. m.]

455. 1. Japanese authorities have stated to the press that as their troops stationed at Fengtai were returning from maneuvers last night about 6 o'clock the Chinese sentry in front of the Chinese barracks made an insulting remark or gesture to one of the Japanese officers commanding the troops. An altercation immediately ensued and the Chinese barracks which are situated near the railroad station and house 120 troops or 1 company of the 37th Division of the 29th Army and constitute all of the Chinese troops stationed in Fengtai itself were kept under siege without shooting during the night and early morning. Meanwhile negotiations were carried on between Chinese and Japanese authorities and according to good authority the following agreement was reached at 10 this morning when the siege was raised :

(a) A public apology before the troops of both countries to Colonel Mutaguchi of the Japanese Embassy Guard by the Chinese general in command.

(b) The immediate withdrawal of all Chinese troops in Fengtai to a point 2 miles south of railroad.

(c) The eventual withdrawal of all Chinese troops in Fengtai region to Nanyuan or Hsiyuan.

Reliable American informants say the first two requirements being carried out this week. They were informed by Chinese officers on the spot that they were unable to resist the Japanese in view of General Sung Che Yuan's standing instructions that they were not to fight in any event.

2. According to the press, precautions were taken throughout China yesterday to avoid unfortunate incidents on the fifth anniversary of the Mukden incident. No such incidents have been reported.

By mail to Tokyo.

JOHNSON

793.94/8166 : Telegram

The Chargé in Japan (Dickover) to the Secretary of State

TOKYO, September 22, 1936—3 p. m.
[Received September 22—9 : 10 a. m.]

190. 1. Vernacular press reports that after Hankow incident unanimity in Japanese Government circles has been reached regarding fundamental principles to be followed in dealing with the China situation and that attitude has become stronger. *Yomiuri*

enumerates four demands being considered, namely, (1) organization of a completely autonomous regime in five northern provinces; (2) perfection of communications between Japan and China; (3) reduction of Chinese import tariff and, (4) employment of as many Japanese advisers as possible. These demands are in addition to those relating to eradication of anti-Japanese activities.

2. Yesterday the Navy Department issued communiqué enumerating the recent incidents and announcing that as navy might be compelled to take measures in self-defense it had decided to despatch landing forces to augment its Third Fleet in Chinese waters.

3. Press reports also indicate navy is skeptical about Nineteenth Route Army's evacuation from Pakhoi and favors fixing with National Government a time limit after which navy would take independent action to enable Japanese investigation if in the meantime Nineteenth Route Army's evacuation has not been completed.

4. I gathered from a conversation with the Counsellor of the Chinese Embassy on the 19th that he did not consider the present situation in the relations of the two countries necessarily serious as he thought it unlikely that Japan would push matters too far for fear of becoming embroiled with other powers. He thought that Japan's policy for the next 5 years pending the completion of its armament program was to advance its position in China one step at a time and to avoid drastic measures.

5. A responsible official of the Foreign Office yesterday stated to me that the newspaper accounts of the Japanese Government's attitude in regard to the situation vis-à-vis China were greatly exaggerated and that the Japanese Government hoped to settle amicably the incidents and also some of the outstanding general problems between the two countries.

6. In view of these two opinions it appears probable to the Embassy that the Japanese Government while using the leverage afforded by these incidents to gain as much as possible along the lines enumerated in paragraph 1 will not push matters with China to a critical point at this time.

7. In relation to possible developments growing out of Pakhoi incident it is of interest that, according to the Embassy's information, the French Ambassador at Tokyo has reminded the Japanese Minister for Foreign Affairs of the declaration of 1897 concerning the non-alienation of the Island of Hainan.[7]

Repeated to Peiping.

DICKOVER

---

[7] For text of declaration of March 15, 1897, see John V. A. MacMurray (ed.), *Treaties and Agreements With and Concerning China, 1894–1919* (New York, 1921), vol. I, p. 98.

793.94/8169 : Telegram

The Consul General at Canton (Linnell) to the Secretary of State

CANTON, September 22, 1936—4 p. m.
[Received September 23—8 a. m.]

Official information has now been received from Pakhoi that the Nineteenth Route Army are evacuating that port and Kwangtung forces under General Wu Chien Hsiung have been sent to take control. It is reported that at least five and possibly seven Japanese naval vessels including one cruiser and four destroyers are near Pakhoi. No confirmed reports have yet been received that Dr. Ling Shih Feng [and] Japanese investigators have landed.

It is officially stated that Kwangsi forces will be reorganized into the Fifth Route Army with Li Tsung Jen as Commander-in-Chief and Tsai Ting Kai of the Nineteenth Route Army as Vice Commander-in-Chief. Between six and eight divisions will be allowed for whose maintenance Central Government will make appropriation. Reports from Nanning, Kwangsi, are that Pai Chung Hsi is well satisfied with the outcome of Chiang Kai Shek's conferences with Li Tsung Jen and Huang Shao Hsiung at Canton. Pai is working on the reorganization of the Kwangsi forces and is expected to come for a conference with Chiang Kai Shek before he goes abroad as it is now settled he will do. It is stated that division leaders Liao Lei and Hsia Wei will accompany him overseas. Their expenses will be paid out of the National Treasury.

Sent to the Department, Peiping and Nanking.

LINNELL

793.94/8170 : Telegram

The Consul at Hankow (Jarvis) to the Secretary of State

HANKOW, September 23, 1936—10 p. m.
[Received September 23—2:50 p. m.]

Two Japanese destroyers arrived from Shanghai yesterday and last night disembarked fully equipped landing force of 180 men. I was informed at the Japanese Consulate General that this force has been sent here temporarily and will be relieved shortly by larger contingent from Japan and that it is the Japanese intention to keep a permanent landing force at Hankow.

2. Miura, the Japanese Consul General, had a lengthy conference yesterday afternoon with Yang Yung Tai, the Hupei Governor. From Chinese and Japanese official sources I learn that Miura demanded that the Chinese accept full responsibility for the killing of the Japanese policeman and that the Governor declined to do so. Miura pressed

for acceptance of his theory (see first paragraph of my telegram of September 21, 4 p. m.[8]) that the policeman was killed in the so-called Japanese extension and that the Chinese are responsible for patrolling this area, to which the Governor replied by producing a letter written by one of Miura's predecessors refusing a joint survey of the concession boundary and stating that the limits [of] the concession include the so-called extension. Most of the conversation was given over to a discussion of the status of this area and the responsibility for policing it, and the question of who killed the policeman appears to be of less interest than where he was killed.

3. I saw Miura this morning. He was tired and anxious. He reiterated the Japanese version of the shooting, already mentioned. This theory is contradicted by the evidence of the Norwegian lady, referred to in the second paragraph of my September 21, 4 p. m., who states that she heard two shots and saw the policeman fall at his post in the Japanese concession. Miura has been informed of her statement (which was made in writing to the Norwegian Vice Consul yesterday) and has been shaken by it. The lady was questioned by the Mayor of Hankow in the Norwegian Consulate this afternoon; Miura was invited to be present or send a representative to interrogate her but refused.

4. The Japanese concession is quiet. The landing force was not in evidence this morning.

Sent to the Department, Peiping, Nanking, Shanghai.

JARVIS

793.94/8171 : Telegram

The Consul General at Shanghai (Gauss) to the Secretary of State

SHANGHAI, September 24, 1936—11 a. m.
[Received September 24—7:20 a. m.]

509. Four Japanese bluejackets attacked last night about 8:30 p. m. by Chinese in Hongkew district within settlement. One bluejacket killed and two injured. One Chinese gunman arrested on the spot. He has since been turned over by Japanese to the Shanghai municipal police.

Japanese landing party promptly threw cordon around the area, stopped all traffic and in conjunction with Shanghai municipal police searched pedestrians and houses in the vicinity. Patrols were also posted in the Hongkew and Chapei area[s] and a considerable force of Japanese reservists called up and concentrated at Japanese headquarters. Five hundred and fifty sailors also reported to have been landed from the troop ship *Muroto* which arrived during the night.

---

[8] Not printed.

The Japanese community is greatly aroused and very tense. Japanese naval authorities have issued a statement to the effect that the special naval landing party will proceed "armed for the protection of Japanese lives within and outside the Settlement according to its own judgment". Statement made by Japanese Embassy here expresses intense indignation at this latest outrage and continues "we can no longer trust Chinese assurances that anti-Japanese movements and activities will be suppressed and we must regretfully take upon ourselves the task of protecting the lives and property of our nationals in China by whatever means we consider suitable".

No unusual demands made so far by Japanese upon the Settlement authorities who report that the Japanese cordon was withdrawn this morning and that only a few extra patrols remain in the Hongkew and Chapei areas. Shanghai municipal police incline to the belief that shooting was done by terrorist or Communist group. Japanese are understood to be of the same opinion but are fast losing patience over these frequently recurring incidents. Settlement and Chinese authorities taking special precautions. Situation quiet but tense.

GAUSS

793.94/8175 : Telegram

The Counselor of Embassy in China (Peck) to the Secretary of State

NANKING, September 24, 1936—2 p. m.
[Received 2:47 p. m.[9]]

279. Our 278, September 24, 9 a. m.[10]

1. We are reliably informed that the Ministers of Industry and Education are proceeding today by plane to Canton to confer with Chiang Kai Shek concerning the negotiations between the Japanese Ambassador and the Minister for Foreign Affairs and that they have been sent by the National Government because the Government believes that the negotiations so far have been fruitless and have reached or will reach a deadlock. From reliable information available to us, we are convinced that Kawagoe has presented no demands or threats to Chang Chun but the Chinese Government has conceived from the three conversations here, from reports from the Chinese Minister at Tokyo and from Japanese news sources (which most probably have had tacit approval of some Japanese Government officials) what it considers to be the present objectives of the negotiations which the Japanese Ambassador initiated September 15 ostensibly over the Chengtu incident. These objections [*objectives?*], as reportedly conceived by the Chinese Cabinet ministers are: (1) the alienation of

---

[9] Telegram in three sections.
[10] Not printed.

China from dependence upon foreign countries other than Japan and specifically an open stand on the part of the Chinese Government in favor of Japan against Communism and, by implication at least, Soviet Russia; (2) Sino-Japanese economic cooperation in North China to be developed within a political framework which will virtually create a five province buffer region; Chinese administrative organs will, independently of Nanking, control such Chinese troops as are necessary to maintain peace and order in that area.

2. In an informal discussion incident to a call by myself and Atcheson upon the new British Ambassador [11] and his Chinese counselor this morning the two latter stated that last night at a dinner for the British Ambassador given by Chang Chun there was some discussion among Chinese Cabinet Ministers of a possibility they envisaged that a deadlock in the Sino-Japanese negotiations would result in a break with and Chinese resistance to Japan. The Ministers felt that the Japanese were segregating the incidents from the main [part of?] the negotiations and that the former could probably be settled one by one but China could not passively allow Japan to achieve the two objectives outlined in paragraph 1.

3. The British officials stated to us that British interests in the Far East made it plain that their own role should be to calm the Chinese at this time with a view to warding off a definite break between China and Japan or the development of any major Sino-Japanese hostilities since British as well as other foreign persons and property would suffer in such case. The British Ambassador had therefore advised Chang Chun to meet Japanese wishes to the last point possible.

4. There has been during recent months so much talk by Chinese of armed resistance against Japan that we are inclined to believe that (1) too much importance should not be attached to what the British Ambassador was told, (2) this information may have been given him in the expectation that it might through him reach the Japanese Embassy and possibly influence the Japanese Ambassador to continue the attitude of obvious caution with which he has been approaching Sino-Japanese problems.

5. The Japanese Ambassador informed an American newspaper correspondent at midnight last night that (1) the Shanghai murders greatly increased the gravity of the situation and it would now be necessary for Japan to adopt a much stronger attitude in order to achieve Japanese desires; (2) it now depended largely upon the Minister for Foreign Affairs whether the conversations with him would be continued.

6. To Department and Peiping.

PECK

---

[11] Sir Hughe M. Knatchbull-Hugessen.

793.94/8174 : Telegram

The Consul General at Shanghai (Gauss) to the Secretary
of State

SHANGHAI, September 24, 1936—6 p. m.
[Received September 24—1 : 32 p. m.]

511. Further to my 509, September 24, 11 a.m., the Consulate General has learned confidentially from Secretary General of municipality of Greater Shanghai that Mayor Wu lodged written protest this morning with the Japanese authorities regarding incursion of Japanese naval units into Chapei area last night and pointed out that the appearance of fully armed Japanese units was causing much apprehension among the Chinese [in] that district. The Mayor further pointed out some Japanese units have been posted in areas where there are no Japanese residents and requested that these and all other units be withdrawn forthwith. No reply has been received to this protest thus far. It was further stated that when Japanese bluejackets proceeded into Chapei last night strict instructions were issued to all Chinese police not to oppose them in any way but that their continued presence was provocative and might lead to further trouble.

Wakasugi, Acting Japanese Consul General, called on Mayor Wu this morning and urged the cooperation of the Chinese authorities in apprehending the perpetrators of the shooting and requested that every possible effort be made to give the fullest protection to Japanese lives and property. Wakasugi further informed the Mayor that he reserved the right to present any new demands (it is understood that instructions from Tokyo are being awaited). The Mayor is understood to have assured him that everything possible would be done. Wakasugi also called on the Chairman of the Shanghai Municipal Council [12] this afternoon and similarly urged the Settlement authorities to apprehend the murderers and to protect fully Japanese residents. His attitude was surprisingly conciliatory. I am informed that Shanghai municipal police are functioning normally in the Hongkew area without Japanese opposition. For a time last night, however, their functioning was considerably restricted by Japanese naval cordon.

I was informed last night that Japanese naval authorities desired declaration of state of emergency. As a matter of precaution I advised Commanding Officer United States Marine Corps that the situation as reported did not justify such a measure. He concurred. I learn today that no formal request was received from any responsible Japanese authority for declaration of state of emergency.

---

[12] H. E. Arnhold, British businessman.

It is learned that the one Chinese arrested on the spot was probably a bystander and not one of the culprits who are generally thought to have been hired gunmen operating for political purposes.

Thus far the attitude of the Japanese as indicated by their representatives to both the Chinese and Settlement authorities and the measures taken by the Japanese Navy, with the exception of their penetration into Chapei, indicates a surprising measure of restraint.

GAUSS

793.94/8179 : Telegram

The Counselor of Embassy in China (Peck) to the Secretary of State

NANKING, September 25, 1936—noon.
[Received 2 : 55 p. m.]

281. My 280, September 25, 10 a. m.[13]

1. Conveyed informally at reception given by Kung for the British Ambassador, Senior Vice Minister Hsu Mo told an officer of the British Embassy and me that at the first conference between the Minister of Foreign Affairs and the Japanese Ambassador held September 15th the Ambassador outlined proposals for fundamental settlement of Sino-Japanese difficulties; at second conference held September 16 the Chinese Minister for Foreign Affairs directed conversation mainly to China's proposals for settlement of the Chengtu incident and such settlement was of pressing importance; at the third conference held September 23 the Chinese Minister for Foreign Affairs gave China's proposals for fundamental settlement of Sino-Japanese difficulties. Hsu Mo complained that the Japanese Ambassador had consistently refused to accelerate settlement of the murders on [of?] Japanese territory [nationals?] and he hinted that that settlement was being deliberately obstructed in order that they may be utilized as alleged unredressed grievances as excuse for reprisals if China definitely rejects Japanese terms for fundamental solution. He said the Chinese Government was ready and eager to settle these incidents in accordance with international law. Before I could verify from Hsu Mo the truth of current reports that Japanese proposals relate principally to economic cooperation and what would amount to practical alienation of five northern provinces, Suma, Secretary of the Japanese Embassy, arrived and rather ostentatiously held Hsu Mo in private conversation until both of them left the reception. Kung privately confirmed both reports and added that economic cooperation on lines proposed by the Japanese would result in excluding other nations from China. Both Hsu Mo and Kung were very guarded regarding exact nature of the discussions.

2. To the Department and Peiping.   PECK

---

[13] Not printed.

793.94/8176 : Telegram

The Chargé in Japan (Dickover) to the Secretary of State

Tokyo, September 25, 1936—6 p. m.
[Received September 25—9 : 33 a. m.]

193. 1. Consensus of conservative vernacular press opinion today is that Japan's fundamental policy for dealing with Chinese situation remains unchanged and that Japan will continue to press Nanking for settlement of pending questions but that navy will take measures for protection of Japanese residents. Foreign Office spokesman is quoted by *Japan Times* as voicing disappointment with "insincere" attitude so far manifested by Chinese in Nanking negotiations and as declaring that if negotiations prove futile Japan will be obliged to take other measures.

2. Vice Minister for Foreign Affairs confirmed to Ballantine [14] this morning that Japan's policy remained unchanged. He said, however, that Navy Department was assigning warships at various ports for the protection of Japanese residents.

3. Naval Attaché was today informed by his contact in the Navy Department that the Third Fleet was not being augmented from Japan for the present; that a naval landing party comprising one battalion 500 strong was landed today at Shanghai from a naval transport and that at Pakhoi there were now two cruisers, one gunboat and five destroyers.

Repeated to Peiping.

DICKOVER

793.94/8180 : Telegram

The Chargé in Japan (Dickover) to the Secretary of State

Tokyo, September 26, 1936—11 a. m.
[Received September 26—12: 35 a. m.]

194. All vernacular papers report this morning that after a Cabinet meeting yesterday the Minister for Foreign Affairs sent for the Chinese Ambassador and pointed out that the failure so far of the negotiations at Nanking to make progress which he ascribed to a lack of understanding of the present situation on the part of the National Government had caused dissatisfaction in Japanese official and unofficial circles and had evoked a demand that the negotiations be broken off. The Minister for Foreign Affairs therefore impressed upon the Ambassador the urgency of Chiang Kai Shek's return to Nanking to be personally present at these important negotiations.

Repeated to Peiping.

DICKOVER

---

[14] Joseph W. Ballantine, First Secretary of Embassy in Japan, temporarily.

793.94/8181 : Telegram

The Consul General at Shanghai (Gauss) to the Secretary of State

SHANGHAI, September 26, 1936—noon.
[Received September 26—7 a. m.]

515. My 513, September 25, 4 p. m.[15] Japanese naval landing party has still further curtailed its activities and as a result conditions in Hongkew, Chapei and adjoining northern area in Chinese territory are gradually returning to normal.

Japanese Counselor of the Embassy informed me yesterday evening that the Sino-Japanese negotiations at Nanking had come to a stand-still and that unless the Ministers of Education and Industry who flew to Canton yesterday to see General Chiang brought back satisfactory instructions, negotiations would probably be broken off. He also told me that Japanese are taking a very strong attitude but gave no inkling of the nature of their demands.

Copy to Nanking by mail.

GAUSS

793.94/8188 : Telegram

The Counselor of Embassy in China (Peck) to the Secretary of State

NANKING, September 26, 1936—noon.
[Received 3 : 25 p. m.[16]]

282. My 281, September 25, noon.

1. A responsible official of the Foreign Office today in reply to questions outlined to me the general Sino-Japanese situation.

2. He said that it is true that the Japanese Foreign Office is adopting a much milder attitude in the present discussions than it took, for example, at the time of the Kuramoto case in 1934[17] and milder than that advocated by the Japanese Ministries of War and Navy. Nevertheless, the restraint followed in negotiation is at variance with the serious character of the proposals the Japanese Foreign Office is presenting to China. If the Japanese Government were to insist upon acceptance of these proposals with threat of force a rupture of diplomatic relations would necessarily follow. Informant reiterated Japanese refusal to discuss several recent numerous murders of Japanese and said that this was apparently based on the theory that if the Chinese Government accepted Japanese proposals for fundamental solution of mutual relations the incidents

---

[15] Not printed.
[16] Telegram in two sections.
[17] Japanese consular student interpreter at Nanking; he disappeared and was found uninjured.

would be settled easily whereas rejection of the proposals would at once impart to the incidents an aspect of utmost gravity. Informant believed that the slower mild attitude of the Japanese Foreign Office was inspired by caution rather than good will. In the secrecy maintained concerning the nature of the Japanese proposals he said the situation did not resemble that obtaining when the 21 demands were presented for no written demands had been formulated and no pledge of secrecy exacted; secrecy followed from tacit agreement on both sides. While the Japanese proposals were fundamentally grave they were wide in scope and many. The Japanese Ambassador from the first interview on September 15 had indicated wish to talk with Chiang Kai Shek but in latter's absence he would probably take up discussions with the Minister for Foreign Affairs again about September 28. Indications are that Chiang will return from Canton shortly before October 10. The Pakhoi incident was investigated jointly by the Japanese and Chinese representatives but no general report was adopted at the conclusion of the investigation.

To Department and Peiping.

PECK

793.94/8184 : Telegram

The Ambassador in China (Johnson) to the Secretary of State

PEIPING, September 26, 1936—3 p. m.
[Received 3 : 25 p. m.]

465. Reference Embassy's 459, September 21, 6 p. m.[18] It now appears that the establishment of the proposed "inspectorate" has been abandoned at least for the time being. The representative of the Ministry of Finance who was sent to Tientsin to investigate the local situation, particularly with a view to the establishment of the "inspectorate", after several conferences with General Sung Che Yuan and the local customs authorities, is said to have made a report to Nanking but no information is available regarding his recommendations.

Due to the very effective interference by the customs with the transport of smuggled goods by the Tientsin–Pukow and Pieping–Hankow Railways, large quantities of smuggled goods are now being sent from Tientsin to the interior by motor trucks as far as Tsinanfu and through Central and South Hopei. It is reported that this trade is so profitable that the motor trucks used pay for themselves within 2 weeks.

The Consulate General at Hankow which itself never appears to have been seriously affected, reports that the authorities there are confident that their preventive measures have effectively checked

---

[18] Not printed.

the movement of smuggled goods on the Peiping–Hankow Railway. With North China flooded with smuggled goods, however, any action that tends to weaken the effectiveness of the customs measures will be viewed with concern by American and foreign merchants there.

Copy by mail to Tokyo.

JOHNSON

793.94/8185 : Telegram

The Consul General at Shanghai (Gauss) to the Secretary of State

SHANGHAI, September 28, 1936—noon.
[Received September 28—4 : 20 a. m.]

517. Abend, *New York Times* representative, has just informed me confidentially that Japanese Ambassador has presented seven demands to the National Government which must be completely agreed to before any settlement can be effected of the Chengtu and other incidents. From a source he described as "unimpeachable" he has learned three of these demands. They are (1) establishment of an independent regime in North China to include Hopei, Shantung, Shansi, Chahar and Suiyuan over which the National Government will retain only nominal suzerainty; (2) stationing of Japanese troops with Chinese troops in all areas where Communist armies are active; (3) the placing of Japanese advisers in all departments and services of the National Government.

Abend also informed me that from recent interviews with Japanese Military and Naval Attachés he has gained the definite impression that these demands are in the nature of an ultimatum and that nonagreement will result in definite action by the Japanese. He states that a press telegram to his paper recounting the above has been passed by the Chinese press censor at Shanghai.

Repeated to Peiping and Nanking.

GAUSS

793.94/8186 : Telegram

The Chargé in Japan (Dickover) to the Secretary of State

TOKYO, September 28, 1936—7 p. m.
[Received September 28—6 : 20 a. m.]

197. 1. At a press conference this afternoon with foreign correspondents conducted personally by the Minister for Foreign Affairs, he emphasized that China was at the cross roads and declared that the Japanese Government was now in the course of deciding what steps it must take to protect its nationals.

2. According to vernacular press, conferences between Foreign Office and Defense Ministries continue to be held from day to day. *Kokumin* yesterday reported that army has decided to insist that the National Government be pressed at this opportunity for the settlement of the question of the autonomous regime in the five northern provinces.

Repeated to Peiping.

DICKOVER

793.94/8189 : Telegram

The Consul General at Shanghai (Gauss) to the Secretary of State

SHANGHAI, September 28, 1936—7 p. m.
[Received September 28—1:35 p. m.]

520. Situation in Shanghai quiet but Japanese community tense. Few Japanese patrols still being maintained in Chinese territory. With reinforcements landed from five Japanese destroyers which arrived yesterday, strength of Japanese naval forces ashore estimated to be 2400 men supplemented by civilian reserves now five to six thousand. Three Japanese cruisers anchored off Woosung, five destroyers and Japanese flag ship at Shanghai. Repeated to Peiping and by mail to Nanking.

GAUSS

793.94/8281

The Consul at Kobe (Scott) to the Secretary of State

No. 22
KOBE, September 28, 1936.
[Received October 19.]

SIR: I have the honor to report that an economic mission sponsored by the Osaka Chamber of Commerce and Industry and supported by the Fourth Division Army Headquarters, Osaka, left that city on September 10, 1936 for Manchuria and North China.

The mission is headed by Yakichi Ataka, President of the Osaka Chamber of Commerce and Industry, and is composed of some sixty-one business leaders representing various trades and industries. Its stated purpose is to investigate economic conditions in "Japan's first line of defense". While ostensibly sponsored by the Osaka Chamber of Commerce and Industry, all arrangements for travel and investigation have been made by the Fourth Division Headquarters. Major Odashima attached to the Fourth Division Headquarters will conduct the party on its tour. It will pass through Hsingking, Kirin, Mukden, Tientsin, Tsingtao, returning to Japan via Dairen on October 2, 1936.

The sending of this mission is in no sense a routine commercial gesture. Several points of interest may claim our attention. First, the army, that is to say in this case the Fourth Division Headquarters, is publicly supporting a movement of this sort for the first time. Previously such missions had received little more than the good-will of the army authorities on the spot. Second, its members are made up of outstanding business leaders from the city of Osaka, figures of first magnitude in the cotton piece goods, rayon, and railway supply industries, as well as representatives of important banking interests. Third, the personnel has been drawn from elements known to have been very outspoken in their criticisms of the army at the time of the February 26th incident. It is significant also that with but a few exceptions the members of the mission have not been primarily interested in the China trade.

It is apparent that the army for the first time has become convinced of the desirability of enlisting the sympathy of industrial leaders towards its military adventures on the continent. This represents an important departure from the hysterical type of policy which characterized the revolt of the young officers in the February incident. The Fourth Division officers appear to feel that fostering closer relations between the Osaka business world and the army will avoid much of the misunderstanding that has arisen in the past and forward the smooth fulfilment of the army's aims.

Respectfully yours,

WINTHROP R. SCOTT

793.94/8194 : Telegram

The Counselor of Embassy in China (Peck) to the Secretary of State

NANKING, September 29, 1936—2 p. m.
[Received September 29—10:35 a. m.]

285. My 282, September 26, noon.

1. This office has obtained from an authoritative source not in the Foreign Office the following partial account of the interview between the Minister for Foreign Affairs and the Japanese Ambassador on September 23:

2. The Japanese Ambassador recapitulated measures which the Japanese Government believed it would be necessary for the Chinese Government to take if Sino-Japanese relations were to be materially improved including (1) elimination of anti-Japanese sentiments from Chinese text books and the suppression of indications of anti-Japan feeling (in this connection the Japanese Ambassador expressed the belief that the dissolution of the Kuomintang would ultimately be necessary but he would not press this at the moment) : (2) cooperation

of Japanese with Chinese military forces in the suppression of Communist armed forces: (3) the use of Japanese advisers in many departments of the National Government: (4) establishment of direct air communication between Japan and Shanghai. (Informant did not confirm or deny the report I mentioned to him that the Japanese Ambassador demanded creation of completely autonomous government for maintaining the northern provinces,—see Shanghai's September 28, noon to Peiping.)

3. The Minister for Foreign Affairs replied that the suppression of Communist armed forces was an internal matter which China could handle itself and, moreover, the problem had practically disappeared and that the establishment of air communication with Japan was a matter of routine business which should be discussed with the Ministry of Communications and not made a matter of diplomatic negotiations.

6 [4]. The Minister for Foreign Affairs then said that in the view of the Chinese Government the improvement of Sino-Japanese relations required the taking of certain measures by the Japanese Government including (1) the cancellation of the Shanghai military agreement of May, 1932 and of the Tangku truce of May 30th [31st], 1933; [19] (2) elimination of the East Hopei autonomous government; (3) Japanese support of Chinese measures to check smuggling activities in North China; (4) cessation of indiscriminate flights by Japanese air planes over Chinese territory, and (5) cessation of Japanese interference in East Suiyuan and Inner Mongolia generally.

5. The Japanese Ambassador appeared deeply incensed at these counterproposals and said that evidently there was no use in continuing the interview. The atmosphere was very strained when the two officials parted.

6. Informant said that Chiang Kai Shek flew from Canton to Kuling yesterday and may come to Nanking today.

7. Sent to the Department, Peiping, Shanghai.

PECK

793.94/8193 : Telegram

The Ambassador in China (Johnson) to the Secretary of State

PEIPING, September 29, 1936—4 p. m.
[Received September 29—9 : 15 a. m.]

470. Assassination of a Japanese sailor in the Hongkew area, reported in Shanghai's 509, September 24, 11 a. m., is the ninth incident of its kind since the fall of 1935 when it was announced that Hirota

---

[19] For texts, see *Foreign Relations, Japan, 1931-1941*, vol. I, pp. 217 and 120 respectively.

would seek an understanding with Nanking generally based upon three points mentioned in my telegram from Nanking, No. 80, November 15, 3 p. m., 1935.[20]

Peck's recent messages from Nanking, notably his 279 of September 24, 2 p. m., and 281 of September 25, noon, indicate his growing conviction that Japanese are determined to use incidents as leverage for compelling an agreement along the lines of Hirota's three points.

I believe that sentiment of Chiang Kai Shek and his supporters and of Chinese in general would be opposed to any agreement along this line. The fact that both sides fear publicity regarding demands indicates this.

Situation is still uncertain. I do not believe that either Chinese or Japanese want war.

. . . .

. . . Whichever eventuality results from present negotiations at Nanking, I feel that present situation is more serious than any which we have thus far had, and will require great self-control on both sides if actual hostilities are to be avoided.

Repeated to Tokyo.

JOHNSON

793.94/8191 : Telegram

The Chargé in Japan (Dickover) to the Secretary of State

TOKYO, September 29, 1936—6 p. m.
[Received September 29—10 a. m.]

198. 1. The tone of today's reactions to the China situation has been dominated by Arita's press conference of yesterday which apparently marks the beginning of a more determined effort at solution by the Foreign Office of pending questions with China. His statement is notable for its firmness and comprehensiveness in enumerating outstanding issues and for his refusal to define or limit the scope of the negotiations desired with China.

2. So far there have been no editorial comments in the vernacular press or reports of further developments here in the situation except that the Prime Minister has postponed his departure for the maneuvers and that it has been suggested that he may now not go at all.

3. *Yomiuri* today ascribes Japan's insistence upon Chiang Kai Shek's presence at Nanking to the conviction that further negotiation with the Foreign Minister would be futile in view of the unsatisfactory temporizing reply alleged to have been received by the Japanese Ambassador on September 23 to four demands previously presented.

---

[20] *Foreign Relations*, 1935, vol. III, p. 417.

These demands were identically enumerated as those mentioned in paragraph 1 of the Embassy's 190, September 22, 3 p. m.

Repeated to Peiping.

DICKOVER

793.94/8202

Memorandum by the Assistant Chief of the Division of Far Eastern Affairs (Hamilton)

[WASHINGTON,] September 30, 1936.

The British Chargé, Mr. V. A. L. Mallet, called by appointment. The Chargé met Mr. Grew just outside Mr. Hamilton's office and suggested to Mr. Grew that, as the subject which he had in mind related to the Far East, perhaps Mr. Grew would care to be present. Mr. Hamilton had previously arranged with Mr. Grew that, should the British Chargé's call relate to the present state of relations between the Chinese and Japanese Governments, Mr. Grew would come in during the call of the British Chargé. Accordingly, Mr. Grew was present throughout the entire interview.

The Chargé left with Mr. Hamilton the attached *aide-mémoire* dated September 30 [21] informing the Department of the instructions which the British Government had issued to the British Ambassadors at Tokyo and at Peiping to approach the Japanese and Chinese Governments respectively, in regard to the present state of Sino-Japanese relations. Mr. Grew and Mr. Hamilton read the *aide-mémoire*. Mr. Hamilton then commented that, while we had received substantially the same information as that contained in the first paragraph of the British *aide-mémoire*, the Chinese Government had not officially given this information to the American Embassy in China. Mr. Hamilton gave the British Chargé to read Nanking's confidential telegram 285, September 29, 2 p. m., wherein Nanking reports information in regard to the proposals of the Japanese Government and the counter-proposals of the Chinese Government as obtained "from an authoritative source not in the Foreign Office".

Mr. Hamilton then commented that the British *aide-mémoire* did not suggest that the American Government take action similar to that taken by the British Government. The Chargé replied that this was accurate and that his telegram, which he had received yesterday afternoon, merely asked him to inform the State Department.

Mr. Hamilton then called the Chargé's attention to an item in the *New York Times* of today's date from Tokyo to the effect that "Japan's Military Seek New Control". Mr. Hamilton said that, if this report were true, it would appear that the Japanese military were

---

[21] Not printed.

attempting to force the hand of and bring pressure upon Premier Hirota.

Mr. Grew and Mr. Hamilton then informed the Chargé that we appreciated the courtesy of the British Government in communicating this information to us; that we were following the situation carefully; that our Ambassador at Peiping considers that the situation is very serious; that we were of course desirous of protecting American interests and rights and of fulfilling our obligations; that the Department realized the importance of registering our position at each step and not allowing matters to go by default; and that in considering the matter of approaching the Japanese Government the time element and the form of approach were very important. We said that we wished to avoid action which would not only have no good effect but might be likely to have an adverse effect.

During the course of the interview Mr. Hamilton took occasion to point out to the British Chargé tactfully but clearly that we recognized the desirability of cooperating with the British (and other) Governments in situations where there were involved common interests, rights, and obligations, especially when provisions in regard to those common interests, rights, and obligations had been embodied in treaties to which both governments were party, but that, when the British Government merely informed us of action which it had already taken and gave no opportunity for an advance exchange of views as to the advisability of such action, we were sometimes placed in the position of having to choose between apparent non-support of the principle of cooperation and taking action which might seem inopportune. The Chargé stated that he appreciated this point.

Mr. Hamilton said that the Department would probably wish to telegraph our Embassy at Tokyo the substance of the British Embassy's *aide-mémoire* and to ask for an expression of the Chargé's opinion as to the desirability of the Embassy approaching the Japanese Foreign Office. Mr. Hamilton said that he could not say whether the Department would go further in the matter at this time until the matter had been referred to the Secretary.

Mr. Grew and Mr. Hamilton commented in regard to the possibility that the British Ambassador at Tokyo might not carry out his instructions immediately but might prefer first to consult his Government and to advance his own views. Mr. Grew and Mr. Hamilton pointed out that this had happened in the past in similar instances. The Chargé asked whether we would care to have him suggest to the British Government that his Government inform us of the British Ambassador's views as to the arguments which might influence the Japanese attitude". Mr. Grew and Mr. Hamilton indicated that information on this point would be appreciated.

M[AXWELL] M. H[AMILTON]

793.94/8203a : Telegram

The Secretary of State to the Chargé in Japan (Dickover)

WASHINGTON, September 30, 1936—6 p. m.

125. 1. Associated Press despatch from Tokyo states that rejection by the Cabinet of extensive administrative reforms advocated by the army and navy might lead to the resignation of the Minister of War and consequently result in resignation of the entire Cabinet.

2. Having in mind recent developments in Sino-Japanese relations, your comments by telegraph on the subject of the above-mentioned press report would be of interest.

HULL

793.94/8201 : Telegram

The Secretary of State to the Chargé in Japan (Dickover)

WASHINGTON, September 30, 1936—7 p. m.

126. 1. This morning the British Chargé called at the Department and left an *aide-mémoire* [22] stating that the Chinese Government had informed the British Ambassador in China that recently the Japanese Ambassador had pressed for a general settlement of Sino-Japanese relations, the principal points in which would be the reduction of tariffs on specific articles of interest to Japanese trade, Chinese cooperation with Japan against communists throughout China, joint air service between Japan and Shanghai, the setting up of an area of economic cooperation throughout all of China, and the employment of Japanese advisers in Chinese Government departments. The *aide-mémoire* states that it is understood that the Chinese gave reasonable replies but that when the Chinese indicated that they regarded consideration of their own grievances essential to any general settlement the Japanese Ambassador broke off the interview. The *aide-mémoire* states that the British Ambassador at Tokyo has been instructed to express to the Japanese Government the concern of the British Government and the desire of the British Government to see Sino-Japanese relations established on a genuinely peaceful basis; also that the British Ambassador at Tokyo has been asked to submit to the British Foreign Office his views as to the arguments which might influence the Japanese attitude. The *aide-mémoire* states further that instructions had been issued to the British Ambassador in China to bring to the attention of the Chinese Government the danger which would be likely to result from any alarmist attacks on Japanese nationals in China, and to express the hope that if possible such developments will be prevented. The *aide-mémoire* concludes with the statement that

[22] Not printed.

the British Government intends to inform the Chinese Government that the British Government is urging moderation in Tokyo and to inform the Japanese Government of the diplomatic action taken in China.

2. In bringing this information to the attention of the Department, the British Government has not made any request that the American Government take similar action.

3. Please consult the British Ambassador and ascertain whether he has as yet approached the Japanese Government and, if so, the nature and form of his approach. Also ask the British Ambassador to be so good as to inform you of the substance of the views which he is submitting to his Foreign Office as to the arguments which might influence the Japanese attitude. An expression of the Embassy's views on this subject would also be welcomed, together with an expression of the Embassy's opinion whether an approach by this Government to the Japanese Government and to the Chinese Government at this time would serve any useful purpose.

4. Recalling the statement made to Ballantine by the Vice Minister for Foreign Affairs as reported in paragraph 2, first sentence, of your 193 of September 25, 6 p. m., you may wish to consider the advisability of Ballantine's calling upon the Vice Minister, informally and as upon his own initiative and without reference to the British Government's *démarche*, and inquiring whether the Vice Minister could comment upon the accuracy of press reports (which are approximately along the general line indicated in the first sentence of this telegram) with regard to recent developments in relations between Japan and China. Please bear in mind, however, that we leave entirely to your judgment and discretion whether such a call should be made.

5. Report promptly and completely by telegraph, repeating your telegrams to Peiping.

6. Repeat to Peiping with request that Ambassador Johnson cable the Department as soon as practicable his view as to whether an approach at this time by this Government to the Japanese and Chinese Governments would serve any useful purpose and, if his reply be in the affirmative, his suggestions as to the form and substance of such approach.

HULL

793.94/8205 : Telegram

The Counselor of Embassy in China (Peck) to the Secretary of State

NANKING, October 1, 1936—2 p. m.
[Received October 1—1 : 10 p. m.]

287. 1. We are reliably informed that the Foreign Office intended yesterday to issue a statement in reply to Arita's press statement of

September 28th but had not yesterday afternoon done so. Ho Ying Chin and director of Asiatic Affairs Department of Foreign Office flew yesterday to Kuling to see Chiang Kai Shek who left Canton September 28th, stopped September 29 at Nanchang, and yesterday flew to Kuling. It seems likely that the officials mentioned have taken the statement to Chiang for his approval.

2. It is generally believed here that (1), Chiang will shortly come to Nanking and will see Kawagoe although it is problematical whether he will discuss issues with the Japanese Ambassador and (2), he went first to Nanchang and Kuling in order to avoid impression that he was hastening to the capital pursuant to Japanese desire that he come down to undertake negotiations.

3. Sent to the Department and Peiping. By mail to Tokyo, Shanghai.

PECK

793.94/8206 : Telegram

The Consul General at Shanghai (Gauss) to the Secretary of State

SHANGHAI, October 1, 1936—4 p. m.
[Received October 1—1:20 p. m.]

525. My September 28, 7 p. m. Japanese forces very active today. They have taken up 1932 defense positions in Hongkew and Chapei areas and erected movable barbed wire entanglements at the majority of such posts. Japanese civilian reservists have also been called out [to form?] strong Japanese patrols in Chapei. Reported that these measures have been taken in anticipation of a decision being rendered by the First Special District Court in the Nakayama case; measures are said to be precautionary but may also be intimidatory. Information just received indicates that court today announced judgment would be rendered 2 p. m. tomorrow.

With respect to rumored concentration of Chinese troops in the general vicinity of Shanghai, intelligence officer of the Fourth Marines states that from best information available it appears Chinese troops totalling 10 to 15,000 men have recently arrived in Hangchow but that these units are largely replacements. He estimates an equal force has arrived at Kashing (halfway between Shanghai and Hangchow) which represents a very considerable increase; and about 3500 men at Sungkiang (an entrance to Shanghai and Hangchow).

It is reliably reported that Chinese banks are transferring their funds to foreign banks; silver shipments to the United States are being made on American steamers on their outbound voyages. Such ships proceed to Manila before returning here en route to the United States.

GAUSS

793.94/8204 : Telegram

The Chargé in Japan (Dickover) to the Secretary of State

Tokyo, October 1, 1936—9 p. m.
[Received October 1—11 : 35 a. m.]

199. Department's 125, September 30, 6 p. m.

1. Administrative reform has been widely advocated for many months, particularly since the February 26 incident.

[2.] The War Minister on September 22 apparently presented to the Premier a plan of administrative reform including (*a*) the consolidation of certain departments; and (*b*) the consolidation of the various existing investigation and legislative bureaus for the formulation of national policies under a Cabinet Minister without portfolio.

3. September 30 the Vice Minister of War in a statement to the press said that the plan was proposed by the War Minister as a Cabinet member and cannot be considered to be the plan of the Japanese Army. He added that the War Minister will not make approval of the proposal in its original form an absolute demand.

4. Although administrative reform will undoubtedly be a large question in the run of political issues in the approaching months in Japan, the Embassy believes that the present proposal made while Sino-Japanese relations are strained will have no significant influence on Japanese policy in China. There is no present indication that any proposal of administrative reform will result in resignation of the Cabinet.

DICKOVER

793.94/8208 : Telegram

The Chargé in Japan (Dickover) to the Secretary of State

Tokyo, October 1, 1936—10 p. m.
[Received October 1—4 : 02 p. m.]

200. Department's 126, September 30, 7 p. m.

1. British Ambassador, Clive, has informed the Embassy as follows: He saw Arita at Arita's home this morning and orally expressed the concern of the British Government and the desire of the British Government to see Sino-Japanese relations established on a genuinely peaceful basis; Clive told Arita that the British Ambassador in China was calling the attention of the Chinese Government to the danger which would be likely to result from any alarmist attacks on Japanese nationals in China and expressing the hope that such developments would be prevented; speaking personally to Arita, Clive dwelt upon the likelihood that pressure on the part of Japan to gain far-reaching

demands would force Chiang Kai-shek to armed resistance, with consequences so serious that no one could foresee the end; in the course of the interview Arita, in reply to Clive's references to press reports, stated that the demands were not unconditional but subject to discussion and denied after apparent hesitation that they included the detachment of the five northern provinces involving separate customs administration and separate currency; Arita begged Clive that neither Clive's official approach to Arita or his personally expressed sentiments be made known to the Chinese Government to which Clive agreed.

2. Because of this request of Arita's, Clive requested that his statements to the Embassy be kept in strict confidence.

3. Clive informed the Embassy that he knew of no arguments which would be likely to influence the Japanese Government other than that of the serious consequences that would arise from China's being forced in desperation to resist.

4. In the present temper of the Japanese defense forces (possibly not shared by the Foreign Office), I do not think that an approach by the American Government to the Japanese Government will serve to lessen pressure upon China. I feel that such an approach would only serve to stiffen Japanese determination to proceed. I do not believe that the Japanese are prepared at this time to take drastic action in China but believe they will utilize the present situation to obtain concessions along the path of their larger objectives. This impression is supported by Arita's statement to the British Ambassador that the present demands are not unconditional.

5. At the same time, it is my opinion that it will be well to let the Japanese Government know by informal conversations, such as the Department suggests in its numbered paragraph 4, that the American Government is watching the situation constantly and with interest. As I can now receive visitors and as the Vice Minister for Foreign Affairs has expressed a desire to visit me, it might be possible in this way to arrange the desired interview without the risk of press publicity, or the Department's suggestion of Ballantine's calling on the Vice Minister might serve the same purpose.

6. The Embassy invites the Department's attention to Clive's statement to the Embassy that Clive agreed to Arita's request that the British Government's present approach to the Japanese Government be not divulged to the Chinese Government. This assurance apparently nullifies the intention of the British Government as expressed in the conclusion of the *aide-mémoire*.

Repeated to Peiping.

DICKOVER

919456—54——27

793.94/8211 : Telegram

The Minister in Switzerland (Wilson) to the Secretary of State

GENEVA, October 1, 1936—midnight.
[Received October 1—8 : 30 p. m.]

374. Wellington Koo and Quo Tai Chi [23] arranged a meeting with me. At the risk of repeating information which you already possess and because they expressly requested that you be informed, I repeat their statements.[24] They told me that they had asked their Government for information respecting the Japanese demands. The Government furnished this information and authorized them to convey it confidentially to representatives of "friendly governments". They said they had conveyed the information to Halifax,[25] Delbos [26] and Litvinov,[26a] in addition to myself.

The demands were presented approximately September 15, orally by the Japanese Ambassador to the Chinese Minister for Foreign Affairs at Nanking; the Chinese countered by suggesting that the various incidents in which Japanese nationals were involved should be discussed and liquidated first. This, the Japanese were unwilling to do and pressed for the discussion of the demands. The Chinese then countered by: (1) abolition of the Tangku truce, (2) cancellation of the Eastern Hopei autonomous government, (3) cessation of Japanese smuggling, (4) cancellation of a military agreement which compelled the withdrawal of Chinese troops from the two northern provinces.

They stated that the Japanese Ambassador then suspended negotiations on the grounds that the Minister for Foreign Affairs lacked plenipotentiary powers.

The demands are not in the form of an ultimatum. No date is fixed before a reply must be received but severe pressure is being brought upon the Chinese for quick action, including Arita's recent threat before the foreign correspondents.

The demands follow: (1) the autonomy of the five northern provinces, (2) an economic cooperation with the whole of China, similar to that now existing in the North, (3) agreement for joint measures for defense against Communism, (4) appointment of Japanese advisers in the Central Government, (5) establishment of air communications between Japan and China, particularly with Shanghai and Foochow, (6) a special or preferential tariff agreement, (7) complete suppression of anti-Japanese propaganda including the revision of

---

[23] Chinese Ambassadors in France and the United Kingdom, respectively.
[24] The Department replied that this report "is helpful and is appreciated."
[25] Viscount Halifax, Lord Privy Seal and leader of the British House of Lords.
[26] Yvon Delbos, French Minister for Foreign Affairs.
[26a] Soviet Commissar for Foreign Affairs.

school texts and special restrictions upon Koreans naturalized in China, including their expulsion from military schools.

In terminating Koo stated that he learned on "good authority" that the French and British had discussed the matter here and intended to instruct their Ambassadors in Tokyo to make representations. They hope that our Government as well, will take some step to bring about a *détente* in the Sino-Japanese relations.

WILSON

793.94/8272

The Chargé in Japan (Dickover) to the Secretary of State

No. 2061　　　　　　　　　　　　　　　TOKYO, October 1, 1936.'
[Received October 19.]

SIR: I have the honor to submit the following report upon Sino-Japanese relations, supplementing that contained in Embassy's despatch No. 2041 of September 17, 1936.[27]

The apprehensions which had prevailed in Japan that the anniversary of the September 18 incident in Mukden might be made the occasion for further attacks upon Japanese in China were realized when there occurred in close succession the Swatow, Fengtai, Hankow and Shanghai affairs.

[Here follows résumé of recent incidents and Japanese public reaction thereto.]

Summary.

The developments in Sino-Japanese relations during the past two weeks have served to gain support in Japanese political circles for the advocate of a strong China policy and to strengthen the force of public opinion behind them. Japan's objectives in addition to the immediate settlement of the incidents appear to be (1) the eradication by China of anti-Japanese activities which would incidentally have the effect of embarrassing Chiang Kai-shek with the Kuomintang and weaken his position; and (2) the creation of an autonomous regime under Japanese influence in North China. There would appear to be also other minor objectives, such as the reduction of China's customs duties and the appointment of Japanese advisers to the National Government. In this connection, it is well to bear in mind Hirota's three points which underlie Japan's objectives in China.

There are evidences that it is Japan's policy to press China to give in to the Japanese demands, as far as can be done short of resort to outright military coercion, using to the best advantage the leverage afforded by the series of incidents that have occurred. Should China

---

[27] Not printed.

refuse to accede to the demands relating to the suppression of anti-Japanese activities, there will probably be an increase in the naval protection for Japanese residents in port cities. If Nanking refuses to give way to the demands relating to North China, the Japanese army will probably pursue a policy of slow and steady penetration advancing towards the goal as opportunities present themselves.

Respectfully yours,   E. R. DICKOVER

793.94/8209 : Telegram

The Consul General at Shanghai (Gauss) to the Secretary of State

SHANGHAI, October 2, 1936—3 p. m.
[Received October 2—10:10 a. m.]

527. My October 1, 4 p. m. No substantial change in measures adopted yesterday by Japanese forces though a few barricades are reported to have been removed. Slight exodus of Chinese from Chapei and Hongkew districts.

First Special District Court today rendered decision in the Nakayama case, two suspects being sentenced to death and the third accused being found not guilty. Verdict which is pleasing to the Japanese, though resented in some Chinese circles, may now result in relaxation of strong "precautionary" measures taken by the Japanese.

Repeated to Department and Peiping. By mail to Nanking.

GAUSS

793.94/8207 : Telegram

The Ambassador in China (Johnson) to the Secretary of State

PEIPING, October 2, 1936—3 p. m.
[Received October 1—7:30 p. m.]

471. Department's 126, September 30, 7 p. m. to Tokyo.

1. Considering situation outlined in my 470, September 29, 4 p.m. I do not believe that any useful purpose would be served by an approach by us at this time either to the Japanese or to the Chinese Government.

2. British Ambassador informed me this evening that he had instructed his Counsellor at Nanking to visit Foreign Office and urge prevention further provocative incidents. I believe Chinese Government to be doing everything in its power to accomplish this, but I am convinced that situation is beyond their control and I am at a loss to know what else we could recommend except complete surrender.

[3?]. British Ambassador also informed me that Kawagoe had seen his Military Attaché who recommended that he leave Nanking. Kawagoe, however, is remaining in Nanking to prevent situation falling completely into the hands of the military. British Ambassador stated that Kawagoe is reported by Chinese Foreign Office representative to have urged Chinese acceptance as refusal would result in fall of Japanese Cabinet and coming into power in Tokyo of a much more extreme government.

4. In my opinion a direct approach from us at this time at Tokyo, considering present temper of Japanese military, would harm rather than help. I yield in this regard, however, to Tokyo's opinion as to whether an expression of concern made to the Japanese without simultaneous representations at Nanking might aid Hirota Cabinet in facing pressure from military.

5. I still entertain views set forth in my 191, December 2, 3 p. m.[28] Repeated to Tokyo, Nanking.

JOHNSON

793.94/8210 : Telegram

The Chargé in Japan (Dickover) to the Secretary of State

TOKYO, October 2, 1936—7 p. m.
[Received October 2—9:10 a. m.]

202. 1. According to Domei, the Foreign Office authorities commenting upon a London report circulated by Reuter containing a purported revelation attributed to "diplomatic sources" of Japanese demands, among which was mentioned the right to station troops along Yangtze, the right to edit Chinese school texts, and autonomy of the five northern provinces, declared that the alleged demands were malicious propaganda aimed at alienating Japan and China and stated that the Consulate General at Nanking had on September 26 filed with the Chinese Foreign Office a strong protest in which it was pointed out that the spread of such reports was contrary to an arrangement between the two Governments not to reveal the contents of the negotiations.

2. Foreign Office spokesman today, according to *Japan Times*, announced that as the Japanese Government was conducting its negotiations with a careful attitude it had decided to despatch the director of the Asiatic Bureau of the Foreign Office to Nanking immediately in order to convey the intentions of the Government to Ambassador Kawagoe.

Repeated to Peking.

DICKOVER

---

[28] *Foreign Relations*, 1935, vol. III, p. 460.

793.94/8212 : Telegram

The Ambassador in China (Johnson) to the Secretary of State

PEIPING, October 2, 1936—7 p. m.
[Received October 2—9 : 35 a. m.]

472. My 470, September 29, 4 p. m., and my 471, October 2, 3 p. m. Major Imai, Japanese Assistant Military Attaché, in conversation with foreign press correspondents here this morning stated that he was pleased that in this area there had thus far occurred no such unfortunate incidents as have taken place in the "South". He said that the Japanese authorities had taken measures to prevent such incidents here in the North but that if such an incident should occur it would be "seized upon". He did not specify what action would be taken by the Japanese but the American correspondents present gained the definite impression that he took it for granted that an "unfortunate incident" would inevitably occur and that stern action would follow.

In view of the provocative and truculent attitude of the Japanese military it will be surprising if an "unfortunate incident" does not occur here in the North or in other regions in China despite all preventive action now being taken by the Chinese authorities arising out of the open rejoicing of the Japanese on the occasion of the anniversary of the Mukden incident, the constant exhibition in Peiping and surrounding regions of Japanese soldiers and military equipment, the forthcoming maneuvers of Japanese forces between here and Tientsin, the continual maneuvers of the Japanese landing forces in Shanghai, all invite such incidents, unaltered by the danger inherent in the enmity toward Chiang Kai Shek of political opponents, intellectuals and radical elements. The situation continues to be definitely and increasingly alarming.

Repeated to Tokyo.

JOHNSON

793.94/8215

Memorandum by the Secretary of State

[WASHINGTON,] October 2, 1936.

The Chinese Ambassador called and urged that the American Government take action similar to that taken by the British Government at Tokyo in asking the Japanese Government to be moderate and conciliatory toward China. I replied that we are following developments in relations between China and Japan with care and genuine interest; that we very much regret the serious conditions; that we will give every attention and consideration to each phase as it develops;

that we are mindful of all phases; that in thus giving attention it will be necessary for us to avoid any step which might do more harm than good.

The Ambassador then inquired as to the attitude of the United States in the event of a clash, to which I replied again that our country is, of course, intensely interested in peace and that we earnestly hope no clash will occur.

C[ORDELL] H[ULL]

793.94/8266

Memorandum by the Assistant Chief of the Division of Far Eastern Affairs (Hamilton)

[WASHINGTON,] October 2, 1936.

The French Ambassador, Mr. André de Laboulaye, called by appointment. He said that this morning he had received a cable from his Government stating that the French Government had been informed in London that the British Government had made an informal approach in Tokyo to the Japanese Government urging that the Japanese Government adopt a moderate and conciliatory attitude in its present relations with China. The Ambassador said that his cable asked him to call at the Department and inquire, in the light of the circumstance that the American Government was the "custodian" of the Washington Conference treaties, as to the attitude of the Department of State in the matter and whether the American Government planned to make an approach to the Japanese Government. The Ambassador said further that his cable indicated that the receipt of information in regard to the attitude of the American Government would be helpful to the French Government in itself reaching a decision in the matter.

Mr. Hamilton said that we were of course following developments in the situation with especial care and concern and that we were endeavoring to assemble all possible information which would be helpful to us in adequately understanding the situation. Mr. Hamilton said that the Ambassador would realize that due to the position of leadership which the American Government took in the Sino-Japanese controversy in 1931 and the immediately ensuing years, in relation to a situation where there were involved rights, interests and obligations common to this and many other Governments, the American Government now, in order that any approach made by it to the Japanese Government might not have an adverse rather than a good effect, had to move perhaps more circumspectly than other governments: at least the American Government had to weigh very carefully the question whether any diplomatic action which it might take would be likely to do more harm than good.

The Ambassador stated that if and when the Department should reach a decision whether to make an approach to the Japanese Government, he would appreciate being informed of the nature of the decision. Mr. Hamilton said that he would be glad to do this.

M[AXWELL] M. H[AMILTON]

793.94/8208 : Telegram

The Secretary of State to the Chargé in Japan (Dickover)

WASHINGTON, October 2, 1936—9 p. m.

127. Your 200, October 1, 10 p. m.

1. The Department is continuing to study the situation in the light of all available reports. In the meanwhile the Department desires that the Embassy act along the lines of the suggestion contained in paragraph 5 of your telegram under reference, namely, to let the Japanese Government know by informal conversations that the American Government is watching the situation constantly and with solicitous interest. In so doing the Embassy should act as upon its own initiative, and the Embassy will of course endeavor to avoid publicity and to choose as soon as practicable appropriate occasions for such conversations.

2. We suggest that you (or alternatively Ballantine) say to the Vice Minister that you had for some time been observing with concern the press reports of the differences lying between the Japanese Government and the Chinese Government, but that you had refrained from approaching the Foreign Office lest undesirable publicity ensue; that the press reports are now assuming so serious a tone that you consider it advisable to seek authoritative information with regard to the developments to which the press reports refer; and that you accordingly invite the Vice Minister to comment on these reports in order that you may be in position to keep your Government adequately and accurately informed of developments in a situation which of course commands its interest and concern.

3. Please continue to report promptly and fully by cable.

4. The Department appreciates the promptness and comprehensiveness of your telegram under reference.

5. Referring to paragraph 6 of your telegram under reference, a telegram from Wilson at Geneva indicates that the Chinese Ambassadors to Great Britain and to France had knowledge that the British Government intended to instruct its Ambassador in Tokyo to approach the Japanese Government.

HULL

693.94244/151 : Telegram

The Ambassador in China (Johnson) to the Secretary of State

PEIPING, October 3, 1936—11 a. m.
[Received 8 p. m.]

473. The representative of the Ministry of Finance has returned to Nanking. Nothing definite can be learned regarding the plans of the Chinese authorities relative to the smuggling situation, but it is rumored that a new committee will be formed composed of members of the Chinese Maritime Customs, Hopei-Chahar Political Council, and the Ministry of Finance, the function of which will be the disposal of the accumulation of smuggled goods in Tientsin.

It is reported that smuggled merchandise continues to move out of Tientsin to the interior by roads and canals, but that only very small quantities of these goods now pass into Shantung and Honan due to interference by the authorities. Tsinanfu reports that 12 truck-loads of such goods (mainly rayon, sugar and cigarette paper) are said to have arrived there on September 23, and that on the same day 60 truckloads left Tientsin for Tsinanfu. The trucks are said to be driven by Chinese and carrying Japanese guards who are armed with rifles and machine guns. Tsinanfu understands, however, that the Chinese authorities have instructed the natives living along the route followed by the trucks to dig ditches across the roads and create other obstructions. This may result in decreased smuggling but will also ruin motor roads in Shantung.

JOHNSON

793.94/8216 : Telegram

The Counselor of Embassy in China (Peck) to the Secretary of State

NANKING, October 3, 1936—noon.
[Received October 3—10 : 15 a. m.]

290. My 285, September 29, 2 p. m.

1. I called on Vice Minister Hsu Mo this morning on a purely social matter and he took the opportunity to give me an extensive review of the discussions between the Japanese Ambassador and the Chinese Minister for Foreign Affairs differing slightly from my September 29, 2 p. m. He said proposals made by the Japanese Ambassador were (1) reorganization of the five northern provinces with arrangements for economic cooperation therein, (2) joint defense against Chinese communistic military activities, (3) convention for direct air communication between Japan and Shanghai, (4) Japanese advisers in many departments of the Chinese Government removing disparity

between numbers of Japanese and advisers of other nationalities, (5) customs convention specifically lowering rates on certain items.

2. The Chinese Minister for Foreign Affairs replied to the Japanese Ambassador that China was quite willing to effect economic cooperation with Japan but wished to begin with two economic conditions only, namely, Hopei and Chahar; suppression of Chinese Communist forces was a purely internal matter; China would be willing to conclude air convention on reciprocal basis recognizing China's sovereignty; China has already one Japanese adviser but would be willing to engage more in purely technical but not political or military capacities; China has not adopted any reciprocating customs conventions but would be willing to revise the customs tariff with both increases and decreases and having regard to necessity for maintaining customs receipts.

3. The Chinese Minister of Foreign Affairs then enumerated points which China regarded as requiring action by Japan if relations were to be improved. Briefly they were (1) elimination of the East Hopei autonomous regime, (2) Japanese cooperation in suppressing smuggling in North China, (3) cessation of indiscriminate flights by Japanese airplanes in disregard of China's sovereignty, (4) revision or cancellation of the Shanghai and Tangku military arrangements of 1932 and 1933. The last interview on September 23 ended abruptly and in a strained atmosphere.

4. The Vice Minister told me that substantially this outline had been sent to the Chinese Ambassador for communication to the Department of State but there was another matter he would be grateful to have me transmit. He said that the British Ambassador in Tokyo under instructions from his Government had called on the Japanese Minister for Foreign Affairs to urge moderation on the Japanese Government in what was currently regarded as a crisis in Sino-Japanese relations; the French Ambassador in Tokyo had received similar instructions. The Vice Minister wondered whether the American Government would be willing to take a like step through the American Chargé d'Affaires in Tokyo. He said that I might have heard a comment which he said is being made by many persons today, namely, that in reference to the present crisis Great Britain and the United States have interchanged positions as compared with their positions during a similar crisis in 1931 and 1932. I referred to newspaper reports that the British Ambassador in Tokyo had informed the Japanese Foreign Office that Great Britain was not intervening in the present discussions between China and Japan. The Vice Minister said that his information was that these newspaper reports were not true.

5. I said that I would telegraph the purport of his remarks to the American Ambassador and to the Department.

6. My telegram No. 287, October 1, 2 p. m., paragraph 1. The Vice Minister said the Chinese Government has no present intention to issue a statement. The two officials mentioned returned from Kuling yesterday. The director of the Asiatic Department will call on the Japanese Ambassador I presume today. The Vice Minister said General Chiang's duties would require his early return to Nanking but the date was uncertain. Other sources state Chiang will return October 5th.

7. Sent to the Department and Peiping.

PECK

793.94/8218 : Telegram

The Chargé in Japan (Dickover) to the Secretary of State

TOKYO, October 3, 1936—7 p. m.
[Received October 3—1 : 10 p. m.]

203. Embassy's 200, October 1, 10 p. m.

1. This morning Ballantine called on Vice Minister for Foreign Affairs at the Vice Minister's request. Vice Minister stated in view of misleading and mischievous press reports abroad regarding Sino-Japanese relations he wished to say that discussions with the Chinese Government to solve pending questions and adjust relations had not reached substantial stage when Chengtu incident occurred, and that this and other incidents interfered with progress of negotiations. Vice Minister said that Japan desires in connection with the settlement of these questions that China take effective steps to eradicate anti-Japanese movements, and that at the same time Japan desires to clear up other questions which he could not enumerate but which he emphasized are Japanese desires to be attained by discussion and are not unconditional demands. The Vice Minister said there are no new points in the negotiations. Referring to press reports he denied that Japan is asking for the right to station troops along the Yangtze or for the rights of North China involving fiscal, administrative, diplomatic autonomy. In reply to a question the Vice Minister said that a press interview by Kuwashima, director of Asiatic Bureau, was substantially correct except alleged statements defining scope of demands. In conclusion the Vice Minister emphasized Japan's desire for a solution of issues by diplomacy and express[ed] the hope that the Embassy would inform the American Government of the situation.

2. The Kuwashima interview referred to in paragraph 1 has been reported by the Associated Press. In view of the Vice Minister's remarks and in view of the care of Foreign Office representatives not to divulge the actual points under discussion with China the Embassy believes that the report of the Kuwashima interview is of no value as defining the demands.

3. In conversation this afternoon with me at the hospital the Vice Minister for Foreign Affairs stated that the present discussions with China are in no respect like the 21 demands and that Japan has no intention of using force or other military operations to obtain Chinese agreement to Japanese desires. He said that the only demand upon which the Japanese will insist is the suppression of anti-Japanese propaganda and agitation because of the danger of further incidents. Other matters will be discussed but they will be simply desiderata subject to negotiation and designed to promote more healthy and normal relations. He said that the discussions will be based on Hirota's three points. In regard to sending Kuwashima to China the Vice Minister said the object is to convey the real purposes of the Japanese Government to Kawagoe and added that "the deer hunter does not see the mountain" implying that Japanese representatives in China are unable to maintain perspective. When asked what steps are contemplated if China refuses compliance the Vice Minister stated "we shall not cross that bridge until we reach it". He deplored the inaccuracy of *New York Times* reports presumably coming from Hallett Abend.

4. Since these conversations the Embassy has received Department's 127, October 2, 9 p. m.

5. In spite of reports of the alarming attitude of Japanese representatives in China the Embassy believes that the Government in Tokyo is still in command of the situation and is confining its efforts to objectives less sweeping than those reported in the press abroad.

Repeated to Peiping.

DICKOVER

793.94/8220 : Telegram

The Consul at Hankow (Jarvis) to the Secretary of State

HANKOW, October 3, 1936—8 p. m.
[Received October 3—5 : 40 p. m.]

Hankow is quiet but there is considerable nervousness among the Chinese. Officials regard the situation as very grave and are preparing for a possible conflict. Troops continue to arrive and to move north through Hankow, their ostensible destination being Shensi, Kansu and the anti-Communist front. Large consignments of silver have been shipped from Hankow during the past few days to places of greater safety.

2. The Japanese landing party has been increased to about 300 men. In addition there are several hundred reservists among the local residents. There are two Japanese destroyers and one gunboat here now.

3. Changsha is reported to be undisturbed.

Sent to the Department, Peiping, Nanking, Shanghai.

JARVIS

793.003 Manchuria/11

The Secretary of State to the Belgian Ambassador (Van der Straten-Ponthoz)

WASHINGTON, October 3, 1936.

EXCELLENCY: I have the honor to acknowledge the receipt of Your Excellency's note, and enclosure, of September 9, 1936, in which inquiry is made concerning the attitude of the American Government with regard to the declaration made on July 1, 1936, by the Minister for Foreign Affairs of "Manchukuo".

It is recalled that the Minister for Foreign Affairs of "Manchukuo" stated in substance that "Manchukuo" had decided to abolish by gradual steps the extraterritorial rights enjoyed by foreign nationals residing in "Manchukuo" and is prepared to consider proposals for opening negotiations toward reaching agreement with interested governments with regard to the status of their respective nationals resident in each others' territory.

The enclosure to your note has been read with interest and care, and attention has been given to the various considerations set forth therein which have received the attention of the Belgian Government.

This Government has not overlooked the substance and purport of the declaration of the "Manchukuo" Minister for Foreign Affairs. With regard to the intended gradual abolition of extraterritorial rights in Manchuria, this Government is not disposed at this time to take any action. However, should there occur, as a result of the policy under reference in "Manchukuo", cases of injustice, of unreasonable taxation or of discrimination adversely affecting American nationals, this Government would expect to give appropriate consideration to the problems thus and then created.

It is the opinion of this Government that the suggestion of the "Manchukuo" Minister for Foreign Affairs that negotiations be held on the subject of the status of foreign nationals does not require a reply, and that any treatment of the question of extraterritorial rights in Manchuria, as a question distinct from the question of extraterritorial rights throughout China, could be expected, as matters stand at this time, to lead to complications of an embarrassing character.

I appreciate the spirit in which your Government has given me the benefit of its reflections with regard to this matter and has sought the views of my Government. Your Government's exposition of the subject is helpful and I trust that the foregoing statement of my Government's views will be found adequately responsive to your Government's inquiry.

This Government will expect to treat as confidential this exchange of communications and the contents thereof and assumes that your Government will desire to follow a similar course.

Accept [etc.] CORDELL HULL

793.94/8219 : Telegram

The Chargé in Japan (Dickover) to the Secretary of State

TOKYO, October 4, 1936—1 p. m.
[Received October 4—4:19 a. m.]

204. 1. Press gives wide publicity to an interview yesterday between the Minister for Foreign Affairs and Chinese Ambassador. Arita is said to have emphasized the importance of the present negotiations for adjusting Sino-Japanese relations and to have expressed the conviction that Japan's true intentions would become known when Kawagoe meets Chiang Kai Shek.

2. There has been no recent allusion in press to any interview on Sino-Japanese relations by the Foreign Office with any other diplomatic representative.

3. Press states that Prime Minister left yesterday for Hokkaido to report developments in Sino-Japanese situation to the Throne.

Repeated to Peiping.

DICKOVER

793.94/8218 : Telegram

The Secretary of State to the Chargé in Japan (Dickover) [29]

WASHINGTON, October 4, 1936—2 p. m.

128. Your 203, October 3, 7 p.m.

1. Department desires that Ballantine call as soon as practicable upon the Vice Minister for Foreign Affairs and, referring to the conversations reported in your telegram under reference, read to the Vice Minister, as under instruction, a statement substantially but in close paraphrase reading as follows:

"The American Government is gratified to have the benefit of this information direct from the Japanese Government as communicated by the Vice Minister for Foreign Affairs. The situation to which it relates has from its inception had the interest and careful attention of the American Government. This Government has naturally observed with concern the alarming and sensational reports which have appeared in the press in the United States and other countries, and therefore appreciates sincerely the initiative taken by the Japanese Government in acquainting this Government with information contributory toward an understanding of the present state of relations between Japan and China. The American Government is especially gratified to receive the assurance that the Japanese Government desires to obtain a solution of the issues lying between Japan and China by diplomacy. This Government will follow developments in the situation as it unfolds with solicitude, and it would be

---

[29] Repeated to the Ambassador in China on the same date as telegram No. 235.

helpful if the Japanese Government would from time to time and as circumstances make such action useful, continue to give this Government information toward clarifying the situation."

2. Ballantine should not leave with the Vice Minister a copy of the statement, which should be regarded as an oral one.

3. Report by cable when action has been taken.

4. The developments reported in your telegram under reference and this reply obviate the need of the Embassy taking action at this time along the lines contemplated in the Department's 127, October 2, 9 p.m.

HULL

793.94/8221 : Telegram

The Counselor of Embassy in China (Peck) to the Secretary of State

NANKING, October 5, 1936—1 p. m.
[Received October 5—7 a. m.]

293. The Chinese press, October 3, carried long statement over the names of numerous prominent Chinese newspapers.[30] There follow two excerpts from translation published by Central News Agency under date October 2nd:

(1st excerpt) "For China's present foreign relations are in no way similar to those of several years ago. Once she breaks off with another country, it would be tantamount to gambling the existence of the nation to the last straw and there is no way of retracting.

Should a rupture occur between China and Japan the situation would be as serious as just pictured. Once hostilities were started, and should China be forced to surrender, it would mean her endorsing a pledge of giving up her own independence. In that event, posterity would be left to suffer and the chances of a national revival would be nil.

It is therefore imperative that we should consider the rupture of diplomatic relations as the last resort. Meanwhile, we should still entertain the hope that some satisfactory solution to the deadlock may be reached. But should the last resort fail, the whole populace would not hesitate to lay down their lives for their fatherland."

(2d excerpt) "Mincing no words, the Nanking and Shanghai dailies remind their Nipponese colleagues that should no efforts be made to fundamentally readjust the Sino-Japanese relations, gravity of the future situation would far exceed that of the Shanghai war and the Great Wall fighting.

Driven to desperation, China would have to make her last sacrifice in a last effort to maintain her independence. Chinese public opinion,

---

[30] The Counselor of Embassy in his telegram No. 294, October 5, 2 p. m., reported that the statement "was drafted by the Chinese Ministry of Foreign Affairs and was approved by General Chiang Kai Shek. The first intention was to publish it as an official communiqué but considerations of policy later prompted its issue as a statement by the Chinese press." (793.94/8222)

it says, has reached the point whereby it will not tolerate the Government accepting humiliating terms in order to preserve peace. China might have to suffer untold sacrifices but could Japan escape from such a disastrous whirlpool in the Orient?"

PECK

793.94/8223 : Telegram

The Counselor of Embassy in China (Peck) to the Secretary of State

NANKING, October 5, 1936—4 p. m.
[Received October 5—1:12 p. m.]

295. General Chiang Kai Shek arrived Nanking this afternoon. No interview with the Japanese Ambassador arranged as yet so far as can be learned. Kuwashima,[31] special emissary of the Japanese Foreign Office to the Japanese Ambassador, is expected in Nanking morning of October 6.

Sent to the Department and Peiping.

PECK

793.94/8231 : Telegram

The Chargé in Japan (Dickover) to the Secretary of State

TOKYO, October 6, 1936—3 p. m.
[Received October 6—7:36 a. m.]

206. 1. Instructions contained in Department's 128, October 4, 2 p. m. carried out at 2 o'clock this afternoon. Vice Minister made no comments; he informed Ballantine, however, that there were no further developments in the situation.

2. *Chugai* says that the Foreign Office authorities made the following announcement yesterday in connection with a Domei London report that the British Ambassador here has made representations to the Japanese Government in regard to its China policy:

"Recently in response to a request by British Ambassador Clive for information regarding Sino-Japanese negotiations Foreign Minister Arita gave him an explanation of the present status of Sino-Japanese relations. The Ambassador's request was not based upon instructions from his Government but was on his own initiative. Consequently it is not true that the British Government has made any representations to the Imperial Government regarding Chinese questions. Furthermore, the Foreign Office authorities made to a member of the American Embassy a similar explanation; no representations have been made by the American Government."

The other newspapers publish similar reports.

Repeated to Peiping.

DICKOVER

---

[31] Kozue Kuwashima, director of the East Asiatic Bureau, Japanese Foreign Office.

793.94/8233 : Telegram

The Counselor of Embassy in China (Peck) to the Secretary of State

NANKING, October 6, 1936—4 p. m.

[Received October 6—9 : 20 a. m.]

296. 1. Franklin Ho, director of the Political Department of the Executive Yuan, questioned by me today gave the following considered views regarding Sino-Japanese relations :

2. Negotiations ended on September 23 with complete deadlock. This deadlock cannot be broken unless Kuwashima, who arrived in Nanking this morning, brings instructions to the Japanese Ambassador to be more conciliatory.

3. Chinese informed popular opinion is that further yielding to Japan would be futile because Japan is never satisfied. Not only do the military classes and academic circles advocate armed resistance unless the Japanese demands are greatly modified but even banking circles which would feel the destructive effect of warfare most quickly and disastrously. Informant admits that the Government is not financially equipped to wage war with Japan but he believes that the Government could not retain its authority if it capitulated to the Japanese demands. With apparent sincerity he expressed the opinion that it would be preferable for the Government to meet a glorious end rather than consent to the gradual dismemberment of the country.

4. Informant felt some hope that the Japanese would realize that China had been pushed to the last extremity and would moderate their demands because he could not see what advantage Japan could expect to gain from a complete overthrow of the National Government with ensuing chaos in China.

5. Informant naturally inquired what the attitude of the American Government was toward this crisis. I replied that I had no information about this but I recalled that the Washington Conference and other past events showed the hope of the American Government that a strong and independent China would emerge. Informant observed that the present crisis calls for thoughtful and far seeing statesmanship in other countries as well as in China.

6. Sent to the Department and Peiping.

PECK

793.94/8254

Memorandum by the Chief of the Division of Far Eastern Affairs (Hornbeck)

[WASHINGTON,] October 6, 1936.

The British Chargé called by appointment and stated that he had received instructions to inform the Department of the report which the British Ambassador at Tokyo had made to the British Government in regard to the British Ambassador's conversation on October 1 with the Japanese Minister for Foreign Affairs and to say that the British Government felt that the "time for concerted action had not yet arrived". The Chargé then proceeded to read the report of the British Ambassador's conversation with the Japanese Foreign Minister which may be summarized as follows:

On October 1 the British Ambassador called on the Japanese Minister for Foreign Affairs and referred to a previous conversation wherein the British Ambassador had said that the British Government would, he was sure, without in any way attempting to act as mediator in the Sino-Japanese situation, be glad to impress upon the Chinese Government the danger of anti-Japanese incidents in China. The British Ambassador then said that he wished to inform the Japanese Foreign Minister, under instruction, that the British Government desired to see Sino-Japanese relations established on a peaceful basis and that the British Ambassador in China was speaking to the Chinese Government in regard to attacks on Japanese nationals in China. Continuing, the British Ambassador said that, speaking personally, he wished to point out to the Foreign Minister that if the Japanese pressed the Chinese too hard the Japanese would force the Chinese to resist. The Foreign Minister said that the Japanese Army realized that the Chinese might possibly offer armed resistance as well as the danger of pushing the Chinese too far. The Foreign Minister commented that the part of the Kuomintang in which Feng Yu-hsiang was outstanding, which part had communistic tendencies, was a dangerous factor in the situation and responsible for much of the anti-Japanese agitation in China. The British Ambassador then remarked that in view of these factors it would seem that the Japanese Government would not wish to press Chiang Kaishek too hard. The Foreign Minister then referred to Chang Hsuehliang and said that this general was very active in anti-Japanese agitation. The British Ambassador commented that one could hardly blame a defeated Chinese general for attempting to "save his face" by now being active in anti-Japanese agitation; also that there were usually two sides to every quarrel. The Foreign Minister replied "somewhat ominously" that "the Japanese could not be expected to give consideration to the Chinese point of view." The Foreign Minister said that Japan was determined to make North China safe for "Manchukuo". He denied that Japan's proposal with regard to North China provided for separate customs and separate currency for North China. He also said that Japan's proposals were not unconditional demands but were subject to discussion. The British Ambassador requested that the Japanese give no publicity to his call on the Japanese Foreign Minister and the Japanese Foreign

Minister in turn requested that the Chinese Government not be informed of the British Ambassador's approach to the Japanese Foreign Minister.

Mr. Hornbeck said that he would like to have Mr. Hamilton hear the substance of the information which the British Chargé was communicating and upon Mr. Hamilton's entry the Chargé read again the substance of the cablegram which he had received from the British Foreign Office.

Mr. Hornbeck then handed the British Chargé the Department's *aide-mémoire* of October 6,[32] informing the British Embassy of the interchange of communications between the American Embassy at Tokyo and the Department subsequent to the morning of October 3. Mr. Hornbeck also handed to the Chargé, to read, Tokyo's telegram No. 206, October 6, 3 p. m.

There then followed a brief discussion of the general situation, wherein Mr. Hornbeck commented that it seemed apparent that the Japanese Government wished to keep from the Japanese people the fact that representations, even of a very informal character, had been made by the British and the American Governments; that it might be just as well that the Japanese Foreign Office was taking this attitude; and that the record revealed that the Japanese Government had made to the Chinese Government certain proposals or demands which it did not intend to reveal to the British or to the American Governments. When the Chargé asked whether it would seem that the control of the military in Japan was lessening, Mr. Hornbeck replied in the negative.

S[TANLEY] K. H[ORNBECK]

793.94/8216 : Telegram

*The Acting Secretary of State to the Counselor of Embassy in China
(Peck)*

WASHINGTON, October 7, 1936—7 p. m.

65. Your 290, October 3, noon. For the Ambassador's confidential information and guidance.

1. Referring to paragraph 4 of the telegram under reference, first sentence, the second matter touched upon was presented here and an appropriate reply, indicating our genuine interest and concern but containing no commitment, was made. A copy of the memorandum of conversation [33] has been sent to the Embassy by pouch.

2. Tokyo's No. 206, October 6, 3 p. m., to the Department, copy of which was repeated to Peiping, indicates in paragraph 2 that the

---

[32] Not printed.
[33] Memorandum of October 2 by the Secretary of State, p. 330.

Japanese Foreign Office desires to avoid disclosing to the Japanese public the fact that any representations, even of an informal character, have been made to the Japanese Government. In the light of this indication and inasmuch as the Department is of the opinion that the approach made by the American Government to the Japanese Government is more likely to have a constructively helpful effect if it is not made known to the Chinese Government, at least at this time, the Department desires that no intimation be given to the Chinese Government at this moment that such an approach has been made. The Department realizes that, this being the case, there may be need for very tactful action toward preventing possible development of a prejudicial effect upon Sino-American relations. With this in mind, the Department offers certain comments and suggestions which may be helpful to you and to Peck in making appropriate oral and confidential response to any questions that may be put by responsible Chinese officials, as follows:

The attitude and position of the American Government with regard to treaty rights and obligations have in no way altered. The American Government has been following, and continues to follow, closely, developments in relations between China and Japan. The American Government is giving attention and consideration to each phase of the situation as it develops, bearing in mind all its phases. Inasmuch as there are involved rights, interests and obligations common to a number of governments, the American Government has made a practice of discussing developments and exchanging information in regard thereto with other interested governments. The American Government has taken in the past and will continue to take such steps as seem to it appropriate and feasible. It wishes to avoid the taking of any action which would be likely to have a harmful rather than a beneficial effect. The American Government intends to attempt to exert its influence quietly and unobtrusively and to avoid giving any countenance to measures or situations contravening any legitimate interests or treaty rights and it desires, in any action that it may take, to be constructively helpful.

3. Referring to the statement in paragraph 4 of Nanking's telegram under reference, the Department expects that officers of the American Government will make appropriate and tactful replies to any comment calculated to misrepresent the attitude or action of the United States or to place these in an unfavorable light as compared with those of any other countries. It should be realized and admitted by anyone not adversely prejudiced—and it may so be discreetly pointed out—that the American Government has consistently endeavored in relations with the Far East, while serving the interests of the United States to avoid and avert disservice to the interests of China. At the present moment we are in no way forgetful of either

of these objectives and we are intent upon both. We desire to be constructively helpful where possible and as appropriate, but we naturally are exercising our own best judgment as to what contribution on our part may be most practicable, opportune and appropriate.

CARR

793.94/8245 : Telegram

The Counselor of Embassy in China (Peck) to the Secretary of State

NANKING, October 8, 1936—2 p. m.
[Received October 8—10 : 40 a. m.[34]]

297. My 296, October 6, 4 p. m.

1. Interview between the Japanese Ambassador and General Chiang Kai Shek occurred October 8, 10 a. m. Results have not been ascertained. Social exchange of visits will take place between the British and Japanese Ambassadors this afternoon and between the British Ambassador and Chiang tomorrow.

2. An American news correspondent states that Suma this morning emphatically denied reports attributed to Chinese sources that the visit of the Japanese Ambassador this morning was purely social. He asserted that it was a "business interview". Suma protested against nature of American press despatches which describe the present negotiations as mainly concerning "Japanese demands". He stated that the only fundamental requirement of Japan is the eradication of the ungovernable causes of the recent outrages against Japanese and he minimized the so-called proposals.

3. Leighton Stuart, president of Yenching University, informs me that he has consulted extensively with Chinese intellectuals in this area during the last few days and had half hour discussion with Chiang Kai Shek yesterday. Stuart told Chiang Kai Shek yesterday he felt that if the National Government under Japanese pressure segregated North China there would be a strong movement there to declare independence on the ground that if the North is to be abandoned to Japan it can obtain the best terms eithers by resistance or by its own independent negotiations. Stuart expresses the belief that the most prevalent Chinese popular sentiment advocates resistance to Japan on the ground that yielding would be more disastrous than even unsuccessful resistance. Another view, held by a minority whose typical representatives are bankers, advocates conciliation, for example, by regarding North China as differentiated from China in general though constituting an inseparable part of the country. This view envisages even the possibility that Manchuria might again coalesce with China in a similar status. The minority advocating

_____

[34] Telegram in three sections.

conciliation of Japan are influenced by the belief that unless the hands of the civilian element in the Japanese Government are strengthened the imperialistic element among the younger military officers aided by profound economic discontent among the soldiers and the masses will seize control and bring about disaster possibly to both countries. Stuart says that Chiang is much harassed by proponents of these two policies in his entourage. Among his personal advisers his wife and W. H. Donald are strongly urging resistance and the other group is thought to include Chang Kia Ngau, former banker, present Minister of Railways, and Wu, Nanking manager of the Bank of China. Stuart inclines to the belief that a preliminary conference between Japanese and Chinese representatives yesterday agreed upon some forms of compromise.

4. *London Times* editorial released by Reuter's and *North China Daily News* editorial yesterday have strongly pro-Chinese tone in the present controversy.

5. Sent to the Department and Peiping.

PECK

793.94/8246 : Telegram

The Consul General at Shanghai (Gauss) to the Secretary of State

SHANGHAI, October 8, 1936—4 p. m.
[Received October 8—2 : 10 p. m.]

535. A renewed and heavy exodus of Chinese from the Hongkew and Chapei districts of Shanghai commenced yesterday and continues unabated today. It is reported that this exodus is due (1) to special measures by Chinese Government approximating martial law in districts around Shanghai, (2) to spread of wild rumors, (3) to continued precautionary measures on the part of Japanese landing party and (4) to the rumored gradual penetration of peace preservation units, wearing civilian clothes and avoiding business centers, into Chapei and the Chinese native city. Situation otherwise quiet.

Repeated to Peiping and by mail to Nanking.

GAUSS

693.94244/156 : Telegram

The First Secretary of Embassy in China (Merrell) to the Secretary of State

PEIPING, October 9, 1936—3 p. m.
[Received October 9—9 : 45 a. m.]

491. Embassy's 473, October 3, 11 a. m. No official announcement has been made relating to plans for disposing of smuggled goods now held in Tientsin, regarding which the authorities concerned have held numerous conferences in Tientsin during the last 2 weeks, but the

Consulate General at Tientsin has received information which it believes to be reliable to the effect that a certain Japanese firm in Tientsin now collects a tax of 48 cents per unit on kerosene smuggled into Tientsin, following which the kerosene is distributed freely in eastern Hopei and Chahar. It is said that the proceeds of the tax are paid over to the Chairman of the Hopei-Chahar Political Council.

By mail to Tokyo.

MERRELL

793.94/8248 : Telegram

The Ambassador in China (Johnson) to the Secretary of State

NANKING, October 9, 1936—4 p. m.
[Received October 9—1 : 05 p. m.]

298. Embassy's 297, October 8, 2 p. m. from Nanking.

1. I saw Donald this morning who informed me that Japanese Ambassador at his interview with Chiang Kai Shek on October 8, 10 a. m., mentioned outrages against Japanese subjects but that this was the only concrete question discussed. He stated that Chiang had assured Kawagoe of China's willingness to settle these cases in accordance with international law but added that there were various other matters outstanding between China and Japan and that he would instruct the Chinese Minister for Foreign Affairs to be ready to resume negotiations with the Japanese Ambassador for a settlement of these issues on the basis of regard for China's territorial and administrative sovereignty.

2. Donald stated that he had urged Chiang to bring up question of Japanese violation of China's sovereignty but that Chiang had replied to Donald in a sense permitting the inference that he was convinced that the Japanese wished to moderate their position and that he did not wish to do anything which might make this difficult for the Japanese. Donald said he did not know how Chiang had reached this conviction but that there could be no doubt that he was so convinced.

3. I saw the Minister of Foreign Affairs this morning who described the position of his Government saying that on September 23 the discussions with Kawagoe reached a deadlock. He commented on the arrival of Kuwa Shima stating that it was believed that he was sent by Tokyo to give revised instructions intended to moderate the previous attitude of the Japanese Ambassador and that China was now waiting for the Japanese Ambassador to discover the nature of this alleged new attitude. The Minister for Foreign Affairs confirmed Donald's description of the interview between Chiang and Kawagoe and stated that no concrete proposals were brought up by Kawagoe.

4. The Chinese Minister for Foreign Affairs asked me pointblank whether the American Embassy in Tokyo had approached the Japanese Ministry of Foreign Affairs and discussed the Sino-Japanese negotiations. I replied that no such approach had been made. Replying to his question regarding my personal reaction and regarding the American Government's reaction to the current situation I stated that it was difficult to determine just what was taking place in view of the confusion of information available concerning surface as well as inner considerations involved. I said that insofar as the American Government was concerned its attitude in regard to matters here in the Far East was well known from statements which have been made in the press by responsible American authorities and that this attitude and policy had not changed. At conclusion of the conversation I thanked the Minister for the information which he had given me regarding developments up to date and stated that concerned as it was over the situation my Government welcomed any information which either side might volunteer to give it in regard to the course of events.

5. In subsequent interviews either with the Minister for Foreign Affairs or with the Vice Minister I propose to make use of the opportunities offered to pursue the line laid down in the Department's No. 65 of October 7, 7 p. m.

6. Sent to the Department and Peiping.

JOHNSON

893.01 Inner Mongolia/84 : Telegram

The First Secretary of Embassy in China (Merrell) to the Secretary of State

PEIPING, October 9, 1936—5 p. m.
[Received 8 : 50 p. m.]

492. Embassy's 429, September 1, 2 p. m. Reports appearing in the Chinese press for the past few days indicate a possible renewal of warlike activities on the Chahar–Suiyuan border. According to this information, a conference began at Chapsur on October 5 between the important Chahar military leaders Teh Wang, Pao Yueh Ching, Li Shou Hsin, Wang Ying and others, in regard to important questions affecting Chahar and Suiyuan. Previous reports alleged that an airdrome and a wireless station have recently been established under Japanese initiative and control at Tingyuanying, northwest of Ninghsia, but that a similar project at Paotow was halted under pressure from Fu Tso Yi, Suiyuan Chairman, and the interested Japanese forced to withdraw to Kalgan. The current press reports now allege that additional military forces, presumably Mongol or Manchukuo in complexion, have moved into Chahar from Jehol, and that

Wang Ying's units at Shangtu have been strengthened in numbers and in addition furnished with four airplanes and four tanks; minor clashes are stated in the press to have been occurring in the past few days between these troops and the regular Suiyuan forces on the Chahar–Suiyuan border, and more important developments are alleged to be impending.

The *Shanghai Shenpao* of October 5 in a lengthy analysis of the current Sino-Japanese situation considers the political status of North China to be one point of focus, with the Japanese objective being the detachment of the five northern provinces from the authority of the National Government. The newspapers believe that overt action will temporarily be withheld pending the conclusion of the conversations between Chiang Kai Shek and Kawagoe, but that the Japanese will appeal to force if necessary to achieve their ends in Hopei, where the expulsion of the 29th Army is desired, and in Suiyuan; the force applied would so far as possible wear a Chinese aspect to avoid unfavorable reaction in China and abroad. The newspapers conclude, however, that the spirit of the troops of the 29th Army and the close relationship between Suiyuan and Shansi, qualified as these factors would inevitably be by the character of the National Government's policy, put substantial difficulties in the way of the Japanese program in North China. This supposition is supported by a report obtained by the Consulate General at Tientsin from a source having connections in Inner Mongolia to the effect that the Silingol Mongols and those from the west are opposing the present forward move in Suiyuan, and that any fighting will have to be done with Jehol or other Manchukuo Mongols or by "bandit" Chinese groups.

The Embassy considers that (1) the potentialities of the Suiyuan situation may largely be viewed as a threat which the Japanese side will use in the present negotiations at Nanking, (2) important developments will probably be postponed pending the reaching of an agreement or a breakdown in the negotiations, but that a "demonstration" may be staged in an effort to influence those negotiations, and (3) in the event of such breakdown, the Suiyuan situation may logically be expected to take on a more threatening aspect.

By mail to Tokyo.

MERRELL

793.94/8326

Memorandum by the Chief of the Division of Far Eastern Affairs (Hornbeck) of a Conversation With the French Ambassador (Laboulaye)

[WASHINGTON,] October 10, 1936.

The French Ambassador called and, referring to the conversations which he has had previously with Mr. Hamilton on this subject, said that he wished to inform me of developments so far as the French Government was concerned. He said that, in Paris, the Japanese Ambassador had called on the Minister for Foreign Affairs and had given an outline of Japan's views and desiderata in regard to China: the Japanese Ambassador had referred to the violent acts against Japanese nationals and the necessity for Japan's making an effort to put a stop to such things, had referred to the menace of communism and Japan's desire to combat it, and had emphasized Japan's wish to arrive at settlements of questions with the Chinese by amicable processes. The Minister for Foreign Affairs had replied that the French Government was always desirous that difficulties and disagreements between nations be settled by amicable processes and always wished to cooperate with other countries toward that end. He told the Japanese Ambassador of instructions which had been sent to the French Ambassador in Tokyo.

The French Ambassador here continued to the effect that the instructions to the French Ambassador in Tokyo had been along lines similar to those given by the American Government, as outlined to him (M. de Laboulaye) by Mr. Hamilton; they had been to the effect that the French Ambassador to Japan should consult with the American and the British Embassies and should use his discretion in proceeding on lines similar to those on which the other embassies were proceeding. The Ambassador had not yet been informed with regard to action taken by the French Ambassador in Tokyo, but if and when informed thereof he would give us information thereof. He wished us to know at this point that the French Government had taken action and given instructions similar to ours.

The Ambassador then inquired whether there had been any new developments so far as we were concerned. I referred to the information given him by Mr. Hamilton in their last conversation and I repeated the substance of what our Chargé in Tokyo had said to the Vice Minister for Foreign Affairs. The Ambassador asked what the Vice Minister had replied. I said that the Vice Minister had apparently had little to say on that occasion, having before that "spoken his piece." I then inquired regarding the date on which the Japanese Ambassador in Paris had talked with the Minister for Foreign Affairs. M. de Laboulaye said first that it must have been on October 5th or 6th, and then he said that he was quite sure that it was the 6th.

The Ambassador said that when he had further information he would try promptly to inform us and that he hoped that we would tell him promptly of any new developments which came to our attention of which we might inform him. I said that we would be very glad to hear from him and very glad to keep him informed.

There followed some discussion, led by the Ambassador, of the situation in China, of the motivation of Japan's action, etc. The Ambassador said that the account given in this morning's *New York Times* of Japan's demands seem to coincide substantially with what the Japanese Ambassador in Paris had told the Minister for Foreign Affairs. I pointed out that, whereas the reports hitherto have indicated that Japan was demanding that Japanese troops be permitted to cooperate with Chinese troops where the latter are fighting communism in China, the newspaper report of this morning to which the Ambassador referred made it appear that the demand was for military cooperation in fighting the "menace of communism from a third country." The Ambassador said that this latest newspaper report on that point coincided with the representation of the Japanese objective which had been made by the Japanese Ambassador in Paris.

The Ambassador made certain observations with regard to what seemed to him to be similarities between the Chinese political psychology, with which he said he was not acquainted at first hand, and the Russian psychology, with which he had had first-hand experience and observation.

The conversation ended with reciprocal assurances with regard to exchanging of further information when and as received.

S[TANLEY] K. H[ORNBECK]

793.94/8258 : Telegram

The Ambassador in China (Johnson) to the Secretary of State

NANKING, October 14, 1936—11 a. m.
[Received October 14—7 : 37 a. m.]

300. My 298, October 9, 4 p. m.

1. Sino-Japanese situation remains calm and probability is that present lull will continue. Hsu Mo informs me that at yesterday's preliminary conversation between Suma and Kao Tsung Wu, chief of the Asiatic Affairs section of the Foreign Office, the latter explained to Suma the Chinese attitude which he presumed Kawagoe was communicating to his Government and that now they were awaiting further approach from the Japanese.

2. Hsu Mo states that present negotiations differ radically from those which characterized the presentation of the twenty-one demands [35] in that whereas in that case the demands were specific in this case the Japanese have laid down general principles subject to diverse interpretations. He informed me that the Chinese had asked the Japanese to bring to them a detailed statement of their desires, explaining to me that certain of these general principles were on the surface innocuous. He said that there was no truth in published reports that the Japanese desired to station troops along the Yangtze or that the Japanese demanded the independence of North China.

---

[35] See *Foreign Relations*, 1915, pp. 79 ff.

With reference to North China he said that the Japanese had merely asked the Central Government to give the local authorities a free hand in negotiations there but that the Chinese Government hesitated as it was unwilling to give blanket authority. He said that the Japanese had objected to the preponderance of European and American foreign advisers over Japanese advisers and that the Chinese Government in reply had indicated willingness to use Japanese advisers in technical lines if it were left free to hire and discharge Japanese at will as it had been free to do in the case of advisers of the other nationalities. Mr. Hsu expressed himself as feeling that the situation was dangerous as there was no leadership in Japan able to control ambitions of military who apparently were committed to a program intended to place China under the complete control of Japan.

3. In concluding our conversation Hsu Mo asked whether I had any information from the Department or from our Embassy at Tokyo in regard to our attitude in these matters. I said to Hsu Mo that our interest in conditions here in the East was crystal clear; that it had been amply covered and explained in times past and that there was no change in attitude now. I said we were deeply interested in developments and that I would be grateful to him if he could keep Mr. Peck and myself currently informed in order that we might adequately inform the American Government.

4. To the Department, copy to Peiping by hand of the Ambassador.

JOHNSON

793.94/8346

The Ambassador in China (Johnson) to the Secretary of State

No. 778   PEIPING, October 15, 1936.
                                                  [Received November 16.]

SIR: I have the honor to transmit herewith a copy of despatch No. 66 of October 9, 1936, from the Consulate at Tsinan [36] in which Consul Allison reports the opinion of the Secretary of the German Embassy in Tokyo to the effect that Japan is not ready to engage in war at this time for the following reasons:

1. The economic and financial situation in Japan is extremely serious.
2. The Japanese Army is not in sufficiently good condition.
3. Japan has no international agreements which would be of assistance in case of war.

Respectfully yours,
For the Ambassador:
GEORGE R. MERRELL, JR.
First Secretary of Embassy

---

[36] Not printed.

CHAPTER IV: OCTOBER 16–DECEMBER 31, 1936

Possibility of break in relations between China and Japan over excessive demands by latter; improvement of Japanese-Soviet relations; authorization of North China–Manchuria air service; unlikelihood of neutralization of Shanghai; defeat of pro-Japanese forces in Suiyuan; German-Japanese accord against Communist International and setback to Japanese-Soviet relations; Japanese-Italian agreement on Ethiopia and "Manchoukuo"; Japanese demonstration at Tsingtao by temporary landing of marines; forced detention at Sian of Generalissimo Chiang, December 12–25; surrender of Chang Hsueh-liang, a ringleader in Sian mutiny; settlement of Chengtu and Pakhoi incidents.

793.94/8264 : Telegram

The Counselor of Embassy in China (Peck) to the Secretary of State

NANKING, October 16, 1936—7 p.m.
[Received October 16—11:10 a.m.]

304. 1. Government department is reliably reported to be packing archives preparatory to removal of the Government from Nanking possibly to Changsha.

2. Responsible officers of the Government have just informed me, however, that although minute plans have been prepared to effect removal when hostilities seem unavoidable this crisis does not seem imminent. One of these informants stated that in the most recent conversations between Suma and the director of the Asiatic Department the former has strongly insisted on joint military operations against Communistic menace in Hopei-Chahar and Suiyuan and on joint economic activities in Shantung, Shansi and Suiyuan and has placed lessened emphasis on the other proposals. The other informant did not think the Japanese would press negotiations to the point of open break at the moment possibly because of unstable condition of the Japanese Cabinet but he asserted that "anything might happen." It is confirmed that Han Fu Chu is arriving at Hangchow October 17 to confer with Chiang Kai Shek.

Repeated to Peiping, by mail to Tokyo.

PECK

761.94/931

The Chargé in Japan (Dickover) to the Secretary of State

No. 2091 TOKYO, October 16, 1936.
[Received November 2.]

SIR: With reference to the Embassy's despatch No. 2069 of October 2, 1936,[37] I have the honor to report that Soviet-Japanese relations have shown a tendency to slight but steady improvement during the past two weeks, the chief contributions to this improvement being the

---

[37] Not printed.

reported settlement of two outstanding causes of friction, namely the fisheries treaty question and the extension of the Japanese oil concessions in North Saghalien.

According to reports here the agreement regarding the fisheries question was reached at Moscow on October 2, 1936. As will be recalled the present treaty expired in May, 1936, and had been extended to provide further time for negotiations. It has now been agreed that the new treaty will run for eight years, which is a compromise between the Japanese demand that it be valid for twelve years and the Soviet Government's desire to limit it to a five year period. The treaty, which it is predicted will be concluded by the middle of November, will provide for the continuation of the system of bidding for fishery grounds in certain areas, restrictions upon the amount of fish to be taken in the open sea, the protection of fish, and the prohibition of fishing in Kamchatka rivers. The value of the rouble for the payment of rentals on fishery grounds, a subject of great controversy heretofore, has been settled at 32.5 sen, but this provision is effective for only five years of the treaty, the rate being subject to revision by agreement at the expiration of that period.

The negotiations regarding the extension of the Japanese oil concessions in North Saghalien were successfully concluded at Moscow on October 10, 1936, between Vice-Admiral Masazo Sakonji, President of the North Saghalien Oil Company, and Mr. Lukinovitch, Vice-Chairman of the People's Heavy Industries of Soviet Russia. The details of this agreement have not yet reached here but it is understood that it will run from [for?] five years from January 1, 1937.

With the fisheries and the oil questions apparently settled the attention of the Japanese is next turning to the question of the establishment of a commission for the settlement of border disputes and a clear definition of the Soviet-"Manchukuo" frontier.

There has been a disposition in the press lately to comment with satisfaction and at some length upon the "brighter and more cheerful aspect" of relations between Japan and Soviet Russia. The superficial and temporary improvement cannot be doubted and the elimination for a certain period, at least, of the troublesome fisheries and oil questions admittedly makes the conduct of pleasant relations more hopeful. The only untoward incident which has occurred between the two countries during the past two weeks is another border skirmish between a "Manchukuo" patrol and O. G. P. U. troops on October 11 at two points on the "Manchukuo"-Soviet eastern frontier; one halfway between Yangkuanping and Chiushaping on the Tumen River, and the other near Matita, near Hunchun, both points in the province of Cheintao. There were several casualties, including one Japanese soldier killed. On the following day a small Japanese detachment, searching for the body of this soldier missing in the previous day's engagement, was met with further fire from Soviet troops and the Japanese officer leading the detachment did not return. While a protest was filed by the Soviet Government with the Japanese Chargé d'Affaires at Moscow and it is expected that similar action will be taken by the Tokyo Foreign Office, there appears to be no intention on the part of the Kwantung Army authorities to let the matter assume serious proportions. An official communiqué in the matter was issued by the headquarters of the Korean Army at Seoul which stated, in part: "The case will be transferred for diplomatic settlement to the Foreign Office authorities upon conclusion of the investigation on the spot. The army headquarters judge from the present circumstances that it will not assume proportions".

Although the foregoing is evidence that the Japanese authorities were at first disposed to minimize the importance of these incidents, a few days later a further statement was issued by the Kwantung Army calling attention sharply to the evident purpose of the Soviet authorities to interfere with the pursuit of amicable relations between the two countries. A possible reason for this apparent change of attitude may be found in the *Yomiuri's* Hsinking correspondent who, in reporting the Kwantung Army's communiqué, suggested that the reason why the Soviets provoked the most recent incidents was to embarrass the Nanking negotiations which in the view of the Soviet Government were progressing too smoothly and might therefore lead to the establishment of a Sino-Japanese arrangement for the joint defense against communism.

To revert, however, to the recent comments in the Japanese press on the brighter aspects of relations between Soviet Russia and Japan, many reasons are advanced for this state of affairs; the Japanese take the view that the Soviet Government is beginning in general to display a more conciliatory attitude due to the developments in Europe which are tending to expose Russia to the threat of military action in the West. Added to this is the revelation this summer of the anti-Stalinist plots and the dangers to the internal structure of the Soviet political machinery.

One paper, the *Nichi Nichi* of October 8, 1936, says that the failure of the Soviet authorities to take a positive attitude in the question of border incidents is taken by the Foreign Office as proof that Soviet Russia has at last come to understand the real intentions of Japan's continental policy. There is, however, no evidence that the Foreign Office authorities believe this; on the contrary this very point is one of the two main outstanding difficulties in the way of a real and basic improvement of relations between the two countries. It will be recalled that in his address before the Diet on May 6 last, the Foreign Minister, Mr. Arita, stressed the fact that the main obstacles to the conduct of peaceful relations with Soviet Russia were (1) the lack of clear border demarcation and, (2) the lack of comprehension on the part of Soviet statesmen of Japan's position in East Asia, coupled with their baseless fears and suspicions. While there is talk at present, as stated before, of beginning negotiations regarding the border demarcation the presence of the large number of Soviet troops along the "Manchukuo" frontier together with the supposed number of airplanes and submarines at Vladivostok and the general militarization of the Eastern Provinces are proof enough that Soviet Russia is far from willing to abandon either their fears and suspicions of Japan or to alter their understanding of what Japan's position in East Asia signifies.

Despite the disposition on the part of the Japanese press to credit the Russians with displaying a more conciliatory attitude at the present time, impartial observers are more inclined to feel that it is the Japanese who are contributing to the present generally easier situation because they wish to avoid trouble in the Far East for the next few years until their army program shall have reached completion.

Respectfully yours,   E. R. DICKOVER

793.94/8258 : Telegram

The Secretary of State to the Ambassador in China (Johnson)

WASHINGTON, October 17, 1936—2 p.m.

248. Your 298, October 9, 4 p.m., and 300, October 14, 11 a.m., from Nanking. The particular occasion of your visit to Nanking was the diplomatic reception on October 10. In the telegrams under reference you report in regard to three conversations held by you while there. Department would appreciate having reports by radio or cable of attendance on [at?] the diplomatic reception and on any additional conversations which you may have had with other representative persons, of whatever nationalities, the substance of which would be of interest to Department, on such subjects as, for instance, the views of Chinese officialdom in regard to British or other foreign diplomatic endeavors in regard to present Sino-Japanese relations; Chinese income tax law, the Hukuang and Chicago Bank loans, American claims against China,[38] your detailed estimate of the present situation between China and Japan, etc. Department assumes that you are sending some reports by mail, but Department needs summary reports for current purposes.

HULL

------

[38] For correspondence concerning claims against China, see pp. 574 ff.

793.94/8269 : Telegram

The Counselor of Embassy in China (Peck) to the Secretary of State

NANKING, October 17, 1936—3 p. m.
[Received October 17—7 : 16 a. m.]

308. My 305, October 16, 9 p. m.[39]

1. The director of the Publicity Department of the Foreign Office this morning informed me that Suma and the director of the Asiatic Department have had two conferences since October 8th preparatory to another meeting between the Japanese Ambassador and the Chinese Minister for Foreign Affairs. He said the Ambassador had received fresh instructions from Tokyo since the visit of Kuwashima and that another meeting will almost certainly take place next week. Informant seemed to withhold much information and was obviously constrained.

2. The confidential aide to the Minister of War this morning assured me that the present obscure situation would be clear to me "in a very short time". A German military adviser told an officer of the Embassy last night that the Chinese military are considering the possibility of an attempt by the Japanese to provoke a decisive campaign in the Shanghai–Hangchow–Nanking area the object of which would be to crush the pick of the Chinese forces. Informant was of the opinion that the Chinese would accept such a challenge if made counting on difficult terrain to counteract Japanese tanks. The Chinese alternative strategy would of course be to revert to their former plan of abandoning this area in order to conduct protracted guerrilla warfare in the interior.

3. Sent to the Department and Peiping.

PECK

793.94/8273 : Telegram

The Ambassador in China (Johnson) to the Secretary of State

PEIPING, October 19, 1936—3 p. m.
[Received October 19—10 a. m.[40]]

507. Department's telegram 248, October 17, 2 p. m.

1. I arrived in Nanking about midnight October 8 and on morning of October 9 I called upon Minister and Vice Minister for Foreign Affairs. I attended diplomatic reception given by President at 11 a. m. October 10. Twenty-one nationalities were represented, including the Soviet, Italian, American, French, Japanese and British Ambassadors; the Polish, Dutch and Brazilian Ministers. Others were represented by Chargés. The President received us formally

---

[39] Not printed.
[40] Telegram in two sections.

in groups and conversed informally with each group, individually. This was followed by refreshments attended by all of the high officials of the Government present in Nanking, including Chiang Kai Shek and Feng Yu Hsiang and H. H. Kung and Wang Chung Hui. The conversation was general and informal after drinking to the prosperity of the Government. In the evening of October 10th the Minister for Foreign Affairs gave a state dinner to the diplomatic representatives who were present at the reception in the morning.

2. My telegram referred to in Department's telegram under acknowledgment reported conversations with Donald, Minister of Foreign Affairs and with Vice Minister Hsu. I had no conversations with anyone regarding Chinese income tax law, the Hukuang and Chicago Bank loans or American claims against China.

3. On October 12, 13 and 14 I called upon or had visits from Sun Fo, C. T. Wang, the Minister of the Navy, the Minister of War, Wang Chung Hui and Dr. Lo Chia Lun. Conversations were general and nothing developed which seemed worthy of reporting. C. T. Wang and Wang Chung Hui expressed an interest in the attitude of the United States and Russia. But all left me with an impression that the Government was, and is, prepared to meet Japanese force with force and is resigned to the consequences, being convinced that to concede all that Japan appears to wish would mean complete Japanese domination and elimination present Chinese Government. Military disposition to that end was being made including concentrations between Hangchow and Shanghai and despatch of Central Government forces into Shantung and into Shansi. Orders had apparently been issued and were being complied with to remove all silver to points of safety and all agencies in Nanking were acting upon instructions to prepare to remove valuable documents and records away from Nanking in the direction of Hunan.

4. Chiang left Nanking October 10 for Hangchow. He was to have been accompanied by H. H. Kung. I was informed by Mrs. Kung and by Donald that Kung is ill and was trying to resign. Mrs. Chiang is on the verge of a nervous breakdown. Chiang was not returning to Nanking, but according to Donald was to go shortly to Sianfu and the Northwest.

JOHNSON

793.94/8282 : Telegram

The Counselor of Embassy in China (Peck) to the Secretary of State

NANKING, October 20, 1936—2 p. m.
[Received 2 : 10 p. m.]

309. My telegram No. 308, October 17, 3 p.m.

1. Vice Minister Hsu Mo informed me this morning that the Japanese Ambassador and the Minister of Foreign Affairs in a 3-hour

conversation held on October 19 exchanged views on Sino-Japanese matters but arrived at no agreements. The Japanese Ambassador devoted his attention mainly to the North China proposal and joint resistance to Communistic activities which apparently was widened to include joint measures against the spread of Communistic propaganda. The Japanese Ambassador continued to talk in general terms as heretofore. The Vice Minister said no third person was present during the interview and he himself had received as yet only an outline from the Minister for Foreign Affairs. Further discussion between the Ambassador and the Minister for Foreign Affairs being planned but no date has been set. I remarked that the tension of the last few days seemed to have relaxed. The Vice Minister made no comment but observed that no agreement had been reached on any point discussed during the interview. He asked me not to communicate to my colleagues especially the Japanese anything he had said but to use all the information only officially. I gave him an assurance and said that the Department is continuing its keen interest in these matters and is following Sino-Japanese situation both in Tokyo and Nanking.

2. An American news correspondent reports that Suma this morning compared the present discussions to the ascent of a mountain and expressed the belief that progress toward an understanding although slow was actual. American informant said that a Japanese newspaper representative intimate with the Japanese Ambassador had told him that the Ambassador was determined to bring about an understanding between the two countries through discussion and persuasion rather than by military threats.

3. It may be expected that both negotiators will defend themselves against popular criticism in their respective countries by denying that an agreement has been reached until this becomes an actual fact. Nevertheless, a lessening of the tension is distinctly perceptible in Nanking.

4. Chiang Kai Shek returned to Nanking yesterday.

5. Sent to Peiping and Shanghai.

PECK

893.79694/13a : Telegram

The Secretary of State to the Ambassador in China (Johnson)

WASHINGTON, October 21, 1936—2 p. m.

252. Associated Press under Shanghai date line October 18 reports as follows:

"Japan's long-held wish to establish airlines to China was reported today by Chinese newspapers to have been fulfilled.

Gen. Sung Cheh Yuan, Chairman of the Political Council governing the semiautonomous Hopei and Chahar Provinces, signed an agreement at Peiping with Japanese representatives providing for establishment of air routes between several North China points and Japan, the newspapers said."

Please telegraph such information as may be available in regard to this matter and keep Department currently informed.

HULL

793.94/8287 : Telegram

The Counselor of Embassy in China (Peck) to the Secretary of State

NANKING, October 22, 1936—5 p. m.
[Received October 22—11 : 25 a. m.]

311. My 309, October 20, 2 p. m.

1. Reliable informant in the Government states that the lengthy conversation between the Japanese Ambassador and the Chinese Minister for Foreign Affairs yesterday afternoon was devoted almost exclusively to the Japanese proposal for joint cooperation against Communistic menace and no agreement was reached. Informant said the Japanese Ambassador at the last two interviews had adopted a manner of friendly discussion rather than peremptory demand and had asked only for agreement in principle leaving military experts to decide details later. Nevertheless even the basic proposal included stationing of Japanese troops in Chinese territory and the employment of Japanese advisers in the Chinese military organization which would amount to practical Japanese domination of the Chinese Army. The proposal is not only entirely unacceptable to China for this reason but also because Japan clearly contemplates its utility if war between Japan and Russia should occur. China would earnestly desire to keep aloof from such a conflict as far as possible.

2. Suma departed for Tokyo last night presumably to report and seek fresh instructions. Informant thought discussions would probably continue but with little hope of agreement and with great uncertainty regarding Japanese activities in China in the meantime.

3. Sent to the Department, Peiping, Tokyo.

PECK

893.79694/14 : Telegram

The Ambassador in China (Johnson) to the Secretary of State

PEIPING, October 22, 1936—6 p. m.
[Received October 22—3 : 55 p. m.[41]]

510. Department's 252, October 21, 2 p. m. I was informed this morning by the Chairman of the Foreign Affairs Commission of the

---

[41] Telegram in three sections.

Hopei-Chahar Political Council that the reported agreement has actually been signed.

He said that the Huitung Company, which is being established as the competent organization, is in the nature of a private enterprise, with the chairman of the board of directors to be appointed by the afore-mentioned Political Council. The capital of the enterprise, 2,500,000 yuan dollars, will be 50% Chinese and 50% Japanese; however, the value of the land furnished by the Chinese side for landing fields and other installations will be computed as part of the Chinese capital and likewise the value of the airplanes, which are to be Japanese and will be figured in the total of the Japanese capital. (This arrangement would probably relieve the Chinese side of the necessity of paying more than a moderate sum.) The technical personnel, including pilots according to my informant are to be Japanese. The vice chairman of the company it is anticipated will be Kodama, vice president of the "Manchuria Air Transport Company". According to the terms of the agreement the route will be Peiping, Tientsin, Dairen, Mukden, Hsinking, and my informant stated that the present agreement did not envisage the extension of the service to other points in North China. The service, he stated, will probably begin the first part of next year. The agreement as signed is general in nature, and the particular procedure remains to be worked out.

According to a report appearing in today's press the Chairman of the Economic Commission of the Political Council has denied that any agreement has been signed, but admits that the Huitung Company is to be organized "to deal with through air traffic". He stated that the organization would accord to Chinese company law and would be on the lines of the China National Aviation Corporation.

According to the original press report, the agreement was signed by Sung Che Yuan and Horiuchi, Japanese Consul General at Tientsin, on October 17 in Peiping.

A Japanese official connected with the military confidentially informed a member of the Embassy that agreement in actuality gives legal sanction to flights that are now being made. It will permit of the establishment of additional landing fields, and is intended to lead to the extension of the projected airline into other parts of North China, more particularly to such important points as Taiyuan, Shansi; Kalgan, Chahar; and Paotow, Suiyuan. News despatches from Nanking would seem to indicate that the National Government has no official knowledge of the matter, and that it is planned to repudiate the agreement if signed. It has been alleged, however, without confirmation, that in actual fact the permission of the National Government was obtained by the Political Council in advance. It is to be noted that Ke Ting Yuan, Secretary General of the Council, participated in the recent discussions at Hangchow, evidently in the capacity of delegate of Sung Che Yuan.

Repeated to Nanking.   To Tokyo by mail.

JOHNSON

793.94/8290 : Telegram

The Counselor of Embassy in China (Peck) to the Secretary of State

NANKING, October 23, 1936—10 a. m.
[Received October 23—7 : 14 a. m.]

312. Source believed reliable states that Chiang Kai Shek proceeded from Nanking to Sian, Shensi, by airplanes yesterday accompanied by about 20 officers. Press announces purpose as inspection of the bandit suppression activities but there is a rumor that the Communist leaders Chu Teh and Mao Tse Tung have again offered to submit to the National Government in order to fight the Japanese and that Chiang intends to negotiate terms leading to inclusion of the Communist forces in the Chinese Army. I will endeavor to ascertain possible basis of this rumor.

Sent to Peiping.

PECK

793.94/8294 : Telegram

The Ambassador in China (Johnson) to the Secretary of State

PEIPING, October 23, 1936—4 p. m.
[Received October 24—8 a. m.[42]]

514. The following telegram has been received from Shanghai:

"October 23, 11 a. m.   I am informed confidentially that the Japanese Counselor of Embassy who serves concurrently as Consul General at Shanghai states that the Sino-Japanese negotiations at Nanking have almost reached a deadlock. He is also quoted to the effect that the Japanese authorities are annoyed that while these negotiations have been proceeding Chiang Kai Shek has been making military dispositions which are not consonant with a desire for a peaceful settlement of the outstanding issues.

Abend has informed Consulate General [at] Shanghai that T. V. Soong recently expressed the view that as China and Japan had gone to such lengths in the present negotiations in making demands and counter demands, it would be extremely difficult for either side to retreat from its present position without irreparable loss of prestige and face.[]"

JOHNSON

---

[42] Telegram in two sections.

793.94/8292 : Telegram

The Ambassador in China (Johnson) to the Secretary of State

PEIPING, October 23, 1936—5 p. m.
[Received October 23—7 : 28 a. m.]

511. Following from Nanking:

"October 21, noon. While the tension has eased considerably dur- ing the past 24 hours, I feel, after discussing protection plans with Captain Maynard of the USS *Guam*, our present station ship, that it would be highly desirable at this time to transfer temporarily from the station ship to the Embassy a small quantity of arms, uniforms and pyrotechnics for possible emergency use. I believe that this could be done without attracting any attention.

In making this suggestion I have in mind particularly the possi- bility of civil disorder and looting. A request for an armed landing force would hardly be justified except under hazards of actual crisis, and under such circumstances the landing party would doubtless face heavy odds in its attempt to reach the Embassy. On the other hand if a certain amount of equipment were now to be transferred to the Embassy, I believe that this action would provide a certain degree of protection as we could probably bring unarmed enlisted men in civilian clothes to the Embassy whenever circumstances might make this desirable. This action could be taken without attracting par- ticular attention and could therefore precede conditions of actual crisis.

If you concur will you request the approval of the State and Navy Departments?"

I do not see how any harm can be done, and I therefore concur and request necessary approval.

JOHNSON

793.94/8291 : Telegram

The Ambassador in China (Johnson) to the Secretary of State

PEIPING, October 23, 1936—6 p. m.
[Received October 23—9 : 40 a. m.]

512. Following from Nanking:

"October 23, 9 a. m. Bond [43] this morning told me Bixby [44] is very apprehensive that the Chinese military authorities may utilize planes of the China National Aviation Corporation for military purposes thereby affecting status of the American pilots. Such action might cripple the activities of the corporation if hostilities were to begin. To protect both the status of the American pilots and the American capital invested in the corporation, Bond inquires on behalf of Bixby

---

[43] W. L. Bond, vice president of the China National Aviation Corporation.
[44] H. M. Bixby, president of China Airways Federal Incorporated, U. S. A., holding company for the American interest in the China National Aviation Corporation; also director of the latter.

whether I would be authorized to make informal oral request of the Chinese military authorities on behalf of American interests involved that purely commercial character of the corporation's plane service be preserved in view of possible eventualities.

I respectfully suggest I might speak informally to the Minister of War and the Acting Minister of Communications. Please instruct by telegraph.["]

I informed Peck October 23, 9 a. m. that I approve action suggested in the last paragraph of his telegram.

JOHNSON

793.94/8292 : Telegram

The Secretary of State to the Ambassador in China (Johnson)

WASHINGTON, October 24, 1936—noon.

255. Your 511, October 23, 5 p. m. Department and Navy Department approve. Navy Department states that captain possesses authority to make such transfer. Please take complete and effective precautions that there be no publicity.

HULL

793.94/8295 : Telegram

The Counselor of Embassy in China (Peck) to the Secretary of State

NANKING, October 24, 1936—2 p. m.
[Received October 24—9 : 25 a. m.]

314. My 312, October 23, 10 a. m.

1. The Minister of War insisted to me today that the object of the journey of General Chiang to Sian was really bandit suppression and was occasioned by the congregation of most of the Communist forces in the Northwest. He ridiculed the idea that any peaceful arrangement might be reached with the Communist leaders although he himself recalled that some time ago they issued manifesto announcing willingness to fight the Japanese under the direction of the National Government. The Minister of War seemed uncertain how long General Chiang would remain in Sian. The Minister of War said it was impossible that an airfield had been prepared at Paotow for the Japanese (see my October 23, 11 a. m.[45]) since "Provincial Chairman Fu Tso Yi is not that kind of man". He said recently the Japanese sent about 100 workmen including many Koreans and Japanese to Paotow to prepare a landing field but meeting with obstruction recalled the party to Tientsin.

2. I have seen a letter quoting Donald as saying on October 22, that General Chiang had been talking war with Japan for some weeks

---

[45] Not printed.

which indicated a great change in attitude. Donald stated that General Chiang when leaving for Sian told his close friends that if everything went well they should celebrate his birthday October 31 in Kuling but that otherwise they must come to Sian. Donald interpreted the second alternative as indicating that Chiang foresaw the possible necessity of remaining at Sian in connection with actual or prospective hostilities with Japan. Unofficial but apparently reliable information is that if Chinese or Manchukuo troops invade Suiyuan Province local forces will resist but if Japanese troops take part National Government forces will immediately join resistance.

3. Sent to the Department, Peiping.

PECK

893.506 Manchuria/24 : Telegram

The Ambassador in China (Johnson) to the Secretary of State

PEIPING, October 27, 1936—noon.
[Received October 27—8 a. m.]

517. Department's 3, January 4, 7 p.m., 1935; [46] Legation's despatch 3702, July 22, 1935.[46] The Consulate General [at] Mukden reported by despatches Nos. 29 and 32 of September 25 and October 3,[47] respectively, that a life insurance monopoly was evidently shortly to be established in Manchukuo. Copies of these despatches were sent to the Department and Tokyo. A news item appearing in the Manchuria Daily News for October 20 reports that an imperial ordinance was issued on that date authorizing the establishment of the "Manchuria Life Insurance Company" at Hsinking; the formal establishment was set for October 22. The capital is fixed at 3,000,000 yuan, one-half of which will be taken up by the Government.

The tenor of the news item indicates that existing life insurance interests in Manchuria will not be eliminated from the field by this development, and this would accord with the information given in Mukden's despatch of October 3, but the Consulate General also reported that the state enterprise would receive a degree of protection from private competition and that the business of private companies, Japanese and others, would be subjected to restrictions.

The Consulate General stated that the West Coast Life Insurance Company of San Francisco is the only American interest likely to be affected. In view of the prior unprotested establishment in Manchuria of numerous monopoly enterprises (note Mukden's despatch of September 25), and the circumstance that private enterprises apparently have the technical right of competing with the state enter-

---

[46] Not printed.
[47] Neither printed.

prise for business, the Embassy considers it improbable that a protest would prove effective. It therefore recommends that no action be taken, unless it subsequently develops that the right of co-existence is to be denied to private companies.

By mail to Tokyo, Mukden and Hankow [Harbin?].

JOHNSON

793.94/8300 : Telegram

The Counselor of Embassy in China (Peck) to the Secretary of State

NANKING, October 28, 1936—9 a. m.
[Received October 28—3 : 20 a. m.]

315. My 311, October 22, 5 p. m.

1. Responsible Foreign Office official yesterday informed me that no progress was made toward adjustment of Sino-Japanese relations in the sixth conference between the Japanese Ambassador and the Chinese Minister for Foreign Affairs which was held October 26. He expressed fear that an agreement would be impossible unless Suma returned from Japan with instructions changing Japanese attitude on those proposals which it is impossible for China to accept. I inferred the proposals in question related to reorganization of the five northern provinces and joint military action against Communist menace.

2. Sent to the Department and Peiping.

PECK

793.94/8292 : Telegram

The Secretary of State to the Ambassador in China (Johnson)

WASHINGTON, October 28, 1936—7 p. m.

260. Reference your 511, October 23, 5 p.m., and Department's 255, October 24, noon, in reply thereto.

The Department has noted Nanking's reference in second paragraph of Nanking's telegram of October 21, noon, to Peiping, to possible action in a possible situation of "actual crisis". In this connection, the Department requests that numbered paragraph 1 of the Department's telegram No. 19 of February 3, 1932, 7 p.m., addressed to the American Consul at Nanking,[49] for the Minister, be brought to the attention of Nanking. The Department is confident that, should there appear imminent a situation imperiling the lives of members of the American community and Embassy staff in Nanking, the Embassy at Nanking would take appropriate steps in the light of that instruction. The Department of course expects that in any situa-

---

[49] Not printed.

tion of crisis officers and staffs will remain at their posts as long as practicable for the purpose of safeguarding and assisting American nationals and interests but does not desire that officers and staffs be exposed unduly and beyond a point of reasonableness to serious danger of life.

The foregoing is brought to your attention not in the thought that any action along the line indicated is likely to be needed at this time but as of possible assistance and guidance if and when there should arise a situation of crisis.

HULL

793.94/8345

The Chargé in Japan (Dickover) to the Secretary of State

No. 2107 TOKYO, October 29, 1936.
[Received November 16.]

SIR: I have the honor to submit the following report on Sino-Japanese relations supplementing that contained in my despatch No. 2086 of October 16, 1936.[50]

[Here follows summary of events reported in the Japanese press.]

From what has transpired during the last two weeks in connection with the developments in the China situation it is apparent that the Japanese Government perceives no alternative for the present to the continuation of its efforts to seek its ends through diplomatic means. Although the press still contains intimations of "independent action" to be taken if China persists in its refusal to accede to the demands in regard to North China and joint defense against communism, these intimations sound less ominous than the allusions to the "steps which Japan has prepared in reserve", of which so much was heard a few weeks ago. The continuation of a deadlock like the present for so long without ultimatums or other forms of intimidation is a new phenomenon in Sino-Japanese diplomacy. It can only mean that Japan has become aware of a change in the Chinese temper and that Japan does not wish to risk the consequences of action which would be almost certain to lead to armed resistance. Although there are advocates in Japan of breaking off the negotiations at Nanking and pursuing an "independent course" in North China, which means a resumption of the old tactics of seeking to gain ground by intrigue with local leaders and abandonment of the effort to legalize the Japanese position by dealing with Nanking, it is obvious that to break off the negotiations would mean not only the sacrifice of an agreement with Nanking on those points on which China has indicated a willingness to make terms but also the end of hope for future reconciliation and cooperation with the National Government.

---

[50] Not printed.

Japan has probably already lost much prestige in China with corresponding gains for Chiang Kai-shek as a consequence of the stiff front that has been put up against the Japanese demands. There are indications from the press comments in Tokyo that the Japanese Government, fearing that further protraction of the negotiations will render the situation increasingly disadvantageous to obtaining favorable terms, is approaching, if it has not already reached, the point where it would be willing to make the best bargain obtainable. As it is clear that China will not yield on the two points to which Japan professes to attach the most importance, the outcome at Nanking may be an agreement on the other proposals with these two points left in abeyance for the time being or covered by face-saving formulae. This would mean a continued impasse on the North China and anticommunist defense questions, as it is not likely that Japan would withdraw its proposals.

The foregoing observations from the very nature of the situation can be offered only as tentative. Further incidents may occur involving Japanese in China which might bring sudden changes in the aspect of affairs, or again the Chinese becoming over confident over the apparent success that has already attended their tactics might take so strong an attitude as to force Japan to decisive measures in defense of its prestige on the continent.

Respectfully yours,

E. R. DICKOVER

893.506 Manchuria/24 : Telegram

The Acting Secretary of State to the Ambassador in China (Johnson)

WASHINGTON, October 30, 1936—5 p. m.

262. Your 517, October 27, noon. The Department concurs in the recommendation contained in the last paragraph that at this time no action be taken.

Please continue to keep the Department informed of developments, including the attitude of other interested governments.

CARR

693.94244/161 : Telegram

The Ambassador in China (Johnson) to the Secretary of State

PEIPING, October 30, 1936—5 p. m.
[Received 7 : 10 p. m.]

523. Embassy's 506, October 19, 11 a. m.[51] Consulate General [at] Tientsin reports that according to good authority smuggling into the East Hopei autonomous region reached considerable proportions during September, duty which is set at one-fourth Chinese duty having

---

[51] Not printed.

been collected on only about three-fourths of goods entering that region, East Hopei thus collecting only $750,000 during September instead of $1,000,000 and the Chinese Government losing thereby $4,000,000.

Smuggled goods continued to pass out of Tientsin by roads and canals to the interior in large quantities and the real authority for such traffic continues to be the guards composed of Japanese subjects who accompany trucks and boats, the traffic apparently being handled principally by a Japanese firm, the Gitaiyoko.

The Commissioner of Customs, Tientsin, has informed Berger that an office for the prevention of smuggling on the railways will be established in Tientsin about November 1st. Service of such an office appears doubtful however since local authorities are making use of situation for their further financial benefit. Private Japanese interests are reliably reported to have paid over $26,000 last week to a subordinate of General Sung. Local authorities could undoubtedly terminate distribution of smuggled goods from Tientsin by cooperating with customs but such action would involve them in conflict with Japanese and would cut off considerable income.

Consulate [at] Tsinanfu reports serious dispute last week between large group of alleged Korean smugglers and local customs unit over two truckloads of rayon and cigarette paper which were seized near Tsinanfu and brought into that city, goods finally being returned smugglers none of whom received any punishment. Tsinanfu businessman, who recently returned from motor trip in northern Shantung, states that he twice passed groups of 20 or 30 trucks carrying smuggled goods south.

Consul General Gauss has learned from an official source that the Chinese Maritime Customs has recently despatched three Chinese customs preventive cruisers north to waters along the Chinese coast where they have heretofore been forbidden by Japanese to function with instructions to make seizures of smuggling vessels. This is unconfirmed but if true represents a stiffening of the attitude of the Central Government toward smuggling in the demilitarized zone.

JOHNSON

741.94/75

The Chargé in Japan (Dickover) to the Secretary of State

No. 2113   TOKYO, October 30, 1936.
[Received November 16.]

SIR: I have the honor to enclose a translation [52] of the essential portions of an article which appeared in the *Kokumin* of October 29, 1936,

---

[52] Not printed.

in which it is indicated that the Japanese Government has now given up the idea which has been favored in certain political circles of entering into a political arrangement with Great Britain for cooperation.

It is not known what the authority of the *Kokumin* is for the views attributed to the Japanese Government, but as the *Kokumin* often voices the opinions of certain groups in the Japanese Army, it is possible that the views expressed can be attributed to military sources. There is no doubt that the view is widely held in Japan, especially among the more chauvinistic elements, that so long as Japanese goods are subjected to restrictions in British territory an arrangement for cooperation with Great Britain would be a one-sided affair of little benefit to this country. Although there is a liberal element which recognizes the disadvantages of international isolation and the value from the point of view of national prestige which association with Great Britain would afford, these considerations apparently do not appeal forcibly to the military group, which, however, might be disposed to make concessions to Great Britain in return for some form of recognition of Japan as "the sole stabilizing force in East Asia".

Respectfully yours,   E. R. DICKOVER

793.94/8303 : Telegram

The Counselor of Embassy in China (Peck) to the Secretary of State

NANKING, October 31, 1936—9 a. m.
[Received October 31—7 a. m.]

316. The Foreign Office informed the press last night that it had on October 30th lodged three protests with the Japanese Ambassador against (1) the extensive maneuvers of Japanese troops in the Tientsin area which, it was charged, infringed upon China's sovereign rights and violated international law and practice, (2) the forcible occupation by Japanese citizens of a Chinese house in Taiyuan, Shansi, and incorrect Domei press reports that there was an anti-Japanese demonstration in Taiyuan and that local officials had evicted a Japanese merchant from his premises, (3) malicious speculation in the Japanese press regarding the death of Provincial Chairman Yang [53] which speculation was described as an insult to the Chinese people.

Sent to the Department and Peiping.

PECK

---

[53] Yang Yung-tai, Chairman of the Hupeh Provincial Government.

793.94/8304 : Telegram

The Ambassador in China (Johnson) to the Secretary of State

PEIPING, October 31, 1936—3 p. m.
[Received October 31—10:33 a. m.]

524. Your October 28, 8 p. m.[54]

1. My approval was based on two considerations: (*a*) use of corporation's planes for military purposes would unquestionably result in the withdrawal of American pilots from the service (see section 4090 and 5281 of the Revised Statutes of the United States). This would impair if not completely extinguish operating rights of the American company at least temporarily and be a serious loss likewise to American pilots. (*b*) See Shanghai's No. 71, February 18, 1932, 5 p. m., to the Department [55] which seemed to warrant informal action to protect rights of American aviators and incidentally operating rights of American company.

2. The Embassy exerted particular care to make its representations informal and oral, the Embassy purposely avoided taking the matter up with the Foreign Office. It will be observed that Peck discussed the question informally only with the Minister of War. The Embassy would not be disposed to make formal representations on this question and in that case would first seek the Department's authorization.

The Department's 261, October 28, 8 p. m., and this reply have been repeated to Nanking.

JOHNSON

793.94/8397

The Consul at Tsinan (Allison) to the Ambassador in China (Johnson)[56]

No. 1   TSINAN, November 3, 1936.

SIR: I have the honor to refer to an interview with Han Fu-chu, accredited to Domei, Japanese official news agency, published in the *North China Daily News* for October 30, 1936, and to report that General Han has personally confirmed this interview and that he stated the version published in the above mentioned newspaper was a good translation of remarks made by him to a group of Japanese newspaper men brought to see him by a representative of the local Japanese Consulate General.

In this interview, a copy of which is enclosed,[55] General Han said

---

[54] Not printed; it requested "a brief outline of the reasoning upon which Peck's suggestion and your approval were based" as reported in telegram No. 512, October 23, 6 p. m., last two paragraphs, p. 363 (793.94/8291).

[55] Not printed.

[56] Copy transmitted to the Department by the Ambassador in China in his despatch No. 833, November 6; received November 30.

that a war between China and Japan would be one of attrition with both countries emerging from the struggle in a weakened condition. He stressed the point that events happening within the Great Wall have a much greater significance to the Chinese than affairs in Manchuria, and that if Japan should use force in Hopei or Shantung, China will have no alternative but to fight. At the same time he expressed himself as in favor of Sino-Japanese cooperation if such were possible.

In conversation with the writer, General Han amplified this interview somewhat. He said that China did not want to fight and would not do so unless compelled, but that the patience of the people was almost exhausted and that if Japan continued its policy of aggression he could see no alternative. When asked whether the display of national unity made at the Hangchow conference recently and the military preparations known being made throughout the country, together with the fact that Japan has not as yet made any active step toward using force to gain her ends, might not indicate that Japan would be willing to reach a compromise of some sort, General Han shook his head. He said he believed the present period of negotiation and peaceful activity on the part of Japan could not last and that there was definite trouble ahead. He indicated that preparations were being made for any eventualities and that he was wholeheartedly behind the Central Government in whatever might be done. Throughout the interview General Han maintained a very serious attitude and the impression was gained that he was convinced war was the only solution of the present crisis.

Respectfully yours,

JOHN M. ALLISON

793.94/8333 : Telegram

The Counselor of Embassy in China (Peck) to the Secretary of State

NANKING, [November 7, 1936—1 p.m.]
[Received November 7—12 : 15 p.m.]

322. 1. Leighton Stuart informed me this morning that on November 3 he met Chiang Kai Shek in Loyang at latter's request. Chiang asked what Stuart thought about the attitude of Sung Che Yuan toward Japanese aggressive plans. The salient points in the lengthy reply made by Stuart were that Sung has only mediocre ability but would prefer to resist the Japanese if assured of moral and military support by Nanking. Sung is apprehensive of criticism for having signed the aviation agreement with the Japanese falsely claiming that it had received Nanking's sanction and is also sensitive because of the subservient attitude toward Japan of which he is accused. Stuart said to Chiang that the development of events in the

North depended almost entirely on the mental attitude of Sung and that he should be handled with extreme tact. At this interview Chiang personally wrote letters to Sung and to Han Fu Chu asking that the latter visit Sung in Tientsin in order to inform him of the position of the local government as conveyed to Han by Chiang recently in Hangchow. Stuart said this project is extremely secret but he thought that a visit by Han to Sung on some plausible pretext might be expected in the near future.

2. Sent to the Department, Peiping.

PECK

893.01 Inner Mongolia/87 : Telegram

The Ambassador in China (Johnson) to the Secretary of State

PEIPING, November 9, 1936—5 p. m.
[Received November 9—8 : 50 a. m.]

537. Embassy's 492, October 9, 5 p. m. Reports of a disturbing nature have been appearing in the press during the past few days in regard to the Chahar–Suiyuan situation, but it is possible that some of the more threatening reports are being issued by interested parties for political purposes. Despite the fragmentary reports, however, it would appear reasonably certain that (1) in the course of the last month there has been an increase in number of pro-Manchukuo and Mongol forces in Chahar, (2) those forces hope to extend their influence into Suiyuan, and (3) the Suiyuan authorities have been making definite defense preparations with the evident determination to resist any hostile incursion into their territory. Current reports are to the effect, however, that the forces mentioned in (1) above are now in part moving into Pailingmiao, North Suiyuan. Although that place has remained under the influence of Teh Wang, Mongol leader, since his defection from the National Government, the stationing of any considerable hostile force at Pailingmiao would constitute a threat to both Kweisui and Paotow. Tokyo by mail.

JOHNSON

793.94/8334 : Telegram

The Counselor of Embassy in China (Peck) to the Secretary of State

NANKING, November 10, 1936—1 p. m.
[Received November 10—11 : 05 a. m.]

325. My 322, November 7, 1 p. m.

1. Responsible official of the Foreign Office informs me that the seventh conference will take place between the Japanese Ambassador and the Minister for Foreign Affairs today but that there is little

hope of an agreement because the attitude of the two Governments has not changed since the sixth interview October 26th.

2. Suma is reported as stating to an American press representative that the Japanese Government has not receded from any of its proposals to the Chinese Government and that no importance should be attached to current reports of Chinese preparedness to resist Japan by force. This professedly optimistic attitude may be contrasted with a statement made by another Foreign Office official to the same press representative that the Japanese Government now realizes the strength of the determination of the Chinese Government to resist Japanese encroachments and that the position of the Japanese Ambassador is "pathetic" in view of the failure of his efforts. A third informant in the Foreign Office has told an American Embassy official that the Japanese are obviously more moderate and seem to be seeking a face-saving retreat.

3. Sent to Peiping.

PECK

793.94/8335 : Telegram

The Counselor of Embassy in China (Peck) to the Secretary of State

NANKING, November 11, 1936—noon.
[Received November 11—10 : 15 a. m.]

326. My 325, November 10, 1 p. m. Japanese Embassy has informed news representatives that the interview yesterday dealt with proposals as a whole and although no specific agreement was reached the viewpoints of the two parties were perceptibly closer. Suma has informed one American press representative since his return from Japan that he found the Chinese leaders had passed through their mood of self-confidence and uncompromising rejection of Japanese proposals and were again taking the proposals seriously. Suma thought this change might have been occasioned by his warning to them not as an unlooked for but as a plain fact that if these negotiations terminated through futility an incident might occur which could not be handled diplomatically.

Sent to Peiping.

PECK

793.94/8337 : Telegram

The Consul General at Shanghai (Gauss) to the Secretary of State

SHANGHAI, November 12, 1936—11 a. m.
[Received November 12— 7 a. m.]

581. A Japanese merchant seaman was shot and killed last evening in the Hongkew area of the International Settlement, allegedly by a

Chinese who escaped. A small Japanese Navy landing party force established a cordon around the place of the killing but there was no general mobilization and occupation of the Hongkew district by the Japanese such as followed the killing of the Japanese blue jacket on the night of September 23rd. Situation quiet. Municipal police and Japanese authorities are cooperating in the investigation.

GAUSS

793.94/8338 : Telegram

The Counselor of Embassy in China (Peck) to the Secretary of State

NANKING, November 12, 1936—noon.
[Received 1 : 15 p. m.[58]]

328. Suma said to American press correspondent today with reference to killing of a Japanese in Shanghai November 11, 8 p. m. that irrespective of what terroristic organization may have been behind it the Chinese Government would be held responsible for the anti-Japanese feeling throughout the country of which such acts were the result. The Japanese Embassy has not decided on any definite action following the latest murder and will await full report.

Same informant was told by a responsible Chinese official confidentially and not for publication that at the last conference the Chinese Minister for Foreign Affairs had told the Japanese Ambassador that if the Japanese would abolish East Hopei autonomous regime and would withdraw support from the irregular troops threatening Suiyuan, the Chinese Government would be willing to consider restricted joint operation against Communists. Chinese informant said that this proposal was made only because the Chinese Government was convinced it would not be accepted and that it would be most unfortunate if the offer received publicity because the Russian Government, unfamiliar with the background, might misunderstand it and take offense.

Sent to the Department, Peiping.

PECK

693.94244/165 : Telegram

The Ambassador in China (Johnson) to the Secretary of State

PEIPING, November 12, 1936—3 p. m.
[Received November 12—10 : 50 a. m.]

539. The Consulate General at Tientsin has been informed by an officer of the Chinese Maritime Customs that an order has been issued

---

[58] Telegram in two sections.

by General Sung Che Yuan's headquarters for the detention of customs preventive service officers at two places on the Tsinanfu road just outside Tientsin and that instructions from the same quarters were also received on November 4 by the Commissioner of Public Safety in Tientsin that the police were no longer to assist the customs in the seizure of smuggled goods. It seems reasonably certain that Tientsin authorities possibly at Japanese instigation are prepared to block Nanking's efforts to suppress the smuggling of goods into and out of Tientsin. This belief is strengthened by the fact that the "customs chief inspection bureau for the prevention of smuggling by railroads" is not yet functioning.

Tientsin was informed by the above-mentioned source yesterday that a group of more than 200 Koreans and Japanese, reported to be armed with 2 machine guns, pistols, clubs, and knives, have gathered in Taku with the intention of landing smuggled goods there. A boat bringing smuggled goods from Dairen is expected to arrive off Taku bar about noon today. The customs authorities have brought this to the attention of the Tientsin Japanese Consul General who is said to have called leaders of the gang to his office where they stated, it is alleged, that their activities were being carried on with the approval of the 29th Route Army units stationed in the vicinity of Taku. It is understood that the Consulate General has sent reenforcements to its police station at Taku but whether these are for the purpose of protecting the smugglers or to restrain them is not known to the customs.

At the request of the Tientsin Customs, a customs cruiser has been sent from Chefoo. In addition, the customs have two armed launches. Several sailing junks (one belonging to a British firm) which it is thought the smugglers expect to use to bring smuggled cargo ashore from Taku bar have been seized by the smugglers.

By mail to Tokyo.

JOHNSON

793.94/8339 : Telegram

The Ambassador in China (Johnson) to the Secretary of State

PEIPING, November 13, 1936—5 p.m.
[Received 5 : 10 p.m.]

545. Embassy's 537, November 9, 5 p.m. Fighting is reported by press to have broken out on the Chahar–Suiyuan border on November 11 when an attack was launched on Suiyuan by the pro-Manchukuo forces of Li Shou Hsin at Shangtu, west of Chahar. Confirmation or details are not available.

Repeated to Tokyo, Nanking.

JOHNSON

793.94/8389

The Chargé in Japan (Dickover) to the Secretary of State

No. 2127   Tokyo, November 13, 1936.
                                          [Received November 30.]

SIR: [Here follows summary of events reported in the Japanese press.]

There is enclosed a memorandum of a conversation [59] which Mr. Ballantine and I had with the Counselor of the Chinese Embassy at an informal dinner given by the latter on November 8. He gave reasons which he thought were responsible for a moderation of the Japanese stand in the negotiations, but he felt that the crisis over the Japanese demands in relation to North China and the anti-communist defense question had only been deferred until next spring or summer, when he anticipated that war was inevitable.

The only thing that occurs to me now to add to the comments contained in my previous despatches on the subject is that it is even more pronounced that Japanese public opinion evinces a steadily calmer and less truculent attitude toward the Chinese questions. This may be attributed to the following causes: (1) the public feels that it has not been taken into the confidence of the Government in regard to the objectives sought by Japan in China; this renders the public apathetic to the outcome at Nanking; there has been no intelligent discussion in the press, due to lack of authoritative information, of what is involved in the North China and anti-communist defense issues and why Japan is so intent upon them. (2) Among the more thoughtful of the public there is a dawning realization that the North China and anti-communist defense questions have nothing to do with eliminating the cause of anti-Japanese outrages in China, which renders this group unsympathetic with the Japanese conduct of the negotiations. That is to say, there is an opinion, suggested by the continued recurrence of anti-Japanese incidents, that the Japanese Government made a serious error in judgment at the outset of the Nanking negotiations in insisting that its demands be dealt with as a whole, and that the negotiations should have disposed first of the settlement of the incidents and of the demands having a direct relationship to them, such as the elimination of anti-Japanese propaganda movements, and leaving the other questions to be taken up at a later day. (3) For a long time past the public has been kept at a high tension by the army through its activities on the continent and its propaganda at home to keep the nation alive to the necessity of preparing for a national crisis, which seems to come no nearer. Public feeling has become apparently jaded to a point where it would

---

[59] Not printed.

require some unusual stimulant to revive interest in Chinese questions. (4) The army, furthermore, in an effort to recover ground lost as a result of the February 26 incident, has been trying to consolidate its position in domestic politics by a campaign for a so-called "purification of national politics" which calls for far reaching changes in the administrative and legislative structure under which the Cabinet would be organized and function like an army general staff. This campaign coupled with the new defense estimates, which are of staggering proportions and which necessitate a sharp increase in the already heavy tax burden, has resulted in diverting public attention to domestic politics.

Respectfully yours,   E. R. Dickover

762.94/79 : Telegram

The Ambassador in Italy (Phillips) to the Secretary of State

Rome, November 16, 1936—4 p. m.
[Received November 16—1 : 35 p. m.]

465. With reference to the possible alignment of Japan with Germany and Italy (Tokyo's telegram No. 232, November 13, 5 p. m.[60] and my 446, November 6, 6 p. m.[61]) the Soviet Ambassador here told me he had heard from his Government that Italy had approached Japan with a project of recognition of Manchukuo in exchange for recognition by Japan for Ethiopia but had been unable to obtain confirmation thereof. In this connection he referred to the Gayda article (my telegram #432, October 26, noon[61]) in which a relation of Manchukuo and Italy's Ethiopian problem was intimated. He also said that certain of the Paris press had published indications that the Italian Government was acting in this sense.

In the course of a later conversation with the Under Secretary for [of] State and [for] Foreign Affairs I asked him whether there was any truth in this rumor and he explained that some months ago the Japanese Ambassador had approached him for the purpose of securing the permission of the Italian Government to install a Consul at Addis Ababa. The Ambassador was told that this could be arranged provided the Japanese Government would follow the usual course of asking for an exequatur whereupon the Ambassador had said that he was not in a position to make this request. Bastianini had then suggested that a member of the Japanese Embassy staff could be sent from Rome without the necessity of requesting an exequatur but nothing further had been heard from the Japanese on this subject.

---

[60] Vol. I, p. 391.
[61] Not printed.

Since that time the Italian Government had been obliged to change its Consul in Manchukuo but that in sending out the new man no steps have been taken to change his status as regards the Manchukuo authorities.

Bastianini then said that this situation remained unchanged "at present" and thought possibly that the Paris press reports to which I had alluded were in the nature of a trial balloon.

PHILLIPS

793.94/8357 : Telegram

The Ambassador in China (Johnson) to the Secretary of State

PEIPING, November 17, 1936—3 p. m.
[Received November 17—10 : 50 a. m.]

551. Embassy's 545, November 13, 5 p. m. The fighting of November 11 was confirmed by subsequent news despatches. It is further reported, and confirmed by independent sources, that an attack was launched on November 15 north of Taolin, East Suiyuan, by pro-Manchukuo forces operating with the assistance of airplanes and tanks. Fighting was still in progress yesterday at the time of the last report.

Repeated to Nanking and Tokyo.

JOHNSON

793.94/8364 : Telegram

The Ambassador in China (Johnson) to the Secretary of State

PEIPING, November 18, 1936—6 p. m.
[Received November 18—9 : 23 a. m.]

556. Embassy's 551, November 17, 3 p. m. Member of the Naval Attaché's staff returning from Suiyuan yesterday reports that, although some fighting has occurred on the Suiyuan–Chahar border, press reports have been highly exaggerated; that the pro-"Manchukuo" forces have not the strength and equipment reported; that neither troops nor airplanes have been sent into the province by the National Government with exception of small number of specialized troops, chiefly anti-aircraft men. He believes that no serious developments will occur in immediate future, although trouble may be expected intermittently for some time.

A British military officer reports along essentially same lines. He states that Chinese side seems to be exaggerating seriousness of situation in order to embarrass Japanese program; he considers, as did I in my 492, October 9, 5 p. m., that whole matter intimately connected with course of Sino-Japanese negotiations at Nanking.

A local Japanese military officer is quoted as having stated that important developments may be expected in Suiyuan within 10 days. Like predictions have been appearing in the press.

Langdon [63] reports in a telegram received today that "This office accidentally learned from the air station that all aircraft excepting sufficient for skeleton Manchurian service have left for Mongolia, presumably Inner Mongolia".

Repeated to Nanking and Tokyo.

JOHNSON

893.102S/1427

The Consul General at Shanghai (Gauss) to the Secretary of State

No. 482   SHANGHAI, November 18, 1936.
                                           [Received December 16.]

SIR: I have the honor to inform you that some weeks ago when Sino-Japanese tension was particularly critical, and when foreign business and banking interests were concerned as to a possible Sino-Japanese conflict and the status of Shanghai in event of such a situation, I requested Consul E. F. Stanton to prepare for me a memorandum examining the available material on the subject of the possible neutralization of Shanghai in event of a Sino-Japanese conflict. Mr. Stanton has submitted to me the enclosed memorandum. I concur with his conclusions.

I am aware that there has been considerable discussion in foreign business and banking circles as to the possibility that the Powers might seek to bring about the neutralization of Shanghai in event of serious difficulty between China and Japan approaching a state of war. I have carefully abstained from discussing this subject, but I have been interested to note the feeling amongst non-official British circles that the British Government would be likely to move in an attempt to neutralize Shanghai in event of Sino-Japanese hostilities. It is not possible to say whether there is any foundation for this non-official British opinion.

Respectfully yours,   C. E. GAUSS

[Enclosure]

Memorandum by the Consul at Shanghai (Stanton)

[SHANGHAI,] October 6, 1936.

[Here follows a historical summary of the development of the foreign Settlement at Shanghai.]

It will thus be seen that the conception of the exclusion of the International Settlement from the operations incidental to either internal

---

[63] William R. Langdon, American Consul at Mukden.

or external warfare had its origin in the necessity which existed early in the life of the Settlement to protect the lives and property of its residents and the inability of the Chinese authorities to fulfill their recognized obligations in this regard. Necessity gradually assumed the characteristics of a recognized "right" not only to protect life and property but to maintain, by force if necessary, the integrity and neutrality of the Settlement as such. Paralleling this development there has been recognition by the foreign powers of that necessity, of the right of the constituted authorities of the Settlement to defend the lives and properties of its residents and of the obligation to assist in such measures of protection when necessary; to this end the powers have from time to time warned opposing Chinese factions engaged in internecine warfare that the Settlement must be excluded from the area of war-like operations. With a few exceptions, where there has been war between China and a foreign country in the past there has also been recognition by the foreign belligerent of the extensive international interests in the Settlements and of the desirability of leaving those areas undisturbed.

POSSIBILITY OF EFFECTING THE PERMANENT NEUTRALITY OF SHANGHAI

It would thus appear that the neutrality of the International Settlement and French Concession has been based upon contingencies rather than definite international agreement. It has been maintained for the most part against the country which by virtue of the sovereign rights it continues to claim over these areas is charged with the primary responsibility of protection. It has been maintained by force and has been contingent therefore upon the inability or unwillingness of China to oppose such force with greater force. It has been maintained upon the further contingency of the interests of the concerned powers being coincident, for experience has shown that where there is any deviation of interests independent and unneutral action may easily follow. The neutrality of the Settlement, therefore, rests on a precarious and uncertain basis. What are the possibilities of placing neutrality on a more permanent and secure basis through the medium of collective international agreement?

The more important factors underlying this question appear to be (1) the scope of such neutralization including (a) area and (b) such questions as municipal and national services, taxation, revenue and related fiscal matters, and (2) the attitude of the interested powers and more particularly China and Japan.

(1) *Scope of Neutrality:*

(a) *Area:* The experience of the past few years has clearly demonstrated that effectively to maintain the neutrality of the Settlement there should be excluded from the field of military operations not only the Chinese city but an area of from ten to fifteen miles around the entire city and port of Shanghai. Modern weapons and modern methods of warfare which are now being utilized by Chinese as well as foreign armies have made the defense of the Settlement and French Concession a hazardous and difficult undertaking where the Chinese city or the territory immediately adjacent thereto is available as a base of operations. To protect adequately the Settlement it seems vitally necessary that a sufficiently deep neutral zone be created from which defensive operations when necessary might be conducted without serious risk to the Settlement. There is the added consideration that much of the residential property occupied by foreigners and representing an investment of approximately twenty-five million dollars is located beyond the limits of the Settlement; there has been a growing tendency for the past few years to occupy these areas even more extensively. It, therefore, seems essential to include the whole area embraced by the Municipality of Greater Shanghai and to establish a neutral zone around the whole city.

(b) *Services and Facilities within Neutral Area:* It would also seem desirable that there be agreement to completely neutralize the essential municipal services such as light, power, water, systems of transportation, telephones, harbor facilities, et cetera—and all national services such as radio, radio telephone, telegraph cables, railways, bus lines, et cetera, located within the neutral area created. During the Sino-Japanese hostilities in 1932 there was constant use by the Japanese forces of docks, wharves, and other facilities, as well as such municipal services as light, power, water, et cetera. In other words it appears essential to specifically delimit not only the area to be neutralized but also to attempt definitely to neutralize all municipal or national services and facilities of whatever nature existing within the neutralized area and thus make impossible its use as a base of operations.

In the event of China being at war with a foreign country there would also arise the question of the neutralization or disposition of the revenues which are ordinarily remitted to the Chinese treasury. The continued remittance of such funds to the Chinese Government in time of war might naturally be objected to by a nation at war with China, as might the flotation by the Chinese Government of loans with Chinese banks or similar fiscal transactions. It is obvious that the drawing of revenues from the largest and most important commercial city in China and the flotation of loans in that city in time of war, if permitted, would be of vital assistance to a belligerent. The belligerent not so favored might rightfully complain that there existed neutrality in name but not in fact since its enemy was deriving vital succor from the so-called neutral area.

On the other hand to deprive China of this very important source of revenue and to deny her the right to protect that source from seizure by an enemy would appear to be equally questionable. This is a point the satisfactory adjustment of which is surrounded by formidable obstacles and yet the failure to resolve it by satisfactory formula would render neutrality largely nugatory. A possible solution might be the holding in trust by the neutral powers of all Chinese national revenues collected within the neutral area and the return of such revenues to the Chinese or other legally constituted and internationally recognized government upon the termination of hostilities. However, it is obvious that such a procedure bristles with difficulties and complications and might not prove acceptable to the parties concerned.

(2) *Probable Attitude of Interested Countries:*

The more important foreign powers have indicated in the past a very keen interest in the question of protecting and defending their interests in this great commercial port in which their nationals reside and in which they have built up or acquired interests. It should be noted that this natural interest of the powers, with the exception of Japan, has not been accompanied in the past by any manifestation of an ulterior intent. It may perhaps be assumed therefore that their attitude in any international discussions regarding the neutralization of Shanghai would be reasonable, considerate of China's sovereign rights, and would be common rather than individual as to objective.

The probable attitude of China and Japan toward proposals of neutralization appears more uncertain and conditional. It is obvious that the participation of these two countries in any scheme is vital to its successful implementation unless neutrality is to be maintained by strong armed forces and without regard to either China or Japan; the latter is a solution which would unquestionably be found to be wholly unsatisfactory and quite impracticable, certainly for any extended period.

China:

It is not easy to gauge China's attitude toward the neutralization of Shanghai or the extent to which she would participate in such a scheme, but perhaps this phase of the question may be most conveniently considered under (a) complete refusal to participate and (b) participation.

(a) *Refusal to participate:* It is wholly conceivable if not highly probable that China would refuse to participate in any scheme for the neutralization of either the Settlement or a more extensive area. Looking back over the history of the port there appear to have been no indications that the Chinese would welcome or assent to the neutralization of any part of Shanghai. On the contrary, Chinese opposition to suggestions regarding the neutralization of Shanghai has been immediate and strong in the past, a case in point being Chinese suspicions of the neutralization proposals made by the Secretary of State in 1927.[64] There has been acquiescence in the armed neutrality effected by foreigners in Shanghai from time to time, but that acquiescence has been based on necessity and not volition. It might be remarked parenthetically, however, that this official attitude has not prevented either Chinese officials or private citizens from availing themselves of the security which that armed neutrality has made possible.

Chinese reluctance to recognize or to participate in effecting the neutrality of Shanghai is unquestionably predicated upon the fear that any scheme of neutralization must inevitably result in loss or derogation of sovereign rights and in the relinquishment of control over the richest and most important commercial city in the country. These fears appear to be not without foundation for it is not improbable that to effect the complete neutralization of Shanghai and a broad zone around the city, which is what adequate protection for foreign life and property seems to dictate, there would be some curtailment, if not outright loss, at least temporarily, of certain sovereign rights and certain administrative, judicial and fiscal prerogatives corollary to those rights.

(b) *Participation:* To induce China to participate in the neutralization of Shanghai it is believed the foreign powers including Japan would unquestionably be called upon to give the most solemn and definite assurances affirming recognition of China's sovereign rights over the area neutralized. It is also probable that China would insist upon such questions as the control and use of the customs and other revenues of the port, which would be of such vital concern to her in time of war, being definitely resolved in her favor. She might also desire specific assurances that any temporary assumption of sovereign rights, including administrative, judicial and fiscal rights would be relinquished immediately upon the conclusion of hostilities. An international guarantee covering these points might induce Chinese agreement but agreement is scarcely conceivable without.

In the event that an international guarantee along the lines indicated in the preceding paragraph could not be given by the interested powers because of the refusal of one or more to bind itself or because of disagreement on other issues, would it be possible to induce China to participate in a very limited neutralization? It seems unlikely, for while China might be more agreeable to the limitation of neutraliza-

---

[64] For proposals, see telegram No. 31, January 28, 1927, 3 p. m., to the Minister in China, *Foreign Relations*, 1927, vol. II, p. 59; for correspondence, see *ibid.*, pp. 59–78, *passim.*

tion to the International Settlement and French Concession, she would probably insist in any event upon the favorable solution of such important questions as control within the neutralized zone of national revenues, particularly customs revenues, affirmation of her sovereign rights, et cetera. However, neutralization of the Settlement and French Concession areas alone would be of little practical value so long as contiguous Chinese territory remained available as a base of operations; anything less than the neutralization of the entire city of Shanghai, including a protective zone, would be of doubtful value.

In view of these considerations it is difficult to escape the conclusion that the obstacles surrounding the securing of Chinese assent to any scheme of neutralization are formidable and susceptible of realization only upon certain definite conditions.

Japan:

The attitude of Japan towards neutralization is dependent, it is believed, upon the policies activating her at the time such a proposal is advanced. In the past her views on this subject appear to have been characterized by a desire to bring about the complete neutralization of the entire Shanghai area. This desire received a definite impetus from the Sino-Japanese hostilities of 1932 which resulted in something in the nature of a demilitarized zone being created to the west of Shanghai by the provisions of the agreement of May 5, 1932, terminating hostilities. There is reason to believe, however, that there had also been germinating in the minds of Japanese officials a scheme more comprehensive than the neutralization of Shanghai. The plan is understood to have contemplated the conversion of Shanghai and a considerable area around the port into a free and independent territory and was given considerable newspaper publicity following the conclusion of hostilities in 1932. It is not known whether it was ever officially brought to the attention of the interested foreign governments but the Japanese Government is understood to have sounded out our government and other governments regarding the convening of a "Round Table Conference" to consider the future status of Shanghai and related questions. It seems not improbable that a proposal for the creation of a free and independent city would have been broached if such a conference had been convened.

It should be noted, however, that in the event Japan's policy is one committed to territorial expansion by military conquest, she would probably avoid making any commitments regarding the future status of Shanghai which might hamper her in any way, for in pursuance of this policy she might conceivably determine upon the seizure of Shanghai, including the International Settlement and French Concession, regardless of possible international reprecussions.

Japanese participation in the neutralization of Shanghai is thus likely to be predicated upon conditions and purposes completely antithetical to those entertained by China. In view of this fact the finding of a formula common to both countries would doubtless prove to be a most difficult if not impossible task.

Conclusion:

One is, therefore, reluctantly forced to the conclusion

(1) that the neutralization of Shanghai by an international agreement subscribed to by both China and Japan is only remotely possible since it is dependent upon too many conflicting political aspirations;

(2) that without the cooperation and participation of both China and Japan, neutrality could only be maintained by a large, well equipped international force, inasmuch as the volunteer corps now being supported by the Shanghai Municipal Council at great expense to the taxpayer is largely obsolete;

(3) that in view of the tense and unstable political situation in Europe and the disinclination of our own and other governments to dispatch large forces abroad, it is highly problematical whether an international force could be assembled in Shanghai sufficiently powerful to maintain the neutrality of the port in the face of determined Chinese opposition or serious Japanese aggression;

(4) and finally that the problems involved in the defense of the International Settlement and the French Concession and the maintenance of the neutrality of these areas are likely to remain subordinated in the minds of the powers to more pressing and seemingly important political questions.

E. F. S[TANTON]

793.94/8382 : Telegram

The Ambassador in China (Johnson) to the Secretary of State

PEIPING, November 20, 1936—7 p. m.
[Received November 20—4:27 p. m.]

563. Embassy's 556, November 18, 6 p. m. Information purportedly given by a Chinese officer who participated in the fighting is to the effect that the Suiyuan forces had about 200 casualties in the fighting near Taolin; airplanes belonging to the attacking Chahar forces were reported active in bombing and observation. A foreign source reports the despatch of seven trains of troops from Tatung, North Shansi, evidently en route to the two fronts of Pingtichuang and Paoting [*Pailingmiao?*]. The troops were thought to be Shansi forces, and their equipment included some tanks.

A foreigner who arrived from Suiyuan today reports that fighting took place again on the 18th, with a reported attempt made by the Chahar attackers to cut the railway line. This informant stated that no National Government forces had been observed in the province, despite the rumors that 100,000 troops were being sent, and that the current press reports seem to be highly exaggerated. Various missionaries have evacuated from the province, Japanese nationals are also reported leaving points along the railway line for Peiping and Tientsin, but this informant stated that informed foreigners in Suiyuan were not yet seriously perturbed by the course of events.

Today's Chinese press reports that the attacking forces were defeated and driven back by the Suiyuan defense forces, but that a new attack is expected.

Circular letters, purporting to be signed by Wang Ying and other rebel Chahar leaders, have appeared in Peiping; they strongly denounce Chiang Kai Shek and the Nanking Government.

Conferences in the last day or two between Sung Che Yuan and Han Fu Chu at Nanking, South Hopei, between Chiang Kai Shek and Yen Hsi-shan at Taiyuan, and between Chiang ad Han at Tsinanfu, are all presumed to be in connection with the North China situation; it is possible that they also have reference to the negotiations at Nanking. Sung announced yesterday, in regard to the meeting at Nanking, that he and Han "were both of the opinion that in view of the proximity of Shantung and Hopei we should cooperate closely for the maintenance of local peace and order and cultivate the friendship of our neighboring power (Japan) under the guidance of the fixed policy of the Central Government".

A great deal of interest in the Suiyuan situation is being evinced by all articulate groups in China, and campaigns are already being started to collect money, clothing and comforts for the Suiyuan troops.

To Tokyo by mail. JOHNSON

893.00/13740 : Telegram

The Ambassador in China (Johnson) to the Secretary of State

PEIPING, November 24, 1936—4 p. m.
[Received November 24—3 : 50 p. m.]

572. Embassy's 569, November 23, 6 p. m.[65] Today's Chinese press reports that an attack was launched yesterday on Wuchuan and Kuyang, North Suiyuan, by Chahar forces operating from Pailingmiao, and that additional Chahar forces are moving up from the rear by motor truck. (A foreigner recently returned from Jehol reports having seen between 100 and 200 new heavy trucks lined up in a terrace yard at Chengteh, and states that he was informed that about 2,000 trucks are in service in Jehol and Chahar.) A foreign source confirms the report that National Government troops have arrived at Tatung, North Shansi, but numbers and destination of the troops are unknown.

Information from Tungchow purports that new flag, said to be the five-barred flag of the Republic, will be raised there tomorrow on the

---

[65] Not printed.

occasion of the celebration of the first anniversary of the East Hopei autonomous government. A circular telegram allegedly signed by Teh Wang and Cho Shih Hai was issued under date of November 17 and announced the formal assumption by Teh Wang of the post of Commander-in-Chief of the Mongol banner armies. That telegram in general accuses the National Government of faithlessness in dealing with the Mongols, and states that on November 9 the Mongols, "having reached the limit of their patience", communicated to the Suiyuan Provincial Government five demands:

(1) Return to the jurisdiction of the Chahar Mongol Council of the four Mongol banners now under Suiyuan control;
(2) Destruction of the military defenses which have been erected by the Suiyuan authorities in East Suiyuan and south of Pailingmiao, and cessation of the "economic blockade" against the latter place;
(3) Return of the munitions seized by the Suiyuan authorities from mutinied Peace Preservation Corps troops from Pailingmiao last spring;
(4) Payment by Suiyan of $200,000 due for the expenses of the Pailingmiao Mongol Council; and
(5) Punishment of those involved in the Pailingmiao mutiny.

The telegram states in conclusion that there is no intention of rebellion, but that the oppressions of Suiyuan must cease.

By mail to Tokyo.

JOHNSON

893.00/13741 : Telegram

The Ambassador in China (Johnson) to the Secretary of State

PEIPING, November 25, 1936—4 p. m.
[Received November 25—10 : 40 a. m.]

574. Embassy's 572, November 24, 4 p. m. The Chinese press reports that counterattacks by the Suiyuan forces threw back the Chahar irregulars along the Wuchuan-Kuyang front, and that 4 regiments of Suiyuan troops captured Pailingmiao yesterday morning with about 300 casualties on their side. There is no independent confirmation of this report, but the news is reported with substantial agreement from various quarters. The report alleges that a large number of Japanese officers were with the Pailingmiao forces, which would accord with the statements made in the interview with Kita as said to have been printed in the *New York Times* on November 23, but which if true would seem to be at variance with reports emanating from Tokyo that the Japanese Government is not concerned with Suiyuan matter.

The press further reports that the National Government has sent a telegram to Teh Wang directing him to withdraw from Pailingmiao and criticizing him for starting warfare.

By mail to Tokyo.

JOHNSON

762.94/97 : Telegram

The Ambassador in the United Kingdom (Bingham) to the Secretary of State

LONDON, November 25, 1936—7 p. m.

[Received November 25—3:42 p. m.]

570. Your 416, November 23, 3 p. m.[66] When complying with your 418, November 24, noon,[66] the Embassy had an opportunity to get Craigie [67] to expand further his remarks contained in the third from the last paragraph of my 546, November 19, 9 p. m.,[66] and it was possible to refer in the course of the conversation to the excerpt from the *Morning Post* editorial quoted in my 544, November 19, 7 p. m.[66] Craigie said the word "proposals" did not accurately describe Yoshida's talks with the Foreign Office which were more in the nature of "soundings". Yoshida has come to London with high hopes of arriving at a satisfactory settlement of Anglo-Japanese differences and as recently as a few days ago had again talked with the Foreign Secretary on this subject. Craigie said that personally he did not think that Yoshida's hopes would be realized and that in any event should the talks give promise of fruition he felt sure that the Foreign Secretary would deem it as important as he did that the American Government be informed.

Craigie expressed the view that since the murder in Tokyo the civilians had gained back a little ground from the military but he greatly doubted whether the same element in Japan would be strong enough to conclude any worthwhile agreement with Great Britain. Craigie said that this was the general view held in the Foreign Office.

However, in this general connection reference is made to my 569 of November 25, 6 p. m.[66]

BINGHAM

793.94/8448

The Chargé in Japan (Dickover) to the Secretary of State

No. 2147

TOKYO, November 25, 1936.

[Received December 15.]

SIR: I have the honor to report that during the past two months there has been in Japan a very noticeable decrease in expressions of belligerency against Soviet Russia and China. This decrease has manifested itself in various ways; principally, however, in the unofficial utterances of members of the defense forces and in the tone of

---

[66] Not printed.
[67] Sir Robert Leslie Craigie, British Assistant Under Secretary of State for Foreign Affairs.

the Japanese press. After the Chengtu, Pakhoi and Hankow incidents the Japanese defense forces gave press interviews in which they threatened to take "direct" or "independent" action in China to protect Japanese nationals and interests, should the Chinese Government fail to afford such protection. The Japanese newspapers at that time generally supported the fighting forces. Since then several further incidents have occurred in China in which Japanese nationals were killed or their property destroyed, but in Japan the defense forces are no longer taking advantage of these opportunities for pugnacious talk. The newspapers, moreover, have given little news space to the incidents and have completely ignored them in their editorial columns.

In regard to the Soviet Union, moreover, the Japanese nation seems to have lost much of the belligerency which characterized its relations with the country until recently. Frontier incidents no longer arouse excitement and resentment in the Japanese press and even the recent refusal of the Soviet Union to sign the new fisheries agreement has been received calmly by the people and the defense forces of the country.

It is difficult to state whether this apparent loss of pugnacity is real or is inspired by the Government for reasons of its own. A survey of conditions both internal and external leads observers to believe that this change is largely due to existing domestic and external circumstances, with perhaps some official inspiration. Following are some of the causes which appear to have led to a loss of belligerency on the part of the Japanese nation, as collected from numerous sources of information in Tokyo.

1. *Internal Conditions.*

The Japanese army is not at all certain of its political position in Japan. It has had to endure several political defeats since the first of the year. In the February 26 incident the army was compelled by the pressure of public opinion to execute the ring leaders of the rebellion, although it will be remembered that in the incident of May 15, 1932, light sentences only were imposed upon the ring leaders of that incident. In the cases of the Diet reform and other administrative reform issues, the Army, after sending up what appeared to be trial balloons advocating drastic measures, was compelled by the outburst of public resentment to withdraw the statements unofficially made. There appears to be a strong under-current of feeling against the military among the people of Japan—a feeling which is not usually manifested and which lacks leadership but which is strong enough to cause the army to withdraw from its advanced position from time to time. Moreover, the Army is still divided within itself. General Terauchi, the Minister of War, has carried out extensive reforms designed to purge the Army of the more radical elements, but rumors which have reached the Embassy indicate that the younger officers of both the Army and the Navy are still as radically opposed to the present political system in Japan as they were before the purge took place. With this division within itself, and the popular feeling opposed to the imposition of the military will upon the nation, the Army does not feel in a position to take any drastic steps in China or Russia at the moment.

The people of Japan, for their part, seem to have lost interest in military adventures. For many months past the Army has been holding up the difficulties in Sino-Japanese and Russo-Japanese relations as indications of the crisis which was to come in 1935 and 1936. The crisis has not materialized and, until recently, it appeared that the difficulties in the relations between Japan and China and Japan and the Soviet Union would be settled by diplomatic means. It was to be expected, under such circumstances, that the people of the country would gradually lose interest in the war-scares of the military. The people cannot be kept at a high tension indefinitely. Too many cries of "Wolf!" cause them to disbelieve in the existence of the wolf. Another factor contributing to the indifference of the people toward Sino-Japanese problems arises from the censorship on news of the negotiations. The exact nature of the Japanese demands on China, their scope and the extent to which the Japanese Government is prepared to go in enforcing those demands, have been kept from the people of Japan. Public opinion is therefore unformed in regard to the question, and the press is unable to reflect the sentiments of the public. The public is better informed in regard to Russo-Japanese relations, but here again there seems to be no very definite indication of public opinion.

Moreover, the attention of the people has been distracted from external affairs by pressing domestic problems. The taxation increase and taxation reform schemes, the increase in the military budget demands, the plans for administrative reform and the quarrel between the Army and the political parties over the reform of the Diet have occupied the attention of the Japanese people to the exclusion of Sino-Japanese and Russo-Japanese affairs. There is also a feeling of unrest among the people of Japan. The heavy increase of taxation planned for the coming fiscal year is not being favorably received by the nation, and the slowly-developing struggle between parliamentarism and Fascism in Japan is causing a feeling of insecurity among the financial and industrial elements.

Under these conditions it is not surprising that the military have dropped war-like talk for the time being. On the other hand, it is quite probable that the military have deliberately tried to calm the nation and to prevent outbreaks of anti-Chinese or anti-Russian feeling which might get out of hand and force the nation into war. For the above-mentioned domestic reasons, and for external reasons which will be discussed later, it appears that the Japanese Army is not prepared to engage in a major war on the Asiatic continent, and consequently it is not only possible but probable that the military have desired that the Japanese nation lose interest in the minor incidents on the continent which formerly were exaggerated in order to fan the war-like ardor of the people.

2. *External Conditions.*

Perhaps chief among the external circumstances causing Japan to exhibit less pugnacity in its relations with its neighbors on the Asiatic continent is the strength and determination against further aggression shown by both China and Soviet Russia during recent months. The Soviet Union has indicated unmistakably that while it does not desire war with Japan, it will fight to the extent of its ability to preserve every inch of its territory or territory which it believes should be under its control. This determination, as the Japanese Army knows, is backed by military force probably superior to any which Japan could put into the field of conflict within a reasonable period. At the same time the rapidly growing unification of China and that country's determination not to concede further loss of sovereignty have given the Japanese cause for thought. A war with China would undoubtedly result in early victories for Japan, whereby the Japanese Army and Navy could hold the Chinese coastal provinces, but it is not believed, even in Japan, that the war would be so soon resolved. It is considered more probable that the war would last in a guerilla form for years and would impose such a severe financial strain on Japan that the economic structure might collapse. In order to proceed further with its expansion schemes on the continent, therefore, it appears that it will be necessary for Japan to use force, and the country is not apparently prepared for this step.

It is also quite probable that the Japanese Army had expected another world war to break out in Europe as a result of the Spanish civil war and the growing tendency to divide into leftist and fascist blocs. Anticipating that such a war would give Japan a free hand in Asia, the fighting forces indulged in expansionist sentiments until recent months, but as the European war did not materialize, the fighting forces considered it best to drop their expansion schemes for the moment. The Japanese nation also realizes that it is more or less isolated in a world of conflicting ideas and policies. A need for a friend is being felt, and the possibility also exists that the military decided to relax its pressure on China and to discontinue its threats against the Soviet Union until such time as the pending agreement with Germany should be concluded.

A survey of the domestic causes of the apparent lessening of the belligerent spirit among the people of Japan reveals the fact that they are largely temporary in character, or of such a nature as to be readily overcome by an inspired outburst of patriotic fervor. From this viewpoint the loss of pugnacity cannot be considered as permanent; it is rather a temporary phenomenon subject to change at any time. The external causes of the lessening of belligerency, however, are more fixed in character and are more liable to act as a permanent restraint on Japanese pugnacity in the Far East.

Respectfully yours,   E. R. DICKOVER

793.94/8384 : Telegram

The Counselor of Embassy in China (Peck) to the Secretary of State

NANKING, November 26, 1936—10 a. m.
[Received November 26—9 : 30 a. m.]

333. 1. Hsu Mo told the British Ambassador yesterday morning that the Japanese Kwantung army had warned Fu Tso Yi that an agreement between Doihara and Sung Che Yuan prevented sending of Chinese troops into Chahar. Hsu Mo said there is an opinion growing in the Chinese Government that the Government should issue a statement denying validity to any agreement with the Japanese not concluded by direct emissaries of the National Government as in the case of the Shanghai and Tangku truces. My British informant said Hsu Mo inquired whether the British Ambassador thought the Japanese Government would support the Kwantung army in its intrigues in Chahar and explained that Chiang Kai Shek might go to Suiyuan in person, the implication being that he might then pursue the irregular forces into Chahar thus challenging the Kwantung army.

2. Informant said that the lack of frankness of the Chinese Government regarding the obligations it has incurred was illustrated by a recent remark of Sung Che Yuan to the British Ambassador that he was obliged to sign the aviation agreement because the Tangku truce provided for it and that there were other concessions attached to the same document so "shameful" that he dared not reveal them.

3. Reuter despatch dated Tokyo November 25 quotes *Nichi Nichi* assertion that Great Britain and China are negotiating offensive and defensive alliance. The press carries denial of this report by the Chinese Government which describes it as fantastic. There have been indications here that the British Ambassador has consulted various Chinese authorities concerning their difficulties with Japan and has even tendered advice. I have several times reminded Hsu Mo that the Department is interested in the progress of events but

when he has shown himself reticent I have refrained from pressing him for information because of my impression that the Department would prefer that I carefully avoid any implication of a joint American-Chinese interest in China's struggle against Japanese encroachment.

Repeated to Peiping.

PECK

761.94/938

The Chargé in Japan (Dickover) to the Secretary of State

No. 2160   TOKYO, November 26, 1936.
                                                  [Received December 15.]

SIR: I have the honor to report that Soviet-Japanese relations, which during the past few weeks had been showing marked improvement due to the progress made toward the settlement of the outstanding issues between the two countries, have now received a severe set-back following the news of the German-Japanese accord.[69] The details of this accord which are discussed in another despatch* are not important for the purpose of this discussion; the fact, however, that Japan has seen fit to join with Germany in a common front against the Soviet ideology, if not the Soviet Government itself, has apparently satisfied the USSR that the Japanese Government has thus sacrificed any claim it might have had to good-will and cooperation in the settlement of the questions which have been and are up for discussion between Moscow and Tokyo. Consequently negotiations on pending issues have been summarily suspended by Moscow and the prospects for their resumption have become remote.

It will be recalled that during the past few months Premier Hirota has been taking up one by one the outstanding issues between Japan and Soviet Russia in accordance with the policy which he has pursued ever since he became Foreign Minister and which he has continued through Mr. Arita while Prime Minister. After the transfer of the Chinese Eastern Railway was accomplished in March, 1935, the remaining questions have been the following: 1. The extension of the Japanese oil concessions in North Saghalien; 2. The new Fisheries Treaty to supplement the treaty which expired in May of this year; 3. The establishment of two commissions, one for the demarcation of the "Manchukuo"-Siberian border and the other for the settlement of border disputes between Japan-"Manchukuo" and the USSR. While there may be said to remain several other problems, such as the crea-

---

[69] See vol. I, pp. 390 ff.
*Embassy's despatch No. 2159, November 26, 1936. [Footnote in the original; for despatch see *Foreign Relations*, Japan, 1931–1941, vol. II, p. 153.]

tion of a demilitarized zone along the Manchurian-Siberian border and a non-aggression pact as well as the fundamental question of supremacy over Mongol peoples and pastures† only the first three mentioned have been the subject of actual negotiations up to the present. Of these the agreement extending the North Saghalien oil concessions was successfully concluded at Moscow on October 10, last; whether the Soviets will now create any difficulty in the way of enforcing these concessions remains to be seen.

The draft of the new Fisheries Treaty had been actually completed and on November 18 was formally approved by the Privy Council at a Plenary Session at the Palace in the presence of the Emperor and later accepted by the Cabinet. Instructions to sign it had been cabled to the Japanese Chargé d'Affaires at Moscow but on the date set for signature, November 20, the Soviet Foreign Office informed the Japanese Chargé that "in view of the threatening developments in relations" the Soviet Government would be unable to sign the new Fisheries Convention until the atmosphere had changed.

On November 16, 17, and 18 the Soviet Ambassador conferred at length with the Japanese Minister for Foreign Affairs, Mr. Arita, concerning the establishment of the border demarcation commission and the commission for the settlement of border disputes, and while little progress was apparent in the direction of settling the points at issue at least a real effort was being made to this end. Indications now lead to the belief that these negotiations will be broken off entirely, at least for an indefinite period.

In addition to these, and possibly as an indirect result of Soviet pressure and indignation over recent developments, it is reported that the preliminary border negotiations between the Governments of Outer Mongolia and "Manchukuo", which recently opened at Manchuli, have been temporarily postponed "because of the illness of the chief Mongolian delegate, Mr. Samboa."

The reaction of the Soviet Government to the German-Japanese pact cannot have come as a surprise to the Japanese Government; there is, however, some question as to whether the premature discussion in the press of this pact was not disappointing to Mr. Hirota who undoubtedly hoped that at least the Fisheries Treaty would be signed before the news of the German agreement became known. Indications lead to the belief that the draft of the Fisheries Treaty was hurried through the Privy Council and the Cabinet in the hope that it could be signed on November 20, that is, six days before the publication of the German agreement.

Reverting to the negotiations regarding the border commissions it may be stated for purposes of record that Mr. Yurenev is reported to

†Embassy's despatch No. 1236, April 5, 1935. [Footnote in the original; for despatch see *Foreign Relations*, 1935, vol. III, p. 106.]

have made at the last conference with Mr. Arita the following contentions based upon his most recent instructions from Moscow:

1. That the border disputes commission should extend its jurisdiction, as early as possible, to the entire Soviet-"Manchukuo" border from the eastern frontier.
2. That the proposed commission deal with all border incidents dating from the Chingchangkou affair of January 20.
3. That Japan and "Manchukuo" should operate as a single responsible unit in the proposed commission.

Thus it will be observed, by reference to a recent despatch ‡ on the subject, that the Soviets have made a slight concession on point 1 mentioned above in that instead of holding out for the establishment of the dispute settlement commission within two months after the establishment of the commission dealing only with the eastern frontier, the Soviet Government wishes that the commission be established "as early as possible" afterward. With regard to points 2 and 3 above, there has been no concession. Furthermore, if the reports are correct, the Soviet contentions have been reduced from the six points mentioned in the despatch under reference, to only three.

In conclusion it may therefore be observed that Japan must look for a period of considerable uncertainty in her relations with Soviet Russia in the near future and that Mr. Hirota's policy of settling the outstanding issues between the two countries one by one will suffer at least temporarily due to resentment and retaliation on the part of Moscow because of Japan's new liaison with Germany.

Respectfully yours,   E. R. DICKOVER

793.94/8462

The Ambassador in China (Johnson) to the Secretary of State

No. 879   PEIPING, *November 27, 1936.*
[Received December 23.]

SIR: I have the honor to submit, as of possible interest to the Department, the following comment on the subject of the expansion of Japanese activities as observed in the everyday life of Peiping.

The number of Japanese soldiers which one sees appears to be the thing which most impresses foreign visitors to Peiping. The permament residents have, on the other hand, become so accustomed to seeing the north glacis of the Legation Quarter thronged with Japanese infantry and cavalry indulging in their daily exercises and maneuvers, that they almost fail to note how very many more Japa-

---

‡ Embassy's despatch No. 2114, October 30, 1936. [Footnote in the original; despatch not printed.]

nese soldiers are in evidence now than was the case two or even three years ago. Japanese troops are constantly on the march, usually to the accompaniment of shrill bugling, and one rarely walks along Legation Street, especially in the early morning or evening, without meeting a number of Japanese officers, often mounted, their orderlies trotting along behind on foot. It is a noticeable fact that Japanese officers are now more often seen on their mounts on the main streets outside of the Legation Quarter than was formerly the case.

Officers' motor cars bearing the flag of the Rising Sun are much in evidence and it is a daily occurrence to see Chinese coolies dragging truck loads of military supplies from the Chien Men Station to the barracks of the Japanese Guard.

There are several officers' messes in the Legation Quarter situated outside of the Japanese Embassy compound. One is in the former Chinese-Eastern Railway Building. (See Embassy's despatch No. 3130 [*3530*], April 23, 1935 [70]). Others are situated in the Ewo Building (Jardine Matheson & Company) on Legation Street, the ex-Belgian Bank Building and several houses in the Customs Compound on Rue Marco Polo.

The influx of Japanese has created a shortage of houses in Peiping. In many of the hutungs, especially those east of Hatamen Street, one observes a profusion of Japanese flags. Japanese flags have been observed flying over small farms east and particularly to the south of the Chinese city in the direction of Nan Yuan. Recently a Japanese interested in producing cotton in the province of Hopei called at the Embassy in regard to a certain farm in this district which he had been informed belonged to an American citizen. He stated that he was very anxious to rent the property in question for the purpose of cotton cultivation.

On Morrison and Hatamen Streets, and in the environs thereof, as I have previously reported, numerous Japanese shops and cafes have opened, not to mention Korean opium dens and brothels.

The Japanese civilians are quite as much in evidence as the military and not only frequent their own cafes and hotels but also the larger hotels such as the Grand Hotel de Pekin, the Wagons-Lits Hotel and the Hotel du Nord.

There has been a noticeable increase in the number of civilians and tourists traveling on the trains arriving in and departing from Peiping, and the First Secretary of the Japanese Embassy in Peiping informed a member of my staff that he is kept constantly on the go entertaining important visitors from his homeland, business delegations and numerous other Japanese who flock here for reasons ranging from mere curiosity to search for investment opportunities. During

---

[70] Not printed.

the past summer a visitor to the Temple of Heaven, Summer Palace or any of the tourist landmarks would have encountered groups of Japanese school children here on conducted tours the itinerary of which as a rule included Manchuria, Jehol, and Peiping. As the Department is aware, the Japanese bus service now runs daily between Peiping and Jehol and the recently inaugurated airline (see Embassy's telegram No. 555, November 18, 12 noon [71]) between this city and points in "Manchukuo" will undoubtedly augment Japanese travel to and from North China, as will also the newly constructed streamlined trains which have been placed on the through service between Peiping and Mukden. These trains, of which there are three, were constructed by the South Manchuria Railway Company and are the latest in de luxe air conditioned equipment.

The Japanese residents do not mingle freely in the community life of Peiping, presumably finding their own colony sufficient unto itself for social diversion and recreation. However, the men, at least, appear to enjoy the golf course at Pa Pao-shan where by far the predominating number of playing members are Japanese. This also is true of the Tientsin golf course.

Respectfully yours,

NELSON TRUSLER JOHNSON

893.00/13743 : Telegram

The Counselor of Embassy in China (Lockhart) to the Secretary of State

PEIPING, November 28, 1936—noon.
[Received November 28—7 : 05 a. m.]

577. Embassy's 572, November 24, 4 p. m. The Suiyuan situation has remained quiet since the capture of Pailingmiao, but both sides appear to be making preparations for future eventualities. The irregular forces at Shangtu are reported to have been reenforced. Chen Cheng, one of Nanking's most important generals, is reported to be proceeding from Taiyuan to Kweisui for an important conference with the military leaders there. The Military Attaché's office has been informed that three Nanking divisions have arrived in Suiyuan but have not yet proceeded to the front; and that six Suiyuan and Shansi divisions and two artillery regiments are stationed on the defense line running from Paotow east to Pingtichuan and south to Fengchen.

Upon the occasion of the Tungchow ceremonies (see paragraph 2 of the Embassy's 572, November 24, 4 p. m.) the five-barred Republican flag was raised. Handbills were dropped from airplanes denouncing the Kuomintang rule and threatening Chiang Kai Shek with the fate

[71] Not printed.

which overtook Yuan Shih Kai [72] and Chang Hsun.[73] A proclamation was issued on the same day over Yin Ju Keng's signature, castigating Communism, alleging that the Kuomintang is still allied with Communism, and calling for various reforms and economic reconstruction on the basis of local autonomy; a call was issued to the people of China to throw off the Kuomintang rule.

By mail to Tokyo.

LOCKHART

762.94/105 : Telegram

The Ambassador in China (Johnson) to the Secretary of State

NANKING, November 30, 1936—noon.
[Received November 30—8 a. m.]

335. The German Ambassador on November 27 called on the Chinese Minister for Foreign Affairs and an official communiqué announced that the Ambassador promised to apply to his Government for information desired by the Minister for Foreign Affairs concerning the German-Japanese anti-Communist agreement.[74] The communiqué added that the attention of the Ambassador was drawn to the reaction on the Chinese people and to the fixed policy of the Chinese Government to rely on its own strength to suppress Communism.

The Italian Ambassador will call on the Minister for Foreign Affairs November 30, 4 p. m. to discuss the recent Italian-Japanese agreement which press reports state relates to the recognition of the present status of Ethiopia and Manchuria.

JOHNSON

865d.01/210 : Telegram

The Ambassador in Japan (Grew) to the Secretary of State

TOKYO, November 30, 1936—2 p. m.
[Received November 30—7 : 40 a. m.]

245. 1. No official announcement has yet been made in Tokyo in regard to the subject matter of the Italo-Japanese agreement now being negotiated but the spokesman of the Foreign Office has stated that the negotiations are not connected with the recently concluded German-Japanese anti-Comintern agreement.

2. From the best information available to the Embassy it appears that the Italo-Japanese agreement will contain trade clauses whereby

---

[72] President of the Republic, 1912–16, and unsuccessful in his attempt to become Emperor.

[73] Unsuccessful in July 1917 in his attempted restoration of the Manchu dynasty.

[74] See vol. I, pp. 390 ff.

Japan will obtain raw material concessions in Abyssinia; will provide for the *de facto* recognition by Japan of the Italian possession of Abyssinia by the reduction of the Japanese Legation there to a consular office and for the Italian *de facto* recognition of Manchukuo by the accrediting of consular officers to that country; and will provide for Italian technical and material assistance to Japanese aviation (the information in regard to aviation was obtained from an officer of the Italian Embassy and therefore may be considered as authentic).

3. I shall see the Italian Ambassador tomorrow and shall telegraph further information if obtained.

GREW

765.94/33 : Telegram

The Ambassador in Japan (Grew) to the Secretary of State

Tokyo, December 1, 1936—4 p. m.
[Received December 1—9 : 15 a. m.]

247. Embassy's 245, November 30, 2 p. m.

1. The Italian Ambassador this morning told me that the emphasis given by the press to the recent Italian-Japanese negotiations was due to the fact that they followed so closely the conclusion of the German-Japanese agreement and that this emphasis was out of proportion to the facts. He said that for at least a year Italy had desired to reopen her Consulate General in Mukden, closed since the great war, because most of the other great powers had such Consulates while Italy possesses a Consulate only in Harbin and that this arrangement had finally been made by the Japanese Government acting as intermediary with Manchukuo. Japan at the same time had sent a Consul to Abyssinia after a similar arrangement with the Italian Government. He said he knew nothing about any signed agreement.

2. The Ambassador said that commercial conversations were also proceeding in Rome between the Japanese Ambassador and the Italian Foreign Office but that he had not been kept informed of their progress and knew only what he had seen in the press. He said that so far as he himself was aware the question of Italian technical assistance to Japanese aviation had not arisen. (The information on this point contained in my No. 245 was received from his Naval Attaché.)

3. The *Nichi Nichi* this morning states that the Japanese Foreign Office is displeased with the intimations emanating from Rome that an Italian-Japanese political agreement is being negotiated. These intimations are blamed on excessive desire for propaganda on the part of the Italians. It appears that the Japanese authorities wish to avoid the implication that a German-Italian-Japanese Fascist bloc is being formed.

GREW

762.94/110 : Telegram

The Counselor of Embassy in China (Lockhart) to the Secretary of State

PEIPING, December 1, 1936—4 p. m.

[Received 5 : 05 p. m.]

521. 1. According to press despatch from Loyang, Chiang Kai Shek declared yesterday in a speech to the Loyang branch Military Academy that in his opinion the new Japanese-German agreement does not affect the general situation in the Far East. He is said to have expressed the view that the agreement contains no secret clauses, and that there still remained remnants of the Communist armies in China which would be exterminated at all costs, and that this is a domestic problem which "brooks no foreign interference". The Generalissimo is also reported to have said that the capture of Pailingmiao has not only roused the spirit of the people and the army but has strengthened the conviction of the people that if they unite and act together there should be no loss of national territory. He described the capture of Pailingmiao as the turning point of national independence.

2. The Chinese press generally has been warm in its praise of Fu Tso Yi and the defenders of Suiyuan and the view is expressed that China has now come to the point where it may be expected that further foreign aggression will be opposed by a united military front. The Embassy believes that it is too early to evaluate the Pailingmiao victory, but that victory has at least demonstrated that the Chinese are now more definitely unified and have a new determination and that the malcontents who have been aided and abetted by intriguers within and without the country may expect a more difficult time henceforth.

3. It seems probable that Chinese officialdom will be much more concerned over the Japanese-Italian agreement regarding Abyssinia and "Manchukuo" (if concluded) than over the Japanese-German agreement. Any agreement which would actually or by implication sanction Japanese action in Manchuria in 1931 and since that time is certain not to be well received. Such an agreement strikes directly at sovereign rights which China does not admit have been surrendered, whereas the Japanese-German agreement is an instrument which might or might not have any direct bearing on China. In any event the popular view is that the latter is directed solely against Russia. The *Hua Pei Jih Pao* in an editorial today states that Germany, Italy and Japan have many things in common and that "they have trampled under foot international agreements and have been pursuing a very aggressive policy in foreign affairs" and on the point of recognition it states that the "*de facto* or *de jure* recognition of the illegal gains

of the two countries" is a serious matter and most deplorable from the standpoint of international morality and righteousness. Concluding, the editorial states: "For her (Italy) to accord moral support to a group of rebels at this juncture betrays not only a wanton disregard of Chinese sovereignty but also means that she sets no store by Chinese friendship".

By mail to Tokyo.

LOCKHART

762.94/111 : Telegram

The Ambassador in China (Johnson) to the Secretary of State

NANKING, December 2, 1936—11 a. m.
[Received December 2—10 : 15 a. m.]

337. My 335, November 30, noon.

1. Responsible official of the Foreign Office stated today to Peck that neither the German nor Italian Ambassador could return informative replies to questions asked by the Minister for Foreign Affairs regarding the German and Italian agreements with Japan but promised to submit the questions to their Governments.

2. Informant stated that the Chinese Government understands that the arrangement with Japan was negotiated by Ribbentrop as confidential representative of Hitler with the Japanese Ambassador in Berlin and that even the German Foreign Office was not kept informed of the nature of the negotiations. Informant said that the Chinese Government is uneasy over article 2 of the published text of the agreement which carries the implication, especially in the Japanese text, that Germany and Japan will take measures against Communists who, in their opinion, threaten them even outside the limits of their respective countries. The Government is apprehensive also regarding the possibility of a secret military rider and questioned the German Ambassador concerning both of these points.

3. Informant said that the Italian Ambassador asserted that so far as he knew the Italian understanding with Japan was concluded orally and provided only for the substitution of a Japanese consular office in Addis Ababa for a legation and for the setting up of an Italian consular office in Mukden and that specifically it did not involve recognition of "Manchukuo". The Minister for Foreign Affairs inquired why, if the understanding included only these measures, Italy wished to bring Japan into the German-Italian Fascist bloc and the Italian Ambassador replied that he inferred that this bloc felt the necessity of obtaining the support of a large navy.

4. Responsible official of the Executive Yuan yesterday informed an officer of the Embassy that while the Chinese Government is still ignorant of the precise contents and significance of the German and Ital-

ian agreements with Japan these agreements had again impressed the Chinese Government and people with the fact that for protection from aggression China cannot rely on effective help from any other nation or exterior agency but must depend entirely on its own exertions. Informant said that he thought the Chinese would not forget this lesson and he evidently intended this observation as a guide to understanding of China's policies in the future.

5. Sent to the Department and Peiping.

JOHNSON

793.94/8405 : Telegram

The Ambassador in China (Johnson) to the Secretary of State

NANKING, December 2, 1936—noon.
[Received December 2—7 : 42 a. m.]

338. Nanking's telegram November 26, 10 a. m.

1. Responsible Foreign Office official stated to the Embassy today that the Chinese Government is convinced of Japanese instigation of the attacks on Suiyuan by irregular forces and has made several oral protests to the Japanese Embassy. The Government believes that forces are massing in Chahar to attempt recapture of Pailingmiao in northern Suiyuan and is convinced that it can repel such invasion but has not decided whether the Chinese Government troops, if successful, shall continue eastward into Chahar Province. Informant referred to the alleged Doihara–Sung Che Yuan agreement of December last but said the Chinese Government knows of no such agreement and in any event is absolved from obligation to respect it by the official announcement made following the Mukden incident denying recognition to any agreement not concluded under sanction of the National Government.

2. Sent to the Department and Peiping.

JOHNSON

865d.01/213 : Telegram

The Ambassador in Italy (Phillips) to the Secretary of State

ROME, December 2, 1936—2 p. m.
[Received December 2—10 a. m.]

504. My 497, November 28, 5 p. m.[75] The following official communiqué has just been issued:

"Count Ciano received the Japanese Ambassador who communicated to him the decision of his Government to transform the Legation in Addis Ababa into a Consulate General asking the exequatur therefor of the Government of His Majesty the King of Italy and Emperor of Ethiopia.

---

[75] Not printed.

Count Ciano after having assured him that the Japanese interests in Ethiopia will be the object of particular attention on the part of the Italian authorities expressed to His Excellency Sugimura his pleasure at the decision of the Imperial Government at Tokyo."

It is understood that a communiqué affecting Italian relations with Manchukuo will be issued in Tokyo and subsequently published here.

The explanation given in Italian official circles for the delay in issuing this communiqué is to the effect that owing to the world wide reaction to the German-Japanese anti-Communist agreement the Italian Government felt that if the Italo-Japanese undertakings affecting Ethiopia and Manchukuo should be published at the time of the publication of the German-Japanese agreement it might be construed that these two accords were closely connected and consequently erroneous inferences might be drawn as to the intentions of the governments concerned.

PHILLIPS

793.94/8409 : Telegram

The Counselor of Embassy in China (Lockhart) to the Secretary of State

PEIPING, December 3, 1936—3 p. m.
[Received December 3—7 a. m.]

583. Following telegram has been received from Tsingtau:

"December 3, 11 a. m. Japanese merchant marine landed 800 armed sailors during night to protect 9 Japanese cotton mills which declared lockout yesterday.

The City Hall was surrounded by Japanese sailors who withdrew from this one place this morning.

The Japanese landing party arrested and are still questioning nine Chinese among whom are local officials, Tangpu officers and newspapermen.

Situation on all streets normal.

Labor situation did not appear to outside observers so serious as to warrant lockout."

Repeated to Nanking and Tokyo.

LOCKHART

793.94/8412 : Telegram

The Ambassador in China (Johnson) to the Secretary of State

NANKING, December 4, 1936—noon.
[Received 6 : 50 p. m.]

341. Tsingtau's December 3, 11 a. m. to Peiping.[76]

1. The Foreign Office has released a statement that the Minister for

[76] See *supra*.

Foreign Affairs invited the Japanese Ambassador to the Foreign Office at 7 : 30 December 3 and orally and strongly protested landing of sailors at Tsingtau, demanding withdrawal of sailors, release of persons illegally arrested and return of documents illegally seized. Another Foreign Office press release states that the oral protest was confirmed by note to the Japanese Embassy dated December 3 charging the Japanese naval authorities with flagrant violation of Chinese sovereign rights; accusing the Japanese of aggravating the labor trouble by declaring a lockout and landing sailors; and reserving the right of the Chinese Government to make such demands as are relevant to the situation.

2. The Japanese Ambassador regarded the request for him to call on the Minister for Foreign Affairs as reply to his standing request for another interview concerning settlement of outstanding issues, and following the discussion about the Tsingtao incident of December 3, presented to the Minister for Foreign Affairs a long *aide-mémoire* recapitulating the previous seven discussions. The Minister for Foreign Affairs seems to have glanced at this document and found portions unsatisfactory whereupon he returned it to the Ambassador. In fact, the authorized release from the Foreign Office states that the Minister for Foreign Affairs referred to the situation in Suiyuan and said he was not prepared to discuss any Sino-Japanese question that had been under negotiation. However, the Ambassador insisted upon leaving the *aide-mémoire* with Minister for Foreign Affairs.

3. An American news representative states that the Japanese Embassy informed him this morning that the Ministry of Foreign Affairs returned the *aide-mémoire* by messenger to the Japanese Embassy December 4, 4 a. m., but that the Embassy has again sent it to the Ministry of Foreign Affairs. The informant reports Japanese Embassy officials as asserting that the reason why the Minister for Foreign Affairs was unwilling to receive the *aide-mémoire* was because it recorded statements which he actually made, but now regrets, and not because its contents "were quite at variance with the facts" as asserted in the press release from the Foreign Office. Japanese Embassy officials reported that return of the *aide-mémoire* by the Foreign Office to the Embassy was insulting and that the proper course would have been to point out in a written reply any features to which objection was taken.

4. Sent to the Department, by mail to Peiping.

JOHNSON

793.94/8410 : Telegram

The Counselor of Embassy in China (Lockhart) to the Secretary of State

PEIPING, December 4, 1936—3 p. m.
[Received December 4—1:17 p. m.]

588. Embassy's 583, December 3, 3 p. m. Following telegram has been received from Tsingtau:

"December 4, 10 a. m. Situation remains quiet. Chinese who were arrested have been released. Chinese authorities regard Japanese action as designed to force out present Mayor and his administration."

Nanking informed.

LOCKHART

702.6593 Manchuria/12

The Consul at Harbin (LaMont) to the Ambassador in China (Johnson) [77]

No. 286
HARBIN, December 4, 1936.

SIR: I have the honor to refer to despatch No. 284 of this office of December 1, 1936,[78] entitled "Report of Italian Recognition of 'Manchukuo' " as well as previous despatches on this subject and Italian consular representation in Manchuria.

There is enclosed an extract [79] from the Dairen *Manchuria Daily News* reporting that the Italian Ambassador in Tokyo requested permission through the "Manchukuo" Ambassador to establish a Consulate General in Mukden and that the request was granted.

According to Mr. A. Maffei, the local Italian Consul, this report is true. Such negotiations as took place in this matter were carried on in Tokyo and Mr. Maffei had no part in them. This action probably constitutes *de facto* recognition of "Manchukuo" inasmuch as the permission of the "Manchukuo" government was formally requested to establish the new Consulate General. Mr. Maffei does not believe that his government plans to fully recognize "Manchukuo" and establish a legation at Hsinking at present.

Respectfully yours,
GEORGE D. LAMONT

---

[77] Copy transmitted to the Department by the Consul at Harbin in his despatch No. 443, December 4; received January 5, 1937.
[78] Not printed.
[79] Not reprinted.

893.01 Inner Mongolia/92 : Telegram

The Counselor of Embassy in China (Lockhart) to the Secretary of State

PEIPING, December 8, 1936—1 p. m.
[Received December 8—7 : 40 a. m. [80]]

592. Following from Mukden:

"December 7, 6 p. m. Concordia Society today made following [statement?] through its [president?] Premier Chang [of Manchoukuo].

'In order to give concrete expression to its wholehearted spiritual support of the Inner Mongolia volunteer army which has taken up arms to destroy bandit Communism, this society, which has declared itself against Communism, had decided to campaign far and wide among Japanese and Manchurians for donations to aid the said army'.

"An acquaintance reported seeing at Mukden station last week special train of 19 cars of wounded Japanese, enroute presumably to the local base hospital, adding that 100 severely wounded are being treated in the South Manchuria Railway Hospital and that Japanese wounded arrive daily in great numbers evidently from Suiyuan front."

Report on "Manchukuo Concordia Society" was made in Mukden's despatch No. 304, of July 28, copies of which were sent directly to the Department.[81]
Nanking informed.

LOCKHART

793.94/8421 : Telegram

The Ambassador in Japan (Grew) to the Secretary of State

TOKYO, December 8, 1936—6 p. m.
[Received December 8—9 : 40 a. m.]

254. 1. Some observers in Tokyo believe that the landing of Japanese marines in Tsingtau has a political rather than a defensive background. They base their opinion on the following facts and theories: (a) a landing force of 800 men appears to be excessive under the circumstances; (b) the Sino-Japanese diplomatic negotiations having been suspended, the landing of marines in Tsingtau may be the first step in a policy of bringing stronger military pressure to bear on China, possibly with a view to forcing the reopening of the negotiations; and (c) Tsingtau being a vital strategic point for any Japanese military action against China, the Japanese may have used the strike as an excuse to take over control of the city. The Naval and Military Attachés of the Embassy are inclined to concur in these views.

---

[80] Telegram in two sections.
[81] Not printed.

2. Without ruling out the possibilities implied in paragraph 1 (*c*), the Embassy considers it also possible that the landing of the unusually large force at Tsingtau may have been intended as a demonstration to the Chinese of the reported determination of the Japanese to take "self-defensive" measures for the protection of Japanese nationals and interests should all diplomatic negotiations to this end definitely cease.

3. The Military Attaché of the Embassy in a conversation with the assistant Liaison Officer of the War Office today was told that the tension in Tsingtau had relaxed, the Chinese forces having been withdrawn from contact with the Japanese forces; that the Mayor of Tsingtau had been instructed by Chiang Kai Shek not to aggravate the situation; that the Mayor was showing "sincerity" in complying with the Japanese demands; and that the Japanese demands on the Mayor were substantially as published in the press. (The demands as reported by Domei were: (*a*) the dissolution of the Tsingtau branches of the Kuomintang; (*b*) punishment of municipal officials who have been backing the strikers; (*c*) apology by the Mayor, and (*d*) expulsion of "irregular" Koreans from the city.)

Repeated to Peiping.

GREW

793.94/8427 : Telegram

The Ambassador in Japan (Grew) to the Secretary of State

TOKYO, December 9, 1936—9 p. m.
[Received December 9—1: 15 p. m.]

255. Embassy's 252, December 5, 6 p. m., paragraph 2.[82]

1. Sentiment favoring the resignation of the Hirota Cabinet is accumulating. Increasingly outspoken opposition to the international position into which Japan has been led by the agreement with Germany is being expressed throughout the country. The general policy in China does not seem to be a dominant factor in the dissatisfaction with the Cabinet but the disapproval of the failure of the Foreign Office to obtain satisfactory results appears to predispose the military and the leaders of the political parties toward the overthrow of the Hirota Cabinet.

2. This afternoon the Minister for Foreign Affairs is appearing before the Privy Council to defend the Cabinet's foreign policies. The press predicts difficulties for the Government.

3. Apart from political maneuvering in the Cabinet situation the serious interest of leaders is partially concerned with the advisability of the overthrow of the Cabinet at this juncture for the effect of such a step on world opinion. In other words the question at issue is

---

[82] Not printed.

whether the enforced resignation of the Cabinet would assist in quieting foreign apprehensions that the Japanese Government intends to develop the recently concluded agreement with Germany in the direction of a sweeping new orientation of Japanese foreign policy.

4. The Embassy inclines to the opinion that while the German-Japanese agreement may be used as a means of attack on the Cabinet, the actual underlying cause of any such attack will be the loss of face involved in the failure of the Japanese negotiations with China.

Repeated to Peiping.

GREW

893.00/13751 : Telegram

The Counselor of Embassy in China (Lockhart) to the Secretary of State

PEIPING, December 10, 1936—5 p. m.
[Received December 10—2 : 30 p. m.[83]]

601. Embassy's 586, December 4, 1. p. m.[84] Today's Chinese press reports the capture by Suiyuan forces of Tamiao (Sharramuren), an important point of strategic importance northeast of Pailingmiao. A foreigner upon whom great reliance can be placed has returned from Suiyuan and states that Tamiao was the first objective of the Suiyuan forces in their countermovement against Chahar, and that the present plans of the regulars envisage the capture of Shangtu and Chapatante. He states that three Nanking divisions are on the line from Pingtichuan to Tatung, but says no Government planes are at the front. The regular forces have suffered somewhat from bombing attacks in which, according to chairman Fu Tso Yi, 20 and 60 pound bombs were commonly used. This informant stated that some of Wang Ying's subordinates have apparently been bought over to the Government side, and that in view of the adverse weather conditions and other factors, it is difficult to conceive of any important Manchukuo supported countermove before spring.

A Chinese official in conversation stated yesterday that there is in fact an oral agreement, such as is mentioned in Nanking's 342, December 4, 1 p. m.[84] He gave it as his opinion that it was concluded about June 1935 while Ho Ying Chin was still in Peiping and that it provided for the effective extension of the demilitarized zone to include the six districts of Southeast Chahar.

He stated in addition that Sung Che Yuan, under orders from Chiang Kai Shek, has moved two divisions to be ready to enter Chahar

[83] Telegram in two sections.
[84] Not printed.

in a flanking movement should reenforcements be sent from Jehol to meet a Chinese thrust into Chahar, which he also forecasts.

By mail to Tokyo.

LOCKHART

793.94/8481

The Ambassador in China (Johnson) to the Secretary of State

No. 277

NANKING, December 10, 1936.
[Received January 4, 1937.]

SIR: I have the honor to transmit a self-explanatory memorandum of conversation which I held on December 3, 1936, with Mr. Suma, Japanese Consul General and First Secretary of Embassy in Nanking.

The Department's attention will doubtless be drawn to Mr. Suma's statement to the effect that until recently the Chinese and Japanese negotiators had found themselves ninety per cent in material agreement in regard to the questions under discussion. I may observe in this connection that possibly Mr. Suma was able to envisage agreement on ninety per cent of the total number of points under discussion, counting all minor points, but there has at no time appeared any evidence indicating even a remote understanding as regards the several vital matters at issue. This statement by Mr. Suma may have been dictated by a desire to make it appear that the breakdown in negotiations resulted from a sudden reversal of position on the part of China. It will be recalled that the recent incident which took place when the Chinese Minister for Foreign Affairs refused to accept an Aide-Mémoire from the Japanese Ambassador, was explained, according to the Chinese version, by the assertion that the Aide-Mémoire represented the Chinese Foreign Minister as having gone further than he could or would admit, in meeting the Japanese point of view.

Mr. Suma struck what to me was a surprising note in his statement that he had long entertained the thought that Japan and the United States should do something to bring about political stability in the Pacific. It will be observed that he coupled this remark with the statement that he had recently, during his visit to Japan, had occasion to discover that the same thought was in the minds of "a number of very important people in Japan."

Mr. Suma's observations suggest the possibility that there may be a growing tendency in Japanese official circles to seek American cooperation and understanding, as the means toward a breathing space, until such time as she is more sure of herself than at present.

Respectfully yours,

NELSON TRUSLER JOHNSON

[Enclosure]

Memorandum by the Ambassador in China (Johnson)

NANKING, December 3, 1936.

Mr. Y. Suma, Consul General and First Secretary of the Japanese Embassy, called, and in the course of conversation he remarked that the situation between China and Japan had not materially improved. He stated that during the last month or so he had noticed a distinct change for the worse in the attitude of the Chinese toward the Japanese, and that even the soldiers and officers of General Chiang's own troops were now urging a more anti-Japanese attitude. He ascribed this to several causes, among which he gave first place to the suspicions raised in China by the Japanese-German agreement recently signed in Berlin; but he also mentioned the Suiyuan situation which he described as very serious and very embarrassing to Japan.

He stated that the Japanese Ambassador had had seven or eight meetings with the Minister for Foreign Affairs, but that he and other members of the staff had had many meetings with the Chinese, and he could say that up to recently they had found themselves ninety per cent in material agreement in regard to the questions under discussion. However, the Chinese were now hesitating going any further in the matter because of the complications above referred to. He said they were now awaiting the report of an officer who had been sent by the Ministry of Foreign Affairs to Suiyuan to investigate the situation on the spot.

With reference to the agreement between Germany and Japan calling for cooperation against the Comintern, Mr. Suma stated that this had been negotiated and signed in Berlin. From the way he referred to it I inferred that he felt the agreement had complicated matters very much for Japan here in China, for he stated that, although the Japanese Foreign Office had made a very positive statement to the effect that Japan would alone take steps to meet any threat from the Comintern, the Chinese seemed to be very suspicious. In this connection he also mentioned the Italian-Japanese agreement.

Referring to the Suiyuan situation, he stated that this was very serious; that, whereas Chiang Kai-shek had not made up his mind in regard to the matter, he was being urged by a considerable part of his supporters to send the national forces now at Suiyuan into Chahar. He said that if these forces went into Chahar the situation would become most difficult.

Mr. Suma's attitude seemed to be pessimistic. After a pause he branched out upon a line which, for him in his conversations with me, was very strange, and maybe significant. He said that on his recent visit to Tokyo, whither he had gone for the purpose of making a report to the Cabinet Council on Chinese conditions, with particular reference to their negotiations, he had had opportunity to talk with a number of very important people in Japan, during which conversations he had discovered that there was a great deal of sentiment in favor of an idea which he had long held. This idea was one which he had had in mind when he was in the Foreign Office and had charge of American affairs. Briefly put, his idea was that the very bad situation in the Pacific and in Asia should be stabilized, and he thought that America should do something to bring about such stabilization. He mentioned the League as a product of American idealists, and the fact that America had withdrawn; stated that he thought America and Japan might find it possible by some very simple agreement to stabilize the situation; referred to the Lansing–Ishii notes [86] as an example of what he had in mind; mentioned the Pacific, the Philippines, as the area which he believes will be covered. He was careful to state that these were his personal thoughts and that he was astonished that the higher authorities in Tokyo were not laboring to accomplish something along these lines, and asked what my personal opinion was.

I stated that I felt sure the United States wished to live at peace with all of its neighbors; that it sought only their friendship and good will, being prepared to give its friendship and good will in return. I remarked that the stabilization of the situation in the East and in the Pacific by an arrangement such as Mr. Suma had in mind might be a very complicated matter. I referred to the fact that attached to the naval agreement [87] there was a four-power arrangement [88] under which the signatory powers, which included Japan and the United States, agreed to consult one another about their mutual interests (in their insular possessions) in the Pacific area. I stated that I was in some doubt as to the present status of the naval agreement and those agreements ancillary thereto, but that I thought they offered the approach necessary. They were at least recorded efforts to do the very thing which Mr. Suma presumably had in mind. I said that doubtless a great deal would have to be discussed preliminary to any stabilizing understanding. Mr. Suma agreed.

The conversation then dwindled off and he made his departure, but I was somewhat puzzled by his approach. He left me feeling that the Japanese are not as sure of themselves as they have seemed to be, and that there appear to have been in official circles discussions of a possibility of Japan enlisting American support for an understanding which would establish the *status quo* as Japan had succeeded in building it up, thus giving her breathing space for a time.

NELSON TRUSLER JOHNSON

---

[86] Dated November 2, 1917, at Washington, *Foreign Relations*, 1917, p. 264.
[87] Treaty signed at Washington, February 6, 1922, *Foreign Relations*, 1922, vol. I, p. 247.
[88] Treaty signed at Washington, December 13, 1921, *ibid.*, p. 33.

693.94244/180

The Ambassador in China (Johnson) to the Secretary of State

No. 913
PEIPING, December 10, 1936.
[Received January 4, 1937.]

SIR: I have the honor to enclose a copy of despatch No. 13 of December 7, 1936, from the Consul at Tsinan [89] in which he reports the seizure by the Shantung Provincial authorities of a number of trucks in various parts of the Province, operated by armed Japanese and Korean smugglers. The smugglers are reported to have been arrested and turned over to the Japanese Consul General at Tsinan, while the trucks were detained at the Governor's Yamen. This is described as the first serious attempt on the part of the Governor to stop smuggling in Shantung Province. Consul Allison states that although all the elements are present for a real crisis, it is his opinion that there is no immediate danger of Sino-Japanese trouble.[90]

Respectfully yours,
For the Ambassador:
F. P. LOCKHART
Counselor of Embassy

711.0012 Anti-War/1516

Memorandum by the Ambassador in China (Johnson) [91]

NANKING, December 12, 1936.

During the course of conversation to-day Sir Hughe [92] stated that he had a matter of some delicacy which he wished to communicate to me, and expressed the hope that if I saw Hsu Mo I would not mention it to him. He said that during a call which he had made at the Foreign Office, Mr. Hsu Mo, Vice Minister for Foreign Affairs, had made a suggestion to him which he, Hsu Mo, said was purely an idea of his own. He wondered what Sir Hughe's personal reaction was to a proposal or suggestion that the powers join in a kind of a joint statement in support of the Kellogg Pact. He had in mind a statement to be made perhaps by the British, the Americans, the Japanese, and the French, and in fact, all interested powers. His interest in such a suggestion arose out of a recently published agreement between Germany and Japan.

---

[89] Not printed.
[90] On December 23 the trucks with contents were turned over to the Japanese Consul General at Tsinan after he had given oral assurance "that no more smuggling by Japanese or Koreans would occur in Shantung." (693.94244/196)
[91] Copy transmitted to the Department by the Ambassador in China in his despatch No. 285, December 15; received January 14, 1937.
[92] Sir Hughe Montgomery Knatchbull-Hugessen, British Ambassador in China.

Sir Hughe said that he told Mr. Hsu Mo that there were difficulties in such a proposal; that as far as the British Government was concerned Sir Anthony Eden [93] had already made its position clear vis-à-vis the German-Japanese agreement by a statement in Parliament deprecating national blocks.

He asked Mr. Hsu Mo whether he had mentioned this proposition to any one else. Hsu Mo stated that he intended to talk to the American Ambassador about it. His idea was that the statement would include as many powers as possible, even Japan.

I told Sir Hughe that of course I was in no position whatever to anticipate the reaction of the United States to such a suggestion; that the difficulties were obvious; that we had made our position quite clear in regard to the Kellogg Pact from time to time; that of course I would be interested in hearing whatever Mr. Hsu Mo might have to say on the subject and would report it to my Government.

NELSON TRUSLER JOHNSON

893.00/13756 : Telegram

The Ambassador in China (Johnson) to the Secretary of State

NANKING, December 13, 1936—10 a. m.
[Received December 13—8 a. m.]

349. Reuter this morning carries following official statement issued at 5 a. m.:

"Telegraphic communications with Sian were interrupted this morning. Later reports were received that Chang Hsueh Liang with his troops had rebelled against the Central Government. Meanwhile, a circular telegram was issued advocating the overthrow of the Government. In this telegram it was clearly stated that he was offering 'the final advice to General Chiang Kai Shek' and was temporarily detaining General Chiang at Sian. At an emergency meeting of the Government leaders, it was decided that: (1) H. H. Kung will be in charge of the Executive Yuan; (2) The Standing Committee of the National Military Council will have from five to seven members. Ho Ying Chin, Chen Chien, Li Lieh Chun, Chu Pei Teh, Tang Sheng Chi, and Chen Shao Kuanz will be members of the Standing Committee; (3) Feng Yu Hsiang and members of the Standing Committee will be in charge of the Military Council's meetings; (4) General Ho Ying Chin will be in charge of troops movements and military operations; (5) Chang Hsueh Liang shall be dismissed from all posts and handed to the National Military Council for punishment. His non-commissioned officers shall be placed under the command of the National Military Council."

Vice Minister for Foreign Affairs Hsu Mo with whom I talked this morning confirms reports stating that Chang Hsueh Liang to whom

---

[93] British Secretary of State for Foreign Affairs.

was entrusted the Government's campaign against the Communists has apparently made common cause with them and is withdrawing his troops who were opposing them. Hsu Mo states that Government feels that it can control situation.

Reuter reports that Chang Hsueh Liang in a circular telegram advocates resistance against Japan, Chinese treaty with Soviet Russia and the formation of democratic government.

Nanking is quiet.

Sent to the Department, Tokyo, Peiping.

JOHNSON

893.00/13754 : Telegram

The Counselor of Embassy in China (Lockhart) to the Secretary of State

PEIPING, December 13, 1936—1 p. m.
[Received December 13—7 a. m.]

604. Embassy's 603, December 13, 11 a. m.[94] Apparently under the initial stimulus offered by the funeral services of Tuan Chi Jui,[95] some 400 Peiping students met yesterday afternoon upon the invitation of Sung Che Yuan after previous demonstrations which threatened some disorder and in which several students received injuries. The gates of the meeting place were first locked and troops put in position. Sung did not arrive but the Mayor came instead and spoke to the students in a conciliatory manner. The meeting apparently had anti-Japanese aspects and hand bills were distributed. These demand the breaking off of relations with Japan; resistance to Japanese troops in Suiyuan and Tsingtao; attack on the East Hopei regime of Yin Ju Keng; retrieving of North Chahar and Manchuria; support of the 29th Army and other patriotic defense organizations.

It is reported without confirmation that a demonstration along somewhat the same lines and incorporating the same general demands occurred at Sian on December 9 and that Chang Hsueh Liang "gave his acceptance" to the program of the meeting after which the demonstrators made a long march to present to Chiang Kai Shek the demands for an anti-Japanese policy.

Repeated to Tokyo.

LOCKHART

---

[94] Not printed; it reported the same information as telegram No. 349, December 13, 10 a. m., *supra.*
[95] Provisional Chief Executive at Peking, 1924–26.

893.00/13755 : Telegram

The Counselor of Embassy in China (Lockhart) to the Secretary of State

PEIPING, December 13, 1936—3 p. m.
[Received December 13—9 a. m.]

605. My 603 [96] and 604. 1. Chang Hsueh Liang's troops whose mutiny against the Central Government seems to have been the cause of the detention of Chiang Kai Shek by Chang are said to have made certain demands of Nanking among them being: 1, war against Japan; 2, an alliance with Soviet Russia; 3, admission of Communists to Kuomintang; and 4, moderation of formal constitution instead of dictatorship.

2. Reuter reports Madame Chiang Kai Shek has received at Nanking personal message from Chang Hsueh Liang guaranteeing her husband's safety.

3. There has been dissension between Chiang and Chang for sometime over the latter's failure to deal effectively with the Communists in the Northwest and it is possible that the present difficulty is the outgrowth of that failure as well as personal animosity especially in view of the reported appointment by Chiang Kai Shek on December 11 of General Chiang Ting Wen as Commander in Chief of bandit suppression in the Northwest in succession to Chang Hsueh Liang. Marshal Chang has from time to time been charged with sympathetic leanings towards the Communists troops.

4. The revolt and detention of Chiang has created a tremendous sensation in Peiping and it is known that there is great activity in Chinese circles. It is understood that Sung Che Yuan's attitude towards Nanking has not changed and that his attitude towards communism in the Northwest has not been altered by the new turn of events. Repeated to Tokyo and Nanking.

LOCKHART

793.94/8436 : Telegram

The Counselor of Embassy in China (Lockhart) to the Secretary of State

PEIPING, December 13, 1936—4 p. m.
[Received December 13—1 : 30 p. m.]

606. The Consulate at Tsingtao by mail despatch dated December 11 [96] confirms report that the strike there has been amicably adjusted on the following terms:

---

[93] Not printed.

1. Punishment of the principal offenders among the bad labor elements who have been discharged.

2. The foregoing bad labor elements to be deported from Tsingtao.

3. Beside the deporting of bad labor elements a strict watch over and control of other discharged laborers to be exercised by the Chinese authorities. In the event there is a recurrence (of the labor trouble) the Chinese authorities will be held strictly responsible.

4. Agitators of present labor trouble are to be deported.

5. The Chinese authorities are not only not to place obstacles in the way of laborers who wish to resume work but the authorities by proclamation and other appropriate means are positively to encourage and urge the resumption of work by the laborers.

6. The discharged bad labor elements must not be employed by the Municipal Administration.

7. The Chinese police are to exercise vigilance over bad elements among the laborers so as to preserve peace and order.

Some of the Japanese landing party have already returned to their ships according to press reports and the remainder will be withdrawn by December 15, but this is not confirmed by Tsingtao Consulate.

Repeated to Nanking, by mail to Tokyo.

LOCKHART

893.00/13759 : Telegram

The Ambassador in China (Johnson) to the Secretary of State

NANKING, December 14, 1936—10 a. m.
[Received December 14—7:30 a. m.]

350. 1. Nanking continues quiet. Kung on assuming duties as Acting President of the Executive Yuan issued an appeal to the people to support the Government, the text of which is not being telegraphed as I assume it is carried by the press. Hsu Mo informed me this morning that Central authorities had received telegrams supporting the Government from Sung Che Yuan and other provincial governments and expressed confidence that Government can control situation. Donald is in Loyang trying to get in touch with Chang Hsueh Liang. Hsu Mo also told me that the central authorities are in touch with Sian by radio.

2. Central News Agency under date of December 13 carries a long appeal from Feng Yu Hsiang to Chang Hsueh Liang offering amnesty if he will release Chiang and discuss matters frankly with Government; offers himself as hostage as evidence of his sincerity. In this appeal Feng expressed belief that Chiang will accede to Chang Hsueh Liang's request and added "thus, your difficulties will be solved and your wish of fighting Japan may be expressed."

3. By mail to Peiping.

JOHNSON

793.94/8437 : Telegram

The Ambassador in Japan (Grew) to the Secretary of State

TOKYO, December 14, 1936—noon.
[Received December 14—10 a. m.]

258. 1. The British Ambassador has told me that Eden had called on the Chinese Ambassador in London and had strongly advised him to urge his Government not to overplay its hand. As matters stand at present the Japanese Cabinet finds itself in a precarious position owing to the adverse public reaction to the agreement with Germany, the consequent holding up of the Fisheries Treaty by Soviet Russia and the failure of the negotiations with China. The British Government believes that China has everything to gain by making such unessential concessions as will save Japan's face. If on the other hand Nanking proves completely recalcitrant to all overtures the result will tend to solidify and unify Japanese public opinion in favor of stronger measures.

2. I am informed that Moscow has made similar recommendations to Nanking.

3. The Chinese Ambassador here, after describing to me the various Japanese demands presented in the recent conversations in Nanking, the replies given to those demands and the counterdemands presented by the Chinese Government, said that no further negotiations would be possible until the Chinese troops in Suiyuan had driven out the Japanese-supported Mongolian forces but that the Chinese forces would stop at the frontier in order not to invite direct attack from the Kwantung army. He said that the Mongolian forces were now surrendering in large numbers and that there was no question as to the early suppression of the entire movement. The impression derived from his talk and manner was that China is at present "feeling its oats" and is very likely to overplay its hand in resisting Japanese overtures.

4. Sir Charles Addis of the Hong Kong [and] Shanghai Bank told Eden that the Japanese representative of the Yokahama Specie Bank in London had said to him that the Japanese military had definitely given up for the present any thought of separating North China from Nanking.

5. The foregoing telegram was drafted prior to the reported rebellion of Chang Hsueh Liang.

Repeated to Peiping.

GREW

893.00/13760a : Telegram

The Acting Secretary of State to the Ambassador in China (Johnson)

WASHINGTON, December 14, 1936—1 p. m.

79. Department desires that, unless you perceive objection (in which event you should promptly cable the Department to that effect, citing reasons), you call on the Minister for Foreign Affairs or on the Acting Chairman of the Executive Yuan, or both, and express orally, as under instruction, the American Government's solicitude with regard to the safety of the person of Chiang Kai-shek, Chairman of the Executive Yuan.

Please inform the Department by telegram when you have carried out this instruction.

MOORE

893.00/13764a : Telegram

The Acting Secretary of State to the Ambassador in China (Johnson)

WASHINGTON, December 14, 1936—2 p. m.

80. In view of the important political implications, both internal and international, of the present situation and possible developments at and connected with Sianfu, I desire that you give most solicitous attention to those matters, making full report of outstanding facts in the immediate situation and of related facts; and that you maintain close contact with Chinese officialdom and your diplomatic colleagues, especially the British. There may exist or may arise an opportunity for appropriate use of influence by representatives of foreign governments in the best interest of all concerned. It stands to reason that interference with the normal functioning of the National Government in China, especially if this should involve procedures of unlawful violence among and against high officials and perhaps a domestic military conflict, would impair and impede the progress which China has been making toward establishing political stability and economic well-being, would impose new hardships on the Chinese people, would create a new menace to foreign lives and property and interests in general in China, and would add to the danger of international conflict in the Far East. The situation therefore is of concern to the world. It is, as you know, the policy of this Government not to interfere or intervene in the internal affairs of foreign countries. At the same time, we cannot be indifferent to developments anywhere which jeopardize the interests of nations which are earnestly seeking political and economic stability and which may inject new hazards into an international situation already delicate. We are not prepared at this moment to say or to suggest that any action might appro-

priately be taken by this or other governments in relation to the situation under reference; but we will be carefully observing developments therein and studying the question of possible helpful action. I therefore desire that you give us the benefit of careful observation and study on your part, consultation with your colleagues, and, promptly and continuously, any comments or suggestions which you may formulate.

MOORE

893.00/13763 : Telegram

The Counselor of Embassy in China (Lockhart) to the Secretary of State

PEIPING, December 14, 1936—4 p. m.
[Received December 14—3 : 27 p. m.]

608.   1. Chinese officials interviewed today appear to be in a very confused state of mind regarding events in Shensi, and are apparently without information except that which comes from Nanking. It is very evident that at least some of them have come to the conclusion that Chiang Kai Shek is dead although they have no direct information to sustain that conclusion. Information coming from Nanking seems to indicate that Chiang is alive but it is pointed out that some significance may be attached to the fact that no direct word seems to have been received from him by the Chinese officials and that there has been a reorganization of the Military Council at Nanking.

2. A well-informed foreigner (See first paragraph Embassy's despatch No. 869, November 18 [98]) gives it as his opinion that the present move has been in contemplation for some time between Chang Hsueh Liang and a number of his commanders and that it is designed to force Chiang Kai Shek's hand for the formation of a constitutional government with all factions participating and with a united front against the Japanese. He believes that there is little foundation for the report that Chang Hsueh Liang will attempt to establish a separate government in the northwest.

3. It is well known that Chang Hsueh Liang's troops have for a year been subjected to nationalistic propaganda of Chinese Communism. In November, before the capture of Pailingmiao from the irregulars, Chang proposed to Chiang that the Northeastern troops should be despatched to the Suiyuan front to resist the irregulars, but Chiang refused the request as premature. Previously the animosity between the two men had been increased as a result of ill-feeling between Chang and Yang Yung Tai (Chiang's right hand man, the Governor of Hupeh, recently assassinated).

The recent convocation of high officials at Sian was for the nominal

_____
[98] Not printed.

purpose of discussing the proposal for direct united action of all Chinese factions against Japan, but at the meeting Chiang is said to have adopted a strong attitude against Chang and all proposals for military action against Japan in conjunction with the Communist forces. A Northeastern army man is quoted as stating that the Chang Hsueh Liang group reached the final decision that Chiang Kai Shek actually has an agreement with Japan, that Chiang intended to eliminate Chang and the Northeastern troops from the scene, and that with consolidation of his power Chiang would have definitely joined the so-called Fascist front of Japan, Germany and Italy. The convocation of many important Nanking officials at Sian offered the desired opportunity, and the demonstration of December 9 (See Embassy's telegram No. 604, December 13, 1 p. m.) provided the immediate stimulus. A certain unit of Chang's troops sometime subsequently is reported to have surrounded Chiang's place of residence, and some fighting is said to have occurred before his bodyguard surrendered. (Some reports have it that all of the bodyguard were killed). One local newspaper reports that more than 50 important figures of Chiang's group were taken in custody including Yu Hsueh Chung.[99]

Student organizations meeting yesterday in Peiping declared themselves as definitely opposed to civil war while they declared themselves in favor of propositions similar to those allegedly announced by Chang Hsueh Liang. At the same time it is announced that Sung Che Yuan, Han Fu Chu and Yen Hsi Shan have already issued a joint statement to the effect that they are opposed to civil war and to alliance with the Communists.

A telegram sent by Feng Yu Hsiang to Chang is couched in conciliatory terms. It requests the release [of] Chiang Kai Shek in return for which hostages will be sent "as guarantee" if necessary, suggests that Chang's proposals would thereupon receive adequate consideration and promises that the telegram castigating Chang and relieving him of his posts would be withdrawn if Chang accepts the proposals.

4. The immediate objective of the Chinese officials judging by press reports is to obtain the release of Chiang Kai Shek, the suppression of the rebellion and the discussion of demands being a secondary consideration.

5. Tientsin reports that freight service is practically suspended on Tientsin–Pukow and Lunghai lines to give way to transportation of troops (presumably westward).

By mail to Tokyo.

LOCKHART

---

[99] Commander of Peace Preservation forces in Szechwan and Kansu.

793.94/8502

The Ambassador in China (Johnson) to the Secretary of State

No. 917   Peiping, December 14, 1936.
                                               [Received January 14, 1937.]

Sir: I have the honor to enclose a copy of despatch No. 536 of December 8, 1936, from the Consulate General at Shanghai,[1] in which there is given a translation of a statement covering Sino-Japanese issues reported to have been dictated by General Huang Fu, former high Chinese Government official prior to his death on December 6, 1936. In the statement General Huang advises the Chinese people to support General Chiang Kai-shek in his work of rejuvenating the country and advises Japan that unless it desists from its activities in North China and its support of the bogus regime of "Manchukuo" *rapprochement* between the two oriental countries will be impossible.

Mr. Gauss states that he believes that General Huang's statement reflects the attitude of the most enlightened Chinese regarding the present Sino-Japanese situation.

Respectfully yours,   For the Ambassador:
                                                  F. P. Lockhart
                                                  Counselor of Embassy

---

893.00/13765 : Telegram

The Counselor of Embassy in China (Lockhart) to the Secretary of State

                                               Peiping, December 15, 1936—3 p. m.
                                               [Received December 15—8 a. m.]

612. 1. General Sung Che Yuan sent principal assistant to see me this morning to say, on behalf of the General, that: (1) General Sung will be responsible for the declaration of peace and order in Hopei and Chahar; (2) no matter whether Chiang Kai Shek returns to Nanking or is detained in Sian General Sung will continue to obey the orders of the Nanking Government, and (3) General Sung will not alter his policy of anti-Communism.

2. General Sung's office does not yet have definite information of the release of General Chiang Kai Shek.

3. General Sung's representative informed me that Yin Ju Keng, head of the East Hopei Anti-Communist Autonomous Government, left 4 days ago for Changchun, Manchuria, for conference with the Manchukuo authorities. He seemed to think some important negotiations may be going on in Changchun.

Repeated to Nanking, by mail to Tokyo.

                                                                      Lockhart

---

[1] Not printed.

893.00/13767 : Telegram

The Ambassador in China (Johnson) to the Secretary of State

NANKING, December 15, 1936—4 p. m.
[Received December 15—9 : 35 a. m.]

352. Your 79, December 14, 1 p. m. I expect to see Minister for Foreign Affairs at 4 p. m. today and convey Department's message. Nanking quiet. Situation unchanged. Government anxiously awaiting news of Donald's visit Sian. Troops continue to move north.

JOHNSON

793.94/8438 : Telegram

The Counselor of Embassy in China (Lockhart) to the Secretary of State

PEIPING, December 15, 1936—6 p. m.
[Received December 15—9 : 25 a. m.]

613. Embassy's 600, December 10, 4 p. m.[2] Following from Tsingtau:

"December 15, 3 p. m. Three hundred members of Japanese landing party have been withdrawn to their ships. Remainder have been withdrawn from cotton mills to billets in Tsingtau.
City is very quiet".

To Tokyo by mail.

LOCKHART

893.00/13774 : Telegram

The Ambassador in China (Johnson) to the Secretary of State

NANKING, December 16, 1936—noon.
[Received 4 : 55 p. m.]

354. Department's 80, December 14, 2 p. m.

1. Situation created by detention of General Chiang Kai Shek has been rendered exceedingly obscure by lack of any information from Sian as to purposes of Chang Hsueh Liang. Either of following may be true (*a*) Chang Hsueh Liang controlled by disaffected officers from among own discontented northeastern troops may have seized Chiang Kai Shek and his entourage for the purpose of coercing Central Government to meet pay requirements and adopt a stronger attitude toward Japan (*b*) Chang Hsueh Liang and his troops may have made common cause with the Communists and therefore seized Chiang and his entourage for the purpose of compelling Central Government to

---

[2] Not printed.

desist from attacks against Communists and adopt recent declared policy of Communist forces for more active opposition to Japan, a revival of revolutionary policy of Government and the adoption of a more friendly policy toward Soviet Russia.

2. I called on Minister for Foreign Affairs yesterday and conveyed to him our Government's solicitude for the safety of General Chiang. Foreign Minister thanked me for message and told me that the action of Chang Hsueh Liang came as a complete surprise and shock to the Government and that Government was now undertaking to do everything possible to obtain release of Chiang but that in any case, with the support of the provinces and the people, who had been unanimous in condemning Chang Hsueh Liang, the Government purposed continuing routes hitherto adopted by them. The Minister for Foreign Affairs was much worried because no news had been received from Donald who was reported to have arrived at Sian at 2 p. m. on Monday. Later in the evening I learned confidentially from a newspaper source that Madame Chiang Kai Shek had received a message from Donald reporting Chiang's safety. Newspaper source stated that source of his information close to Madame Chiang intimated that Communists were not in control of Sian and seemed to feel cheerful as to outcome in view of terms which Donald was supposed to have communicated as from Chang Hsueh Liang. This morning Vice Minister Hsu Mo confirmed receipt of message from Donald at Loyang by Madame Chiang. Vice Minister stated situation had not changed, that Government troops were nearing Sian. He did not communicate to me contents of message or its nature other than to say that Chiang Kai Shek was safe.

3. I have maintained close contact with my British, French and German colleagues since Sunday. We are all agreed that situation is serious but perceive no beneficial action which we can recommend or take. Hsu Mo reported that Donald was returning to Sian which would indicate that negotiations of some kind are under way.

4. For some time it has been known that the northeastern troops now in Shensi and Chang Hsueh Liang were discontented with their lot and with the Government's policy vis-à-vis Japan. It is known that while [Chang] Hsueh Liang was withdrawing his forces which had been sent against Communist forces that the Northeastern troops have been the object of propaganda from student and radical agitators. Chiang knew this when he went to Sian. I foresee that any negotiations which may result in Chiang's release may result in a change in the Government's policy but it is difficult yet to forecast events.

5. Sent to the Department, code text by mail to Peiping.

JOHNSON

893.00/13770 : Telegram

The Counselor of Embassy in China (Lockhart) to the Secretary of State

PEIPING, December 16, 1936—2 p.m.
[Received December 16—6 : 30 a.m.]

615. 1. Except for the growing belief, apparently now well-founded, that General Yang Hu Cheng has not actually staged a revolt and that General Chiang Kai Shek is still under restraint, the situation at Peiping vis-à-vis the Sian imbroglio remains unchanged with a welter of misinformation being circulated, some for political, some with a view, apparently, to influencing the Chinese bond and stock market (notably of Chiang's release and return to Nanking which had its origin, it is now learned, in Chinese banking circles) and some based on mere hope and speculation. The only encouraging aspect of the whole unfortunate situation, as I see it, is the remarkable capacity of the Chinese for extricating themselves from critical situations. Whether the present one is beyond their customary resourcefulness remains to be seen but the possibility of settlement by negotiation and compromise rather than by military operation offers perhaps the best prospect of releasing Chiang and solution of the problem, which unquestionably has shaken the whole of China as no other incident in recent years has done.

Repeated to Tokyo.

LOCKHART

793.94/8450 : Telegram

The Counselor of Embassy in China (Lockhart) to the Secretary of State

PEIPING, December 16, 1936—3 p.m.
[Received December 16—2 p.m.]

616. Berger [3] reports that there have recently occurred several robberies of American and British property at Peitaiho Beach, now under the control of the "East Hopei Anti-Communist Autonomous Government". Berger states that the British Consul General at Tientsin has made representations to the Chief of Police at Peitaiho and he requests instructions regarding the advisability of his addressing similar representations to that official. The Embassy considers that Berger might appropriately address an informal communication to the "Chief of Police, Peitaiho Beach", on strictly police matter and that this action would not be likely to imply any recognition of the East Hopei regime.

---

[3] David C. Berger, Consul at Tientsin.

2. Berger also reports that the "East Hopei Anti-Communist Autonomous Government" has issued an "instruction" to the three foreign oil companies operating in North China, directing them to pay import duties on all goods shipped into territory controlled by that regime. Standard Vacuum Oil Company has protested to the Commissioner of Customs at Tientsin against this additional taxation on the ground that the East Hopei regime is not recognized by the Chinese Government and that its territory is still under the jurisdiction of the Chinese Maritime Customs. No reply has been received to that protest and it does not seem likely that any effective action can be taken by the Chinese Government. The Standard Vacuum Oil Company has requested the assistance of the American authorities, but the Embassy does not feel that representations to the East Hopei regime in a matter affecting its revenue would be effective, and it likewise entertains doubt of the advisability of doing so lest its representations on so important a matter be construed as recognition of regime by the American authorities.

The Department's instructions by radio on the two matters abovementioned are respectfully requested.

LOCKHART

761.94/942

The Ambassador in Japan (Grew) to the Secretary of State

No. 2188   TOKYO, December 16, 1936.
                    [Received January 4, 1937.]

SIR: With reference to the Embassy's last despatch on the subject*, I have the honor to report that the reluctance of the Soviet Government to sign the new Fisheries Treaty, the draft of which was approved by the Privy Council on November 18, last, and which was to have been signed at Moscow on November 20, has become an issue of such importance in Soviet-Japanese relations as not only to overshadow all other outstanding issues but to strike a blow at the Hirota Cabinet itself. This situation has arisen out of the resentment shown by Moscow when the news of the German-Japanese agreement became known and the consequent retaliation on the part of the Soviet Government which took the form of refusing to sign the Fisheries Pact and of suspending all negotiations on other pending questions.

Leaving aside the wisdom of Japan's step vis-à-vis Germany, the Japanese Foreign Minister must be found guilty of a major tactical error in having imparted the fact to the Soviet Ambassador only a few days before the date set for the signature of a treaty settling the most pressing and immediate question at issue between Japan and the USSR. The swift reaction of the Soviet Government and its conse-

---

*Embassy's despatch No. 2160, November 26, 1936. [Footnote in the original.]

quences, coupled with the breakdown of the recent negotiations at Nanking over North China, caused an attack to be launched against the Hirota Cabinet which has not only severely shaken it but leaves its future uncertain.

On December 9 Mr. Arita was forced to face the Privy Council and among other things to explain the refusal of Moscow to sign the Fisheries Pact. During the course of the questioning it came out that Mr. Arita had informed the Soviet Ambassador of the German-Japanese agreement, under a pledge of secrecy, a few days before November 20, the date set for the signature of the Fisheries Treaty. Mr. Arita said that it was a matter of regret if Mr. Yurenev had communicated the matter to his home government and was pressed no further on this question. When asked what step was to be taken in case the new Fisheries Treaty was not signed, the Foreign Minister replied that there was no other way except to enforce free fishing on the strength of the rights acquired by Japanese under the Portsmouth Treaty.[4] The Council then remarked that this would be a very grave step and one which would concern the Army and Navy.

Attacks in the press continued and the *Nichi Nichi* said the following day that while the (Privy) Councillors "regard with sympathy the present mistake which Mr. Arita seems to have made in the Soviet Fishery Treaty affair, as a pitfall into which an individual easily falls, the Foreign Minister is to be censured as a diplomat for lack of foresight". The *Jiji Shimpo* a few days later predicted that "the Foreign Minister's resignation is inevitable because of general diplomatic failure", referring specifically to the Sino-Japanese negotiations and the Fisheries Pact.

At first the attitude was taken here that the Soviet Government, after recovering from its first irritation, would sign the new Treaty before the end of the year the argument being that (1) if the Pact, already approved by the Privy Council, is not signed, it will affect the fate of the Hirota Cabinet. Not only are there no prospects of a new Cabinet more friendly to the USSR than the present one but there are prospects of the opposite, and (2) if greater pressure is brought to bear upon Japan the result would be a nationwide resentment against Soviet Russia. Therefore, in order to avoid either of the two foregoing contingencies as well as to keep the faith, the Soviet Government will sign the Treaty.

However, a detailed report has reached here of Ambassador Shigemitsu's recent interview with Litvinov and the attitude of the Soviet Foreign Commissar, if correctly reported, was apparently such as to render the signing of the Fisheries Pact before the end of the year virtually impossible. Mr. Shigemitsu, under instructions, is said to have

---

[4] Russo-Japanese peace treaty signed September 5, 1905, *Foreign Relations,* 1905, p. 824.

attempted to explain the "true meaning" of the German-Japanese agreement and to have expressed a wish to seek an early settlement of various pending issues. In reply Mr. Litvinov is reported to have severely criticized the anti-Comintern Pact and to have said that it was so clearly directed against the Soviet Union that the Government could not possibly respond favorably to the Ambassador's proposals for the solution of the various pending problems.

Hope has therefore been practically abandoned that the Fisheries Treaty will be signed before the end of the year and the question is now arising as to what the situation will be regarding Japanese fisheries. If so-called "free-fishing" is declared, under the rights accruing by the terms of the Treaty of Portsmouth, the result will be a virtual rupture of diplomatic relations between the two countries because the Japanese fishing fleet will have to be supported by Japanese armed vessels and the opportunities for conflict will be frequent and unavoidable. It is however being pointed out in the press here, for the attention of the Soviet Government, that the Japanese deep sea fisheries could inflict enormous damage upon the Soviet fishery industry in Soviet territorial waters by the simple use of so-called floating nets by which salmon and trout could be entirely cut off, for instance, from the coast and rivers of Kamchatka. One paper remarked that since 1934 the number of Japanese vessels engaged in deep sea fisheries has been reduced by one half in the interest of protecting certain species of fish; but that if the Japanese fishery industries cared to do so, they could increase their activities to such an extent as to deal the salmon and trout fisheries in Soviet waters a fatal blow.

There is no doubt a great deal of truth in these contentions and, in view of the similar threat which could at any time be made to the Alaskan and Canadian salmon fisheries, the matter is of more than academic interest to the United States.

At any rate, to return to the question of Soviet-Japanese relations, the prospect for anything but an increase in friction and danger in the near future appears to be remote. Despite the feeling that the German pact may have been unskilfully handled by Mr. Arita, the knowledge that Japan has at last emerged from the isolation which followed her departure from the League of Nations and has acquired a powerful friend and ally in Germany has undoubtedly made a deep impression upon the Japanese public. If, in addition, the Hirota Cabinet with its "Hirota diplomacy" should be turned out, any succeeding Government would probably be less favorably inclined to attempt the patient negotiations with Soviet Russia followed by Mr. Hirota during the past few years which, when all is said and done, have removed many obstacles to the improvement of relations between the two countries.

Respectfully yours,   JOSEPH C. GREW

693.94244/186

The Consul at Tientsin (Berger) to the Ambassador in China (Johnson) [5]

No. 377   TIENTSIN, December 16, 1936.

SIR: I have the honor to refer to this Consulate General's weekly despatches concerning current developments in the smuggling situation in this area and to state that I have received information, through what I believe to be absolutely reliable channels, from the Japanese Military Headquarters in Tientsin that these Headquarters have been, and still are, engaged in the duty free importation of passenger automobiles and motor trucks in considerable numbers, which vehicles are not intended for the immediate use of the Japanese military. About two hundred and fifty cars have already been brought in under Japanese military *huchaos* and *huchaos* to cover the importation of an additional one hundred passenger cars and five hundred truck chassis have been issued during the past week.

The Japanese military, in return for the issuance of the *huchaos*, require that the importer (who needless to say must be a Japanese subject or firm) build bodies on the truck chassis according to the specifications of the military and also require that both trucks and passenger cars be made available for use by the Japanese military in an emergency.

Aside from the patent rascality of the whole scheme, the pertinent points are that Japanese operators of motor vehicles in North China are being subsidized at the expense of the Chinese Government, which government is also assisting in providing the Japanese military with transportation.

I have also received information from what I believe to be a reliable source, that the South Manchurian Railway recently forwarded two hundred Japanese Toyoda motor trucks through Tientsin to Kalgan under *huchao* issued by the local Japanese military, which trucks were turned over to the bandits for use in their operations against Suiyuan.

Respectfully yours,   DAVID C. BERGER

---

[5] Copy transmitted to the Department by the Consul at Tientsin in his unnumbered despatch of December 16; received January 11, 1937.

893.00/13776 : Telegram

The Ambassador in China (Johnson) to the Secretary of State

NANKING, December 17, 1936—noon.
[Received December 17—9 : 25 a. m.⁶]

355. My 354, December 16, noon.

1. Situation unchanged; Nanking quiet. Yesterday Government announced punitive expedition against Chang Hsueh Liang headed by Ho Ying Chin, Minister of War. Military situation is as follows: Chang Hsueh Liang at Sian has two to three divisions poorly disciplined and poorly equipped. He has one division on highway connecting Sian with Tungkuan with outposts at approximately Weinan. He has a further two divisions on highway running north of Sian which are reported to be north of Taohsien but marching south presumably followed by Communist forces with which they have fraternized. He also has some troops in Kansu but present status of these troops unknown, presumably coming southward on great highway through Pinhsien.

National Government has one division understood to be the thirteenth at Sienyang at the junction of the highway connecting Sian with Kansu and the highway running north to Ninghsia and Suiyuan. These troops have been ordered to hold Sienyang against Chang Hsueh Liang's troops coming south. At a place called Puafeng south of the Sian–Kansu road National Government has five divisions which have been engaged in railway and road construction. They are understood to be under orders to reenforce division at Sienyang and also to cross over to Sian–Kansu highway to cut off approach from Kansu. National Government also has a division at Lantien on road connecting Sian southward with Honan and Hupeh. National Government troops including division with complete modern mechanized equipment, artillery, tanks and trucks, now concentrating at Tungkwan on Sian–Loyang highway and marching west, part of them going northward to cut Sian–Ninghsia highway at Sanyuan. Modern equipment being advanced along road to Sian and capable of traveling very fast. Military dispositions intended to isolate and impress Chang Hsueh Liang and his troops.

(2) Political situation. Donald is in Sian and negotiations proceeding in the hope that, backed by military display, Government will succeed in relieving the situation. Elder,⁷ representing Chang Hsueh Liang, understood to have arrived last night, now closeted with Kung and T. V. Soong.

Sent to the Department; code texts mailed Tokyo, Peiping.

JOHNSON

---

⁶ Telegram in two sections.
⁷ James C. Elder, British national.

893.00/13780 : Telegram

The Counselor of Embassy in China (Lockhart) to the Secretary of State

PEIPING, December 17, 1936—3 p. m.
[Received December 17—1 : 05 p. m.]

620. Embassy's 601, December 10, 5 p. m. A current newspaper report, not yet confirmed, states that fighting "of a serious nature" began again on December 14 on the eastern Suiyuan front in the vicinity of Hsingho. An observer from the Military Attaché's office and Victor Keen (China correspondent of the New York *Herald Tribune*), both of whom have just returned from the Suiyuan front, are nevertheless in agreement in stating that the situation there is quiet. Keen, who left Peiping almost immediately for the South, is quoted in the press today as stating that the morale of the Chinese troops is good, that considerable stores of meat were obtained by the Chinese with the capture of Pailingmiao (which he visited), and the damage done there "by Japanese bombing planes" has been exaggerated.

He confidentially stated to a foreign Military Attaché, and not for publication, that a surrendered staff ["irregular"?] officer of Wang Ying's cavalry [*forces?*] in a personal interview stated as follows: Some 40 Japanese officers and [technicians] attached to the brigade were killed before its surrender to the Suiyuan [forces] on December 10 at Ulanhua (southwest of Tamiao; all but a few hundred of Wang Ying's forces have now surrendered, but Li [Shou] Hsin with some 10,000 Mongolian and Manchukuo "irregulars" is at Changpei; about one quarter of Teh Wang's forces, which consisted of about 4000 Mongol cavalry, surrendered to the Chinese at Tamiao on December 11 (the actual date of capture) ; the casualties and captured and surrendered of the "irregulars" total to date about 7000; Pailingmiao is now garrisoned by between 2000 and 3000 Shansi and Suiyuan forces, supplemented by a Nanking anti-aircraft unit of about 100 men.

According to the same source, " 'irregulars' military expedition was planned, officered and financed by Kwantung army. All military units received their pay direct from Kwantung army. Expedition was commanded by former colonel in Kwantung army who was killed at Tamiao". Surrendered officer is also alleged to have stated that the Kwantung army donated 12 planes, 5 tanks, 3 trucks and about 100 lorries, ammunition and provisions.

The above information may be of doubtful value since it originated from a surrendered "irregular" officer and it is therefore submitted for what it may be worth. It seems improbable, even with the affair in Sian, that any effective attack can be launched on Suiyuan by the "irregulars" in the near future.

By mail to Tokyo.

LOCKHART

893.00/13779 : Telegram

The Ambassador in China (Johnson) to the Secretary of State

NANKING, December 17, 1936—4 p. m.
[Received December 17—1:30 p. m.]

357. General Chiang Ting Wen, who was among those detained by Chang Hsueh Liang in Sian, has been released and is expected shortly in Nanking with a personal letter from General Chiang Kai Shek. Sources close to Kung express optimism over the situation. There has been a noticeable division of opinion here as to method of handling the matter, the younger army group believing in forceful measures while older group, and this includes Kung and Madame Chiang Kai Shek, favor negotiation.

Sent to the Department; code text to Peiping by mail.

JOHNSON

893.00/13782 : Telegram

The Ambassador in China (Johnson) to the Secretary of State

NANKING, December 18, 1936—noon.
[Received December 18—8:45 a. m.]

360. I have just seen Dr. Kung and have conveyed to him our Government's concern over safety of General Chiang. Dr. Kung asked me to express to the President and to you his thanks. Dr. Kung expressed himself as hopeful of a solution which would result in the safety of General Chiang although he admitted that the situation was still very serious. He told me that he expected General Chiang Ting Wen in Nanking this morning.

Sent to the Department; code text mailed to Tokyo and Peiping.

JOHNSON

893.00/13787 : Telegram

The Ambassador in Italy (Phillips) to the Secretary of State

ROME, December 18, 1936—noon.
[Received December 18—9:30 a. m.]

536. Count Ciano told me yesterday that in view of his long friendship with Chang Hsueh-liang he had sent him a personal message appealing to him to free Chiang Kai Shek. He allowed me to read this message which, though in friendly terms, was strong. He told me furthermore that the Italian Ambassador in China had been instructed officially to communicate a similar message to Chang Hsueh-liang which in part pointed out the risks of any cooperation with Moscow on Chang's part.

Although Ciano did not indicate that he had any proof that Chang was acting under the influence of Moscow, the Minister said he was convinced of it. He also felt sure that Chang himself had been governed by his personal hatred of Chiang Kai Shek.

In the only press comment on the situation the Government spokesman in an editorial on December 17th indicates that Moscow had a hand in the capture and is covering up its own traces by accusing Japan of inspiring the revolt. He maintains that the policy of seeking an agreement between Japan and China is the only wise course for China.

PHILLIPS

893.00/13786 : Telegram

The Ambassador in China (Johnson) to the Secretary of State

NANKING, December 18, 1936—4 p. m.
[Received December 18—10:30 a. m.]

361. Following is based on press releases at Nanking.

Donald has returned by plane to Sian to continue mediation efforts. T. V. Soong and Madame Kung are attending a Soong family conference at Nanking with Madame Chiang and Kung regarding safety of Chiang. Yu Yu Jen,[8] aged statesman, telegraphed Chang Hsueh Liang and Yang Hu Cheng to send delegates to meet him at Loyang for discussion for settlement of the issue. Chang Hsueh Liang telegraphed wife of Chen Cheng, Vice Minister of War, that Chen is safe. Rebels have started attack on Government troops moving against Sian, destroyed railroads and bridges west of Huahsien. Kung stated in a broadcast in English that Chiang was in good health, that the new life movement had aroused national consciousness against internal strife which would weaken defense of Suiyuan, that strong action against rebels would prove solidarity of China, that Government will proceed with vigor along policies formulated by Chiang, that a new national unity has arisen out of the crisis. Kung further stated: "Our attitude is that the personal safety of Government's one man should not be allowed to interfere with normal conduct of the Government." Government mandate ordered Ho Ying Chin to launch punitive campaign against Chang and appointed him Commander-in-Chief thereof. General Chiang Ting Wen arrived Nanking 11:45 a. m. He reported Generalissimo well and all other Government leaders safe. Kao Tsung Wu and Suma continue Sino-Japanese conferences in Nanking.

To Peiping by mail.

JOHNSON

---

[8] President of the Chinese Control Yuan.

893.00/13794 : Telegram

The Acting Secretary of State to the Ambassador in China (Johnson)[9]

WASHINGTON, December 18, 1936—7 p. m.

84. 1. This afternoon the Counselor of the British Embassy called at the Department and left an *aide-mémoire* stating that it has occurred to the British Government that if Chang Hsueh-liang could be assured of his own personal safety he might be persuaded to release Chiang Kai-shek: that for instance Chang might be removed by air to Shanghai or to Tientsin whence he could leave China; and that possibly there could be made locally arrangements to this effect. The British Government inquires whether the American Government would cooperate and states that the British Government is also taking the matter up with the Japanese, French and Italian Governments. The *aide-mémoire* concludes with the statement that the British Government are only offering their good offices in the hope that they might be of assistance in the carrying out of any arrangements which may be reached by the parties and that they do not propose any intervention in negotiations that may be taking place.

2. Please confer with your British colleague, discuss the practicability and expediency of action on the line suggested, make no commitment on behalf of your Government, and report promptly with your comments. In your conversation with your British colleague, you should discuss not only possible advantages and possible disadvantages and difficulties which would attend procedure such as the British Government suggests but any possibility of measures whereby foreign governments might contribute helpfully and without impropriety toward averting tragic developments and further political disturbance potential within the Sian situation.

MOORE

793.94/8510

The Consul at Harbin (LaMont) to the Ambassador in China (Johnson)[10]

No. 291   HARBIN, December 18, 1936.

SIR: With reference to the deadlock in the Nanking negotiations, and the recent coup at Sian, I have the honor to submit an estimate of the way in which people of the Chinese race here would react to a Sino-Japanese conflict.

[9] Notation by the Chief of the Division of Far Eastern Affairs: "Approved in principle by the Acting Secretary and the President."
[10] Copy transmitted to the Department by the Consul at Harbin in his despatch No. 451, December 18; received February 19, 1937.

It is difficult to obtain information concerning the reactions of the native population. For one thing, there is no officer stationed here who speaks the Chinese language, and even if there were, he would experience great difficulty in frank and open conversation with thinking Chinese because they would be afraid to risk the danger of being seen in the company of a foreigner. Although frequently "Manchukuo" officials are met in a social way, these people are either renegades or mere figure-heads, and a frank expression of opinion from them would not be forthcoming even if one had the temerity to embarrass them with questions. The local Chinese language press, of course, is useless, as it is completely owned by Japanese, and under military censorship. There is not a single inch of printed material which is free, directly or indirectly, from Japanese propaganda.

From such contacts as have been possible, however, it has been disclosed that the native population almost unanimously would welcome the return of Chinese control. This is in spite of increasingly favorable economic conditions, a stable currency, perhaps a lessening of extortion on the part of officials, and a uniform rate of taxation. It is natural that the rural population should welcome the return of the Chinese, for not only have the farmers been the last to benefit by the "improvements", but they have received brutal and soul-killing treatment far in excess of the city dwellers. Their farms have been destroyed and they have been forced into concentration areas, as part of the drive against outlaws; in many cases they have been driven off their farms, or have received but a fraction of their value to accommodate Korean and Japanese immigrants; their traditional cash crop, poppy, has been made illegal except in a few areas; and the 1930–34 economic depression in Manchuria was intensified because of the chaotic conditions which prevailed, and in their ignorance the farmers are apt to blame the Japanese for all the misfortunes which have befallen them.

Most important of all, of course, is the inherent hatred any race has for alien dominance. This has been noticed in many parts of the world, where the rules frequently were more tactful with the native population than has been the case in Manchuria. This dominance involves a loss of "face" which is almost insupportable, and which causes even the relatively well-to-do city merchants to look with longing for the return of a government of their own kind, even though they have received some economic benefits from the present regime and have not suffered the extreme hardships of their compatriots on the farms.

If the recent coup in Sian should lead to extensive Sino-Japanese hostilities, however, there is no reason to suppose that the present authorities would experience any particular difficulties with the population. For one thing, the people are to a large extent disarmed, and have not the means to procure weapons. For another, there is no leader with sufficient initiative, funds, or backing. Finally, the Chinese are notoriously apathetic to matters political and military, which, coupled with the fear of the efficiently organized system of secret police whose activities would undoubtedly be redoubled, would in all likelihood preclude the possibility of a serious uprising.

The greatest trouble would probably come from so-called bandits who are in reality patriotic Chinese in touch with Nanking or communists in touch with the U. S. S. R. The activities of these bands would in all probability increase, and perhaps many recruits would join them. Only recently one such band, numbering about 400 (according to official report) captured the town of Foshan, on the Amur north of Chiamussu, and was not dislodged for a week. It is hardly likely, however, that such bands would prove a serious menace in the rear to Japanese operations in China, although sporadic raids would doubtless continue and lawlessness as a whole increase. The possibility of an increase in covert Soviet assistance to these bands would be offset by the undoubted disappearance of assistance from China which is coming at the present time.

The situation in the event the U. S. S. R. should abandon neutrality is another question, beyond the scope of this report. The Chinese population, if left to its own devices, would not be likely to be a serious menace to the Japanese, at least in north Manchuria.

Respectfully yours,   GEORGE D. LAMONT

893.00/13792 : Telegram

The Ambassador in China (Johnson) to the Secretary of State

NANKING, December 19, 1936—1 p. m.
[Received December 19—7 : 50 a .m.[11]]

362. Chiang Ting Wen arrived Nanking yesterday with following letter addressed by Chiang Kai Shek to Ho Ying Chin:

"Informed of the bombing of Weinan by squadrons yesterday, I am writing to request you to order the immediate cessation of the air raids. As far as I can tell from the present circumstances, I may be able to return to Nanking before the end of this week, and therefore hostilities should not break out and bombing should be discontinued until after Saturday. (Signed) Chung Cheng".[12]

Foregoing letter in Chiang Kai Shek's handwriting was written by Chiang in the presence of Chang Hsueh Liang. It is interpreted here as an ultimatum to Chang Hsueh Liang by Chiang. Ho Ying

---

[11] Telegram in two sections.
[12] Signature of Chiang Kai-shek.

Chin ordered cessation of hostilities until 6 p. m. tonight. Authorities here are anxiously awaiting results without too much optimism as to outcome. No report here yet as to Chiang's release.

In my opinion letter indicates possible break in Chang Hsueh Liang's stand and opens some hope of settlement. It is significant that Chang Hsueh Liang made no objection to time limit.

Negotiations apparently are continuing but there is no information available here as to direction negotiations are taking. It is understood that Government desired to arrange discussion with Chang Hsueh Liang at Taiyuan. Nanking is quiet with martial law effective nightly after midnight.

T. V. Soong left this afternoon for Loyang and presumably for Sian.

Sent to Department, code texts to Peiping and Tokyo by mail.

JOHNSON

893.00/13797 : Telegram

The Ambassador in China (Johnson) to the Secretary of State

NANKING, December 19, 1936—4 p. m.
[Received 5 p. m.]

363. Following is based on press releases at Nanking:

Holograph letters brought from Generalissimo to Madame Chiang and Ho Ying Chin by Chiang Ting Wen request delay of bombing air raids until after Saturday as he anticipates return by that time. Consequently active hostilities have ceased but Government troops are still concentrating east of Sian. Chiang Ting Wen reported that Generalissimo had four times been approached by the young marshal for a reply to demands but was each time rebuffed on the basis that latter should release Chiang Kai Shek or otherwise might as well admit treachery and kill him.

Sun Fo replied to a telegram of December 13 from rebels asking him to proceed to Sian, strongly demanding prompt return of Generalissimo to Nanking before any discussion.

Feng Yu Hsiang received telegraphic information from Sian that Shao Yuan Chung,[13] reported to have been killed in the revolt Saturday, was only slightly wounded.

Central Publicity Department man issued manifesto giving the following reason for punitive expedition against Sian rebels: (1) to pledge national loyalty to Generalissimo; (2) to uphold discipline of the state; (3) to exterminate remaining bandits for benefit of the people; (4) to preserve uniformity and complete national recovery;

---

[13] Kuomintang Central Executive Committee member.

919456—54——34

(5) to adhere to policy of national salvation. It states further that Sian revolt will not prevent rejuvenation of the country or impair great task accomplished by Generalissimo and asks full national support to Government for further resistance against foreign aggression, removal of traitors and continuous support to Suiyuan defenders.

Troops of Chang Hsueh Liang from North Shensi and East Kansu are taking up defensive positions at Sua-hsien east of Sian but mobilization in the west is proceeding with difficulty.

Irregulars heavily attacked Chinese lines in eastern Suiyuan but were repulsed. A further drive expected soon.

Sent to the Department, to Peiping by mail.

JOHNSON

893.00/13798 : Telegram

The Ambassador in China (Johnson) to the Secretary of State

NANKING, December 19, 1936—11 p. m.
[Received December 19—4:30 p. m.]

365. Department's 84, December 18, 7 p. m.

1. I have discussed matter with British Ambassador and we are agreed upon the following.

2. We have explored possible actions which foreign powers might take in present contingency but are agreed that except for the suggestion of the British Government there is no action which powers could profitably take at this juncture in a situation so peculiarly affecting the stability of the National Government.

3. British Ambassador sounded Kung yesterday on present proposal and found him disposed to accept it if laid before him.

4. We are of the opinion that it will be better for all concerned if the Chinese Government is able to find a solution for itself without bringing in the powers. But we believe that the fact that certain powers are prepared to guarantee safe departure of Chang Hsueh Liang, and, if necessary, of Yang Hu Cheng might be of value.

5. We, therefore, suggest that we be instructed to inform Dr. Kung that the American and British Governments are prepared to take all proper steps to ensure the safe departure from China of Chang Hsueh Liang and if necessary of Yang Hu Cheng. This undertaking would be given also by such of the other three powers approached as may be willing.

6. With reference to the method of performance we believe that the only feasible plan would be for the Chinese Government to be responsible for safe passage of either or both generals to some place where the powers would be in a position to undertake their safe departure

from Chinese soil. The obvious and nearest port would be Tientsin where they would be accommodated on a warship until safe passage could be arranged.

7. If this suggestion is accepted, would you be willing to proceed in concert with one or more of the powers consulted, or would you act only if all agree. Opportunity may come suddenly and Department's instructions would be welcome.

8. British Ambassador is reporting to his Government in the same sense.

9. It is my opinion that situation, although very serious, is not entirely hopeless yet as negotiations continue behind the scene. I am completely in the dark as to the direction which these negotiations are taking. If the Chinese Government can possibly work its way out without outside help it will, I believe, emerge with increased prestige. If it fails it is difficult to say what will happen. Up to the present it has had an undivided public opinion behind it, but if Chiang should be killed it seems to me inevitable that personal jealousies will once more rend the country.

10. According to Central News, Ho Ying Chin has ordered bombing to begin again in the morning. No news out of Sian tonight. Soong will probably remind [*remain?*] overnight at Loyang.

Sent to the Department, repeated to Tokyo, code text by mail to Peiping.

JOHNSON

893.00/13798 : Telegram

The Acting Secretary of State to the Ambassador in China (Johnson)[14]

WASHINGTON, December 19, 1936—midnight.

86. Your 365, December 19, 11 p. m., especially paragraphs 5, 6 and 7. It is the view of this government that representatives of this and other foreign governments should proceed very cautiously in this matter and should make no guarantees which would make their governments responsible in case Chinese interference caused failure of an attempt by them to save lives and to guarantee security of lives, but you are authorized to collaborate with your British colleague in informing Kung of the willingness of this government in cooperation with the British Government and other governments, if any, to attempt to effect safe conduct of generals Chang Hsueh-liang and Yang Hu Cheng from, say, Tientsin to some point outside of Chinese soil, with the understanding that, if and when this safe conduct shall have been

---

[14] Notation by the Chief of the Division of Far Eastern Affairs: "This has the approval in principle of Mr. Carr [Assistant Secretary of State] and the President."

completed, the responsibility of this government in relation to the safety of lives of the persons thus evacuated would of course cease. Within the principles indicated above, details left to your discretion.

MOORE

893.00/13803 : Telegram

The Counselor of Embassy in China (Lockhart) to the Secretary of State

PEIPING, December 20, 1936—5 p. m.
[Received December 20—12 : 15 p. m.]

627. Embassy's 626, December 19, 3 p. m. [15] The following is a translation of the circular telegram (which incidentally has not been published locally so far as known) allegedly issued by Chang Hsueh-liang on December 12 at Sian and signed by him and 18 other generals and one civilian leader, some of whom are, however, now apparently detained by Chang at Sian:

[Here follows introductory section of the circular telegram.]
The military and civilians in the Northwest unanimously maintain the following demands: (1) Reorganize the Nanking Government and admit all parties to share the joint responsibility for saving the nation. (2) *All [stop all]* kinds of civil wars. (3) Immediately release the patriotic leaders arrested in Shanghai. (4) Release all political prisoners throughout the country. (5) Emancipate the patriotic movement of the people. (6) Safeguard the political freedom of the people to organize and call meetings. (7) [Actually] obey the words [*will*] of Dr. Sun Yat Sen. (8) Immediately call the National Salvation Conference. The above-mentioned eight items are the points of national salvation unanimously maintained by us and by all the military and civilians throughout the Northwest.

We, therefore, hope you gentlemen will stoop to mention [*meet*] public sentiment and sincerely adopt these demands, so as to open one line of life for the future, and cleanse your past guilt in ruining the country. The great cause is before us. It does not permit glancing backwards. We only hope to carry out thoroughly the policies [*policy*] maintained for national salvation and benefit to the country. As to merit or guilt, we leave this to the judgment of our fellow countrymen.

In sending this telegram we urgently await legislative action [*await your*] order." [16]

---

[15] Not printed.
[16] This statement bore the names of the following: Chang Hsueh-liang, Yang Hu-cheng, Chu Hsiao-liang, Ma (Hung-kuei?), Yu Hsueh-chung, Chen Chen(g?), Shao Li-tze, Chiang Ting-wen, Tung Ying-pin, Wei Li-huang, Chien Ta-chun, Ho Chu-kuo, Feng Chin-tsai, Sun Wei-ju, Chen Chi-cheng, Wang I-che, Wan Yao-huang, and Miao Cheng-liu, some of whom were in the party of Generalissimo Chiang at Sian.

I am inclined to vouch for the authenticity of the above telegram, but [*sic*] I believe it to be the circular issued by Chang since it was obtained from a northeastern army spokesman in Peiping. The spokesman is authority for the statement that the terms "startling changes in the international situation" and "nations are intriguing between one another" relate to the German-Japan-Italian agreements.

Inasmuch as text of telegram has apparently not been published here, I suggest that it be not given out for publication.

Seemingly authentic news releases from Canton indicate that Li Tsung Jen, Pai Chung Hsi and Li Chai Sum and others in Kwangsi have pledged their complete support to Nanking Government. It is believed that Chang Hsueh-liang expected sympathy from them in his objectives.

By mail to Tokyo.

LOCKHART

893.00/13806 : Telegram

The Counselor of Embassy in China (Lockhart) to the Secretary of State

PEIPING, December 21, 1936—3 p. m.
[Received December 21—5 : 04 a. m.]

628. 1. The Japanese military authorities in North China continue to maintain an attitude of watchful waiting vis-à-vis Shensi revolt. Contrary to the general practice they are giving out but few interviews and these are quite moderate in tone. The representative of Sung Che Yuan who called at this and some other Diplomatic Missions (see my No. 612, December 15, 3 p. m.) did not call at the Japanese Embassy.

2. It does not appear that either Japan or Russia had any direct connection with instigating the Shensi revolt. It may ultimately develop that the revolt arose in large part either from petty jealousies among the military leaders, short rations and back pay, false information circulated among the troops, or lack of understanding of policy of Chinese Government in dealing with Japanese situation.

3. The longer Chiang Kai-shek is detained the more complicated the situation will become. It is becoming increasingly evident that Chang Hsueh-liang is not the only one with whom the Nanking Government will have to deal. Other recalcitrant military leaders in the Northwest will necessarily have to be brought back into line.

By mail to Tokyo.

LOCKHART

893.00/13804 : Telegram

The Ambassador in China (Johnson) to the Secretary of State

NANKING, December 21, 1936—4 p. m.
[Received December 21—9 : 04 a. m.]

368. Shanghai's telegram of December 20, 4 p. m., especially paragraph 5.[17]

At my request Dr. Kung undertook on December 19 to send a telegram to Donald as from me asking if latter could make arrangements with the Young Marshal for evacuating American missionaries at Sian. I suggested that this be effected by airplane if possible and that other foreigners be included in the arrangement.

Repeated to Peiping, Shanghai, Hankow.

JOHNSON

893.00/13809 : Telegram

The Consul General at Shanghai (Gauss) to the Secretary of State

SHANGHAI, December 21, 1936—4 p. m.
[Received December 21—12 : 05 p. m.]

662. 1. Local interest today centers in activities of T. V. Soong at Sian where he is reported endeavoring in private capacity to effect release of Generalissimo and also in flight yesterday of General Huang Shao Hsiung to Taiyuan to enlist aid of Yen Hsi Shan in solving Sian crisis. Meanwhile Nanking Government appears to be maintaining firm attitude towards settlement of issues.

2. Japanese Ambassador Kawagoe who left Shanghai yesterday for Nanking under instructions to interview Chinese Foreign Minister will according to Japanese press reports express deep interest of Japanese Government in terms of any compromise that may be negotiated between Nanking and Sian, pointing out that Japan could not remain unconcerned should such settlement provide for adoption by Nanking of policy of cooperation with Communists to oppose Japan. At present however the Japanese continue to maintain an attitude of watchful waiting.

3. Local stock, bond and exchange markets remain steady and trade continues uninterrupted.

4. Repeated to Nanking by mail; to Peiping by airmail.

GAUSS

---

[17] Not printed.

793.94/8450 : Telegram

The Acting Secretary of State to the Counselor of Embassy in China (Lockhart)

WASHINGTON, December 21, 1936—4 p. m.

302. Your 616, December 16, 3 p. m.

1. The Department perceives no objection to Berger addressing an informal communication to the "Chief of Police, Peitaiho Beach" in regard to the robberies of American property.

2. With regard to the question raised in paragraph 2 of your telegram under reference, the Department concurs in the view expressed by the Embassy that no useful purpose would be served in discussing with the "East Hopei Anti-Communist Autonomous Government" a matter affecting its revenue. The Department feels, therefore, that it is not advisable to make any representations to that regime in regard to this matter.

For your information it may be observed that informal efforts on the part of American consular representatives with a view to protecting American interests in the territory controlled by the "East Hopei Anti-Communist Autonomous Government" would not warrant any implication of recognition by this Government of the regime in question.

3. As a matter of record, it is suggested that the Embassy give consideration to bringing, at an appropriate time and in an appropriate manner, the case to the attention of the Chinese Foreign Office.[18]

MOORE

893.00/13805 : Telegram

The Ambassador in China (Johnson) to the Secretary of State

NANKING, December 21, 1936—5 p. m.
[Received December 21—8 : 25 a. m.]

369. T. V. Soong has sent a holograph letter from Loyang to Young Marshal demanding that he release Generalissimo without delay. He enclosed editorial "Open Letter to Sian Troops" from *Ta Kung Pao*, December 18, copies of which are also being scattered among Sian forces by airplane. Editorial contains following points:

1. Generalissimo should be escorted back, not merely allowed to escape from Chang; 2. He need not leave but may remain in Sian to direct national affairs from that place but this must be approved

---

[18] The Embassy in China, in its despatch No. 958, January 5, 1937, reported that "two shipments of petroleum products have recently been made by the Standard-Vacuum Oil Company to its agents in the East Hopei area without molestation and that, as the situation now stands, Mr. Berger does not consider that any action by the American authorities is required." (793.94/8514)

by him and concurred in by repentant mutineers in a circular telegram; 3. No guarantees other than integrity of Generalissimo and public opinion of nation should be sought for their pardon if they repent and their proposals will be adopted on his release if he deems them useful; 4. At request of Generalissimo punitive action is temporarily postponed so that they may prove their loyalty. Rebels are also reminded of folly of talk of national salvation when all Government and military machinery has been halted by their action.

Resumption of Government bombing air raids on December 20 has caused heavy losses and stopped rebel movements near Sian.

Sent to the Department; by mail to Peiping.

JOHNSON

893.00/13808 : Telegram

The Counselor of Embassy in China (Lockhart) to the Secretary of State

PEIPING, December 21, 1936—5 p. m.
[Received December 21—11 : 35 a. m.]

629. 1. The Shensi revolt has had the effect, perhaps temporarily only, of suspending the agitation of students at Peiping, although it is understood that rather pronounced differences have arisen among them on the question of the advisability of despatching a punitive expedition to Shensi. Although professing to believe that a more aggressive policy towards Japan is needed, the sympathy of the students on the whole appears to be with Chiang Kai-shek notwithstanding the huge demonstration staged at Peiping on December 12 (see Embassy's No. 604, December 13, 1 p. m.)

2. There are signs that Yen Hsi Shan may emerge from the present trouble with increased power and prestige. If Chiang Hsueh-liang is finally ousted from authority there would seem to be a good prospect for the expansion of Yen's authority since it is believed that he might be satisfactory to both factions if a drastic reorganization of the military establishment in the northwest area should become necessary as now seems inevitable. The defection of Yu Hsueh Chung from Lanchow, reports of which are persistently reported but not yet confirmed, are most disturbing as he has long been one of Chiang Kaishek's most steadfast adherents.

3. Reports, apparently well-founded, continue to circulate that defections from the "irregulars" in Suiyuan to the Government side are occurring almost daily.

By mail to Tokyo.

LOCKHART

893.00/13807 : Telegram

The Ambassador in China (Johnson) to the Secretary of State

NANKING, December 21, 1936—6 p. m.
[Received December 21—11 a. m.]

370. Department's 86, December 19, midnight.

1. I communicated Department's message to British Ambassador this morning. He was without instructions from his Government and we will await further eventualities.

2. French Ambassador called upon me this morning and inquired about British proposal. Apparently French Government had completely misunderstood, for it described it as a proposal for the offer of mediation by the powers. I read to the French Ambassador Department's 84 of December 18, 7 p. m.; my 365, December 19, 11 p. m.; and Department's 86, December 19, midnight, and explained to the French Ambassador that the proposal contemplated merely offering Chang Hsueh-liang, Yang Hu Cheng sanctuary and safe conduct out of China after his [*their?*] arrival at a port, preferably Tientsin. I explained to him that both the British Ambassador and I were in agreement that it would be highly dangerous and very improper for us to offer any mediation under present circumstances.

5 [*3*]. Suma called upon me this afternoon and inquired regarding British proposal. I explained to him as I explained to the French Ambassador. Suma stated that his Government had not made up its mind but was seeking information and advice.

6 [*4*]. I called on the Minister for Foreign Affairs this afternoon to inquire concerning developments. He stated that Soong was still in Sian and that they hoped for some news tomorrow. I found them expecting Donald to arrive in Nanking this afternoon. There is no change in local situation. All are anxiously awaiting outcome of present negotiations.

Sent to the Department; code texts by mail to Peiping and Tokyo.

JOHNSON

893.00/13811 : Telegram

The Ambassador in China (Johnson) to the Secretary of State

NANKING, December 22, 1936—11 a. m.
[Received December 22—2:26 a. m.]

371. T. V. Soong accompanied by Donald returned to Nanking by air yesterday. It is believed that T. V. is returning to Sian today possibly accompanied by Madame Chiang Kai-shek.[19] Neither Don-

---

[19] Mr. Soong, Mme. Chiang, and W. H. Donald left by airplane for Sian that day.

ald nor T. V. brings very good news from Sian.   Donald is reported to have said that real power at Sian is Yang Hu Cheng; that question of Chiang's release might be settled except for the uncertainty of Yang's attitude and those under him. .

Sent to the Department, code texts to Peiping and Tokyo by mail.

JOHNSON

893.00/13812 : Telegram

The Ambassador in China (Johnson) to the Secretary of State

NANKING, December 22, 1936—noon.
[Received December 22—2 : 38 a. m.]

372. Please inform Military Attaché that I think that he or Assistant Military Attaché or a responsible student officer should be sent to Loyang to watch situation and consider whether anything may be done as regards safety of American citizens in Shensi.   It may be necessary for you to consult Department regarding this matter. British Embassy is similarly instructing British Military Attaché.

Sent to Peiping, repeated to Department.

JOHNSON

893.00/13821 : Telegram

The Counselor of Embassy in China (Lockhart) to the Secretary of State

PEIPING, December 23, 1936—noon.
[Received December 23—7 a. m.]

633. Nanking's 372, December 22, midnight [*noon?*]. A representative of the Military Attaché's office, probably Colonel Stilwell himself, will leave for Loyang tonight.   I told Colonel Stilwell that he should strongly urge evacuation of American citizens from Shensi if evacuation is possible.

Nanking and Shanghai informed.

LOCKHART

893.00/13827 : Telegram

The Ambassador in China (Johnson) to the Secretary of State

NANKING, December 23, 1936—6 p. m.
[Received December 23—11 : 18 a. m.]

377. British Ambassador, who has just seen Kung, reports Kung as stating that there will be no developments within next 2 or 3 days but hopeful that private negotiations now proceeding will result

in something by that time. Military operations have been suspended pending result.

Sent to the Department, code text by mail to Peiping, Tokyo.

JOHNSON

893.00/13829 : Telegram

The Counselor of Embassy in China (Lockhart) to the Secretary of State

PEIPING, December 23, 1936—7 p. m.
[Received December 23—5 : 10 p. m.]

637. Embassy's 631, December 22, 3 p. m.[20] On a radio broadcast, of which at least a part was in English, from Sian last night the verbal attacks of the rebels on the National Government and Chiang Kai Shek were continued. Ho Ying Chin in particular was condemned for his actions, while a warning was issued to Yu Yu Jen, now at Loyang, not to proceed to Sian unless he was prepared to accept the eight points of Chang Hsueh Liang's program. Anti-Japanese sentiment was prominent, and it was stated that the "Northwest National Salvation uprising" is being organized. It was announced that the Northeastern Army now regarded the Chinese Communists as brothers in the common cause against Japan, and it was stated that a regiment of infantry had arrived at Sian from a point about 100 li west of Sian and that they had discarded all insignia of rank and were holding meetings throughout city.

The Shensi forces of Feng Chin Tsai are reported moving toward the north bank of the Wei River against the rebels in conjunction with the deployment of National Government troops, which are said to have captured Weinan yesterday, apparently without fighting of consequence. Four divisions belonging to Yu Hsueh Chung are reported en route from Kansu to Sian to assist the rebels.

Announcement was made of the death of a German, Dr. Philipi (or Wrumsch) during the uprising on December 12 by a stray bullet.

By mail to Tokyo.

LOCKHART

893.00/13830 : Telegram

The Ambassador in China (Johnson) to the Secretary of State

NANKING, December 24, 1936—noon.
[Received December 24—6 : 50 a. m.]

379. Following is based on press releases at Nanking:

H. H. Kung as Acting Executive Yuan President has issued circular

---

[20] Not printed.

telegraphic instructions to provincial and local authorities to following effect: (1) suppression of rumors and censorship of press to be carried out; (2) student agitation to be discouraged; (3) radicalism in factories to be suppressed; (4) commodity prices to be regulated; (5) food supplies to be controlled.

Yu Yu Jen, Control Yuan President, is consolidating support of the Government policies in East Shensi by conferences with prominent local officials.

Discord over power is reported between Chang Hsueh-liang and Yang Hu Cheng. Reds are advancing in East Kansu as rebels fall back on Sian. Both forces are preparing for a struggle for Weinan now held by rebels.

By mail to Peiping.

JOHNSON

893.00/13831 : Telegram

The Counselor of Embassy in China (Lockhart) to the Secretary of State

PEIPING, December 24, 1936—noon.
[Received December 24—7 : 35 a. m.]

638. Generals Sung Che Yuan and Han Fu Chu issued a circular telegram last night suggesting the convocation of a national conference of Government leaders and retired elder statesmen to evolve measures to deal with the Sian trouble. Their stated aims are to preserve the nation, prevent the suffering of the people and safeguard the life of Chiang Kai-shek. The inference is that the two generals are opposed to a punitive expedition.

By mail to Tokyo.

LOCKHART

893.00/13837 : Telegram

The Ambassador in China (Johnson) to the Secretary of State

NANKING, December 25, 1936—7 p. m.
[Received December 25—9 : 25 a. m.]

380. Foreign Office states Chiang Kai Shek reached Loyang safely afternoon December 25. It is also reliably reported that Chiang Kai Shek, accompanied by Chang Hsueh Liang, will come to Nanking, December 26.

Sent to the Department, Peiping, Shanghai and Tokyo.

JOHNSON

893.00/13837 : Telegram

The Acting Secretary of State to the Ambassador in China (Johnson)

WASHINGTON, December 25, 1936—11 p. m.

90. Your 380, December 25, 7 p. m. If news of Generalissimo Chiang Kai-shek's release is confirmed and his safety assured, please express appropriately to Foreign Office this Government's gratification.

MOORE

893.00/13836 : Telegram

The Ambassador in China (Johnson) to the Secretary of State

NANKING, December 26, 1936—2 p. m.
[Received December 26—7:21 a. m.]

381. The Generalissimo in company with Madame Chiang and Donald reported to have arrived Nanking by plane at 6:20 today and to have made a circuit for recognition by the people. T. V. Soong is reported to have arrived by later plane with the Young Marshal. Sent to the Department, repeated to Peiping, Tokyo and Shanghai.

JOHNSON

893.00/13841 : Telegram

The Counselor of Embassy in China (Lockhart) to the Secretary of State

PEIPING, December 28, 1936—noon.
[Received December 28—7 a. m.]

641. My 633, December 23, noon. Colonel Stilwell returned to Peiping this morning and reports that the consensus of opinion in Loyang is that the release of Chiang Kai-shek practically ends the possibility of trouble in Shensi and that in his opinion there is no present need for the evacuation of Americans from that province.

Nanking informed.

LOCKHART

893.01 Manchuria/1390 : Telegram

The Counselor of Embassy in China (Lockhart) to the Secretary of State

PEIPING, December 29, 1936—10 a. m.
[Received December 29—7:12 a. m.]

643. The following telegram has been received from Mukden:

"December 28, 11 a. m. A source recently attached to Japanese forces in Jehol confidentially stated: there is in Jehol one Japanese division and in Inner Mongolia one and a half Japanese divisions;

their detail is being extended from December to next May and will be further extended in case of serious hostilities; troops have been ordered to be prepared for resumption of operations during the first half of January."

By mail to Tokyo.

LOCKHART

893.00/13843 : Telegram

The Counselor of Embassy in China (Lockhart) to the Secretary of State

PEIPING, December 29, 1936—3 p. m.
[Received December 29—9: 50 a. m.]

644. 1. Service on the Lunghai Railway between Loyang and Sian will be restored today. Telegraph service to Sian has been restored.

2. Military Attaché reports a very heavy concentration of Government troops on the Lunghai. There was wild jubilation among these troops when news of Chiang Kai Shek's release reached them.

3. From various sources it would appear that foreign lives in Shensi and Kansu are not now endangered.

4. Small group of radicals in Peiping universities have been attacked and their headquarters ransacked during the past few days by student sympathizers of Chiang Kai Shek. Authorities of universities concerned have taken situation in hand and it is believed that trouble between the two factions will now cease.

5. Reports are published almost daily of further defections in the ranks of the irregulars in Suiyuan and of dissension among the leaders of those forces. It is very doubtful whether any major operations will take place in Suiyuan in the near future.

By mail to Tokyo.

LOCKHART

893.00/13844 : Telegram

The Ambassador in China (Johnson) to the Secretary of State

NANKING, December 29, 1936—4 p. m.
[Received December 29—9: 40 a. m.]

382. The following is reported from newspaper sources: Chiang Kai-shek today tendered his resignation from all concurrent offices to the Central Executive Committee. It was rejected by the Standing Committee and he is this morning in all offices. The question of reorganization of the Government will be considered at or after third plenary session of the Fifth Central Executive and Supervisory

Committees now set for February 15, 1937. Chang Hsueh-liang was handed over to the Military Affairs Committee for appropriate discipline.

Sent to the Department, repeated to Peiping.

JOHNSON

893.00/13849 : Telegram

The Counselor of Embassy in China (Lockhart) to the Secretary of State

PEIPING, December 30, 1936—6 p. m.
[Received December 30—9 : 20 a. m.]

646. An American newspaper correspondent who returned today from Loyang stated that the impression is general there that the *quid pro quo*, in part, for Chiang's release is the acceptance of most of the points set forth in Chang Hsueh-liang's circular telegram (see Embassy's 627, December 20, 5 p. m.). The correspondent also states that young officers have now largely supplanted older men in Chang's army; that the "feudal dead wood", as they were described, have (presumably) been dismissed or allowed to resign; that the young officers have been undergoing intensive political and military training for many months and that they now dominate Chang Hsueh-liang. It is entirely possible that this element may have been a dominating factor in Chang's recent coup. Correspondent reports that the Central Government has an extremely firm hold on Shansi and that the movements of all foreigners in Loyang and thereabouts are closely watched. He reports an extremely strong military line along the Lung-Hai Railway.

By mail to Tokyo.

LOCKHART

761.94/943

The Ambassador in Japan (Grew) to the Secretary of State

[Extracts]

No. 2203
TOKYO, December 30, 1936.
[Received January 14, 1937.]

SIR: With reference to the Embassy's despatch No. 2188, dated December 16, 1936, on the subject of Soviet-Japanese relations, I have the honor to report that the question of the failure of the Soviet Government to sign the fisheries treaty has outshadowed all others in Soviet-Japanese relations during the past two weeks. A solution to the disturbing problem has finally been found in the extension for one year of the 1928 Fishery Treaty, which expires December 31 of this year. Although this greatly relieves the actual situation, the tension which accompanied the slight to Japan continues but little abated.

. . . .

The final agreement was signed in Moscow on December 28, and was given out by the Foreign Office here the next day. The Protocol as published in the *Japan Advertiser* of December 30 reads as follows:

"Whereas the term of duration of the fishery convention between Japan and the Union of Soviet Socialist Republics, signed on January 23, 1928, and prolonged by the protocol signed on May 25, 1936, comes to an end on December 31, 1936; and

"Whereas a new convention will not be concluded before December 31, 1936;

"The Governments of Japan and the Union of Soviet Socialist Republics hereby agree that the fishery convention between Japan and the Union of Soviet Socialist Republics as well as the documents annexed thereto, signed on January 23, 1928, shall remain in force until December 31, 1937.

"In witness whereof the undersigned, duly authorized by their respective Governments, have signed the present protocol.

"Done in public in the City of Moscow on the 28th day of the 12th month of the 11th year of Showa, corresponding to December 28, 1936.

M. Shigemitsu
B. Stomoniakov."

. . . .

In spite of suspicion, therefore, neither country seems willing to let relations lapse into a really dangerous state.

Respectfully yours,   JOSEPH C. GREW

793.94/8478 : Telegram

The Ambassador in China (Johnson) to the Secretary of State

NANKING, December 31, 1936—noon.
[Received December 31—7 a. m.]

387. Exchange of notes between the Chinese Foreign Office and the Japanese Embassy dated December 30 settling the Chengtu and Pakhoi incidents have been released in Chinese and English. Chinese Government expressed regret in both instances and listed following actions taken with reference thereto:

Chengtu incident. Garrison commander and chief of the Bureau of Public Safety relieved of their posts. Two principal culprits executed and four others sentenced to various terms of imprisonment. Families of the two Japanese killed reimbursed for actual damages suffered and given adequate compassionate grants. Two Japanese injured given medical expenses and compensated for actual damages suffered. Total paid by Chinese Government in settlement of Chengtu incident yuan $98,887.10.

Pakhoi incident. Two officers in charge of garrison dismissed. Those found guilty have "received punishment in accordance with the degree of their complicity". Compassionate grant of yuan $30,000 given relatives of the deceased Japanese. JOHNSON

893.00/13989

The Ambassador in China (Johnson) to the Secretary of State

No. 975   PEIPING, January 12, 1937.
                                          [Received February 20, 1937.]

SIR: I have the honor to refer to the Embassy's despatch No. 552 of July 3, 1936,[20a] reviewing the political, military, economic, and financial developments in China during the first six months of 1936, and to submit a similar review of the last six months of the year just ended.

Whereas the outstanding developments during the first half of 1936 increased the precariousness of China's position, the significant events of the second half, in their larger aspects, have had the opposite effect. The following factors have definitely tended to unify and strengthen the Republic and even to cause the Japanese, at least temporarily, to adopt a decidedly less aggressive policy towards China: the *dénouement* of the Southwestern crisis whereby recalcitrant Kwangtung and Kwangsi Provinces were taken into the Central Government's fold and the scope of Chiang Kai-shek's authority accordingly widened; the abortive attack on Suiyuan by Japanese directed and supported Mongol "irregulars" under the leadership of General Li Shou-hsin, the bandit Wang Ying, and Prince Teh, which brought practically the entire nation enthusiastically to the support of the Suiyuan defenders and evoked an amazing manifestation of nationalism; and the outcome of the detention at Sian of Chiang Kai-shek by Chang Hsueh-liang from December 12 to December 25 which fostered another spontaneous outburst of nationalism throughout the country and caused universal rejoicing when the Generalissimo was released on Christmas day. Each of these crises at their inception gave promise of disastrous results for the progress of China; in the end each in turn, with the possible exception of the aftermath from the Sian affair, proved a political asset to the country and an enhancement of the power of Chiang Kai-shek.

There continued to exist during the first days of July the pessimism which had deepened during the last days of June because of the fear that the difficulties between Nanking and the Southwest, whose primary purpose was to overthrow the Generalissimo and perhaps, secondarily, to wage war against Japan, could not be settled without resort to civil war. If the rebellion could not be quashed there was the possibility of a complete breakdown in authority with attendant

----

[20a] *Ante*, p. 231.

political impairment of Nanking's authority and economic bankruptcy and consequent encouragement to Japan for further aggression. However, at the Second Plenary Session of the Fifth Central Executive Committee of the Kuomintang (July 10 to 14), which had been called in an endeavor to place the Southwestern leaders in the position of traitors if they should disobey the Session's mandates and to open the way for conciliation, decisions were made which constituted a decided political victory for Chiang Kai-shek. The Executive Committee abolished the legality of the semi-independent political organs in the Southwest and removed General Ch'en Chi-t'ang from his position. They offered the Southwestern leaders a means of obtaining absolution by cooperating with the Central Government. The decisions made also confirmed the Generalissimo's policy toward Japan and enabled him to continue to avoid taking an open and definitive stand regarding armed resistance to Japanese aggression and interference in political affairs in China. General Chiang, through his skill in political maneuvering and the threat of military action, succeeded in bringing Kwangtung under his control.

During July and August General Chiang was unable to liquidate the Kwangsi situation. Negotiations and military preparations went on simultaneously. During the first half of September, however, after protracted negotiations an agreement was reached whereby Kwangsi also came under the control of the Central Government. The Southwestern rebellion was thus ended, leaving the country more completely unified than it had been at any time since the establishment of the Nanking Government.

The threat against Suiyuan, although existent for some time, was late in materializing. The situation in Northern Chahar, where General Sung Che-yuan appeared reluctant to interfere, remained obscure even throughout October, but there seemed little doubt that "pro-Manchukuo" Mongol and bandit forces based on Shangtu, Changpei, Pailingmiao and Chapsur were continuing preparations for an attack on East Suiyuan, in which preparations Japanese planes and armaments formed a part. General Fu Tso-yi, Chairman of the Suiyuan Provincial Government, had been endeavoring for many months to perfect the defense of his Province. In October Central Government troops were despatched to his support. Hostilities were finally opened by the "irregulars" on November 15, and by November 24 the Suiyuan forces had successfully repulsed the invaders and had taken Pailingmiao, the strategically important base of the "irregulars" and the capital of the Inner Mongolian Autonomous Political Council. This caused national rejoicing. Great popular support was given the defenders of Suiyuan as a fresh wave of patriotism swept the country. The failure of the "irregulars'" drive became obvious in December with the unsuccessful attempt to retake Pailingmiao, the defection of some of the "irregular" leaders and troops, and the capture by Suiyuan forces of Tamiao, the principal "irregular" base some 60 miles northeast of Pailingmiao.

On December 12 General Chang Hsueh-liang and General Yang Hu-cheng, the Pacification Commissioner of Shensi, revolted against Nanking and forcibly detained Chiang Kai-shek and other important Central Government officials who were in Sian with the Generalissimo. The leaders of the rebellion issued a statement demanding a reorganization of the Government to include all factions, presumably even the Communists, and for a united front against Japan. Shensi and Kansu responded to the plea, but the rest of the country loudly proclaimed its adherence to the Generalissimo and voiced the bitterest contempt for Chang Hsueh-liang and the revolt. The Generalissimo's release on Christmas day was greeted with enthusiasm throughout the country which had again become more closely knit through common patriotic zeal.

A very regrettable aftermath of the Sian coup was the reported alliance between the mutineers and the communists who had been concentrated for some time in the vicinity of Sian. At the end of the year, in the absence of knowledge as to what agreement, if any, had been made for the release of Chiang, the Central Government was at a loss to know whether further trouble was to be expected from that source. Chang Hsueh-liang who requested punishment was sentenced by court martial to ten years' imprisonment but was pardoned. His civil rights, however, have not been restored.

Other less important occasions which also fostered Chinese nationalism were the celebration of the National holiday on October 10, with a diplomatic reception (for the first time since the Mukden incident) and of the anniversary of Chiang Kai-shek's birthday on October 31 at which time a large number of airplanes bought with funds publicly subscribed were presented to the Generalissimo.

It would appear that, at least partially due to the above indicated expansion and strengthening of the Chinese national consciousness, and to the failure of the Sino-Japanese negotiations at Nanking, the Japanese have lessened their pressure on China. Since the large October military maneuvers and the founding in October of the Hui T'ung Aviation Company, whose planes now furnish through service between Manchuria and Tientsin and Peiping with Japanese pilots and Japanese planes, the Japanese have been relatively quiescent in North China. Whereas smuggling in this region has continued on a vast scale and is still causing a great loss in revenue to the Chinese Government, the Japanese authorities have recently shown less ardor in endeavoring to protect Japanese and Korean smugglers when their activities are interfered with by Chinese officials.

The replacing of General Matsumuro last month by Colonel Matsui as the Japanese resident officer of the North China Garrison in Peiping is also believed to be of considerable political significance, as indicating the gradual recession of Japanese influence in North China which became particularly noticeable during the last half of December. A further indication of this recession is the reported decision of the Hopei-Chahar Political Council to enter upon a general program of retrenchment.

There are also indications that the East Hopei Anti-Communist Autonomous Government presided over by Yin Ju-keng may be on its descendency. Rumors of serious dissension within the administration of the bogus regime continued to circulate during December. It is becoming more apparent that Yin's hold is highly tenuous, and it is altogether possible that the elaborate and costly celebration of the regime's first birthday on November 25 and its reported donation of $1,600,000 to the support of the "irregular" forces attacking Suiyuan may be the harbingers of its demise.

The improvement of China's position vis-à-vis Japan developed despite ill feeling which sometimes was brought to a dangerous pitch through a long series of Sino-Japanese incidents varying from murder to trivialities. This improvement developed notwithstanding the failure of the negotiations held in Nanking between the Japanese Ambassador and the Minister for Foreign Affairs and their subordinates during the last four months of the year. The negotiations were disrupted by China's conviction, allegedly, that Japan had been aiding the "irregular" forces in their attack on Suiyuan. The Ministry of Foreign Affairs on December 6 issued a statement outlining the present position of the Chinese Government relative to the subjects which had been under negotiation. This release has been briefly summarized by the Embassy at Nanking as follows:

"1. The Chinese Government is prepared to inaugurate a civil air line between Shanghai and Fukuoka as soon as the unauthorized and illegal flights of Japanese airplanes over Chinese territory are stopped.

"2. The revision of China's tariff is a domestic affair. When tariff readjustment is studied the suppression of smuggling and the freedom of the Customs Preventive Service will be the first questions studied.

"3. With reference to the unlawful anti-Japanese activities of Koreans in China, the Chinese Government does not like to see these acts committed on Chinese soil. At the same time the Japanese Government should suppress the other unlawful activities of its subjects, Koreans, Formosans and others, committed on Chinese territory under Japanese protection.

"4. The employment of foreign advisers depends upon their ability, not their nationality. Should Sino-Japanese relations improve, it would not be impossible for China on its own initiative to employ Japanese technical experts.

"5. Orders have repeatedly been issued stressing the necessity of maintaining friendly relations with foreign nationals. However, cognizance must be taken of the fact that much cause exists inciting the people against Japan."

Other unfavorable circumstances were: (1) the presence of the Communist troops in the Northwest against whom the Government troops confined their offensive mainly to "pushing"; (2) the wholesale North China smuggling by Japanese and Koreans; and (3) the Japanese cotton mill strikes in Shanghai and Tsingtao and the landing of Japanese forces at the latter port, against which action the Chinese Government protested.

At a meeting on October 15 the Standing Committee of the Central Executive Committee decided to postpone indefinitely the convocation of the National People's Congress which was to have met on November 12.

Economic and financial conditions in Kwangtung began to improve in August under the direction of General Chiang Kai-shek. In the same month resumption of service was offered on the Lung-hai Railway loans and Canton–Kowloon Railway bonds.

In September decision was made to revise the law governing the encouragement of shipbuilding. Through train service was inaugurated on the Canton–Hankow Railway, and definite plans were made to construct a modern port at Whampoa.

During October it was announced that the British Government in order to promote British exports to China had decided to guarantee credits advanced by British firms to Chinese importers. Chinese officials and business leaders publicly expressed gratification on this decision. It was believed that this action was intended to demonstrate Great Britain's desire to advance its commercial relations with China and to serve as a warning to Japan that Great Britain was not disinterested in China's future. China also expressed her approval of the monetary agreement recently concluded between the United States, France and Great Britain. The Ministry of Finance viewed the accord as a stabilizing influence in international exchange which would tend further to strengthen China's currency. He pointed out that China had profited by more than U. S. $1,000,000 through the sale of a part of its gold reserves abroad, and that China would be assisted in the discharge of its foreign loan obligations. (Chinese currency remained stable during the period under review except for slight and brief fluctuations at the time of the Sian coup).

During November it became obvious that the continuation of the shipping strike in the United States was injuring trade relations with the United States and adversely affecting American prestige and good will. The service of the China National Aviation Corporation was extended to Hong Kong, a Pan American Clipper having made its first call at Hong Kong the month before.

A number of loan operations in connection with the financing of the construction of the Nanking–Kiangsi Railway, which will link Nanking with the Canton–Hankow line and thus make a direct connection between Nanking and South China, were concluded during December. It was announced on December 16 that a loan contract for Yuan $34,500,000 for the construction of the Chengtu–Chungking Railway had been signed by the Szechuan–Kweichow Railway Corporation and a French banking syndicate. Indications at the end of the year were that the United States, notwithstanding the American shipping strike, would continue to enjoy the largest share of Shanghai's foreign trade, with Germany showing the greatest gain over 1935.

During the period under review there were no marked changes in the relations between China and the western nations. There were indications, however, of an increasing *rapprochement* between China and Great Britain. Great concern, moreover, was shown by Chinese officials and the public regarding the conclusion of the anti-Communist pact by Japan and Germany and the reported *de facto* recognition of "Manchukuo" by Italy. Chinese officials and the Chinese press expressed gratification over the election of China to a non-permanent seat on the Council of the League of Nations. The reelection of President Roosevelt was accepted by the Chinese newspapers and public with great enthusiasm.

Respectfully yours,

For the Ambassador:

F. P. Lockhart,
Counselor of Embassy

CHINA

PROBLEM OF CHINA'S ECONOMIC RECONSTRUCTION AND THE ATTITUDE OF THE UNITED STATES AND OTHER GOVERNMENTS RESPECTING FINANCIAL ASSISTANCE TO CHINA [1]

893.48/1034

Memorandum by Mr. Raymond C. Mackay of the Division of Far Eastern Affairs

[WASHINGTON,] January 3, 1936.

Conversation: The Chinese Ambassador, Mr. Sao-Ke Sze;
       Mr. Hornbeck [2];
       Mr. Mackay.

The Chinese Ambassador called at the Department and, after referring to recent negotiations in regard to payments due on the wheat credit of 1931 and the cotton and wheat credit of 1933, affirmed that the Chinese Government had been "penalized" by the effecting on December 31, 1935, of payment in full of the sum of $3,000,000 plus then owing the Farm Credit Administration. The Ambassador further stated that the situation had resulted from his having placed "all his cards on the table" and that therefore there devolved on him the "guilt" for China's loss of the accommodation which had been sought. Mr. Hornbeck said that he could not agree either as to there being any "guilt" (or fault) or as to the contention that the Chinese Government had been "penalized" by the effecting of a payment in full of the amount due on the given due date.

The Ambassador then said that he hoped he might be able to obtain from the Farm Credit Administration a refund of $2,750,000 and from both the Farm Credit Administration and the Reconstruction Finance Corporation more liberal terms covering payments on those portions of the credits under reference which remain outstanding.

The Ambassador asked whether Mr. Hornbeck would, in case the Ambassador should succeed in obtaining by direct approach to the F. C. A. and the R. F. C. the concessions which he had indicated,— whether Mr. Hornbeck would refrain from opposition. Mr. Hornbeck said that he doubted whether it would be possible by any process

---

[1] Continued from *Foreign Relations*, 1935, vol. III, pp. 526–664.
[2] Stanley K. Hornbeck, Chief of the Division of Far Eastern Affairs.

to effect a refund such as the Ambassador had mentioned; that he personally would not view with favor any procedure to that end, although the Ambassador was of course at liberty to canvass the situation; that neither he nor the Department could in advance give a blanket assurance as to a future position in regard to such a matter; and that, if at some future time there were submitted to the Department a new project or plan for revised schedules of payments on the obligations of the Chinese Government under reference, such projects or plans would be given thoughtful consideration at the time in the light of the then existing circumstances.

There followed a lengthy and detailed discussion of recent developments in the matter under consideration. It was suggested and was agreed that the existing situation called primarily for consideration of possible future action rather than of developments in the past. The Ambassador, however, again referred to "errors" made and faulty tactics employed by representatives of the Chinese Government in their recent negotiations for a postponement of payments due on the credits under reference. Mr. Hornbeck expressed the opinion that in the scale of importance there rested far above such matters as tactics and strategy the all-important question of the attitude of the Chinese Government. Mr. Hornbeck further stated that, expressed in simplest terms, the situation under discussion was one in which the Chinese Government had requested of the American Government material concessions; that the American Government, in indicating to the Chinese Government the extent to which it might be in position to comply with such request, had sought an indication of a definite disposition on the part of the Chinese Government to take appropriate steps toward the liquidation of various of its long outstanding obligations to American private creditors; that the only response which the Chinese Government had made, as contrasted with the eminently satisfactory spirit of cooperation displayed by Ambassador Sze, were indications of dissatisfaction with the concessions which the American Government had indicated that it might be in position to make and a statement emanating from the Chinese Minister of Finance implying that it was the Chinese Government's view that nothing could or would be done by the Chinese Government to meet the wishes of the American Government; and that in view of such indicated attitude on the part of the Chinese Government there had followed, as a natural consequence, the action of the American Government in accepting on December 31, 1935, payment in full of monies then due to it by the Chinese Government.

893.48/1036a

The Department of State to the Chinese Embassy [3]

ORAL STATEMENT

In reply to the Ambassador's observations in reference to events on and immediately preceding December 31,—

It does not seem to us that any very useful purpose is to be served by an endeavor to attribute to any one act or to any person or agency involved a special or precise measure of responsibility for the *dénouement* of December 31.

The simple facts are that the Chinese Government asked of the American Government certain favors in the nature of accommodations with regard to adoption of new schedules, involving deferring of payments, in connection with financial obligations in effect. The American Government indicated a willingness to consider this request favorably but at the same time asked of the Chinese Government an indication of a definite disposition to give appropriate consideration to certain matters of outstanding obligations of that Government. Thereafter, although the Chinese Ambassador gave clear evidence of an attitude sympathetically responsive to the American Government's request, such evidence as came to the American Government of the Chinese Government's attitude was indicative of a disinclination if not a flat refusal on the Chinese Government's part to do anything effective by way of response to the American Government's request. In addition, it was indicated to the American Government that the Chinese Government would not be satisfied with the plan of deferred payments which the American Government had tentatively suggested in response to the Chinese Government's request and that the Chinese Government intended to ask for a further revision still more favorable to it. Under these circumstances and with no agreement having been reached, it was logical that the American Government expect full payment by the Chinese Government on the due date of the amount due on that date. The Chinese Government made on the due date the payment due.

It is not perceived that the Chinese Government was in any way "penalized".

There still remains to be considered the possibility of readjustments in schedules of payments involving an aggregate sum of $17,000,000 plus, as compared with the sum of $3,000,000 plus paid by the Chinese Government on the due date, December 31, 1935.

The American Government is prepared to give further consideration to the question of making readjustments in regard to what remains to

---

[3] Handed by the Chief of the Division of Far Eastern Affairs to the Chinese Ambassador "for his personal record of conversation."

be paid. The American Government feels warranted in expecting that the Chinese Government will give further consideration to the request which was made by the American Government in connection with the Chinese Government's request. The American Government awaits some indication of the Chinese Government's attitude.

[WASHINGTON,] January 3, 1936.

893.515/968 : Telegram

The Consul General at Shanghai (Davis) to the Secretary of State

SHANGHAI, January 6, 1936—5 p. m.
[Received January 6—6 : 33 a. m.]

11. Reliably informed Sir Frederick Leith-Ross [4] has advised the Chinese Government to abandon present standard of 880 for silver coinage in favor of alloy used in Great Britain understood to be 500 silver, 400 nickel, 50 copper and 50 zinc. He has telegraphed London inquiring whether blanks for one dollar and 50 cent pieces can be supplied promptly and dies have been or are about to be ordered from Philadelphia. Purpose is to have coins that will not meet melting point unless world price of silver reaches approximately 1.29 United States currency.

DAVIS

893.515/972 : Telegram

The Consul General at Shanghai (Davis) to the Secretary of State

SHANGHAI, January 11, 1936—10 a. m.
[Received January 11—9 : 55 a. m.]

24. All foreign banks in Shanghai except Japanese have now made arrangements to surrender silver to Central Bank either in accordance with the terms mentioned in my 751, December 11, 5 p. m.[5] or on basis of mutual deposits with Central Bank and foreign bank concerned in place of deposit of securities equal to two-thirds of face value of silver surrendered, the foreign bank's deposit with the Central Bank to bear 6% interest while the Central Bank's deposit with foreign bank will draw 1%. Understand slightly under 26,000,000 silver dollars surrendered while Japanese banks still hold about 14,000,000.

Repeated to Peiping. Mail to Nanking.

DAVIS

---

[4] Chief Economic Adviser to the British Government, assigned temporarily as financial adviser to the British Embassy in China.
[5] Not printed.

893.515/1001 : Telegram

The Counselor of Embassy in China (Peck) to the Secretary of State

NANKING, February 6, 1936—3 p. m.
[Received February 6—9 : 10 a. m.]

31. McDaniel [6] was informed by Jabin Hsu,[7] February 6, 11 a. m. that Suma [8] has just told him that when in Shanghai February 5 he had personally told Leith-Ross that in view of the imminent *rapprochement* between Japan and China it would not be fitting for any other nation to offer advice or otherwise intervene in China's currency or fiscal matters. Suma said he had called to tell Kung [9] about this. However, Suma told Hsu the Japanese Government does not disapprove of the recent bond conversion scheme and believes there was nothing else for the Chinese Government to do.

Repeated to the Embassy and the Department.

PECK

893.48/1044 : Telegram

The Consul General at Shanghai (Gauss) to the Secretary of State

SHANGHAI, February 17, 1936—4 p. m.
[Received February 17—9 : 25 a. m.]

107. [From the Ambassador.] My October 27 [*29*], 7 p. m. from Shanghai [10] and subsequent telegrams regarding suggested reinstatement of cotton and wheat loan. While making social call on Kung today accompanied by Gauss, Kung asked C. T. Wang [11] to be present and asked Wang to communicate to me the following. Wang stated that while on the ship with the congressional party between Shanghai and Yokohama he discussed with Leslie L. Biffle [12] and possibly others the question of reinstatement of uncompleted part of wheat and cotton loan. He stated that there had since been an exchange of communications on this subject and that he had been referred to Hunt [13] in the matter. He described the proposal very generally without going into detail and said that he had referred the matter to Dr. Kung. Kung stated that he was interested and that he had instructed the Chinese Ambassador to make inquiry as to whether the proposal

[6] C. Yates McDaniel, Associated Press correspondent at Nanking.
[7] Director of General Affairs, Chinese Ministry of Finance.
[8] Yakichiro Suma, First Secretary of the Japanese Embassy in China.
[9] H. H. Kung, Chinese Minister of Finance.
[10] Not printed.
[11] Former Chinese Minister for Foreign Affairs.
[12] Secretary to the Democratic majority in the Senate.
[13] William P. Hunt, American businessman.

would be received favorably by the American Government if application were made by the Chinese Government for reinstatement of loan. He stated that the Chinese Ambassador's reply was vague as he had been unable to see Jones.[14] He said that they did not wish to apply unless assured that the application would be favorably received and asked me to telegraph you and inquire as to this point stating that this information was urgently needed here. Without other comment I promised to make the inquiry.

2. From the very broad and general statements made by Kung and Wang I infer that the proposal is along lines described in my November 24, 2 p. m. from Shanghai,[15] China proposing to sell cotton to Germany obtaining 25 percent in cash and credits for the balance payable within a year, the Chinese obligation to the American Government to be liquidated in installments over a period of from 2 to 5 years. Kung remarked that credits would aid in plans for stabilizing currency but made no other statement regarding use of funds. I still hold the opinion expressed in the last paragraph of my November 24, 2 p. m.[16] Can Department give me a reply to Kung's question which either I or Gauss can communicate to Kung. [Johnson.]

GAUSS

893.48/1044 : Telegram

The Secretary of State to the Counselor of Embassy in China (Peck)

WASHINGTON, February 21, 1936—5 p. m.

15. For the Ambassador. Shanghai's 107, February 17, 4 p. m. You or Gauss may inform Kung orally, with appropriate reference to his conversation with you on February 17, as follows:

The American Government, after careful consideration of the many factors involved, would not be prepared, if requested as indicated, to reinstate the canceled portion of the cotton and wheat credit of 1933 under reference.

HULL

893.51/6082 : Telegram

The Consul General at Shanghai (Gauss) to the Secretary of State

SHANGHAI, February 24, 1936—5 p. m.
[Received February 24—10:30 a. m.]

113. 1. Press today reports that last week Central Political Council approved Minister of Finance Kung's economic policy for China and

---

[14] Jesse H. Jones, Chairman of the Reconstruction Finance Corporation.
[15] Not printed.
[16] In this telegram the Ambassador concluded: "I think the consummation of such a transaction at this time would have grave repercussions in Japan and I am doubtful whether China can ever repay." (893.48/1018)

enjoined Executive Yuan to take effective steps within 1 month looking toward the execution of the plan.

2. Kung's plan refers to success of Italy, Russia and Japan and calls for China to "pledge ourselves to enforce the policy of economic self-sufficiency" "according to a designed program".

3. Plan provides practical primary education, thrift, utilization wasteland, Government subsidies to banks to enable agricultural and industrial loans at low interest, promotion and nationalization domestic industries, 3 days annual conscripted labor or head tax in lieu thereof, establishment quality standards exports and balancing of imports and exports with import trade under "direct as well as indirect control of Government" "measures should be adopted to arrange for the enforcement of exchange by barter or by a quota system with the various foreign powers".

4. Editorial comment thus far limited to brief laudatory remarks of the China press.

Repeated to Embassy, Peiping and mail to Nanking.

GAUSS

893.48/1049

Memorandum by the Chief of the Division of Far Eastern Affairs (Hornbeck)

[WASHINGTON,] February 25, 1936.

Conversation: Mr. Sao-Ke Alfred Sze, Chinese Ambassador;
Mr. Hornbeck;
Mr. Mackay.

The Ambassador called and said that he had a telegram from H. H. Kung in which Kung instructed him to inquire whether it would be agreeable to the American Government, pending negotiation, as the Chinese Government was sending someone to this country to negotiate on the subject, to let stand in abeyance the payment of $420,000 which will be due from the Chinese Government on March 1 on the RFC credit.

Mr. Hornbeck called Mr. Mackay in. Mr. Hornbeck inquired on what ground the Chinese Government wished that the payment be held in abeyance. The Ambassador replied that Kung had not informed him but that he supposed that they were "hard up". Mr. Hornbeck said that we would have to submit the question to the RFC.

S[TANLEY] K. H[ORNBECK]

893.48/1050 : Telegram

The Consul General at Shanghai (Gauss) to the Secretary of State

SHANGHAI, February 27, 1936—4 p. m.
[Received February 27—7 : 25 a. m.]

120. Reference Department's 16, February 26, 5 p. m., to Nanking.[17] The Department's reply [18] was communicated by me to Kung on the morning of February 24th. He received the information without comment.

From other sources I learn quite confidentially that K. P. Chen, Shanghai banker, is to leave for Washington early in March to confer on monetary matters with the Secretary of the Treasury on behalf of the Minister of Finance, and that he has been advised to familiarize himself with the flood relief loan and the cotton and wheat credit. It is the expectation of those interested in the reinstatement of the cotton and wheat credit that the proposal will be revised and reinstatement consummated during Chen's visit to Washington.

Repeated to Nanking.

GAUSS

893.48/1057

Memorandum by the Chief of the Division of Far Eastern Affairs (Hornbeck)

[WASHINGTON,] March 4, 1936.

I called up the Chinese Ambassador this morning and inquired whether he had any new information with regard to Mr. K. P. Chen's mission.

The Ambassador said that Mr. Chen is scheduled to sail from Shanghai on March 9, for Honolulu; at Honolulu he will transship and will arrive on the steamship *Lurline* at San Francisco on March 26. He will be accompanied by Mr. Y. C. Koo, a banker and an expert on monetary matters, and Mr. P. W. Kuo (Kuo is well known in this country; he is an educator and publicist and was for some time connected with the China Foundation, with his offices in New York).

I asked whether the Ambassador had any new specifications with regard to Chen's mission. The Ambassador said that Chen was coming on the invitation of the Secretary of the Treasury; that Mr.

---
[17] Not printed.
[18] See Department's telegram No. 15, February 21, 5 p. m., p. 464.

Morgenthau had at first asked that T. V. Soong[19] come; that Soong had countered by suggesting that C. T. Wang be sent; that Mr. Morgenthau had said that he wanted not a diplomat or politician but a financial expert; that the Chinese had then offered K. P. Chen and it had been arranged that Chen should come; that Mr. Chen was to talk with Mr. Morgenthau about monetary matters but that he, the Ambassador, had been informed that in addition Mr. Chen would be prepared to talk about matters relating to the outstanding credits and that he, the Ambassador, had suggested to his Government that Mr. Chen be informed about certain of China's outstanding financial obligations. The Ambassador said that Mr. Morgenthau had informed him that he, Morgenthau, was keeping Mr. Phillips[20] informed.

I inquired whether Mr. K. P. Chen would have an official status. The Ambassador replied that Mr. Chen had been given an official passport but not an official title, and that it had been agreed that there should be no publicity. I said, "Is it to be understood that Chen will be regarded by his Government as an official?" The Ambassador replied, "Yes".

The Ambassador then said that Mr. Bartz[21] had called on him recently, subsequent to a conversation which Mr. Bartz had had with me. See memorandum entitled: "Proposed reinstatement of canceled portion of the cotton and wheat credit of 1933."[22]

893.48/1050 : Telegram

The Secretary of State to the Counselor of Embassy in China (Peck)

WASHINGTON, March 4, 1936—7 p. m.

18. For the Ambassador. Shanghai's 120, February 27, 4 p. m., last paragraph.

Background: Department has been given to understand that Chen is coming here on the invitation of the Secretary of the Treasury to give the Treasury information with regard to monetary matters; that the Chinese Government has given Chen an official passport but no official title; and that no publicity is to be given at either end.

Action: Referring expressly to the information given in Shanghai's telegram under reference, Department feels, in the light of conversations with Reconstruction Finance Corporation officials, that interested Chinese officialdom should be discouraged from entertaining any expectation of reinstatement of canceled portion of cotton and

---

[19] Former Chinese Minister of Finance.
[20] William Phillips, Under Secretary of State.
[21] C. F. Bartz & Co., cotton merchants.
[22] Dated February 18; not printed.

wheat credit. Chen presumably will be permitted to raise any appropriate questions and make any appropriate inquiries which his Government may wish to authorize him to put forward, but Department feels it would be neither to this Government's nor to the Chinese Government's advantage for him to arrive here with any preconceived expectation of success in seeking loans or credits. Such questions as possible revision of schedules of payments on outstanding obligations may perhaps be susceptible of discussion.

Department desires that you discreetly communicate the substance of the above orally, informally and in friendly manner to Kung and that you suggest to him that these considerations should be fully understood by the Chinese official personnel most concerned.

You are authorized to do this yourself or through Peck or Gauss. Telegraph Department when you have acted.

HULL

893.48/1062 : Telegram

The Ambassador in China (Johnson) to the Secretary of State

SHANGHAI, March 6, 1936—1 p. m.
[Received March 6—4 : 33 a. m.]

139. Your 18, March 4, 7 p. m., to Nanking.

1. According to press reports in connection with Chen's departure on Monday [23] on a tour of inspection of the United States and Europe he has been appointed High Adviser to Ministry of Finance.

2. I communicated orally Department's message to Kung yesterday at Nanking. I inferred from the way he received the message that he was disappointed as he inquired casually in the course of the conversation as to whether Treasury Department or State Department was responsible for deciding question of loan. I replied that ultimate responsibility would lie with the President in considering financial policies of the Government.

3. Gauss tells me that he has learned in confidence from Hunt that K. P. Chen received advice from the Treasury Department that he should come prepared not only to discuss monetary matters but that he should also familiarize himself with the Flood Relief Loan and cotton and wheat credit. This may explain Kung's attitude.

JOHNSON

---

[23] The Consul General at Shanghai in his telegram No. 156, March 14, 10 a. m., reported that K. P. Chen and party had sailed the night before on the S. S. *President Pierce*, accompanied by P. W. Kuo, Director of Bureau of Foreign Trade of the Ministry of Industries; Y. G. Koo, submanager of the Chung Foo Union Bank and Counselor of the Executive Yuan; and Mrs. Koo (893.48/1066).

893.51/6126

Memorandum by the Chief of the Division of Far Eastern Affairs
(Hornbeck)

[Extract]

[WASHINGTON,] March 26, 1936.

. . . .

This brings us back to the question raised earlier in this memorandum: Would a dissolution of the China Consortium [24] be of advantage, or of no concern, or of disadvantage to the United States?

The advantage, concern, or disadvantage of the United States should be considered in terms of policy and of political and diplomatic interest and concern in the field of our Far Eastern relations.

The chief advantages to us of the Consortium Agreements have been, first, that they are in line with one of the underlying principles for which we have contended, that of cooperative action and individual and collective self-restraint on the part of the powers in the carrying on of public business in and with regard to China where there exist certain rights and obligations which are common to the powers; second, that, whereas if the field of making loans to China and of doing business in and with China of types which require special action by the Chinese Government be left to free and unrestricted competition, the United States and American nationals stand little chance (because of the more emphatic methods used by foreign governments and foreign nationals supported by their governments in dealing with the Chinese Government), by contrast, where the principles of cooperative action and of individual and collective self-restraint are agreed upon and observed the United States and American nationals stand an approximately equal chance of doing with and in China some of this type of business; and, third, the assumption of a collective interest and responsibility by the banking groups of the several major powers which groups constitute the membership of the Consortium has effectively prevented irresponsible loaning (with a mixture of economic and political objectives) by certain powers to China and acquisition by irresponsible groups of politicians in China of funds borrowed by such irresponsible groups in the name of China and applied by the borrowers to wasteful enterprises (sometimes of greater or less public interest and sometimes of purely personal interest). The American Government and the American people sincerely believe in the principle of equality of commercial opportunity; they also believe that the achievement by China of real political and economic progress, in the direction of stability of national strength, would be in the best

---

[24] See agreement signed at New York, October 15, 1920, *Foreign Relations*, 1920, vol. I, p. 576.

interest of all concerned; they do not believe in and they try to discourage action calculated toward or tending to perpetuate and increase civil strife and economic disorder in China; they do not believe in cut-throat competition among the powers toward the securing of special political or economic advantages in or at the expense of China; they believe in an effort on the part of all the powers to be helpful to the Chinese and to promote progress in China.

Ever since the early 1850's, the American Government, having from time to time experienced and observed the relative difficulties of régimes in which the principle of free competition has prevailed and régimes in which the principle of cooperative action has prevailed, among the powers, in relations with China, has weighed the advantages and disadvantages of the two régimes and has decided repeatedly in favor of the principle of cooperative action. Since the days of John Hay, thirty-five years ago, the American Government has most of the time been the foremost proponent of the principle. At the Washington Conference this Government played a leading part in bringing about general agreement that that principle was desirable and should prevail. Since then each Administration in this country has been guided by and has made frequent reference to the Washington Conference treaties and agreements. The present Administration for more than three years has persevered on the same line. The long and the short of the matter is, there is no other possible course which the American Government might follow with any prospect of advantage and with any likelihood of other than disadvantage. Free and unrestricted competition among the powers in relations with China cannot possibly be to our advantage. Already, activities of Japan in disregard of the cooperative principle and the Washington Conference agreements in regard to China has resulted in political difficulties and economic disadvantage to this country. Already, activities of the British Government, more forceful than the methods which the American Government—American commercial interests being somewhat apathetic and American public opinion being adverse to a vigorous diplomacy for the promotion of American interests in the Far East—is in position to use, have obtained for British commercial interests in China a position of technical advantage in competition with American commercial interests. If the principle of cooperative action passes into the discard, it is going to be increasingly difficult for American commercial interests to hold their own, to say nothing of making progress, in China.

The break-up of the China Consortium would be a step in that direction.

The moment is fast approaching when the banks, both in this country and in others, which have had their confidence if not their foundations shaken by the economic and financial debacle which set in in

1929 and from which we are just beginning to emerge—the banks, which have their vaults full of money which they have been afraid to put to work—will begin to respond to the demands of new opportunities. It will probably not be long before they will be eagerly looking about for opportunities. They will again scan not only opportunities in their own countries but opportunities abroad. With the Consortium gone, China will appear a field unattractive indeed for the investment of funds. Yet the traditional concept of China as a great potential market will continue to prevail. The Far East in general will still have a lure for merchants and financiers. The doctrine which Japanese propagandists have been preaching for twenty years: that the Occident should do business with China through Japan: will sound increasingly attractive. Wanting to place funds somewhere in the Far East, foreign bankers and merchants will tend to give ear to that idea. The Japanese will be encouraged to reiterate that business with China can be done, if at all, with promise of success only if done through Japan. If foreign funds be withheld from investment in China and be supplied in considerable amount to the Japanese—for no matter what purpose—the way of Japan toward the establishing of a Japanese hegemony in the Far East will have been made easier and the "open door" into and in China will have been narrowed and will be tending toward a shrinkage into nonexistence.

Hence, it is believed that a break-up of the Consortium would be to the disadvantage of the United States in that it would contribute toward a weakening of our general position as regards policy in relation to the Far East and would facilitate the attainment by other countries of ends which, if achieved, would put our trade with China in a position of increasing disadvantage. With regard to trade, the contention may be made that we would gain more by having our trade with Far Eastern countries pass through or be under the control of Japan than by having it continue in the natural channels which it now follows. That contention is one which must rest on considerations which are largely matters of opinion. In the opinion of the undersigned and his immediate associates in the Department, the adoption of and action in accordance with such a view would not be warranted. Experience of the past thirty years has shown that when control of commerce in any area in the Far East outside of Japan falls into Japanese hands, Japanese interests prosper relatively and the foreign interests, while there may accrue to them some absolute gains, do not prosper relatively and often are at last squeezed out entirely. Japanese trade, from point of view of production and export, is coming increasingly into competition with the trade of other nations, everywhere. Once make Japan a channel for trade to and from China, the tendency will be for Japanese interests to get the cream and most of the milk of that trade.

It is believed that, as between China and Japan, the American Government should still proceed on the principle of playing no favorites. This country has of course no intention of using force for the preservation of the "open door" in China. At the same time, there would be nothing to be gained by our giving up of our advocacy of the principle of equality of commercial opportunity, in application to that region as elsewhere. We need not discontinue our diplomatic efforts on behalf of American policy and interests in the Far East. The existence of the Consortium is in line with our general effort on behalf of the principle of equality of commercial opportunity. The Consortium is an instrument in support of the principle of cooperative action. As between a break-up or a continuance in existence of the Consortium, our influence, if exerted, should be on the side of continuance.

It is believed that it would be warrantable and advisable for this Government to discuss this question informally with representatives of the American banking group in the Consortium. It is believed that in such a discussion we might reasonably intimate that we would regret seeing the Consortium broken up.

It is suggested that the Chief of the Far Eastern Division be authorized to discuss this matter in the sense indicated with Mr. Thomas Lamont.[25]

S[TANLEY] K. H[ORNBECK]

893.51/6128

Memorandum by the Chief of the Division of Far Eastern Affairs (Hornbeck)

[WASHINGTON,] March 31, 1936.

At the close of a conversation which the Chinese Ambassador had initiated in regard to another matter, I took occasion to ask the Ambassador whether he had received anything new regarding negotiations in relation to Hukuang Railway bonds.[26] The Ambassador replied that he had not.

I then said that I wanted to make an entirely informal and unofficial inquiry: I merely wanted the Ambassador's impression: what is the thought and feeling of Chinese officialdom nowadays in regard to

---

[25] The Secretary and Under Secretary of State on March 30 authorized Mr. Hornbeck to discuss this matter with Mr. Lamont, of J. P. Morgan & Co., representing the American Group of the China Consortium.

[26] For correspondence concerning the Hukuang loan, see section entitled "Efforts for consideration of American Claims Outstanding Against China", pp. 576–594, *passim.*

the China Consortium: do the Chinese still view the Consortium with antipathy: what would be their feeling if it were to go out of existence. I said that this must be regarded as an inquiry just between myself and the Ambassador and that his reply would be simply for the purpose of orienting me with regard to current Chinese thought. The Ambassador replied that he had not given this subject much consideration; that in the early days the Chinese had felt objection to the Consortium because of the restrictions which it tended to impose on their freedom of action in regard to borrowing; they had gradually come to look upon it as a negative instrument; in later years it had seemed to them an obstacle to any borrowing on their part—because the Japanese, being in the Consortium, always imposed some kind of a veto; but that, with regard to what they might think of a disappearance of the Consortium, he felt that such a disappearance at this time would have an upsetting and harmful effect on China's interests and he believed that many other Chinese would feel the same way about it.

_____

893.51/6129

Memorandum by the Chief of the Division of Far Eastern Affairs (Hornbeck) of a Conversation With Mr. Thomas W. Lamont of New York

[WASHINGTON,] April 1, 1936.

Reference, FE [27] memorandum of March 26, subject: "China Consortium, Hukuang Bonds, Divergence of View between British and American Groups, and Questions of Major Policy", and Mr. Phillip's memorandum to Mr. Hornbeck of March 30.[28]

I talked with Mr. Lamont on the telephone yesterday morning, and, being in New York last evening, I had a few minutes' conversation with Mr. Lamont.

In the course of these conversations Mr. Lamont and I were in agreement that the American Group in the Consortium and the American holders of Hukuang bonds have warrant for dissatisfaction with the manner in which British interests and the Chinese Government have been proceeding in regard to the matter of the Hukuang bonds. Mr. Lamont said that if the British bondholders accept the proposal which the Chinese Government has made, the American interests will probably have no alternative but to accept the same terms. He read to me a cable from Morgan, Grenfell and Company, London, which, together with copies of previous correspondence which he has sent us, shows that since some time in January the American Group has

_____

[27] Division of Far Eastern Affairs.
[28] See footnote 25, p. 472.

been given more or less information, from Chinese and from British sources, with regard to developments in this matter. This correspondence also shows that the British interests and the American interests are now conferring with regard to the matter. Mr. Lamont also showed me a copy of a telegram which he had prepared but not yet sent, to London, indicating the views of the American issuing and Consortium groups regarding the Hukuang bonds.

In the course of the first conversation, I took the opportunity to say to Mr. Lamont that, in view of information which we had received from London indicating that there was some threat of a possible break-up of the Consortium, the question of this Government's attitude had been canvassed and I was authorized to say that we were not indifferent and that we would in fact view with regret a break-up of the Consortium. In the course of the evening conversation, I said that, the political situation in the Far East being what it is, and various problems of cooperation being what they are, it would seem to us that a break-up of the Consortium at this time might have unfortunate implications and occasion unsatisfactory inferences. Mr. Lamont indicated that he was of the same view. He said however that various of the American banks were skeptical if not indifferent with regard to Far Eastern possibilities and impatient of the expense which was involved in the American membership in the Consortium with, over a period of many years, none but negative effects, and that, with the irritation over the way the Hukuang matter is being handled, there would be an inclination on the part of some of them to advise letting the Consortium go to the board. He said that if the Government felt that it was worth while to have the Consortium continue, he wondered whether the Government would be willing in connection with the current developments to give a little assistance on behalf of the American Group. He was proposing to London some changes to be considered for proposal to the Chinese Government in that Government's offer. He said that all concerned felt that it would be better to have a new arrangement with regard to the bonds than to have no new arrangement; but, the American Group felt that the Hukuang bonds were entitled to better terms than the Tientsin–Pukow bonds. He thought it would be very helpful if the State Department would instruct Ambassador Johnson to give support to the suggestion, if and when made by the groups on behalf of the bondholders, in that sense. He wanted to ask me to give consideration to that idea. I said that it sounded to me reasonable in principle but that I could not say just how far the Department might be willing to go: I would report the suggestion to the Secretary.

Mr. Lamont said that the British Bondholders Committee had inquired whether the American Group would have any objection to their conferring with Mr. Reuben Clark of the Foreign Bondholders Protective Council, Incorporated, and that reply had been made that the American interests would have no objection. I asked Mr. Lamont whether this meant that the American interests merely would make no objection or that they felt no objection. Mr. Lamont replied that they were perfectly willing to have that procedure followed. I inquired what effect that might have in regard to use of channels of communication. Mr. Lamont replied that he had not thought about that. He said that he did not know whether Mr. Clark would be willing to take on this task, but that he and his associates saw no reason for replying otherwise than affirmatively to the British inquiry. I remarked that we had received a telegram in which it was stated that the British interests intended to confer with Mr. Clark.

Mr. Lamont gave me copies of papers, which are here attached.[29]

S[TANLEY] K. H[ORNBECK]

893.48/1062 : Telegram

The Secretary of State to the Ambassador in China (Johnson)

WASHINGTON, April 9, 1936—7 p. m.

84. Reference Ambassador's message as contained in Shanghai's 139, March 6, 1 p. m. K. P. Chen and party have arrived in Washington and begun conversations with officials of the Treasury Department in regard to, as announced by press, "mutual monetary problems."

When there is clarification or particularization of subjects and as developments of importance occur, Department will expect to inform Embassy.

Please inform Nanking and Shanghai.

HULL

893.48/1078

Memorandum by the President of the Export-Import Bank of Washington (Pierson)

[WASHINGTON,] April 13, 1936.

The Chinese Ambassador, Mr. Sze, accompanied by Messrs. Tswenling Tsui [30] and T. G. Koo, called at the Export-Import Bank this afternoon.

The Ambassador stated that it was the desire of his Government to arrange a modification in the payments due upon the loans assigned to the Bank by the Farm Credit Administration ($3,070,942.20 plus accrued interest at the rate of 4% per annum) and by the Reconstruction Finance Corporation ($13,537,387.79 plus accrued interest at the rate of 5% per annum).

---

[29] None printed.
[30] Second Secretary of the Chinese Embassy.

The Ambassador further stated that his Government hoped that the Bank would consent to the following proposals:

1. To consolidate the two loans upon a uniform interest basis, presumably at some rate less than 5% per annum;
2. To secure the consolidated loan by a first charge against the consolidated taxes for which provision is made in the contract between the Government of the Republic of China and the Reconstruction Finance Corporation;
3. To discontinue the customs surtax against which the Reconstruction Finance Corporation now has a second lien;
4. To discontinue further payments upon principal until the end of 1940;
5. To amortise the balance of principal from 1940 to 1950.

When asked what the attitude of the Bank would be to his suggestions, I replied that it would be necessary for me to discuss them with other officers of the Bank and with the Bank's Policy and Loan Committee. In addition to that I indicated that in my own opinion an extension of the loans and particularly the Farm Credit Administration loan would be difficult to arrange; and that the proposal generally contemplated too extended a period for amortization.

The Ambassador requested that we give the matter our most sympathetic consideration and then advise him as to our conclusions.

Thereafter we conversed in general terms about our trade with China, during the course of which I expressed the hope that American exports to China might be increased.

As he was leaving, Mr. Koo remarked that one of the greatest problems faced in connection with China's new monetary policy was finding the necessary foreign exchange with which to meet the Government's requirements, and that the modifications requested in connection with the obligations held by the Export-Import Bank would, if arranged, be of great benefit to China.

I concluded our conversation by assuring the Ambassador and his two companions that we would act on their request within the near future.

WARREN LEE PIERSON

893.51/6143 : Telegram

The Consul General at Shanghai (Gauss) to the Secretary of State

SHANGHAI, April 17, 1936—2 p. m.
[Received April 17—9:07 a. m.]

211. 1. Kuomin despatch dated Nanking, April 11, reports interview with Ma Yin Chu, Chairman of the Finance Committee of the Legislative Yuan. Despatch concludes as follows:

"In conclusion, Doctor Ma said that personally he is of the opinion that during the period of extraordinary national emergency the Government should depend for its main source of revenue upon the income tax which he hoped the Government would immediately put into effect. Besides authorizing a limited currency inflation and issuing a few domestic loans, the Government may also utilize foreign capital to meet its financial needs or declare a moratorium on existing foreign loans."

2. According to a Kuomin Nanking despatch April 16, a spokesman of the Ministry of Finance states Ma's views were personal and not those advocated by the Government. Same despatch states Finance Minister Kung in an interview said China is still on the silver standard and that prior to November 3rd, 1935, China was on a free silver standard whereas now China is on a managed silver standard.

3. Above may be of interest in connection with the Department's 84, April 9, 7 p. m., to the Embassy.

GAUSS

893.515/1100

Memorandum by the Chief of the Division of Far Eastern Affairs (Hornbeck)

[Extract]

[WASHINGTON,] April 22, 1936.

Conversation: The Secretary of the Treasury, Henry Morgenthau, Jr.

Mr. Yutaro Tomita, Financial Commissioner of the Japanese Government and Financial Attaché of the Japanese Embassies at Washington, London and Paris.

Present: The Japanese Ambassador, Mr. Hirosi Saito.

Mr. Harukage Ukawa, Assistant Financial Attaché of Japanese Embassy, Washington.

Mr. Hornbeck.

. . . .

Mr. Tomita said that, before Sir Frederick Leith-Ross went to China, he had talked with Reith-Ross. As an aside, he remarked that he, Tomita, had been in charge of Japan's financial relations with China for a period of twenty years. He said that Leith-Ross had said that China might pursue a financial course such as has been followed in "Manchukuo". He, Tomita, had told Leith-Ross that this was not possible, as the situations were different: that in Manchuria there was a strong central bank which Japan had backed and with which Japanese banks cooperated; that in China there was no such situation. Nevertheless, he said, the Chinese had tried to proceed on the line which had been followed in Manchuria; and, he remarked, the attempt at monetary reform in China was not proving successful. It looked to be successful in the neighborhood of Shanghai, but in other regions, especially in the interior, such was not the case. "Shanghai currency" did not circulate in the interior. Mr. Morgenthau suggested that it was "Nanking currency". Mr. Tomita said that "Nanking currency" was in fact Shanghai currency, and he repeated that the monetary reform was not succeeding. Mr. Morgenthau said that in his opinion it had gotten on remarkably well, considering the short time—since November 4, 1935—that it had been under way. He pointed out that the banks of other countries had turned in their silver—with the exception of the Japanese banks. Mr. Tomita said that the Japanese banks had not turned their silver in because they were convinced that the monetary reform would not succeed. Mr. Morgenthau remarked that the Japanese banks are holding out about $10,000,000. Mr. Tomita turned to the Japanese Ambassador and said: "They have not made up their minds".

At that point the Japanese Ambassador indicated that he thought it was time to bring the call to an end.

There followed the usual exchange of courtesies and departure of the Japanese guests.

Mr. Morgenthau held Mr. Hornbeck back. He requested that Mr. Hornbeck make a memorandum of the conversation. He asked for Mr. Hornbeck's opinion of the interview. Mr. Hornbeck said that he thought that Mr. Morgenthau had said just those things which would produce the to-be-desired impression; that he had brought out in vigorous relief the strength of our public financial situation and position. Mr. Morgenthau remarked that he had had to "give it to" Mr. Tomita on the matter of the Chinese monetary reform. Mr. Hornbeck replied that such was the case but that Mr. Tomita "had asked for it" and that it was well for him to have been given the clear indication that the sympathy of the Secretary of the Treasury of the American Government is with the Chinese in their effort at monetary reform and that we look with disfavor on Japan's placing of obstacles.

Mr. Morgenthau said that he had told the Chinese bankers of Mr. Tomita's impending appearance in Washington and that the Chinese bankers had pressed him yesterday for a commitment, which he had refused to make. He said that they were apparently nervous over Tomita's approach. Mr. Hornbeck told Mr. Morgenthau the story of the arrival of Tang Shao-yi and the signing of the Root–Takahira Agreement—in 1908.[31]

---

[31] For exchange of notes at Washington, November 30, 1908, see *Foreign Relations*, 1908, pp. 510–512.

There followed some discussion of the purpose of Tomita's visit to Washington. This visit may have been timed deliberately to take place while the Chinese bankers are here; but Mr. Tomita apparently has no message to deliver on behalf of his Government and no proposals to make; he may desire to make a certain impression through the publicity which may be given in the Far East to the fact of his being here and making certain calls at this moment; he is on his way home from London to Tokyo; he is here for two days only; he of course desires to be able to say at home that he has made contacts with high officials here, and he of course desires to pick up any information which may be of use to him either from a technical or from a political point of view. (Note: In the earlier stages of the conversation, the Japanese Ambassador remarked that Mr. Tomita had been talked of as a possible head for the Ministry of Commerce and Industry.) Mr. Morgenthau asked for Mr. Hornbeck's opinion in regard to his having held this interview at his home rather than at his office. Mr. Hornbeck said that he felt that it had been very good strategy; he felt that the Japanese would feel that special courtesies had been shown them, and, at the same time, publicity would be avoided.

(Note: At one point in the conversation—while the question of balancing the United States budget was under reference—, Mr. Morgenthau made the observation that in Japan about one-half of the Japanese Government's expenditures goes to military matters.)

893.515/1053 : Telegram

The Consul General at Shanghai (Gauss) to the Secretary of State

SHANGHAI, April 25, 1936—11 a. m.
[Received April 25—7 : 40 a. m.]

231. Finance Minister Kung yesterday informed press that time limit for exchanging silver for legal tender notes which expires on May 3 would probably be extended several months. I am informed by reliable source that there is developing in China an increasing tendency to surrender silver and that since November 3 when managed currency was established 175,000,000 silver dollars exchanged for notes making the total of Government's stocks of silver about 400,000,000 silver dollars.

Repeated to Peiping. Nanking by mail.

GAUSS

893.48/1088

*Memorandum by Mr. Eugene H. Dooman, of the Division of Far
Eastern Affairs, of a Conversation With the Counselor of the
Japanese Embassy (Yoshizawa)*

[WASHINGTON,] April 30, 1936.

I saw Mr. Yoshizawa yesterday during the reception at the Japanese
Embassy and said to him that we are not now in position to give him
information beyond that given to the press in regard to the negotiations between the Treasury and the group of Chinese officials and
bankers.

Mr. Yoshizawa said that he hoped that he would be called in whenever the Department felt that it could tell the Japanese Embassy
anything in regard to the negotiations.

893.515/1063

*The Chief of the Division of Far Eastern Affairs (Hornbeck) to the
Secretary of State*

[WASHINGTON,] May 14, 1936.

MR. SECRETARY: In the opinion of FE, the arrangement which the
Treasury is prepared to consummate with the Chinese bankers, insofar as indicated and dealt with in the memoranda hereunder [32]
(which were read and explained to you by Mr. Taylor [33]), may be regarded as satisfactory and gratifying.

With regard to the plan of the Treasury for an agreement—facts
and terms of which not to be made public—for purchase of silver, it
is believed that this Department will need to regard that matter as
essentially Treasury business.

Our principal concern, of course, in both connections, is, as Mr.
Phillips pointed out to Mr. Taylor, that of the political effects in the
Far East, including the reactions of the British and the Japanese
Governments. It is a definite feature of our Far Eastern policy at
present that (1) we do not wish to inject new elements of irritation
into that situation; (2) we do not wish to assume new responsibilities
of initiative or leadership in regard to matters of general international
interest in the Far East; (3) we favor cooperation with Great Britain
and we do not wish to give Japan ground for a contention that she is
being discriminated against or being deliberately left out in the cold.

---

[32] None printed; they dealt with "increasing the use of silver in China", "increasing the liquidity of the cash reserve against note issues of the Chinese
Government banks", and "the question of the independence of the Chinese currency". (893.515/1065–67)
[33] Wayne Chatfield Taylor, Fiscal Assistant Secretary of the Treasury.

It is believed that the proposed arrangements in this case give no warrant for criticism or objection by the British and/or the Japanese. But, national and international susceptibilities being what they are, effort should be made in the handling of this matter to be as completely tactful as may be possible and to have the British and the Japanese Governments taken into confidence as far as may be practically possible. A suggestion along that line might perhaps to advantage be made to the Chinese.

Mr. Taylor tells me that, in case this Department wishes to offer any comments or suggestions, the Treasury Department would appreciate having word from us promptly. Might it not be well for Mr. Phillips or for me to inform Mr. Taylor of this Department's views along the lines of the entries which I have made hereinabove.

S[TANLEY] K. H[ORNBECK]

893.515/1064

Memorandum by the Under Secretary of State (Phillips)

[WASHINGTON,] May 14, 1936.

Mr. Wayne Taylor called me on the telephone today to say that the Treasury had acted on the State Department's suggestion and had intimated to the Chinese financial representatives that it might be wise for their Government to inform the British and Japanese of the arrangements just made with the American Treasury before making any official announcement; the Treasury had emphasized that this was entirely up to the Chinese Government to do or not to do as they saw fit, but that, nevertheless, in the opinion of the United States Treasury, it might be a helpful step to take.

According to Mr. Taylor, the Chinese representatives received the suggestion very favorably. Furthermore, Mr. Taylor advised me that the exchange of "notes" between the Treasury and the Chinese would probably take place on Monday next, but there was a possibility of the exchange on Saturday next.

WILLIAM PHILLIPS

893.515/1062 : Telegram

The Consul General at Shanghai (Gauss) to the Secretary of State

SHANGHAI, May 18, 1936—4 p. m.
[Received May 18—10 : 30 a. m.]

270. The following appears in today's press as a Kuomin release at Nanking, May 17th.

"Dr. H. H. Kung, Minister of Finance, issued the following statement today:

'During the past 6½ months the Government has earnestly devoted its efforts to developing and strengthening the measures of monetary reform adopted November 3, 1935, which have resulted in the attainment of exchange stability at a level adopted [adapted?] to China's economic life.

The Minister of Finance now announces that in the light of experience and of additional knowledge of monetary conditions obtaining in China and abroad, the Chinese Government deems it desirable to make known the following measures of monetary reform in accordance with the decree of November 3, 1935.

(1). It will continue to be the policy of the Government at all times to maintain adequate reserves against note issue consisting of gold, foreign exchange, and silver, the silver portion of the reserves to have a value equivalent to at least 25 percent of the note circulation.

(2). For the purpose of completing the reform of the Chinese coinage system, the Government will issue silver coins of 50 cents and 1 dollar denominations.

(3). For the purpose of further strengthening the position of the Chinese currency, definite arrangements have been made to increase the gold and foreign exchange portion of the note issue reserve.

The Minister expresses the firm belief that these supplementary measures of monetary reform and the arrangement made will assure the continued maintenance of an independent currency system not linked to any foreign monetary unit and the permanent stability of the Chinese currency which will inevitably lead to greater economic improvement and prosperity of the Chinese people.' "

Repeated to Peiping, mail to Nanking.

GAUSS

893.515/1062 : Telegram

The Secretary of State to the Ambassador in China (Johnson)

WASHINGTON, May 19, 1936.

120. Reference Shanghai's 270, May 18, 4 p. m., to Department. Treasury Department on May 18 issued to the press a statement by Secretary Morgenthau reading as follows:

"The representatives of the Chinese Ministry of Finance who have been in the United States to make some studies of our monetary and banking system, and to exchange views on monetary problems of mutual interest, have completed their mission and are returning to China.

Our conversations with them have been mutually instructive. I feel confident that the monetary program being pursued by the National Government of China is not only along sound lines, but constitutes an important step toward the desired goal of stability of world currencies.

To supplement their efforts toward that objective and to cooperate with them in their program of monetary reform and currency stabilization, and in accordance with our silver purchase policy, we have definitely indicated our willingness, under conditions mutually acceptable, to make purchases from the Central Bank of China of substantial amounts of silver, and also to make available to the Central Bank of China, under conditions which safeguard the interests of both countries, dollar exchange for currency stabilization purposes.

The mission headed by Mr. Chen has been instrumental in bringing about a more complete understanding of our mutual monetary problems.

I believe that only through full and frank exchange of views similar to that which has just taken place between the representatives of the Chinese Ministry of Finance and ourselves will it be possible to improve the internal stability of national currencies and with this achieve a greater international stability.

Please repeat to Nanking and Shanghai.

HULL

893.515/1062 : Telegram

The Secretary of State to the Ambassador in China (Johnson)

WASHINGTON, May 20, 1936—1 p. m.

121. Department's 120, May 19. Treasury Department requests that the Embassy at Peiping and Nanking and the Consulates General at Shanghai, Tientsin, Hankow, Hong Kong and Canton submit by naval radio on May 23 reports not exceeding 100 words each covering the reaction in the areas indicated to (*a*) the measures of monetary reform recently announced by the Chinese Government and (*b*) the explanatory statements issued on May 18 by the Chinese Minister of Finance and the United States Treasury Department in regard to the measures under reference.

Please issue appropriate instructions and indicate that reports should be sent direct to this Department on the date indicated.[34]

HULL

893.515/1072 : Telegram

The Consul General at Shanghai (Gauss) to the Secretary of State

SHANGHAI, May 20, 1936—1 p. m.
[Received 3:25 p. m.]

277. 1. As of possible interest, a prominent Chinese banker of Shanghai in discussing with me the press reports of the silver agreement at Washington expressed concern as to how far K. P. Chen had

---

[34] Reports from Consulates in China indicated in reply a generally favorable reaction at Chefoo, Hankow, Hong Kong, and Shanghai but a mixed reaction at Amoy, Canton, Foochow, Swatow, Tientsin, Tsinanfu, and Tsingtao. (893.515/1075, 1076, 1078, 1079, 1080, 1089, 1092.) On May 23 at Canton it was noted that "A few intelligent observers feel Sino-American agreement increases prospects of open Sino-Japanese hostilities." (893.515/1080)

committed the Chinese. This concern apparently arose out of the fact, admitted by him confidentially but perhaps indiscreetly, that the Nanking Government has no control over the silver accumulations in Canton. He said that Canton has repeatedly threatened to sell independently of Nanking, and if Canton should sell then the more or less independent regime in the North would also be likely to take an independent attitude.

2. Referring to the minting of subsidiary silver coins, another source expressed concern lest similar coins might be minted in Japan and smuggled into circulation in China. This same source stated confidentially that China had agreed to mint token dollars with not less than 138 grains of silver but weight and fineness had not been stipulated. Repeated to Peiping and Nanking by mail.

GAUSS

893.515/1081 : Telegram

The Counselor of Embassy in China (Peck) to the Secretary of State

NANKING, May 23, 1936—11 a. m.
[Received 5 : 20 p. m.]

154. Department's 121, May 20, 1 p. m. to Peiping; my 144, May 18, 2 p. m.; [35] Shanghai's 270, May 18, 4 p. m.

1. Kung's announcement published 18th omits mention of agreement at instance, I am informed, of State Department. Morgenthau's published 20th.

2. Kung's: Official reaction and controlled press extremely favorable and optimistic; no other local reaction.

3. Morgenthau's: Foreign Vice Minister, former banker, states that agreement has not materially advanced China toward solution currency problems and that there is no general relief or interest presumably because magnitude of agreement is not known; press comment meager and either lukewarm or suspicious; only journal making specific comment sees American attempt to assist China with resulting control over Chinese currency.

4. To Peiping and Shanghai by mail.

PECK

893.515/1077 : Telegram

The Ambassador in China (Johnson) to the Secretary of State

PEIPING, May 23, 1936—1 p. m.
[Received May 23—6 : 28 a. m.]

254. Department's 121, May 20, 1 p. m.

(a). There has been no reaction in Peiping to the monetary reforms

[35] Telegram No. 144 not printed.

recently announced. Exchange rates and Government bonds have remained constant.

(b). Opinion in Chinese banking circles is that Kung's statement of May 18 is confusing and unnecessarily disturbing, especially since Chinese had already adjusted themselves to the new stabilized currency. Doubt was expressed that new token coins would be acceptable to the people. Actually there has been no reaction to Kung's announcement, but the psychological effect has been bad. There has been no reaction in Peiping to the Treasury Department's announcement.

JOHNSON

893.515/1077 : Telegram

The Acting Secretary of State to the Ambassador in China (Johnson)

WASHINGTON, May 23, 1936—3 p. m.

125. Your 254, May 23, 1 p. m.

1. Has there been press comment in regard to the measures of monetary reform and the statements of May 18 made by Kung and the United States Treasury Department? If so, please summarize.

2. Please amplify statements that "Kung's statement is confusing and unnecessarily disturbing" and that "the psychological effect has been bad".

3. Reports from Hankow and Shanghai indicate that the measures of monetary reform were well received there.

4. Report promptly by radio.

CARR

893.515/1082 : Telegram

The Ambassador in China (Johnson) to the Secretary of State

PEIPING, May 24, 1936—6 p. m.
[Received May 24—10:50 a. m.]

255. Department's 125, May 23, 3 p. m.

1. There have been no comments in the Chinese or foreign press in Peiping on the monetary reforms or the two statements of May 18.

2. A Chinese banker with whom this was discussed by a member of my staff on May 23 stated that Kung's statement was confusing because it was impossible to tell from the statement just how Kung proposed to carry out these reforms. He said that the statement was unnecessarily disturbing since the stabilized currency program of the National Government was regarded satisfactorily and that the statement had raised doubt in the minds of some people (who do not understand reserves to back currency are maintained) as to the sta-

bility of the currency which they are now using and which they have accepted as sound. This background of uncertainty in the minds of some people he considered unfortunate. Local manager of the National City Bank with whom same member of staff discussed question same day expressed similar views. Bankers themselves do not appear perturbed.

It is my own personal belief that above represents not so much opinion as lack thereof due to present almost complete financial separation of this area from Central China.

JOHNSON

893.48/1096 : Telegram

The Counselor of Embassy in China (Peck) to the Secretary of State

NANKING, May 25, 1936—9 a. m.
[Received May 25—1 : 21 a. m.]

156. Your 35, May 21, 2 p. m.[36] The Embassy has received a formal note dated May 23, 1936, addressed to the American Ambassador by the Chinese Minister for Foreign Affairs over the official seal of the Ministry of Foreign Affairs which states that the Chinese Ambassador at Washington under instructions from the Chinese Government has negotiated with the second Export-Import Bank [37] a draft agreement for the revision of the schedule of payments of the flood relief loan of 1931 and the cotton and wheat loan of 1933, and that the Chinese Ambassador has received authority to sign this agreement on behalf of the Chinese Government. This constitutes adequate evidence of the authority of the Ambassador to sign. Note proceeding in the next pouch.[37a] By mail to Peiping.

PECK

893.515/1103a : Telegram

The Secretary of State to the Consul General at Shanghai (Gauss)

WASHINGTON, June 5, 1936—7 p. m.

154. At request of Treasury Department, please report not later than morning of June 8 information available at Shanghai in regard to the currency situation in South China and the financial and mone-

---

[36] Not printed.

[37] The Counselor of Embassy in China in his telegram No. 160, May 29, 9 a. m., reported that the Chinese Ministry for Foreign Affairs had replaced the above-mentioned note with another of the same date using the name "Export Import Bank of Washington." (983.48/1098)

[37a] Dated May 29, not printed.

tary aspects of the recent conference held at Canton between the Nanking delegation and Southwest leaders.

HULL

893.515/1106 : Telegram

The Consul General at Shanghai (Gauss) to the Secretary of State

SHANGHAI, June 8, 1936—11 a. m.
[Received June 8—10 : 15 a. m.]

316. Reference Department's telegram No. 154, June 5, 7 p. m. There is little information available here in regard to South China currency situation. Canton business is usually done through Hong Kong. Transactions in Canton exchange are small in Shanghai. Bank of China transactions over the counter only and for accommodation of customers. Rates recently subject to wide fluctuation and no local desire to buy Canton exchange.

Understand that discussions thus far between National Government and Southwest authorities have not produced tangible results. Will report again when further information obtainable. It is rumored in Shanghai that British Government recently started to purchase by Hong Kong and Shanghai Banking Corporation of large amounts of silver from Southwest authorities.

GAUSS

893.515/1107 : Telegram

The Consul General at Canton (Spiker) to the Secretary of State

CANTON, June 8, 1936—4 p. m.
[Received June 8—11 : 10 a. m.]

Referring to Department's telegram June 5, 6 [7] p. m., requesting new developments in matter reported in first two sentences of paragraph 3 of my telegram of June 1, 10 a. m.[38] Subsequent fluctuations in local exchange have been reported in my telegrams of June 3, 6 p. m., June 4, 4 p. m., June 5, 5 p. m.,[39] and June 6, noon.[40]

2. All reports received from reliable sources to date indicate that negotiations between Nanking and local authorities for adoption locally of national currency have thus far been productive of no results since the matter is rather hopelessly controlled by politics rather than by the crying needs of the present situation.

3. As evidence of present confused situation, the national Depart-

---

[38] *Ante,* p. 184.
[39] None printed.
[40] *Ante,* p. 195.

ment of Finance has sought to control situation by fiat, yesterday announcing that speculation in Hong Kong dollars should be curtailed from today and that outstanding accounts should be settled at a rate not exceeding $1.72 to the Hong Kong dollar while future transactions between merchants shall be at rates determined by usual exchange factors. Banks find it increasingly difficult to continue business and are frankly seeking to avoid exchange transactions. Exchange shops today quoted rate 1.80 on Hong Kong dollars. Business is dead. Prominent local banker today informed this office he considers wholesale bankruptcies inevitable unless drastic measures taken within next 3 weeks to relieve situation.

Repeated to Embassy and Shanghai.

SPIKER

893.515/1112 : Telegram

The Consul General at Shanghai (Gauss) to the Secretary of State

SHANGHAI, June 9, 1936—11 a. m.
[Received 3 : 55 p. m.]

320. Reference my 316, June 8, 11 a. m., which was mailed Nanking and Peiping, following has been handed me in confidence by reliable source:

"Reliably informed Canton asked for help in currency reform and Government stated it was prepared to help if they would cease excessive note issue, turn over their silver to branch Currency Reserve Board and agree to adoption of the currency system based on the national dollar in accordance with plan to be approved by the Government. It was understood Canton was to send here for conference but before this could be done came Southwest anti-Japanese action."

Repeated to Peiping, paraphrase to Nanking by mail.

GAUSS

893.51/6184 : Telegram

The Chargé in the United Kingdom (Atherton) to the Secretary of State

LONDON, June 12, 1936—5 p. m.
[Received June 19—11 : 55 a. m.[41]]

309. Your 206, June 12 [11], 5 p. m.[42] Reuter despatch from Nanking, June 7th, which was generally published in the British press

---

[41] Telegram lost in transmission.
[42] Not printed.

and doubtless available likewise to the Department, reported: "The Chinese Minister of Railways has announced that a 6% sterling loan for the completion of the Shanghai–Hangchow–Ningpo Railway will be floated very shortly with the aid of a syndicate composed of British and Chinese corporations."

I understand this loan is to be issued in the Shanghai market for 1,130,000 pounds. The object of the loan is as stated and it will be remembered the outstanding bonds amounting to 300,000 pounds of the previous Shanghai-Ningpo Railway loan were repaid at par last June. Two weeks ago a Chinese 6% indemnity loan was placed in Shanghai but that was a private issue whereas the present loan will be publicly floated. Moreover, it is understood here that application may be made to the London Stock Exchange for a quotation of the new loan. The Foreign Office generally confirms the above and hazards the suggestion that a great deal of the loan may have to be taken by the banks.

ATHERTON

893.48/1102

Press Release Issued by the Export-Import Bank of Washington, June 20, 1936

Mr. Warren Lee Pierson, President of the Export-Import Bank of Washington, today made the following announcement:

The Export-Import Bank of Washington has recently taken over the credits made available by the Reconstruction Finance Corporation and The Grain Stabilization Corporation to the Chinese Government to finance the purchase of American cotton, wheat and flour. In order to simplify their handling, the two credits have now been consolidated.

Of the original sum of $17,105,385 advanced by the Reconstruction Finance Corporation, there remains a balance of $13,537,387. The Grain Stabilization Corporation credit, known as the 1931 Flood Relief Loan, was originally $9,212,826 and has been reduced to $3,070,942. Payments of instalments of principal amounting to $9,709,882 have been duly met.

The consolidated obligation is payable in quarterly instalments over a period of six years. The security for the consolidated obligation is the same as that provided by the original agreements, namely, a first charge against China's consolidated taxes consisting of the rolled tobacco tax, the flour tax, and others, together with a first charge upon the 5% flood relief customs surtax.

893.515/1141

The British Embassy to the Department of State [43]

STATEMENT ISSUED BY SIR F. LEITH-ROSS TO THE PRESS ON LEAVING CHINA

His Majesty's Government in the United Kingdom sent me out to examine the financial and economic difficulties of China and the possibilities of our assisting her, in conjunction with the other Powers interested, to overcome these difficulties. I have spent nearly nine months here and have done my best to investigate conditions as I found them, without prejudice or preconceptions. A large part of my time has necessarily been spent in Shanghai, but I have visited Nanking, Tientsin, Peking, Hankow, Chungking, Amoy and Canton, and have met representatives of the Government authorities and local banking and trading communities in all these centres. It had been the hope of my Government that the United States of America, Japan and France would appoint experts to collaborate with me, but this did not prove possible. However, an important Economic Mission from the United States recently visited China and I have found their Report [44] of great interest. I have maintained contact with Japanese Government representatives and bankers here and have paid two visits to Tokyo so as to obtain first-hand information on the views of the Japanese Government.

2. The considered report on my mission will have to be presented in due course to my Government, but it may be useful, before I leave China, to give some outline of my impressions.

3. The first question to which my attention was directed was naturally the position of the currency. Silver has for many centuries been the currency of China, and the sudden and sharp rise in the value of silver during 1934 caused a similar rise in the exchange value of Chinese currency. Chinese produce became too dear in relation to world prices, exports fell off and silver had to be exported to meet the adverse balance of trade. This, in turn, caused a contraction of credit and an acute deflationary crisis: prices began to fall, debts could not be met and the banks became more and more "frozen", particularly in Shanghai where the collapse of the real estate boom created a special problem. By October 1934 the situation had become so serious that the Chinese Government imposed a variable export tax on the export of silver, thereby divorcing the Shanghai dollar from the free silver standard. But this measure, while it mitigated the extreme effects of the rise in silver, did nothing to remedy the difficulties which

---

[43] Handed to the Chief of the Division of Far Eastern Affairs, by the British Ambassador, June 25.
[44] See *Report of the American Economic Mission to the Far East: American Trade Prospects in the Orient* (New York, National Foreign Trade Council, 1935).

that rise had already caused: and when I reached Shanghai last September, it was evident that further positive measures had to be evolved. China had abandoned silver, without adopting any alternative currency basis. I did not bring any cut and dried scheme out with me to "put over" the Chinese Government. There were several possible alternatives, and the decision between them, depending as it did largely on Chinese psychology, could only be taken by the Chinese Government. I was examining the situation with a view to the preparation of a detailed programme with adequate safeguards and if possible with international support. But before any such scheme could be devised, the exchange market became dangerously weak and the Chinese Government decided to adopt an inconvertible managed currency on the basis of their own resources.

4. I had no responsibility for this bold step, but I have of course closely followed the situation, and I have no hesitation in saying that the action taken has been fully justified by the success which it has achieved. It was accepted throughout China without any serious difficulty. The notes of the Government Banks have been steadily replacing the silver dollars in circulation. Their exchange value has been firmly maintained and the resources at the disposal of the Government Banks for this purpose have substantially increased. The rate of exchange fixed has tended to encourage exports and the resulting increase of agricultural prices should, in due course, lead to improvement in the purchasing power of agricultural producers. The adverse balance of trade has been greatly reduced, and it seems probable, so far as can be judged from the statistics available, that the international receipts and expenditures of China on income tax are now evenly balanced. Thus the fundamental economic conditions for a stable currency are fulfilled.

5. I think the Chinese Government are to be congratulated on the progress which their policy has achieved. Already much has been done to re-establish sound financial and economic conditions. Confidence in the currency is growing. But much has still to be done before it can be solidly assured as a basis for long-term trading and investment plans. The currency reform had to be put into force at short notice, and the various measures necessary to make it watertight have had to be drafted piecemeal and fitted together gradually. The unification of the note issue and the reorganisation of the Central Bank as an independent Reserve Bank has not yet been carried through effectively. There have been unfortunate speculative movements of a non-commercial character which have disturbed sentiment. There is a large Budget deficit entailing constant recourse to Government borrowing. The domestic bond market is depressed and Government credit low. Though the market is now comparatively easy many of the commercial banks are far from liquid. Meanwhile, both in the

Southern Provinces and in the North, there have been political difficulties in carrying through the currency reform, as it should be done, on a national basis. Lastly, the sharp fall in the price of silver, following the suspension by the United States Treasury of silver purchases on the world market, aroused temporary misgivings. But, all things considered, there would appear to be every reason, so far as economic factors are concerned, for confidence in the present currency system, provided that the Chinese Government complete and carry through efficiently the programme of internal reforms, including especially the re-organisation of the Central Bank and the reform of the Budget.

6. The prospects of the currency, and indeed of the whole financial situation of China for the future will depend firstly on the maintenance of peace and order in the interior of China and secondly on a settlement of the special situation in North China. In particular the customs revenues are a vital factor in Chinese finance and every effort should be made to put an end to the difficulties in the way of their collection in east Hopei. These difficulties cannot be removed without a better political understanding between China and Japan. During my last visit to Japan I was assured that the Japanese Government desires such an understanding: that it favours the maintenance of the Chinese customs administration and will give no support to the creation of special tariffs by any local authority in China; and that it has no wish to interfere with internal administration of China. It is greatly to be hoped that a solution of the present difficulties will be reached which will restore general confidence and security for trade and investment.

7. I have dealt at length with the currency position because financial security is the basis of trade. Erratic exchanges and the contraction of credit strangle enterprise. The currency reform has laid the foundation for an increase of trade activities. Exports are expanding and the adverse balance of trade has been greatly reduced. But the export trade could be still further stimulated if the burden of local taxes, interport duties and export duties could be reduced and if the standards of production, manufacture and handling could be improved. It rests with the Chinese themselves to promote exports by such means. But I would sound a note of caution in regard to the tendency to create a control by monopoly or anything resembling a monopoly of national exports of China. As regards imports, the immediate prospects may not seem encouraging. But it is no use importing goods that cannot be paid for, and the export trade of China must improve before progress in imports can be looked for. If however present tendencies are maintained, there is every reason to expect a gradual and steady improvement in the import trade. I hope that

British exporters will take advantage of the turn in the tide when it comes. They must expect to face keen competition and enterprise and expert salesmanship will be required, as well as readiness to take some risks. Needless to say, they must make a careful study of market requirements and establish the closest possible contact with their Chinese customers. Indeed, in every field of business, co-operation with Chinese interests should be aimed at. The establishment of Sino-British Trade Councils in Shanghai and Hankow will, I hope, help in this direction.

8. Imports, of course, are largely affected by the tariff, and I hope that the Chinese Government will consider whether the present tariff cannot be revised in a downward direction so far as this is possible without reducing revenue. During the depression a number of the tariff rates have been pushed up to a point at which they produce no revenue and merely prohibit legitimate trade. These rates require to be reconsidered in the light of the present exchange position. Industrial interests will no doubt press strongly for the maintenance of the highest possible protective tariff, but the advantages they obtain will be at the expense of the agricultural population. It is the duty of the Government to strike a fair balance between the interests of industry and agriculture, but I believe that in China the restoration of rural economy should have first consideration. In my opinion, therefore, a downward revision of the present tariff would be advantageous to China both in its financial and in its economic effects. The Maritime Customs is the basis of Chinese Government credit and it is in the first interests of China both to maintain that service in all its traditional efficiency and to adjust the tariff so as to secure the maximum revenue.

9. The development of China will require the importation of much capital goods and this is probably the most promising field for British exports. Such exports would be greatly facilitated by a flow of credit to China, where capital is scarce and the yield under proper management should be fully remunerative. In the past the United Kingdom has done much to develop the Railway system of China, but unfortunately many of the loan obligations thus incurred have not been fully met. These defaults have seriously prejudiced the credit of China, and her efforts to secure finance for new development purposes have been correspondingly hampered. The national Government appear genuinely anxious to settle outstanding obligations, within the limits of their financial possibilities, and also to remedy the serious defects in the administration and management of the Railways, with a view to enabling them to meet their charges. It must be borne in mind that the defaults are, in the main, a heritage of years of civil strife and social disorganisation. If a reasonable

settlement could be reached in regard to these old debts, the way would be open for financing extensions to the present railway system and opening vast stretches of country to foreign trade. No other form of enterprise could be more beneficial both to China and to the United Kingdom, and every effort should be made to overcome the difficulties.

10. Apart from railway financing, which calls for long-term credit, the possibilities of arranging middle-term credits deserves exploration. Such credits would be of particular value for financing public utility schemes. I have been impressed by the energy and capacity with which the municipal authorities are developing local projects of this character and I think the British manufacturers and exporters should consult the Banks operating in China, as well as the Government Departments concerned, with a view to obtaining finance for soundly planned projects.

11. There are also many openings for the investment of private capital in properties or undertakings in China: but if investors are to be attracted to such ventures, confidence must be re-established by abrogating any measures that have the effect of discriminating against foreign capital, and as regards real estate, by securing that the legal rights of mortgagees are fully protected. Foreign capital cannot be expected to assist China unless it is assured of fair treatment.

12. I fully agree with the observations of the American Economic Mission, viz: "A vast change is coming over China: a modernisation that as compared with ten or even five years ago, marks many centuries". I believe that this change will make China not a less but a more fruitful field for British enterprise—commercial, industrial and financial. Our principal interest here is to promote the peace, the prosperity and the trade of China, and in working for this, it seems to me we are working in the interests of all countries trading with China. The reconstruction of China is a vast task which will take years to accomplish and there is room for all to assist her in this task. The present Chinese Government has, despite conditions of peculiar difficulty, made remarkable progress in the restoration of law and order, the resettlement of the devastated regions and the development of communications. Their recent currency reform was, in my opinion, planned on sound lines and it is in the interests of everyone that it should succeed.

13. In conclusion, I should like to express on behalf of my colleagues and myself to the Chinese Government and their officials and to the Chinese and foreign bankers and traders whom we have met our warm thanks for the assistance and hospitality extended to us wherever we went.

893.515/1176

The Ambassador in China (Johnson) to the Secretary of State

No. 571   PEIPING, July 9, 1936.
                                                         [Received August 10.]

SIR: I have the honor to refer to despatch No. 1897 of June 12, 1936, from the Embassy at Tokyo [45] concerning the recent visit to Japan of Sir Frederick Leith-Ross, and to enclose a copy of a memorandum of conversation [45] which I had with Mr. Y. Suma, Counselor of the Japanese Embassy on June 29, at Nanking, on that subject. Mr. Suma was in Japan at the time of Leith-Ross' visit there and has himself just recently returned to China.

Mr. Suma stated that Sir Frederick in conversation with Japanese officials in Tokyo had expressed opinions on the subject of international cooperation in the form of loans to China for currency and reconstruction purposes, even mentioning a possible sum for railway construction in Szechuan and Kweichow. The reply to this, according to Mr. Suma, was that whereas the Japanese Government was prepared to cooperate in international assistance to China, particularly in supplying materials, it felt that it was not safe at present to grant financial assistance to the Chinese Government because of the unstable and uncertain political situation now existing. Mr. Suma implied that the Japanese were not willing to encourage political stability which might make it possible for any one but Japan to invest money in China, and I therefore inferred that Mr. Suma was telling me that the Japanese had served notice upon England through Sir Frederick that Western Powers would lend money to China at the present time at their own peril and at the further risk of Japan's displeasure.

Respectfully yours,   NELSON TRUSLER JOHNSON

893.515/1162 : Telegram

The Ambassador in Japan (Grew) to the Secretary of State

                                                         TOKYO, July 21, 1936—1 p. m.
                                                         [Received July 21—4 : 52 a. m.]

160. 1. Vernacular newspapers this morning feature a Domei news despatch from Shanghai dated July 20 reporting the conclusion of an agreement allegedly negotiated in the United States by Chen, Director of the Bank of China, providing for purchase of Chinese silver by the United States; American assistance in the unification of Chinese currency and revenues, and assistance in tariff revision and control of foreign trade; purchase by China of American railway ma-

---
[45] Not printed.

terials, automobiles, airplanes, et cetera; guarantees by the American Government to syndicates selling to China; a pledge of the American Government to refrain from selling arms to local regimes opposed to Nanking; and special licenses to be issued by the Treasury for shipments to China under the agreement.

2. The newspapers refer to the above as an American credit to China to finance purchase of munitions and give the alleged attitude of the Foreign Office as being opposed to economic assistance to China by any of the powers and as being inclined to inquire of the Nanking Government concerning details of the alleged agreement.

To Peiping by mail.

GREW

893.515/1162 : Telegram

The Secretary of State to the Ambassador in Japan (Grew)

WASHINGTON, July 21, 1936—5 p. m.

96. Your 160, July 21, 1 p. m. Complete statements covering results of conversations between Chen and Treasury Department were issued in this country and in China before Chen left Washington.

American assistance in unification of Chinese currency and revenues consisted of advice only.

For the remaining items in the story which you report, as regards American assistance, there is no basis in fact.

There have been no conversations or agreement subsequent to Chen's visit here.

We regard this story as planted for political purposes and to elicit information.

Suggest you relay your telegram and this to Peiping.

HULL

893.48/1111

Memorandum by the Chief of the Division of Far Eastern Affairs (Hornbeck) of a Conversation With Mr. William P. Hunt

[WASHINGTON,] July 21, 1936.

The record states that Mr. Hunt stated that he was "acting on behalf of the Chinese Government".   Query: As we have been given no information with regard to this from Chinese sources, there is warrant for presuming that, if "acting on behalf of the Chinese Government", Mr. Hunt's authorization is on a commission or contingency basis.

Mr. Hunt's project amounts to this: that the American Government advance China a credit of $30,000,000; that, against this credit, China purchase American cotton; that this American cotton be shipped directly from the United States to Germany, on sale of it by China to Germany; that German interests pay the Chinese Government, probably on a thirty-day basis, for the cotton; and that the Chinese Government pay the American Government, on a credit extended, over a period of six or seven years, with interest at four and one half or five per cent, with Chinese consolidated taxes as the security.

This project, if consummated, would constitute in effect a loan by the American Government to the Chinese Government of $30,000,000 (Chinese $90,000,000). It would contribute toward sale abroad of American cotton to the amount of $30,000,000.

China would get the $30,000,000; Germany would get the cotton; the United States would get China's promise to pay.

Any loan to China at this time from abroad would, as to proceeds, go directly or indirectly into the military exchequer of the Nanking Government. It would arouse the antipathy of those factions in China which are opposed to that Government. It would be regarded as a taking sides by the lending country in China's internal affairs. It would probably elicit criticism from various quarters in each of the countries which have been interested in the principle of international cooperation for public financing in China, especially the Consortium powers. It would most of all meet with disapproval in Japan and probably elicit angry criticism from that country. It would have a tendency to cause the Japanese military to increase the pressure and hasten the tempo of their activities against and toward coercion of the Nanking Government.

Thus, approval of this project by the American Government, and the consummation of this loan (a loan in fact though a credit in form), would be likely to have unsatisfactory political consequences both for the United States and for China.

Additional pressure by Japan upon China would have a tendency to undermine the ability to pay of the present Chinese Government in regard both to the outstanding financial obligations of that Government and to newly incurred obligations thereof. Long since badly impaired, the ability to pay of the Chinese Government has been constantly subjected during the past three or four years to increasing strains. No one can with warrant say today that a loan to the Chinese Government, no matter what the security, would be a good risk for any lender not in position to collect by use or threat of force. Any loan which might be made in disregard of objections by Japan would be in itself a very bad "risk" and would tend to encourage developments in consequence of which China's ability to pay would be further diminished. We have definite knowledge that high Japanese officials have stated that any rendering of financial assistance to China from abroad without approval (and participation?) by Japan will be regarded with disfavor by Japan. It therefore would seem that, as a business proposition (or from the economic point of view), a transaction such as is under reference would not be a sound business transaction.

The question arises: What advantage does a three-cornered transaction like this offer to the German interests concerned as compared with a direct purchase of cotton by them from the United States? A reasonable surmise would be that the Chinese expect to offer the Germans this cotton at a price less than that which the Germans would have to pay if making the purchase direct. There is also the question: What advantage does the project offer to Mr. Hunt? It is a reasonable surmise that, if consummated, it would give him a substantial commission. If these surmises are correct, the transaction would be expensive to China: the discount given to the Germans and the commission given to Mr. Hunt would diminish the amount received by the Chinese Government as compared with the $30,000,000 of indebtedness to the United States which it would incur. Might it not seem that, if the American Government wishes to loan money to China, it would be better to make the loan direct and let the Chinese receive the full benefit (?) of the full amount thereof?

Reference is made to various memoranda here attached [46] in which there has been discussed in earlier stages the project, in slightly different form, which Mr. Hunt now brings to our attention in a somewhat simplified form. In these memoranda it is shown that various agencies of this Government have not been in favor in principle of a transaction of this type. Reference is also made to Tokyo's despatch No. 1905, June 16, 1936,[47] in which there is given us the latest evidence with regard to the attitude of Japan on the question of financial assistance to China.

Reference is also made to an item which appears in the *Washington Post* of July 21, by the Associated Press, with date line Tokyo, July 21, which gives an indication of Japanese attitude in the presence of a report that the United States is extending a credit to China.

It is believed that this Department should take a definite position of categorical opposition to this project. This could be done in a negative form: "This Department believes that this Government should not become involved in this project." [48]

---

[46] Not attached to file copy.
[47] Not printed.
[48] The Secretary of State said he would not approve any such project, and he authorized the Department's taking the position stated in this paragraph. Dr. Herbert Feis, Economic Adviser, concurred in this view.

893.515/1188

The Chief of the Division of Far Eastern Affairs (Hornbeck) to the Secretary of State

[WASHINGTON,] July 29, 1936.

MR. SECRETARY: The Consul General at Shanghai has sent me the memorandum here attached.[49]

It occurs to me that it might be wise for this Department to have a more complete knowledge than has been given us by the Treasury of the conversations held between Mr. Morgenthau and Mr. K. P. Chen a few weeks ago. There is reason to believe that there was more agreed upon than is indicated by and in the press release which the Treasury made and the press release which the Chinese Government made. It would be altogether warrantable for the Secretary of State to ask the Secretary of the Treasury for texts of any agreements or agreed-upon memoranda that may have been signed or initialed by the Secretary of the Treasury and the representative of the Chinese Government (Ministry of Finance).

At the same time, it is realized that there might in some situations be advantage inherent in the fact that the Department of State could disclaim knowledge of the fact of the contents of any such agreements. I lean toward the view, however, that the balance of advantage would be on the side of our having adequate knowledge of the facts.

I submit this statement without recommendation.[50]

S[TANLEY] K. H[ORNBECK]

893.51/6213 : Telegram

The Consul General at Shanghai (Gauss) to the Secretary of State

SHANGHAI, July 30, 1936—4 p. m.
[Received July 30—1 : 45 p. m.]

419. Reuter under London date line July 29th states rumors persist China seeks 20,000,000 pounds loan for economic development from Great Britain, France, Belgium and Japan. Also reports Japanese press extending feelers for revival Anglo-Japanese friendship. Repeated to Peiping, by mail to Nanking.

GAUSS

---

[49] Not printed.
[50] No record of action has been found in Department files.

893.48/1112

Memorandum by the Chief of the Division of Far Eastern Affairs (Hornbeck)

[WASHINGTON,] August 26, 1936.

Mr. Mackay brought Mr. Hunt to my office and left Mr. Hunt with me. Mr. Hunt gave me a résumé of developments, including conversations, relating to his project for a purchase by China of cotton, on credit, in this country and sale by China of that cotton to German interests, payment to be made to China by German interests. He mentioned the inquiry which he had made sometime ago whether, in the event of favorable action elsewhere in the Government upon this proposal, the project would, when it got to the State Department, meet with objection. After an exchange of comments on the subject of "hypothetical questions", wherein Mr. Hunt gave evidence of considerable familiarity with that subject, I said that, in order to save time and to be perfectly frank, I would have to say that: "We have thus far not discovered that any agency of the executive branch of the Government is in favor of this proposal."

Mr. Hunt then asked whether he might inquire what objections were advanced to the proposal. I said that it seemed to me that the burden of convincing the Government that the proposal should meet with favor rests with the proposers; and that it is not incumbent upon those who have not been convinced to advance reasons in explanation of their not having been convinced. I said that the burden of the argument, if any, should fall on the affirmative side. Mr. Hunt said that he felt that my feeling was fully warranted and that he did not wish to press the point, but he would appreciate it if I could give him any indication as to whether the doubt was in regard to the economic or in regard to the political aspects of the project. I replied that, to be frank, it seemed to be with regard to both aspects. Mr. Hunt then said that he had talked with Mr. Jesse Jones and he felt that Mr. Jones was favorably disposed although he (Hunt) was fully aware that in January Mr. Jones had been definitely unfavorable. At that point I made no comment.

Mr. Hunt then went on to tell me about some other of his business projects in China, especially the contract with regard to which he had had difficulty with the Mayor of Nanking. The conversation continued for a half hour and Mr. Hunt gave no evidence of feeling badly over the indication which I had given him that his cotton credit project was not regarded with favor. In parting, Mr. Hunt said that he would doubtless wish to come to see me from time to time. I replied that I would be glad to see him at any time. He intimated that he was going to talk further with Mr. Jones. I asked him to remember that what I had said to him with regard to the cotton credit project was that "We have thus far not discovered that any agency of the executive branch of the Government is in favor of this proposal." [51] Mr. Hunt said that he clearly understood.

S[TANLEY] K. H[ORNBECK]

893.51/6240a : Telegram

The Secretary of State to the Ambassador in the United Kingdom (Bingham)

WASHINGTON, October 14, 1936—6 p. m.

375. Today's press under London date line October 13 states "The British Treasury has agreed in principle to grant Government credits to China" and that "Premature disclosure that the British Government's export credits guarantee department was contemplating granting credits to facilitate British trade with China has delayed official announcement of the scheme, which may not now be revealed in detail before next week".

Report by telegraph such information as may be available in regard to foregoing and keep Department currently informed.

HULL

893.51/6241 : Telegram

The Secretary of State to the Ambassador in China (Johnson)

WASHINGTON, October 17, 1936—noon.

247. Press of October 15 under Shanghai date line October 14 carried United Press and Havas reports to the effect that Kung has confirmed that a loan to China (a) is now under consideration (b) will soon be granted by British Government.

London Embassy, commenting upon reports in regard to this subject appearing in the American press under London date line October 13, states "informal enquiries at the Export Credit Guarantee Department revealed that whereas Leith-Ross had urged the granting of a materials credit to China, the matter is still under discussion within that Department which maintains that no contact has yet been made with the Chinese authorities since the proposal has not yet taken precise form."

Telegraph available information in regard to foregoing and keep Department currently informed.

HULL

---

[51] Raymond C. Mackay's memorandum of October 28, 1936, initialed by the Secretary of State, stated that under existing conditions the American Government should refrain from extending to the Chinese credits of the nature indicated above (893.48/1113).

893.51/6246 : Telegram

The Counselor of Embassy in China (Peck) to the Secretary of State

NANKING, October 20, 1936—3 p. m.
[Received October 20—8:55 a. m.]

310. Your 247, October 17, noon, to Peiping. Foreign Office states that reports of a loan or of export credit from Great Britain are premature since neither plan has taken definite form. Foreign Office has received inquiries from the German Embassy likewise.

British Embassy, Nanking, confirms Reuter's message dated London, October 20, stating that a representative of the Export Credits Department will come to China in accordance with the new scheme working with British official trade representatives; that the scheme will operate on a commercial basis and that no loan to China is contemplated.

Sent to the Department and Peiping.

PECK

893.51/6274

Memorandum by the Chief of the Division of Far Eastern Affairs (Hornbeck)

[WASHINGTON,] December 29, 1936.

Mr. Lamont called me on the telephone from New York. He referred to a letter of a few weeks ago (October 9, 1936)[52] in which he had informed me of views imparted to him by Sir Charles Addis[53] with regard to a proposed rescinding of a resolution relating to the China Consortium Agreement which provides that when loans are made to the Chinese Government that Government shall be free to make purchases with the proceeds in the open market. Mr. Lamont said that he had written to Sir Charles Addis expressing the views of the American Group in the Consortium in opposition to the proposal. Now, however, he had received from Sir Charles Addis a letter saying that the British Government will not permit the making of a loan which is under consideration to China unless provision be made that the proceeds shall be spent in Great Britain (British Empire?). Mr. Lamont said that he and his associates feel that the rescinding of the resolution under reference would put an end to any and all hope that the Consortium may ever function for the purpose for which it was intended; that the Chinese had never become reconciled to the idea of the Consortium; and that the rescinding of this proviso would make the idea conclusively unacceptable to them. It seemed to him that it would be preferable to suggest to the British Group that the member

---

[52] Not printed.
[53] Representing the British Group of the China Consortium.

Groups vote to make an exception in the case of a proposed loan such as the British have in contemplation. I said that I concurred in the view which Mr. Lamont had expressed that a rescinding of the resolution would be fatal to the idea of the Consortium: it would take the foundation right out from under the whole Agreement; it seemed to me that his suggestion of an alternative was sound; I still hoped that the Consortium idea might some day prove useful and I would deprecate seeing the Consortium dissolved. Mr. Lamont said that neither the American Group nor any of its members is in position now to make any loans to China and that they are simply holding together the framework. I said that this was true, but that the time might come when the whole situation would be such as to make a resort to the Consortium machinery seem desirable on the part of most or all of the parties especially concerned. Mr. Lamont intimated that he would submit his proposed alternative to Sir Charles Addis (or the British Group). I suggested that it might be well to call attention, for the benefit of the British Government, to the fact that the British Government along with the other governments had given its blessing to the Consortium idea and had contributed, in influence, to the creation of the Consortium, and that it seemed not altogether appropriate that the British Government should take a position toward compelling British banks to pursue a course inconsistent with or destructive of the Consortium Agreement. Mr. Lamont said that he thought that a good suggestion and that he would incorporate in his communication to his British associates some observations to that effect.

Best wishes for the New Year were exchanged, and the conversation there ended.

S[TANLEY] K. H[ORNBECK]

MEASURES TAKEN BY THE UNITED STATES FOR THE PROTECTION OF AMERICAN LIVES AND PROPERTY IN CHINA [54]

893.00/13356 : Telegram

The Consul General at Canton (Spiker) to the Secretary of State

CANTON, January 29, 1936—4 p. m.
[Received 5 : 45 p. m.]

Referring to my telegram of January 20, 4 p. m.,[55] local military charge [*authorities?*] have just confirmed yesterday's press reports that about 20,000 Communists under command of Hsiao Ko [56] and Ho Lung [57] moved southward from Wengan and after heavy fighting with

---

[54] Continued from *Foreign Relations*, 1935, vol. III, pp. 664–700.
[55] Not printed.
[56] Member of the Kweichow Branch Communist Military Commission.
[57] Chairman of the Kweichow Branch Communist Military Commission.

Government forces succeeded in occupying Pingyueh and Maping-chang on the 26th, thus controlling main route from east to Kweiyang toward which Central Government troops have retired. Today's press quotes Kweiyang reports that Kweiting has been taken and that enemy is now attacking Lungli, 70 li east of Kweiyang, which is defended by only two divisions. Yunnan authorities allegedly rushing aid to Kweiyang where populace is terror stricken and assisting garrison in digging entrenchments east of railway. Communist objective believed to be juncture with Communist forces in Szechuan. Kwangsi forces reported to be remaining aloof from fighting and to be holding defensive positions in southern Kweichow in areas described in my telegram of January 15, 10 a. m.[57a]

Recent advices from American missionaries in Kweichow show no Americans in Kweiyang and that two in Kiensi and one each in Pingpa, Anping and Anshun were, in accordance with this Consulate General's previous advices, very carefully watching developments preparatory to evacuation if situation warrants. Further telegraphic warning has been sent missionaries concerned. Department, Peiping, Nanking, Hankow informed.   SPIKER

893.00/13359 : Telegram

The Consul General at Canton (Spiker) to the Secretary of State

CANTON, February 4, 1936—9 a. m.
[Received February 5—9 : 35 a. m.]

Referring to my telegram of January 29, 4 p. m., last paragraph. Mr. and Mrs. Crofts from Kiensi, Kweichow, have telegraphed from Tating that they are escaping to Szechuan.

Reports available locally indicate that during the past 3 days Communists have been repulsed by Kweiyang Garrison after sanguinary fighting at Lungli and some have moved north to Honghoaifeng from which they threaten the capital. Northern aeroplanes from Chungking and Yunnan reinforcements are alleged to have assisted materially in repulse of enemy. Kwangsi forces apparently still holding.   SPIKER

893.00/13361 : Telegram

The Counselor of Embassy in China (Lockhart) to the Secretary of State

PEIPING, February 10, 1936—7 p. m.
[Received February 10—9 : 07 a. m.]

57. Following telegram has been received from Yunnanfu:

"February 10, 11 a. m. Red Army reached Tating on the 5th and Pichieh on the 8th, crossing the border into Yunnan the following day.

[57a] Not printed.

The local authorities are deeply concerned over the safety of Chaotung. Doctor and Mrs. Tucker, American citizens resident at Chaotung, up to the present time have not heeded my telegram urging evacuation.

Repeated to Nanking."

LOCKHART

893.00/13364 : Telegram

The Counselor of Embassy in China (Peck) to the Secretary of State

NANKING, February 17, 1936—noon.
[Received February 17—9 : 40 a. m.]

34. Following telegram has been sent Yunnanfu and repeated to Department, Peiping and Hankow.

"February 17, noon. Your February 17, 11 a. m. was communicated to Foreign Office with request that telegraphic instructions be sent to local authorities to afford protection to Americans at Chaotung and any others in places of danger. Foreign Office now states that requested instructions have been issued and that Yunnan Provincial Government has telegraphed in reply that Communists have not entered that Province and are still in western Kweichow."

PECK

893.00/13365 : Telegram

The Consul General at Canton (Spiker) to the Secretary of State

CANTON, February 17, 1936—10 p. m.
[Received February 17—10 : 55 a. m.]

Referring to my telegram of February 13, 2 p. m.,[58] leading Hong Kong paper on February 13 published missionary letter recently written from Kweiyang and stating that whereabouts of certain American and British missionaries then evacuating mission stations were unknown. Telegraphic inquiry was made at once by this office and assurances since received indicate that all Americans in Kweichow Province evacuated to places of safety. Reports available locally indicate main body of Communists now over Yunnan border with smaller body possibly still in occupation of Pichieh border area, Kweichow.

SPIKER

893.00/13383 : Telegram

The Counselor of Embassy in China (Lockhart) to the Secretary of State

PEIPING, March 4, 1936—5 p. m.
[Received March 4—2 : 10 p. m.]

110. In view of the reported movements of considerable Communist forces into western Shansi Province, the Embassy suggested to Con-

---

[58] Not printed.

sul General Caldwell at Tientsin [59] on February 29 that it might be advisable to issue warnings to Americans in Fenchow and other apparently dangerous areas. Caldwell telegraphed on that day to American Board Mission at Fenchow and to James Mellow at Siaoyi, advising their removal to place of greater safety, unless conditions were definitely safe at their posts. He also addressed warning letters to missionaries in Hungtung, Kiehsiu and Pingyao.

Consul General Caldwell telegraphed on February 29 to General Yen Hsi Shan, Pacification Commissioner of Shansi at Taiyuan, requesting that adequate measures be taken to protect Americans in areas affected by incursion of Communist troops. General Yen telegraphically replied saying that adequate measures would be taken. Caldwell has furnished General Yen a list of Americans known to be in affected area.

American Board Mission, Peiping, received letter this morning, dated at Taiku, March 1, from an American missionary, reporting that four American women, one man and two children of the Fenchow Mission had arrived at Taiku. Three men and five women apparently still remain in Fenchow. The writer stated that the latest information received in Taiku indicated that the Communists, who were reported on February 28 to be at Wucheng (30 miles west of Fenchow) had been driven back and that 3,000 troops of General Shang Chen had arrived at Siaoyi.

Chinese reports from Taiyuan, dated March 3, state that seven districts in western Shansi are now in the hands of the Communists, whose strength is estimated at between 10,000 and 20,000 men. Officials at Taiyuan admitted severe reverse at the hands of the Communists but stated that a counterattack was being launched.

Repeated to Nanking.

LOCKHART

893.00/13384 : Telegram

The Counselor of Embassy in China (Lockhart) to the Secretary of State

PEIPING, March 4, 1936—6 p. m.
[Received March 4—2 : 20 p. m.]

111. Embassy's 110, March 4, 5 p. m. American Board Mission, Peiping, has just received a telegram from its station at Fenchow, despatched at 3 p. m., today, stating Fenchow is safe. The mission has closed its school as there is fighting near the city and the situation

[59] John Kenneth Caldwell.

gives cause for concern. Some Chinese are leaving city. Communications remain open. Following Americans remain in Fenchow: Dr. Judd, Carl B. Huber, the Misses Josie E. Horn, Mary L. McClure, Emma B. Noreen, Louise Meebold, and Harold B. Matthews, wife and two children.

Mrs. Marian Judd and two children, Mr. and Mrs. Myron Burton and two children, and Mrs. Bertha Brown are at Taiku. Miss Bernice Brown is due to arrive in Peiping tomorrow.

Repeated to Nanking.

LOCKHART

893.00/13388 : Telegram

The Counselor of Embassy in China (Lockhart) to the Secretary of State

PEIPING, March 7, 1936—6 p. m.
[Received March 7—8 : 55 a. m.]

120. Following from American Consul General at Hankow.[60]

"March 7, 1 p. m. Recent activity of a force of about 800 Communist bandits in East Hupeh has resulted in threat to Hwangshihkong according to American Catholic missionaries there who telegraphed last evening asking that naval vessel be despatched if possible. This request was referred to Admiral [Allen][61] who is sending U. S. S. *Tutuila* from Hankow to investigate and report."

Repeated to Nanking.

LOCKHART

893.00/13393 : Telegram

The Ambassador in China (Johnson) to the Secretary of State

PEIPING, March 10, 1936—4 p. m.
[Received March 10—8 a. m.]

123. Embassy's 115, March 6, 4 p. m.[62] The Military Attaché of the Embassy has returned from a short trip to Taiyuanfu and Fenchow. It is his opinion that Fenchow will not be occupied by the Communists, although there are Communist troops in occupation of villages in the vicinity of Fenchow. According to the report of the military commander at Fenchow, some 27,000 Communist forces have crossed from Shensi into Shansi, but this is believed to be exaggerated. He does not believe that the Communist activity in Shansi has any direct

---

[60] Paul R. Josselyn.
[61] Admiral W. H. Allen, Commander of the U. S. Yangtze Patrol.
[62] Not printed.

relation to Sino-Japanese affairs. He reports that six Americans (4 women and 2 men) are now at Fenchow.

JOHNSON

893.00/13394 : Telegram

The Ambassador in China (Johnson) to the Secretary of State

PEIPING, March 11, 1936—9 a. m.
[Received March 10—11 : 50 p. m.]

124. Following from American Consul General at Hankow.

"March 10, 6 p. m. My March 7, 1 p. m. Situation in vicinity Hwangshihkong has cleared and *Tutuila* returned Hankow today."

JOHNSON

393.11/1832

The Ambassador in China (Johnson) to the American Consular Officers in China [63]

Circular No. 26   PEIPING, March 18, 1936.

SIRS : In connection with several incidents which have occurred in China during recent months involving relations between the Government of the United States and another government, the Department of State has recently informed the Embassy that in cases in which it is clear that American responsibility exists it would appear appropriate, as well as helpful in reaching a prompt and satisfactory settlement, for the Consular Officer in charge, when such cases arise, to call on the representative of the foreign government concerned for the purpose of giving assurance that an adequate and prompt investigation would be made, and also to express regret if, in the judgment of the officer concerned, the facts then known warrant such action. If doubt exists on the last-named point, the instructions of the Embassy should immediately be requested.

The Department of State also considers that cases involving an infraction of the personal or property rights of foreigners in which American citizens are in any way involved should be promptly reported to the Embassy, with all the facts and pertinent comment, whether or not the cases are likely to become diplomatic issues.

The above is communicated to you for your information and future guidance in cases which may complicate the relations between the United States and another country.

Very truly yours,   NELSON TRUSLER JOHNSON

---

[63] Copy transmitted to the Department by the Embassy in China without covering despatch ; received April 20.

893.00/13411 : Telegram

The Consul General at Shanghai (Gauss) to the Secretary of State

SHANGHAI, March 19, 1936—4 p. m.
[Received March 19—11: 15 a. m.]

165. Informed by China Inland Mission that it has received a telegram [from?] Shansi superintendent dated Hungtung, March 18, 4 p. m., decoding [*decoded*] as follows:

"It is reported here and generally believed that Communists quite unexpectedly arrived yesterday Hwochow[?]–Chaocheng. Cannot give even approximate number of [Communists?]. Railway services suspended. Hungtung missionaries inside city. (S. G. D.) Trudinger."

In that area are Americans, Claude H. Thomas, wife, two children. Repeated to the Department, Peiping, Nanking and Tientsin.

GAUSS

893.00/13412 : Telegram

The Counselor of Embassy in China (Peck) to the Secretary of State

NANKING, March 20, 1936—noon.
[Received March 20—7 a. m.]

58. Shanghai's 164 [*165*], March 19, 4 p. m. Embassy is informing Foreign Office and requesting that military authorities be directed to afford adequate protection to Americans at Hungtung. Shanghai informed of action taken.

PECK

893.00/13413 : Telegram

The Consul General at Shanghai (Gauss) to the Secretary of State

SHANGHAI, March 21, 1936—noon.
[Received March 21—7: 30 a. m.]

170. My 164 [*165*], March 19, 4 p. m. Shanghai office China Inland Mission now states has received messages from Linfen (Pingyangfu) and Taiyuan that Hungtung communications cut. Missionaries at Linfen are British and have requested evacuation by airplane. Repeated to Peiping, Nanking and Tientsin.

GAUSS

893.00/13416 : Telegram

The Ambassador in China (Johnson) to the Secretary of State

PEIPING, March 22, 1936—4 p. m.
[Received March 22—6 : 48 a. m.]

144. Shanghai's 164 [*165*], March 19, 4 p. m. The following Americans who left Taiku, Shansi, March 20th arrived Peiping last night : Mrs. Judd and two children, Mrs. Brown, Mr. and Mrs. Burton and two children, Mr. Huber, Miss Munger and mother, and Mrs. Williams. Mrs. Judd reports following Americans still in Taiku : Dr. and Mrs. Wilbur, Miss Heebner, Miss Hemingway, Miss Williams, Miss Cade, Mr. Strong, Miss Cheny, and Miss Hamilton. She also reports following Americans still in Fenchow : Dr. Judd, Mr. Matthews, Miss Horn, Miss Meebold, Miss McClure, and Miss Noreen. Moyer family due to arrive Peiping tonight.

No information available here regarding Thomas family referred to in Shanghai's 164 [*165*], March 19, 4 p. m. Tientsin informed by telephone.

Telegraph Administration reports inability to deliver telegrams to Fenchow.

JOHNSON

893.00/13417 : Telegram

The Ambassador in China (Johnson) to the Secretary of State

Peiping, March 23, 1936—9 a. m.
[Received March 22—11 : 20 p. m.]

145. Embassy's 144, March 22, 4 p. m. Misses Hamilton, Cade and Cheny arrived in Peiping last night.

This telegram and Embassy's 144, March 22, 4 p. m. have been repeated to Nanking and Shanghai.

JOHNSON

893.00/13422 : Telegram

The Counselor of Embassy in China (Peck) to the Secretary of State

NANKING, March 24, 1936—10 a. m.
[Received March 24—6 : 30 a. m.]

62. Tientsin's telegram March 22, 10 a. m. On March 23, 4 p. m. the Foreign Office informed me that on the evening of March 21 it had telegraphed to the Shansi Provincial authorities regarding the Thomas family at Hungtung and not having received any [reply?]

again telegraphed on March 23rd. I called attention to Reuter telegram dated Peiping, March 22, stating that Government troops were near Chiehhsien, 74 miles south of Linfen, and urged that orders be sent to these troops to rescue the Thomas family. The Foreign Office promised to ask the Military Affairs Committee to send such orders. An attempt here to telegraph to Hungtung, March 23, 4 p. m. failed and notification was received from Taiyuan that both telegraph and postal communications were still interrupted.

Repeated to Peiping, Tientsin and Shanghai.

PECK

893.00/13423 : Telegram

The Counselor of Embassy in China (Peck) to the Secretary of State

NANKING, March 24, 1936—noon.
[Received March 24—10 : 10 a. m.]

63. My 62, March 24, 10 a. m. to the Department. The Foreign Office has just telephoned that the Shansi Provincial Government has reported that instructions have been issued to the military forces in the Hungtung area to take special measures for the protection of foreign residents and that it is expected that the Communists in that area will be suppressed shortly. The Foreign Office on the evening of March 23 sent an urgent request to the Military Affairs Committee that it issue instructions to Government troops in South Shansi to rescue foreign residents threatened by Communist bands.

The Foreign Office promised to telegraph immediately to the Shansi Provincial Government for a brief report and explanation of the report contained in telegram from Shanghai to the Department No. 178, March 23, 7 p. m.[64]

PECK

893.00/13424 : Telegram

The Consul General at Tientsin (Caldwell) to the Secretary of State

TIENTSIN, March 24, 1936—4 p. m.
[Received March 24—9 : 50 a. m.]

Following telegram received today from Matthews, Fenyang: "The six of us living in Fenyang are not in danger, please don't worry."

It is believed that the six are Dr. Walter Henry Judd, or [*and?*] Harold Shepherd Matthews, Miss Josie Elinor Horn, Miss Louise Meebold, Miss Louise McClure, and Miss Emma Bertha Noreen.

CALDWELL

---

[64] Not printed.

893.00/13429 : Telegram

The Counselor of Embassy in China (Peck) to the Secretary of State

NANKING, March 26, 1936—9 a. m.
[Received March 26—6 : 33 a. m.]

64. My 63, March 24, noon.

1. March 25, 4 p. m., I discussed with Vice Minister Hsu Mo[65] Reuter's report dated Peiping, March 25 that Hungtung had been occupied by Communist forces. He said the Foreign Office had received no information to this effect.

2. March 25, 7 p. m., the Foreign Office telephoned that the Military Affairs Committee thought it most unlikely that Hungtung and Linfen where there are many British missionaries had been occupied by such forces and that the report had been inspired from "certain source." The Committee stated that four divisions of Government troops are in the area affected and that no anxiety need be felt for the safety of American citizens at Hungtung. Special instructions had been issued by the Committee to commanders in Shansi to rescue foreigners. I replied that the Embassy still felt great concern and pointed out that for about 1 week no reliable information concerning the fate of Hungtung had been received. I suggested that a military plane reconnoitering could at least ascertain whether Hungtung had been seized by the Communist forces and urged that accurate information be obtained. The Foreign Office assured me the Government was doing its utmost to safeguard foreign lives.

3. March 26, 9 a. m., the Foreign Office telephoned that a telegram had been received from the Shansi Provincial Government that there was absolutely no foundation for the report of the capture of Hungtung by the Communists; that the Communists had no equipment with which to make such an attack; that the Communist forces between Linfen and Hungtung were being "squeezed out" by Government troops approaching from the north and south; and that no serious anxiety need be felt for American citizens at Hungtung. The Foreign Office said that apparently Linfen was not mentioned because the telegram was in reply to a specific inquiry concerning Hungtung.

Repeated to Peiping, Shanghai and Tientsin.

PECK

---

[65] Chinese Vice Minister for Foreign Affairs.

893.00/13431 : Telegram

The Counselor of Embassy in China (Peck) to the Secretary of State

NANKING, March 27, 1936—9 a. m.
[Received 9:20 a. m.]

66. 1. My 64, March 26, 9 a. m.

1. Central News Agency late March 26th published a statement which was issued by the Foreign Office, substance being as follows:

Reports of capture of Hungtung and Linfen (Pingyangfu) by Communists are denied by authoritative quarters which state that the 2nd, 4th, 6th and 25th Divisions have already arrived at Lingshi to assist Provincial forces and that with this large concentration of troops the Government can adequately cope with the situation. Reports of the fall of Hungtung and Linfen probably arose from "temporary suspension of passenger traffic on a section of the Tung Pass–Pu [Chow] Railway south of Lingshi due to heavy demand on its rolling stock". The Shansi Provincial Government has telegraphed that: The Southern and Northern Route Armies (presumably Shansi armies) have been ordered to launch simultaneous attacks on the Communists between Hungtung and Linfen; that strong precautions have been taken to guard the two walled cities; and that since the Communists do not possess artillery there is no cause for alarm as to safety of residents. Nanking authorities are paying the greatest attention to the safety of foreign missionaries in menaced areas and the Shansi Provincial authorities have been instructed to take necessary measures to ensure the safety of foreign missionaries, and to utilize the best means to evacuate them if necessary.

2. The agency despatch goes on to say that it has confirmed from official sources that Hungtung and Linfen are still occupied by Government troops; and that a telegram from Yangku (Taiyuanfu) received the morning of March 26 states that two columns of Government troops are closing on the Communists between Hungtung and Linfen and speaks of the certainty of soon raising the siege of the two cities.

3. The communiqué's explanation of the interruption of the railway is obviously not to be credited. It is known that postal and telegraph communications with Hungtung and Linfen are interrupted and that trains are not proceeding south of Yangku beyond Nankwan (just south of Sukow). So far as is known no messages have been received from residents of the two cities or from the troops which are allegedly occupying them although such troops would probably possess radio sending apparatus.

4. Repeated to Peiping, Tientsin, Shanghai.

PECK

893.00/13434 : Telegram

The Second Secretary of Embassy in China (Atcheson) to the Secretary of State

NANKING, March 30, 1936—3 p. m.
[Received March 30—12 : 10 p. m.]

71. My 66, March 27, 9 a. m. and previous.

1. I have been informed over the telephone by the Foreign Office that despatch from the Military Affairs Commission just received states that (1) further telegraphic instructions have been sent Yen Hsi Shan directing the military in Shansi to give particular attention to the problem of protecting foreigners and to evacuate foreigners from danger zones if necessary; and (2) a plane has been despatched to reconnoitre the Hungtung–Linfen area.

2. I replied that the Embassy's concern for the safety of Americans at Hungtung continued because of the lack of definite information concerning their welfare and suggested that a message be dropped into the city asking for some signal indicating the Americans' condition. Citing reports of successful Soviet experiments in dropping military equipment from air planes, I also suggested that a radio-sending apparatus might be dropped into Hungtung by parachute without undue risk to a plane since the Foreign Office communiqué of March 26 stated that the Communist forces lack artillery. The spokesman said the Foreign Office would consult with the Military Affairs Commission as to these suggestions and other possible means of obtaining definite information.

3. According to the spokesman's understanding, a large body of Communists is still operating between Hungtung and Linfen and these cities continue to be under siege. A Central News Agency sheet [from?] Taiyuanfu dated March 28 states that Chiaokou and Shihlou near Suitouchen, 60 miles northwest of Hungtung, were captured by Government troops March 27.

ATCHESON

893.00/13438 : Telegram

The Second Secretary of Embassy in China (Atcheson) to the Secretary of State

NANKING, March 31, 1936—noon.
[Received March 31—9 : 15 a. m.]

73. My 72, March 31, 11 a. m.[66]

1. I am informed by British Embassy that a telegram just received from its Military Attaché at Taiyuan states that (1), according to official despatch, Government troops have reoccupied Shihlou and

---

[66] Not printed.

Homa (the press reported the reoccupation of Shihlou March 27, Homa March 28) ; (2), the Government's 4th Division and one brigade of the 6th Division have entered northern Shansi; (3), the situation at Hungtung is serious but Government troops will shortly close upon the Communists in that area; and (4), foreign women and children have evacuated Luanfu (Changchih) in southeast Shansi.

2. Tientsin's January 1st list names following Americans: (all of China Inland Mission) at Luanfu: Dr. Paul Ernest Adolph, wife and two children; Eber J. Hazelton, wife and two children; and James E. Kester. The press reports that five foreign men are remaining at Luanfu and that an anticipated march upon that place by Communist forces has not developed.

3. Repeated to Peiping, Tientsin, Shanghai.

ATCHESON

893.00/13439 : Telegram

The Ambassador in China (Johnson) to the Secretary of State

PEIPING, April 1, 1936—5 p. m.
[Received April 1—8 : 50 a. m.]

158. Nanking's 73, March 31, noon. The British Military Attaché, who returned last night to Peiping from Taiyuan, states that (1) in all, seven National Government divisions or parts of divisions have entered Shansi, as follows: 2nd, 4th, 6th, 25th, 141st and 142nd Divisions; (2) Hungtung and Linfen (Pingyang) are still surrounded by Communist forces but are holding out while Government forces are converging on the area from north and south; and (3) the Government forces would seem to have the situation well in hand in the Province.

Repeated to Nanking, by mail, to Shanghai and Tientsin.

JOHNSON

893.00/13443 : Telegram

The Counselor of Embassy in China (Peck) to the Secretary of State

NANKING, April 3, 1936—10 a. m.
[Received April 3—7 a. m.]

78. This office's 75, April 1, 11 a. m.[67]

1. Foreign Office has telephoned that, in accordance with this office's suggestion and as reported in the press, General Yen Hsi Shan presumably on April 1 sent a plane over Hungtung and Linfen which dropped messages arranging a signal code with result that the missionaries in those two towns signaled that they are safe and well. A telegram received from Yen in this connection stated that Government

---

[67] Not printed.

troops were "relieving the siege" of Hungtung and Linfen and expected shortly to occupy both places.

2. Repeated to Peiping, Tientsin, Shanghai.

PECK

893.00/13454 : Telegram

The Counselor of Embassy in China (Peck) to the Secretary of State

NANKING, April 9, 1936—10 a. m.
[Received April 9—2 : 05 a. m.]

86. This office's 81, April 6, 11 a. m.[70]

1. Foreign Office states that it has this morning received a telegram from Shansi authorities stating that the sieges of Linfen (Pingyang) and Hungtung were raised on April 2 and 4, respectively. The foreign missionaries at those places are "quite safe" and continued protection is being afforded them.

2. Repeated to Peiping, Tientsin, Shanghai.

PECK

893.00/13493

The Vice Consul at Yunnanfu (Ringwalt) to the Secretary of State

No. 186   YUNNANFU, April 9, 1936.
[Received May 18.]

SIR: I have the honor to enclose copies of this Consulate's Despatch No. 162, dated April 9, 1936,[70] reporting on the latest invasion of Yunnan by the communists under Hsiao K'o and Ho Lung. Although they passed only thirty-five miles to the north of Yunnanfu, and although there is at the present time an indecisive engagement in progress shortly to the northwest of here, it is believed that this city is in no danger. American residents of exposed outlying areas have all been safely evacuated.

Respectfully yours,   ARTHUR R. RINGWALT

393.11/1837

The Ambassador in China (Johnson) to the Secretary of State

No. 467   PEIPING, May 20, 1936.
[Received June 15.]

SIR: I have the honor to refer to the Department's telegraphic instruction No. 60 of March 19, 12 noon,[70] relative to the question of

---

[70] Not printed.

United States naval protection for American citizens at Foochow, and to enclose for the information and files of the Department copies of the following correspondence on the matter:

[Here follows list of enclosures; none printed.]

The discussion of this matter between Consul Burke [71] and various United States naval officers appears to have grown out of a feeling on the part of Mr. Burke that current instructions governing the actions of the United States Navy in rendering protection to American citizens and their property in foreign lands are in some way at variance with Paragraph 113 of Section 11 of the Consular Regulations which governs the action of consular officers in determining when the presence of a naval force is necessary for the protection of American citizens and their property.

The Embassy informed Consul Burke in its instruction of May 20, 1936,[72] that it does not perceive any contradiction between the instructions issued to the two independent services. Paragraph 113 of the Consular Regulations specifically requires that the Consul, having determined when the public exigencies absolutely require the presence of a naval force at his port, will then give the officers in command of the naval forces the reasons in full why the request is made and then "leave with them the responsibility for action". The responsibility for the safety of the lives and property of American citizens at the port, and of the officers and men under the command of the naval officer called to the port in question, rests entirely with the naval officer in command. It is his duty to lay down the conditions under which protection can be given, and it is the Consul's duty to assist the naval officer in obtaining the cooperation of the American citizens in making the protection effective. The commanding officer concerned naturally must not be bound by too limiting a plan, for conditions and circumstances change, and his responsibility under the circumstances is very great.

The Department will note from Mr. Burke's despatch No. 445 of April 27, 1936,[72] that the matter has now been satisfactorily settled through the receipt by Mr. Burke of a letter, dated March 11, 1936, from the Commander-in-Chief, United States Asiatic Fleet, and of a letter, dated March 28, 1936, from Commander Hall of the U. S. S. *Asheville*, with which Commander Hall enclosed a copy of the "Evacuation and Defense Plan for Foochow, China, dated February 1, 1936", duly approved by the Commander of the South China Patrol. Mr. Burke was informed in the Embassy's instruction of May 20 that, in the present instance, it appeared to the Embassy that the plan above-mentioned adequately meets the requirements of the port of

---

[71] Gordon L. Burke, Consul at Foochow.
[72] Not printed.

Foochow considering its distance from deep water, and that the situation will be definitely met when he has worked out with American nationals resident at Foochow the concentration plans required by Paragraph 3 of that defense plan.[74]

Respectfully yours,   NELSON TRUSLER JOHNSON

893.00/13528 : Telegram

The Ambassador in China (Johnson) to the Secretary of State

PEIPING, June 11, 1936—1 p. m.
[Received June 11—8 a. m.]

299. Following telegram has been received from the Consul General at Hankow:

"June 10, 5 p. m.   Press reports from Sian state that Reds under Mao Tse-tung, Peng Teh-huai and Hsu Hai-tung have entered Kansu from northwestern Shensi, that on June 4th they were north of Hwanhsien on the Kwan River in eastern Kansu and south of Tingpien, Shensi and that they would move westwards into Kansu or northwestwards into Ningsia. My latest information is contained in a telegram dated June 10th from Scandinavian Alliance Mission at Pingliang, Kansu, in reply to a telegram from me warning the mission that the Shensi Reds were moving into Kansu; this telegram reads

'Red movement direction confirmed, main force northward travelling westward Tsingning, Americans in Pingliang city safe.'

I have sent telegrams of warning to all Americans known to be in or en route to Kansu or Chinghai."

JOHNSON

893.00/13533 : Telegram

The Consul General at Hankow (Josselyn) to the Secretary of State

HANKOW, June 12, 1936—noon.
[Received June 12—6:45 a. m.]

Substance of Nanking's June 11, 9 a. m.,[75] and June 11, 11 a. m.,[76] is being communicated to Navy to be forwarded to Admiral Allen. U. S. S. Monocacy will leave Hankow for Changsha morning of June 13th.

Repeated to Department, Peiping and Nanking .

JOSSELYN

---

[74] Paragraph 3 provided inter alia that the concentration plans should be prepared and circulated by the Consulate, a copy of such Consulate concentration plan to be furnished the Commander of the South China Patrol.
[75] Ante, p. 202.
[76] Not printed.

893.00/13552 : Telegram

The Consul General at Hankow (Josselyn) to the Secretary of State

HANKOW, June 16, 1936—3 p. m.
[Received 3 : 35 p. m.]

My June 14, noon.[77] Following telegram sent from U.S.S. *Monocacy* at Changsha to Yangtze Patrol Commander received today:

"Changsha quiet. Obtained reliable information that conference between Nanking and Southwestern representatives now taking place at Hengchow. Result of this conference will determine possible hostilities or amicable relations held with American businessmen who have representatives in and south of Hengchow. The consensus of their opinion is that at present there is no cause for alarm. Strong rumor is current Changsha that the price for withdrawal of Southern forces now being discussed. British Consul and senior naval officer are not in accord with above opinions. British Consul has withdrawn all nationals south of Changsha to Changsha and has strongly urged that Americans now south of Changsha be withdrawn. He feels that in the event of hostilities anti-foreign feeling will develop and it may then be impossible to withdraw nationals. No large number troops present Changsha, estimates of Central Government troops south of Changsha vary between 5 and 15 divisions. Central Government troops reported to be entrenching just south of Hengchow. Will issue detailed evacuation plan to all American nationals present Changsha. This plan based on cooperating with British naval forces present, no instructions issued to American nationals other than those in Changsha pending definite decision from American Consul General, Hankow".

I have today despatched following telegram to American Presbyterian Mission stations at Chenchow, Hengyang and Siangtan and to Evangelical Mission at Siangtan

"Future developments uncertain, exercise caution and withdraw if conditions make it advisable telegraph".

Admiral Allen informed.
Repeated to Peiping, Nanking.

JOSSELYN

893.00/13554 : Telegram

The Consul General at Hankow (Josselyn) to the Secretary of State

HANKOW, June 17, 1936—11 a. m.
[Received 11 : 45 a. m.]

My June 16, 3 p. m. Replies have been received to my telegrams to Presbyterian Mission stations at Chenchow, Hengyang and Siangtan. These all state that the situation is quiet and indicate that the mission-

---

[77] Not printed.

aries are not withdrawing for the present. Evangelical missionaries have left Siangtan. Chenchow states Kwangtung troops retired south night of June 15. Hengyang reports numbers of Central Government troops are increasing and that nearest opponents are 40 miles away. Siangtan reports conditions there normal. Commander U.S.S. *Monocacy* at Changsha reports June 16, no change in the general situation; that rumor is current of imminent failure of conference at Hengyang; that Hunan Provincial troops are reported withdrawing from western Hunan with orders to occupy position south of Changsha; that fairly reliable estimates place number of Central Government troops now in Hunan at six divisions with more en route. Americans arriving from Changsha state Governor Ho Chien has remained loyal to Nanking notwithstanding representations from Southwest delegates who went to Changsha last week.

Repeated to Department, Peiping, Nanking, Canton.

JOSSELYN

393.11/1843

The Ambassador in China (Johnson) to the Secretary of State

No. 523   PEIPING, June 17, 1936.
                                                    [Received July 13.]

Subject: United States naval protection for American citizens at Foochow.

SIR: I have the honor to refer to the Embassy's despatch No. 467 of May 20, 1936, relative to the above-mentioned subject, and to enclose for the information of the Department a copy of despatch No. 451 of June 8, 1936, from the Consul at Foochow.[78] Mr. Burke reports therein that the complete defense plan for Foochow includes an evacuation and concentration plan worked out by the Consulate with American nationals resident at Foochow, known as the "Consulate Concentration and Evacuation Plan". He states that this plan is separate and distinct from the plans worked out by the naval authorities and includes a scheme for transport by water from Nantai Island, the main concentration point, to Pagoda Anchorage. Mr. Burke adds that the plan is on record with the naval authorities.

Respectfully yours,   NELSON TRUSLER JOHNSON

121.5493/150 : Telegram

The Acting Secretary of State to the Ambassador in Japan (Grew)

WASHINGTON, June 26, 1936—2 p. m.

84. Department yesterday released to the press portions of text of a telegram received from Peiping [79] reporting presentation by Ameri-

---

[78] Not printed.
[79] Department of State, *Press Releases*, June 27, 1936, p. 653.

can Embassy there to Japanese Embassy of three memoranda testifying to certain acts of Japanese military personnel in Peiping.[80] Certain American newspapers published this morning stories sensational as to text and headlines indicating that Embassy had delivered "protests" and that Department was considering more emphatic follow-up. Department has informed Japanese Ambassador here of the simple and complete facts regarding all that has thus far been done on this case. There is no warrant for and no good purpose to be served by sensationalizing of the case. You may make any use that you see fit of this information.

PHILLIPS

121.5493/152 : Telegram

The Acting Secretary of State to the Ambassador in Japan (Grew)

WASHINGTON, July 1, 1936—5 p. m.

86. Department's 84, June 26, 2 p. m. On the basis of a telegram of June 30 from the Embassy at Peiping [81] the Department on June 30 released to the press a statement as follows:

"The Department has received from the American Embassy at Peiping a telegram reporting that the Japanese Embassy there has given the American Embassy a memorandum making satisfactory reply to the memoranda which the American Embassy gave the Japanese Embassy on June 25 in regard to incidents which occurred in Peiping on June 21 and June 23 involving Japanese military personnel and American citizens and premises."

Department is asking Peiping to forward you by mail the text of its telegram of June 30.

PHILLIPS

893.00/13590 : Telegram

The Consul General at Canton (Spiker) to the Secretary of State

CANTON, July 4, 1936—6 p. m.
[Received July 4—6 p. m.]

Referring to my telegram July 3, 5 p. m.,[82] American resident in Wuchow, Kwangsi, in June 30 letter reports that official families from

---

[80] The acts consisted of rough treatment by Japanese military of American citizens in Peiping: an American officer in civilian clothes was pushed in the stomach with a bayonet by a Japanese sentry, an American woman was threatened with a saber for refusing to leave the sidewalk, and American property was violated by Japanese troops.
[81] Embassy's telegram, No. 330, June 30, 4 p. m., stated that the Japanese "expression of regret" conveyed to the American Embassy would not be given to the press by the Japanese Embassy as "it would hurt the feelings of the Japanese Military."
[82] Not printed.

Nanning, Liuchow and elsewhere in Province are pouring through Wuchow en route to Hong Kong; that Nanking bombers have been making daily flights over Nanning, Liuchow and Kweihsien from where most of the populace have fled; that there is underlying fear in event of defeat Pai [83] "will turn Red"; that Kwangsi currency reached new low on June 3 when it suddenly dropped to four to Hong Kong dollar; and that Kwangsi Bank remained closed. Wuchang, however, remained quiet.

Missionaries express serious fears that popular indignation over soaring food prices and forcible enlistment for unpopular civil war may precipitate uprisings and conversion of Province to Communism. Such information is of interest in the light of a missionary's previously expressed conviction that Red influence in Kwangsi is much stronger than is generally believed, as evidenced by increasing percentage of Moscow trained aviators and technical personnel, radical literature and other signs, and also of various fragmentary information suggesting the 19th Route Army elements associated with Kwangsi have been working for alliance with Reds as in 1933 Fukien rebellion.

Sent to Peiping, Nanking, Shanghai, Hankow.

SPIKER

893.00/13596 : Telegram

The Consul General at Canton (Spiker) to the Secretary of State

CANTON, July 6, 1936—4 p. m.
[Received July 6—2 : 50 p. m.]

Further reports from Kwangsi indicate increasingly serious situation there with marked bandit activity in southwestern corner of province. Latest advices indicate all Americans except two evacuated from Nanning and all Americans from Kweilin area where authorities have ordered evacuation of women and children of the populace and are fortifying the city. Government rationing foodstuffs in Wuchow and elsewhere in Province and have fixed food prices with the result that farmers are not bringing foodstuffs into cities and towns. Most foreigners in Kwangsi now concentrated in Wuchow which remains quiet. Have advised Americans still remaining in interior of Kwangsi to evacuate to place of safety. Have also requested Commander of the South China Patrol to send U.S.S. *Mindanao* to Wuchow where one British gunboat now stationed. He is referring the matter to Commander-in-Chief of Asiatic Fleet. If *Mindanao* proceeds to Wuchow, U.S.S. *Tulsa* will come here from Hong Kong.

2. Sent the Department, Peiping, Nanking, Shanghai and Hankow.

SPIKER

---

[83] General Pai Chung-hsi, Kwangsi military leader.

893.00/13645 : Telegram

The Ambassador in China (Johnson) to the Secretary of State

PEIPING, August 1, 1936—11 a. m.
[Received August 1—8 : 35 a. m.]

386. The following telegram has been received from the Consulate General at Canton.

"July 31, 6 p. m.   Nanking troops have been arriving at Canton to reenforce Kwangtung units in drive up West River against Kwangsi rebels.   Reliable information from Wuchow confirms that Kwangsi military expects such an attack and indicates that while preparing for a provisional defense at Wuchow they are withdrawing principal base up river.   U. S. S. *Mindanao* left Canton this morning for Wuchow."

Sent to Nanking.

JOHNSON

893.00/13655 : Telegram

The Consul General at Canton (Linnell) to the Secretary of State

CANTON, August 6, 1936—5 p. m.
[Received 11 : 30 p. m.]

Advice received from Commander South China Patrol now at Wuchow, Kwangsi, that all American women have left Wuchow for Hong Kong.   Americans in Kwangsi now consist of nine men at Wuchow, including five Catholic priests, and the Catholic priests in the interior.   The latter refuse to leave their posts at present but could get to Wuchow in 10 to 20 hours in case of necessity.

2. Information from reliable sources indicate that the Central Government, having won over Tsai Ting Kai, Teng Shih Tseng and other Nineteenth Route Army leaders, is employing them to overcome Kwangsi *intransigeance* through pressure of Li Chi Shen,[84] whose influence in Kwangsi councils is apparently considerable through his potential value as a rallying point for Nineteenth Route Army personnel and other anti-Nanking-Kwangtung elements.   Interesting instances are today's press reports that Li Chi Shen has secretly left Nanning and that Li Tsung Jen and Pai are preparing to capitulate.

Sent to the Department, Peiping, Nanking, Shanghai and Hankow.

LINNELL

[84] Also known as Marshal Li Chai-sum.

893.00/13671 : Telegram

The Consul at Hankow (Jarvis) to the Secretary of State

HANKOW, August 12, 1936—4 p. m.
[Received August 12—2 : 45 p. m.]

I despatched warnings yesterday by telegraph or airmail to all American missionaries known to be in Kansu south and east of the Yellow River pointing out that the return to northwestern Szechuan from Sikang of a large group of Communists who may try to combine forces with the Communists now occupying part of eastern Kansu on the Ningsia border constitutes a serious threat to Kansu and urging the exercise of the utmost caution.

Sent to the Department, Peiping, Nanking.

JARVIS

893.00/13694 : Telegram

The Consul at Hankow (Jarvis) to the Secretary of State

HANKOW, September 5, 1936—11 a. m.
[Received September 5—11 a. m.]

My August 23, 11 a. m.[85] The Communists in southern Kansu are moving north through Changhsien, Lungsi and Weiyuan districts. It is uncertain whether Minhsien is still infested. In eastern Kansu the Communists are still based on Hwanhsien, and Yuwang in Ningsia, but rove the countryside to within a short distance of Kuyuan.

2. All Americans in Kansu (including West Kansu) have evacuated to Lanchow or into Shensi except Miss Bertha Roberson at Taochow old city and Mr. James Vigna at Siaho (both of Assemblies of God) and Mr. Earl Peterson, Miss Jennie Wedicson and Miss Anna Madsen at Pingliang and Miss Edith Johnson at Kingchwan (all of Scandinavian Alliance Mission) ; Marshal Chang Hsueh Liang's [86] headquarters in Sian has sent special instructions to both the Kansu Governor and the Kansu Pacification Commissioner to afford them protection. The Lanchow-Pingliang-Sian motor road is again open.

Sent to the Department, Peiping, Nanking, Shanghai.

JARVIS

893.00/13733 : Telegram

The Ambassador in China (Johnson) to the Secretary of State

PEIPING, November 12, 1936—4 p. m.
[Received November 12—10 : 30 a. m.]

540. Following received late last night from Nanking:

"November 11, 2 p. m. The following is quoted from translation of a formal note dated November 10 from the Foreign Office.

---

[85] Not printed.
[86] Vice Commander in Chief, Bandit Suppression Forces for the Northwest.

'I have the honor to inform you that a bandit suppression campaign is now in progress in Suiyuan, Ningsia, and Chinghai Provinces and in several places in Inner Mongolia, and that necessary military steps are being taken. With a view to protecting the safety of foreigners, the Chinese Government has issued a circular letter suspending the issuance of visas and travel documents to these places and requesting that all foreign residents thereat be promptly withdrawn, as otherwise the Chinese Government can assume no responsibility for their protection.

'I have the honor to indite this note for your information and to request that instructions be issued to the parties concerned for their compliance.' "

Telegram has been repeated to Tientsin and Hankow for their information and for such action as they may deem advisable in the light of their knowledge of conditions in that part of the area which lies in their respective consular districts.

See registration lists for names of Americans in area described.

JOHNSON

893.00/13734 : Telegram

The Ambassador in China (Johnson) to the Secretary of State

PEIPING, November 19, 1936—11 a. m.
[Received November 19—6 : 50 a. m.]

558. Embassy's 540, November 12, 4 p. m. Tientsin communicated notice to Americans resident in Suiyuan and Ningsia and advised them if they found themselves endangered, or if the situation gave promise of developing in such a way as to threaten their position, they should withdraw to a place of safety. Several Americans have already withdrawn from Suiyuan. No report from Hankow.

JOHNSON

893.00/13858

The Consul at Tientsin (Berger) to the Ambassador in China (Johnson) [87]

No. 350 TIENTSIN, November 20, 1936.

SIR: I have the honor to refer to this Consulate General's despatch No. 348, dated November 19, 1936,[88] concerning the action taken by this office in connection with the request by the Chinese Foreign Office that Americans be withdrawn from Suiyuan, Ninghsia, Chinghai, and Inner Mongolia, and to report that information given me by Consul Ward [89] of this office, who returned this morning from a trip into

---

[87] Copy transmitted to the Department without covering despatch; received January 4, 1937.
[88] Not printed.
[89] Robert Spencer Ward, Consul at Tientsin.

Inner Mongolia, is to the effect that the Misses Sara Heinrichs, Elizabeth Hofer, and Helen Willems, of the Krimmer Mennonite Brethren Mission at Chotzeshan, Suiyuan, left that place on November 18 for Peiping, and were followed the next day by Mr. and Mrs. Abraham K. Wiens, the only other Americans at Chotzeshan; that Mr. and Mrs. A. G. Lindholm and their two children from Patsebolong, are understood to be on their way to Kueisui, where they intend to stay for the time being with Mr. Ekblad; and that Mr. and Mrs. Stuart Gunzel and their infant daughter have taken up temporary residence at Kalgan, Mr. Gunzel having, it is understood, returned alone to Kueisui on November 18 to proceed from there to Chaoho to collect certain personal belongings at that place, whereafter he will return to Kalgan.

The Embassy will note that all American citizens known to be or to have been resident in the Province of Suiyuan are now accounted for.

The Consulate General does not contemplate any further action at present in connection with the withdrawal of those Americans still in Suiyuan.

Respectfully yours,   DAVID C. BERGER

893.00/13775 : Telegram

The Counselor of Embassy in China (Lockhart) to the Secretary of State

PEIPING, December 16, 1936—5 p. m.
[Received December 16—2 : 45 p. m.]

618. Hankow's December 15, 5 p. m.[90] Embassy here telegraphed this morning to an American missionary in Sian, requesting him to report by telegraph concerning safety and welfare of American citizens in Sian and vicinity.[91] Telegraph office here accepted message and will endeavor to ascertain whether it is delivered. Telegraph line is reported open to Sian but messages are subject to delay in delivery and censorship.

Sent to the Department, Nanking, Shanghai and Hankow.

LOCKHART

---

[90] Not printed.
[91] This request followed the seizure of Generalissimo Chiang Kai-shek by mutinous military leaders at Sian.

893.00/13801 : Telegram

The Consul at Hankow (Jarvis) to the Secretary of State

HANKOW, December 20, 1936—2 p. m.
[Received December 20—8 a. m.]

My December 14, 6 p. m.[92] I have just received the following telegram, filed at Sian at 2:10 p. m. yesterday, from Herman Swenson, American missionary there: "Americans safe".

2. A telegram from Pingliang, eastern Kansu, filed at 7 o'clock last night and received here at 1 p. m. today reports that Americans there and at Tsingning are safe and the situation is somewhat easier, with communications uncertain and further developments depending upon the situation at Sian. I have not yet heard from Lanchow. Sent to the Department, Peiping, Nanking, Shanghai.

JARVIS

893.00/13810 : Telegram

The Counselor of Embassy in China (Lockhart) to the Secretary of State

PEIPING, December 22, 1936—noon.
[Received December 22—3:07 a. m.]

630. Following telegram has been sent to Hankow:

"December 22, noon. Reference paragraph 2 of your December 20, 2 p. m. The following telegram has been sent to Chairman of the Kansu Provincial Government:

'December 22. Please afford every possible protection to American citizens at Lanchow and throughout Kansu. Please also afford them facilities to evacuate from Lanchow and other places pending return to settled conditions in the Northwest. The favor of a reply is requested.'

Please get in touch with Americans in Kansu and Chinghai directly, if possible, or through their Mission Headquarters and advise evacuation."

Sent to the Department and Nanking.

LOCKHART

893.00/13817 : Telegram

The Consul at Hankow (Jarvis) to the Secretary of State

HANKOW, December 22, 1936—5 p. m.
[Received December 22—4:19 p. m.]

My December 20, 6 [2] p. m. The situation in Kansu is obscure. Unconfirmed reports are that: (1) Yu Hsueh-chung, the Kansu Chair-

---

[92] Not printed.

man and adherent of Chang Hsueh Liang, has made himself master of Lanchow, after seizing the headquarters of Pacification Commissioner Chu Shao-liang, who is detained in Sian; (2) Chang Hsueh Liang's troops are withdrawing towards Sian from northeastern Kansu, leaving the Province open to the main Communist force now occupying the Kansu–Ningsia–Shensi border, and (3) there is fighting between Yu Hsueh-chung's men and loyal troops of Hu Tsung-nan. There are 30 Americans stationed or temporarily residing in Lanchow and 12 other towns in eastern and southern Kansu and 14 Americans in or near Sining, Chinghai, any or all of whom may be put in jeopardy by a Communist attack or a conflict between rebel and loyal troops.

2. I am still without direct news from Americans in Lanchow. I have sent an urgent telegram to the Kansu Chairman requesting information concerning Americans in Lanchow, elsewhere in the Province and asking that protection be afforded them. I hope it will be possible for the Embassy to reenforce this request.

3. My information is meager and uncertain. I think Americans should evacuate Kansu and Chinghai but may not be possible or safe for them to do so except by air. Could the Embassy make arrangements (similar to those outlined in Nanking's telegram No. 368 of December 21, 4 p. m. to this office [93]) to evacuate Americans from such central points in Kansu as Lanchow and Pingliang? Sent to Nanking; repeated to Department, Peiping, Shanghai.

JARVIS

893.00/13822 : Telegram

The Ambassador in China (Johnson) to the Secretary of State

NANKING, December 23, 1936—2 p. m.
[Received December 23—7 : 15 a. m.]

374. Hankow's December 22, 5 p. m., paragraph 3. Investigations thus far made by the Embassy have not shown that it would be possible to obtain permission to send airplanes to Sian and other affected areas, because there would be no assurance that they would not be detained by the local forces. Moreover, the question of expense probably about 2000 dollars Chinese currency per diem would have to be met.

The Embassy is giving urgent attention to the matter of safety of American citizens. It desires to have all possible information and will welcome any helpful suggestions.

Repeated to Peiping, Hankow, Shanghai.

JOHNSON

[93] *Ante,* p. 442.

893.00/13825 : Telegram

The Consul at Hankow (Jarvis) to the Secretary of State

HANKOW, December 23, 1936—4 p. m.
[Received December 23—8 : 35 a. m.]

Peiping's December 22, noon. Mission offices here, with whom the Consulate General is in close touch, have heard nothing since the coup from their stations in Sian or Kansu. The only communications the Consulate General has received are the two telegrams mentioned in my telegram of December 20, 2 p. m. As directed by Peiping's December 22, noon, I have despatched urgent telegrams to the heads of missions in Kansu and Chinghai advising Americans to evacuate and informing them of the Embassy's request to the Kansu Chairman to afford them facilities and protection. Sent to Peiping, Nanking, Shanghai.

JARVIS

893.00/13826 : Telegram

The Ambassador in China (Johnson) to the Secretary of State

NANKING, December 23, 1936—8 p. m.
[Received December 23—11 : 14 a. m.]

378. Hankow's December 23, 4 p. m. and December 20, 2 p. m. Telegrams have been received today from Swenson and Fitch, American representative of Texas Company in Sian, stating that Americans are safe. Sent to the Department. Repeated to Hankow by mail. To Peiping, Shanghai.

JOHNSON

893.00/13835 : Telegram

The Consul at Hankow (Jarvis) to the Secretary of State

HANKOW, December 25, 1936—9 a. m.
[Received December 25—6 : 50 a. m.]

My telegram of December 24, 9 a. m.[94] I have received the following telegram from the China Inland Mission, Lanchow, Kansu:

"Your telegram received Sunday 20th. All Lanchow foreigners safe, immediate tension relieved. No accurate news of other centers but believe safe. Communications difficult. Kindly inform missions."

This telegram was filed at Lanchow at 7 : 10 p. m., December 20th and received Hankow 6 : 15 a. m. today. My telegram to the mission was sent December 16.

[94] Not printed.

2. I am informing missions here and my interested colleagues.
Sent to the Department, Peiping, Nanking, Shanghai.

JARVIS

893.00/13834 : Telegram

The Consul at Hankow (Jarvis) to the Secretary of State

HANKOW, December 26, 1936—5 p. m.
[Received December 26—11 : 40 a. m.]

The news of Chiang Kai Shek's release, first report of which
reached here yesterday evening,[95] has been received with striking mani-
festations of popular joy and relief.

2. I have received a telegram from the Kansu Provincial Government which states that Kansu is peaceful and quiet, order is being
preserved as usual, all Americans at Lanchow and other points are
safe and the Provincial Government has issued orders for their protection. This telegram was sent from Lanchow at 1 : 20 p. m., December 24th and received at Hankow at 2 : 15 p. m. yesterday.

3. Peterson, American missionary in Pingliang, eastern Kansu has
telegraphed that all Kansu Scandinavian Alliance Missionaries are
going to Lunghsien, Shensi, the first party leaving today. His telegram was sent yesterday afternoon at 5 and arrived here via Sian this
morning.

Sent to the Department, Peiping, Nanking, Shanghai.

JARVIS

893.00/13840 : Telegram

The Consul at Hankow (Jarvis) to the Secretary of State

HANKOW, December 28, 1936—9 a. m.
[Received December 28—2 : 15 a. m.]

My December 26, 5 p. m. Seventh Day Adventist Mission at Sining,
Chinghai, has telegraphed me that the local government is loyal, the
situation is quiet and evacuation is difficult owing to lack of facilities.

2. I telegraphed yesterday to missions in Chinghai and Kansu
(except Pingliang) that the situation had eased and to advise Americans to use their own discretion in the light of local conditions.

Sent to the Department, Peiping, Nanking, Shanghai.

JARVIS

[95] See telegram No. 380, December 25, 7 p. m., from the Ambassador in China,
p. 448.

893.00/13852 : Telegram

The Consul at Hankow (Jarvis) to the Secretary of State

HANKOW, December 31, 1936—6 p. m.
[Received December 31—10 : 15 a. m.]

My telegram of December 28, 9 a. m. Missionaries report and military authorities here confirm that area west of Sian is disturbed. American missionaries there are evacuating to Nancheng, southwestern Shensi. Sent to the Department, Peiping, Nanking, Shanghai.

JARVIS

OPPOSITION OF THE DEPARTMENT OF STATE TO PROPOSED WITHDRAWAL OF AMERICAN ARMY FORCES FROM NORTH CHINA; RETENTION OF AMERICAN EMBASSY IN PEIPING [96]

893.0146/479

The Secretary of State to the Secretary of War (Dern)

WASHINGTON, February 7, 1936.

MY DEAR MR. SECRETARY : Reference is made to the letter of November 19, 1935, from the Acting Secretary of War (and to my letter of acknowledgment of November 20, 1935) [97] in which the Acting Secretary of War refers to a letter, under date April 9, 1931, addressed by the Secretary of War to the then Secretary of State, [98] recommending the withdrawal of the American garrison from Tientsin, and states that, in view of current developments in North China, he renews that recommendation.

This Department, in the light of changes in the situation in North China, has given constant thought and study to this question and offers below for the consideration of the War Department its present views. In this connection, attention is called to this Department's letter of February 17, 1933, [99] addressed to General Douglas MacArthur, Chief of Staff, enclosing a copy of a memorandum entitled "Foreign Armed Forces in the Peiping–Tientsin Area of China", in which were set forth the facts in regard to the circumstances under which American armed forces were originally sent to North China and the purpose for which they are at present maintained there.

The foreign armed forces maintained at Peiping and Tientsin and at various points along the railway between Peiping and Shanhaikwan

---

[96] For previous correspondence regarding these questions, see *Foreign Relations*, 1935, vol. III, pp. 700 ff. and pp. 508 ff.
[97] *Ibid.*, pp. 701 and 702.
[98] Not printed ; for the reply thereto, see *ibid.*, 1931, vol. III, p. 1015.
[99] Not printed.

under the provisions of the Boxer Protocol [1] were (as reported by the Military Attaché at Peiping under date September 27, 1935) on September 1, 1935, as follows:

United States	1256
Great Britain	1004
France	1763
Italy	390
Japan	1838
Total	6251

(The American forces comprise two battalions of the Fifteenth Infantry stationed at Tientsin—a detachment of which was on September 1 at the summer encampment near Chinwangtao—and a Marine Corps detachment at Peiping.)

Under existing conditions, it would seem that the original mission of this force (that of providing, in cooperation with similar forces of other countries, special protection for the lives and property of foreign nationals, including the legations at Peiping and, in case of emergency that may call for evacuation, making available an armed escort to the sea) has been substantially modified by the fact that the presence of this force along with similar forces of other countries is regarded as having a psychological influence of a reassuring and stabilizing character. We feel that it should be kept in mind at all times, in thinking of this force, that its mission has not been and is not combat or coercion but has been and is guard duty and potential escort.

The presence of American and Japanese armed forces in juxtaposition presents, of course, during periods of tension between Japan and the United States possibility that incidents may arise between members of these armed forces. At present this danger is, in the opinion of the Department and its representatives in China, not great, and there appears to be little reason to expect that the situation in this respect will greatly change.

On the basis of renewed consideration of all facts and factors known to it, military, political and diplomatic, this Department is of the opinion that the withdrawal at this time of the American detachment at Tientsin would not be to the best interests of the United States.

In the first place, the precipitate withdrawal of this force would contribute toward a further breaking down of what remains of the system of cooperative or collective action which has been an objective of American policy in regard to the relations of the principal treaty powers with each other in China and in their dealings with the Chinese Government. This system, which is typically exemplified in the

---

[1] Signed at Peking, September 7, 1901, *Foreign Relations*, 1901, Appendix (Affairs in China), p. 312.

several agreements relating to China entered into during the Washington Conference,[2] has been, in our opinion, of advantage to the United States and might well be to the best interests of the other "foreign" powers as well as of China. Moreover, the American Government has certain responsibilities to the other signatory powers of the Boxer Protocol and certain responsibilities as a consequence of our long association with these powers in maintaining armed forces at Tientsin. If a decision were reached to withdraw from these responsibilities it would be desirable, prior to such termination, to consult with or give notice to the interested powers.

In the second place, the precipitate withdrawal of American troops from Tientsin at a moment when China is confronted with a new and serious impairment of its administrative integrity, and when Chinese rule in North China although already attenuated is still indeterminate,[3] might be expected to be misinterpreted by both the Chinese and the Japanese. Coming closely after developments which occurred in China subsequent to the establishment of our silver purchasing policy and after recent bankruptcies of American firms (including one bank) in Shanghai, the withdrawal of this detachment might be expected to encourage an unfavorable reaction against American nationals in China and their interests. Japanese propaganda could be expected to encourage these reactions. The taking of this step by us might even encourage the Japanese to enlarge the scope and increase the tempo of their militaristic advance in China.

In summary, it appears to the Department that the danger of the United States becoming embroiled with Japan because or in consequence of the continued presence of a detachment of American troops at Tientsin is not greater today than it has been in the past, while the precipitate withdrawal of this contingent would in all probability be misunderstood and be used to the disadvantage of the United States and of the principle of cooperative action in China of which the American Government has been a leading advocate.

This Department is desirous that all American troops be withdrawn from China whenever the advantages of their being there become outweighed by the disadvantages and when their withdrawal can be effected without embarrassment to American interests. For the time being we feel that very useful purposes are served by their being and their remaining there.

It is suggested that the Commandant of the American detachment at Tientsin might in view of recent developments care to consult with the American Ambassador at Peiping in regard to the advisability of discontinuing the use of the summer encampment near Chinwangtao.

---

[2] See *Foreign Relations*, 1922, vol. I, pp. 1 ff.
[3] See *ante*, pp. 1 ff.

If at any time there is in contemplation any substantial reduction or substantial alteration in the organization or equipment of the force under reference, this Department would appreciate being informed well in advance that such matters are under consideration, in order that it may have opportunity to confer with the War Department in regard to political aspects and, if need be, to communicate in confidence with other governments most concerned in relation thereto.

Of course, in case other powers maintaining garrisons in North China should indicate an inclination or intention to withdraw their armed forces from the area under reference, or in the event that developments occur substantially altering the situation with regard to the maintenance of American armed forces in that area, this Department would expect at any moment to reconsider the whole question in consultation with the War Department and any other Departments concerned.

Sincerely yours,   CORDELL HULL

124.9318/194

The Chief of the Division of Far Eastern Affairs (Hornbeck) to the Ambassador in China (Johnson)

WASHINGTON, February 21, 1936.

DEAR NELSON: Referring further to your letter of October 9, 1935, and my acknowledgment of November 11,[4] especially the last paragraph of your letter (wherein you mention the matter of possible gradual reduction of our Guard at Peiping and of the 15th Infantry at Tientsin),—

The Department has sent you, I understand, copies of a letter from [5] and the Department's reply [6] to the War Department, recently, on the subject of possible withdrawal of the 15th Infantry. Subsequent to the sending of our reply, there has been brought to our attention a report by General Kilbourne,[7] dated Manila December 28, 1935, entitled "Observations Concerning Situation in North China",[7a] in the course of which General Kilbourne makes statements which indicate that his reasoning with regard to the usefulness of the presence of the Protocol Forces in North China is in line with ours, and he makes in particular this statement:

"2. My former opinion was that our troops should be given a definite mission or withdrawn; I felt that their presence was more liable

---

[4] Neither printed.
[5] Dated November 19, 1935, *Foreign Relations*, 1935, vol. III, p. 701.
[6] *Supra.*
[7] Maj. Gen. Charles Evans Kilbourne.
[7a] Not printed.

to cause international friction than to prevent it. However, after close contact with the local situation, I believe this is a danger we must accept, and that the troops should remain. The Legation Guard in Peiping is an absolute necessity."

Although I understand that some officers in the War Department are not entirely convinced, I think that we may rest assured that the War Department will not make any new moves or recommendations in this matter without first conferring with us.

We have not failed to give thought to the question of possible "gradual reduction", but our conclusion is to the effect that it would not be advisable.

The idea now is to proceed on the principle of maintenance of the *status quo*.

Yours sincerely,

STANLEY K. HORNBECK

124.93/324

Memorandum by the Chief of the Division of Far Eastern Affairs
(Hornbeck)

[WASHINGTON,] March 19, 1936.

The question asked is: Why not move the American Embassy in China from Peiping (presumably to Nanking)?

Officers of the Division of Far Eastern Affairs, having previously given this question consideration at intervals during the past eight years, have, in response to this inquiry, given the question renewed consideration; have, in doing so, given renewed consideration to the co-related question, why not withdraw the American armed forces stationed at Peiping and Tientsin; have, in connection with both questions, conferred with appropriate officers of the Army and of the Navy; and have produced memoranda setting forth the facts and stating their conclusions. The memoranda, separate but closely inter-related, are attached hereunder.[8]

The conclusions arrived at are that the Embassy should not be moved from Peiping at this time and that the American armed forces stationed at Peiping and Tientsin should not be withdrawn at this time.

With regard to the Embassy, it is shown that, since the removal of the Chinese capital from Peiping to Nanking in 1928, the majority of the foreign governments, including the American Government, have made various readjustments in their diplomatic "set-up" in China in accordance with and to meet the needs of changes in the situation there, as those changes have occurred. It is shown that there is a measure of uncertainty with regard to the continuance of the

---

[8] Memoranda not printed.

seat of the National Government at Nanking; that the provisions of certain treaties and agreements have to be taken into consideration; and that political implications and possible consequences of a removal, if made, at this time are factors to be considered. It is shown that the difficulty of obtaining adequate housing facilities at Nanking (or at Shanghai) together with the question of expenditures which would have to be made were the diplomatic establishment to be removed to either of those cities have been and are obstacles to such a removal. It is pointed out that, even if the Embassy establishment were removed, it would still be desirable or necessary for this Government to have official representation at Peiping, and that, therefore, removal of the Embassy would not put an end to certain hazards which may attend the presence in Peiping of American official representation. It is stated, in conclusion, that:

"Under these circumstances, the preponderance of factors seems still to point to the inadvisability of removing the Embassy establishment at this time and *in toto* from Peiping. It seems preferable to 'carry on' as at present, with the Embassy headquarters in Peiping and the sub-embassy at Nanking, continuing to make readjustments gradually and with due consideration of common interests and methods and of changes in the situation as they occur." [9]

Impossible of disassociation from the question of the removal of the Embassy establishment from Peiping is the question of the withdrawal of the American armed forces stationed at Peiping and at Tientsin.

In the memorandum discussing that question, it is pointed out that up to the present time all who have studied the question have repeatedly arrived at the conclusion that, although it is desirable that these forces be withdrawn at the earliest possible moment, such withdrawal would at the existing moment be not advisable. There is given an account of the history of the presence and the mission of these armed forces, of the legal authority under which they were sent, beginning in 1900, and by which they have been maintained. There is given an account of the present "set-up", under which the American contingents have a total of 1,256 men (officers and enlisted men). It is pointed out that the mission of these forces has not been and is not combat or coercion but has been and is guard duty and potential escort. It is indicated that these forces play a part in the system of cooperative action which has been an objective of American policy in regard to the relations of the principal treaty powers with each other in China and in their dealings with the Chinese Government; that precipitate withdrawal of these American forces at this time

---

[9] The Ambassador in China in his despatch No. 442, May 12, concurred in this conclusion (124.93/330).

might be expected to be misinterpreted both by the Chinese and by the Japanese; and that the Chinese Government and people do not now object to the presence of these forces but look upon these forces as a stabilizing element in a critically disturbed political situation. There is cited testimony by Major General Kilbourne, in a report written in December last,[10] strongly expressing, in reversal (after investigation) of an earlier opinion of his, the opinion that these forces should not at this time be withdrawn. Facts and opinions are adduced to the effect that the question of cost of maintenance is negligible.

In conclusion it is stated that: it is the opinion of officers of the three Departments who have recently studied the matter that the danger of complications with Japan through the continued presence of these American forces in North China is not substantially greater now, or likely to be, than it has been in the past; that a precipitate withdrawal of them would in all probability be misunderstood and be used to the disadvantage of the United States and of American policy; that the Department is desirous that all American troops be withdrawn from China whenever the advantages of their being there become outweighed by the disadvantages and when their withdrawal can be effected without embarrassment to American interests; that for the time being very useful purposes are served by their presence there; and that, in case any other powers maintaining such forces in China should indicate an inclination to withdraw their forces, or if developments occur substantially altering the situation with regard to this question, the Department would expect promptly to reconsider the whole question in consultation with the War and Navy Departments.[11]

124.93/326

Memorandum by the Chief of the Division of Far Eastern Affairs (Hornbeck)

[WASHINGTON,] March 30, 1936.

WHY NOT MOVE THE EMBASSY FROM PEIPING?

The principal reason for moving would be that it is usual to have diplomatic missions at capital cities: Peiping is no longer the capital city; Nanking is now the capital of China.

But, in China the conditions are exceptional. Nanking has not long been the capital, and it is by no means certain that it will remain

---

[10] Not printed.
[11] The Ambassador in China in his despatch No. 442, May 12, agreed with the views expressed in this concluding paragraph (124.93/330).

the capital: the Chinese themselves hastily moved a part of their Government offices from Nanking in 1932 and they have plans for a removal at any moment to a point in the interior (as far west as Szechwan Province).

As matters stand, a considerable removal of our Embassy from Peiping to Nanking has since 1928 gradually been effected. We have at Nanking a substantial working Embassy. We retain in Peiping the principal residence of the Ambassador, the records, the wireless station, the establishments of the Military Attaché and the Naval Attaché, and the Marine Guard.

Complete removal from Peiping would entail not only the removal of the diplomatic establishment but withdrawal of the wireless station and of our armed forces in North China. It is doubtful whether we would be permitted to transfer the wireless station to Nanking. That station is run by the Marine Guard at the Embassy. It is practically certain that we would not be permitted to transfer the Guard to Nanking. Moreover, if we were to withdraw the Guard from Peiping, it would follow that we ought to withdraw our Army force from Tientsin.

But, in addition to the Embassy staff, there are in and around Peiping and Tientsin some 1,300 American nationals (with their various interests). Withdrawal of the Marine Guard and the Army force would deprive these people of the sense of security (comparative) which the presence of the armed forces gives them.

Our Embassy in Peiping (located in the Legation Quarter) and our military forces at Peiping and Tientsin are a part of the international system, created under treaty provisions, for promoting security and, indirectly, stability in the situation in China. We have in connection with them certain legal and certain moral obligations to the other powers, including China. The Chinese do not at present urgently desire that the powers give up the rights and obligations involved in this situation. None of the powers (except Japan) desires that such a removal and withdrawal be now consummated, and most of the powers which have major interests in China (including *inter alia* the United States, Great Britain and France) have not effected such removal and withdrawal. We ought not make such moves independently and without consideration of the interests and the opinions of the other powers.

Complete removal of our Embassy and withdrawal of our armed forces would by just that much diminish the political hazard of our position in China.

But, while possibly diminishing a political hazard in one respect (physical), it would increase that hazard in another respect (psychological). While decreasing our points of contact, it would increasingly expose to assault and abuse those of our points of contact (nationals and property) which remain *in situ quo*. Moreover, it would bring upon us reproaches of the Chinese and other powers (except the Japanese) and would tend to confirm the view of many foreign critics of the United States that this country has no feeling of responsibility in regard to rights and obligations which it possesses in common with other powers and that we cannot be relied on in situations of general international concern. It would encourage and facilitate more "positive" action on the part of Japan in the direction of applying armed pressure in prosecution of her China policy.

The presence at Nanking of our whole diplomatic establishment would give some advantage in the field of contacts with Chinese officialdom.

But, it would deprive us of the advantage of contacts with the personnel of the diplomatic establishments of other nations which remain at Peiping; and it would weaken the principle of cooperation among the powers in defense of common interests.

As matters stand, we have both at Nanking and at Peiping establishments which meet the needs of the situation. From each and from the position of both we derive certain advantages. Adjustments we are constantly making. An abrupt and complete removal of the Peiping establishment would deprive us of a part of the advantage which the present system gives us.

If there were available at Nanking adequate housing for our whole diplomatic establishment, and if it were certain that the Chinese Government is firmly seated at Nanking, delay in completing the removal of our establishment to that city might be difficult to defend.

But, there is not available there adequate housing and it is by no means certain that the Chinese will not some day precipitately move their Government to some other point.

To move, we would have to have a Congressional appropriation; and when we move we will probably incur a substantial loss in disposing of our Government property at Peiping.

If we could make this move without adversely affecting the political situation in China and the Far East in general, the case for moving might be made very strong.

But, this Administration has been proceeding in the field of Far Eastern relations and policy on the principle of making what contributions we can to the stabilizing of the situation and of avoiding action or gestures which would tend, by injecting new factors of uncertainty, of suspicion, of nervousness and of friction into it, to disturb the situation.

It is the belief of the officer personnel of FE that we should be governed in the conducting of our Far Eastern relations by the same principles that govern our conducting of relations with other parts of the world and that we should as rapidly as possible make our agencies and our methods in that field the same as those which we employ elsewhere. It is necessary, however, to deal with situations as we find them. The Far East is still in many respects a "special" region. The agencies and methods which have been used and which are in use there are in many respects "special". These we want to change—as rapidly and as effectively as may be. The changes should, however, be made gradually—as the situation changes. We try to keep up with —in fact we try to keep a little ahead of—changes in the situation; but we feel that it would not be sound policy and it would not be to anybody's interest for the United States to proceed in regard to this situation as though the situation had already been changed, and so completely changed, as to be no longer special and to call no longer for special agencies and methods.

We feel that the removal of the Embassy to the Chinese capital and the withdrawal of our Marine Guard from Peiping and our Army force from Tientsin should be consummated at the earliest opportune moment. But we believe that the moment has not yet arrived when it would be in the best interests of the United States to make these moves. In this view we have the concurrence of officers of the Navy and of the Army who have made special study of these questions.

893.0146/493

Memorandum by the Ambassador in China (Johnson) of a Conversation With the Commanding Officer of the United States Army Troops in China (Lynch) [12]

PEIPING, April 13, 1936.

Colonel Lynch called by arrangement this afternoon. He brought with him a copy of a letter addressed by the State Department to the War Department in regard to the keeping of the 15th Infantry Regiment at Tientsin, in which the suggestion was made that Colonel Lynch might consult with me as to the advisability of retaining the summer camp of the 15th Infantry at Chingwantao. Colonel Lynch had been instructed by the Commanding General of the Philippine Islands to discuss this matter with me.

I told Colonel Lynch that in our opinion we should not discontinue the camp of the 15th Infantry at Chingwantao. I said that the maintenance of that camp was necessary for the health of the 15th Infantry at Tientsin; that it was interfering with no one; that I had heard no objections to its being there, nor did I know of any one who had any right to object to its being there; that its status was legal

---

[12] Copy transmitted to the Department by the Ambassador in China in his despatch No. 393, April 22; received May 18.

under the Protocol of 1901, and therefore on all fours with the legal status of the Japanese troops in the same area. I stated that I could see no objection whatever to keeping this camp going as long as we maintained a Guard at the Embassy and the 15th Infantry at Tientsin.

NELSON TRUSLER JOHNSON

124.93/326

Memorandum by President Roosevelt to the Secretary of State

WASHINGTON, April 14, 1936.

In regard to this problem of the Embassy in Peiping, I think you might confidentially discuss the subject with the Chinese Ambassador here and get his thought and perhaps that of his Government. I still think that the advantages of moving the Embassy to Nanking outweigh the disadvantages. This does not mean that we should precipitately make the move but at least the Chinese Government would know of our suggestion and if they approve the general thought it would be a definite advantage to our relations.

Your conversation with the Ambassador and his inquiries should, of course, be kept highly confidential.

F[RANKLIN] D. R[OOSEVELT]

124.93/326

The Chief of the Division of Far Eastern Affairs (Hornbeck) to the Secretary of State

[WASHINGTON,] May 15, 1936.

MR. SECRETARY: In accordance with the suggestion which you made to me a few days ago that I solicit the views of the Chinese Ambassador on the subject of the possible removal of the American Embassy from Peiping to Nanking and withdrawal of the American armed forces from North China, I today brought this subject up with the Chinese Ambassador. I said to the Ambassador that I realized that these were matters about which it might be embarrassing to him to have asked officially and formally a direct question, but that I would like to have informally and unofficially an expression of his opinion. The Ambassador said that it was quite true that it would be embarrassing to him to have to make officially and formally a reply to such a question and that, in what he would say unofficially and informally, he must request that we treat the matter as strictly confidential. He then said that, on the occasion of the President's reception of himself and the Chinese bankers on Monday last (May 11), at tea, the President had made a casual reference to this subject and had remarked that the Ambassador understood his, the President's, attitude with regard to the matter. That had occurred in the presence of the Secretary of the Treasury. Thereafter, last evening (May 14), at the conference at Mr. Morgenthau's house between Treasury officials and the Chinese, Mr. Morgenthau had asked the Ambassador what the Chinese really thought about the question of moving the Embassy. He, the Ambassador, had then stated to Mr. Morgenthau that, although Chinese officialdom had for sometime after the establishing of the Nanking Government desired that the foreign Missions leave Peiping and come to Nanking, and that the foreign armed forces be removed, conditions have changed and, in view of the situation which now prevails, Chinese officialdom is inclined to be gratified at the presence of the foreign diplomatic establishments in Peiping (that is, in North China). The Ambassador said that I might say to you, in expression of his opinion, but in strict confidence, that he believes that Chinese officialdom would prefer that, as matters stand, there be made no step toward moving our Mission away from Peiping or taking our armed forces out of North China, and that it is his own feeling that the effect of any such step, if taken, would be the opposite of helpful.

Comment: This reply by the Ambassador is entirely in keeping with and gives confirmation to the conclusions arrived at in the study recently made by this Division, in consultation with officers of the Army and of the Navy, of this subject, as reported to you in this Division's memoranda.[13] It also confirms the opinion which I expressed to you in estimate of the probable Chinese view.

In the light of the facts under reference as regards what has been presented on this subject, taken together with the events which have recently transpired in connection with the attack upon the American Legation at Addis Ababa,[14] the precaution taken by the British Government in providing a guard for its Legation there, the service which that guard was called upon to perform, the resort of our Legation to the assistance of and protection by that guard, questions which have been asked and criticism which has been made subsequently in Congress, it would seem to me that there is little if any ground for doubting the wisdom of the successive decisions which have been made on the basis of which we have continued to maintain in Peiping a part of our diplomatic establishment in China and to maintain the armed forces which are related to and which go with the maintaining of that establishment; and, it seems to me that it clearly would be inadvisable for us to take at this time any step toward altering the physical set-up of our total establishment in North China.

S[TANLEY] K. H[ORNBECK]

---

[13] See memorandum of March 19, p. 535.
[14] See vol. III, pp. 254 ff.

701.4193/68 : Telegram

*The Chargé in the United Kingdom (Atherton) to the Secretary
of State*

LONDON, June 30, 1936—noon.
[Received June 30—9 : 05 a. m.]

329. Under Secretary for Foreign Affairs in response to a question in the House of Commons whether seeing that the Government of the Chinese Republic had been established in Nanking it was intended to move the British Embassy there, stated "His Majesty's Government consider that the time has now come for this change and they intend, subject to the provision by Parliament of the necessary funds, to remove the Embassy to Nanking as soon as fitting premises can be erected in that capital. His Majesty's Chargé d'Affaires is now negotiating for the acquisition of a suitable site in the new city."

ATHERTON

701.4193/71

*Memorandum by the Chief of the Division of Far Eastern Affairs
(Hornbeck)*

[WASHINGTON,] July 2, 1936.

With authorization by the Under Secretary, Mr. Phillips, I called on the British Ambassador by appointment today.

I made reference to conversations which the Ambassador and I had had in the past when the subject of raising the diplomatic missions in Peiping to the grade of embassy was under consideration. I said that there was now another matter somewhat related which I hoped might be talked over in the same informal manner, namely, the question of plans, if and when, for removal of the embassies in China from Peiping to Nanking. I then handed the Ambassador the text, minus superscription and signature, of London's telegram 329, June 30, noon. The Ambassador read this text. I said that we in the Department assumed that the reply made by the Undersecretary for Foreign Affairs in response to the question put in the House of Commons was a replying statement of principle and general intention rather than an indication of a conclusive decision intended to be carried out in the immediate or near future. The Ambassador made a general comment with regard to questions and answers in the House of Commons, pointed to the reference which the Undersecretary for Foreign Affairs had made to the precedent need for provision of necessary funds by Parliament and to the fact that the British Chargé in China is "now negotiating for the acquisition of a suitable site." He said that he thought that this was to be read like provisions in party platforms.

I told the Ambassador that we have considered from time to time the questions both of removal of the Embassy and withdrawal of the armed forces in North China and that we have regularly come to the conclusion that the opportune moment has not arrived. I said that we had gone over the matter recently. There followed some discussion of the considerations pro and contra. I said that so far as the Department is concerned, our view at present is that the considerations contra outweigh those pro—both as to Embassy and as to armed forces. I said that I could not speak in a sense binding the Administration, but that it was our hope in the Department that the Ambassador would be able to give us an interpretation of the statement under reference and an indication of the thought of the British Foreign Office; also, that we hoped that, if and as the situation changes and opinion or policy either in Washington or in London change, it will be possible for the Foreign Office and the Department reciprocally to initiate consultation or give information of probable or impending action. The Ambassador said that he appreciated and reciprocated that attitude. I pointed out again that in what I had said I was expressing the thought and desire of the Department and did not want to be understood as affirming any future view or intent or course of action on the part of the Administration as a whole. The Ambassador said that he clearly understood.

The Ambassador concluded the conversation with the remark that the maintenance of the agencies which the two countries possess in North China stands as a sign of our rights and interests.

S[TANLEY] K. H[ORNBECK]

701.4193/76

The Ambassador in China (Johnson) to the Secretary of State

No. 565 PEIPING, July 6, 1936.
[Received August 10.]

SIR: I have the honor to enclose herewith copy of a letter dated June 30th [15] which I have just received from the British Chargé, Mr. R. G. Howe. Mr. Howe informs me of the British Government's decision to build new premises at Nanking capable of housing the entire staff of the British Embassy, and states that negotiations have already been set on foot for the acquisition of a suitable site at Nanking. He concludes by stating that the British Government have clearly expressed their intention of retaining the existing British property at Peiping.

This letter was written on the very day that an item appeared in the Shanghai papers reporting that an announcement had been made in Parliament by the Under Secretary of State for Foreign Affairs to

---

[15] Not printed.

the effect that the British Embassy was to be moved from Peiping to Nanking, and that the British Chargé was negotiating for an Embassy site at Nanking. According to a statement made to Mr. Peck [16] by Mr. Howe in Nanking on July 1st, it is the expectation of the British that the British Ambassador will spend a portion of each year in North China.

Naturally, this step on the part of the British Government brings forth the question as to whether the United States Government should not similarly interest itself in the acquisition of an Embassy site at Nanking. It is my personal belief that this is not necessary at the present moment.

We are about to take over on a six-year lease a very desirable place at Nanking, upon which are now being finished five houses to accommodate myself and members of my staff, and the office of the Embassy. I expect that these houses will be ready for occupancy in September of this year, and it is my present intention to move myself and my family to Nanking in October at the latest and establish a permanent residence in Nanking, keeping the residence here sufficiently furnished to enable me to use it during the summer months if that seems possible or feasible. I believe that once I am settled in Nanking we can then examine the situation more judiciously and determine upon a policy in regard to the acquisition of a new site.

The latest information regarding sites which the Nationalist Government at Nanking was prepared to sell to foreign Governments for Embassy use indicated a desire on its part to put the Legations and Embassies over into the northeastern section of the city, just inside the wall from Lotus Lake, an area that is very low, filled with ponds and known to be within the malarial mosquito area of the city. Personally I would be opposed to the purchase of a site in such a location under present conditions.

During a recent visit to Nanking I talked with Mr. Suma, First Secretary of the Japanese Embassy and Japanese Consul General at Nanking. Mr. Suma stated that the Japanese were meeting with considerable difficulty in their desire to obtain an Embassy site at Nanking. It has been my understanding that the Japanese desire to purchase land near the present site of their buildings at Nanking, long occupied by their Consulate. The newly-arrived Japanese Ambassador is, I understand, taking over the main residence of the old Japanese Consulate at Nanking, relegating Mr. Suma who has hitherto occupied that building to a more modest edifice within the compound. It is a matter of local gossip in Nanking that the Chinese are opposed to the Japanese acquisition of a site for their Embassy at the present site of their buildings because it is located on high ground.

---

[16] Willys R. Peck, Counselor of Embassy in China, at Nanking.

In my opinion, with the completion of the buildings now being erected for lease to the American Government at Nanking, the American Embassy at Nanking will be well taken care of for the time being, and we can afford to wait a while before deciding to purchase a site for the Embassy.

Respectfully yours,   NELSON TRUSLER JOHNSON

701.4193/77

Memorandum by the Chief of the Division of Far Eastern Affairs (Hornbeck)

[WASHINGTON,] July 24, 1936.

The British Ambassador came to my office and opened the conversation with reference to a conversation which we had had at his Embassy on July 2, 1936. He said that he had informed his Foreign Office of that conversation and had received from them a statement that the removal of the British Embassy from Peiping to Nanking would not take place in the near future. Plans were under way for an ultimate removal, as indicated in the answer given to the question in the House of Commons. The Ambassador said that the question and answer relating to this matter in the House of Commons had been in the category called "printed questions" and that this indicated that the matter was regarded in London as in no way of any urgent importance.

I asked whether the Foreign Office had said anything in reply to my suggestion about keeping in close touch in regard to plans or decisions in relation to the subject of changes in the establishments in North China. The Ambassador replied that they had said nothing on that point but that he assumed that the two foreign offices would proceed in the spirit of reciprocal and mutual helpfulness in that connection.

S[TANLEY] K. H[ORNBECK]

893.0146/515

Memorandum by the Counselor of Embassy in China (Lockhart), Temporarily in Washington

[WASHINGTON,] August 3, 1936.

Conversation: Brig. General Stanley D. Embick, Deputy Chief of Staff, War Department;
Mr. Hornbeck;
Mr. Lockhart.

Mr. Hornbeck opened the conversation by showing to General Embick a clipping from the *North China Star* (Tientsin) indicating that the lease for the barracks and other property occupied by the United States 15th Infantry at Tientsin had recently been renewed. Mr. Hornbeck stated that, inasmuch as the matter of the retention of the 15th Infantry in North China had recently been under discussion, he had brought along Mr. Lockhart, Counselor of the Embassy at Peiping, so that he might give to General Embick his views on the situation in North China, especially with regard to the need for keeping the 15th Infantry at Tientsin. General Embick stated that there had been some recent discussion of the question of withdrawing the 15th Infantry because the War Department felt that the troops were not serving any useful military purpose at Tientsin. He stated that in the event of any war involving North China the troops would be awkwardly situated and that there would be no possibility of their participating in any successful military activity. Mr. Lockhart stated that from the point of view of military operations it could be said that the troops are perhaps of no military value but that from the point of view of providing protection in case of the need of evacuating American nationals from North China, incident to Sino-Japanese disturbances or arising from other causes requiring their removal, they would be of the very greatest value. Mr. Lockhart stated that it would be difficult to foresee when an emergency might arise and cited the suddenness with which the disturbances arose at Hankow in 1927 and the fact that the American Navy was at hand to render protection to the American nationals at that place; [17] that the absence of the Navy at that time would have placed American citizens in a much more dangerous position at Hankow and that a similar situation might conceivably arise, with equal suddenness, in Tientsin or Peiping; that Peiping was considerably removed from the sea and that the object of keeping the Infantry at Tientsin and the Marines at Peiping was to keep communication open to the sea. Mr. Lockhart cited one instance when this had become necessary and it was stated that the Chinese authorities could not be relied upon to perform this function in an emergency. Mr. Hornbeck referred to the disturbances in Spain and to the need for protection for American nationals until they could reach a place of evacuation.[18] Mr. Lockhart remarked that a failure on the part of the Chinese authorities in similar circumstances to render protection would make it necessary for American troops and Marines to step into the breach and that they would unquestionably do so. Mr. Lockhart stated that the troops had manned barricades during the Sino-Japanese troubles of 1931 at Tientsin and prevented bad elements from passing into the foreign residential areas, and that the situation in North China is such that they might be called upon

---

[17] See *Foreign Relations*, 1927, vol II, pp. 236 ff.
[18] See vol. II, pp. 626 ff.

again in similar circumstances or to give protection to Americans should it become necessary to evacuate them. General Embick again referred to the awkward situation in which the 15th Infantry would be placed in case of a Sino-Japanese war and stated that in any kind of war in North China the 15th Infantry would have no military value. Mr. Lockhart remarked that it was his impression that it was the plan of the Commandant of the 15th Infantry, in case fighting should be adjacent to the barracks or should involve the regiment in some conflict with the opposing factions, to have recourse to internment in the British or French Concessions at Tientsin. Mr. Lockhart stated that the barracks were located on Chinese soil immediately adjoining the British Concession.

Mr. Hornbeck suggested that Mr. Lockhart might tell General Embick the attitude of the American Ambassador, Mr. Johnson, on the subject of the removal of the Embassy and armed forces from Peiping. Mr. Lockhart stated that as he understood the matter the Ambassador favors the retention of the main part of the Embassy at Peiping and that he also favors the retention of the 15th Infantry at Tientsin and the Marine detachment at Peiping; that he sees no need to change the present American diplomatic and military set-up in North China with the exception that the Ambassador expects to spend more time in Nanking after his residence at that place has been completed. Mr. Lockhart said that in his view the presence of the troops in North China, as well as the retention of the Embassy at Peiping, had the effect of deterring the Japanese and that he felt that the Japanese were not anxious to have any trouble with any foreign military contingents in North China although, as pointed out, there were evidences that the Japanese were not so friendly in that area to foreign nationals as they once were. Mr. Lockhart stated that there was increasing signs of dislike of foreigners on the part of the Japanese soldiery who, after all, are somewhat more arrogant in a foreign land than they are in their own country. He expressed the view, in reply to a question from General Embick, that the Japanese have no immediate objective south of the Peiping-Tientsin area but that ultimately, having more or less settled in the area between the Great Wall and Peiping and Tientsin, they might elect to extend their dominance down to the Yellow River. He remarked that this was guesswork and he also stated, in reply to an inquiry from General Embick, that he felt the Chinese could not put up any substantial resistance unless and until they were more thoroughly trained in a military way, better equipped and better officered than at present. Mr. Lockhart, in reply to a question by General Embick, stated that he believed that Japan's interests in North China are based on two considerations: (1) military strategy in a possible armed conflict between Russia and Japan (which he regards as not imminent) and (2) economic exploitation by Japan of North China. Mr. Lockhart in closing his part of the conversation referred to the responsibility shared with other nations under the Protocol in protecting foreigners in North China and said that it seemed to him necessary to consult the interested powers before taking any definite steps in the direction of withdrawing troops and in conclusion remarked that he hoped no change would be made at this time in the present arrangements.

The conversation was closed by a brief discussion between Mr. Hornbeck and General Embick on the relative position of the United States and Great Britain in affairs in the Far East. Mr. Hornbeck expressed the view that the United States has much more ultimately at stake in events that take place in the Pacific Ocean than has Great Britain and General Embick advanced the view that Great Britain's interests exceeded those of the United States but it appeared that this view was based largely on the theory that Japan would ultimately take possession of the Philippines, the Dutch East Indies, the Mandated Islands in the South Seas and then would threaten India and Australia, which ultimately might end in a break-up of the British Empire. Mr. Hornbeck remarked that this was taking the conflict out of the Pacific and into the Indian Ocean and that so long as the question is confined to the Pacific Ocean the ultimate concern of the United States is greater than that of Great Britain in that region.

124.93/333a : Telegram

The Acting Secretary of State to the Ambassador in China (Johnson)

WASHINGTON, August 22, 1936—1 p. m.

204. 1. Scripps-Howard newspapers printed August 20 a story by Philip Simms which begins "Led by the United States and Great Britain, the great powers are quietly preparing to abandon Peiping and move their embassies to Nanking, seat of China's Nationalist government." The article states "What is happening is that the great powers, as well as China, are retreating before the advancing Japanese."

Such is not the Department's view.

2. With reference to recent reports relating to the proposed removal of the British Embassy from Peiping to Nanking, the British Foreign Secretary on July 27, in reply to a question in the House of Commons, stated, *inter alia*, "I should like to make it clear that the abandonment of the present Embassy at Peiping is not contemplated. There are important British interests in North China which render its retention desirable."

This parallels the Department's views.

3. The Department desires and we are assured that British Foreign Office desires that there be frank and continuous exchange of information relating to contemplated or decided upon changes in our respective diplomatic establishments, also armed forces, in North China.

It is important that there be no misconstruction, especially by the British, of our action or intention with regard to our establishments.

4. In light of the foregoing and in view of your impending occupation of residence at Nanking, Department desires that Embassy take special pains to avoid any implications and discourage any inferences that your entry into residence at Nanking has any ulterior or broader significance.

Department suggests that you inform British Chargé of this.

5. Inform Nanking and Shanghai.

PHILLIPS

124.93/334 : Telegram

The Ambassador in China (Johnson) to the Secretary of State

PEIPING, August 25, 1936—1 p. m.
[Received 4:40 p. m.]

415. Department's 204, August 22, 1 p. m. Both Peck and I have carefully kept Cadogan [19] and Counselor Howe informed of every step of our decisions regarding Nanking. We have been particularly careful to keep nothing concealed. I say this because of implication in Department's telegram that we may have failed in some way in this manner. In discussing matter with newspapermen, private individuals, and Chinese authorities, we have been equally scrupulous. I have at all times tried to make it abundantly clear that American Government has never had any idea of abandoning its position here in Peiping.

I regret to state that I cannot say the same either for Cadogan or for Howe, although our relations are, and have been, most cordial and they have always been willing to give us information in reply to direct questions. At some time, still unknown to this Embassy, but believed to have been prior to Cadogan's departure, the British Embassy or Board of Works [*Consulate General?*] at Shanghai began negotiations with Chinese for purchase of a site for British Embassy at Nanking. I learned of this indirectly from third parties, and only accidently, a short while ago. Inquiries have confirmed fact, but have produced little or no personal reasons; however, it would appear from information obtained from third parties that negotiations have proceeded to the point where a site has been chosen on road leading to Ho Ping

[19] Sir Alexander M. G. Cadogan, British Ambassador in China.

Men north of Central Party Headquarters in Nanking; that the site is a fairly large one and that plans for Embassy buildings have been drawn and are now under consideration. It is understood that check for site has not yet been handed over. It is knowledge of these negotiations which has given rise to reports through both press and statement in Parliament on July 27. Recent statements by subordinate officers of British Embassy to subordinate members of this Embassy indicate that it is not expected that necessary Embassy buildings in Nanking will be ready within 5 years. Before Cadogan left he told me in a conversation which I had with him that it was going to be necessary for him to take most of his staff to Nanking. At that time, however, our conversation concerned the renovation, then completed, of the old quarters of the British Consulate General and Customs owned houses at Nanking which were being made over for the residence and accommodation of the British Ambassador and staff. Cadogan stated that it was his understanding that British Ambassador will continue to use Peiping dwelling from time to time.

German Embassy moved to Nanking last fall and is now permanently located there, maintaining a junior staff officer here in Peiping.

Japanese Embassy has moved and for some time has been trying to purchase a site in Nanking without success. Japanese Ambassador told me the other day that he expected to continue to use residence in Shanghai at least for the time being.

German Government has for some years owned a large plot of land near the present Railway Ministry site at Nanking. They are now negotiating for the purchase of a small plot to connect the old plot with the Chung Shan Road, but they have no immediate plans for building.

JOHNSON

123J634/408 : Telegram

The Secretary of State to the Ambassador in China (Johnson)

WASHINGTON, August 28, 1936—4 p. m.

209. Reference your telegram 413, August 24, noon,[20] and mail despatch 565, July 6. In the light of 4th paragraph of your despatch under reference and final sentence of your telegram under reference, there arises doubt whether Department's conception and yours regarding Peiping and Nanking establishments, and the question of Ambassador's seat of residence in relation thereto, completely coincide.

Toward making Department's conception absolutely clear to you:

(*a*) As to policy: It is felt here that no change should be made for

---

[20] Not printed.

the present in our establishments in north China, both diplomatic and military. It has been and is assumed here that you will maintain residences in both Peiping and Nanking and that your periods of residence as between the two will be determined by considerations of policy and needs as situations develop. It is desired that such be regarded the procedure at present intended. It therefore is desired that your entry into residence in Nanking shall not be regarded as constituting or implying in any way an abandonment of your Peiping residence or an altering of the existing status of our establishments in Peiping.

(*b*) As to action: In light of the above and communications that have preceded, Department feels that special pains should be taken by Embassy as is being done by the Department to avoid any implication and discourage any inference that your impending occupation of house in Nanking constitutes a change of the Ambassador's seat of residence from Peiping to Nanking. It should be generally understood that your residing at Nanking for a portion of the year is simply for the purpose of facilitating the performance of your official functions and does not alter the character or location of our Embassy establishment. It seems desirable that nothing be said or done suggesting a distinction between or fixity of the periods of time which the Ambassador will spend in residence in either Peiping or Nanking, for instance, mention of "permanence" or a given number of months or a season in connection with either.

HULL

124.93/334 : Telegram

The Secretary of State to the Ambassador in China (Johnson)

WASHINGTON, August 28, 1936—5 p. m.

210. Reference your 415, August 25, 1 p. m. Department's 204, August 22, 1 p. m., was for your information and guidance and should not be construed as implying anything not stated in its text. It gives you in the first three numbered paragraphs new and latest information and was occasioned by the developments reported in its paragraph 1 and in the fifth and following words of its paragraph 3. Please reread carefully, especially first sentence of paragraph 3 and last sentence of paragraph 4, the latter of which sentences applies to all that precedes it in that telegram. See also Department's 209, August 28, 4 p. m.

Department is glad to have all the information given in your telegram under reference.

HULL

701.4193/83

The Ambassador in China (Johnson) to the Secretary of State

No. 704   PEIPING, September 11, 1936.
                                           [Received October 5.]
SIR: I have the honor to refer to the last sentence of paragraph 4 of the Department's telegram No. 204 of August 22, 1 p. m., instructing me to inform the British Chargé d'Affaires of the Department's views in regard to the changes contemplated in the diplomatic establishment of the United States in China. I have noted that it is the desire of the Department that there be a frank and continuous exchange of information between my British colleague and myself on this subject and in regard to any contemplated changes in the armed forces of Great Britain and the United States in North China. Bearing this in mind I called on September 3, 1936, on Mr. Howe, the British Chargé d'Affaires ad interim, and I enclose a memorandum of my conversation with him.[21] It will be noted that Mr. Howe stated that the British Government had no intention of changing the status of its Embassy in Peiping; that it was their intention to go on as before with the Ambassador and most of his staff residing in Nanking and the Counselor in Peiping, the latter residing in Nanking when the Ambassador was in residence in Peiping; that even when their new Embassy establishment in Nanking was completed, about 3 or 4 years hence, they expected to continue to use the Peiping residence as a summer Embassy.

Respectfully yours,   NELSON TRUSLER JOHNSON

ATTITUDE OF THE DEPARTMENT OF STATE ON THE EXPORT TO CHINA OF ARMS OR MUNITIONS, INCLUDING MILITARY AIRCRAFT [22]

893.113 Airplanes/116

The Secretary of State to the Ambassador in China (Johnson)

No. 85   WASHINGTON, January 27, 1936.

SIR: Reference is made to despatch No. 99 of September 24, 1935, addressed to the Embassy by the American Vice Consul at Yunnanfu,[21] which relates in general to the sale of American aircraft in the Province of Yunnan and in particular to the information communicated to the American Consulate by the French Consulate at Yunnanfu to the effect that the Yunnan Railway will refuse to accept American aircraft and aircraft equipment for delivery at Yunnanfu.

---

[21] Not printed.
[22] Continued from *Foreign Relations*, 1935, vol. III, pp. 711–738.

In the absence of additional reports in regard to the subjects under reference it is assumed that no developments of importance have occurred. The Department desires, however, that the situation at Yunnanfu be followed closely with a view to obtaining, if possible, additional evidence confirming the aforementioned attitude of the French consular authorities to the effect that the facilities of the Yunnan Railway would not be available for the shipment to China of American aircraft and accessories.

As previously made known to American diplomatic and consular officers, it is not the policy of this Government to encourage the export trade in arms, ammunition and implements of war, including aircraft. Such trade, however, when carried on in conformity with existing law and regulations, is entirely legitimate. Thus the Department would not wish to acquiesce in any situation wherein goods of American manufacture, including aircraft and aircraft accessories, would be subject to discriminatory treatment.

Very truly yours,   For the Secretary of State:
                                                    WILLIAM PHILLIPS

893.113/1627

The British Ambassador (Lindsay) to the Secretary of State

No. 31   WASHINGTON, January 31, 1936.

SIR: I have the honor to invite reference to the note which you were good enough to address to me on the 1st August last,[24] and to explain, under instructions from His Majesty's Principal Secretary of State for Foreign Affairs, that His Majesty's Government in the United Kingdom have given careful consideration to the suggestion there put forward that they should exercise over the export to China of aircraft and the component parts thereof a control similar to that exercised by the United States Government, and that the two Governments should agree to make their lists of arms and implements of war conform more closely to the list prepared by the Committee for the Regulation of the Trade in and Private and State Manufacture of Arms and Implements of War.[25]

His Majesty's Government do not, however, feel that bilateral action, affecting the United States and Great Britain only, would provide a satisfactory solution. Moreover, in their view, the present time is

[24] *Foreign Relations*, 1935, vol. III, p. 733.
[25] See League of Nations, Conference for the Reduction and Limitation of Armaments, *Conference Documents*, Annex 5, vol. II, p. 559.

unfortunately not favourable for an attempt to secure general international agreement on the adoption of the provisions of the draft convention.[26]

I have [etc.] R. C. LINDSAY

711.00111 Armament Control/724 : Telegram

The Counselor of Embassy in China (Peck) to the Secretary of State

NANKING, February 6, 1936—8 p. m.
[Received February 6—12 : 50 p. m.]

32. 1. Reuter telegram dated Washington, February 6, published here today, states that Department of State has released figures of over 3 million dollars worth of airplanes, bombs and machine guns purchased by representative from the United States in January.

2. Kung, Minister of Finance, this afternoon asked me to ascertain whether it is true that the State Department issued this statement. I inferred that he desires, if possible, to issue some sort of statement minimizing the importance of the report. When speaking to me he was greatly agitated and said the Government was seriously disturbed by this announcement. He observed that if such publicity were to be the settled policy of the Department he would be obliged to give consideration to the advisability of placing future orders outside the United States. He said previous purchases had not been made public by the American Government and pressed me for an explanation of the present action. I suggested that perhaps the munitions control law required that statistics of munitions purchases be published.

3. An Official of the Ministry of Finance informed me confidentially February 4, 4 p. m. that the recent purchase of 80 bombing planes from the Intercontinent Company involved $11,000,000 Chinese currency of which 5,000,000 were to be paid in cash, February 5. He said all details of the transaction were being kept as secret as possible. However, an American businessman told me, January 25, that many persons in Shanghai knew about this aeroplane purchase.

4. Does the Department desire that I convey any comment to the Minister of Finance?

Repeated to Peiping.

PECK

---

[26] For text of draft convention, see *Conference Documents*, vol. III, p. 788. For correspondence concerning provisions of the convention, see *Foreign Relations*, 1935, vol. I, pp. 1 ff.

711.00111 Armament Control/724 : Telegram

The Secretary of State to the Counselor of Embassy in China (Peck)

WASHINGTON, February 10, 1936—6 p. m.

12. Your 32, February 6, 8 p. m. The figures referred to in paragraph 1 appeared in a routine press release issued on February 5,[27] giving a summary of information in regard to export licenses for arms, ammunition and implements of war issued during January covering proposed exports to all countries. These figures indicated that licenses had been issued to cover proposed shipments to China of "machine guns, automatic rifles and machine pistols of all calibers, and their barrels" valued at $125,500, and proposed shipments of military aircraft valued at $2,799,000. Similar press releases had been given out previously in regard to licenses issued in December and in November, but the figures in respect to proposed shipments to China were not sufficiently large to attract attention. The practice of making public information in regard to licenses issued was adopted in the light of the provisions of Section 2 of the Neutrality Act of August 1935,[28] under which the system of licenses was established, and of the intent of Congress as expressed in discussions in the Congressional Committees which considered the Act.

I regret that the publication of such information in this instance has caused embarrassment to the Chinese Government. Since the receipt of your telegram, the matter has been discussed with the Chinese Ambassador who stated that he would telegraph an explanation to his Foreign Office.

I am considering the problem of obviating embarrassment to the Chinese Government or other Governments in connection with the publication of information in regard to licenses issued in the future.

In this connection, it may be pointed out that all arms producing countries publish at intervals—some monthly and some annually—information in regard to exports. Furthermore for some years the League of Nations has published an annual detailed tabulation of information in regard to the international traffic in arms. Thus more detailed information than that which has been released in our monthly statements concerning licenses issued would be made public at least annually in respect to any purchases of arms which the Chinese Government might make in any country.

The above is for your information and for communication orally in your discretion to Kung.

HULL

---

[27] Department of State, *Press Releases*, February 8, 1936, p. 146.
[28] Approved August 31, 1935 ; 49 Stat. 1081.

893.113/1627

The Secretary of State to the British Ambassador (Lindsay)

WASHINGTON, February 10, 1936.

EXCELLENCY: I have the honor to acknowledge the receipt of Your Excellency's note of January 31, 1936, with further reference to the procedures which our two Governments are following in respect to the export of aircraft to China. I note that your Government does not feel that bilateral action in respect to the enumeration of arms, ammunition and implements of war affecting the United States and Great Britain only, would provide a satisfactory solution of the difficulties which have been the subject of recent correspondence between us. In this connection, I enclose, for your information, two copies of *Laws and Regulations Administered by the Secretary of State Governing the International Traffic in Arms, Ammunition, and Implements of War.* I invite your attention particularly to Section VII of this pamphlet.[29] You will note that the arms, ammunition and implements of war enumerated in Categories III and V of the President's Proclamation of September 25, 1935,[30] are almost identical with the enumeration contained in Category III in the list of arms, ammunition and implements of war which your Government, in common with the other Governments of the League of Nations, has adopted in connection with the embargo on the exportation of arms which it has put in effect in respect to Italy. Both of these lists conform closely to the list prepared by the Committee for the Regulation of the Trade in and Private and State Manufacture of Arms and Implements of War. In view of the fact that your Government has adopted such a list in respect to exports from Great Britain to Italy, I again venture to express the hope that it may find it possible to adopt a similar list in respect to exports to China. Such action which would bring the procedure of our two Governments into harmony would, I believe, even if followed by our two Governments only, do much to achieve the objectives of preventing the development or the continuance in China of conditions of domestic violence and of co-operating with the Chinese Government in its efforts to maintain an effective control of the import into China of arms, ammunition and implements of war which both of our Governments desire to achieve.

Accept [etc.]   For the Secretary of State:
R. WALTON MOORE

---

[29] Department of State Publication No. 794, 2d ed., p. 15.
[30] See proclamation No. 2138, Department of State, *Press Releases*, September 25, 1935, p. 222.

893.113/1636

Memorandum by the Chief of the Office of Arms and Munitions Control (Green)

[WASHINGTON,] April 22, 1936.

The Chinese Ambassador called at my office this afternoon by appointment. Mr. Hamilton of FE [31] was present.

I explained to the Ambassador that although under the regulations in effect prior to October 10, 1935, export licenses were required to cover proposed shipments to China of military aircraft and engines and accessories for the same, no export licenses were required for aircraft engines and accessories when they were presumably intended for non-military uses. I pointed out that under the new regulations which became effective on October 10, no distinction was made on the basis of presumptive use in respect to aircraft engines and accessories, and that export licenses were now required to cover proposed shipments of all aircraft and aircraft engines and of certain specified parts. I pointed out that, in respect to proposed shipments to China, licenses were not granted until the Department had been informed by him that the Chinese Government desired that the shipment be authorized; that this procedure would appear to conform entirely to the interests of the Chinese Government; and that it enabled the Chinese Government to exercise control over all importations of aircraft into China from this country. I said that recently representatives of the Bendix Products Corporation and the Kinner Airplane and Motor Corporation and also the President of the Aeronautical Chamber of Commerce of America had called at the Department to complain of difficulties encountered by American exporters of aircraft in obtaining authorization to import into Canton aircraft engines and accessories for non-military uses. I said that from their statements, it appeared that the Cantonese authorities applied regularly to the Central Government for *huchaos* to cover the importation of aircraft for military uses, but that they had on occasion been refused *huchaos* to cover importations of aircraft for non-military uses and had, therefore, decided not to make further applications for such *huchaos*. I pointed out that the apparent failure of the Chinese authorities to bring their procedure in regard to the granting of *huchaos* into conformity with the new American export regulations was having the unintentional result that American exporters were discriminated against in favor of exporters from other countries which did not apply export restrictions to aircraft intended for non-military uses. I told the Ambassador that Mr. Leighton W. Rogers, President of the Aeronautical Chamber of Commerce of America, had informed me that when he was in China,

---

[31] Maxwell M. Hamilton, Assistant Chief of the Division of Far Eastern Affairs.

he had had a conversation with Dr. Kung, in regard to this matter, and that Dr. Kung had told him frankly that the Central Government had used applications for *huchaos* made by the Cantonese authorities as trading points in its dealings with those authorities, but that Mr. Rogers had gained the impression that there would be no difficulty in regard to the granting of *huchaos* requested by the Cantonese authorities in the future.

The Ambassador said that he would communicate with his Government, but that the answer would probably be to the effect that the Chinese Government would put an end to the difficulties complained of if the American Government would cease to publish monthly statements of exports of arms to China.

I told the Ambassador what I had told him in my conversation with him on March 23,[32] viz: that we were considering the possibility of ceasing in the near future to issue monthly statements of exports of arms and of substituting quarterly statements for the monthly statements heretofore issued.

The Ambassador replied that if the statements were issued quarterly they would probably not result in the embarrassments of which his Government had complained.

The Ambassador repeated that he would communicate with his Government, requesting that some arrangement be made to obviate the difficulties which the Cantonese have had in obtaining *huchaos* for aircraft presumably for non-military uses.

The Ambassador suggested that a communication direct from Mr. Rogers to Dr. Kung might be more effective in the premises than anything which he might be able to do.

Mr. Hamilton stated that we were hardly in a position to suggest to an American citizen that he communicate directly with the Chinese Minister of Finance in regard to such a matter.

After the Ambassador's departure and after consultation with Mr. Hamilton, I called Mr. Rogers by telephone. I told him briefly of our conversation with the Ambassador and that the Ambassador had said that he would communicate with his Government. I suggested that if representatives of the American aircraft industry in China were to take up the question simultaneously with Dr. Kung, such action might serve to expedite a solution of the difficulties.

Mr. Rogers thanked me for the suggestion and said that he would immediately telegraph to the committee of representatives of the American aircraft industry which had its headquarters in Shanghai, and that undoubtedly the Committee would communicate immediately with the appropriate Chinese authorities.

J[OSEPH] C. G[REEN]

___

[32] Memorandum of conversation not printed.

893.113/1637

Memorandum by the Assistant Chief of the Division of Far Eastern Affairs (Hamilton)

[WASHINGTON,] May 5, 1936.

The Chinese Ambassador telephoned and referred to his call at the Department on April 22 at which time Mr. Green of CA[33] had brought to the Ambassador's attention the reports received by the Department indicating difficulties experienced by American exporters in connection with attempted sales to South China of aircraft and aircraft parts intended for non-military uses. The Ambassador stated that he had telegraphed his Government, as requested, and that he was now in receipt of a reply from the Chinese Foreign Office to the effect that the Foreign Office had referred the matter to the Aviation Commission; that the Aviation Commission had replied to the Foreign Office that all provinces in China were accorded equal treatment and that the American Government should be assured that there was no discrimination against American exporters or American products.

The Ambassador said that he would be at our disposal in the event that we wished him to take any further action in the matter. Mr. Hamilton replied that he thought the fact that the Ambassador had brought this matter to the attention of his Government might serve a useful purpose and Mr. Hamilton said that he would bring to the attention of Mr. Green the reply received by the Chinese Ambassador from his Government.

M[AXWELL] M. H[AMILTON]

846G.113/260

The Secretary of State to the British Ambassador (Lindsay)

WASHINGTON, June 24, 1936.

EXCELLENCY: I refer to Mr. Osborne's [34] note of September 4, 1935,[35] and previous correspondence, in regard to the regulations governing the exportation of arms, ammunition and implements of war destined to China, and have the honor to inform you that I am in receipt of information which would appear to indicate that the pertinent regulations of several governments cannot be considered wholly satisfactory if judged by the criteria set forth in our former correspondence on this subject.

---

[33] Office of Arms and Munitions Control.
[34] F. D. G. Osborne, then Counselor of the British Embassy.
[35] Not printed; it informed the Secretary of State that the information regarding the reported Czechoslovak shipment had been communicated to the British Government; cf. *Foreign Relations*, 1935, vol. III, p. 735.

It would appear that German manufacturers have been exporting large quantities of arms and implements of war—particularly military planes—to Belgium whence they have been shipped on through bills of lading to Canton via Hong Kong, and that they have entered China without a *huchao* from the Central Government.

It would appear further that French manufacturers have shipped to Canton or are proposing to ship to that city arms, ammunition and implements of war—including tanks and field guns—without securing a *huchao* from the Central Government.

Furthermore it would appear that the Cantonese authorities entered into contracts with the German and French manufacturers referred to above rather than with British or American manufacturers, for the specific reason that the former would be able to make delivery of the articles contracted for without obliging the Cantonese authorities to obtain *huchaos* from the Central Government.

If the information which I have received is accurate—and I have reason to believe it to be so—it would appear that British and American exporters and exporters of other nationalities whose governments comply with the regulations of the Chinese Government, in respect to the importation of arms into China, are placed at a disadvantage by the action of the Belgian, French and German Governments in permitting these shipments. Unless the Czechoslovak Government has modified its regulations since I addressed to you on August 31, 1935 a note,[36] in regard to a shipment of machine guns and ammunition to China from Czechoslovakia, it would appear that the Czechoslovak Government should be added to the list of those governments whose regulations in respect to the exportation of arms to China are not wholly satisfactory.

In my note of April 15, 1935,[37] I informed you that, in compliance with your request, I had instructed the representatives of this Government in Brussels and Bern to cooperate with their British colleagues, with a view to obtaining practical uniformity of procedure by all the governments concerned in the matter of the exportation of arms to China. Should your Government see its way clear to bring this matter to the attention of the Czechoslovak, French and German Governments and once more to the attention of the Belgian Government, I should be pleased to instruct the representatives of this Government in Prague, Berlin, Paris and Brussels to cooperate with their British colleagues with a view to achieving that degree of uniformity in the regulations of the several governments which is necessary to accomplish the purposes on which your Government and this Govern-

---

[36] *Foreign Relations*, 1935, vol. III, p. 735.
[37] *Ibid.*, p. 721.

ment are in substantial agreement as indicated by our previous correspondence on this subject.

Accept [etc.]   For the Secretary of State:
                                                        R. WALTON MOORE

711.00111 Armament Control/976

Memorandum by the Assistant Chief of the Office of Arms and Munitions Control (Yost)

[WASHINGTON,] July 8, 1936.

Mr. Lao, First Secretary of the Chinese Embassy, called this morning to make inquiry in regard to certain matters of procedure concerning the issuance of export licenses and to repeat once more his Government's concern over our publication of statistics of arms exported from this country. I showed Mr. Lao the draft of the press release covering export statistics for the month of June, in which month China stood second on the list. I informed Mr. Lao that the Department had been contemplating for some time the possibility of publishing these statistics every three months instead of every month and that I felt that it was very likely that this would be the last monthly press release which would be issued. Mr. Lao expressed the belief that this change would be highly agreeable to his Government, but nevertheless suggested that a complete cessation of publication might be even more agreeable.

C[HARLES] W. Y[OST]

711.00111 Armament Control/978

The Secretary of State to the Ambassador in China (Johnson)

No. 224   WASHINGTON, July 23, 1936.

SIR: I enclose a copy of a note of July 16, 1936, from the Chinese Ambassador in Washington,[38] in regard to the regulations governing the exportation of arms, ammunition, and implements of war to the International Settlement in Shanghai. There are also enclosed two copies of the pamphlet, *Laws and Regulations Administered by the Secretary of State Governing the International Traffic in Arms, Ammunition, and Implements of War and Other Munitions of War,* to Section VII of which the Ambassador refers.

You will observe that the Ambassador objects to an alleged discrimination in favor of the International Settlement embodied in the regulation which he quotes. It is possible that the Ambassador mistakenly believes that the regulation applies to arms shipped to the

---

[38] Not printed.

International Settlement for commercial sales. This is not the case. The permission of the Chinese Government is required before licenses are issued for the export to the International Settlement of arms intended for commercial sale. The regulation quoted applies only to shipments to the Municipal authorities in the International Settlement for the use of their own police forces. As these authorities are not under the direction or control of the Chinese Government, it was felt that they should not be obliged to request permission from that Government for the exportation of arms from the United States.

The regulation is one which has been followed for a number of years by the Department in its administration of the President's Proclamation of March 4, 1922,[39] without any objection having been raised. In point of fact, exports of arms from the United States to the Shanghai Municipal authorities rarely occur. There has been but one export license issued for such a shipment since the publication of the first edition of the above-mentioned pamphlet on October 10, 1935.

You are requested to bring the enclosed note from the Chinese Ambassador, together with the considerations presented in this instruction, to the attention of the Consul General in Shanghai, and to report to the Department such comment as you or he may wish to make in the premises. It would be of especial interest to discover what procedure was followed by the British and French Governments in the issuance of licenses for the export of arms to the Municipal authorities of the International Settlement, and what procedure was followed by the French in connection with the importation of arms into the French concession for the use of the local police.

Very truly yours,   For the Secretary of State:
WILBUR J. CARR

711.00111 Armament Control/1010

Memorandum by the Chief of the Division of Arms and Munitions Control (Green)

[WASHINGTON,] August 18, 1936.

After consultation with Mr. Hornbeck,[40] I called the Chinese Ambassador by telephone at his summer residence at Blue Ridge Summit, Pennsylvania, last evening. I told him that after careful consideration, it had been decided that we could not properly at this time cease publishing the monthly summaries of export licenses issued for arms, ammunition and implements of war. I said that for various reasons we had not found it possible to comply with the wishes of his Government in this matter. Among those reasons I mentioned the possi-

---

[39] *Foreign Relations*, 1922, vol I, p. 726.
[40] Stanley K. Hornbeck, Chief of the Division of Far Eastern Affairs.

bility that should we cease publishing the monthly statistics at this particular time, our action might possibly be construed as motivated by a desire to prevent shipments to Spain from becoming known. I told the Ambassador that export licenses had been issued in July covering proposed shipments to China to the value of only $660,924.40, whereas export licenses had been issued to cover proposed shipments to Netherlands Indies to the value of $1,288,027.51.

The Ambassador asked when the statistics for July would be published. I told him that they would probably be published today. He expressed his regret that the Department considered it necessary to continue the publication of monthly statistics, but he added that he recognized that, in view of the present situation in Spain, it might be unwise to discontinue publication at this time. He thanked me for communicating with him in advance of publication and for giving him the information in regard to the value of proposed shipments to China, saying that, in view of the fact that the proposed shipments to China were greatly exceeded by the proposed shipments to Netherlands Indies, he did not believe that the publication of the July statistics would result in any unfavorable publicity.

I told the Ambassador that the question of substituting at a later date quarterly publication for monthly publication was still under consideration.[41]

J[OSEPH] C. G[REEN]

846G.113/272a

The Secretary of State to the British Chargé (Mallet)

WASHINGTON, September 14, 1936.

SIR: I refer to the Ambassador's note of July 1, 1936,[42] and previous correspondence, in regard to the regulations governing the exportation of arms, ammunition and implements of war destined to China, and have to inform you that I am in receipt of information which would appear to indicate that the pertinent regulations of the French Government are still unsatisfactory if judged by the criteria set forth in our former correspondence on this subject.

The information which I have received—and I have reason to believe it accurate—is to the effect that the Yunnan Provincial Government placed an order on June 12 with the Groupe de Chine for the following:

---

[41] On October 23 the Chinese Ambassador, under instruction, again requested cessation of publication of license statistics; but the Department found it necessary to adhere to the issue of monthly summaries (711.00111 Regis. Lic./268).

[42] Not printed; it acknowledged receipt of the Secretary of State's note of June 24 (846G.113/271).

```
      12 mountain guns, 75 millimetre calibre
  12,000 shells for these guns
      40 trench mortars, 81 millimetre calibre
  10,000 shells for these mortars
       4 trench mortars, 120 millimetre calibre
     400 shells for these mortars
     100 machine guns (Hotchkiss)
       4 light tanks (Renault), two of which are equipped with
            one light machine gun each, and two of which are
            equipped with one gun each of 37 millimetre calibre
       6 motorcycles with side-car
       6 motorcycles with side-car, equipped with one light ma-
            chine gun each
         Optical instruments for the direction of the artillery fire
  10,000 rifles (Belgian)
10,000,000 cartridges for these rifles (Belgian)
```

It appears that no *huchao* covering this proposed shipment was obtained from the Central Government; that the Yunnan Provincial Government has not requested a *huchao* for it; and that the Groupe de Chine has not insisted that it do so.

The report of this proposed shipment reinforces the misgivings which I expressed in my note on this subject addressed to the Ambassador on June 24. I should appreciate it, therefore, if you would inform me as to whether your Government desires to take the action which I proposed in that note, or proposes to take any other action to accomplish the purposes on which your Government and this Government are in substantial agreement as indicated by our previous correspondence on this subject.[43]

Accept [etc.]
                              For the Secretary of State:
                                   R. WALTON MOORE

PROBLEM OF CONTROLLING THE TRAFFIC IN OPIUM AND NARCOTIC DRUGS IN CHINA, INCLUDING MANCHURIA AND JEHOL [44]

893.114 Narcotics/1460

The Ambassador in China (Johnson) to the Secretary of State

No. 172   PEIPING, January 14, 1936.
                                          [Received February 10.]

SIR: I have the honor to refer to the Embassy's despatch No. 149 of December 27, 1935,[45] regarding the regulations governing the im-

---

[43] The British Chargé d'Affaires in his note No. 298, September 16, informed the Secretary of State that the above information had been communicated to his Government (846.G113/273). There was no further reply from the British Government on this point; however, negotiations on the general subject of shipment of arms to China continues in 1937.

[44] Continued from *Foreign Relations*, 1935, vol. III, pp. 739–753.

[45] Not printed.

port into China of narcotics, and to enclose for the information of the Department copies [47] of 1) the Embassy's note of December 2, 1935, to the Ministry of Foreign Affairs requesting to be informed regarding the nature of certain provisional regulations for the control of the purchase of narcotics as reported by the Consulate at Foochow; and 2) the Ministry's reply of December 30, 1935.

It will be observed that these regulations, which are transmitted in English translation as an enclosure with the note from the Ministry of Foreign Affairs, are largely concerned with purely administrative procedure. The Embassy in its instruction of December 11, 1935, to the Consulate at Foochow had already instructed that office that Americans could properly be advised to give general adherence to the administrative provisions in question, but that the American authorities, having maintained that it lies within the discretion of American medical institutions and practitioners in China to register or not as they may see fit, could not admit the right of Chinese administrative organs to restrict the supplies of such of those institutions and persons as may have refused to register, merely by reason of the fact of non-registration. A copy of that instruction is also enclosed.[47]

Pending the receipt of such observations as the Department may wish to make, no circular instruction is being sent out to the other consular officers in China.

Respectfully yours,   NELSON TRUSLER JOHNSON

893.114 Narcotics/1453 : Telegram

The Secretary of State to the Ambassador in China (Johnson)

WASHINGTON, January 29, 1936—noon.

19. Your despatch No. 149, December 27.[47] If you have not already done so

(1) Please submit your comment on this proposal which purports to preclude American citizens from dealing in and American physicians, dentists and hospitals from importing not only drugs covered by the Narcotics Limitation Convention of 1931 [48] but also strychnine.

(2) Report the attitude adopted in regard to the matter by other governments which enjoy extraterritoriality.

(3) Request the American Consul General at Shanghai to report fully to the Department the probable effect on American commercial and professional interests and the attitude of those interests toward the proposal.

<hr>

[47] Not printed.
[48] *Foreign Relations*, 1931, vol. I, p. 675.

(4) Endeavor to ascertain and report why it is proposed to limit strychnine in the manner outlined.

HULL

893.114 Narcotics/1473

The Consul General at Shanghai (Davis) to the Ambassador in China (Johnson) [49]

No. 115 SHANGHAI, February 1, 1936.

SIR: I have the honor to transmit for the confidential information of the Embassy a copy of a report prepared by the Municipal Advocate's office of the Shanghai Municipal Council concerning the opium and narcotics regulations promulgated by the Chinese authorities under date of October 28, 1935. For convenient reference a translation of the first set of regulations referred to is also enclosed.[50] This translation has been obtained from the Shanghai Municipal Police but a copy of the Chinese text could not be obtained in time to accompany this despatch. It will be noted that the Municipal Advocate calls attention to the serious and drastic punishments prescribed, expresses the view that the regulations in question are not applicable to the International Settlement under the provisions of the Rendition Agreement of February 17, 1930,[51] and Chinese law and recommends that the Council protest to the Consular Body against any steps that may be taken by the Chinese authorities to enforce the regulations in the Settlement. Particular attention is called to the statement that the regulations are an attempt "to create an opium monopoly under the supervision and control of the Military Affairs Commission rather than an endeavor to suppress opium and narcotics."

The Secretary General of the Shanghai Municipal Council is said to fear that the long prison sentences provided by the new regulations, if applied in the International Settlement, would place an unduly heavy burden on the taxpayers and result in congestion in the jails, and to be apprehensive lest the Chinese authorities attempt to license establishments in the foreign settlements. Although not disposed to raise any question regarding the legality of the regulations in so far as the Chinese are concerned, he does intend to ask that persons convicted under them serve their sentences in Chinese prisons and that no opium establishments be licensed in the Settlement.

Respectfully yours, MONNETT B. DAVIS

[Received February 24]

---

[49] Copy transmitted to the Department by the Consul General at Shanghai in his despatch No. 126, February 1; received February 24.
[50] Enclosures not printed.
[51] Foreign Relations, 1930, vol. II, p. 333.

893.114 Narcotics/1461 : Telegram

The Counselor of Embassy in China (Lockhart) to the Secretary of State

PEIPING, February 18, 1936—2 p. m.
[Received February 18—11 a. m.]

69. 1. The Peiping–Tientsin Opium Suppression Inspectorate was inaugurated January 14, similar organs in the area allegedly being abolished at the same time. Sale of opium in Hopei has heretofore been illegal. The new inspectorate, however, issued rules on February 10 for the licensing of shops for dealing in opium, purchases and sales to be made only through licensed shops. Licenses for wholesalers are to cost $5000 local currency per annum and a wholesaler must have not less than $50,000 capital. There are two classes of retail shops, annual licenses ranging from $400 to $2400 and required capital ranging from $800 to $6000.

2. This development, for which the Hopei–Chahar Political Council is responsible, appears to have no object other than that of increasing revenue, in which it [concurs in] the example set by the National Government. There is no evidence of Japanese direction or [association]. Despatch [52] with regulation[s] follows. By mail to Tokyo.

LOCKHART

893.114 Narcotics/1471 : Telegram

The Secretary of State to the Consul General at Shanghai (Gauss)

WASHINGTON, February 20, 1936—5 p. m.

40. Telegraph whether Chinese Courts in the International Settlement and in the French Concession now apply in opium and narcotic drug cases the laws of 1934 and 1935 or the old opium suppression law.

HULL

893.114 Narcotics/1474 : Telegram

The Consul General at Shanghai (Gauss) to the Secretary of State

SHANGHAI, February 25, 1936—noon.
[Received February 25—10 : 40 a. m.]

115. Department's 40, February 20, 5 p. m. Shanghai Municipal Advocate advises Chinese courts in International Settlement and

---

[52] Dated March 21, not printed.

French concession are applying new laws in opium and narcotic drug cases over objection of the Shanghai Municipal Council and the French authorities. The former regard the new laws as too drastic, fear possible congestion in jails and think attempt may be made to establish licensing system in the Settlement. It is understood that the Shanghai Municipal Council will ask that persons convicted under new laws be incarcerated in Chinese prisons and that no opium establishments be licensed in the International Settlement. See despatch 126, February 1, 1936.[53] There has been an attempt in certain quarters to place the Municipal Council in a bad light for objecting to the new laws on these grounds. See despatch No. 162, February 7, 1936.[54]

GAUSS

893.114 Narcotics/1509

The Ambassador in China (Johnson) to the Secretary of State

No. 272   PEIPING, February 28, 1936.
[Received March 23.]

SIR: I have the honor to acknowledge the receipt of the Department's telegram No. 19 of January 29, 12 noon, with regard to Customs Notification No. 1480 of December 9, 1935,[55] limiting to the Central Health Laboratory the importation into China of narcotics, similar poisonous substances, and strychnine.

In compliance with the Embassy's telegraphic instruction of February 5, 5 p. m., a copy of which is enclosed,[54] the Counselor at Nanking reported in a despatch of February 7, 1936, addressed to the Embassy, a copy of which is enclosed,[54] that Mr. Peck [56] called on Dr. J. Heng Liu, Director of the National Health Administration and, in reply to his inquiries, was told that the importation of narcotics, similar poisonous substances, and strychnine is now a Government monopoly, that any persons or organizations in China requiring these substances will in the future be obliged to purchase them from the National Health Administration, "purchase permits" being issued to permit the transportation in China of the articles purchased, that strychnine was added to the list of narcotic drugs because it is used in the manufacture of heroin pills, that the statement in the Customs Notification No. 1480 to the effect that importations of these poisonous substances must be covered by certificates issued by the Ministry of the Interior

[53] Not printed; for enclosure transmitted with this despatch, see p. 567.
[54] Not printed.
[55] Copy sent as enclosure to despatch No. 149, December 27, 1935, from the Ambassador in China; neither printed.
[56] Willys R. Peck, Counselor of Embassy in China.

probably referred to purchases by departments of the National Government other than the National Health Administration, and that a great effort was being made to restrict the importation of various substances used in the manufacture of heroin pills and other harmful narcotics.

The Embassy also, in compliance with the Department's instruction, directed the Consulate General at Shanghai to report fully to the Department the probable effect on American commercial and professional interests and the attitude of those interests, in reply to which the Consulate General stated in despatch No. 155 of February 11, 1936 (copies of which were forwarded direct to the Department),[57] that a full report on this subject was in the course of preparation for transmission to the Department.

An officer of the Embassy made inquiries of the British, French, and Japanese Embassies to ascertain their attitudes toward this apparent monopoly of the importation of the substances in question. Neither the French nor Japanese Embassies appeared to have given the question any consideration, seeming not to have knowledge of Customs Notification 1480. An officer of the British Embassy stated that a report had been made to its Government, that there had as yet been no reaction, and that it was probable that no action would be taken as long as imports of the substances in question were not being interfered with, as was the case, and that consideration had not yet been given to what might be done if such imports were interfered with.

Following the receipt of a copy of the report of the Shanghai Consulate General with regard to the probable effect on American commercial and professional interests and the attitude of those interests, the Embassy will submit further comment.

Respectfully yours,   For the Ambassador:
F. P. LOCKHART
Counselor of Embassy

893.114 Narcotics/1526

The Ambassador in China (Johnson) to the Secretary of State

No. 299   PEIPING, March 11, 1936.
[Received April 6.]

SIR: I have the honor to refer to the Embassy's despatch No. 272 of February 28, 1936, regarding the restrictions imposed upon the import into China of strychnine and other narcotics by virtue of Cus-

---

[57] Not printed.

toms Notification No. 1480, and to observe that, according to the information supplied by the Consulate General at Shanghai in its despatch No. 22 of February 21 to the Department,[58] American interests in China are evidently very little concerned by the application of the new regulations, excepting as regards the monopolistic features of the regulations which might have undesirable effects on prices and quality of the materials purchased. The despatch continues with the observation that "there is a general feeling amongst the American interests concerned that the Chinese should not be hindered in their endeavor to effect control of the narcotics trade, and the tendency of the American interests is to cooperate with the Chinese Government in carrying out the regulations provided they are enforced in an impartial manner and onerous restrictions are not imposed on American persons or firms having a legitimate use for narcotics." This attitude, the Embassy believes, is in general an accurate counterpart of the Department's policy regarding the question of control of trade in narcotic drugs in China.

The important point in this connection would seem to be the question of whether American practitioners of medicine and surgery are to be required to register with the Chinese authorities in order to obtain needed supplies of strychnine and other narcotic drugs. The Department has previously indicated, in its instruction No. 129 of June 5, 1930,[58a] that it considers American practitioners in China to be subject to the jurisdiction of American laws and courts and therefore not required to conform to Chinese regulations which would subject them to control by Chinese authorities. The Department further stated in its telegram No. 198 of June 16, 1931, 4 p. m.,[59] however, that, in the absence of American laws and regulations specifically applicable to American practitioners in China, it considered it advisable to cooperate as fully as possible with the Chinese authorities in efforts directed toward the establishment of reasonable regulations on the subject. The sense of that instruction was communicated by the Legation to the Minister for Foreign Affairs by a formal note dated June 27, 1931,[58] with the express limitation that the proffered cooperation was "subject to the understanding that jurisdiction over American citizens in China must be retained by the appropriate American officials."

The Department observed in its aforementioned instruction of June 5, 1930, that the problem was then primarily one of evolving a suita-

[58] Not printed.
[58a] *Foreign Relations*, 1930, vol. II, p. 541.
[59] *Ibid.*, 1931, vol. III, p. 1011.

ble policy to be followed in the existing circumstances. The question seems to be essentially the same at the present time. In this connection, it is to be noted that, although certain undesirable factors certainly still persist, nevertheless the situation as regards the administration of health services and the practice of medicine has undergone a marked improvement since 1930 (due in no small part, it should be said, to the influence of League experts and other foreign advisers). Questions of the permanence of the existing regime in Nanking quite apart, the inevitable tendency in China, as a whole, is toward the exercise of ever more control by the Chinese authorities over Chinese administrative processes. It would appear to be the better wisdom to shape American policy to fit that tendency, and in this particular matter the Embassy would therefore recommend that American citizens in China should be directed to conform to the regulations laid down in Customs Notification No. 1480. This would require their registration with the Chinese authorities, it will be observed, but this fact would not appear to involve directly the principle of extraterritorial jurisdiction by American officials over citizens of the United States.

Respectfully yours,   NELSON TRUSLER JOHNSON

893.114 Narcotics/1524 : Telegram

The Ambassador in China (Johnson) to the Secretary of State

PEIPING, April 2, 1936—8 p. m.
[Received April 2—7:20 p. m.]

166. Embassy's 69, Feb. 18, 2 p. m. It is reported in the Chinese press that 2 opium wholesalers in Peiping commenced business on March 25, and that 12 opium retail shops have been "ordered" to begin trade as of April 1. It is also reported that a certain opium wholesaler in Tientsin has recently put in an order for a large consignment.

It is understood that two factors have operated to delay the institution of the proposed monopoly control in North China: (1) The power exercised by existing illegitimate dealers who hold large opium stocks, and (2) the doubt in the minds of potential operators as to whether the business will, under the present circumstances, so flourish as to warrant the payment of the comparatively large stamp fees. The program is, nevertheless, evidently going through.

By mail to Tokyo.

JOHNSON

3.114 Narcotics/1537 : Telegram

The Secretary of State to the Ambassador in China (Johnson)

WASHINGTON, April 10, 1936—7 p. m.

89. Your despatch No. 172, January 14. Your despatch No. 272, ebruary 28. Your despatch No. 299, March 11. In view of the pro- isions of Articles 5 and 6 of the Narcotics Limitation Convention of)31,[60] the Chinese Government is considered to be within its rights 1 limiting to a single organ of the national government the importa- ion and distribution of the drugs to which that Convention applies nd to be entitled to take adequate steps under that Convention, which pplies Article 7 of the Geneva Drug Convention of 1925,[61] to limit elivery to or possession by authorized persons of such drugs in order o limit the use of such drugs exclusively to medical and scientific urposes. The Department, therefore, is not disposed to object to the equirements of Customs Notification No. 1480 or of the regulations, ranslations of which accompanied your despatch No. 172 of January 4, 1936, insofar as they relate to the drugs to which the Narcotics imitation Convention of 1931 applies.

The Department accordingly approves the recommendation con- ained in your despatch No. 299 of March 11 and requests that Ameri- an citizens in China to whom the Customs Notification and regula- ions are intended to apply be informed of this Government's desire o cooperate with the Government of China for the more effective ccomplishment of the purpose of the Narcotics Limitation Conven- ion, namely, to prevent the use, for other than medical or scientific urposes, of the drugs to which the Convention has application; that n order to make this cooperation effective the American citizens con- erned should be advised to conform to Customs Notification No. 1480 nd the provisional regulations, translations of which accompanied our despatch of January 14, subject to the understanding that ex- lusive jurisdiction over American citizens in China must be retained y the appropriate American authorities and that necessary supplies f narcotic drugs shall not be withheld from any American national n China who is recognized by the Government of the United States s lawfully entitled and qualified to dispense, prescribe or use the lrugs solely for medical and scientific purposes.

The substance of this telegram may be communicated to the Foreign Office if occasion should arise for replying to the Foreign Office note of December 30, 1935.[62]

HULL

---

[60] *Foreign Relations*, 1931, vol. I, p. 675.
[61] League of Nations Treaty Series, vol. LI, p. 337.
[62] Not printed.

EFFORTS FOR THE CONSIDERATION OF AMERICAN CLAIMS OUTSTANDING AGAINST CHINA [63]

893.48/1037

Memorandum by the Chief of the Division of Far Eastern Affair (Hornbeck) of a Conversation With the Chinese Ambassador (Sze

[WASHINGTON,] January 21, 1936

The Chinese Ambassador called, and the conversation began with discussion of miscellaneous phases of the current situation in China There was then brought up the subject of the conversation held on January 3 [64] and the views exchanged at that time. The Ambassador said that since then he had exchanged a number of communications with the Chinese Minister of Finance, H. H. Kung, urging upon Kung adoption of the suggestions which the Ambassador had made with regard to procedure in relation to the Chicago Bank Loan.[65] He said that as recently as yesterday he had received a telegram from Kung in which Kung advanced certain views and asked for the Ambassador's opinion, and that he (the Ambassador) had telegraphed back again urging adoption of his (the Ambassador's) suggestions. He said that he was convinced that the thing to do was to begin the making of payments and that the Chicago Bank Loan was the obligation with regard to which the beginning should be made. He said that he could not understand the failure of his Government not to see the matter in the light in which he saw it. He said that he would keep on the line which he was pursuing.

I asked the Ambassador whether he had any information with regard to a rumor to the effect that H. H. Kung is likely to retire from the Ministry of Finance and that there are divergencies of view between Kung and T. V. Soong.[66] The Ambassador said that he had not had quite that information, but that he had had in a personal letter information to the effect that Kung was becoming very tired of his "job" and would like to go abroad as an Ambassador.

The Ambassador asked me whether I had heard anything about the Hukuang Loan.[67] I told him that I had, and I gave him the substance of the information which we have in Peiping's mail despatch No. 117, December 4, 1935,[68] on the Hukuang Loan. I made the comment that

---

[63] Continued from *Foreign Relations*, 1935, vol. III, pp. 753–767.

[64] See Memorandum by Mr. Raymond C. Mackay of the Division of Far Eastern Affairs, p. 459.

[65] See *Foreign Relations*, 1919, vol. I, pp. 505 ff.

[66] Former Chinese Minister of Finance, Executive Member, National Economic Council of China.

[67] Final agreement for a railway loan from a four-power banking group (American, British, French, German), signed at Peking, May 20, 1911; John V. A. MacMurray (ed.), *Treaties and Agreements With and Concerning China, 1894–1919* (New York, 1921), vol. I, p. 866.

[68] Not printed; for enclosure, see memorandum from the Chinese Ministry for Foreign Affairs to the American Embassy, *Foreign Relations*, 1935, vol. III, p. 765.

ᴇ Chinese Government's reply to the joint memorandum of the ᵣᵢtish, the French and the American Ambassadors of August last ᵣas unsatisfactory and was regarded as another evidence of the dis-ᵢclination of the Chinese Government to deal effectively with such ᵢatters.[69] The Ambassador shook his head with a gesture of despair. I deliberately avoided inquiring expressly whether the Ambassador ᵤd been taking any further steps toward obtaining readjustment of ᵗhe R. F. C.[70] and the F. C. A.[71] obligations, as regards schedule of ᵤayments; but I gained the impression both from what the Ambassa-ᵤor said and from what he omitted saying that he has not recently ᵤeen active in that connection. I took occasion to throw out the sug-ᵣestion that if in the future officials of other departments choose to ᵤake statements to the Ambassador affirming or implying that the ᴧmerican Government will pursue a particular course of action with ᵣegard to those obligations or other obligations, it might be well for ᵤhe Ambassador to let this Department know of the such assurances ᵣr intimations upon which, when conferring with this Department, ᵤe relies. The Ambassador indicated that he welcomed the suggestion ᵤnd regarded it as one which might prove helpful.

The Ambassador then reverted to the efforts which he is making ᵤn connection with the Chicago Bank Loan. He said that he was ᵤressing the matter so hard that perhaps some of his own people ᵤight suspect that he himself had a personal interest, which, he said ᵤmphatically, he had not. He said that he nevertheless would keep ᵣight on urging the soundness of his view and his plan. I expressed ᵣratification that he was thus being active in the matter.

93.51/6087

The Ambassador in China (Johnson) to the Secretary of State

ᴺo. 73

NANKING, January 21, 1936.
[Received February 25.]

SIR: I have the honor to refer to a despatch addressed to the De-ᵤartment by the American Consul General at Shanghai, No. 107 ᵤf January 20, 1936,[72] on the subject "Slump in Chinese Government Bonds Causes Alarm". On January 15, in the course of a conversa-ᵢon I held with Dr. H. H. Kung, Minister of Finance, in reference ᵤo another subject, he told me that he had been trying to do some-thing in the direction of liquidating British and American loans now ᵢn default. He said that he had proposed to the British and Ger-

[69] For joint memorandum see *Foreign Relations*, 1935, vol. III, p. 763; for Chinese reply see *ibid.*, p. 765.
[70] Reconstruction Finance Corporation.
[71] Farm Credit Administration.
[72] Not printed.

mans the replacement of Tientsin–Pukow Railway bonds in defau
with new bonds redeemable in thirty years and at a lower rate c
interest than the present bonds. The plan would provide for th
payment of interest only for the first five years and thereafter fo
payment of interest and gradually increasing payments on capital.

Dr. Kung said to me that the object of his plan was to protect th
interests of holders of bonds now in default and that he had prc
posed a similar plan for adoption in the case of the Hukuang Railwa
bonds, one semi-annual payment of interest on which bonds has bee
in default for a long time. This proposal, he said, had been hande
to Mr. Charles R. Bennett of the National City Bank in Peiping, wh
had just landed in Shanghai after a journey to the United States an
intended to remain in Shanghai for a few days. The Minister o
Finance said, also, that he had directed the Chinese Ambassador a
Washington to discuss with the Chief of the Division of Far Easter
Affairs of the State Department and with Mr. John Jay Abbott o
the Continental-Illinois National Bank and Trust Company, a simila
plan to take care of the "Chicago Bank Loan" of 1916.

Dr. Kung made it appear that these schemes were praiseworth
efforts to make good existing deficiencies in the handling of its foreig
obligations by the Chinese Government, but apparently these effort
are at the bottom of the rumors of tampering with Chinese bonds anc
have occasioned the public uneasiness which is described in the des
patch of January 20, 1936, from the American Consul General a
Shanghai.

My conversation with Dr. Kung has been reported elsewhere, but i
seems desirable to invite special attention to his remarks concerning
the bond situation, as is done in the present despatch.

Respectfully yours,

For the Ambassador
WILLYS R. PECK
Counselor of Embassy

893.48/1040

Memorandum by the Chief of the Division of Far Eastern
Affairs (Hornbeck)

[WASHINGTON,] January 30, 1936.

The Chinese Ambassador called and stated that he regretted having
to say that the Chinese Minister of Finance, H. H. Kung, after much
effort on the Ambassador's part, had decided that the Chinese Government could not adopt the plan which the Ambassador had been
urging for the handling of the payment of the Chicago Bank Loan.

I said that I received this news with great regret.

The Ambassador said that Kung takes the position that he must
handle this obligation in the same manner in which he is dealing with

the others". I made the observation that, with regard to most of the others", this meant "doing nothing about them", whereas, with egard to some of "the others" the Chinese Ministry of Finance has een making special arrangements of particular character. I said hat Kung's reported position amounted to a refusal to be responsive o the request which the Department had communicated in the form f the suggestion which I had made to the Ambassador in conversations held in December, our request having been occasioned by and aving been made in response to the Chinese Government's request nade to this Government in relation to the FCA and the RFC obligations of the Chinese Government. I said that it amounted to a "no" y the Chinese Government. The Ambassador said that he felt that was putting it a little too strongly.

The Ambassador said that he had informed Mr. Abbott, of the Chicago Bank, of Kung's position and that Mr. Abbott would be assing through Washington tomorrow and would confer with the Ambassador about the situation. It was assumed that Mr. Abbott while here would call on me. I said that if the Ambassador would explain to Mr. Abbott what the method was by which Kung was contemplating dealing with "all" of the obligations in some one manner, Mr. Abbott might be able to explain the matter to me.

I said that, so long as it remained Kung's position that he would not be responsive to the suggestions which we had made, I hoped 'that the Chinese Ambassador would make no further move toward requesting concessions in connection with the FCA and the RFC payments". The Ambassador said that this would put him in a difficult position. I said that I realized that he himself had been doing everything possible to move his Government in the right direction and that the last thing that I would wish to do would be to put him in an embarrassing position, but that nevertheless the hope which I had expressed was a hope which I entertained.

It was agreed that the Ambassador would try to make clear to Mr. Abbott points which thus far I had been unable to understand.

S[TANLEY] K. H[ORNBECK]

893.51 Con. Ob. Ault and Wiborg/13

The Ambassador in China (Johnson) to the Secretary of State

No. 110   NANKING, March 5, 1936.
[Received April 6.]

SIR: In reference to the debt owed by the Bureau of Engraving and Printing at Peiping to the Ault and Wiborg Company, I have the honor to state that the Embassy, under date of January 6, 1936. received a letter from the Ault and Wiborg Company (Far East)

enclosing a copy of its letter of January 5, 1936 to the Bureau of E
graving and Printing, which contained a statement of the outstand
ing indebtedness. The Company desired that the Embassy continu
its efforts to bring about a settlement of this account. There is en
closed herewith a copy of the Company's letter of January 6, 1936.

I took this matter up on March 2, 1936 with Mr. Chang Ch'un
Minister for Foreign Affairs, having given him advance notice o
my intention to do so.

A memorandum of my conversation with the Minister for Foreig
Affairs is enclosed.[74]   There is enclosed, also, a copy of a letter on thi
subject, written by the Counselor of Embassy at Nanking, to Di
Hsu Mo, Vice Minister for Foreign Affairs, on January 27, 1936.[74]

It will be noted from the memorandum of conversation that th
Minister for Foreign Affairs had written to the Ministry of Finance
urging that the debt be settled, but had not received a reply.   Th
Minister for Foreign Affairs stated, erroneously, that the Bureau o
Engraving and Printing had been closed. He also stated that th
Bureau had a great number of debts, and that he did not know wha
plans had been undertaken in regard to these debts.

In this connection, I have the honor to refer to the Embassy's des
patch No. 84, of November 13, 1935, from Peiping,[74] on the subjec
"Nishihara Loans",[75] in which I had the honor to report that th
Bureau of Engraving and Printing was reorganized and had recentl
resumed operations after a stoppage lasting through the summe
months, and that the Ministry of Finance had authorized th
Bureau to make an arrangement for the repayment of a loan o
Yen 2,000,000.00 negotiated with the Peking Government in 1918 by
Mr. Nishihara [76] on behalf of Japanese banks; the amount to be re
paid, including interest, was Yen $4,500,000.00 payable in three
hundred equal monthly instalments.

In his conversation with me the Minister for Foreign Affairs did
not mention these facts and, I assume, was ignorant of them.

The Embassy will continue to press this matter with the Ministry
of Foreign Affairs, in the hope of bringing about the payment of the
debt to the Ault and Wiborg Company.[77]

Respectfully yours,

                                NELSON TRUSLER JOHNSON

---

[73] Not printed. The indebtedness amounted to a total of U. S. $48,556.27.
[74] Not printed.
[75] See *Foreign Relations*, 1918, pp. 122–123, 130–133, 147–148, and 155–159.
[76] Kamezo Nishihara, Japanese banking group representative at Peking for 1918
loan negotiations with the Chinese Government.
[77] The Ambassador in China in his despatch No. 1421, October 5, 1937, reported
as follows: "A reply dated July 5 was received from the Director of the Bureau
of Printing and Engraving that as the amount owed to Messrs. Ault and Wiborg
and various other concerns by the Bureau was extremely large the Bureau at
the moment was unable to take any action with a view to liquidating the
indebtedness." (893.51 Con. Ob. Ault and Wiborg Co/15)

93.51/6099 : Telegram

The Secretary of State to the Ambassador in China (Johnson)

WASHINGTON, March 7, 1936—2 p. m.

52. Shanghai's 128, February 29, 5 p. m.,[78] transmits Commercial Attaché's report to Commerce "232, February 29. Supplement to Weekly Economic" which reads in part as follows:

"Finance Minister appointed by National Government mandate to head the commission for readjustment of domestic and foreign loans which now consists of nine members of Ministerial rank from Government yuans including also chairman of board of Bank of China."

Department desires to receive by naval radio such additional information as you may have in regard to the commission under reference and would appreciate being kept fully and currently advised of all developments of importance in regard thereto.

HULL

93.11/1983

The Ambassador in China (Johnson) to the Secretary of State

No. 113

NANKING, March 7, 1936.
[Received April 6.]

SIR: I have the honor to refer to the Department's telegraphic instruction No. 226, of July 29, 6 p. m. (1935),[79] directing that the Embassy continue to urge strongly the setting-up of a Sino-American Claims Commission.

In this relation there is enclosed a memorandum of a conversation on this subject held by the American Ambassador with the Minister for Foreign Affairs on March 2, 1936.[80] The feature in this memorandum to which the attention of the Department is particularly invited is the statement of the Minister for Foreign Affairs that the Committee for the Readjustment of Domestic and Foreign Loans had been re-organized and that the Committee would go into the whole question of internal and foreign debts, although he was non-committal on the point whether it could deal with "diplomatic claims" arising from internal disturbances. It was the evident desire of the Minister for Foreign Affairs that the American Embassy should take some solace from the fact of the reorganization of the Committee for the Readjustment of Domestic and Foreign Loans and should, on this account, refrain from pressing for the formation of a Sino-American

---

[78] Not found in Department files.
[79] *Foreign Relations*, 1935, vol. III, p. 762.
[80] Not printed.

Claims Commission. Other arguments, also, were advanced again the proposal.

It will be noted that, in order to soften the iterated refusal of tl Chinese Government to set up a Claims Commission, or its desire th this step be at least postponed until all other methods had failed, tl Minister for Foreign Affairs insisted that the Ministry was active investigating those American claims which had been reported to i that efforts were being made to make settlements of claims concer ing which no doubt existed; and that the Ministry would do what could to urge settlement of the various matters as soon as settleme should become possible.

On March 5 at a luncheon given for the Ambassador by the A ministrative Vice Minister for Foreign Affairs, the Counselor of En bassy at Nanking [81] discussed this general subject with Mr. T. I Tseng, Administrative Vice Minister of Railways, who has long bee Secretary General of the Committee for the Readjustment of Dome tic and Foreign Loans. Mr. Tseng has always been frank and inforn ative on the subject of China's obligations when questioned by office of the Embassy.

The gist of replies made by Mr. Tseng to questions put by Mr. Pec follows:

Mr. Tseng said that he would continue as Secretary General of tl reorganized Committee for the Readjustment of Domestic and Fo eign Loans. He said frankly that he did not think that the Commi tee as reorganized would accomplish anything more in the way c concrete progress than had the former Committee. His reasons wer (1) the immensity of the problem and (2) the existence of th "Nishihara" loans.

As for the first reason, the Committee would still fear that if th Chinese Government were to attempt to settle some of the smalle debts, the Government would have the question of similar treatmer of larger debts, beyond its capacity to deal with at the present tim raised in an acute form. His own idea was that some sort of begir ning should be made, both by paying off some small, undisputed for eign obligations, and also by deciding on a few principles of repay ment and the adjudication of other debts in accordance therewith.

In reference to the second reason, he said that the "Nishihara" loan offer some points of difference which make the formulation of uniforn rules for repayment difficult. There is the question whether some o these loans are, in fact, obligations binding on the Chinese Govern ment. Mr. Tseng said that, for his own part, he felt that it was n concern of the creditor whether the proceeds of loans ostensibl negotiated, say, for railways, were actually used for railways; tha

---

[81] Willis R. Peck.

was a domestic matter and should not affect the question of the obligation of the Government to repay the loans. Again, whereas bond issues are often issued at a considerable discount, the "Nishihara" loans were for the most part paid to the Chinese Government at a rate of 100%. Although the Chinese Government might conceivably decide to repay bond issues at a rate scaled down to what the Government received, it would be somewhat unfair to scale down the "Nishihara" loans, yet if they were not scaled down other creditors might demand payment of the face value of their loans.

Mr. Peck mentioned that he had been reliably informed that a Japanese diplomatic official had recently stated that Japanese firms had claims against Chinese railways, based on unpaid loans, aggregating $500,000,000 Chinese currency and he asked Mr. Tseng whether he thought such claims could conceivably amount to that sum.

Mr. Tseng said that it was possible that, from the Japanese viewpoint, Japanese claims against Chinese railways reached this high figure. He pointed out that a loan at eight per cent (8%) compounded for twenty years more than quadrupled in amount, and he thought it possible that Japanese loans ostensibly for railway purposes aggregated more than $100,000,000.

I have the honor to explain that the remark quoted above as having been made by a Japanese official was reported by Mr. C. Yates McDaniel, of the Associated Press. Mr. McDaniel when conversing with Mr. Y. Suma, Secretary of the Japanese Embassy, on or about February 29, had been told by the latter that the Japanese Government viewed with grave concern the reports of other than Japanese foreign railway projects in China, because Japanese firms held claims against Chinese railway revenues more than $500,000,000 in amount.

Mr. Peck called attention to the fact that the Ministry of Finance had recently authorized the Bureau of Engraving and Printing in Peiping to negotiate with Japanese creditors an arrangement to pay them Yen 4,500,000 in settlement of a loan of Yen 2,000,000, made in 1918 (See Embassy's despatch from Peiping No. 84, of November 13, 1935, entitled "Nishihara Loans" [82]). Mr. Tseng said he thought that probably the amount to be repaid was not more than twice the amount of the loan, since the Ministry of Finance had made it a rule not to recognize accretions to a loan amounting to more than 100% of the loan itself.

Respectfully yours,

For the Ambassador:
WILLYS R. PECK
Counselor of Embassy

---

[82] Not printed.

893.51/6100 : Telegram

The Ambassador in China (Johnson) to the Secretary of State

PEIPING, March 12, 1936—2 p. m.
[Received March 12—10 : 50 a. m.]

127. Department's 52, March 7, 2 p. m. Besides the appointment of Kung as chairman of the committee the Government's mandate of February 28 also designated the following persons as committee members: T. V. Soong, Foreign Minister Chang Chun, Minister of Communications Ku Meng Yu, Minister of Railways Chang Kia Ngau, Minister of Industries Wu Ting Chang, Minister of Education Wang Shih Chieh, Yeh Chu Tsang (Secretary General of the said committee of the Central Executive Committee) and Chiang Ting Fu (director of the Political Affairs Department of the Executive Yuan).

The Department's telegram has been repeated to Nanking and Shanghai with the request that the matter be given the close attention of those two offices.

JOHNSON

893.51/6101 : Telegram

The Counselor of Embassy in China (Peck) to the Secretary of State

NANKING, March 14, 1936—10 a. m.
[Received March 14—5 : 36 a. m.]

54. Department's 52, March 7, 2 p. m. to Peiping concerning committee for readjustment of foreign and domestic loans.

A member of the reorganized committee informed me yesterday that the committee would immediately set to work on plans to meet outstanding debts especially bond issues but would not attempt a comprehensive plan covering the entire indebtedness of China. He mentioned the Chicago Bank Loan, but did not specify what steps were being taken in that connection. He was not sure whether the committee would handle diplomatic claims and I took the opportunity to urge the desirability of a Claims Commission.

Repeated to Peiping.

PECK

893.51/6127

Memorandum by the Chief of the Division of Far Eastern Affairs (Hornbeck) of a Conversation With Mr. Thomas W. Lamont, of New York

[WASHINGTON,] April 1, 1936.

Mr. Lamont[83] called me on the telephone. He said that he and his associates were contemplating sending a telegram to the representative of the American Group in China, Mr. Charles R. Bennett, instructing Mr. Bennett to talk to the Chinese setting forth the American Group's view with regard to the proposed arrangement for the Hukuang bonds; and he felt that it would be desirable to tell Mr. Bennett that he might expect some action in support by the American Ambassador. He wanted to have our opinion before taking this step.

I said that I appreciated his having thus informed me of what he had in mind. I said that I had not yet had opportunity to report to the Secretary on our conversations of yesterday[84] but that I had been talking the matter over with one of my immediate associates and there had come up a query with regard to possible and probable lines of procedure: it had been my impression from what Mr. Lamont had said yesterday that the American and the British Groups are now actively conferring and that the American Group is in the act of expressing to the British Group its view regarding modifications that might advantageously be made in the proposed arrangement for the Hukuang bonds. Mr. Lamont said this was correct. I said that it then seemed to me that it would be desirable to arrive at the establishing of a common front, with the American and the British Groups in agreement upon an approach to be made to the Chinese Government. Mr. Lamont said that he felt that the best chance of producing such a common front would be for the American Group with the support of the American Government to inform the Chinese Government of the American Group's view that the present proposal is not entirely satisfactory. There followed some discussion of the relative merits of these possible lines of procedure. In the course of this, Mr. Lamont stated that the British Group in the Consortium is standing aside and that the matter has taken the form of an effort merely by the representatives of the bondholders of the various nationalities interested in the Hukuang loan. It happens that these representatives are also among the principal signatories of the Consortium Agreement,[85] but the business of the Hukuang bondholders

---

[83] Of J. P. Morgan & Co., representing the American Group of the China Consortium.

[84] Memorandum of conversations not printed.

[85] Signed at New York, October 15, 1920, by British, French, Japanese, and American banking groups, *Foreign Relations*, 1920, vol. I, p. 576; for minutes of conferences, October 11–15, see *ibid.*, pp. 581–589.

and the business of the Consortium are separate matters. Mr. Lamont felt very strongly that it would be to the advantage of the American interest involved for the representatives of the American bond-holders at this time to speak, with governmental support, to the Chinese on behalf of the American interest. I inquired how urgent the matter should be considered. Mr. Lamont replied that a matter of 2 days or so of delay would do no harm. I said that I would see that the question was given consideration. Mr. Lamont inquired whether it would be helpful if he were to have someone in his office prepare an outline of the facts which need most to be considered. I said that I thought it would be exceedingly helpful. Mr. Lamont said that he would send me informally a memorandum showing what he had in mind. I thanked him, and the conversation there ended.

S[TANLEY] K. H[ORNBECK]

893.51/6120a : Telegram

*The Secretary of State to the Ambassador in the United Kingdom
(Bingham)*

WASHINGTON, April 5, 1936—8 p. m.

115. Please confer informally with the Foreign Office on the following:

1. The American Government has on several occasions joined with the British and the French Governments, usually upon the initiative of the British Government, in joint representations through the missions of the three countries in China, to the Chinese Government, urging that the provisions of the Hukuang loan contract looking to substitution of customs revenue for abolished likin be carried out. These representations have been based on the obvious adequacy of the customs surplus to pay the full current loan service and clear up the arrears of overdue interest; they were not predicated upon reductions in the regular service called for by the loan contract.

The Department is advised that an adjustment has recently been proposed by the Chinese Government with regard to the service of the Tientsin–Pukow loan, and that such adjustment has been recommended to the British bondholders by the British Bondholders Committee formed at the instance of the Bank of England, but that, with regard to this adjustment, the British Group of the Consortium has taken no official position. The Department is further advised that, following the proposal with regard to the Tientsin–Pukow loan, representatives of the British interests, without previous agreement among the various national Groups as to procedure, undertook to negotiate with the Chinese Government a proposal with regard to the Hukuang loan, and that these negotiations resulted in the making by the Chinese Ministry of Finance of a proposal, later amended and somewhat improved, the terms of which in the amended form are substantially identical with the offer in regard to the Tientsin–Pukow bonds in the form recommended to the British bondholders by the above-mentioned British Committee.

While there are substantial foreign holdings of both groups of bonds, there was no American issue of the Tientsin–Pukow loan and, so far as the Department is aware, there are no American holdings of importance. American investors hold, however, a substantial amount of Hukuang bonds, and the issuers of the Hukuang loan, who are largely identical with the managing committee of the American Group of the Consortium, urge that on the basis of existing security the Hukuang bonds are entitled to receive more favorable treatment in a readjustment than the Tientsin–Pukow bonds. The American Group contends that the superior position of the Hukuang bonds has been consistently recognized through payment of one-half the interest annually, as contrasted with complete default on the Tientsin-Pukow bonds, and through the market price for Hukuang bonds, almost double that of the Tientsin–Pukow bonds. It contends, therefore, that these differentials in favor of Hukuangs should be given recognition, on a basis which it has outlined, through its representatives in London, to the British interests concerned.

While ordinarily the details of a financial settlement between American bondholders and the Chinese Government might not come within the Department's province, the Department feels that, in the light of the antecedents to this situation, neither the American Government nor the British Government can disregard the issues and implications involved in the possibility of there being concluded between the bondholders of the one nationality and the Chinese Government without due consideration of the interests and views of the bondholders of the other nationality an agreement satisfactory to one Group but not to the other, there having been hitherto common action and there being throughout involved common interests.

The American Group has presented to the British Group its views on these and other points and has invoked the cooperation of the British Group. The members of each of the Groups are of course entirely free to arrive at their own decisions. In the belief, however, that the interests of all concerned will be best served by the continued maintenance of the cooperative attitude and practices that have heretofore largely prevailed, the Department feels it highly desirable, and it believes that the British Foreign Office will share the view, that careful consideration be given by the British Group and Committee members to the views expressed by the American Group. The Department therefore ventures the hope that the British Foreign Office will see its way clear to suggest to the British interests involved the desirability that those interests give consideration as sympathetically as possible to the views of the American interests, in order that the spirit and practice of cooperative action in support of common rights and a common objective may not be impaired and may in fact be strengthened.

2. In case rejoinder be made by the Foreign Office that the American Government failed to act on the principle of cooperation in that it did not respond favorably to the British Government's suggestion that each of the interested governments send to China a financial attaché, you should say that the American Government gave the British Government's suggestion full consideration on its merits and in the light of then existing circumstances, and that all that we now ask is that the British Government give to the suggestion made above consideration on its merits and in the light of now existing circumstances and future possibilities.[86] The British Government's suggestion upon which this Government was not able to act favorably related to a new and affirmative step; the suggestion which the American Government now makes relates to continuation of an attitude and a practice long since agreed upon and effective in defense of common rights and interests.

3. You should say that your Government requests an indication at an early date of the British Government's views and intention with regard to the above suggestion.

4. The Department suggests that Atherton [87] handle this matter in person and report action when taken.

HULL

893.51/6124 : Telegram

The Ambassador in the United Kingdom (Bingham) to the Secretary of State

LONDON, April 7, 1936—6 p. m.
[Received April 7—2 : 15 p. m.]

186. Atherton discussed Department's 115, April 5, 8 p. m., this afternoon with Sir Victor Wellesley [88] and Orde.[89] The contents of section 1 were admitted to be substantially correct, and it was added

[86] For correspondence with reference to sending a financial attaché to China, see *Foreign Relations*, 1935, vol. III, pp. 591–646, *passim*.
[87] Ray Atherton, Counselor of Embassy in the United Kingdom.
[88] Sir Victor A. A. H. Wellesley, Deputy Under Secretary of State, British Foreign Office.
[89] Charles William Orde, Counselor and Head of the Far Eastern Department, British Foreign Office.

with reference to paragraph 2 of section 1 that Leith-Ross[90] had, after an unofficial survey on the spot, recommended to the bondholders the acceptance of the proposed adjustment for the Tientsin–Pukow loan. Foreign Office informally claimed that the security and provisions behind the Hukuang loan agreement were no better than those behind the Tientsin–Pukow agreement . . .

Part 2 did not arise.

As for part 3, both Wellesley and Orde were reluctant to hazard an opinion as to whether the Foreign Office would agree to undertake to make suggestions to the Bondholders Committee in their direct and purely unofficial negotiations with the Chinese Government over obligations which had been a long time in default. However, they would endeavor to give the Embassy a reply as soon as possible after the forthcoming holidays.

BINGHAM

893.51 Con. Ob. Continental/123

Memorandum by Mr. Raymond C. Mackay of the Division of Far Eastern Affairs of a Conversation With the Chinese Ambassador (Sze)

[WASHINGTON,] April 9, 1936.

The Ambassador said that he wished to acquaint the Department "very informally" with certain recent developments in connection with the so-called "Chicago Bank Loan"; that Mr. John Abbott of the Continental Illinois National Bank and Trust Company of Chicago had, in the course of a long distance telephone call, informed him (the Ambassador) of the receipt of an inquiry from a New York bank, presumably J. P. Morgan and Company, in regard to the nature of the call made on Mr. Abbott by Mr. K. P. Chen, Mr. P. W. Kuo and Mr. Y. C. Koo while the latter were in Chicago en route to Washington;[91] that Mr. Abbott had replied to the effect that Mr. Chen and party had called purely as a matter of courtesy and in order to convey to Mr. Abbott the cordial greetings of Finance Minister H. H. Kung.

The Ambassador said that he had used the opportunity thus presented to inform Mr. Abbott of the receipt, through Mr. Chen, of instructions from Minister Kung to assume responsibility for negotiations in regard to a possible settlement of the Chicago Bank Loan; that Minister Kung was prepared to offer to holders of Chicago Loan bonds terms similar to those offered to holders of Tientsin–Pukow

---

[90] Sir Frederick Leith-Ross, Chief Economic Adviser to the British Government and temporary financial adviser to the British Ambassador in China since 1935; see *Foreign Relations*, 1935, vol. III, p. 591.

[91] For correspondence concerning the Chinese Economic Mission to the United States, see pp. 465–498, *passim*.

Railway bonds; that a detailed statement of the proposed Tientsin–Pukow agreement had been forwarded by mail to Mr. Abbott and that the Department would be provided with a copy thereof (subsequently received and attached hereto) ; [92] that he (the Ambassador) had suggested to Mr. Abbott that the views of at least most of the Chicago Loan bondholders in regard to such a proposal might be obtained by issuance on the part of the bank of notification to those individuals whose names appear on the records of the bank; and that some sort of arrangement would have to be effected whereby authority to enter into final agreement would be delegated by the bondholders to Mr. Abbott or the Continental Illinois Bank or a bondholders' committee. The Ambassador said that Mr. Abbott, after indicating some of the difficulties involved, had stated that he would write a letter of explanation to all bondholders of record.

The Ambassador said that, although he was charged with responsibility for effecting negotiations in regard to not only the Chicago Bank Loan but also the wheat and cotton credits of 1931 and 1933, Mr. Chen and party were under instructions to assist in such negotiations and that he (the Ambassador) therefore wished to "push" matters while Mr. Chen and party are still in Washington. The Ambassador inquired whether he might with propriety, in view of his understanding that both of the credits under reference have been transferred to the Export-Import Bank, discuss these matters directly with the bank's president, Mr. W. L. Pierson.

Mr. Mackay, in reply, stated his opinion to the effect that matters relating to the outstanding obligations of the Chinese Government to American creditors should, with the possible exception of the F. C. A. credit of 1931 and the R. F. C. credit of 1933, be discussed with the Department but that subject to confirmation by Mr. Hornbeck (later obtained and conveyed to the Ambassador) there would seem to be no objection to a direct approach by the Ambassador to Mr. Pierson in regard to the particular credits named.[93]

893.51/6124 : Telegram

The Secretary of State to the Ambassador in the United Kingdom
(Bingham)

Washington, April 11, 1936—2 p. m.

123. Your 186, April 7, 6 p. m., final paragraph. In view of (a) the reported activities of Leith-Ross in connection with the proposed

[92] Not printed.
[93] The Chinese Ambassador in his covering letter of April 28 to the Chief of the Division of Far Eastern Affairs enclosed a copy of a proposal for the settlement of the Chicago Bank Loan, which he handed to Mr. Abbott on the same day (893.51 Con. Ob. Continental/131).

settlements of both Tientsin–Pukow and Hukuang loans, (b) the intimate association of Leith-Ross with the British Treasury and Foreign Office, and (c) the considerations outlined in Department's 115, April 5, 8 p. m., particularly ultimate and penultimate paragraphs of section 1 thereof, Department would be at a loss to understand a refusal, if made by the Foreign Office on the score that this is purely a private business matter, to offer to those British interests concerned with the Hukuang loan a suggestion that sympathetic consideration be given to the views of the American interests.

Department suggests that Atherton, unless you perceive objection thereto, convey discreetly and orally to the appropriate British officials the substance of the foregoing.

HULL

893.51/6137

Memorandum by the Under Secretary of State (Phillips)

[WASHINGTON,] April 11, 1936.

Mr. Cameron Forbes [94] showed me this morning a cablegram just received from Mr. C. H. French of Anderson and Meyer, Shanghai, which has recently been acquired by the International General Electric.

Speaking for prominent local Chinese closely in touch with the situation there, Mr. French advises that the liquidation of the claims of material American creditors would be greatly facilitated if the American Government expresses an interest at this time, especially in view of Mr. K. P. Chen['s] present mission in Washington; Mr. French believes that now is the most opportune time to achieve results; the designation by the American Government of Mr. Forbes as an executive of the Import and Export Bank would be welcomed.

W[ILLIAM] P[HILLIPS]

893.51/6141 : Telegram

The Consul General at Shanghai (Gauss) to the Secretary of State

SHANGHAI, April 16, 1936—4 p. m.
[Received April 16—2:21 p. m.]

209. Department's 52, March 7, 2 p. m., to Embassy.

1. I am reliably informed [95] that the Minister of Finance through the Chinese Ambassador in Washington is initiating discussions, presumably with Continental Illinois Bank and Trust Company, Chicago, looking toward servicing the 6% 3 year gold loan Treasury notes of

[94] Chairman of the American Economic Mission to the Far East in 1935.
[95] By Arthur N. Young, American adviser to the Chinese Ministry of Finance.

1919. Apparently no such action is being taken in regard to so-called Pacific Development loan of 1919. Also reliably informed that definite proposition has been made by Chinese Government for resumption service on Hukuang loan along general lines of recent agreement for resumption service on Tientsin–Pukow Railway loans. Other loans which are having the attention of the Ministry of Finance are the Vickers loan of 1919, the Pukow loan of 1914, and the so-called Marconi loans of 1918 and 1919.

2. Also reliably informed that Ministry of Finance is actively working on reorganization Central Bank of China along lines Federal Reserve Bank. Rogers of Leith-Ross party is one of those engaged in drawing up the plans.

GAUSS

893.51/6144 : Telegram

The Ambassador in the United Kingdom (Bingham) to the Secretary of State

LONDON, April 18, 1936—1 p. m.
[Received April 18—9 a. m.]

212. Your 123, April 11, 2 p. m. In the absence of Atherton, substance of the Department's views was communicated informally to Orde yesterday by Johnson.[96] Orde made no comment except to say that they were still waiting for advices from the Treasury in the matter and he reiterated that it was not Leith-Ross who was conducting the negotiations, that Leith-Ross had only given advice.

BINGHAM

893.51/6141 : Telegram

The Secretary of State to the Consul General at Shanghai (Gauss)

WASHINGTON, April 22, 1936—6 p. m.

111. Your 209, April 16, 4 p. m. Please on behalf of Department thank your source orally for this information and say that the Department has noted with gratification manifestation of the Chinese Government's interest and activity in regard to the general question of making arrangements for servicing its outstanding obligations. State also that the Department desires that your source know that in a number of quarters here, both private and official, there is a feeling that the terms offered by the Chinese Government envisage such extensive diluting of the creditors' rights as to render such terms unduly favorable to the debtor government; and that the terms offered on the

---

[96] Herschel V. Johnson, First Secretary of Embassy in the United Kingdom.

Tientsin–Pukow bonds, if applied to some of the other obligations mentioned, will appear far from generous; and that there prevails here the view that solicitous consideration should be given by the debtor to each of its various obligations on the individual merits thereof.

HULL

893.51/6156 : Telegram

The Ambassador in the United Kingdom (Bingham) to the Secretary of State

LONDON, May 1, 1936—2 p. m.
[Received May 1—8:30 a. m.]

239. Foreign Office asked that Atherton call today with reference to my 186, April 7, 6 p. m., and stated that the Treasury which is handling this matter was unwilling to assume the responsibility involved by making any suggestions to British bondholders in the settlement of this issue that had been negotiated unofficially, although Leith-Ross had been kept informed of the course of the negotiations. It was confidentially added that Leith-Ross had some 2 months ago suggested that he might well return to England but the Chancellor of the Exchequer felt on the contrary that his presence in the East continued to be useful. In conclusion Foreign Office stated it was understood British and American Bondholders Committees were in communication.

BINGHAM

893.51/6158 : Telegram

The Consul General at Shanghai (Gauss) to the Secretary of State

SHANGHAI, May 5, 1936—10 a. m.
[Received May 5—6 a. m.]

245. 1. Department's 111, April 22, 6 p. m. Orally conveyed to source who expressed appreciation and stated that views indicated would be taken into account. He agrees each obligation should be considered on its own merits and stated that he is doing all practicable promote settlements consistent with capacity to pay under present and prospective conditions and avoidance of unjustified discrimination.

2. My telegram No. 209, April 16, last sentence paragraph 1. Source states those loans are not now subject of actual negotiations and probably will not be for some time.

Repeated Peiping, Nanking by mail.

GAUSS

893.51/6179

Memorandum by the Third Secretary of Embassy in China (Lyon)[97]

PEIPING, May 12, 1936.

This morning I interviewed Mr. Hutchison, Commercial Secretary of the British Embassy, in regard to the question of the Hukuang Loan. I told him that we were interested in the statement contained in his letter of March 27, 1936, to Mr. Merrell[98] in which he said, "We are assuming that this minor issue will be arranged in the general settlement of the Chinese Government's indebtedness under the loan which is now under negotiation". I told him that our interest in this statement arose from the fact that we knew of no loan under negotiation for the general settlement of the Chinese Government's indebtedness. Mr. Hutchison said that his letter must have been very badly worded and that what he meant was the general settlement of the Hukuang loan question, a proposal for which has been made by the Chinese Government and referred to the American, British, French, and German banks of issue (I understand that the German interest in the loan has been taken over by Chinese banks). I asked Mr. Hutchison if this proposal of settlement had been the result of Leith-Ross' negotiations. He was evasive in his reply, but said that the settlement plan was one of the Chinese Government. Mr. Hutchison said that at the time of writing his letter of March 27 he assumed, of course, that we knew all about this and he took it for granted that Leith-Ross had discussed the whole question with the Ambassador. He said that Mr. Bennett of the National City Bank knew all the details of the settlement. Mr. Hutchison also said that he understood from Leith-Ross that the reason we did not know about it was "due to the American system of Government", for the United States Treasury knew all about these negotiations and apparently had failed to notify the State Department. Mr. Hutchison read to me part of a memorandum of a conversation with Leith-Ross, somewhat as follows: "As regards the Hukuang Loans, the proposal for the settlement has been referred to the banks of the issuing countries. The American banks apparently refuse to accept the settlement, it being against their principle to settle except dollar for dollar". Mr. Hutchison informed me that he understood that it was the American banks' refusal to agree to the settlement offered by the Chinese Government which was at present holding up the successful conclusion of the negotiations.

---

[97] Copy transmitted to the Department by the Ambassador in China in his despatch No. 458, May 16; received June 15.
[98] George R. Merrell, Jr., Second Secretary of Embassy in China.

893.51 Con-Ob Continental/135

Memorandum by the Chief of the Division of Far Eastern Affairs (Hornbeck) of a Conversation With the Vice President of the Continental Illinois National Bank and Trust Company (Abbott)

[WASHINGTON,] May 19, 1936.

Mr. Abbott called me on the telephone from Chicago. He said that he had been present at a meeting of representatives of interested banks, in New York, on May 14, presided over by Mr. Thomas Lamont, in discussion of the China Consortium and financial indebtedness of the Chinese Government. In consequence of the discussion then held, together with discussion with his associates in Chicago, he had decided to ask the help of the Foreign Bondholders Protective Council in relation to the Chicago Bank Loan. He had just now talked with the Chinese Ambassador, by telephone, and had told the Ambassador that he and his associates were not satisfied with the offer made by the Chinese Government for an adjustment of the Chicago Bank Loan contract, and that this matter would be taken up by the Foreign Bondholders Protective Council. He wanted the Department to know of this. His next move would be to inform Mr. Reuben Clark [99] and Mr. Francis White.[1]

893.51/6182 : Telegram

The Acting Secretary of State to the Ambassador in China (Johnson)

WASHINGTON, June 26, 1936—2 p. m.

161. Reference proposed settlement of Hukuang Loan. Department is sending you by mail a copy of a memorandum of June 11 [2] prepared by Thomas Lamont for Lord Alness, chairman, British Chinese Bondholders Committee, and a copy of the reply of Lord Alness of June 15 [2] which in effect accepts the suggestions of Lamont that the British Committee join in an endeavor to obtain for holders of Hukuang bonds terms which are at least equal to those offered in connection with the Tientsin–Pukow Loan. The reply of Lord Alness states that the British representative in Shanghai (Cassels) has been instructed to cooperate with the American representative "in approaching the Chinese Minister of Railways along these lines."

PHILLIPS

---

[99] J. Reuben Clark, Jr., president of the Foreign Bondholders Protective Council, Inc.
[1] Executive vice president and secretary of the Foreign Bondholders Protective Council, Inc.
[2] Not printed.

893.51/6215

The Ambassador in China (Johnson) to the Secretary of State

No. 578   PEIPING, July 16, 1936.
                                          [Received August 10.]

SIR: I have the honor to refer to the Department's strictly confidential instruction No. 177 of May 16, 1936, in regard to the
Hukuang Railway loan of 1911, and to enclose copy of a memorandum
of conversation which I had on July 1, 1936,[3] in Shanghai with Dr.
Arthur N. Young, Adviser to the Chinese Ministry of Finance, in
regard to the Chinese Government's offer for settlement of arrears of
this loan.

When I pointed out to Dr. Young that there was a feeling in the Department and among interested Americans that the Chinese Government was apparently not as considerate of its obligations toward
Americans as it appeared to be toward its obligations to other nationals, Dr. Young expressed his regret at this and invited my attention to the fact that Article IX of the Tientsin–Pukow Railway agreement of 1908 contained the same provision for a contingent lien upon
the Customs revenues in favor of the Tientsin–Pukow bonds, should
likin be decreased or abolished, as was provided under Article IX of
the Hukuang agreement, and expressed the hope that any misunderstanding in regard to these matters would have been cleared up by
his letter of May 12 to Mr. Francis White, Executive Vice President
and Secretary of the Foreign Bondholders Protective Council, a copy
of which he had communicated to the Chief of the Far Eastern Division of the Department of State under date of May 18, 1936.[4]

Respectfully yours,   NELSON TRUSLER JOHNSON

893.51 Con. Ob. Andersen, Meyer and Co./28

The Secretary of State to the Ambassador in China (Johnson)

No. 246   WASHINGTON, August 24, 1936.

SIR: The Department refers to the Embassy's despatch No. 3740 of
August 13, 1935,[5] and to the Department's instruction No. 23 of November 2, 1935,[4] in regard to the financial condition of the Peiping-
Hankow Railway, and encloses, for consideration and appropriate
action by the Embassy, a copy of a letter under date August 19, 1936,[4]
together with its enclosures, received by the Department from The
Baldwin Locomotive Works.

---

[3] Neither printed.
[4] Not printed.
[5] Not printed; for an enclosure transmitted with this despatch, see *Foreign
Relations*, 1935, vol. III, p. 760.

It will be noted that, with reference to the agreement of October 31, 1933, by and between the Ministry of Railways of the National Government of the Republic of China on the one hand and the General American Car Company, Andersen, Meyer and Company, Limited, and The Baldwin Locomotive Works on the other hand, the American creditors named are of the opinion that the financial condition of the Peiping–Hankow Railway has so materially improved as to warrant implementation of that portion of the agreement under reference which provides that, "as and when there is an improvement in the financial condition of the Peiping–Hankow Railway", the amount of the monthly payments specified in paragraph 2 of the agreement ($50,000 Chinese currency) shall be increased.

Based upon such information as is now available to the Department, particularly that contained in the enclosures to the aforementioned letter of August 19, 1936, from The Baldwin Locomotive Works, the Department is of the opinion that the Embassy, unless it perceives objection thereto, should seek by the use of all appropriate and practicable means to cause the Chinese Ministry of Railways to fulfill the obligations incurred by it in connection with the terms of the abovementioned agreement of October 31, 1933.[6]

Very truly yours,   For the Secretary of State:
                                          R. WALTON MOORE

893.51 Russian Issue/44

The Secretary of State to the Ambassador in China (Johnson)

No. 252   WASHINGTON, September 5, 1936.

SIR: The Department refers to its instruction No. 229 of July 31, 1936,[7] and to previous correspondence in regard to the Russian issue of the Chinese Government Five Per Cent Reorganization Gold Loan of 1913 and, in this connection, encloses, for the information of and appropriate action by the Embassy, a copy of a letter under date August 28, 1936, from J. G. White and Company,[7] and, with the exception of the detailed lists of bonds sold by J. G. White and Company and Paine, Webber and Company, copies of the enclosures as mentioned therein.[7]

It will be noted from the copies of correspondence attached hereto that, although certain details are lacking, there would appear to

---

[6] The Ambassador in China in his despatch No. 783, October 14, stated: "This is the policy which the Embassy has been pursuing for the last year." (893.51 Con. Ob. Andersen, Meyer and Co./32)
[7] Not printed.

exist no doubt that a settlement was made by the Chinese Government with a British bondholders committee; that the settlement provided for a cash payment, against delivery in Shanghai with all overdue coupons attached, of thirty per cent of the principal amount of British-owned bonds of the Russian issue under reference; and that payment was actually made to British owners of such bonds as were deposited with the British bondholders committee. There would further appear to exist at least a possibility that about six years ago Japanese holders of bonds of the Russian issue under reference received from the Chinese Government terms of settlement similar to those recently accorded to British bondholders.

In consideration of the above, it is the Department's desire that the Embassy, unless it perceives objection thereto, bring this subject to the attention of the appropriate authorities of the Chinese Government with a view to obtaining for American holders of the issue under reference an opportunity to receive from the Chinese Government, if they so desire, payment for their bonds on terms no less favorable than those granted to bondholders of other nationality.

In this connection, it is the Department's understanding that bonds in principal amount of £55,660 were sold by J. G. White and Company and in principal amount of £11,600 by Paine, Webber and Company.

Very truly yours,   For the Secretary of State:
                                     R. Walton Moore

893.51 Con. Ob. Continental/151 : Telegram

The Secretary of State to the Ambassador in China (Johnson)

Washington, September 15, 1936—11 a. m.

223. 1. Under date September 3 the Foreign Bondholders Protective Council, in continuation of discussions with the Chinese Ministry of Finance in regard to the so-called Chicago Bank Loan, cabled the Minister of Finance stating that the Council had reluctantly come to the point where it might consider some proper solution other than immediate payment and offering certain suggestions as a basis for settlement. Under date September 8 the Minister of Finance cabled a reply which the Council characterizes as "most disappointing".

2. In its correspondence with the Ministry of Finance the Council has emphasized the special position of this loan and its view that the terms of settlement offered by the Chinese Government are inequitable if not actually discriminatory. The Council now informs the De-

partment that it proposes to send a further telegram to the Minister of Finance urging that the Chinese Government give further study to the matter with a view to offering terms which would represent more adequate consideration of the interests and rights of American noteholders. The Council has requested that the Department support its further communication to the Chinese Minister of Finance.

3. Please telegraph Peck or Gauss (depending on whether Kung is at Nanking or at Shanghai) to seek an early interview with the Minister of Finance and to express to him orally, as under instruction from the Department, the earnest hope of the American Government that the Chinese Government will see its way clear to giving careful and sympathetic consideration to the general intent of the Council's further cable, when received, to the end that the Chinese Government and the Foreign Bondholders Protective Council may be able to reach a mutually satisfactory agreement appropriately considerate of the rights and interests of the American noteholders as well as of the interests of the Chinese Government. Peck or Gauss should avoid supporting any specific suggested terms of settlement. Peck or Gauss might take occasion to express the gratification of the Department that the Chinese Government considers improvement of its credit to be an important phase of its program of reconstruction and that that Government is making substantial efforts toward effecting settlement of its debts in arrears.

4. Inform Department immediately by telegraph when approach has been made to Kung.

HULL

893.51 Con. Ob. Continental/152 : Telegram

The Counselor of Embassy in China (Peck) to the Secretary of State

NANKING, September 17, 1936—6 p. m.
[Received September 17—8:50 a. m.]

269. Department's September 15, 11 a. m. to Peiping. I communicated to Kung September 17, 1 p. m. message contained in paragraph 3. He assured me he would give careful and sympathetic consideration to the new proposals and he recapitulated efforts made by him on behalf of Chicago Bank Loan including conversations with Abbott in 1926 and 1931. I inferred main points of disagreement are now interest rates and period of amortization. Kung urged that the bondholders be lenient in these respects and pointed out that with the announcement of redemption agreement market value of bonds would inevitably rise. Repeated to Peiping.

PECK

893.51 Con-Ob Continental/154 : Telegram

The Ambassador in China (Johnson) to the Secretary of State

PEIPING, October 4, 1936—5 p. m.
[Received October 4—10 : 40 a. m.]

477. Reference Department's No. 223 of September 15, 11 a. m. Gauss reports that Lockhart, adviser to Ministry of Finance,[9] told him confidentially and [privately] that Kung was somewhat exercised over what he considered strong representations made by Peck as reported in Nanking's September 17, 6 p. m. Other information conveyed by Lockhart was:

1. Contrary to the apparent assumption of the Bondholders Council, China was adopting no definite formula for loan settlements and would be in a further unfortunate position if she were forced to do so in the adjustment of loans carrying high interest rates such as the Japanese share of the "$96,000,000 loan". The negotiations for the adjustment of this are apparently being conducted by the Ministry of Foreign Affairs and not by the Finance Ministry, the American financial advisers to the Finance Ministry know little of these negotiations.

Gauss points out that under pressure Japan might be able to induce China to grant better interest rates on the readjustment of her loan than those granted on other foreign loans and suggests that this might make desirable an appropriate reservation by the Bondholders Council or the Department under which, in event of any such arrangement, American loan settlements might be reopened for equally favorable revision.

2. The Vickers Marconi settlement was on the basis of cancellation of interest in arrears and then 1½ percent interest for 1936–37, increasing one quarter percent annually until it reaches 3 percent in 1942 and subsequently until fully paid.

3. Dr. Arthur Young, now on leave in Los Angeles, has been asked to proceed to Washington to discuss the Chicago Bank Loan with the Department jointly with Ambassador Sze. He has been told that Dr. Kung regrets his inability to accept the percentage principle and increase of current interest to 3 percent and 6 percent. However, Kung is prepared to pay 1.3 percent on arrears and also to reimburse the bank for the November 1920 coupon advance. If absolutely necessary China will pay the November 1921 coupon as a matter of expedience but much prefers to shorten the period of amortization to 18 instead of 20 years.

---

[9] Oliver C. Lockhart, also American Associate Chief Inspector of the Chinese Government Salt Revenue Administration. This conversation at Shanghai on September 23 was reported in detail by the Embassy's despatch No. 757, October 6. (893.51 Con. Ob. Continental/162)

4. Minister of Finance told Sze, presumably as a gesture of security of the salt revenue in foreign loan adjustments, that he might mention that the Associate Chief Inspector of the Salt Revenue Administration was an American. In view of the fact that the future of foreign participation of the Salt Revenue Administration seems to be gravely threatened, Gauss suggests that the Department or the Bondholders Council may wish to consider whether they should not ask for some indication of the intentions of the Chinese Government with reference to the reorganization of the Salt Administration and the continuance of responsible foreign representation in the control of this revenue agency.

JOHNSON

893.51 Russian Issue/50

The Ambassador in China (Johnson) to the Secretary of State

No. 840   PEIPING, November 6, 1936.
                                         [Received November 30.]

SIR: I have the honor to refer to the Department's instruction No. 252 of September 5, 1936, in regard to the Russian issue of the Chinese Government Five Per Cent Reorganization Gold Loan of 1913 in which the Department expressed its desire that, unless the Embassy perceived objection thereto, it bring this subject to the attention of the appropriate authorities of the Chinese Government with a view to obtaining for the American holders of the issue under reference an opportunity to receive from the Chinese Government, if they so desire, payment for their bonds on terms no less favorable than those granted to bondholders of other nationality. In compliance with the Department's wishes, I instructed the Counselor of Embassy at Nanking to bring this matter to the attention of the appropriate Chinese officials, suggesting to him that in my opinion it would be advisable that he first do so in informal conversation. I enclose a copy of my instruction of October 16, together with Mr. Peck's reply of October 30, 1936.[10] It will be observed that Mr. Peck discussed the matter with Dr. S. S. Liu, Director of the Department of European and American Affairs of the Ministry of Foreign Affairs, who assured Mr. Peck that he would be glad to communicate the latter's observations to the Ministry of Finance and again take the matter up with Mr. Peck. I shall continue to press this matter on all appropriate occasions and shall keep the Department informed of any developments.

Respectfully yours,   NELSON TRUSLER JOHNSON

[10] Neither printed.

893.51 Salt Funds/153 : Telegram

The Acting Secretary of State to the Ambassador in China (Johnson)

WASHINGTON, December 1, 1936—3 p. m.

74. Reference Ambassador's telegram 575, November 25, 5 p. m., from Peiping,[12] in regard to Salt Administration. You are authorized to cooperate with your principally interested colleagues in an informal endeavor to persuade the Chinese Government to refrain from such action as would lessen the extent of foreign participation in the administration of the Salt Gabelle. Department is of the opinion that such approach should be not in the interest of the continued efficient functioning of the Salt Gabelle, which *per se* would seem to be a matter solely of Chinese concern, but rather in the interest of those foreign bondholders whose security for loans made to the Chinese Government might be affected adversely by elimination or curtailment in the effective functioning of foreign employees of the Salt Gabelle.

As the contemplated action of the Chinese Government would if taken apparently affect British, French, Japanese, and German interests equally if not more than American interests, you are authorized to cooperate but not to take the lead in this matter.[13]

MOORE

REPRESENTATIONS BY THE UNITED STATES AGAINST THE ESTABLISHMENT OF MONOPOLIES IN CHINA [14]

893.659 Matches/10

The Ambassador in China (Johnson) to the Secretary of State

No. 190   PEIPING, January 27, 1936.
                                                     [Received February 24.]

SIR: I have the honor to refer to despatch No. 58 of December 30, 1935, from the Consulate General at Shanghai to the Department,[12] with regard to the proposed match monopoly, and to enclose for the information of the Department copies [15] of: 1) a memorandum, dated January 3, 1936, of a conversation between Third Secretary O. Edmund Clubb and an officer of the British Embassy; 2) telegram No. 25, January 11, 11 a. m., from the Shanghai Consulate General to

---

[12] Not printed.
[13] The Ambassador in China in his despatch No. 318, January 19, 1937, reported informal representations to the Chinese Government by the American Ambassador and the British Ambassador in conversations with Dr. Hsu Mo, Chinese Vice Minister for Foreign Affairs, in December 1936. Dr. Hsu Mo gave assurance that the Chinese Government had no intention whatever of doing anything that would impair the efficiency of the Salt Administration. (893.51 Salt Funds/156)
[14] Continued from *Foreign Relations*, 1935, vol. III. pp. 767–789.
[15] None printed.

the Embassy; 3) a memorandum, dated January 17, of a conversation between Mr. Clubb and the aforementioned British official; 4) the Embassy's instruction of January 18 to the Consulate General at Shanghai; and 5) the Embassy's communication of January 18 to the Embassy at Nanking.

It will be observed that the American and British Embassies are in agreement in the opinion that the proposed organization would in actual fact be a combine with a monopolistic policy and that this Embassy has therefore instructed the Consul General at Shanghai that he should not associate himself with the negotiations at present in progress. The American company concerned has been considering the proposition with the view of joining the combine, but difficulties have arisen by reason of the fact that, although the Japanese interests have apparently reached a satisfactory agreement with the Chinese side (the precise terms of that agreement evidently not being known to the American interests), the arrangement proposed to the American side would seem to give to all intents and purposes actual control over the company's production and finances to the monopoly. It is at this point that there is discovered the very practical danger which would await any American company should it associate itself with a monopoly project in which it would have but little, if any, control. The voluntary association of American business interests with such a combine as the one outlined in the proposition for a match monopoly would be a definite invitation to their competitors promptly to impose restrictions which would redound to the benefit of the latter group; the acquiescence of the American authorities in any such arrangement would perhaps irreparably injure their technical position were they to desire to protest at a later date when the character of the combine became somewhat more apparent and American interests were confronted with a concrete threat.

In these circumstances, the Embassy does not intend to offer any support whatsoever to the American company for the purpose of enabling that enterprise to obtain favorable concessions in its negotiations with the monopoly group. As will be noted from the enclosures, it has, contrariwise, requested the Counselor at Nanking [16] to take steps to obtain additional information regarding the proposed combine and—if he thinks it desirable at this juncture—to point out to the Chinese authorities the attitude which the American authorities have consistently maintained as regards the general subject of monopolies in China. Where, as in this case, foreign interests are definitely involved and the pertinent provisions of the Nine Power Treaty [17] seem clearly applicable, the circumstances seem to warrant the taking

---

[16] Willys R. Peck.
[17] Signed at Washington, February 6, 1922, *Foreign Relations*, 1922, vol. I, p. 276.

of a strong stand for the maintenance of the important principle involved. This the Embassy proposes to do if Mr. Peck's investigations indicate the necessity. The Embassy will follow the matter closely and keep the Department informed.

A copy of the Embassy's instruction of January 18 to the Embassy at Nanking has been sent informally to the British Embassy for its information. It would seem highly desirable to obtain the fullest cooperation from the British authorities for the maintenance of the integrity of the treaty provisions involved in the proposal herein discussed.

Respectfully yours,   NELSON TRUSLER JOHNSON

893.659 Matches/12

The Ambassador in China (Johnson) to the Secretary of State

No. 103   NANKING, February 27, 1936.
                                          [Received March 25.]

SIR: I have the honor to refer to my despatch No. 98, of February 21, 1936,[19] in reference to the proposed match monopoly and to enclose herewith, for the files of the Department, a memorandum of a conversation[19] which took place regarding this subject between Mr. Blackburn, of the British Embassy, and Mr. Peck, Counselor of Embassy at Nanking.

It will be noted that Mr. Blackburn stated that the British Embassy has taken very little action in reference to this proposed match monopoly, because the British financial interests involved are slight. It will be noted, also, that in reply to a question asked by Mr. Blackburn, Mr. Peck said that the American Government takes the position that all American economic enterprises in China are by treaty protected from monopolistic interference, although he admitted that Article XV of the American-Chinese Treaty of 1844[20] deals only with the rights of "citizens of the United States engaged in the purchase or sale of goods of import or export".

I have thought it advisable to inquire whether the American Consulate General at Shanghai has any information calculated to supplement or revise the finding of the American Commercial Attaché that practically no American capital is invested in the two American companies involved in the discussions for the proposed match monopoly.

I should be glad to receive from the Department any advice which it may be moved to give me, on the basis of information already submitted, in reference to the extent to which the Embassy should continue its opposition to the proposed match monopoly. The British

---

[19] Not printed.
[20] Signed at Wang Hiya, July 3, 1844; Hunter Miller (ed.), *Treaties and Other International Acts of the United States of America*, vol. 4, p. 559.

Embassy appears to have no intention of taking active steps in the matter, because the British financial interests involved are slight. The policies of the Chinese Government in reference to the development of manufacturing industries in China will, if present indications are taken into account, have a dual object, the bringing about of conditions which will foster the expansion of such manufacturing industries and the devising of methods whereby the Government may be enabled to derive revenue therefrom. It seems to be taken as a foregone conclusion in the Ministry of Finance that the match monopoly will come into being, despite all obstacles and if any foreign company were to seek to maintain an independent business in manufacturing and selling matches, beyond doubt it would require the most active assistance on the part of a foreign government to enable it to succeed in its endeavor. The Chinese Government feels that in placing the manufacture and sale of matches in China under monopolistic government control it is following respectable precedents abroad, e. g., that of France.

Respectfully yours, NELSON TRUSLER JOHNSON

893.659 Matches/12 : Telegram

The Secretary of State to the Ambassador in China (Johnson)

WASHINGTON, March 28, 1936—noon.

67. Nanking's despatches Nos. 98 [21] and 103 of February 21 and 27 in regard to proposed match monopoly. On the basis of the information contained in the Embassy's despatches, the Department is inclined to concur in the view expressed in the penultimate paragraph of Nanking's No. 98 under reference.[22] In this connection, the Embassy should bear in mind Department's instruction No. 1745 of September 4, 1935,[23] on the subject of monopolies.

HULL

893.61331/43 : Telegram

The Ambassador in China (Johnson) to the Secretary of State

PEIPING, May 19, 1936—5 p. m.
[Received May 19—3:30 p. m.]

250. Following from Shanghai:

"May 19, 10 a. m. American leaf tobacco interests at Shanghai have reported to me that a proposal is now under consideration by the

---

[21] Not printed.
[22] The Ambassador in China stated that it was his intention "to take no further step in connection with the discussions relating to the formation of a match monopoly unless it shall seem necessary to emphasize further the opposition of the American Government to monopolies." (893.659 Matches/11)
[23] *Foreign Relations*, 1935, vol. III, p. 786.

Executive Yuan of the National Government to establish a Chinese Government monopoly of tobacco leaf grown in China from American seed and at the same time to increase the duty on imported tobacco leaf sufficient to protect the proposed domestic leaf monopoly.

This proposal if adopted would vitally affect the American leaf trade and at the same time the monopoly would throw out of business the same American leaf tobacco interests which are engaged in distributing seed and buying, curing and selling Chinese leaf in China to supply the market for low grade leaf at cheap prices, which market cannot be reached by American grown leaf.

I am mailing a report on this subject.[24] Might I respectfully make the suggestion that the foregoing should be communicated to the Department of State which may wish to take advantage of the present negotiations with K. P. Chen in Washington to make it clear that the American Government disapproves this and other plans of the Chinese Government to establish monopolies which would seriously affect American trade and American business interests in China."

JOHNSON

893.61331/43 : Telegram

The Acting Secretary of State to the Ambassador in China (Johnson)

WASHINGTON, May 22, 1936—6 p. m.

124. Your 250, May 19, 5 p. m. Department has received from the Universal Leaf Tobacco Company and from members of Congress inquiries in regard to the situation outlined in your telegram under reference.

Please initiate a thorough investigation not only in regard to the proposed monopoly but also the reported intention of the Chinese Government to increase duties applicable to imported leaf tobacco.

Bearing in mind the position of the American Government in regard to the creation of Chinese private and Government monopolies (see in particular Department's instruction No. 1745 of September 4, 1935)[25] and the ever increasing difficulties and handicaps to which during recent years foreign tobacco interests operating in China have been subjected, the Embassy should take all appropriate and practicable steps with a view to safeguarding American interests. To that end the Department desires that the Embassy, unless after investigation it perceives objection, bring the subject to the attention of the appropriate Chinese authorities. Also, as the proposals under reference, if implemented, would in all probability affect adversely not only American but also British tobacco interests, the Department suggests that you may wish to discuss the matter with your British colleague.

Please keep Department promptly and fully informed.

PHILLIPS

[24] Dated May 19, not printed.
[25] *Foreign Relations*, 1935, vol. III, p. 786.

893.6583/1a : Telegram

The Secretary of State to the Consul General at Shanghai (Gauss)

WASHINGTON, May 27, 1936—4 p. m.

144. Your 266, May 16, 11 a. m., and 286, May 25, 1 p. m.[26] If you have not already done so please repeat to Peiping and Nanking section 2 of Commercial Attaché's report 313 of May 16 and all of report 325 of May 25 [26] in regard to proposed vegetable oil refinery.

In transmitting the reports under reference please include a statement of the Department's desire that the Embassy, as in the case of the proposed tobacco monopoly, initiate a thorough investigation of the situation under reference; that it takes such steps as may be deemed appropriate and practicable with a view to safeguarding concerned American interests; and that it keep the Department promptly and fully informed.

HULL

893.61331/45 : Telegram

The Ambassador in China (Johnson) to the Secretary of State

PEIPING, June 2, 1936—6 p. m.
[Received June 2—10 : 25 a. m.]

274. Department's 124, May 22, 6 p. m. Following telegram has been received from Nanking:

"May 28, 11 a. m. [*noon?*]. Your May 26, 4 p. m., penultimate paragraph. I have confirmed from an official of the Executive Yuan that the Yuan has approved and referred to the Central Political Committee a plan for a Government tobacco leaf monopoly. Informant specifically confirmed the following features set down in despatch of May 1 [*19?*] from Shanghai: the committee composed of the Ministers of Foreign Affairs, Finance and Industries had already reported to the Executive Yuan with the result just mentioned; tobacco raised from American seed in the provinces of Honan, Anhwei and Shantung will be monopolized and tobacco curing plants and warehouses will be established; private manufacturers of cigarettes in China will necessarily buy China grown tobacco as described above from the Government monopoly; tobacco grown from Chinese seed will likewise be monopolized ultimately; import duties on foreign leaf tobacco will be increased so that Government monopoly's sales may receive no injury from this source. Informant expressed the opinion that considerable time must elapse before the monopoly can be put into operation.
Copy mailed to Shanghai".

The Embassy is filing written protest with the Ministry of Foreign Affairs against projected monopoly and proposed raising of the im-

---

[26] Neither found in Department files.

port duty on leaf tobacco. British Embassy has already made informal oral representations to the Ministry of Foreign Affairs against the monopoly.

JOHNSON

893.6583/2 : Telegram

The Ambassador in China (Johnson) to the Secretary of State

PEIPING, June 10, 1936—1 p. m.
[Received June 10—11 : 05 a. m.]

296. Department's 144, May 27, 4 p. m. to Shanghai concerning proposed vegetable oil monopoly.

1. Hankow Consulate General has reported fully on reaction there to proposed monopoly.[27] Josselyn [28] states that wood oil exporters of all nationalities, including Chinese, are extremely apprehensive of the effect which the scheme will have upon their business. It is believed by them that the scheme involves a monopoly either of the trade as a whole or of the storage and preparation of wood oil. Josselyn states that American exporters at Hankow seem to be unanimously of the opinion that if the scheme goes through it will put them out of business. And that he is inclined to concur in this opinion. American investments in the wood oil trade appear to be substantial. The two American firms which handled nearly half of the 1935 exports which passed through Hankow (69,000 short tons valued at United States dollars 12,000,000) maintain installations and equipment at Hankow and at Chungking and Wanhsien in Szechuan and Changteh in Hunan. Indirectly the Socony Vacuum Oil Company with which the American companies have storage facilities and transportation arrangements, and the Hankow branch of the National City Bank of New York through which most of the transactions are cleared by American exporters may be expected also to suffer by the establishment of the proposed monopoly.

2. Peck reports from Nanking [29] that he has received confirmatory reports of a great many features of scheme as contained in the press and that it is his opinion that in spite of the reluctance of officials in Nanking to discuss the details of the proposed plan, sufficient evidence has been accumulated to show beyond a doubt that the Chinese Government has the intention to monopolize the refining, storing and sale of wood oil, and possibly of other vegetable oils. I am instructing Peck to call on the Minister of Industry and make known to him the extent of American interests engaged in the wood oil trade and the opposition

---

[27] Despatches from the Consulate General at Hankow on this subject not printed.
[28] Paul R. Josselyn, Consul General at Hankow.
[29] Despatch No. 182, June 6, not printed.

of the American Government to any restrictions placed in the way of American business enterprises in China under the treaties. Formal protest will be filed against the proposed vegetable oil monopoly if Peck's interview with the Minister of Industry is unsatisfactory, and if such a course at the time appears desirable.

3. In discussing with Dr. Hsu Mo, the Vice Ministry for Foreign Affairs, on June 6 the matter of our positions the proposed leaf tobacco monopoly (see my 274, June 2, 3 [6] p. m.), Mr. Peck observed while the American Government had positive convictions in regard to its treaty rights as against Government monopolies in China, there were other considerations of great importance distinct from the legal aspect, such as the equilibrium in the trade between the two countries, which merited serious attention. Referring to the legal aspect of Government monopolies in China, Dr. Hsu said the Ministry of Foreign Affairs had in the past replied in detail to the arguments of the American Embassy against the principle embodied in the idea of Government monopolies in certain lines of activity, arguments based in part on article 14 [15] of the treaty with the United States of 1884 [1844], on the French Treaty of 1858 [30] and on the Washington Conference Treaty [31] on principles and policies. He recalled that the Chinese Government in these replies had taken the position that in the treaty of 1844 the Chinese Government had undertaken not to grant monopolistic rights to any Chinese individuals engaged in foreign trade, but to permit American citizens to enter into business relations with any Chinese citizen they might select. He reiterated that in the opinion of his Government this did not preclude the legality of Government monopolies such as the salt gabelle. He stated that it would be of advantage to various lines of business to receive guidance and improvement of those industries at the hands of the Government, as for example, in the tea export business which had fallen off badly of late, and that he thought it would be of general benefit if the Government took over control of the production and sale of certain important commodities. When Mr. Peck inquired whether it was to be inferred that China was tending to become a corporate state like Italy, Dr. Hsu replied that he would not undertake to say that this tendency existed in China but that it seemed to be the tendency in the world at large for governments to intervene in commercial matters in the way described.

4. Peck ventures the opinion based on recent conversations and observations in Nanking that the Chinese Government has deliberately embarked on a policy of controlling the production and sale of a number of important commodities in the belief that this will result in bene-

---

[30] Signed at Tientsin, June 27, 1858, *British and Foreign State Papers*, vol. LI, p. 636.
[31] Signed at Washington, February 6, 1922, *Foreign Relations*, 1922, vol. I, p. 276.

fit to these industries and develop attractive revenues for the Government. I concur in Mr. Peck's opinion.

5. Copy to Shanghai by mail.

JOHNSON

893.6583/3 : Telegram

The Ambassador in China (Johnson) to the Secretary of State

PEIPING, June 18, 1936—2 p. m.
[Received June 18—11 a. m.]

309. My 296, June 10, 1 p. m. The following telegram has been received from Peck at Nanking:

"June 13, 1 p. m. Your June 10, 11 a. m. The net result of interview this morning with the Minister of Industries regarding the 'Chinese Vegetable Oil Company Limited' is as follows:

(1) Existing facilities for storing and refining tung oil may continue in use but new facilities for pressing wood oil by machinery may be erected only by the company in question and the government is now giving consideration to the question whether private firms may be allowed to erect additional storage tanks.

(2) When the new system is in operation the Chinese Vegetable Oil Company, Limited, will offer all necessary financial facilities entailed in the sale, shipping and insuring of oil stored in its tanks even to the extent of effecting sales direct to foreign purchasers but owners of oil thus stored will be at full liberty to arrange all such matters with other parties. There will be no limitation on the freedom of American merchants to purchase oil from native producers.

(3) The object of the Government in setting up the new system is to prevent the wood oil industry from falling into a slump as the silk industry has done and to produce a supply of wood oil for export dependable in quality and quantity at a low price not subject to fluctuations. Success of the project requires willing cooperation of Chinese and foreign merchants and the Government has continuously and frankly consulted them.

(4) I opened the conversation with detailed statement of importance of the wood oil trade to American merchants and industries and the American Government's objection to any limitation violating treaty rights. The Minister of Industries in explaining the desire of the Chinese Government to improve and regulate the wood oil business referred with evident satisfaction to the conversations reported in the Department's instruction No. 181, May 18, to Peiping [32] and said that the Chinese Government had been embarrassed by lack of authority which would enable it to comply with the request of the American Government."

The Consul General at Hankow has obtained further evidence that the scheme actually contemplates the monopoly control of the wood oil business. This evidence is contained in letters addressed by the Chairman of the Preparatory Committee of the "China Vegetable

---

[32] Not printed.

Oil Corporation (Limited)" to the Hankow Wood Oil Exporters Association and the foreign owners of wood oil tank installation. These letters do not confirm the innocuous nature of the scheme as described by the Minister of Industry to Peck. The Embassy is therefore filing written protest against the formation of the vegetable oil monopoly along the lines followed in the protest against the tobacco leaf monopoly.[33]

To Shanghai and Hankow by mail.

JOHNSON

893.6583/3 : Telegram

The Acting Secretary of State to the Ambassador in China (Johnson)

WASHINGTON, June 24, 1936—5 p. m.

157. Your 309, June 18, 2 p. m., and previous. As it would appear that the proposed "Chinese Vegetable Oil Company Limited" contemplates monopoly control of the wood oil trade in which American interests are largely concerned, the Department notes with approval the intention of the Embassy to file written protest with the Chinese Government. Department desires that this matter be pursued energetically and suggests that, as other foreign interests in addition to American interests would in all probability be affected adversely by the creation of such a monopoly, your concerned colleagues may also wish to lodge formal protest with the appropriate Chinese authorities.

PHILLIPS

893.6583/8

The Ambassador in China (Johnson) to the Secretary of State

No. 560   PEIPING, July 1, 1936.
                                          [Received July 28.]

SIR: I have the honor to refer to the Embassy's despatch No. 530 of June 18, 1936, with which there was enclosed a copy of the Embassy's note of the same date addressed to the Ministry of Foreign Affairs protesting against the formation of the proposed vegetable oil monopoly, and to enclose a copy of a letter from Counselor Peck at Nanking, dated June 24, 1936,[34] in which he recounts his conversation with an official of the Ministry of Foreign Affairs on the subject. It will be noted that Mr. Peck pointed out to that official that the Embassy's note of protest should not be regarded as a formality, but as indicating a very real concern felt by the Embassy on behalf of

---

[33] Protest addressed to the Chinese Minister for Foreign Affairs, June 18, not printed.
[34] None printed.

the American businessmen concerned. There is also enclosed a copy of a memorandum of a conversation Mr. Peck had on June 24, 1936,[35] with the Director of the National Bureau of Industrial Research and concurrently head of the Section of Industrial Planning and Promotion of the Ministry of Industry, at which time mention was made of the proposed vegetable oil monopoly. This official denied that the project is in effect a monopoly.

The Consulate General at Hankow continues to report the concern felt by the Hankow wood oil dealers that the project is in fact a monopoly which when established will eliminate them from the trade. There are enclosed copies of its despatches No. 302 of June 19, No. 304 of June 24, and 306 of June 26, 1936,[36] on the subject. It is apparent that the Chinese wood oil dealers, as well as the foreign dealers, dislike the scheme, and also that some of the Provincial governments, which under the regulations are to supply part of the capital, are not enthusiastic about it. The conversations between the delegates of the Hankow Chamber of Commerce (Chinese) and the Minister of Industry, as reported in despatch No. 306, apparently had a beneficial effect and it appears that the Minister might now be more willing to consider the wishes of the wood oil dealers. However the Consulate General does not feel that the fundamental difficulties presented by the scheme have been solved by these conversations. It is hoped that the Embassy's note of June 18 will help to bring about an abandonment, or at least a substantial modification of the scheme. The Department will be informed as soon as a reply to the Embassy's note is received from the Ministry of Foreign Affairs.

Respectfully yours,   For the Ambassador:
                                          GEORGE R. MERRELL, JR.
                                          First Secretary of Embassy

---

893.6359 Wolfram Ore/42

The Ambassador in China (Johnson) to the Secretary of State

No. 585   PEIPING, July 16, 1936.
                                          [Received August 10.]

SIR: I have the honor to refer to the Embassy's despatch No. 111 of November 30, 1935,[37] concerning the activities of the tungsten monopoly in Kiangsi Province, and to enclose a copy of despatch No. 273

---

[35] Not printed.
[36] None printed.
[37] *Foreign Relations,* 1935, vol. III, p. 789.

of April 28, 1936, from the Consul General at Hankow [38] in which he reports a rumor to the effect that the Central Government is maneuvering to obtain control of the trade in tungsten mined in Kiangsi, and that, as a means to that end, it has established an office in Changsha, Hunan, to control the export of Kiangsi tungsten through that port. He reports that it is also rumored that the Central Government intends to set up in Nanking a refinery to which it will divert ore formerly exported and from which it will export the refined products.

Counselor Peck was instructed to make inquiries at Nanking in regard to these rumors, and there is enclosed a copy of the memorandum of his conversation on the subject with the Vice Minister of Industries on May 22.[38] It will be noted that the Vice Minister stated that not only had the above-mentioned control bureau been established at Changsha, but a control bureau had also been established on the Kwangtung–Kiangsi border to prevent the smuggling of tungsten ore from Kiangsi into Kwangtung.

The time would appear opportune again to make some form of representations against the establishment of the Kiangsi wolfram monopoly, as authorized in the Department's instruction No. 1745 of September 4, 1935,[39] but before doing so I desire to have more recent information from the Consulate General at Hankow on the activities of the monopoly organization. As requested by the Department in its above-mentioned instruction, I shall endeavor to induce the British to make a simultaneous protest.

In this connection there is enclosed a copy of a letter dated May 19, 1936,[38] addressed by the Commercial Attaché at Shanghai to the Metals and Minerals Division of the Department of Commerce, transmitting a World Trade Directory Report on the National Resource Commission, the National Government organization in charge of the monopoly of wolfram ore mined in all provinces except Kwangtung and Kwangsi. It appears that at the same time that the Embassy is objecting to the activities of the Chinese Government in forming various monopolies the Commercial Attaché is assisting one of these monopoly organizations to make contacts in the United States. I am bringing this matter to the attention of the Commercial Attaché, and enclose a copy of my letter to him of today's date.[40]

Respectfully yours,   NELSON TRUSLER JOHNSON

---

[38] Not printed.

[39] *Foreign Relations*, 1935, vol. III, p. 786.

[40] Not printed. Department's instruction No. 253, September 5, indicated the Department's approval of the Embassy's action in this matter and asked that the Commercial Attaché be requested to refrain from further activity. (893.6359 Wolfram Ore/44)

893.6583/13

The Ambassador in China (Johnson) to the Secretary of State

No. 659   PEIPING, August 20, 1936.
                                                 [Received September 21.]

SIR: I have the honor to refer to the Embassy's despatch No. 637 of August 10, 1936,[42] with regard to the proposed establishment of a vegetable oil monopoly in China, and to enclose for the information of the Department copies of a note received from the Ministry of Foreign Affairs under date July 25 and despatch No. 320 of August 6, 1936, from the Consulate General at Hankow.[43]

It will be observed that the Minister for Foreign Affairs quotes the Ministry of Industry as stating that the establishment of the China Vegetable Oil Corporation is intended for the regulation of production and promotion of trade, and that no restrictions are imposed upon the legitimate commerce in tung-oil and other oil products;

"The legal commerce of the present enterprises of Chinese and foreign merchants may of course be carried on as they wish, and will not be subjected to restrictions."

The despatch from the Hankow Consulate General points out the fact that the China Vegetable Oil Corporation plainly intends to engage, through the provision of financial facilities, in the sale, shipment and insurance of tung-oil belonging to its clients; and that, moreover, additional private plants may evidently be erected only with the permission of the Ministry of Industry. Consul Jarvis[44] observes that it is obviously possible for the Government, while observing the letter of the assurances of the Minister of Industry to the delegation from the Hankow Chamber of Commerce, to drive foreign merchants out of business by the use of indirect methods; this the foreign merchants believe to be the intention of Mr. C. C. Chang, the Minister's lieutenant, and as proof of this they point to Mr. Chang's statement that he had received no new instructions from the Minister and was proceeding with the original plan.

Mr. Jarvis agrees with the opinion of the majority of the foreign merchants that the situation is unsatisfactory, especially in view of various statements made by Mr. Chang during a recent trip to Hankow. He suggests, therefore, that certain formal and specific assurances be obtained from the National Government for the protection of the interests of American tung-oil merchants. In view of the explicit character of the Foreign Minister's assurances in his aforementioned note of July 25, the Embassy feels that, instead of sending an-

[42] Not printed.
[43] Neither printed.
[44] Robert Y. Jarvis, Consul at Hankow.

other formal communication to the Foreign Office on essentially the same subject of policy, it would probably be preferable first to obtain informally an interpretation in detail of certain of the points under discussion. It is therefore requesting Counselor Peck, in an instruction under today's date, to take up with the appropriate authorities at Nanking the matters discussed by Mr. Jarvis, and in particular to obtain the views of those authorities as regards the four items listed by Mr. Jarvis as being aspects of the problem requiring specific assurance from the National Government for the protection of American interests. Mr. Peck is also being requested to call to the attention of the Chinese authorities the circumstances, emphasized by Mr. Jarvis, that the National Government, contrary to the assertion of the Minister of Industry, has not endeavored to consult at all times with Chinese and foreign merchants with regard to its proposal to establish a vegetable oil monopoly. A copy of the Embassy's instruction is enclosed.[45]

Respectfully yours, NELSON TRUSLER JOHNSON

893.6583/16

The Ambassador in China (Johnson) to the Secretary of State

No. 692 PEIPING, September 4, 1936.
[Received October 5.]

SIR: I have the honor to refer to the Embassy's despatch No. 659 of August 20, 1936, with regard to the proposed establishment of the China Vegetable-Oil Corporation, in which it was stated that Counselor Peck was being requested to take up with the appropriate Chinese authorities at Nanking the questions raised by the Hankow Consulate General in connection with certain monopolistic aspects of the organization's program, and to enclose a copy of a despatch received from Mr. Peck under date August 26, 1936, in reply.[45]

It will be observed that, although Dr. Wong Wen-hao, Secretary-General of the Executive Yuan, in conversation with Mr. Peck expressed the opinion that the scheme which the Government is now attempting to carry out does not include any intention to limit in any way the activities of foreign merchants engaged in exporting vegetable-oils, his assurance seemed too general to be of any value as regards the points in which the tung-oil merchants are most interested— the storage and refining of oil-products and the financing of shipments, as well as the actual buying, sale and transportation of such products.

---

[45] Not printed.

The Embassy is therefore sending a new note to the Foreign Office under today's date in an attempt to obtain official assurances that legitimate American trade in oil-products will not be excluded from the benefits of trade by the imposition of restrictions through the medium of an organization having exclusive and monopolistic characteristics. A copy of that note is enclosed for the information of the Department.[47]

There is also enclosed, as of possible interest in connection with the general subject of state control of industrial and commercial enterprises in China, a copy in English translation [47] of an item appearing in the *Central Daily News* (semi-official Chinese-language organ, Nanking) under date July 3, 1936, reporting the convening on July 2 of the first meeting of the "Section for National Operation of Foreign Trade of the Central People's Economic Planning Committee". In this connection it is recalled that, as reported by the Assistant Commercial Attaché in report No. S–90 of May 25, 1936,[48] page 3, some sentiment evidently exists in Chinese official circles for the adoption of state economic control and the elimination of so-called economic individualism. It is conceivable that, in the absence of political and economic distractions, the next few months will see definite developments in the direction of the state control of industrial and commercial enterprises. It seems probable that the Government leaders will be overly sanguine regarding the prospect of achieving favorable results from such a policy, so that they may perhaps be led to undertake enterprises beyond their technical and financial capacity, but this can hardly be expected to cause the eventual abandonment of the drive toward state control in China. If the present tendencies continue—and they probably will, barring the intrusion of elements of grave social disorder—apparently the best that individual foreign entrepreneurs can hope to retain is the right of co-existence side-by-side with state enterprises. China's need for capital and modern technical skill will probably force at least temporary compromises of its program for complete state control, and the exercise of pressure from foreign commercial groups would be an additional factor of protection, under certain circumstances, for American trade interests in the country. It would appear, however, that the extension of Japan's political control in China would constitute an immediate threat to various established commercial interests even if, by hypothesis, it were to be of general benefit to international trade in the long run.

Respectfully yours,   NELSON TRUSLER JOHNSON

---

[47] Not printed.
[48] Not found in Department files.

893.61331/53 : Telegram

The Secretary of State to the Ambassador in China (Johnson)

WASHINGTON, September 9, 1936—6 p. m.

216. Reference Department's 124, May 22, 6 p.m., and Shanghai's 373 [*473*], September 1, 4 p. m. to Department.[49] Representatives of the Universal Leaf Tobacco Company and the Export Leaf Tobacco Company, both companies of Richmond, Virginia, have called at the Department and stated they had reports from China that the Chinese Minister of Finance had sanctioned a proposal for the formation of a semi-official company for the purchase and sale first of the Honan flue-cured leaf tobacco crop and later of the Shantung and Anhwei crops. They expressed the view that the proposed plan, if implemented, would inevitably lead to discrimination against American exports of tobacco to China, would adversely affect the operations in China of the Universal Leaf Tobacco Company and others engaged in handling Chinese tobaccos and would in a short time lead to a monopolistic control of the entire tobacco business in China. They expressed the hope that the present plan be abandoned or at least postponed until further study.

The Department desires that the Embassy make a thorough investigation into this matter and on the basis of the Department's instruction under reference take all appropriate and practicable steps with a view to safeguarding American interests. It is suggested that you obtain details from local representatives of American interests involved. It has been suggested to Department that you might get valuable opinions from Lockhart [50] of the Salt Administration.

Please keep the Department promptly and fully informed.

HULL

893.61331/55 : Telegram

The Ambassador in China (Johnson) to the Secretary of State

PEIPING, September 12, 1936—noon.
[Received September 12—7 a. m.]

443. Department's telegram No. 216, September 9, 6 p. m., has been transmitted to Shanghai with the request to follow the matter closely. Instructions have been sent to Nanking by the Embassy's September 12, noon as follows:

"Shanghai has been instructed to follow the matter closely. Please ⅃pproach those officials of the Ministry of Finance who would pre-

---

[49] Latter not found in Department files.
[50] Oliver C. Lockhart, Associate Chief Inspector, Salt Revenue Department of the Chinese Government.

sumably be informed of the project with a request for authoritative information regarding the matter. In conferring with Chinese officials in this connection, the instructions contained in the Department's telegram No. 124, May 22, 6 p. m., should be borne in mind. You should make an initial oral protest at the Foreign Office if it seems that various current reports of a monopoly project are essentially correct. Please keep the Department, Embassy and Shanghai currently informed of developments."

The Embassy is studying the problem and will make formal protest should Nanking's information warrant such action.

JOHNSON

893.61331/57 : Telegram

The Counselor of Embassy in China (Peck) to the Secretary of State

NANKING, September 17, 1936—5 p. m.
[Received September 17—4:43 p. m.]

268. The Department's 216, September 9, 6 p. m.

1. During informal conversation with Kung, Minister of Finance, September 16, 6 p. m., he confirmed plan to organize company to take over exclusive control of the raising and curing of tobacco leaf in China and its sale to cigarette manufacturers. He said that the Government's objectives are to foster this domestic industry by the application of scientific methods and the elimination of harmful competition and to protect Government revenue derived from taxation of cigarettes by preventing leaf tobacco from falling into the hands of illicit cigarette manufacturers. He also confirmed that a majority of the stock in the new company would be offered to Chinese and foreign tobacco companies, thus placing the control of the operations of the company in the hands of the trade. He said that this proves that the Government has no hidden motive in organizing the company and aside from protection is giving revenue desired only to promote tobacco raising in China. He referred to complaints hitherto filed with him by the American Embassy on behalf of American tobacco companies against inroads on legitimate business by illicit manufacturers and pointed out that American sellers of cigarettes would benefit by this measure to suppress such unfair competition. He asserted that in principle he was personally opposed to taking away business enterprise from private initiative and vesting it in the hands of "politics" but he frankly stated that he hoped through the present measures to raise tobacco growing in China to a point where it would be able not only to supply domestic needs but would be able to compete in world markets.

2. I did not present any treaty arguments against this scheme and said that my instructions were merely to seek authoritative informa-

tion. However, I anticipate that it may be difficult to apply article XV of the Treaty of 1844 prohibiting limitations on business in this connection because these measures seemed designed merely to foster a domestic industry and article XV specifically gives protection to merchants known to have been importing or exporting. The question presumably will arise whether we have treaty basis for objecting to protective tariffs on imported leaf if imposed (see my May 28, noon [*11 a. m.?*], to Peiping [51]).

3. In compliance with the Ambassador's instruction September 12, noon,[52] directing initial oral protest to the Foreign Office, if reports of a more precise project were found to be essentially correct, I have called today on the director of the Department of European and American Affairs of the Foreign Office and urged that reply be sent to the Embassy's note of June 1st.[53] I stated that the report that the change in plan whereby a semi-official company would be formed to monopolize handling of leaf tobacco raised in China did not allay fears of American tobacco companies that ultimately their business would be taken from them.

4. Since my conversation with the Minister of Finance was informal I suggest that his statements should not be quoted publicly.

5. Sent to the Department and Peiping. Copy to Shanghai by courier.

PECK

893.61331/58 : Telegram

The Ambassador in China (Johnson) to the Secretary of State

PEIPING, September 20, 1936—noon.
[Received September 20—9 a. m.]

457. Nanking's 268, September 17, 5 p. m. The following telegram has been received from Shanghai:

"September 17, 11 a. m. Embassy's telegram, September 12, noon.

1. From source referred to in my despatch 365, September 3,[53] it has been learned that during course of recent informal conversation he had with Director General of Internal Revenue Administration, distinct impression was gained that Director General is under pressure from buyers to carry through the scheme and in particular to inaugurate the proposed semiofficial leaf tobacco company. In reply to a question, Director General stated he believed larger Chinese cigarette companies were in favor of the formation or [*of?*] such a company and added significantly 'the smaller ones will fall in line.'

---

[51] See telegram No. 274, June 2, 6 p. m., from the Ambassador in China, p. 605.
[52] See *supra*.
[53] Not printed.

2. Also informed by above source that his company has learned from reliable sources that Commissioners of Finance and Reconstruction of Honan Province are in Shanghai trying to induce Internal Revenue Administration to agree to establishment of provincial monopolies of leaf tobacco or failing this a joint national provincial monopoly.

3. Lockhart states he is not in touch with those interested in this scheme and therefore has no inside information. He added, however, that present Minister of Finance is and has been an advocate of state monopolies and that he is undoubtedly pushing this and similar proposals.

4. Representatives of B.A.T.[55] conferred September 15th with British Ambassador and other British officials and outlined their opposition to these proposals. They understand British authorities will make representations very shortly."

It was stated at the Japanese Embassy yesterday that, although no formal protest had been made by the Japanese in regard to the tobacco monopoly, they were opposing the project and Suma[56] at Nanking had on several occasions, in meeting with Chinese officials, taken the opportunity to make oral protest in the premises. The Embassy official stated that no changes of treaty provision had been made, the ojection being thus far based upon "practical considerations", but that any changes would be made in the event of formal protest. It was further suggested by the official that a united front of Japanese, British and American interests would possibly prove effective in checking that monopoly project.

British Embassy officials in Nanking and Peiping are concerned regarding the project. It was stated at the British Embassy yesterday morning that the British Ambassador has informed the Foreign Office that the matter should be protested and that he proposed to confer with his American and Japanese colleagues in an effort to obtain their support.

It is my present reaction that, despite the obvious difficulties faced in resisting the formation of a domestic combine, as outlined by Peck, the Embassy should nevertheless take action directed against any monopolistic features of the proposed organization; although a sympathetic attitude should be adopted toward the efforts of the Chinese to strengthen their industrial and commercial enterprises, the weakness of their project due to financial and technical factors at the present time makes it improbable that those projects can be carried through to the general benefit of those concerned. In the particular case at point, where exclusive monopolistic features characterize the proposed organization, established American and British interests of considerable importance are threatened for ends which are still questionable. (The Japanese interests seem to be confined largely to

---

[55] British-American Tobacco Co.
[56] Yakichiro Suma, First Secretary of the Japanese Embassy in China.

certain drying plants, and perhaps mooted projects, in Shantung). It is therefore my belief that the American Government should endeavor to maintain the right of American commercial enterprises to coexist and function side by side with such experimental Chinese Government enterprises, pending such time as both the economic and political situations may have become more stabilized and a new agreement may have been reached regarding the function of foreign enterprise in China.

The Embassy proposes to wait several days for a reply to its note of June 1,[57] and to see what line of action the British and Japanese propose to take.

By mail to Shanghai.

JOHNSON

893.61331/60 : Telegram

The Ambassador in China (Johnson) to the Secretary of State

PEIPING, September 25, 1936—3 p. m.
[Received September 25—2 : 45 p. m.]

463. Embassy's 457, September 20, noon. The following telegram has been received from Shanghai:

"September 19, noon. Following message sent to Hankow regarding difficulties being experienced by Lienhwa Leaf Tobacco Company in the purchase of leaf tobacco at Hsuchang, Honan, is being repeated to Embassy. Inasmuch as the reported attitude of the Honan Provincial authorities may be result of attempt of National Government to establish leaf tobacco monopoly 'Lienhwa Leaf Tobacco Company Federal Incorporated', China subsidiary of Universal Leaf Tobacco Company report that their American and Chinese representatives sent to Hsuchang, Honan for the purpose of buying Honan leaf tobacco are being obstructed by local authorities at Hsuchang presumably on instructions of Provisional Government. They have apparently been told that there is objection to foreigners doing business at Hsuchang. The American company is not establishing branch office in Honan. Its representatives are there temporarily only for the purpose of buying leaf tobacco and shipping it to Shanghai. They are entitled to do this under the treaties, and with particular reference to section 3, article 6, Sino-Japanese treaty of 1895 [58] they may temporarily rent or hire warehouses for the storage of the leaf tobacco purchased for transportation. Consulate General understands local authorities have stated that protection will be refused when representatives start buying. A more complete statement of facts is expected by mail. Meanwhile I send you foregoing and suggest that you communicate by telegraph with Honan Provincial Government reciting report, requesting investigation and making reference to treaty rights.

---

[57] Not printed.
[58] Signed at Shimonoseki, April 17, 1895; John V. A. MacMurray (ed.), *Treaties and Agreements With and Concerning China*, 1894–1919 (New York, 1921), vol. I, p. 18.

American representatives now at Hsuchang are G. W. Macon and J. F. Malone, their telegraphic address is Li Wat Hsuchang".

The Consulate General at Hankow reported in its telegram of September 20, noon, that a telegram had been sent to Honan Provincial Government as suggested in Shanghai's September 19, noon.

The following telegram has been received from Nanking:

"September 24, 10 a. m.   Telegram September 19, noon, Shanghai to Peiping, first sentence.   Your attention is respectfully invited to article in first column page 11 *North China Daily News* of September 23 quoting Shanghai Tobacco Leaf Dealers Association as stating that control of tobacco leaf sales shall be first effected at Hsuchang, Honan as an experiment."

In these circumstances, the Embassy has sent the following instruction to Nanking:

"September 25, 2 p. m.   Your September 24, 9 a. m. Shanghai's despatch No. 392, September 22.   Please call at the Foreign Office, invite attention to the circumstances of the reported interference of the Honan officials with the right of the American company to purchase leaf tobacco in the Province in the pursuit of its trade, and request that appropriate instructions be issued to the Honan authorities to cease such interference.   You should state that the Hankow Consulate General has already protested to the Honan Government direct.

It is noted that the right to purchase leaf tobacco in the interior is enjoyed as an established practice, but the Sino-Japanese treaty of 1895 may be cited as legal basis for your request should there exist any disposition on the Chinese side to deny that right.
By mail to Shanghai, Hankow".

Shanghai's despatch No. 392, September 22, is being forwarded to the Department.[59]

JOHNSON

───────────

893.61331/59 : Telegram

The Ambassador in China (Johnson) to the Secretary of State

PEIPING, September 25, 1936—5 p. m.
[Received September 25—8 a. m.]

464. Embassy's 457, September 20, noon. The First Secretary of the Japanese Embassy states that Suma at Nanking on September 24 delivered a verbal protest to Kung opposing the proposed establishment of a leaf tobacco monopoly.
By mail to Shanghai.

JOHNSON

───────────

[59] Not printed.

893.61331/66

The Ambassador in China (Johnson) to the Secretary of State

No. 763

Peiping, October 7, 1936.
[Received November 2.]

Sir: I have the honor to refer to the Embassy's despatch No. 744 of September 25, 1936, in regard to the leaf-tobacco monopoly, and to enclose for the information of the Department a copy of despatch No. 382 of September 15, 1936, from the Consulate General at Shanghai,[60] reporting the grant in July 1936 by the Ministry of Industry to the Philippine Chinese Tobacco Company, Ltd., (a Chinese corporation) of exclusive rights to manufacture mentholated and anisated cigarettes.

It will be observed from the enclosures to the despatch that the Yee Tsoong Tobacco Company Ltd. (British) considers this move to be a result of the operation of the policy laid down in the Industrial Encouragement Act of 1934. It appears to have more immediate relationship to the National Government's present program for the establishment of monopoly control in the tobacco industry, and it is with reference to this matter that the Embassy is requesting Counselor Peck at Nanking to invite the attention of the National Government authorities to the circumstances that the grant of monopoly rights to the aforementioned Chinese tobacco company appears to be a part of the general monopoly program which faces the opposition of the American Government. It is nevertheless appropriate to remark the fact that the Foreign Office in its note of February 25, 1935,[61] transmitted the assurances of the Ministry of Industry that the Industrial Encouragement Act "is simply a necessary arrangement for domestic industry and will result in not the slightest detriment to the interests of foreign merchants. During successive years all commercial interests acquired by foreign merchants under treaties have without exception been respected and protected by the Government, and there is really no discrimination." (Cf. Legation's despatch No. 3422, March 7, 1935.[62])

A copy of the above-mentioned instruction to Mr. Peck is enclosed.[61]

Respectfully yours,

Nelson Trusler Johnson

---

[60] Neither printed.
[61] Not printed.
[62] See *Foreign Relations*, 1934, vol. III, p. 569, footnote 32.

893.61331/62 : Telegram

The First Secretary of Embassy in China (Merrell) to the Secretary of State

PEIPING, October 12, 1936—5 p. m.
[Received October 12—10:20 a. m.]

495. Embassy's 463, September 25, 3 p. m. Peck at Nanking reported on October 1 [65] that he was informed on the same date by the Foreign Office that a telegram had been sent to the Honan Provincial Government on September 26 "advising" that American merchants be permitted to purchase leaf tobacco. He further reported under date of October 5 that the Lienhwa Leaf Tobacco Company had received a telegram dated September 30 from the Honan Commission of Reconstruction stating that, if the company takes no action contrary to the treaties, it may purchase leaf tobacco in Honan Province. He now states, in a communication dated October 7,[65] that he has been informed by the director of the Political Department of the Executive Yuan that, from what the latter had heard, it was his judgment that the project for a leaf tobacco company has been dropped. Peck endeavored to obtain further particulars, but the director appeared unwilling to go into details. It is presumed, however, on the basis of Peck's conversation with the Director on September 15, that the latter had reference to the whole leaf tobacco monopoly project for the purchase and sale of leaf tobacco, and that the assurance he gave may be considered semiofficial.

MERRELL

893.61331/65 : Telegram

The Ambassador in China (Johnson) to the Secretary of State

PEIPING, October 24, 1936—2 p. m.
[Received October 24—8 a. m.]

513. Embassy's 495, October 12, 5 p. m. The Consulate General at Shanghai telegraphed October 14, noon, as follows:

"President of the Lienhwa Company informs me that they are still unable to do business at Hsuchang for the reason that the Chinese from whom they are renting temporary warehouse is unable to give possession of the premises presumably due to the non-withdrawal of the confidential circular letter of the Hsuchang Chamber of Commerce, a copy of which was enclosed with my despatch number 433 of October 9.[65] Company inquires whether it would be possible to send officer from Hankow (perhaps Stevens)[66] to Kaifeng and Hsuchang to make representations to provincial and local authorities and endeavor to facilitate matter. Company willing to bear expense."

[65] Not printed.
[66] Harry E. Stevens, Consul at Hankow.

The Embassy October 15, 5 p. m. informed Shanghai and Hankow that it considered it unnecessary at this stage to send a consular officer to Honan, and instructed Nanking as follows:

"October 15, 5 p. m. Shanghai's October 14, noon. Please bring to the attention of the Foreign Office the circumstances of the case reported Shanghai, and request that prompt steps be taken to give effect to the assurances received that there will be no interference with the legitimate activities of American leaf tobacco merchants in Honan".

Nanking reported October 17, 2 p. m. as follows:

"I described to the Director of the European American Department of the Foreign Office Oct. 17, 11 a. m. the present difficulties of the Lienhwa Tobacco Company and he promised that the Foreign Office would telegraph the Honan Provincial authorities to attempt to remove obstacles to the renting of warehouse."

The Embassy next instructed Hankow as follows:

"October 20, 9 a. m. Nanking's October 17, 2 p. m. Kindly telegraph the Honan Provincial authorities, noting the obstructions which are evidently being offered to American leaf tobacco buyers in Honan (Shanghai's October 14, noon) despite the Provincial Government's assurances that there would be no interference with the legitimate activities of American leaf tobacco merchants in the province, and ask that the Hsuchang authorities be directed to conform strictly to the tenor of those assurances and that you be informed promptly by telegraph as soon as this has been done."

No report has yet been received from Hankow, and the Embassy is now requesting Shanghai to ascertain from the Lienhwa Company whether the obstructions have been removed. If difficulties still exist, the Embassy plans to instruct Hankow to send a consular officer to Hsuchang to deal with the matter direct.

Nanking, Shanghai and Hankow have been kept currently informed.

JOHNSON

893.659 Matches/18

Memorandum by Mr. Myrl S. Myers of the Division of Far Eastern Affairs

[WASHINGTON,] October 30, 1936.

Conversation: Mr. Atterberg, New York Match Company, New York;
Mr. Mackay; [67]
Mr. Myers.

Mr. Atterberg stated that he was calling in the interest of the American Far Eastern Match Company, Federal Incorporated, and

[67] Raymond C. Mackay, of the Division of Far Eastern Affairs.

the River Trading Company, Federal Incorporated, both of Shanghai, which companies were owned by the Swedish Match Company, and that American interests owned approximately twenty percent of the last-named company. He referred to the Chinese "Match Sales Union" at Shanghai which he stated was expected to have control of the sale of tax stamps and the issuance of permits for the importation of match materials, and said that although these American companies had had no difficulty in securing permits for the importation of chemicals in the past, it was feared that they might be refused import permits in the future. He stated that he had been given the impression that the American Consulate General at Shanghai or the American Embassy had intimated to these above-mentioned firms in Shanghai that if they joined the union the American Government would not give them assistance.

Mr. Mackay and Mr. Myers glanced through the recent files on this case and pointed out that there appeared to be no basis for such a statement. They explained the situation in regard to this matter as it was set forth in the files and referred to this Government's attitude of opposition to monopolies. Mr. Atterberg was informed to the effect that, with regard to the question whether, in the light of all the factors involved, it would be advisable for the aforementioned Federal Incorporated Companies to effect a working arrangement with the "Match Sales Union", it would appear that decision should rest solely with the companies concerned. Mr. Atterberg was also informed to the effect that, in the event the companies under reference should be subjected to discrimination by agencies of the Chinese Government, American authorities in China, bearing in mind, however, the admitted fact that in neither of the companies does there exist a direct American interest, would render such assistance as may be deemed appropriate and practicable.

893.61331/68 : Telegram

The Ambassador in China (Johnson) to the Secretary of State

PEIPING, November 4, 1936—11 a. m.
[Received November 4—6 : 38 a. m.]

529. Embassy's 513, October 24, 2 p. m. The Embassy October 24, 2 p. m., directed Shanghai to ascertain from the Lienhwa Company whether the obstructions at Hsuchang had been removed. Hankow reported October 28, 11 a. m. as follows:

"Following is translation of telegram received today from Honan Provincial Government in reply to my telegram of October 20th:

'Your telegram of the 20th has been noted. In connection with the temporary leasing of a warehouse at Hsuchang by the Lienhwa Leaf Tobacco Company, this Government has instructed Administrative Inspector Hsu at Hsuchang to afford protection in accordance with his instructions. A special reply.'"

Shanghai reported as follows:

"October 28, 1 p. m. My October 26, noon. Lienhwa Company today received telegram from representative that Hsuchang magistrate approved lease of premises but cannot give permission for company to commence operations until Honan Provincial Government at Kaifeng approves company's buying procedure. Lienhwa Company accordingly requests that consular representative be detailed to join company's representative, Macon, at Hsuchang to proceed to Kaifeng in order to expedite matters".

The Embassy instructed Hankow as follows:

"October 31, 9 a. m. Your October 28, 11 a. m; Shanghai's October 28, 1 p. m. The American authorities in this case are concerned only with obtaining for the Lienhwa Company the right, guaranteed by the Sino-Japanese treaties of 1895 and 1896,[68] of purchasing leaf tobacco in Honan and obtaining temporary warehouse facilities for use in that connection; the American authorities would not desire to become concerned with negotiations which the company [69] in regard to its buying procedure except in so far as treaty rights are involved. In the light of these circumstances, and in view of the Hsuchang magistrate's acquiescence, as reported in Shanghai's October 28, 1 p. m., your opinion is requested as to the desirability of sending a consular officer to Hsuchang and Kaifeng. Is there still legitimate assistance to be rendered to the company of such importance as to justify such a detail?"

Hankow replied as follows:

"November 1, 2 p. m. Peiping's October 31, 9 a. m. From the information that has been furnished to this office it seems clear that there is strong local opposition to the Lienhwa Company buying and shipping leaf tobacco at Hsuchang and that the Honan authorities are not anxious to have the company commence operations there. Although some progress has been made towards removing the obstacles placed in the way of the company there is nothing to show that either the Honan authorities or the local interests opposed to the Lienhwa Company are reconciled to the company doing business at Hsuchang and that the company will not encounter further obstruction and delay. I believe it would be useful to send an officer to Hsuchang to investigate the situation on the ground. If the Embassy approves, I shall send Stevens there on November 4th (he cannot be spared sooner) with instructions to proceed to Kaifeng if as a result of his investigation he finds that direct conversations with the Provincial Government are necessary or desirable in order to obtain for the Lienhwa Company the rights to which they are entitled by treaty. He will, of course, be guided, in his decision to proceed to Kaifeng and in any conversations he may have with the authorities there or elsewhere, by the principles laid down in the Embassy's telegram of October 31, 9 a. m."

---

[68] Treaty of Commerce and Navigation, signed at Peking, July 21, 1896, MacMurray, *Treaties*, 1894–1919, vol. I, p. 68.
[69] Sentence apparently garbled at this point.

The Embassy, November 2, 1 p. m., instructed Hankow that the proposed detail of Stevens to Honan was approved under the instructions as outlined. Stevens will arrive at Hsuchang November 5.[70]

JOHNSON

893.61331/80

The Ambassador in China (Johnson) to the Secretary of State

No. 890   PEIPING, November 28, 1936.
                                          [Received December 23.]

SIR: I have the honor to refer to my despatch No. 729 of September 16, 1936, in regard to the proposed leaf tobacco monopoly, and to enclose for the information of the Department a copy in English translation of a formal note received from the Foreign Office under date November 9, in reply to the Embassy's note of June 1, 1936,[71] denying the validity of the arguments adduced by the Embassy against the establishment of the monopoly organization.

The attitude of the British and Japanese Embassies in regard to the matter will be ascertained, and the Consulate General at Shanghai is being instructed to report on recent developments. A copy of that instruction is enclosed.[72]   A new note will be sent to the Foreign Office if the information obtained makes that line of action appear desirable.

Respectfully yours,   For the Ambassador:
                                          F. P. LOCKHART
                                          Counselor of Embassy

893.6583/26

The Ambassador in China (Johnson) to the Secretary of State

No. 946   PEIPING, December 30, 1936.
                                          [Received February 20, 1937.]

SIR: I have the honor to refer to the Embassy's despatch No. 692 of September 4, 1936, on the subject of the formation of a vegetable oil monopoly, with which there was enclosed a copy of the Embassy's note of the same date to the Ministry of Foreign Affairs on this subject.[73]   The Department will recall that the Embassy requested assurances that the legitimate trade of American firms engaged in the

---

[70] The Ambassador in China in his despatch No. 881, November 27, reported that Mr. Stevens' interview with the Hsuchang magistrate bore favorable results, as the Lien Hwa Company could commence buying operations (893.61331/79).
[71] None printed.
[72] Not printed.
[73] Enclosure not printed.

vegetable oil business would not suffer restraints as the result of the formation of the China Vegetable Oil Corporation, the officially sponsored organization. A reply has now been received from the Ministry of Foreign Affairs under date of December 15, 1936, a copy of the translation of which is enclosed.[73a]

The Department will note that the reply merely states that no restrictions have been imposed upon the legitimate trade of American citizens. In view of the representations already made by this Embassy and by the British Embassy, and the nature of the enclosed reply from the Ministry of Foreign Affairs, I feel that nothing further need be done until we have actual evidence of restraints upon American firms engaged in the vegetable oil business. I have accordingly requested the Consulates General at Hankow and Shanghai to follow the situation closely and to notify the Embassy of any evidence that the business of American firms is suffering on account of the monopolistic activities of the China Vegetable Oil Corporation.

Respectfully yours,   For the Ambassador:
                                                            F. P. LOCKHART
                                                        Counselor of Embassy

---

893.61331/82

The Ambassador in China (Johnson) to the Secretary of State

No. 953   PEIPING, January 4, 1937.
                                            [Received February 20.]

SIR: I have the honor to refer to the Embassy's despatch No. 824 of November 5, 1936, with which there was enclosed a copy of an *Aide-Mémoire* delivered on October 30, 1936, to the Ministry of Foreign Affairs at Nanking by Counselor Peck on the subject of monopoly rights granted to a Chinese corporation to manufacture mentholated and anisated cigarettes from certain recipes, and to enclose a copy of the translation of the Ministry of Foreign Affairs' undated third person note in reply thereto.[74]

The note states that exclusive patent rights to use certain recipes in the manufacture of mentholated and anisated cigarettes have been granted to the Philippine Chinese Tobacco Company for a period of five years, but adds that other mentholated and anisated cigarettes, the recipes for which differ from those used by the Philippine Chinese Tobacco Company, are not affected by the exclusive rights granted to this company. The note goes on to state that "There is no intention to effect monopoly control over the tobacco industry".

Since there is a technical question involved concerning which the Embassy is not competent to express an opinion, I am instructing

[73a] Not printed.
[74] None printed.

the Consulate General at Shanghai to request the representatives of the American interests concerned in this matter to give the Embassy the benefit of their views as to whether the granting of an exclusive right to use these recipes will adversely affect the interests of the American firms already in the field. It is the Embassy's present opinion that if the recipes referred to in the enclosed note differ from those used by the American firms, then no question of monopoly of the market for mentholated and anisated cigarettes would appear to be involved. This situation would, however, be changed if the Chinese Government should grant to a native manufacturer of cigarettes the exclusive patent rights to use the identical recipes used in American mentholated and anisated cigarettes manufactured in China.

Respectfully yours, For the Ambassador:

F. P. LOCKHART

Counselor of Embassy

REJECTION BY THE UNITED STATES OF APPLICATION OF CHINESE INCOME TAX TO AMERICAN CITIZENS

893.5123/6 : Telegram

The Ambassador in China (Johnson) to the Secretary of State

PEIPING, August 11, 1936—4 p. m.
[Received 5 : 20 p. m.]

401. The Embassy at Nanking has transmitted under cover of a despatch dated July 31 a translation of the Chinese "Provisional Income Tax Regulations." Copies of the despatch were sent directly to the Department and should be received within the next week or 10 days.[75]

The regulations were promulgated by a National Government mandate dated July 21 of this year. The date of enforcement has not yet been fixed but it is understood that the Chinese authorities plan to enforce the regulations as of September 1. No communication on the subject has yet been received from the Foreign Office by this Embassy or the other diplomatic missions here, but it is understood that the Foreign Office will shortly address the various missions, requesting that the tax be paid by the foreign nationals concerned.

The British Embassy by authority states that it is suggesting to the British Chargé d'Affaires, now at Peitaiho, that, if a communication is received from the Foreign Office, he reply that the matter has been referred to the British Foreign Office. The British Embassy here is suggesting to the Chargé d'Affaires that he recommend to the British Foreign Office that the Chinese authorities be informed that the British Government cannot consent to the payment of the tax by British

---

[75] Not printed.

subjects unless it is also paid by other foreign nationals. I believe that we might adopt a similar attitude.

I will telegraph the Department any further information received concerning the views of the various diplomatic missions and will report if and when a note is received from the Foreign Office. I will appreciate receiving the Department's instructions when it has received and considered Nanking's despatch mentioned above.

JOHNSON

893.5123/7 : Telegram

The Ambassador in China (Johnson) to the Secretary of State

PEIPING, September 3, 1936—2 p. m.
[Received September 3—9 : 48 a. m.]

430. Embassy's 401, August 11, 4 p. m., concerning Chinese income tax law. Rules for enforcement of provisional income tax regulations were adopted by the Executive Yuan on August 25 and published in the National Government *Gazette*. According to these rules, the regulations are to be effective October 1, but no mandate has been issued. According to press reports, collections from the public functionaries and on bank deposits and bonds will commence October 1, but collections on other categories will not commence until January 1, next. It is understood that exemption from the payment of the tax will be granted diplomatic officials of countries which accord similar treatment to Chinese diplomatic officials.

This Embassy has received a note dated August 25 from the Foreign Office, transmitting copies of the regulations and requesting that American nationals be instructed to comply therewith. Similar notes have been received by the other diplomatic missions.

French Embassy replied September 1 to the Foreign Office, pointing out that under article 40 of the Treaty of Tientsin of 1858 [76] no obligation of this nature could be imposed upon French nationals in China.

Japanese Embassy is understood to have instructed Japanese subjects to ignore the regulations.

British Embassy is merely acknowledging the receipt of the note with the statement that the matter is being referred to the British Foreign Office. British Embassy believes that the British Foreign Office will take the position that the British Government cannot consent to the payment of the tax by British subjects unless it is also paid by other foreign nationals.

I respectfully recommend that this Embassy reply to the Foreign Office, stating that the American Government cannot acquiesce in the

---

[76] Signed June 27, 1858, *British and Foreign State Papers*, vol. LI, pp. 636, 650.

payment of the tax by American nationals unless it is paid by other foreign nationals. The Department's telegraphic instructions will be appreciated.

Atcheson [77] reported September 2, 9 a. m., that an American correspondent was informed by an official of the Ministry of Finance that the Chinese Government anticipated opposition by treaty powers and was merely placing the matter on record for future use in the event of favorable replies from diplomatic missions to the Foreign Office note of August 25.

JOHNSON

893.5123/8 : Telegram

The Ambassador in China (Johnson) to the Secretary of State

PEIPING, September 5, 1936—1 p. m.
[Received September 5—6 : 30 a. m.]

436. Embassy's 430, September 3, 2 p. m. Following mandate dated September 2d was published in National Government *Gazette* September 3d:

"October 1, 1936 is hereby designated as the date for the enforcement of the provisional income tax regulations.

The collection of the income tax on salaries and emoluments of public service functionaries and on interest accrued on Government bonds and deposits, referred to in the regulations as income under classes B and C, respectively, shall commence on January 1, 1937".

JOHNSON

893.5123/10 : Telegram

The Secretary of State to the Ambassador in China (Johnson)

WASHINGTON, September 16, 1936—6 p. m.

224. Your 401, August 11, 4 p. m.; 430, September 3, 2 p. m.; 436, September 5, 1 p. m.; and 444, September 12, 3 p. m.,[78] in regard to the Chinese income tax law.

1. The Department, in its instruction No. 405 of May 22, 1923,[79] stated, in regard to taxation in China, that between the extremes presented by the French Treaty of 1858 (the provisions of which accrue to American nationals by virtue of the most-favored-nation clause in American treaties with China), and our treaty of 1903 [80] an equitable medium might be found which would allow a reasonable exercise by China of the ordinary sovereign rights in fiscal matters, and at the same time prevent abuse of power through the imposition of undue

---

[77] George Atcheson, Jr., Second Secretary of Embassy in China.
[78] Telegram No. 444 not printed.
[79] *Foreign Relations*, 1923, vol. I, p. 582.
[80] Signed at Shanghai, October 8, 1903, *ibid.*, 1903, p. 91.

burdens upon foreigners residing or doing business in China. Having in mind the concluding clause in the preceding sentence in relation to the character of the Chinese income tax, the Department feels that it would not be advisable or practicable to reply to the Foreign Office in the sense recommended in your telegram of September 3, 2 p. m.

2. In view of the character of the income tax, its high rates on average incomes, the difficulty of orderly and impartial administration, and considerations connected with the collection of the tax from American nationals, the Department at this time is disinclined to indicate approval, even by implication, of the income tax regulations in their present form or conditional acquiescence in their application to American nationals.

3. The Department desires therefore that you inform the Chinese Foreign Office, in reply to its note of August 25, enclosing copies of the provisional income tax regulations, that the regulations cannot be considered applicable to American nationals.[81]

HULL

893.5123/11 : Telegram

The Counselor of Embassy in China (Peck) to the Secretary of State

NANKING, September 17, 1936—7 p. m.
[Received September 17—5 : 35 p. m.]

270. 1. The Minister of Finance [82] today discussed with me Chinese income tax enforcement. He asked me to convey to the American Government his earnest hope that the American Government would be generous in its attitude toward payment of this tax by American citizens in China. I told him the Embassy had not yet received the Department's instruction in regard to this subject. Kung said there was no reason in law or equity why foreigners in China should not pay that tax. Foreigners residing in other countries pay the local income tax and the Chinese rates are relatively low. He was especially anxious that American firms should deduct the income tax from salaries of Chinese employees in accordance with the law and that American banks should deduct the tax from income derived by Chinese from deposits in such banks.

2. Kung alluded to the moral obligations resting on foreigners to pay income tax in consideration of privileges attached to their residence. He said that although the United States was traditionally China's foremost friend apparently in the matter of this tax Great Britain had shown the way to other nations, since the new British Ambassador arrived in China broadly said British subjects would pay

---

[81] See footnote 83, p. 632.
[82] H. H. Kung.

the tax if all other foreigners did so. Kung emphasized that unless the tax were actually collected from all other nationalities including Japanese no effort would be made to collect from Americans.

3. Sent to the Department and Peiping.

PECK

893.5123/12 : Telegram

The Secretary of State to the Ambassador in China (Johnson)

WASHINGTON, September 19, 1936—3 p. m.

226. Nanking's 270, September 17, 7 p. m. to Department; Department's 224, September 16, 6 p. m.; and your 453, September 18, 6 p. m.,[83] in regard to the Chinese income tax law.

In the event you feel that Kung's approach to Peck, as reported in Nanking's telegram under reference, calls for a reply, you are authorized to instruct Peck to call informally on Kung (at a convenient time after the delivery to the Foreign Office of your note of September 22) and make an oral reply in the sense of paragraph 2 of the Department's instruction above mentioned. Peck may add that our decision in regard to the tax was reached after careful and sympathetic consideration but that the Department would be prepared to give further consideration to the matter in the event that all other governments concerned should acquiesce in the imposition of an income tax on their respective nationals.

With regard to the last sentence in paragraph 1 of Nanking's telegram, Peck should explain to Kung that American firms could not be expected to act as agencies of the Chinese Government in the collection of the tax from Chinese citizens.

HULL

893.5123/13 : Telegram

The Counselor of Embassy in China (Peck) to the Secretary of State

NANKING, September 23, 1936—9 a. m.
[Received 3 : 30 p. m.]

276. Department's 226, September 19, 3 p. m., to Peiping and Peiping's September 21, 11 a. m. to Nanking.

1. Note to Foreign Office dated September 18 stating that the regulations governing income tax cannot be considered as applicable

---

[83] The Ambassador in China in his telegram No. 453, September 18, 6 p. m., reported that the Embassy was addressing a note to the Chinese Foreign Office in compliance with paragraph 3 of the Department's No. 224, the note to be delivered September 22.

to American nationals was delivered morning of 22nd and I called on the Minister of Finance September 22, 6 p. m.

2. I told Kung that the Ambassador had just sent to the Foreign Office a reply concerning income tax and I repeated its phraseology. I then said that I had been directed to deliver a reply to the oral message he asked me to transmit on September 17. Following this I gave in informal language the purport of the observations set down in the Department's September 19, 3 p. m.

3. There ensued a rather lengthy discussion the upshot of which was that Kung felt disappointed and hurt [84] at the boldness of the Ambassador's reply which was a simple assertion that "the regulations cannot be considered as applicable to American nationals". Kung again referred to the press item quoting an oral statement by the newly arrived British Ambassador (See my September 17, 7 p. m.) which, although conditioning payment of the income tax by British nationals on its payment by all other nationals, nevertheless gave him some moral support in initiating this new tax. Part of the *China Press* September 14 stated in effect that the British Ambassador informed a reporter that Great Britain was not opposed to the measure *per se;* that similar taxes were collected by other governments and that the British Government saw no reason for objecting to the tax if it were paid by citizens of other countries. Kung observed that the attitude of the American people toward China had always been characterized by fair play and generosity and he had not expected that in connection with the income tax the United States would evince a less friendly attitude than Great Britain. He remarked that he quite understood that the American Government might entertain objections to features of the income tax law itself such as its comparatively heavy incidence on incomes in very low brackets, which features were occasioned by standards of living peculiar to China, but having regretted the public impression which would be created by the statement made in the Embassy's notifications to the Foreign Office without explanation or qualification that the law could not be considered as applicable to American nationals. Kung said that he personally had endeavored to frame an equitable tax law which would not be oppressive in its rates or mode [of] collection and he stressed the urgent need of the Chinese Government for additional funds wherever [possible?] to carry out vital projects such as currency reform. He explained that tax declarations regarding incomes would be accepted at face value and demands for documentary evidence would be exceptional.

---

[84] The Acting Secretary of State in his telegram No. 229, September 24, 6 p. m., to the Ambassador in China stated: "It is regretted that Kung felt disappointed and hurt at the tone of the Embassy's note." (893.5123/15.)

4. In connection with Kung's apparently strong feeling on this subject I venture the explanation that he believes his reputation is closely involved in the success of the income tax as a measure widely used, the justice of which is almost universally acknowledged. He evidently attaches great importance to the arguments referred to in paragraph 2 of my September 17, 7 p. m. He apparently overlooks the fact that rejection of the application of the law to American nationals on grounds of imperfections in the law would hardly have benefited his situation, although he insists he would have had no objection to an acceptance conditioned on actual application to all nationalities. I was appropriate in my comments but the interview ended with Kung apparently feeling much less agreeable than at the beginning.

5. Sent to the Department and Peiping.

PECK

893.5123/14 : Telegram

The Counselor of Embassy in China (Peck) to the Secretary of State

NANKING, September 23, 1936—2 p. m.
[Received September 23—2 p. m.]

277. My 276, September 23, 9 a. m.

1. So far as this office can learn the only formal replies sent by foreign diplomatic missions to the Foreign Office regarding application of income tax to foreign residents have been from the French and American Embassies (see Peiping's September 3, 2 p. m., paragraph 3).

2. Chargé d'Affaires of Belgium expressed to me yesterday the personal view that although the treaty of November 22, 1928,[85] might be interpreted as requiring payment of the tax by his nationals, nevertheless he felt that the treaty would warrant their claim to most-favored-nation treatment. He had received no instructions.

3. The German Chargé d'Affaires yesterday told me he had sent in no reply but that although without extra territorial jurisdiction Germany would claim exemption on the ground of an oral assurance given by Foreign Minister C. T. Wang[86] some years ago that surrender of extraterritorial jurisdiction would not subject German nationals to discriminatory treatment in matters of this sort.

4. Sent to the Department and Peiping.

PECK

[85] Treaty of Amity and Commerce, signed at Nanking, November 22, 1928, League of Nations Treaty Series, vol. LXXXVII, p. 288.
[86] C. T. Wang, Chinese Minister for Foreign Affairs at Peiping, 1924–25, and at Nanking, 1928–31.

RESERVATION OF AMERICAN RIGHTS IN PROPOSED CHANGES FOR
CONTROL OF PILOTAGE AT SHANGHAI [87]

893.825/81

The Ambassador in China (Johnson) to the Secretary of State

No. 658

PEIPING, August 19, 1936.
[Received September 21.]

SIR: I have the honor to refer to the Legation's despatch No. 3655
of July 2, 1935,[88] concerning the Shanghai pilotage question, and to
enclose for the information and records of the Department copies
of the following further correspondence on the matter:

[Here follows list of enclosures; none printed.]

Consul General Gauss [89] reported in his despatch No. 165 of May 5,
1936,[88] that at a Consular Body meeting held on that day the Senior
Consul distributed copies of a confidential memorandum which was
being communicated by the Inspector General of Customs, through
the Commissioner of Customs at Shanghai, to the Shanghai Licensed
Pilots Association. This memorandum proposed a settlement of the
impasse in the pilotage question on the following basis:

1. That consent will be given to filling the existing vacancies by
the appointment of two British and one German candidates, in accordance with the pilotage fee percentage arrangement, provided:

2. That in yielding to the Association in this instance China does
not prejudice her position in the final settlement of the pilotage question and is not to be construed as relinquishing the Government's
title to fill vacancies in the ranks of Government licensed pilots with
properly qualified Chinese candidates, irrespective of the amount of
pilotage fees paid by Chinese shipping; and

3. That in view of the fact there are at present certain countries
whose quota of pilots is in excess of the number allowable according
to the percentage of pilotage fees paid by these countries, it is to be
understood that, as a temporary expedient pending the final settlement of the pilotage question, whenever vacancies occur in the case
of a country the number of whose pilots happens to be in excess of the
quota allowable according to the percentage of pilotage fees paid,
such vacancies shall be filled by qualified Chinese pilots so as to bring
China's quota of pilots temporarily to a total of six.

Mr. Gauss stated that it was explained that acceptance of this arrangement would cause no disturbance of the quotas then in operation,
except when a vacancy occurred in the case of a country whose quota
was in excess of that to which it was entitled by the percentage of
pilotage fees paid.

---

[87] Continued from *Foreign Relations*, 1935, vol. III, pp. 797–800.
[88] Not printed.
[89] Clarence E. Gauss, Consul General at Shanghai.

The Japanese Consul General took exception to the proposed arrangement and the French Consul General made a reservation of decision in the matter. The British Consul General was disposed to accept the arrangement, pointing out that it represented a practical solution of the matter for the present and that it would take some few years before the total of six Chinese pilots would be reached. Mr. Gauss doubted whether the pilots were entitled to accept such an arrangement without the assent of the interested consular representatives, and stated that he was prepared to submit the matter to his Embassy with the recommendation that the solution be accepted. The British Consul General having questioned whether it would not be better to have the acceptance come from the pilots rather than from the interested powers, Mr. Gauss stated that he had no objection to that procedure but he believed that the pilots should not be expected to accept the proposal without the acquiescence of their interested consular representatives.

Mr. Gauss requested in his despatch referred to above that he be instructed whether the Embassy approved acceptance of the solution proposed and also if he should indicate acceptance of the solution so far as American pilots were concerned, whether or not the Japanese and French were prepared to do so with reference to their pilots. He stated that he believed that instructions so to accept should be issued, to be followed in the event that the British Consul General and the majority of the other interested consular representatives were prepared likewise to accept with reference to their pilots independently of the Japanese and French attitude. Mr. Gauss added that he had been informed that the Inspector General of Customs had encountered great difficulty in persuading the Nanking Government to agree to the solution proposed in his memorandum and that he (the Inspector General) felt that it was the best that could be obtained under the circumstances. The proposal would provide for an eventual increase of Chinese pilots from three to six, out of a total of thirty-six pilots.

The Embassy informed Mr. Gauss in its telegraphic instruction of May 11, 3 p. m.[91] that it approved the acceptance of the proposed solution along the lines indicated by him.

Mr. Gauss reported in his telegram of May 26, 2 p. m.[91] that all interested consular representatives favored acceptance of the proposed solution except the Japanese and the French, the latter's attitude being indefinite. Mr. Gauss stated that, confronted with this fact, the Japanese Consul General said that he could of course not prevent his colleagues from accepting the proposal but that at the right time he would negotiate with the Chinese authorities with a view to maintaining and even increasing the present number of Jap-

---

[91] Not printed.

anese pilots, and that he would proceed without regard to the quota system which now determines the nationality of the foreign pilots. Mr. Gauss discussed this matter in his despatch No. 204 of May 26,[92] stating that he felt that the Japanese Consul General had overplayed his hand in the threat he had made to move for more Japanese pilots and to disregard the quota arrangement. He considered that the British pilotage association and pilot company were in a good position to offset any Japanese effort to that end in view of the fact that, while the Japanese might be able to force the Chinese authorities to appoint more Japanese pilots, it did not follow that such Japanese pilots would be entitled to the use of the floating equipment of the pilot boat company or that they would be entitled to membership in the (British) pilots association. Furthermore, it did not follow that, with their appointment as licensed pilots, foreign flag vessels would be required to employ them as pilots for their vessels. So long as the pilots association remains in existence and is recognized, the foreign flag vessels may apply to the association for the assignment of pilots.

Mr. Gauss reported in his telegram of June 12, 10 a. m. and his despatch No. 237 of June 12 [93] that the British Consul General had on June 11 addressed a letter to the manager of the Shanghai Licensed Pilots Association, requesting him to advise the British members of the association that he had received instructions from the British Foreign Office through the British Embassy to advise acceptance of the arrangement for filling vacancies in the association offered in the memorandum handed to the association by the customs authorities on May 5, 1936, the acceptance to contain the reservation that it was without prejudice to a final settlement of the pilotage question by the national authorities concerned. Mr. Gauss regretted that the British Consul General had not consulted with his colleagues before giving his advice to the British pilots, but stated that the action taken conformed in general to that which he had recommended should be taken by the American authorities. Mr. Gauss requested that he be authorized to give similar advice to the American pilots and, this having been granted in the Embassy's telegraphic instruction of June 13, 10 a. m.,[92] he addressed the following letter under date June 13 to the American members of the Pilots Association:

"With the approval of the American Embassy, I write to advise acceptance of the arrangement for filling vacancies in the Association offered in the memorandum of the Commissioner of Customs of May 5th last. The acceptance should contain the reservation that it is without prejudice to a final settlement of the pilotage question by the national authorities concerned."

---

[92] Not printed.
[93] Neither printed.

Mr. Gauss reported in his despatch No. 237 of June 12 that the Inspector General of Customs had agreed unofficially and informally that the matter would be considered settled if the Pilots Association would address the Commissioner of Customs as follows:

"The members of the Shanghai Licensed Pilots Association for their part, accept the arrangement for filling vacancies in the Association embodied in the memorandum received from the Commissioner of Customs on May 5, 1936, without prejudice to a final settlement of the pilotage question by the national authorities concerned."

Mr. Gauss enclosed with his despatch No. 259 of June 24 a copy of the Senior Consul's circular of June 22,[95] from which it will be noted that the members of the Pilots Association agreed "unanimously" to accept the arrangement for filling vacancies proposed in the memorandum of May 5 from the Commissioner of Customs.   Mr. Gauss stated that this meant that the Japanese pilots had joined with their American, British, German and other associates in accepting the proposed solution. He added, however, that it was known that the Japanese Consul General continued to maintain his views in opposition to the settlement.[96]

Further developments will be reported to the Department.

Respectfully yours,   NELSON TRUSLER JOHNSON

ASSISTANCE TO PAN AMERICAN AIRWAYS IN SECURING RIGHTS NEEDED TO EXTEND ITS UNITED STATES-PHILIPPINE SERVICE TO CHINA [97]

811.79690 Pan American Airways/47a : Telegram

The Secretary of State to the Ambassador in China (Johnson)

WASHINGTON, February 27, 1936—5 p. m.

17. On February 14 an anonymous news item appeared in *Washington Post* under headline "U. S. Negotiates on Clipper Ship Base in China: Diplomats Seek to Overcome Japan's Objections in Orient," in which, after considerable detail, the writer states "Postoffice and airline officials, however, are confident that Japanese objections to the Manila–China link can be smoothed out 'within a month'. Whatever the outcome of these diplomatic efforts to pour oil on

---

[95] Neither printed.
[96] The Ambassador in China in his despatch No. 1201, April 22, 1937, reported that "the Japanese have shown no disposition during the past ten months to break away from the present quota system and to press for an increase in the number of Japanese pilots, although it was intimated by Consul General Ishii in May of last year that such a course of action was being considered." (893.825/85)
[97] For previous correspondence on the subject of civil aviation in China, see *Foreign Relations*, 1935, vol. III, pp. 800 ff.

troubled Oriental waters, Pan American, it was stated, would go through with its plans to link the Philippines and China".

Far Eastern Division inquired of Pan American officials and was told that the latter thought Post Office Department was pressing Chinese postal administration. Conference with Post Office officials discloses that Post Office Department has made no such move; and it has been agreed that neither Post Office Department nor this Department will make any move in the matter without previous consultation.

Department requests such information as you can give with regard to any conversations or negotiations in China out of which the newspaper story referred to above might have arisen.

For guidance, Department desires that American official representatives in China make no moves in this matter without previously consulting Department.

HULL

811.79690 Pan American Airways/48 : Telegram

The Ambassador in China (Johnson) to the Secretary of State

NANKING, February 29, 1936—noon.
[Received February 29—9 : 50 a. m.]

45. Your 17, February 27, 5 p. m.

1. The press in China has carried announcements of the arrangements made for Pan American planes to fly to the Portuguese controlled port of Macao but I have heard of no objection made by the Japanese to this project nor do I know of any negotiations for a "clipper ship base in China".

2. On January 13 Bixby, vice president of Pan American Airways, called on me in Peiping and handed me a letter from himself stating that his company had concluded arrangements with the Portuguese colony for operating rights and an air mail contract which entitled the company to transport mail originating in Macao from Macao to the Philippines and the United States and mail from the United States and the Philippines to Macao. Contract does not cover air mail from places in China to the United States or to the Philippines. The letter stated that the Chinese Government had made an arrangement with the French for an air line between Canton and Hanoi (see Nanking telegram 26, October 4, 11 a. m.[98]) and that the Chinese were unwilling to make similar arrangements with Portugal whereby air mail might be exchanged in Macao between China mail planes and the Pan American planes and complained of the discrimination. The letter asked that I take informal action to obtain Chinese consent to such an arrangement. Bixby informed me orally that the Portuguese at Macao would

---

[98] Not printed.

welcome such an exchange whether or not the mail passed through the Macao post office.

3. I wrote to Peck [99] on January 14 asking him to say to Kung, Minister of Finance, in my name that Pan American had made arrangements to connect San Francisco with Macao and to ask him to use his influence in the Government to bring about calling of Chinese planes at Macao to make possible exchange of mail. Kung told Peck October [*January*] 15 that he thought it would not be difficult to get authorization for the pacts in view of the fact that the proposal of the American company did not involve landing American planes in China. On January 25 Peck inquired about the matter incidentally at the Ministry of Communications and found it was at a deadlock. On January 26th he talked with Kung again and Kung suggested that the easiest way to achieve the result would be for the Portuguese Government first to inform the Chinese Government that it would have no objection to the arrangement. Peck conveyed this idea to Bixby. Peck suggested to me that he be authorized to see the Minister for Foreign Affairs in order to acquaint him with the status of the company's application and I said I saw no objection to this. On February 8 Bond of Pan American told Peck that Pan American had instructed its agent at Lisbon to present to the Portuguese Government the plan suggested by Kung and fearing that this might be carried out and find the Foreign Office without information regarding it Peck called on Vice Minister Hsu Mo the same day and described the situation. Hsu Mo said that if the Portuguese Government gave the suggested notification the Chinese Government would consider it. On February 13 I thanked Kung for his helpful cooperation and he showed a desire to have project succeed. No further conversation[s with] Chinese officials have occurred. As the matter stands the Chinese Government is awaiting an approach from the Portuguese Government.

4. The Department will note that this whole project is one for which Pan American Airways, a private American company, is attempting to gain the approval of the Chinese authorities. Discussions have been in progress between company officials and Chinese officials for several months. The informal and exclusively oral discussions between Embassy officials and Chinese officials have been intended merely to assist the company in its efforts to bring about contact between the Chinese Government's planes and its own planes at Macao a port not under Chinese jurisdiction through making Macao a landing station for Chinese planes already flying between Shanghai and Canton.

---

[99] Willys R. Peck, Counselor of Embassy in China at Nanking.

Full reports of above will be forwarded the Department by mail.[1]

JOHNSON

811.79690/Pan American Airways/63

The Ambassador in China (Johnson) to the Secretary of State

No. 473   PEIPING, May 22, 1936.
[Received June 15.]

SIR: I have the honor to refer to despatch No. 163 of May 14, 1936, to the Department from the Embassy at Nanking,[2] with regard to the delay of the Portuguese Government in authorizing the exchange of air mail at Macau between planes of the China National Aviation Corporation and planes of the Pan American Airways, and to enclose a copy (received at Peiping May 19) of a memorandum of a conversation [2] which took place on April 18, 1936, at Nanking, between the Counselor of Embassy and Mr. Harold Bixby, Director of the China National Aviation Corporation, in which Mr. Bixby expressed the surmise that the delay of the Portuguese Government was the result of pressure exerted by the British Government and that the New York office of Pan American Airways had learned that the British authorities would continue such pressure until the Chinese Government should give the British Imperial Airways the right to fly its planes over Chinese territory.

Respectfully yours,   NELSON TRUSLER JOHNSON

811.79690 Pan American Airways/68

The Ambassador in China (Johnson) to the Secretary of State

No. 188   NANKING, June 15, 1936.
[Received July 13.]

SIR: I have the honor to refer to my despatch No. 163, of May 14, 1936,[2] in which I submitted information received from Mr. W. L. Bond, of China Airways, Federal Incorporated, and of the China National Aviation Corporation, concerning the prospects for an exchange of airmail between Pan American Airways and the China National Aviation Corporation at Macau.

I have the honor to state that Mr. Bond called on me on June 11, 1936, and gave information tending to show that it is now probable

---

[1] None printed. Department's telegram No. 19, March 6, 6 p. m., stated: "Department appreciates having this information and has informed Post Office Department."
[2] Not printed.

that this exchange will take place at Hong Kong, rather than at Macau. There is enclosed a Memorandum of my conversation with Mr. Bond, dated June 11, 1936,[4] which will indicate that Mr. Bond reported that the Ministry of Communications had informed the Director of the China National Aviation Corporation that the British Chargé d'Affaires [5] had recently proposed to the Ministry of Foreign Affairs that the planes of the China National Aviation Corporation call at Hong Kong, there to effect traffic arrangements with the planes of the British Imperial Airways. The British Chargé d'Affaires had attached certain conditions to this offer. The message stated that the Executive Yuan had decided to accept this offer, but to reject all the conditions, except the stipulation that British airplanes, in conditions of *force majeure*, might land in Chinese territory.

After his conversation with me Mr. Bond called on the British Chargé d'Affaires, in order to verify the facts, and subsequently told me that Mr. Howe, the Chargé d'Affaires, had informed him that the British Government had, as stated, invited the Chinese Government to send the planes of the China National Aviation Corporation to Hong Kong. Mr. Howe said, however, that the Chinese Government had stated that in accepting this offer it did so without agreeing to any conditions whatsoever, the permission granted to British planes to land in China in circumstances of *force majeure* being merely a voluntary act on its part. Mr. Bond inferred that the British Government would not object to the deletion of the "conditions", since the connection between Chinese planes and Air France at Hanoi was effected without any conditions. Mr. Bond said that Mr. Howe had been puzzled by the apparent misunderstanding in regard to "equal rights", mentioned in the enclosed memorandum, and had not succeeded in solving the mystery.

Mr. Bond seemed to think that if the China National Aviation Corporation planes actually commenced calling at Hong Kong, Pan American Airways would change its proposed China terminal from Macau to Hong Kong.

The Department may be interested in the statement made by Mr. Bond (see bottom of page 3 of the Memorandum) that the Chinese Government had granted permission to the Southwestern Aviation Corporation to conduct the connecting air line between Canton and Hanoi, via Nanning and Luchow.

Respectfully yours,

For the Ambassador:
WILLYS R. PECK
Counselor of Embassy

---

[4] Not printed.
[5] Robert George Howe.

811.79690 Pan American Airways/67

The British Ambassador (Lindsay) to the Secretary of State

No. 213   WASHINGTON, July 11, 1936.

SIR: I have the honour to inform you under instructions from His Majesty's Principal Secretary of State for Foreign Affairs that a formal application has been received by His Majesty's Government in the United Kingdom from Pan-American Airways Company for permission to extend to the Colony of Hong-Kong their proposed air service between the West Coast of America and the Philippine Islands. Copies of the letter addressed by the Company to the Secretary of State for Air and of the reply returned by the Air Ministry are enclosed herein.[6]

2. It will be observed from the latter document that His Majesty's Government have decided not to enforce for the time being the normal requirement of reciprocity in return for the granting of these facilities, but have nevertheless felt obliged to state that the grant to the Company of operating facilities in Hong Kong for a period of five years is on the understanding that, if during this period facilities are afforded by the United States Government to other nations to operate air services on the trans-Pacific route, similar facilities will automatically be afforded for the operation of British air services on that route. It is in view of the fact that the fulfilment of this understanding does not lie in the hands of Pan-American Airways but is necessarily dependent on the decisions of the United States Government that I have been instructed to communicate to you the terms of the present arrangement.

I have [etc.]   R. C. LINDSAY

811.79690 Pan American Airways/73

Memorandum by the Assistant Chief of the Division of Protocol and Conferences (Holmes)

[WASHINGTON,] August 24, 1936.

The other evening at a dinner party, I had an opportunity to discuss personally and quite unofficially with Mr. Mallet, the British Chargé d'Affaires, the British Ambassador's note of July 11, 1936, No. 213, with regard to the granting to Pan American Airways Company permission to operate an air service into, through, and away from the colony of Hong Kong.

I told Mr. Mallet that I did not quite understand the British note, in that it was not clear to me personally whether they were simply notifying us of the terms on which they had granted permission to

---

[6] Neither printed.

Pan American Airways or whether they were asking us to agree to the extension of automatic facilities in the event that we should grant rights to some third power to fly over the transpacific route during the period of five years covered by the permit to be issued by the Governor of Hong Kong to Pan American Airways. Mr. Mallet said that he would look into it and let me know. He called me the next day to say that he had studied the matter thoroughly and that the purpose of the British in sending the note was simply to notify us of their understanding with Pan American Airways. He said categorically that they were not asking us for commitment now, they only wanted us to understand that if, during the period of five years covered by the permit to Pan American Airways, we should grant flying facilities to some third power and decline a British request for reciprocal privileges, the permit of Pan American Airways would be cancelled.

811.79690 Pan American Airways/67

The Secretary of State to the British Chargé (Mallet)

WASHINGTON, August 29, 1936.

SIR: The receipt is acknowledged of the Ambassador's note No. 213, of July 11, 1936, with which was enclosed a copy of a communication addressed to Pan American Airways Company by the Secretary of State for Air,[7] in which there are set forth the conditions upon which that company is granted permission to operate an air service into, through, and away from the colony of Hong Kong.

My Government is appreciative of the courtesy of His Majesty's Government in bringing to its attention the terms of the permission granted to this American company.

In the second paragraph of the Ambassador's note the following statement is made:

"It will be observed from the latter document that His Majesty's Government have decided not to enforce for the time being the normal requirement of reciprocity in return for the granting of these facilities, but have nevertheless felt obliged to state that the grant to the Company of operating facilities in Hong Kong for a period of five years is on the understanding that, if during this period facilities are afforded by the United States Government to other nations to operate air services on the trans-Pacific route, similar facilities will automatically be afforded for the operation of British air services on that route."

In this connection, I wish to state that, if during the period under reference facilities are afforded by the United States Government to

---

[7] Latter not printed.

other nations to operate air services on the route under reference, this Government will of course be prepared to give sympathetic consideration to an application, if made, for operation by a British company of an air service on that route; but, as this Government desires to consider each such action on its merits as it arises, I am not in position at the present time to give an assurance that such facilities will automatically be afforded.

Accept [etc.]   For the Secretary of State:
R. WALTON MOORE

811.79690 Pan American Airways/76

The Ambassador in China (Johnson) to the Secretary of State

No. 697   PEIPING, September 11, 1936.
[Received October 5.]

SIR: I have the honor to refer to previous correspondence relative to the Pan American Airways, Inc., and to report that a member of my staff was informed confidentially by Mr. Harold M. Bixby, chief American executive of the China National Aviation Corporation, in Shanghai on September 3 last, that negotiations for facilities for the Pan American Airways, Inc., at both Macao and Hong Kong making possible the linking of that company's service with that of the China National Aviation Corporation would culminate favorably within a short time.

Mr. Bixby said that due to British pressure the contract which the Pan American Airways had submitted to the Portuguese Government, which had been approved by the Governor of Macao, had been rejected at Lisbon, and that the proposal made by the Portuguese authorities in return contained so many unacceptable provisions that it was impossible to revise it into a compromise draft. Mr. Bixby had assisted in drafting an entirely new contract when he arrived in New York recently after a seven-day flight from Manila, and that contract had been submitted to the Portuguese Government with virtually no hope on the part of the Pan American Airways officials that it would be accepted. They feared that an impasse in the negotiations with Portugal had been reached. Much to their astonishment, however, the British pressure apparently having been relinquished, possibly due to the British authorities' decision to invite China to send planes to Hong Kong and to Great Britain's preoccupation with the situation in Spain, the draft was accepted *in toto*. This action was particularly gratifying to the Pan American Airways since the draft included provisions for rights in the Azores even more important to the trans-Atlantic service than the rights in Macao to the trans-

Pacific service. Mr. Bixby said that it only remained now for the Portuguese authorities to invite the Chinese Government to send planes to Macao to connect with the service of the Pan American Airways, Inc. He understood that such action would be taken.

The Pan American Airways, Inc., are glad to have this link as an auxiliary or reserve and so as to maintain a stronger position vis-à-vis the British. Mr. Bixby said, moreover, that the China National Aviation Corporation would probably establish some sort of service with Macao despite the fact that its main terminus would be in Hong Kong.

The British in their negotiations with China had held out for three privileges: most-favored-nation treatment, the right to fly over China, and permission to land in Chinese territory in case of emergency. The Chinese authorities had finally been persuaded to grant the first and last of these privileges but were not willing to grant permission in writing for British aircraft to fly over Chinese territory in view of their reluctance to grant the same right to the Japanese. Upon an intimation from an American source, however, that the Chinese authorities would in fact have no objection to the flight of British planes over Chinese territory provided the right to do so did not have to be stated publicly or in writing, the new Governor of Hong Kong consented to relinquish this point in the negotiations, and arrangements have already been made for the inauguration of the China National Aviation Corporation service with Hong Kong.

Mr. Bixby felt, moreover, that as soon as the Governor, who is ill at present, is able to give consideration to the final details of the agreement providing for air facilities for the Pan American Airways, Inc., in Hong Kong the whole matter would be satisfactorily concluded.

Mr. Bixby remarked incidentally that trans-Pacific passenger service between Manila and San Francisco would be inaugurated on or about November 1, 1936.

Respectfully yours,   NELSON TRUSLER JOHNSON

811.79690 Pan American Airways/83

The Consul at Hong Kong (Donovan) to the Secretary of State

No. 430   HONG KONG, December 8, 1936.
[Received January 4, 1937.]

SIR: I have the honor to enclose herewith the articles of incorporation of the "Aeorportos Pan Americana de Macau, Limitada",[8] a company which the Pan-American Airways was compelled under Portu-

---

[8] Enclosures not printed. The Consul General at Hong Kong in his telegram of January 20, 1937, 3 p. m., stated: "The Crown Colony of Hong Kong and the Pan-American Airways have signed an agreement for the direct air transport of first class mail matter to and from the United States via the Philippines." (811.79690 Pan American Airways/84.)

guese law to organize at Macao in order to operate their airport there. The capital of the company is HK$40,000.

Under the articles of incorporation the Aeroportos Pan-Americana de Macau is empowered to construct, establish, and operate airports, aerodromes, hangars, workshops, and all ground facilities pertaining thereto, in the territory of Macao. The Society "may also engage in the representation, either through the means of agency or through other contracts, of commercial airlines as well as in their advertising, and also engage itself in the operation of airlines where such may promote its principal objects or its commercial interests."

There is nothing unusual in the articles of incorporation which are routine under Portuguese law. The full text taken from the *Boletim Oficial De Macau* of October 31, 1936, is enclosed herewith.

It is learned from reliable sources in Hong Kong that Japan is still desirous of establishing an air line from Japan to Bangkok but that their inability to obtain landing facilities at some point between Formosa and Bangkok is a stumbling block.[9] It is difficult to see, however, how the British can refuse them facilities at Hong Kong when such privileges have been accorded to the United States and China, according to the same informant.[*]

It is also understood that Great Britain would like to have landing facilities on Hainan Island but how actively they are pushing the matter cannot be ascertained.

Respectfully yours, HOWARD DONOVAN

ATTITUDE OF THE DEPARTMENT OF STATE WITH RESPECT TO THE APPLICATION OF CHINESE LAWS TO AMERICAN INSURANCE COMPANIES DOING BUSINESS IN CHINA

893.506/36

The Secretary of State to the Ambassador in China (Johnson)

No. 111 WASHINGTON, March 9, 1936.

SIR: The receipt is acknowledged of the Embassy's confidential despatch No. 20 (from Nanking) of October 17, 1935,[10] in regard to a request made by the representatives in China of American insurance companies that representations be made to the Chinese Government with a view to obtaining certain modifications of the Insurance Enterprise Law, promulgated on July 5, 1935, which modifications the companies allege are essential for the proper conduct of insurance business in China by foreign companies. There are enclosed [11] with the des-

---

[9] For information regarding the establishment of Japanese civil aviation service with North China, see pp. 359–364, *passim*.
[*] Mr. H. M. Bixby, Vice-President, Pan American Airways. [Footnote in the original.]
[10] Not printed.
[11] Enclosures not printed.

patch copies of letters from the representatives of the American insurance companies giving their views on this legislation; a copy of a letter from the British Embassy transmitting copies of a note and a memorandum from the British Ambassador to the Chinese Foreign Office; and a copy of a memorandum, prepared by Counselor Peck,[12] reviewing the position and rights claimed by the American insurance companies under existing treaties and setting forth his conclusions. The Embassy states that it is in substantial accord with the conclusions reached on Counselor Peck's memorandum which are to the effect that the treaties do not confer on American insurance companies the right to operate in China in disregard of Chinese laws and it requests the Department's instructions as to the nature of the rights which may be claimed by the American insurance companies in China and as to the nature of the recommendations, if any, which the Department desires that the Embassy make to the Chinese Government in the matter.

It is observed that the request of the American companies appears to be based on the contention that under existing treaties they "are under no legal obligation to comply with any regulations issued by the Chinese central or local authorities" and that although they do not request complete exemption from the application of the Insurance Enterprise Law they have registered definite objection to the application to them of certain provisions of the law, particularly the provisions relating to registration, guarantee deposits, limitations of activities of insurance companies to treaty ports, et cetera.

The companies have not cited any particular treaty or treaty provisions in support of their claim to exemption from Chinese regulation of their business. With a view to determining whether their claim has any treaty basis, the Department has examined all treaties between the United States and China which are in force. This examination has disclosed that there is no treaty provision which specifically confers any rights on or grants any exemption to American insurance companies as such in China. However, Article III of the Treaty of 1903 [13] contains the following provision which seems to be pertinent to the question under consideration:

"Citizens of the United States may frequent, reside and carry on trade, industries and manufactures, or pursue any lawful avocation, in all the ports or localities of China which are now open or may hereafter be opened to foreign residence and trade; . . ." [14] (underscoring by Department).

It is clear from the Chinese text of the treaty that the word "avocation" is used in the sense of vocation, or regular or habitual employment.

---

[12] Willys R. Peck, Counselor of Embassy in China at Nanking.
[13] Signed at Shanghai, October 8, 1903; Foreign Relations, 1903, p. 91.
[14] Omission indicated in the original instruction.

While the Department has taken the position that it will not assert in behalf of American nationals in China rights which are not conferred by the treaties either expressly or by clear implication, the Department does not consider that treaty rights or immunities must be held to be limited to enterprises which are specifically named in the treaties. In Article III of the Treaty of 1903 above quoted, insurance business is not named specifically, but it will not be questioned that insurance is included in the English and Chinese texts of the phrase "all other lawful avocations" and that it was so recognized at the time the treaty was concluded, as insurance business was then well established in China and throughout the world as a legitimate business activity. It should be noted, however, that the right granted by this treaty is limited to the treaty ports of China, and in the absence of a more extensive grant in a treaty between China and some other power to the benefits of which the United States would be entitled by virtue of the most-favored-nation clause, insurance companies could not claim the right to conduct their business beyond the limits of the ports opened to foreign trade. It appears, therefore, that American insurance companies may properly claim a treaty right to carry on insurance business in the treaty ports of China. In the event the companies produce satisfactory evidence in support of their contention that they are entitled to do business in the interior through native brokers or agents, the Embassy would be warranted in asserting such a right in their behalf. This conclusion suggests the query whether the exercise of the right conferred by the treaty is subject to any control or regulation by the Chinese Government or whether the Government of China, having surrendered jurisdiction over American nationals in China, must be held to have relinquished the right to exercise any control over business authorized by the treaties and conducted by American nationals.

It appears to be true, as stated by Counselor Peck, that the Department has never taken the position that extraterritorial status confers on American citizens in China the right to engage in any unspecified variety of activity they desire, free of any form of Chinese control. The Department has, however, consistently maintained the position that American citizens in the conduct of activities permitted by the treaties could not be made subject to Chinese laws and regulations, the effect of which would be to deny or materially impair their extraterritorial status or to nullify a right granted by treaty to carry on an authorized activity. While the Department has always stressed the importance and desirability of cooperation with the Chinese authorities so as to give the fullest recognition to legitimate Chinese interests affected by American activities and to facilitate the intercourse of Americans and Chinese, it has, nevertheless, insisted on the right of American citizens to exemption from the compulsory application of Chinese laws and regulations involving control of American activities by Chinese authorities.

The excerpts from the Department's instructions which are quoted in Counselor Peck's memorandum seem to confirm the views expressed herein, particularly the instruction of August 2, 1922 [15] (to the Legation at Peking), relating to fire insurance companies in Canton; the instruction of August 28, 1923,[15] relating to American practitioners of medicine; and the instruction of June 5, 1930,[16] relating to hospitals. The case of the China Searchlight Publishing Company,[17] cited by Mr. Peck as an indication that the Department did not consider the activities of American citizens immune from interference by the Chinese Government, involved the grossly improper activities of an American citizen in conducting a campaign of vilification against the Chinese Government and officials and was regarded by the Department as a gross abuse of the hospitality of China which could not be countenanced by this Government, although unfortunately there appeared to be no American law under which any effective action by American representatives could be taken. In this situation the Chinese Government was informed that the Government of the United States would interpose no objection to the suppression by the Chinese authorities of the publication of the company mentioned. This case clearly was exceptional and could hardly be regarded as an admission by the Department of the right of the Chinese authorities to control American activities.

While the Department is, therefore, unable to concur fully in the views expressed by Mr. Peck as to the Department's attitude with respect to the question of Chinese control of American authorized activities in China, it recognizes the force of his observations that the insurance business affects in a particular manner the rights and interests of Chinese citizens and that the conduct of this class of business should be subject to adequate governmental control and that in the absence of effective American supervision of American insurance companies in China this Government could not in good faith question the right of the Chinese Government to take reasonable measures to protect the public, particularly Chinese citizens, and to prevent abuses which might result from the operation of insurance companies not subject to any governmental control.

In summary, it appears from the above that the American insurance companies may properly claim a treaty right to conduct insurance business in treaty ports and that they may possibly be able to establish a right to do business in the interior; and that the Department has consistently maintained the position that American citizens in the

---

[15] Not printed.
[16] *Foreign Relations*, 1930, vol. II, p. 541.
[17] See telegram No. 247, September 8, 1932, 6 p. m., to the Consul General at Shanghai, *ibid.*, 1932, vol. IV, p. 660.

conduct of activities permitted by the treaties could not be made subject to Chinese laws and regulations, the effect of which would be to deny or materially impair their extraterritorial status or to nullify a right granted by treaty to carry on an authorized activity. Therefore, with a view to conserving our treaty position and obtaining a modification of the objectionable features of the Insurance Enterprise Law in the interest of the American companies, the Department desires that appropriate oral representations be made to the Chinese Foreign Office. The Department suggests that the Embassy should bring out in its conversations with the Foreign Office that this Government considers that certain provisions of the law, if enforced, would be inconsistent with the treaties and would be unduly burdensome to the companies and that as this Government desires to cooperate with the Chinese Government with a view to obtaining the proper conduct of the insurance business carried on by American concerns this Government trusts that the Chinese Government will appropriately modify the law in order to eliminate the conflict between the law and the treaties and to enable the foreign companies to cooperate with the Chinese authorities charged with the administration of the law.

Before approaching the Chinese Foreign Office, the Embassy may care to discuss with the American insurance companies the matter of the proposed oral representations to the Foreign Office and the desirability of their effecting a satisfactory arrangement with the Chinese authorities which would enable them voluntarily to comply with the law. Also, the Embassy may find it profitable before taking any steps whatever to inquire of the British Embassy in regard to the progress of the negotiations initiated by that Embassy with the Chinese Government.

The Department desires that the Embassy keep it informed of developments.

Very truly yours,

For the Secretary of State:
R. WALTON MOORE

893.506/38 : Telegram

The Ambassador in China (Johnson) to the Secretary of State

PEIPING, May 9, 1936—11 a. m.
[Received May 9—7 a. m.]

235. Department's instruction No. 111 of March 9 concerning new Chinese insurance law. Counselor Peck conferred with representatives of American insurance companies at Shanghai on April 30. They indicated a hope that the Chinese legislation might be so modified and guided as to make it possible for American insurance companies to register and otherwise conduct their business in China in

conformity with Chinese law and with the approval of the Chinese authorities without, however, waiving their legal position as extraterritorial persons. They did not think that necessity existed for any action by the Embassy for the time being but they hoped that the Embassy would be authorized to present to the Foreign Office at an opportune time written representations expressing the views of the Embassy and transmitting as from the American insurance companies a memorandum drafted by those companies setting forth features which would be desirable in Chinese legislation controlling insurance business. I respectfully suggest that the Department authorize the Embassy to act in this way.

JOHNSON

893.506/38 : Telegram

The Secretary of State to the Ambassador in China (Johnson)

WASHINGTON, May 11, 1936—6 p. m.

112. Your 235, May 9, 11 a. m. in regard to new Chinese insurance law. The Department perceives no objection to the Embassy acting in the manner indicated. It is assumed, of course, that the Embassy will avoid giving its support to any representations of the American companies which may not accord with the views expressed in the Department's instruction No. 111 of March 9.

HULL

893.506/40

The American Embassy in China to the Chinese Foreign Office [18]

The American Embassy has the honor to recall that an Insurance Business Law was approved by the Legislative Yuan on June 17, 1935, and was promulgated by the National Government on July 5, 1935.

The text of this law has been carefully studied by the representatives of American firms transacting insurance business in China and they have come to the opinion that it would be to the interest of the Chinese public and of insurance companies of various nationalities engaged in the insurance business in China if certain sections of the law were modified. There is transmitted herewith a Memorandum prepared by the American Chamber of Commerce at Shanghai [19] setting forth the recommendations in this respect made by the American insurance companies already mentioned.

The American Embassy observes that American insurance companies, in consonance with the treaties in force between the United States

---

[18] Copy transmitted to the Department by the Ambassador in China in his despatch No. 857, November 13; received December 15.
[19] Not printed.

and China, have been conducting their business in China over a long period of years with mutual benefit to the parties concerned. The American authorities desire to cooperate with the Chinese Government with a view to obtaining the proper conduct of the insurance business carried on by American firms and they believe that it would be to the general interest if the Insurance Business Law were to be modified in such way as to enable the American companies to cooperate with those Chinese authorities charged with the administration of the law.

With this object in mind the American Embassy has the honor to invite consideration by the appropriate authorities of the Chinese Government of the recommendations for the modification of the Insurance Business Law embodied in the enclosed Memorandum.[20]

NANKING, November 5, 1936.

RE-REGISTRATION OF TITLE DEEDS TO REAL PROPERTY OF AMERICANS IN CHINA [21]

893.52/379

The Ambassador in China (Johnson) to the Secretary of State

No. 163   PEIPING, January 13, 1936.
                                           [Received February 10.]

SIR: I have the honor to refer to Despatch No. 86 of December 24, 1935, from the Consulate General at Canton to the Embassy [22] on the subject of the acceptance by American land holders at Canton of new title deeds issued through the instrumentality of a special investigation office opened on Shameen last summer, a copy of which despatch was sent directly to the Department, and to enclose for the Department's information a copy of the Embassy's telegram of January 8, 6 p. m.,[22] authorizing the filing of a formal protest. Similar action was taken simultaneously by the British Embassy.

The Department will note that the new title deed differs considerably from the land ownership certificate issued at Shanghai (see Shanghai's despatch to the Legation No. 6804 of February 19, 1931, for text [22]), upon which the Consulate General at Canton was led to believe it would be based. It would be more accurate to state that, in spite of assurances given to the contrary, the new title deed is based upon obnoxious Articles 55 and 56 of the Kwangtung Land Regulations (see Legation's despatch No. 1649 of July 27, 1932, for text [22]) since Articles 3 and 4 of the regulations quoted in the deed (see Legation's despatch

---

[20] This memorandum was transmitted promptly by the Chinese Foreign Office to the Legislative Yuan, but there were no further results.
[21] Continued from *Foreign Relations*, 1935, vol. III, pp. 802–814.
[22] Not printed.

No. 1023 of June 10, 1931, for text of those regulations [23]) provide for a procedure which is almost identical with that specified in Articles 55 and 56 aforementioned. The deed as it now stands is not satisfactory on account of the restrictions placed upon the transfer of land, and Consul General Spiker [24] was accordingly authorized by the Embassy to file a formal protest as outlined on page 8 of his despatch No. 86 of December 24.

The British and American Consulates-General at Canton have made every effort to cooperate in liquidating a highly unsatisfactory land situation at Canton. The failure to obtain the desired results must be laid partly to the general confusion that exists throughout China in regard to land matters . . . However, it may be expected that two benefits will result, namely, foreigners who have thus far not been able to get deeds stamped in the past will have the required documents albeit they may not be satisfactory in every respect, and, those who have obtained new deeds can no longer be refused building permits, et cetera, on the grounds that title deeds are not in order.

Respectfully yours,   NELSON TRUSLER JOHNSON

893.52/395

The Ambassador in China (Johnson) to the Secretary of State

No. 353   PEIPING, April 7, 1936.
                                             [Received May 4.]

SIR: I have the honor to refer to the Legation's despatch No. 3557 of May 10, 1935,[25] with reference to the question of the re-registration of land titles at Nanking. This question has arisen specifically in reference to the re-registration of land titles to property belonging to several missionary societies who own and use land in Nanking. But it is of wider import, because the Embassy is convinced that the attitude of the municipal authorities at Nanking represents the attitude of the National Government and may be expected to be applied to the question of the use and ownership of land by American citizens throughout the territory of China. The Embassy has not yet received a reply to its communication addressed to the Chinese Foreign Office under date of April 26, 1935, (copy of which was enclosed with the Legation's despatch above referred to [23]), but a number of developments have occurred which indicate that the Nanking Municipality continues to maintain the policy in regard to land holding by American missionary societies which was objected to in the Legation's note to the Foreign Office of April 26, 1935.

---

[23] Not printed.
[24] Clarence J. Spiker, Consul General at Canton.
[25] *Foreign Relations*, 1935, vol. III, p. 809.

I enclose a memorandum handed to Mr. Atcheson [26] at Nanking on March 7, 1936,[27] by Mr. Blackburn [28] of the British Embassy, which quotes an extract from the *North China Daily News* dated February 25, 1936, purporting to describe a form for the lease of land for use by foreign missions or residents at Nanking. This newspaper item contained the following statement:

"When the lessee no longer wishes to continue a lease, the property may be taken back by the Land Bureau at its assessed value."

[Here follow extracts from the British memorandum.]

Under date of March 13 the Embassy suggested to the Consulate General at Shanghai, under whose jurisdiction Nanking land matters now belong, that formal notice of this Government's attitude to the Mayor at Nanking was in order, in view of an item which appeared in the *Central Daily News* of February 24, 1936, which was apparently similar to the one referred to in Mr. Blackburn's memorandum above quoted. A copy of this despatch is enclosed.[27]

On March 19 the American Consul General at Shanghai despatched a note to the Mayor at Nanking along the lines suggested by the Embassy. Copy of that note with covering despatch No. 84 of March 19, 1936, to the Embassy from the Consulate General at Shanghai is enclosed herewith.[27] In this connection the Consul General at Shanghai brought up an interesting question, namely, as to what effect the enforcement of the Land Law and the Law for the Enforcement of the Land Law as from March 1, 1936, would have upon such measures as those apparently proposed by the Municipality at Nanking. The Consul General pointed out that the Land Law required that land in China be registered or re-registered under the provisions of that law. The Consul General stated:

"But an examination of the pertinent sections of the Land Law and the Law for the Enforcement of the Land Law failed to disclose any stipulation curtailing the right of owners or lessees of land to dispose freely of their holdings, nor that such land be required to be surrendered to the Chinese Government except by expropriation. In such circumstances, apart from the question of unilateral treaty abrogation, it is not discerned just how the Nanking Municipal Government can enact municipal land regulations that appear to be contrary to the Land Laws of the National Government."

Under date of March 27, 1936, Mr. Peck, Counselor of this Embassy, made certain comments upon the observations of the Consulate General at Shanghai in regard to the effect of the Land Law and the Law for the Enforcement of the Land Law upon such regulations

---

[26] George Atcheson, Jr., Second Secretary of Embassy in China at Nanking.
[27] Not printed.
[28] A. D. Blackburn, Chinese Secretary of the British Embassy in China at Peiping.

as might be issued by the Municipality at Nanking in regard to the re-registration of land. A copy of these comments is enclosed for the information of the Department.[30]

I feel that Mr. Peck's comments in this regard are important and deserve serious consideration. In general he points out that the Chinese have taken the position that the system of "perpetual lease" is a legal anomaly based originally on the theory that the Emperor of China was the lord of the soil and that as a consequence the Chinese Government at the time when the treaties were negotiated was unwilling to grant title to real property to foreigners who were not under the jurisdiction of the Government. He follows this statement by saying that if this explanation is sound the Chinese would doubtless insist that the reversionary right and ownership vests in the Chinese Government, or a subdivision thereof, since the original owner or lessor divested himself of his own right in perpetuity.

I have not had time to explore all of the records for the purpose of determining just how and when the term "perpetual lease" came into use in regard to the holding of property by foreigners in China. The first use of the term in a treaty occurs, I believe, in Article 14 of the Treaty of October 8, 1903, between the United States and China,[31] and it has generally been used in all title deeds covering land acquired by American citizens and juridical persons since that time, although I remember, in a somewhat extended experience with Chinese title deeds to land acquired by American citizens, to have seen occasionally the term "sale" used, which I believed was an inadvertence. Title deeds to property owned by Chinese are fee simple deeds, the term "perpetual lease" only coming into use when the property passes from Chinese hands into foreign hands. I have always supposed that the term "perpetual lease" was a legal device for getting around the theory that foreigners might not own Chinese land in fee simple and was not intended to estop a holder of such title of disposing of it at will, for in the past, in so far as I have been aware, no objection has been made by the Chinese authorities when foreigners have desired to dispose of their perpetual lease by sale at the current value of property held in fee simple. I am of course aware that, since 1903 at least, property purchased by missionaries in the interior has in practice always been described in the perpetual lease as "kung ch'an", or "common property", to indicate, as I have always assumed, that the property was the common property of the mission or the juridical person named in the deed, and not the property of an individual.

The theory that the Emperor was lord of the soil in China is a theory of ancient standing in China. All land not registered as the

---

[30] Not printed.
[31] Signed at Shanghai, October 8, 1903; *Foreign Relations*, 1903, p. 91.

property of an individual is presumed to be the common property of the Emperor or the Government. This is evidenced by the methods used when an individual desired to obtain title to foreshore accretions, or hitherto uncultivated forest or mountain land. Evidence of occupation, use or ownership was by title deed and payment of the land tax, and under ancient practice an individual could obtain a prescriptive right to land after thirty years' unquestioned payment of taxes. It is possible, of course, that the taxes were looked upon as rent paid to the lord of the soil, thus supporting the idea that the user of soil was a lessor under the Emperor and not an owner in fee simple.

The point, however, is that the only title which an American citizen can obtain for land in China is in the form of a perpetual lease. This is recognized by Article 14 of the Treaty of October 8, 1903, between the United States and China. The difficulty that faces American citizens, and, in the case under discussion, specifically American missionary societies, concerns their right to transfer property so held. For the position of the Chinese Government now is that if a lessee in perpetuity, specifically an American missionary society, no longer desires to exercise its right to use the property "for missionary purposes", as stipulated under Article 14 of the Treaty of October 8, 1903, the property must revert to the Government, which has replaced the Emperor as the lord of the soil. Mr. Peck states:

"It will be noted that Article 33 of the Land Law definitely provides for the acquisition, establishment, transfer, modification or extinction of the right of perpetual lease. Article 117 of the same Law prescribes what data shall be supplied in the application form. In the Law for the Enforcement of the Land Law, Article 10 specifically refers to treaty stipulations granting rights to foreigners, but Article 31 makes clear the position now taken by the Chinese Government toward perpetual leases held by foreign persons and institutions. Article 31 states that land leased to foreigners in accordance with the treaties must be registered as 'public land', although it provides that the lessee shall be responsible for taxes and 'all the other requisite obligations of owners'."

To give point to this attitude on the part of the Municipal Government at Nanking, Mr. Peck refers to the case of Mr. James H. McCallum which is covered in a copy of a letter addressed by Mr. Atcheson to the Director of the Department of European and American affairs of the Ministry of Foreign Affairs, Dr. Liu, under date of March 26, 1936, enclosed with this despatch.[32] Mr. McCallum received from the Municipal Government at Nanking a notice which he was instructed to hang at the entrance to certain property owned by

---

[32] Not printed.

the United Christian Missionary Society. This notice stated that as the time limit for the registration of the property in question had expired, the property would be regarded as ownerless. The notice invited any person who had claim to any cadastral rights over the land in question to raise objection to the registration, in default of which the land was to be given "hypothetical registration" (*chia ting teng chi*) by the Land Administration. An interesting point is that the notice, in describing the boundaries of the land in question, states that the property extends "south to municipal land" and "west to municipal land". Now, the "municipal land" referred to as bounding this property on the south and west is land leased in perpetuity by the University of Nanking, an American juridical person. As Mr. Peck points out, the phraseology used in the notice is clearly dictated by Article 31 of the Law to Enforce the Land Law.

Mr. Peck states in conclusion:

"Summed up, the situation seems to be that the two laws in question do actually seek to give effect to the treaties by permitting foreigners to acquire, establish and even transfer rights of perpetual lease. There seems to be no question, therefore, but that an American missionary organization would be allowed under the Law to transfer its perpetual lease to another person or organization permitted under the treaties to hold a perpetual lease. This would seem to follow, in any event, from the right to 'establish' the right of perpetual lease.

"Certain questions arise, however, from the requirement of the Law that property leased in perpetuity shall be registered as 'public land', e. g. in the case of the United Christian Missionary Society property as 'Municipal Land'. If the lessees may dispose of their property only by transferring their leases to other organizations entitled to acquire perpetual leases, it is clear that there will be, practically speaking, no such thing as a market value for such property. There have been indications that it is the wish of the Chinese authorities that land held by foreign organizations under perpetual lease, especially land inside the city of Nanking shall revert to Chinese ownership as soon as possible. Consequently, it may be that the municipal authorities would permit Chinese to purchase such land and would register their titles. On the other hand, the land being recorded as 'Municipal Land' there may be formalities which would preclude transfers in this manner. If the lessees elect to avail themselves of the privilege, now reported, of surrendering their property to the Municipal Government, what will be the basis of appraising its value?"

Mr. Peck states that the question which chiefly concerns American missionary organizations here is the question of their right to dispose of their property at its market value, and he asks that he be authorized to ask the Ministry of Foreign Affairs in writing to reply to the following questions:

"(1) Is it the intention of the Chinese authorities, under the new procedure, to permit American missionary organizations and other persons and organizations authorized to hold property under perpetual lease, to sell or lease their property to any persons or organizations, Chinese or foreign, who may wish to purchase or lease it?

"(2) Will such purchasers or lessees be given, without impediment, certificates of ownership or lease, as the case may be?"

These were the questions which we put to the Foreign Office in the Legation's note of April 26, 1935, and instead of putting these questions in the way that Mr. Peck has put them, I am addressing a note to the Foreign Office requesting a reply at an early date to the Embassy's note of April 26, 1935. A copy of my note of today's date is enclosed.[34] In the meantime, however, the Embassy will appreciate some expression of opinion from the Department as to the evident interpretation which the Chinese Government seeks to place upon Article 14 of the Treaty of October 8, 1903, between the United States and China, which article appears specifically to limit the right of missionaries and missionary societies to acquire land for missionary purposes only. More specifically, would this article in the opinion of the Department estop an American missionary organization from disposing of its land to a Chinese for purposes other than missionary and at the current market value of land held in fee simple?

Respectfully yours,   NELSON TRUSLER JOHNSON

893.52/398

The Ambassador in China (Johnson) to the Secretary of State

No. 404   PEIPING, April 24, 1936.
                                 [Received May 18.]

SIR: I have the honor to refer to the Embassy's despatch No. 353 of April 7, 1936, on the subject of the re-registration of title deeds to property held by American citizens or organizations at Nanking, and to enclose for the information of the Department a copy of despatch No. 108 of April 2, 1936, from the Consulate General at Shanghai,[34] reporting on a conversation held between Vice-Consul Jenkins [35] and the Mayor of Nanking regarding the policy to be followed in that city. It will be observed that, according to the information submitted in that despatch, the Nanking municipal authorities are prepared to admit the right of holders of leases in perpetuity to transfer their holdings to Chinese citizens and to others entitled to hold such leases. These oral assurances, however, would not seem of themselves

---

[34] Not printed.
[35] Douglas Jenkins, Jr., Vice Consul at Shanghai and Third Secretary of Embassy in China at Nanking.

to constitute adequate guarantee of the nature of the policy to be followed in future by the Nanking Municipal Government and other administrative authorities as regards the matter under discussion, and the Embassy proposes to wait for a reply to its note of April 7, 1936, to the Foreign Office,[36] before instituting any change in the present procedure of not advising American title-holders to apply for re-registration of their deeds until such time as there may have been a basic clarification of the question of right of transfer.

Respectfully yours,　　　　　　　　　　NELSON TRUSLER JOHNSON

893.52/398

The Secretary of State to the Ambassador in China (Johnson)

No. 185　　　　　　　　　　　　　　　WASHINGTON, May 29, 1936.

SIR: Reference is made to your despatches Nos. 3557,[37] 353 and 404 of May 10, 1935, April 7, 1936, and April 24, 1936, respectively, in regard to the reregistration of land titles at Nanking involving a new lease agreement which the Nanking municipality proposes to issue to foreign holders of perpetual leases in exchange for the title documents which they now hold. The new lease agreement contains the following provision: "Owner: If the land is leased in perpetuity, and when in future the perpetual lessee does not need to use the land or when he dies and has no heir, the Nanking municipal government will purchase the land at the original price."

You refer to apprehension felt by American missionary societies holding property under perpetual lease that the new lease agreement might involve impairment of the right long enjoyed by them to dispose of their leases to Chinese citizens or associations authorized to hold them under perpetual lease at the price obtainable by agreement of the parties. You express the view that the action taken by the municipal authorities at Nanking represents the attitude of the national government and may be expected to be applied to the question of the use and ownership of land by American citizens throughout the territory of China and you request an expression of opinion by the Department as to the rights possessed by American missionary societies holding land under perpetual lease by virtue of the provisions of Article XIV of the Sino-American Treaty of 1903, the pertinent part of which reads as follows:

"Missionary societies of the United States shall be permitted to rent and to lease in perpetuity, as the property of such societies, buildings or lands in all parts of the Empire for missionary purposes . . ."

---

[36] Not printed.
[37] *Foreign Relations*, 1935, vol. III, p. 809.

The Department appreciates that the situation disclosed by the Embassy's despatches of May 10, 1935, and April 7, 1936, and their enclosures, reasonably warranted the apprehension felt by the missionary societies and the Embassy. However, the situation appears to have been materially changed by the facts reported by the Consulate General, Shanghai, in its despatch of April 2, 1936, to the Embassy, Peiping [38] (enclosed with your No. 404, April 24, 1936), from which it appears that the Mayor of Nanking has given definite oral assurances to American consular representatives that holders of leases in perpetuity covering property in Nanking will be permitted to transfer their holdings to Chinese, who upon such transfer will be given valid Chinese title deeds, and that holders of such leases will also be permitted to transfer their rights to others entitled to hold leases in perpetuity, and that the only circumstance under which the municipal government will insist upon purchasing the land will be where the municipality desires the land for some specific purpose, in which event it will be expropriated. It also appears that written confirmation of these assurances was being drafted by the municipal authorities and would soon be despatched to the Consulate General. As stated by the Consul General at Shanghai, these admissions on the part of the municipal authorities at Nanking would appear to place the rights of American holders of perpetual leases on substantially the basis claimed by the leaseholders, and if those admissions are confirmed in writing in accordance with the Mayor's oral promise or, irrespective of such written confirmation, by the action of the municipal authorities, there would not appear to be any further ground for apprehension respecting the effect of the new lease agreement on the rights of missionary societies holding land under perpetual lease.

For this reason and because of uncertainty as to the precise legal rights claimable by missionary societies under the provisions of Article XIV of the Sino-American Treaty of 1903, the Department is of the opinion that it would be inadvisable to insist at this time on a reply to the Embassy's notes to the Foreign Office of April 26, 1935, and April 7, 1936, or to encourage perpetual lease holders to refrain from reregistering their titles in accordance with the municipal regulations under reference, unless, of course, the action of the municipal authorities should not substantially conform with their declarations.

For the purpose of complying with the Embassy's request for its views as to the rights possessed by American missions holding land under perpetual leases, the Department has made a fairly comprehensive examination of available material on the subject, but its examination has not disclosed a satisfactory basis for consideration of the question of legal grounds. The Department is not aware of any Chinese law or regulation which defines perpetual leases or the extent

---

[38] Not printed.

of the rights or obligations incident to such documents.   Neither the treaty provision quoted herein nor the texts of perpetual leases throw any clear light on the question.   There appears to be no express grant of a right of alienation of such lease nor any express prohibition of such right.   The limitations or conditions stated in the treaty article might be held to be incorporated by reference in any perpetual lease issued to an American missionary society, and the continued validity of the lease might, therefore, be held to depend on the strict observance of the stated limitations or conditions with right of reversion in the lessor upon failure or violation of those conditions.   From this point of view the treaty article in question does not seem to afford a very strong basis for claiming the right of free alienation of title, but a determination of this question on legal grounds is rendered difficult by the apparent absence of authoritative provisions establishing how or in whose behalf any possible reversionary right may be exercised.   However, the repeated approval by the Chinese authorities over a long period of time of transfers of perpetual leases from missionary societies to Chinese citizens or foreign associations and the issuance of valid deeds of sale or of perpetual leases to the transferees reasonably warrants the conclusion that the Chinese authorities have never regarded such transfers as raising the question of reversion and accordingly it would seem reasonable to hold that the long-continued practice of the Chinese authorities constitutes clear recognition of the right of free alienation of perpetual leases held by American missionary societies.   Since that now seems to be the attitude of the municipal authorities at Nanking, it would seem prudent to avoid any further discussion of the question at this time.

Very truly yours,   For the Secretary of State:

WILLIAM PHILLIPS

893.52/407

The Ambassador in China (Johnson) to the Secretary of State

No. 494   PEIPING, June 5, 1936.

[Received June 29.]

SIR: I have the honor to refer to the Embassy's despatch No. 447 of May 12, 1936,[39] regarding the re-registration of title deeds to property held by American citizens and organizations at Nanking, and to enclose for the information of the Department a copy of a despatch received from the Embassy at Nanking under date of May 27, 1936, forwarding a note received from the Ministry of Foreign Affairs under date of May 22 in reply to the Embassy's note of May 12 [40] on the subject.

[39] Not printed.
[40] None printed.

It will be observed that the Nanking Municipal Government, as quoted in the aforementioned note from the Foreign Office, gives an undertaking that there will be eliminated from the new form of lease-certificate the present stipulation regarding the purchase of land from the perpetual lessee by the Municipal Government, and states in addition that any transfer of title to land leased by missions must be by sale to Chinese citizens or by lease to another mission for missionary purposes.

It is to be noted that the Foreign Office's note does not constitute an adequate reply to the Embassy's note of May 12, which requested of the National Government a reply to the Embassy's previous note of April 26, 1935,[41] and a definitive regularization, in accord with existing treaty rights, of the administrative procedure as regards land tenure by American citizens and organizations in general throughout the country. Some concession has been made by the Nanking Municipal Government, it is true, but neither is that concession without its ambiguities nor has the Foreign Office committed the National Government to any policy of general applicability. In these circumstances, the Embassy is instructing Counselor Peck that American citizens and organizations in Nanking should not be advised to file application for re-registration of their property until it has been ascertained that the new form of certificate actually no longer contains any of the features which were formerly protested as being contrary to established procedure and treaty rights. A copy of that instruction, under today's date, is enclosed for the information of the Department.[41] It is of course clear that, in any event, the procedure laid down for the Nanking Municipality cannot be taken as applicable to the country as a whole. The general problem therefore remains unsolved.

As regards the current proposal of the American missionary societies to turn over their property titles to Chinese holding organizations, as referred to in Counselor Peck's despatch of May 27,* it is to be observed that such action would automatically eliminate many of the troublesome questions that arise for American Foreign Service Officers in connection with the administration of land-tenure matters, inasmuch as such property would no longer be in the legal possession of American organizations. The Embassy does not feel that it is in any position gratuitously to offer advice to the interested missionary societies one way or the other as regards the advisability of those organizations' so acting, and proposes not to concern itself in the matter.

---

[41] Not printed.
*Cf. also despatch No. 167 of May 21, 1936, from the Embassy at Nanking to the Department, and despatches No. 184 and No. 213 of May 15 and May 29, 1936, respectively, from the Shanghai Consulate General to the Embassy. [Footnote in the original; despatches not printed.]

It is apparent that a further request to the Foreign Office for definitive action regarding the general problem of land tenure by American citizens and organizations in China would probably not be productive of satisfactory results; until there occur new basic developments, therefore, the Embassy intends to limit itself to following the subject with attention and dealing with local questions as they arise.

Respectfully yours,   NELSON TRUSLER JOHNSON

893.52/410

The Ambassador in China (Johnson) to the Secretary of State

No. 540   PEIPING, June 19, 1936.
                                                [Received July 13.]

SIR: I have the honor to refer to the Embassy's despatch No. 519 of June 16, 1936,[44] regarding the re-registration of title deeds to property held by American missionary organizations at Nanking, and to enclose for the information of the Department a copy in English translation of a note received from the Minister for Foreign Affairs under date June 6, 1936,[44] transmitting the substance of a communication received from the Nanking Municipal Government. It will be observed that the Municipal Government repeats its former assurance that the application and lease-certificate forms have been revised, and states in addition that the time-limit for the re-registration of land by foreign missions has been extended from June 10 to August 30, 1936. The Foreign Minister requests that the Embassy take note and act accordingly.

There is also enclosed a copy of a despatch received from the Embassy at Nanking under date June 11, 1936,[44] transmitting communications from organs of the Presbyterian Mission embodying the request of officials of that organization that they receive as soon as possible information in regard to reported changes made by the Municipal Government in the system of foreign land tenure in Nanking.

The Embassy plans to hold up action in this matter until after receiving the opinion of the Shanghai Consulate General as requested in its instruction of June 12, 1936.[44] A copy of this despatch is being sent to the Consulate General for its information.

It is the belief of the Embassy that, although action on the part of the Chinese authorities against the foreign rights of land tenure is threatened for some future date, in the present political circumstances the National Government will not be inclined to take precipitate action along those lines. It would appear advisable, that is, for the Embassy

---

[44] Not printed.

to endeavor to maintain its original position and make no concessions which might admit an infringement of treaty and customary rights in the matter of land tenure on the part of American citizens and organizations. As of possible interest in this general connection, there is enclosed a copy in English translation of a despatch addressed by the Ministry of the Interior to the Kiangsu Provincial Government,[45] as printed in the *Internal Affairs Gazette* of December 1935 (Vol. 8, No. 22), regarding the request of a district magistrate for instructions in the matter of an application by a Catholic mission for a perpetual lease. It will be observed that the Ministry instructed the Provincial Government that "The term of the lease of land by foreign missions in the interior is, before the treaties are abolished, regarded as unlimited, and agreements for leases in perpetuity may be concluded. The Executive Yuan issued on September 7, 1933, an instruction No. 4162 to the various provincial and municipal governments to this effect."

Respectfully yours, NELSON TRUSLER JOHNSON

893.52/412

The Ambassador in China (Johnson) to the Secretary of State

No. 569 PEIPING, July 8, 1936.
[Received August 10.]

SIR: I have the honor to acknowledge the receipt of the Department's instruction No. 185 of May 29, 1936, in regard to the re-registration of title-deeds to property held by American missionary organizations at Nanking, and to enclose a copy of despatch No. 254 of June 20, 1936, from the Consulate General at Shanghai [46] on this subject.

As stated in the Embassy's despatch No. 494 of June 5, 1936, the Nanking Municipal Government, according to a note received under date May 22 from the Ministry of Foreign Affairs regarding the matter, has now recognized the principle that foreign missionary societies possess a qualified right of alienation of perpetual leases which are held by them. As noted in the Embassy's instruction of June 12, 1936, to the Consulate General at Shanghai,* however, the new term- and perpetual-lease certificate forms as obtained by the Embassy at Nanking were not without their objectionable features. The Consulate General in its aforementioned despatch of June 20 agreed with this point of view. The Embassy at Nanking therefore sent under date June 30 a new note to the Ministry of Foreign Affairs

---

[45] Not reprinted.
[46] Not printed.
*Embassy's despatch No. 519 of June 16, 1936, to the Department. [Footnote in the original; despatch not printed.]

requesting official copies of the new lease-certificate forms and outlining the Embassy's objections to the ambiguous features still reputedly remaining in the forms. A copy of that note is enclosed.[47]

There is also enclosed for purposes of record a copy of the Embassy's instruction of today's date to the Consulate General at
Shanghai,[47] transmitting copies of the Department's aforementioned
instruction of May 29 and the Embassy's note of June 30, 1936, to
the Foreign Office. This instruction records the Embassy's belief
that, the Nanking Municipal Government having thus recognized the
right of alienation, the elimination by the Nanking Municipal Government of the final objectionable features found in the lease-certificate
forms would satisfactorily terminate the present phase of the discussions so that American missionary organizations could be advised
that they might safely apply for re-registration.

The importance of effecting a satisfactory settlement of the question
as it exists in Nanking is of course discovered in the circumstance that
the principles established there will probably prove to be the basic
precedents used in subsequent negotiations regarding similar questions
in other parts of the country.

Respectfully yours,   NELSON TRUSLER JOHNSON

893.52/415

The Ambassador in China (Johnson) to the Secretary of State

No. 625   PEIPING, August 4, 1936.
                                             [Received September 8.]

SIR: I have the honor to refer to the Embassy's despatch No. 569
of July 8, 1936, in regard to the re-registration of title-deeds to
property held by American missionary organizations at Nanking, and
to enclose copies [48] of a note (in English translation) from the Foreign
Office under date of July 23, 1936, a despatch from the Embassy at
Nanking under date of July 28, a telegram to the Consulate General
at Shanghai under date of August 1, 3 p. m., a note from the Embassy
to the Foreign Office and an instruction to the Consulate General at
Shanghai under today's date.

It will be observed that the Foreign Office in its note gives what
appear to be satisfactory explanations regarding the points raised
in the Embassy's note of June 30, 1936.[47] On the basis of the assurances received, but without recognition of the validity of the time-
limit imposed by the Nanking Municipal Government, the Embassy,

[47] Not printed.
[48] None printed.

in accord with the general observations made in the Department's instruction No. 185 of May 29, 1936, instructed the Consulate General at Shanghai that American missionary organizations may be informed that no objection is perceived to their applying for re-registration of their land-titles.

The provision under the heading "Remarks" of the new lease-certificate forms for the payment of a land-tax would not seem to introduce any new element into the question: if it is thought desirable, the land-tax may still be paid by the mission concerned as a "voluntary contribution" as heretofore. The Shanghai Consulate General was instructed, however, that the Embassy was not expressly accepting the principle of the payment of the land-tax.

Respectfully yours, NELSON TRUSLER JOHNSON

393.1163/724 : Telegram

The Ambassador in China (Johnson) to the Secretary of State

PEIPING, September 8, 1936—11 a. m.
[Received September 8—6 : 50 a. m.]

438. Reference last paragraph Embassy's despatch number 600, July 24.[49] The Consulate General at Shanghai in a despatch dated August 28 transmits a news item to the effect that the Nanking Municipal Government will begin on October 1 next the collection of land value taxes on property at Nanking; the collection of such taxes is considered to be the natural step following upon the current re-registration of title deeds. No official notice has been received by the Consulate General regarding the tax. Gauss [50] observes that the land value taxable [*tax?*] is apparently being paid at Shanghai by American and British owners of land in Chinese administered areas, by the former as a "voluntary contribution", but apparently is not being paid by the Japanese. He states:

"I have no particular objection to the rates of proposed land value taxes as reported to have been adopted for Nanking, or as authorized by the land law (section 4) ; but when we shall have submitted to 'land value' taxes, we will next be confronted with the 'increased value' land taxes (as distinguished from the land tax) as provided for in article 305 of the land law".

The instructions of the Department are requested with regard to the policy to be adopted as to the land value tax.

JOHNSON

---

[49] Not printed.
[50] Clarence E. Gauss, Consul General at Shanghai.

393.1163/724 : Telegram

The Secretary of State to the Ambassador in China (Johnson)

WASHINGTON, September 12, 1936—3 p. m.

221. Your 438, September 8, 11 a. m. and despatch No. 625 of August 4, in regard to the collection of land value taxes on property at Nanking.

Although the Department understands that the treaty powers in China have generally recognized the application to their nationals in China of the principle that the ownership of land is subject to the *lex loci*, the Department is not aware of any authoritative judicial decision by an American or other court as to the enforcement of the Chinese land tax against extraterritorial nationals in China. However, pending an authoritative judicial decision of the question, the Department is of the opinion that American-owned property in China (perpetual leaseholds) should properly be subject to the Chinese land tax, provided the tax is reasonable in amount and applied without discrimination and without violation of any treaty right. It is believed that the land tax has for years been paid by many American citizens in China either as a "voluntary contribution" or as a tax.

The substance of this instruction may be communicated to American citizens who request the advice of the American authorities in regard to the payment of the land tax.

HULL

893.52/425

The Ambassador in China (Johnson) to the Secretary of State

No. 718   PEIPING, September 15, 1936.
[Received October 19.]

SIR: I have the honor to refer to the Embassy's despatch No. 625 of August 4, 1936, regarding the re-registration of title-deeds to property held by American missionary organizations at Nanking, and to enclose a copy in English translation of a note received from the Foreign Office under date September 4, 1936,[53] transmitting a communication from the Nanking Municipal Government in which it is stated that the time-limit for application for re-registration has been extended one month to September 30 of this year.

The Embassy is sending a new note to the Foreign Office under today's date, reiterating its refusal to recognize the validity of any time-limit which may be imposed as it might affect established rights of land-tenure. A copy of this note is enclosed for the information of the Department.[53]

---

[53] Not printed.

There is also enclosed, for purposes of record, a copy of an instruction being sent under today's date to the Consulate General at Shanghai.[54]

Respectfully yours,   NELSON TRUSLER JOHNSON

393.1163 P 92/50

The American Ambassador in China (Johnson) to the Chinese Minister for Foreign Affairs (Chang Ch'un) [55]

No. 103   PEIPING, October 27, 1936.

EXCELLENCY: I have the honor to refer to the general subject of the rights of American citizens to acquire title to land in China, and to inform you that the Municipality of Greater Shanghai, apparently acting on the basis of a misinterpretation of Articles II and VI of the Provisional Regulations Governing the Lease of Land and Buildings by Foreign Missionary Societies in the Interior, has recently refused to issue a lease in perpetuity for land recently acquired by the American Presbyterian Mission, North, in Nantao, Shanghai. The position of the Municipal Government was outlined in its letter No. 7336 of September 18, 1936, replying to a letter from the American Consulate General at Shanghai dated August 3, 1936. Copies of these two letters are enclosed for Your Excellency's ready reference.[56]

It is observed that there exists no question of the right of American missionary organizations to lease land in perpetuity in China for missionary purposes. As noted in Your Excellency's formal note of May 22, 1936,[57] in regard to the allied question of the re-registration of land belonging to American missions in the Nanking Municipality, the last section of Article XIV of the Sino-American Treaty of 1903 [58] clearly provides that "missionary societies of the United States shall be permitted to rent and lease in perpetuity, as the properties of such societies, buildings or lands in all parts of the Empire for missionary purposes." It was in recognition of this fact that the Ministry of the Interior, in its communication under date December 9, 1935, instructed the Kiangsu Provincial Government that the term of the lease of land by foreign missions is regarded as unlimited, and that agreements for leases in perpetuity therefore might be concluded. As noted in that communication, which was printed in the *Internal Affairs Gazette* of December 1935 (Vol. VIII, No. 22), the Executive

---

[54] Not printed.
[55] Copy transmitted to the Department by the Ambassador in China in his despatch No. 813, October 27; received November 30.
[56] Neither printed.
[57] Not found in Department files.
[58] Signed at Shanghai, October 8, 1903; *Foreign Relations*, 1903, p. 91.

Yuan issued on September 7, 1933, an instruction (No. 4162) to the various provincial and municipal governments to this effect.

Inasmuch, therefore, as the above-mentioned case at Shanghai has evidently arisen merely from a misconception of the significance of the Provisional Regulations on the part of the local authorities, who have neglected to give appropriate consideration to the treaty provisions and the position of the National Government in regard to the subject, it is respectfully requested that Your Excellency cause an appropriate instruction to the Municipal Government to be issued, directing that the desired lease in perpetuity be issued to the American Presbyterian Mission.[59]

I avail myself [etc.]   NELSON TRUSLER JOHNSON

CHINESE CENSORSHIP RESTRICTIONS UPON AMERICAN MOVING PICTURES IN CHINA [60]

893.4061 Motion Pictures/189

The Ambassador in China (Johnson) to the Secretary of State

No. 572   PEIPING, July 9, 1936.
                                                  [Received August 10.]

SIR: I have the honor to enclose a copy of despatch No. 253 of June 19, 1936, from the Consulate General at Shanghai [61] in regard to the confiscation of two films belonging to American motion picture companies. The two films in question are "The Cat's Paw" distributed by Fox Film, Federal Incorporated, U. S. A., and "Oil for the Lamps of China" belonging to Warner Brothers First National Pictures, Incorporated. The National Motion Picture Censorship Committee took exception to the pictures on the grounds that they were derogatory to China and the Chinese and refused to permit them to be exhibited. The companies thereupon requested the return of the films for re-exportation but they were informed by the committee that the films had been confiscated and would not be returned.

I discussed this matter with Counselor Peck [62] recently in Nanking and came to the conclusion that there was not adequate reason for the confiscation of the above-mentioned films by the censorship committee. I therefore directed Mr. Peck to take up the matter with the censorship committee or other appropriate Government department with a view to bringing about the return of the films to the American owners.

---

[59] The Ambassador in China in his despatch No. 966, January 8, 1937, reported that "in accordance with the instructions received from the Ministry of Foreign Affairs, the Chinese authorities have expressed themselves as prepared to issue the perpetual lease in question." (393.1163P92/51.)
[60] Continued from *Foreign Relations*, 1934, vol. III, pp. 620–625.
[61] Not printed.
[62] Willys R. Peck, Counselor of Embassy in China at Nanking.

A copy of a memorandum on the subject dated June 28, 1936, prepared by Mr. Peck, is enclosed.[63] There is also enclosed a copy of a despatch dated July 2, 1936, from Mr. Peck [63] informing me of the action taken by him. The Department will note that Mr. Peck called on the Director of the Motion Picture Censorship Committee on July 1, and, although the release of the films was not effected at that time, he has hopes of ultimate success.

The Department will be informed of further developments.

Respectfully yours,   NELSON TRUSLER JOHNSON

893.4061 Motion Pictures/191

The Ambassador in China (Johnson) to the Secretary of State

No. 220   NANKING, August 14, 1936.
                                                [Received September 8.]

SIR: I have the honor to refer to despatch No. 572 of July 9, 1936 from the American Embassy, Peiping, to the Department on the subject: "Confiscation of Motion Picture Films by the Censorship Committee".

Mainly for purposes of record I have the honor to recount below the course of the informal attempts made by the American Embassy, Nanking, to obtain a reversal of the order of confiscation. Acting under the instructions given by the American Ambassador, as reported on page 2 of the latter's despatch of July 9, Mr. Peck continued his discussion with Mr. Lo Kang, Director of the National Motion Picture Censorship Committee. On July 23 Mr. Peck held another long conversation with Mr. Lo Kang in which he largely reiterated the arguments advanced on July 1, as already reported to the Department.[64] At one stage Mr. Lo Kang attempted to justify the confiscation of the films by saying that a warrant was supplied by practice in other countries, for example in Soviet Russia any printed material or films, or even photographs, were confiscated by the authorities if they were prejudicial to Soviet interests. Mr. Peck admitted that this was probably true and added that it would be very interesting to learn whether Chinese practice in such matters followed usage obtaining in the Soviet Union, based upon a Party dictatorship superior to all law, or democratic principles as followed in the United States, where private persons have rights protected by law, even as against the American Government. The question was presented, Mr. Peck observed, whether China is being governed as a party dictatorship or as a democracy under the control of law. This presentation of the

---

[63] Not printed.
[64] See Embassy's despatch No. 572, *supra;* memorandum of conversation not printed.

implications involved in confiscation seemed to nonplus Mr. Lo Kang and he asked that he be allowed, as a favor, to discuss the matter further with his colleagues.

Another interesting development from this conversation was the assertion that, according to Mr. Lo Kang, one reason the Chinese authorities feel themselves justified in taking strong action against American motion picture producers lies in the fact that the American Government has openly admitted its inability to exercise any legal restraint over the production of motion pictures and is, therefore, unable to accompany its protests with any assurances for the future.

On July 30 Mr. Peck made another attempt to get a decision from Mr. Lo Kang, but without success, and at this time Mr. Lo Kang left Nanking for a vacation of one week. In view of the apparent failure of the efforts at informal settlement in conversation with Lo Kang, Mr. Peck on August 4, called on the Director of the Department of International Affairs of the Foreign Office.[65] A memorandum of the conversation is enclosed.[66] It will be noted that Mr. Peck said that the American Embassy strongly protested against this confiscation of American property and pointed out that so far as the circulation of these pictures throughout the world was concerned, the confiscation of one copy of each would have no appreciable effect. Mr. Wu promised to look into the matter and communicate with Mr. Lo Kang. On August 8 Mr. Peck. telephoned to Mr. Wu and was informed that the views of the Embassy as explained on August 4, 1936, had been communicated to the National Motion Picture Censorship Committee "for its consideration", but that no reply had been received from the Committee. On August 10 Mr. Peck again talked with Mr. Wu Sung-kao, Director of the Department of International Affairs, and was informed by Mr. Wu that in writing to the National Motion Picture Censorship Committee, the Ministry of Foreign Affairs had urged the Committee to revise the two films in such a way as would permit of their being exhibited in China. Mr. Peck said that he appreciated this effort to bring about the granting of permission for the exhibition of the pictures in China, but he emphasized that the Companies had not made this the main issue in the present case. The main issue was the confiscation of property.

On August 13 Mr. Peck telephoned to Mr. Wu and was informed that the National Motion Picture Censorship Committee had not yet returned any reply to the Foreign Office communication concerning the confiscation of these two films. Mr. Peck said that the American Ambassador had authorized him to endeavor to settle this difficulty through friendly informal conversations, but had instructed him to

---

[65] Wu Sung-kao.
[66] Not printed.

write formally to the Ministry of Foreign Affairs if such endeavors proved fruitless. Mr. Wu said that he agreed with the position taken by the American Embassy in regard to the confiscation of the films and he would continue his efforts to persuade the National Motion Picture Censorship Committee to rescind its confiscation order. Mr. Peck inquired whether it would assist, or hinder, Mr. Wu's efforts if the Embassy were to address the Foreign Office formally in the matter and Mr. Wu replied that he thought a formal communication would be a good thing. Mr. Peck then addressed a note to the Foreign Office in the name of the American Ambassador [67] setting forth the protest of the Embassy against the arbitrary and illegal seizure of American property, as represented by the confiscation of these films.

In explanation of the difficulty encountered in handling a matter of this sort it may be pointed out that the Censorship Committee is not a department of the National Government, but functions under the control of the Nationalist Party Central Headquarters (Kuomintang). The Party is, in theory, quite distinct from and even superior to, the Chinese Government. In many cases it is evident that the amenities of international intercourse have no weight with the authorities of the Party, who keep themselves in seclusion. In an attempt to overcome this attitude Mr. Peck has tried to make Mr. Lo Kang feel that in managing motion picture matters he is dealing with a subject which has an important bearing on the cordiality of relations between the people of China and the people of the United States. Mr. Lo Kang seemed to react favorably to this appeal. . . .

Although without direct bearing on the subject under discussion it is relevant to remark that the American Embassy, Nanking, is constantly having occasion to emphasize the view of the American Government that officials of the Nationalist Party are not from that circumstance officials of the Chinese Government. This is often disconcerting to the officials of the Party, especially when it becomes a matter of inability to obtain an official visa on a passport. Mr. Peck has had occasion to point out to Party and Government officials that neither the Chinese Government nor the Nationalist Party have ever officially taken the position that the Nationalist Party is a part of the Government, even though the highest officials of the Government owe their appointment to the highest organs of the Party. Government officials apparently are not above taking a certain satisfaction in the discomfiture of Party officials when denied recognition which is accorded to officials of the Government.

Respectfully yours,

For the Ambassador:
WILLYS R. PECK,
Counselor of Embassy

---

[67] Not printed.

893.4061 Motion Pictures/194

The Ambassador in China (Johnson) to the Secretary of State

No. 748   PEIPING, September 29, 1936.
                                           [Received November 2.]

SIR: I have the honor to refer to despatch No. 220 of August 14, 1936, from the Embassy at Nanking to the Department, in regard to the confiscation of American motion picture films by the Chinese National Motion Picture Censorship Committee, and to enclose for the information and consideration of the Department copies of the following further correspondence [68] on the matter:

1. Embassy's note of August 13, 1936, to the Ministry of Foreign Affairs.
2. Foreign Office's note of September 1, 1936, to the Embassy.
3. Counselor Peck's despatch of September 15 to the Embassy.
4. Shanghai's despatch No. 379 of September 15 to the Embassy.

In its note of August 13 to the Foreign Office the Embassy reviewed the circumstances surrounding the confiscation of the two films concerned, "The Cat's Paw" and "Oil for the Lamps of China", which are the property of Fox Film, Federal Incorporated, U. S. A., and Warner Brothers First National Pictures, Incorporated, respectively. The Embassy pointed out that the two American companies had not protested against the refusal to grant exhibition permits in the case of these two films, but that they had emphatically objected to the retention of the films as an arbitrary and illegal procedure. The Embassy stated that it concurred in this view as it was evident that the owners of the films, in submitting them to the National Motion Picture Censorship Committee for inspection, had manifested their complete good faith. The Embassy stated that there had been no attempt at concealment of the nature of the films and that no offense had been committed which would justify seizure of their property; moreover, when the companies were notified that the pictures could not be exhibited in China they had expressed their willingness to re-export the films from the country. The Embassy did not enter into the question whether these two films were, or were not, derogatory to China and the citizens of China, but stated that if the Chinese Government department concerned wished to supply the Embassy with a statement of its reasons for objecting to the two films, the Embassy would be willing to report the matter to the American Government. The Embassy stated that, apart from this aspect of the case, it must insist that the American property represented by these films be returned to the owners, and that the retention of the films by the Censorship Committee would be regarded by the Embassy as an arbitrary and illegal act for which no authority exists in the treaties now in force between the two nations.

---

[68] None printed.

The Embassy therefore requested that steps be taken to bring about the early restoration of the films to their owners.

The reply of the Foreign Office to the Embassy's note is most unsatisfactory in that it formally endorses and approves the confiscation of American property without due process of law and in a wholly illegal and arbitrary manner, and, as stated by Consul General Gauss [69] in his despatch No. 379 of September 15, the Ministry's action constitutes a precedent which is of serious concern to American interests. As pointed out by Counselor Peck in his despatch of September 15, the Foreign Office completely ignores the charge made by the Embassy that confiscation of the films is "an arbitrary and illegal act for which no authority exists in the treaties now in force between the two Nations". I concur in Mr. Peck's view that the question of whether confiscation of these films is or is not a legal measure has no relation to the question whether the films are, or are not, objectionable or whether producers have been guilty of wrongful practices.

As I do not wish the Foreign Office to gain the impression that the Embassy acquiesces in the action of the Censorship Committee in confiscating these films, I have addressed a further note to the Foreign Office, a copy of which is enclosed. [70] I state therein that I have forwarded a copy of the Foreign Office's note of August 13 [September 1?] to the Department but that I must insist that the films be returned without further delay to their owners, as I consider that their retention is an arbitrary and illegal act for which no authority exists in the treaties in force between China and the United States.

It seems to me that a deadlock has been reached in this matter and I will therefore appreciate receiving any instructions or observations which the Department may care to make on the subject. I commend to the particular consideration of the Department, in its study of the matter, the able despatch addressed to me by Counselor Peck on September 15.

Respectfully yours,   NELSON TRUSLER JOHNSON

893.4061 Motion Pictures/196 : Telegram

The Acting Secretary of State to the Ambassador in China (Johnson)

WASHINGTON, November 11, 1936—3 p. m.

271. The Department has received a letter under date November 9 [70] from Motion Picture Producers and Distributors of America, Inc., New York City, in regard to the ban which has been placed by the Chinese Government on the distribution in China of Paramount

---

[69] Clarence E. Gauss, Consul General at Shanghai.
[70] Not printed.

motion picture "The General Died at Dawn" and of all other Paramount pictures. The letter states *inter alia* that when Paramount started production of the motion picture "The General Died at Dawn", it obtained the help of a General Tu [72] who had been loaned by the Chinese Government to Metro [73] (in connection with the production of their picture "The Good Earth"); that in accordance with the suggestions which he made certain portions were removed from the picture, and that the picture as approved by him was released for general circulation. The letter also states that prior to the showing of the picture in Manila a foreword was added to the effect that the story was laid before the establishment of the Nationalist Government at Nanking, that that Government had freed the Chinese nation from oppression and that the story and characters were fictitious; that the Chinese Consul and the Chinese Chamber of Commerce in Manila after seeing the picture issued statements to the Chinese press and the Paramount representative to the effect that in their opinion the picture was not in any way offensive to the Chinese and that with the approval of the Chinese Consul and the Chinese Chamber of Commerce the picture was then shown in the Capitol Theatre at that place, which theatre is partly owned by Chinese; and that Paramount is willing to have this foreword placed on all copies of prints throughout the world if such is the desire of the Chinese Government. The letter states further that the Chinese Vice Consul at Los Angeles made a report on this picture to his Government objecting to its protrayal of Chinese people and situations and that as no copy of the picture has as yet reached China it was not possible for the Chinese Government to have seen it before issuing the ban (the inference being that that Government's action was taken on the basis of the Vice Consul's report).

The Department desires that the Embassy investigate this matter and in the light of Department's instruction No. 1138, August 3, 1933,[74] make such representations to the concerned authorities as may appear appropriate in the circumstances.

Report promptly by radio.

MOORE

893.4061 Motion Pictures/194 : Telegram

The Acting Secretary of State to the Ambassador in China (Johnson)

WASHINGTON, November 16, 1936—6 p. m.

278. Your despatch No. 748, September 29, 1936, concerning confiscation of American motion picture films by the Chinese National

---

[72] General Tu Ting-hsiu.
[73] Metro-Goldwyn-Mayer.
[74] *Foreign Relations*, 1933, vol. III, p. 694.

Motion Picture Censorship Committee. The Department approves the action taken by the Embassy in regard to this matter.

The Department has carefully reviewed this case and concurs in the view expressed by the Embassy that the confiscation of the two films in question is clearly in contravention of Sino-American treaties and that the question of confiscation has no relation to the question whether the films are, or are not, objectionable, or whether producers have been guilty of wrongful practices. It is suggested, accordingly, that the Embassy, unless it perceive objection, informally approach the appropriate Chinese authorities for the purpose of informing the Chinese Government of this Government's view and obtaining, if possible, the return to the owners of the films and that in the event this move does not achieve the desired result the Embassy lodge, as under instruction, a formal protest with the Foreign Office against the arbitrary and illegal retention of American property in contravention of treaty and request the immediate return of the property in question to the owners.

MOORE

893.4061 Motion Pictures/199 : Telegram

The Ambassador in China (Johnson) to the Secretary of State

PEIPING, November 17, 1936—5 p. m.
[Received November 17—1 : 57 p. m.]

553. Your 271, November 11, 3 p. m. Peck reports under date of November 13 a conversation with Mr. Kao, sales manager for Paramount, who reported that question of ban on "The General Died at Dawn" had been compromised by him with Lo Kang, Chairman of the Censorship Committee, as follows: the Censorship Committee will allow Paramount 40 days to bring to China a positive and a negative of the picture, the company to guarantee that if the committee disapproved of the picture all existing prints would be destroyed, the company to furnish satisfactory guarantee that this action would be taken. In the meantime the committee will resume censoring of Paramount pictures. Peck had not been informed whether the parent company had accepted this solution or not.

Kao told Peck that while the company conceded the right of the Chinese Government to ban a picture from China, it did not concede the right of the Government to demand its suppression all over the world. Peck replied that if it was conceded that China had the right to ban a picture in China it seemed to follow as a matter of course that the Government might ban the showing of all pictures in China of a given company as a means of compulsion.

I shall await developments to determine whether further steps seem advisable. Peck protested orally to Wu, Director of the Department of International Affairs of the Foreign Office, on November 11, against the arbitrary treatment meted out to Paramount.

Repeated to Nanking.

JOHNSON

893.4061 Motion Pictures/200 : Telegram

The Counselor of Embassy in China (Peck) to the Secretary of State

NANKING, November 18, 1936—noon.
[Received November 18—8 a. m.]

329. Embassy's 553, November 17, 5 p. m. from Peiping.

1. I have received call today from Perkins [75] representing Paramount, Hagar [76] representing Cathay Finite [*Grand?*] Corporation, Shanghai, and Sellett, Attorney for the latter. Perkins denies emphatically that he even accepted any compromise proposal made by the Censorship Committee. He states moreover that this proposal as reported by Kao was only that positive and negative of "The General Died at Dawn" [be?] brought to China and did not include any undertaking by Paramount that the decision of the Censorship Committee after viewing the picture would be accepted without question. The proposal has been referred to Paramount, New York, but no reply has been received. Perkins believes that Paramount will be willing to come to amicable arrangements if reasonable.

2. These representatives of a major motion picture distributor and of the Cathay Grand Corporation, which was formed by order of the United States Court for China to liquidate the affairs of the United Theatres, Chesterton [*sic*] an American Corporation, represent that if the ban on Paramount films is enforced there is every indication that one of these theatres would have to close and the Cathay Grand Corporation would be obliged to operate at a loss and would therefore be obliged to cease operations, involving loss to the substantial American interests involved in the corporation and its creditors. They deny any right of the Motion Picture Censorship Committee either under the treaties or under the Chinese motion picture censorship law of 1930 or regulations issued in 1935 in pursuance thereof, to ban all Paramount pictures pending adjustment of the dispute over "The General Died at Dawn". They assert that the principle at issue is of the utmost importance because several motion pictures now in production by major American producers contain matter relating to China and if this precedent is now established practically the entire American motion picture business in China will be involved and imperiled. The representatives therefore urgently request that the Em-

---

[75] J. E. Perkins, Paramount Films of China, Inc.
[76] A. R. Hagar, president, Cathay-Grand Corporation.

bassy take the strongest measures to bring about the immediate withdrawal of the present ban on Paramount films which is equally as important as the principle described above.

3. I have indicated to the representatives my complete readiness to ask for interview with Vice Minister of Foreign Affairs Hsu Mo, to argue this matter but I believe my representations would be much more effective if reinforced by direct instructions from the Department and I shall therefore defer action for 1 day in the hope of receiving them.

4. Sent to the Department and Peiping.

PECK

893.4061 Motion Pictures/200 : Telegram

The Acting Secretary of State to the Ambassador in China (Johnson)

WASHINGTON, November 18, 1936—6 p. m.

73. Your 329, November 18, noon. The Department feels that the action of the Chinese authorities in banning all Paramount pictures pending adjustment of the dispute over the motion picture "The General Died at Dawn" is arbitrary and without justification and authorizes you to make appropriate representations in regard to the matter.

MOORE

893.4061 Motion Pictures/202 : Telegram

The Counselor of Embassy in China (Peck) to the Secretary of State

NANKING, November 19, 1936—2 p. m.
[Received November 19—1 : 30 p. m.]

331. Embassy's 329, November 18, noon, from Nanking.

1. During informal conversation today at the Foreign Office I was told that as early as April last Vice Consul Kiang at Los Angeles informed Paramount that "The General Died at Dawn" would be offensive to the Chinese in its then existing form and subsequently gave other warnings but that Paramount returned a written reply that modification of the film was impossible. It was represented to me that the present ban of all Paramount pictures is therefore the effect of a long controversy between Paramount and the Censorship Committee with the Vice Consul and the Foreign Office serving as channel of communication. Since the Foreign Office brought up this subject for discussion I took the opportunity to object to the banning of other films to bring about suppression of the film in dispute since this was at best an extra legal measure and might be regarded as illegal infringement on the rights of innocent third parties, for example, the

theatres concerned. The Foreign Office official volunteered to try to settle this controversy at least to the extent of withdrawal of the ban until the film in dispute could arrive in China and be inspected by the Censorship Committee.

2. Sent to Peiping.

PECK

893.4061 Motion Pictures/203 : Telegram

The Ambassador in China (Johnson) to the Secretary of State

PEIPING, November 20, 1936—3 p. m.
[Received November 20—7 a. m.]

562. Nanking's 329, November 18, noon. The following telegram has been sent to Nanking:

"November 19, noon. Your 329, November 18, noon. Unless you receive different instructions from the Department within the indicated period of time, you should make strong representations to the Foreign Office against the action of the Motion Pictures Censorship Committee, which the Embassy considers to be arbitrary and unwarranted. I believe that you should not concede to the committee in this event any other authority than to deal with American motion pictures as they are to be shown in China, and you should contend that in equity the committee should limit itself to taking action in regard to the particular film in question. You may convey to the Foreign Office my belief that the adherence of the committee to the extreme position it has taken would have an unfavorable reaction in the publicity it would receive in the United States."

JOHNSON

893.4061 Motion Pictures/204 : Telegram

The Counselor of Embassy in China (Peck) to the Secretary of State

NANKING, November 21, 1936—11 a. m.
[Received 2 : 25 p. m.[77]]

332. Department's 73, November 18, 6 p. m., to Nanking.

1. I interviewed Vice Minister Hsu Mo November 20, 4 p. m. for 1 hour. I informed him that the Department regarded the banning of all Paramount films as arbitrary and unwarranted especially in view of the fact that the Censorship Committee had not itself seen the film "The General Died At Dawn" and the fact that associate American financial interests in no way connected with the production of the film would be involved in heavy loss (see my 329, November 18, noon, paragraph 2). I conveyed the assurance of Paramount (as stated to the Embassy in writing) that the company was anxious to

[77] Telegram in two sections.

settle the matter amicably. In the course of the long interview I also advanced other arguments.

2. The Vice Minister, however, adhered firmly to his contentions that the producers had repeatedly and obstinately refused to heed advice and warning given by the Chinese Vice Consul Kiang at Los Angeles; that the committee was justified in relying on the judgment of the Vice Consul as a Chinese official regarding the offensive nature of the film and that the banning of all the films of an offending company was the only "sanction" available to the Chinese Government with which to defend China from defamatory films and that this measure was therefore justified.

3. I again pointed out that the Department was willing to give consideration to any specific objections which the Foreign Office might convey to the Embassy and I inquired whether the Foreign Office would not be willing to intervene in the present case to the extent at least of attempting to get the ban lifted until the film in dispute could be brought to China for inspection by the committee. The Vice Minister inquired what authority the Department exercised in such matters and whether the company would be willing to give an indication that the offending film would be withdrawn from all countries. I refused to attempt any definition of the Department's authority or influence in matters of film production and I said I could give no assurances on behalf of Paramount; moreover, I refused to accept the committee's assumption that the Vice Consul's opinion of the film was infallible, particularly in view of the fact that the Chinese Consul and Chamber of Commerce in Manila were reported as finding it unobjectionable.

4. The Vice Minister would not admit that the banning of Paramount films was in any way unwarranted or arbitrary and on the contrary steadily maintained it was warranted by the indifference of Paramount to Chinese opinions and the heavy responsibility resting on the committee to protect China from the injury of world wide disparaging film publicity.

5. I subsequently encountered the Vice Minister at a reception and inquired whether he would not recede from his uncompromising position in view of the danger that the dispute of the American film company with the censorship committee might develop into a serious conflict between them. He replied that such a development would be regrettable and that he would have the Director of the International Affairs Department talk with me again next week.

6. My opinion is that the Vice Minister sympathizes entirely with the Censorship Committee and feels that it is in a strong tactical position but that because of the present Sino-Japanese tension he may refrain from pressing his advantage in order to avoid causing further irritation to the Embassy and the Department. It is unlikely, how-

ever, that he would concede any weight to our arguments and such a compromise would not obviate further difficulties (see my November 18, noon, paragraph 2, sentence 3). Sent to Peiping.

PECK

893.4061 Motion Pictures/205 : Telegram

The Acting Secretary of State to the Ambassador in China (Johnson)

WASHINGTON, November 25, 1936—3 p. m.

288. Your 571, November 24, 2 p. m.[78] The Motion Picture Producers and Distributors of America, Incorporated, New York City, in a letter under date November 23, states

"The Paramount office in New York have a cable from their office in China stating that the Chinese Government there has allowed them a period of 40 days in which they can go ahead and distribute their pictures and, during which period they are expected to show a print of the above-mentioned picture ('The General Died at Dawn') to the Chinese censors to see if some conclusion cannot be worked out to the satisfaction of all parties concerned."

As the Embassy has already made oral representations and as the above offers a possible basis for reaching a satisfactory solution of the matter, the Department feels that it would be advisable to await developments before giving conclusive consideration to the making of a formal protest.

MOORE

893.4061 Motion Pictures/209 : Telegram

The Ambassador in China (Johnson) to the Secretary of State

NANKING, December 1, 1936—11 a. m.
[Received 5 : 50 p. m.[79]]

336. Your 288, November 25, 3 p. m., to Peiping.

1. It appears that the Shanghai office of Paramount was over-sanguine in regard to the terms on which the Censorship Committee offered to resume temporary censoring of Paramount films. On November 24 Peck wrote informally to the Director of the Department of International Affairs of the Foreign Office quoting a letter dated November 23 from the Paramount office, Shanghai, stating that a print of "The General Died at Dawn" was being sent to Nanking and stating that a formal petition had been sent to the Censorship Committee asking that censorship of other films be resumed. Peck inquired [when] resumption would begin. On the same day Peck was informed by

[78] Not printed.
[79] Telegram in two sections.

the director that the committee had stated that censorship would be resumed at once provided Paramount guaranteed arrival of the film within 40 days and undertook to discuss with the committee what action should be taken on this picture. After discussing these terms with the Paramount office, Shanghai, on the telephone Peck wrote again to the director on November 25 saying that Paramount willingly accepted the terms and wished to know when censorship would be resumed. Matters dragged until November 27 when Paramount informed Peck that the committee's terms as communicated directly to that office were more onerous than those transmitted through Peck in that they included action on a second film "Klondike Annie", required that negatives as well as positives of both films be sent to Nanking and required a guaranty of $1,000 which would be forfeited if the films did not arrive within 40 days. In reply to request for advice Peck suggested that while responsibility for decision rested solely on Paramount, it might be well to accept these terms under protest in order to save from heavy financial loss another American firm, the Cathay-Grand Corporation in Shanghai which depended upon receiving Paramount films. On November 28, the representative of Paramount, then in Nanking, informed Peck that after accepting the more severe version of the committee's terms Paramount had been told by the committee that before censoring could be resumed all copies of "The General Died at Dawn" must be withdrawn immediately from circulation. When the representative protested that this requirement had not been made heretofore the committee replied that it had been "understood".

2. The Director of the Department of International Affairs has now written Peck as follows under date of November 30:

"I take pleasure to inform you that the Central Motion Picture Censorship Committee will continue to issue certificates to the Paramount Films Company in the immediate future. It is to be understood that the suspension of the original decision will last for a period of 40 days pending the arrival of the negative of the picture 'General Died at Dawn'.

"It is reported, however, the picture in question 'General Died at Dawn' is shortly to be shown in Japan and some other different countries, and this, I believe, will render the situation more difficult. In order to avoid any further aggravation of friction in the present case, you are requested to use your good intermediary in persuading the company to withhold the show of the picture until some settlement of the controversy has been secured. Kindly let me know the result when you receive a reply from the company."

A copy of the letter has been sent to Paramount, Shanghai. In view of the loss which American interests say they are suffering because of failure to receive Paramount films (see the Embassy's November 18, noon, from Nanking) I venture to suggest that if Paramount, New York, asks advice the Department reply by representing the possible advisability of acceding to the request of the Chinese authorities for withdrawal of this film.

3. Sent to the Department, by mail to Peiping.

JOHNSON

893.4061 Motion Pictures/220

The Ambassador in China (Johnson) to the Secretary of State

No. 898   PEIPING, December 3, 1936.
                                    [Received January 4, 1937.]

SIR: I have the honor to refer to the Department's telegram No. 278, November 16, 6 p. m., in regard to the confiscation of American motion picture films by the Chinese National Motion Picture Censorship Committee, and to enclose for the information of the Department a copy of a despatch received from Counselor Peck at Nanking regarding this subject under date November 20, 1936.[80] In that despatch Mr. Peck reports that the Director of the Department of International Affairs of the Foreign Office in an interview with Mr. Peck stated that the Ministry of Foreign Affairs shares the opinion of the Embassy that there exists no legal provision authorizing the Censorship Committee to confiscate films; and, the Director promised that the Ministry would send a communication to the Censorship Committee in regard to the matter.

Respectfully yours,   For the Ambassador:
                                    F. P. LOCKHART
                                    Counselor of Embassy

893.4061 Motion Pictures/215 : Telegram

The Counselor of Embassy in China (Peck) to the Secretary of State

NANKING, December 7, 1936—1 p. m.
[Received 2 p. m.]

346. Embassy's 336, December 1, 11 a. m. from Nanking concerning ban on Paramount films.

1. Letter dated December 4 from Perkins stated that the two pictures which were being held by the Censorship Committee had been released with permits for showing and that Paramount had submitted three other films which Perkins believed were being considered.

2. Letter stated that Perkins could not comment on the letter of November 30 from the Director of the Department of International Affairs until he had consulted New York but observed that it would

---

be impossible to withdraw the film from circulation immediately since this would expose Paramount to damage suits for violation of contracts.

3. Perkins requested in letter that the Embassy advise the Foreign Office only that he was taking up with the New York office the matter of international withdrawal of this film.

4. To Peiping for the Ambassador.

PECK

893.4061 Motion Pictures/219 : Telegram

The Ambassador in China (Johnson) to the Secretary of State

NANKING, December 30, 1936—5 p. m.
[Received December 30—10:10 a. m.]

385. Herron, foreign manager Motion Picture Producers and Distributors of America, New York, has telegraphed asking information concerning situation Paramount Pictures. Please inform him Paramount films are again being censored but when films of "General Died at Dawn" and "Klondike Annie" reach Nanking, about January 9, whole matter will be reviewed.

JOHNSON

AMERICAN INTEREST IN PROBLEMS AFFECTING THE INTERNATIONAL SETTLEMENT AT SHANGHAI [81]

893.102S/1388

The Consul General at Shanghai (Gauss) to the Ambassador in China (Johnson) [82]

No. 169   SHANGHAI, May 6, 1936.

SIR: I have the honor to inform you that, following the recent difficulty over the Municipal election in the International Settlement at Shanghai, when the Foreign Treaty Consuls set aside the ballot as invalid and ordered a new election, the German Consul General inquired of the Senior Consul why he had not been invited to attend the meeting of the Foreign Treaty Consuls which took the action indicated. The Senior Consul replied that he was following the precedent established for some years that matters affecting the International Settlement and the Land Regulations are dealt with by the extraterritorial Consuls. Thereupon the German Consul General asked that there should be put on the agenda of the next Consular Body meeting the question of an invitation to "all consular represent-

[81] For previous correspondence, see *Foreign Relations*, 1934, vol. III, pp. 607 ff.
[82] Copy transmitted to the Department by the Consul General at Shanghai in his despatch No. 180, May 6; received June 1.

atives at Shanghai to meetings of the Consular Body when matters of general interest are to be discussed."

This move by the German Consul General arises out of some dissatisfaction felt in the German community that they are invited to support the substantial British-American control of the Settlement but have no representation in the consular group dealing with Settlement matters, and that notices on Municipal matters issued by the Foreign Treaty Consuls are published over the signatures of the extraterritorial Consuls, thus publicly emphasizing the non-participation of the German Consul General in consular deliberations.

The action of the German Consul General has, so far, become known only to the Senior Consul (Norwegian), the British Consul General, and myself. The British Consul General and I agree that it is desirable that, so far as possible, an international community of interests in respect of the International Settlement should be recognized and emphasized and that some means should be found of including the German Consul General, as the representative of a substantial German element in the community, in the deliberations of the Consuls on Settlement matters. At the same time, however, we recognize that if the German Consul General were to be accepted as a "Foreign Treaty Consul" under the Land Regulations, an embarrassing situation might arise later if the consular representatives of some other non-extraterritorial treaty power (such as Soviet Russia) fundamentally opposed to the present position of the other powers in China, should demand recognition in the consular meetings on Settlement affairs. There might also be involved in the situation a possible demand by non-career honorary Consuls of non-extraterritorial powers . . . to be consulted in Settlement matters in which they have no real interest.

As a result of a study of the matter, I have proposed informally to the Senior Consul and the British Consul General that we might seek a solution of the difficulty along the following lines:

(1) That we continue to take the view that the Land Regulations, when referring to the "Foreign Treaty Consuls" and to the "Consuls of Foreign Powers having Treaties with China", contemplate the exercise of the prescribed functions by the Consuls of the extraterritorial powers.

(2) That, at the same time, we recognize a community of interest in Settlement affairs on the part of all foreign nationals, and that on that basis, the German community being substantial, we, the extraterritorial Consuls, might "invite" the German Consul General to "meet and consult" with us on Settlement matters.

(3) That, in order to overcome that situation in which the German Consul General is so obviously excluded from "Foreign Treaty Consul" notices on Municipal affairs, the extraterritorial Consuls adopt the practice of not publishing such notices over their signatures but that, instead, they cause the Senior (extraterritorial) Consul to communicate to the Municipal Council texts of notices which the Council

shall publish as "by direction of the Foreign Treaty Consuls", all signatures being omitted from the published notices.

My colleagues, the Senior Consul and the British Consul General, have welcomed these suggestions as providing a happy solution of the difficulty. The Senior Consul will approach the German Consul General in the matter. It is believed that he will find the solution satisfactory. It will then be necessary to consult the Japanese and other extraterritorial Consuls.

I believe that the position that, under the Land Regulations, the extraterritorial Consuls alone have status in connection with Settlement matters, is technically correct. At the same time, it does not seem desirable that that situation be emphasized unduly, either in the foreign community or before the Chinese. The system of administration of the International Settlement at Shanghai is closely interwoven with the system of extraterritoriality, and is largely but not entirely dependent thereon.

Respectfully yours,   C. E. GAUSS

893.102S/1395

The Ambassador in China (Johnson) to the Secretary of State

No. 646   PEIPING, August 13, 1936.
                                           [Received September 8.]

SIR: I have the honor to enclose for the information of the Department copies of Consul General Gauss' unnumbered despatch of July 26, 1936, to the Embassy, my instruction to him of July 30, his unnumbered despatch of August 3, and my instruction of August 13,[83] relating to the establishment of Japanese naval patrols in certain sections of the American and British defense sectors at Shanghai without notification to the Shanghai Municipal Police or to the commanding officer of the American and British forces.

Mr. Gauss reported in his despatch of July 26 that there were numerous Japanese residents in the areas where the Japanese patrols were functioning and that the patrols were undoubtedly sent into those areas to assure the Japanese residents of adequate protection additional to that provided by the Municipal Police following the excitement caused by the recent killing of a Japanese subject named Kayau. Mr. Gauss stated that courtesy should have dictated that the Commanding Officer of the Japanese Naval Landing Party notify the Shanghai Municipal Police or the American and British commanding officers of his intention to establish patrols in sections of their defense areas and of his reasons therefor. Colonel Price of the Fourth Ma-

---

[83] None printed.

rines consulted Mr. Gauss on July 24 and informed him that he proposed, subject to the approval of the Commander-in-Chief, United States Asiatic Fleet, to address a courteous letter to the Commanding Officer of the Japanese Naval Landing Party requesting information as to the reasons for the presence of the Japanese patrols in the American sector. Mr. Gauss told Colonel Price that he would be in accord with his proposal if he would preface his inquiry with the statement that, while no state of emergency existed under which he had taken up the defense of the sector assigned to the American forces under the defense plan, he was, nevertheless, interested at all times to know of military dispositions in that sector and for that reason made his inquiry. Colonel Price accepted the suggestion.

The Embassy informed Mr. Gauss in its instruction of July 30 that it approved his suggestion to Colonel Price.

Mr. Gauss reported in his despatch of August 3 that the proposed letter was sent by Colonel Price, under authorization of Admiral Murfin,[84] to the Commanding Officer of the Japanese Naval Landing Party and resulted in a visit from the Chief of Staff of the Japanese force, who explained the reason for the establishment of the patrol— the uneasiness in the Japanese community following the killing of Kayau and the desire on the part of the Japanese naval authorities to make a gesture of reassurance to Japanese nationals—and stated that the Japanese authorities regretted that they had overlooked giving the Marines information on the subject. Mr. Gauss stated that he had been informed by the Intelligence Officer of the Fourth Marines that the Japanese patrol had been withdrawn from the American sector but that a patrol at the Toyoda Mill, adjoining the British sector, continued to be maintained. Mr. Gauss said that the action taken by Colonel Price seemed to have had the desired effect of reminding the Japanese that they were intruding on the American sector without the usual polite notification and of inducing an expression of regret over their omission.

Respectfully yours,
NELSON TRUSLER JOHNSON

893.102S/1397

The Ambassador in China (Johnson) to the Secretary of State

No. 661   PEIPING, August 20, 1936.
                                               [Received September 21.]

SIR: I have the honor to enclose for the information and consideration of the Department copies of despatch No. 333, dated August 12, 1936, from the Consul General at Shanghai, in regard to Chinese representation on the Shanghai Municipal Council.[85] Mr. Gauss en-

---

[84] Rear Adm. Orin Gould Murfin, Commander in Chief, U. S. Asiatic Fleet.
[85] Not printed.

closes with his despatch a copy of Consular Body Circular No. 178–M–XII of August 6, 1936, in which there is quoted a letter from the Mayor of the Shanghai Municipal Government transmitting a request from the Chinese Ratepayers' Association for an increase, effective in 1937, of Chinese representation on the Municipal Council of the International Settlement at Shanghai.

Mr. Gauss recalls that the Land Regulations for the International Settlement make provision for not more than nine foreign members of the Municipal Council. In 1928 a "temporary arrangement" was effected by which three Chinese members were added to the Council and in 1930 a further arrangement increased the Chinese membership from three to five. Mr. Gauss states that the Chinese now desire a further increase to nine members, in order to have equal representation with the foreign community. He states that he understands that the Chinese request has been made known informally to the Municipal Council and that the senior Chinese member of the Council has approached the Chairman of the Council on the subject. He adds, however, that the impression seems to prevail that the Chinese application will not be pushed vigorously at this time.

I concur in the views expressed by Mr. Gauss and respectfully commend his despatch to the careful consideration of the Department.[86] I will appreciate receiving any comments the Department may desire to make on the subject.

Further developments will be reported to the Department.

Respectfully yours, NELSON TRUSLER JOHNSON

893.102S/1402

The Ambassador in China (Johnson) to the Secretary of State

No. 701 PEIPING, September 11, 1936.
[Received October 5.]

SIR: I have the honor to refer to despatch No. 169 of May 6, 1936, from the Consul General at Shanghai, concerning the status of non-extraterritorial consuls in connection with the Land Regulations and International Settlement at Shanghai, copies of which were forwarded by Mr. Gauss to the Department under cover of his despatch No. 180 of May 6.[87]

The course of action suggested by Mr. Gauss in his despatch under reference was approved in the Embassy's instruction to him of May 14th. Mr. Gauss has now reported in his despatch No. 349 of

---

[86] Mr. Gauss expressed the view that the Chinese had adequate representation on the Shanghai Municipal Council, but if there should be a general disposition to agree to a further increase in Chinese representation we should be disposed to acquiesce in such an arrangement. At the same time, the American Consul General should not take the initiative in any such proposal.
[87] Not printed.

August 22, copies of which are enclosed,[88] that the Senior Consul ascertained from the German Consul General that the proposals outlined in his despatch No. 169 would be acceptable to him and then circulated the proposals to the extraterritorial consuls, who appear to have accepted them. The British Consul General has not yet recorded his opinion in writing but he approved the proposals before they were laid before the German Consul General. Mr. Gauss states that, in circulating the proposals to the extraterritorial consuls, the Senior Consul suggested that the arrangement "might be extended if it is so desired, to include all the heads of non-extraterritorial consulates of countries having treaties with China". This suggestion was not accepted.

Respectfully yours, NELSON TRUSLER JOHNSON

893.102S/1411

Memorandum by the Chief of the Division of Far Eastern Affairs (Hornbeck)

[WASHINGTON,] September 25, 1936.

The port of Shanghai is one of the world's great trade centers. At that port there is located an "International Settlement". In that Settlement there reside some 66,000 "foreigners" and about a million Chinese. Among the "foreigners" there are some 3,800 Americans. That Settlement is administered by a Municipal Council which is elected by the local taxpayers, which is of mixed (international) personnel, and which has among its members American nationals. The municipality maintains a police force which is of mixed personnel and maintains a volunteer armed force which is made up of several units of foreign nationalities, recruited from among the foreign residents, subject to active duty for general policing and defense duties in event of "emergencies". On the police force there are usually a few Americans, and in the volunteer forces there is an American unit. Foreign governments regularly have present at Shanghai some naval vessels, and, since 1927, several foreign governments have had at Shanghai temporarily landed armed contingents. Among the naval vessels present (regularly) are some American vessels, and among the landed forces there is an American contingent which at present consists of marines to the number of approximately 1,100.

Among the responsibilities of the American Government in regard to Shanghai the first is the ordinary responsibility of affording appropriate protection to American interests. These interests are in particular the security and the general rights of 3,800 American nationals,

---

[88] Not printed.

a physical property and investment interest aggregating $90,000,000, and a participation interest in the trade which is carried on through that port. (Note: About one-half of the foreign trade of China centers at Shanghai.) Second, we have a responsibility which arises out of and relates to the unusual (quasi-international) character of the port of Shanghai, the historical and actual facts in the "set-up" of the International Settlement, and the special treaties with and in regard to China. The rights, obligations, and interests of the various nationalities represented in the make-up of the local population, together with those of the various countries concerned there, are substantially and tenaciously interwoven. The web is one in the weaving of which the American Government and American nationals have from the very beginning of the life of the Settlement, more than ninety years ago, taken part. The American Government at the outset insisted and has throughout nearly a century insisted that this country should enjoy equal rights (and "privileges") with other countries at Shanghai and equal rights of participation in the affairs, the administration, the defense, etc., of the International Settlement. We have responsibilities with and toward the other nations in regard to the situation at and the future of Shanghai. While we might at any moment by a political act turn our backs upon our political responsibilities in regard to Shanghai, it is questionable whether we could thus get away from our legal obligations there, and it is certain that we could not thus dispose of our moral obligations.

The landed armed forces which the various foreign powers, this country included, have since 1927 maintained at Shanghai were landed for the purpose of contributing to the maintenance of order in and to the security of the International Settlement. Each foreign power of course envisaged the protection of its own nationals, especially as regards life; but, it was and is realized that the maximum of assurance with regard to the lives of individuals could best be obtained through defense of the area within which these individuals in the aggregate are resident. Disorder in or an invasion of the Settlement from outside would endanger all foreign nationals and therefore endanger individual foreigners of each and every nationality. The theory, therefore, upon which the police and the volunteer armed units and the landed forces of each and several nationalities are maintained and do function at Shanghai, is that local, foreign national and foreign international interests are both separately and collectively involved, and that the municipality and each of the foreign governments concerned have and shall have both separate national and collective international responsibilities in relation to the problem of order and security. There exist no treaties or formal international commitments providing that the various political authorities concerned shall maintain these armed forces, or prescribing the proportions or limitations which shall prevail among these forces, as to numbers, disposal, etc.; but, the presence and the plans with regard to the functioning of these forces rest on considerations of experience and of informal commitment to the idea of cooperation, over a period of years, among and on the part of the major powers concerned.

The Shanghai International Settlement has been and is a going quasi-international enterprise. All of the powers enjoy rights and benefits by virtue of its existence and of the various agencies which contribute thereto. All of them have obligations to each other, severally and collectively, in connection therewith.

In 1927, the presence of the foreign landed armed forces effectively discouraged the threatened invasion of the Settlement by highly excited and none too well disciplined Chinese "nationalists" troops. In 1932, the presence of these foreign landed armed forces contributed enormously toward the maintenance of order in the Settlement in the presence of a migration of many thousands of Chinese refugees from an outlying portion into the main area of the Settlement; also, contributed toward preventing (or insuring against) a retreat into the main area of the Settlement of Chinese soldiery who were in conflict with Japanese troops and who, but for the operation of the "defense plan" (which involved a disposal on certain agreed-upon lines of the various foreign armed contingents), might easily have retreated in disorder into that area. In neither of these cases was the presence of nor were the acts of the foreign landed armed contingents (with the exception of the Japanese) provocative; in neither instance did they lead to armed clashes; and in both instances they contributed effectively to the maintenance of order, the giving of a sense of security, protection of life, and prevention of destruction of property. In the 1932 instance, both the British and the American Governments hastily reenforced their landed armed contingents, the British with troops from Hong Kong, the Americans with troops from Manila. The Japanese and the Chinese had begun fighting, in a part of and on a border of the Settlement. There came from no source, so far as the undersigned is aware, any criticism of the action of the American Government in the playing of its part in thus contributing to the meeting of the situation of emergency and of danger to the lives of the foreign, including American, residents of the International Settlement.

It is believed that with due regard for its existing responsibilities and for general and particular considerations incident to the "good neighbor policy," the American Government could not and should not at this time make any withdrawal of any of its armed forces at Shanghai; and that we should expect, in the event of there developing at Shanghai a critical situation—which does not now seem likely—

even to have to give consideration to the possibility of increasing, as we did in 1932, those forces.

S[TANLEY] K. H[ORNBECK]

893.0146/520 : Telegram

The Ambassador in China (Johnson) to the Secretary of State

PEIPING, October 2, 1936—1 p. m.
[Received October 3—10 : 40 p. m.]

475. Reference Shanghai's 374, September 11 to the Embassy concerning Shanghai Volunteer Corps, copies of which were mailed direct to the Department.[89] Following is a brief summary of my instruction of October 1 to Gauss.

1. I agree that the Department will hardly wish to reply to the question concerning its attitude toward desire of the rate payers to curtail cost of present volunteer corps, as I feel that this is a matter for the decision of the rate payers themselves.

2. I am recommending to the Department that it may care to discuss the whole question of the International Settlement and its protection with the British Government with the idea of possible exchange of views with the French and Japanese Governments.

3. I agree that the Fourth United States Marines should be retained in Shanghai for such time as may be necessary for the protection of American life and property, but within such limits as responsible American naval authority may consider compatible with the military question involved and with a clear understanding on the part of the Settlement authorities that our Marines are in Shanghai for that purpose and not for the defense of the political and territorial integrity of the Settlement against armed attack from any quarter.

4. I agree as to the falsity of Fessenden's [90] assumption of the purpose [of] the Volunteer Corps and regarding purpose of the foreign powers, certainly the United States, in maintaining landing forces at Shanghai.

5. I consider that the whole purpose of the Volunteer Corps, which after all consists of the armed residents of the Settlement, is to supplement the efforts of the paid police force in cooperating with the sovereign authority (the Chinese Government) in maintaining peace and order in the Settlement.

6. With regard to the distinction between limited functional activities of the volunteers and police in comparison with those of a naval

---

[89] Not printed.
[90] Stirling Fessenden, American Secretary General of the Shanghai International Settlement Municipal Council.

force, I feel that the question of the use of the American landing force at Shanghai to protect American citizens in their homes beyond the Settlement borders is a military question which I consider must be left to the senior American naval officer concerned. Fundamentally those Americans beyond the Settlement borders are living under Chinese police protection and, if that protection is withdrawn or fails, such Americans must choose whether they will remain at their own risk or withdraw into the area policed by the Settlement, for it is doubtful whether the allied armed forces would care to substitute themselves for the police power of the sovereign Government, and in case of direct attack it is believed that the military arm would not care to expose its limited force over a large area or by concentration at a point beyond protection of its ships.

Copies of my instruction to Gauss are being taken to Shanghai by courier today and will be mailed by first boat.[92]

JOHNSON

893.0146/520 : Telegram

The Secretary of State to the Ambassador in China (Johnson)

WASHINGTON, October 14, 1936—1 p. m.

243. Embassy's 475, October 2, 1 p. m.

1. Department assumes that your instruction to Shanghai, summarized in the telegram under reference, does not contemplate that Gauss shall make definitive reply to the letter of September 1 addressed to him by the Chairman of the Municipal Council pending the receipt by the Embassy of an expression of the Department's views. It is suggested that Gauss, unless he has already done so, merely acknowledge the receipt of the Chairman's letter and state that the subject matter is receiving consideration by the appropriate agencies of the American Government. The Department assumes also that the matter is not so urgent as to require immediate consideration, and accordingly the Department, while it concurs in general with the views expressed in your telegram under reference and in Gauss' despatch, will await, before reaching a definite conclusion, receipt of a copy of the full text of the instruction to Gauss which you are sending by pouch.[92]

2. Should you or Gauss receive any indication of the attitude of the British Government or of the character of the reply which the British Consul General at Shanghai may make or makes to the letter under discussion, please report promptly and fully thereon to the Department by cable.

3. Repeat to Nanking for the Ambassador.

HULL

---

[92] Not printed.

893.0146/522 : Telegram

The Ambassador in China (Johnson) to the Secretary of State

PEIPING, October 16, 1936—6 p. m.
[Received October 16—8 : 55 a. m.]

504. Department's 243, October 14, 1 p. m. Gauss reports that he does not consider that for the time being any acknowledgment is necessary of the letter from the Chairman of the Council but that he may take an opportunity to inform the Chairman orally that the matter has been referred for the consideration of the Department. I am sending to Shanghai by courier today code text of the Department's telegraphic institution [*instruction*] under reference and am instructing Gauss that if the Chairman desires written acknowledgment he reply as suggested by the Department.

Attitude of the British Government and action taken by the British Consul General at Shanghai will be reported when ascertained.

Gauss reported October 5 that steps had been taken by the Council to disband artillery units of the Volunteer Corps which should effect saving of $95,000 Chinese currency.

JOHNSON

893.102S/1413

The Ambassador in China (Johnson) to the Secretary of State

No. 790
PEIPING, October 17, 1936.
[Received November 16.]

SIR: I have the honor to enclose for the information of the Department a copy of despatch No. 408 of September 28, 1936, from the Consul General at Shanghai, with which he transmitted a copy of a letter dated August 12, 1936, from the Secretary General of the Shanghai Municipal Council to the Senior Consul,[93] requesting that the Consular Body approve the decision of the Council to reprint the Land Regulations with certain amendments to provide for the Chinese members of the Council and the Chinese members of the Land Commission.

Mr. Gauss recalled in his despatch that, when arrangements were made to provide for Chinese members of the Council, no textual amendment of the Land Regulations was proposed or adopted. When arrangements were made to add two Chinese to the Land Commission, certain textual changes in the Land Regulations were proposed, but the Chinese authorities avoided recognition of the Land Regulations, merely approving the arrangement for two Chinese Land Commis-

---

[93] Neither printed.

sioners. He stated that, in discussing the matter with the British (and Senior) Consul General, he expressed to Sir John Brenan the opinion that as there had been no agreement for the textual amendment of the Land Regulations it would seem desirable simply to annotate the Regulations to show the arrangements made in accordance with the procedure prescribed in Land Regulation XXVIII to provide for the Chinese members of the Council and the Chinese Land Commissioners. His British colleague, however, was disposed to establish the amendments to the Land Regulations as drafted by the Council and communicate them to the Mayor, leaving it to the latter to agree, reject, or remain silent. He had so recommended to his Embassy and had discussed the matter with the British Ambassador when he visited Shanghai. Sir John felt that textual amendments of the Land Regulations were necessary in order that the reprint might be annexed to a King's Regulation which is necessary to make the amended Land Regulations binding upon British subjects in China. Mr. Gauss stated that, while he believed that this end might just as easily be accomplished by the publication of annotated Land Regulations, he informed Sir John that, in an effort to meet his wishes as far as possible, he would be disposed to agree that the Council be informed that the Consular Body approved the reprinting of the Land Regulations with the textual amendments as drafted by the Council, but that such amendments should appear in italics and that an appropriate note should be added to explain that the amendments had been established in accordance with arrangements made by the competent authorities under Land Regulation XXVIII to provide for the Chinese members of the Council and the Chinese members of the Land Commission. A copy of the reprinted Land Regulations when so published would be transmitted to the Mayor by the Senior Consul. This proposal was accepted by the British Consul General who stated that he would approach the Japanese Consul General informally for his concurrence before the matter was put before a meeting of the Consular Body.

Mr. Gauss reported in his subsequent despatch No. 438 of October 12, 1936, a copy of which is enclosed,[94] that at a meeting of the interested consular representatives held on October 6 it was agreed that the Shanghai Municipal Council should be informed that the Consuls approved the reprinting of the Land Regulations with the textual amendments as drafted by the Council, but that it should be suggested to the Council that such amendments should appear in italics and that an appropriate footnote be added in each case to explain that the amendments had been established in accordance with arrange-

---

[94] Not printed.

ments made by the competent authorities under Land Regulation XXVIII to provide for the Chinese members of the Council and the Chinese members of the Land Commission. It was further agreed that the Council should be requested to draft a pertinent footnote in each case for the purpose mentioned and to submit the drafts to the Consular Body for approval. Mr. Gauss stated that some of his colleagues felt that the footnotes should include the full text of the articles of the Land Regulations before amendment, but he considered that the footnotes as drafted by the Council could be made sufficiently explanatory to avoid the necessity of reprinting the full text of the articles before amendment.

A copy of the communication sent by the Senior Consul to the Council under date October 7, 1936,[95] is enclosed with Mr. Gauss's despatch No. 438 of October 12.

Further developments will be reported to the Department.

Respectfully yours, NELSON TRUSLER JOHNSON

893.102S/1414

The Ambassador in China (Johnson) to the Secretary of State

No. 791   PEIPING, October 17, 1936.
                                                [Received November 16.]

SIR: I have the honor to refer to the Embassy's despatch No. 661 of August 20, 1936, in regard to Chinese representation on the Shanghai Municipal Council, and to enclose for the information of the Department copies of two despatches from Consul General Gauss on the subject, Nos. 407 and 437, dated September 28 and October 12, 1936, respectively.[96]

Mr. Gauss reported in his despatch No. 407 that the British and Senior Consul General had prepared a draft reply [95] to the Mayor's communication of July 27, 1936. Mr. Gauss stated that:

"The British draft despatch points out that the International Settlement was established primarily for the purpose of residence and trade by foreign nationals, that under the authority delegated by the Chinese Government in the Land Regulations the administration of the Settlement was entrusted to a foreign Council elected by the foreign ratepayers, that in the course of time agreement was reached to add five Chinese members to the Council to represent the interests of Chinese who for various reasons have come to live in the Settlement, that in addition to these five Chinese councillors, there are also two Chinese members of the Land Commission, that the Consuls are of the opinion that the Chinese residents of the Settlement are already well repre-

[95] Not printed.
[96] Neither printed.

sented and there is no danger of the Chinese side of any question remaining unheard for lack of spokesmen, and that 'so long as the International Settlement at Shanghai remains a place for foreign residence and trade under the treaties' the Consuls 'are unable to agree to any changes in the Land Regulations which might endanger the foreign control of the administration'."

After examining this draft Mr. Gauss informed his British colleague that he would be disposed to accept his proposal provided the last paragraph were amended to modify the assertion that the Consuls were unable to agree to any changes which might endanger the foreign control of the administration. Mr. Gauss suggested that, while this might be a policy which could be supported in principle, he did not believe that it should be announced in the note to the Mayor. It was enough, he considered, to point to the character of the Settlement as an area of foreign residence and trade and to emphasize that the Chinese were already well represented. The British Consul General requested Mr. Gauss to suggest changes in the draft and a copy of the British draft with the changes suggested by Mr. Gauss is enclosed with his despatch in question.

Mr. Gauss reported in his despatch No. 437 of October 12 that on October 6 the interested consular representatives approved the despatch of a communication which conformed to the amended draft. In this communication, which was sent to the Mayor on October 7, the Senior Consul stated that, while the interested Consuls noted with appreciation the keen interest taken by the Chinese community in the affairs of the International Settlement and had much sympathy with their desire for further cooperation in the municipal administration, it was felt by the Consular Body that the Chinese ratepayers were under a misapprehension in claiming as a right that Chinese representation on the Council should be proportionate to the amount of taxes paid by Chinese residents. The interested Consuls wished to point out, he stated, that the International Settlement was established primarily for the residence and trade of foreign nationals and, in pursuance of that purpose, the Chinese Government had delegated certain administrative powers by means of the Land Regulations to a Council composed of foreign members elected by the foreign ratepayers. The Senior Consul said that in the course of time it was considered desirable to admit Chinese representation in the international administration in order that due importance should be given to the wishes and sentiments of the Chinese population, who for various reasons had come to reside within the Settlement area. The foreign ratepayers and their national authorities had accordingly agreed at different times to the addition of five Chinese members to the Council to assist their foreign colleagues in the work of administration and, in addition to these five Chinese councillors, there were eleven Chinese members of municipal committees and two land commissioners who were all chosen for the purpose of voicing the Chinese point of view and Chinese wishes in municipal questions. The Senior Consul stated that the interested Consuls were therefore of the opinion that the Chinese residents in the Settlement were already well represented and that there was no danger on the Chinese side of any question remaining unheard for lack of spokesmen; for these reasons the Consuls regretted that they were unable to support the proposal made by the Chinese Ratepayers' Association and they requested that the Mayor be good enough to so inform the Association.

I am pleased that the Senior Consul and the other interested Consuls accepted the revisions in the original British draft suggested by Mr. Gauss.

Further developments will be reported to the Department.

Respectfully yours,   NELSON TRUSLER JOHNSON

893.102S/1397

The Secretary of State to the Ambassador in China (Johnson)

No. 283   WASHINGTON, October 29, 1936.

SIR: The receipt is acknowledged of the Embassy's despatch No. 661 of August 20, 1936, enclosing a copy of despatch No. 333 of August 12, 1936, from the Consul General at Shanghai,[97] in regard to a request, transmitted by the Mayor of the Shanghai municipal government in a letter addressed to the Senior Consul, from the Chinese Ratepayers' Association for an increase, effective in 1937, of Chinese representation on the Municipal Council of the International Settlement at Shanghai. It is noted that in Shanghai's despatch under reference the Consul General discussed various aspects of this question and added that the impression seemed to prevail that the Chinese application would not be pushed vigorously at this time.

The Department is in general agreement with the views expressed by the Consul General and concurred in by the Embassy and desires that the Consulate General, as it has suggested, should not take the initiative in matters of this kind nor take an advanced position in support of or in opposition to them.

It is assumed that the Embassy will continue to keep the Department informed of developments.

An extra copy of this instruction is enclosed for transmission to the Consulate General at Shanghai.

Very truly yours,   For the Secretary of State:
                                         R. WALTON MOORE

---

[97] Despatch No. 333 not printed.

893.0146/527 : Telegram

The Acting Secretary of State to the Ambassador in China (Johnson)

WASHINGTON, November 11, 1936—2 p. m.

270. Your telegrams 475, October 2, 1 p. m., 504, October 16, 6 p. m., and despatch 749, October 3, and Shanghai's despatches 387, September 11, and 416, October 5, 1936,[98] concerning the Shanghai Volunteer Corps.

The Department is in general agreement with the views expressed in the communications under reference, both in regard to the Shanghai Volunteer Corps and the retention, for such time as may be necessary for the protection of American life and property, of the American Landing Force at Shanghai. The Department agrees with the Embassy's view that the question of the practicability of using the American Landing Force to protect American residents beyond the settlement borders must be left to the Senior American Naval Officer concerned.

As it is neither practicable nor advisable for the Department to make any definite response to the inquiry of the Chairman of the Council in regard to the retention of the American Landing Force at Shanghai, it is suggested that Gauss, as on his own initiative, informally reply (orally or in writing) to the Chairman to the effect that questions relating to the size or maintenance of the Volunteer Corps are matters for the municipality to decide and that as the American Landing Force at Shanghai was originally sent there for the purpose of protecting the large number of American citizens residing in that port from the dangers incident to serious disorders beyond the control of the local authorities and continues to be maintained as a temporary measure for the protection of American citizens and their property it would obviously not be possible to give any assurance as to how long the Force might be retained there. The Department, however, perceives no objection to Gauss informally discussing the matter with the Chairman of the Council in greater detail.

With regard to the recommendation contained in paragraph 2 of your telegram No. 475, the Department seriously questions whether the present is an opportune time for the American Government to take the initiative of approaching the British or other interested Governments for the purpose of discussing the whole question of the international settlement and its protection.

The Department raises for your and Gauss' consideration the question of the advisability of Gauss deferring the making of his reply until the British Consul General has made a reply.

MOORE

---

[98] Despatches not printed.

893.102S/1417 : Telegram

The Consul General at Shanghai (Gauss) to the Secretary of State

SHANGHAI, November 21, 1936—4 p. m.
[Received November 21—9:45 a. m.]

604. Secretary General of the Shanghai Municipal Council has informed the British Consul General and me that the Japanese Consul General recently called on the Chairman of the Council and, stating that he was acting under instructions of his Government, "demanded" that the police of the Hongkew area of the International Settlement be placed under the control of a Japanese Assistant Commissioner of Police and that the heads of the principal police stations in Hongkew and Yangtze Poo areas be Japanese. He is stated to have asked for a reply within a week and also to have insisted that no publicity be given to the matter.

British Consul General who is also Senior Consul has asked the Commissioner of Police to submit a memorandum on the subject. This should be forthcoming on Monday next.[99]

I have discussed this matter with my British colleague and we are in agreement that when we have an exact report on the present police arrangements and the measures which might reasonably be taken to meet Japanese wishes, we should go together to the Japanese Consul General and inquire as to the exact representations he has made to the Council and the Japanese desires concerning police arrangements in Hongkew.

Personally, I feel that it would be unwise and dangerous to place the control of the police in the Hongkew and Yangtze Poo areas under Japanese officers. Few of these officers have had any substantial experience in the Shanghai police force; few of them understand English; they would certainly be under the influence of the Japanese Navy and consular authorities; and they would be likely to deal with Chinese in an arbitrary Japanese fashion which would soon place the authorities of the International Settlement in an embarrassing situation.

Furthermore, there are heavy Chinese interests and a very large Chinese population in the area; also very extensive British interests, and such substantial American interests as the Shanghai Power Plant, a number of factories and warehouses, the American Government consular site, various American missionary interests and an American resident population of several hundred. The introduction of Japanese control of the police in the area would be likely seriously to affect the morale of the white and Chinese police acting under such

---

[99] Not printed.

officers. It might also result in the exodus of the Chinese from the area. And certainly the present period of tense Sino-Japanese relations is no time to consider placing Japanese officers of the municipal police in control of the area. This might well be the first step toward the establishment of the area as a Japanese settlement.

On the other hand, in view of the large Japanese interests and the Japanese population in the area, I believe that the Council would be wise to provide as large a number as possible of Japanese police under reasonably high-ranking Japanese who acting in cooperation with equally high-ranking white officers under the direction and supervision of a white assistant commissioner or perhaps under co-assistant commissioners, one of whom might be a Japanese. There is already a substantial number of Japanese in the municipal police force in the area stationed principally in the area of Japanese residence.

I will report promptly all developments.

GAUSS

893.102S/1418 : Telegram

The Ambassador in China (Johnson) to the Secretary of State

PEIPING, November 22, 1936—noon.
[Received November 22—10 a. m.]

565. Following telegram has been sent to Shanghai:

"November 22, noon. Your 604, November 21, 4 p. m. I agree with your views in this matter and approve action you and British Consul General propose to take. I believe also that secrecy should be combated."

JOHNSON

893.102S/1420 : Telegram

The Consul General at Shanghai (Gauss) to the Secretary of State

SHANGHAI, November 25, 1936—noon.
[Received November 26—3 : 10 p. m.]

613. Referring to my telegram No. 604, November 21, 11 a. m. [*4 p. m.*]. Yesterday afternoon the British Consul General and I called upon the Japanese Consul General [1] who confirmed that under instructions of the Japanese Government he had made representations of [*to*] Chairman of the Shanghai Municipal Council for increased Japanese participation in the policing of the Settlement and for the appointment of a Japanese Assistant Commissioner to the command-

---

[1] Memorandum of conversation not printed.

ing officer Hongkew division and the appointment of Japanese as heads of three important police stations in the Hongkew and Yangtze Poo divisions. Japanese Consul General stated that these represented "minimum demands". The Japanese colony and the Japanese Navy had desired greater demands. Japanese dissatisfaction with Settlement police arises out of alleged lack of adequate protection against such attacks on Japanese nationals as have occurred within recent months in the Settlement.

British Consul General outlined the history of the Settlement and the development of police administration along British lines. He pointed to the heavy Chinese and other foreign resident population and interests in the northern and eastern divisions of the Settlement, the necessity for a homogeneous police administration well coordinated under central control, the lack of experienced and trained Japanese officer personnel in the police force to take the positions indicated by Japanese Consul General, the disruption of the administration which would result from the introduction to these positions of police officers from Japan, et cetera.

I supported my British colleague and added that the preferment by [of?] Japanese officers or that introduction of such officers from Japan would destroy the morale of the force; that in the present Sino-Japanese tension, any measures to place Japanese officers in control of the police in the northern and eastern divisions would result in much disquietude amongst the Chinese of the areas and perhaps in an exodus of Chinese therefrom; and that even the fact of the Japanese demands having been made, if it became known, would serve to disturb the situation.

British Consul General stated frankly that there is considerable feeling that Japanese in command of police in the areas indicated would be under the influence or control of the Japanese authorities and navy landing force rather than the Commissioner. Japanese Consul General insisted there is no foundation for such apprehension.

We pointed to the heavy increases in Japanese personnel of police force already made and further contemplated for 1937 budget, stating that there is of course no objection on the basis of nationality to Japanese as officers in command of divisions and stations but there is at present a lack of such personnel experienced and trained in the Shanghai methods.

Japanese Consul General promised that he would study the whole subject further in the light of our views and later confer with us and with the Chairman of the Council. Repeated to Peiping. By mail to Nanking.

GAUSS

893.102S/1433

The Consul General at Shanghai (Gauss) to the Secretary of State

No. 507   SHANGHAI, December 3, 1936.
[Received January 5, 1937.]

SIR: With reference to my despatch No. 496 of November 28, 1936,[2] concerning the Japanese demand for control of the police of the northern and eastern districts of the International Settlement at Shanghai, I have the honor to report that Mr. Stirling Fessenden, the (American) Secretary General of the Shanghai Municipal Council, informed me this morning that he had been invited to attend a meeting at the British Consulate General yesterday at which were present the British Ambassador, the British Consul General, the British Consul, the Chairman of the Shanghai Municipal Council (Mr. H. E. Arnhold, a British subject) and the Commissioner of the Shanghai Municipal Police (also a British subject), who discussed the situation which has arisen in connection with these Japanese demands.

Mr. Fessenden tells me that the British Ambassador expressed himself as in agreement with the proposal that the officials of the Council should discuss this matter with the Japanese consular authorities with a view to seeking some arrangement which might meet the Japanese in a reasonable measure.

Mr. Fessenden said that he had expressed the opinion, which is in accord with my own, that an effort should be made to arrive at some compromise arrangement with the Japanese; the object of the discussions to be a reduction of the Japanese demands and an arrangement which will not disrupt the police administration of the Settlement.

He told me, however, that the British Consul General appears to be very much concerned over the Japanese demands, and seems to feel that they must be met in large measure. Sir John Brenan has also told me recently that he feels that the Japanese are determined to accomplish their ends. He seems to feel that any opposition to the Japanese demands will be charged principally to the British since the police organization of the Settlement is largely British and the municipal administration principally under officials who are British subjects.

I am of the opinion that my British colleague takes too serious a view, at present, of the Japanese demands. My impression from my discussions with the Japanese Consul General is that the Japanese will accept very much less than they have demanded; and I believe that my proposal for the appointment of "co-officers" would go a long way toward meeting the Japanese wishes. The authority of the Japanese "co-officer" should, so far as possible, be restricted, and confined to Japanese affairs.

---

[2] Not printed.

I do not believe that the anxiety of the British Consul General is fully shared by the British and American members of the Council, who are likely to seek to reduce the Japanese demand to a minimum. While it is not possible to say at this time what course will be followed in event a compromise arrangement cannot be made with the Japanese, it seems—if I interpret correctly the attitude of the officials of the Council as explained to me by the Secretary General—that the whole question of the Japanese demands and the attitude of the police administration in regard to them, will be exposed to the full membership of the Council, including the Chinese. I have emphasized with my Japanese colleague that if the Japanese demands should become known to the full Council—and they must become known if the Municipal authorities are unable to make some mutually satisfactory arrangement with the Japanese—there will likely be strong Chinese opposition to the Japanese demands, and the present difficult situation in regard to Sino-Japanese relations at Shanghai will not be improved.

In his telegram to me of November 22, 12 noon, the American Ambassador, in expressing agreement with my views as set out in my telegram No. 604 of November 21, 4 P. M., to the Department and the Embassy, stated that he believed that the secrecy imposed by the Japanese should be combated. I have held that suggestion in mind, and believe that it should be followed in event that no satisfactory compromise arrangement can be reached with the Japanese to continue substantial foreign (non-Japanese) control of the police in the eastern and northern districts of the Settlement. I am not disposed, however, to urge that any publicity be given to the Japanese demands so long as there exists any possibility of a reasonable and satisfactory arrangement. I feel that if the Japanese demands were given publicity at this time, there might be serious repercussion amongst the Chinese, particularly in the northern and eastern districts, and, perhaps, a renewal of attacks on Japanese in those areas. It seems to me desirable that the matter should take its natural course between the officials of the Council and the Japanese, and then, if there is a breakdown that it should be referred formally to the full Council, with probable resulting publicity.

My British colleague has said nothing to me of the meeting held by the British Ambassador; my information comes confidentially from the (American) Secretary General of the Council who says that he was invited to attend the meeting in that capacity.

Respectfully yours,

C. E. GAUSS

JAPAN

POLITICAL DEVELOPMENTS IN JAPAN; THE ASSASSINATIONS OF FEBRUARY 26 [1]

894.00/560

The Ambassador in Japan (Grew) to the Secretary of State

No. 1630
Tokyo, January 7, 1936.
[Received January 27.]

Sir: During my recent visit to Washington the Department emphasized the importance and helpfulness of including in our current despatches an "evaluation of forces". So far as such evaluation entails prophesy of future developments, it is perhaps trite to say that predictions in this part of the world are generally unwise because the unexpected can always happen—a fact often demonstrated in past and recent history. Nevertheless current trends and their contributing factors may be gauged without commitment as to the turn which these trends may take in future owing to the injection of new factors into the situation. It is on this basis that the Embassy submits the following discussion of the general situation facing Japan at the opening of the year 1936.

ECONOMIC AND FINANCIAL

The year 1935 was in general a very prosperous and successful year for Japanese commercial and financial circles. Corporation earnings for the first half of the year amounted to 14.8 per cent of the paid-in capital plus reserves and unexpended balances, showing an increase of .9 per cent over the earnings of the previous half-year. No doubt these increased earnings were in part due to the so-called "munitions boom", but they were also due in large measure to the general prosperity of the country. The average dividends against paid-in capital amounted to 7.8 per cent (per annum rate), or an increase of .5 per cent over the previous half-year. Over half of the earnings were placed to reserves, indicating not only a cautious attitude but a surplus of earnings over dividend necessities. Although the figures for the second half of 1935 are not available as yet, the available trade returns indicate that corporation earnings for the latter half will exceed those for the first half.

---

[1] For previous correspondence, see *Foreign Relations*, 1935, vol. III, pp. 821 ff.

In foreign trade the country had the best year since the Great War. Both exports and imports registered large increases over those for 1934, and the excess of imports for the Empire dropped from Yen 123,000,000 in 1934 to about Yen 19,000,000 in 1935 (complete figures are not yet available but the above calculations are based on figures to December 25, 1935). The invisible trade balance, according to preliminary figures, was slightly unfavorable for the year, showing an excess of payments over income of Yen 44,500,000, as compared with an excess of income of Yen 8,700,000 in 1934. In 1935, however, the Japanese redeemed the outstanding South Manchuria Railway sterling bonds and made large investments in Manchuria, including the purchase of the Chinese Eastern Railway, which account for the excess of payments over income. Combining the visible and invisible balances, moreover, it will be noted that the combined adverse balance in 1935 was Yen 63,500,000, as compared with an adverse balance in 1934 of Yen 114,300,000. If, therefore, Japan is exporting its capital, as some economists claim, it is doing so at a decreasing rate.

Money remained easy in Japan throughout 1935, with steady increases in both bank deposits and in loans outstanding, indicating increasing business activity. Bank deposits increased considerably faster than loans, however, and during the year there was an increase of about Yen 700,000,000 in the spread between deposits and loans, which naturally resulted in an easy money market. On the other hand, although the Government finances appeared sound, there seemed to be some doubt among the Japanese as to Government credit toward the year-end. During the year the Government issued large quantities of so-called "red-ink" bonds, or bonds issued for the purpose of covering budgetary deficits, and in the latter part of the year the private banks and individual investors appeared somewhat reluctant to absorb more of these bonds. Although exact figures are not yet available, it is believed that the total outstanding debt of the Government passed the ten billion yen mark by the close of the year—a record debt for Japan. The Governor of the Bank of Japan, however, in his New Year message, stated that the Bank was able to take up all further Government issues until the close of the present fiscal year (March 31, 1936), and appealed to the Japanese people to uphold the credit of the Government.

Although the Japanese nation had an unusually favorable year, economically and financially, in 1935, there is little reason to believe that 1936 will be any less favorable—in fact, practically all students of Japanese economics and finance predict a steady continuance of Japan's prosperity. Their predictions are based largely on the fact that better financial conditions exist in the farming districts, due to higher prices for rice and raw silk, and that further large sums will be spent during the year by the Army and Navy for modern military equipment, both of which factors will ensure continued and perhaps increased activity in the industries of the nation. Foreign trade will, according to the predictions, continue to flourish during 1936, and may be considerably increased by the conclusion of a trade agreement with Canada, which will restore trade with that country to normal, and by the further opening of North China through the establishment of an autonomous government there which will be favorably disposed toward Japan. Moreover, the economic recovery of the United States will undoubtedly create a larger market for Japanese goods, while the war-nervousness in Europe will cause an unusual demand for such war supplies as Japan produces.

On the other hand, there are various factors which are not so favorable and which, in the opinion of this Embassy, may cause disturbances in Japan's economic and financial circles during the year. The principal unfavorable factor consists of the uncertain position of Government credit. It is true that during the coming fiscal year (April 1, 1936 to March 31, 1937) the Government plans to issue a considerably smaller amount of "red-ink" bonds than in the present fiscal year, but even so the amount (about Yen 680,000,000) may be larger than the capacity of the market, in which case there may be serious dislocations of credit and serious financial disturbances. The Japanese, however, have proved themselves very able financiers and probably will find means to overcome the possible financial difficulties of the Government.

Another possible disadvantageous factor is the erection of further and higher trade barriers against Japanese goods. The Japanese Government is now fighting against the erection of such trade barriers by voluntarily restricting the exportation of goods to countries where it appears that opposition to the flood of Japanese goods is growing. Whether or not this means of combating the tendency throughout the world to restrict the importation of Japanese goods will be effective remains to be seen. The Japanese Government also has another weapon which was used effectively in the case of trade with Canada. This is the Trade Protection Law, which authorizes the imposition of greatly increased duties on goods imported from countries which impose discriminatory measures against Japanese goods.

Another factor which may militate against increased Japanese prosperity during 1936 is the extreme economic nationalism now apparent in Japan. This economic nationalism, principally promoted by the military for purposes of national defense, was illustrated in 1934 and 1935 by the passage and enforcement of the Petroleum Industry Law, which is designed to develop oil refining within Japan and to provide large stores of petroleum for use in time of emergency.

The effect will be greatly to restrict the operations of the American and British oil companies in this field, and perhaps to eliminate them from the field altogether.[2] In 1936 the Government plans to enact an Automobile Industry Law, which would have much the same effect upon the two large American automobile assembling and distributing organizations in Japan.[3] The American and British oil firms have already been eliminated from the Manchurian field, and it is expected that in 1936 steps will be taken to eliminate the foreign automobile companies, turning the trade over to Japanese interests.

This rampant economic nationalism is apt to invite reprisals from other nations, which might seriously interfere with the further growth of Japan's foreign trade. This fact is not generally understood in Japan, but the Embassy is aware that some of the leaders of the Government understand the dangers of the movement and are trying to curb it. The military, however, with their dominant influence in the Government, apparently do not understand the effect which their policies may have on Japan's foreign economic relations and continue to insist upon the enforcement of their ideas of what is best for the nation.

POLITICAL

DOMESTIC

The domestic political field has been largely occupied by discussions over what has been called the "Emperor organ" theory, a question which has been discussed in several despatches from the Embassy. The "fundamentalists" object to any attitude on the part of public officials to regard the Emperor as in any sense an instrument or organ of the State. He is to be considered Heaven's Regent, the descendant of the Sun Goddess, and as such far above such mundane position as the Head of a State or the organ whereby the body politic makes its decisions known. Paradoxically this vigilance has been accompanied by agitation on the part of these same elements to remove all "non-fundamentalists" from positions in the Imperial Court which would have the effect of rendering such officials as the Minister of the Household, the Grand Master of Ceremonies, the Keeper of the Seals and perhaps the President of the Privy Council, responsible to the Government for their political views. Up to the present time these officers have been men of experience and prestige who have been considered as non-political appointees and have held office regardless of political changes in the Government. The agitation in effect is against the influence which these older men surrounding the Emperor have been

[2] See pp. 786 ff.
[3] See pp. 981 ff.

able to exert without accompanying political responsibility. It is probable that the agitators do not see the results which would flow from the success of their efforts.

The Government has continued to be "national" or non-party in character, and has managed to stay in office. It has, however, been unable to control the Diet to the extent of obtaining much new legislation. The Diet adjourned last spring with most of the Government's bills on the calendar.

In 1936 the Government will be confronted with a general election, as the four year term of office of members of the House of Representatives will expire, but it is not yet known whether the Government will dissolve the Diet, or allow the legislature to complete its session and then hold the election. This question will be decided by the political exigencies of the moment. There seems no doubt that this year as last, the Government will be able to put through the budget because the influence or fear of the military will probably be sufficient to accomplish it. There is no doubt, however, that the latter has not now the political prestige that it had when the present Diet members were elected four years ago. Besides, the Seiyukai have seized upon the "Emperor organ theory" as a political slogan and threaten to make a campaign issue of it. It will be interesting also to see the character of the new Diet, the first to be elected under the rigid rules of the Corrupt Practices Act, because the members will be less subject to the charge of owing their election to bribery or other sinister activities.

FOREIGN

Abroad, the main arena of Japanese interest and activity for the moment centres in North China, Mongolia and the Manchukuo-Siberian frontier.[4]

North China.

Few observers will be found who fail to see in Japan's announced policy of constituting herself the "stabilizing influence" in East Asia the thought of eventual domination of North China and Mongolia with exclusive Japanese influence therein. The conquest of Manchuria, as Mr. Owen Lattimore has pointed out in his article on "The Inland Gates of China" in the December issue of *Pacific Affairs*, could not be isolated or limited but was of necessity the beginning of a process. "Japanese control in North China" he considers "is in fact an inevitable corollary of the conquest of Manchuria; and this involves Mongolia, because military domination of North China cannot be made good without a solid strategic position in Mongolia, as the Manchus discovered in the seventeenth century. . . ."[5] While

---

[4] See pp. 1 ff.
[5] Omission indicated in the original despatch.

the soundness of Mr. Lattimore's theory may be open to argument, this is undoubtedly the view held by the Japanese military, and the only question at issue is how far and how fast the military will be permitted to proceed with this strategic program, and the extent to which the control of the Government in Tokyo can or will be exerted in restraining this movement. Herein lies the nub of the situation.

One fact is evident: the orders of the General Staff issued last June forbidding troops of the Kwantung Army from moving below the Great Wall without Imperial sanction is still in force and at least informal assurances have been given by the Vice Minister for Foreign Affairs to the British Ambassador that the order would remain in effect and that there would be no occupation of North China by Japanese military forces.* From its observations and from all information available, the Embassy believes that these assurances genuinely represent the intentions of the Government in Tokyo including the higher army officers responsible for military policy. In the domination of North China, military occupation is not envisaged. Quite apart from any question of treaty commitments or of international ethics, there are important practical considerations opposing such procedure, particularly the financial expense and the disadvantage of using troops now stationed in Manchuria, thereby weakening the defenses against Soviet Russia. The exertion of control by other methods is believed to be more effective and cheaper. This view is substantiated by current comment in Japanese military magazines and by officers with whom foreign contact has been established; they declare categorically that not a square foot of territory in North China will be occupied. The general conception abroad that Japanese troops have recently invaded North China—based on the activities of the garrison troops already there—are, so far as this Embassy is aware, incorrect, and save for a few additional staff officers the Embassy has no knowledge of recent increases in the North China Garrison forces. Domination of North China, as well as Chahar and possibly Suiyuan, the Army is determined to obtain as a defense against Soviet Russia and Russian and Chinese communism, and as a protection of sources of essential raw materials and Japanese trade and economic expansion, but the present military program aims to achieve this purpose by methods other than by military occupation. It is therefore believed that the Army authorities in Tokyo recommended and welcomed the "Imperial Sanction" restriction as perhaps the only effective means of restraining irresponsible and hot-headed officers looking south from the Great Wall.

---

*Embassy's telegram 128, June 11, 1935, 6 [5?] p. m., paragraph 3. Embassy's telegram 245, December 19, 1935, 11 a. m., paragraph 1. [Footnote in the original; for telegram No. 128, see *Foreign Relations*, 1935, vol. III, p. 230; telegram No. 245 not printed.]

For the purposes of this discussion it does not appear necessary to go into the details of the so-called autonomy movement in North China, and the part played by the Japanese military therein, which have been fully reported by my colleague in Peiping. The Embassy wishes to deal here only with the broader aspects of the situation. Recent developments have however afforded a fairly clear conception of the methods by which the Japanese propose to establish control in the northern provinces, namely by the setting up of Chinese officials who at least to some degree will do their bidding. If these methods fail it will remain to be seen what other methods will be adopted, but for the present at least it is not believed that the intention exists to create an independent buffer state and to place Pu Yi [6] on a newly-created throne, for that presumably would require military occupation.

Mongolia.

If, as Mr. Lattimore believes, the conquest of Manchuria could not be isolated but was of necessity the beginning of a process, we should in 1936, four years after that conquest, be able to recognize further steps in the process. These have, in fact, not been lacking. During 1935 skirmishes along the border between "Manchukuo" and Outer Mongolia led to the unsuccessful Manchuli Conference, an ill-disguised attempt on the part of Japan to open Outer Mongolia. Moreover, to the south in Inner Mongolia, notably in the province of Chahar, the Japanese have been increasingly active and at the present time there appears to be emerging an autonomous regime acceptable to the Military.

The fact is then that the westward process has begun. In Inner Mongolia it is largely indistinguishable in aim and method from the process which is proceeding concurrently in North China. In both regions autonomous movements aiming at the concentration of authority in the hands of individuals subservient to the Japanese are being created. It matters little who the individuals are; the fact of importance with respect to Inner Mongolia is that the Japanese now dominate Chahar. Nor will the westward process end there. On the contrary, one new factor at least has appeared which tends to accelerate, if anything, the westward momentum and that is the increasing preoccupation of the Japanese military with Chinese communism. One hears much at present of Japan's duty to save China from the Communists. The reported spread of communism in Kansu, Northern Shensi, and the Ordos region is undoubtedly a source of concern to the Japanese military who perceive that it is not far from these districts to revolutionary Outer Mongolia and that an avenue of

---

[6] "Emperor Kang-teh of Manchoukuo."

easy communication between the Communists in China and those to the north may thus be created. This factor may spur Japanese agents to greater activity, but the same considerations which militate against military conquest in North China and which were discussed earlier in this despatch apply here as well.

There remains then the question of the vast desert region of Outer Mongolia. Japan's efforts to gain a foothold here can not be ascribed to any desire for economic opportunity for little opportunity exists in this inhospitable region. No section of the Japanese people can be vitally interested save the Military and their interest is primarily strategic. Lately the "Manchukuo" authorities have deplored the failure of the Manchuli Conference, which proved that Outer Mongolia was not to be opened by diplomatic means, and have voiced their intention of dealing with the problem of determining the frontier towards Outer Mongolia independently and to their own satisfaction. Although on December 19 and again on December 24 there were clashes on the border between "Manchukuo" and Outer Mongolian forces, the fears of serious trouble which have been expressed in certain quarters seem unnecessarily grave. The Mongolian winter is not favorable to extensive military operations.

To date Japan has only made it clear that she would like to open Outer Mongolia. There is no evidence that she is as yet prepared to back up this desire with any considerable expenditure of money or resources. In fact, according to report, the War Office professes to have little knowledge of events in the northwest and there is no available evidence that an effort to penetrate this region and to flank Baikal and the Transiberian from the south is being planned. Nor is it possible to secure from the local Soviet officials any expressions of opinion on this situation. The Soviet Ambassador will say nothing and, despite the reported presence of the Mongolian Prime Minister in Moscow for the last month, it is likely that he has little or no information. Accordingly, although a gradual increase in Japanese interest in Outer Mongolia has been fostered by the Manchuli Conference of last year, by border incidents, and by mutual recriminations between "Manchukuo" and Outer Mongolia, it is not possible to say that the issue is becoming critical or that it has left the province of military strategists concerned with possible but distant future developments.

"Manchukuo"–Siberia.

At the beginning of 1936 no serious trouble between Japan and Soviet Russia is foreseen in the near future. The Soviet Ambassador here professes to be thoroughly optimistic and remarked to me several days ago that the Japanese would not dare to attack the USSR because the latter's preparations along the border were so formidable. He has taken the same attitude with several of my colleagues. Doubtless the "Manchukuo"-Siberian border will remain a danger spot and incidents will occur. But there appears to be nothing in this situation nor in the unsettled fisheries case nor in that involving the oil leases of North Saghalien comparable in gravity to the Chinese Eastern Railway issue which at this time a year ago remained unsolved. That problem, involving the final elimination of the Soviets from Manchuria, was considered vital by the Japanese; to replace it no issue equally vital has as yet appeared. In the more or less remote future one can picture the further westward spread of Japan as a continental power presenting a serious threat to Russia's security in Siberia, but such forebodings belong to the realm of speculation rather than to an appraisal of existing trends. For the present, the danger of Japanese aggression in Siberia, believed two years ago to be imminent, appears to be in abeyance.

Having in mind the foregoing brief survey of the program and activities of the Japanese military in bringing to bear Japan's "stabilizing influence" in East Asia, we may return to an evaluation of the forces which may influence the Government in Tokyo in restraining or accelerating the inevitable movement westward.

First of all, the weight of the personal influence of the Emperor himself in shaping policy and procedure is extremely difficult for any foreign observer to gauge. Few Japanese are willing to touch upon that subject, but the consensus of opinion is that such influence as the Emperor does exert, having in mind the varied interests and viewpoints within the country which he must so far as practicable conciliate, is pacific. The Vice Minister for Foreign Affairs,[7] who is generally regarded as an ardent nationalist with somewhat chauvinistic leanings, in recent conversation with one of my colleagues confirmed this fact and added that the development of the Emperor's personality, mental attributes and grasp of public affairs during recent years has been little short of amazing; indeed Mr. Shigemitsu went so far as to predict that the present Emperor would go down in Japanese history, in point of enlightened outlook, as on a plane with the Emperor Meiji himself, a statement somewhat surprising to a foreigner in view of the fact that the present ruler's personality, influence and constructive activity have been hidden behind a veil of secrecy which few have had an opportunity to penetrate. Mr. Shigemitsu is, however, a direct and hard-headed official not given to weaving fanciful theories and his opinion may therefore be listened to with reasonable respect.

If it is true that the leanings of the Emperor himself are in principle pacific—or perhaps a better word is moderate—it can with equal truth

---

[7] Mamoru Shigemitsu.

be held that his principal advisers, notably Prince Saionji, Count Makino, Viscount Saito, Baron Ikki, and probably the present Prime Minister [8] and Minister for Foreign Affairs,[9] would prefer to achieve gradually and by peaceful means what certain elements in the Army would accomplish by force. While they unquestionably support the doctrine of Japan's "stabilizing influence" in East Asia, her strategic security, her protection against communism and her economic development westward, it is believed that their views as to the methods of consummating such a position differ from the views of the more radical school of chauvinists. Despite the bluster of the occasional utterances of the spokesman of the Foreign Office and other officials, Japan's reputation in the world at large is to them far from inconsequential, nor do they desire to risk unnecessary embroilment with foreign Powers even while convinced that those Powers are highly unlikely, either from policy or because they are occupied elsewhere, to fight. In other words, statesmanship is not wholly lacking in Japan today, and at least for the moment the more moderate elements in the Government appear to have control of the general situation. There is a feeling that the military have recently overplayed their hand in North China, and at a given moment the curbing rein was pulled from Tokyo just as it was last June.†

As for the Japanese military themselves, they are no longer riding on the crest of the wave to the same degree as in 1931 and 1932. As one of the two bulwarks of the nation, the Army can hardly become unpopular within Japan, yet it may be said with assurance that the Army does not command the same extravagant enthusiasm and support which it enjoyed during and immediately after the Manchurian adventure. More and more Japan is developing into a commercialized and industrialized nation; business is becoming paramount; money talks; the worker who was content with 30 sen a day is beginning to reach out for a higher standard of living; the whole social aspect of the country is gradually changing from the old feudal conception. In this state of the public mind the extravagant military budget, in spite of intensive propaganda, cannot be popular. Apart from its strategic value, the economic advantages of the conquest of Manchuria are not yet apparent; the costs of its development and defense are enormous; as an outlet for the over-population of the home country it has failed; the promised financial returns from the investment are not yet in sight and will not appear for many a day. While the thought of eventually commanding the raw materials,

---

[8] Admiral Keisuke Okada.
[9] Koki Hirota.
† Embassy's telegram 128, June 11, 1935, 6 [5?] p. m., paragraph 5. Embassy's telegram 132, June 18, 1935, 1 p. m., paragraph 2. Embassy's telegram 143, June 29, 1935, 11 a. m. [Footnote in the original; for telegrams see *Foreign Relations*, 1935, vol. III, pp. 230, 262, and 283.]

industries and markets of North China no doubt appeals to the Japanese business man as a pleasing future prospect, the outlook for the steady development of business in the home land, in industry, commerce, shipping, banking, is not as yet sufficiently cramped to inspire a public demand, or indeed a public desire, for further military conquest in the present day. The financial and economic status of the country is sound and active; domestic and foreign business is steadily developing and expanding; an inherent urge towards new fields of military conquest does not at present predominate. Economic conquest more aptly describes the stimulus.

Other considerations may conceivably influence Japan's future course of action. The stiffening attitude in China, as manifested especially by the student movement in Peiping and other cities, has not been lost upon the statesmen in Tokyo. My British colleague is informed that the solidarity of the movement has taken the military by surprise and that it has given them "furiously to think". My own information is that the movement is discounted and that army circles believe that it will soon lapse. More attention is given to the sanctions against Italy,[10] the ostensibly growing influence of the League of Nations and especially the force of public opinion in Great Britain against an aggressor, as palpably demonstrated in the recent public outburst against Sir Samuel Hoare[11] and his enforced resignation arising out of the obvious effort to conciliate Italy in the Hoare–Laval[12] peace proposal.[12a] These things are being carefully weighed in Japan. Now comes the President's address to Congress,[13] and whatever may be its effect in Europe, I am of the opinion that it has come at a timely moment to influence Japanese thought and policy. While Japanese officials and the press have carefully avoided fitting the Presidential shoe to their own foot, the implications of the address and especially the words (as reported in the press here) "The point has been reached where the peoples of the Americas must take cognizance of a growing ill will marked by trends toward aggression, of increasing armaments, of shortening tempers—or a situation having many of the elements that lead toward the tragedy of a general war", must inevitably sink deep if tacitly into the consciousness and conscience of the Government and public of Japan.

There is another element in the situation which, if no unexpected incidents occur, I am inclined to believe may play a not unimportant part in influencing Japanese policy during the next few years. The

---

[10] See vol. III, pp. 34 ff.
[11] British Secretary of State for Foreign Affairs, June–December 1935.
[12] Pierre Laval, President of the French Council of Ministers (Premier).
[12a] See *Foreign Relations*, 1935, vol. I, pp. 699–723, *passim*.
[13] For text of address of January 3, see *Congressional Record*, vol. 80, pt. 1, p. 27.

Japanese, as is well known, are rapidly and effectively becoming a race of first-rate athletes; their interest in sport is nation-wide and the public enthusiasm for baseball especially, and in hardly less degree for track athletics, swimming, skiing, golf, tennis, and other sports, is quite as intensive as in our own country. Their outstanding champions and winning teams in the various sports are acclaimed as public heroes quite as extensively as their outstanding soldiers. Here is a healthy and emotional channel into which, if the Government plays its cards wisely, public interest can be directed and concentrated with the Olympic Games of 1940 in view. The Department is aware of the efforts which are being made to secure the meeting for Japan; Italy, we are informed, has definitely waived her claim in favor of Tokyo, and it appears that only the claim of Finland remains to be overcome. In 1940 will be celebrated in Japan the 2600th anniversary of the founding of the Empire by Jimmu Tenno. If the Olympic Games can be secured for that year, the preparations for the meet and for the synchronous celebration of the national anniversary will tend to eclipse all other matters in popular interest. The Government, too, may appreciate the opportunity which such an occasion will offer for bringing Japan more intimately into the international circle from which, inevitably, she feels temporarily on the periphery. The *Asahi*, in an editorial, has already given a hint in that direction. "The crisis that did not come in 1935", it says, "is not likely to come in 1936, but the 2600th anniversary of the accession of Emperor Jimmu is certain to come. Preparations for it are necessary. . . ."[14] Preparations are already in full swing for the big international exposition and the Olympic Games to be held here at that time. . . it is questionable whether there is need for reckless crisis propaganda. In this sense we wish to bury 1935 and look forward with hope to the 2600th anniversary of the accession to the Throne of Emperor Jimmu, which is four years away. . . ."

Let us hope that the Government and the statesmen of Japan will recognize in this a goal upon which to rivet the attention and interest of the country during the next few years.

But since this despatch deals with trends rather than with events, and must therefore give consideration to the long future pull together with the immediate outlook, I quote the following paragraphs from *The Price of Peace* by Frank H. Simonds and Brooks Emeny (page 230) which seem to me to be sound alike in fact and reasoning:

"As the situation stands today, despite an enormous expansion of industry, Japan is still, as in the past, confronted by two facts of ominous import, a rising standard of living and a rapidly expanding population. For the moment it is still possible to foresee the preservation of that parity in progress and population. Doubtless there

---

[14] Omissions indicated in the original despatch.

will be further gains in foreign trade, alike in textiles and in rubber goods, electric appliances, novelties, and in certain other directions. An adequate supply of cheap labor is also assured, and costs of production may therefore for the present fall rather than rise.

"Nevertheless, Japanese exports are already encountering constantly multiplying obstacles in the way alike of competition from India and China and tariff barriers amongst the Western nations as the march of economic nationalism continues uninterruptedly. The further advantage of the depreciated yen, to which no inconsiderable part of recent trade expansion has been due, is patently transitory. Thus, so far as Japan and her Korean and Formosan possessions are concerned, it is plain that these cannot long continue to support their growing population under existing conditions."

These are facts, not theories, and should be given due weight in any evaluation of forces influencing the probable trends in Japanese policy and action during the years ahead. The procedure to be followed and the methods to be pursued are open to influence by some or all of the factors suggested in this despatch, but the expansionist urge is fundamental, and I think there is no doubt that whether quietly and gradually or openly and aggressively Japanese energies will be found, from now on, steadily directed towards consolidating Japan's control in North China and Mongolia as a primary axiom of her future strategic safety and economic welfare.

Respectfully yours,   JOSEPH C. GREW

894.00/565 : Telegram

The Ambassador in the Soviet Union (Bullitt) to the Secretary of State

Moscow, February 25, 1936—6 p. m.
[Received February 25—3 : 56 p. m.]

64. In the course of a brief conversation today Litvinov [15] expressed some surprise and great satisfaction at the results of the Japanese elections. He said that he believed the victory of the Minseito Party indicated that the sentiment of the Japanese people was clearly against the policy of military adventures and that he now expected a considerable improvement in Russian-Japanese relations and a cessation of provocative border incidents.

Dr. Yen, Chinese Ambassador, commenting on the Japanese elections said that while he was sure they would produce no fundamental change in Japan's attitude toward China they might produce a more suave method of procedure.

Yen expects to leave Moscow for China about March 20th.

BULLITT

---

[15] Maxim Litvinov, Soviet Commissar for Foreign Affairs.

894.00/563 : Telegram

The Ambassador in Japan (Grew) to the Secretary of State

TOKYO, February 26, 1936—10 a. m.
[Received February 26—2 : 22 a. m.]

36. The military took partial possession of the Government and city early this morning and it is reported have assassinated several prominent men. It is impossible as yet to confirm anything. The news correspondents are not permitted to send telegrams or to telephone abroad.

This telegram is being sent primarily as a test message to ascertain if our code telegrams will be transmitted.

GREW

894.00/564 : Telegram

The Ambassador in Japan (Grew) to the Secretary of State

TOKYO, February 26, 1936—noon.
[Received February 26—4 : 52 a. m.[16]]

37. Embassy's 36, February 26, 10 a. m.

1. It now appears fairly certain that former Premier Admiral Saito, former Lord Keeper of the Privy Seal Count Makino, Grand Chamberlain Admiral Suzuki, and General Watanabe, Inspector General of Military Education, have been assassinated. It is also reported that Finance Minister Takahashi and the Chief of the Metropolitan Police Board have been wounded.

2. The Military have established a cordon around the district containing the Government Administration Offices and the Imperial Palace and do not permit ingress without army passes. Telephonic communication with the administrative offices has also been stopped. The stock exchange has been closed.

3. It has been reported that Premier Okada, Home Minister Goto and former War Minister Hayashi were also assassinated and that Finance Minister Takahashi has died of his wounds. The Embassy cannot confirm any of these rumors.

4. So far there has been no disorder and no street fighting as far as the Embassy is aware. The troops taking part in the uprising appear to be under perfect discipline and are not interfering with normal affairs of the people. Until the nature and probable results of the uprising are better understood by the Embassy however the Embassy is advising those who ask to remain at home. There appears to be absolutely no anti-foreign feeling involved in the affair.

---

[16] Telegram in four sections.

5. A mimeographed statement was left by groups of soldiers at each of the principal newspaper offices this morning. The statement alleged that the present Government had been drifting away from the true spirit of Japan and that it had usurped the prerogatives of the Emperor. As evidence of this statement cited the signing of the London Naval Treaty [17] and the dismissal of General Masaki. It continued rather vaguely with an expression translated by the United Press about as follows: "If this condition is permitted to continue, the relations of Japan to China, Russia, Britain and the United States will become 'explosive in nature'". The statement was signed by Captain Nonaka and Captain Ando, both of the Third Infantry Regiment stationed in Tokyo. According to the soldiers who delivered the statement, another announcement will be made at 5 o'clock this evening and at that time "a new law of state" will be promulgated. The Embassy's informant believes that certain constitutional prerogatives will be suspended. He likened the existing situation to the Batista *coup d'état* in Cuba.[18]

6. As far as the Embassy has yet been able to ascertain, the uprising is in the nature of a *coup d'état* engineered by the young Fascist element in the army and intended to destroy the entire group of elder statesmen who have been advisers to the Throne and thereby to effect the so-called "Showa restoration". The Emperor himself is apparently being held incommunicado in the Palace presumably to prevent anyone from obtaining access to him and securing an Imperial mandate which would interfere with the plans of the army group. The immediate causes of the uprising appear to have been the recent election which returned an unexpectedly large number of the more liberal candidates and the trial of Aizawa, murderer of General Nagata, which has excited the feelings of the Fascist element in the army.

Latest reports indicate that General Masaki is the leading spirit in the affair and that Admiral Osumi, Minister of the Navy, has assumed the position of Acting Prime Minister. The movement appears to have been thoroughly organized in advance down to the last detail.

7. The Embassy has just learned from a fairly reliable source that Count Makino is safe.

GREW

---

[17] Signed April 22, 1930, *Foreign Relations*, 1930, vol. I, p. 107.
[18] See *ibid.*, 1933, vol. v, pp. 361 ff.

894.00/563 : Telegram

The Secretary of State to the Ambassador in Japan (Grew)

WASHINGTON, February 26, 1936—5 p. m.

25. Unless you perceive objection, please communicate to the Japanese Minister for Foreign Affairs as from me a message reading as follows:

"On behalf of the American Government and people I assure you of the deep regret with which we have learned of the death of distinguished officials of the Japanese Government and I extend to you our sincere condolences."

Report action by telegraph.

HULL

894.00/566 : Telegram

The Ambassador in Japan (Grew) to the Secretary of State

TOKYO, February 26, 1936—7 p. m.
[Received February 26—12:15 p. m.[19]]

38. Embassy's 37, February 26, noon.

1. Up to this point the Embassy has endeavored merely to keep the Department promptly apprised of current reports emanating from the most reliable contacts available but not susceptible of definite confirmation. In the existing nebulous atmosphere the wildest rumors have naturally been passed around in Tokyo. The following information was received confidentially this afternoon in conversation with a friendly and trustworthy official.

2. "It appears that the attempted *coup d'état* was the work of a few companies of the First and Third Regiment of the First Division with headquarters in Tokyo. These soldiers amounting to perhaps 1000 men, led by officers of junior rank, left their barracks in the night with arms and ammunition. Some of the men seized the Prime Minister's residence, the police headquarters, the Home Office, the War Department, and the office of the General Staff of the Army. The rest armed with machine guns proceeded to the residences of Viscount Saito, Admiral Suzuki, Finance Minister Takahashi, General Watanabe and others and murdered them. Attempts were also made upon Prince Saionji and Count Makino residing in the country but both appeared to have been forewarned and to have escaped although their safety is not yet definitely confirmed. The exact list of the assassinated officials is not available and the Government has banned all news regarding the matter. The uninjured members of the Cabinet and of the War Council are meeting at the Palace in lieu of other

---

[19] Telegram in two sections.

available meeting place. Admiral Osumi, Minister of the Navy, is reportedly acting Prime Minister. The Government believes itself in command of the situation and apparently no new units have joined the insurgents who are still in possession of the buildings they seized last night. The approaches to these buildings as well as the Palace entrances are guarded by soldiers from loyal units not affiliated with the revolutionary troops. The higher military officers have not taken drastic action against the latter because they do not wish further bloodshed or street fighting."

3. This afternoon a meeting was held between the Emperor, Imperial Princes, members of the Cabinet and members of the War Council at which discussions were held regarding the Acting Premier. It is reported by newspaper men (who are not allowed to publish the news) that at the meeting it was proposed that Prince Konoye [20] or General Araki [21] be appointed as Premier but the insurgents stated that they wanted either Admiral Kanji Kato [22] or Baron Hiranuma; [23] otherwise they will resume their insurgency. The Embassy has not yet been able to ascertain who has been appointed Acting Premier but official sources have mentioned to the Embassy Osumi and Goto. Negotiations are proceeding between the Army High Command and the insurgents but the latter refuse to surrender the buildings they occupy. Additional loyal Government troops have been brought into Tokyo from nearby towns.

4. Latest reports indicate that Home Minister Goto and former War Minister Hayashi were not assassinated.

5. At the present moment there is no indication or prospect of anti-foreign demonstrations in Tokyo. The Embassy's statement in paragraph 4 of telegram No. 37 [24] that there appears to be absolutely no anti-foreign feeling involved in the affairs referred primarily to the absence of anti-foreign demonstrations. Obviously a chauvinistic discontent with the so-called liberal policies of the late Government was the basis of the *coup d'état* involving dissatisfaction with its foreign, no less than its domestic, policies and measures.

6. The report of General Masaki's implication in the revolt is not confirmed. The restricted size of the movement so far as we can now see indicated fairly clearly that it was the work of junior officers. The Embassy has been given to understand that there will be no further developments of the situation tonight.

GREW

---

[20] President of the House of Peers.
[21] Former Minister of War.
[22] Former Chief of the Naval General Staff.
[23] Vice President of the Privy Council.
[24] Dated February 26, noon, p. 719.

894.00/570 : Telegram

The Ambassador in Japan (Grew) to the Secretary of State

TOKYO, February 26, 1936—11 p. m.
[Received February 26—2 p. m.]

39. 1. The Tokyo *Nichi Nichi* in an extra tonight states that Home Minister Goto has been appointed as temporary acting Premier.

2. The Embassy has learned from a reliable informant who talked with Count Makino this evening that Makino was neither killed nor wounded.

GREW

894.00/571 : Telegram

The Ambassador in Japan (Grew) to the Secretary of State

TOKYO, February 27, 1936—noon.
[Received February 27—1 : 37 a. m.]

40. Department's 25, February 26, 5 p. m. As the Minister for Foreign Affairs expects to be all day in conference at the Palace, I have communicated your message to his secretary who undertook to deliver it textually to Hirota this morning.

GREW

894.00/572 : Telegram

The Ambassador in Japan (Grew) to the Secretary of State

TOKYO, February 27, 1936—1 p. m.
[Received February 27—9 : 30 a. m.[25]]

41. Embassy's 39, February 26, 11 p. m.

1. The deaths have now been confirmed of Premier Okada, Admiral Saito, General Watanabe and Finance Minister Takahashi, although Takahashi's death has not been officially announced, probably to avoid disturbing financial circles. Admiral Suzuki is still alive although seriously wounded. Prince Saionji is safe.

2. Martial law was proclaimed by Imperial Ordinance at 3 this morning embracing the entire City of Tokyo and commanded by General Kashii. It is indicated that the martial law will restrict traffic in certain areas and establish a strict censorship over newspapers, telegraphs and telephones in order to minimize misleading rumors and to calm the situation.

3. None of the stock or commodity exchanges opened today. The banks are open but doing little business, the situation being still too

---

[25] Telegram in two sections.

nebulous. The yen rates are approximately normal, [being] held to normal by the pegging operations of the Yokohama Specie Bank. The death of Takahashi is expected by bankers to have an adverse effect on the market for Japanese bonds and may cause serious disturbances in the Japanese money market.

4. The newspapers are permitted to publish only the meager official statements which are obviously designed to minimize the affair as much as possible. The foreign press correspondents are now able to send messages abroad but they expect that under martial law their telegrams will be strictly censored.

5. According to the best information available to the Embassy, about half of the insurgent troops have returned to their barracks; the other half has been gradually evacuating the Government buildings occupied yesterday and has been concentrated in the Premier's official residence. Martial law was proclaimed largely to enable the army to negotiate with the insurgents on an entirely legal basis without involving other interests. It is within the power of the General in command of the martial law area to order the arrest of the men who refuse to return to their commands but it is not likely that this will be done except as a last resort when all other methods fail. From the Premier's residence the young officers who directed the uprising are negotiating with the present Government and the army authorities. Exact facts in regard to these negotiations are impossible to obtain but it is understood that at first the insurgents demanded a military dictatorship for Japan. This demand was immediately rejected by the Government (then meeting in Council at the Palace) which suggested Prince Konoye or General Araki as Premier. The insurgents recommended Admiral Kanji Kato or Baron Hiranuma. The negotiations are continuing and will probably result in a compromise Premier. General Araki, Prince Higashi Kuni and Admiral Eisuke Yamamoto, Supreme War Councilor[s], are being most prominently mentioned at the moment.

6. No forceful measures are being taken nor, as far as the Embassy is aware, are being contemplated against the insurgent troops. It is explained that to arrest them would involve fighting in the heart of Tokyo and might result in the destruction of buildings and loss of life among the civilian population; that the use of force against political insurgents is opposed to Japanese custom; that no Japanese Army officer would order the Emperor's soldiers to fire on other soldiers of the Emperor; that the fighting if it took place would be too close to the Palace of the Emperor; and that in any case there is considerable sympathy among the people for the motives which animated the misguided young men and consequently a certain amount of consideration must be shown them or the army will find itself possessed of a crowd of martyrs which must be avoided at almost any cost.

7. The Embassy feels that until the present emergency situation is further clarified and settled there is not sufficient ground to justify diagnosis of the full import of the affair or conjecture as to its bearing on future policy.

Repeated to Peiping.

GREW

894.00/573 : Telegram

The Ambassador in China (Johnson) to the Secretary of State

NANKING, February 27, 1936—2 p. m.
[Received February 27—9 : 45 a. m.]

42. A Japanese Embassy spokesman here has told a foreign news correspondent that the officials killed were Okada, Takahashi, Saito and Watanabe.

2. The news of the coup was at first received in local Chinese official circles with considerable pessimism as probably portending increased Japanese pressure upon China by a military controlled government. The Minister for Foreign Affairs,[26] however, last night gave me his opinion that Japanese pressure and chauvinistic activities in China would probably lessen for a time because of the need for the Japanese to concentrate upon keeping the domestic situation in hand. Rather strangely, his principal concern seemed to be over the harm the uprising presaged for Japan. He said that the military clique had successively removed trusted advisers from around the person of the Emperor in order to control the Emperor themselves.

3. Telegraphic messages which he received from Japan while I was with him and which he showed to me were similar to Reuter's despatches. Information from foreign news sources in Shanghai indicates that because of rigorous censorship in Japan confirmation of the various reports is still lacking, actual details are not known and doubt exists even as to the identity of all officials killed or wounded. The reports in general agree that at least Okada, Saito and Watanabe are dead.

4. Repeated to the Department, Peiping and Tokyo.

JOHNSON

894.00/576 : Telegram

The Ambassador in the Soviet Union (Bullitt) to the Secretary of State

Moscow, February 27, 1936—7 p. m.
[Received February 27—3 p. m.]

71. Stomoniakoff, Assistant Commissar for Foreign Affairs in charge of Far Eastern Affairs, stated to me this evening that he

[26] General Chang Chun.

919456—54——52

had just received telegrams from Tokyo reporting the following facts:

1. The mutinous officers supported by soldiers of the 3rd and 6th Regiments of the First Division are still occupying the War Ministry and police headquarters but have announced that they are ready to surrender under certain conditions.

2. The entire Government spent the night in the Imperial Palace afraid to leave.

3. Goto, after being appointed Prime Minister ad interim and resigning, was again appointed Prime Minister ad interim.

4. The Soviet Ambassador in Tokyo believes that the Emperor is weakening in his opposition to the militarists and that it is possible that a general will be appointed Prime Minister.

Stomoniakoff said that in his opinion the general would be either Araki or Masaki. He added that he feared that appointment of Masaki would produce the gravest consequences. He alleged that the Soviet Government had information which indicated that Masaki might be behind the present mutiny and said that the Soviet Government considers him the most dangerous of all Japanese militarists.

Stomoniakoff also said that he considered the summoning of Prince Chichibu [27] to Tokyo an ominous sign and alleged that Chichibu was more friendly to the Japanese militarists than any other member of the Imperial Family.

In commenting on the whole situation Stomoniakoff said that he expected an immediate brutal advance of the Japanese Army against China. He said that he would not be surprised if there should be a similar advance against Outer Mongolia but that he considered an advance against the Chinese more likely because it would meet with less resistance than an advance against the Mongolians and would give the militarists an easy victory to display to the Japanese populace.

Stomoniakoff added that he did not anticipate any attack under any circumstances by Japan on the territory of the Soviet Union until the Japanese had made considerable further advances in North China and Outer Mongolia.

BULLITT

894.00/574 : Telegram

The Ambassador in Japan (Grew) to the Secretary of State

TOKYO, February 27, 1936—11 p. m.
[Received February 27—11:05 a. m.]

43. Embassy's 41, February 27, 1 p. m. Latest intelligence indicates that an ultimatum was issued at 8 o'clock tonight by the Govern-

---

[27] Younger brother of Emperor Hirohito.

ment to the insurgents and that at least a temporary compromise was reached, the nature of which has not been revealed.

There are many rumors of possible military action tonight probably based on considerable movements of troops and machine guns throughout the city but up to the present moment there appears to be no grounds to justify serious apprehension. The Embassy is heavily guarded by Government troops.

Repeated to Peiping.

GREW

894.00/577 : Telegram

The Ambassador in Japan (Grew) to the Secretary of State

TOKYO, February 28, 1936—noon.
[Received February 28—6 : 58 a. m.]

44. Embassy's 43, February 27, 11 p. m.

1. Loyal Government troops with tanks are being concentrated in the vicinity of the British Embassy. Other dispositions indicate preparations for a possible attack from the east on the Premier's official residence and the Sanno Hotel where the insurgent troops now are.

2. This morning a general staff officer attached to the martial law headquarters called at the Embassy and stated that the Embassy is situated in a zone which may possibly become dangerous during the day from flying bullets should fighting take place; and that therefore the martial law authorities had arranged to transfer the personnel of the Embassy to the Military Academy as a place of safety if I should consent to such a move. He added that similar arrangements were being made for other Embassies and Legations situated in the danger zone. I have declined the offer with thanks but have warned all members of the staff and their families not to expose themselves needlessly. There is adequate protection in the Embassy in case of necessity.

3. Everything indicates that some sort of an ultimatum has been given by the Government to the insurgents and that in all probability it expires sometime today.

Repeated to Peiping.

GREW

894.00/580 : Telegram

The Ambassador in China (Johnson) to the Secretary of State

NANKING, February 28, 1936—noon.
[Received February 28—7 : 15 a. m.]

44. My 42, February 27, 2 p. m. Comment on recent events in Japan among important Chinese officials with whom I have talked is gen-

erally to the effect that action of Japanese Army presages a more drastic attitude toward China and Russia by Japan. Chinese now as in the past are speculating upon probabilities of an early outbreak of hostilities between Japan and Russia. Russian Ambassador expresses confidence that Japan will hesitate to attack strongly fortified and armed Russian position in Siberia and believes Japan will concentrate upon a China that is weak and disunited. He expresses belief that further aggression by Japan in China will precipitate a revival of civil war. He looks upon recent events in Japan as a natural Fascist evolution which will bring inflation, increased trade and larger military expenses.

By mail to Peiping and Tokyo.

JOHNSON

894.00/577 : Telegram

The Secretary of State to the Ambassador in Japan (Grew)

WASHINGTON, February 28, 1936—noon.

27. Your 44, February 28, noon, paragraph 2. I appreciate very much the high sense of official responsibility and duty which you and your staff are displaying during the present emergency situation; also the timely and helpful telegrams which you are sending the Department. I realize that the information contained in these telegrams has been difficult to obtain. We have complete reliance upon the soundness of your judgment in deciding whether or not the personnel of the Embassy should be temporarily transferred to a place removed from the danger zone. You will of course keep in mind that we would not wish that the Embassy staff be exposed unnecessarily to danger.

Should any moves of persons or property be needed involving expenditures, a special allowance will be granted upon telegraphic request therefor.

HULL

894.00/582 : Telegram

The Ambassador in the Soviet Union (Bullitt) to the Secretary of State

Moscow, February 28, 1936—5 p. m.
[Received February 28—1:25 p. m.]

73. Litvinov has just informed me that he has received today the following reports from the Soviet Ambassador in Tokyo:

Prince Saionji advised the Emperor to have no negotiations with the mutineers but to treat them with the utmost severity.

The troops loyal to the Government are in complete control of Tokyo.

There is no chance whatever that Masaki will become Prime Minister.

It is now believed in Tokyo that Prince Konoye, President of the House of Peers, will become Prime Minister.

Litvinov said that from the point of view of the Soviet Union the whole situation looked brighter than yesterday as it now seemed unlikely that an extreme militarist could become Prime Minister.

Dr. Yen, Chinese Ambassador, expressed the opinion to me that increased pressure on China was not to be expected for several weeks.

BULLITT

894.00/578 : Telegram

The Ambassador in Japan (Grew) to the Secretary of State

TOKYO, February 28, 1936—6 p. m.
[Received February 28—7 : 50 a. m.]

45. Embassy's 44, February 28, noon.

1. The day has passed with many conflicting rumors but without armed combat. Obviously the diplomatic and other foreign communities have exhibited much anxiety during the day but present indications point to a relaxation of the tension.

2. I have just been informed by a responsible official of the Foreign Office that the Commander of the First Division approached the insurgents this afternoon with an order that they obey the commands of the Emperor. The insurgents thereupon agreed to obey the Emperor's commands and to return to their barracks but are negotiating as to when and under what conditions they will return. The flag of the insurgents still flies over the official residence of the Prime Minister and the loyal troops still occupy strategic positions throughout the area around the residence.

3. Censorship on news despatches abroad was relaxed during the morning and foreign correspondents were able to talk freely by international telephone. This privilege was rescinded this afternoon and it is not known when free foreign communication will again be permitted.

4. The death of Finance Minister Takahashi on the 26th has now been officially announced. As yet there has been little perceptible effect in financial circles, as the stock and bond markets are closed, but the newspapers report that there have been heavy withdrawals from deposits in banks throughout the country.

5. One light cruiser and eight destroyers from Yokosuka tied up at Shibaura yesterday morning and the First Fleet arrived in Tokyo

Bay this morning for guard duty. No bluejackets or marines have been landed except to guard the Ministry of the Navy.

6. Several vernacular newspapers this morning commented in regard to the next Premier and Cabinet. The opinion was expressed that it would be difficult for Prince Saionji to advise the Throne in the present circumstances, as the apparent purpose of the uprising was to dispose of the "senior statesmen bloc" surrounding the Throne, but that it was most necessary to appoint a really national Cabinet composed of men of ability and headed by a man of great influence and upright character in order to correct the present emergency situation. No attempt has yet been made to forecast the name of the next Premier.

Repeated to Peiping.

GREW

894.00/583 : Telegram

The Ambassador in Japan (Grew) to the Secretary of State

TOKYO, February 28, 1936—midnight.
[Received February 28—3 : 15 p. m.]

46. Embassy's 45, February 28, 6 p. m.

1. A friendly Japanese in high position has informed me that an ultimatum "from the highest source" was delivered the insurgents at 3 o'clock this afternoon ordering them to disband and return to barracks and that the insurgents have chosen to disregard the order. Our informant states that in these circumstances the Government has decided to proceed with military measures early tomorrow morning probably at daybreak and that in view of the determination of the insurgents this may mean fighting until the last man has been wiped out.

2. It is reported that the insurgents demand that General Masaki shall be named Prime Minister; that a portion of the revenues of the big financial interests such as Mitsui and Mitsubishi shall be given to the Government; and that Colonel Aizawa (the murderer of Nagata) shall be freed. They indicate that having drawn the sword for these principles they must carry through to the end.

3. Subsequent to my receipt of the foregoing communication, three radio announcements were made this evening to the effect that the Tokyo Garrison would take "a certain step" against the three or four hundred insurgent troops now stationed in Kojimachi. These official announcements would seem to corroborate the report of my informant.

4. The Embassy's observers find that the disposition of the Government troops in this vicinity and near the British Embassy this evening are precisely the same as when the General Staff officer this

morning predicted that fighting might take place as set forth in paragraph 2 of my 44, February 28, noon.

5. All of the foregoing information indicates that unless a last hour surrender occurs or unless the insurgent officers adopt the classic way out by suicide there will be fighting in Tokyo early tomorrow morning. It is believed that the number of insurgent troops are at present considerably greater than the number mentioned in the radio announcements.

Repeated to Peiping.

GREW

894.00/621

The Consul at Dairen (Grummon) to the Ambassador in Japan (Grew) [28]

DAIREN, February 28, 1936.

SIR: I have the honor to submit a summary of a conversation between Mr. Matsuoka, president of the South Manchuria Railway Company and Mr. Golubtsov, the Soviet Consul, held in the presence of the officers of this Consulate, at the Dairen Club, the evening of February 26th on the occasion of a dinner held in honor of Mr. Matsuoka.

At the time the conversation took place no definite information had been received as to the actual extent of the military rebellion in Tokyo. Rumors had been prevalent all day and there was even some doubt as to whether, under the circumstances, Mr. Matsuoka would appear at the dinner. The conversation reported below took place in the lobby of the Club prior to the dinner itself. It should be borne in mind that Mr. Matsuoka was talking to a Communist and used language which he probably considered would be intelligible to one versed in communist ideology.

Mr. Golubtsov asked Mr. Matsuoka what information he had in regard to the day's events in Tokyo. The latter replied that his information, which he would not guarantee to be accurate, was that the Premier, the Minister of the Imperial Household, and the Finance Minister had been killed and that other members of the cabinet had been attacked. He stated that it was a revolution of the young army officers and that 3,400 troops had rebelled in Tokyo. The center of unrest was said to be the Third Regiment in Azabu, Tokyo, and the rebelling troops were believed to have taken possession of the building of the Colonial Ministry and made it their headquarters. All cabinet ministers who were still alive were reported to have taken refuge in the Imperial Palace.

---

[28] Copy transmitted to the Department without covering despatch; received March 23.

The Soviet Consul asked if the rebellion was against the Emperor and Mr. Matsuoka replied that it definitely was not. "It is actually against capitalism," he said. He went on to say that in the view of the young army officers all property in Japan belongs to the Emperor and the political parties and large business and financial houses had been diverting the wealth of the nation to their own ends. The only remedy is violence which will get rid of the politicians. Then Mr. Matsuoka added, "Maybe they are right." Mr. Golubtsov asked if it was the intention of the rebels to abolish private property and Mr. Matsuoka then went into an interesting exposition of what he termed "moral communism" in Japan, as opposed to material communism as it exists in Russia. He said that the Japanese state could not be organized as if it were a machine as the spiritual side of the Japanese people must be given expression. Each nation must work out its salvation according to its own inner psychology. "We had a revolution about 70 years ago to throw out the Tokugawa Shoguns, perhaps the time has come for another revolution to overthrow the present rulers of Japan and again return the country to the Emperor." The above statement is believed to be almost the exact words used by Mr. Matsuoka. Later, in answer to a question as to the danger of disorder spreading, Mr. Matsuoka said that if Prince Higashi-Fushimi [29] and Prince Chichibu were called on, as they probably would be, the army would be kept under control.

The Soviet Consul made the comment later that he believed Mr. Matsuoka knew much more than he had told and that he would not be surprised if Mr. Matsuoka were called back to Tokyo to take a leading part in whatever new government is set up.

Respectfully yours,   STUART E. GRUMMON

894.00/586 : Telegram

The Ambassador in Japan (Grew) to the Secretary of State

TOKYO, February 29, 1936—11 a. m.
[Received February 29—4:20 a. m.]

47. Embassy's 46, February 28, midnight; Department's 27, February 28, noon.

1. The staff and I sincerely appreciate your message. Members of the staff and their families living in the danger zone are staying with us in the residence which is still heavily guarded with troops, outposts and sandbag barricades below the Chancery, also three detectives and two soldiers within. I believe that the only danger is from flying bullets and that in case of necessity the basement of the residence and Chancery will afford the best possible protection.

---

[29] Reference here is probably to General Prince Naruhiko Higashi-Kuni, Supreme War Councilor.

2. According to a radio announcement this morning, about 300 of the insurgent troops from the vicinity of the Sanno Hotel have surrendered and returned to their barracks. At 5 a. m. this morning an appeal to the remaining insurgents was broadcasted, ordering them to obey the Emperor's command that they return to the barracks, asking them to reconsider their position and stating that they would be considered as revolutionists if they refused to obey. Leaflets to the same effect and stating that all revolutionists would be killed are being dropped over the insurgents positions from airplanes. It is significant that these leaflets are addressed only to insurgent soldiers and not to the insurgent officers. At 10 o'clock this morning a radio announcement stated that 30 of the insurgents with machine guns from near the General Staff office surrendered to the loyal troops, and that the Government expected the remaining troops to surrender. All traffic has been stopped in the martial law area and as far as Yokohama. Barricades have been thrown across all streets in the vicinity of the insurgents positions and the residents have been evacuated from the danger zone. The people have been warned by radio to keep out of the lines of fire and to avoid stray bullets by sitting on the floor. Telegraphic and telephonic communications abroad have been stopped, except for Government messages. No newspapers are being published.

3. All the naval vessels in or near Tokyo except one light cruiser and three destroyers have left for Yokohama indicating that the loyal troops are considered sufficient to quell the disturbance.

4. The atmosphere throughout the night and early this morning was tense and every indication existed that combat was imminent. During the course of the morning, however, a relaxation of this tense atmosphere was noticeable probably due to the radio announcement and leaflets. It is evident that the Government is using patience and making every possible effort to persuade the insurgents to disband without resorting to armed attack.

Repeated to Peiping.

GREW

894.00/585 : Telegram

The Ambassador in Japan (Grew) to the Secretary of State

TOKYO, February 29, 1936—4 p. m.
[Received February 29—4: 02 a. m.]

49. The announcement has just been made that all the revolting troops have surrendered, and that normal conditions will be restored at 4: 10 this afternoon.

Reported to Peiping.

GREW

894.00/584 : Telegram

The Ambassador in Japan (Grew) to the Secretary of State

TOKYO, February 29, 1936—6 p. m.
[Received February 29—7 : 19 a. m.]

50. Excellent order has been maintained in Tokyo throughout the recent incident and no injury or molestation to American citizens has been reported to the Embassy except the inconveniences necessarily caused by the precautionary measures of the authorities.

GREW

894.00/588 : Telegram

The Ambassador in Japan (Grew) to the Secretary of State

TOKYO, February 29, 1936—7 p. m.
[Received February 29—9 : 30 a. m.]

51. I am informed by Baron Hayashi, former Grand Master of Ceremonies, who has just returned from the Palace, that Prime Minister Okada is alive and uninjured. It appears that his brother-in-law who somewhat resembles him was killed by mistake and that the Premier escaped and has been under cover since the night of February 25th. It is said that he suddenly announced himself to the Emperor whereupon Acting Prime Minister Goto resigned the Premiership which was resumed by Okada. The Emperor is officially reported to have expressed great pleasure at Okada's reappearance.

The implications of this dramatic turn of events are too obvious to need comment. Our first reaction to the circumstances of the past 4 days is that they may well cause a revulsion of feeling against the military throughout the country and that the final results may be salutary.

We learn that from 15 to 20 officers not higher than the rank of captain were involved in the insurgency. Their fate is unknown but it is generally thought from the tone of the announcement that they may have been allowed to commit suicide.

Repeated to Peiping.

GREW

894.00/591 : Telegram

The Ambassador in Japan (Grew) to the Secretary of State

TOKYO, March 1, 1936—6 p. m.
[Received March 1—9 : 35 a. m.]

52. 1. Although martial law has not yet been lifted, virtually normal conditions prevail in Tokyo once more. The barricades have all

been removed, the police have replaced soldiers in patrolling the city, and few troops are to be seen except in the neighborhood of the martial law headquarters. A considerable proportion of the troops called into the city during the emergency have apparently departed.

2. According to an official announcement, only one of the insurgent officers, Captain Nonaka, committed hara-kiri and the others are in prison under arrest. They and five additional officers of low rank have been dismissed in disgrace from the army. Their dismissal without trial is believed to indicate a more drastic policy than has hitherto been followed in dealing with incidents of this type.

3. No announcement has yet been made concerning the formation of the new Cabinet and the appointment of a new Lord Keeper of the Privy Seal.

GREW

894.00/593 : Telegram

The Ambassador in Japan (Grew) to the Secretary of State

TOKYO, March 2, 1936—noon.
[Received March 2—3 : 34 a. m.]

53. 1. The Vice Minister for Foreign Affairs speaking confidentially told me this morning that in the conferences now taking place looking to the formation of a new Cabinet the primary and fundamental consideration under discussion is that a government shall be chosen which will not only maintain but constructively improve Japan's relations with foreign countries. Obviously we must await concrete evidence to support these indications. He said that he himself knew nothing more definite at the present moment and he thought it might take 2 or 3 days to form the Cabinet but that he would keep me apprised of any definite developments in order that I need not rely on the press for information.

2. I have today written a letter to the Minister for Foreign Affairs requesting him to convey to the competent authorities my sincere appreciation of the thoroughness of the measures taken by various departments to ensure the safety of ourselves and the personnel and property of the Embassy during the recent uprising. The situation was admirably handled.

GREW

894.00/594a : Telegram

The Secretary of State to the Ambassador in Japan (Grew)

WASHINGTON, March 3, 1936—5 p. m.

28. Department assumes that Embassy is preparing and will in due course forward by mail to the Department for purposes of present

study and future reference a comprehensive account, as authentic as possible and citing where possible official or authoritative statements, of last week's coup. In your preparation of this, Department suggests that, in view of highly conflicting press reports regarding circumstances of attack on Okada and his reappearance, of action taken against insurgents, and of fate of insurgent leaders, special attention be given to those subjects.

HULL

894.00/596 : Telegram

The Ambassador in Japan (Grew) to the Secretary of State

TOKYO, March 4, 1936—noon.
[Received March 4—6:34 a. m.]

56. Embassy's 53, March 2, noon. Prince Saionji arrived in Tokyo on March 2 and is reported to have called various national leaders into consultation preparatory to formulating his recommendations to the Throne in regard to the composition of the next Cabinet. Many of the important Japanese newspapers editorially demand the formation of a really strong national Cabinet capable of stabilizing the situation. Conditions are still too nebulous, however, to permit any prediction as to the personnel of the next Cabinet. In the meantime, the Okada Cabinet which resigned *en bloc* on February 26 assuming responsibility for the insurrection is carrying on its duties as a provisional government.

Repeated to Peiping.

GREW

894.00/595 : Telegram

The Ambassador in Japan (Grew) to the Secretary of State

TOKYO, March 4, 1936—1 p. m.
[Received March 4—1 a. m.]

57. Department's 28, March 3, 5 p. m. The Embassy is now compiling a despatch containing all available official announcements, official radio broadcasts, leaflets, et cetera, which will be transmitted in the pouch due Washington March 21.[30] It is improbable, however, that all the official details desired by the Department will be available for some time to come owing to continued censorship and the fact that even the officials of the Foreign Office are not yet certain of all the details. The whole subject will be fully covered in due course.

GREW

[30] Despatch No. 1721, March 6, not printed.

894.00/604

Memorandum by the Secretary of State

[WASHINGTON,] March 4, 1936.

The Japanese Ambassador [31] called and handed me the following note in writing from Foreign Minister Hirota:

"I am most grateful to you for your kind message of condolence transmitted to me by the American Ambassador in Tokyo, and, on behalf of the Japanese Government, I wish to convey to you and through you to the United States Government our most sincere thanks for this manifestation of sympathy."

The Ambassador and I exchanged a few general statements about the restoration of international trade, in the course of which I emphasized the broad program which this Government was pursuing, and, without referring to Japan, I endeavored to point out the necessity for the restoration at the earliest possible date of the normal processes of international finance and commerce. The Ambassador suggested that our two nations had similar views on this general subject. He then added that there were some small minor troubles in our trade situation which had been the subject of more or less discussion and misunderstandings.[32] I replied that this Government was carrying all the political load possible in its efforts to go forward with our program of liberalizing commercial and general trade policies; that the small overflows of imports with respect to given commodities were very combustible politically; and that it was necessary that we should compose the troubles which they presented by amicable agreements, if and when at all possible; otherwise, we were obliged to take other necessary steps.

The Ambassador seemed agreeably disposed towards special agreements, such as we had been making. I replied further that it was either this or a possible cessation of our trade restoration movement and the still further increase of tariff that would soon follow, with the result that Japan would be much worse off than if she entered into these special agreements, restricting voluntarily certain quantities of exports from Japan to the United States.

The Ambassador volunteered the suggestion that the recent explosion in Japan, planned at the instigation of certain young army officers with the result that a number of Japan's statesmen were assassinated, was not a controversy between the ultra-radical and conservative elements in the military group, but that it was the reaction of the soldiers to seriously discriminatory economic treatment of farmers and small business men in Japan by what we would call big

---

[31] Hirosi Saito.
[32] See pp. 806 ff.

business in this country. The Ambassador said that these officers, without the knowledge of their superiors, sought to resent the action of the Government in playing into the hands of what we would call the big predatory interests at the expense of the farmers and small business men whose suffering was growing steadily worse. The Ambassador went on to say that seven generals had resigned because they were in charge of the military forces of which the rebellion companies were a part; he said that the generals knew nothing about the plans for this uprising and the systematic assassination, but that, of course, the generals were chargeable with the responsibility for the results, and hence their resignation.

The Ambassador stated he felt now that conditions were comparatively calm and normal the Government unquestionably would work out a list of cabinet members who would make up a satisfactory government, and by that the Ambassador said he meant a government more considerate of the rights and interests of the farmers and the small business men and less under the domination of big business in Japan, which he said had rapidly accumulated wealth by trading, while the other classes mentioned suffered correspondingly.

C[ORDELL] H[ULL]

894.00/625

The Ambassador in Japan (Grew) to the Secretary of State

No. 1706   TOKYO, March 5, 1936.
                                        [Received March 23.]

SIR: The results of the Diet election held on February 20 appear to have been one of the immediate causes of the uprising that broke out six days later with the murder of Admiral Viscount Saito, Finance Minister Takahashi, General Watanabe, and Colonel Matsuo, the Premier's brother-in-law.* However, the fundamental causes beneath the outbreak date back several years and are bound up with a feeling of discontent in the Army over political and social conditions in Japan.

In their campaigning before the election the two principal political parties were at variance in several important points. Although both appeared to stand for a "positive foreign policy", for the improvement of agricultural interests, and for the relief of local finance, the Seiyukai advocated political reform for the abolishment of bureaucracy and insisted upon the resignation of the Okada Cabinet, which the Minseito continued to support. The Seiyukai was reported to be desirous of the abolition of the "senior statesmen bloc", while there was no evi-

---

*Embassy's telegram No. 37 of February 26, 1936. [Footnote in the original.]

dence that the Minseito was opposed to consultation of the senior statesmen by the Emperor and the Government, a practice maintained during the incumbency of the Saito and Okada Cabinets.† In a speech delivered on February 3, Mr. Chuji Machida, President of the Minseito Party and Minister for Commerce and Industry, stated that in the belief of the Party the Japanese people had sufficient political ability to solve Japan's problems; that the situation could not be handled by a single faction, but that the whole nation must set its mind to it; and that to show its conviction in this belief and to carry out its function as a national party the Minseito had supported the Saito Cabinet and later the Okada Cabinet. As a part of its platform the Kokumin Domei advocated consistency between military and diplomatic action, and promotion of public health. The Showakai, the newly organized pro-Government party, had the slogans "Down with those who disturb national unity" and "From Takahashi finance springs business prosperity." The Shakai Taishuto, or Social Mass Party, was said to favor establishment of democratic parliamentary politics, opposition to higher taxes on the masses, immediate adoption of the national pension system, and State management of important industries as opposed to capitalistic management. Various members of the Cabinet made speaking tours during the last week of the Diet campaign and on February 17 the Premier addressed a public meeting at the Hibiya Public Hall held under the auspices of the Cabinet, an action which the *Asahi* termed unprecedented in the history of Japan. Premier Okada reiterated the platform of the Government adopted at the formation of the Cabinets‡, set forth the Government's reasons for dissolution of the Diet on January 21, and attributed the sound basis of Japan's finances to the untiring efforts of Finance Minister Takahashi.

The Army and the Navy were reported to desire as a result of the election the resignation of the Cabinet and the formation of a "stronger" Government. According to the *Nichi Nichi* of February 12, both services hoped for the emergence of a strong cabinet "reflecting the prevailing international situation" and held the belief that the nation could not solve its present difficulties so long as the Okada Cabinet failed to grasp the emergency nature of the international situation and remained under the restraint of the political parties "and other forces at odds with national defense and the execution of the national polity." It was reported by *Nippon Dempo* on February 19 that the military insisted that regardless of the outcome of the election the Government should resign because "it was too weak".

---

†Monthly Report for January, Section III (*c*). [Footnote in the original; report not printed.]

‡Embassy's despatch No. 918 of August 3, 1934. [Footnote in the original; despatch not printed.]

Before February 20 observers generally were of the opinion that the Seiyukai would maintain its position in the House of Representatives and that the Government would be forced to resign. In any case, the pronounced gains of the Minseito came as a surprise. The election reduced the Seiyukai Diet seats from 242 to 174 and increased the Minseito seats from 127 to 205. According to the figures published by the *Japan Times* of February 24, which are believed to be official, the candidates elected were as follows:

Minseito	205
Seiyukai	174
Showakai	19
Shaki Taishuto	18
Kokumin Domei	15
Others	35

The election thus resulted in giving no party a majority in the Diet. In addition to the relative good fortune of the Minseito, the other surprises afforded by the election were the defeat of Dr. Kisaburo Suzuki, President of the Seiyukai, and the success of the Shakai Taishuto, whose representation was increased from 3 members to 18. In this connection it is pertinent to remark that this political party is in no way communistic and that the closest parallel to it in foreign countries would appear to be the British Labor Party.

Shortly after the election results became known, Mr. Adachi, President of the Kokumin Domei, was reported to have proposed to Premier Okada the resignation of the Cabinet "en bloc" and its reconstruction in cooperation with the Seiyukai for the purpose of forming a national coalition government. According to the *Japan Advertiser* of February 26, the Government decided on February 25 to reject Mr. Adachi's suggestion and to defer consideration of the question of Cabinet reconstruction until after the adjournment of the extraordinary session of the Diet, scheduled to convene on April 20. This newspaper also stated that at the same time the Cabinet had arrived at the belief that the Government would be able to control the Diet without having to rely on the support of the Kokumin Domei.

For the most part, public opinion appeared to be optimistic over the results of the Diet election. There was nevertheless a noticeable difference of opinion as to whether the political situation would be stabilized by the election. The *Japan Times* of February 24 stated that financial and economic circles were sanguine over the election results on the ground that Mr. Takahashi's financial policy would be maintained by the continuance in office of the Okada Cabinet through the support of the Minseito. On the other hand, the Tokyo *Asahi* of February 25 and the *Osaka Asahi* of February 26 attributed the victory of the pro-Government parties to popular disgust with the

Seiyukai and expressed doubt that the policy of the Okada Cabinet had won the confidence of the nation.

Amid all this speculation the outbreak of February 26 occurred. It is probable that the plot of the younger Army officers was carried out at this juncture partly because of despair over the Minseito victory, coupled with the knowledge that the Okada Government would continue in power. There is little likelihood that the plotters were alarmed over the success of the Shakai Taishuto, or so-called proletarian party. On the contrary, some of the aims of this Party were known to coincide with the objectives of the radical element in the Army, such as control of industry by the State rather than by capitalists, less taxation of the masses, and increased taxation of the capitalists. The position of the Shakai Taishuto was later made clearer with the issuance of a statement on March 2 by Mr. Hisashi Aso, a Diet member of the Party. According to Domei (news agency), after stating that hasty comment on the February 26 incident would be withheld, Mr. Aso repeated the party platform as follows: (1) State management of important industries and State control of finance, insurance and foreign trade; (2) State management of land, with the right of tillage remaining with the holder of the land; (3) State control of staple agricultural products; (4) A fundamental reform in taxation to increase the levy on capitalists; (5) Creation of a national pension system; (6) Establishment of credit institutions or smaller industrialists and businessmen; (7) Radical readjustment of agrarian debts; (8) Enactment of a labor union Law and a tenancy law; and (9) Public management of medical institutions. A comparison of the Party's platform with the desiderata of the Army, as expressed in the various Army pamphlets, reveals the fact that both have very similar socialistic aims.§

To return to the question of the Minseito, it may be reiterated that this Party had not expressed opposition to the senior statesmen while the Seiyukai, like the insurgents, desired the abolition of the whole senior statesmen system. In the announcement of the War Office issued on the evening of February 26, it was stated: "According to the written documents of these officers, the purpose of the uprising was to eliminate those perpetrating the destruction of the national polity, such as the Genro, the statesmen close to the Throne, financial magnates, the military cliques, the bureaucrats, and the political parties at this moment of serious crisis at home and abroad in order to clarify great principles and to protect and make manifest the national polity".

Respectfully yours,

JOSEPH C. GREW

---

§ Embassy's despatch No. 1031 of November 1, 1934. [Footnote in the original; despatch not printed.]

894.20/155

The Ambassador in Japan (Grew) to the Secretary of State

No. 1707   Tokyo, March 5, 1936.
                                                        [Received March 23.]

Sir: I have the honor to submit a report on the trial of Lieutenant-Colonel Saburo Aizawa for the murder of Major-General Nagata*, with particular reference to its bearing on the recent uprising and on the political views of the discontented element in the Army.

On August 12, 1935, Lieutenant-Colonel Aizawa stabbed to death Major-General Nagata, Director of the Military Affairs Bureau of the War Ministry, who was then in his office. Aizawa, of Samurai family, had as a result of the August 1 Army shifts been transferred from his post in Northern Japan to Formosa and was on his way to Formosa when he assassinated Nagata. He was detained and questioned by the *gendarmerie* and later placed in the Tokyo Military Prison where he remained until his trial.

The public trial was opened at the Court Martial of the First Division in Tokyo on January 28. The counsels for the defense were Lieutenant-Colonel Sakichi Mitsui and Dr. Somei Uzawa, a member of the House of Peers and of the Seiyukai political party, and President of Meiji University. Mr. Tomosaburo Shimada, in charge of the judicial affairs of the First Division, was the chief prosecutor and was assisted by Mr. Kotaro Sugihara, a judicial official attached to the Army. The presiding judge was Major-General Shozaburo Sato, Commander of the First Infantry Brigade.

There was never any question of Aizawa's guilt, since this was admitted by him at the very start. The manner in which the trial was conducted from the beginning showed conclusively that the fate of Aizawa was only a minor consideration. It transpired with increasing clarity as the trial proceeded that the important aspects of the case were the political ideas entertained by a section of the Army and reports that a large number of prominent men were involved in the affair, either directly or in some nebulous way. That which began as the cold-blooded murder of a high-ranking Army officer by one of his subordinates developed into an intensely dramatic episode that affected almost all phases of Japan's political life.

In the formal indictment against Aizawa it was stated that since about 1930 he had been worrying about the future of Japan; that he had become convinced in June, 1933, of the necessity of reforming the War Ministry, as the Army had failed to unite for the clarification of the national polity spirit; that he had taken an antipathy for General Nagata in the belief that the General was hindering the national

---

* See Embassy's telegram No. 166, August 13, 1935, and despatch No. 1450, August 23, 1935. [Footnote in the original; telegram and despatch not printed.]

reformation under the pretext of control of the Army; and that his antipathy had become more intense when General Masaki was relieved of his post of Director General of Military Education since he believed General Nagata responsible for the dismissal. The trial proceeded for nearly a month and was indefinitely postponed on February 27, the day after the murder of Viscount Saito, General Watanabe, Finance Minister Takahashi, and Colonel Matsuo, the Prime Minister's brother-in-law.

This trial has unusual significance because the revelations brought out during its course are closely associated with the feeling in military circles that prompted the May 15 incident and subsequent plots and incidents. The names of the persons mentioned in the Aizawa trial figured prominently in the trial of the officers connected with the murder of Premier Inukai on May 15, 1932. In November, 1934, there was discovered a plot of younger Army officers for the "renovation of the country" and the assassination of Prince Saionji, the Genro, as well as Dr. Suzuki, President of the Seiyukai. Since this plot was alleged to have been frustrated by Major-General Nagata, it came up for frequent mention in the trial of Aizawa and was referred to as the "secret incident of November." On July 16, 1935, General Jinsaburo Masaki, Inspector General of Military Education, was removed from office and General Watanabe was appointed in his place.† In view of the suspicion held by Aizawa and others that Nagata had been largely responsible for Masaki's dismissal, this event occupied a great deal of attention in the trial. Shortly after Masaki's dismissal Captains Kaji Muranaka and Asaichi Isobe issued a pamphlet defending Masaki and accusing Nagata of being connected with the large business interests and also of being a spy for the senior statesmen. It was disclosed during the hearings that Muranaka and Isobe had been associates of Aizawa. Their pamphlet was referred to in the trial as the "secret evidence" of Nagata's guilt and was apparently considered to have influenced Aizawa in this action. The mystery which surrounds this document is indicated by the fact that the Embassy's Military Attaché was unable to obtain a copy of it.

Perhaps the most significant development of the trial is the revelation of a desire held by various Army officers and persons outside the Army for a "renovation of the nation" to destroy the influence of the senior statesmen and the big industrialists and of the bureaucrats and Army officers affiliated with them. This feeling was made clear both by Aizawa's testimony and by the statements of Colonel Mitsui and Dr. Uzawa, the defense counsels. Aizawa himself defined the renovation of the nation, otherwise known as the Showa restora-

---

† Embassy's telegram No. 151 of July 16, 1935, and despatch No. 1414 of July 26, 1935. [Footnote in the original; for telegram No. 151 see *Foreign Relations*, 1935, vol. III, p. 314; despatch not printed.]

tion, as "the return of political and financial powers to the Emperor." In the light of all the other testimony this rather vague phrase could probably be interpreted as follows: "The Showa Restoration will be achieved when the Emperor has ceased to be influenced by the senior statesmen and their backers, the financial magnates." In addition, Aizawa admitted that he had desired to carry out a reformation by removing present civil officials and effecting perfect control of the Army by the Emperor. When asked to explain more concretely the practical method for bringing about the "Showa Restoration", Aizawa replied that the Minister of Education could not properly educate the general public and that this should be done by Army reserve men. Lieutenant-Colonel Mitsui supported and amplified Aizawa's statements by asserting that the national impasse was characterized by Japan's international isolation, the chaotic condition of national thoughts, poverty among the people, and political instability; that the real cause of the Aizawa-Nagata incident was the conflict between the financial interests and the conservative forces close to the Throne on the one hand, and the radical elements desirous of the "Showa Restoration" on the other; that the conservatives had the upper hand and as a result had nearly "poisoned" the Imperial Army.

As stated above, the names of a number of prominent men were brought into the hearings of the Court Martial. Viscount Saito was charged by the defendant and his counsels with having been instrumental in Japan's accepting the London Naval Treaty; with responsibility for the "illegal dismissal" of General Masaki from the post of Inspector General of Military Education and General Watanabe's appointment in his place; with having guaranteed the future status of General Hayashi (then Minister for War) and Major-General Nagata if they would bring about the removal of Masaki; with having induced Prince Saionji to respond to the Emperor that Admiral Okada was the suitable man for the post of Premier; and with having asked Premier Okada to suppress those who aimed at the Showa Restoration. Aizawa accused Generals Minami, Hayashi, and Ugaki of having schemed with the senior statesmen, bureaucrats, and financial leaders to persuade General Nagata to cause the removal of General Masaki. In addition, he said: "General Ugaki is the Ashikaga Takauji (i. e., the embodiment of disloyalty in the Japanese mind) of the Showa era." The defendant also believed, according to certain statements found in his diary, that Count Makino and Prince Saionji were also responsible for obstructing the Showa Restoration. At the tenth and last hearing on February 25, Lieutenant Colonel Mitsui, defense counsel, stated that he wanted to summon Mr. Seihen Ikeda of the Mitsui interests; Mr. Ijuro Ota, Ikeda's relative; Marquess Koicho Kido; Major General Saburo Inouye; Mr. Sakichi Shimozono, personal secretary of Count Makino; and Mr. Toshiki Karasawa, Director of the Police

Affairs Bureau of the Home Office. In connection with his desire to question Ikeda and Ota, Lieutenant Colonel Mitsui said that he wanted to find out whether they had conferred with General Nagata on the suppression of the Showa restoration movement and whether they had extended financial assistance to him. Among other men mentioned for summoning to the trial before its adjournment were General Ugaki and Lieutenant-General Hajime Sugiyama, Vice Chief of Staff. On February 25 General Masaki appeared for questioning in camera, the public not being admitted for fear that the proceedings would tend to injure the interests of the Army. According to Domei (news agency), after remaining for fifty minutes General Masaki left the court room abruptly and apparently in indignation. The reasons for General Masaki's sudden departure from the Court Martial are not known, although the news agency quoted above stated that he had refused to give concrete evidence on the ground that in so doing he would violate Article 235 of the Court Martial Regulations, which provides that testimony involving official secrets may not be given by members of the Supreme War Council without Imperial Sanction.

A great part of the questioning and testimony had to do with Aizawa's motives, probably on account of the prosecution's desire to ascertain whether higher officers had influenced the assassin. According to his testimony, Aizawa's motives were: his belief that Nagata was a "source of evil incarnate" and the principal obstructionists of the "Showa Restoration"; his despair over the corruption in the Army; and his conviction that elements in the Army were consorting with senior statesmen. Although Aizawa insisted throughout the trial that the murder was purely a case of direct action, suspicion would naturally fall on the Army officers with whom he admitted having had contact for several years past. These associates in the Army, as far as can be gathered from the testimony published by the newspapers, were Captains Asaichi Isobe and Koji Muranaka, the joint authors of the "secret pamphlet" referred to above; Captain Okishi; Zei Nishida; two naval officers involved in the May 15 incident; former Army Captains Sone, Eichi Okura, Ando, Sato, and Koda; Captain Tsuji; and one Kazutero Kita. Although some observers suspected General Masaki of direct complicity in the murder, there is no evidence of this. All that is known, according to the defendant's statements, is that he was an admirer of Masaki and killed General Nagata on account of the latter's alleged connection with Masaki's "disgrace". Aizawa was also closely questioned as to whether he had been aware of the guilt attached to the murder of a superior officer and the punishment which might be administered to him. The prosecution's reason for insisting upon this point was doubtless that of discovering whether Aizawa had received from higher officials a promise of clemency. The defendant's answers were vague, namely, that he had not thought of punishment because his inspiration had come from "on high"; that he had anticipated that he would be questioned for a few days by the *gendarmerie* and subsequently tried by officers in his regiment who would understand his motives and thus condone him; and that perhaps he would be allowed the honor of pleading his case before the Emperor. It will be remarked that many of Lieutenant-Colonel Aizawa's statements were extremely illogical. However, the force of his emotional convictions is aptly exemplified by a statement attributed to him in connection with his indictment. When asked if he had thought how the renovation of the nation must he effected he replied: "I did not 'think'; I acted. It (the indictment) also claims that I was moved by the 'words' of my associates. It was not their words but the communion of their souls that moved me".

As already reported to the Department, the developments that came to light in the Aizawa trial were probably one of the immediate causes of the February 26 uprising.‡ The revelations of the trial, whether true or not, undoubtedly excited the feelings of the plotters and perhaps forced them to act on February 26 instead of later. There is no doubt of Masaki's influence, passive at least, on the officers who took part in the rebellion. Evidences of this influence are the following: his known opposition to the moderate element in the Army, comprised of such men as General Hayashi, ex-Minister for War, and General Watanabe, Masaki's successor in office; the coincidence that he was admired by the younger chauvinist officers, as revealed by the trial; and the fact that as Inspector General of Education he went a long way toward moulding the chauvinist ideals of the younger officers. It may also be pointed out that Captains Ando and Nonaka, two of the ringleaders in the attempted *coup d'état*, were cadets at the Military Academy during the time that both Masaki and Aizawa were instructors there. Also, Nonaka was a member of the Aizawa Court Martial and must have heard Masaki's testimony at the secret session of February 25. And it is very significant that former Captains Koji Muranaka and Asaichi Isobe, who were close associates of Aizawa, were among those who took part in the revolt, according to the communiqué of Martial Law Headquarters issued on the afternoon of March 1, which contained the statement: "The majority of the remaining officers and Koji Muranaka, Asaichi Isobe, and Zensuke Isobe, who participated in the revolt, were put in the military prison." Perhaps the insurgents were also inspired by the following statements made by Lieutenant-Colonel Mitsui at the second hearing of the trial on January 30: that the spirit of the Showa Restoration was about to be manifested through Lieutenant-Colonel Aizawa; that a large majority of the younger officers in the Army were determined to oust outside influences; that the nation desired sincerely that the

‡Embassy's telegram No. 37 of February 26, 1936. [Footnote in the original.]

Army should prove itself to be the Army of the Emperor; and that if the Court failed to understand the spirit which guided Aizawa, a second Aizawa and even a third would appear.

As no official record of the trial has been available, the statements made during its proceedings were obtained by the Embassy from several newspapers. However, as the trial (except for one session in camera) was open to reporters and as the newspapers consulted by the Embassy were generally in agreement, it is thought that the testimony and statements recorded in this despatch can be relied on.

Respectfully yours,　　　　　　　　　　　　　JOSEPH C. GREW

894.00/611

Memorandum by the Chief of the Division of Far Eastern Affairs (Hornbeck)[33]

[WASHINGTON,] March 6, 1936.

The explanation given by the Japanese Ambassador, as recorded in the paragraph which begins at the bottom of page 2 of the memorandum under reference,[34] of the assassinations which occurred in Tokyo last week is altogether too "easy" and tends to throw the whole matter out of perspective. Economic factors unquestionably contribute to the feeling among certain large classes in Japan of discontent and unrest, as well as to the feeling of antipathy toward the commercial giants and their associates which notoriously is widespread in Japan. But these factors are, as regards the occurrences of last week, background factors. Extreme chauvinism exists in the Army and has been by no means confined to one regiment or to the so-called younger officers. The chauvinistic element in the Army has resented the moderates' policy of restraint, for which the influences around the Emperor were considered (by them) responsible. The chauvinistic element in the Army believes, apparently sincerely, that the policy of restraint is not in the best interests of the country. In this view it has widespread support throughout the people of Japan. Political assassination is, in Japan, a well recognized—one may almost say a time honored—method of expressing political resentment and disposing of officials who are felt to be pursuing a mistaken policy. The perpetrators of last week's assassination were expressing a view and making a political move which was not original with or exclusive to them. They represented the desire of many people, in many walks of life, that the restrictions on the military favored by such men as, for instance, Takahashi, be done away with, and the views of the military be given the ascendancy.

S[TANLEY] K. H[ORNBECK]

---

[33] Copy transmitted to the Ambassador in Japan, March 21.
[34] See memorandum of March 4 by the Secretary of State, paragraph beginning "The Ambassador volunteered . . .", p. 737.

894.00/602 : Telegram

The Ambassador in Japan (Grew) to the Secretary of State

Tokyo, March 6, 1936—9 p. m.
[Received March 6—10:20 a. m.]

61. Hirota is now endeavoring to form a Cabinet but has met certain difficulties, apparently with the army, and has not yet succeeded.

The appointments of Yuasa [as] Lord Keeper of the Seals, and of Matsudaira, formerly Ambassador to Great Britain, as Household Minister have been announced.

GREW

894.00/623

The Ambassador in Japan (Grew) to the Secretary of State

No. 1718   Tokyo, March 6, 1936.
[Received March 23.]

Sir: I have the honor to submit the following report on the basic and immediate causes leading to the outbreak of the junior officers of the Japanese Army on February 26, 1936, in which Admiral Viscount Saito, Finance Minister Takahashi and General Watanabe were killed and various other prominent statesmen were attacked. The precise causes impelling the young officers will not be known until they are disclosed at the trials of the officers (if they are made public even then), but in the meantime the Embassy will attempt to describe such of the factors leading to the outbreak as are known to the staff of the Embassy.

In any attempt to analyze the causes leading to the insurrection of February 26, 1936, it is necessary to take into consideration the fact that Japan, despite its well-known national unity in times of emergency, is in fact composed of many different and oftentimes warring factions. Moreover, the fact must be taken into consideration that, in order to understand the motives of modern Japan, one must examine the customs and procedure of ancient Japan, especially the Japan of the Tokugawa Shogunate, when Japanese conventions and modes of thought were largely crystallized.

1. Basic Causes

a. Mental Unrest.

The mental unrest in Japan, according to a high Japanese official, dates back to the time of the World War which, in Japan as in other countries, disturbed the usual ordered processes of thought and substituted therefor vague questionings and ill-formed ideas. In Japan the disturbance of thought was especially intensified by the industrialization of the country which resulted from the War. The mode of life of the Japanese was to a considerable extent altered by industrialization; a wealthy and influential class came into being; and new influences and abuses appeared in governmental circles. The Japanese nation was not entirely prepared for the transition from a predominantly agricultural state to a modern industrial and commercial nation, with the natural result that certain factions of the nation found difficulty in adjusting themselves to altered conditions. This difficulty was particularly apparent in the military and reactionary factions, which, accustomed as they were to government by military oligarchies, could not understand or appreciate the new and powerful elements in the Japanese Government. The mental unrest was intensified by the results of the Washington Conference of 1921–22,[35] which appeared to the Japanese to relegate Japan to a position as a second-rate Power, and later was further intensified by the American Immigration Act of 1924,[36] which, the Japanese believe, stigmatized the Japanese as an inferior race. A large part of the Japanese nation has been able to adapt itself to changed conditions and to interpret truly the meaning behind the seeming slights to Japan, but the remaining part is bewildered and resentful and, perhaps, to some extent desirous of a return to the old and more understandable days of feudalism. This disturbance of thought, caused by the breakdown of the old standards and the non-assimilation of the new standards, is believed by many observers to account in part, not only for the recent incident, but also for the incident of May 15, 1932, and for the more recent murder of Lieutenant-General Nagata.

b. Economic Mal-Adjustment.

Another basic cause of the incident of February 26 (as well as that of May 15, 1932) lies in the economic situation. It appears undeniable that a considerable section of the Japanese Army is distinctly opposed to capitalism as a system of economics. To understand this one must again remember the Tokugawa and previous eras, when wealth was considered largely in terms of returns from agriculture and when capitalism, as it is known today, did not exist. A considerable part of the Japanese nation (consisting largely of the military and unpropertied classes) does not understand the part played by the capitalists in the world of today and resents the growth of the financial and industrial interests, which they believe are battening on the common people. As an indication that the resentment is directed only against the modern capitalists, it might be pointed out that the resentment does not extend to the great landowners of the old aristocracy, who acquired their lands and wealth in the feudal days. The feeling only applies to the modern capitalists, and principally against the

---

[35] See *Foreign Relations,* 1922, vol. I, pp. 1 ff.
[36] Approved May 26, 1924; 43 Stat. 153.

Mitsuis, Iwasakis, Sumitomos, Yasudas and Okuras. The Army officers feel this resentment especially keenly (according to a Japanese official) because, during the Hamaguchi Cabinet, at the start of the world depression, the salaries of Government officials, including Army officers, were drastically reduced, for purposes of retrenchment. The reductions did not create trouble at the time, because all the Japanese were poor together. Then the industrialists took advantage of the Governmental action to reduce the wages of their employees, while the continued depression reduced the earnings of the farming class. Later the yen was devaluated, export trade increased tremendously, and the industrialists became very wealthy. But this prosperity was not passed on to the poorer classes, and the farmers and the military officers remain poor today. As a result of their resentment of this condition some of the Army officers have evolved a curious conception of state economy, consisting, as far as the Embassy can ascertain, in a sort of state socialism or collectivism, with the Emperor as absolute owner of all property and with the people as administrators. There is also a unique admixture of what might be called "samurai-ism", whereby all are to work together with loyalty to the Emperor for the good of the state. Naturally, capitalism is opposed to any such conception of state economy, and therefore the radical group in the Army is opposed to the capitalists. As will be explained later, this opposition extends to the "senior statesmen bloc", which the radical military group believes to be the tool of the capitalists.

c. The Emperor's Prerogatives.

Probably the most powerful factor in the situation is the political factor bound up with the so-called "Minobe Theory" dispute, which, in brief, is a dispute as to whether the Emperor is simply an administrator of the law or is The Law itself. The young officers who engineered the insurrection believed, and undoubtedly most sincerely, that the group of senior statesmen surrounding the Throne were relegating the Emperor to the position of being simply an administrator of the law and that they were usurping his prerogatives. This is indicated in the written statement which, according to the War Office announcement, the insurgents distributed on February 26 and which has been translated as follows:

"The purpose of the uprising was to eliminate those destroying the national polity, such as the Genro, statesmen close to the Throne, financial magnates, the military clique, bureaucrats and political parties, at the present crisis at home and abroad, in order to clarify great principles and to protect the national polity."

The "national polity" in this case is understood to mean the theory that the Emperor is The Law. The inference is that the Genro (Prince Saionji), the statesmen close to the Throne (Count Makino,

Admiral Suzuki, Admiral Saito, Admiral Okada, Baron Ikki [37] and others), the financial magnates (the Mitsuis, Iwasakis, Sumitomos, Okuras, Yasudas and others), the military clique then in power (General Kawashima, General Watanabe, General Hayashi and others), the bureaucrats (Mr. Takahashi, Mr. Goto, Mr. Machida and others) and the political parties were usurping the authority of the Emperor and thereby destroying the national polity. The reactionary element in the Army and outside believe not only that these groups are usurping the authority of the Emperor, but also that they are using the Emperor and even the Army itself to further their own selfish interests. They believe that the Genro, the senior statesmen surrounding the Throne and the moderate element in the Army are in league with the great financial interests, and that they are using their power in the Government to further those interests at the expense of the great mass of the people. This point of view is well brought out in an interview which Captain Weckerling,[38] Assistant Military Attaché and Mr. J. G. Parsons,[39] of the Embassy, had with Dr. James A. B. Scherer, a friend of General Jinzaburo Mazaki, whose opinions Dr. Scherer is presumed to have expressed during the interview. A memorandum of this conversation is enclosed.[40] The Embassy can by no means agree with all of Dr. Scherer's statements, some of which seem almost fantastic. For example, Dr. Scherer implied that Finance Minister Takahashi was the tool of the capitalists, who fattened off the profits made on munitions. But it is undeniable that Mr. Takahashi tried by every means in his power to reduce the military budgets. Again, Dr. Scherer implied that the campaigns on the Asiatic continent were sponsored or instigated by the capitalists, whose tools the senior statesmen are. But again it is undeniable that the campaigns into North China by the Kwantung Army were stopped by command of the Emperor, presumably on the advice of the same senior statesmen. Despite these obviously illogical implications, however, it is believed that Dr. Scherer's statements contain a germ of truth and undoubtedly represent the opinions of a section of the Japanese Army.

It will be noted that the insurgent officers, on February 26, attacked principally the senior statesmen surrounding the Throne. Viscount Saito, Lord Keeper of the Privy Seal, was killed; Admiral Suzuki, Grand Chamberlain, was wounded; Premier Admiral Okada was attacked but escaped; Count Makino, now not in high office but probably the most disliked (by the chauvinistic element) of any statesmen in Japan, was attacked but escaped; and an attack was planned on Prince Saionji, the Genro, according to reports, but the insurgents were arrested on the train en route to the resort where the Prince

---

[37] President of the Privy Council.
[38] Capt. John Weckerling was also Assistant Military Attaché for Air.
[39] Secretary to Ambassador Grew.
[40] Not printed.

was spending the winter. The assumption therefore is that the insurgent officers considered the senior statesmen surrounding the Throne to be the most destructive element in the Japanese Government and decided to eliminate them first. They apparently did not attempt to assassinate any of the great financial magnates. According to a Japanese official, however, the insurgents had a second program, which was designed to eliminate some of the more prominent financiers, but lack of support from the people and the prompt measures taken for the suppression of the insurgents prevented them from carrying out the second program.

d. Dissatisfaction with the External Political Situation.

The military believe that the treaties concluded as a result of the Washington Conference of 1921–22 were well-intentioned, but in the end did more harm than good. In effect, they say that the treaties gave China a "blank check" which China believed could be used at any time to obtain help from Great Britain and the United States. The Chinese therefore not only did not help themselves out of the morass into which they had fallen, but became arrogant toward Japan. According to a Japanese official, they refused to recognize Japan's interests in Manchuria, which brought on the Manchurian Incident of 1931. The same factor applies to China proper. China has diligent and intelligent people, like the Japanese, but whereas the Japanese have made a great deal out of little, the Chinese have made nothing out of much, due primarily to poor government. The Chinese are using their "blank check" of the Washington treaties to keep the Japanese from developing China, and the Japanese themselves are more or less estopped by those same treaties. The military are resentful of this fact and the resentment leads to direct action against those considered responsible for the treaties.

e. Indiscipline in the Japanese Army.

Another very serious basic factor in the situation lies in the fault in the training of the officers of the Japanese Army which impels them to take direct action whenever they feel that they should correct some real or fancied abuse. To understand this peculiar tendency to take direct and violent action, one must again go back to feudal days in Japan. Then the samurai, the soldiers, were loyal only to their feudal lords. When attempts were made to organize an Imperial Army after the Meiji Restoration, it was found that the soldiers, accustomed as they had been to giving loyalty only to their clan chiefs, tended to transfer this loyalty to their immediate superior officers, with the result that insurrections occurred and there was little loyalty to the Empire. To correct this defect, the Emperor Meiji, in 1882, issued an Imperial Rescript to the Army and Navy, emphasizing the necessity of complete loyalty to the Emperor. The following passages from the Rescript will serve to illustrate the emphasis placed upon this point:

"The supreme command of Our forces is in Our hands, and although We may entrust subordinate commands to Our subjects, yet the ultimate authority We Ourself shall hold and never delegate to any subject."

"Soldiers and Sailors, We are your supreme Commander-in-Chief. Our relations with you will be most intimate when We rely upon you as Our limbs and you look up to Us as your head."

The Rescript accomplished its purpose of transferring the loyalty of the soldiers from their immediate chiefs to the Emperor, but the trouble today arises from the fact that the Rescript was not allowed to sink into obscurity after it had accomplished its purpose but remains today, in a modern state, as the Bible of the Army. The Japanese Army places great importance upon the "spiritual training" of its soldiers, and uses the Imperial Rescript for the purpose of such training. The result has been to over-emphasize the officer's direct connection with the Emperor and his loyalty to the Emperor, and to under-emphasize the necessity of absolute obedience to his superior officers. Consequently the young officers feel that, if their conception of their duty to the Emperor conflicts with orders received from their superior officers, they can, with a clear conscience, disregard the orders and act according to their lights. This fact was well illustrated by the advance upon North China by the Kwantung Army in 1935. It will be remembered that the units of the Kwantung Army could only be stopped at the Great Wall by the issuance of an Imperial order to the effect that the Army should not move south of the Wall without Imperial sanction. In any other country, a simple order from the general commanding the army would have been sufficient to stop the advance, but in the case of the units of the Kwantung Army, an Imperial command was required to stop the young officers in command of the units. This tendency toward direct and individual action lay behind the recent incident of February 26, 1936, as well as behind the previous one of May 15, 1932, and behind the murder of General Nagata in 1935. In the recent incident, the young insurgent officers refused to obey the repeated commands of their superior officers that they return to their barracks, and eventually an Imperial command was issued. The privates obeyed the Imperial command and surrendered, but the officers held out for some time longer, refusing to surrender until their demands had been met. The inconsistency of refusing unquestioning obedience to the Emperor, while professing to be fighting to restore the Emperor's authority, does not seem to have occurred to the insurgent officers.

2. Immediate Causes

There were several minor causes which impelled the insurgent officers to take direct action at this particular time, but, as was expressed by a Japanese official, they constituted only the fuse which touched off the powder, the powder (the basic unrest) being already there.

a. The Transfer of the 1st Division to Manchuria.

The 1st Division, stationed in and near Tokyo, was recently ordered to Manchuria as replacements for another division which has served its time in the Kwantung Army. Some of the regiments of the 1st Division were scheduled to start for Manchuria within a few days, and the dissatisfied young officers felt that they were compelled to act quickly, before their departure, if they hoped to attempt to correct the abuses which they believed existed in the Government. Moreover, having been equipped with ammunition and other supplies for active duty in Manchuria, they were in a position to make an effective attack on the Government.

b. The Aizawa Trial.

The hearings in the trial of Lieutenant-Colonel Aizawa, who murdered Lieutenant-General Nagata last year, have been proceeding for the past month and have served to excite the group of younger officers in sympathy with Aizawa. It developed at the trial that Aizawa held much the same ideas in regard to the national polity and abuses in the Government as did the insurgent officers, and that he had killed General Nagata because he believed him opposed to the best interests of the State. The rumor became current that Aizawa was not being given a fair trial, the court martial being composed of officers not in sympathy with Aizawa's views, and on February 25, General Mazaki, who had been called as a witness, is reported to have walked out of the courtroom in indignation at the methods used in the trial. It is possible that this precipitated the revolt of the troops, as it is rumored that one of the demands of the insurgent officers was that Aizawa be freed. The Aizawa trial has now been indefinitely postponed, undoubtedly in order to avoid further exciting the Army. This trial is discussed more fully in despatch No. 1707 of March 5, 1936.

c. The Results of the Recent Diet Election.

As was reported in despatch No. 1706, of March 5, 1936, the recent election of Diet members resulted in the return of an unexpectedly large number of Minseito and Shakai Taishuto members and the defeat of the Seiyukai, the party opposed to the Okada Government. The Okada Cabinet was thus assured of support during the coming special session of the Diet. The young, radical officers of the Army were bitterly opposed to the Okada Cabinet, which they believed to be corrupt and weak, and apparently decided to overthrow it by force if it could not be overthrown by orderly constitutional methods.

3. CONCLUSIONS

While it is yet too early to venture any definite predictions in regard to the effects of the recent uprising in the Army, it seems fairly certain, according to the observations of this Embassy, that certain specific results will flow therefrom. The first, and perhaps the most important, will be definite attempts to instil a better sense of discipline into the Army. It is not known how this will be done, but it is possible that less emphasis will in the future be placed upon the high-flown "spiritual" teachings of men such as General Araki and General Mazaki, and more upon the soldier's practical duty to the State.

There will almost undoubtedly be attempts to organize a "Japanese New Deal" and to correct the economic maladjustments which lie at the root of much of the present unrest. In Japan there is, in the opinion of many students of the situation, too great a spread between the very rich and the very poor. The distribution of wealth is too unequal, and as long as this condition lasts the nation will be in danger of further outbreaks similar to those of May 15, 1932, and February 26, 1936. There is a limited public sympathy and support for the young officers who engineered the recent uprising, but one frequently hears it said that there is a considerable amount of truth in the accusations of the young officers and their clique in the Army in regard to maldistribution of wealth and corruption in high places. It is believed that most of the farming class and a considerable section of the Army are in sympathy with the ideals of the insurgents, and it is freely predicted that there will be other and perhaps more serious outbreaks unless something is done to remedy the conditions giving rise to the unrest. There is therefore little doubt that the new Government, whatever its complexion may be, will strive to evolve concrete policies which will tend to accomplish the same purposes as the New Deal in the United States has as its aims.

It is also possible that the recent incident will cause a swing in popular feeling toward the left. It will be remembered that at the time of the great earthquake of 1923, Osugi and other persons with socialistic tendencies were murdered in cold blood by police officers. The brutality of the murders shocked the public and caused a swing to leftist sentiments in Japan. Later several communist plots were discovered by the authorities, and there was a revulsion of feeling in Japan, resulting in the popularity during recent years of the reactionary elements. The public is now becoming fatigued with the numerous plots and uprisings of the extreme right elements, culminating in the recent incident, and it is predicted that there will be a decided swing toward the left in public feeling, although the swing will not reach to socialism or communism.

Respectfully yours,   JOSEPH C. GREW

894.00/606 : Telegram

The Ambassador in Japan (Grew) to the Secretary of State

TOKYO, March 7, 1936—9 p. m.
[Received March 7—2 : 33 p. m.]

63. Following is part summary of a statement made today to the Military Attaché by an officer of the General Staff. Insisted that he came as a personal friend and not officially but there is no doubt that he was directed to explain the situation to Lieutenant Colonel Crane.[41]

1. The incident of February 26 was planned and executed by officers forming the ignorant radical fringe of the nationalistic group to which all officers belong. Non-commissioned officers and men knew nothing of the officers' real purpose as they were told they were to take part in a night maneuver.

2. The total number of extreme radicals among officers is not known but is believed to be small. Strenuous efforts are being made throughout the country by the police and military police to locate and round up "direct actionists" among civilians and officers. The same small group of radicals was responsible for the May 15th and all subsequent incidents.

3. Our informant does not believe that any rebel officers who escaped are still at large. Three officers committed suicide. More suicides are expected later when opportunity is afforded. At present while under investigation by the military police they are unable to harm themselves.

4. The retirement of the senior army members of the Supreme Military Council (including Araki and Masaki) is due to their assumption of responsibility for the incident. General Minami, the senior general in the army, will also retire on his return from Manchuria.

5. General Terauchi's selection as the next Minister of War and General Ueda's designation as Minami's successor were dictated by their seniority, all men senior to them having retired.

6. The army approves of Hirota as Premier and of his foreign policy but dislikes the type of "*status quo*" Cabinet indicated by his first selection. In particular the army wants a non-political man as Home Minister. The army has no ambition to form a strictly military

---

[41] Lt. Col. William C. Crane, Military Attaché in Japan.

Cabinet, realizing that it is not qualified for the task. It insists on a progressive, vigorous Cabinet.

7. The army's position is expressed clearly in General Terauchi's statement yesterday: "the Government must have determination and courage to effect radical reforms, to do away with traditional evils, to carry out a strong and positive policy in providing adequate national defense, et cetera. It must not be compromising, leaning toward the *status quo* and tinged with liberalism. There must be a renovation of national administration through positive policies. Anything compromising or reactionary would not only fail to meet the situation but would aggravate it, creating an everlasting source of evil." Repeated to Peiping.

GREW

894.00/607 : Telegram

The Ambassador in the Soviet Union (*Bullitt*) to the Secretary of State

Moscow, March 8, 1936—1 a. m.
[Received March 9—7: 11 a. m.]

80. Litvinov expressed the opinion to me this evening that the elements in Japan opposed to war were definitely in control of the situation and that the Soviet Union would have nothing to fear from Japan in the immediate future.

Marshal Tukhachevsky [42] who is equally well informed and somewhat more frank on the other hand stated that he believed the army officers of the Araki, Masaki, Hayashi school would prove to be more dangerous out of command than in command and that he thought peace in the Far East would continue to be at the mercy of an incident.

BULLITT

894.00/608 : Telegram

The Ambassador in Japan (*Grew*) to the Secretary of State

TOKYO, March 9, 1936—10 p. m.
[Received March 9—12: 45 p. m.]

65. Hirota has succeeded in forming a Cabinet. He will at least temporarily continue as Foreign Minister owing to the army's disapproval of Yoshida.[43] Other Ministers of importance are Baba, Finance; Count Terauchi, War; Nagano,[44] Navy; Ushio, Home Affairs; Hayashi, Justice.

---

[42] Soviet Vice Commissar for Defense.
[43] Shigeru Yoshida, traveling Ambassador in 1935.
[44] Japanese chief delegate to the London Naval Conference, 1935.

Baba is a well-known banker of conservative leanings who has been President of the Hypothec Bank for several years. The choice is generally considered a good one as he has no strong affiliations with any political or financial groups, knows the agricultural land situation and is thoroughly familiar with long-term financing.

General Terauchi is the son of the late Count Terauchi and has the reputation of being independent and allied with no faction in the army. He has no known political affiliations and is said to be popular in army circles and to have no prejudices in regard to foreign countries.

Admiral Nagano is well known to the Department.

Ushio is a member of the House of Peers and has held a number of administrative positions of importance including the post of Vice Minister of Home Affairs. He is highly respected and appears to have been chosen because of his knowledge of administration. He will be concurrently Minister of Education.

Hayashi has had a distinguished career in the Ministry of Justice having served as Vice Minister, as Procurator General, and as presiding judge of the Court of Cassation.

Full reports on these and other members of the new Cabinet will be sent by mail.[45] The Cabinet appears to have the support of the two principal political parties as members of each of them have portfolios. The choices for Home and Justice posts indicate an investigation of these Departments which the public has long demanded.

It seems probable that separate Ministers for Foreign Affairs and Education will be appointed subsequently when Hirota has had time to canvass the situation more at leisure.

GREW

894.00/609 : Telegram

The Ambassador in Japan (Grew) to the Secretary of State

TOKYO, March 9, 1936—11 p. m.
[Received March 9—3 : 05 p. m.]

66. Embassy's 53, March 2, noon.

1. The choice of Hirota as Prime Minister and his determination to hold the direction of foreign affairs in his own hands owing to the army's disapproval of Yoshida tends to support the statement made to me by the Vice Minister on March 2nd to the effect that the improvement of Japan's foreign relations was given careful consideration in the selection of the new Cabinet.

---

[45] Despatch No. 1736, March 18, not printed.

2. The primary causes of the recent insurrection were domestic rather than international issues. The incident was an expression of basic social and economic maladjustments in Japan having root in the poverty of the masses of the people especially in certain rural districts, the absence of the stabilizing influence of a large powerful middle class and the alleged exploitation of the nation by the very wealthy who assertedly use the politicians and statesmen as their tools.

3. While the "direct action" group of younger officers in the army responsible for the recent incident is comparatively small, a considerable section of the army as a whole believes that it has a duty under the Emperor to relieve the alleged exploitation of the people to abolish political corruption and to unify the nation in a manner which they vaguely relate to ancient Japanese conceptions. They desire *inter alia* "new deal" and in this they are supported by the great mass of the people. To achieve this "new deal" will be the task of the new Government, the third "emergency Cabinet" organized since May 15, 1932. As no government in Japan can long exist under the opposition of the army the new Cabinet will have to deal drastically and effectively with the root causes of the recent insurrection or be forced out of office with the possibility of further violence.

4. Predictions as to foreign policies would be premature but it is logical to assume that in concentrating on essential domestic problems and readjustments the tendency of the Government as long as Hirota is in control will be to tranquilize Japan's foreign relations. Only time will show whether Hirota will be strong enough to curb the dangerous tendencies of the army in China and on the borders of Manchuria.

Repeated to Peiping and Moscow.

GREW

894.00/613 : Telegram

The Ambassador in Japan (Grew) to the Secretary of State

TOKYO, March 13, 1936—7 p. m.
[Received March 13—1: 30 p. m.]

74. 1. The Prime Minister received me today.

2. He said that his former policy as Minister for Foreign Affairs would continue without any change whatsoever and that it would now always prevail owing to his position as head of the Government. He added that all members of the Cabinet were in accord with his policy and that he would eventually select a Foreign Minister equally in sympathy with that policy.

3. I observed that the press was constantly talking about the new Government following a "positive diplomacy" and I asked if he would define this term. Hirota said that the term applied exclusively to Soviet Russia and China and simply meant the speeding up of the policy already enunciated.

4. As regards Soviet Russia, the army desired the establishment of defensive forces in Manchuria more nearly equalling the Soviet forces in Siberia. He said, however, that there would be no war while he was in office. A Japanese war with Soviet Russia would be stupid because both parties would have everything to lose and nothing to gain.

5. As regards China, the Japanese Government would proceed on the basis of the three points already enunciated. I asked him to define these three points. He did so as follows.

(*a*) Cessation of anti-Japanese propaganda and activity.
(*b*) Recognition of the existence of Manchukuo and regularization of factual relations such as communications, transit, customs, et cetera. This need not imply *de jure* recognition.
(*c*) Sino-Japanese c o o p e r a t i o n to combat the spread of Communism.

These three points he said had been accepted in principle by the Chinese Government and would form the basis for negotiations.

6. I said that I would be glad if the Prime Minister could authorize me to reassure my Government concerning the protection of foreign rights and interests in connection with the pursuance of Japan's policy in China including the preservation of the principle of the open door. The Prime Minister said that the principle of the open door would not be injured by Japan. The only possible result of Japan's policy in China which might indirectly affect foreign rights and interests so far as he could see would be the possible relinquishment in his opinion of her extra-territorial rights in China as an eventual result of future negotiations.

7. The Prime Minister said that he saw no serious problems existing between Japan and the United States. In this connection I took occasion on my own initiative and after stating that I was not speaking under instructions to mention the difficulties encountered by the Government in Washington arising out of the increasing flow of cheap Japanese goods into the American markets. I spoke of the cooperative steps of our Government to solve the problem through friendly and informal discussions with the Japanese Embassy in Washington and the mutual efforts to find equitable and practical solutions of the difficulties. Nevertheless pressure on our Government from domestic industrial interests was becoming increasingly heavy and I might eventually have to appeal to him for more restrictive

efforts on the part of the Government of Japan. I labeled these observations as entirely informal but thought it best to leave this thought in the Prime Minister's mind.

Paragraphs 1 to 6 inclusive repeated to Peiping.

GREW

894.00/626

Memorandum by the Under Secretary of State (Phillips)

[WASHINGTON,] March 17, 1936.

During the call of the Japanese Ambassador at my office this afternoon I asked him whether he had any information about a new Minister of Foreign Affairs, and said that I supposed the Premier would not be able to occupy both offices for very long. Mr. Saito said that according to his latest information Mr. Arita, the present Japanese Ambassador to China, would be named Minister of Foreign Affairs. He felt that the Japanese political situation resembled somewhat a boil which had now burst and which would quiet down for a considerable time.

W[ILLIAM] P[HILLIPS]

894.00/634

The Ambassador in Japan (Grew) to the Secretary of State

No. 1735   TOKYO, March 19, 1936.
[Received April 6.]

SIR: I have the honor to report that the outbreak of February 26–29 has had the effect of stimulating the Government to the adoption of many of the reforms which the insurgents demanded.

I. AIMS OF THE INSURGENTS WHICH MET WITH SUBSTANTIAL SUCCESS

It is true that the insurrection was successfully quelled in a military way, that the radical or "direct action" group in the Army and its civilian sympathizers are at present in disfavor and are being rounded up by the authorities for eventual trial*, that several of the revolting officers have committed suicide, and that the remainder have been expelled from the Army. On the other hand the actions of the younger officers who took part in the revolt have definitely borne fruit in line with the program of grievances of these officers. It has been stated recently by Army leaders now in control that not only must stricter discipline in the Army be established but that also the "fundamental causes" of the insurrection must be wiped out. For example, General Terauchi, the newly appointed War Minister, issued a statement on

---

*Embassy's telegram No. 63, March 7, 1936. [Footnote in the original.]

March 9 in which, among other things, he said: "As for the Incident, the causes of it were widespread and deeply rooted. It should be made the occasion for endeavors to clarify the principles of the foundation of the Army and remove the evils with which it is affected. Efforts must be made to make it manifest that the Army is under the direct command of the Emperor." Incidentally, an "Army under the direct command of the Emperor" was one of the battlecries of the insurgents and the banners flown from their headquarters stated: "Loyalty to the Emperor and up with the pure Army."† General Terauchi went on to state that when discipline in the Army had been perfected, efforts should be made to clarify the national polity, promote the welfare of the people, make administrative reforms and strengthen national defense. The adoption of such a program was an important part of the rebels' plans.

Furthermore, according to the *Asahi* of March 7, on that day General Terauchi told Mr. Hirota that the Army insisted upon utilizing the February 26 incidents as a turning point in Japanese policy and on establishing a fundamental policy based on state control and complete reform of the national administration, with the rejection of the liberal policy pursued since the Meiji Restoration. There are distinct indications that the Army's desires as expressed by the War Minister will meet with fulfilment at the hands of the Cabinet. Mr. Hirota has reportedly stated that his views are not at variance with those of the War Minister. In his "verbal statement" of March 9, Mr. Hirota implied that the "present unfortunate incident" was fundamentally connected with past laxity in administration and lack of a positive and independent foreign policy. Finally, many of the ideals of the defeated younger officers, later endorsed by the loyal Army, are embodied in the statement of policy issued by the new Government on March 17.‡ A parallel can be drawn between these developments and the actions since September, 1931, of the more intemperate Army officers in Manchuria and North China which, as "faits accomplis", received the endorsement of the Japanese Government.

Before analyzing the aims of the insurgent officers in connection with the success or failure of these aims, it is pertinent to remark that a large section of the Army and of the civilian population were and are in sympathy with the ideals that prompted the February 26 affair, though opposed to the violent and undisciplined methods adopted. This fact helps to explain the fundamental success of the insurgent movement.

---

†Embassy's despatch No. 1721 of March 6, 1936. [Footnote in the original; despatch not printed.]

‡Embassy's despatch No. 1733 of March 19, 1936. [Footnote in the original; despatch not printed.]

The motives and plans of the "direct action" group in and outside the Army are revealed by the actions and statements of this group since the Incident of May 15, 1932, by the mimeographed statement left by the insurgent soldiers at newspaper offices on the morning of February 26 last, and by the official document issued by the War Office on the evening of February 26. According to the statement of the insurrectionists, they desired the fall of the Okada Government because it had "been drifting away from the true spirit of Japan and had usurped the prerogatives of the Emperor." The Okada Government fell owing to its responsibility for the Incident. Evidences given for the above charge against the Okada Cabinet were the signing of the London Naval Treaty,[46] for which Viscount Admiral Saito was alleged to have been largely responsible,§ and the dismissal of General Masaki as Inspector General of Military Education on July 16, 1935, for which Saito was also blamed. Saito was one of the victims of the recent outbreak. The insurrectionaries also desired the abolition of the system whereby the senior statesmen offered counsel to the Emperor and to the Government without being responsible for their actions. In this connection it is interesting to note that the Hirota Cabinet is reported to be seriously considering abolishment of the Cabinet Deliberative Body, which since its organization on May 10, 1935,‖ had been largely under the influence of such senior statesmen as Admiral Saito, its President, and Mr. Takahashi, its Vice President. The official statement of the War Office issued on the evening of February 26,¶ gave among the purposes of the uprising the elimination of statesmen close to the Throne (Saito was killed, Admiral Suzuki, Court Chamberlain, was seriously wounded and at any rate deprived of political influence, and Baron Ikki resigned from his post of President of the Privy Council on March 11). Also listed for "elimination", according to the War Office announcement, were the military clique (General Watanabe, Inspector General of Military Education of the War Office, was killed), and bureaucrats (Mr. Takahashi, Finance Minister, was killed). A partial motive for the assassination of these men was the need felt by the younger officers to "clarify great principles and to protect and make manifest the national polity." Clarification of the national polity and the extinction of ideas incompatible with national principles (such as the Minobe theory) are set forth as the first principles of the new Government's policy in the official statement issued on March 17.

[46] Signed April 22, 1930, *Foreign Relations*, 1930, vol. I, p. 107.
§ Embassy's despatch No. 1707, March 5, 1936. [Footnote in the original.]
‖ Embassy's despatch No. 1332, May 31, 1935. [Footnote in the original; for despatch see *Foreign Relations*, 1935, vol. III, p. 858.]
¶Embassy's despatch No. 1721, March 6, 1935 [*1936*]. [Footnote in the original; despatch not printed.]

Also among the known aims of the radical army element and of a great part of the Army as well was the establishment of a kind of state socialism, with the imposition of higher taxes on capitalists, the reduction of taxes on the poorer people, and general administrative measures for the welfare of the masses, particularly in the rural communities. These objectives were touched on in the Army pamphlet of October 1, 1934, which contained such phrases as: "So long as economic profits, and especially unearned incomes, are enjoyed by one section of the nation alone the majority of the people will be left in utmost misery and distress. . . ."** A program of state reform resembling that desired by the Army is now under consideration by the Hirota Cabinet as evidenced in general terms in the Hirota Cabinet's policy statement of March 17.††

After the assassinations of February 26, according to information received by the Embassy, the insurgents demanded of the provisional Government the appointment of either Baron Hiranuma or Admiral Kanji Kato as Premier.‡‡ While Baron Hiranuma was not made Premier, he was appointed to the post of President of the Privy Council on March 13 and formally installed in office on that day. It will be recalled that Hiranuma has long been known as a chauvinist, an anti-liberal, and a favorite of the radical group in the Army; that the appointment of Baron Ikki as President of the Privy Council on May 3, 1934, was made in violation of the precedent that the Vice President of the Council be promoted to the Presidency upon the resignation of the former incumbent; and that the supporters of Baron Hiranuma were greatly annoyed because, although Vice President of the Council, he had not been appointed to the Presidency.§§

The younger officers who engineered the insurrection wanted larger defense appropriations and a stronger policy against Soviet Russia. Judging from current reports and the present Cabinet's statement of policy, an increase in defense appropriations seems assured. As stated above, on March 9 Mr. Hirota mentioned the necessity of positive and independent readjustment of international relations. Four days later, in a conversation with me, Mr. Hirota stated that the "positive diplomacy" frequently mentioned in the press applied exclusively to Soviet Russia and China and simply meant the expediting of his former policy as Minister for Foreign Affairs.‖‖

**Embassy's despatch No. 1031, November 1, 1934. [Footnote in the original; despatch not printed.]

†† Embassy's despatch No. 1733, March 19, 1936. [Footnote in the original; despatch not printed.]

‡‡Embassy's telegram No. 41, February 27, 1936. [Footnote in the original.]

§§ Embassy's despatch No. 776, May 5, 1934. [Footnote in the original; despatch not printed.]

‖‖ Embassy's telegram No. 74, March 13, 1936. [Footnote in the original.]

II. Aims of the Insurgents Which Failed

Prince Saionji, the Genro, escaped assassination and in fact subsequently recommended to the Emperor the appointment of Mr. Hirota as Premier. However, in choosing a candidate for Premier, the Genro avoided consulting the other elder statesmen near the Throne, a custom which had been established by him immediately after the May 15 Incident and which was distasteful to the radical element in the Army. On February 27 the leaders of the rebellion were reported to have demanded a military dictatorship for Japan. This demand was immediately rejected by the Government.¶¶ However, the establishment of a military dictatorship was not among the objectives of the insurgents as disclosed by their mimeographed statement of February 26 and by the official statement of the War Office on that day. The probable reason for the issuance of this demand was to enable the insurgents to make a better bargain with the Government in accordance with the well-known Japanese habit of demanding more than can be obtained for the purpose of striking a future compromise. Seven Army members of the Supreme War Council resigned on March 3, assuming responsibility for the incident. Among those who resigned were Generals Masaki and Araki, who had been an inspiration to the plotters and whose ideas undoubtedly influenced the latter. However, General Hayashi, a member of the military clique which the insurgents wanted to get rid of, also resigned from the Supreme War Council.

In return for certain concessions mentioned elsewhere in this despatch, General Terauchi is reported to have agreed with Mr. Hirota to establish stricter control in the Army. The disciplinary measures thus far taken by the Army have already been mentioned. In addition, more than one hundred civilians are said to have been arrested by the Tokyo *gendarmerie* and the Metropolitan Police for alleged complicity in the February 26 Incident. If the Army and the Home Office continue to take vigorous steps against the "direct actionists" and if the Government supplements these steps by carrying out the reforms desired by the Army, the danger of another uprising in the near future will probably be greatly lessened.

III. Conclusion

From an examination of the foregoing considerations it would appear that the aims of the insurgents which failed are outweighed by those that succeeded. In general, the insurgents wanted a liquidation of the *status quo*. The Okada Cabinet, which had been upheld at the polls on February 20, gave no indication of any intention to alter its policy or to adopt a reform program similar to the one announced by the Hirota Cabinet on March 17. While the changes

¶¶ Embassy's telegram No. 41, February 27, 1936. [Footnote in the original.]

desired by the insurgents have not all come about, measures toward effecting them gradually are under definite consideration. It is probably true that the reforms desired would have had to be adopted in the course of time owing to widespread popular sympathy for the Army's ideas. Nevertheless, it can be safely said that the insurrection of February 26 hastened that break-up of the *status quo*.

Respectfully yours,   JOSEPH C. GREW

894.00/635

The Ambassador in Japan (Grew) to the Secretary of State

No. 1746   TOKYO, March 20, 1936.
[Received April 6.]

SIR: Supplementing the Embassy's despatch No. 1707 of March 5, 1936, concerning the trial of Lieutenant-Colonel Aizawa for the murder of Major-General Nagata, I have the honor to submit a report on developments that have come to light since the writing of that despatch, with particular reference to the relation between the trial and the Incident of February 26.

Recently the Embassy's Military Attaché was informed by an official of the War Office that former Captains Koji Muranaka and Asaichi Isobe, former Lieutenant Zei Nishida and Kazuteru Kita (once a "ronin" in China), all of whom were prominently mentioned in the Aizawa trial as close associates of the defendant, had been the real ringleaders in the revolt although the nominal and active leaders had been Captains Ando and Nonaka. This information was substantiated by an announcement of the Martial Law Headquarters on March 11.

According to newspaper reports, Kazuteru Kita was a Socialist during the early part of his career and later became converted to out-and-out nationalism. About 1920 he published a book in Shanghai entitled *Japan's Reconstruction* which was prohibited from distribution in Japan on account of its pernicious intermingling of leftist and rightist ideas and its insistence upon direct action. It is said that the book, *Japan's Reconstruction,* had a great influence on the men accused of perpetrating the May 15 assassination. Zei Nishida resigned as a lieutenant in the Army in 1924 on account of illness and subsequently joined the chauvinist movement, becoming a member of several ultra-nationalist societies. In 1926 he was arrested in connection with a plot against the life of Count Makino and others and was sentenced to five months' penal servitude in 1930. For the past five years he has been working closely with Kazuteru Kita.

Furthermore, according to the *Asahi* of March 5, ex-Captain Muranaka and Zensuke Shibukawa, a graduate of the Military Academy and one of the civilians arrested for participation in the February 26 Incident, attended seven sessions of the Aizawa trial, carefully taking notes, and on February 17 ceased to appear at the hearings. The disclosures made during the trial may thus have influenced the conspirators in the choice of the date on which to act and of the persons to be assassinated.

It was reported by the *Asahi* of March 12 that Lieutenant-Colonel Aizawa would have to be completely retried because his trial had already been suspended fifteen days, the legal limit under the Court Martial Law. Domei (News Agency) stated that no date for a new trial had been set and that it would be postponed indefinitely. In this connection it is of interest to note, according to newspaper accounts and to the Military Attaché's informant mentioned above, that the trial of the officers and civilians involved in the February 26 Incident will be distinctly different from the trial of the men involved in the assassination of Premier Inukai on May 15, 1932, and from the Aizawa trial in that it will be held strictly in camera, the accused will be denied the benefit of counsel, the decisions given will be final with no appeal allowed, and there will be less airing of political views and more attention paid to establishing the guilt of and the punishment for the defendants.

A five-day conference of Army and Division Commanders is scheduled to begin at Tokyo on April 7. Although such conferences of Army and Division Commanders are routine matters and take place from time to time under ordinary circumstances, the newspapers report that the purpose of the coming conference is to strengthen Army discipline and to unify the control of the Army. It remains to be seen whether any extraordinary measures will be taken at the scheduled conference.

Respectfully yours,   JOSEPH C. GREW

894.032/152 : Telegram

The Ambassador in Japan (Grew) to the Secretary of State

TOKYO, May 6, 1936—6 p. m.
[Received May 6—8 : 20 a. m.]

95. 1. In his speech before the House of Peers this morning Premier Hirota said that in removing the causes of national unrest he would avoid extremes and would adhere to constitutional government under the Emperor. He avoided concrete expressions of policy but said that the Government would clarify the national policy; would perfect national defense while watching developments in China and Soviet Russia, would meet new expenditures by strengthening national

finances and improving the taxation system; would take drastic steps if need be to overcome the barriers being erected against Japanese trade; and would if desirable abolish some governmental organs or merge them with others in order to effect administrative reforms.

2. The Foreign Office states that the speech of the Minister for Foreign Affairs was transmitted practically *in toto* to the Japanese Embassy in Washington where it will be available to the Department.

3. Contrary to expectations the Minister for War did not give a detailed account of the causes of the recent incident but stated that the causes would be made public at the proper time. He stated that the discipline of the army as a whole was not affected by the affair and that the trouble was caused by radicals working behind the scenes.

GREW

894.20/165

The Ambassador in Japan (*Grew*) to the Secretary of State

No. 1821

Токуо, May 12, 1936.
[Received June 1.]

SIR: With reference to the Embassy's despatches No. 1450 of August 23, 1935,[47] No. 1707 of March 5, 1936, and No. 1746 of March 20, 1936, concerning the murder on August 12, 1935, of Major General Nagata by Lieutenant Colonel Aizawa and the trial of the assassin from January 28 to February 26, 1936, I have the honor to report that the War Office announced on May 9 that Aizawa had been sentenced to death on May 7 by the Court Martial of the First (Tokyo) Division.

It will be remembered that Lieutenant Aizawa's first trial, which had a direct bearing on the recent insurrection, was indefinitely postponed on February 26; that subsequently his trial was suspended fifteen days, which necessitated a complete re-trial under the provisions of the Court Martial Law;* and that the military authorities have during recent weeks reportedly been seriously considering the elimination of all "direct actionists" from the Army.† On April 7 Dr. Somei Uzawa, who in the first trial had exerted his utmost efforts to bring out the patriotic motives of the accused, resigned as a counsel for Aizawa, possibly because of his responsibility for the manner in which the trial had been handled and hence for the February 26 Incident. Aizawa's second trial was opened on April 22 and there were five hearings in camera. The date of the resumption of the trial was not publicly known until the War Ministry's announcement of the

---

[47] Not printed.
*Embassy's despatch No. 1746 of March 20, 1936. [Footnote in the original.]
†Embassy's despatch No. 1784 of April 17, 1936. [Footnote in the original; despatch not printed.]

death sentence was made. In the following statement of the War Office, issued on May 9, it will be noted that the reason given for holding the hearings in camera was that public hearings would have been disturbing to public order:

"The Aizawa case was for some time under examination by the court-martial of the 1st Division. With the outbreak of the February 26 incident, a change was made in the presiding judge, and the retrial was opened on April 22. There were five hearings. The presiding judge suspended public hearings because the proceedings, if published, would be disturbing to public order. On May 7, the judge announced the decision, and on May 8, Lieutenant General Aizawa appealed."

In accordance with the provisions of the Army Criminal Code, the higher Court Martial for Aizawa must be held within thirty days of his appeal, which was made on May 8. The War Office authorities issued an interesting statement concerning the sentence of the Court Martial, a translation of the text of which is enclosed,[48] as published by the *Japan Times* of May 11.

While it is impossible to predict whether the higher Court Martial will uphold this decision and Aizawa will actually meet his death as a result of the murder, the death sentence laid down in this case may be considered as highly significant in view of the lenient sentences passed on the perpetrators of similar political assassinations in the past and also in view of the fact that the first trial of Lieutenant Colonel Aizawa, which was held before the occurrence of the February 26 Incident, seemed to have little or no connection with his confessed guilt and seemed to be much more concerned with sympathy for his political motives. There may be an indication in the Court Martial's decision of May 7 that the War Minister is, as he himself has asserted in recent Diet sessions, seriously intent upon establishing rigid discipline in the Army and punishing those guilty of direct action methods.

Respectfully yours, JOSEPH C. GREW

894.00/651

The Ambassador in Japan (Grew) to the Secretary of State

No. 1833 TOKYO, May 14, 1936.
[Received June 1.]

SIR: With reference to the Embassy's despatch No. 1784, dated April 17, 1936,[48] concerning the results flowing from the incident of

---

[48] Not printed.

February 26, 1936, I now have the honor to report the following developments in the situation.

POSITION OF THE ARMY

The Japanese Army, and particularly that portion of the Army which has been concerning itself with political questions and advocating ultra-nationalistic principles, does not appear to be in favor in Japan at the moment. Since the convening of the special session of the Diet on May 1, numerous critical interpellations have been directed at the Minister for War, the most striking one being that of Mr. Takao Saito, a Minseito member of the Lower House, delivered on May 7 (Embassy's despatch No. 1826, dated May 13, 1936 [50]). In the course of his interpellation, Mr. Saito criticized the tendency of young Army officers to meddle in political affairs and described their ideas as "naive", "laughable" and "simple and pure but puerile". He condemned the Army authorities for not having taken steps at an earlier date to eliminate erroneous ideas in the Army and declared that the May 15 and February 26 incidents could have been prevented if the higher authorities in the Army had endeavored from the first to remove the causes of the evil. He further declared that extreme rightists were as dangerous to the State as extreme leftists and advised the higher military authorities to guide properly the younger officers, in order to prevent the growth of dangerous ideas. His speech was greeted with loud and prolonged applause and was later commented upon most favorably by several newspapers, indicating clearly that the general sentiment in the country is favorable to the critics of the Army and opposed to that section of the Army which has advocated extreme reactionary principles.

The Army has been somewhat embarrassed by these demonstrations of lack of sympathy, and consequently is apparently taking strong measures to eliminate from the Army those elements which have called down upon the Army the wrath of the public. The most striking example of these measures is the sentencing to death of Lieutenant-Colonel Aizawa, the murderer of Lieutenant-General Nagata in August last (see Embassy's despatch No. 1821, dated May 12, 1936). This sentence, imposed by the First Division Court Martial (held in camera) on May 7, 1936, is much more severe than the sentences imposed upon the young Army and Navy officers involved in the murder of Premier Inukai on May 15, 1932. It will be remembered that the young officers involved in that affair received prison sentences of from one to fifteen years, with, of course, commutation of sentence

---

[50] Not printed.

for good behavior and by Imperial clemency, although the civilian participants in the May 15 affair, who were tried in the civil courts, received life sentences. The sentence imposed upon Colonel Aizawa [51] is also an indication of the severity of the sentences which will be imposed upon the young officers involved in the incident of February 26 and of the determination of the Army to rid itself of those who are subjecting the organization to the criticism of the public.

At the same time, the Army does not seem to be greatly worried over the criticisms in the Diet and the newspapers. It is proceeding calmly and smugly on its way, believing thoroughly in its mission as the savior of Japan. It continues to keep Tokyo in the grip of martial law, has asked for larger appropriations than ever, has formulated and proposed bills for the mobilization of industries, for the preservation of national industrial mobilization secrets and for the control of "seditious literature". These measures, if passed, obviously would increase the power of the Army to control the internal administration of the country. In addition there have been inaugurated so-called "Three-Minister Conferences", composed of the Ministers for Foreign Affairs, War and Navy, for the purpose of discussing Japan's foreign policies. The Three-Minister Conferences have received criticism in the Diet, but the Army and Navy maintain that, from the broad viewpoint of national defense, their Ministers should have the right and opportunity to express their views in regard to foreign policy as well as to internal administration.

It would appear, therefore, that the military, rather than being crushed by the shame of the February 26 incident, have in fact taken advantage of the incident to tighten their hold upon the Japanese Government and to further the so-called "Showa Restoration" (which in fact means the restoration of some form of government resembling the Shogunate). At the same time, it should not be forgotten that the military sincerely believe that the nation stands in grave danger of involvement in a serious war in the not distant future and that it is therefore of pressing necessity that the defense forces be augmented and the nation unified under the Emperor (with, of course, the leadership of the military). The military's insistence upon dominance in the Government can be ascribed quite as well to the immediate necessity, real or fancied, of defense, as to the more vague idea of a return of military government in Japan.

ECONOMIC, SOCIAL AND ADMINISTRATIVE REFORMS

As will be observed from a perusal of the addresses of the Premier and the Ministers for Foreign Affairs, Finance and War before the

---

[51] The execution was carried out July 3.

Diet on May 6 (Embassy's despatch No. 1830, dated May 14, 1936 [52]), no concrete measures were announced for the execution of the economic, social and administrative reforms promised the nation by the Hirota Cabinet upon its inauguration. The policies outlined in the speeches before the Diet were vague and not very convincing, and the Cabinet has not introduced any reform measures of importance, the bulk of the bills introduced having been carried over from the previous government. The only social reform bill of importance introduced by the Hirota Cabinet is one compelling industrialists to build up retirement allowance funds for their employees. This lack of concrete reform measures has disappointed the nation, which apparently had expected much of the present national or "transcendental" Cabinet. Several of the prominent newspapers, including the *Asahi*, the *Kokumin*, the *Yomiuri* and the *Jiji*, have commented editorially upon the vagueness of the speeches of the Ministers, the unsatisfactory nature of their replies to interpellations and the failure of the Cabinet to carry out the promised administrative reforms. The Tokyo *Nichi Nichi* of May 13 stated that the Army also is dissatisfied with the lack of zeal for administrative reform in the civilian government. The Army, according to the newspaper, feels this especially strongly because the Army itself has been endeavoring, with success, to purge itself of the elements leading to unrest and indiscipline. It believes that the civilian authorities should show the same zeal in effecting reforms, instead of issuing vague promises only.

Mr. Hirota's announced policy, however, was to undertake economic and administrative reforms slowly and gradually, in order to avoid any great disturbance of the life of the people, and in reply to interpellations in the Diet, the Cabinet Ministers involved have stated that administrative reforms and changes in the economic system will be studied after the present session of the Diet. Observers of the situation are becoming of the opinion, however, that the Hirota Cabinet is deliberately procrastinating in regard to reform measures, in the expectation that the agitation for such measures will die out, and that the Government then will be able to maintain the *status quo*, with only such minor reform measures as may be forced upon the Government by discontented elements in and out of the administration. The possibility always exists, however, that if the Government adopts such procrastinating and half-way tactics, and instead of earnestly endeavoring to correct the maladjustments and abuses in Japan, attempts to suppress by use of force all symptoms of unrest and discontent, there will arise other and perhaps worse incidents than those of May 15, 1932, and February 26, 1936.

Respectfully yours,

JOSEPH C. GREW

---

[52] Not printed.

894.002/292

The Ambassador in Japan (Grew) to the Secretary of State

No. 1864   Tokyo, May 28, 1936.
                                              [Received June 15.]

Sir: I have the honor to transmit herewith the Embassy's translations of Imperial Ordinance No. 63, which appeared in the *Official Gazette* of May 18, 1936, and No. 64, which appeared in the *Official Gazette* of May 19, 1936.[53] These two ordinances are amendments of the regulations governing the organization of the Army and Navy Departments, respectively, and provide that appointment to the posts of Minister and Vice Minister of the Army and Navy Departments shall be confined to generals and admirals on the active list.

By an ordinance issued in 1913, permission was granted for the appointment of officers in the first and second reserves to the abovementioned posts. Aversion of the military to the ordinance of 1913, coupled with the fact that no reserve officer was ever appointed either War or Navy Minister under its authorization, appears to have induced the decision to limit formally by Imperial Ordinances, the choice of Army and Navy Ministers to officers on the active list.

Respectfully yours,   Joseph C. Grew

894.20/166

The Ambassador in Japan (Grew) to the Secretary of State

No. 1876   Tokyo, May 29, 1936.
                                              [Received June 15.]

Sir: I have the honor to report that the introduction to the Diet by the Hirota Cabinet of the Seditious Literature Emergency Control Bill and the Mobilization Secrets Preservation Bill aroused stubborn opposition both within the Diet and among the public to regimentation and the invasion of individual freedom by repressive legislation. The struggle against these bills provided the most outstanding feature of the 69th Diet session.

The Seditious Literature Bill was introduced to the Lower House on May 14 and the Mobilization Secrets Bill on May 18. The Government sought by the former bill further power to suppress pamphlets, "secret documents", and the distribution of unsigned or uncensored literature tending to subvert army discipline, disturb the existing financial organization of Japan, or provoke public unrest. By the latter bill which was to supplement the Fortified Zone Act and the Military Secrets Preservation Law it sought further power to safeguard military and important industrial secrets against the perils

---

[53] Neither printed.

of international espionage. This latter bill failed of passage, being abandoned without a vote, whereas the former passed only after considerable revision lightening the penalties for its violation and renaming it so as to brand it as temporary, emergency legislation. All parties were opposed to these bills while the minority parties, the Kokumin Domei and the Social Mass party were most uncompromising.

The Embassy will transmit a translation of the authentic text of the Seditious Literature Emergency Control Bill when available. Meanwhile there is enclosed with this despatch a clipping from the *Japan Advertiser* of May 26 [54] setting forth the terms of the amended bill as given by the Domei news agency and including two resolutions attached by the Seiyukai and Minseito parties which emphasize the emergency nature of the law and enjoin the Government to respect freedom of speech and personal rights in applying it.

The Hirota Cabinet attached great importance to these bills. As evidence of the pressure which it brought to bear on the legislators and which they in considerable measure resisted, it may be mentioned that on two occasions, one shortly after the introduction of the bill and the other while it was in committee in process of revision, rumors were circulated that the Army would seek an emergency Imperial Ordinance to effect the purposes of the Seditious Literature Bill if it failed of passage; that the Cabinet Ministers from the Seiyukai and Minseito parties were sent to implore their respective parties to modify their attitude towards the bills; that the Prime Minister, as well as the Home Minister, the Justice Minister, and the War Minister reiterated the Government's desire for the passage of the bills; and that the Diet Session was twice prolonged (for a day each time) in order to allow time for the passage of the amended Seditious Literature Control Bill. At the same time it does not appear that the Government ever elucidated the precise meaning of the bills before the Diet as a whole or that it ever dispelled the conviction that it was legislating concerning offenses against which ample remedies had already been provided by law.

The nature of the controversy and the sincere as well as searching examination to which the bills were put may best be indicated by reference to points brought out by interpellators and by rebuttals on the part of the Cabinet Ministers. On May 14 Mr. Toshiyuki Hisayama of the Seiyukai stated in a lengthy interpellation on the Seditious Literature Bill that if there were freedom of speech in Japan deleterious pamphlets would cease, that if army reform took place an effective end would be put to the circulation of subversive pamphlets, that if army discipline were good, the army would be proof

---

[54] Not reprinted.

against the effects of subversive literature, that if the bill were passed Japan would revert to the underground politics of the closing years of the Tokugawa Shogunate, and that if it were passed the public would be at the mercy of policemen making arrests in the hopes of securing promotion. He further asked who it was that the War Minister imagined was circulating pamphlets to disturb the control of the army and whether the Government imagined that public uneasiness could be dispelled simply by law. Others emphasized that there were already enough laws and that the Government should concern itself instead with root causes while the Social Mass party, claiming seditious literature to be the reflection of prevailing social unrest, said that to legislate against it without stopping the source of the evil would only intensify the public uneasiness. Opposition to the bill was rendered especially intense by a virtual admission on the part of the Director of the Police Bureau of the Home Office that advocacy of the overthrow of the Hirota Cabinet would be regarded as sedition under the bill. Further opposition and ridicule was aroused by the Government's claim that in applying the bill the presence or absence of seditious intent on the author's part was the test of criminality; mere awareness that public disorder might result from his writings did not incriminate an author but intent to incite it would.

The principal rebuttals on the part of Cabinet Ministers were brief and were repeated again and again. The Home Minister freely admitted that it was inevitable that freedom of speech and the liberty of the press should be restricted to a certain extent but declared that the bill would be carefully administered. The War Minister claimed that pamphlets were circulated for the purpose of disturbing the control of the army, not because the control of the army was lax. The Prime Minister stated that the bill was to restore peace to the public mind and prevent a repetition of the recent deplorable incident. Existing circumstances, he reiterated, made it necessary. It may be supposed that further explanations by the Government were advanced in secret committee sessions. In the foregoing paragraphs, however, is set forth the nature of the developments which terminated in the passage of the amended bill during the closing hours of the session, by the Lower House late on May 25, by the House of Peers on May 26.

In reviewing the Cabinet's struggle with the Diet over these two bills it is at once obvious that large issues were involved. The Government claimed that the whole state of the nation, whose stability was called into question on February 26, needed the remedy provided by these measures. The Diet on the other hand, while fighting to preserve individual liberties from encroachment, was also aware that the rival forces of bureaucracy and militarism were arrayed in veiled but nevertheless real opposition to liberal government. In a sense the

Diet was fighting to justify its existence and it acquitted itself creditably. In so doing it identified the Government in the public mind with regimentation while it clamored itself for reform not repression. The two bills considered in this despatch were the subject of great publicity and the public and press stood squarely behind the Diet in opposition to them. The following which appeared in the *Yomiuri* on May 28 is by no means unique and, in the light of the struggle over the sedition bill, the reference to the Government is inescapable.

"There have been few times in the past at which the people were called upon in a greater degree than at present to become intelligent and display their power of unity. But on the other hand, the unpatriotic evil hand is being extended all the more to suppress speech and interfere with efforts designed to awaken the people to become more intelligent."

It is still too close to the event to tell whether there is in prospect a continued damming up of natural forces which will render the national stability more precarious but, it may be pointed out, the Japanese have in the controversy over these bills, demonstrated that, subject to regimentation as they are, there is a limit to their docility. They have held out stubbornly for the preservation of their individual prerogatives. When, during a discussion of the unsuccessful Mobilization Secrets Bill, a Diet member claimed that the sanctity of conversation in that great Japanese forum, the public bath, was threatened, the bill was doomed forthwith. The Government leaders were made to realize that they could go no further. Whether this implies a change of trend cannot be predicted but the developments and considerations set forth in this despatch suggest at least that the public mind since February 26 is more healthful than the Government's projects would lead one to suppose.

Respectfully yours,

JOSEPH C. GREW

894.00/661 : Telegram

The Ambassador in Japan (Grew) to the Secretary of State

TOKYO, July 7, 1936—noon.
[Received July 7—1 : 25 a. m.]

149. Embassy's 140, June 24, 7 p. m.[55]

1. War Office announcement made at 2 o'clock this morning states that of 19 officers, 75 non-commissioned officers, 19 privates and 10 civilians indicted and tried for complicity in the February 26 incident the following have been sentenced : 13 officers and 4 civilians to death; 5 officers to life imprisonment; 1 officer, 17 non-commissioned officers

---

[55] Not printed.

and 6 civilians to imprisonment of from 2 to 15 years; 27 non-commissioned officers and 3 privates to imprisonment of from 18 months to 2 years but with stay of execution for 3 years.

2. The judgment states that sentences of death and life imprisonment were pronounced upon certain officers because they had employed the Imperial Army without Imperial sanction. Some of the non-commissioned officers and privates were found to have participated knowingly in the incident but the others were acquitted because they had only obeyed the orders of their superior officers.

3. The newspapers state that no appeal will be granted. The time of execution of the death sentences was not announced but the military criminal law provides for execution by shooting within 5 days from confirmation of the sentence by the Minister of War.

GREW

894.00/662 : Telegram

The Ambassador in Japan (Grew) to the Secretary of State

TOKYO, July 13, 1936—2 p. m.
[Received July 13—3 : 08 a. m.]

154. Embassy's 149, July 7, noon. War Office announcement 6 p. m., July 12, names 15 persons as executed July 12 for participation in February 26 incident. These persons are the 13 officers and 2 of the 4 civilians whose death sentences were announced July 7. The two remaining civilians are presumably being held for evidence in further investigations. The press generally approves the executions and no disturbances have been reported.

GREW

894.00/663 : Telegram

The Ambassador in Japan (Grew) to the Secretary of State

TOKYO, July 18, 1936—11 a. m.
[Received July 18—2 : 44 a. m.]

158. Tokyo martial law repealed by Imperial ordinance effective today.

GREW

894.00/668

The Ambassador in Japan (Grew) to the Secretary of State

No. 1955
TOKYO, July 23, 1936.
[Received August 10.]

SIR: I have the honor to submit the following study of the political consequences of the incident of February 26, 1936.

As reported to the Department in numerous telegrams and despatches, on the morning of February 26 at Tokyo a group of young officers in the Japanese Army led several hundred troops to the residences of a number of the highest officials of the country, several such officials were assassinated, the insurgents seized a number of public buildings, martial law was declared by the Government, a few days later the insurgents surrendered and submitted to arrest, they were tried by court martial extending over several months, the leaders were sentenced to death, other conspirators were sentenced to various terms of imprisonment, on July 12 most of those sentenced to death were executed, and on July 18 martial law was lifted.

Confusion was the first effect of the incident. The people were at a loss to know what had occurred and what was about to occur, particularly inasmuch as a strict censorship made them susceptible to rumors as their source of knowledge of what was actually going on. There were frequent expressions of resentment against the censorship, and one newspaper went so far as to say that the incident itself would not have occurred in a community enjoying freedom of speech.

But the populace quickly regained its composure by virtue of its political inertia, its general indifference to political ideas. Although the insurgents began their operations by assassinations, their use of terrorism ended there. Confining their use of violence to this dramatic opening they expected that a simple statement of their motives and program would call forth widespread popular support and lead to the changes which they advocated. They addressed the people through printed statements. Quietly and confidently they harangued the passers-by in front of the buildings which they seized. They explained that they were opposed to privilege, whether of wealth or of big business or of the misguided advisers close to the Emperor or of those Army leaders who gave in to favoritism in military promotions; they advocated a restatement of the fundamental structure of the state; they favored stabilization of the livelihood of the people of Japan; they argued for recognition of the needs of adequate defense of the country. They urged a Showa restoration in the year 1936 as brilliant and comprehensive as the Meiji restoration. But several circumstances materially weakened the appeal of the insurgents to the country. The people did not like the killing of old men in cold blood; they were opposed to the commanding of Imperial troops contrary to orders from above; they resented the threat to the Imperial palace and the Emperor in the movements of the troops controlled by the insurgents; and for the first time they were awakened to the necessity of putting a stop to the long series of political assassinations which have taken place in Japan in recent years.

Stunned that the ideas of the insurgents were not sweeping the populace, and faced by inevitably heavy bloodshed if choosing resistance to the overwhelming loyal force sent against them, the insurgents capitulated. The uprising was at an end. There remained its punishment and the prevention of the recurrence of similar danger in the future. The situation called for the formation of a new cabinet.

At this point the Army stepped forward to assert a leadership which it has successfully maintained up to the present time. Through its well-known power of preventing the formation of a cabinet by forbidding any officer to become Minister of War the Army was able to exact from the new Premier, Hirota, definite concessions to the wishes of the Army. The Army vetoed the appointment of Yoshida as Foreign Minister. More important, the Army undoubtedly required that the new cabinet undertake fundamental political reform. What is especially startling to the foreign observer is that the fundamental reforms which the Army has pushed during the tenure of office of this cabinet are practically those reforms advocated by the insurgents of February 26. Soon after the formation of the Hirota cabinet the Army stated to the press that in the cabinet-forming negotiations it had insisted on Hirota's recognition of the need for action on the national polity, livelihood of the people, national defense, and positive foreign policy. The details which appeared in this Army statement to the press are now, in retrospect, astonishingly accurate as a prospectus of what has in fact occupied the Government in the months since. The Army took the whip hand and has kept it.

So serious a shock as the incident of February 26 could not pass without causing many intelligent people doubts of Japanese stability. Deposits in the Japanese banks associated with clearing houses fell two and a half per cent between the end of January and the end of February 1936. Pressure to remove investments from Japan to foreign countries resulted in preventive restrictions by the Finance Ministry, and many wealthy Japanese were thereby checked in their plans. Concurrently the Government recognized danger in the covert circulation of politically disquieting documents (such had been discovered to have had a part in all the recent political assassinations of Japan) and new measures were consequently put into force to control dangerous and seditious literature.

A direct consequence of the changed public state of mind following upon the February 26 incident was decisive action in the trial of Aizawa, the Army officer who assassinated General Nagata in August 1935. Previous to the incident Aizawa's trial had dragged out inconclusively with astonishing explanations of patriotic motive admitted as evidence in his defense. After February 26 a new trial was launched for him and he was sentenced to death. On July 1 [*3*] he was executed.

When sentences of imprisonment and death were pronounced July 7 on the conspirators of the February 26 incident popular approval was practically unanimous.   The conviction was wisely based on the insurgents' use of Imperial troops without Imperial authority.   This ground of conviction in a way justified the punishment meted out, so heavy by comparison with that of the conspirators of May 15, 1932. It had the further virtue of explaining the severe penalties imposed without reflecting upon the reform measures advocated by the insurgents.   This was desirable from the Army's point of view because of the great similarity of the reform measures which the Army is backing.

The Army has gained rather than lost by the incident and its sequel. At first, to be sure, the fact that the insurgents were Army men had its reaction, and there was a noticeable resistance to military service in some districts.   But the Army itself has been the executor of the measures taken against the insurgents and has discharged the responsibility with finality in a manner which is approved by the people.   In addition, the Army has succeeded in maintaining itself in the role, under the present administration, of trustee for fundamental reform.   No organization realizes as well as the Army itself how widespread is military sentiment in favor of basic political change.   The movement promoted by the February 26 insurgents was no passing fancy.   That General Masaki himself was much more than a passive sympathizer of the insurgents is scarcely open to doubt.   The urge to political change is ingrained in the Army, and in spite of the failure of cabinet national policy discussions (these discussions degenerated into special requests by the various departments for increased appropriations, and were abandoned in July after a few sessions) the Army, which is still the crucial factor in the future of Japan, can confidently be expected to continue in its search for a new political order for this country.

The settlement of the incident of February 26, 1936, has strengthened government in Japan without in any way weakening the movement for social and political reform which has been gaining weight in the Army over a period of years.   The incident was in large part a protest against privilege—privilege enjoyed by the wealthy, privilege within the Army, privilege close to the Throne, privilege in economic life.   It was a protest drawn in the terms of the military code.   The incident was decisively put down, but it was put down as a disciplinary measure only, without prejudice to the cause protested.   It was put down by the Army itself which has not failed to reiterate the same protest.   As a result of the incident, the country's stand on any political assassinations that might occur in the future is clear and will no doubt serve as a check on conspiracy; but at the same time the increasing adoption of the principles advocated by the disturbers of the peace of the last years has become a more active issue, and an Army-guided expansion of government control of industry at the expense of private property is not only likely but also appears to be expected by most intelligent Japanese.

The lack in Japan of liberal institutions, as is particularly evident in the absence of those guarantees grouped in Anglo-Saxon countries under the heading of civil liberties, should not blind the foreign observer to the great possibility, even the probability, of fundamental political change in this country. What is most solidly established in Japanese political psychology is not a belief in one particular form of government economically and sociologically defined, but is a belief in the necessity and authority and rightness of government itself. The acceptance of the authority of the Emperor is something that can be counted upon to remain; but along with that acceptance ideas are changing on the subject of what the government should bring to the people. Japan's constitution itself is a definition rather of structure of government than of function of government, and will prove adaptable to functional changes.

From the February 26 incident, government in Japan emerges strong and the Army emerges strong. Previous to the incident there was noticeable a trend under Army leadership toward increasingly powerful state control of the economic mechanism. That trend has not suffered by the incident; rather it has increased.

Respectfully yours, JOSEPH C. GREW

894.00/666 : Telegram

The Ambassador in Japan (Grew) to the Secretary of State

TOKYO, August 1, 1936—11 a. m.
[Received August 1—12 : 58 a. m.]

165. The War Office issued a communiqué last night to the effect that the Army Court Martial now sitting in Tokyo has sentenced six other military officers to varying terms of imprisonment from life in one case to 4 years for their connection with the February incident.

The Embassy is informed on what seems to be reliable authority that the investigation will continue and that other officers probably including General Masaki will be brought to trial.

GREW

711.94/1120

Memorandum by the Ambassador in Japan (Grew) [56]

[TOKYO,] August 25, 1936.

In calling today to take leave of the Prime Minister I asked him if there were any observations which he would wish me to take back

---

[56] Copy transmitted to the Department by the Ambassador in Japan in his despatch No. 2005, August 26; received September 21.

to the President and the Secretary of State. Mr. Hirota said that although he was no longer Foreign Minister he felt that the relations between Japan and the United States were proceeding smoothly. He said that so far as China was concerned, Japan would in no way interfere with American trade in that country and that he could specifically give me assurances to that effect.

As regards domestic affairs the Prime Minister asked me what I thought of the present situation. I told him that after the incident of February 26th I had told my Government that I thought the net result of the incident would be salutary and present conditions made me feel that I was right in this prognostication. Mr. Hirota said that this was perfectly true and that his whole effort at present was one of conciliation. There were naturally difficulties to be overcome, but he was happy to say that the civil government and the army and navy were working together in entire accord. The thing that bothered him most both in the world at large in general and in China in particular was the spread of bolshevism and that in China Japan must make efforts to stem the tide of the communist menace. He added that he appreciated very much the policy of President Roosevelt toward the Far East and Japan.

J[oseph] C. G[rew]

DISAPPROVAL BY THE AMERICAN GOVERNMENT OF THE EMPLOYMENT OF AMERICAN CITIZENS BY A FOREIGN GOVERNMENT AS PROPAGANDA AGENTS

893.01B11 Manchuria/17

Memorandum by Mr. Eugene H. Dooman of the Division of Far Eastern Affairs

[Washington,] November 28, 1936.

On the occasion of a call at the Japanese Embassy today on various official matters, I saw the Japanese Ambassador.[57] I said to the Ambassador that I should like to present certain views which we had long held with regard to the employment by foreign political authorities of propangandists in the United States. I ventured the opinion that the moment was timely for presentation of these views, for the reason that, upon the recent death of George Bronson Rea, the Japanese Government would perhaps be giving thought to the appointment of a successor to Rea. I said that for purposes of clarity and convenience the views which I wished to communicate had been put on paper; and I handed the Ambassador as a record of an informal oral presentation a copy of the paper which is hereto attached.[58]

---

[57] Hirosi Saito.
[58] *Infra.*

The Ambassador read this paper and remarked that Rea had been recalled last year to "Manchukuo" as the result of a recommendation made by the Ambassador, who believed that the cause of "Manchukuo" might better be presented in the United States by a Manchurian than by an American citizen. He stated that he would communicate with Ohashi, "Manchukuo" Vice Minister for Foreign Affairs, in the sense of the statement which I had just presented.

I stated to the Ambassador that our views with regard to the employment of propagandists by foreign political authorities applied, not only to the "Manchukuo" government, but to the Japanese Government or to any other government employing propagandists in the United States.

I went on to say that there were, of course, various kinds of propaganda. The United States is constantly being visited by Britishers prominent in various walks of life who endeavor to present to the American public in as favorable a light as possible certain cultural aspects of British life. For the most part they refrain from touching upon political matters in controversy between the United States and Great Britain, and so far as we know they come to the United States on their own initiative and not as paid agents of the British Government. Propaganda could take, however, another and more objectionable form, and that is when efforts are made by a foreign government through the instrumentality of paid agents to persuade the people of the United States to bring pressure to bear upon the American Government to alter, to the advantage of the foreign government concerned, a position that has been taken with regard to a political situation.

The Ambassador again stated that the Japanese Government could do nothing to prevent the "Manchukuo" government from sending a publicity agent to the United States. I replied that this Government has endeavored during the past few years to avoid the raising of issues over the political situation in the Far East, and that it is our understanding that Mr. Hirota [59] agrees with us in the belief that the cause of promoting friendly relations between the United States and Japan would not be served by permitting incidents to arise which would emphasize the political differences between the two countries.

The Ambassador stated that he did not look with favor upon the employment of American citizens as propagandists, but that if the "Manchukuo" government decided to send to the United States a Manchurian for publicity purposes there was nothing that the Japanese Government could do in the matter. I pointed out that if a "Manchukuo" publicity agent were sent to the United States and this Government felt disposed to refuse him entry, a most unfortunate

---
[59] Koki Hirota, Japanese Prime Minister.

situation would arise. The Ambassador seemed taken back for a moment, but he smiled and said that he understood.

As I rose to leave, the Ambassador expressed his appreciation of the informal and personal manner in which the matter under discussion had been presented to him.

893.01B11 Manchuria/17

The Department of State to the Japanese Embassy [60]

The American Government has throughout viewed with disapproval the presence in this country of an American citizen acting in the capacity of a salaried spokesman for the unrecognized political régime in Manchuria. It has been our assumption that this spokesman has been here with the approval if not the express authorization of the Japanese Government, or at least that without the approval of the Japanese Government he would not have been here in that capacity.

In probably no other country is the principle of freedom of speech more completely observed in practice than in this country. The American Government places few restrictions upon and makes little objection to free expression of opinion. However, we regard as anomalous and undesirable the employment of American citizens by foreign countries in the endeavor to influence public opinion in the United States in the direction of modification of views or policies or of adoption by the United States of views and policies differing from those to which the American Government is giving effect. It is felt to be particularly objectionable that advantage is taken by such persons of the freedom of speech in the United States to carry on propaganda in behalf of and at the instance of governments which would not regard with indulgence similar activities in their territories on the part of the employees of foreign countries.

Adverse criticism by a citizen or subject in the employ of a foreign government of an attitude or policy of his government cannot be expected to cause a change in his government's attitude or policy: such criticism usually serves merely as an irritant and to becloud understanding of, and to render more difficult a friendly and frank approach to, problems in relations between governments. The activities of such persons therefore are a disservice to both governments concerned.

This Government, seeking to promote amicable relations between the United States and all countries with which this country has relations, doubts the wisdom of employment by foreign political authorities of American nationals as spokesmen for such authorities and would certainly view with regret any further use by such political

---

[60] Handed to the Japanese Ambassador by Eugene H. Dooman of the Division of Far Eastern Affairs, November 28.

authorities of American nationals as their spokesmen or "unofficial representatives" in this country.

893.01B11 Manchuria/17

The Chief of the Division of Far Eastern Affairs (Hornbeck) to the Ambassador in Japan (Grew)

WASHINGTON, November 28, 1936.

DEAR MR. GREW: I refer to my letter of September 10, 1934,[61] to previous correspondence on the subject of George Bronson Rea, and to our conversation during your recent visit to Washington on the subject of propagandists.

We had prepared a memorandum on the subject of the employment as propagandists of American citizens by foreign political authorities, which we intended to send to you as reference material in considering what might appropriately be said to Arita on that subject. However, before we had got around to sending you the memorandum, Rea died, a few days ago. At about the same time, evidence came to hand that the Japanese Government is casting about for some one to continue with certain of Rea's activities, and we came to the conclusion that any action that might be taken toward discouraging the appointment of an American citizen as a paid propagandist for "Manchukuo" should for maximum of potential effectiveness be taken as soon as possible. We came to the further conclusion that there would be advantage in our making an early approach here to Saito. The memorandum was accordingly appropriately modified and in the course of a conversation was this morning handed to Saito as a memorandum of an informal oral statement. A copy of that statement is enclosed.[62]

Saito's first comment after reading the statement was that the cause of "Manchukuo" might be better presented in the United States by a Manchurian than by an American citizen, and that for that reason he had recommended last year that Rea be recalled to Manchuria. However, we made it clear to him that the views which we had expressed to him are applicable, not only to "Manchukuo", but to Japan or to any other country which places itself in a like position in the matter of propaganda. Saito made the further observation that, if the "Manchukuo" government should decide to send to the United States a Manchurian for publicity purposes, the Japanese Government could do nothing in the matter. We replied that, in our opinion, no useful purpose would be served by the occurrence of incidents which would emphasize the differences between the American Government and the

---

[61] Not printed; see letter of August 20, 1934, from the Ambassador in Japan, *Foreign Relations*, 1934, vol. III, p. 679.

[62] *Supra.*

Japanese Government rising out of the political situation in the Far East, and that, if the "Manchukuo" Government were to send an agent to the United States for publicity purposes, and if this Government should feel constrained to refuse him entry, a situation might arise which would not serve the cause of promoting friendly relations between the United States and Japan.

We further emphasized to Saito the point made in the penultimate paragraph of the memorandum.

We assume that the matter of our approach will be reported to Tokyo by Saito. We believe that it would be helpful if you would, if you feel so disposed and have favorable opportunity, reenforce our action here by making some appropriate observation to Arita.

Yours sincerely,   S. K. HORNBECK

REPRESENTATIONS ON ESTABLISHMENT OF OIL MONOPOLIES IN JAPAN AND MANCHURIA [63]

894.6363/239 : Telegram

The Ambassador in Japan (Grew) to the Secretary of State

TOKYO, January 7, 1936—1 p. m.
[Received January 7—6 : 30 a. m.]

3. Embassy's 246, December 19, 3 p. m.[64] I discussed the situation of the oil companies today with the Vice Minister for Foreign Affairs [65] on the basis of paragraph 4 of Embassy's 240 December 13, 6 p. m.[66] The Vice Minister made no comment except to say that the Government had no intention to deprive the foreign companies of a reasonable economic return and that he would see what if anything could be done.

The Dutch Minister recently made similar representations.

GREW

894.6363/243 : Telegram

The Ambassador in Japan (Grew) to the Secretary of State

TOKYO, January 15, 1936—11 a. m.
[Received January 15—1 : 27 a. m.]

12. Embassy's 253, December 28, noon.[67]

1. At a recent conference of the representatives of the foreign oil companies with Kurusu [68] the latter stated that the Vice Minister for

---

[63] Continued from *Foreign Relations*, 1935, vol. III, pp. 877–939.
[64] *Ibid.*, p. 937.
[65] Mamoru Shigemitsu.
[66] *Foreign Relations*, 1935, vol. III, p. 935.
[67] *Ibid.*, p. 939.
[68] Saburo Kurusu, Chief of the Commercial Affairs Bureau, Japanese Foreign Office.

Commerce and Industry [69] agrees in principle with the plan of giving the oil companies governmental guarantees covering quotas over an extensive period, reasonable profit and maximum stock holding obligation as well as equal treatment with Japanese refiners should the oil companies desire to refine in Japan. Kurusu therefore requests the oil companies to propose definite terms upon which they will comply with the stock holding provision of the law and the question has been referred to New York and London for consideration.

2. The Embassy and the local representatives of the oil companies are of the opinion that the Japanese authorities are now sincerely endeavoring to find some solution of the problem which will permit opposing oil companies to continue in business in Japan although it appears highly improbable that they will be able to allow stock holding obligation. It, therefore, appears desirable that the Japanese proposal outlined above be carefully considered.

GREW

893.6363 Manchuria/281

Memorandum by Mr. Raymond C. Mackay of the Division of Far Eastern Affairs of a Conversation With Mr. Claude A. Thompson, General Counsel of the Standard-Vacuum Oil Company, New York

[WASHINGTON,] January 24, 1936.

Mr. Thompson called the Department by telephone from New York and was referred to Mr. Mackay.

Mr. Thompson said that he wished to inform the Department that his proposal (see memorandum of January 9, 1936 [70]), to the effect that an endeavor be made to cause the Japanese Government to use its good offices with a view to causing the authorities in Manchuria to compensate the oil companies for losses incurred as a result of the creation in that area of an oil monopoly, had met with the approval of the Standard-Vacuum Oil Company; that it had also met with the approval of the Shell interests in London to whom the matter had been explained by Mr. Walden [71] who is now in England; that both companies, however, are of the opinion that it would be inadvisable to initiate any new action in regard to the oil situation in Manchuria until such time as a definite decision has been reached in regard to the oil situation in Japan; that, at least for the moment, no further assistance is required; and that the company will keep the Department informed of all developments of importance.

---

[69] Shinji Yoshino.
[70] Not printed.
[71] G. S. Walden, chairman of the board of directors, Standard-Vacuum Oil Co.

Mr. Mackay thanked Mr. Thompson for his kindness in keeping the Department currently and fully informed in regard to the oil situations in Manchuria and in Japan.

894.6363/247 : Telegram

The Ambassador in Japan (Grew) to the Secretary of State

Tokyo, February 24, 1936—8 p. m.
[Received February 24—10 : 10 a. m.]

34. Embassy's 12, January 15, 11 a. m., American oil interests in Japan.

1. Kurusu informed the Embassy on February 22 that the Vice Minister for Commerce and Industry had just called on him and had stated that:

(*a*) It would be impossible to change the law and regulations and consequently the 6 months' storage provisions would have to stand.

(*b*) It might be feasible to place a maximum on the amount of oil to be stored but any proposal to this effect must come from the foreign oil interests. The Vice Minister could then discuss the proposition with the military and other interests.

(*c*) The quotas for the second quarter of this year must soon be considered and if the foreign companies definitely and finally refuse to store 6 months' stocks, it will be necessary to reduce their quotas.

(*d*) Mitsubishi and Nippon Oil have applied for permission to add to their refining facilities, probably having in mind an eventual refusal of the foreign oil interests to comply with the law and consequent reduction of their quotas. The Vice Minister is now holding up these applications but will be compelled to grant them if the foreign oil companies do not agree to carry 6 months' stocks.

(*e*) Therefore, the Vice Minister recommends that the foreign oil interests present a concrete proposal offering to store 6 months' stocks under the following or somewhat similar conditions:

(1) that 6 months of 1934 or 1935 be taken as the maximum storage requirement;
(2) that adequate compensation be paid by the Government;
(3) that adequate guarantees of future business be given.

(*f*) If the Vice Minister has some such proposal, he can continue the present quotas, at least until June 30, 1936, and can refuse the applications for additional refining capacity, on the ground that the foreign oil companies have not refused to comply with the law but on the contrary have agreed to store the oil under certain conditions. The foreign oil companies' objections to the establishment of a precedent of 6 months' storage will be overcome by the fact that they have agreed only to store a fixed quantity in gallons and not half of their previous year's sales.

2. The local representatives of the foreign oil interests have telegraphed the substance of the above to their respective head offices,

recommending that the suggestion of the Vice Minister be adopted and that some scheme of Government financing of the non-commercial stocks be embodied in the concrete proposal.

GREW

894.6363/254 : Telegram

The Ambassador in Japan (Grew) to the Secretary of State

TOKYO, March 9, 1936—5 p. m.
[Received March 9—7 : 46 a. m.]

64. Embassy's 34, February 24, 8 p. m.

1. The local representatives of the Standard and Shell interests have received telegrams from their head offices proposing that the oil interests will carry fixed maximum quantities of oil with indemnification and guarantees of future business and provided that Japanese capital finance the stock holding. Full details can be obtained from Standard Vacuum, New York. The telegram concludes: "We suggest that you have formal talk with Kurusu and Yoshino in conjunction with both Embassies to explore the foregoing".

2. The Embassy has never yet participated directly in the oil negotiations except to introduce the special request [*representatives?*] for the oil interests in December 1934 and to transmit messages from one side to the other. To participate directly in the proposed conference would imply official sanction of the proposed plan.

3. The Embassy will not therefore participate in the conference unless instructed.

GREW

894.6363/254 : Telegram

The Secretary of State to the Ambassador in Japan (Grew)

WASHINGTON, March 10, 1936—2 p. m.

30. Your 64, March 9, 5 p. m. Department has received from New York office of Standard-Vacuum text of its cable to Japan of March 7.

Based upon such information as is now available, Department is of the opinion that the proposal outlined in the company's cable under reference merits careful consideration by the Japanese Government. Therefore, although concurring in your opinion that it would not be advisable for Embassy to participate directly in proposed conference, Department would suggest that, unless you perceive objection, you and your British colleague orally and informally make known to appropriate Japanese officials the desire of the foreign oil interests to present and discuss a plan designed to meet the needs of both parties. You may also express the hope that there will flow from the negotiations under contemplation a solution of this problem which will prove mutually satisfactory to all concerned.

HULL

894.6363/258 : Telegram

The Ambassador in Japan (Grew) to the Secretary of State

TOKYO, March 13, 1936—4 p. m.
[Received March 13—7 : 03 a. m.]

73. Department's 30, March 10, 2 p. m.

1. American and British Embassies today made oral and informal representations to Kurusu along the lines suggested by the Department. The representations were not made at an earlier date as the British Embassy had not received instructions. On March 11, however, as a conference had been arranged, the local representatives of the oil companies presented the plan of their head offices to Kurusu and the Vice Minister for Commerce and Industry. The local representatives did not desire to postpone their conference until the British Embassy had received instructions and believed that the diplomatic representations would be as effective if not more effective as a follow up rather than as a paving of the way.

2. Today Kurusu seemed decidedly pessimistic. He said that the Vice Minister for Commerce and Industry was examining the companies' proposal to ascertain if it were worth while to endeavor to continue the conversations; that it would be necessary to reach final decision before March 20 when the quotas for the next quarter would be set; and that he did not think that an independent storage company would be feasible because of lack of adequate compensation. He said that he would inform the Embassies as soon as the Vice Minister for Commerce and Industry had formulated his reply.

GREW

894.6363/259 : Telegram

The Ambassador in Japan (Grew) to the Secretary of State

TOKYO, March 20, 1936—8 p. m.
[Received March 20—10 : 45 a. m.[72]]

77. Embassy's 73, March 13, 4 p. m., American oil interests in Japan.

1. The American oil interests have informed the Embassy that they are about to enter into negotiations with the Mitsui interests for some solution of the oil problem in Japan. Details of the plan can be obtained from Standard Vacuum in New York. In view of the

---

[72] Text printed from corrected copy received at the same time.

fact that the deadline for announcement by the oil interests of acquiescence with the law was supposed to be today, the Standard Vacuum has requested the Embassy to urge the suspension of the regulations until negotiations are completed.

2. This has already been done informally by the Embassy through Kurusu without mentioning the nature of the transaction. However, I propose to see the Vice Minister for Foreign Affairs on Monday and to say to him that as very important negotiations are now taking place I would wish to see the regulations in regard to the storage of oil suspended until the negotiations are completed. The British Ambassador, who has consulted with me, will take the same action.

3. Unless otherwise instructed I shall take the indicated action on Monday.

GREW

894.6363/259 : Telegram

The Acting Secretary of State to the Ambassador in Japan (Grew)

WASHINGTON, March 20, 1936—6 p. m.

33. Your 77, March 20, 8 p. m. Officers of American oil interests showed to and discussed with officers of Department last evening texts of cablegrams sent earlier yesterday by Standard-Vacuum and Shell giving identical instructions to their respective representatives in Japan.

These texts indicate and conversation confirmed that the oil interests concerned are in complete agreement regarding approach to the Mitsui interests and that this approach is to be a common undertaking looking toward a common agreement. Texts do not disclose details of plan to be proposed to Mitsui, nor did spokesman of interests, though asked, appear to have any details worked out.

Department approves the informal action taken by you, as reported, but feels that great care should be taken to see that action taken by the two interests and action by the two Embassies in support thereof be closely and discreetly synchronized.

Referring to your projected call on the Vice Minister for Foreign Affairs, might it not be more appropriate first for representatives of the oil interests to make request to Japanese authorities that suspension of the regulations be authorized, and then for Embassies to give support to this request? Will you be in position on Monday to affirm that "very important negotiations are now taking place"? Department has full confidence in the Embassy's judgment and discretion, but, in view of lack of knowledge regarding method, content and moment of projected approach by oil interests to Mitsui, suggests that Embassy feel its way very carefully and avoid getting out ahead of interests or of British Embassy.

PHILLIPS

894.6363/262 : Telegram

The Ambassador in Japan (Grew) to the Secretary of State

TOKYO, March 23, 1936—7 p. m.
[Received March 23—10 : 05 a. m.]

78. Department's 33, March 20, 6 p. m.

1. The local representative[s] of the oil interests this afternoon communicated to Kurusu and Yoshino (Vice Minister for Commerce and Industry) the outline of the proposal of their head offices to cooperate with Japanese capital in some form. The proposal was apparently well received by the Japanese officials. Yoshino stated that for the next 3 months the foreign oil companies would receive the same quotas as hitherto and that he would continue to hold up the pending applications for additional refining capacity. Asked if penalties would be enforced after July 1, should it be found impossible for the new merger or arrangement (if it materializes) to complete the required oil storage by that time, Yoshino said, "Speaking unofficially I shall do my best".

2. Under these favorable circumstances my British colleague and I agree that it will not be necessary at the present moment officially to urge suspension of the regulations and that it will be better to reserve our ammunition for use later should it be found desirable to request suspension of the regulations after July 1st. Unless otherwise instructed, therefore, I shall not make the authorized representations.

3. Third sentence of paragraph 1 of the Embassy's 77, March 20, should have read as follows: "In view of the fact that the deadline for announcement by the oil interests of acquiescence with the law was supposed to be today, et cetera."

GREW

893.6363 Manchuria/288

The Consul at Dairen (Grummon) to the Ambassador in Japan (Grew)[73]

DAIREN, May 22, 1936.

SIR: Referring to the Consulate's despatch dated April 13, 1936,[74] concerning the reported defection of the Texas Company from the

---

[73] Copy transmitted to the Department without covering despatch; received June 22.

[74] Not printed.

position hitherto assumed by it, jointly with the two other foreign oil companies concerned, of refusing to supply the Petroleum Monopoly with their products, I have the honor to report that it now appears certain that the Company has definitely abandoned that position. On April 16th last the press announced that following protracted negotiations, an agreement had been effected whereby the Texas Company on the previous day sold 100,000 cases of gasoline out of "stock" to the Monopoly. I am reliably informed however that actually the sale amounted to 114,000 cases, of which only about 15,000 cases were from stock, while the balance—some 99,000 cases—consisted of newly imported products. It is estimated that this new stock will permit the Monopoly to carry on fairly well for approximately one month. It was acquired just in time to avert a serious shortage which would have ensued but for these opportune arrangements. The urgent need for this material is indicated by the fact that before the end of the present month a total of 67 carloads of refined products are required to be delivered in 2 and 3 carload lots to the various agencies of the Monopoly at Harbin, Hsinking (Changchun), Tsitsihar, Ssupingkai, Newchwang, Shahochen and Antung.

In this connection it is of interest to note that the Standard-Vacuum Oil Company, together with the other foreign companies prejudiced by the Monopoly, have consistently refused to bid on gasoline for the Japanese Military in North China owing to lack of assurance that the Army would not divert purchases made by it to the Monopoly. Repeated requests for their products have been received from Army sources, the latest, a few days ago, for 200,000 cases to be delivered to Tientsin. The future attitude on this subject of the Texas Company is now a matter of anxiety to the other two companies, although there would seem no reason why it should maintain its united front as regards the Army, having relaxed it with respect to the Monopoly.

The total shipments of crude oil received by the Monopoly thus far for this year amount to approximately 27,000 tons, divided as follows:

January	2	From San Francisco Per S. S. *Nore* 11,243 metric tons Casinghead Gas.
February	26	From San Francisco Per S. S. *Nore* 1,490 kilo liters untreated Kerosene.
February	27	From Yokohama Per S. S. *Kuisaku Maru* 1,259.76 metric tons Crude Oil.
March	12	From Yokohama Per S. S. *Kuisaku Maru* 1,239.854 metric tons Crude Oil.
April	2	From Estero Bay Per S. S. *Yeiyo Maru* 11,582 metric tons Crude Oil.
April	26	From Elwood Per S. S. *Toyo Maru* 12,398 metric tons Crude Oil.
May	22	From Wilmington Per S. S. *Evita* 8,900 metric tons Gasoline.

In addition, 12,000 tons of Persian oil are now en route from Bahrein. They were purchased there from the wells of the Standard Oil Company of California. The previous report that they were Roumanian products is unfounded.

Two officers of this Company, Messrs. J. U. Landes and B. Randanne Vazeille, who have recently visited the Company's refineries in Europe and the Near East, arrived in Dairen last night en route to California via Tokyo. Although one might assume their visit to Dairen to be for the purpose of discussing future supplies with the Monopoly authorities, Mr. Landes, in the presence of an officer of the Consulate, denied that he had come for that purpose and stated that he did not expect to see any one connected with the Monopoly. In support of this statement, Mr. Landes indicated that as his Company has just erected a new refinery at Bahrein, it is not desirous of selling further crude petroleum at present.

Respectfully yours,   Stuart E. Grummon

894.6363/279

Memorandum by Mr. Raymond C. Mackay and Mr. Eugene H. Dooman of the Division of Far Eastern Affairs

[Washington,] June 11, 1936.

Mr. Mackay called Mr. Parker [75] at New York by telephone.

Mr. Mackay referred to Mr. Parker's letter of June 8,[76] in regard to the above-mentioned subject, and said that due to Mr. Parker's absence from New York yesterday afternoon an endeavor to reach him by 'phone at the time indicated had proven unsuccessful. Mr. Mackay said that Ambassador Kurusu [77] had called at the Department on June 10; [78] that there had followed a discussion of commercial relations between the United States and Japan and of problems in connection therewith, including that resulting from the Japanese Petroleum Control Law; and that as Mr. Dooman was present at the discussion he (Mr. Dooman) would endeavor to acquaint Mr. Parker with the substance of that portion of the conversation which related to the oil situation in Japan.

Mr. Dooman then stated to Mr. Parker that, in the course of an extended conversation between Mr. Kurusu and an officer of the Department when various commercial problems lying between the United States and Japan were discussed, opportunity was had to explain to Mr. Kurusu in clear language the dissatisfaction of the

---

[75] P. W. Parker, president of the Standard-Vacuum Oil Co., New York.
[76] Not printed.
[77] En route to Belgium as Japanese Ambassador.
[78] For memorandum of June 10, see p. 897.

American Government over the manner in which American oil interests in Japan were being dealt with by the Japanese Government. Mr. Kurusu had replied that unfortunately the issue had been brought about by the enactment of a law, with regard to which law he would reserve his opinion. Mr. Kurusu had expressed confidence that difficulties would be amicably adjusted. He had pointed out that the American oil interests in Japan had put forward three desiderata: first, a guarantee that they would be permitted to operate in Japan for a stipulated period of time; second, a guarantee that they be permitted to sell each year a definite quantity of petroleum products; and third, the raising of the price in Japan of gasoline. Mr. Kurusu had stated that the Japanese Government had met the foreign oil companies at once on the first two points, and that although there had been certain difficulties in increasing the price of gasoline he had heard shortly before leaving Japan that decision had been made to increase the price of gasoline.

Mr. Parker stated that apparently Mr. Kurusu had not been frank with regard to the second point; that although it is true that the Japanese Government has agreed to guarantee that the foreign oil companies be permitted to market each year a definite quantity of petroleum products, the foreign companies had in fact insisted that they be permitted to share in meeting the growing demand in Japan for petroleum products; and that this demand had not been met by the Japanese Government.

Mr. Dooman stated that the general principle of American interests being permitted to expand their business in Japan as there is increasing demand for the products handled by these American interests had in fact been emphasized to Mr. Kurusu.

Mr. Dooman added that Mr. Kurusu had expressed optimism in regard to certain negotiations which were taking place between the foreign oil concerns and Japanese interests, and that he (Mr. Kurusu) had given the impression that as soon as the various parties concerned had agreed upon a place for negotiation the negotiations would be brought rapidly to a successful conclusion.

In response to Mr. Dooman's question whether Mr. Parker desired that any further points be discussed by officers of the Department with Mr. Kurusu, Mr. Parker stated that he would appreciate the hope being expressed to Mr. Kurusu that he would urge his Government to persuade Mitsui to send their representatives to New York to enter into negotiations with representatives of the foreign oil interests. Mr. Parker stated that the company's representative in Japan had recently cabled that oil quotas for the second half of the year would be allotted by the Japanese Government on July 1, but that the terms of the petroleum law with regard to stocks would have to be complied with on or before June 30. It was Mr. Parker's thought that if the Japanese Government could be assured that the negotiations with Mitsui were progressing satisfactorily, no penalties would be exacted for non-fulfillment of the stock keeping requirements. It is therefore very urgently desired that Mr. Kurusu do what he can to induce Mitsui to despatch representatives to New York as soon as possible. Mr. Dooman said that he would see Mr. Kurusu this morning, and that he would be glad to discuss the matter with him.

Mr. Parker expressed appreciation of the information which had been made available to him and stated that he did not expect that any further acknowledgment would be made of his recent letter to Mr. Hornbeck [79] on the subject of Mr. Kurusu's visit.

894.6363/280 : Telegram

The Ambassador in Japan (Grew) to the Secretary of State

Tokyo, June 23, 1936—7 p. m.
[Received June 23—2: 50 p. m.]

137. Embassy's 78, March 23, 7 p. m.

1. Yesterday the local representatives of the foreign oil interests were requested by the Ministry of Commerce and Industry to submit immediately a statement along the following lines.

"(a) The two companies will fulfill the obligation of stock holding;

(b) Accordingly, they are now in process of discussing special arrangements to that end".

The local representatives believe it impossible for their principals to agree to part (a) of the statement.

2. Today, in the course of an informal conversation, in the presence of Sansom [80] and Dickover,[81] Yoshino, Vice Minister for Commerce and Industry, stated that he would accept a statement as follows:

"The companies are now negotiating a special arrangement to enable them to fulfill their obligations under the petroleum law and have reached an agreement in principle".

This is believed to be the minimum which Yoshino can accept in order to give unreduced trade quotas from July 1st to the foreign oil interests and to continue the postponement of the granting of additional refining permits.

---

[79] Stanley K. Hornbeck, Chief of the Division of Far Eastern Affairs.
[80] Sir George B. Sansom, British Commercial Counselor in Japan.
[81] Erle R. Dickover, First Secretary of Embassy in Japan.

3. The local representatives are telegraphing the foregoing statement to their principals and in view of the urgency are pressing for an early reply.

4. Yoshino also stated that it would be impossible further to postpone enforcement of the stock holding provision of the law. I therefore do not believe it advisable to make the representations authorized in the Department's 33, March 20, 6 p. m., except as a last resort.

GREW

894.6363/286

The President of the Standard-Vacuum Oil Company of New York (Parker) to the Chief of the Division of Far Eastern Affairs (Hornbeck)

NEW YORK, July 14, 1936.

DEAR DR. HORNBECK: The reason we have not written you recently on the Japan situation is that we have deliberately marked time in our negotiations during the last few weeks, awaiting the critical date of July 1st, on which the Japanese Government were to allocate the third quarter quotas. On June 29th we were forced to give the Government some assurance that we had in mind a proposal whereby technically at least, we would be meeting the storage provision of the law. This we did, and on July 3rd, we received a telegram from Yokohama announcing the third quarter quotas. While our allotment of trade for the next three months does not permit us to participate in the natural increase, we are pleased to say that at least we received quotas on all products equal in volume to those allocated for each of the previous quarters.

The assurance we gave the Government in regard to meeting the storage provision, is predicated on a joint proposal of our British friends and ourselves, that a Japanese storage company comprising Japanese capital, be formed in Japan for the purpose of holding for our account, the non-commercial stock requirements, and on terms which are now being negotiated. It will be seen from this that we are continuing the policy of presenting a united front with the British.

We have also, in conjunction with London, offered to make available to the Japanese, certain hydrogenation processes controlled by our associates. While the Japanese have undoubtedly made considerable progress themselves in hydrogenation, nevertheless it seems that the Government is interested in acquiring our processes. We are hoping that our offer will be of material value in the negotiations regarding the storage company.

Sincerely yours,   P. W. PARKER

894.6363/293

The President of the Standard-Vacuum Oil Company of New York (Parker) to the Chief of the Division of Far Eastern Affairs (Hornbeck)

NEW YORK, October 20, 1936.

DEAR DR. HORNBECK: When I say that I just returned from Europe this week and that when I left New York early in September, our negotiations in Japan had not materially advanced beyond those described in my letter of July 14th, I am sure you will understand why I have really had no occasion to write before this.

The first part of this month while I was in London, our British friends and we were able to reach a clear understanding of the course we should pursue, and consequently, I am now pleased to advise you that the Japanese Government has accepted in principle a plan whereby Mitsui & Company will store, on behalf of both of us, the non-commercial stocks obligatory under the Petroleum Control Law. The final details are now being worked out in Japan and we anticipate these will very shortly be settled to the satisfaction of all concerned.

Briefly, it is contemplated that Mitsui will build sufficient tankage and purchase sufficient stocks to meet these requirements and in return will receive the Government subsidy plus a commission from us on a small amount of business we will cede them, thus providing for an adequate return against their investment.

When the negotiations are definitely concluded, we shall have pleasure in advising you, but we wish to take this opportunity now of expressing our deep appreciation to you personally, and to the State Department, and also of course to the American Embassy in Tokyo, for the most valuable assistance constantly rendered us during this rather difficult and complicated period.

Sincerely yours,

P. W. PARKER

894.6363/294 : Telegram

The Secretary of State to the Chargé in Japan (Dickover)

WASHINGTON, November 6, 1936—3 p. m.

140. Your despatch No. 2076, October 14, in regard to oil interests in Japan.[82] Proposed action, as outlined in concluding paragraph of your despatch under reference, has Department's approval. De-

---

[82] Not printed; in the final paragraph the Ambassador in Japan stated that confirmation of previous oral assurances by the Japanese Government had not yet been given, but "there is little doubt that the confirmation will be given in due course." He suggested that the Embassy request "oral or written confirmation" of a memorandum of previous assurances to be presented to the Chief of the Commercial Affairs Bureau of the Japanese Foreign Office.

partment suggests that, in your discretion, Embassy endeavor to obtain written rather than oral confirmation of Japanese Government's assurances.

HULL

894.6363/295 : Telegram

The Ambassador in Japan (Grew) to the Secretary of State

TOKYO, December 14, 1936—1 p. m.
[Received December 14—9:45 a. m.]

259. For the Acting Secretary. Embassy's despatch No. 2076, October 14, 1936.[83]

1. The Standard Vacuum Oil Company will shortly approach the Department to request that diplomatic efforts be made to assist them in view of the present impasse in their negotiations with the Japanese Government.

2. After 2 years of unremitting effort on the part of the oil interests the negotiations have reached a critical moment due to the fact that the Ministry of Commerce and Industry has failed to give satisfactory written confirmation of the oral assurances previously given in regard to the security of the future trade of the oil interests in Japan. Moreover, recent actions of the authorities of the Ministry of Commerce and Industry particularly the unwarranted decrease of the foreign companies, kerosene quotas for 1936 and the proposed revision of the petroleum tariff which will discriminate against importers indicate that if matters are left exclusively in the hands of the Ministry of Commerce and Industry the authorities cannot be relied upon to adhere in good faith to those assurances.

3. My British colleague[84] feels that the time has come for strong diplomatic representations and he is cabling today to London to recommend that Eden[85] send for the Japanese Ambassador to express the anxiety of the British Government as to the future of British oil interests in Japan, to ask for a categorical statement of the intentions of the Japanese Government because its present attitude arouses the suspicion that the Japanese Government wishes to drive the foreign oil companies out of Japan; and to request that if such is not the case the Japanese Government give the written assurances required by the oil interests.

4. I concur in the British Ambassador's judgment that such action is fully warranted and I furthermore believe that the present moment

---

[83] See footnote 82, p. 798.
[84] Sir Robert H. Clive, British Ambassador in Japan.
[85] Anthony Eden, British Secretary of State for Foreign Affairs.

is psychologically favorable for such a step. In view of the preoccupation of the Japanese Minister for Foreign Affairs [86] with foreign and domestic complications it appears that the best results might be obtained if you would have a frank and forceful talk with Saito [87] along the general lines of the proposed British representations in London. Details of the situation will be supplied to the Department by the oil company.

GREW

894.6363/296 : Telegram

The Ambassador in Japan (Grew) to the Secretary of State

Tokyo, December 17, 1936—11 a. m.
[Received December 17—2:40 a. m.]

261. Embassy's 259, December 14, 1 p. m.

1. The *Asahi* this morning reports that the Japanese oil companies are agitating against the granting of any increases in the gasoline sales quotas by the Ministry of Commerce and Industry to the foreign oil companies because (*a*) the purpose of the petroleum industry law is to protect the Japanese oil industry and therefore the quotas of foreign companies should not be increased and (*b*) the foreign oil companies have as yet failed to fulfill the oil storage obligation. The newspaper adds that the question is expected to become an issue in the coming session of the Diet.

2. The above is transmitted as a further indication of the situation with which the foreign oil interests are faced in Japan.

GREW

894.6363/296 : Telegram

The Acting Secretary of State to the Ambassador in Japan (Grew)

Washington, December 17, 1936—2 p. m.

160. 1. Reference Department's 140, November 6, 3 p. m. Has any action been taken under this authorization?

2. Reference your 259, December 14, 1 p. m., and 261, December 17, 11 a. m.

Mr. Coe of Standard Vacuum has called at Department this morning and supplied details, confirming last sentence your telegram 259, and the present problem has been discussed at length. Department

---

[86] Hachiro Arita.
[87] Hirosi Saito, Japanese Ambassador at Washington.

concurs in your view and that of your British colleague that diplomatic representations should be made at this time, but feels that, rather than to follow the procedure suggested of conversations in Washington and London respectively, it would be more expedient to have conversations held by you and your British colleague respectively with the Japanese Prime Minister.[88] We feel that ambassadors on the spot are more completely familiar with the facts antecedent and present and have a more effective feel of the situation and of what might most appropriately and effectively be said than could officials in Washington and in London. We doubt the advisability of "strong representations" in a positive sense at this stage, as we estimate that such representations would not be effective. We therefore envisage an approach in the form of an expression of anxiety regarding the future in Japan of the foreign oil interests concerned, respectively, with request for a clear indication that it is not the desire of the Japanese Government to drive the foreign oil companies out and an express request that the assurances sought by these oil interests be given in writing.

Department desires that you discuss this matter along lines suggested above immediately with your British colleague and that, if you and he agree that this line of approach is practicable, you ask him to suggest this line to his Government and to seek from it authorization, such as the Department now gives you for parallel action, so to proceed. Department desires that action taken by the two Governments be approximately simultaneous and substantially identical in character. You therefore will take action vis-à-vis the Japanese Government only when your British colleague is prepared to take similar action. Department strongly feels that such procedure at Tokyo would have distinct advantages over the suggested procedure of approaches at London and Washington.

MOORE

894.6363/295 : Telegram

The Acting Secretary of State to the Ambassador in the United Kingdom (Bingham)

WASHINGTON, December 18, 1936—8 p. m.

452. Reference Department's mail instruction 1478 of November 10 in regard to oil situation in Japan.[89] Grew informs Department that, in view of failure of Japanese Ministry of Commerce to confirm in writing oral assurances previously given in regard to security of

---

[88] Koki Hirota.
[89] Not printed.

future trade of foreign oil interests in Japan, British Ambassador at Tokyo has recommended to his Government that Eden discuss situation with Japanese Ambassador at London, and Grew suggests that Department take similar action in Washington. Department, strongly of opinion that suggested action would not be as expedient as direct approach in Tokyo by British and American Ambassadors to Japanese Prime Minister, has so informed Grew for his consideration in consultation with his British colleague.

MOORE

894.6363/298 : Telegram

The Ambassador in Japan (Grew) to the Secretary of State

TOKYO, December 19, 1936—6 p. m.
[Received December 19—10:35 a. m.]

264. Department's 160, December 17, 2 p. m.

1. I have discussed with my British colleague the question of representations concerning the oil situation along the lines suggested by the Department.

2. In view of the attitude of the Department, Clive will recommend to his Government that a further diplomatic approach approximately simultaneous and substantially identical in character be made by us in Tokyo. He, however, feels very strongly that a further approach of this nature would be ineffective and insufficient to secure results. During the past 2 years we have repeatedly supported our oil companies by diplomatic representations here with almost negative results. The present Minister and Vice Minister for Foreign Affairs [90] have probably never familiarized themselves with the details of the situation and would merely pass on to the Ministry of Commerce copies of the *aides-mémoires* which we would present. In the Ministry of Commerce the matter is handled by an official [91] who is known to be anti-foreign in his attitude while the new Vice Minister is less helpfully inclined than was his predecessor Yoshino. The polite written inquiry (sent after oral assurances had been given) from the oil companies in regard to assurances for future trade evoked a reply of which the Japanese text was offensive in tone. Clive, therefore, feels that the time has come for a new method of procedure and believes that our representations here would be given emphasis if a day or two prior to our representations, the anxiety of our two Governments regarding the future in Japan of the foreign oil interests and their desire that assurances as to the intentions of the Japanese Govern-

[90] Hachiro Arita and Kensuke Horinouchi.
[91] Chief of the Fuel Section, Bureau of Mining Industry (Sakai).

ment be given in writing were appropriately presented to the Japanese Ambassadors in Washington and London.

3. After the most careful consideration I incline to the opinion that representations from both ends of the line would serve to emphasize the unsatisfactory nature of the situation.

4. Our recommendations for "strong representations" did not envisage anything further than a formal approach such as was suggested in the Department's 160.[92] We feel, however, that unless the situation is now presented with marked emphasis our representations will be dealt with by the Foreign Office as a matter of diplomatic routine with only negative results. We obviously do not envisage anything in the nature of "demands" which would defeat their own purpose.

5. We doubt the advisability of an approach to the Prime Minister. Such procedure is not understood in Japan and by going over the head of Foreign Office and, therefore, causing the Foreign Minister a loss of face the result might be more harmful than helpful to the oil interests. If the Department approves, however, I could take a favorable opportunity after the formal representations have been made to the Minister for Foreign Affairs to discuss the situation informally with the Prime Minister.

6. As we are now on the threshold of the holidays when only the most pressing business is dealt with by the Departments of the Japanese Government, we feel that no step should be taken until after January 8. My British colleague will probably recommend that, in the meantime, the British Ambassador in Washington be instructed to discuss the matter with the Department.

7. No action has been taken under the authorization in the Department's 140, November 6, 3 p. m., as the request for this authorization contemplated only the confirmation by the Foreign Office of such assurances as the oil interests might receive from the Ministry of Commerce. The oil interests have received no satisfactory assurances for confirmation.

GREW

894.6363/299 : Telegram

The Ambassador in Japan (Grew) to the Secretary of State

TOKYO, December 22, 1936—8 p. m.
[Received December 22—12 : 13 p. m.]

265. Embassy's 264, December 19, 6 p.m., paragraph 6.

1. The local representatives of the oil interests have today asked that at least some preliminary diplomatic approach to the Japanese

---

[92] Dated December 17, 2 p. m., p. 800.

Government be made either in Washington and London or in Tokyo before the holidays—(a) because not having fulfilled the storage promises the foreign oil companies are in the position of lawbreakers and are liable as penalization to have their 1937 sales quotas reduced unless they are supported by diplomatic measures and—(b) because the anticipated approval by the Tariff Investigation Commission of the proposed revision of the petroleum tariff should be forestalled. Any discriminatory tariff revision as the Department is aware would be contrary to the oral assurances given the oil companies. It is expected that the 1937 quota will be allotted and the tariff revision examined within the next few days.

2. I shall, however, take no action here without the Department's authorization and unless the British Ambassador takes an approximately simultaneous and similar step. Clive informs me that he is cabling similarly and urgently to London tonight.

GREW

894.6363/300 : Telegram

The Ambassador in Japan (Grew) to the Secretary of State

TOKYO, December 23, 1936—7 p. m.
[Received December 23—9 : 35 a. m.]

266. Embassy's 265, December 22, 8 p. m.

1. My British colleague informs me that he has just received his instructions to the effect that Eden agrees with your views and that Clive is to concert with me and to proceed as soon as possible to joint representations to the Japanese Government. Clive proposes that the two Embassies prepare an identic memorandum to be communicated tomorrow, the 24th, to the Minister for Foreign Affairs, either personally or in some other manner if the Minister cannot see us.

2. Please rush instructions if not already sent. I feel that our representations should be approximately simultaneous and substantially identical not joint and identic.

3. According to the telegram received by Clive, Eden also took advantage of an interview with Yoshida[93] to draw attention to the difficult position of the British oil interests because of the failure of the Japanese Government to live up to its promises.

GREW

---

[93] Shigeru Yoshida, Japanese Ambassador in the United Kingdom.

894.6363/300 : Telegram

The Acting Secretary of State to the Ambassador in Japan (Grew)

WASHINGTON, December 23, 1936—1 p. m.

164. Your 264, December 19, 6 p. m., and 265, December 22, 8 p. m., and 266, December 23, 7 p. m.

1. Department approves of procedures suggested in concluding sentence paragraph 5 of your telegram 264 and you may so proceed if and when your British colleague is prepared to take similar action.

For your guidance: The Department has not shared the view of your British colleague that there should be made "strong" diplomatic representations, for the reason *inter alia* that Standard-Vacuum, we understand, and Shell, we presume, have not decided on a definitive course of action in the event that the assurances desired are not forthcoming. It has seemed to us (see Department's 160, December 17, 2 p. m.) and we continue of that opinion, that circumspection is called for in the tone of representations until the companies are prepared to make such decision. Apparently, however, Department and Embassy are now in agreement as to the tone of the representations which should next be made to the Japanese Government.

In view of the foregoing and after further careful consideration of the points raised in your telegrams under reference we do not, at least at this time, favor the making of representations to the Japanese Ambassadors at Washington and London.

2. Your 266, December 23, 7 p. m., just received. You are authorized, as per Department's telegram 160, December 17, 2 p. m., to proceed in accordance with the view expressed in paragraph 2 of your telegram 266.

MOORE

894.6363/301 : Telegram

The Ambassador in Japan (Grew) to the Secretary of State

TOKYO, December 24, 1936—6 p. m.
[Received December 24—6 : 34 a. m.]

268. Department's 164, December 23, 1 p. m. I carried out the Department's instructions in an interview with the Minister for Foreign Affairs this afternoon and after an oral presentation of the details of the situation I left with him an *aide-mémoire* based on the Department's telegram No. 160, December 17, 2 p. m., paragraph 2. The Minister said that he was unfamiliar with the subject but would study it and would reply as soon as possible. The Minister received

my representations and the reading of the *aide-mémoire* in a wholly friendly way and his attitude remained thoroughly cordial throughout the interview.

The British Ambassador made similar representations a few moments earlier.

GREW

TRADE RELATIONS BETWEEN THE UNITED STATES AND JAPAN; FURTHER DISCUSSION OF VOLUNTARY RESTRICTION BY THE JAPANESE OF EXPORTS TO THE UNITED STATES AND THE PHILIPPINES [94]

611B.9417/159

Memorandum by Mr. Roy Veatch of the Office of the Economic Adviser of a Conversation With the Counselor of the Japanese Embassy (Yoshizawa)

[WASHINGTON,] January 7, 1936.

Mr. Yoshizawa called to say that the Embassy had received instructions from Tokyo in reply to the Ambassador's [95] cable (dispatched following the Ambassador's conversation with Mr. Sayre [96] on December 27 [97]) respecting an adjustment of the agreement covering imports into the Philippines of Japanese cotton piece goods. The Japanese Government had secured the agreement of the exporters to withhold shipments until after the end of January, and the Japanese Government had no objection to announcement of this fact by this Government.

The Japanese Ambassador and Mr. Yoshizawa would like to call upon Mr. Sayre and discuss the rest of the instruction which they had received from Tokyo. Mr. Yoshizawa could offer only a hint of the nature of this instruction:—the Japanese Government would urge Japanese exporters to limit their shipments into the Philippines during the second six months period of the agreement to a total of 19,000,-000 square meters rather than the 23,500,000 square meters which the exporters felt they were entitled to ship during this period (the Government's figure of 19,000,000 square meters is arrived at by subtracting the total of arrivals in the Philippines during the first four months of the agreement from the normal total of 45,000,000 square meters for the year, whereas the exporters' figure of 23,500,000 is

---

[94] For previous correspondence, see *Foreign Relations*, 1935, vol. III, pp. 940 ff.
[95] Hirosi Saito.
[96] Francis B. Sayre, Assistant Secretary of State.
[97] For memorandum of December 27, 1935, see *Foreign Relations*, 1935, vol. III, p. 1045.

arrived at by subtracting the 26,000,000 from the maximum of 49,500,-
000 for one year, including a transfer of 10 percent from the second
year.)

As he left, Mr. Yoshizawa asked if any particular thought had
been given to the problem of transshipments via Hong Kong and
Shanghai, and he gave the impression that the Japanese exporters
are still anxious about this part of the arrangement since they cannot
control such shipments and in their opinion they threaten to upset
the allotment of their total quota among the members of the Exporters
Association.

I replied that apparently it was impossible to find any way to
handle this problem or the parallel problem of possible increases in
imports into the Philippines of cotton goods from Shanghai mills
without special quota legislation in the Philippines. I asked if Mr.
Yoshizawa saw any other method and he replied in the negative. I
then asked what his Government would think of action by the Philippine Government setting up quotas for all countries other than the
United States, the Japanese quota to be based upon figures established
by the voluntary agreement.

Mr. Yoshizawa expressed his own opinion that his Government
would have no objection to such an arrangement and would, in fact,
favor it. He was of the impression that earlier instructions to the
Embassy, stating that his Government would favor action by the
Philippine Government to prevent the importation of Japanese goods
transshipped via other ports, was intended to cover also the possibility of like action by the Philippine Government respecting imports of goods manufactured in Chinese ports. It was his opinion,
and he was sure also the opinion of his Government and Japanese
exporters, that increasing shipments from Shanghai mills, whether
Chinese-owned or Japanese-owned, would be harmful to Japanese
interests and to the successful working of the agreement.

In order to be certain of the point, I asked if Mr. Yoshizawa was
of the opinion that his Government would agree to such action by the
Philippine Government (placing quotas upon direct shipments from
all countries and transshipments of Japanese goods) if it were requested for an opinion. In reply Mr. Yoshizawa said that such action
was clearly within the power of the Philippine Government and he
saw no reason why it should not take such action independently and
without any reference to Tokyo. I then put the question in another
way and said that if action of this nature were contemplated the
Embassy might be asked to inquire if the Japanese Government had
any objection to such action, and he said that he was sure no objection would be raised. He then reiterated his belief that his Government and Japanese exporters do now favor such action and he made
it particularly clear that he included direct shipments from Shanghai

mills in this judgment. Japanese exporters have no more control over exports from these mills than they do over transshipments of their goods from other ports and they would like to have some arrangement made which would remove these complicating factors.

611B.9417/116

Memorandum by Mr. Roy Veatch of the Office of the Economic Adviser

[WASHINGTON,] January 9, 1936.

Conversation: The Japanese Ambassador,
Mr. Seijiro Yoshizawa, Counselor, Japanese Embassy,
Mr. Sayre,
Mr. Turner,[98]
Mr. Veatch.

The Ambassador called to deliver the response of his Government to the problem placed before the Ambassador by Mr. Sayre in their conversation of December 27, 1935.[99] First, he was authorized to say that exports of cotton piece goods to the Philippines would not be resumed by Japanese exporters until after the end of January and an announcement to that effect might be made by the American Government.

He was further authorized to say that the Japanese Government had secured the agreement of the Exporters Association to limit their quotas of shipments to the Philippines for the second half of the agreement [1] period to a total of 19,000,000 square meters. This agreement represented a concession on the part of the exporters, since they considered it to be their right to export a total of 23,500,000 square meters during this period, taking advantage of the allowable transfer of 10 percent of the quota for the second year.

Mr. Sayre expressed the opinion that this arrangement apparently represented no concession on the part of the Japanese from their position that the entire quota should be measured by arrival statistics only. He asked whether the Ambassador had received any response to the Ambassador's suggestion that 14,000,000 square meters should be deducted from the quota for the rest of the two year period and the Ambassador replied that his Government had made no mention of his proposal in its cable.

Mr. Sayre referred again to the statistical basis of the agreement, i. e., the Philippine customs statistics of imports, based on liquida-

---

[98] William T. Turner, of the Division of Far Eastern Affairs.
[99] For memorandum of December 27, 1935, see *Foreign Relations*, 1935, vol. III, p. 1045.
[1] For agreement, see memorandum of October 11, 1935, *ibid.*, p. 1007.

tions. The Ambassador then said that it was "problematical" or "controversial" as to whether the agreement should be interpreted as referring to the Philippine statistics of liquidations or to Philippine statistics of arrivals. The Ambassador then called attention to Paragraph I of a typewritten statement which he handed to Mr. Sayre [2] in which was quoted a certain section of the Philippine Customs Regulations referring to importations. He also read a quotation from Section 1248 of the Philippine Customs Regulations defining importations as beginning when goods enter the waters under Philippine jurisdiction and as being completed when the duty on these importations has been paid or when a deposit has been made and the goods cleared through the customs. These quotations had been furnished the Japanese Government by the Japanese Consul General in Manila and it was apparent that the Japanese Government had been making special effort to establish its contention that Philippine statistics of arrivals, whether or not they were in existence at the time the agreement was reached, were the statistics to which reference was made.

In discussion of the rest of the typed statement presented by the Ambassador it became apparent that although the Japanese contended that the measure of importation should be on the basis of arrival statistics the Ambassador was not speaking of a shift from the present liquidation statistics to arrival statistics. When this point was raised he replied that he felt it would be difficult or undesirable to shift from the liquidation statistics to arrival statistics in the middle of the agreement period—having started with one set we should continue through to the end with it. He did agree that strict adherence to the basis of liquidation statistics would make it impossible for the Japanese exporters to ship any more cotton goods to the Philippines before June, 1936. He contended, however, that insofar as the total quota was concerned the Japanese would not fare badly upon the liquidation basis since their shipments into the Philippines during the last three months of the two year period would not be recorded as imports during the period under limitation—they could, therefore, ship into the Philippines during May, June and July, 1937, as much as 28,000,000 square meters and therefore cancel off the amount shipped into the Philippines before August 1, 1935, which has been charged against the quota because it has been liquidated during the quota period.

After discussion the Ambassador agreed, however, it would not be desirable for the Japanese to make such heavy shipments at the end of the two year period since they would wish to maintain a stabilized position in the Philippine market and probably would be unable to secure an extension of the agreement if they made such unusual shipments.

---

[2] *Infra.*

Mr. Sayre sketched again his understanding of the positions of the two Governments. The United States Government had offered to recede from the rigid position which it might take of insisting upon strict adherence to the letter of the agreement. To be quite frank, he was unable to see that the Japanese Government had made any approach to a compromise, however,—in effect they still held strictly to their interpretation of the agreement.

Mr. Sayre then called attention to the wide-spread impression in the United States that the Japanese have broken the agreement and have already over-shipped their quota very substantially. This Government regrets this impression and wishes to clear up the whole situation through a press release as soon as possible. It is unable, however, to explain the statistical difficulties, and therefore to clear the Japanese of blame for intentional evasion of the agreement, until it can announce at the same time a readjustment of the agreement.

Mr. Sayre had made frequent reference to the Ambassador's proposal during their conversation on December 27. The Ambassador now sought to clarify what his proposal had meant, saying that it was about the same as the present proposal of the Japanese Government. He had not had in mind a shift from liquidation statistics to arrival statistics and he had meant that the 14,000,000 square meters, to be accepted by the Japanese in the quota (rather than the entire 28,000,000 square meters awaiting liquidation on August 1) should be carried over as an unliquidated amount at the end of the two year period.

Mr. Sayre returned to the present Japanese proposal, based entirely upon actual arrivals of Japanese goods in the Philippines since the opening date of the agreement and said that he could not present this proposal to his committee and to the textile people and hope for acceptance. He had been ready to place before them some such compromise as that which he had understood the Ambassador had suggested during their last conference and he had felt that he could carry through an agreement upon that basis. He wished to say also that he did consider it desirable to shift to arrival statistics as a basis for the agreement from February 1st. This would be advantageous to the Japanese and make it possible for them to carry out the agreement smoothly and to stabilize the position for their textiles in the Philippines rather than to run the danger of the recurrence of wide fluctuations in their shipments.

The Ambassador again stated that his proposal had not been fully understood, that he had not had in mind a shift to arrival statistics. Therefore it had been his expectation that there would be a normal carry-over of an unliquidated amount at the end of the two year period. He had not intended to suggest, however, that necessarily the entire amount of 14,000,000 square meters should be carried over at the end of the period.

The Ambassador went on to say, however, that the situation was now very clear to him. He understood the suggestion that the agreement be measured by arrival statistics from February 1st on, but he was of the opinion that his Government would wish to have the entire two year period measured by arrival statistics if any shift was to be made in the statistics. In any event, he was quite sure that Japanese exporters would not absorb the whole of the 14,000,000 square meters, representing the "bulge" which so concerned the American Government. Perhaps some compromise could be reached, however, so that a part of this amount would be absorbed by the Japanese.

Mr. Sayre restated the position of this Government so that it might be repeated clearly to the Japanese Government. He suggested that that Government be informed that we have two points to propose. First, that arrival statistics shall be used to govern the agreement after February 1, and, second, that if this shift is made the 28,000,000 square meters awaiting liquidation on August 1, or some part of it, should be apportioned during the remaining eighteen months. This Government would be glad to consider suggestions of the Japanese Government as to how this apportionment might be made.

The Ambassador then asked if it would not be possible for the American Government to agree that, if the Japanese Government should accept the entire amount of the 14,000,000 square meters as included in the quota, some amount less than 14,000,000 square meters could be carried over at the end of the agreement.

In reply Mr. Sayre said that this Government might be able to make a considerable sacrifice, along this line, if the Japanese Government could arrange for some limitation on the shipments of rayon goods to the Philippines. Rayon shipments had increased inordinately during the last few months, being three times as large in November as in August, the rate of increase apparently continuing during December. It is probable that present shipments of rayon are in excess of the demand in the Philippines and that Japanese exporters would sacrifice very little, if anything, in reality by agreeing to shipments limited to a monthly figure much below this level.

Mr. Yoshizawa expressed the opinion that it would be very difficult to secure any such agreement. The suggestion is psychological more than it is economic. The Japanese rayon industry is very proud of the fact that it now leads the world in production and it would be loath to accept any limitation on its exports. Furthermore, the impression is growing in certain quarters in Japan that Japanese exports to the United States or American territories are being limited too much, especially in view of the present trade balance between the two countries.

After further discussion the Ambassador said that he understood the importance of rayon shipments to the Philippines in their effect upon the cotton textile agreement. He asked if it was the intention of this Government to bring up the question of rayons even apart from the present discussion of the cotton textile agreement.

In reply Mr. Sayre said that rayons were becoming an increasingly difficult question to handle since heavy Japanese shipments afforded American exporters an opportunity to charge that the spirit of the cotton textile agreement was being broken. On the other hand, he would wish to bow to the judgment of the Ambassador and Mr. Yoshizawa as to whether it would be wise at the present time to mention the subject of rayons in their communications with their home Government. He would be quite willing to keep rayon out of the discussion until a satisfactory agreement had been reached on cotton textiles.

Mr. Sayre showed the Ambassador and Mr. Yoshizawa, copies of the statement, which it was proposed to release to the press,[3] concerning the intention of the Japanese exporters to withhold shipments to the Philippines until after February 1. The Ambassador and Mr. Yoshizawa found no objection to the proposed release.

611B.9417/160

The Japanese Embassy to the Department of State [4]

1. The Japanese Government in entering upon the Gentlemen's Agreement had in mind only arrivals after August 1, 1935, according to Philippine statistics.

The Japanese Government considers that its stand in this respect is supported by the Philippine laws and practices. The Philippine customs regulations (September 18, 1909, No. 574, Section 2) provide: "The dutiability of and the rates of duty applicable to merchandise imported into the Philippine Islands shall be determined by the arrival of the carrying vessel within the jurisdictional waters of the first port of entry in the Philippine Islands entered by the said vessel with the intention to unload any portion of her cargo thereat." It is understood to have been the practice of the Philippine Government to apply new tariffs, when tariffs are changed, upon the arrival basis above referred to.

2. Arrivals from August 1 to December 1, 1935 amounted to 26,000,-000 square meters, making the arrivable amount for the second semester, beginning February 1, 1936, 19,000,000 square meters on the basis

---

[3] For text of statement, see p. 813.
[4] Handed by the Japanese Ambassador to Assistant Secretary of State Sayre, January 9.

of the annual quota of 45,000,000 square meters, and 23,500,000 square meters on the basis of the annual quota plus the transfer standing at 49,500,000 square meters.

3. The United States Government interprets "Philippine statistics" as liquidation statistics. The result is that 28,700,000 square meters which stood unliquidated on August 1, 1935 is to be included in the liquidable amount allotted to Japanese importation. On that basis by the end of November, 1935, 34,500,000 square meters had been liquidated leaving the liquidable amount for the rest of the twelve months to be (45,000,000 minus 34,500,000 equals) 10,500,000 square meters on the basis of the annual quota or (49,500,000, minus 34,500,000, equals) 15,000,000 square meters on the basis of the annual quota plus the transfer.

4. The United States Government has suggested that 14,000,000 square meters should be added to the liquidable amount for the first twelve months. Add to this amount 15,000,000 square meters (liquidable amount on the basis of the annual quota plus the transfer) the total will be 29,000,000 square meters.

5. The Japanese Government now proposes that the shipments will be controlled during the semester beginning on February 1, 1936, to the amount of 19,000,000 square meters, namely the annual quota amount remaining on the basis of the arrival statistics. And there still remains, it is said, 20,000,000 square meters to be liquidated. The total will therefore be 39,000,000 square meters.

6. Therefore it appears that the 39,000,000 square meters in the second semester can, to the figures of 29,000,000, be taken care of by the remaining liquidable amount, the excess being 10,000,000. This amount has to be carried over for the second twelve months unliquidated.

7. If the customs practices of the Philippine Government should be so altered while the Gentlemen's Agreement is in effect, as to bring about a great change in the relation of the amount of arrivals and the amount liquidated, that fact, it seems, shall be taken into due consideration so as not to affect the arrivable quota of Japanese shipments.

An understanding like the following may be advisable;—The arrivable amount may be in excess of the liquidable amount to the figures of 10,000,000 square meters at the end of each semester.

611B.9417/113

Press Release Issued by the Department of State, January 9, 1936

The Japanese Ambassador called upon Mr. Francis B. Sayre, Assistant Secretary of State, today to inform him that no cotton piece goods will be shipped from Japan to the Philippines until after the first of February. In conformity with the provisions of the voluntary agreement between the Japanese Government and the United States Government, shipments of cotton piece goods to the Philippines were suspended by Japanese exporters on November 16.

Conversations are now in progress with respect to adjustment of the amount of Japanese goods to be imported into the Philippines after the fifteenth of February (approximately two weeks are required to transport freight from Japanese ports to Manila). An exact adjustment of these imports for the remaining eighteen months covered by the agreement has not yet been reached but average monthly imports during this period will be considerably less than during the first few months of the agreement.

611.946 Rag Rugs/123

Memorandum by Mr. Roy Veatch of the Office of the Economic Adviser of a Conversation With the Attaché of the Japanese Embassy (Kuroda)

[WASHINGTON,] January 10, 1936.

Mr. Kuroda called to report upon his Government's expression of opinion with respect to the points raised in our previous conversation of December 21, 1935.[5]

The Japanese Government is of the opinion that there is no necessity of forcing all cotton rug manufacturers into the Exporters Association since the few manufacturers not now members of the Association are quite insignificant in size and importance.

The Government will instruct the Exporters Association to cooperate fully with the American Consulate General at Kobe and it has expressed the hope that the Consulate may find some way of assisting the Association in minimizing exports by non-members. Mr. Kuroda mentioned again (evidently reflecting his instructions) the possibility of the Consulate denying certificates to shippers outside the Exporters Association. Mr. Veatch replied, as in the former conversation, that it probably would be impossible for the Consulate to take any such action. Certainly it would be helpful, however, for representatives of the Consulate and the Exporters Association to discuss this problem.

---

[5] See telegram of December 24, 1935, 2 p. m., to the Consul General at Shanghai, *Foreign Relations*, 1935, vol. III, p. 1040.

611.943 Gloves/27

Memorandum by Mr. Roy Veatch of the Office of the Economic Adviser

[WASHINGTON,] January 23, 1936.

Conversation: The Japanese Ambassador,
              Mr. Seijiro Yoshizawa, Counselor of the Japanese
              Embassy,
              Mr. Sayre,
              Mr. Turner,
              Mr. Veatch.

Mr. Sayre explained that he had asked the Ambassador and the Counselor to call in order to place before them the problem of imports into the United States of wool-knit gloves manufactured in Japan, and also to inquire further regarding the subject of cotton velveteens imported into the United States from Japan.

The Ambassador said that he welcomed the opportunity to talk with Mr. Sayre since for a day or two he had intended to request an opportunity to present to Mr. Sayre the reply which his Government had made to the Ambassador's last cable respecting the Philippine cotton textile agreement. He had received a cable from his Government earlier in the week but had been cogitating the best way of presenting the situation to Mr. Sayre.

Mr. Sayre explained that in accordance with the Ambassador's earlier request he was now able to bring to the attention of the Ambassador a case in which rather severe restriction of United States imports from Japan was impending. An investigation of the differences in costs of production of wool-knit gloves in Japan and in the United States, under Section 336 of the Tariff Act of 1930,[6] which had been called for by a Senate resolution,[7] was practically complete and Mr. Sayre had found it possible to ascertain what the findings of this investigation probably would be and, therefore, the nature of the report which must soon be made to the President. In order to place the case before the Ambassador clearly, Mr. Sayre handed him a typed statement,[8] which was then read and discussed in detail.

The Ambassador remarked that he supposed the Commercial Attaché of the Embassy, Mr. Inouye, would be better informed upon this problem than anyone else in the Embassy and that he would get in touch with him, perhaps asking him to come to Washington tomor-

[6] Approved June 17, 1930; 46 Stat. 590, 701.
[7] Senate Resolution 178, 74th Cong., 1st sess., agreed to August 19, 1935: *Congressional Record*, vol. 79, pt. 13, p. 13616.
[8] *Infra.*

row. Mr. Yoshizawa called attention to Mr. Sayre's statement that it probably would be impossible to hold up the Commission's report past the 1st of February unless action were taken by the Japanese, and he and the Ambassador then agreed that it would be necessary for them to get a cablegram off to Tokyo tonight.

Mr. Yoshizawa said that this further request for voluntary restriction by the Japanese of their shipments to the United States appeared to justify further the prediction which he had made when the case of cotton rugs had been brought up, i. e., that any action by Japanese exporters to limit shipments of one commodity would encourage American competitors in other lines to demand similar restrictions upon other commodities.

Mr. Sayre said that it was true, of course, that we had found it necessary to bring more than one commodity to the attention of the Japanese Government, but he called attention to the fact that the American Government had by no means requested restriction of Japanese exports of all commodities against which complaint had been made in the United States. This Government has acted as a sieve and has strained out practically all of the complaints that have been made against Japanese goods. This Government had brought the situation to the attention of the Japanese only in the few cases where competition had become alarming and where it was likely that more extreme restrictions would be set up as a result of the pressure of the affected economic interests in the United States. He reminded the Ambassador that there was one other situation which he had called to the attention of the Ambassador—the case of cotton velveteens. Although in view of the Supreme Court decision on certain aspects of the Agricultural Adjustment Act, action to limit imports of velveteens probably would not proceed under Section 22 of the AAA,[9] if the duty on imports of wool-knit gloves should be increased radically as a result of the investigation under Section 336 of the Tariff Act, then it was quite possible that action on velveteens would be urged by the American industry under Section 336. From the standpoint of the Japanese industries themselves, it was important that voluntary control of exports of these two commodities should be exercised in time to prevent action here under Section 336.

PHILIPPINE TEXTILE AGREEMENT

The Ambassador said that he would like to take this occasion to report instructions which he had received from his Government a day or two previously with respect to the proposed adjustment of the Philippine cotton textile agreement. He had not asked to see Mr.

---

[9] The Agricultural Adjustment Act was approved May 12, 1933; 48 Stat. 31, 42.

Sayre immediately upon receipt of this cable because he had been at a loss to know just how to present the situation. His Government apparently had paid no attention to his arguments in favor of a compromise and held rigidly to its original position, insisting that the Japanese exporters should proceed to ship a maximum of 19,000,000 square meters up to August 1, 1936. His Government still maintained that it held strictly to the wording of the original agreement and it referred again to the definitions of "importations" contained in documents of the Philippine Customs Service.

Mr. Sayre said that the textile people in this country were already convinced that Japan has broken the agreement. It was Mr. Sayre's desire to clear up this matter and to remove all blame from the Japanese. Unfortunately the attitude of the Japanese Government and exporters cut the ground from under his feet, however, and made it impossible for him to make a good case to the American textile people.

The Ambassador said that he understood the difficulties and that he had been trying to persuade his Government to reach a compromise agreement in order to help the American Government to meet these difficulties. He felt the present difficulties had arisen out of a misunderstanding when the agreement was first put into operation, however. And he was bound to say that in spite of the fact that he could well understand the position of the American Government, he felt that his Government had assumed a position which could be justified on more or less "legal" grounds. He wondered if Mr. Sayre would agree that there is involved no question of bad faith on the part of the Japanese Government or Japanese exporters. If it could be made clear to his Government that there was no accusation of bad faith involved but merely a desire to reach a compromise between the positions of the two Governments in order to make the agreement work, then he felt that it might be possible to get something done. He had a feeling that his Government was particularly concerned about this question of bad faith.

Mr. Sayre said that he had, of course, maintained this position from the first and had no intention whatever of creating the impression that this Government charged the Japanese Government with bad faith. He then said that he had had in mind the possibility of sending a cable to the American Embassy in Tokyo and asking that the question be presented to the Japanese Foreign Office there. He wanted to have the Ambassador's advice as to the advisability of proceeding in this way.

In reply the Ambassador said that he thought such an approach to his Government would be helpful, particularly if the case as presented emphasized the fact that there was no charge of bad faith and only a desire to secure a practical adjustment of the problem.

It was agreed, therefore, that this Government should request the American Embassy in Tokyo to take the matter up with the Foreign Office and to explain in some detail the position of this Government and the reason for desiring an adjustment of the original agreement or a clear understanding as to the way in which that agreement should work. Mr. Sayre made it clear that he appreciated fully what the Ambassador had done in seeking an understanding between the two Governments and he certainly would not approach the Japanese Government through the American Embassy in Tokyo unless the Ambassador felt that this move might assist in securing the desired understanding. The Ambassador in turn assured Mr. Sayre that he was in complete agreement with this procedure. It was understood, however, that it was not the intention of this Government to transfer to Tokyo detailed negotiations on this or on similar problems.

611.943 Gloves/2

The Department of State to the Japanese Embassy [10]

UNITED STATES IMPORTS OF WOOL-KNIT GLOVES FROM JAPAN

1. An investigation of wool-knit gloves and mittens under Section 336 of the Tariff Act of 1930 was instituted on August 20, 1935 by the United States Tariff Commission in accordance with Senate Resolution 178 of the 74th Congress. In this investigation, as in others under Section 336 of the Tariff Act of 1930, the Tariff Commission is directed to ascertain the differences in the costs of production of the domestic article and the imported foreign article and to specify, in a report to the President, what changes in duty, if any, would be required to equalize such differences in costs of production.

2. The report of the Tariff Commission upon wool-knit gloves is nearing completion. In accordance with the request of the Japanese Ambassador, it is possible to give this advance indication of the probable findings or conclusions of the Commission with respect to this case so that the Japanese Government may have an opportunity, if it so desires, to consider remedial action before it will become incumbent upon the President under the provisions of the law to proclaim such changes in the rates of duty on imports of this article as will be specified in the report of the Commission.

3. Although the Commission's report is not yet complete, it seems likely that the facts brought to light by its investigation will necessitate a shift from the foreign valuation to the American valuation as a basis for levying duties upon imports of wool-knit gloves and

---

[10] Handed to the Japanese Ambassador by Assistant Secretary of State Sayre, January 23.

mittens. Specifically, that would mean a recommendation that the duty on knit gloves and mittens, finished or unfinished, wholly or in chief value of wool, valued at not more than $1.75 per dozen pairs, provided for in paragraph 1114(b) of the Tariff Act of 1930 at the rate of 40¢ per pound and 35 percent ad valorem on foreign value, be changed to 40¢ per pound and 35 percent ad valorem on the American selling price.

4. It appears, therefore, that under the provisions of the law, the President will be faced with the necessity of issuing a proclamation providing for this change in duty on imports of wool-knit gloves and mittens unless definite steps have been taken amply to protect the American industry before the Tariff Commission report has been submitted to him.

5. It is impossible to say exactly how long it will be before the Tariff Commission will make its report to the President, but the report is practically complete and it should be ready for submission to the President before the end of January. Furthermore, the condition of uncertainty in the market is such that some definite action with respect to imports of wool-knit gloves will be necessary before the first of February if action by the President, under the law and in conformity with the findings of the Tariff Commission's investigation, is to be avoided.

611B.9417/119a : Telegram

The Secretary of State to the Ambassador in Japan (Grew)

WASHINGTON, January 29, 1936—6 p. m.

12. When the Department reached agreement with the Japanese Government, through the Japanese Ambassador, restricting the amounts of Philippine imports of Japanese cotton textiles for 2 years (see Department's 863 of October 22, 1935 [11]), it was hoped that the groundwork was well laid for a mutually satisfactory settlement of this troublesome question.

However, this hope is now imperiled by various developments. . . . Certain difficulties have arisen in connection with the working of and the interpretation of the agreement. The agreement, embodied in the memorandum of conversation of October 11, 1935, initialed by the Japanese Ambassador, provided that "the statistics of imports compiled by the Philippine Customs will be used as the basis of determining the volume of imports of Japanese cotton piece goods". At that time, the only available Philippine Customs statistics of imports were

---

[11] This instruction transmitted a copy of the memorandum of agreement initialed October 11, 1935; for memorandum see *Foreign Relations*, 1935, vol. III, p. 1007.

recorded as of the date of liquidation of duty. The liquidation customarily takes place some 3 or 4 months after the arrival of the goods in Philippine ports. As a result, duties were liquidated after August 1, the effective date of the agreement, on a large part of the unusually heavy arrivals of Japanese textiles during several months prior to August. The customs statistics of imports based on liquidation since August 1 include these amounts and show a total of nearly 42,000,000 square meters up to January 1, 1936 (although actual arrivals between these two dates were only 26,000,000 square meters). Estimates based on Japanese export statistics indicate that this total will reach 54,000,000 when all the goods now in the Philippines are liquidated. When compared with the limitations established by the agreement, this statistical record gave rise to a popular impression that the Japanese had violated the agreement.

The marketing of these large quantities of Japanese cotton textiles has meant that the American cotton textile exporters have to date secured no apparent advantage from the agreement. There still remain in the Philippines considerable stocks of most lines of Japanese cotton piece goods in spite of the reduction in shipments from Japan since November, and the American exporters foresee no opportunity for satisfactory future business if these stocks are replenished to any substantial extent during the next few months.

This situation has been discussed repeatedly with the Embassy here but the Japanese Government has maintained throughout that it interpreted the agreement to refer only to arrivals of Japanese goods in the Philippines; it has shown no disposition to compromise along the lines suggested by the Department.

This rigid attitude has blocked all of our efforts to reach a reasonable and mutually satisfactory readjustment of the cotton goods agreement to meet the practical difficulties of the situation which the two Governments sought to remedy by the agreement. In the meantime, the position of American exporters of cotton goods has become much less favorable due to the unusually heavy arrivals of Japanese rayon goods, in direct competition with American cotton goods, since the agreement was put into operation. This development makes it increasingly difficult to secure any support in this country for the cotton textile agreement and endangers the success of the entire undertaking. We fear that if the agreement loses the support of American textile interests they will make every effort through legislation and otherwise to restrict Philippine imports from Japan and this would react unfavorably upon the entire problem of United States imports of competing Japanese products.

In the light of the foregoing circumstances, it appears essential to the Department that the Japanese Government and exporters should agree to such an adjustment of the situation as will offer some expectation of moderate improvement in the position of American cotton textiles in the Philippine trade in the near future. This apparently is the only way to attain the objectives which the two Governments had in mind when they set up the original agreement last October. The Department has consistently maintained the view that the agreement was based on liquidation statistics rather than arrival statistics, and considers that it would be justified in asking that Japanese shipments during the remainder of the agreement be limited in accordance with the letter of the agreement. As it has already indicated to the Japanese Ambassador, however, the Department does not wish to hold rigidly to this position and prefers to work out a mutually satisfactory compromise.

Will you please, unless you perceive objection, seek an interview with the Minister for Foreign Affairs,[12] and such other interested officials as may be concerned, and explain the situation along the lines set forward in the preceding. In these explanations please make it completely clear that we are in no way accusing Japan of any attempt to evade the agreement, or attributing blame to it for the existing circumstances. On the contrary, we seek completely to dissipate any such misapprehension as may have arisen following the publication of the Philippine import statistics. However, the difficulties faced by the Department and the American textile trade are genuine, and if they are to be handled with mutual satisfaction, some measure of compromise will have to be shown by the Japanese Government. The Department therefore greatly hopes that the Japanese Government will see its way clear to transmit instructions to its Ambassador in Washington which might form the basis of a compromise settlement of the difficulties that have arisen. It may be that such a settlement could be reached most easily by reaching an understanding on rayon as a part of or as a supplement to the original agreement. The Department has already placed this problem before the Japanese Embassy in a general way and it would be prepared to discuss a definite arrangement. It probably will be possible to go much further in meeting the Japanese point of view with respect to the amount of cotton goods to be imported into the Philippines during the next 18 months if a mutually satisfactory arrangement on rayon can be worked out. Such an arrangement need not be unreasonably restrictive and need not block normal expansion of the rayon market in the future.

It is not desired to transfer general negotiations on this whole field from Washington to Tokyo, and it will therefore not be necessary for you to negotiate on details. The Department looks to you for

---

[12] Koki Hirota.

making a full presentation of the problem to the Japanese authorities with the idea that the position of the Japanese Government in the future negotiations in Washington may become more constructive.

In order to give a further opportunity for working out the details of an adjustment, the Japanese Ambassador at our request has just cabled his Government the proposal that shipments of cotton goods to the Philippines be delayed until March 1 or be limited for the month of February to something like 2,000,000 square meters. The Ambassador has also informed his Government that you will present the American position to the Foreign Office. Further discussion here will await your full and prompt report.

HULL

611B.9417/121a : Telegram

The Secretary of State to the Ambassador in Japan (Grew)

WASHINGTON, January 30, 1936—6 p. m.

13. The Japanese Embassy has been informed of the Department's appraisal and view of the situation explained in Department's No. 12, January 29. The Department believes the Japanese Embassy considers these views and suggestions reasonable and practicable but apparently the Embassy has not transmitted to the Japanese Government the proposal dealing with February shipments. Contrary to the Department's understanding, the Embassy merely informed the Foreign Office that it should expect such a proposal from the American Embassy in Tokyo. You are requested, therefore, to seek immediately agreement with the Japanese Government along the following lines: Suspension of shipments of cotton goods to the Philippines until March 1 or control by Japanese exporters of their shipments so that arrivals in the Philippines will not exceed 2 million square meters between February 15 and March 15, such arrangement to be announced by the Japanese Government or, with its consent, by this Government.

It is feared that without some definite limitation, Japanese exporters will be inclined to make heavy shipments beginning February 1, an eventuality which undoubtedly would arouse American and Philippine business interests and which would make it more difficult to carry forward the cotton goods agreement in a satisfactory manner. Announcement of the intention of holding February shipments to moderate levels would serve to allay fear and to create a favorable atmosphere for reaching agreement regarding the entire problem.

HULL

611B.9417/120 : Telegram

The Ambassador in Japan (Grew) to the Secretary of State

TOKYO, January 31, 1936—8 p. m.
[Received January 31—9:45 a. m.]

20. Department's 12, January 29, 6 p. m., and 13, January 30, 6 p. m.

1. I called on the Minister for Foreign Affairs at 2:30 today and made the desired representations in detail. The Minister stated that he was unfamiliar with situation and that the Chief of the Bureau of Commercial Affairs [13] would handle the matter. He said that he would instruct Kurusu to "endeavor to conciliate".

2. The Commercial Attaché [14] and the First Secretary [15] called on Kurusu this afternoon and discussed the matter thoroughly. According to Kurusu, the Japanese position is that the Philippines customs import statistics are extremely inaccurate for the purpose of recording actual monthly importations because liquidation of duty often takes place long after the goods have been cleared through customs and have entered into consumption. He also denied that there were unusually large stocks in the Philippines when the agreement became effective. In order to quiet possible opposition, however, he made the following tentative counterproposal subject to the approval of the Osaka cotton exporters: that the Japanese renounce for this semester the 10 percent flexibility privilege and that instead of shipping the remaining 19,000,000 square meters of their quota during the rest of the quota year they will ship only 15,000,000 square meters or at the rate of 2,500,000 per month. However, because of contracts already concluded and accumulated since November when shipments were stopped he cannot promise that the February shipments can be held within 2,500,000. Thereafter, however, every effort will be made to equalize the monthly shipments over the 6 months' period. He said that they could not possibly agree to the proposal to stop shipments during February because of contracts already concluded.

3. Kurusu hopes to obtain the approval of the cotton exporters to the above proposal tomorrow as well as their consent to publication of the arrangement in the United States if approved. The Embassy, of course, has in no way indicated that the Department would accept this counterproposal.

4. The risks of adverse moves by the American textile interests were fully set forth both to Hirota and Kurusu.

GREW

---

[13] Saburo Kurusu.
[14] Frank S. Williams.
[15] Erle R. Dickover.

611B.9417/120 : Telegram

The Secretary of State to the Ambassador in Japan (Grew)

WASHINGTON, January 31, 1936—7 p. m.

15. Your 20, January 31. It will be appreciated if you will impress upon Kurusu the following points:

(1) This Government would like to have whatever proposal the Japanese Government is able to make in definite form as soon as possible. If a definite offer is made following the lines of Kurusu's tentative proposal, we would suggest that it include the following details:

(*a*) Philippine customs statistics of arrivals in the Philippine Islands of Japanese cotton piece goods rather than liquidation figures will be used as the basis for determining the volume of imports of such goods.

(*b*) The total amount of Japanese cotton piece goods to be imported into the Philippines between February 15 and August 1, 1936 will not exceed 15 million square meters.

(*c*) So far as possible, the total amount of Japanese cotton piece goods to be imported into the Philippines during this period will be distributed proportionately over the entire period.

(*d*) Japanese exporters will limit importations (measured as arrivals) into the Philippines of Japanese cotton piece goods for the 12 months following August 1, 1936, to a maximum of 45 million square meters, the total amount imported to be distributed so far as possible proportionately over the 12 months of the year. (It may be necessary to reach agreement upon a definite arrangement of this distribution throughout the year.)

(2) To make the position of this Government tenable in accepting such an adjustment of the original agreement, it is essential that the Japanese offer should include an agreement upon the regulation of Philippine importations of Japanese rayon goods or, at the very least, a statement of the intention of the Japanese Government to join with this Government immediately in establishing a mutually satisfactory method of regulating such importations.

(3) The Department recognizes the difficulties in restricting shipments to the Philippines during February, in fulfillment of contracts already concluded, but it considers it most important that the Japanese Government should urge the Japanese exporters very strongly to find a way of surmounting these difficulties so as to hold February shipments to moderate levels. Heavy shipments in February would militate against the acceptance of an adjustment of the agreement along the lines suggested by Kurusu and it is believed that aside from this, a concentration of Philippine imports of Japanese goods at this time would weaken the prices to be obtained for Japanese textiles as well as for American textiles.

(4) In view of the period of time during which the future of the cotton textile agreement has been uncertain and in view of the possibility that heavy Japanese shipments may be made in the early part of February, it is extremely desirable that an announcement be made at the earliest possible time of agreement between the two Governments upon this entire question and that, as indicated above, this announcement should include at least a statement that the two Governments will negotiate a mutually satisfactory agreement on rayon. Continuation of present abnormally heavy rayon shipments would reinforce the general feeling of the textile trade and of the public here that the spirit of the original agreement has been violated by Japanese exporters and that that agreement is a failure.

If the question again arises as to the amount of Japanese cotton piece goods in the Philippines on August 1, you may wish to refer to the Japanese statistics of exports of such goods to the Philippines, indicating that such exports from March to July were decidedly higher than at any time during 1934.

Hull

611.943 Gloves/28

Memorandum by Mr. Roy Veatch of the Office of the Economic Adviser

[Washington,] February 1, 1936.

Mr. Yoshizawa telephoned Friday evening, January 31, to say that the Embassy had received instructions from Tokyo with respect to the possibility of voluntary restriction by Japanese exporters of their shipments of wool-knit gloves and mittens to the United States. It was then too late for him to prepare a statement to bring to the Department but he wished to call upon Mr. Sayre late Saturday morning. When it was learned that Mr. Sayre would not be in the office again until Monday, Mr. Yoshizawa suggested that he bring the statement to Mr. Veatch so that the Department might study it before he saw Mr. Sayre on Monday.

Mr. Yoshizawa presented a typed statement to Mr. Veatch (copy attached)[16] and explained briefly the situation in which the Japanese manufacturers found themselves.

It was his understanding that the industry had been created largely, if not entirely, to supply the American market; there was no considerable demand as yet for wool-knit gloves in Japan, although the vogue of winter sports had created recently a small demand. The possibility of supplying wool-knit gloves and mittens to the American

---

[16] *Infra.*

market had been brought to the attention of the Japanese by American jobbers and the prospect of a good market in the United States had led the Japanese to install new machinery and, in fact, to create a new industry in Japan. As a result, these manufacturers and their workers (the industry is carried on largely on a household basis although evidently small machines must be installed in the household) would be faced with great losses.

Mr. Veatch commented upon this situation as a good example of the desirability of checking such rapid expansion of production primarily for the American market when it is almost certain to create unusual difficulties with American manufacturers already supplying that market and thus give rise to strong agitation against Japanese trade. Some method should be found of warning Japanese manufacturers in time to prevent investment in equipment which in all probability could only be used a short time due to the almost certain agitation in the United States for restriction against such destructive competition.

Mr. Yoshizawa agreed that it was desirable to find a means of doing this. The difficulty at present is that individuals or small concerns are drawn into enterprises of this nature by the promise of an attractive American market and they have no way of knowing the conditions in that market other than the reports given them by the American dealers who urge them to supply that market. Ordinarily American jobbers appeal to small manufacturers and bring great pressure upon them to cut prices and enter into competition with each other. Without organization, the individual manufacturers do compete strongly with each other and drive prices down to the lowest possible level with the result that quality also is very low. An effort has been made in the manufacture of wool-knit gloves to organize the industry and to make it possible for them to improve prices and quality with the hope that the American market could be stabilized.

611B.9417/133

The Japanese Embassy to the Department of State [17]

1. The minimum prices of wool-knit gloves and mittens to be exported to the United States will be fixed as hereunder stated:

        (a) Gloves and mittens for children,
               (No. 1–3) .... ¥ 2.50 per dozen pair
        (b) Gloves and mittens for junior misses,
               (No. 4–6) .... ¥ 3.00 per dozen pair
        (c) Gloves and mittens for ladies,
               (No. 7–9) .... ¥ 4.20 per dozen pair

---

[17] Handed by the Counselor of the Japanese Embassy to Roy Veatch, of the Office of the Economic Adviser, February 1.

The prices fixed above shall be maintained as effectively as possible by the Association of Exporters of the said articles.

(It is desired, however, that those goods already contracted and to be shipped from Japanese ports by March 15 should be exempted from the above price regulation.)

2. The Association will take, besides the maintenance of the minimum prices above stated, measures for the exercise of stricter inspection and improvement of the quality of the goods for exportation.

3. The Association is prepared to consider the voluntary control of the quantity to be exported.

611.946 Rag Rugs/124 : Telegram

The Consul General at Shanghai (Davis) to the Secretary of State

> SHANGHAI, February 3, 1936—4 p. m.
> [Received February 3—1: 25 p. m.]

72. Following from Kobe: [18]

"January 30, 11 a. m. Referring to your December 24, 2 p. m., via Shanghai,[19] I have to report that at a conference on January 29th between myself, the chief executive of the Rug Export Association and Messieurs Waring and Dorfman [20] it was agreed:

(1) The association will notify the Consulate of each permit it issues for a shipment which will not require a consular invoice, that is less than $100 value.

(2) The association will notify the Consulate whenever any permit is canceled or the amount altered.

(3) At the end of each month the association will bring to the Consulate customhouse figures identifying the shipments which have actually been exported rather than merely under permit or invoice awaiting shipment which condition has been a source of disagreement in consular and association figures for any specific month in the past. This will also enable us to check shipments which never leave Japan.

(4) The Consulate will cooperate with the association in endeavoring to have non-members of the association report their shipments, if any, to the association.

(5) The association will send its representative to the Consulate at the end each month to reconcile its figures with those of the Consulate.

The association states that it is not now permitting shipments from any port except Kobe and that it believes no shipment can be exported without the association's knowledge as association representatives are checking actual shipment at the pier with the exception that possibly

---

[18] From Kenneth C. Krentz, Consul at Kobe.
[19] *Foreign Relations*, 1935, vol. III, p. 1040.
[20] Frank A. Waring and Ben D. Dorfman, of the U. S. Tariff Commission staff.

goods falsely declared on consular invoice the Japanese customs export declaration might escape notice; for example, a shipment invoiced as cotton rags instead of cotton rugs. To contravene such practices the association requests the cooperation of the Department in promptly notifying to the Consulate any cases where the American customs report that a shipment misleadingly invoiced has been entered.

Figures for January and subsequently will be prepared in accordance with the foregoing and reconcilement of association and consular figures for June–December 1935 period now under way will be telegraphed the Department early in February.

Consulate General informed. Krentz."

DAVIS

611B.9417/122 : Telegram

The Ambassador in Japan (Grew) to the Secretary of State

TOKYO, February 3, 1936—6 p. m.
[Received February 3—9 : 35 a. m.]

23. Department's 15, January 31, 7 p. m.

1. The Commercial Attaché and the First Secretary called on Kurusu this afternoon. Kurusu said that the Osaka cotton textiles exporters had accepted his proposal on the following conditions:

(*a*) That they be allowed to carry over to the 1936–37 quota year the 4 million square meters not to be shipped this quota year, thus giving them a quota of 49 million next quota year.

(*b*) That the Philippine or American Governments endeavor to control transshipments from Hong Kong which in the past have interfered greatly with control of shipments from Japan to the Philippine Islands.

(*c*) That no agreement whatsoever be made to control or restrict shipments of rayon to the Philippine Islands.

2. The Department's proposals as contained in the Department's No. 15 were then presented to Kurusu. He accepted 1 *a*, *b* and *c*, and 3, but could not accept 1 *d* because of 1 *a* above, or 2 because of 1 *c* above.

3. In regard to the rayon question, Kurusu said that he positively could not agree even to negotiate the question as he had used the possible restriction of Japanese rayon imports into the Philippines as a weapon with which to induce the Osaka textile exporters into acceptance of his cotton textiles proposal and to agree now even to negotiate the rayon question would inevitably defeat the present compromise proposal concerning textiles which he had obtained only with great difficulty. He was asked if he would negotiate the rayon question if no adjustment were made of the cotton textiles question (i. e., if the Japanese were permitted to ship 19 million square meters during the second semester of this quota year and were allowed the 10 per

cent flexibility privilege) but he replied that he could not negotiate on the rayon question under any circumstances. His attitude at both interviews was that the Japanese textile exporters while willing to negotiate on the cotton textiles question were determined to quote "draw the line" at control of rayon exports.

4. Kurusu said that his proposal as given in the Embassy's 20, January 31, 8 p. m. and amended in paragraph 1 above is definite and if accepted by us can be published by the Department in Washington provided that the arrangement be not called an "agreement" but instead be called a "voluntary adjustment by the Japanese exporters".

5. Kurusu further indicated that in case of non-acceptance of his proposal as amended and resultant tariff legislation he could see no outcome other than that the Japanese textile trade would have to "fight it out" in unrestricted competition.

GREW

611B.9417/134

Memorandum by Mr. Roy Veatch of the Office of the Economic Adviser

[WASHINGTON,] February 4, 1936.

Conversation: Mr. Seijiro Yoshizawa, Counselor of the Japanese Embassy,
Mr. Sayre,
Mr. Turner,
Mr. Veatch.

Mr. Yoshizawa had been asked to call to discuss the statement of his Government regarding wool-knit gloves which he had left with Mr. Veatch on Saturday, February 1. In view of the fact that he had spoken with Mr. Veatch over the telephone on Monday, February 3, with regard to future negotiations regarding adjustment of the Philippine cotton textile agreement, this matter was taken up first.

PHILIPPINE TEXTILE AGREEMENT

Mr. Yoshizawa repeated what he had said to Mr. Veatch on the telephone, that the cable he had received February 3 from Kurusu in the Foreign Office stated that the Foreign Office had been informed by the American Commercial Attaché in Tokyo that in the future negotiations regarding the textile agreement would be handled through the American Embassy in Tokyo. The cable to Mr. Yoshizawa had referred then to information contained in Mr. Yoshizawa's cable to the Foreign Office some days earlier, in which he had repeated the statement contained in the Department's instructions to the American Embassy in Tokyo to the effect that it was not intended to transfer negotiations from Washington to Tokyo. Mr. Yoshizawa merely wished to straighten out the matter so that he and his Government might know the wish of this Government.

Mr. Sayre confirmed Mr. Yoshizawa's understanding of the instructions to Tokyo and said that it had been our intention to continue to handle arrangement of the details of such agreements through the Embassy here. It was probable that the misunderstanding had arisen out of the fact that the Department had considered it necessary to ask the Embassy in Tokyo to negotiate a definite agreement regarding February shipments when the Department had learned January 30 that the Embassy had not transmitted the suggestion of the Department with regard to this matter.

Mr. Yoshizawa wished to explain the action of the Embassy with respect to the suggestion regarding February shipments. He said that he had not failed to inform his Government of the suggestion but he had not stated in his cable that the American Government asked for such an agreement—he had merely referred to the probability that such a request would be made through the American Embassy in Tokyo.

Mr. Yoshizawa was asked if the cable he had received from Tokyo clearly stated that the American Commercial Attaché had said that "in the future" all negotiations regarding this matter would be handled in Tokyo. Mr. Turner and Mr. Yoshizawa then examined the Japanese text of this cable and agreed that this was clearly the meaning of the statement contained therein.

In response to an inquiry, Mr. Yoshizawa said that Kurusu was clearly the one person in the Japanese Government who could secure the sort of voluntary action on the part of Japanese exporters in which this Government was interested, if such agreements could be secured at all. It was desirable to handle the matter through him. There had been much talk recently of his appointment as Ambassador to Brussels.

United States Imports of Wool-Knit Gloves

With respect to the statement which Mr. Yoshizawa had left with Mr. Veatch on Saturday, Mr. Sayre said that he was going to be frank and even blunt and to make no attempt to be diplomatic. The time had already dragged on to the point where action must be taken very quickly if the Tariff Commission's report under Section 336 were not to be presented to the President and acted upon by him. He had had prepared a statement setting forth the problem and a definite proposal, which he handed to Mr. Yoshizawa (copy of which is attached to this memorandum.) [21] This statement was read out loud.

---

[21] *Infra.*

Mr. Yoshizawa's comment was that this ultimatum would be very hard for the Japanese exporters to swallow. He was informed that they already had contracts for 1936 which would require the delivery to the United States of at least double the proposed quota.

Mr. Sayre emphasized the fact that there was no alternative between action along these lines and recommendation by the Tariff Commission of a shift to the American selling price in the collection of duty on imports of wool-knit gloves and mittens. This Government had done everything possible to present the case to the Japanese at the earliest possible moment, in conformity with the promise Mr. Sayre had made to the Japanese Ambassador several months ago, and it had gone just as far [as] possible in making a liberal offer to the Japanese. Furthermore, it was understood that this whole matter had not come suddenly to the attention of the Japanese since the Commercial Secretary [22] in New York had been informed of it last summer or fall.

Mr. Yoshizawa confirmed the fact that Mr. Inouye had learned of the situation (Mr. Yoshizawa thought toward the end of September 1935) and had reported it to Tokyo. (Mr. Yoshizawa then repeated the description of the industry and its problems which he had included in his conversation with Mr. Veatch on February 1.)

Later in the afternoon Mr. Yoshizawa telephoned Mr. Veatch to clarify the use of words under paragraph 4 on page 2 where it was stated that the limitation for the calendar year 1936 was to be based upon "actual arrivals in this country (general imports)". In response Mr. Veatch explained the meaning of "general imports" and of "imports for consumption", making the point that basing the arrivals from Japan upon general imports would not require the inclusion in the maximum amount of the 34,000 dozen pairs of Japanese gloves in bonded warehouses on December 31, whereas imports for consumption would make it necessary to include these gloves in the year's total if they were entered through customs.

At the suggestion of Mr. Fox,[23] Mr. Veatch called Mr. Yoshizawa still later in the afternoon to make it entirely clear that all wool-knit gloves and mittens arriving in the United States from Japan were to be included in the agreement and no gloves appearing under different classifications in the tariff were to fall outside of the limitation.

A copy is attached of the statement handed to Mr. Veatch by Mr. Yoshizawa February 1, 1936.[24]

---

[22] Toyoji Inouye.
[23] A. M. Fox, director of research, U. S. Tariff Commission.
[24] Ante, p. 826.

611B.9417/134

The Department of State to the Japanese Embassy [25]

1. The Tariff Commission is about to report to the President the result of its investigation on wool-knit gloves under Section 336 of the Tariff Act of 1930. Indications are that this report will call for a shift in valuation from the foreign to the American selling-price basis, which means a great increase in duty. Action under section 336 will proceed unless a satisfactory alternative is adopted within the next few days. This is the season during which orders for wool-knit gloves are usually placed; early decision in the case is, therefore, vital to all parties interested in the wool-knit glove industry.

2. It appears that wool-knit gloves are being rushed into the United States in anticipation of the results of the Tariff Commission investigation. In the four years preceding 1935, imports during the first five months of the year were very small, varying from 1 to 3 percent of annual imports. Even in the year 1935 imports in these months did not exceed 6 percent. From all accounts, imports during January of this year, however, will be exceptionally large. Moreover, imports of wool-knit gloves actually entered for consumption in December 1935 were about 75 percent of such imports in November of that year, whereas December imports were about 33 percent of November imports in 1931, 12½ percent in 1932, 45 percent in 1933, and 17 percent in 1934. In addition, at the end of December, 34,000 dozen pairs of wool-knit gloves were in bonded warehouse available for entry.

3. Price limitations and improvement of inspection proposed in points 1 and 2 of the statement handed to the Department of State February 1, 1936 are both of only incidental interest to the United States Government. The primary interest of this Government is in a limitation of shipments that will assure a reasonable improvement in the competitive situation in the wool-knit glove industry in the United States. From no imports from Japan in 1933, imports of wool-knit gloves rose to 27,000 dozen pairs in 1934 and to 489,000 dozen pairs in 1935. The large importation in 1935, which is continuing in 1936, creates a very serious competitive situation, particularly in view of the fact that the domestic industry produces only about 700,000 dozen pairs annually.

4. The average of imports of wool-knit gloves from Japan during the three years 1933–1935 is about 172,000 dozen pairs and this figure would seem to afford a reasonable basis for an agreement for the limitation of shipments of wool-knit gloves from Japan to the United

---

[25] Handed by Assistant Secretary of State Sayre to the Counselor of the Japanese Embassy, February 4.

States. But in order to prevent the necessity for action under section 336, the United States is willing to accept a basis more favorable to Japan. The most liberal agreement which the United States can accept in lieu of action under section 336 would be an undertaking so to regulate shipments of wool-knit gloves from Japan to the United States that actual arrivals in this country (general imports) during the calendar year 1936 shall not exceed 225,000 dozen pairs. This amount equals approximately one third of production in the United States in 1934 and in 1935; considering the 34,000 dozen pairs of Japanese wool-knit gloves in bonded warehouse at the end of 1935, it will permit a total entry for consumption of 259,000 dozen pairs of gloves, or slightly in excess of the average annual import for consumption of 258,000 dozen pairs in the two-year period 1934–1935.

5. The suggestion, contained in the preceding paragraph has been made as liberal as the existing situation will permit in the hope that a mutually satisfactory arrangement can be reached.

The shortage of time, however, makes it imperative that if action under Section 336 is not to proceed immediately, the suggestion must be accepted without amendment not later than February 8.

611.943 Gloves/9

Memorandum by Mr. Roy Veatch of the Office of the Economic Adviser

WASHINGTON, February 7, 1936.

Mr. Yoshizawa called on Mr. Veatch late in the morning to deliver his Government's response to the Department's position respecting wool-knit gloves set forth in a statement handed to Mr. Yoshizawa by Mr. Sayre on February 4, 1936.

Mr. Yoshizawa reported that members of the Exporters Association met on the 7th for a lengthy discussion "in deadly earnest". The meeting had been unable to reach a definite decision, however, and the Japanese Government requested four or five days more of grace so that members of the industry in outlying cities and towns might be consulted before a final decision was reached with respect to the proposal of the Department.

Nothing was said in the cable which the Embassy had received from Tokyo to indicate whether the exporters were likely to set up the voluntary restriction mentioned in the Department's statement of February 4. Mr. Yoshizawa was requested to place certain additional facts before this Government, however. A check-up in Japan had disclosed the fact that contracts had already been concluded with American firms for the delivery of 800,000 dozen pairs of wool-knit gloves and mittens this year and some 230,000 or 240,000 dozen pairs were already in the process of manufacture for delivery on these contracts. Many, if not most, of these contracts had been made with Americans in Japan representing American importers. Mr. Yoshizawa indicated that the Japanese manufacturers considered that there would be great difficulties in limiting their shipments to the volume suggested by this Government, entailing the breaking of many contracts and possible court action resulting therefrom and also real financial loss due to the number of gloves already made or in process of manufacture and to the amount of machinery which has been installed to supply this market. In any event, it would take some time to make the necessary arrangements in Japan, including the allotment of a quota if it be accepted.

The manufacturers of wool-knit gloves are rather widely scattered in Japan, although they are chiefly in four important cities. It would take four or five days to get their views and thus to give the American suggestion due consideration.

Mr. Veatch spoke of the considerable delay that this Government had already agreed to and of the difficulty of securing further delay by the Tariff Commission, especially in view of the situation in the trade and the pressure for early action. He would place the Japanese request before American officials just as Mr. Yoshizawa had presented it, however, and would be able to give Mr. Yoshizawa a reply before evening so that a cable might be gotten off to Tokyo the same day.

As soon as possible Mr. Veatch conferred with Mr. Ryder of the Tariff Commission and he in turn discussed the matter with others in the Commission, including Mr. Fox and Mr. Durand. It was decided in the Tariff Commission that so far as the Commission was concerned, the Japanese Government might be given the following statement: The Tariff Commission will proceed as it had planned to make its report to the President, probably the first of the week. Since it will take some time for the President to study the matter and to refer it for comment to certain agencies of the Government, however, it will be possible for the President to take no action upon the Tariff Commission's report until after Thursday, February 13. Should the Japanese Government inform this Government on or before February 13 that the Japanese exporters would institute the measure of control as suggested by this Government, then the President would be advised to refrain from proclaiming increases in the tariff upon imports of wool-knit gloves and mittens.

This suggestion of members of the Tariff Commission was placed before Mr. Phillips [26] and he authorized Mr. Veatch to make the suggested statement to Mr. Yoshizawa.

At 5:00 o'clock Mr. Veatch telephoned Mr. Yoshizawa and communicated the statement set forth above.

---

[26] William Phillips, Under Secretary of State.

611B.9417/122 : Telegram

The Secretary of State to the Ambassador in Japan (Grew)

WASHINGTON, February 7, 1936—6 p. m.

18. Your 23, February 3. The Department is prepared to accept the suggestion of the Japanese Foreign Office regarding a voluntary adjustment by the Japanese exporters of the agreement reached October 11, 1935 to the effect that importations into the Philippines of Japanese cotton piece goods between the present time and August 1, 1936 shall not exceed 15,000,000 square meters. In conveying this information to the Foreign Office, however, you are requested:

(1) To make it clear that this Government cannot consider the Japanese proposal to be a satisfactory adjustment of the agreement. Furthermore, it is felt that the Japanese Government and the Japanese exporters can themselves hardly expect the agreement, so adjusted, to attain fully the objectives which the two Governments had in view when the original understanding was reached last October.

(2) To urge Kurusu very strongly to make every effort to lead the textile exporters to agree that the maximum limitation of 45,000,000 square meters for the second year of the agreement shall not be increased by 4,000,000 square meters.

(3) To secure agreement upon some method of distributing the total amount to be imported into the Philippines during the second year of the agreement proportionately so far as possible over the 12 months of the year, perhaps through monthly or quarterly limitation, with the possibility of a transfer of as much as 20 percent from one period to another to meet seasonal demands if necessary.

(4) To inform Kurusu that it will be impossible, at least for the present, to take the action suggested in 1 (b) of his proposal as submitted in your 23. This Government has no means of controlling such transshipments or arrivals in the Philippines and the Philippine Government has no executive power to take such action. Legislative action in the Philippines would be required to set up the necessary controls, and the Philippine Assembly will not meet again until October 1936. It may be possible later for the Philippine Government to establish some means of controlling arrivals of Japanese goods which have been transshipped. Until some such alternative means of control can be established, however, it is essential that no change be made in the original agreement with respect to the inclusion of transshipped goods in the total amount of imports from Japan; the removal of all control would create new and perhaps insuperable obstacles to the satisfactory operation of the agreement. This Government is of the opinion that general knowledge by the trade that the agreement will continue to cover transshipments will prevent or hold to inconsequential volume such transshipments since this provision removes any advantage which might be gained by rehandling goods in an intermediate port.

(5) To impress upon Kurusu the importance of Japanese rayon shipments to the Philippines in relation to the working of the cotton textile agreement. If the Japanese textile exporters refuse to negotiate any agreement on rayon, then at least it should be made clear

to them that their own policy with respect to shipments of rayon goods to the Philippines will be a very important factor in determining whether or not the cotton textile agreement is to work satisfactorily and in determining the attitude of American and Philippine interests with respect to the policy of the Philippine Government regarding textile imports.

(6) To inform the Japanese Government that in agreeing to this adjustment of the original agreement, this Government will adhere strictly to its stated intention to take no initiative toward securing an increase in the Philippine tariff rates on cotton piece goods, and that, as in the case of the original agreement, the agreement as modified implies in no way any limitation upon the full liberty of action of the Philippine Government or upon the freedom of this Government to consider without prejudice any action taken by the Philippine Government.

The Japanese Embassy here has been informed by Kurusu that representatives of the American Embassy have asserted that negotiations on trade matters will in the future be handled through the Embassy in Tokyo. To avoid confusion, please assure Kurusu (in conformity with Department's No. 12, January 29) that it is not the intention of the Department to transfer to Tokyo general or detailed negotiations in this field. In view of the advanced stage of your negotiations with Kurusu on the present problem, however, it is considered wise for you to arrange the details of a final adjustment.

HULL

611B.9417/123 : Telegram

The Ambassador in Japan (Grew) to the Secretary of State

TOKYO, February 8, 1936—8 p. m.
[Received February 8—9 : 35 a. m.]

25. Department's 18, February 7, 6 p. m.

1. The Embassy has informed Kurusu of the Department's suggestions and wishes, all of which were favorably received except that Kurusu could not bind himself to fulfill the suggestion contained in numbered paragraph 2. He said that he would have to consult with the Vice Minister for Commerce and Industry [27] on Monday as to the feasibility of the suggestion and would inform the Embassy later.

2. Kurusu also most strongly urges that the American and Philippine Governments make every possible effort to control transshipments from Hong Kong to the Philippines which he said are the disturbing factor in the situation.

3. The Embassy again brought to Kurusu's attention the fact that there is no intention to transfer from Washington to Tokyo the nego-

[27] S. Yoshino.

tiations in regard to this question. Kurusu did not indicate from whom he obtained the impression that the negotiations had been transferred. Representatives of the Embassy have given no such impression.

GREW

611.943 Gloves/10

Memorandum by Mr. Roy Veatch of the Office of the Economic Adviser of a Conversation With the Counselor of the Japanese Embassy (Yoshizawa)

[WASHINGTON,] February 13, 1936.

Mr. Yoshizawa said that the Embassy had just been informed that the exporters of wool knit gloves to the United States had met on Wednesday and had decided that it was technically impossible to comply with the request of the United States Government. Among the reasons for this decision were the following:

1. There were shipped from Japan to the United States during December, 90,000 dozen pairs of wool knit gloves and mittens.
2. Shipments of 60,000 dozen pairs were made in January and further shipments during the early part of February.
3. Consequently, there would be little of the proposed quota left for the Japanese exporters to exercise control over during the rest of the year. By the time control could actually be set up in Japan it is probable that no further shipments could be made this year. It would be necessary to secure from each manufacturer the facts regarding the amount produced last year, the amount shipped since the first of January, the amount contracted for for the current year, and the amount on which work had already been started. Only after this information had been secured could quotas be allotted to the different manufacturers.
4. If there were in fact any quota left to be allotted to the Japanese exporters they would have to meet unreasonable difficulties. For instance, they now have under manufacture many more gloves than could be delivered, probably they would have to meet damage claims because of the broken contracts and the exporters or the Government would have to take steps to bring all exporters into the association.

The Japanese Government agrees with the exporters that it would be impossible to carry out exactly the suggestion made by the United States. Although it recognizes that the American offer was in the form of an ultimatum, the Japanese Government hopes that the American Government will understand the unusual difficulties which would be created. In order to save time the Japanese Government offers an alternative to which the Japanese exporters would be willing to agree—the Japanese Government has made every effort to make this offer as liberal as possible and feels that the exporters would be making considerable sacrifices in agreeing to such an arrangement. This offer follows:

1. The Japanese exporters should be given sufficient time to set up their controls, therefore, the period of limitation of arrivals in the United States should begin on March 1, 1936.

2. The agreement should cover the 12 months from March 1, 1936.

3. Arrivals in the United States should be limited to 225,000 dozen pairs for this period (arrivals before this time, presumably the 150,000 dozen pairs shipped from Japan during December and January, would not be included in the quota).

In support of this proposal the Japanese Government calls attention to the following points:

1. That the 225,000 dozen pairs would be only one-fourth of the total production in the United States in 1935 (the figures of the Department of Commerce showing some 990,000 dozen are used by the Japanese).

2. It is understood that the Japanese gloves have developed to a large extent a new market in the United States in which Japanese gloves are not competitive with American wool knit gloves.

3. Japanese exporters will be sacrificing nearly three-fourths of the orders for which they have already signed contracts.

It was agreed that from the standpoint of both Governments a final disposition of this matter was desirable as quickly as possible. Mr. Veatch said that he would bring the matter before the appropriate officials immediately and call Mr. Yoshizawa later in the evening, if possible. At least he would report upon the matter later in the evening and try to get final word to Mr. Yoshizawa by the afternoon of Friday the 14th.

611.943 Gloves/11

Memorandum by Mr. Roy Veatch of the Office of the Economic Adviser

[WASHINGTON,] February 14, 1936.

Conversation: Mr. Seijiro Yoshizawa, Counselor of the Japanese
Embassy,
Mr. Feis,[28]
Mr. Veatch.

Mr. Yoshizawa had called Mr. Veatch during the afternoon to say that he would be leaving for Cleveland that evening and that if the American reply to the Japanese statement regarding wool-knit gloves was not yet ready, Mr. Veatch could communicate with Mr. Hayama [29] about it on Saturday. Mr. Yoshizawa said that he would be at the

---

[28] Herbert Feis, Economic Adviser, Department of State.
[29] Tsuneo Hayama, Third Secretary of the Japanese Embassy.

Embassy until after six o'clock, however, and it was arranged that Mr. Veatch would call him there if anything further could be said by that time regarding the American reply.

Mr. Feis presented a statement regarding the American proposal to the President and secured the President's O. K. about five o'clock, so Mr. Veatch telephoned Mr. Yoshizawa and it was arranged that he should come to the Department and talk with Mr. Feis and Mr. Veatch about the matter.

Mr. Feis explained to Mr. Yoshizawa that a statement of the best offer which the Department could make to the Japanese had not yet been prepared and could not be presented to representatives of the Japanese Embassy until Saturday morning. He could give Mr. Yoshizawa the main outlines of the American position, however. He proceeded then to state in some detail the argument and the specific proposals contained in the American statement to be handed to Mr. Hayama of the Japanese Embassy on Saturday morning.

Mr. Yoshizawa repeated his understanding of the various points in the American proposal and then, as he left, said that he would send a cable to Tokyo immediately setting forth these principal points and then would send a further cable on Saturday after the Embassy had received the American statement.

611B.9417/127 : Telegram

The Ambassador in Japan (Grew) to the Secretary of State

TOKYO, February 14, 1936—7 p. m.
[Received February 14—10 a. m.]

28. Embassy's 25, February 8, 8 p. m. Philippine imports of Japanese cotton textiles.

1. Kurusu stated today to a member of the staff that after consultation between himself and the Vice Minister for Commerce and Industry the replies to the suggestions contained in the Department's 18, February 7, 6 p. m. were decided upon as follows:

Department's numbered paragraph 1. The Japanese Government wishes it understood that the adjustment does not imply any change in the original agreement nor does it establish any precedent. The arrangement consists of a voluntary amicable adjustment by the Japanese exporters undertaken to meet the wishes of the American side.

Department's numbered paragraph 2. The Japanese Government will transmit the desire of the American Government to the Exporters Association but it should be understood that the Japanese Government undertakes no new obligation in this connection.

Department's numbered paragraph 3. The Japanese Government and the Exporters Association will endeavor to fulfill this suggestion provided that the Japanese Government statistics of exports be used as the basis of computation of volume of shipments or if Philippine arrival statistics are used, that some attempt be made to restrict transshipments from Hong Kong which defeat all efforts of the association to equalize shipments over the 12 months.

Department's numbered paragraph 4. The Japanese Government again most strongly urges that the American and Philippine Governments make every effort to control transshipments from Hong Kong. Such transshipments double the difficulties of the Japanese exporters as in addition to their voluntary curtailment of shipments they are obliged to meet the price competition of the transshipments from Hong Kong, thereby reducing their profits.

Department's numbered paragraph 5. The Japanese Government wishes it understood that the rayon question has no connection with the cotton agreement. It will, however, transmit the implied warning of the Department to the rayon exporters who probably will be inclined to listen as their export business of recent months has not been done at profitable prices.

2. The adjustment of the agreement interpreted in the sense conveyed in the above may be published in the United States but probably will not be published in Japan.

GREW

611.943 Gloves/5

The Department of State to the Japanese Embassy [30]

WOOL-KNIT GLOVES

This Government regrets that the Japanese exporters consider it to be impossible to restrict their shipments so that arrivals in the United States of wool-knit gloves and mittens manufactured in Japan should not exceed 225,000 dozen pairs during the calendar year 1936. This Government has given the most careful thought to the circumstances to which the Japanese Government has referred, however. Recognizing the difficulties created for Japanese exporters this year by the volume of shipments that have already been made since December 1, 1935, it has made every effort to formulate some arrangement which would take account of these difficulties and which would at the same time give to the American industry the protection which has been made necessary by the very rapid increase in imports of competitive wool-knit gloves from Japan.

[30] Handed to the Third Secretary of the Japanese Embassy by Mr. Veatch, February 15.

The report of the Tariff Commission upon its investigation under Section 336, made in compliance with a resolution of the Senate of the United States, has already been submitted to the President. Unless by the voluntary action of the Japanese industry immediate assurance can be given that the position of the American industry will be adequately safeguarded in the future, the President has no alternative under the law than to give immediate effect to the recommendation of the Tariff Commission, under Section 336 of the Tariff Act of 1930, that the base for the tariff upon imports of these goods should be shifted to the American selling price.

In spite of the considerable delay already occasioned in the efforts to secure a settlement of this matter, this Government is able to offer this final suggestion to the Japanese Government:

1. In recognition of the shipments of wool-knit gloves and mittens already en route to the United States, voluntary restriction by the Japanese exporters shall become effective applying to arrivals in the United States as of March 1, 1936. It is understood from the information presented by the Japanese Embassy that the arrivals in American ports of all Japanese wool-knit gloves and mittens between January 1 and March 1, 1936 will approximate 150,000 dozen pairs.

2. The Japanese exporters will undertake to restrict their shipments of wool-knit gloves and mittens to the United States so that total arrivals in the United States of wool-knit gloves and mittens manufactured in Japan, of all varieties, from March 1, 1936 to January 1, 1937 shall not exceed 200,000 dozen pairs.

3. If it should eventuate that the arrivals of all Japanese wool-knit gloves and mittens in American ports between January 1 and March 1, 1936 should exceed the estimated 150,000 dozen pairs, the Japanese exporters will undertake to restrict their shipments so that arrivals in the United States between March 1, 1936 and January 1, 1937 shall not exceed 200,000 dozen pairs less the amount by which arrivals between January 1 and March 1, 1936 exceed 150,000 dozen pairs.

4. Japanese exporters will so restrict their shipments to the United States of all grades and varieties of wool-knit gloves and mittens manufactured in Japan that the total arrivals in the United States during 1937 and 1938 shall not exceed 225,000 dozen pairs each calendar year.

It is in our judgment essential that the voluntary restriction undertaken by the Japanese interests should extend to at least three years in order that the American industry may have a permanently safeguarded position. Only an arrangement running at least this long could possibly assure a situation permitting the Executive to find action on the Tariff Commission's report unnecessary. For this reason this Government cannot consider any voluntary restriction arrangement covering merely 1936 adequate, and must suggest that the Japanese exporters undertake this longer-range control program if the alternative of voluntary restriction is to be adopted.

The market position of the American industry is such that if that industry is to operate with assured prospects during 1936, it is essential that some form of effective restriction of imports should begin to operate at the earliest possible date and, therefore, no time is available for a prolongation of the discussions between the Japanese Government and the American Government of the possibility of voluntary restriction. For the sake of stabilizing the American wool-knit glove market to the advantage of the industry in both countries and for the wider interests of Japanese-American trade, this Government sincerely hopes that the Japanese Government and the Japanese manufacturers and exporters concerned will be able to accept, no later than Wednesday February 19, the specific compromise suggestions of means of regulating this trade presented above. In the event that the Japanese interests cannot indicate by that date their acceptance of this proposal, action on the report of the Tariff Commission will become essential.

[WASHINGTON,] February 15, 1936.

611.943 Gloves/12

Memorandum by Mr. Roy Veatch of the Office of the Economic Adviser

[WASHINGTON,] February 15, 1936.

Conversation: Mr. Tsuneo Hayama, Third Secretary of the Japanese Embassy,
Mr. Feis,
Mr. Veatch.

Mr. Veatch called Mr. Hayama during the morning and asked if a decision had been reached at the Embassy as to whether the Ambassador would wish to come to the Department to receive the typed statement[31] prepared for the Embassy and to discuss the matter further or whether Mr. Hayama would come to the Department to receive this statement. Mr. Hayama said that the matter had been discussed after Mr. Yoshizawa's visit to the Department last evening and that it was agreed that Mr. Hayama should come for the statement.

Mr. Hayama came in to see Mr. Veatch, who handed him the Department's typed statement. Mr. Hayama read this statement carefully and repeated his understanding of the points made. He then said that he would like to raise one question which had occurred to him, although he had no instructions to bring up this point. Since the American Government was now proposing a three-year agreement, he wondered what commitment or responsibility of the American Government was implied for the entire period. Would the Japanese exporters be justified in assuming that there would be no fear of in-

[31] *Supra.*

crease of tariffs or taxes on imported wool-knit gloves during the three-year period? Mr. Veatch suggested that he would like to have Mr. Feis come in and express his opinion on this point.

Mr. Feis joined the discussion, and after hearing Mr. Hayama's question, he explained in some detail the division of authority in the American Government and the inability of the Executive to pledge the legislative branch with respect to future action or to pledge a subsequent administration even with respect to executive action. So far as this administration was concerned, however, the suggestion contained in the statement handed to Mr. Hayama included the pledge that the Executive during this administration would not proceed with the tariff action recommended in the Tariff Commission's report on wool-knit gloves if the Japanese exporters should agree to the proposed limitations. Furthermore, it might be assumed, in his opinion, that this administration would seek to discourage any tariff increases on wool-knit gloves during the life of the agreement and that probably in line with this policy the President would veto any such increases if by chance they were enacted by Congress. There would exist, of course, the possibility that Congress might pass such an act over the President's veto. Mr. Veatch and Mr. Feis were in agreement, however, that the purpose of the proposed agreement with the Japanese for voluntary restriction by Japanese exporters would be to discourage or prevent tariff increases on wool-knit gloves, and it was the opinion of the administration that control of shipments in the manner proposed in this statement would have the effect of removing the pressure for tariff action, not only now but during the life of the agreement.

Mr. Hayama said that after Mr. Yoshizawa's return from the Department of State the night before, they had sent a cable to Japan stating the main points of the American proposal. He would now make certain that those points agreed with the written statement just handed to him and he would dispatch a supplementary cable setting forth the details contained in this statement.

611.943 Gloves/16

Memorandum by Mr. Roy Veatch of the Office of the Economic Adviser

[WASHINGTON,] February 18, 1936.

Conversation: Mr. Tsuneo Hayama, Third Secretary of the Japanese Embassy,
Mr. Feis,
Mr. Veatch.

Mr. Hayama came to the Department shortly before one o'clock to inform us immediately of a cable which had come from Tokyo just a half hour earlier. This cable suggested certain changes in the American proposal and he had come to the Department quickly so that a reply could be sent to Tokyo later in the day, since Tokyo was under the necessity of giving a final answer to this Government by tomorrow, February 19.

The cable from Tokyo instructed the Japanese Embassy to offer what in effect was a counter-proposal. This proposal covered the following points:

(1) Japanese exporters to restrict shipments from Japan from March 1, 1936 to January 1, 1937, to 200,000 dozen pairs. This shift from arrivals in the United States to shipments from Japan was requested in order to allow the Japanese to set up their controls effectively and also to provide for accuracy and speed in compiling the statistics so that the exporters might exercise control more effectively.

(2) All shipments made from Japan prior to March 1, 1936 should fall outside of the limitation—this provision to serve as a substitute for the American proposal that only arrivals in the United States between January 1 and March 1, 1936, up to a maximum of 150,000 dozen pairs should be exempted from limitation.

(3) Agreement should be reached now only upon the first year with details of a second and third year to be settled at a later time when the facts regarding the probable effect of limitation upon the American market and the welfare of the American industry, and the facts regarding the total trade between the United States and Japan could be taken into consideration more adequately.

Mr. Hayama agreed to send a written statement of the Japanese counter-proposals [32] to the Department later in the afternoon.

Mr. Feis assured Mr. Hayama that he would bring the Japanese proposals to the attention of the Under Secretary of State as quickly as possible and that full consideration would be given the matter this afternoon—he saw no reason why a definite reply could not be given to the Japanese Embassy before evening.

As he left, Mr. Hayama said that he was somewhat embarrassed by the necessity of presenting these proposals but, of course, he had been instructed to do so. He felt personally that the people in Tokyo were a little stubborn and that they wanted to get everything they possibly could. He took it for granted, however, that the American reply to these counter-proposals could be given instantly and that it would have to be negative. He was assured, however, that the matter would be considered sympathetically here and that the considerations presented in the Japanese cable would be weighed carefully.

---

[32] Not printed.

611.943 Gloves/18

The Department of State to the Japanese Embassy [33]

Wool-Knit Gloves

The suggestions presented to the Department today regarding details of the proposed agreement have been given careful consideration. It would be impossible for the President to withhold action on the report of the Tariff Commission if voluntary restriction assumed by Japanese exporters should offer less adequate safeguards to the American industry than the arrangement set forth in the Department's statement of February 15.

This Government made the most liberal offer it could possibly make with respect to the period between March 1, 1936 and January 1, 1937. To shift to shipments from Japan during this period as a substitute for arrivals in the United States would have the effect of increasing considerably and to an indeterminate amount the total volume of imports of wool-knit gloves into the United States during this year. It is essential that arrivals in the United States of all wool-knit gloves manufactured in Japan for the period March 1, 1936 to January 1, 1937 shall be limited to 200,000 dozen pairs provided that arrivals of such gloves between January 1 and March 1, 1936 shall not exceed 150,000 dozen pairs, any excess over 150,000 dozen pairs during this two-month period to be subtracted from the limit of 200,000 dozen pairs during the ten months following.

It is essential also that the agreement cover at least three years and that it should definitely limit arrivals in the United States of all wool-knit gloves and mittens manufactured in Japan to 225,000 dozen pairs for each of the calendar years 1937 and 1938, and that definite announcement of this agreement and its terms should be made if the President is to be justified in refraining from the action recommended in the report of the Tariff Commission.

Should the circumstances determining the position of the American industry develop subsequently in such a way as to warrant increased importation consistently with the welfare of the American industry, and should the Japanese Government then wish to propose in the light of this situation that the voluntary limitation on arrivals in the United States for the subsequent calendar year be made more liberal, this Government would, of course, give consideration to any such proposals.

[Washington,] February 18, 1936.

---

[33] Handed to the Third Secretary of the Japanese Embassy by Mr. Veatch, February 18.

611.9417/79

The Ambassador in Japan (Grew) to the Secretary of State

No. 1690   Tokyo, February 19, 1936.
                                                   [Received March 9.]

SIR: I have the honor to report that Mr. Dickover of this Embassy had a conversation with Mr. Saburo Kurusu, Chief of the Bureau of Commercial Affairs of the Foreign Office, on February 16, 1936, in which Mr. Kurusu expressed a certain amount of disagreement with the policy of the Department of State in considering seriously the various petitions from American manufacturers for the restriction by informal trade agreements of small items of Japanese exports to the United States. Without attempting to reproduce the entire conversation, which lasted some two hours, a summary of Mr. Kurusu's argument is given below.

Mr. Kurusu said that formerly, when American manufacturers who might actually represent very insignificant interests wanted protection from the competition of foreign goods, they approached their Congressmen with petitions for higher tariff rates on the competing articles. The Congressmen, obliged to consider the interests of their constituents, usually succeeded in obtaining the tariff increases by the "log-rolling" system, even though only a very small group of people might be benefitted by the tariff increases, at the expense of the rest of the nation. This system, however, naturally resulted in excessively high tariff walls and apparently has been abandoned by the United States, which has substituted trade agreements for tariffs as a means of restricting competition from abroad. American manufacturers now go to the Department of State with their petitions for the restriction of imports of competing goods from foreign countries.

Mr. Kurusu said that the dissatisfaction in Japan now arises because the Department apparently, like the Congressmen in former days, gives consideration to every petition which comes in, even though the industry in question may only give employment to five or six small factories in New Jersey. Therefore the result is the same as it was in the days of tariff legislation. The Japanese are faced with the restriction or prohibition of the imports of their goods, even though the items in question may be small, such as velveteen or woolen gloves, which the Department has brought up recently. The imports of velveteen from Japan into the United States amount only to around a quarter of a million dollars per annum, and the imports of woolen gloves amount only to around $125,000. These are insignificant items as compared with the total foreign trade of the United States, and are especially insignificant when the fact is taken into consideration that the United States has a large excess of exports to Japan over imports from Japan.

Mr. Dickover remarked that the American excess of exports was due largely to the Japanese purchases of American raw cotton, and that it was a well-known fact that the Japanese were searching eagerly, in North China, the Philippines, Siam, Brazil and elsewhere, for other sources of a supply of cotton than the United States. If Japan succeeded in reducing its imports of cotton from the United States, the United States would have to look for other markets for its cotton and would have to conserve its domestic market for cotton textiles. That was one reason why we were trying to protect our domestic markets.

Mr. Kurusu ridiculed the idea, held by many Japanese, that Japan could in the near future find other sources of raw cotton than the United States. The development of cotton growing in North China or Brazil would take twenty years or more. In Japan, however, the restriction of exports of small items to the United States creates present difficulties. Not only are the people becoming restive under the pin-pricks of requests from the Foreign Office for voluntary restriction of their exports to the United States, but the Foreign Office itself is hampered in its work of trying to assist the American manufacturers of and dealers in petroleum products and automobiles. The importation and sale of American petroleum products have already been put upon a quota basis by the Petroleum Industry Law, and the importation of American automobile parts and their assembly in Japan will be restricted as soon as the Diet passes the proposed Automobile Industry Law. He (Mr. Kurusu) has been fighting to obtain more liberal treatment for American oil and automobiles, but now his efforts are being met with the argument that the United States is restricting, or asking the Japanese to restrict, all sorts of Japanese commodities, including cotton textiles, canned tuna, pencils, porcelains, matches, cotton rugs, velveteen and woolen gloves. These are small items, but their restriction is encouraging the Japanese to ask their Government for restriction of large items of exports from the United States to Japan, such as petroleum products and automobiles, the Japanese purchases of which amount to many millions of dollars annually. Mr. Kurusu therefore was of the opinion that if we hoped to obtain more liberal treatment of our large items of export to Japan, we should not irritate the Japanese by asking them to restrict their exports of small items to the United States.

The *Asahi* of February 15, 1936, contained an article (which may have been inspired by the Foreign Office) to the effect that, although Japanese imports from the United States exceeded Japanese exports to the United States in 1935 by Yen 274,000,000, the United States is trying to check imports from Japan, such attempts having become more and more frequent recently. The Japanese Foreign Office, fearing friction in American-Japanese commercial relations over these minor matters, has been endeavoring to exercise control over the exports of sundry articles, but despite these efforts, the tendency in the United States to restrict imports from Japan is growing stronger. The indications now are that the Foreign Office has decided to adopt the firm attitude of refusing further American demands of this nature, in view of the present excess of imports from the United States over exports to that country.   (The article continues with the statement that when Mr. Grew, the American Ambassador, left Japan recently on leave of absence, Mr. Hirota proposed to him an adjustment of trade relations between the United States and Japan, but that the Ambassador returned to his post from leave without having secured any definite opinion from the American Government, as his attention while at home was occupied with the Presidential election which was then taking place!)

There is enclosed a clipping from the *Osaka Mainichi* and *Tokyo Nichi Nichi*, English Edition, of February 13, 1936,[34] containing an editorial on the subject of American-Japanese trade. The newspaper states that the moves in the United States to restrict the imports of Japanese cotton textiles cannot be understood in Japan, in view of the large excess of exports to Japan over imports from Japan. The newspaper advises the conclusion of a reciprocal economic agreement (presumably similar to that concluded between Japan and British India), whereby in return for guaranteeing the purchase of a stipulated amount of raw cotton, the Japanese will be permitted to sell a stipulated amount of cotton textiles in the United States. Such an agreement is advocated "so as to solve the basic problem and seal forever the sources of American complaint".

These two articles, taken in connection with Mr. Kurusu's conversation with Mr. Dickover, indicate a very real and growing resentment in Japan against continued requests from the United States that the Japanese exporters voluntarily restrict their shipments to the United States. The Embassy is also inclined to share the opinion of Mr. Kurusu that it may become increasingly difficult to obtain liberal treatment for American manufactured goods in Japan if we continue to ask the Japanese to restrict their exports to the United States.

Respectfully yours,   JOSEPH C. GREW

---

[34] Not reprinted.

611.943 Gloves/25

The Secretary of State to President Roosevelt

WASHINGTON, February 20, 1936.

MY DEAR MR. PRESIDENT: I return herewith the report of the United States Tariff Commission on its investigation of wool knit gloves and mittens, under the provisions of Section 336 of the Tariff Act of 1930, which you referred to me on February 12, 1936, for recommendation.

On the basis of its investigation, the Commission finds that the existing rate of duty on knit gloves and knit mittens, finished or unfinished, wholly or in chief value of wool and valued at not more than $1.75 per dozen pairs, does not equalize the difference in costs of production, as defined in Section 336, of the domestic articles and the like or similar foreign articles produced in the principal competing country, Japan. The Commission finds that within the limits permitted by law, the duty necessary to equalize such costs can be achieved only by shifting from foreign value to American selling price. It accordingly recommends that the rates of duty upon this class of wool knit gloves and mittens be increased to forty cents per pound and 35 percent ad valorem based upon the American selling price as defined in Section 402 (*g*) of the Tariff Act of 1930, of knit gloves and knit mittens, finished or unfinished, wholly or in chief value of wool, manufactured or produced in the United States. The effect of this action would be to increase the existing rate of duty very substantially, roughly an increase from 70 to 150 percent ad valorem.

In anticipation of the nature of the finding which would be indicated by the Commission's investigation, and in view of the expressed desire of the Japanese Government to be afforded an opportunity for its exporters voluntarily to control exports to the United States of commodities in which the United States would be forced to take restrictive action in the absence of such control, the Executive Committee on Commercial Policy recommended that the Japanese Government be approached to discover whether that Government or the Japanese exporters could undertake to control exports of wool knit gloves to this country so as to remove the excessive threat to the domestic industry offered by the large imports of recent months.

Negotiations have accordingly been conducted to this end. I have to inform you, however, that the Japanese Government has found itself unable to agree to the most liberal terms which this Government feels to be consistent with the welfare of the domestic industry. The

Executive Committee on Commercial Policy believes that in view of the fact that now is the time when orders for these gloves are customarily placed, these negotiations cannot be further prolonged and indeed a prolongation would appear to offer no chance of a satisfactory agreement. It therefore recommends that the findings of the Tariff Commission be approved as promptly as possible.

The method of American valuation recommended in the report of the Tariff Commission is an extreme measure which almost amounts to an embargo with regard to the specific goods to which it is made applicable. In my judgment, therefore, it should not be used except where the matter is most urgent and no alternative possible. I do not wish, therefore, in any sense to commit myself to this use of American valuation as a permanent or frequently employed policy with respect to any set of conditions.

The present instance, however, seems to present such immediate conditions of exigency as to call for affirmative action, especially in view of the present indisposition or inability of the Japanese industry to undertake any reasonable voluntary adjustment of their exports of wool-knit gloves to this country. This unusual and extreme step may be necessary to induce Japanese industry to deal more effectively with such situations as this. I, therefore, concur in the recommendation of the Tariff Commission.[35] I sincerely trust, however, that this method of valuation can be avoided in dealing with all other situations.

Faithfully yours,   CORDELL HULL

611B.9417/135

Memorandum by Mr. Roy Veatch of the Office of the Economic Adviser

[WASHINGTON,] February 26, 1936.

Mr. Yoshizawa came in late in the afternoon with an instruction from Tokyo. Before discussing the points raised in this despatch, he asked if it was the understanding of the Department that an adjustment of the Philippine textile agreement had been finally arranged. In response Mr. Veatch said that apparently the two Governments were in agreement on at least two of the main points, restriction of imports during the second half year of the agreement of 15,000,000 square meters and the use of arrival statistics from now on. Mr. Sayre had just returned and it was probable that he would wish to call the Ambassador on Thursday or Friday to discuss the final understanding of this adjustment.

---

[35] The President issued a proclamation dated February 21; 49 Stat. 3497.

Mr. Veatch mentioned the fact that one feature of the proposed adjustment apparently remained uncertain since the American Embassy in Tokyo had been informed by Mr. Kurusu that he would transmit to the Exporters Association the American suggestion that the quota of 45,000,000 square meters for the second year should not be increased by 4,000,000 square meters. No further word had been received regarding this matter.

Mr· Yoshizawa at first stated that information which the Embassy here had received from the Foreign Office indicated that the exporters were willing to agree to the American suggestion regarding this point, but then he apparently feared that he had gone too far and stated that the information the Embassy had received was along the same lines as that received by this Government through the American Embassy in Tokyo.

Mr. Yoshizawa said that the point which he was instructed to raise with the Department was again the question of control of shipments of Japanese goods via Hong Kong. He said that the Japanese position from the beginning had been that the United States should control arrivals of such transshipped goods and that the Japanese exporters themselves were in no position to exercise control over these transshipments. Imports into the Philippines of Japanese goods from Hong Kong had increased rapidly in recent weeks, reaching a total of 2,000,000 square meters, and the problem was becoming so important that something must be done about it. If this development were allowed to take its course it would nullify the agreement. Japanese exporters are not satisfied with the present situation and are making strong complaints. In connection with this last point Mr. Yoshizawa made the following statement: "That means that at any time they may be compelled to take some action to cope with the situation."

The difficulty is being caused by importations into the Philippines from Hong Kong by Chinese dealers in the Philippines. Not much difficulty was experienced in this way at first because the Chinese importers fully expected that the Philippine Government or the United States Government would prevent or control goods arriving from Hong Kong. Now that they have come to realize that such shipments are not to be controlled by the Philippines or the United States they have begun to buy large amounts of goods in Hong Kong and will be able to import any quantity that they desire. The fact that the Japanese exporters have limited their shipments to the Philippines has decreased stocks and created a greater demand for these goods so that the Chinese merchants are able to sell in a better market and are encouraged to bring in goods from Hong Kong.

The Chinese importers and the Chinese dealers in Hong Kong have resorted to various forms of subterfuge to cover up part of this trade. The original marks of origin have been torn off in Hong Kong and new ones put on the goods, and in some cases goods have been put through some form of processing in Hong Kong so that they might be imported into Manila as Chinese goods.

The Japanese exporters and the Japanese dealers in the Philippines have attempted to increase prices so that they might take some advantage of the better market created by the limitations they have placed upon the supply of their own goods. Their efforts to profit by this situation have been checked, however, by the competition of cheaper goods brought in from Hong Kong by the Chinese dealers. Furthermore, the Japanese fear that they will lose the foothold which they had gained in the wholesale and retail business in the Philippines, following the Chinese boycott of Japanese goods in 1932. Japanese exporters to the Philippines favor Japanese dealers in the Philippines and, if part of the quota is used up by Chinese importing through Hong Kong, then the Japanese dealers will have their supplies further restricted.

The Japanese Government again wishes to urge very strongly that the United States do something about this problem.

Mr. Veatch explained the feeling here that the problem was primarily a matter to be dealt with by the Japanese exporters. In any event, the Americans had gained the impression that the Japanese exporters were not being forced to make any sacrifice by this development. If more Japanese goods were brought in from Hong Kong, limiting the quantity of Japanese shipments directly to the Philippines, then the market for Japanese goods in Hong Kong was increased to a like extent.

After discussion Mr. Yoshizawa agreed that the Japanese were really concerned only over the following two points.

1. They are unable to raise the prices of their goods in the Philippines to any great extent and thus are hampered in their efforts to prevent loss by restriction of the quantity of their exports to the Philippines.

2. Japanese dealers in the Philippines are threatened with loss of business to their Chinese competitors.

Mr. Yoshizawa stressed again the fact that the Japanese themselves are not seeking in any way to evade the agreement by shipping goods through Hong Kong. Japanese importers in the Philippines have been urged not to purchase goods through Hong Kong, and Mitsui and Company, the only Japanese concern which had brought in goods through Hong Kong, had discontinued this practice some months ago. The whole difficulty was caused by the activities of Chinese importers in the Philippines.

Mr. Veatch explained that the best informed officials in Washington had been called in to conferences to study this problem but that no method for controlling arrivals in the Philippines of Japanese goods transshipped through Hong Kong or other ports had been discovered short of legislation in the Philippines to embargo or restrict such arrivals. The Philippine legislature does not meet again until June. Of course, there is no way of telling whether the Philippine Government would wish to institute such control even then, but at least in the meantime there appeared to be no way of handling the situation in the Philippines. Our only suggestion was that Japanese exporters might be able to control this trade through agreements with the dealers in Hong Kong.

Mr. Yoshizawa thought that it would be impossible for the Japanese exporters to arrange any such understanding with the dealers in Hong Kong. If these dealers saw this opportunity for increased business and profits the Japanese exporters could hardly bring sufficient pressure to bear upon them to lead them to give up this business.

Mr. Yoshizawa asked if this Government had considered the possibility of controlling shipments of Japanese goods from Hong Kong by means of denying consular invoices for such shipments. He said that Dr. Waring had had a long conference with people concerned in Japan (It was not clear whether he meant exporters or Government officials) and that the Japanese had gained the impression that Dr. Waring would propose this method of controlling shipments when he arrived in Washington.

Mr. Yoshizawa took this opportunity to mention again the fact that there was increasing discussion in Japan of the desirability of balancing strictly the commodity trade between the United States and Japan and at the same time increasing irritation caused by the number of separate requests for restriction of Japanese exports to the United States or its possessions. Some weeks ago in a despatch to the Japanese Embassy here the Foreign Office had mentioned the possibility of reaching some general agreement with the United States covering trade problems. The Foreign Office had again referred to this possibility and had now requested the Ambassador to report his ideas regarding such a possibility.

Mr. Yoshizawa suggested that in the event Mr. Sayre does request the Ambassador to call upon him in order to discuss the Philippine agreement it is quite possible that the Ambassador will refer to this possibility of an agreement or an understanding regarding trade matters along more general lines. Mr. Yoshizawa requested, therefore, that Mr. Sayre be informed of the interest of the Japanese Government in this possibility so that he might be prepared to discuss the matter at least in a preliminary way with the Ambassador.

Mr. Yoshizawa asked also that his discussion of the transshipment problem be laid before Mr. Sayre in detail so that he might be prepared to discuss this matter with the Ambassador.

611B.9417/140

Memorandum by Mr. Roy Veatch of the Office of the Economic Adviser

[WASHINGTON,] March 3, 1936.

Conversation: The Japanese Ambassador,
            Mr. Seijiro Yoshizawa, Counselor of the Japanese Embassy,
            Mr. Sayre,
            Mr. Coville,[36]
            Mr. Veatch.

Mr. Sayre explained that he had asked the Japanese Ambassador to come in for a further discussion of readjustment of the agreement concluded October 11, 1935, regarding voluntary limitation by Japanese exporters of importations into the Philippines of Japanese cotton piece goods. It was his impression that the two Governments might now be ready to agree upon the final adjustment. The suggestions of the Japanese Government had been discussed with the American textile people and with the Interdepartmental Committee on the Philippines and Mr. Sayre believed that this Government is now ready to accept these suggestions.

Mr. Sayre then handed the Japanese Ambassador and Mr. Yoshizawa copies of a draft of a memorandum of conversation,[37] which might be initialed by the Ambassador and Mr. Sayre, and this draft was read aloud.

The Ambassador's first remark upon the draft was to the effect that it did not mention the question of transshipments of Japanese goods via Hongkong or other ports. The Ambassador and Mr. Yoshizawa then spoke at some length of this problem. Their extensive remarks on this subject may be summarized in the following points:

1. Japanese cotton goods shipped by Japanese exporters to the Philippines via Hongkong or by means of transshipments in Hongkong can be limited or controlled by the Japanese exporters in the same manner that direct shipments to the Philippines are controlled;

2. Goods which are exported from Japan for the Hongkong market and which may then be resold by dealers in Hongkong (chiefly Chinese dealers) to Chinese importers in the Philippines create a very special problem with which the Japanese exporters cannot deal. These exporters know of no effective way of controlling or limiting the resale and reshipment to the Philippines of such goods;

---

[36] Cabot Coville, Second Secretary of Embassy in Japan, temporarily in Washington.
[37] *Infra.*

3. From the very beginning the Japanese Embassy, particularly through Mr. Yoshizawa, has stated that Japanese exporters could not be held responsible for shipments to the Philippines which they could not control;

[4.] Japanese exporters have considered that Japanese goods reshipped from Hongkong into the Philippines by dealers in Hongkong are not covered by the agreement and are not to be included in the quota of Philippine imports of Japanese goods which the Japanese exporters accepted under the agreement.

5. At the time the agreement was made Japanese goods transshipped via Hongkong formed a negligible part of the entire Philippine importation of Japanese cotton piece goods. Recently, however, Chinese importers in the Philippines have begun to bring in large amounts of Japanese goods from Hongkong.

6. Japanese exporters and the Japanese Government have recognized that this development would endanger the market for American cotton textiles in the Philippines since they considered these shipments to be made outside of the limits which they had accepted and the Japanese Embassy had, therefore, warned the American Government repeatedly that the American Government or the Philippine Government would have to control such transshipments. The Japanese Government and the Japanese exporters are entirely willing to have the Philippine Government restrict or prevent entirely arrivals of Japanese goods transshipped through Hongkong or other ports—Japanese exporters have no desire whatever to evade the agreement by encouraging such transshipments.

7. The only practical suggestion that the Japanese Government is able to make to the Government of the United States with respect to handling this problem is the possibility of denying American consular invoices for the reshipment of Japanese goods from Hongkong to the Philippines.

Mr. Sayre explained in some detail the definite understanding of this Government regarding the way in which the question of transshipments was handled in the original agreement. He reminded the Ambassador that they had discussed the problem before the agreement was reached and that at the time the memorandum of conversation regarding the agreement was read and initialed by the Ambassador Mr. Sayre had called particular attention to the fact that the agreement provided that Japanese goods transshipped via Hongkong or other ports were included in the total amount of Japanese goods to be imported into the Philippine Islands under the agreement. The agreement refers specifically to the fact that the Philippine customs statistics of imports of Japanese goods are to be used as the measure of the amounts of Japanese goods to fall under the limitation established by the agreement. Mr. Sayre had explained to the Ambassador at the time that the Philippine customs statistics included as Japanese goods all goods originating in Japan no matter what the route of shipment or transshipment might be. Mr. Sayre said that he had understood that there had been no disagreement about this provision of the agreement and no misunderstanding as to its meaning and he supposed that the Japanese Government was not now questioning that provision of the agreement.

The Japanese Ambassador and Mr. Yoshizawa were a little uncertain in their response to Mr. Sayre's direct questioning as to their understanding of the agreement on this point. The Ambassador nodded his head frequently in agreement with Mr. Sayre's statements and Mr. Yoshizawa said that in view of the fact that transshipments via Hongkong were negligible at the time the agreement was reached last October the Japanese Government had not objected then to the American suggestion although it did insist that no special mention be made in the agreement to the effect that Japanese goods transshipped via Hongkong would be included in the total amounts of Japanese goods to be imported into the Philippines. These statements of Mr. Yoshizawa left some uncertainty as to his exact meaning, but later in the discussion he made the following statement: "I want you to understand, Mr. Sayre, that I have stated frequently, and you have agreed, that we shouldn't be held responsible for shipments we could not control", and Mr. Yoshizawa's further discussion left no doubt of the fact that he was referring to Japanese goods shipped for the Hongkong market and resold there by Hongkong dealers to the Philippines.

Mr. Sayre took occasion at this point to inform Mr. Yoshizawa that neither Mr. Sayre nor anyone else in this Government had agreed to the exclusion from the limits of the agreement of any Japanese goods transshipped via Hongkong. The agreement was based on the Philippine customs statistics which included all such goods.

Mr. Yoshizawa expressed his belief that there should be inserted in the draft memorandum of conversation which had just been read a statement that the Japanese Ambassador had said that the Japanese Government and Japanese exporters could not accept any responsibility for Japanese goods reshipped from Hongkong or some other port to the Philippines.

In reply Mr. Sayre said that this Government could not consider for a moment excluding transshipped goods from the limitations established by the agreement. Such exclusion would defeat the purpose of the agreement. If the agreement were to be nullified by such a demand on the part of the Japanese then the only alternative would be more extreme action by the Philippines, placing even greater restrictions upon the importation of Japanese textiles into the Philippines. This Government had opposed such extreme measures and had sought this voluntary arrangement which was designed to have the effect of dividing equally between Japanese and American textile exporters the total Philippine market for Japanese and American cotton goods.

The Japanese Ambassador and Mr. Yoshizawa agreed that the Japanese Government would have no objection to a system of quotas to be imposed by the Philippine Government upon imports of cotton piece goods from all sources, so that imports of cheap cotton goods from Hongkong, Shanghai, British India, or other sources, would not capture the market created by limitations of Japanese exports to the Philippines and thus prevent the recapture of some of the Philippine market for American cotton goods. The Ambassador and Mr. Yoshizawa were warned, however, that once the question of quotas be raised in the Philippines it would be difficult to control the action of the Philippine Government upon such a proposal. There probably would be great pressure to set a quota for Japanese goods much below that established by the present agreement. Furthermore, quota action by the Philippine Assembly on this question might create the demand for quotas on many other commodities imported into the Philippines and might lead to ever increasing restrictions upon imports of Japanese goods.

The conversation returned repeatedly to the question of whether or not the agreement provided that all Japanese goods transshipped via Hongkong should be included in the reckoning of the amounts of Japanese goods to be imported into the Philippines under the limits established by the agreement. When the Japanese Ambassador and Mr. Yoshizawa were asked specifically if they had the intention of denying that such transshipments were not covered by the agreement they found it difficult to reply directly. They did leave no doubt, however, that the Japanese exporters have no intention of having such transshipments charged against the total which they have accepted as the limit of their imports into the Philippines. The "legal" question was not finally settled in the discussion but it was agreed that whatever the conflicting interpretations of the agreement might be the question of transshipments was a practical question which should be handled if possible.

Mr. Yoshizawa had stressed particularly the way in which inclusion of considerable amounts of transshipped goods in the quota which the Japanese exporters accept would upset their method of allocating this quota to the various exporters for an entire half year in advance. In view of this situation and the fact that no one knows how much Japanese goods will be shipped into the Philippines from Hongkong during the next few months, Mr. Sayre suggested that the Japanese exporters might shift from the system of allocating quotas by six months periods to an allocation month by month so that the amount of goods shipped into the Philippines from Hongkong in any one month might be subtracted from the total to be allocated to the exporters who will ship directly from Japan to the Philippines during the succeeding month or the second month succeeding.

Mr. Yoshizawa said that of course the Ambassador would submit this suggestion to his Government but Mr. Yoshizawa doubted that the exporters would be able to accept it.

Mr. Sayre asked the Ambassador what he felt should be done next. He wondered if the Ambassador would be able to transmit the text of the draft memorandum of conversation to Tokyo with the suggestion that he be authorized to initial it and that then both governments would continue to make every effort to find a solution to the transshipments problem.

To this suggestion the Ambassador was somewhat noncommittal. He would be glad of course to transmit the draft memorandum but both he and Mr. Yoshizawa seemed to feel that it would be necessary to do something about the transshipment problem before the draft could be initialed in its present form—if there were no direct solution of that problem then the Japanese would find it necessary to insert in such a memorandum of conversation the statement that the Japanese exporters would not be held responsible for shipments of Japanese goods into the Philippines over which they had no control. It was apparent that the proposed readjustment of the agreement, set forth in this memorandum, would be unsatisfactory, if not entirely meaningless, without a clear understanding as to the inclusion of all transshipped goods in the quota to be accepted by the Japanese exporters.

The Japanese Ambassador said that he would refer to his Government the draft memorandum which had been given to him and would report fully upon the point of view and the opinions of this Government. Mr. Sayre in turn said that this Government recognized that transshipments were a practical difficulty and that this Government would explore every possibility of assisting in some way or other in meeting this problem. If in the meantime it proved impracticable to initial such a memorandum as he had presented to the Japanese Ambassador he hoped that the Japanese exporters would hold their shipments to the Philippines to moderate levels. He assumed that in spite of the difficulties over transshipments and the practical problem that had arisen there was no question as to the meaning of the original agreement with respect to such transshipped goods.

In his final comment on this last point, Mr. Yoshizawa said that the instruction which the Embassy had received from Tokyo on the transshipment problem did not make any specific statement as to the wording or the interpretation of the wording of the agreement. It merely instructed the Embassy to get the United States Government to corroborate the understanding of the Japanese Government that the Japanese exporters should not be held responsible for any shipments of Japanese goods into the Philippines over which they could exercise no control and to suggest that the American Government or the Philippine Government take steps to control such transshipments.

611B.9417/140

The Department of State to the Japanese Embassy [38]

[WASHINGTON,] March 3, 1936.

The Japanese Ambassador, accompanied by Mr. Yoshizawa, Counselor of the Embassy, called on Mr. Sayre, Assistant Secretary of State on March 3, 1936.

The Japanese Ambassador stated that he was authorized by his Government to inform the Government of the United States that the Association of Japanese Exporters of Cotton Piece Goods to the Philippine Islands has agreed to the following voluntary adjustments of certain details of the arrangement* instituted by the Association to limit imports of Japanese cotton piece goods into the Philippine Islands for the two-year period August 1, 1935 to July 31, 1937:

1. The total amount of Japanese cotton piece goods to be imported into the Philippines during the period February 1, 1936, to August 1, 1936, will not exceed fifteen million square meters.

2. Statistics of arrivals in the Philippines of Japanese cotton piece goods compiled by the Philippine customs service will be employed as the measure of Japanese cotton piece goods imported into the Philippines from February 1, 1936, to the termination of the agreement.

3. The total amount of Japanese cotton piece goods to be imported into the Philippines between the present time and August 1, 1936, will be distributed evenly so far as possible over the intervening period.

4. The total amount of Japanese cotton piece goods to be imported into the Philippines for the twelve months following August 1, 1936, as measured by Philippine customs statistics of physical arrivals, will not exceed forty-five million square meters.

5. It will be the intention of the Japanese exporters to distribute evenly insofar as possible over the twelve months period the total amount of Japanese cotton piece goods to be imported into the Philippines during the second year of the agreement, August 1, 1936, to July 31, 1937. Furthermore, some definite limitation of the amounts to be imported monthly or quarterly during this period will be established as soon as possible. In any event imports will not exceed twenty-six million square meters in either semester of this year.

---

[38] Handed by Assistant Secretary of State Sayre to the Japanese Ambassador, March 3, for reference to the Japanese Government.

*The Department was informed of this arrangement, through Mr. Sayre, by the Japanese Ambassador on October 11, 1935, and the details of the arrangement were set forth in a memorandum of conversation of that date initialled by the Japanese Ambassador and Mr. Sayre. [Footnote in the original; for memorandum, see *Foreign Relations*, 1935, vol. III, p. 1007.]

Mr. Sayre stated on behalf of the Secretary of State that the Government of the United States was pleased to accept these adjustments of the original agreement and that in doing so it would adhere strictly to its stated intention to take no initiative during the life of the agreement toward securing an increase in the Philippine tariff rates on cotton piece goods. Mr. Sayre made the further statement that the agreement implies in no way any limitation upon the full liberty of action of the Philippine Government or upon the freedom of the Government of the United States to consider without prejudice any action taken by the Philippine Government, and the Japanese Ambassador assured Mr. Sayre that this statement was clearly understood.

Mr. Sayre agreed fully to the understanding of the Japanese Government that the agreement referred only to cotton piece goods but he voiced regret that Japanese exporters had not agreed to similar limitations upon Philippine imports of Japanese rayon piece goods, and he expressed the opinion that the policy pursued by Japanese textile exporters with respect to shipments of rayon goods to the Philippines will be a very important factor in determining whether or not the cotton textile agreement is to work satisfactorily. With reference to this point, the Japanese Ambassador informed Mr. Sayre that the opinions and concern expressed by the American Government had been placed clearly before the Japanese exporters of rayon goods

---

611.9417/81

Memorandum by Mr. Roy Veatch of the Office of the Economic Adviser

[WASHINGTON,] March 9, 1936.

Conversation: Mr. Seijiro Yoshizawa, Counsellor of the Japanese Embassy,
Mr. Feis,
Mr. Veatch.

Mr. Feis handed Mr. Yoshizawa copies of a table of statistics [39] showing the United States imports of countable cotton cloth from Japan monthly during 1935 and during January, 1936. He pointed out that the January statistics, both of imports for consumption (goods actually entered through customs) and general imports (goods arriving in American ports), were much higher than at any time during the last six months of 1935. Imports for consumption in January were almost fifty percent higher than during any month of 1935

---

[39] Not printed.

and general imports for January were exceeded only in the month of February, 1935. It was quite apparent that imports in January again showed the abnormal increase which had characterized imports of such goods from Japan during the early part of 1935.

Mr. Feis explained that the Department was bringing these statistics to the attention of the Japanese Embassy at the earliest possible moment so that the Japanese Government and the Japanese exporters might have an opportunity to take some action regarding this trade if they felt it wise to do so. This rapid increase in imports was almost certain to arouse again the strong opposition of the American industry to such imports and to create great pressure upon the Government to set up some drastic means of restricting these imports. These figures had just been received from the Commerce Department and had not yet been published and, with the desire of being foresighted in this instance, the Department was bringing them to the attention of the Japanese Embassy so that they might be cabled to Tokyo if the Embassy so desired.

Mr. Yoshizawa agreed that the increase in imports of these goods into the United States during January was very marked. He said that he understood that they were being brought to the attention of the Japanese Embassy as a warning to the Japanese Government.

Mr. Feis said that in a way this was true but it was not that the State Department wished to warn the Japanese Government. Rather, the Department merely wished to give the Japanese Government the advantage of an understanding of the circumstances. Mr. Yoshizawa was reminded of the campaign of the cotton textile industry in New England during the early part of 1935 against Japanese competition and it was pointed out that opposition to imports from Japan had been growing in the South as well as in New England so that if occasion were given for new protests it was probable that the industry would be united in such protests and would thus be able to bring much greater pressure to bear upon the Government.

Mr. Feis said that of course he was not authorized to make any promises whatsoever but that he believed that if imports from Japan had continued at the levels at which they had been held during the latter half of 1935 it would be possible for this Government to avoid placing further restrictions upon imports of cotton piece goods from Japan. If the heavy importations of January continue, however, it would be very difficult, if not impossible, for the Government to withstand the pressure for action. Undoubtedly it would wish to prevent added restrictions but pressure would be very difficult to withstand, especially during this election year. As Mr. Yoshizawa knew, the Tariff Commission has been engaged in investigation of the cost of production of cotton piece goods for some months. A report on this investigation will be ready some time in the near future.   Action with respect to this report would necessarily be influenced by the course of imports of cotton piece goods from Japan.

Mr. Yoshizawa said that he would transmit to his Government the statistics which had been handed him as well as the statement which Mr. Feis had made.

611B.9417/190

Memorandum by Mr. Roy Veatch of the Office of the Economic Adviser

[WASHINGTON,] March 13, 1936.

Mr. Yoshizawa called by on his way to an appointment in the Department and said informally that the Embassy had received a cable from Tokyo regarding the memorandum which Mr. Sayre had handed to the Ambassador on March 3.   This cable from Tokyo had merely requested clarification of certain points, however, and the Japanese Embassy was able to answer the questions raised.

No final word has been received from Tokyo as yet, but Mr. Yoshizawa said that he might tell me confidentially that the Japanese exporters were willing to agree that the quota for the second year should not be increased by 4,000,000 square meters (the amount by which they agreed to reduce the quota, based on arrivals, for the first year) provided that the American Government or the Philippine Government should do something about transshipments.

611B.9417/146

Memorandum by Mr. Roy Veatch of the Office of the Economic Adviser of a Conversation With the Counselor of the Japanese Embassy (Yoshizawa)

[WASHINGTON,] March 23, 1936.

IMPORTS INTO THE UNITED STATES

Mr. Yoshizawa said that the Embassy had received no comment from the Foreign Office in Tokyo upon the information which had been cabled to the Foreign Office regarding the statistics of imports of Japanese cotton piece goods into the United States in January. Mr. Yoshizawa was in New York over the last week-end, however, and he found that on Friday night the importers of Japanese cotton textiles had planned a dinner to discuss their interests and he asked, therefore, if he might attend and discuss the matter with them.   They welcomed him and he talked at some length with this group, which included two representatives from each of the important import firms.

At this dinner Mr. Yoshizawa attempted to explain carefully the attitude of the Department of State and the concern of the Department over the pressure which would be brought upon the American Government to take restrictive action as a result of heavy importations of cotton piece goods from Japan. He urged upon the importers, therefore, the desirability of not importing "in a rush" and he explained to them the fact that the Japanese Government had given assurances to this Government (he commented that they were informal but, nevertheless, assurances) that it would be unlikely that imports of Japanese cotton piece goods should again be as high as they were during the first months of last year. (Mr. Yoshizawa used practically these exact words and left no doubt but that the interpretation of the assurances expressed by the Ambassador to Mr. Sayre on December 21 [40] were interpreted by the Japanese Embassy in the same way that they have been interpreted in the Department.)

Mr. Yoshizawa said that he would be very glad to send another cable to the Foreign Office stating that this Department was feeling the pressure of the domestic textile interests as a result of the publication of the January import statistics. It was agreed, however, that it probably would be better to withhold such a cable until after the Ambassador calls upon Mr. Sayre.

PHILIPPINE TEXTILE AGREEMENT

Mr. Yoshizawa said that the Embassy had received several days ago a reply from the Foreign Office discussing the memorandum of conversation which Mr. Sayre had proposed for initialing by the Ambassador and himself. This reply from Tokyo had raised a number of questions regarding which Mr. Yoshizawa had then sent a further cable. Mr. Yoshizawa now had the final comment of his Government upon this matter and wished to place it before Mr. Veatch so that the Department might have an opportunity to discuss it before the Ambassador and Mr. Sayre should go into the matter again.

The Foreign Office felt that there had been some misunderstanding between the American Embassy in Tokyo and the Department of State because the Foreign Office had the impression that the discussions had not reached a stage in which a memorandum of agreement could be initialed. The Foreign Office had succeeded in securing the agreement of the Japanese exporters to a limitation of imports into the Philippines during the six month period ending July 31, 1936, to a total of 15,000,000 square meters, but this agreement was on the condition that the American Government would do something regard-

---

[40] See memorandum of December 21, 1935, *Foreign Relations*, 1935, vol. III, p. 1037.

ing the imports into the Philippines from Hong Kong and that the 4,000,000 square meters which they would sacrifice by accepting such limitation should be added to their quota for the second year of the agreement. The Foreign Office had passed on to the Exporters Association the American proposal that the 4,000,000 square meters be sacrificed but it had received no definite response from the Association. He might say, however, (and I took this statement down almost verbatim) that the Foreign Office understands that the Exporters Association might be agreeable to the American suggestion that the 4,000,000 square meters should not be transferred to the quota for the second year if the whole agreement can be carried out satisfactorily, particularly if transshipments from Hong Kong can be dealt with satisfactorily. The Japanese Government and the exporters are making an effort to satisfy the "requirements" of the American position and they feel that the American Government should try to do something to meet the difficulties Japanese exporters are experiencing because of the transshipment problem.

In discussing again the draft memorandum of conversation which Mr. Sayre had handed to the Japanese Ambassador and which had been transmitted to Tokyo, Mr. Yoshizawa said that, of course, at that time neither the Department of State nor the Japanese Embassy here knew that the question of the 4,000,000 square meters and the question of transshipments were interdependent. This remark emphasized the point that the Japanese exporters have made this direct suggestion although no formal proposal of this sort has yet been presented to this Government by the Embassy. The Embassy appears to be informed of this position but not instructed to present the proposal in so many words.

Mr. Veatch asked if Mr. Yoshizawa had secured any information regarding the effect of the working of the agreement upon the wholesale and retail textile trade in the Philippines. Mr. Yoshizawa replied that he did have information on this point. The Exporters Association had pointed out that in the course of the natural working out of the agreement importers in the Philippines having direct connection with Japanese exporters had been "benefited." The Exporters Association allots quotas to the exporters and exports cannot be made without permits secured from the Association. Naturally, therefore, importers in the Philippines who have established direct connections with the exporters in Japan holding these permits have been the first ones to secure goods—thus Mitsui, Mitsubishi and a few other large firms handle a considerable part of the business with the Philippines directly with their own representatives. The Exporters Association stressed the fact, however, that one or two Chinese firms with headquarters in Osaka and Kobe have been given export permits.

Mr. Yoshizawa stressed the fact that it would not be correct to say that Chinese merchants have been deprived of Japanese goods "altogether". He recognized that probably many Chinese dealers had found it impossible to secure cotton textiles directly from Japan but this was not the result of any deliberate attempt on the part of the exporters to discriminate against them. Even small Japanese traders in the Philippines who do not have direct connections with exporters have been "complaining" and now are probably looking for chances themselves to import goods from Hong Kong. When asked for his opinion, Mr. Yoshizawa said that he did suppose that the natural working out of limitation of shipments under the agreement probably was an important reason for the growing demand of Chinese importers for Japanese goods in Hong Kong.

During the discussion Mr. Yoshizawa brought out one point which serves to clarify the reason for the strong interest of Japanese exporters to the Philippines in cutting off the trade from Hong Kong. Although he did not have official information from the Japanese Exporters Association, he said that he understood that exporters had to pay the Association 4 sen, 5 rin per square meter for permits to export to the Philippines. (This amounts to about $1\frac{1}{3}$ cents per square meter and if Mr. Yoshizawa is correct in this figure it would represent an important item in the exporters' calculations.) As a result, the exporters are particularly concerned about market conditions in the Philippines and they are irritated when their attempts to raise prices in the Philippines are defeated or endangered by the importation of Japanese goods from Hong Kong at lower prices.

Mr. Yoshizawa said that he did not wish to say this officially or to make the statement to Mr. Sayre, but he thought it might be helpful to be perfectly frank and to say to Mr. Veatch that the Japanese Government was having considerable difficulty in getting the exporters to be reasonable about the agreement since they have been calculating that they would be able to sell as much as 90,000,000 square meters to the Philippines in one year (rather than 90,000,000 square meters in two years as provided by the agreement) if the normal trends of the trade had continued uninterrupted. Hence, now that transshipments via Hong Kong have become an important factor and one which the exporters feel they cannot control in any way, many of them are inclined to counsel letting the agreement go into the discard, taking their chances without voluntary restriction. Mr. Yoshizawa then said that, of course, his Government joined with this Government in a sincere desire to avoid this eventuality. Mr. Yoshizawa himself had been greatly relieved when the agreement had been initialed last October because he thought the matter was then settled. It was very unfortunate that the agreement had not worked well. He felt that it was neither the fault of this Government nor of his Government nor of the Japanese exporters. The original difficulty was a lack of understanding of Philippine statistics and now this difficulty with transshipments, which he was bound to admit, appeared insoluble.

611B.9417/144

Memorandum by Mr. Roy Veatch of the Office of the Economic Adviser

[WASHINGTON,] March 25, 1936.

Conversation: The Japanese Ambassador,
     Mr. Seijiro Yoshizawa, Counselor of the Japanese Embassy,
     Mr. Sayre,
     Mr. Turner,
     Mr. Veatch.

In view of a number of unsettled questions requiring further discussion and of the desire which the Japanese Ambassador had expressed previously to discuss general trade relations between Japan and the United States, Mr. Yoshizawa had informed Mr. Veatch on March 23 that the Japanese Ambassador would be glad to call upon Mr. Sayre at his convenience.

PHILIPPINE TEXTILE AGREEMENT

Mr. Sayre explained that officers of the Department and experts from other agencies in the Government had been wrestling with the transshipment problem. These officials had been forced to come to the conclusion that both this Government and the Philippine Government were powerless to do anything about this problem, at least at the present time. No legal authority exists for the restriction or denial of consular invoices and there is no administrative authority in the Philippines to take any action regarding imports from Hong Kong. Even if it were possible to deny consular invoices to Japanese goods transshipped from Hong Kong, such action undoubtedly would be considered discrimination against Hong Kong.

In view of the fact that this Government has been unable to do anything about the problem of transshipments, a problem which is giving concern to the Japanese exporters, an effort has been made to meet the Japanese position as far as possible in other ways. Therefore, this Government is willing to accept the Japanese point of view regarding the statistics to be used as a measure of imports of Japanese goods into the Philippines, accepting statistics of arrivals for the entire period of the agreement rather than the usual statistics of the Philippine customs, based on liquidations of duty. By this interpretation there would be charged against the Japanese quota for the first six months of the agreement the actual amount of Japanese goods which arrived in the Philippines during that period, approximately 26,000,000 square meters. According to the terms of the agreement there would remain, therefore, 19,000,000 square meters to arrive in the Philippines during the second half-year period. This Government would, therefore, not insist upon any alteration of the quotas as measured by arrival statistics, although Mr. Sayre personally felt that this was a little unfortunate because this arrangement would ignore entirely the unusually heavy arrivals of Japanese cotton goods in the Philippines in the few months prior to the effective date of the agreement, August 1, 1935.

The Japanese Ambassador wished to clarify the matter of transshipments as affected by Mr. Sayre's proposal. He said that although the Japanese exporters had known that they could not exercise any control over reshipments of Japanese goods from Hong Kong to the Philippines, the Japanese Government had not stressed that problem when the agreement was reached because transshipments at that time were very small and no great increase was expected. Now that these transshipments have become heavy, however, they have created large difficulties for the exporters from Japan, since these exporters can have no way of knowing how much they can ship to the Philippines under the quota. The Ambassador understood the inability of this Government or of the Philippine Government at the present time to control these transshipments.

Mr. Sayre said that he supposed there was no disagreement regarding the fact that Japanese goods transshipped via Hong Kong or other ports on the way to the Philippines were clearly included in the quotas established by the agreement. This had been the only basis on which the agreement was workable, he said, and he was sure there had been no misunderstanding about the way in which the agreement handled the transshipment problem. The only comment the Japanese Ambassador made to these statements was an affirmative "yes".

Mr. Yoshizawa asked if Mr. Sayre's statement implied that the American Government was dropping the consideration of a reduction of the Japanese quota for the second six months by 4,000,000 square meters. In reply, Mr. Sayre said that it had been decided to drop this matter because it was desired to give the Japanese exporters a sufficient margin to make it possible for them to take care of the transshipment problem.

Mr. Sayre said that he recognized that it had been difficult to make the Philippine textile agreement work satisfactorily and that transshipments via Hong Kong were giving Japanese exporters concern, but he hoped that it would be possible for the Japanese Government to appreciate the efforts of this Government to agree to a liberal interpretation of the agreement. He believed it would be greatly to the interest of the Japanese exporters to make the agreement effective so that the American textile people should not go on a rampage, seeking more extreme restrictions upon the Japanese market in the Philippines, a result which he feared would follow if it became necessary for this Government to announce that the agreement had broken down or that the Japanese had not lived up to the terms of the agreement.

Mr. Sayre then asked the Ambassador what he thought of the American proposal. In reply the Ambassador and Mr. Yoshizawa said that the proposal seemed to them "quite fair".

Mr. Sayre then said that of course we hoped that the Japanese exporters would refrain from making use of the ten percent leeway in their quota this year, since to ship that much more goods before August 1 would make the situation very much worse. In response to this suggestion the Ambassador and Mr. Yoshizawa said that they also thought that it would be undesirable for more than 19,000,000 square meters to enter the Philippines during the second half year of the agreement.

United States Imports of Cotton Piece Goods from Japan

Mr. Sayre asked if the Embassy had received any word from Tokyo in response to the statement regarding the heavy importations into this country in January of cotton piece goods from Japan. In response, Mr. Yoshizawa explained that following his discussion with Mr. Feis on March 9 he had cabled the information to Tokyo with the indication that it was in the nature of a warning from this Government. He had not worded that cable so as to require a reply. He had intended to send a further cable as soon as the figures had been published in this country but since he was out of town most of last week he had not realized that they had been released on March 18. After talking with Mr. Veatch on Monday, March 23, he had sent a further cable.

Mr. Sayre explained the increasing pressure that was being brought upon this Government following the release of the January figures. A great many people were writing in and the industry seemed to be united in demanding action on this subject. It would help the Department of State a great deal in dealing with this strong pressure for new restrictions upon Japanese trade if some reassuring word could be secured from the Japanese Government as quickly as possible. (At Mr. Feis' suggestion Mr. Veatch improved the opportunity of a telephone call from Mr. Yoshizawa later in the day to remind him of Mr. Feis' statement on March 9 that the Tariff Commission has had under way for some months an investigation of cotton piece goods under Section 336 of the Tariff Act. Undoubtedly there would be pressure upon the Tariff Commission and upon the President to bring out a report on this investigation and to take action upon it unless there was some reassurance regarding the volume of continuing imports of cotton goods from Japan. He mentioned also the fact that Section 22 of the Agricultural Adjustment Act had been made applicable to the new Soil Conservation Act,[41] empowering the President to impose quantitative limitations upon imports affecting the agricultural programs under either Act. A demand for action on cotton textiles had been placed before the Secretary of Agriculture under Section 22 of the A. A. A. before a portion of that Act had been found unconstitutional in the Schechter decision.[42] If the domestic industry continues its drive against cotton imports from Japan, it is quite probable that it will again demand action under this provision of law.)

Mr. Yoshizawa said that he would put all this information before his Government and urge that a reply be made as soon as possible.

GENERAL QUESTIONS OF JAPANESE-AMERICAN TRADE RELATIONS

Mr. Sayre recalled the statement that the Japanese Ambassador had made a few weeks ago that he would like to discuss with Mr. Sayre more general questions of the trade relations between the two countries than had been possible during their recent conversations on particular commodities.

The Japanese Ambassador explained that he had had an opportunity to talk with the Secretary of State recently about such general trade problems and he would appreciate an opportunity to talk the matter through. He did wish to report to his Government upon any possibilities that might exist for a more general trade understanding. Perhaps they might talk about a possibility of the two Governments entering into a trade treaty or something like that if it seems feasible.

In reply Mr. Sayre said that by all means he would like to discuss these matters with the Ambassador. He wondered if the Ambassador had anything in particular in mind, and in reply the Ambassador said that he did not but merely wished to explore the general question.

Mr. Sayre then referred to a despatch of February 19 from the American Embassy at Tokyo reporting upon a conversation between Mr. Kurusu of the Foreign Office and Mr. Dickover of the Embassy. This conversation had indicated that Mr. Kurusu misunderstood very important aspects of the policy of the Department regarding the competition in the United States of imports from Japan. Mr. Sayre

---

[41] Approved February 29, 1936; 49 Stat. 1148.
[42] May 27, 1935; 295 U. S. 495.

then read, for the Ambassador's information, those parts of the despatch (most of pages two and three) which set forth Mr. Kurusu's views and called particular attention to Mr. Kurusu's belief that at the present time American economic interests desiring increased protection against imports brought their problems to the Department of State and got it to act for them in securing such added protection.

Mr. Sayre then emphasized the fact that this Department has brought particular situations to the attention of the Japanese only when they had become quite severe and had given rise to such strong pressure for action in this country that the Executive was to be forced to take action under existing provisions of law or new restrictive legislation was in prospect. Mr. Kurusu had called attention to the fact that most of the items which this Government had brought to the attention of the Japanese Government, requesting voluntary restriction of shipments by the Japanese, had been rather unimportant items in the total trade between the United States and Japan and frequently had involved only a few plants and a few hundred workers in the United States. Mr. Sayre said that in his opinion it was fortunate that the few lines in which some restriction had become necessary were small and relatively unimportant items of trade, since restriction would not greatly affect the volume of Japanese exports to this country. When the very existence of these small industries might be threatened by rapidly mounting imports from Japan they became sore spots and unless these spots could be healed, at least to a certain extent, the broader and more important trade interests of the United States and Japan might be threatened by greater restrictions forced through the legislature by economic interests in this country.

Mr. Sayre said that he was sure the Ambassador realized that the desire of this Government was to protect the common economic interests of the two countries. He felt that these interests were largely complementary—Japan was our chief cotton customer and the United States was the principal market for Japanese silk. In our efforts to protect the trade relations between the two countries we wished to appreciate the psychological problems in Japan just as we had to give attention to the psychology of the situation in this country. We did not want to ask any action by the Japanese Government or Japanese exporters which would cause anti-American feeling in Japan, just as we hoped the two Governments could take such action regarding trade as to prevent the growth of anti-Japanese feeling in this country.

Mr. Sayre called attention also to the similarity of the general interests of the two countries in international trade. Both countries are much interested in international trade and both are dependent to a great extent upon triangular trade. It is in the interest of the United States that the freedom of triangular trade be undisturbed, particularly to protect the foreign market for American cotton. On the other hand, we realize that the Japanese are much concerned about their markets in South America. This Government has leaned over backward in refraining from placing pressure upon Latin American countries who sell more to us than they buy from us, pressure to discriminate in their tariff treatment or other trade regulations so as to favor American goods. American exporters have urged the Government to secure these special favors for American goods but the Government has refused to take any action of this nature. Confidentially, he could say that the Government of Brazil had actually made offers to the American Government for special arrangements favoring American goods in the Brazilian market, but this Government had refused these offers. American textile people may have gone to certain Latin American countries seeking special action to favor American textiles in those markets, but they certainly have received no encouragement from this Government. As a matter of fact, Mr. Sayre wrote a very strong letter to one representative of the textile interests whose activities in certain Latin American countries had come to his attention and this gentleman had never forgiven Mr. Sayre.

Mr. Sayre said that this Government would be glad on its part to try to touch up any sore spots in the trade relations between the two countries wherever it could. Of course, tariff reductions were a matter for Congress to deal with and he didn't believe that there would be anything to be gained in discussing tariff rates. It was his opinion that the Japanese Government would not profit by any direct trade agreement. Tariff concessions being made to other countries in connection with trade agreements that this Government is negotiating are being extended to Japanese goods and he felt that Japan would profit most through continuing to enjoy these concessions.

Mr. Sayre said that this Government would be happy to discuss any adjustment of trade problems with the Japanese and he wondered if the Ambassador had anything in mind at the present moment.

The Japanese Ambassador said that in his opinion it would be very useful if Mr. Sayre could put down in writing the things that he had said regarding triangular trade.

In reply to this suggestion Mr. Sayre said that he would be very glad to consider the possibility and to talk it over with his associates. He wondered if the Ambassador had in mind merely a statement to the Japanese Government or if he had thought of a statement which could be made public; obviously, a statement would have to be drafted somewhat differently if it were to be made public.

The Ambassador said that he thought it would be particularly helpful if his Government could have a statement on this subject which could be made public so that the Japanese people might know clearly the attitude of the American Government. Mr. Sayre said that he supposed that the Japanese Government would be particularly interested in being able to make clear the attitude of this Government regarding the Latin American market for Japanese goods, and the Ambassador said that he thought that was the most important point.

The Japanese Ambassador, in response to Mr. Sayre's question regarding any situations in this country affecting Japanese trade which he would like to discuss, referred to the possibility of adoption by Congress of the proposed processing tax on silk. His Government was much concerned about this possibility.

In reply Mr. Sayre said that as the Ambassador knew a similar proposal to this had been brought up last year and that it had been blocked. The present proposal was not receiving the hearty support of the subcommittee on taxes in the House, and Mr. Sayre said he had a hunch that it would not go through. In any event, if adopted it was indicated that this tax would not be directed specifically at silk but would be merely in the nature of a compensating tax on silk in connection with a processing tax on cotton and rayon. It was probable that even if adopted these taxes would not be of a permanent nature.

611B.9417/144

Memorandum by Mr. Roy Veatch of the Office of the Economic Adviser

[WASHINGTON,] March 25, 1936.

At Mr. Sayre's request I telephoned Mr. Yoshizawa following the conversation between Mr. Sayre and the Japanese Ambassador and asked Mr. Yoshizawa if I might make one further point which Mr. Sayre had intended to bring to the attention of the Ambassador. Mr. Yoshizawa agreed to include the following information in his memorandum of the conversation between Mr. Sayre and the Ambassador and to incorporate it in his report to Tokyo:

A shipment of 25 cases of Japanese cotton goods cut in short lengths, under six feet, had arrived in the Philippines from Japan, these goods being classified as semi-manufactured and the importers expressing willingness to pay the surcharge for semi-manufactured goods. It is possible that this shipment has been made as a test case and that certain exporters from Japan or importers in the Philippines will be inclined to follow this practice as a means of importing cotton goods into the Philippines outside of the quota on cotton piece goods. It was Mr. Sayre's desire to place this information before the Japanese Ambassador with the expectation that he would wish to bring it to the attention of the Exporters Association since the Association probably would wish to guard against any extension of this practice as a means of evading the agreement.

Mr. Yoshizawa said that he was sure the Association would not countenance a practice of this sort and that he would see that this information was brought to its attention.

Mr. Veatch said that he supposed Mr. Yoshizawa had the same feeling that Mr. Sayre had about the present status of the Philippine textile agreement. It was Mr. Sayre's feeling that it would not be necessary to initial any understanding regarding an adjustment of that agreement since this Government had offered to accept the Japanese suggestion regarding measurement of imports of Japanese goods from the beginning of the agreement. He would like to have, however, some indication of the position of the Japanese Government regarding a final understanding on this matter. Mr. Yoshizawa said that this was also his understanding and that he was framing his cable to Tokyo with the idea of eliciting some response from his Government.

Mr. Yoshizawa said that he had found a further despatch from Tokyo waiting for him when he returned to the Embassy from the conference with Mr. Sayre this morning. This despatch had given figures of arrivals of transshipped goods in the Philippines from Hong Kong for the month of February and for the first 15 days of March, these figures having been furnished by the Japanese Consul General in Manila. In view of the heavy importations of Japanese goods from Hong Kong in February and March, Mr. Yoshizawa was somewhat concerned about the reception that Mr. Sayre's proposal would receive in Tokyo. Both he and the Ambassador felt that that proposal was very fair and they appreciated the spirit in which it had been made, but in view of the fact that twelve months' importations from Hong Kong at the rate of the February arrivals would exceed 10,000,000 square meters, he was somewhat worried over the ability of the Foreign Office to get the textile exporters to agree to this Government's offer. He intended to present the offer in as favorable a light as possible in his despatch.

611.946/277

Memorandum by Mr. Roy Veatch of the Office of the Economic Adviser

[WASHINGTON,] April 3, 1936.

At Mr. Sayre's direction, Mr. Veatch asked Mr. Yoshizawa to come to the Department to receive the latest United States statistics of imports of cotton piece goods from Japan and to discuss the information which Mr. Yoshizawa had placed before Mr. Veatch on March 30, 1936.[43]

---

[43] Not printed.

When Mr. Yoshizawa arrived, he said that he had brought with him a translation of the points contained in the despatch from the Foreign Office which he had discussed with Mr. Veatch on March 30 and also a table of Japanese exports of cotton piece goods to the United States in January and February 1936 and monthly during 1935 (copies attached).[44] These statements he left for the Department's files.

Mr. Veatch then handed Mr. Yoshizawa a statement (copy attached)[44] regarding this Government's statistics of imports of cotton piece goods from Japan during the same period, pointing out that the American statistics were considerably higher during January and February 1936 than the Japanese export statistics for the months of December 1935 and January 1936. He called attention to the second paragraph in the statement which he had handed to Mr. Yoshizawa, which apparently gave the full explanation of this discrepancy.

Mr. Yoshizawa asked a number of questions regarding shipments of Japanese goods directly to Puerto Rico, and Mr. Veach showed him statistics of the Japanese shipments directly to Puerto Rico, statistics taken from Japanese reports, which indicated that direct shipments had increased considerably during the last two or three months. Mr. Veatch said that we were looking into this trade and that he would hazard a guess that considerable amounts of Japanese goods which were used in the embroidery trade in Puerto Rico and shipped to the United States in manufactured form had formerly been secured through New York and were now being brought in directly, possibly due to improvement in Japanese freight service and marketing in the Caribbean area. Mr. Yoshizawa agreed that the fact that a portion of Japanese exports to the United States went to Puerto Rico, most of it then coming into continental United States in manufactured form, did not change the importance of this trade since Japanese goods in Puerto Rico evidently supplanted American goods. Mr. Veatch made it clear that American statistics had always included imports into any area inside the United States customs system and that our import figures included imports into Puerto Rico and Hawaii as well as into continental United States.

Mr. Veatch said that Mr. Sayre had been of the opinion that neither the figures cited in the despatch from the Foreign Office which Mr. Yoshizawa had translated for Mr. Veatch on March 30 nor the United States statistics of imports during January and February 1936 could afford a basis for any release or any action on the part of this Department designed to allay the alarm over increased importations of

---

[44] Not printed.

Japanese cotton goods. Mr. Yoshizawa said that he had to admit that personally he agreed with this conclusion and that he had been of the opinion that even the statistics cited in his instructions, not including shipments to Puerto Rico and Hawaii, did not warrant a statement on the part of the American Government that the Japanese Government was living up to the assurances given this Government on December 21, 1935.[45] He recognized the importance of the fact pointed out by Mr. Veatch that statistics of imports into the United States for consumption were the important figures and that these statistics for January and February 1936 showed total imports exceeding the imports for consumption for the first three months of 1935, months when imports were the highest on record at that time. He recognized the alarm of the American industry in view of the fact that imports during these two months were at the rate of over 75,000,000 square yards a year.

Mr. Veatch then mentioned again the extent of the pressure which was being placed upon this Government and the embarrassment in which we were placed in that we were not yet able to give any assurance to the American industry that the Japanese exporters were going to be able to control the situation satisfactorily. We had made an effort to delay or discourage the development of demands for restrictive action by this Government on the score that the January increases in imports had been brought to the attention of the Japanese Government, that the Japanese Government was giving serious consideration to the situation and that a reply to our representations was expected soon. In spite of these efforts the agitation was growing and already pressure was being brought for restrictive action of one sort or another by this Government.

Mr. Yoshizawa asked Mr. Veatch if he would describe to him in some detail the character of this agitation so that he might include this information in his despatch to Tokyo and therefore emphasize the necessity for action. In response to this request Mr. Veatch detailed the way in which the Cotton Textile Institute, representing the entire industry, was taking the lead in the movement for protection against increasing imports from Japan. This movement was likely to be much stronger this year than last because the industry in the South was joining with the New England industry in supporting the demand for action. He referred to the letters which were being sent out by the Cotton Textile Institute and to the activity of other groups, such as the National Association of Cotton Manufacturers, in bringing the situation to the attention of members of Congress and also various departments of the Government. Mr. Yoshizawa said that it would be helpful if he could get a copy of the letters being circulated by these

---

[45] See memorandum of December 21, 1935, *Foreign Relations*, 1935, vol. III, p. 1037.

groups.   Mr. Veatch said that Senator Walsh [46] had read into the *Congressional Record* on March 27 the text of the letter which the National Association of Cotton Manufacturers had addressed to members of Congress and also the text of the very full letter and of tables sent out by the Cotton Textile Institute.[46a]   Mr. Yoshizawa recalled these letters and said that he would make use of them in preparing his despatch to Tokyo.

Mr. Veatch emphasized the fact that the drive against importations of Japanse cotton textiles apparently was only in its early stages. Leaders of the cotton textile industry had indicated to the Department that they wished to cooperate with the Department and would not press for restrictive action by this Government if the situation could be handled voluntarily by the Japanese.   In view of the fact that importations in January and February have been so completely out of line with the assurances given by the Japanese Government on December 21 and that the State Department had not been able to announce any new assurances or any adjustment of the situation by the Japanese exporters, the movement was now getting under way to demand other action.   First, there was now pressure upon the Tariff Commission to get out as quickly as possible the report on its investigation of the cost of production of bleached cotton goods in Japan and the United States, the investigation inaugurated under Section 336 of the Tariff Act of 1930.   Second, the Department of Agriculture was being approached (as evidenced by the letter from the Cotton Textile Institute read into the *Record* by Senator Walsh) with the purpose of securing restrictions upon the quantities of cotton textiles which might be imported from Japan, and finally, of course, the whole problem was being placed before members of Congress and in recent days Senator Walsh and Representative Martin [47] have brought the problem onto the floor and into the *Record*.

After further discussion, Mr. Yoshizawa reviewed the points which he intended to place before his Government, including the following:

(1) The statistics for the first two months of 1936, even the Japanese statistics of direct shipments to continental United States, do not form a basis for discouraging agitation for restrictive action by the American Government.

(2) Japanese exports for February indicate that United States statistics of imports for March will again be heavy.

(3) Imports for consumption are the important matter to be watched and this would require not only control of shipments from Japan but also control of sales from existing stocks in bonded warehouses in the United States, which total over 11,000,000 square yards.

(4) Unless some action can be taken or definite assurance of action

---

[46] David I. Walsh, Democrat, of Massachusetts.
[46a] *Congressional Record*, vol. 80, pt. 4, p. 4459.
[47] Joseph W. Martin, Jr., Republican, of Massachusetts.

given by the Japanese Government very soon, the movement for direct action by the American Government will gain such headway that it will be difficult to handle. In view of the fact that the assurances given by the Japanese Government on December 21 have turned out to be very poorly founded, some more definite action or assurances of some more definite form are now needed if the American textile industry is to be impressed.

611.946 Rag Rugs/147

Memorandum by Mr. Roy Veatch of the Office of the Economic Adviser

[WASHINGTON,] April 14, 1936.

Conversation: Mr. Tsuneo Hayama, Third Secretary of the Japanese Embassy,
Mr. Otoshiro Kuroda, Attaché of the Japanese Embassy,
Mr. Veatch.

Mr. Hayama and Mr. Kuroda presented a typed statement requesting the extension for another year (that is, from June 1, 1936 to May 31, 1937) of the existing agreement with regard to the export of cotton rugs from Japan to the United States. They were instructed to say that the Japanese Government desires a continuation of the agreement in its present form although the Japanese exporters had been urging the Government to seek an increase in the amounts of rugs of each class which might be shipped during the coming year. Exporters have received orders which they have not been able to fill this year inside of the limits of the agreement to the following amounts:

Chenille rugs . . . . 350,000 square yards
Hit-and-miss rugs . . . . 150,000 square yards
"All other" cotton rugs . . . . 200,000 square yards

To be sure, the Japanese Government would like to secure as liberal figures for the Japanese exporters as possible and their statement, therefore, was phrased to say that they desired limits "at least" as liberal as those agreed upon for the present year. Mr. Hayama said that he did not want to "negotiate" or "bargain", however, so that he stated frankly that they would be glad to agree to the present figures for next year.

Mr. Veatch said that he would place this request before the Department immediately. Undoubtedly inquiry would have to be made as to the present state of the market for rag rugs and the prospects in the future. In this regard he said that some complaints had been made by manufacturers of rag rugs and rag carpets against what was claimed to be increasing competition of Japanese rag carpets in this market. Mr. Veatch stressed the fact that he did not know to what extent this complaint was justified and only mentioned it in passing. Since it appeared that cotton rag carpets were manufactured at least to some extent by the same concerns that manufacture cotton rugs, the market for rag carpets might have some effect upon the rag rug situation. In any event, the proposal of the Japanese Government would be looked into immediately and Mr. Hayama would be informed just as soon as this Government was able to say what arrangement could be made.

(A copy of the statement handed to Mr. Veatch by Mr. Hayama is attached.[48])

611.946/285

Memorandum by the Assistant Secretary of State (Sayre) and Mr. Eugene H. Dooman of the Division of Far Eastern Affairs

[WASHINGTON,] April 27, 1936.

The Japanese Ambassador called with the Counselor, Mr. Yoshizawa, at Mr. Sayre's office by appointment at 3:30 p. m. The Ambassador was taken by Mr. Sayre into the Secretary's office in order to discuss the question of Japanese importation of cotton piece goods into the United States.

The Secretary, after a few preliminary remarks, began by speaking of the fight which he and this Government have been making for the liberalization of the trade of the world. The Secretary spoke of his efforts in London and in Montevideo.[49] He went on to say that the program for trade liberalization which so vitally concerns the economic recovery and the welfare of the world is growing in strength and gaining in support in various quarters of this country and of Europe. Just at the present time, however, the Secretary pointed out, a political crisis is upon us and we are in a critical and serious situation. If the Japanese Government should not cooperate with us in helping to stabilize the trade situation, it might well cause a commotion which would prove disastrous. This Government therefore finds itself in a situation where it must appeal to the Japanese Government to make its own contribution for the furtherance of our program for the liberalization of world trade. The United States Government is making considerable sacrifices to promote the program and to secure support both in this country and in Europe. As a matter of fact, Japan has an equal interest, we feel sure, in the development of the

---

[48] Not printed.
[49] For correspondence concerning these conferences, held in 1933, see *Foreign Relations*, 1933, vol. I, pp. 452 ff., and *ibid.*, vol. IV, pp. 1 ff., respectively.

program. The program calls for a reduction of trade barriers throughout the world and the insistence upon the maintenance of triangular trade. If the program fails, it can mean only the victory of the present movement toward bilateral balancing of trade, and this would mean commercial disaster for Japan as well as the United States. After all, Japan and the United States are fighting the same fight as to excessive trade barriers. This Government therefore feels justified in asking the Japanese Government to support us in the present critical situation.

The Japanese Ambassador at this point asked whether he could correctly report to his Government that the United States Government is asking for a reduction in Japanese exports to the United States,— a step which is superficially inconsistent with the general trade program sought by the United States,—in order to withstand political pressures so as to gain strength to successfully promote its trade program to secure ultimate reduction of trade barriers all along the line. The Secretary replied in the affirmative. The Secretary added that he did not want this critical situation to pass without bringing this matter to the attention of the Japanese Government so that, should there come failure of our liberalizing program, the Japanese Government would not feel they had not been given the opportunity to support the program during the crucial period when it was either to be made or broken. The Secretary then asked the Ambassador to discuss the concrete and technical situation with which we are confronted with Mr. Sayre.

The Ambassador then returned to Mr. Sayre's office, where Mr. Yoshizawa and Mr. Dooman were waiting, and the conversation was resumed between the four of them.

Mr. Sayre then proceeded to read the following memorandum to the Japanese Ambassador, stopping to comment as he went along in order to explain and slightly amplify some of the passages. The memorandum which he read is as follows:

"More than two years ago, the Japanese Government expressed to the American Government the wish that, in those instances where the American Government contemplated the taking of action designed to restrict imports of a particular commodity from Japan, the Japanese Government be given an opportunity to adjust, if possible, the conditions giving rise to the need for the contemplated restrictive action. In accordance with that wish, the American Government has subsequently approached the Japanese Government whenever instances of dislocations of industrial or market conditions have been caused by imports from Japan, and it has been very gratifying to us that in nearly every one of these instances some arrangement has been made which has satisfactorily adjusted the disturbing conditions. I refer, for example, to the pencil and cotton rug arrangements, which are now approaching the end of their second year. It is in the light of the great measure of success which has been attended by these two arrangements that, in approaching the Japanese Embassy last year, we hoped that it might be possible to conclude a further arrangement, this time in regard to imports of Japanese cotton textiles into the United States.

"We regretted that, after extended negotiations, the Japanese Government could not see its way clear to enter into another gentlemen's agreement in regard to this trade. However, we appreciated the assurance given us on December 21, 1935, that exports of cotton piece goods from Japan to the United States would be held down to last year's figures, and we were hopeful that if the rapidly rising curve of imports from Japan were flattened out the agitation in the United States for the taking of some restrictive action against Japanese piece goods would subside.

"Unfortunately this expectation is not being fulfilled. During the first three months of 1936, imports of cotton piece goods from Japan were on a higher level than ever before. This is particularly true of imports for consumption which total 21,530,000 square yards for the quarter as compared with 12,769,000 square yards for the corresponding quarter of 1935 and 36,000,000 square yards for the whole of 1935. General imports (actual arrivals) from Japan for the first quarter of 1936 were 17,886,000 square yards as against 16,730,000 square yards for the corresponding quarter of 1935. Stocks in bonded warehouses were reduced from 11,000,000 square yards at the end of December to 7,165,000 square yards at the end of March.

"These conditions have brought about a recrudescence in an even more persistent and extended form than ever before of the agitation for the taking by this Government of action against imports of Japanese cotton textiles. As I have already remarked to you on several occasions, this Government does not associate itself with that school of thought which takes the stand that the domestic market be denied to all foreign products competing in any way with products of domestic manufacture; nor has the American Government encouraged the movement for placing restrictions upon importations of specific commodities merely because those commodities have increased in volume or because they compete in the American market with the products of American industries. The rapidly mounting volume of imports from Japan of textiles offered for sale at much lower prices than those at which corresponding American products can be marketed, is, however, causing a dislocation of conditions which is entirely disproportionate to the volume of imports as compared with the total production. The disturbing effects of these rapidly mounting Japanese imports is further accentuated by the fact that they are confined to a relatively narrow field. Although imports of countable cotton cloth were equivalent to only about one-half of one percent of the total volume of domestic production in 1935, these imports were confined largely to print cloths, especially bleached print cloths. The ratio of imports from Japan of bleached print cloths to domestic production was 12.6 percent in 1935.

"A complaint was filed on the basis of Section 336 of the Tariff Act with the Tariff Commission, and I may say to you in strict confidence, in the light of the various facts which were brought out after investigation by the Tariff Commission, the Tariff Commission has been obliged to recommend moderate increases in duty in order to equalize cost differences between American and Japanese cloths.

"It would not be in line with the general economic policy of this Government to increase duties. In this particular instance, however, it has been found that cotton textiles are being imported from Japan on such terms, and at such a rapidly increasing rate, that the very existence of established American industries is being endangered and the organization of the cotton industry and the trade in cotton textiles have been greatly disturbed. Notwithstanding these facts, this Government does not wish unilaterally to impose new restrictions upon Japanese imports, or indeed to determine what action should be taken, without full consultation with your Government.

"We fully appreciate the circumstances which prevented your Government from entering into a gentlemen's agreement last year with regard to imports of cotton piece goods. The situation at this moment is, however, far more pressing than it was last year, and we, therefore, urgently hope that it may be possible for the Japanese Government to reconsider its decision, and that it may be possible to arrange to limit total imports to last year's figures of approximately 36,000,000 square yards.

"There is, of course, another alternative, and that is promulgating the very moderate tariff increases recommended by the Tariff Commission. It is, of course, impossible to predict exactly the effects of tariff changes, but it is our expectation that a moderate increase in the duties on Japanese cotton textiles will tend to maintain imports from Japan at about last year's level. We consequently hope that it may be possible for the Japanese Government to see its way clear to entering into a gentlemen's agreement along the lines that have been suggested, but if this is found impracticable we sincerely hope that the Japanese Government will appreciate our sincere and friendly endeavor to collaborate in every way possible with the Japanese Government with a view to the friendly adjustment of this problem."

Mr. Sayre emphasized the fact that his proposal was of a most informal kind, made in a personal way as a constructive suggestion and was not to be considered as a formal legal offer. He added that the Tariff Commission's report is now on the President's table; and that he had personally requested that the President take no action with regard to that report until he (Mr. Sayre) had had an opportunity to discuss with the Japanese Ambassador the possibility of concluding a gentlemen's agreement. He added that time was of the essence, and that we should hope to have a definite reply within, say, ten days.

The Japanese Ambassador asked whether Mr. Sayre envisaged an agreement featured with other details than those which he had specified. Mr. Dooman stated that we had in mind certain other details which the Japanese would find very little difficulty in accepting once they had reached the decision that they could, in principle, accept a gentlemen's agreement. These details, broadly speaking, contemplated that Japanese textiles imported into the United States should be distributed over a wider range of goods than their present restricted range. He stated that Japanese textiles come into competition with American textiles on a relatively narrow front. It was contemplated that they should continue to market those particular lines of textiles which at present are sold in the United States, but that it would be expected that shipments up to the maximum amount to be agreed upon would be more evenly spread out, both in regard to time and lines of goods, than at present.

Mr. Sayre added that the United States would expect the agreed upon figures to be those of imports for consumption.

Mr. Yoshizawa stated that the Japanese Government could not control the trade once shipments left Japan. He feared that the Japanese Government could not accept responsibility for imports for consumption being exceeded. Mr. Dooman thought that Mr. Yoshizawa's point was well taken, and he suggested to Mr. Sayre that, if the Japanese were asked to limit imports for consumption to 36,000,000 square yards, it would be necessary for the Japanese Government to restrict exports from Japan for the next twelve months to about 29,000,000 square yards which, with the 7,000,000 square yards in bonded warehouses in the United States, would make a total of 36,000,000 square yards.

Mr. Yoshizawa observed that he had had frequent conversations with officers in the Department and that he thought he was fairly well conversant with the whole problem confronting us. He had previously discussed with several of these officers the possibility of the duty on cotton textiles being increased. He could not, however, suppress the feeling that the Japanese Government was now being confronted with an "ultimatum". Mr. Sayre took exception to the use of this word and stated that what both Governments were called upon to do at this moment was to face the facts. He wondered whether the Japanese Government could suggest an additional alternative to those of a gentlemen's agreement and an increase in duties. He added that if the Japanese Government had any third alternative in mind it might rest assured that the American Government would give it the most careful and sympathetic consideration.

In concluding the conversation, Mr. Sayre again stated that the American Government is most anxious to collaborate with the Japanese Government in working out problems of mutual concern and he had placed before the Ambassador in all frankness and sincerity the facts which make the present situation a most difficult and critical one.

611.946/296

Memorandum by Mr. Eugene H. Dooman of the Division of Far Eastern Affairs

[WASHINGTON,] May 1, 1936.

Conversation: The Japanese Ambassador;
    Mr. Seijiro Yoshizawa, Counselor, Japanese Embassy;
    Mr. Sayre; and
    Mr. Dooman.

The Japanese Ambassador began the conversation by saying that he did not bring with him any good news. He stated that he had received on April 28 a telegram from his Government which had crossed the telegram he had sent to Tokyo immediately after his conversation with Mr. Sayre on April 27. The instruction which he had received stated that the Japanese Government is endeavoring to hold exports to the United States to a monthly maximum of 5,000,000 square yards, the Japanese Government's expectation being that the volume of exports during a certain proportion of the next twelve months would be substantially less than the figure mentioned. The Ambassador stated that the plan proposed by his Government was obviously one which would not be responsive to the wishes of the American Government as explained to the Ambassador by Mr. Sayre on April 27. The Ambassador had therefore immediately telegraphed his Government and requested that the matter be reconsidered in the light of his telegram of the previous day. He had, the Ambassador continued, received today fresh instructions, directing him to lay before Mr. Sayre the Japanese Government's suggested plan, which, the Japanese Government thought, would probably be satisfactory to Mr. Sayre.

Mr. Sayre stated that the question was not whether the plan would be satisfactory to him: the question was whether the plan would meet the situation now confronting both Governments. He himself had no hesitation in saying that he considered the plan of limiting Japanese exports to a monthly maximum of 5,000,000 square yards would, if made public, result in an outburst and probably lead to some form of Congressional action. He stated that he had been approached within the last day by several prominent Members of Congress in regard to the cotton textile situation, and he could say from personal knowledge that the "situation on the Hill is boiling".

Mr. Sayre then stated that this Government could not conclude any arrangement with Japan whereby total annual imports from Japan would exceed 36,000,000 square yards; that any amount over that would not "permit a pick-up" in those mills which are most seriously affected by Japanese textile competition.

Mr. Yoshizawa stated that he had been checking with the Japanese Commercial Attaché the figures of imports compiled by the Treasury Department, and he had ascertained that our figure of 36,000,000 square yards of imports from Japan in 1935 included imports into Puerto Rico, the imports into Puerto Rico alone exceeding in many months 1,000,000 square yards. He observed that the Japanese exports to Puerto Rico could not be controlled by the association that had been organized to regulate exports to the United States, for the reason that exporters to Puerto Rico were not included in the association. Mr. Yoshizawa added that, in any event, Japanese textile exports to Puerto Rico consisted for the most part of sheetings, and were not, therefore, of great concern to the American industry.

Mr. Sayre reminded Mr. Yoshizawa that Puerto Rico is within the United States customs area, and that there are no customs barriers between the United States and Puerto Rico. In his opinion, it would be impossible for various reasons to set up a gentlemen's agreement to be applicable only to imports into the continental United States and to be exclusive of imports into Puerto Rico. It was obvious to him that if such an agreement were put into effect the transshipment problem which we are now having in connection with the Philippine agreement would recur. Furthermore, he did not believe that it would be politically practicable to separate for customs purposes Puerto Rico from the United States.

The Japanese Ambassador asked Mr. Sayre whether it would be possible for us to agree to increasing the maximum Japanese shipments. Mr. Sayre stated that the situation is now so critical that some form of action had to be taken without delay and that, therefore, there is no time for bargaining. He also stated in strict confidence to the Japanese Ambassador that the Executive Committee on Commercial Policy had fixed the maximum at 36,000,000 square yards and he could hold out no hope whatever of the Committee agreeing to any increase in that figure.

Mr. Sayre asked the Ambassador whether his instructions had given him any indication of the attitude of the Japanese Government in regard to the increase in tariff recommended by the Tariff Commission. The Japanese Ambassador said that his Government would prefer that a gentlemen's agreement be concluded. Mr. Sayre again expressed grave concern over the situation created by the agitation for the taking of action by Congress, and he thought it not unlikely that there might be presented almost any day in Congress a bill aimed at Japanese textiles. The President had granted him an opportunity to arrive at some understanding with the Japanese Embassy, but he (Mr. Sayre) could not affirm with any degree of confidence that the President could hold off much longer the pressure being brought to bear on him by Members of Congress. It seemed to Mr. Sayre that time was of the essence.

The Japanese Ambassador stated that he would at once telegraph to his Government the purport of the present conversation; that a conference is to be held next Monday, May 4, between representatives of the Japanese Government and representatives of the cotton industry, and he expected that he would receive further instructions by Thursday, May 7.

611.946/297

Memorandum by Mr. Eugene H. Dooman of the Division of Far Eastern Affairs of a Conversation With the Counselor of the Japanese Embassy (Yoshizawa)

[WASHINGTON,] May 4, 1936.

Mr. Yoshizawa said that the Japanese Embassy had received from Tokyo instructions to inform the Department of the final position of the Japanese Government in regard to the restriction of imports of Japanese cotton textiles; that he had been directed by the Ambassador to make known the Japanese position to Mr. Dooman; and that, if the Department were of the opinion that "there is room for further discussion", the Ambassador would be glad to call on Mr. Sayre.

Mr. Yoshizawa further stated that the meeting planned to take place today in Japan between Japanese officials and representatives of the textile industry had taken place, and that the final position, beyond which no concession could be made, was as follows:

1. Owing to the opposition in Japan to the conclusion of further gentlemen's agreements, any arrangement that might be made should take the form of a unilateral declaration by the Japanese Government.
2. Japan will agree to a limitation of 40,000,000 square yards for the year begun April 1. This limitation is to apply to "imports for consumption".
3. The restriction shall apply only to those textiles covered by Item 904–B of the Tariff Schedule.
4. The previous Japanese proposal that there should be no restriction on imports into Puerto Rico is withdrawn.

Mr. Dooman informed Mr. Yoshizawa that he would at once make a report to Mr. Sayre. Mr. Yoshizawa expressed the hope that it might be possible to give him a reply today, so that he could telegraph to Tokyo this evening and receive a reply by tomorrow morning.

There then took place a brief discussion in regard to the terms proposed by the Japanese. Mr. Dooman stated that it had been found about a year ago that no recovery could be made by those American mills particularly affected by Japanese competition if Japanese imports were substantially in excess of 35,000,000 square yards, and that he believed that it would be difficult, if not impossible, to justify the American Government agreeing to any such figure as that proposed. Mr. Yoshizawa agreed that the terms which he had presented were not responsive to the American proposal of annual limitation to 36,000,000 square yards. He wished, however, to stress the fact that the report of the Cabinet Committee on Textiles published last summer stated that imports from Japan would, if not regulated, exceed 42,000,000 for 1935, whereas the actual imports were 6,000,000 square yards less—which fact, in his opinion, was due to the control exercised by the Japanese Government.

611.946/298

Memorandum by Mr. Eugene H. Dooman of the Division of Far Eastern Affairs of a Conversation With the Counselor of the Japanese Embassy (Yoshizawa)

[WASHINGTON,] May 5, 1936.

Mr. Dooman stated that the proposal in regard to imports of cotton textiles from Japan which Mr. Yoshizawa had presented on May 4 would be finally acted upon by the Cabinet at its meeting on Thursday, May 7. He added that in all probability the Cabinet would not view with favor the Japanese proposal and that it would recommend to the President that he accept the findings of the Tariff Commission and promulgate an increase of 50 percent on cotton textiles found to be unduly competitive with American goods.

Mr. Dooman then explained the effects which the Japanese proposal, if accepted, would have:

1. it would increase the proposed maximum allotment on bleached goods from 30,000,000 square yards to 40,000,000 square yards;
2. it would probably stimulate imports in the unrestricted lines, notably printed dyed or colored goods; and
3. it would probably stimulate imports of manufactured handkerchiefs.

Mr. Dooman then added that an arrangement such as that proposed by the Japanese could not be justified before the American public. The American Government could on logical and reasonable grounds defend an arrangement limiting Japanese imports to 36,000,000 square yards, but any maximum figure substantially in excess of 36,000,000 square yards would be open to the valid objection that it would operate still further to depress American industries that had been depressed by Japanese competition.

Mr. Yoshizawa stated that he was glad to get the statement of our position. He would report by telegraph to Tokyo today, in order that the Japanese Government might know as soon as possible that there is strong probability of its proposal being rejected. He said that, of course, very little time remained before next Thursday for the Japanese Government to attempt to bring the Japanese cotton industrialists into line if the Japanese Government considered it desirable to accept the American proposal of a limitation of imports of 36,000,000 square yards. He expressed the hope, therefore, that, in the event of the Cabinet recommending to the President that the duties be raised, such action be held in abeyance "for a day or two". Mr. Dooman said that he would be glad to bring this request to the attention of Mr. Sayre.

611B.9417/188 : Telegram

The Consul General at Hong Kong (Hoover) to the Secretary of State

Hong Kong, May 5, 1936—5 p. m.
[Received 7 : 45 p. m.]

Shipments of cotton textiles to the Philippines which are invoiced as China and Hong Kong products are rapidly increasing, 416,074 yards in January, 906,026 yards in February, 1,854,681 yards in March, 1,464,363 yards in April. Chinese manufacturers' associations in both Canton and Hong Kong declare that large quantities of Japanese goods are coming to Hong Kong and are reshipped from here as local products. The manufacturers themselves declare that their sales to local wholesalers have fallen off about 50 percent during the past 4 months, and that when they sell goods to wholesalers the latter demand two signed blank bills which the wholesalers evidently fill in and present at the Consulate with the invoices. Full report is being made by mail,[50] but in the meantime the seemingly illicit shipments are continuing. Manufacturers here declare that there is collusion between the shippers here and the Customs employees in Manila.

Hoover

---

[50] Not printed.

611.946/289

Memorandum by Mr. Eugene H. Dooman of the Division of Far Eastern Affairs

[WASHINGTON,] May 8, 1936.

Conversation: The Japanese Ambassador;
Mr. Seijiro Yoshizawa, Counselor, Japanese Embassy;
Mr. Sayre;
Mr. Ryder of the Tariff Commission; and
Mr. Dooman.

The Japanese Ambassador stated that he had been directed by his Government to call at the Department and to make perfectly clear the final position of the Japanese Government in regard to the restriction of imports of Japanese cotton textiles into the United States. The Ambassador then read in translation the text of his Government's instructions, which were substantially as follows: the Japanese Government is prepared to limit imports for consumption of textiles classified under item 904–*b* of the Tariff Act for a period of twelve months beginning April 1, 1936, to 30,041,422 square yards. The Japanese Government cannot undertake to regulate imports of textiles classified under 904–*c* of the Tariff Act.

The Ambassador, still setting forth his instructions, stated that the latter category of goods were exported from Japan largely to Puerto Rico by small manufacturers and merchants who are not members of the association of Japanese textile exporters to the United States.

The Ambassador went on to say that he was directed by his Government to declare that the Japanese cotton industry is greatly aroused over the reported intention of the American Government to increase duties on Japanese textiles in the event that no gentlemen's agreement can be reached, and that if the American Government should decide to impose increased duties on Japanese textiles the Japanese Government would have to reserve its right to take any appropriate action in the premises.

Mr. Sayre stated that he regretted that the reply of the Japanese Government was not favorable. He went on to say that the Cabinet had on May 7 recommended to the President that he issue an order increasing the duty on certain types of textiles, as advised by the Tariff Commission, but that the Cabinet had further recommended that the President take no action in this regard before noon Saturday, May 9. Mr. Sayre stated that the Ambassador could understand that the decision as to whether or not the last Japanese proposal should be accepted was no longer in his hands—that that decision lay in the hands of the President; that he would get in touch with the President as soon as possible; and that he would let the Ambassador know as soon as possible in regard to the President's decision.

Mr. Yoshizawa expressed the opinion that no great difficulty should be anticipated in regard to cloths coming under 904–c. He stated that the greater part of this cloth went to Puerto Rico, where there was a limited market; that the exporters in Japan had very little capital; that there is little likelihood of the Japanese being able to increase their market in the United States for printed cloths, for the reason that before current designs can be sent out to Japan to be copied the fashions change. Mr. Yoshizawa added that his Government would expect to have the Japanese allotment credited with re-exports on which a drawback had been granted.

Mr. Sayre observed that although the facts might be as stated by Mr. Yoshizawa, an announcement indicating that this Government had overlooked this category of Japanese goods would open the Government to severe attack. References would be made to the heavy increase in shipments of rayon from Japan to the Philippine Islands as an example of the ability of the Japanese to find loopholes.

Mr. Yoshizawa replied in the latter connection that his Government had instructed the Embassy to state to the Department that no parallel could be drawn between cotton goods and rayon goods.

After further discussion along the foregoing lines, Mr. Dooman advanced the suggestion that it might be possible to work out an agreement if the Japanese Government could see its way clear to proposing that an agreement be reached to limit imports of goods coming under 904–b to 30,041,422 square yards, but that this Government would have complete freedom of action to impose duties on goods coming under 904–c if imports for consumption should exceed last year's figures. Mr. Sayre stated that he would be disposed to consider favorably such a proposal if it were advanced by the Japanese Government, but that he could not, in the present circumstances, advance such a proposal himself. The Japanese Ambassador stated that he would report this suggestion to his Government and ask that a reply be telegraphed to him by tomorrow morning.

Mr. Ryder stated that he wished to raise the question of imports of manufactured handkerchiefs. It was realized that it would not be practicable to reach an agreement in regard to imports of this commodity, but in view of the fact that it was the increasing amount of imports of bleached goods used to manufacture handkerchiefs in the United States which had led to all the agitation, Mr. Ryder thought that some definite understanding should be reached in regard to this matter. The Japanese Ambassador replied that he understood the facts, and that he assumed that it would be our wish that, if an agreement were reached, the question of manufactured handkerchiefs would not be raised by increased imports over last year.

611.946/290

Memorandum by Mr. Eugene H. Dooman of the Division of Far Eastern Affairs

[Washington,] May 9, 1936.

Mr. Yoshizawa began the conversation by stating that he was "fed up". The Embassy had received instructions this morning to inform the Department that the Japanese Government could not advance the proposal suggested by Mr. Dooman, for the reason that it would lead to an agreement which the Japanese Government considered objectionable. The Japanese Government, Mr. Yoshizawa continued, would, however, agree to limit imports for consumption of goods coming under 904–*b* to last year's figures; that it did not expect that there would be any appreciable increase in imports of goods coming under 904–*c*, but that if the American Government anticipated that last year's figures of such imports would be exceeded, the Japanese Government would expect the American Government to consult with it before raising the duties on this category of textiles.

Mr. Yoshizawa added that the Embassy was further directed to emphasize the importance attached by the Japanese Government to the American Government agreeing to deduct from the figures of imports for consumption the figures of re-exports of Japanese cloths on which a drawback had been granted.

Mr. Dooman said that unfortunately Mr. Sayre could not be reached at once, and that he would therefore endeavor to place before the Secretary the terms of the Japanese reply, and that he would later communicate with Mr. Yoshizawa by telephone.

Note: Mr. Dooman saw the Secretary and explained the terms of the latest Japanese proposal. In response to an inquiry from the Secretary, he expressed the opinion that the terms seemed to warrant acceptance, and he thought that the White House should be informed that a new proposal had been received from the Japanese Embassy which made advisable the postponing of issuance by the President of an Executive Order increasing duties on cotton textiles. The Secretary consulted over the telephone with the President, who gave his approval to the Department giving consideration to the latest proposal.

Mr. Dooman then telephoned Mr. Yoshizawa that no action would be taken during the week-end to increase duties on cotton cloths, and he requested that Mr. Yoshizawa call on him next Monday, May 11.

611B.9417/196

Memorandum by the Assistant Secretary of State (Sayre)

[WASHINGTON,] May 12, 1936.

I had lunch today with Mr. Murchison [51] and talked over with him quite informally the textile situation both with respect to Japanese imports into the Philippines and Japanese importations into the United States.

With regard to imports into the Philippines, I gave Mr. Murchison a copy of the accompanying memorandum showing the Japanese importations during April.[52] As is apparent from this memorandum, the Japanese cut their direct shipments of February, 1936 (amounting to 4,504,000 square meters) in half during March; and they again cut the March shipments in half during April. As a result, for the first time during the period of the agreement (with the exception of December, 1935 and January, 1936, when the Japanese made practically no shipments), arrivals of United States cotton goods in the Philippines exceeded arrivals of Japanese cotton goods. Mr. Murchison was very pleased with these figures. He asked me whether, in consequence, he had better advise textile representatives in the Philippines to make no further move in approaching Filipino leaders with a view to securing Filipino legislation during the coming session of the Legislature to restrict Japanese shipments. I replied that I did not feel I was in a position to advise the textile groups on what action they should take; but I added that so far as I myself am concerned I had decided to follow a course of watchful waiting since it seemed likely to me that the Japanese were taking active steps to cut down their shipments of textiles so as not to exceed the quotas provided for in the Gentlemen's Agreement.

With regard to Japanese importations into continental United States, I first told Mr. Murchison that we had been carefully weighing the comparative advantages and disadvantages of limiting Japanese imports (*a*) by a tariff increase and (*b*) by quantitative restrictions. I said that we had reached the conclusion that restriction by a tariff increase would not be as advantageous to American textile interests as a limitation by quantitative restriction, for the reason that an increase in tariff would cause considerable uncertainty in the textile business since no one could tell in advance just what the Japanese importations would be under a tariff increase. I also said that a tariff increase might not give sufficient protection to domestic textile interests since the Japanese might manage to go over the tariff wall by means of cheapened production or otherwise. Mr. Murchison

---

[51] Claudius T. Murchison, president of the Cotton Textile Institute and former director of the Bureau of Foreign and Domestic Commerce.
[52] Not printed.

responded that the textile industry thoroughly agreed that quantitative restriction would be far more advantageous than a tariff increase.

I then said that in view of this conclusion we had approached the Japanese to secure, if possible, a voluntary agreement on their part to restrict imports for consumption to a definite figure. I went on to say that although no definite agreement had been concluded we hoped to secure a voluntary agreement from the Japanese to restrict their imports for consumption during the year April 1, 1936 to April 1, 1937 covering bleached goods (the most competitive goods), under Section 904(b) of the Tariff Act, to a figure not to exceed imports during 1935, namely 30,000,000 square yards. With respect to printed, dyed or colored goods (coming under Section 904(c) of the Tariff Act), I explained that in order to save the face of the Japanese we were not demanding a specific undertaking but that we were urging an understanding that if Japanese imports should exceed the 1935 figures (namely some 6,000,000 square yards) we would then be free to take action at once under Section 336.

I said that I wanted to explain these matters to Mr. Murchison before the agreement was buttoned up so as to secure his reaction as representing the textile groups.

Mr. Murchison replied that he was delighted to hear of the proposed agreement. He said that we deserved the sincere thanks of the textile interests and that he felt they would thoroughly approve the agreement. At the conclusion of our discussion he became almost enthusiastic about the proposed agreement.

He suggested that if I desired, he would be glad to issue a public statement when we put out our press release endorsing the agreement and adding any particular thoughts which I would like to have added. I promised accordingly to send him our proposed press release a day or two before its release with a suggestion of what I would like to have him say.

F[RANCIS] B. S[AYRE]

611.9417/138

Memorandum by Mr. Eugene H. Dooman of the Division of Far Eastern Affairs

[WASHINGTON,] May 21, 1936.

Mr. Yoshizawa called me on the telephone at my house last night at about 11:30. He said that the Japanese Ambassador and he had just completed a trans-Pacific telephone conversation with the Foreign Office at Tokyo, and that to his great regret he was directed to say that the Japanese Government could not proceed toward the conclusion of a gentlemen's agreement covering the imports into the United

States of cotton piece goods, so long as the American Government is not in position to direct American consuls in Japan to refuse certification of consular invoices covering shipments of cotton piece goods not covered by Japanese export permits.

Mr. Yoshizawa expressed his deep personal regret that the long and arduous efforts made by the Japanese Ambassador and himself, as well as by officers of the Department, had been fruitless. He expressed the appreciation of the Ambassador for the sympathetic consideration and attitude shown by officers of the Department and of the Tariff Commission. I reciprocated these sentiments, and further expressed the thought that it was fortunate from the point of view of relations between the United States and Japan that the Japanese Government had come to the decision, before concluding the arrangement, that it could not be made to work. Mr. Yoshizawa concurred.

With mutual expressions of regret the conversation ended.

611.9417/137a : Telegram

The Secretary of State to the Ambassador in Japan (Grew)

WASHINGTON, May 21, 1936—6 p. m.

63. For the past 3 weeks we have been discussing with the Japanese Embassy in Washington the terms of a proposed "gentlemen's agreement" with regard to imports into the United States of Japanese cotton piece goods. Although agreement had been reached with regard to the general terms of such an arrangement, it was not found possible to dispose of certain technical difficulties. Accordingly, the President today issued a proclamation [53] increasing, as recommended by the Tariff Commission, the rates of duty on certain types of cotton textiles.

HULL

611.946 Rag Rugs/155

Memorandum by Mr. Roy Veatch of the Office of the Economic Adviser

[WASHINGTON,] May 22, 1936.

Conversation: Mr. Tsuneo Hayama, Third Secretary of the Japanese Embassy; and
Mr. Otoshiro Kuroda, Attaché of the Japanese Embassy;
Mr. Veatch.

Mr. Hayama and Mr. Kuroda came to the Department on May 20 to receive the reply of this Government to the request which they

---

[53] 49 Stat. 3518.

presented on April 14, 1936, for an extension of the existing agreement covering the export of cotton rugs from Japan to the United States. Mr. Veatch informed them that he was authorized to say that after a study of the market conditions in the United States and after discussions with representatives of the American manufacturers and of the importers, the Government of the United States agreed to the Japanese proposal, namely, that Japanese exporters will limit their shipments of cotton rugs to the United States during the twelve-month period June 1, 1936 to May 31, 1937, to the following amounts:

(1) Chenille rugs wholly or in chief value of cotton—700,000 square yards.
(2) Hit-and-miss rag rugs wholly or in chief value of cotton—3,350,000 square yards.
(3) Rugs wholly or in chief value of cotton (except grass and rice straw), other than chenille, imitation oriental, and hit-and-miss rag rugs—4,070,000 square yards.

Mr. Hayama expressed his pleasure at this response of the American Government.

Mr. Veatch called attention to the fact that grass and rice straw rugs chief value of cotton are excluded from limitation in this agreement under category No. 3 in spite of the fact that they were included in the third category when the agreement was first reached in 1934. It was his understanding that imports of rice straw rugs chief value of cotton had reached considerable proportions and he merely took this opportunity of mentioning the fact that although the American Government had no intention now of asking that rice straw rugs be included in the limitations upon shipments of cotton rugs, it was conceivable, of course, that if rice straw rugs were pushed in the American market and entered into competition directly with domestic cotton rugs, it would be necessary to discuss the inclusion of rice straw rugs in connection with extension of the rag rug agreement. At the present time there was no particular reason for fearing this eventuality and it was to be hoped that it would not arise.

Agreement was then reached upon the text of a press release to be handed out before the end of the month. Mr. Hayama took the original of this draft with him (copy attached).[54] He said he was sure that there would be no objection to anything included in the draft.

On May 21 Mr. Hayama telephoned Mr. Veatch to say that he had transmitted to his Government a statement that the American Government had agreed to the Japanese proposal and also the text of the proposed press release. In response he had received the acknowledgment of this information by the Foreign Office. His

---

[54] Not printed; for text released to the press, see Department of State, *Press Releases*, May 30, 1936, p. 556.

Government had found no objection to the press release but had suggested that the release should be made a few days later.

611.946/306

Memorandum by Mr. Eugene H. Dooman of the Division of Far Eastern Affairs of a Conversation With the Counselor of the Japanese Embassy (Yoshizawa)

[WASHINGTON,] May 26, 1936.

Mr. Yoshizawa stated that early this morning he had received a telephone call from a Japanese correspondent in New York, who invited Mr. Yoshizawa to comment with regard to an article which was being carried by the *New York Times*. The article intimated among other things that the recent tariff action on Japanese cotton textiles was in large measure taken in retaliation for the smuggling situation in North China,[55] and suggesting that Japanese textiles would be excluded from the Philippine Islands as a further act of retaliation. Mr. Yoshizawa stated that he had informed the correspondent that he would make no comment until he had seen the article. He further went on to say that he had discussed the article this morning with the Japanese Ambassador, who had concluded that, as the article made no direct affirmation prejudicial to Japanese interests, it would not be appropriate for him to make an inquiry at the Department, but that he desired that Mr. Yoshizawa call at the Department and ascertain whether there were any basis in fact for the *New York Times* "story".

Mr. Dooman stated that the Department had also noticed the *New York Times* article, and that it was concerned by the implication contained therein that the recent tariff action on cotton textiles had in any way been caused by the smuggling situation in North China. He observed that, as Mr. Yoshizawa well knew, the conversations with the Japanese Embassy on the cotton textile situation had started as long ago as the summer of last year, and the action taken was the conclusion of a series of developments initiated months ago. He further pointed out that official information from the Philippines indicated that the gentlemen's agreement with Japan on cotton textiles imported into the Philippine Islands was on the whole working satisfactorily.

Mr. Yoshizawa asked whether he could inform his Government definitely that there was no relation whatever between the tariff action recently taken, or the recently announced silver arrangement with China [56] (which is also mentioned in the article under reference), and the smuggling situation in North China. Mr. Dooman said that he was authorized to make to Mr. Yoshizawa an oral statement, and he

---

[55] For correspondence concerning this situation, see pp. 110–230, *passim*.
[56] See pp. 459 ff.

read and then handed to Mr. Yoshizawa the text of such statement (copy attached).[57]

After Mr. Yoshizawa read the statement, he said that he supposed that the substance of the *New York Times* article had already been telegraphed to Japan by Japanese correspondents, and he thought that the statement which he had just received would be very helpful to his own Government in explaining to the Diet, which is now in session, the real attitude of the American Government.

At this point in the conversation, Mr. Dooman received a copy of the record of the press conference of Monday, May 25.[58] He invited Mr. Yoshizawa's attention to the reply by the Secretary to a question put by a correspondent with regard to possible future action by this Government on the North China situation. Mr. Yoshizawa read over several times the Secretary's statement, but made no comment.

The conversation then passed on to other matters.

611.946/306

The Department of State to the Japanese Embassy [59]

A press despatch under a Washington date line suggesting that the American Government has taken tariff action on Japanese goods, or is giving consideration to the taking of further action affecting Japanese goods, because of an economic and political situation external to the United States, is entirely without basis in fact.

The article under reference states that "steps were being considered looking toward cooperation with the Philippines and closing the Philippine textile market to Japan", and that "reports from Manila that transshipments of textiles, particularly from Hong Kong, have exceeded the provisions of the gentlemen's agreements are held to give the United States a lever for further action". As the most recent authoritative figures from the Philippine Islands indicate that imports of Japanese cotton textiles have not reached a quantity in excess of the terms of the gentlemen's agreement with Japan, no occasion has arisen for giving consideration to any action designed to exclude Japanese textiles from the Philippine Islands.

It may be stated in general that any action taken by the American Government to restrict imports from any foreign country has been based solely upon economic considerations and only after a careful collection and examination of factual data. Each case (or situation) is dealt with on its own merits.

---

[57] *Infra.*
[58] Not printed.
[59] Handed to the Counselor of the Japanese Embassy, May 26; released to the press by the Department the same day.

611.9431/115

Memorandum by Mr. Eugene H. Dooman of the Division of Far Eastern Affairs

[Washington,] June 10, 1936.

Conversation: Mr. Saburo Kurusu, Japanese Ambassador to Belgium;
Mr. Sayre;
Mr. Dooman.

After an exchange of amenities, Mr. Kurusu stated that he had looked forward to an opportunity to meet Mr. Sayre, whose book, *America Must Act*, he had repeatedly read. He associated himself with Mr. Sayre in virtually all of the views expressed in that book, and he felt confident that there would be no important difference of opinion between the two with regard to international economic problems.

Mr. Kurusu went on to say that, although the economic policies of the United States and of Japan are identical, unfortunately there had occurred developments which had created in Japan a feeling that the United States was acting with less generosity toward imports from Japan than the facts seemed to warrant. He referred to the fact that the United States is plentifully endowed with natural resources and is less dependent upon outside trade than is Japan, which is obliged to import most of the raw materials necessary for industry and to export the products of its labor. It had seemed to him that it would be essential for Japan to oppose, as does the United States, the tendency towards bilateral trade balancing, for the reason that trade balancing has the effect, not of increasing trade, but of decreasing trade.

Mr. Kurusu stated that Japan was being faced on all sides with barriers designed to limit and reduce Japanese imports. He referred to the quotas established against Japanese textiles in the British colonies and to the various measures adopted for such purpose by countries in Latin America. Nevertheless, he said, those countries that were busily engaged in restricting imports from Japan are at the same time demanding of Japan that she increase her purchases from those countries. There were, Mr. Kurusu observed, several countries which enjoyed a considerable and favorable trade balance against Japan, and it was the general feeling in his country that Japan could reasonably and with warrant expect those countries to refrain from taking action to restrict imports from Japan. Mr. Kurusu remarked that the circumstances would serve to explain the dissatisfaction which had been created in Japan by the successive acts of the American Government toward curtailing imports of Japanese commodities.

Mr. Sayre stated that he was glad to receive from Mr. Kurusu this frank statement of views. He welcomed this opportunity to make known to Mr. Kurusu that this Government does not look with disfavor upon increased purchases by Americans of Japanese goods, and that it would, in line with its basic economic policy, welcome increased imports from Japan, provided that such increased imports do not seriously harm or endanger established American industries. This Government has strenuously opposed the tendency toward bilateral balancing, for the reason that, as Mr. Kurusu had remarked, the effect of such a policy is to reduce the volume of international trade. He cited as an example of multilateral trade the excess of exports of the United States to European countries, of European countries to Latin America, and of Latin American countries to the United States, and he showed how the trade between these three areas would be reduced if the principle of bilateral balancing were effectively carried out.

Mr. Sayre then reviewed the numerous conversations which he had had with Mr. Saito during the past two years with regard to Japanese competition. He had explained to the Japanese Ambassador that it was the fundamental policy of this Government to liberalize trade throughout the world, but that practical considerations made necessary certain exceptions to this policy; that in certain cases goods had come in from Japan in such quantities and at such low prices as to endanger the existence of established American industries; and that in such instances it had been necessary to approach the Japanese Government with a view to shipments from Japan being regulated in such manner as to relieve the pressure upon affected American industries. Where the Japanese Government had found itself unable to exercise the necessary measures of control, this Government had reluctantly imposed additional duties.

Mr. Kurusu remarked that Japan is in a difficult position. Most countries which had an unfavorable balance of trade with Japan made no effort to find markets for their products in Japan, insisting that Japan come to them and buy more of their products. Mr. Kurusu said that Japan is carrying a double burden—it is endeavoring to expand its exports, and at the same time it is making every effort to increase its purchases from those countries that are insisting upon the principle of bilateral balancing. He added that certain Latin American countries followed the practice of raising a hue and cry over Japanese competition; that merchants closely associated with government officials would rush to buy Japanese goods and restrictions would be imposed as soon as a large stock of Japanese goods had been accumulated; and that the effect of restrictions would be an immediate increase in the value of such stocks, thus giving the merchants an opportunity to make unwarranted profits. Mr. Kurusu added that as soon as the stocks showed signs of depletion, proposals would be made to the Japanese Government with regard to a fresh start.

Mr. Kurusu then referred to the various items of Japanese imports into the United States upon which restrictions had been imposed, and he wondered whether the American Government understood how the Japanese people as a whole had reacted to the restrictions. He stated that the amounts involved were small in most of the instances to which he referred, and that the Japanese people could not understand why they should be repeatedly called upon to forego opportunities to cut down the large amount owing to the United States on trade balance. As to cotton cloths, Mr. Kurusu stated that the amount involved is negligible when compared with Japan's purchases of raw cotton. He said that about five-ninths of Japan's total textile output is sold to foreign countries, and that if the restrictions that are being imposed on all sides against Japanese cotton textiles continued Japan will have no alternative but to reduce its purchases of raw cotton. He referred again to the large favorable balance of trade of the United States with Japan, and he stated that the imposition of restrictions by the United States on Japanese goods placed Japan in an awkward position when dealing with countries, with unfavorable balances of trade with Japan, which are restricting imports of Japanese goods. He stated that very frequently representations of the Japanese Government to governments of such countries were met by the rejoinder that Japan had a more serious grievance against countries like the United States.

Mr. Sayre remarked that the Japanese viewpoint with regard to recent American action on cotton cloths as presented by Mr. Kurusu did not seem to take sufficiently into account the discussions which had extended over more than a year between the Department and the Japanese Embassy before the action was finally taken. He said that he had urged Mr. Saito to persuade his Government to regulate exports to the United States of cotton cloths, and that toward the end of last year the American Government had received an assurance which had been interpreted to mean that exports to this country would be kept down to last year's levels. Unfortunately, however, the figures for imports for consumption for the first three months of the present year were far in excess of the figures for the corresponding period of last year. Mr. Sayre then showed to Mr. Kurusu a table of statistics. Mr. Sayre went on to say that in all fairness to the Japanese he should say that the actual arrivals of cotton cloths were not much larger than they were for the corresponding period of last year, but that as the Japanese had overshipped last year there were in bonded warehouses substantial stocks, which were drawn upon and added to the amounts arriving from Japan. The result was that the amount of cotton cloth cleared through the customs was so great as to profoundly agitate the American textile industry. The Tariff Commission had been directed to make an investigation on the basis of Paragraph 336 of the Tariff Act to determine costs of production in the United States and in Japan, and the Tariff Commission had found that additional duties were required in order to equalize such costs of production. Before taking action on the report of the Tariff Commission, a final opportunity was given the Japanese Government to regulate shipments from Japan, and when the Japanese Government found itself unable to enter into any arrangement, this Government reluctantly increased the duties on competitive cotton cloths.

Mr. Sayre said that unfortunately in instances of this character there are available only the two alternatives either of an arrangement being concluded with the Japanese Government or higher duties. It might appear to the Japanese that a gun was being held to their heads, in fact the Japanese Ambassador had remarked in the case of cotton cloths that the American Government was issuing to the Japanese Government an ultimatum. Mr. Sayre said that such was not in fact the case. The circumstances required that some form of action be taken at once.

Mr. Sayre said that there was another case now before the American Government. There had been in recent months a large influx of snap fasteners [60] from Japan, and he feared that it would be necessary that action be taken. The position taken by the Japanese Government in the cotton cloth case did not hold out much promise of the Japanese Government responding favorably to a proposal, if made, with regard to the conclusion of a gentlemen's agreement on snap fasteners, but no decision had been taken whether or not the Japanese Government would be approached. Mr. Sayre said that there are now in the offing a considerable number of other cases which involve the possibility of further action against Japanese goods.

Mr. Kurusu stated that the procedure followed by the American Government is of such character as to accentuate the difficulties caused by Japanese competition. He stated that as soon as reports appear that there is possibility of the American Government taking cognizance of imports from Japan, the tendency of exporters in Japan and importers in the United States is to rush in a large volume of the commodities concerned, and at any price which may yield a profit, before duties are raised or before any restriction as to quantity

---

[60] Also known as zippers or slide fasteners.

has been imposed. It is his opinion that most of the damage was done before restrictive action has been taken. He had come to the conclusion that the only satisfactory method of dealing with questions of this kind would be to prevent the difficulties from actually arising, and with that purpose in mind he believed that it would be advantageous if there were set up in the United States some governmental agency whose primary function it would be to watch market prices and trends of imports from Japan, so that the business men concerned would be apprised beforehand of the possibility of Japanese imports unduly affecting the American market.

Mr. Dooman said that thought had been given on the American side to the setting up of some such body as that suggested by Mr. Kurusu, but that the weight of opinion seemed to be that the body should be non-governmental in character. He explained to Mr. Kurusu that there had been set up a few years ago an association to protect American holders of foreign bonds. It had been determined that the functions of such an association could not be properly carried out by the Government, but that the Government could give such an association its "blessing" and render it assistance in various ways. Similarly, it is thought that the American Government could properly place the information available to it at the disposal of a private agency whose function it would be to render advice to merchants engaged in trade between the United States and Japan.

Mr. Sayre remarked that before the conversation was concluded there were certain points affecting American interests which he desired to bring to the attention of Mr. Kurusu.

Mr. Sayre then explained briefly the situation with regard to the red salmon fishing industry in Alaska.[61] He expressed the hope that Mr. Kurusu could see his way clear to advise his Government how this Government is concerned over future developments and hopes that the Japanese Government can enter into some arrangement which would serve to preserve the red salmon for American interests. Mr. Kurusu said that the matter lay outside the scope of the Commercial Bureau of the Foreign Office, but that he had some knowledge of the conversations which had taken place during the past few years between officials of the American and Japanese Governments. He recalled that several years ago the American Embassy, in collaboration with Japanese officials and private individuals, had formulated a certain arrangement, and Mr. Kurusu thought it a pity that the arrangement had not gone through. He said, however, that he would transmit to his Government the remarks of Mr. Sayre in this connection.

---

[61] See pp. 942 ff.

Mr. Sayre then referred to the recently enacted Japanese law for the control of the automobile industry.[62] He said that in the gentlemen's agreements concluded with Japan it was the intention of the American Government to assure to the Japanese a share in the American market. When the cotton rug agreement was renewed, the American Government had taken cognizance of the beneficial effects of that agreement and had voluntarily offered the Japanese an increased share of American business. He thought it important that the Japanese Government should similarly grant to American business increased participation in Japanese markets as such markets developed. He could realize that the Japanese Government would naturally try to foster a native automobile industry, but at the same time he thought it important that the Japanese Government should not restrict for all time the American automobile industry to its present share of the Japanese market, but that as the demand in Japan for automobiles increased American manufacturers should be permitted to supply a portion of that increase. Mr. Kurusu remarked that the point of view expressed by Mr. Sayre interested him very much, and that he would not fail to present it to Tokyo.

The next point presented by Mr. Sayre was the Japanese Petroleum Control Law.[63] Mr. Sayre stated that it was the view of this Government that several features of that law would operate to affect adversely and inequitably American interests, and that although this Government had not thus far made any representations to the Japanese Government on a basis of the legal considerations involved he thought it necessary that the Japanese Government should realize that developments with regard to the petroleum situation in Japan were being followed by this Government attentively and with much concern. He hoped that the Japanese Government would realize that important American interests were involved and that the manner in which the controversy is dealt with by the Japanese Government will inevitably affect the thought and feelings of the American people toward Japan. Mr. Kurusu stated that he was on the whole optimistic with regard to the final outcome. He said that the foreign oil interests had stressed three desiderata: first, that they be given a guarantee that they will be permitted to operate in Japan for a specified period of time; second, that they be given a guarantee as to the quantity of petroleum products that they will be permitted to sell; and, third, that the price of gasoline be increased. Mr. Kurusu went on to say that the Japanese Government had no difficulty in meeting the first two of these points, but it was reluctant to raise the price of gasoline for the reason that the livelihood of taxicab drivers would

[62] See pp. 981 ff.
[63] See pp. 786 ff.

be adversely affected. He understood, however, that just prior to his departure from Japan it had been decided that the price would be raised. Mr. Kurusu added that certain negotiations were in process between the foreign oil interests and certain private Japanese interests, and that he had reason to anticipate that the negotiations will be brought to a successful conclusion without any great difficulty.

As the conversation had continued for almost two hours, Mr. Sayre suggested that Mr. Kurusu accompany him to lunch.

611.9417/146

Memorandum by Mr. Roy Veatch of the Office of the Economic Adviser

[WASHINGTON,] June 11, 1936.

Conversation: Mr. Toyoji Inouye, Commercial Secretary of the Japanese Embassy,
Mr. Tsuneo Hayama, Third Secretary of the Japanese Embassy,
Mr. Otoshiro Kuroda, Attaché of the Japanese Embassy,
Mr. Veatch.

Mr. Inouye suggested that I lunch with him and Mr. Hayama and Mr. Kuroda in order to discuss particularly the details of a possible joint Japanese-American committee to study and advise upon the solution of problems arising out of Japanese competition in the United States. Mr. Kurusu had mentioned the possibility of such a joint committee to Mr. Sayre and Mr. Dooman and he had suggested that Mr. Inouye might attempt to get some agreement upon details of the plan before Mr. Inouye returns to Japan this summer. In addition to discussion of this plan, Mr. Inouye took the occasion to state strongly his feelings with respect to the expected action of the President increasing the rates of duty on importations of slide fasteners.

PROPOSED JOINT COMMITTEE ON JAPANESE-AMERICAN TRADE

Mr. Inouye outlined his scheme as follows: A committee would be set up in Washington, meeting perhaps regularly once a month, to include the officials of the United States Government who deal with Japanese competition and representatives of the Japanese Government in the Embassy in Washington, including Mr. Inouye, who would come from New York for the meetings. A somewhat similar committee would be set up in Tokyo, to be composed of officials of the Japanese Government who deal with the problem, including probably a representative of the Departments of Commerce and Agriculture and perhaps a representative of the Federation of Industries, and, on the American side, representatives of the American Embassy, including the Commercial Attaché, Mr. Williams.

At the meetings of these committees, including special meetings when necessary, the latest information regarding the trends of Japanese-American trade would be reported and discussed. In Washington an attempt would be made to have for meetings of this committee the fullest possible information regarding new developments in the importation of Japanese products into the United States, especially those which would be competitive with American products. In Japan developments affecting American interests or trade would be brought to the attention of the committee and the American representatives would have an opportunity to secure information regarding any such developments. Each committee would make full reports upon the problems considered, including recommendations of action to be taken either by the Governments or by the private commercial interests in the two countries. These reports would be exchanged by the two committees and they would be presented to the two Governments.

Mr. Inouye felt that his Government would be greatly assisted by this sort of advice and that it would be able to call upon Japanese industry to take the necessary steps to prevent the creation of difficult problems in connection with the sale of Japanese commodities in the United States. Mr Inouye himself now makes an attempt to keep his Government informed regarding developments here and to suggest where action should be taken by Japanese industry in order to prevent the creation of difficult problems. Under the new scheme such warnings would be more likely to be effective since they would have the prestige of the committee behind them, they might be much better prepared and substantiated than is possible at present and he felt that the recommendations of action would probably receive serious consideration by both Governments in time to secure favorable results.

I raised the question of the cooperation of private business in both countries, which in most instances would appear to be necessary in order to prevent the necessity of restrictive action by either Government. Mr. Inouye agreed that the cooperation of business would be necessary but said that at least in the case of Japan he felt that effective cooperation could be secured only as a result of approach by the Government to the private interests concerned. He repeatedly stated that in his opinion all business interests, whether in Japan or in the United States, were essentially selfish and shortsighted and that it is necessary to exercise governmental pressure upon them to lead them to take action which will be in line with the interests of all. To his mind, all business interests are shortsighted and interested only in immediate advantages.

SLIDE FASTENERS

Mr. Inouye said that he had understood that the Tariff Commission had completed its investigation of slide fasteners and that the Commission's report was now somewhere in the neighborhood of the White House. He had gone to the Tariff Commission yesterday, therefore, to learn as much as he could about the situation and to find out if there was anything which the Japanese might do to remedy the situation or at least to make possible delay in increasing the tariff rates on slide fasteners.

Mr. Inouye asked if I didn't see some way to save the situation, which he thought was very unfortunate. I then explained the difficulties of our position and stated that I had had the feeling that probably the best possible action from the standpoint of the Japanese would be a moderate tariff increase since I understood it would be very difficult, if not impossible, for the Japanese industry to exercise effective control of its exports to the United States.

Mr. Inouye showed a realistic understanding of the problems in this country but in a very serious mien he sought to impress me with the dangerous position in Japan. He spoke of the manner in which certain sections of the press in Japan had played up the action of this Government in increasing the rates of duty on cotton cloth and he said the journalistic treatment of that action in this country had been widely commented upon in Japan. There was the greatest danger that the more sensational press in Japan would give such emphasis to further tariff increases in the United States directed specifically against Japanese goods, following so closely the action on cotton textiles, that the Japanese Government might be forced to take a "strong position" toward such increases and retaliation of some sort be decided upon. He himself is planning to go to Japan in July. He has had great hopes of being able to make considerable progress this summer in educating the Japanese to view with favor the action which he considers Japanese industry must take in order to allay the alarm aroused by Japanese competition in this country. In his opinion action now to increase the tariff on slide fasteners would make it practically impossible for him to make any progress in this direction.

I emphasized the fact that if action was taken by the President to increase the duty on slide fasteners it was practically certain that that action would be very moderate and would in no sense be a prohibitive tariff. In Mr. Inouye's opinion, however, the extent of the tariff increase would have little importance because the press comments, both in the United States and in Japan, would emphasize merely the fact that the tariff was increased and that this was another step in jacking up the rates generally against Japanese products.

611.003 Oils/63

The Japanese Ambassador (Saito) to the Secretary of State

No. 127　　　　　　　　　　　　　　WASHINGTON, June 13, 1936.

The Japanese Ambassador presents his compliments to the Honorable the Secretary of State and, in pursuance of his note No. 113 [*123*], dated June 6, 1936,[64] has the honor to inform the Secretary that the proposed imposition of customs duty on Rapeseed oil would affect the importation of such oil adversely as in the case of Perilla oil if the Revenue Tax Bill now under consideration by the Congress in conference be enacted in the present form. Both Perilla and Rapeseed oil are not only special products of Japan which are exported to the United States to the amount of ¥21,000,000 and ¥11,000,000, respectively, in 1935, but also their cultivation and manufacture are conducted mainly for the United States market.

Now that the proposed duty would be equivalent to 80% and 100% ad valorem, respectively, the bill, if enacted as it is, would prove to be almost prohibitive to the importation of the commodities in question, and further, in view of the fact that these commodities form two important items of Japanese export to the United States the effect on the trade in general between the two countries would not at all be negligible.

In these circumstances, the Ambassador begs leave to express the hope that these two items be eliminated from the list of the proposed new duties so as to avoid creating another hindrance to the Japanese-American trade.

611.946/315

Memorandum by Mr. Eugene H. Dooman of the Division of Far Eastern Affairs

[WASHINGTON,] June 20, 1936.

Conversation:　The Japanese Ambassador;
　　　　　　　　Mr. Seijiro Yoshizawa, Counselor, Japanese Embassy;
　　　　　　　　Mr. Sayre;
　　　　　　　　Mr. Dooman.

Mr. Sayre asked the Japanese Ambassador with a smile whether he had ever heard of "zippers". The Japanese Ambassador replied that unfortunately he had occasion to read about "zippers" in the press.

Mr. Sayre went on to say that the Tariff Commission had recently submitted to the President a report on slide fasteners, and that he

---

[64] Not printed.

could say in strict confidence that the Tariff Commission had found that there was a substantial difference in costs of production in the United States and in Japan. Mr. Sayre stated that the President had indicated that he would take action on the report. The Japanese Ambassador interrupted to inquire whether the President had actually signed the report. Mr. Sayre said that whatever might be the action thus far taken by the President, the fact was that no action could be effective until it had been published in the *Federal Register.* In view of the undertaking given by the Department to the Japanese Ambassador to the effect that no action to restrict imports on Japanese goods would be taken until there had been consultation with the Japanese Government, the President had authorized him (Mr. Sayre) to ascertain whether the Japanese Government would be prepared voluntarily to regulate exports of slide fasteners from Japan.

Mr. Sayre stated that he felt that he should place his cards on the table. He had been disposed at one time to think that, in view of the possibility that any undue delay in obtaining from the Japanese Government a voluntary undertaking to regulate shipments might perhaps lead to a re-opening of the case and to a new recommendation by the Tariff Commission that imports be placed on a basis of American valuation, it might be wise to let matters take their course. He said that there was room for an honest difference of opinion as to what the basis of valuation should be, and that, although the present report of the Tariff Commission recommends a moderate increase in duties, it might be possible to deduce from the available facts that American valuation would be warranted. He had been mindful, however, of the promise given by the Department to consult with the Japanese Embassy, and he had accordingly been authorized to offer the Japanese a choice between voluntary restrictive action by the Japanese or increased duties.

Mr. Sayre expressed the hope that, in view of the efforts he had made to delay the taking of action by the President on the Tariff Commission's report, it would not be thought that he was holding a gun up to the heads of the Japanese, for such was not the case. He sincerely hoped that it would be possible for the Japanese to increase their exports to the United States and in order to help along the development of Japanese trade with the United States he had in the past taken action to remove focal points of agitation. He wondered whether the Japanese appreciated the courageous stand being taken by the Secretary to liberalize trade. It is our hope that when the Secretary's efforts were finally successful it would be possible for each nation to participate in the benefits of this program. The failure of the program would necessarily lead to still further decreases in world trade and it was Mr. Sayre's opinion that a victory for bilateral balancing would very seriously affect Japan.

The Administration, Mr. Sayre continued, was being severely attacked by its political opponents on account of its foreign trade policy, and considerable help was unavoidably given to these political opponents whenever it became necessary to take some measure toward increasing duties, which, of course, is a form of action not consistent with the foreign trade policy of this Government. It would be reasonable, he thought, for people to wonder why then the Administration had taken these measures. The explanation was that duties had been increased in several instances in order to save the larger program; that political pressure had been difficult to withstand in these instances; and that by satisfying the important interests concerned it would be possible to keep their allegiance for the fight to maintain the basic foreign trade program.

The Japanese Ambassador remarked that while he understood the circumstances referred to by Mr. Sayre he hoped that the American Government for its part would appreciate the difficulty which restrictive measures by the American Government created for the Japanese Government, and that was the encouragement given countries with an unfavorable balance of trade with Japan to cut down their imports of Japanese goods.

Mr. Sayre stated that matters were urgent and that there was not sufficient time for bargaining. He hoped that the Japanese Government could see its way clear to offering us terms so liberal that it could be possible for us to resist those who would like to see Japanese manufactured products excluded.

The Japanese Ambassador asked whether he could be given some idea as to the figures which we would consider satisfactory. Mr. Sayre said that there had not been sufficient time to go into the matter of figures. He could say that imports from Japan competed with a certain range of American products equal to fifteen percent of the total production of slide fasteners and that in that range Japanese competition was so severe as to threaten to eliminate American production. He said that during the last six months of 1935 imports from Japan amounted to 9.7 million slide fasteners and that imports during the first four months of the present year amounted to 9.8 million slide fasteners. Here again there was a sharply rising curve of imports from Japan.

Mr. Dooman expressed the opinion that perhaps it might be well for the Japanese Government to consider, in the light of political background so frankly described to the Japanese Ambassador by Mr. Sayre, whether it would not be well to acquiesce in the President proceeding with the report of the Tariff Commission. Mr. Sayre concurred in that view, but he said to the Japanese Ambassador that he hoped that, if the Japanese Government should come to that decision, it would make it completely clear to the Japanese public that the American Government had not taken any action without first consulting the Japanese Government. The Japanese Ambassador thanked Mr. Sayre for his efforts toward removing the possibility of misunderstanding over the matter under discussion, and he stated that he would not fail to report fully to his Government the thoughts and circumstances so frankly presented by Mr. Sayre.

611.946/317

Memorandum by Mr. Eugene H. Dooman of the Division of Far Eastern Affairs

[WASHINGTON,] June 26, 1936.

Conversation: The Japanese Ambassador;
Mr. Seijiro Yoshizawa, Counselor, Japanese Embassy;
Mr. Sayre;
Mr. Dooman.

The Japanese Ambassador stated that he assumed that Mr. Sayre already knew, as a result of informal conversations which Mr. Yoshizawa had yesterday with officers of the Department, what he had been instructed to say with regard to the possibility of there being concluded a gentlemen's agreement on slide fasteners. The Ambassador went on to say that his instructions were to inform Mr. Sayre that, if action is to be taken by the American Government on the basis of section *a* of paragraph 336 of the Tariff Act, the Japanese Government would not deem it practical to proceed with negotiations such as those proposed, but that if action was to be taken on the basis of section *b* of the same paragraph, and "American valuation" declared on imports of slide fasteners, the Japanese Government would be prepared to look into the question of voluntarily regulating exports of slide fasteners from Japan.

Mr. Sayre replied that the possibilities of reaching a satisfactory agreement had been very carefully looked into by the Department, and that we had reached the conclusion that it would be extremely difficult, if not impossible, to find a basis which would be satisfactory to both sides: that any figures which would be acceptable to the Japanese would arouse the domestic industry, whereas any figure satisfactory to the domestic industry would not be acceptable to the Japanese. He hoped that, if the President should take action to increase duties, the Japanese Government would make it clear to the

Japanese public that the American Government had not taken such action arbitrarily but that it had previously consulted with the Japanese Government.

The Japanese Ambassador said that he would, of course, not fail to impress upon his Government the necessity of letting the public in Japan know of the facts.

He wondered whether Mr. Sayre could not assure the Japanese Ambassador that the President would not declare for "American valuation". Mr. Sayre stated that the Department has legally no part in the procedure laid down for the taking of action under paragraph 336 and that the question of the taking of final action can be decided only by the President. After some discussion, Mr. Sayre said that he would endeavor to let the Japanese Ambassador know in the event that the President should decide to return to the Tariff Commission its report for further consideration.

Mr. Sayre stated that during the course of the conversation which he had recently with Mr. Kurusu, Japanese Ambassador to Belgium, Mr. Kurusu had pointed out that once the reports of the Tariff Commission are in the hands of the President, the circumstances are unfavorable for the conclusion of arrangements for voluntary regulation of exports by the Japanese. Mr. Kurusu had suggested that it would be advantageous to have set up a body which would follow trends in shipments from Japan and their effects upon American industries and markets, the body to advise Japanese shippers to regulate their shipments in such manner as to avoid, so far as possible, injuring American interests. Mr. Sayre added that the suggestion with regard to the setting up of a body had been discussed among various officers of the Department, but that it had occurred to him that it might be helpful in the meantime to the Japanese if he were to supply the Japanese Ambassador with a list of Japanese commodities which are now causing trouble, with perhaps a brief memorandum showing the kernel of the problem in each case. He believed that he could have such materials in the hands of the Japanese Ambassador next week. The Japanese Ambassador agreed that it would be extremely helpful to have such information. Mr. Sayre asked Mr. Yoshizawa to express his opinion with regard to the thought which Mr. Sayre had. Mr. Yoshizawa also agreed that it would be most helpful, but he believed that discussions should start as soon as possible with regard to the setting up of a body such as that suggested by Mr. Kurusu.

The conversation then turned to press reports with regard to recent incidents in Peiping (See separate memorandum [65]).

---

[65] Not printed.

611.003 Oils/79

Memorandum by Mr. Roy Veatch of the Office of the Economic Adviser

[WASHINGTON,] June 29, 1936.

Mr. Hayama called to inform the Department of State of a cable which the Japanese Embassy had just received from the Foreign Office in Tokyo. This cable pointed out the very high tax on perilla oil and rapeseed oil and stated that the cultivating industry and oil industry in Japan have been thrown into confusion because of the fear that the tax will prove to be prohibitive on imports of these oils from Japan.[66] Because of the size of this tax and the extensive value of the exports of these oils from Japan (totaling 30,000,000 yen last year) it is the view of the Japanese Government that the effect of the tax upon Japanese exports to the United States will be much more adverse than the tariff increases on cotton cloth and slide fasteners—it is felt that in fact there is no comparison.

The Foreign Office states in the cable to the Japanese Embassy that in view of these circumstances the Japanese Government earnestly hopes that the United States Government will make some allowance for the carrying out of these taxes so as to mitigate the blow which will be given to Japanese exports to the United States, perhaps by means of the regulations which will be promulgated for the enforcement of the Act or by other measures.

Mr. Veatch stated that he was sure the Department would receive this request sympathetically and would immediately have an examination made of the possibility of making some arrangements in line with this request. He feared that there was no discretion left by the language of the Act with respect to the collection of the tax on these oils but there might be some other way in which this Government could assist the Japanese Government in reassuring the industry in Japan with respect to the probable effect of the tax upon the trade in rapeseed oil and perilla oil. He was quite sure that the tax would not prove to be prohibitive and that the industry in Japan might not be as hard hit as was anticipated, although he recognized that planters in Japan and Manchuria must be very uncertain as to the future demand in the United States and therefore as to the supply which will be required from Japan.

Mr. Veatch stated that he would see that information was sent to the Japanese Embassy as soon as possible with respect to whatever measures, if any, this Government would be able to take in order to mitigate the disruptive effects which the Japanese oil industry might feel as the result of the imposition of the new excise taxes or as a result of the fear which these taxes may have engendered.

[66] The Revenue Act of 1936 was approved June 22; 49 Stat. 1648.

611.9417/145

Memorandum by Mr. Roy Veatch of the Office of the Economic Adviser

[WASHINGTON,] July 6, 1936.

Conversation: Seijiro Yoshizawa, Counselor, Japanese Embassy;
Toyoji Inouye, Commercial Secretary, Japanese Embassy;
Tsuneo Hayama, Third Secretary, Japanese Embassy;
Mr. Veatch.

Mr. Inouye spent July 6 in Washington at the suggestion of Mr. Yoshizawa in order to have a final discussion on a number of questions before his departure for Japan on July 9. He had spent most of the morning with Mr. Fox [67] discussing the possibility of an agreement between the American cotton textile industry and the Japanese cotton textile industry with respect to the American Market. Mr. Yoshizawa suggested an informal discussion with Mr. Veatch at luncheon and during the afternoon on a number of points so that the views of Mr. Inouye and of the Japanese Embassy might be made known to the Department of State.

PROPOSED JOINT COMMITTEES ON JAPANESE-AMERICAN TRADE

Mr. Inouye and Mr. Yoshizawa were both particularly interested in a further discussion of the possibility of creating joint Japanese-American committees to attack the trade problems in which the two governments and the two peoples are interested. Mr. Yoshizawa said that he and the Ambassador had gained the impression when they talked with Mr. Sayre on the subject that Ambassador Kurusu had not left with Mr. Sayre a clear understanding of the Japanese suggestion that the two governments join in creating special committees to discuss and to advise upon the best means of handling actual or potential trade conflicts between the two nations. It was Mr. Yoshizawa's suggestion, therefore, that this question be discussed in greater detail.[68]

Mr. Veatch explained that he had written a rather complete memorandum upon his conversation with Mr. Inouye, Mr. Hayama and Mr. Kuroda on June 11, 1936, setting forth in some detail the specific proposals which Mr. Inouye had made regarding the creation of joint official committees in Washington and in Tokyo for the purpose of exchanging information regarding trends in Japanese-American trade and particularly with regard to potential conflicts. He stated that Mr. Sayre had requested that a study be made of this suggestion in

---

[67] A. M. Fox, director of research, U. S. Tariff Commission.
[68] Notation by the Economic Adviser; "I think this deserves encouragement. H[erbert] F[eis]"

the interested divisions of the Department of State and he understood that some action would soon be taken upon the matter in the Department. Undoubtedly Mr. Sayre would be in a position to discuss the subject with Mr. Yoshizawa and the Japanese Ambassador in the near future.

Mr. Inouye pointed out that his proposals would in effect merely continue in a somewhat more definite form the actual practice that has already been followed, since representatives of the Embassy and of the American Government have met frequently in Washington to exchange information and to discuss trade problems, and that similar conferences had been held between representatives of the American Embassy in Tokyo and the Japanese Government. He felt that it was most important, however, to regularize this procedure and particularly to make an effort through such committees to place information in the hands of the Japanese regarding potential conflicts arising out of United States imports from Japan. He himself always made an effort to secure whatever information he could from the Tariff Commission and the Department of Commerce regarding trends in the trade but he felt it would be much easier if this information could be prepared by the American Government and brought to the attention of the Japanese Government at regular intervals. Mr. Inouye dislikes the necessity of having to ferret out information himself and he also feels that when he alone on his own responsibility presents this information to his Government there is not a ready disposition to treat the information as important and as calling for action. If this sort of material could be gone over by the joint committee in Washington and that committee could counsel some action by the two governments in order to meet the situations disclosed, then he felt that the Government in Tokyo would be much more inclined to give serious consideration to the problems presented.

Mr. Inouye discussed at some length his conviction that all of the trade problems in which the two governments were interested should be brought before the proposed official committees and that all information which could be secured from the trades regarding these problems should be collected by the respective governments and brought to the attention of these committees. Mr. Yoshizawa felt, however, that there were many problems affecting Japanese-American trade relations which required attention and action by private agencies before any appropriate action on these problems could be taken by the two governments. He said that it was well known that the American Government did not exercise great control over industry and business. He said it was also true that the Japanese Government frequently was unable to exercise any considerable control over industry and business in spite of the popular idea that the Japanese Government did have the power to control trade as it pleased. It was his feeling, therefore, that most problems of trade conflict between the two countries could appropriately be handled only by private interests in their early stages and it was his opinion that it would be wise to establish, if possible, two parallel sets of joint committees, the official committees suggested by Mr. Inouye to handle or to advise upon acute trade problems and general trade policy, whereas joint committees representing private business and industry should seek ways of handling problems in their early stages so that critical situations should not arise.

After considerable discussion Mr. Inouye, Mr. Yoshizawa and Mr. Veatch agreed that logic seemed to support the desirability of this dual method of handling trade problems between the two countries, if possible. It was further agreed that it would be desirable to proceed first and as soon as possible with the creation of a joint Japanese-American official committee in Washington to consider Japanese-American trade relations and, further, that it probably would be desirable for this committee to consider at its first meeting or at an early meeting the possibility of the two governments giving some impetus to the creation of a joint committee of representative leaders of business, industry and other economic activities in the two countries.

PROPOSED PRIVATE JAPANESE TRADE DELEGATION TO THE UNITED STATES

Mr. Yoshizawa reported that the Japanese Consul General at New York, Mr. Sawada, is now in Japan and has been urging the sending of a private economic mission to the United States partly to return the visit of the Forbes [69] mission to Japan a year ago. Mr. Yoshizawa was informed unofficially that Mr. Sawada had met with success and that things were progressing rapidly for the sending of such a mission to the United States in the near future. Should discussion of some new effort to plan an attack upon trade problems by a joint private committee be undertaken in the near future, it might be possible for the Japanese Government to influence the selection of the personnel of the proposed mission so that that mission might make progress while in this country in discussing such a plan with American business leaders.

Mr. Yoshizawa said that he would make an effort to learn more about the plans for the proposed mission and would pass on to Mr. Veatch whatever information he could secure.

PROPOSED PRIVATE COTTON TEXTILE UNDERSTANDING

Mr. Inouye reported at some length upon his discussions with Mr. Murchison and with Mr. Fox regarding Mr. Murchison's proposal to have the American cotton textile industry seek an agreement or an understanding with the Japanese industry regarding the United States market and other markets in which the two industries find

---

[69] W. Cameron Forbes, former Ambassador in Japan.

themselves in competition. Mr. Inouye had welcomed the suggestion and thought that it held distinct possibilities. He had, however, made some specific suggestions regarding changes in Mr. Murchison's preliminary plans.

Mr. Veatch suggested that probably Mr. Murchison had had in mind the desirability of inviting representatives of the Japanese industry to come to this country as a courteous first move; he might, nevertheless, welcome a suggestion by the Japanese in turn that leaders of the American industry should come to Japan for the discussions. Mr. Inouye said that he had urged upon Mr. Murchison the desirability of the American textile men seeing the Japanese cotton textile industry so that they might know at first hand the conditions about which so much has been said in this country. He was sure that the American group would receive a royal welcome by the Japanese industry and that they would be free to examine thoroughly any part of the Japanese industry. Furthermore, in support of his proposal that the Americans come to Japan, he stated that it would be difficult for the most important figures in the Japanese industry to come to the United States and he felt that a much better discussion would eventuate if the meeting could be held in Japan. Also, in the event that the American group would wish to discuss the Philippine market, he felt that this could be done much better in the Far East. It was his own suggestion that the American group might find it desirable to stop off in Japan for a preliminary discussion, when it might raise with the Japanese group the fundamental questions which would require careful study, that the Americans might then proceed to the Philippines to look over that situation and then return to Japan for more extensive conferences.

Mr. Yoshizawa supported Mr. Inouye's suggestions and said that it would be very pleasant if the American group could arrive in Japan by the first of November so that it might have the advantage of the beautiful fall season in the Orient.

Mr. Inouye had asked Mr. Murchison if he felt that he personally could go to Japan with an American group if the decision were made to hold the conferences in the Far East. In Mr. Inouye's opinion Mr. Murchison gave the impression that he would like very much to be with the American group in such conferences but that he would hesitate himself to suggest that he should make the trip or that he should head the American textile group. Mr. Inouye was of the opinion that it would be wise for Mr. Murchison to head the group because of his background in the academic world and in government service and his understanding of the problems to be considered. It was his opinion, therefore, that the Department of State might wish to exercise some influence in the selection of Mr. Murchison to head the group.

POSSIBLE VISIT OF AMERICAN OFFICIALS TO JAPAN

Mr. Yoshizawa recalled the fact that Mr. Dooman had spoken to him informally some time ago of the possibility of a small delegation of American officials visiting Japan in the near future to study and to discuss possible solutions of trade problems affecting the two countries and also the fact that more recently Mr. Dooman had suggested that it probably would be impracticable to send such a group to Japan before the American elections in November because of the possibility of misinterpretation of the visit. Mr. Yoshizawa and Mr. Inouye wish to urge, however, that if it were at all possible a visit of at least a very small delegation of American officials to Japan at this time should prove to be very helpful. Mr. Veatch pointed out the dangers of misinterpretation of such action because of the political discussions which will continue until the November election [70] and it was agreed that it would be undesirable to take any action which would encourage a political discussion of Japanese-American trade relations. Mr. Veatch explained that even Mr. Fox, who was in no sense a political appointee, had been dragged into the discussion of the trade agreements program through Mr. Peek's articles in the *Saturday Evening Post* and that because of Mr. Fox's activities in the trade agreements program, as publicized by Mr. Peek, it might readily be assumed or be charged that he was sent to Japan by this Government in order to negotiate a trade agreement. Mr. Yoshizawa and Mr. Inouye were strongly of the opinion that Mr. Fox would be an ideal person to go to Japan and they urged that this Government consider sending Mr. Fox alone if a larger group were impracticable and if he could be sent without the danger of creating undesirable publicity. For instance, Mr. Fox might merely go on a vacation and travel to the Orient without any public announcement or discussion. Or this Government might find it desirable to send certain officials to the Philippines to study the situation there and this delegation might in the ordinary course of events stop off in Japan, perhaps going and coming, without exciting comment.

611.9417/150

Memorandum by Mr. Roy Veatch of the Office of the Economic Adviser

[WASHINGTON,] July 13, 1936.

Mr. Veatch handed to Mr. Yoshizawa memoranda [71] on the growth of competition in the American market of cotton hosiery and of cotton

---

[70] Notation by the Economic Adviser: "I agree".
[71] Not printed.

velveteens imported from Japan, stating that these memoranda had been prepared at Mr. Sayre's request so that this information might be placed at the disposal of the Japanese Embassy. Mr. Veatch recalled that in a previous conversation Mr. Sayre had told the Japanese Ambassador and Mr. Yoshizawa that such statements would be prepared for the Embassy with regard to any commodities importations of which were creating an unusual competitive situation in the United States. Memoranda had been prepared only with respect to these two commodities at the present time; data with respect to other commodities might be presented to the Japanese at a later time when more information was available and perhaps through the medium of a joint Japanese-American official committee in Washington should that committee be created.

Mr. Yoshizawa expressed his appreciation of this information and asked certain questions with respect to it. On the authority of Mr. Graham Clark, Chief of the Textile Division of the Tariff Commission, Mr. Veatch informed Mr. Yoshizawa that the Tariff Commission has in progress an investigation of imports of cotton velveteens under its general powers (Section 332 of the Tariff Act of 1930), in response to a Senate Resolution, and that "it might be necessary" to change this investigation into a 336 investigation at some time in the future. On the same authority he was informed that the Tariff Commission has received a request for action under Section 336 with respect to cotton hosiery imported principally from Japan and that the Commission now has under way a preliminary investigation and, on the basis of the facts disclosed by this investigation, will determine whether or not to order an investigation under Section 336.

Mr. Yoshizawa said that he had expected memoranda on more commodities and that he had understood Mr. Sayre to say that a list would be prepared, for the Japanese Embassy, of all commodities imported from Japan against which complaints had been made by American competitors. Mr. Veatch doubted that useful memoranda could be prepared on many commodities at the present time, and Mr. Yoshizawa agreed that this material might appropriately be brought to the attention of the Japanese Embassy through the proposed joint official committee later in the year. He did feel that it would be useful, however, if the Embassy could be given as soon as possible a list of commodities against which complaint had been made, including if possible a statement of whatever investigation or action has been started upon these complaints. Mr. Veatch was of the opinion that this list could be prepared for the Japanese Embassy.

Mr. Veatch also informed Mr. Yoshizawa, at Mr. Sayre's suggestion, that Mr. Sayre had requested that a draft be prepared in the Department immediately regarding the form and functions of the proposed joint official committee representing the Japanese Embassy and the American Government. This draft would then receive immediate attention in the Department and the Japanese Embassy would be informed as soon as Mr. Sayre was ready to discuss the matter.

611B.9417/207

Memorandum by Mr. Roy Veatch of the Office of the Economic Adviser

[WASHINGTON,] July 15, 1936.

At Mr. Sayre's suggestion, Mr. Veatch handed to Mr. Hayama a statement of the arrivals in the Philippines of Japanese cotton piece goods for the month of June 1936 and a summary of arrivals of all Japanese cotton piece goods for the eleven months ending June 30, 1936,[72] expressing the great concern which Mr. Sayre felt because of the fact that the total of 48,916,000 square meters was less than 600,000 square meters under the maximum quota for arrivals of Japanese goods in the Philippines for the full twelve months of the cotton textile agreement dating from August 1, 1935. Mr. Veatch stated that Mr. Sayre would be glad to talk with Mr. Yoshizawa about this situation whenever Mr. Yoshizawa might wish; Mr. Yoshizawa might wish to cable this information to Tokyo and to secure some further information from the Foreign Office before discussing the matter with Mr. Sayre.

611B.9417/209

Memorandum by Mr. Roy Veatch of the Office of the Economic Adviser

[WASHINGTON,] July 17, 1936.

Conversation: Mr. Seijiro Yoshizawa, Counselor of the Japanese Embassy;
Mr. Sayre;
Mr. Veatch.

Mr. Sayre referred to the statistics handed to Mr. Yoshizawa on July 15, 1936,[72] giving arrivals of Japanese cotton goods in the Philippines during the first eleven months of the agreement. Mr. Yoshizawa said that the same statistics had been forwarded to the Foreign Office in Tokyo by the Japanese Consul General in Manila. He indicated, however, that his instructions regarding the attitude of the Japanese

---

[72] Not printed.

Government had not been changed and he proceeded, therefore, to review the course of the discussion between Mr. Sayre and the Japanese Ambassador regarding this entire problem. He recalled that early last spring Mr. Sayre had insisted upon the inclusion of transshipments in the quota as provided for previously in the agreement, but he commented upon the further fact that the American Government had made no attempt to press the Japanese Government for an answer on this point.

Mr. Yoshizawa stated that the Exporters Association had so controlled the allocation of quotas for shipment to the Philippines during the second six months of the agreement that the total shipped directly from Japan to the Philippines during the first year of the agreement should not exceed 45,000,000 square meters. The Association had allocated permits to export only 15,226,430 square meters between February 1 and June 20, 1936, and the total allocation for the period February 1 to August 1 would not exceed 19,000,000 square meters as compared with the 23,500,000 square meters which the Exporters Association maintained it would be justified in exporting to the Philippines during this period under the terms of the agreement. If, during this period, arrivals in the Philippines of Japanese goods transshipped from Hong Kong had not exceeded 4,500,000 square meters, then the maximum quota allowed by the agreement would not have been exceeded even under the interpretation of the American Government.

Mr. Yoshizawa emphasized again the fact that the Japanese Government had warned the American Government that Japanese exporters were unable to control shipments via Hong Kong and the American Government had been requested, therefore, to do something itself to prevent or to limit arrivals of transshipped goods.

Mr. Sayre replied that of course the United States had studied this request very seriously but had been unable to find any means of controlling such transshipments. It had always been the opinion of the American Government, however, that Japanese goods arriving in the Philippines via Hong Kong should be included in the maximum quota for Japanese goods because in the first place Japanese manufacturers did get the advantage of the sale of the goods transshipped via Hong Kong and, conversely, the opportunities for sales of American goods in the Philippines were limited just as much by sales of Japanese goods transshipped via Hong Kong as by goods arriving directly from Japan.

There was considerable further discussion of this problem and of the record of the two Governments in the discussions of the problem during the past several months. Mr. Sayre emphasized the fact that this Government had not in the past and did not now intend to be a stickler for the letter of he agreemnt. He was not wishing to find fault with the Japanese. The real problem regarding the continuance of the agreement for a second year did exist, however. It appeared probable that arrivals of Japanese goods in the Philippines during the full twelve months of the agreement would exceed the maximum of 49,500,000 by three or four million square meters. There probably would be eight to nine million square meters of Japanese goods arriving via Hong Kong, in excess of the 45,000,000 square meters arriving directly from Japan. Mr. Sayre felt that the Japanese Government would not wish to maintain that this large amount of Japanese goods entering the Philippines should be completely overlooked and excluded from the agreement. If this Government is willing to overlook the apparent violation of the terms of the agreement which will result from arrivals in excess of 49,500,000 square meters, then it would appear to be fair for the Japanese Government to agree to a smaller quota of arrivals of Japanese goods in the Philippines for the second year of the agreement, particularly if only goods arriving directly from Japan are to be included in the quota for the second year.

Mr. Yoshizawa emphasized again the disadvantage at which exporters to the Philippines are placed because of the license fee which they pay to the Association on all direct shipments to the Philippines. Chinese importers in the Philippines, therefore, find it possible to compete with these goods by importing Japanese goods from Hong Kong, on which no fee has been collected. Furthermore, he made the point that the greater the reduction in the amount of Japanese goods arriving directly from Japan, the better the market which is created for goods shipped in from Hong Kong.

Mr. Yoshizawa said that if he understood Mr. Sayre to say that either transshipments must be included in the quota or the American Government will consider the agreement as having broken down, then he would wire this information to Tokyo immediately. Mr. Sayre replied, however, that this Government did not wish to take a hard and fast position on this or any other point affecting the agreement. It was the desire of this Government to keep the agreement alive and to make it work as well as possible. He assumed that the Japanese Government had the same desire and he wondered if the Japanese Government could not bring forth some other possibility, perhaps an agreement upon a lower figure for next year if the quota were limited to goods arriving directly from Japan.

Mr. Yoshizawa said that he would be glad to cable this suggestion to Tokyo if Mr. Sayre wished to submit it, but Mr. Sayre assured him that he did not wish to submit any proposal to the Japanese Government. He merely wished to emphasize the serious concern of this Government regarding the working of the agreement and his feeling that a real problem for the serious study of both Governments was created by the present situation and by the desirability of finding a satisfactory adjustment of the agreement for the second year.

Mr. Yoshizawa asked whether it would be possible for the Philippine Assembly, which is now in session, to take action with respect to transshipped goods if the American Government feels that imports of such goods must be included in the agreement. In reply Mr. Sayre said that such action would run counter to the whole trade policy of this Government since it would create direct discrimination against Hong Kong. It would mean the creation of a precedent justifying similar action on the part of other countries.

Mr. Yoshizawa thought the final point of particular significance since it would give a precedent for South American countries to cut Japanese goods out of their markets.

In response to Mr. Sayre's continuing interest in any constructive way in which the present difficulty might be met, Mr. Yoshizawa said that unfortunately he was not in a position, within the scope of his instructions from the Foreign Office, to offer any constructive suggestions. It would be necessary first for him to lay the problem before the Foreign Office and to receive further instructions.

In this connection he asked if he might say in his despatch that in the event that the Japanese Government insists the transshipments must be excluded, the whole agreement will fall through. In response Mr. Sayre said that he would not so word the position of this Government. Rather, he would suggest that Mr. Yoshizawa's despatch should state that if the Japanese Government cannot find some constructive way of meeting the present situation, the American Government will have an exceedingly difficult time in defending the continuance of the agreement to the American cotton textile industry. The agreement had been an attempt to divide 50–50 the joint market for Japanese and American cotton goods in the Philippines. During the period February–June 1936, Philippine imports to American goods had not exceeded 12,000,000 square meters whereas arrivals of Japanese goods had exceeded 23,000,000 square meters; taking account of the embroidery goods sent to the Philippines and reexported to the United States, it was probable that American cotton cloth sold in the competitive Philippine market did not exceed during this period 25 percent of the amount of Japanese cotton cloth sold in that market. In spite of this poor showing for American cotton textiles, however, this Government was not interested in pressing for strict interpretation of the letter of the agreement. It had yielded on many points of interpretation of the agreement in the past and its one interest now was to seek a constructive adjustment of the agreement. Larger issues even than the cotton textile trade itself were at stake.

Mr. Yoshizawa agreed with the desirability of keeping the agreement alive. On the other hand, he said that when his Government yielded to pressure from the American Government, while Japanese imports of American goods greatly exceeded in value American imports of Japanese goods, new difficulties were created for his Government in its efforts to prevent new barriers against Japanese trade in South American markets. When Japan seeks to protect her export trade in those markets, she is asked why she does not insist more strongly upon the extension of her exports to those countries which at present buy less from her than they sell to her. As an example of the attitude which Japan is being forced to take against such countries, Mr. Yoshizawa mentioned the action of the Japanese Government in invoking the trade protection law against Australia since Australia sells much more to Japan than she buys from her.

Mr. Yoshizawa said that many Japanese industrialists and traders could not understand why the Japanese Government yielded to the American Government to the extent of agreeing to control of Japanese exports to the American market or to the Philippines. He said he saw no harm in telling Mr. Sayre that a group of Osaka cotton textile exporters had been in Washington recently and had pressed Mr. Yoshizawa for an explanation of the negotiations regarding an agreement for voluntary restriction of Japanese exports of cotton piece goods to the United States. Following his explanation, these exporters had expressed their gratification that negotiations for such an agreement had broken down since they were convinced that in spite of the recent tariff increases they would be able to ship 100,000,000 square yards of cotton piece goods to the United States before the end of the year. There would be time enough then for negotiation of an agreement. Mr. Yoshizawa insisted that of course these opinions did not express the attitude of the Japanese Government itself; he had called attention to this experience merely as an illustration of the difficulties which the Japanese Government was facing.

Mr. Sayre expressed his hope that the Japanese Government would continue to seek constructive and mutually satisfactory adjustments of the incipient trade conflicts between the two countries. The two Governments must look to the future and try to protect the broad interests, which were more important than any temporary trade advantage. It was important to both Governments that trade wars be avoided since they were inevitably destructive of the best interests of all parties concerned.

611.003 Oils/84

The Acting Secretary of the Treasury (Taylor) to the Secretary of State

WASHINGTON, July 28, 1936.

SIR: Reference is made to your letter of July 9, 1936,[74] relative to a conversation between Mr. Tsuneo Hayama, Third Secretary of the Japanese Embassy, and a member of your Department with reference to the excise tax imposed on perilla oil and rapeseed oil in the Revenue Act of 1936.

You state that Mr. Hayama referred to the concern of his Government over the effect of these taxes upon exports of perilla and rapeseed oil from Japan to the United States and conveyed the hope of his Government that the United States will make some allowance in the administration of these taxes so as to mitigate their adverse effects upon Japanese exports to the United States, perhaps by means of regulations which will be promulgated for the enforcement of the Act or by other measures. You ask that this Department indicate the nature of the reply to be made to the Japanese Government.

Perilla oil is entitled to free entry under paragraph 1732 of the Tariff Act of 1930 (U. S. C. title 19, sec. 1201), and rapeseed oil is dutiable at the rate of 6 cents per gallon under paragraph 53 of the same Act. Section 701, Title V, of the Revenue Act of 1936 (Public, No. 740, 74th Congress) provides the rate of 4½ cents per pound on perilla oil and rapeseed oil in addition to any other taxes or duty imposed by law when imported into the United States, unless treaty provisions of the United States otherwise provide.

This Department knows of no authority for the remission or reduction of these rates with respect to oils imported from Japan and they must be administered as other taxes or duties on imported articles. I am accordingly unable to suggest any way in which importers of rapeseed oil or perilla oil from Japan may be relieved from the payment of the import tax of 4½ cents per pound after the effective date of such tax. There is enclosed herewith a copy of a Circular Letter issued to collectors of customs [74] to advise them concerning the effective date of the new import taxes under consideration.

Very truly yours,   WAYNE C. TAYLOR

---

[74] Not printed.

611.9417/153

Memorandum by Mr. Roy Veatch of the Office of the Economic Adviser of a Conversation With the Counselor of the Japanese Embassy (Yoshizawa)

[WASHINGTON,] August 12, 1936.

Mr. Veatch referred to a recent visit of Mr. Claudius T. Murchison, President of the Cotton Textile Institute, to the Department when he had spoken of his last conversation with Mr. Inouye, Commercial Secretary of the Japanese Embassy, shortly before the latter's departure for Japan. Mr. Murchison had reported that he and Mr. Inouye had agreed at that time that as soon as the American textile industry was ready to support discussions between Japanese and American cotton textile leaders, this information should be brought to the attention of the Japanese Embassy by the Department of State for transmission to Japan. Mr. Veatch then referred to the fact that the projected conversations between the cotton textile leaders themselves had not been brought officially to the attention of the Department of State and that Mr. Sayre had been of the opinion that the matter could be handled best by the private interests without the participation of this Government. In view of the understanding between Mr. Inouye and Mr. Murchison, however, Mr. Veatch had been authorized to pass on to Mr. Yoshizawa quite informally the information regarding this situation which Mr. Murchison had brought to the attention of the Department of State.

Mr. Veatch repeated Mr. Murchison's statement that without exception the leaders of the American cotton textile industry had given their approval to the project of seeking a mutually acceptable adjustment of the competition between Japanese and American cotton textiles in the American market. Mr. Murchison had stated that the American industry would be prepared, therefore, to accept an invitation from the Japanese industry to send a representative delegation to Japan to discuss the matter. If such an invitation were forthcoming soon, the American delegation would prefer to proceed to Japan in October since the American executives could best be spared from their business at that time before the busy winter season had gotten under way.

Mr. Yoshizawa said that he would cable this information to Tokyo and that undoubtedly an invitation from the Japanese industry would be cabled as soon as possible in order to expedite the plans of the American delegation. He stated that he appreciated fully the informal character of this information and that he understood that no reply was expected by the Department. Any invitation forthcoming

from the Japanese industry undoubtedly would be extended directly
to the Cotton Textile Institute and not indirectly through the Department. To assist in expediting such a direct invitation, Mr. Veatch
gave Mr. Yoshizawa the address of the Cotton Textile Institute.

Mr. Veatch then said that Mr. Murchison had mentioned quite
informally an unfortunate occurrence which might tend to embarrass
the projected effort for a *rapprochement* between the cotton textile
industries of the two countries. He had spoken of an interview which
a writer for *Liberty* (an American magazine) had secured with Mr.
Donald Comer, President of the American Cotton Manufacturers
Association, the association of the cotton manufacturers of the South.
This interview had painted Japanese competition in cotton textile
markets as a form of undeclared "warfare" with the United States
and had been highly objectionable. When the text of the article
had come to Mr. Murchison's attention, he had taken up the matter
with Mr. Comer and both had greatly regretted the character of the
reported interview. They had made a strong effort to have the article
in question withheld, but the management of *Liberty* had declared that
the entire issue in which this article was to appear had been set up
and that it would be impossible to withdraw the article at this late
date. The article was to appear, therefore, in the August 29 issue
of *Liberty*. In an effort to counteract the influence of this article,
Mr. Murchison was preparing a careful statement of the whole problem of Japanese-American competition in cotton textiles and it was
his expectation that this article would appear in the Sunday *New
York Times* a day or two before the appearance of the August 29
issue of *Liberty*. Both Mr. Murchison and Mr. Comer greatly regretted this unfortunate occurrence. Mr. Murchison had wished that
their feeling about the matter might come to the attention of the
Japanese so that the article in *Liberty* would not be received as a
true expression of the attitude of the American industry. For this
reason Mr. Veatch had taken this occasion to pass this information
on to Mr. Yoshizawa quite informally.

Mr. Yoshizawa said that assuredly he would see that this information was brought to the attention of the textile leaders in Japan. He
then expressed the hope that, particularly in view of this occurrence,
it would be possible for Mr. Comer to be a member of the American
textile delegation visiting Japan. He felt that it was most important
for such men as Mr. Comer and Mr. Murchison to know the Japanese
industry at first hand in order that there might not be misunderstandings in the future between leaders of the American industry and
leaders of the Japanese industry.

611B.9417/214

Memorandum by Mr. Roy Veatch of the Office of the Economic Adviser

[WASHINGTON,] August 12, 1936.

In connection with a visit to the Department upon another matter, Mr. Hayama took occasion to say that the Japanese Embassy had received from the Association of Cotton Textile Exporters to the Philippines copies of the Association's regulations governing exports of cotton piece goods to the Philippines. These regulations contained a provision, added since the original regulations had been issued, providing that short lengths of cotton piece goods were not covered by the Association's export control and that therefore certificates would not be required for the export of these short lengths to the Philippines.

Mr. Veatch made the comment that apparently this regulation would free exporters from any restriction upon shipments of such cloth to the Philippines and therefore would leave exporters free to ship any amount of cloth in this form outside of the quota to which the Exporters Association had agreed. In Mr. Hayama's opinion this appeared to be a reasonable interpretation, although the Japanese Embassy had received no explanation of this provision. Mr. Hayama recalled the fact that the Department had called to the attention of the Japanese Embassy some two or three months ago arrivals of such cloths in the Philippines, with the suggestion that the exporters from Japan might wish to exercise some control over such shipments so that a new complication in the working of the voluntary agreement could be avoided. Mr. Hayama was unable to say whether the regulation excluding short-length cloths from restriction had been issued before or after the Department's suggestion had been brought to the attention of the Japanese exporters, but he thought it quite possible that the regulation had been issued before that time, perhaps giving rise to the shipments of these cloths which had come to the attention of the Department. The Japanese Embassy had received no response to its communication setting forth the Department's concern regarding these shipments, and it was possible that since that time the Exporters Association had made some change in the regulation to which Mr. Hayama had made reference.

Mr. Veatch pointed out that if ordinary cotton piece goods were to be shipped from Japan to the Philippines without restriction when cut in short lengths, such shipments most probably would increase rapidly and would either nullify the effects of the agreement or force this Government to consider means of dealing with this situation.

It had been the hope of this Government that Japanese exporters voluntarily would refrain from making an issue of this point.

Mr. Hayama said that he thought it was important for the Embassy to bring again to the attention of the Japanese Government the potential difficulties involved in this question and he assured Mr. Veatch that he would see that this was done immediately.

611B.9417/212a

The Department of State to the Japanese Embassy [76]

ARRIVALS OF JAPANESE COTTON PIECE GOODS IN THE PHILIPPINES
IN JULY 1936

(For the ports of Manila, Iloilo
and Zamboanga; other ports not included)

Total	Direct from Japan	Via Hong Kong
	(In thousands of square meters)	
1,911	1,394	517

Total arrivals of Japanese cotton piece goods during the second six months of the agreement exceeded 25,000,000 square meters. The exact amount is not yet available but it is apparent that total arrivals of Japanese goods during the first twelve months of the agreement, August 1, 1935–July 31, 1936, were in the neighborhood of 51,000,000 square meters, or approximately 1,500,000 square meters in excess of the maximum amount to be imported into the Philippines under the terms of the agreement.

611B.9417/218

Memorandum by Mr. Eugene H. Dooman of the Division of Far Eastern Affairs to the Assistant Secretary of State (Sayre)

[WASHINGTON,] August 27, 1936.

With regard to the Philippine cotton textile agreement:

Mr. Veatch and I have had several informal conversations with Mr. Yoshizawa. These conversations were not made a matter of record, for the reason that, during your absence, neither Mr. Veatch nor I felt that we were authorized to make any statement which Yoshizawa could accept as authoritative.

Mr. Yoshizawa showed himself most reluctant to discuss the question of Hong Kong transshipments, and he insisted that if we were to

---

[76] Handed to the Counselor of the Japanese Embassy by Mr. Dooman, August 13.

insist upon reopening the question the Japanese Government would have to insist that those transshipments were not understood by it to be included in the quota. However, we told Mr. Yoshizawa that the question whether the transshipments at Hong Kong are to be included in the total figures is one which must inevitably arrive upon publication of statistics if total imports of Japanese textiles into the Philippines should be maintained at the present rate of importation.

We said further that we could not unduly postpone publication of the figures of imports into the Philippines for the whole year. If the Japanese Government could give us a definite assurance that total imports of Japanese goods would be held down to a reasonable figure, say, between three million and four million square meters per month, in publishing the figures for last year we would stress the difficulties which have attended the efforts of the Japanese Government to control shipments and we would make public some expression of satisfaction with the manner in which the agreement had been carried out. We also informed Mr. Yoshizawa that if no such assurance could be given by the Japanese Government we would have to publish the figures without comment, and if the response in this country to the figures of Japanese imports was adversely critical we would be obliged to give consideration to the question whether the agreement should not be terminated.[77]

Mr. Yoshizawa has said more than once that he believes that we have taken a very moderate position. He promised several weeks ago to present our thoughts to the Japanese Government and to urge it to give the assurance requested. We have no doubt but that he has telegraphed to Tokyo, as promised, but he states that he has thus far received no reply.

611B.9417/215

Memorandum by Mr. Roy Veatch of the Office of the Economic Adviser

[WASHINGTON,] September 2, 1936.

At Mr. Sayre's suggestion, Mr. Veatch telephoned Mr. Yoshizawa and said that Mr. Sayre quite agreed with Mr. Yoshizawa's informal suggestion that a further cable might be sent to the Japanese Foreign Office by Mr. Yoshizawa reporting that upon his return Mr. Sayre was amazed to find that there had as yet been no response from the

---

[77] On August 28 Mr. Dooman handed Mr. Yoshizawa a table of statistics compiled by the Philippine Bureau of Customs (611B.9417/214a).

Japanese Foreign Office to the representations made by this Government with respect to the continuation of the Philippine textile agreement.

Mr. Yoshizawa said that as he had stated the day before, he was disappointed and somewhat chagrined that more than a month had gone by since he had first cabled the Foreign Office with respect to Mr. Sayre's concern over the Philippine cotton textile agreement without a reply from his Government. He had sent two or three further cables on the same subject during the past month but still had secured no response, and consequently he would be very glad to send another cable immediately, expressing Mr. Sayre's concern over the situation and reemphasizing the necessity of clearing up the matter as quickly as possible.

600.0031 World Program/32

Memorandum by the Secretary of State

[WASHINGTON,] September 3, 1936.

After the Japanese Ambassador had concluded briefly presenting me with a Memorandum on another subject [78] during his call this afternoon, I inquired whether his Government was still interested in the development of more suitable world trade relations and a larger volume of international trade generally. He promptly replied in the affirmative. I then briefly reviewed the necessity for the success of the broad program which this Government is pursuing, instead of narrow cut-throat bilateral methods alone, such as are being pursued today, especially in Europe with the result that her international trade will probably be less this year than last, notwithstanding the large volume of purely war trade being conducted. The Ambassador expressed real interest in the success of our program and referred to the fact that his Government had cooperated in several instances with which I was familiar. I thanked him very heartily for this degree of valuable cooperation and again expressed my gratification that his Government is much interested in the success of the program to restore normal world trade, as nearly as possible at least, and I urged that his statesmen on suitable occasions might see their way clear to proclaim this broad doctrine as did Dr. Schacht [79] some weeks ago in Berlin.

C[ORDELL] H[ULL]

---

[78] See memorandum of September 3, by the Secretary of State, vol. I, p. 136.
[79] German Minister of Economics and President of the Reichsbank.

611B.9417/224

Memorandum by Mr. William T. Turner of the Division of Far Eastern Affairs

[WASHINGTON,] September 5, 1936.

Conversation: Mr. Sayre;

    Mr. Seijiro Yoshizawa, Counselor, Japanese Embassy;

    Mr. Turner.

Mr. Yoshizawa called on Mr. Sayre at noon. He stated that he had finally received from his Government a reply to repeated requests that some action be taken in regard to the matter of transshipment at Hong Kong of Japanese textiles to the Philippine Islands. He handed to Mr. Sayre a memorandum [80] containing the proposals of the Japanese Government, which, he said, represented the maximum concession of the Japanese Government and, in his opinion, constituted a definite contribution toward the solution of this problem. Mr. Sayre expressed gratification that the Japanese Government was making such a determined effort toward solving this problem and expressed appreciation of the cooperative attitude of the Japanese Government.

After examining the proposal, Mr. Sayre asked whether, with the proposed measures in force, the Japanese Government would consider transshipments from Hong Kong as included within the total figure of Japanese textile exports to the Philippine Islands. Mr. Yoshizawa replied that he did not think that his Government was prepared to concede on that point. Mr. Sayre then reminded Mr. Yoshizawa that the original textile agreement was based on the principle of sharing equally the Philippine market, whereas the actual result has been that the volume of Japanese textiles, including those transshipped from Hong Kong, is greater than the volume of American textiles entering the Philippine Islands. He handed to Mr. Yoshizawa a sheet containing figures which show the preponderance of Japanese textiles in the Philippine trade.[81] Mr. Yoshizawa replied that while it was of course understood from the first that the basis of agreement was an equal sharing of the Philippine market, yet the Japanese Government was disinclined to negotiate on that basis. He stated that during the negotiations leading up to the agreement emphasis had been focused on figures, that therefore the Japanese Government would not wish that discussions with regard to the agreement revert to the principle of equal sharing of the market.

---

[80] *Infra.*

[81] Presumably statistics as given in a press release of the Department of Commerce, September 22.

Mr. Sayre stated, in regard to the proposals submitted by Mr. Yoshizawa, that he would discuss them with his associates and on a later occasion would again take up with Mr. Yoshizawa the matter of adjustment of the figures of importations into the Philippine Islands. He said that he would be favorably inclined to overlook the excess of Japanese imports already entered on condition that definite arrangements in regard to future importations could be made.

After leaving Mr. Sayre's office, Mr. Turner asked Mr. Yoshizawa whether these proposed measures were already in effect, or whether they were tentative and required acceptance by the American Government. Mr. Yoshizawa replied that the measures were contingent on acceptance by the United States Government.

611B.9417/224

The Japanese Embassy to the Department of State [82]

By means of including Hongkong within the scope of the control exercised by the Association of Exporters of Cotton Piece Goods to the Philippines the following restrictive measures are proposed to govern the exportation of cotton piece goods from Japan to Hongkong and the transhipment at that port of such goods to the Philippines:

1. When the Association of Exporters of Cotton Piece Goods to the Philippines is apprised of a case in which cotton piece goods shipped to Hongkong by a member of the Association is further transhipped to the Philippines either by the consignee of such goods or by any subsequent buyer thereof from the consignee, the Association may, if it finds such transhipment has been made with the knowledge of the consigner, refrain from issuing export permits to such a member. In order to make effective the proposed measure the coöperation of the Office of the Representative of the United States Commerce Department stationed in the Philippines is sought in unofficially furnishing the Association with information with regard to the name and address of a shipper whenever a transhipment of Japanese goods from Hongkong takes place.

2. A premium at the rate of 0.25 sen per one square yard is to be paid on all cotton piece goods which are shipped from Japan to Hongkong. The above premium will be refunded on such goods as have subsequently been transhipped at Hongkong to any other destination than the Philippines.

The rate of the premium payable on goods shipped from Japan directly to the Philippines, which is at present 0.3 sen per one square yard, will be reduced to 0.15 sen as soon as the above measure comes into force.

[82] Handed by the Counselor of the Japanese Embassy to Assistant Secretary of State Sayre, September 5.

611B.9417/224

Memorandum by Mr. Roy Veatch of the Office of the Economic Adviser

[WASHINGTON,] September 10, 1936.

Before I had read the last paragraph of Mr. Turner's memorandum of September 5, I called Mr. Yoshizawa on the telephone and asked if the measures indicated in the statement which he had handed to Mr. Sayre on September 5 had actually been put into operation or if the extension of the Association to cover exporters to Hong Kong had already taken place. In reply Mr. Yoshizawa said that it was his understanding that it had definitely been planned to extend the membership of the Exporters Association and to introduce the measures indicated if the agreement regarding shipments of Japanese cotton goods to the Philippines is to continue. Naturally the Association does not wish to complicate present machinery by taking these further steps if the American Government is of the opinion that the agreement should be abandoned. Hence these steps will not be taken until some response is received from the American Government with respect to the proposed action.

Mr. Yoshizawa did not give me the impression that it would be necessary for the United States to "accept" the proposed action. Neither at this time nor in an informal discussion the afternoon of September 8 did Mr. Yoshizawa give me the impression that continuance of voluntary control by the Japanese was contingent upon any statement by this Government that the proposed measures would settle all questions regarding the operation of the control arrangement for the second year, although it is possible, of course, that the Exporters Association will insist that after the proposed action has been taken, this Government should be agreeable to omitting transshipped goods from the statistics of Japanese goods arriving in the Philippines. Mr. Yoshizawa was strongly of the opinion, however, that the question of the application of the agreement to transshipped goods as well as to those shipped directly should not be pressed by this Government at the present time. It was his opinion that the Japanese exporters would not agree formally to the inclusion of such goods in the statistics but, on the other hand, he did not indicate that the exporters would insist upon the exclusion of these goods. He appeared to be of the opinion that the amounts of Japanese goods arriving in the Philippines probably would fall within the limits suggested by us, at least during the next few months, if we are willing to let the agreement run along. He believed that the Exporters Association had already taken steps to limit shipments during the present months so that there should not occur this fall such a concentration of arrivals of Japanese goods as caused us special concern last fall.

611B.9417/222

Memorandum by Mr. Roy Veatch of the Office of the Economic Adviser

[WASHINGTON,] September 16, 1936.

Mr. Veatch placed before Mr. Yoshizawa a draft of a press statement to be released by the Department of Commerce [83] containing the statistics of Philippine importations of Japanese cotton piece goods during July and August and a summary of importations for the twelve-month period ending August 1, covering the first year of the voluntary restriction by the Japanese exporters. Mr. Yoshizawa suggested certain changes in the paragraph which referred to the plans of the Japanese Exporters Association to institute new measures of control. The original draft had referred to the plan of the Exporters Association to enlarge its membership to include exporters to Hong Kong but Mr. Yoshizawa called attention to the wording of the statement from the Japanese Government, handed to Mr. Sayre September 5, and stated that it was his understanding that exporters to Hong Kong would not actually become members of the Association. Rather, the Association would be empowered under the Safeguarding of Commerce Act, to apply the regulations of the Association to exports to Hong Kong. The draft of this paragraph was revised and approved by Mr. Yoshizawa.

Mr. Yoshizawa then commented upon the inclusion in the draft release of all Japanese goods transshipped via Hong Kong as Japanese goods arriving in the Philippines under the provisions of the agreement. He wished to make it clear that he was not in a position to approve such a statement since his Government still maintained the position that it could not be held responsible for transshipments. He was of the opinion that if the matter were referred to his Government, the Foreign Office would maintain that the only statistics which should be included would be those of arrivals of goods shipped directly from Japan, totaling less than 44,000,000 square meters. Mr. Veatch said that this Government would, of course, be forced to release the statistics of arrivals of all Japanese goods but that this release would be made entirely on the responsibility of this Government and that there was no intention of asking Mr. Yoshizawa to approve the release as a whole. It was necessary only that he advise as to the language which is to be used in reference to the plans of the Japanese Exporters Association. Mr. Yoshizawa accepted this explanation and said in that event he thought it would be unnecessary for him to refer the matter to Tokyo. Mr. Veatch said that he would make it per-

---

[83] Not printed; it was released September 22.

fectly clear in his memorandum of conversation that Mr. Yoshizawa was not in any way expressing approval or any opinion with respect to the release as a whole.

Mr. Veatch then said that this Government also desired to make it clear that no new commitments were involved in connection with the statements to be made in the press release as drafted. Specifically, Mr. Sayre wished to have it made clear that in referring to the plans of the Japanese Exporters Association to exercise some form of control over transshipments from Hong Kong this Government was not in any way changing its position regarding the inclusion of transshipped goods in the quota accepted by the Japanese exporters. Mr. Yoshizawa said that he clearly understood this position and that he would not fail to explain it to his Government.

After agreement had been reached upon the text of the proposed press release, Mr. Yoshizawa expressed the opinion that it would be wise if this Government would not press immediately for any final determination by the two Governments of the total amount of Japanese goods to arrive in the Philippines during the second year of the agreement. He personally felt that his Government and the Japanese exporters could not justifiably urge that the goods transshipped via Hong Kong should be overlooked. His own opinion was that a reasonable solution of the matter would be acceptance by the Japanese of a limitation of 40,500,000 square meters for the second year (the second year quota of 45,000,000 less 10 percent). He felt that if this Government was willing to overlook the 3,000,000 square meters by which arrivals had exceeded the maximum quota of 49,500,000 square meters for the first year, Japanese exporters should be willing to consider the maximum quota for the first year (49,500,000 square meters) as having been exhausted. It was his opinion that the Foreign Office and the Exporters Association could be brought to this position but he would prefer to handle the matter himself and at the most propitious time rather than to have the question raised directly by the American Government.

611B.9417/222a

The Department of State to the Japanese Embassy [84]

1. The United States Trade Commissioner at Manila will be prepared in the future to furnish quite unofficially to representatives of the Association of Exporters of Cotton Piece Goods to the Philippines or to the Japanese Consul General in Manila, the names and addresses of those who transship Japanese cotton piece goods from Hong Kong to the Philippines. Preliminary arrangements have been made for

---

[84] Handed to the Counselor of the Japanese Embassy by Mr. Veatch, September 28.

this information to be furnished confidentially and unofficially to the Trade Commissioner by the Philippine Customs Service. It is essential that this information be furnished confidentially and it is important that the source of the information be held in confidence by the Japanese Exporters Association.

2. It is hoped that the Japanese Exporters Association will be able so to control shipments to the Philippines that the total amount of Japanese goods arriving in the Philippines each month shall be held at moderate levels with no recurrence of the concentration of shipments in a few months which occurred in the fall of 1935.

3. The Philippine customs statistics of arrivals have been based in reality upon statistics of clearances compiled at the time goods are cleared through customs but dated at the time of arrival of each shipment of goods. This method has led to the necessity of some revision of the monthly statistics of arrivals subsequent to their release, since some small proportion of the goods arriving each month is ordinarily not cleared through customs until several weeks later. For the future it may be desirable, therefore, from the standpoint of both the Japanese Government and the American Government, to shift the basis of Philippine statistics to statistics of clearances. It would be possible to compile final statistics based on clearances much more quickly and accurately than is possible so long as they are to be based upon date of arrival of goods. An expression of opinion on this point on the part of the Japanese Government will be appreciated.

611.946/341

Memorandum by Mr. Eugene H. Dooman of the Division of Far Eastern Affairs

[WASHINGTON,] November 2, 1936.

Mr. Yoshizawa said that the discussions between the American velveteen industry and the Japanese velveteen industry had made some progress; that one feature of the proposed agreement with regard to which Mr. Dooman had expressed distaste, namely, the monopoly feature, had been eliminated; and that the two sides are now discussing "quantities". As might be expected there was a large disparity between the figure proposed by the American side and the figure proposed by the Japanese side, the Japanese desiring that the annual allotment be fixed at 4,000,000 square yards, whereas the American side wished to have the allotment fixed at 1,000,000 square yards. In view of that disparity, Mr. Yoshizawa said that the Japanese Government wondered whether interposition by the American and Japanese Governments would not promote a speedy and satisfactory conclusion to the negotiations.

Mr. Yoshizawa then read certain figures, as follows:

Exports from Japan, January to July, inclusive .... 3, 000, 000 sq. yds.
Imports for consumption into the United States, January to July, inclusive...... 1, 973, 000 sq. yds.
Exports from Japan, August 1935 to July 1936 .... 4, 300, 000 sq. yds.
Imports for consumption into the United States.............................. 3, 237, 000 sq. yds.

(Mr. Yoshizawa commented that, after making allowances for normal lag, there seemed to be undue discrepancy between above two sets of figures.)

Exports from Japan	Quantity (sq. yds.)	Value (yen)
1935	2, 425, 000	1, 062, 000
First 9 months, 1936	4, 927, 000	2, 291, 000

Mr. Yoshizawa stated that the Japanese were of the opinion that, in the light of the foregoing figures, an annual allotment of 3,000,000 square yards seems to be a fair one.

Mr. Dooman said that there appeared to be two points raised: (1) should the Governments concerned intervene in the present private negotiations?, and, (2) if the reply to the first question be in the affirmative, would 3,000,000 square yards be a fair allotment?

With regard to the first point, Mr. Dooman said that he would bring the matter to the attention of Mr. Sayre for decision. With regard to the second point, Mr. Dooman felt that he should point out to Mr. Yoshizawa that the figures suggested represented approximately 50% of the total annual consumption, and that speaking for himself he did not think it fair to ask the American industry to surrender approximately one-half of the home market to its Japanese competitor.

Mr. Yoshizawa asked whether Mr. Dooman would have any objection to Mr. Yoshizawa calling on Mr. Fox of the Tariff Commission. Arrangement was made over the telephone for Mr. Yoshizawa to call on Mr. Fox, but before Mr. Yoshizawa left it was agreed that there would be no further or formal discussion of this matter until it had been referred to and acted upon by Mr. Sayre.

611.9417/178a : Telegram

The Acting Secretary of State to the Ambassador in Japan (Grew)

Washington, December 5, 1936—3 p. m.

154. Plans are complete for a private committee representing the American cotton textile industry to sail for Japan on December 24

on the *Chichibu Maru*, arriving in Japan January 8. It is understood the group will call upon the Embassy immediately and will not begin discussions with the Japanese until January 11. This project was initiated entirely by leaders of the American industry, and although this Government has taken no part in formulating the plans, it heartily approves the general purpose. It is understood that the group will confer directly with representatives of the Japanese industry.

The American group will include Dr. Claudius T. Murchison, President of the Cotton Textile Institute, Donald Comer, President of Avondale Mills, Birmingham, Alabama, and President of the American Cotton Manufacturers Association, Cason Callaway, Chairman of Callaway Mills, LaGrange, Georgia, Harry L. Bailey, President of Wellington Sears Company, New York, and Hervey Kent, Treasurer of Exeter Manufacturing Company, Exeter, New Hampshire. Full instructions will follow by mail.

MOORE

611.9417/191

Memorandum by Mr. Roy Veatch of the Office of the Economic Adviser

[WASHINGTON,] December 7, 1936.

Conversation: Dr. Claudius T. Murchison, President, Cotton Textile Institute, Chairman of the Group;

Mr. Donald Comer, President, American Cotton Manufacturers Association;

Mr. Hervey Kent, Treasurer, Exeter Manufacturing Company;

Mr. Robert Philip, Editor of *Cotton* and Secretary to the Group;

Mr. Fred Morrison, Counsel to the Group;

Mr. A. M. Fox, United States Tariff Commission;

Dr. Hornbeck; [85]

Mr. Dooman;

Mr. Veatch.

At the suggestion of Dr. Murchison and Mr. Comer, Mr. Dooman and Mr. Veatch reviewed what this Government had done in its attempts to deal with the problem of the competition of Japanese cotton piece goods in the American market. It was pointed out that last spring the two Governments had reached agreement upon a limitation of 45,000,000 square yards. The conversations had broken down finally, however, because of the fear on the part of the Japanese

---

[85] Stanley K. Hornbeck, Chief of the Division of Far Eastern Affairs.

industry that indirect shipments to the United States, perhaps via Canada or Mexico, could not be controlled by the Japanese Exporters Association and might, therefore, wreck the arrangement; it had been suggested that the American Government should take some action to control such shipments but this Government had been forced to reply that it had no power to take such action. The opinion was expressed that the Japanese Government had been willing to go further than the Japanese industry, just as this Government had reason to expect that the American industry would look with disapproval upon an agreement allowing a total annual importation of 45,000,000 square yards.

Dr. Murchison asked for advice upon the approach to the Japanese. In reply Mr. Dooman stated that on the basis of his experience, he would suggest the following three rules to govern negotiations by the American group:

1. No offer or proposal should be put forth by the American group which would appear to the Japanese to be obviously unfair and outside the realm of consideration by them.
2. On the other hand, the American group should expect the Japanese to take a bargaining position, that is, to advance an offer somewhat below the best terms to which they would be willing to agree. Consequently, the American group should also be prepared to modify the terms first advanced rather than to be unyielding upon the first offer.
3. The American group should close its mind to the possibility of any alternative action by this Government upon this proposal if it is to be successful in securing a direct agreement with the Japanese; it will be difficult to reach agreement with the Japanese in any case and probably impossible if it is felt that the American industry can fall back on some alternative means of protection.

Mr. Fox suggested certain considerations that must be kept in mind by the American group if it is to reach an agreement with the Japanese industry. He stressed particularly the inadequacy of tariff action to check the competition of Japanese goods and expressed the opinion that only quantitative limitation by Japanese exporters themselves could be considered a desirable answer to the present problem.

Mr. Comer stressed the interest of the American industry in the domestic market and his feeling that the Government should give full protection for the industry in that market. If the Government was unwilling to take such action, however, then he wished to know how far the American industry would have to go in granting the Japanese a share of this market—how many spindles would have to be held out of production and how many workers left unemployed.

In reply to Mr. Comer's questions the broad interests of this Government in maintaining peaceful economic and political relations with Japan were given emphasis. It was recognized that the American

Government would not allow the destruction of a major American industry such as cotton textiles but reference was made to Dr. Murchison's opinion that much damage would be done to the American industry before Congress could be convinced that severe restrictions should be placed upon Japanese imports. The desirability of securing an amicable settlement of this problem before the American industry was greatly injured was stressed. Some members of the group expressed the opinion that an agreement between the American and the Japanese industries would serve only as a stop-gap or palliative, since the Japanese industry was likely to expand much further and the situation, therefore, probably would not remain static. Dr. Murchison was of the opinion, however, that an arrangement could be made with the Japanese industry to provide for a constant study and adjustment of the problems arising out of the competition between the two industries and that such an arrangement might be the best possible permanent answer to the problem.

The opinion was expressed that representatives of the two industries probably would find themselves some distance apart even after each group had made what it had considered in advance to be the greatest possible concessions. Probably the American group then would be faced with the necessity of offering to go halfway toward bridging the gap or of giving up the idea entirely. Mr. Fox suggested that the American group might be able to make attractive offers to the Japanese on a number of textiles other than cotton piece goods (for instance, cotton hosiery, underwear, bedspreads and chair coverings) since in a number of these lines Japanese competition is not yet severe. If the Japanese could be given an opportunity for expansion in other lines, they might be willing to restrict their shipments in such lines as cotton piece goods and cotton velveteens, which have already reached important proportions. Dr. Murchison stressed the desire of the industry to prevent the concentration of Japanese competition in any particular lines of American production. On this point it was felt that some arrangement might be reached with the Japanese providing that imports from Japan of any particular line or specialty should not exceed a certain percentage of the American production, say 10 percent. It was also felt that the American industry might avoid the appearance of proposing a static situation for Japanese goods in the American market by agreeing to an expansion of Japanese imports as American consumption might expand.

Some attention was given to the legal problems which might arise out of the efforts of the American industry to lead the Japanese industry to limit and regulate the export of cotton textiles to the United States, and perhaps the marketing of such textiles in the United States. Mr. Murchison mentioned the intention of the American group to secure, if possible, an informal opinion from the Department of Justice before the departure for Japan. In the event that there is uncertainty regarding the legality of such an arrangement between the American and Japanese industries, Mr. Murchison wondered if the two Governments might not be able to set up the agreement themselves after the representatives of the two industries had prepared the groundwork. The officials of the American Government made no attempt to answer this inquiry categorically. They emphasized the hope that had been entertained in the Government that many problems of Japanese competition might be handled by agreements between the Japanese and American industries and that such an agreement on cotton textiles might serve as an encouraging precedent. It was recognized also that the Government itself might be open to attack, under the anti-trust legislation, if it sought restrictive action by the Japanese. The attitude of the Government, as well as the plans of the textile group visiting Japan, clearly were dependent upon advice as to the legal questions involved.

Dr. Murchison said that he was informed quite confidentially that the Japanese industry plans to secure American counsel during the conversations with the American group in Japan. Specifically, he understood that Mr. W. S. Culbertson, counsel for Mitsui and Company, was to be in Japan during the course of the conversations. There was some feeling that the presence of an American lawyer in the picture as an adviser to the Japanese would perhaps add to the difficulties. Dr. Murchison expressed the opinion, however, and many others agreed, that the advice of Mr. Culbertson to the Japanese side might prove helpful rather than obstructive, since his experience as a member of the Tariff Commission and as a diplomatic representative of this Government abroad should have given him a broad point of view on the problems to be considered.

611.9417/178b

The Acting Secretary of State to the Ambassador in Japan (Grew)

No. 1160   WASHINGTON, December 12, 1936.

SIR: Reference is made to the Department's telegram No. 154 of December 5, 3 p. m., informing you that a committee representing the American cotton textile industry is to proceed to Japan to confer with representatives of the Japanese cotton textile industry.

Beginning in the summer of 1935, informal discussions were held between the Department and the Japanese Embassy with a view to the Japanese Government undertaking to exercise control over exports of cotton piece goods from Japan to the United States. Although agreement was reached with regard to the total volume to which such exports should be restricted, the request that the American Government exercise control over imports of cotton piece goods from Japan, for which, of course, this Government has no legal warrant, precluded the making of any arrangement. On May 21, 1936, the President acting on a recommendation from the Tariff Commission ordered a moderate increase in the tariff on certain types of cotton piece goods the principal country of exportation of which is Japan.

Following that action by the American Government, Dr. Claudius T. Murchison, President of The Cotton-Textile Institute, laid before the members of the Institute a proposal that a committee representing the American cotton textile industry visit Japan and place before the Japanese cotton textile industry the possibility of an understanding being reached with regard to the Japanese industry exercising control of shipments of cotton textiles to the American market, and perhaps of the setting up of a joint Japanese-American trade committee to deal with continuing problems affecting the two industries.

This Government looks with decided favor upon the general purpose of the project, which is in all respects a private one. It is understood that the Japanese Government likewise looks with favor upon this effort to obtain, through private initiative, a mutually satisfactory adjustment of a trade problem.

There are enclosed a copy of a confidential circular dated September 18, 1936, addressed by Dr. Murchison to members of the Board of Directors of The Cotton-Textile Institute, and an address on the subject "The Promotion of Japanese-American Trade Relations", delivered on November 19, 1936, by Dr. Murchison at the American-Japanese Trade Council Luncheon of the National Foreign Trade Convention.[86] There is also enclosed a copy of a memorandum [86a] of a conference which took place on December 7, 1936, between Dr. Murchison and members of his committee, and officers of the American Government.

Although the American Government is in no way involved in the project on which Dr. Murchison and the members of his committee are engaged, it is suggested that the Embassy and the consular officers in Japan extend such courtesies and assistance to these gentlemen as may be appropriate.

Very truly yours,
R. WALTON MOORE

---

[86] Neither printed.
[86a] Supra.

DISINCLINATION OF JAPAN TO NEGOTIATE A CONVENTION WITH
THE UNITED STATES REGULATING FISHERIES OFF THE COAST OF
ALASKA [87]

894.628/145

The Ambassador in Japan (Grew) to the Secretary of State

No. 1698   TOKYO, February 21, 1936.
                                                 [Received March 9.]

SIR: I have the honor to refer to Instruction No. 921 of January 11,
1936,[88] in which the Department enclosed a memorandum of conversation between Assistant Secretary of State Sayre and the Counselor of
the Japanese Embassy in regard to a proposal to regulate fishing by
Japanese in certain waters of Bering Sea and Bristol Bay. The instruction stated that although it appears that the conclusion of an
agreement of the kind envisaged is precluded at present by the attitude
of the Japanese authorities, the Department would appreciate further
suggestion or comment from the Embassy.

The Embassy is inclined to the view that the Japanese will not be
willing to undertake negotiations in regard to fishing in northern
waters until the present Russo-Japanese fishing difficulties are
straightened out, which may require some time. Meanwhile, it seems
unlikely that the Japanese Government will encourage salmon fishing
by Japanese interests in waters adjacent to Alaska.

For some years, as the Department is aware, the Japanese have been
dissatisfied with the fur seal treaty,[89] and it is possible that when the
Russian fishery difficulties are out of the way, or in a fair way to
settlement, the Japanese may propose some modification of the present
arrangement and offer restriction of salmon fishing as an inducement.
This is pure speculation, but the Japanese desire to reserve liberty of
action as regards salmon fishing together with their known attitude
towards the present provisions of the fur seal treaty lend some force
to the supposition.

Respectfully yours,   JOSEPH C. GREW

894.628/147 : Telegram

The Secretary of State to the Ambassador in Japan (Grew)

WASHINGTON, March 28, 1936—3 p. m.

37. Embassy's despatch No. 1558, November 20, 1935.[90] The Department of Commerce has received reports from unofficial sources

---

[87] Continued from *Foreign Relations*, 1935, vol. III, pp. 1072–1080.
[88] See *ibid.*, p. 1080, footnote 69.
[89] Convention between the United States, Great Britain, Japan, and Russia,
signed at Washington, July 7, 1911, *ibid.*, 1911, p. 260.
[90] Not printed; see telegram No. 208, November 12, 1935, 5 p. m., from the
Chargé in Japan, *ibid.*, 1935, vol. III, p. 1078.

that Japanese vessels have obtained licenses for salmon fishing in waters adjacent to Alaska and are now engaged in such fishing. It is believed that circulation of such reports might most effectively be discouraged by the Department of Commerce making known to Alaskan salmon fishery interests the assurances given to you last year by the Foreign Office as reported in your despatch above cited.

Please communicate the foregoing to the Foreign Office and inquire whether there would be objection to the procedure above outlined, reporting reply of the Foreign Office promptly by telegraph.

HULL

894.628/148 : Telegram

The Ambassador in Japan (Grew) to the Secretary of State

TOKYO, March 31, 1936—5 p. m.
[Received March 31—6: 49 a. m.]

82. Department's 37, March 28, 3 p. m. The Foreign Office informs the Embassy orally that no licenses to take salmon in waters adjacent to Alaska have been issued to Japanese vessels; that such action is not contemplated at present and that the Japanese authorities have no knowledge of any Japanese fishing craft in Bering Sea at this time. The Embassy is further informed that there would be no objection to giving this assurance to interested persons.

GREW

894.628/151 : Telegram

The Secretary of State to the Ambassador in Japan (Grew)

WASHINGTON, June 3, 1936—2 p. m.

67. Embassy's No. 82, March 31, 5 p. m., and previous. A wireless despatch dated Tokyo, May 29, to the *New York Times* states "A Japanese trawler with experts aboard will be sent to Alaska to investigate the prospects of open sea fishing enterprises there. Hitherto the government has refused permission to operate in Alaskan waters because of American fishing interests . . . It is now considered feasible to extend the Japanese fisheries to Alaska . . ." [91]

The Department would appreciate receipt at your early convenience of your comment and of available information with regard to the project referred to in above-mentioned press despatch.

HULL

---

[91] Omissions indicated in the original.

894.628/153 : Telegram

The Ambassador in Japan (Grew) to the Secretary of State

Tokyo, June 11, 1936—noon.
[Received June 11—12: 30 a. m.]

124. Embassy's 120, June 4, 10 a. m.,[92] Bering Sea fishing. The Embassy is now informed by the Foreign Office that the Department of Agriculture and Forests had arranged for the *Tenyo Maru* 657 tons, with auxiliary motor boat 61 tons, to leave Hakodate about June 15 for the purpose of making investigations concerning manner and density of distribution of salmon and other fishes, fishing grounds and marine and meterological conditions in the North Pacific. Foreign Office states that these vessels are scheduled to return to Hakodate in mid-August, will conduct their investigations on the high seas and will not enter American waters.

Grew

894.628/153 : Telegram

The Secretary of State to the Ambassador in Japan (Grew)

Washington, July 3, 1936—5 p. m.

87. Your 82, March 31, 5 p. m.; 120, June 4, 10 a. m.;[93] and 124, June 11, noon. Department is reliably informed that a Japanese fishing vessel, *Chichibu Maru*, of which the Department had previously no knowledge, has been observed fishing with gill nets for salmon in Bristol Bay.

In view of the assurances mentioned in your 124 the Department would appreciate receipt of your comment and of available information.

Hull

894.628/162

The Ambassador in Japan (Grew) to the Secretary of State

No. 1930   Tokyo, July 7, 1936.
[Received July 28.]

Sir: I have the honor to refer to the Department's telegram No. 87 of July 3, 5 p. m., 1936, and to the Embassy's reply thereto, No. 148 of July 6, noon, 1936,[94] and to enclose a copy of a memorandum of conversation between the Counselor of the Embassy and the Chief of the American Bureau of the Foreign Office in regard to fishing in the

[92] Not printed.
[93] Telegram No. 120 not printed.
[94] Latter not printed.

Bristol Bay region. The discussion on this subject took place during an informal talk which covered a number of other matters.

The Department will note that Mr. Okamoto brought up revision of the Fur Seal Treaty in the course of the conversation. This lends some force to the idea that the Japanese Government may wish to use our apprehensions of Japanese pelagic salmon fishing in Bering Sea to bring about an alteration in the Fur Seal Treaty, a possibility to which the Embassy has previously invited attention.

Respectfully yours, JOSEPH C. GREW

[Enclosure]

Memorandum by the Counselor of Embassy in Japan (Neville)

[TOKYO,] July 6, 1936.

I told Mr. Okamoto that the Embassy had received information from Washington that a Japanese vessel named *Chichibu Maru* had been observed fishing for salmon with gill nets in Bristol Bay, and asked him whether the Foreign Office had any information in regard to this vessel. He sent for the file and the Section Chief in charge of it, and after some conversation with him and an examination of the dossier, Mr. Okamoto said that there was no information on file at all, and that the Foreign Office knew nothing about it. This statement was confirmed by the Section Chief who was emphatic that the Fisheries Bureau had given the Foreign Office no information in regard to this vessel. Mr. Okamoto said that the Foreign Office would investigate the report and give the Embassy what information it could obtain.

Mr. Okamoto then stated that he had first become acquainted with this question when he was Consul at Seattle. He said that the Japanese Government was under some pressure from time to time to grant licenses to fish in Bristol Bay, but so far had refused, because in the first place such action would irritate the Americans and secondly it was doubtful whether such fishing would be profitable. He said that one object of the investigation which the Fisheries Bureau was making was to ascertain the commercial feasibility of fishing off Alaska.

He then said that another question which was brought up from time to time was the problem of fur seals. He said that the Japanese Government had first raised the question of revision of the fur seal treaty some ten years ago, but that the American Government had been unable to consider the matter because it had no diplomatic relations with the Soviets at that time. I told him that I was unable to discuss that question because I had no instructions to that end, and asked him if the Japanese Government wanted to raise the question now. He said that so far as he knew the Japanese were not ready to do so now, but the treaty had expired, was in force only from year to year and there were certain features of it which he understood the Japanese wish modified. He seemed unable to give more detailed information.

E[DWIN] L. N[EVILLE]

894.628/160 : Telegram

The Ambassador in Japan (Grew) to the Secretary of State

TOKYO, July 21, 1936—noon.
[Received July 21—2 : 22 a. m.]

159. Department's 87, July 3, 5 p. m. The Foreign Office states that according to a report from the Ministry of Agriculture and Forestry, the *Chichibu Maru* is a vessel of the Pacific Ocean Fishing Company which is licensed to fish for salmon with drift nets only along the coast of Kamchatka. No license was given that vessel to fish in Bristol Bay. The vessel left Hakodate, May 7, for the Gulf of Anadyr but could not operate owing to drifting ice and turned back from Kamchatka before reaching the Gulf of Anadyr. On July 4 it reported that it had abandoned fishing for the season. It is now operating as a transport ship for the other fishing vessels of the company.

GREW

842.628/512

The Secretary of State to the Minister in Canada (Armour)

No. 546   WASHINGTON, October 9, 1936.

SIR: The receipt is acknowledged of your despatch No. 966 dated September 28, 1936,[95] in which reference is made to the concern of the government of the Province of British Columbia over the effect upon the fishing industry in the north Pacific area of fishing operations by Japanese in non-territorial waters in that area.

The possibility that Japanese fishery interests might operate in waters off the coast of Alaska, especially in the non-territorial waters of Bristol Bay, has engaged the attention for several years past of the Department and of its representatives in Japan. So early as 1931, the desirability was suggested to the Japanese Government of the withholding from Japanese fishing vessels of licenses to fish in Bristol Bay, into which, as you are no doubt aware, flow the rivers where are spawned the highly prized red salmon. Unfortunately,

[95] Not printed.

the Japanese Government did not find it practicable to give this Government a formal undertaking that it would take effective measures to prevent Japanese fishing vessels from operating in Bristol Bay, but informal assurances were given that no licenses would be issued to private Japanese fishing interests to fish for salmon in that area without previous notification having been given to this Government. The Japanese Government further communicated the information that so-called "floating canneries" would be licensed to pack crab in the north Pacific area and that licenses would be issued to a limited number of Japanese fishing vessels to fish for cod, hake and halibut for reduction into fertilizer and for extraction of fish oil.

In view of evidences of increasing interest of the Japanese in the fishery resources of Bering Sea, a further approach was made last year by this Government to the Japanese Government, and renewed assurances were given by the Japanese Government that no licenses would be granted for the time being by the Japanese Government to private vessels to fish for salmon in Bristol Bay. It is understood, however, that one or more vessels belonging to the Bureau of Fisheries of the Japanese Government have recently been conducting experimental operations in Bristol Bay.

The Canadian Legation at Washington has manifested interest with regard to the attitude of this Government in relation to the effect of possible increasing activity by Japanese fishing vessels in the high seas off the coast of Alaska, and it is probable that in the near future opportunity will be found for an informal exchange of the views of this Government and of the Canadian Government. The Department will expect to keep you informed of any discussions which may be had with the Canadian Legation.

Very truly yours,   For the Secretary of State:
                                                    FRANCIS B. SAYRE

711.008 North Pacific/1

Memorandum by Mr. Eugene H. Dooman of the Division of Far Eastern Affairs

[WASHINGTON,] December 16, 1936.

The Canadian Minister, Sir Herbert Marler, called at the Department this morning accompanied by Mr. Hume Wrong, Counselor of Legation, and Mr. Charles Ritchie, Third Secretary of Legation.

The following officers of the Department were present:

Mr. Dooman (FE) [Far Eastern Affairs]
Mr. Hickerson (WE) [Western European Affairs]
Mr. Keating (TD) [Treaty Division]
Mr. Bonbright (WE)

The Canadian Minister stated that his Legation had received from the Canadian Department of Fisheries a memorandum setting forth views with regard to certain fishing problems, and that he thought that it would be helpful to him and to his Government if there could be had an informal discussion on these problems.

Mr. Wrong distributed copies of the memorandum referred to by the Minister (copy attached),[96] the purport of which he outlined and amplified by certain observations. He said that the methods of catching fish and distributing fish had been revolutionized by the development of the so-called "mother" ships and by improvements in refrigeration. He understood that it was now possible for fish to be immersed in brine and frozen without injuring the cell structure of the fish and without materially altering its flavor. It was thus possible for ships now to be sent to all parts of the world to engage in fishing and also to distribute catches in widely separated markets. He thought that there was reason for reviewing the whole problem, with a view to determining new principles calculated to conserve the fishery resources of the various countries.

Mr. Wrong then referred to the specific question of Japanese fishing vessels operating along the coast of North America, and to the fear that operations of this kind would eventually deplete the salmon and halibut of the Pacific.

Mr. Dooman then gave in strict confidence an account of the discussions which have been held between this Government and the Japanese Government over the possibility of action being taken by the Japanese Government to prohibit Japanese nationals from fishing for salmon in the waters of Bristol Bay. He referred to the informal conversations which were held at Tokyo in 1930 and 1931, to the plan which was formulated at that time and which fell through, to the investigations carried out during the last four or five years by vessels of the Japanese Government with regard to the salmon resources of Bristol Bay, and finally to the inquiry made by this Government last year with regard to the possibility of a convention to provide for the exclusion of Japanese fishing vessels from operating in Bristol Bay. The Japanese Government expressed inability to consider any such convention until certain studies which were being conducted of the salmon resources of Bristol Bay were concluded. The Japanese Government had given assurances, however, that Japanese fishing vessels would not be licensed to operate in that area for the time being, and so far as this Government was aware there had been no cases of Japanese packing salmon in the waters of Bristol Bay.

Mr. Dooman went on to say that the studies which were being made by the Japanese Government would, he understood, continue for an-

---

[96] Not printed.

other two or three years, and that he thought it unlikely that the question under consideration would come to a head, either by the conclusion of a convention such as we have in mind or by Japanese operating in Bristol Bay, for several years to come. In the meantime, private suggestions had been put forward by Japanese officials to the effect that it might be desirable for the United States, Canada and Japan to conduct a survey of the fishery resources of the north Pacific with a view to the eventual conclusion of a fishery convention along the lines of the Fur Seals Treaty of 1911.

So far as halibut is concerned, Mr. Dooman did not believe that the possibility is imminent of Japanese being interested in halibut on an extensive scale, although it is true that a few Japanese fishing vessels had been catching certain types of ground fish for reduction into fertilizer and oil.

Mr. Hickerson expressed the thought that problems arising in the Pacific appear to be somewhat less difficult than those arising in the Atlantic, for the reason that in the former area only the salmon appear to be involved—and that only because of the possible interest of one other country—whereas in the Atlantic many types of fish and many countries were involved.

The Canadian Minister pursued that thought and said that it seemed to him that it would be wise to explore the possibility of a convention being concluded between the United States, Canada and Japan. If such a convention were concluded, a precedent and an example will have been created for the setting up of an agreement of the widest possible compass.

It was suggested to the Canadians that our approach to the Japanese might be made easier if it were possible for us to show that we on this side of the Pacific were making an effort to solve our own salmon difficulties through the Sockeye Salmon Convention of 1930.[97] The Canadian Minister agreed and Mr. Wrong expressed the opinion that in the course of the next ten days we would probably know the decision of the Canadian Government regarding the acceptance or rejection of our Senate's reservations to the Convention, which is not yet in operation.[98]

Mr. Dooman said that it did not seem to him that a pessimistic view with regard to the conclusion of a three-power agreement such as that suggested by Sir Herbert was called for at the present time: the salmon resources of Kamchatka were being rapidly depleted, due in large part to the policy of the Soviet Government in farming out the so-called "fishing stations" and the importance of canned salmon in

---

[97] Signed at Washington, May 26, 1930, *Foreign Relations*, 1930, vol. I, p. 505.
[98] For protocol of exchange signed at Washington, July 28, 1937, see *ibid.*, p. 512 (bracketed insertion).

Japan's foreign trade are two reasons which should dispose the Japanese toward cooperating in conserving the salmon resources of the eastern Pacific. It would have to be realized that the conclusion of such a convention would require the making of sacrifices by both Canada and the United States to permit Japanese participation in salmon fishing, and that the uncompromising attitude of the salmon interests on the west coast would have to be taken into consideration.

There then ensued a discussion among the Canadians of the likelihood of the Japanese threat to the salmon resources of Canada being raised in the Canadian Parliament, and there seemed to be a consensus among them that the question would be raised. The Americans made the comment that it also seemed likely that some resolution, probably espousing the view of the American salmon interests that the red salmon found in Bristol Bay are property of the United States, would be introduced at the next session of Congress.

The Canadian Minister observed that the discussion had inclined him to the view that the course to be pursued by Canada and the United States should be to seek with Japan a solution of the Pacific problem, leaving the wider problems presented in the memorandum of the Canadian Department of Fisheries to be resolved at some later date. He added that he would recommend that the Canadian Government endeavor by appropriate means to support and reenforce whatever the American Government might seek to do by way of representations to the Japanese Government. Mr. Dooman said that an instruction to the Embassy at Tokyo is in the course of preparation, and that upon completion he would be glad to confer further with members of the Canadian Legation.

SETTLEMENT OF CASE PRESENTED BY THE JAPANESE GOVERNMENT ON BEHALF OF JAPANESE STEAMSHIP COMPANIES SUBJECT TO UNITED STATES WAR PROFITS TAX FOR THE YEARS 1918 AND 1919 [99]

811.512394 Shipping/54

The Ambassador in Japan (Grew) to the Chief of the Division of Far Eastern Affairs (Hornbeck)

Tokyo, December 20, 1935.
[Received January 21, 1936.]

Dear Mr. Hornbeck: You will recollect that in my talk with the President on September 23rd I took up with him the question of the war profits tax assessed by the Treasury Department against certain Japanese steamship companies and I said to the President that at least as a matter of equity, if not of law, this was an issue in which,

---

[99] For previous correspondence, see *Foreign Relations*, 1934, vol. III, pp. 827 ff.

in my opinion, the Japanese were in the right and we in the wrong. The President showed definite interest in the matter and said that he would take it up with Mr. Coolidge,[1] Under Secretary of the Treasury, with whom he expected to confer on the following day, and that if no satisfaction were obtained in that quarter he would have a bill introduced in Congress with a view to bringing about an equitable solution of the case.

At the time of my visit to Washington it appeared that the Treasury Department looked at the matter purely from the strictly legal point of view which, from the standpoint of that Department, was perhaps a logical position to take as it may not have lain within the province of the Treasury to consider the element of equity. It therefore seems possible that only Congressional action may provide the solution.

I am writing to express the hope that you will think it desirable to follow this matter up and possibly to suggest, either to the Secretary or to Mr. Phillips,[2] that unless action is taken at the commencement of the Congressional session the President be reminded of his promise to me in this connection. The Japanese have not mentioned the matter on my return but it is one of those cases which if equitably settled would, I think, create a favorable basis for appealing to the Japanese Government for equitable treatment in other cases involving our own interests.

If it is felt that it would be helpful and appropriate for me to write to the President myself on this subject at any time please let me know and I shall be glad to do so. You will remember that, in accordance with the President's request, I sent him on September 23rd a one-page memorandum [3] setting forth the principal facts in the case.

Sincerely yours,   JOSEPH C. GREW

811.512394 Shipping/38

The Department of State to the Japanese Embassy [4]

The views of the Japanese Government, as set forth in a memorandum transmitted with the Japanese Embassy's note No. 158 of August 20, 1934,[5] in regard to additional war profits tax asserted by the Treasury Department of the American Government against three Japanese shipping companies, namely, the Nippon Yusen Kaisha, the Osaka Shosen Kaisha, and the Toyo Kisen Kaisha, have received the careful consideration of the American Government.

---

[1] Thomas J. Coolidge.
[2] William Phillips, Under Secretary of State.
[3] Not attached to file copy of covering note.
[4] Handed to the Japanese Ambassador by the Under Secretary of State, April 27.
[5] *Foreign Relations*, 1934, vol. III, p. 830.

The issues involve income tax liability for the years 1918 and 1919 of all three of the companies, and also for the year 1920 in the case of the Nippon Yusen Kaisha. All of the three taxable years involved are governed by the Revenue Act of 1918.[6] That Act provided that in the case of a foreign corporation "gross income includes only the gross income from sources within the United States [Section 233 (*b*)]".[7] The Attorney General held, in an opinion rendered November 3, 1920 [32 Op. Atty. Gen. 336, 345], and published as a Treasury Decision [T. D. 3111], that in the case of a foreign steamship company "income from sources within the United States" means under this Act "income from freight and passenger traffic originating within the United States."

The Revenue Act of 1921,[8] which, of course, had no retroactive effect as to the years 1918, 1919 and 1920, contained detailed provisions as to the method of determining the "income from sources within the United States" of foreign corporations. Under this latter Act, "gains, profits and income from (1) transportation or other services rendered partly within and partly without the United States . . .[9] shall be treated as derived partly from sources within and partly from sources without the United States" and "the portion of such net income attributable to sources within the United States may be determined by processes or formulas of general apportionment prescribed by the Commissioner (of Internal Revenue) with the approval of the Secretary (of the Treasury)". In conformity with the authority granted under the portion above quoted of the Act, the Treasury Department on August 23, 1922, issued Treasury Decision 3387 which provided a detailed and somewhat involved formula for apportioning income as between sources within and sources without the United States.

This formula was much more favorable to the steamship companies as a group than the provisions of the Revenue Act of 1918 as interpreted by the Attorney General; and the representatives of the Japanese steamship companies and of other foreign steamship companies whose cases under the Revenue Act of 1918 had not been closed urgently insisted upon being given the benefit of the formula set out in Treasury Decision 3387. On January 21, 1924, the Attorney General reaffirmed his opinion of November 3, 1920, and expressed the view that the provisions of the Revenue Act of 1921 could not be applied retroactively to the Revenue Act of 1918. However, on July 1, 1927, the Treasury Department informed the Attorney General that the conclusions reached by him in these opinions had never been acquiesced in by the foreign steamship companies, and that the

---

[6] Approved February 24, 1919; 40 Stat. 1057.
[7] Brackets in this document appear in the original.
[8] Approved November 23, 1921; 42 Stat. 227.
[9] Omission indicated in the original.

tax returns of a large number of steamship companies were then pending awaiting the determination by the courts of the proper method of computing tax liability for the years prior to 1921. On July 7, 1927, the Acting Attorney General rendered an opinion which recited the foregoing circumstances and the concluding paragraphs of which were as follows:

"The questions involved are difficult, and there is room for difference of opinion about them and the outcome of the litigation is doubtful, but the opinions referred to stand in the way of your dealing with these cases in the exercise of authority granted to you by law and in a way to serve the best interests of the United States. The questions do not arise under the Revenue Act for 1921 [42 Stat. 227], or any later Revenue Act.

"Under all the circumstances, you should be free to deal with the cases as the conditions seem to require, and, in order that you may do so, the opinions referred to are hereby withdrawn [Acting Attorney General to the Secretary of the Treasury—35 Op. Atty. Gen. 244]."

In computing the taxes to which exception is taken by the Japanese steamship companies, the formula prescribed by Treasury Decision 3387 was used. The application of this formula produces a much smaller aggregate tax than would result from application of the Revenue Act of 1918 as interpreted by the Attorney General, although under such interpretation no part of the Charter hire received by the Japanese steamship companies under the arrangement of 1918 between the American Government and the Japanese Government whereby Japanese vessels were placed at the disposal of the American Government, or subsidies received by the steamship companies from the Japanese Government, would be included as income. On the other hand the formula used in the computation of taxes requires the inclusion as one among many other factors of all income from services performed by vessels whose voyages include United States ports in the total amount to be allocated as "income from transportation and other services rendered partly within and partly without the United States".

It is not possible to explain the formula in a few words, but it may be said that in effect it contemplates as one of its principal factors that the taxable income of a foreign vessel should bear that relation to the entire income derived from that vessel that the time spent by the vessel in American waters bears to the time occupied by it in making a round trip between the foreign terminal port and an American port of call.

It is obvious that a subsidy received by a foreign steamship company from a foreign government is not "income from sources within the United States". However, the view of the Japanese Government that such subsidies "cannot be objects of taxation by the American

Government" and that it is "unreasonable to consider the whole amount of the subsidies as taxable income, while they involve services in other parts of the world", appears to be inconsistent with the previous insistence of the representatives of the Japanese steamship companies that the formula prescribed by Treasury Decision 3387 be used. Both the charter hire and the subsidy payments on the vessels engaged in commerce with the United States are deemed to be "income from transportation or other services rendered partly within and partly without the United States", within the purview of the formula set out in Treasury Decision 3387. There would obviously be no occasion to use a formula to allocate income as between sources within and sources without the United States if there were excluded in the beginning all income other than "income from sources within the United States."

It will be clear to the Japanese Government from a review of the foregoing circumstances that the application to the incomes of the Japanese steamship companies of the formula prescribed in Treasury Decision 3387 was no arbitrary act of the American Government. The fact is, on the contrary, that the formula was made applicable to incomes for the years 1918, 1919 and 1920 at the urgent insistence of the representatives of the foreign steamship companies, including the Japanese companies. The present insistence of the Japanese steamship companies upon the elimination of the items of charter hire and subsidy from a calculation of their income tax liability would seem to indicate their unwillingness to accept the burdens of the formula while enjoying its benefits.

Notwithstanding the fact that the issues relating to subsidies and charter hire would not have arisen had the Japanese steamship companies acquiesced in a settlement of their income tax liability on a basis consistent with the opinion rendered November 3, 1920, by the Attorney General, the American Government has given the most sympathetic attention to the circumstances, as they may affect the tax cases under discussion, arising out of the arrangement of 1918 by which the Japanese Government placed Japanese vessels at the disposal of the American Government. Accordingly, the Treasury Department has proposed to representatives of the Japanese steamship companies a settlement which contemplates a reduction of their income tax liability equivalent to the elimination both of the charter hire and of the subsidies from the formula used in determining taxable income. Such proposal of settlement, if accepted, would effect a reduction of the amount of the total deficiency payments from all three companies from approximately $2,300,000 to approximately $650,000.

As to the deductions for war amortization, there was at first doubt whether the Revenue Act of 1918 permitted war amortization for vessels built by a foreign corporation in a foreign country, but this doubt was resolved in favor of the foreign steamship companies in computing their proposed tax liability in these cases. No amortization was allowed, however, on any vessel which had not actually come into commerce with the United States on or before November 11, 1918. This rule was adopted after careful consideration of voluminous briefs filed by the steamship companies.

It has been the position of the taxation authorities of the American Government that the amortization provision of the Revenue Act of 1918 [Section 234 (*a*) (8)] does not contemplate amortization on vessels constructed after the Armistice except in special cases; for example, where a vessel was in process of construction on the date of the Armistice and its completion was required to carry out existing and uncancelled war contracts.

It is contended by the Japanese Government that amortization should be allowed on vessels built in Japan after the Armistice for the reasons that (1) such vessels were built to replace vessels placed at the disposal of the American Government and (2) a similar concession was made in regard to American vessels.

The suggestion that American vessels were granted the concession in regard to amortization of vessels built after the Armistice which has been denied to Japanese vessels is believed to be erroneous. It is true that in one case [*U. S.* v. *Elliott,* 16 Fed. (2d) 164] the District Court for the District of Maine allowed amortization on a small vessel the construction of which was not begun until after the Armistice, but the information available in that case discloses that the United States defended that case and that, pending appeal of the United States to the Circuit Court of Appeals, the case was settled on the basis of allowing amortization on only forty percent of the cost of the vessel, such forty percent being only that portion of the cost for which the taxpayer had become definitely obligated prior to the Armistice. The amount involved on this issue in the Elliott case was less than one thousand dollars.

With regard to the contention that amortization should be allowed on vessels built in Japan after the Armistice, for the reason that such vessels were built to replace vessels placed at the disposal of the American Government, there are disputed questions of fact. The American Government has no satisfactory evidence that any vessels were built by the Japanese steamship companies after the Armistice to replace vessels under charter to the United States, whereas it has received information to the effect that some or all of the Japanese steamship companies concerned sold vessels during the period of construction of the vessels on which amortization is claimed. There is further information to the effect that some of the vessels sold were disposed of at a large profit, no part of which profit has been included by the American tax authorities as taxable income.

The American Government has been mindful of the spirit of co-operation displayed in 1918 by the Japanese Government in placing Japanese vessels at the disposal of the American Government for the purpose of facilitating the united operations of the Allied and Associated Powers; and with a view to manifesting its sense of appreciation thereof, and to removing the basis of intervention by the Japanese Government in this controversy, the American Government is prepared to exempt the charter hire received by the Japanese steamship companies on account of such vessels from calculation of the income tax liability of such companies, and also to exempt the subsidies granted by the Japanese Government from such calculation; provided, however, that the Japanese steamship companies accept the determination of the Treasury Department with regard to the amortization issue and other minor questions involved in the cases. As previously indicated herein, the willingness of the American Government to make these concessions has been communicated to the Japanese steamship companies in the form of an offer to settle the cases on a basis which would reduce the amount of the aggregate deficiencies from approximately $2,300,000 (the amount now proposed) to approximately $650,-000. The American Government does not, however, accept the contentions of the Japanese Government in regard to the amortization issue, which appears not to be related to any arrangement made between the American Government and the Japanese Government, but to be a matter lying entirely between the Japanese steamship companies, as taxpayers, and the taxation authorities of the American Government.

The American Government is unable to grant to the Japanese steamship companies a privileged position over and beyond that which would be granted in the same circumstances to American steamship companies in regard to an issue the relation of which to any arrangement made between the American Government and the Japanese Government has not been established.

The American Government has, however, presented substantial evidence of its attitude of responsiveness to the procedure initiated by the Japanese Government looking toward adjustment of the present controversy by friendly discussion between the two Governments concerned. The American Government is of the considered opinion that the proposal of settlement made by the taxation authorities to the representatives of the Japanese steamship companies is equitable and this Government commends that proposal to the careful consideration of the Japanese Government.

The Treasury Department is at the present time in position, by exercise of administrative discretion vested in it by law, to give weight to considerations favorable to the Japanese steamship companies which lie more in the field of equity than in the field of law. In the event that the proposal of settlement is rejected by the steamship companies and the cases are litigated, the Treasury Department expects to defend all issues, including both the charter hire and the subsidy issues, and it is probable that any decision rendered by the tribunal before which the cases might come to trial would be based primarily on the legal questions involved.

The cases under discussion are all pending before the Board of Tax Appeals, an independent tribunal created by Congress to hear and determine tax cases. The Japanese steamship companies may, of course, raise before the Board of Tax Appeals all of the points which are at issue, and if the decision there is adverse to them they may appeal to the courts.

WASHINGTON, April 27, 1936.

811.512394 Shipping/56

The Secretary of State to the Ambassador in Japan (Grew)

No. 1030   WASHINGTON, May 7, 1936.

SIR: With reference to your telegram No. 31, February 19, 11 a. m.,[10] there is enclosed a copy of a memorandum, in regard to the question of war profits taxes asserted by the Treasury Department against certain Japanese steamship companies, which was handed on April 27, 1936, to the Japanese Ambassador by the Under Secretary of State.[11]

It will be noted from the enclosure that the Treasury Department has made an offer to the Japanese steamship companies which, if accepted, would effect a reduction of the amount of the total deficiency payments from the Japanese steamship companies concerned from approximately $2,300,000 to $650,000. It will further be noted from the enclosure that the Japanese Ambassador was informed that, in the event that the proposal of settlement offered by the Treasury Department to the Japanese steamship companies is rejected and the cases are litigated, any decision which may be rendered by the Board of Tax Appeals, before which the cases are now pending, or by any court before which the cases may subsequently be brought would probably be based primarily on the legal questions involved.

In the event that further reference to these cases is made to you by officials of the Japanese Government, it is requested that any statement which you may consider desirable to make conform to the sense of the last three paragraphs, or any portion thereof, of the enclosure.

Very truly yours,   For the Secretary of State,
WILLIAM PHILLIPS

---

[10] Not printed.
[11] *Supra.*

811.512394 Shipping/60

Memorandum by Mr. Eugene H. Dooman of the Division of Far Eastern Affairs of a Conversation With the Japanese Ambassador to Belgium (Kurusu)[12]

[WASHINGTON,] June 10, 1936.

Mr. Kurusu said that he had not seen the Department's note of April 27, 1936, on the above subject to the Japanese Embassy until he had arrived in Washington. He had noted that the position of the American Government in this matter could not be reconciled at several points with statements made to him by representatives of the Japanese steamship companies, but that he did not think that any useful purpose would be served by discussion of the differences. He hoped that it would be possible to strike a bargain on some mutually acceptable figure and bring to an end this unfortunate affair. He saw only one other course of action open to the steamship companies, and that would be to contest the tax assessments in the courts. He hoped that matters would not develop in this direction, for the reason that there would be created in Japan the feeling that the American Government had acted arbitrarily against the Japanese steamship companies.

Mr. Dooman stated that he, unlike Mr. Kurusu, felt that it would be useful to review the facts, for the reason that the notes of the Japanese Government in regard to the question under discussion seemed to indicate that the Japanese Government, and probably the steamship companies themselves, were not in possession of all the pertinent facts. Mr. Dooman then reviewed the case as set forth in the Department's note above mentioned to the Japanese Embassy, pointing out that the formula set forth in the Revenue Act of 1921 was actually devised by the representatives of the foreign steamship companies. Mr. Dooman further stated that the principle underlying this formula was the same principle used in assessing the tax on the estimated capital of branches in Japan of foreign corporations.

Mr. Dooman then laid before Mr. Kurusu the information which had been telephoned to Mr. Dooman by Mr. Cox, of the Bureau of Internal Revenue, with regard to the proposed plan of settlement involving the payment by the steamship companies to the Treasury of approximately $650,000. Such plan would involve the payment to the Treasury by the Nippon Yusen Kaisha of $377,674, and by the Osaka Shosen Kaisha of $435,293, or a total of $812,967, and the payment by the Treasury to the Toyo Kisen Kaisha of $154,394, which subtracted from the total figure of $812,967, would leave a balance of $658,573. He stated that the accumulated interest would have to be added to all the foregoing figures, and that he believed that such

---

[12] Formerly Chief of the Commercial Affairs Bureau, Japanese Foreign Office.

interest would run to about seventy-five percent of the principal amounts. Mr. Kurusu uttered an exclamation of surprise and remarked that the addition of interest would involve the net payment by the steamship companies of about one million dollars, which amount he thought would be quite unsatisfactory to the steamship companies. He stated that, as a matter of fact, he had been authorized by the steamship companies to propose a settlement on the basis of payment by them to the Treasury of $500,000. He drew from his pocket tables of figures prepared by the Nippon Yusen Kaisha and the Osaka Shosen Kaisha, which purported to show that if certain counter-claims by the companies against the Treasury were deducted from the Treasury's proposed figures of settlement, there would result an over-assessment of about $300,000. Mr. Dooman stated that the settlement proposed by the Treasury would involve the withdrawal by the steamship companies of all such counter-claims, and he could not therefore admit that the calculations made by the steamship companies were in any way valid.

Mr. Kurusu then asked whether this Government would favorably entertain a counter-proposal of settlement on the basis of the steamship companies paying the Treasury $500,000 and also "taking care" of the counter-claim of the Toyo Kisen Kaisha. Mr. Dooman asked how the figure of $500,000 was arrived at, and Mr. Kurusu said that it was a figure which appealed to the Japanese steamship companies as "fair". Mr. Dooman stated that it had to be borne in mind that there existed three separate cases between each of the three steamship companies and the Treasury, and he did not know whether there would be any warrant in law for accepting such a plan of settlement even if agreement were reached upon a figure.

Mr. Kurusu then asked whether a flat payment of $650,000 would be acceptable to the Treasury, the interest element to be entirely eliminated. Mr. Dooman asked if that inquiry was to be taken as a formal and official counter-proposal of the Japanese Government. Mr. Kurusu replied that it was not to be so taken for the present, but that if Mr. Dooman could ascertain whether there would be any disposition on the part of the American Government to consider such an offer he would recommend to the Japanese Government that such a counter-proposal be made. Mr. Dooman said that he would make inquiries and give Mr. Kurusu such information in regard to that point as he could obtain.

Arrangements were made for Mr. Kurusu to call tomorrow on Mr. Dooman.

NOTE: Mr. Dooman later called on the telephone Mr. Cox of the Bureau of Internal Revenue and described briefly the conversation between Mr. Dooman and Mr. Kurusu.

Mr. Cox informed Mr. Dooman later in the day by telephone that the Bureau of Internal Revenue is desirous that the cases under reference be brought to an end as expeditiously as possible, and that, although no assurance could be given that any counter-proposal such as that above outlined of the Japanese Government would be favorably considered, the "door would not be shut" against consideration of such counter-proposal, if made.[13]

811.512394 Shipping/66

The Japanese Embassy to the Department of State

MEMORANDUM

The Japanese Embassy has transmitted to the Department for Foreign Affairs of the Japanese Government the memorandum of the State Department, dated April 27, 1936, which sets forth the views of the United States Government on the additional war profits taxes asserted by the Treasury Department against three Japanese shipping companies, namely, the Nippon Yusen Kaisha, the Osaka Shosen Kaisha, and the Toyo Kisen Kaisha, and is now authorized to state that the Japanese Government is gratified to note in the memorandum the responsive attitude expressed by the United States Government to the request that friendly consideration be given to the matter in view of the special circumstances in which a number of steamers were placed at the disposal of the United States Government by these shipping companies. The proposal of the Treasury Department made to the companies to effect a settlement of the pending cases on the payment of approximately $650,000 has, therefore, been carefully considered by the Japanese Government as indicative of this responsive attitude taken by the United States Government.

The Japanese Government, appreciative of the conciliatory spirit of the United States Government and desirous of expediting the settlement of this long standing issue, will refrain from submitting its views on various points, particularly on the question of amortization, set forth in the memorandum of the State Department, since any further discussion will inevitably delay such a settlement, and it has endeavored to induce the steamship companies to accept the proposal of the Treasury Department. Now the steamship companies are, it is learned, prepared to accept the proposal above referred to, on the understanding that the amount to be paid as the balance of the deficiencies assessed against the Nippon Yusen Kaisha and the Osaka Shosen Kaisha after deducting the excess assessment

---

[13] On June 11, Mr. Dooman informed Mr. Kurusu that this Government would give consideration to the Japanese counterproposal.

to be refunded to the Toyo Kisen Kaisha will not be more than
$650,000, and further that the payment of interests that may have
accrued from the said deficiencies or excess assessment will not be
claimed in any form.

It is earnestly hoped that the United States Government, which
undoubtedly shares the opinion of the Japanese Government that a
satisfactory settlement of the issue should be reached at as early a
date as possible, will agree to the terms of the settlement as indicated
above.

If they be acceptable to the United States Government, the details
of payment and other necessary procedures will be negotiated between
the Japanese steamship companies and the Treasury Department.

[WASHINGTON,] September 19, 1936.

811.512394 Shipping/65

The Japanese Embassy to the Department of State

MEMORANDUM

In connection with the Memorandum of the Japanese Embassy,
dated September 19, 1936, with regard to the question of the additional war profits taxes asserted by the United States Government
against the three Japanese shipping companies, it is understood that
at the time of a satisfactory settlement of the issue the United States
Treasury Bonds amounting to $120,000 which were deposited by the
Toyo Kisen Kaisha with the United States Government on April 30,
1934 will be returned to the company together with the interest
thereof, and that the amount of $65,756 paid by the Osaka Shosen
Kaisha to the United States Government in excess of the assessment
for the year 1920 will be refunded to the said company.

[WASHINGTON,] September 19, 1936.

811.512394/66

The Department of State to the Japanese Embassy

MEMORANDUM

The Department of State acknowledges the receipt of a memorandum, dated September 19, 1936, from the Japanese Embassy, in
which it is stated that the Nippon Yusen Kaisha, the Osaka Shosen
Kaisha and the Toyo Kisen Kaisha are prepared to effect settlement
of pending cases in which additional war profits taxes are asserted
by the Treasury Department, on the understanding that the amount
to be paid as the balance of the deficiencies assessed against the Nippon

Yusen Kaisha and the Osaka Shosen Kaisha after deducting any excess assessment to be refunded to the Toyo Kisen Kaisha will not be more than $650,000, and on the further understanding that the payment of interests that may have accrued from the said deficiencies or excess amount will not be claimed in any way.

The Department of State is authorized by the Treasury Department to accept the counter-proposal of the Japanese Government, as set forth in the memorandum of the Japanese Embassy under acknowledgment, as a basis for settlement.

As it is necessary that the details of the plan of settlement be worked out in conference between the Treasury Department and representatives of the steamship companies, it is assumed that the Japanese Government will advise the steamship companies to arrange for such conference at an early date.

The attention of the Japanese Embassy is invited to the fact that it will be necessary for the steamship companies to reach an agreement among themselves as to the allocation of the $650,000 payment among the companies; and inasmuch as the counter-proposal of the Japanese Government stipulates that there should be no payment of interest, it is assumed that the amount mentioned will be paid in cash at the time of the consummation of the agreement.

WASHINGTON, October 20, 1936.

811.512394 Shipping/65

The Department of State to the Japanese Embassy

MEMORANDUM

Reference is made to a memorandum dated September 19, 1936, from the Japanese Embassy in which the understanding of the Japanese Embassy is expressed that at the time of a satisfactory settlement of the question of the additional war profits taxes asserted by the Treasury Department against three Japanese steamship companies, certain bonds deposited by the Toyo Kisen Kaisha with the American Government will be returned and certain monies paid by the Osaka Shosen Kaisha to the American Government in excess of the assessment for the year 1920 will be refunded.

A copy of the memorandum under reference was transmitted to the Treasury Department, and there has been received from the Treasury Department a reply under date October 14, 1936, pertinent portions of which are quoted hereunder as follows:

" . . .[14] it is agreeable to this Department that it be understood that at the time of a satisfactory settlement of the issues in the cases before

---

[14] Omission indicated in the original.

the Board of Tax Appeals by the payment of $650,000, the United States Treasury bonds amounting to $120,000 which were deposited by the Toyo Kisen Kaisha with the Anglo California National Bank of San Francisco under escrow agreement dated May 18, 1934 be returned to that company, together with the invested increments thereon, interest, etc., as more particularly provided in the contract. It is also the understanding of this Department that the proposed settlement and payment will completely and finally dispose of all issues relating to the income and profits tax liabilities of all three companies for the years 1918 and 1919, and also for the year 1920 in the case of Nippon Yusen Kaisha. It will not include any settlement of the tax liability of Osaka Shosen Kaisha for the year 1920. It follows, therefore, as suggested in the memorandum of the Japanese Embassy that it will not in any way affect the right of the Osaka Shosen Kaisha to any refund of excess payments made for the year 1920, since the proposed settlement involves only the years 1918 and 1919 in respect of that company. Action on the pending proposed certificate of overassessment in the amount of $65,756.60 has been held up to await the outcome of the case involving the years 1918 and 1919, but it will be given prompt attention with a view to disposing of it at the same time the other years are settled."

WASHINGTON, October 20, 1936.

811.512394 Shipping/68

The Japanese Embassy to the Department of State

MEMORANDUM

The Japanese Embassy acknowledges the receipt of the memorandum of the State Department under date of October 20, 1936, in which it is stated that the Department of State is authorized by the Treasury Department to accept as a basis for settlement the counter-proposal of the Japanese Government, as set forth in the memorandum of the Embassy of September 19, 1936, with regard to the settlement of pending cases concerning additional war profits taxes asserted by the Treasury Department against three Japanese steamship companies. In the memorandum under acknowledgment it is assumed that the Japanese Government will advise the steamship companies to arrange for a conference at an early date between the representatives of such companies and the Treasury Department to work out the details of the plan of settlement; and that the amount of $650,000 will be paid in cash at the time of the consummation of the agreement. It is also stated that the attention of the Japanese Embassy is invited to the fact that it will be necessary for the steamship companies to reach an agreement among themselves as to the allocation of the amount to be paid.

The memorandum of the Department having been duly transmitted to Tokyo, the Japanese Embassy is now in a position to inform the

State Department that the steamship companies are now in readiness to arrange, through their representatives in New York, for such a conference as suggested at as early a date as possible; and that an agreement will be reached among themselves as to the allocation of the $650,000 payment; and that the payment of the said amount will be made in cash at the time of the consummation of the agreement.

[WASHINGTON,] October 31, 1936.

JAPAN'S PROPOSAL THAT PERPETUAL LEASES IN FORMER FOREIGN SETTLEMENTS IN JAPAN BE CANCELED IN FAVOR OF OWNERSHIP RIGHTS

894.52/42

The Secretary of State to the Ambassador in Japan (Grew)

No. 1018   WASHINGTON, April 30, 1936.

SIR: Reference is made to your despatch No. 1269, dated May 1, 1935,[15] in which there is discussed the question of properties in the former foreign settlements in Japan held under perpetual leasehold. It is noted that effort is being made by the British Embassy at Tokyo to devise an arrangement whereby perpetual leaseholders will abandon their claim to exemption from certain taxation and accept deeds in fee simple for their properties in return for sums of money to be paid them by the Japanese Government. It is noted further that the British Ambassador expressed the hope that no definite steps be taken by the Embassy, "as complications might arise should representations be made by the two Embassies along different lines".

The observations hereinafter submitted are based on an examination of the information in the Department's possession on the subject of perpetual leases in Japan, most of which is derived from a pamphlet entitled, *A Survey of the Perpetual Lease Question*, printed by the *Japan Chronicle*, Kobe, Japan, in 1932. This pamphlet will be cited hereinafter simply as *Survey*.

It is the understanding of the Department that in 1894 when agreement was reached between the British and Japanese Governments in regard to the abolition of the extraterritorial rights of British subjects in Japan, it was proposed by the Japanese Government that simultaneously with the abolition of such rights the leaseholds in Japan of British subjects be converted into freeholds; but that the British Government indicated unwillingness to enter into any such arrangement unless provision were made to compensate leaseholders for the loss of exemption from taxation of leasehold property. The Treaty of Commerce and Navigation concluded on July 16, 1894, be-

---

[15] Not printed.

tween Great Britain and Japan,[16] provided that the leaseholds were to be confirmed at the time of the abolition of extraterritorial rights and that "no conditions whatsoever other than those contained in such existing leases shall be imposed in respect of such property". The treaty concluded on April 3, 1911, between Great Britain and Japan[17] contained no analogous provision, but the British and Japanese Governments agreed, as set forth in an annex to that treaty, that

"the contention of either Government regarding the position of the holders of leases in perpetuity in the former foreign settlements, which it was agreed between the two Governments should form the subject of a separate negotiation, was not in any way prejudiced by the omission of reference to that question in the Treaty."

The Treaty of Commerce and Navigation concluded on November 22, 1894, between the United States and Japan[18] contained a clause corresponding to the clause above described of the Anglo-Japanese treaty of 1894. In 1910, the Japanese Government proposed to the American Government the conclusion of a new treaty of commerce and navigation, and on October 19, 1910, the Japanese Embassy at Washington presented to the Department a draft of a suggested treaty[19] which contained no reference to perpetual leaseholds. On January 23, 1911, the Department informed the Japanese Embassy[19] that the American Government would be prepared to enter upon negotiations for a new treaty of commerce and navigation, but it pointed out that there were "certain . . ."[20] matters of prime importance which in the opinion of the Department of State should likewise be considered and settled in principle at the outset of the negotiations". In regard to properties held under perpetual lease, it was proposed that "the present status of the perpetual leasehold property in the former foreign settlements, which have now acquired an established character, will be confirmed and maintained until a mutually satisfactory settlement of the various questions involved be arranged by the parties concerned". At the earnest solicitation of the Japanese Government, however, the American Government did not insist upon insertion in the draft treaty of any clause defining or preserving the rights in regard to leasehold property of American citizens, but there was given by the Japanese Government an undertaking that American leaseholders would be given the benefit of the "superior position" of leaseholders of other than American nationality. Your attention is directed in this connection to the telegram dated February 19, 11 p. m.

---

[16] *British and Foreign State Papers*, vol. LXXXVI, p. 39.
[17] *Ibid.*, vol. CIV, p. 159.
[18] William M. Malloy (ed.), *Treaties, Conventions, etc., Between the United States of America and Other Powers*, 1776–1909 (Washington, Government Printing Office, 1910) vol. I, p. 1028.
[19] Not printed.
[20] Omission indicated in the original instruction.

(1911), from Mr. O'Brien [21] to the Department.[22] (No record can be found of the receipt from the Embassy of a copy of the form which was reported by Mr. O'Brien to have been received by him on February 19, 1911, from the Minister for Foreign Affairs, and it is requested that a copy of that form be furnished to the Department at your early convenience.) At the further solicitation of the Japanese Government, the American Government agreed, as set forth in Article 16 of the Treaty of 1911,[23] that the Treaty of 1894 "shall cease to be binding" upon the coming into effect of the new treaty.

It appears, therefore, that while the existing treaty between the United States and Japan contains no provision relating to the status of perpetual leases in Japan held by American citizens, such a provision was omitted in consideration of the agreement of the Japanese Minister for Foreign Affairs to give American leaseholders any benefits which might be granted to other foreign leaseholders (see telegram from Embassy, February 19, 1911, 11 p. m. and Department's reply of February 21, 1911, 3 p. m.[24]). This Government accordingly has the right to insist that American holders of perpetual leases in Japan shall receive treatment in no respect less favorable than the treatment accorded to other foreign leaseholders in respect of such leases.

The essence of the contentions of the leaseholders appears to be that the land covered by the leases was, in fact, bought outright by the leaseholders from the Japanese Government and that, therefore, ". . .[25] the so-called ground rent is equivalent to nothing more or less than a sum paid as commutation of all present and future taxes" (*Survey*, page 54). The contention that the perpetual leases were, in fact, title deeds conveying the properties to the leaseholders is supported by the language of a sample document covering a certain property in the foreign settlement of Yokohama (*Survey*, page 44). The document is entitled "Title Deed for Lot No. . . .". While the preamble recites that the property is leased in consideration of a stipulated sum of money plus an annual payment of rental, the second, third and fourth paragraphs of the document clearly establish that the so-called leaseholder takes full title to the property with the right of sale subject to certain express conditions. The second paragraph of the document provides "That any transfer of said lot or any portion thereof shall be made to no other person than a subject or citizen of a Power having a treaty with Japan and shall be executed before the Consul of the parties concerned and shall be registered at the Kanagawa Ken-Cho". The third paragraph even more definitely estab-

---

[21] T. J. O'Brien, then Ambassador in Japan.
[22] Not printed.
[23] Signed at Washington, February 21, 1911, *Foreign Relations*, 1911, p. 315.
[24] Neither printed.
[25] Omission indicated in the original instruction.

lishes the document as a deed of sale and not a lease. That paragraph provides "That no portion of said lot or any building which may be erected thereon shall be sold or leased to any Japanese subject, unless both the Japanese and Consular Authorities grant an official act of authorization under their seals of office legalizing such transfer or lease . . .".[26] (Underscoring added.) The fourth paragraph provides in part that "The non-performance of any of the aforesaid conditions will render this Title Deed null and void, and the said lot shall revert to the Japanese Government and the buildings thereon shall become their property".

Assuming that the sample copy is authentic and that it is substantially similar to all the other agreements under reference, there can be no reasonable doubt that the leaseholders are in fact the owners and not merely the lessees of the properties in question. Additional support for this conclusion is found in the wording of the receipts given by the Government Land Office at Yokohama for the "consideration" named in the so-called leases. A sample receipt issued by the office mentioned reads as follows:

"Government Land Office,

Yokohama, ... 186 . .
Received this . . . . . day of . . . . 186 . . from . . . .
. . . . Subject . . . . the sum of Mexican Dollars . . . . in full of Purchase money of Bluff Lot No. . . .
$ . . . . . .

Seal of the Land Office." (*Survey*, page 55)

Inasmuch as the so-called leasehold properties were actually sold to the leaseholders and since the record discloses that the "purchase money" was considerably in excess of the sale value of similar lands in Japan at that time, it would appear reasonable to assume that the "annual rental" was not intended as additional compensation for the property which had apparently already been paid for in full. The questions are therefore presented why the annual rental was stipulated in the leases; on what basis was it computed; and for what purpose or purposes was it intended to be applied.

The agreements concluded in 1867 and 1868 between the leaseholders of Hyogo and Osaka and the Japanese authorities in respect of lands in those foreign settlements are cited by the leaseholders in support of their contention that the annual rental was intended to be in commutation of all municipal charges. Article 7 of the agreement of May, 1867, reads as follows:

"All the ground leased to foreigners at Osaka and Hyogo will be subject to a payment of an annual rent calculated at a rate that will be considered sufficient to meet the expenses of keeping in repair the

---

[26] Omission indicated in the original instruction.

roads and drains, cleansing and lighting of and maintaining orders in the Settlement, and the ordinary land tax payable at the present date to the Japanese Government." (*Survey*, page 20)

Article 5 of the agreement of August 7, 1868, relating to the same settlements, reads as follows:

"The annual rent of the said ground at Osaka and Hyogo shall be 1 bu per tsubo, which shall be paid in advance into the municipal fund of each place and shall be appropriated to the repairs of roads and drains, lighting the streets or other municipal purpose, subject however to a first charge of 1,524 bu at Osaka and 1,641 bu at Hyogo, which sums shall be paid annually to the Japanese Government as the ordinary land tax due on the said ground." (*Survey*, page 20)

The earlier arrangement respecting the foreign settlement of Yokohama is not so explicit as those relating to Hyogo and Osaka. The arrangement concluded between the leaseholders of Yokohama and the Japanese authorities and recorded in a memorandum of December 19, 1864, contains the following provision:

". . .[27] Finally, in order to avoid all further discussion about the keeping of roads, drainage, cleaning of streets and other municipal objects for which hitherto the Japanese local authorities have been held responsible in view of the high rental paid by all foreign leaseholders, it has been agreed that these objects shall henceforth be secured by the foreign land-renters themselves, and towards the expenses that must be incurred anually there shall be a deduction of 20 percent from the yearly rent paid by all land leased to foreigners, to be paid into a municipal fund." (*Survey*, pages 7 and 8)

For three years following this agreement the leaseholders of Yokohama administered the foreign settlement but their only revenue was the 20 percent of the annual rentals remitted by the Japanese Government, plus license fees for publicans (afterwards declared illegal and discontinued), which proved inadequate to cover municipal expenses; and the administration of this settlement was again taken over by the Japanese in 1867 and continued to be administered by them until the settlements were incorporated in the Japanese municipal system in 1899. It also appears that the inadequacy of the 20 percent of the annual rental remitted to the leaseholders of Yokohama was recognized in arrangements made in 1868 for the administration of the foreign settlements of Osaka and Hyogo by which 75 percent of the rental was remitted by the Japanese Government for municipal expenses. It further appears that an additional sum of 25 percent of the proceeds of sales of leases of settlement lots was paid into a municipal fund for the three foreign settlements mentioned. At a meeting of the leaseholders held in Yokohama in April, 1909, a committee report contained the following statement:

---

[27] Omission indicated in the original instruction.

"It is noteworthy that the Settlement of Kobe, which was by far the most efficiently maintained of the foreign quarters in Japan, was able to pay its way out of the 75 per cent of the ground rents retained for municipal purposes." (*Survey*, page 12)

It appears therefore that the agreements relating to Hyogo and Osaka expressly declare that the annual rental was intended to cover the cost of municipal services and the agreement respecting Yokohama and the actual administration of that settlement impliedly warrants the conclusion that the rental collected from the Yokohama leaseholders was computed on substantially the same basis and intended to be applied for the same purposes as the rentals collected from leaseholders in Hyogo and Osaka. It also appears clear that the Japanese authorities recognized exemption of the leaseholders and refrained for a long period of years from imposing any charges or taxes on the leaseholders other than the rental stipulated in the leases, thereby confirming in practice the right of the leaseholders to be exempt from the payment of such charges or such taxes. Evidence of the recognition by the Japanese authorities of the leaseholders right of exemption is contained in the Hague Award in the House Tax Case given on May 22, 1905, holding that buildings on leasehold ground, as well as the land itself, were entitled to the exemptions provided by the treaty of 1894 abrogating extraterritoriality.[28] A pertinent excerpt from the Hague Award mentioned reads as follows:

"Whereas the will of the parties consequently formed the law in the matter, and in order to ascertain how the documents have really been interpreted, one must look at the treatment to which the holders of the lands have in fact been subjected, as regards the taxes in the various localities;

"Whereas, with regard to this, it is an ascertained fact that, following a practice which has not varied, and which has existed for a long series of years, not only the lands in question but also buildings erected on such lands have been exempted from all imposts, taxes, charges, contributions or conditions other than those expressly stipulated in the leases in perpetuity;

"Whereas the Government of Japan contends, it is true, that this state of affairs, as well as the fiscal immunity which foreigners enjoyed in general in the country was only due to the fact that the Consular Courts refused to give the necessary sanction to the fiscal laws of the country;

"Whereas, however, this contention is devoid of proof, and it is not even alleged that the Japanese Government ever made any protests to the Governments of Germany, France or Great Britain, in order to uphold the rights which it says were violated;

"Whereas, although it has been alleged that the immunity which foreigners in fact enjoyed as regards taxes under the governance of the old Treaties was general and extended also to foreigners residing

---

[28] See despatch No. 886, May 25, 1905, from the Chargé in the Netherlands, *Foreign Relations*, 1905, p. 692.

outside the Settlements in question, it nevertheless appears from information furnished with regard to the holders of immovable property, lands and houses, at Hyogo, that the said rule was not universally applied;

"Whereas, in any case, the state of affairs *de facto* is not doubtful in whatever manner it may be explained." (*Survey*, pages 19 and 20)

The treaties concluded between the several powers and Japan in 1894 which provided for the abrogation of extraterritoriality and the incorporation of the foreign settlements in the Japanese municipal system expressly provided that the perpetual leases in question should be confirmed and that "no conditions whatsoever other than those contained in such existing leases shall be imposed in respect of such property". (American-Japanese Treaty of 1894, Article XVII; British-Japanese Treaty of 1894, Article 18.) The provisions of the Franco-Japanese Treaty [29] were even more specific and provided that "no imposts, taxes, charges, contributions, or conditions whatsoever other than those expressly stipulated in the leases in question shall be imposed in respect of such property". (Article 21, Franco-Japanese Treaty)

These treaty provisions raise the question, therefore, whether after the incorporation of the foreign settlements in the municipal system of Japan, the leaseholders retained the right to enjoy the complete exemption from municipal taxes which they enjoyed prior to the incorporation of the foreign settlements in the Japanese municipal system. While the leaseholders contend that the status which they enjoyed prior to the effective date of the treaties abrogating extraterritoriality was intended to be confirmed and continued by the treaty provisions above quoted and that they were, therefore, entitled upon payment of the rental stipulated in their leases to continued exemption from charges or taxes of any kind by the municipalities in which the respective foreign settlements were merged, the Department is inclined to believe that their situation was materially changed by the incorporation of the foreign settlements in the municipal system of Japan and that it would be unreasonable to insist that the immunity which they enjoyed in the former foreign settlements was intended to be perpetual without regard to the changed conditions under which the foreign settlements were administered after the abrogation of extraterritoriality.

This conclusion is based on the following considerations:

(1) There is no express agreement between the Japanese Government and the leaseholders by which the latter are declared perpetually exempt from the payment of every tax or charge except the rental stipulated in the leases.

---

[29] Signed at Paris, August 4, 1896, *British and Foreign State Papers*, vol. LXXXVIII, p. 530.

(2) The fact that such exemption was granted them prior to 1899 may reasonably be explained by the peculiar status of the foreign settlements as isolated communities entirely separate from the Japanese communities and by the fact that the annual rental stipulated in the leases was, for a long period at least, adequate to cover the necessary expenditures by the Japanese authorities in connection with the administration of the settlements.

(3) After the settlements were incorporated in the Japanese municipal system the cost of all municipal services to the foreign settlements areas was considerably in excess of the amount of the annual rental stipulated in the leases and unless it could reasonably be held that the leaseholders were entitled by the treaty provisions of 1894 to continue indefinitely to enjoy the complete exemption from any taxes or charges which they had enjoyed prior to 1899 they should be required to pay their equitable share of the cost of municipal administration.

In point of area and of population each of the former settlements comprises but a small part of the Japanese municipalities into which it was incorporated in 1899. In these circumstances, the contention that the leaseholders, having commuted taxes for the maintenance of the former foreign settlements, have thereby divested themselves of the obligation resting upon them as members of the various municipalities to contribute toward the cost of maintaining municipal services in parts of the municipality other than the former settlements, appears to be inconclusive and unconvincing.

(4) In the Department's opinion the treaties of 1894 do not support the contention of the leaseholders that they are entitled to the complete exemption from municipal taxes or charges which they enjoyed prior to 1899. The treaty provision which is most specific on the question of the exemption granted to leaseholders after 1899 is Article 21 of the Franco-Japanese Treaty, the pertinent part of which reads in translation as follows:

"When said incorporation takes place existing leases in perpetuity under which property is now held in the said settlements shall be confirmed and no imposts, taxes, charges, contributions, or conditions whatsoever other than those expressly stipulated in the leases in question shall be imposed in respect of such property." (Underscoring Added.)

The quoted treaty provision, particularly the underscored portion thereof, seems clearly to establish that the only exemption to which the leaseholders were entitled by virtue of the treaties of 1894 relates solely to taxes or charges "imposed in respect of" the leasehold properties. It is obvious that many modern municipal taxes or charges have no reasonable relation to lands or buildings and it seems clear, therefore, that the leaseholders are not entitled by the treaty provisions in question to exemption from such charges or taxes of this category as are levied against all other residents of the municipalities.

The Department is, therefore, of the opinion that the exemptions expressly admitted by the Japanese Government as applicable to leasehold properties in the former foreign settlements should be regarded by the leaseholders as a reasonable recognition of their rights under the leases and that the taxes and charges which the Japanese Government contend should be paid by the leaseholders who now are residents of the Japanese municipalities should be paid without further opposition. It is believed that an agreement to this effect might reasonably be made with the appropriate Japanese authorities by having the existing lease agreements cancelled and fee simple titles substituted in their stead, on the express condition that the holders of these titles will in the future on the one hand be exempt from the payment of any tax which might be regarded as a direct or indirect charge on the property formerly held under lease and on the other hand be subject to all other municipal charges and taxes on a basis of equality with native or other foreign residents of the municipalities of Japan.

The Department is impressed by the fact that, notwithstanding the efforts made over an extended period of time to find some adjustment which would mutually satisfy the legal rights of all concerned, the emphasis placed in the process of the making of such efforts upon arguments of a legal character has tended to impair the reaching of any such adjustment. It seems to the Department that consideration of the issue from the point of view of equity, there being given thought at the same time to the intent of those party to instruments providing for the establishment of the concessions, to the rights and vested interests of the present leaseholders, and to the rights of the Japanese Government and municipalities, offers at the present time the only reasonable basis of expectation that the issue can be conclusively and satisfactorily disposed of.

The Department has noted with concern reference in your despatch under acknowledgment to the possibility that the Japanese authorities may unilaterally denounce the various agreements and treaty provisions which govern perpetual leaseholds in Japan. It would view with regret the taking by the Japanese Government of any such action, which would in all probability result in arbitrary disposition of the rights of the American leaseholders on a basis less favorable to the American leaseholders than might perhaps be obtained under negotiation by the leaseholders with the Japanese Government.

If the Embassy has received no communication in regard to the matter under reference from the British Embassy subsequently to information conveyed in the course of the conversation on April 14, 1935, between the British Ambassador and Mr. Grew, it would seem to be in order for the Embassy to inquire of the British Embassy whether any progress has been made toward settlement of the matter. With reference to the opinion expressed by the British Embassy "that the British Government would gladly welcome any backing which the American Government may care to give them in regard to this question", you may say to the British Ambassador that the American Government would be prepared to give consideration to any plan which the British Government has formulated looking toward amicable adjustment of the question of leaseholds, but that the American Government is not in position to intervene at the present conjuncture in the issue lying between the Japanese Government and the leaseholders.

The Department desires that after giving careful consideration to statements of fact and of opinion set forth in the present instruction you inform the Department whether or not you concur in them. The Department will expect to communicate further with the Embassy in regard to this matter upon receipt of the Embassy's reply to this instruction.

Very truly yours,   For the Secretary of State:
                                              WILLIAM PHILLIPS

894.52/45

The Ambassador in Japan (Grew) to the Secretary of State

No. 1884   TOKYO, June 10, 1936.
                                                  [Received June 29.]

SIR: With reference to the Department's instruction No. 1018, dated April 30, 1936, which contained an exhaustive and valuable summary of the perpetual lease question in Japan and particularly of the American position in regard to that question, I have the honor to report the following developments in the case.

There have been no formal negotiations, either between the British Embassy and the Japanese Government, or between the lease holders and the local authorities, since the Embassy's despatch No. 1269, dated May 1, 1935,[30] was written. According to a member of the staff of the British Embassy, the British Foreign Office approved of the plan of the British Embassy in Tokyo that some compromise plan be formulated which would be acceptable to both parties and which would dispose of the entire troublesome question. The British Embassy held several informal conversations on the subject last summer

---

[30] Not printed.

and autumn, but it was found that there was so great a spread between the demands of the leaseholders and the wishes of the Japanese Government (which would promise no compensation whatsoever for the relinquishment of the perpetual leases) that a compromise seemed almost hopeless. In December and January the British Embassy was endeavoring to find some new method of approach to the problem, but the February 26 incident [31] and its subsequent disturbances intervened, and the British Embassy has not since undertaken the problem. At the present time, with the changes in the Japanese Government and the lack of experience in the question of those now in the Foreign Office, the British Embassy considers the time inappropriate to reopen the question. In the meantime, the leaseholders, at least in Yokohama, are paying the disputed taxes under protest but are not paying the land and house taxes, which are not in dispute and which have not been collected by the local authorities for years past.

The British Embassy is of the opinion that neither the Japanese municipalities nor the Japanese Government is in a position financially at the present time to adopt the most reasonable plan, namely, that of gradually buying up the perpetual leases and thus eventually disposing of the question. Also because of the lack of sufficient funds, neither the municipalities nor the Government are likely to agree to any plan involving the payment of money to the leaseholders as compensation for the changing of leaseholds to titles in fee simple. Therefore it seems unlikely that the Japanese Government will broach the subject again in the near future.

The British Ambassador, however, has been informed, in accordance with the Department's instruction above referred to, that the American Government would be prepared to give consideration to any plan which the British Government has formulated looking toward amicable adjustment of the question of leaseholds, but that the American Government is not in a position to intervene at the present conjuncture in the issue lying between the Japanese Government and the leaseholders.

In the last paragraph of the Department's instruction under reference, the Embassy is asked whether or not it concurs in the facts and opinions set forth in the instruction. The Embassy concurs in all the statements of fact as set forth in the instruction, excepting the fact that, as the negotiations in connection with the conclusion of the Treaty of 1911 were conducted in Washington, the Embassy has no means of verifying the Department's views in regard to the present position of the American Government vis-à-vis the Japanese Government in connection with the perpetual lease question. The archives of the Embassy contain very few references to the negotiation of this treaty.

---

[31] See pp. 706 ff.

The Embassy also concurs heartily with the Department in its opinion of the equity of the situation and of the rights and duties of the lease-holders. The Embassy, however, does not agree entirely with the Department's view, expressed on page 13 of the instruction under reference, that

"It is believed that an agreement to this effect might reasonably be made with the appropriate Japanese authorities by having the existing lease agreements cancelled and fee simple titles substituted in their stead, on the express condition that the holders of these titles will in the future on the one hand be exempt from the payment of any tax which might be regarded as a direct or indirect charge on the property formerly held under lease and on the other hand be subject to all other municipal charges and taxes on a basis of equality with native or other foreign residents of the municipalities of Japan."

The objection to this solution of the problem would be that it would not greatly alter the present position of the municipalities vis-à-vis the leaseholders. At the present time the leaseholders are not paying the land and house taxes and other charges levied directly in respect of the leasehold properties, but are paying the municipal sur-taxes upon the income and business profits taxes and other municipal taxes under protest and under threat of distraint in case of non-payment. The municipal authorities, however, wish the perpetual leaseholders to be placed in exactly the same position as all other property holders in Japanese cities and to be subject to imposition of the same taxes and levies. The plan outlined by the Department, since it would perpetually exempt the former holders of leases from certain taxes, would not meet the wishes of the municipalities and would not remove the objection of the authorities and the citizens of the municipalities to the presence in their midst of certain privileged property owners.

From this viewpoint it would appear that the better road out of the maze is that advocated by the British Embassy, namely, that the Japanese Government or municipalities pay the leaseholders a lump sum as compensation for the relinquishment in perpetuity of all claims to exemption from taxation of any kind. The objections to this plan are, however, that the Japanese do not appear willing to pay compensation of any sort to the leaseholders, and that it is doubtful if they are financially able to pay such compensation at the present time.

On page 3 of the Department's instruction under reference, the Department requests that the Embassy transmit to the Department a copy of the form received by Mr. O'Brien (then American Ambassador to Japan) from the Minister for Foreign Affairs on February 19, 1911. It is not clear from the records on file in the Embassy which form is referred to, but the Embassy encloses copies of three forms found in the files of the Embassy.[32]   The first would appear to be the form desired by the Department, as it has a notation in ink, "Handed to the Ambassador at Embassy by Mr. Ishii, Feb. 19, 1911". On the other hand, the form appears to be the draft of a proposed second paragraph of Article 16 of the Treaty, preserving the *status quo* for the time being of the perpetual leases, and therefore seems inconsistent with the wishes of the Minister for Foreign Affairs as stated in Mr. O'Brien's telegram.   Moreover, the form bears the pencilled notation "Department draft".   The other two forms, also having connection with perpetual leases, are both labeled "Protocol", one having the pencilled notation "Japan form" and the other the pencilled notation "Department form", while the final paragraph of the latter has a pencilled heading "Japan's last suggestion".   No explanation of these forms exists in the files.

Respectfully yours,   JOSEPH C. GREW

894.52/45

The Secretary of State to the Chargé in Japan (Dickover)

No. 1114   WASHINGTON, October 5, 1936.

SIR: The receipt is acknowledged of the Embassy's despatch No. 1884 of June 10, 1936, with regard to the question of properties in the former foreign settlements in Japan held under perpetual leasehold.   The Department has noted with interest that, whereas informal conversations on this question were held in the summer and autumn of last year between the British Embassy and the Foreign Office, the British Embassy considers the present to be an inappropriate time to reopen the question.

The Department has also noted that the Embassy does not agree entirely with the view set forth on page 13 of the Department's instruction No. 1018 of April 30, 1936, to the effect that an agreement might be made providing for the cancellation of the existing leaseholds and the substitution therefor of fee simple titles, the present leaseholders to have no exceptional privileges other than exemption from payment of any tax which might be regarded as a charge on the property.   The Embassy observes that the objection to this suggested "solution of the problem would be that it would not greatly alter the present position of the municipalities vis-à-vis the leaseholders".   Preference is expressed by the Embassy for the plan put forward by the British Embassy, which is that the Japanese Government or the municipalities compensate the leaseholders, by payment

---

[32] None printed.

of a lump sum, for the relinquishment in perpetuity of all claims to exemption from taxation of any kind.

The Department's suggestion was based on the understanding that, by virtue of the Hague award in the House tax case, handed down on May 22, 1905, the Japanese authorities freely admitted the right of the leaseholders to exemption from taxes on the lands held under lease and the buildings erected on those lands, and the record of the cases available to the Department does not disclose any evidence of an intention on the part of the Japanese authorities to question the right of the leaseholders to such exemption. The record does, however, clearly indicate the determination of the Japanese authorities to refuse to admit that the leaseholders are entitled to any exemption other than exemption from taxes "imposed in respect of such property", that is, leasehold lands and the buildings erected thereon and, as stated in the Department's instruction of April 30, 1936, the position of the Japanese authorities appears to the Department to be reasonably warranted.

The Department feels, therefore, that inasmuch as the claim of the leaseholders to exemption from every form of municipal taxes or charges could not be supported equitably and probably never would be conceded by the Japanese Government, it would appear to be desirable if possible to obtain a formal confirmation by the Japanese Government of the right of the leaseholders to perpetual exemption from taxes or charges imposed in respect of leasehold lands and the buildings erected on those lands with the understanding that the leaseholders would be subject to all other municipal taxes and charges on a basis of equality with all other residents.

It is stated in the despatch under acknowledgment that the Japanese municipal authorities desire that the perpetual leaseholders be placed in exactly the same position as all other property holders in Japanese cities and be subject to imposition of the same taxes and levies. If the municipal authorities are now not willing to concede that the leaseholders are, by the terms of their leases and the Hague award herein mentioned, entitled to exemption from taxes respecting leasehold lands and houses, such a position would appear to represent not only a complete reversal of the position thus far held by the Japanese Government, but to involve a denial of a clear right to which the leaseholders are entitled. As it appears from your despatch to be certain that the Japanese Government and the municipal authorities will reject any plan involving the payment of any compensation to the leaseholders for the termination of the right above mentioned, it would appear that no useful purpose would be served by insistence on the acceptance of the British proposal, for the reason, as the Embassy recognizes, that that proposal appears to be wholly unacceptable to the Japanese Government.

If, as stated in the despatch under acknowledgment, it be the desire of the Japanese municipalities to have extinguished the right of the foreign leaseholders to exemption from taxes on leasehold properties, which in the view of the Department, is a question entirely separate from and independent of the question of the payment by the lease-holders of other municipal taxes, the initiative looking toward the conclusion of an agreement whereby such right would be terminated should properly come from the Japanese Government.

In view of the foregoing considerations, the Department is of the opinion that it would be desirable that its suggested solution of the difficulty be submitted to the Japanese Government, inasmuch as that plan appears to be in accord with the views heretofore expressed by the Japanese Government and would at least offer a basis for dis-cussion toward possible settlement of the dispute. Unless you perceive definite objection to this course, it is requested that you inform the British Embassy that, in the view of your Government, a proposal along the lines of the suggestion under reference appears to offer the only reasonable possibility toward satisfactory adjustment of this vexatious question. You may also state to the British Embassy that your Government is now disposed to present the plan to the Japanese Government at as early a date as practicable and that it would be happy if the British Government, through the British Embassy at Tokyo, could see its way clear to advance an identical proposal. The Department will, of course, be glad to give appropriate consideration to any counter-suggestion or to any proposal toward amendment of its suggested solution which may be advanced by the British Govern-ment, but, in view of a report which appeared in the *Japan Weekly Chronicle* in its issue of July 16, 1936, indicating that some action affecting perpetual leaseholds is about to be taken by the Japanese Government, it desires that further effort be initiated as soon as prac-ticable toward seeking some final solution of this question.

The Department will not suggest what would be a reasonable pe-riod within which the British Government should give word of arrival by it at a definite conclusion with regard to the position which it may decide to take but will expect that some indication in this regard will be given to you by the British Embassy.

Please report to the Department at your early convenience after discussions have been had with the British Embassy.

Very truly yours,   For the Secretary of State:
                                        R. WALTON MOORE

894.52/46 : Telegram

The Secretary of State to the Chargé in Japan (Dickover)

Washington, November 3, 1936—3 p. m.

138. Your despatch No. 2067 of October 2, 1936.[33]

1. Assuming that the third principle (C) of the British proposal contemplates during the 99 year period the continued exemption of leaseholders from payment of taxes on leasehold land and buildings, the Department would be prepared to agree to settlement of the leasehold question on the basis of the British proposal if that proposal should be acceptable to the Japanese Government.

2. Upon receipt of the Department's instruction No. 1114 of October 5, you may in your discretion furnish the Foreign Office informally with an outline of the proposal which this Government had intended to make in the near future, using paragraph 1 of page 13, instruction No. 1018 of April 30, 1936,[34] as basis for such outline. Please add that, although this Government believes, of course, that such intended proposal would offer a basis of settlement of the leasehold question wholly equitable to all concerned, it desires to contribute toward final and amicable solution of this long standing and vexatious question by being prepared to accept settlement on the basis of the proposal which it is understood was submitted to the Foreign Office by the British Ambassador on September 29, 1936.

3. Please inform the Department of action taken. If you have objection to making approach above suggested, please indicate character thereof.

4. For your confidential information and guidance: Any right of American leaseholders which may be legally enforceable in Japan cannot, of course, be compromised by acceptance by this Government of plan of settlement. However, upon acceptance by the Japanese Government of the British proposal, this Government would urge American leaseholders to accept the terms of settlement.

Hull

---

[33] Not printed.
[34] Fifth paragraph from end of despatch, beginning: "The Department is, therefore, of the opinion . . . ," p. 972.

894.52/47 : Telegram

The Chargé in Japan (Dickover) to the Secretary of State

Tokyo, November 11, 1936—4 p. m.
[Received November 11—7: 33 a. m.]

230. Department's 138, November 3, 3 p. m.

1. Third principle of the British proposal contemplated exemption from all land and house taxes and the national income tax, but not the prefectural and municipal surtaxes on the national income tax.

2. Before submitting the Department's proposal to the Japanese Government I again discussed the leasehold question with the British Embassy and learned that that Embassy has recently received a reply from the Japanese Government to its proposal (Embassy's despatch No. 2067, October 2, 1936[35]). The reply states that the perpetual leaseholds constitute an anachronism and cause unequal burdens of taxation upon the Japanese and foreign residents of the municipalities, and that the solution of the problem cannot wait for the expiration of the 99 year period proposed by the British but must be found in the very near future. The Japanese note then makes a counterproposal, as follows: (a) The leases to be canceled and ownership rights substituted therefor in April of next year, (b) as an act of grace the leaseholders to be exempted from payment of the national land tax for a period of 5 years from the date of cancellation of the leases. The note ends with a statement to the effect that if this proposal is not accepted the Japanese Government will take steps to collect arrears taxes from the leaseholders and will take suitable measures to equalize the burden of taxes in the future (it is presumed that this last refers to unilateral cancellation of the leases by the Japanese Government or to the collection by force of all taxes from the leaseholders in the future in disregard of the terms of the leases).

3. The British Embassy has referred the Japanese note to its Foreign Office and to the British leaseholders committees of Yokohama and Kobe, with the request that it be kept confidential for the present.

4. In view of the Japanese reply to the British proposal, I shall not take the action indicated in paragraph 2 of the Department's 138 pending the receipt of further information. It is suggested that action be delayed until the attitude of the British leaseholders is ascertained, when the situation will be more nearly clarified. Expression of opinion from the British leaseholders expected in 1 or 2 weeks. Department will be informed.[36]

Dickover

---

[35] Not printed.
[36] The Department's telegram No. 143, November 12, 7 p. m., gave approval.

JAPANESE AUTOMOBILE LEGISLATION VIOLATIVE OF THE 1911 TREATY OF COMMERCE AND NAVIGATION BETWEEN THE UNITED STATES AND JAPAN [37]

894.797/16 : Telegram

The Ambassador in Japan (Grew) to the Secretary of State

TOKYO, January 9, 1936—11 a. m.
[Received January 9—9 : 25 a. m.]

6. Department's 202, December 24, 1 p. m.[38]   At my direction the Counsellor of the Embassy [39] called yesterday on the Vice Minister for Foreign Affairs [40] and in the course of discussion of the proposed legislation to place the automobile manufacturing industry of Japan under a system of control by means of licenses advised him orally and informally of the American Government's attitude as set forth in the final paragraph of instruction 882 of November 18, 1935.[41]

The Vice Minister said that he had as yet received no draft of the proposed law and was therefore unable to reply but he observed that the treaty of 1911 [42] did not provide for rights of manufacture. The Counsellor replied that irrespective of the specific right of manufacture, assembly and manufacture under present day practice are incidental to and necessary for the trade in automobiles and that a limitation of the right to assemble motor cars under the same conditions as Japanese firms would seriously handicap the American automobile trade and would clearly be discriminatory in contravention of the terms of the treaty.

The Vice Minister said that he would examine the matter and would communicate with the Embassy later. I shall be guided by developments in determining whether representations to the Minister for Foreign Affairs by myself are desirable.

Despatch follows.[43]

GREW

894.797/17 : Telegram

The Secretary of State to the Ambassador in Japan (Grew)

WASHINGTON, January 31, 1936—11 a. m.

14. Your 6, January 9, 11 a. m., second paragraph, and your despatch 1631, January 9.[44]   For your information the Department

---

[37] Continued from *Foreign Relations*, 1935, vol. III, pp. 1048–1052.
[38] *Ibid.*, p. 1051.
[39] Edwin L. Neville.
[40] Mamoru Shigemitsu.
[41] *Foreign Relations*, 1935, vol. III, p. 1048.
[42] Signed at Washington, February 21, 1911, *ibid.*, 1911, p. 315.
[43] No. 1631, January 9, not printed.
[44] Latter not printed.

considers that the use of the word "manufactories" in its context in Articles I and II of the Treaty confers on American citizens the indisputable right to manufacture on terms of complete equality with Japanese subjects.

HULL

894.797/18 : Telegram

The Ambassador in Japan (Grew) to the Secretary of State

Tokyo, February 1, 1936—noon.
[Received February 1—3 : 03 a. m.]

22. Department's 14, January 31, 11 a. m. In a recent conversation the Vice Minister for Foreign Affairs told the Counsellor of the Embassy that the attitude of the Japanese Government towards the treaty of 1911 is that article 1 applies to individuals; that it is not contemplated that any individuals as such would be permitted to operate automobile factories under the proposed law and in that respect there would be no discrimination between Japanese subjects and foreigners resident in Japan. So far as companies or corporations are concerned their position is regulated in article 7 and it therefore seems clear to the Japanese Government that the proposed automobile law would not be inconsistent with the provisions of the treaty.

He said further that while the Foreign Office considers the project unwise there are forces at work beyond its control and that there is a movement on foot to put the bill before the special session of the Diet, probably in the spring, but he did not know whether that could be done. Despite its dislike of the project the Foreign Office would not be in a position to state to other departments that there is a treaty obligation which would stand in the way of the proposed legislation.

Despatch follows.[45]

GREW

894.797/27 : Telegram

The Ambassador in Japan (Grew) to the Secretary of State

Tokyo, July 10, 1936—5 p. m.
[Received July 10—6 : 18 a. m.]

152. Embassy's despatch No. 1891, July [*June*] 11, 1936,[45a] automobile manufacturing industry law.

---

[45] No. 1659, February 5, not printed. The Ambassador's telegram No. 112, May 23, 7 p. m., reported that "the automobile industry law passed the Diet today." (894.797/23)
[45a] Not printed.

1. Imperial ordinance gazetted today fixes date of enforcement of automobile manufacturing industry law as July 11, 1936.

2. At the same time an enforcing ordinance was promulgated defining automobiles to which the law applies as those having engines of more than 750 cubic centimeters capacity and manufacturers to which the law applies as those producing more than 3,000 cars per annum.

3. The Department of Commerce and Industry simultaneously issued an ordinance containing detailed definitions and regulations of little or no interest to American manufacturers. Full text by mail.[46]

4. Inform Commerce.

GREW

894.797/31

The Secretary of State to the Chargé in Japan (Dickover)

No. 1115   WASHINGTON, October 5, 1936.

The Secretary of State encloses a copy of despatch No. 241 dated August 25, 1936, from the American Consul at Yokohama [47] in which it is stated that the manager of the Ford assembly plant at Yokohama has reported to the Consul that Japanese officials appear to be applying the recently promulgated Automobile Industry Control Law with even greater discrimination against foreign companies than is provided for in the law itself.

It is desired that the Chargé d'Affaires direct the Consul to keep the Embassy fully informed with regard to developments adversely affecting American automobile interests in the Yokohama Consular District.

The Department would appreciate the receipt from the Embassy of comment with regard to statements made in the despatch under reference of the Consul and an expression of the Embassy's opinion with regard to the question whether any action in the premises by this Government is called for at the present juncture.[48]

---

[46] Despatch No. 1944, July 14, not printed.
[47] Not printed.
[48] The Department, in telegram No. 118, July 20, 1937, 5 p. m., informed the Embassy that in the absence of new and changed factors affecting the situation, it did not seem advisable to restate its views (894.797/32).

REFUSAL OF JAPANESE GOVERNMENT TO AUTHORIZE VISIT BY UNITED STATES NAVY VESSEL TO PORTS ON ISLANDS UNDER MANDATE TO JAPAN [49]

811.3362i/9a : Telegram

The Secretary of State to the Ambassador in Japan (Grew)

WASHINGTON, June 13, 1936—2 p. m.

75. 1. Each year for the past several years the Japanese Government has requested that this Government extend facilities in American territorial waters off the coast of Alaska to two Japanese public vessels and permit the entry of these vessels into harbors in Alaska and the Aleutian Islands [50] that are ordinarily not open to foreign commerce. It was stated in the case of one of these vessels that its purpose in visiting these harbors and waters was to make studies in connection with the protection of fur bearing seals, but in the case of the other vessel it was not suggested that the visits would be made upon the basis of any treaty or formal arrangement between the United States and Japan. This Government has nevertheless acceded to the requests of the Japanese Government in this regard.

2. For some time past there has been a strong undercurrent of conjecture and suspicion regarding harbor developments or fortifications of the Pacific possessions of both the United States and Japan. The American Government has interposed no objection to the visits of Japanese public vessels to territorial waters and closed harbors of Alaska, in the belief that opportunities thus offered for observation by the Japanese vessels would operate to remove any suspicion which might be held by the Japanese Government that there have been carried out any improvements of such character as would do violence to the spirit or letter of the Washington Naval Treaty.[51]

3. We consider it unfortunate that the Japanese Government has not thus far adopted a similarly liberal attitude in the face of allegations that there are being carried out in the Japanese Mandated Islands [52] various improvements which cannot be reconciled with Japan's treaty obligations to refrain from fortifying such Islands. The reluctance of the Japanese Government to give any countenance to irresponsible allegations is understandable, nevertheless we assume that the Japanese Government shares with the American Government the view that persistence of suspicion in this regard promotes mutual distrust and that such suspicion should, therefore, be removed.

4. The Navy Department plans shortly to despatch the destroyer *Alden* to the Asiatic station. An opportunity will thus be presented

---

[49] For previous correspondence, see *Foreign Relations*, 1929, vol. III, pp. 256 ff.
[50] See *ibid.*, 1933, vol. III, pp. 753 ff.
[51] Signed February 6, 1922, *ibid.*, 1922, vol. I, p. 247.
[52] For Japan's attitude toward this subject, see *ibid.*, 1933, vol. III, pp. 748 ff.

for the Japanese Government to extend to a public vessel of the United States courtesies at the larger unopened ports of the Mandated Islands, as well as at the open ports, and it is our opinion that an invitation by the Japanese Government to the *Alden* to visit such ports would have results highly beneficial from the point of view of relations between the United States and Japan.

5. Please give our views as above outlined your careful and attentive consideration. If you perceive no objection, please be so good as to present these views orally and informally to the Minister for Foreign Affairs[53] and as on your own initiative put forward the suggestion outlined in paragraph 4 above.

6. Please keep the Department currently informed by telegraph.

HULL

811.33621/10 : Telegram

The Ambassador in Japan (Grew) to the Secretary of State

TOKYO, June 16, 1936—9 a. m.
[Received June 16—1 : 45 a. m.]

127. Department's 75, June 13, 2 p. m.

1. While I entirely concur in the Department's premises it should be remembered that the Japanese Government has in the past repeatedly refused permission to American naval vessels to visit the unopened ports in the Mandated Islands (Embassy's telegrams numbers 40, April 19, 4 p. m., 1929;[54] 70, June 29, 10 a. m., 1929;[55] and 236, December 4, 4 p. m., 1930[56]). It seems highly unlikely that the Japanese Government will now change its attitude and I doubt whether even reciprocal treatment of Japanese ships in Alaska would serve to alter its intransigence. In this connection I have before me Department's instruction No. 549, July 19 [*16*], 1934, and enclosures.[57]

2. My carefully studied opinion is that even should the Japanese Government acquiesce in the proposal little or no useful information in regard to naval preparations or fortifications in the Mandated Islands would be obtained while acquiescence would open the way to numerous demands on our Government that Japanese naval vessels be allowed to visit American unopened ports.

3. Moreover, our proposal and the almost certain refusal of the Japanese Government to consider it might find their way into the Japanese press and this would merely serve to intensify public suspicion on both sides of the Pacific.

[53] Hachiro Arita.
[54] See despatch No. 1156, April 25, 1929, *Foreign Relations*, 1929, vol. III, p. 256.
[55] *Ibid.*, p. 258.
[56] See *ibid.*, p. 262, footnote 39.
[57] None printed.

4. Unless, therefore, the Department has some special reasons for wishing to reopen the question at the present moment it would seem questionable whether we ought to risk another rebuff coupled with the official and public irritation that might be caused by our making an issue of the matter.

5. So far as I can see the only likelihood of benefit from the proposed approach lies in the fact that it would serve to determine the present attitude of the Japanese Government in regard to closed ports in the Mandated Islands which might assist our Government in any future discussions of the question of fortifications in the Pacific after the expiration of the Washington Naval Treaty. If such a "show down" is desired our approach would no doubt bring it about.

6. If the Department still desires me to carry out the instructions under reference please specify whether the phrase "as on our own initiative" is intended to cover the whole or only the second part of the second sentence in paragraph 5 of the Department's telegram.

GREW

811.83621/10 : Telegram

The Secretary of State to the Ambassador in Japan (Grew)

WASHINGTON, June 18, 1936—6 p. m.

79. Your 127, June 16, 9 a. m.

1. There are two reasons in particular for the Department's suggestion. First, desire to see something done toward alleviating suspicion and improving relations between the two countries. There is no connection with the problem of future discussion of the fortifications question. Second, the Navy Department, in light of persistent refusal by Japan to permit American vessels to enter harbors in the Mandated Islands, is increasingly inclined to urge refusal to permit Japanese vessels to enter certain of our harbors. In addition, we have in mind that, should the Japanese prove not responsive to the suggestion under consideration, your approach and subsequent evidence of disinclination on their part to adopt the suggestion would create a tactical situation affording a potential point of departure for denying (if such action should later seem advisable) to Japanese vessels permission to enter certain American harbors.

2. Department takes into consideration all points mentioned in your paragraphs 1 and 2. Reference your paragraph 3, Department would not wish that this idea be put forward as a proposal. It would need to be put forward by you in the course of a visit on other business to the Foreign Minister and as a suggestion on your part. You might say that you had obtained permission from the Department but that it was not a proposal from or by your Government. You would point out that an invitation offered by the Japanese Government as of its

own volition would serve toward dispelling suspicion abroad and improving Japan's reputation in quarters where criticism of Japan's attitude and actions prevails. Need it be feared that the fact of your having made such a suggestion would be made public? If Arita should feel it inadvisable to lay the suggestion before other Japanese authorities, would he not probably tell you that he feels the idea impracticable? If he should choose to lay it before them, would he not do it as on his own initiative? Would not this procedure serve toward preventing there arising questions of definitive refusal or rebuff? It is not our thought to make of the matter an issue. But, in course of time, if the Japanese persist in the attitude which you characterize as "intransigence", there may occur a change in the attitude and practice of this Government toward admitting Japanese vessels to certain of our harbors. Would it not be better for them to take some step toward preventing any such possible development?

Please think the matter over with these considerations in mind and telegraph Department your further reaction for our guidance.

HULL

811.3362i/11 : Telegram

The Ambassador in Japan (Grew) to the Secretary of State

TOKYO, June 20, 1936—11 a. m.
[Received June 20—6 : 50 a. m.]

130. Department's 79, June 18, 6 p. m.

1. The Department has made perfectly clear the purposes of its suggestion as well as the method of approach desired.

2. While still believing that the chances of a favorable response from the Japanese tending to alleviate situation and improve relations are small, I do concur in the desirability of the step on the basis of all the considerations now clearly set forth.

3. The risk of premature publicity can be reduced but not necessarily eliminated by my seeing the Minister at his residence instead of at the Foreign Office.

4. It would be helpful to learn just how urgent the matter is regarded so that I may determine whether to seek some ostensible reason for seeing Arita immediately or whether a natural and therefore more favorable occasion for broaching the subject may be awaited. In Japan an Ambassador's visit to the Minister for Foreign Affairs is regarded as a matter of prime importance and periodical calls merely for the purpose of discussing the general situation are seldom understood. The tendency is to look for "the nigger in the woodpile." I see no reason for minimizing the importance of the subject under reference but shall nevertheless be glad to know whether the delay if any

should be a matter of days only or whether it may be a matter of weeks.

5. Obviously I can and shall advance a very strong and logical argument in making the suggestion as on my own initiative.

GREW

811.3362i/11 : Telegram

The Acting Secretary of State to the Ambassador in Japan (Grew)

WASHINGTON, June 25, 1936—noon.

83. Your 130, June 20, 11 a. m. Department, after further consultation with Navy Department, desires you proceed with this matter along lines indicated in Department's 79, June 18, 6 p. m., and previous, and your reply under reference. You should watch for a natural and favorable opportunity such as you suggest. However, the destroyer is scheduled to sail, July 15 and to leave Honolulu on July 21, proceeding to Guam. To have effect at this time, an invitation from the Japanese should be received here before the latter date. Department suggests that you inform us of developments favorable or unfavorable in regard to the making by you of this approach by, say, July 10.

PHILLIPS

811.3362i/13 : Telegram

The Ambassador in Japan (Grew) to the Secretary of State

TOKYO, July 3, 1936—11 a. m.
[Received July 3—1: 50 a. m.]

146. Department's 83, June 25, noon.

1. I have made an appointment to see the Foreign Minister on July 8th, ostensibly to discuss various routine matters and shall take that occasion to broach the subject under reference.

2. Unless the Department perceives objections I believe that it might be helpful on my own initiative, and as a talking point, to call the Minister's attention at that interview to the increasing difficulty met by our Consuls in Japan in obtaining ordinary and customary commercial information due to restrictive measures by the military. The situation in that respect is growing steadily worse. An approach to this subject could be opened by a reference to the Minister's recent appeal to the prefectural Governors to accord greater facilities and courtesies, and to impose fewer restrictions relating to foreigners in Japan.

3. Please instruct.[58]

GREW

---

[58] The Department expressed approval in telegram No. 88, July 6, noon.

811.33621/14 : Telegram

The Ambassador in Japan (Grew) to the Secretary of State

Tokyo, July 8, 1936—10 a. m.
[Received July 8—1:11 a. m.]

150. Department's 83, June 25, noon, and previous telegrams. Informal suggestion as on my own initiative concerning invitation to *Alden* to visit open and unopened ports of the Japanese Mandated Islands was made today to the Minister for Foreign Affairs along the lines envisaged in the telegraphic correspondence.

The Minister indicated marked interest in the situation which I described but professed to know nothing whatever about the subject. He said that he would see what could be done and would endeavor to let me know the result before July 20.

Grew

811.33621/15 : Telegram

The Ambassador in Japan (Grew) to the Secretary of State

Tokyo, July 13, 1936—10 a. m.
[Received July 13—5:56 a. m.]

153. My 150, July 8, 10 a. m.

1. If the Japanese Government decides against favorable action on my informal suggestion that an invitation of its own volition be extended to the destroyer *Alden* to visit the closed ports of the Japanese Mandated Islands, it is quite possible that the Minister for Foreign Affairs will avoid communicating to me the unfavorable reply and will tacitly let the matter drop.

2. If such proves to be the case I can see nothing to be gained by pressing for an answer because failure to extend the suggested invitation would be tantamount to a refusal. Nevertheless, if the Department, having in mind the last sentence paragraph 1 Department's 79, June 18, 6 p. m., feels that a definite even if adverse reply is desirable, it might be well that I should seek a further interview with the Foreign Minister a few days before July 21. I shall not do so unless so instructed.

3. For purposes of record a complete memorandum of my conversation with the Minister [59] has been prepared and will go to the Department in the pouch which leaves tomorrow.

Grew

[59] Not printed.

811.33621/15 : Telegram

The Secretary of State to the Ambassador in Japan (Grew)

WASHINGTON, July 16, 1936—6 p. m.

94. Your 153, July 13, 10 a. m. The Department would not wish to instruct you to seek a further interview but authorizes you, in the event a favorable opportunity should arise, to mention the matter again if such action seems advisable to you.

HULL

811.33621/16 : Telegram

The Ambassador in Japan (Grew) to the Secretary of State

TOKYO, July 28, 1936—1 p. m.
[Received July 28—7 : 27 a. m.]

163. Department's 94, July 16, 6 p. m., and previous telegrams. Counselor [60] called on Vice Foreign Minister [61] at latter's request to discuss questions the Ambassador had broached to Foreign Minister. One concerned proposed visit of *Alden* to Mandated Islands. This was the only opportunity to discuss the matter since the Ambassador's visit of July 8.

Vice Minister said Ambassador's suggestion was referred to Overseas Ministry but that no reply had been received. He said that probably other Government departments would be consulted. In answer to Counselor's query he feared that there was no way of expediting reply to Foreign Office.

His manner though friendly indicated that the Foreign Office was unable to do anything further.

GREW

811.33621/16 : Telegram

The Acting Secretary of State to the Ambassador in Japan (Grew)

WASHINGTON, August 7, 1936—7 p. m.

102. Your 163, July 28, 1 p. m., and previous. Department assumes that there is no prospect of favorable action being taken by Japanese authorities with regard to suggestion made *in re* the *Alden*. Department is today giving to the Japanese Embassy an adverse reply to a request for permission for Japanese government training ship *Shintoku Maru* to enter a harbor in Hawaii not listed as port of entry.

PHILLIPS

---

[60] Edwin L. Neville.
[61] Kensuke Horinouchi.

811.3394/235 : Telegram

The Acting Secretary of State to the Consul General at Shanghai (Gauss)

WASHINGTON, August 11, 1936—4 p. m.

225. Send following message to American Embassy at Tokyo by telegraph:

"Inquire of appropriate authorities whether following proposed visits of the U. S. S. *Gold Star* are agreeable to Japanese Government: Truk, September 10 to September 12; Palau, September 17 to September 19; Miike, October 12 to October 14; Yokohama, October 18 to October 23; Saipan, October 29 to October 31.[62] Inform Department by telegraph of reply of Japanese authorities."

PHILLIPS

811.3394/239 : Telegram

The Chargé in Japan (Neville) to the Secretary of State

TOKYO, September 4, 1936—10 a. m.
[Received September 4—12:01 a. m.]

177. Department's 225, August 11, 4 p. m. via Shanghai. Japanese Foreign Office by note dated yesterday has informed the Embassy that the Japanese Government has no objection to the proposed visit of the *Gold Star* at Miike but regrets it cannot give consent to proposed visits at Truk, Palau and Saipan.

NEVILLE

811.3394/239 : Telegram

The Secretary of State to the Chargé in Japan (Neville)

WASHINGTON, September 19, 1936—3 p. m.

121. Embassy's No. 177, September 4, 10 a. m.

1. Navy Department requests that notification be made in the usual manner to the Japanese Government of the proposed informal visits of the U. S. S. *Gold Star* to certain ports in the Japanese Mandated Islands in accordance with the following schedule: Palau, arrive October 27, depart October 29; Truk, arrive November 2, depart November 4; Saipan, arrive November 7, depart November 9.

2. In making notification to the Foreign Office please state orally that this Government assumes, in view of the numerous instances of the Japanese Government having expressed its willingness for public vessels of the United States to visit any of the open ports of

---

[62] Truk, Palau, and Saipan were located in the Japanese Mandate.

the Mandated Islands, that the objection of the Japanese Government
to the proposed visits of the *Gold Star* at Truk, Palau and Saipan
referred to in the Embassy's telegram above-mentioned was due to
the fact that the dates indicated for such proposed visits were inconvenient to the Japanese Government. It is understood that the
places named were designated by the Japanese Government as open
ports by Ordinance No. 13 of June 1, 1922, and it is further understood that these places are still in the category of open ports.

HULL

811.3394/243 : Telegram

The Chargé in Japan (Dickover) to the Secretary of State

TOKYO, October 13, 1936—3 p. m.
[Received October 13—7 : 05 a. m.]

210. Department's 225, August 11, 4 p. m.; Embassy's 187 [*177*],
September 4, 10 a. m.; and Department's 121, September 19, 3 p. m.
The Japanese Foreign Office by note dated October 12 informed the
Embassy that the Japanese Government was unable for various rea-
sons to give consent to the proposed informal visits of the *Gold Star*
at Palau, Truk and Saipan.

Yesterday the Embassy's Naval Attaché was informed by the British Naval Attaché that on October 10 the Japanese Foreign Office had
replied to the British Government's proposal for the visit of H. M. S.
Lowestoft to open ports in the Japanese Mandated Islands that such
a visit would be inconvenient for some time to come.

DICKOVER

811.79690 Pan American Airways/82

The Chargé in Japan (Dickover) to the Secretary of State

No. 2133   TOKYO, November 13, 1936.
[Received November 30.]

SIR: I have the honor to report that Mr. Ko Ishii, Chief of the
First Section of the American Bureau of the Foreign Office, called on
me today to make inquiries regarding the identity of an airplane
which flew over the Island of Rota, one of the Marianne group of
islands administered by Japan under mandate. According to Mr.
Ishii, on October 26, 1936, a silver-painted airplane flew over the
Island of Rota, which lies just north of Guam and south of the Island
of Saipan, keeping a northeast to southwest course. The airplane
flew at a height of 700 meters and at a speed of about 300 kilometers
per hour. The Foreign Office had no information regarding the

marks and numbers on the airplane and could give no information as to type of plane or the number of motors. There is enclosed a rough chart [63] prepared by the Foreign Office showing the position of the islands in question and the course taken by the airplane in flying over Rota.

Mr. Ishii stated that the Japanese authorities have ascertained that one of the clipper airplanes of the Pan American Airways arrived at Manila on October 27, at 3 p. m., and presume, therefore, that the airplane which flew over the Island of Rota was this clipper ship, en route from Wake to Guam and perhaps blown off its course. The Foreign Office requests the American Government to ascertain if the airplane which flew over Rota was this clipper ship, and, if so, requests that the Pan-American Airways be warned against a repetition of the flight over the island in question.[64]

Respectfully yours,

E. R. DICKOVER

---

[63] Not reproduced.
[64] Department's instruction No. 1351, October 12, 1937, answered the Embassy's despatch (894.0144/29).

SIAM

PROPOSED REVISION OF THE TREATY OF FRIENDSHIP AND COMMERCE BETWEEN THE UNITED STATES AND SIAM, SIGNED DECEMBER 16, 1920[1]

711.922/70

The Siamese Ministry for Foreign Affairs to the American Legation in Siam[2]

MEMORANDUM

Negotiation for treaty revision with U. S. A.

1. In a Memorandum dated October 23rd, 1933,[3] His Majesty's Government put forward proposals[4] for a revision of the present Treaty on the following points:

I. Article 1, paragraph 4: Military exactions or contributions.—It is desired to have these words struck out, so that either Contracting Party may have the right to requisition the property of the nationals of the other Party in its territory in time of war.

II. Article 3: Monopoly.—It is desired to modify this Article so that either Contracting Party should have the right to set up monopolies in its territory.

III. Article 7: Customs duties.—It is desired to modify the Article so that the most favoured nation treatment in regard to customs duties should be reciprocal and not unilateral as it now is.

IV. Article 13, paragraph 3: Consular privileges.—It is desired to have the condition of reciprocity added to the most favoured nation treatment that is now provided for.

The text of the Memorandum is attached herewith. (Annex 1.)[5]

2. On February 1st, 1934, Mr. Stevens,[6] who was entrusted with the negotiation with the Department of State, transmitted the counter-proposals of the Department of State, the text of which is to be found in Annex 2.[5]

---

[1] Continued from *Foreign Relations*, 1935, vol. III, pp. 1105–1111. For text of treaty, see *ibid.*, 1921, vol. II, p. 867.

[2] Handed to Assistant Secretary of State Sayre by the American Minister to Siam, temporarily in Washington, July 2.

[3] Original memorandum not received by the Department, but see telegram No. 17, November 18, 1933, 1 p. m., to the Minister in Siam, *Foreign Relations*, 1933, vol. III, p. 770.

[4] Proposals communicated to the Department by the Siamese Minister, October 16, 1933, *ibid.*, p. 767.

[5] Not printed.

[6] Raymond B. Stevens, American adviser on foreign relations to the Siamese Government.

3. As the proposals regarding (1) military exactions or contributions, (2) customs duties, and (3) consular privileges, concern provisions which are also stipulated in the treaties with other Powers, it was considered desirable to take up the discussion of these points at the time of the general revision of treaties which was due to take place in 1936. As the limitation of the right to set up monopolies exists in the American Treaty only, His Majesty's Government proposed that only Article 3 dealing with monopolies, should be dealt with in the Supplementary Treaty to be concluded, and, on this question, accepted the counter-proposal of the Department of State and, on the 21st of January 1935, authorized the Siamese Minister at Washington to sign the Supplementary Treaty accordingly.[7]

4. The Department of State, however, asked that the revision of Article 3 also should be left in abeyance pending the general revision.

5. Subsequently, in December 1935, through the good offices of Dr. Sayre,[8] the Department of State expressed its readiness to sign the Supplementary Treaty with a new Article 3 as per counter-proposal of the Department of State already accepted by His Majesty's Government, or if His Majesty's Government preferred, the Department of State would accept the provisions of the Article concerning monopolies in the Trade Agreement between the United States of America and Canada[9] (cf. Annex 3), provided however that an exchange of Notes as per drafts in Annexes 4[10] and 5,[11] should take place at the time of the signature of the Supplementary Treaty.

6. As His Majesty's Government hope to be able to start negotiations for the general revision of treaties with the various Powers in June next, it would appear to be desirable to resume the negotiation with the Department of State at that time. Instructions for this purpose will be sent to the Siamese Minister at Washington about June.[12]

7. The Siamese Minister at Washington will also be requested to keep H. E. Mr. Baker[13] *au courant* of the lines along which the negotiation is to proceed.

8. Apart from the points already under negotiation, on which His Majesty's Government will endeavour to find solutions which would

---

[7] See memorandum from the Siamese Legation, February 25, 1935, *Foreign Relations*, 1935, vol. III, p. 1105.

[8] See memoranda by the Assistant Secretary of State, dated December 2 and December 9, 1935, *ibid.*, pp. 1108 and 1110.

[9] Signed at Washington, November 15, 1935; Department of State Executive Agreement Series No. 91, or 49 Stat. 3960. See article VIII on monopolies.

[10] For Department's draft note handed by Mr. Sayre to the Siamese Minister, December 2, 1935, see *Foreign Relations*, 1935, vol. III, p. 1109.

[11] For draft reply from the Siamese Government, see *ibid.*, p. 1111.

[12] Such instructions, if sent to the Siamese Minister, were not conveyed to the Department until November 5, 1936, when the Siamese Minister gave notice of the termination of the treaty. See memorandum by the Chief of the Division of Far Eastern Affairs, November 5, p. 998.

[13] James M. Baker, Minister to Siam, temporarily in Washington.

prove acceptable to the United States Government, it may be mentioned from now on that in view of the promulgation and putting into force as from October 1st, 1935, of all the Codes, His Majesty's Government will take the opportunity, in the forthcoming negotiation for the revision of treaties, to secure the termination of the right of evocation which, according to the existing Jurisdiction Protocol,[14] is to continue for a period of 5 years as from the promulgation and putting into force of all the Codes.

9. His Majesty's Government will be very grateful for any assistance that H. E. Mr. Baker will be so good as to lend them in connection with their negotiations with the United States Government.

[BANGKOK,] 23 April, 1936.

711.922/81

The Chargé in Siam (Chapman) to the Secretary of State

No. 432   BANGKOK, October 14, 1936.
                                           [Received October 28.]

SIR: I have the honor to refer to my telegram No. 14 of October 14, 1936,[15] and to confirm to the Department that I have been confidentially advised of the intention of the Siamese Government to present the draft of a new proposed treaty between the United States and Siam some time within the next few weeks. It is understood that the treaty will include clauses relating to land ownership substantially as quoted in my air mail despatch No. 420 of August 29, 1936.[16] I am informed further that the proposed treaty will incorporate much of the phraseology of model United States treaties of friendship, commerce, and consular rights, that the Siamese Government is particularly anxious to expedite the negotiation and conclusion of a favorable treaty with the United States, if possible, before initiating negotiations with, shall we say, less disinterested countries, and that the Foreign Office will desire to conduct the treaty negotiations at Bangkok.

It is obvious that the Siamese believe that they have a better chance of concluding a favorable treaty with the United States than with certain other countries, and that their hand will be much strengthened if, when negotiating with France, Great Britain and Japan, they can refer to the accepted provisions of a treaty already concluded with the United States.

I shall not fail to keep the Department fully and promptly informed of further developments on this subject.

Respectfully yours,   J. HOLBROOK CHAPMAN

---

[14] Foreign Relations, 1921, vol. II, p. 874.
[15] Not printed.
[16] Missing from Department files.

711.922/82

The Siamese State Councilor for Foreign Affairs (Luang Pradit) to the American Chargé in Siam (Chapman) [17]

No. 7150/2479   [BANGKOK,] 19 October, 1936.

MONSIEUR LE CHARGÉ D'AFFAIRES: You are aware that the Treaty of Friendship, Commerce and Navigation which has governed the relations between the United States of America and Siam has now been operative over the ten year period foreseen in the text, and will continue in force for an additional period of one year after denunciation by one of the Parties. This basic agreement contains many provisions whose usefulness has been proven during the period in question. There are however certain provisions which seem to His Majesty's Government no longer appropriate, some in substance, others in matters of form. Similar remarks apply equally to the existing treaties between Siam and other Powers.

On several occasions the general attitude of His Majesty's Government in these matters has been indicated in public statements. For instance a statement of Government policy made on September 22, 1934 contained the following remarks:

"In regard to the Principle of Independence, there still exist certain treaty provisions which restrict our jurisdictional and fiscal autonomy, and the Government will seek an opportunity for their revision in due course."

The speech of the Council of Regency at the Opening of the Assembly August 1st 1934 contained the following statement:

". . ."[18] at the present time, almost all our treaties with Foreign Powers are nearing expiration. Accordingly, the Government will seek an opportunity of negotiating for their revision in due course, with a view to giving them the form of complete equality."

Even more recently, at the opening of the Assembly 1936, the Council of Regency stated: "As for the treaties with foreign Powers, almost all of which are nearing expiration, steps are being taken by the Government in order to negotiate for their revision, with a view to giving them the form of complete equality."

As thus indicated His Majesty's Government feel it their duty now to initiate measures looking toward a revision of the present treaties, or more exactly stated, the substitution of new texts or instruments for certain of the present ones.

In studying the problem thus presented the Government has come to the conclusion, for its part, that the interests of Siam on the one

---

[17] Copy transmitted to the Department by the Chargé in Siam in his despatch No. 436, October 20; received November 3.
[18] Omission indicated in the original note.

hand, and of foreign States on the other, will be best defined and safe-guarded if the basic treaties are uniform in character. As far as Siam is concerned, such a result will greatly simplify the problem of new legislation and permit interpretation of texts by the courts and ad-ministrative bodies in a way which will secure uniformity in regard to treatment of foreign interests. As no unusual provisions are con-templated, and in general the forms frequently employed in other modern treaties will be proposed, it is not considered that the uni-formity thus suggested will give rise to any especial legislative or administrative problems so far as the other High Contracting Parties are concerned.

With this aim of revising their treaty system to accomplish uni-formity, complete reciprocity and full jurisdictional and fiscal auton-omy, His Majesty's Government propose promptly to communicate a draft of a new treaty, after notice is given at an early date of their wish to terminate the present one. As provided in Article 17 of that document, the existing Treaty continues to have validity for a further one year from the date of such notification, during which time His Majesty's Government will hope to reach full agreement on the terms of the new Treaty and bring it into effect so that no interruption of treaty relationship will intervene.

I avail myself [etc.]   LUANG PRADIT MANUDHARM

711.922/85

Memorandum by the Chief of the Division of Far Eastern Affairs (Hornbeck)

[WASHINGTON,] November 5, 1936.

The Siamese Minister called and, after making some remarks re-garding the interest with which he had observed the political cam-paign and the election, said that his Government had decided to give notice to all of the Siamese "treaty powers" of termination of existing treaties. Such notice was being given today to each of the govern-ments concerned, and therefore he had called to give here the noti-fication contained in his note of this date to the Secretary of State, which note he thereupon handed me.[19]

The Minister stated that his Government hoped to be able to nego-tiate at Bangkok a new treaty with the United States. I asked at what time would the Siamese Government like to have such negotia-tions held. The Minister replied that he had not been informed. He went on to say that he understood that a text of a proposed new treaty would be handed to our Chargé at Bangkok and that he, the Minister,

---

[19] *Infra.*

hoped that his Government would send him a copy. I offered no comment except a remark that it ought to be not difficult to dispose of the question of jurisdictional privilege.

The Minister said that our Minister to Siam, Mr. Baker, had at one time expressed the view that he would like to return to Bangkok for treaty negotiations and that Mr. Baker had at another time expressed doubt whether the state of his health would permit him to return to Bangkok. The Minister said that perhaps Mr. Baker would still "change his mind".

The Minister inquired whether Mr. Sayre was available, as he would like to call on him; and it was shortly arranged that the Minister call on Mr. Sayre at once.

COMMENT: It will probably be deemed desirable to make acknowledgement [20] at an early date of the Siamese Minister's note of November 5, 1936 (here attached).

S[TANLEY] K. H[ORNBECK]

711.922/84

The Siamese Minister (Rajamaitri) to the Secretary of State [21]

WASHINGTON, 5 November, 1936.

SIR: With reference to a note from the Siamese Councillor of State for Foreign Affairs of the 19th October, addressed to your representative in Bangkok, indicating that it is the desire of His Majesty's Government to secure in their treaties a large measure of uniformity, complete equality of form and entire fiscal and jurisdictional autonomy, I now have the honour to inform Your Excellency, under instructions from my Government, that His Majesty's Government hereby give notice for their part of the termination of the Treaty of Friendship, Commerce and Navigation with its Annex between Siam and the United States of America signed at Washington, 16th December, 1920.

It is very earnestly desired, in view of the fact that the Penal Code, the Civil and Commercial Codes, the Codes of Procedure and the Law for the Organization of Courts have been promulgated and have been in force for a certain period of time, to terminate the theoretical and unused right of evocation and to enjoy unrestricted jurisdictional autonomy. His Majesty's Government would therefore request friendly assent of your Excellency's Government to the discontinuation of a jurisdictional privilege which has outlived its time.

---

[20] Acknowledgment was made November 17; for text, see Department of State, *Treaty Information*, Bulletin No. 86, November 1936, p. 19.

[21] Original missing from Department files; reprinted from Department of State, *Treaty Information*, Bulletin No. 86, November 1936, p. 18.

It is however understood that, as provided in Article 17 of the Treaty, all the above-mentioned agreements shall remain in force for one year from the date of the receipt of this notice.

I have [etc.]   PHYA ABHIBAL RAJAMAITRI

711.922/83 : Telegram

The Chargé in Siam (Chapman) to the Secretary of State

BANGKOK, November 6, 1936— 9 a. m.
[Received November 6—4 : 28 a. m.]

16. Foreign Office last night presented draft of treaty to take the place of existing treaty which I am informed was denounced yesterday in Washington. Note of transmittal states "That for practical reasons it would be most acceptable if the negotiations might take place at Bangkok if possible at an early convenient date on the basis of the draft proposed".

Text of draft of treaty will be forwarded air mail 7th.[22] Most important provisions of the treaty from American standpoint are the inclusion of land ownership right subject to reciprocity governed by "laws of the place where the property is situated" and omission of monopoly restrictions.

All treaties with other countries have been simultaneously denounced.

CHAPMAN

---

[22] Missing from Department files.

INDEX

INDEX

INDEX